D1385294

FESTIVALS
SOURCEBOOK

FESTIVALS SOURCEBOOK

A Reference Guide to Fairs, Festivals
and Celebrations in Agriculture, Antiques, The Arts,
Theater and Drama, Arts and Crafts, Community,
Dance, Ethnic Events, Film, Folk, Food and Drink,
History, Indians, Marine, Music,
Seasons, and Wildlife

PAUL WASSERMAN
Managing Editor

ESTHER HERMAN
Associate Editor

ELIZABETH A. ROOT
Assistant Editor

GALE RESEARCH COMPANY   BOOK TOWER   DETROIT, MICHIGAN 48226
―――――――――――― *1977* ――――――――――――

Editorial Staff Manager: Effie Knight
Editorial Assistants: Jacqueline Bernero,
Christine Lundy, Maureen Leshendok

Library of Congress Cataloging in Publication Data

Main entry under title:

Festivals sourcebook.

    Includes indexes.
     1. Festivals--United States. 2. Festivals--
Canada. I. Wasserman, Paul. II. Herman, Esther.
III. Root, Elizabeth A.
GT4802.F47   394.2′0973   76-48852
ISBN 0-8103-0311-6

Table of Contents

Introduction

FESTIVALS SOURCEBOOK has been prepared to give a comprehensive overview of the myriad special occasions celebrated by the people of the United States and Canada in their local communities.

Directories of such events abound, but they tend to center upon specific types of events (such as religious or patriotic events), to cover a limited geographic area (seldom more than a single state), and/or to be limited chronologically to a single month or season. Our intention in the present work has been to provide a thorough compendium of details about recurring fairs, festivals, and community celebrations throughout the United States and Canada, and to organize the material so that several different approaches to the information in the book are possible.

The result of our efforts is a book of more than 3,800 entries covering events with a wide variety of focuses and occurring throughout the continent and throughout the year. This makes FESTIVALS SOURCEBOOK by far the largest collection of factual material in its field of which we are aware.

ARRANGEMENT AND FEATURES

The basic arrangement is by broad general subject with which the event is concerned, e.g., Agriculture, Antiques, Arts and Crafts, Community, Food and Drink, Music, etc.; there are 18 general categories in all.

FESTIVALS SOURCEBOOK features important aids for those who wish to take approaches other than through the broad general subject:

Chronological Index

Event Name Index, in which events are arranged alphabetically by official names

Geographic Index

Subject Index of more than 180 terms, pointing up event themes or subjects which are more narrow than, or in addition to, the 18 broad topics used in the basic organization of the book

Additional details about the book and how to take fullest advantage of the information it contains are given in the sections, "Organization of the Volume" (page ix) and "How to Use This Book" (page xi).

Each entry includes all the descriptive details available at the time of compilation. Thus, a full entry gives information about the name of the event; the geographic location where it takes place; the dates on which it is held; the frequency with which it occurs; the name and address or source of additional information; a description of precisely what transpires during the event; and the date the event was first held. When one or another of these details is not provided, the detail in question was not included in our source material.

RESEARCH SOURCES AND METHODS

The information in this volume has been gathered through a number of approaches, in order to assure coverage which is as nearly complete as the nature of the subject will allow and is as accurate and current as possible. Newspaper and magazine files, indexes, and numerous other sources have been exhaustively reviewed for leads to appropriate events warranting coverage. Hundreds of inquiries have been addressed to state and regional tourism agencies and other government bodies, travel groups, research organizations, trade associations, chambers of commerce, local coordinating bodies, and to subject experts.

Leads established by these and other means were utilized by sending questionnaires requesting information about specific individual events, and in most instances the facts provided are based upon questionnaires completed by the festival sponsors themselves, or from letters and brochures from the sponsors. In some few instances, in spite of repeated follow-ups, no information of any kind was received directly, and the details are based upon descriptions of events gathered from secondary sources.

Certain types of events have been deliberately omitted. For example, celebrations commonly held in virtually every community, such as the Fourth of July and Thanksgiving and their Canadian equivalents, are not covered, as a general practice; exceptions would be those instances where a community carries out a program of unusual scale or importance which far transcends the limits of local or regional concern.

In addition, sporting events, horse shows, county fairs (but not state fairs), holy days and other religious events, rodeos, and beauty pageants have also been left out. Some festivals related to these types of omitted events have, however, been included. Illustrations are the Festival of Roses (which precedes the Rose Bowl Game) and The 500 Festival (which precedes the Indianapolis 500 Memorial Day race).

NEW EDITIONS PLANNED

Despite the editors' intensive pursuit of pertinent information, however, there will doubtless be gaps and omissions even among those types of events the book is intended to cover. Festivals, fairs, and the like are growing ever more popular. New events are coming into being literally every week, and whatever cut-off date for inclusion is employed it is inevitable that newly founded events will evade the zeal of the compilers. Moreover, because the life cycle of many festivals is unpredictable, a number of the festivals described in the present work may no longer exist. Therefore, FESTIVALS SOURCEBOOK will be updated and modified in later editions, and the editors would be grateful to learn about any events which belong in the present work, but which may have been omitted, or which no longer exist and should be deleted from future editions. All suggestions and criticisms from users of the present work will be acknowledged and carefully considered.

We hope the size, scope, and adaptable arrangement of the book make it valuable to all those whose needs have been kept in mind during its preparation - travelers and travel agents, persons with special interests in specific subjects or general areas of activity, public relations and advertising executives, state and local tourism officials and other government executives, feature writers and other journalists, collectors of all kinds, and the many others who can be well served by specific, accurate information about worthwhile and interesting activities.

Just as future editions will benefit from the suggestions and criticisms of users, so the present book could not have been compiled without the cooperation and goodnatured support of innumerable individuals and organizations. Because the numbers are legion, it is not possible to do any more than gratefully acknowledge the assistance and cooperation provided by all those who courteously assisted in making available information about their activities and events. Special thanks are due the FESTIVALS SOURCEBOOK staff, whose names appear elsewhere, for their effort over the protracted period required to compile the book, and particular acknowledgement is due the effort of typists Jeanette Coughlin and Linda Stemmy.

Organization of the Volume

Festivals Sourcebook is composed of five sections:

SECTION I, FESTIVALS AND FAIRS, is the main section of the book. In this section, the recurring festivals, fairs and events are arranged alphabetically within major categories, and are described in serially numbered entries. Each entry includes the following facts, if they have been available:

> Subject – State (or Province) and City where held – Titles of festivals arranged alphabetically – Month of the year – Frequency – Duration – Specific location of event – Contact for further information – Description of the event – Year of origin

SECTION II, CHRONOLOGICAL LISTING OF EVENTS, is arranged by month when the events occur, with the festivals listed alphabetically under each state (or province), then the cities where they take place in parentheses and their entry numbers.

SECTION III, EVENT NAME INDEX, organizes the names of the festivals alphabetically, and includes entry numbers for each to facilitate their location in the main body of the text, Section I, Festivals and Fairs.

SECTION IV, GEOGRAPHIC INDEX, arranges entries by state (or province) and city, followed by the names of the festivals listed alphabetically and the numbers of their entries in Section I, Festivals and Fairs.

SECTION V, SUBJECT INDEX, is to be used for two purposes:

(1) To assist the user to locate festivals under subjects which are narrower than the broad topical subjects under which the main body of the book, Section I, Festivals and Fairs, is organized. An illustration is the subject, 'Jazz,' employed here in this index, compared to the heading 'Music' in Section I, Festivals and Fairs.

(2) Since many festivals cover several important topical themes, and because it is possible to list the festival in the main body of the book, Section I, Festivals and Fairs, under only one subject, this Subject Index provides alternate avenues of access to those festivals which cover more than one theme. As an example, Folk Festivals frequently have Arts and Crafts events as important components. While such events are found in the main body of the book, Section I, Festivals and Fairs, under 'Folk,' in this index the user will be led to the same events using the heading, 'Arts and Crafts.'

How To Use This Book

The content of this work may be approached in a number of ways:

1. To locate festivals on a particular subject:

    (a) Turn to the TABLE OF CONTENTS in order to check the broad headings used for grouping the events in Section I, FESTIVALS AND FAIRS. Then turn to that heading in Section I.

    (b) Refer also to Section V, SUBJECT INDEX. Here you will find alternate subject approaches to the content. Under each subject, festivals are identified. Using the entry numbers, turn to Section I, FESTIVALS AND FAIRS.

2. To find festivals during particular periods of the year:

    Turn to Section II, CHRONOLOGICAL LISTING OF EVENTS, where the festivals are organized by month of the year under each state (or province), with the city where they are held given in parentheses, followed by entry numbers.

3. To locate full details about a particular festival when the name of the festival is known:

    Turn to Section III, EVENT NAME INDEX, which is an alphabetically arranged listing of all of the names of festivals included in the book. In those instances where a name is a very common one, as for example, 'Art Festival,' the city and state (or province) in which the festival is held is also listed before the identifying number.

4. To identify festivals which are held in particular places:

    Turn to Section IV, GEOGRAPHIC INDEX, where the order of listing is under state (or province), and then under city. Under each city there is an alphabetical listing of each festival held there with its identifying number.

> All the festivals are identified in this book by entry number, rather than by page number.

SECTION I
FESTIVALS AND FAIRS

FESTIVALS AND FAIRS

Agriculture
(Includes Flowers and Forest)
See also: STATE FAIRS

ALABAMA

★ 1 ★
Clanton – CHILTON COUNTY PEACH FESTIVAL.
June, 3 days. Contact: Bureau of Publicity,
State of Alabama, Montgomery, Alabama 36104.

Parade, barbeque, selection of Peach Queen,
auction, and selection of prize peaches.

★ 2 ★
Dothan – NATIONAL PEANUT FESTIVAL. Mid
October (third week), annual, 1 week, Houston
County Farm Center. Contact: Mr. John Powell,
Executive Director, National Peanut Festival, Post
Office Box 976, Dothan, Alabama 36301.

Salute to the peanut. Parades, carnival and fair,
beauty pageant, exhibits, concerts, annual Greased
Pig and Calf Scramble, sports events, peanut
recipe contests.

★ 3 ★
Mobile – AZALEA TRAIL FESTIVAL. March,
annual. Contact: Mobile Area Chamber of
Commerce, Post Office Box 2187, Mobile, Alabama
36601.

Tours and festivities celebrate the blooming of
Mobile's azaleas; last week in March is the setting
for the annual America's Junior Miss Pageant.

ARIZONA

★ 4 ★
Phoenix – OLD-FASHIONED HARVEST FESTIVAL.
November (Thanksgiving day), 3 days, Pioneer
Living Museum. Contact: Phoenix Chamber of
Commerce, 805 North Second Street, Phoenix,
Arizona 85004.

Thanksgiving Day celebration in this restored community with a pioneer farm and descriptions of the
life of early settlers. 1800's ambience.

ARKANSAS

★ 5 ★
Clarksville – PEACH FESTIVAL. June. Contact:

Chamber of Commerce, Clarksville, Arkansas 72830;
or Department of Parks and Tourism, 149 State Capitol, Little Rock, Arkansas 72201.

In celebration of the peach crop.

★ 6 ★
Hope – WATERMELON FESTIVAL. August, 1 day.
Contact: Chamber of Commerce, Hope, Arkansas
71601; or Department of Parks and Tourism, 149
State Capitol, Little Rock, Arkansas 72201.

Lots of fun while eating delicious local watermelons.

★ 7 ★
Marshall – STRAWBERRY FESTIVAL. May.
Contact: Chamber of Commerce, Marshall,
Arkansas 72650; or Department of Parks and
Tourism, 149 State Capitol, Little Rock, Arkansas
72201.

Festival celebrating the harvesting of the luscious
strawberry.

★ 8 ★
Nashville – SOUTHWEST ARKANSAS POULTRY
FESTIVAL. May, 1 day. Contact: Chamber of
Commerce, Nashville, Arkansas 71852; or Depart-
ment of Parks and Tourism, 149 State Capitol, Little
Rock, Arkansas 72201.

Festival celebrating the local poultry industry.

★ 9 ★
Springdale – NORTHWEST ARKANSAS POULTRY
FESTIVAL. Mid April. Contact: Northwest
Arkansas Poultry Festival, Executive Vice-President,
Box 166-700 West Emma, Springdale, Arkansas
72764.

Chicken dishes, cooking contest, and barbeques to
celebrate the local poultry farming.

★ 10 ★
Tontitown – TONTITOWN GRAPE FESTIVAL. Mid
August, annual, 3 days. Contact: Chamber of
Commerce, Tontitown, Arkansas 72770.

Festival with grape-judging, dancing, food, and
entertainment.

Agriculture

ARKANSAS (Continued)

★ 11 ★

Warren - PINK TOMATO. Mid June, 3 days. Contact: Chamber of Commerce, 206 North Myrtle, Warren, Arkansas 71671.

All- tomato luncheon, exhibits, and other events highlight this festival.

CALIFORNIA

★ 12 ★

Arroyo Grande - HARVEST FESTIVAL. Early October, 3 days. Contact: California Chamber of Commerce, 455 Capitol Mall, Sacramento, California 95814.

A parade and a carnival are included among the festive events in this seasonal celebration.

★ 13 ★

Beaumont - CHERRY FESTIVAL. Mid June, annual, 5 days. Contact: California Chamber of Commerce, 455 Capitol Mall, Sacramento, California 95814.

A parade, carnival, horse show, art and crafts, dance, and a barbeque to celebrate the harvesting of the cherry crop. The public is invited to pick cherries in the fields and participate in a cherry pie-eating contest.

★ 14 ★

Blythe - CANTALOUPE FESTIVAL. April or May, 4 days. Contact: Chamber of Commerce, Blythe, California 92225; or California Chamber of Commerce, 455 Capitol Mall, Sacramento, California 95814.

Carnival, horse show, civic exhibits, and a parade highlight this celebration in honor of the local crop of cantaloupes.

★ 15 ★

Carmel Valley - FESTIVAL OF THE GRAPE. November, 1 day, Carmel Valley Inn. Contact: Monterey Peninsula Chamber of Commerce and Visitors and Convention Bureau, Post Office Box 1770, Monterey, California 93940.

A traditional festival honoring the grape crop and the wines produced from it.

★ 16 ★

Carpinteria - FLOWER FESTIVAL. Late June, annual, 2 days. Contact: California Chamber of Commerce, 455 Capitol Mall, Sacramento, California 95814.

A variety of flowers are on display and on sale at this community festival.

★ 17 ★

Cloverdale - CITRUS FAIR AND PARADE. Mid February, 4 days, Citrus Pavilion, Fairgrounds. Contact: Chamber of Commerce Office, Owl Plaza on U.S. 101, Cloverdale, California 95425; or Redwood Empire Association, Visitors Information Center, 476 Post Street, San Francisco, California 94102.

Exhibits of arts and crafts, flowers, citrus products, and parade through downtown. The citrus exhibits are often rather fanciful. The fair has a theme each year, but it is always a Western-style legacy of fun.

★ 18 ★

Dinuba - NATIONAL RAISIN FESTIVAL. September or October, annual, 1 week. Contact: California Chamber of Commerce, 455 Capitol Mall, Sacramento, California 95814.

Parade featuring local high school bands and floats from nearby communities. Coronation of queen, barbeque, raisin pie-baking contest, carnival, games, food booths, and art festival. Established for the purpose of bolstering the raisin industry. Begun in 1911.

★ 19 ★

Eureka - RHODODENDRON FESTIVAL. Late April-early May, annual, 9 days. Contact: Information Officer, State of California Department of Commerce, 1400 Tenth Avenue, Sacramento, California 95814; or Eureka Chamber of Commerce, 2112 Broadway, Eureka, California 95501.

Arts and crafts exhibits, horsepitching, bowling and swimming tournaments, Rhododendron Ball, crowning of a floral queen, horse show, and gymkhana. Open house aboard a navy ship, rhododendron parade, and yacht race. Exhibits of native Indian artifacts; ballet and concert performances, a car rally, appearances by the U.S. Army parachute team, square-dance hoe-down, a dairy princess contest, a Scout-o-Rama, and various sports contests. Begun around 1968.

CALIFORNIA (Continued)

★ 20 ★
Garden Grove - STRAWBERRY FESTIVAL. Late May (Memorial Day Weekend), annual, 4 days, Euclid Park. Contact: Garden Grove Strawberry Festival Association, Post Office Box 464, Garden Grove, California 92642.

Strawberry recipe contest, strawberry pie eating contest, cutting of the "World's Largest Strawberry Shortcake", a parade, a celebrity autograph breakfast, and a Miss Garden Grove Beauty Pageant highlight this four day festival to raise funds for civic organizations. Largest community sponsored event in the western states.

★ 21 ★
Holtville - CARROT FESTIVAL. Late January-early February, annual, 10 days. Contact: Chamber of Commerce, Secretary/Manager, Fifth and Holt, Post Office Box 185, Holtville, California 92250.

Events include Carrot Queen contest, Queen's coronation, Carrot Festival Ball, gymkhana show, carrot recipe cooking contest, carrot carnival, fine arts show, arts and crafts fair, and student art contest. Festival parade with drill units, bands, equestrian, and marching units. 4-H and FAA livestock competition, tractor pulling contest, watermelon eating contest, and races. Begun around 1947.

★ 22 ★
Indio - NATIONAL DATE FESTIVAL. Mid February, 10 days, Date Garden Grounds. Contact: Information Officer, State of California Department of Commerce, 1400 Tenth Street, Sacramento, California 95814.

Celebration of the date harvest. Citizens dress up in Arab costumes. Arts and crafts carnival, horse show, ostrich and camel races. Nightly performances of The Tale of the Camel Herder's Daughter. Date and citrus exhibitions, flower and garden displays, and gem and mineral shows.

★ 23 ★
Julian - WILDFLOWER SHOW AND ART MART. May (usually 2nd and 3rd week), annual, 16 days, Community Hall. Contact: Southern California Visitors Council, 705 West Seventh Street, Los Angeles, California 90017; or Chamber of Commerce, Post Office Box 413, Julian, California 92036.

Every day the citizens of Julian gather fresh wildflowers

from the deserts and mountains of the area to put on display in the show. There is also a sale of artwork.

★ 24 ★
La Habra - LA HABRA CORN FESTIVAL. Early August, 2 days. Contact: Chamber of Commerce, La Habra, California 90631; or California Chamber of Commerce, 455 Capitol Mall, Sacramento, California 95814.

A carnival and a parade highlight this tribute to an important local crop.

★ 25 ★
Lancaster - ANTELOPE VALLEY FAIR AND ALFALFA FESTIVAL. Early September, annual, 2 days. Contact: California Chamber of Commerce, 455 Capitol Mall, Sacramento, California 95814.

Carnival, art and crafts, and horse show. Begun around 1943.

★ 26 ★
Lompoc - LOMPOC VALLEY FLOWER FESTIVAL. Late June, annual, 3 days. Contact: Lompoc Valley Chamber of Commerce, 119 East Cypress Avenue, Lompoc, California 93436.

A flower parade, flower show, arts and crafts, barbeque, carnival, horse show, and tours of flower fields.

★ 27 ★
Napa - GRAPE FESTIVAL. Late August, 3 days. Contact: Redwood Empire Association, Visitors Information Center, 476 Post Street, San Francisco, California 94102.

This celebration reflects importance of the grape harvest in this wine producing area.

★ 28 ★
Palmdale - LILAC FESTIVAL. Early April, annual, 2 days. Contact: Southern California Visitors Council, 705 West Seventh Street, Los Angeles, California 90017.

Art show and gem and mineral show in addition to lilac and other floral exhibits.

Agriculture

CALIFORNIA (Continued)

★ 29 ★
Ripon - ALMOND BLOSSOM FESTIVAL. Late
February-early March, 3 days. Contact: Chamber
of Commerce, Ripon, California 95366; or California
Chamber of Commerce, 455 Capitol Mall, Sacramento,
California 95814.

Pancake breakfast, carnival, and two parades highlight
the events of this celebration celebrating the almond
blossoms.

★ 30 ★
Ross - FALL FLOWER FESTIVAL. Late October,
2 days, Marin Art and Garden Center. Contact:
Marin County Chamber of Commerce and Visitors
Bureau, 824 Fifth Avenue, Ross, California 94957.

Traditional festivities in honor of the season and the
flowers.

★ 31 ★
Sacramento - CAMELLIA FESTIVAL. Late February-
early March, annual, 10 days. Contact: Camellia
Festival Association, 724 J Street, Room 101,
Sacramento, California 95814.

Events include Queen's Presentation Breakfast,
Camellia Days at Country Club Plaza (two days), tennis
tournament, Camellia Ball, airport pin-on days, annual
camellia show (begun in 1923), international exhibits,
photographic exhibition, senior citizens day, Macy's
flower show, luncheon, slide show, babies' day,
cheer-up day, parade, ballet, regatta, folkdance
festival and pageant, theme and honored nation,
100-mile marathon and golf tourney. Begun around
1955.

★ 32 ★
San Bernardino - NATIONAL ORANGE SHOW.
Mid March, annual, 11 days. Contact: Southern
California Visitors Council, 705 West Seventh Street,
Los Angeles, California 90017.

Exhibits of many fruits in addition to oranges, including lemons, limes, grapefruit, kumquats and
pomelos. In addition, there are art shows, flower
shows, 4-H fairs, rodeos, queen coronation, rides,
stage entertainment, and livestock exhibits. 61st
in 1976. (Started in 1911, not held during war
years.)

★ 33 ★
San Diego - CARNATION FESTIVAL AND STARVING
ARTISTS' SHOW. June-July, annual, 4 days,
Horton Plaza. Contact: Central City Association,
707 Broadway, Suite 631, San Diego, California
92101.

Display and sale of arts and crafts. Carnations,
the official city flower, are given away on the city
street corners. Begun around 1965.

★ 34 ★
San Gabriel - STEWART'S ORCHID FESTIVAL.
Early April, annual, 4 days, Stewart's Orchids.
Contact: Southern California Visitors Council, 705
West Seventh Street, Los Angeles, California 90017.

A large display of various types of orchids with information on how to grow this lovely flower.

★ 35 ★
San Rafael - GRAPE FESTIVAL. Early October,
annual, 1 day. Contact: Marin County Chamber
of Commerce and Visitors Bureau, 824 Fifth Avenue,
San Rafael, California 94901.

Entertainment, food and drink, handmade and homemade products for sale, and games and prizes for
children. Begun around 1900.

★ 36 ★
Santa Rosa - LUTHER BURBANK ROSE FESTIVAL.
Mid May, 3 days. Contact: Information Officer,
State of California Department of Commerce, 1400
Tenth Avenue, Sacramento, California 95814.

Parade, art and flower shows, tennis tournament,
folkdancing, horse show, boating regattas, and a
carnival throughout the city in celebration of the
Luther Burbank rose.

★ 37 ★
Sebastopol - APPLE BLOSSOM FESTIVAL. Early
April, annual, 3 days. Contact: Information
Officer, State of California Department of Commerce,
1400 Tenth Street, Sacramento, California 95814.

Featuring a drive-yourself tour through blossoming
orchards and a barbeque, Saturday parade, horse
show, and folk dance.

CALIFORNIA (Continued)

★ 38 ★
Sebastopol - APPLE FAIR. August. Contact:
Redwood Empire Association, Visitors Information
Center, 476 Post Street, San Francisco, California
94102.

A community gathering to pay tribute to the important crop of the area.

★ 39 ★
Shafter - POTATO AND COTTON FESTIVAL. Mid
May, annual, 2-3 days. Contact: Chamber of
Commerce, Post Office Box 1088, Shafter, California
93263.

A parade, a barbeque, arts and crafts shows, a
carnival, old-timers day, and a whiskerino highlight
this festival honoring the potato and cotton crop.

★ 40 ★
Smith River - EASTER IN JULY LILY FESTIVAL.
July, 2 days. Contact: Redwood Empire Associations, 476 Post Street, San Francisco, California
94102.

Dance, sun rise service, pancake breakfast, floral
displays and art exhibits (both judged), games,
music, handicraft display, logging show, and 'Ecology
Dive'.

★ 41 ★
South Gate - SOUTH GATE AZALEA FESTIVAL.
Mid March, 10 days, Civic Auditorium. Contact:
Southern California Visitors Council, 705 West
Seventh Street, Los Angeles, California 90017.

Different events every night, including Hobby Night,
Musicale Night, and Art Night.

★ 42 ★
Temple City - CAMELLIA FESTIVAL. Late February
(last weekend), annual, 3 days. Contact: Camellia
Festival of Temple City, 5827 North Temple City
Boulevard, Temple City, California 91780.

A camellia court is chosen from among youngsters in
the first grade, and school children pull flower floats
of their own design and decoration in a parade. A
theme is chosen for each year. The festival was
founded in recognition of the importance of family
life. No commercially produced or motor driven
floats are allowed in the parade. Prizes are awarded,
and entertainers act as grand marshals. Coronation

Ball. Begun around 1945.

★ 43 ★
Three Rivers - THREE RIVERS REDBUD FESTIVAL.
Early April, 2 days. Contact: Southern California
Visitors Council, 705 West Seventh Street, Los
Angeles, California 90017.

Display of red bud trees, arts, crafts, photography,
woodworking, needlework, and baked goods.

★ 44 ★
Wasco - WASCO FESTIVAL OF ROSES. Early
September, 4 days, Wasco Veterans Memorial Building.
Contact: Wasco Festival of Roses, Incorporated, Post
Office Box 220, Wasco, California 93280.

Events include a pageant, parade, barbeque, art and
crafts, dancing, tours, rose show, art show, free rose
tour, queen pageant, and square dancing. Trophies
awarded for parade, roses, and art show.

★ 45 ★
Wilmington - WISTERIA FESTIVAL. Early April,
annual, 1 day, Banning House. Contact: California
Chamber of Commerce, 455 Capitol Mall, Sacramento,
California 95814.

In addition to the floral displays, this celebration includes exhibition of antique cars and reenactment of
four Civil War battles. Begun around 1951.

COLORADO

★ 46 ★
Carbondale - POTATO DAYS. Mid October,
annual, Town Park. Contact: Community Chamber
of Commerce, Box 427, Carbondale, Colorado 81623.

A typical western style celebration of the end of the
potato crop. Celebration includes a parade, picnic,
etc.

★ 47 ★
Denver - NATIONAL WESTERN STOCK SHOW
FESTIVAL. January (3rd week), 9 days. Contact:
Willard Sims, National Western Stock Show, 1325
East 46th Avenue, Denver, Colorado 80216.

Prize livestock are on display such as cattle, hogs,
horses, rabbits and sheep. Entertainment includes
western music performances. Rodeo events include
steer wrestling, barrel jumping and bull riding.

Agriculture

COLORADO (Continued)

There is an award for the Livestock's Man of the
Year. Begun around 1906.

★ 48 ★
Glenwood Springs - STRAWBERRY DAYS CELEBRATION,
Late June, 2 days. Contact: Chamber of Commerce,
1102 Grand Avenue, Box 97, Glenwood Springs,
Colorado 81601.

Square dances, strawberries, rodeo, parade, etc.,
highlight this festival honoring the local crop. Begun around 1899.

CONNECTICUT

★ 49 ★
Bristol - CHRYSANTHEMUM FESTIVAL. Late
September-mid October, 3 weeks. Contact: Bristol
Chamber of Commerce, 81 Main Street, Bristol,
Connecticut 06010.

Paintings, drawings, graphics, and sculpture are on
display and for sale during this festival honoring
the blooming of the chrysanthemums.

★ 50 ★
Durham - CONNECTICUT AGRICULTURAL FAIR.
Late July, 3 days, Durham Fairgrounds. Contact:
Marion W. Beecher, Winchester Center, Durham,
Connecticut 06094.

Cattle-drawing, horse-drawing, professional entertainment, pony-drawing, livestock show, poultry
show, midway, fiddler contest, farm machinery
exhibits, photo and art show, horse show, agricultural
and commercial exhibits, and crowning of fair queen.

★ 51 ★
Fairfield - ANNUAL DOGWOOD FESTIVAL. Mid
May-June, annual, 12 days, Greenfield Hill. Con-
tact: Connecticut Department of Commerce, 210
Washington Street, Hartford, Connecticut 06106.

Amateur musicians entertain at this festival honoring
the blooming of the dogwood trees.

★ 52 ★
Southington - APPLE HARVEST FESTIVAL. Early
October, annual, 9 days. Contact: Connecticut
Department of Commerce, 210 Washington Street,
Hartford, Connecticut 06106.

A community event in honor of the apple crop.
There is an art show in conjunction with this festival.

DISTRICT OF COLUMBIA

★ 53 ★
Washington, D.C. - INTERNATIONAL BONSAI
CONVENTION. Mid July, 2 days. Contact:
James R. Newton, Post Office Box 28308, Washing-
ton, D.C. 20005.

Events include exhibits and lectures on bonsai trees.

★ 54 ★
Washington, D.C. - NATIONAL CHERRY BLOSSOM
FESTIVAL. Early April, annual, 1 week, Tidal
Basin and elsewhere. Contact: National Cherry
Blossom Festival, 1616 K Street, Northwest, Wash-
ington, D.C. 20006.

The festival is an annual event held in early April,
when the cherry blossoms are in bloom, under the
sponsorship of the Washington Convention and Visitors
Bureau. Programs are held out of doors at the
Washington Monument Grounds; the musical portion
of the programs include performances by 53 high
school bands and bands of the military service. A
parade includes floats, bands, and marching units
from around the country, as well as the cherry blossom
princesses. Founded in 1934.

★ 55 ★
Washington, D.C. - SPRING FLOWER FESTIVAL.
Late April-early May, annual, 6 days, U.S. Botanic
Gardens. Contact: U.S. Botanic Gardens, First
and Canal Streets, Southwest, Washington, D.C.
20024.

The Ikebana International, Washington Chapter,
welcomes spring in the Japanese tradition with the
cultural arts of Japan. There are exhibits of
authentic Japanese gardens, bonsai, Japanese dancing,
calligraphy, and music. Ikebana, the art of flower
arranging, is demonstrated as well as on display.
Begun around 1958.

FLORIDA

★ 56 ★
Chipley - PANHANDLE WATERMELON FESTIVAL.
Late June (4th weekend), annual, 2 days. Contact:
Walker Hughen, Chipley, Florida 32428.

Honors watermelon growers of the area. Begins with
a street dance, parade, horse show, and a variety

FLORIDA (Continued)

of children's contests such as seed spitting, pole climbing, etc. Following watermelon auction and awards for largest melons, a queen and junior queen are selected.

★ 57 ★

Inverness - CITRUS COUNTY FAIR. Mid March, 6 days. Contact: Quentin Medlin, Courthouse, Inverness, Florida 32650.

A fair celebrating the citrus crop, the most important of the area.

★ 58 ★

Miami - ROYAL POINCIANA FIESTA. Mid June, annual. Contact: Howard Berger, Miami-Metro News Bureau, 499 Biscayne Boulevard, Miami, Florida 33132.

Salute to the flaming red Royal Poinciana trees. Concerts, parade and selection of the Royal Poinciana Queen, tours and distribution of seedlings.

★ 59 ★

Monticello - JEFFERSON COUNTY WATERMELON FESTIVAL. Late June, annual, 10 days. Contact: Watermelon Festival Association, Post Office Box 401, Monticello, Florida 32344.

Watermelon queen contest, parade and watermelon eating and seed spitting contest, big melon contest, arts and crafts show, horse show, golf tournament, country-western show, and a canoe race.

★ 60 ★

Palatka - AZALEA FESTIVAL. March (first weekend), annual, 3 days, Ravine Gardens State Park. Contact: Gregg Barnard, Post Office Drawer 1358, Palatka, Florida 32077.

A parade, talent contest, beauty contest, three day golf tournament, skeet shoot, and art show highlight this festival honoring the blooming azaleas.

★ 61 ★

Perry - FLORIDA FOREST FESTIVAL. October, annual. Contact: Jim Southerland, c/o Buckeye Cellulose Corporation, Perry, Florida 32347.

Honors Florida's forest industry. Miss Universe, Miss Florida and the Forest Capitol Queen are selected during a beauty pageant. What is billed as the

'world's largest free fish fry' is held at Forest Capitol Park, following the King Tree Parade. Educational exhibits on forestry. Adult and teen dances, Southeastern Chainsaw Championship and forest ecology programs.

★ 62 ★

Plant City - FLORIDA STRAWBERRY FESTIVAL. Early March, annual, 6 days. Contact: Louise Gibbs, Post Office Box 832, Plant City, Florida 33566.

Held in conjunction with the Hillsborough County Fair. Marks the height of the strawberry season. Grand parade, strawberry cookoff, beauty contest, outdoor shows, diaper derby, national horseshoe pitching contests, and coronation of the Strawberry Queen.

★ 63 ★

Starke - STRAWBERRY FESTIVAL. Late March-early April. Contact: John Meyers, Bradford County Fair Association, Post Office Box 116, Starke, Florida 32091.

At the height of the strawberry harvest season, presented in conjunction with the Bradford County Fair. Highlights include the selection of a Strawberry Queen and the Strawberry Invitational Golf Tournament. Exhibits and strawberries.

★ 64 ★

Winter Haven - FLORIDA CITRUS FESTIVAL. Mid February, annual, 1 week. Contact: Robert Eastman, Florida Citrus Showcase, 100 Cypress Gardens Boulevard, Winter Haven, Florida 33880.

Citrus Invitational golf tournament, citrus parade, citrus queen pageant, citrus queen coronation, fruitmen's dinner and governor's citrus luncheon. The Florida citrus showcase presents a comprehensive picture of the citrus industry with special exhibits during the festival week. The Florida Citrus Exposition was organized in 1924 and became the Florida Citrus Showcase in 1965.

GEORGIA

★ 65 ★

Albany - NATIONAL PECAN FESTIVAL. Mid September, 3 days. Contact: Georgia Department of Community Development, Tourist Division, Post Office Box 38097, Atlanta, Georgia 30334.

The city of Albany plays host to the many who celebrate

Agriculture

GEORGIA (Continued)

in honor of the pecan, a crop for which Georgia is widely known.

★ 66 ★
Atlanta - DOGWOOD FESTIVAL. Early April, annual, 9 days. Contact: Atlanta Dogwood Festival, Post Office Box 13996, Station K, Atlanta, Georgia 30324.

Events include official daytime tours of Atlanta, arts and music festival, arts and crafts festival, open gardens, juried art show, flower show, Oriental art exhibit, fashion shows, country fair, farmer's market, gems and minerals show, theatrical performances, antiques, antique cars, and a parade.

★ 67 ★
Blakely - EARLY COUNTY FAIR AND PEANUT FESTIVAL. Early October, 5 days, American Legion Field. Contact: Georgia Department of Community Development, Tourist Division, Post Office Box 38097, Atlanta, Georgia 30334.

A traditional community fair with special emphasis on the important local crop - the peanut.

★ 68 ★
Cordele - WATERMELON FESTIVAL. Early July, annual, 3 days. Contact: Georgia Department of Community Development, Tourist Division, Post Office, Box 38097, Atlanta, Georgia 30334.

In celebration of the watermelon crop, traditional festivities.

★ 69 ★
Cornelia - APPLE HARVEST FESTIVAL. August-September, 3 days. Contact: Georgia Department of Community Development, Tourist Division, Post Office Box 38097, Atlanta, Georgia 30334.

The town of Cornelia pays tribute to the harvesting of the apple - an important local crop.

★ 70 ★
Ellijay - GEORGIA APPLE FESTIVAL. Mid August, 6 days. Contact: Georgia Department of Community Development, Tourist Division, Post Office Box 38097, Atlanta, Georgia 30334.

A gala celebration which pays tribute to the apple harvest.

★ 71 ★
Ocilla - SWEET POTATO FESTIVAL. Mid November, 1 day. Contact: First State Bank of Ocilla, Post Office Box 65, Ocilla, Georgia 31774.

Sweet potato cooking contests, parades, and other events in celebration of the harvest of an important local crop.

★ 72 ★
Smyrna - JONQUIL FESTIVAL. Mid April, 6 days. Contact: Georgia Department of Community Development, Tourist Division, Post Office Box 38097, Atlanta, Georgia 30334.

A community event celebrating the beauty of the jonquils which are in bloom.

★ 73 ★
Stone Mountain - YELLOW DAISY FESTIVAL. Mid September, annual, 3 days, Stone Mountain Park, centered around Coliseum grounds. Contact: Director of Special Events, Stone Mountain Park, Post Office Box 778, Stone Mountain, Georgia 30083.

Arts, crafts, bluegrass music, a standard flower show, American folk dancing, and bluegrass contest. Begun around 1968.

★ 74 ★
Thomasville - ROSE FESTIVAL. Late April, annual, 7 days. Contact: Thomasville Chamber of Commerce, Post Office Box 560, 401 South Broad Street, Thomasville, Georgia 31792.

Thomasville is nicknamed the "City of Roses" for its more than 25,000 rosebushes planted in public places, plus those planted in the yards and gardens of the residents. The south's largest rose show is augmented by plantation tours, parades and a beauty pageant. Sporting events include a horse show and golf tournament. Air shows and music concerts complete the entertainment. Begun in 1922.

★ 75 ★
Waycross - FOREST FESTIVAL. Early May, annual, 1 day, Laura Walker State Park. Contact: Georgia Department of Community Development, Tourist Division, Post Office Box 38097, Atlanta, Georgia 30334.

A celebration of the beauty and wealth of the forests. Begun around 1958.

GEORGIA (Continued)

★ 76 ★
Winterville - MARIGOLD FESTIVAL DAY.   Mid
June, 1 day, Town Square.   Contact: Georgia
Department of Community Development, Tourist
Division, Post Office Box 38097, Atlanta, Georgia
30334.

In celebration of the magnificent marigold, traditional
community festivities.

HAWAII

★ 77 ★
Honolulu - STATE FARM FAIR.   June-July, annual,
11 days.   Contact: Hawaii Visitors Bureau, Honolulu,
Hawaii 96815.

Hawaii International Center Agricultural exhibits, and
country market.   Begun in 1974.

★ 78 ★
Kailua - KONA COFFEE FESTIVAL.   Early Novem-
ber, 4 days.   Contact: Hawaii Visitors Bureau,
Special Events Department, Honolulu, Hawaii 96815.

Pageantry and programs celebrating Hawaii's coffee
capitol and featuring ethnic attractions such as
dances, music, arts and crafts, food. International
bazaar, Polynesian entertainment, coffee products,
queen contest, flowers, bon dancing, coffee recipe
contest, Kona Coffee Blossom Ball, queen's breakfast,
and lantern parade.

IDAHO

★ 79 ★
Deary - STRAWBERRY FESTIVAL.   Mid June (second
week).   Contact: Chamber of Commerce, Deary,
Idaho 83823.

Parade, strawberry shortcake luncheon, dances, old-
time fiddlers' contest, cowboy breakfast and other
events in honor of the local strawberry corp.

★ 80 ★
Emmett - CHERRY FESTIVAL AND SQUAW BUTTE
ROCKHOUNDS.   Late June, 6 days.   Contact:
Chamber of Commerce, 114 North Hays, Emmett,
Idaho 83617.

Saturday parade, square dancing, potluck supper, and
rock show, in honor of the cherry-picking season.

★ 81 ★
Kendrick - LOCUST BLOSSOM FESTIVAL (KENDRICK-
JULIAETTA LOCUST BLOSSOM FESTIVAL).   May
(last Saturday), 1 day.   Contact: Tom Cox, Kendrick,
Idaho 83537.

Parade, races, beef barbeque, old-time fiddlers' contest, dancing, and community get-together.   Also a
picnic lunch, gymkhana show, kids' sack race, flower
show, band concerts, and dance in the evening.   Begun around 1966.

ILLINOIS

★ 82 ★
Barry - APPLE FESTIVAL.   Early October, 3 days,
City Park.   Contact: The Division of Tourism,
Illinois Department of Business and Economic Develop-
ment, 222 South College Street, Springfield, Illinois
62706.

A community celebration at the time of the apple
harvest.

★ 83 ★
Carmi - CORN DAY FESTIVAL.   October, annual,
1 day.   Contact: The Division of Tourism, Illinois
Department of Business and Economic Development,
222 South College Street, Springfield, Illinois 62706.

Corn dishes and many activities highlight this community festival.

★ 84 ★
Cobden - PEACH FESTIVAL.   Mid August, 2 days,
Cobden Ball Park.   Contact: The Division of Tour-
ism, Illinois Department of Business and Economic
Development, 222 South College Street, Springfield,
Illinois 62706.

A host of activities including peach-eating contests.

★ 85 ★
Davis Junction - STEAM AND HORSE POWER
THRESHING SHOW.   Early August, 4 days.   Contact: Chamber of Commerce, Davis Junction, Illinois
61020.

Exhibitions of farm work as performed by steam and
horse-powered antique machinery.

★ 86 ★
Dixon - PETUNIA FESTIVAL.   Early July (associated
with the 4th), annual, 4 days.   Contact: Dixon

Agriculture

ILLINOIS (Continued)

Chamber of Commerce, 74 Galena Avenue, Dixon, Illinois 61021.

Carnival midway, concert, cook-out contests, dances, trail ride, inter-faith sunrise service, parade, drum and bugle corps competition, fireworks, variety show, and N.T.P.A. tractor pull. Begun around 1965.

★ 87 ★
Farmer City - SOYBEAN FESTIVAL. Early September, 2 days. Contact: The Division of Tourism, Illinois Department of Business and Economic Development, 222 South College Street, Springfield, Illinois 62706.

A traditional community celebration which pays tribute to the importance of the soybean crop in this area.

★ 88 ★
Freeport - STEPHENSON COUNTY ANTIQUE ENGINE CLUBS STEAM THRESHING SHOW AND ANTIQUE DISPLAY. Late July, annual, 3 days, Fairgrounds. Contact: The Division of Tourism, Illinois Department of Business and Economic Development, 222 South College Street, Springfield, Illinois 62706.

Numerous large steam traction engines and gas tractors on display. Dozens of gas engines, farm machinery and household antiques on display. Antique tractor pull. Parade sponsored by the Stephenson County Antique Engine Club.

★ 89 ★
Hoopeston - NATIONAL SWEET CORN FESTIVAL. Late August, 5 days, McFerren Park. Contact: The Division of Tourism, Illinois Department of Business and Economic Development, 222 South College Street, Springfield, Illinois 62706.

A celebration reflecting the importance of the corn harvest in the area.

★ 90 ★
Kewanee - HOG FESTIVAL. Late August, 3 days. Contact: The Division of Tourism, Illinois Department of Business and Economic Development, 222 South College Street, Springfield, Illinois 62706.

A pigtail contest, barbeque, and Model T Races highlight this "down home" celebration.

★ 91 ★
Lombard - LILAC FESTIVAL. May, annual, 16 days. Contact: The Division of Tourism, Illinois Department of Business and Economic Development, 222 South College Street, Springfield, Illinois 62706.

The crowning of a queen, flowering parade, and a Lilac Ball are included in the events of this festival honoring the lilac.

★ 92 ★
Mendota - SWEET CORN FESTIVAL. Mid August, annual, 3 days. Contact: The Division of Tourism, Illinois Department of Business and Economic Development, 222 South College Street, Springfield, Illinois 62706.

Crowning of a festival queen, parade, carnival, and free sweet corn are the highlights of this festival in honor of the local crop.

★ 93 ★
Morton - PUMPKIN FESTIVAL. Mid September, annual, 4 days, Downtown area. Contact: The Division of Tourism, Illinois Department of Business and Economic Development, 222 South College Street, Springfield, Illinois 62706.

A giant pumpkin contest, a pumpkin queen pageant, parade, free entertainment, carnival, pumpkin pie eating contest, pumpkin cookery awards, flower and garden, and art shows.

★ 94 ★
Mount Vernon - SWEETCORN-WATERMELON FESTIVAL. Late August, 4 days. Contact: The Division of Tourism, Illinois Department of Business and Economic Development, 222 South College Street, Springfield, Illinois 62706.

A combination festival honoring two important local crops.

★ 95 ★
Murphysboro - APPLE FESTIVAL. Mid September, annual, 4 days, Courthouse square. Contact: The Division of Tourism, Illinois Department of Business and Economic Development, 222 South College Street, Springfield, Illinois 62706.

A carnival, apple peeling contest, parade, drum corps competition, various entertainments, and crowning of the Apple Festival Queen. Begun around 1952.

ILLINOIS (Continued)

★ 96 ★
Newton - WILD FOODS FESTIVAL. Mid May, 2
days, Sam Parr State Park. Contact: Illinois Department of Conservation, Division of Parks and
Memorials, Program Services Section, Springfield,
Illinois 62706.

Edible plant identification tours, a workshop highlighting preparation of these plants, and tours giving
information on the use of medicinal herbs and plants.

★ 97 ★
Pekin - MARIGOLD FESTIVAL. Late August, 5
days, Sunset Plaza. Contact: The Division of
Tourism, Illinois Department of Business and Economic
Development, 222 South College Street, Springfield,
Illinois 62706.

Crowning of a Marigold Queen, a carnival, a parade,
speech contests, foot races, street bazaar, 3 separate
art fairs, an evening of music, a day in the park, an
auto show, and Marigold Ball.

★ 98 ★
Quincy - DOGWOOD FESTIVAL. Early May,
annual, 3 days. Contact: The Division of Tourism,
Illinois Department of Business and Economic Development, 222 South College Street, Springfield, Illinois
62706.

Events include a mini-parade, several auctions, bicycling events, a Mini-500 tricycle race, the Dogwood Grand Prix of Go-Karts and the Dogwood Ball.
Begun around 1970.

★ 99 ★
Sycamore - PUMPKIN FESTIVAL. Late October,
annual, 7 days, Court House lawn. Contact:
Sycamore Pumpkin Festival Committee, George
Beasley, 139 Sacramento, Sycamore, Illinois 60178.

Pumpkin decorating contest. Pumpkins are carved,
painted, etc., and the entrants are displayed on the
Court House lawn. Giant Halloween Parade includes
high school and military bands, queen's and princesses,
kids in wild costumes, spook house, flea market, and
farmers market, pumpkin pie eating and baking contest.

★ 100 ★
Sycamore - STEAM SHOW AND THRESHING BEE.
Early August, annual, 4 days, Taylor Marshall Farm.
Contact: Northern Illinois Steam Power Club, DeKalb,

Illinois 60115.

Steam engines threshing and operating a saw mill.
Large display of gas engines and pork chop barbeque.

INDIANA

★ 101 ★
Aurora - FARMER'S FAIR. Early October, annual,
3 days, Lions Building. Contact: Kenneth Kenworthy, Aurora Lions Club, 502 Second Street, Aurora,
Indiana 47001.

12-15 high school bands participate in a parade.
Farm produce. Demonstrations of canning, cooking,
sewing, and hobby activities.

★ 102 ★
Brownstown - JACKSON COUNTY WATERMELON
FESTIVAL. Early September, 3 days, Court House
Square. Contact: Finance Chairman, Jackson
County Watermelon Festival, Rural Route 1, Brownstown, Indiana 47220.

Music, old-fashioned country square dancing, pet
parade, princess contest, entertainment, flea market,
art show, large general parade, and free watermelon
for everyone.

★ 103 ★
French Lick - ORANGE COUNTY PUMPKIN
FESTIVAL. Late September-early October, 6 days,
Downtown French Lick and Northwood Institute.
Contact: Exchange Club of Springs Valley, Box 276,
West Baden Springs, Indiana 47469.

Pumpkin contests. Also parades, pies, arts and
crafts, shows and sales, talent show, queen contest,
style show, auto show, chess tournaments, band concerts, fish fry, ham-and-bean dinner, etc.

★ 104 ★
Hesston - LIVE STEAM SHOW AND THRESHERMEN'S
REUNION. August-September, annual, 3 days,
LaPorte County Road. Contact: Manager, LaPorte
County Historical Steam Society, 2940 Mount Claire
Way, Long Beach, Michigan City, Indiana 46360.

Antique steam trains, steam threshers, sawmills,
antique gasoline engines, and traction engine rides.
Flea market, antique autos, live-steam model trains, and
electric generating plant.

Agriculture

INDIANA (Continued)

★ 105 ★
Indianapolis - INDIANA ROSE FESTIVAL.   June, annual, 2 weekends, Hillsdale Exhibition Rose Gardens.   Contact: Producer, Indiana Rose Festival, Hillsdale Exhibition Rose Gardens, 7845 Johnson Road, Indianapolis, Indiana 46250.

Festival queen pageant, coronation, band concert, Castleton Rose festival parade, waterball contest, and commemorative address.   Parade includes flowered floats.

★ 106 ★
Kentland - CORN FESTIVAL.   Late June, 3 days. Contact: President, Kentland Lions Club, 204 East Lincoln Street, Kentland, Indiana 47951.

Celebrates the end of the planting season.   Street dancing, food, rides, games, and all the sweet corn you can eat.   Parade, and rock music concert.

★ 107 ★
Kewanna - HARVEST FESTIVAL.   Late August, 3 days, Downtown.   Contact: General Chairman, Kewanna Harvest Festival, Box 115, Kewanna, Indiana 46939.

Queen contest, tractor pull, stage acts, circus, square dance, clowns, bands, artistic displays, food, and tents for browsing in are highlights of the festival events.

★ 108 ★
Leiters Ford - STRAWBERRY FESTIVAL.   June, annual, 1 day.   Contact: Mrs. Judy Stanley, Leiters Ford Strawberry Festival, Post Office Box 86, Leiters Ford, Indiana 46945.

Strawberries prepared in many ways, parade, games, entertainment, square dancing, carnival rides, festival queen, sky diver and stunt pilot.

★ 109 ★
Michigan City - FALL ROSE FESTIVAL.   September, 29 days, Persian Garden of International Friendship Garden.   Contact: Clarence Stauffer, International Friendship Gardens, Pottawatomie Park, Michigan City, Indiana 46360.

Hybrid tea roses and various other breeds of roses are in bloom for the enjoyment of all.

★ 110 ★
Mitchell - PERSIMMON FESTIVAL.   Late September, 4 days, Downtown and Spring Mill State Park.   Contact: Secretary, Mitchell Chamber of Commerce, Post Office Box 216, Mitchell, Indiana 47446.

Home-made persimmon ice cream, persimmon pudding contest, arts and crafts, unique window displays, stage entertainment every night, queen contest, square dancing, carnival area, parade, and candlelight tour of Spring Mill State Park.

★ 111 ★
Orleans - DOGWOOD FESTIVAL.   Late April-early May, annual, 9 days.   Contact: Mrs. Donald Mahan, Orleans Dogwood Festival, 247 East Vincennes Road, Orleans, Indiana 47452.

In honor of the blooming of the dogwood, the festival includes nature tours, and exhibits of arts, crafts, flowers and antiques.

★ 112 ★
Plymouth - MARSHALL COUNTY BLUEBERRY FESTIVAL.   Late August-early September, 3 days, Centennial Park.   Contact: President, Marshall County Blueberry Festival, Incorporated, 1051 Warana Drive, Plymouth, Indiana 46563.

Parade, pony and horse pull, tractor pull, arts and crafts exhibit, car show, Historical Society open house, fireworks, antique and flower shows, waterball fights, softball tourneys, horse show, kiddie rides, and nightly musical entertainment.

★ 113 ★
Richmond - RICHMOND ROSE FESTIVAL.   Mid June, 7 days.   Contact: Mr. William Lowe, Chairman, Richmond Rose Festival, 19 South Ninth Street, Richmond, Indiana 47374.

Roses are the keynote.   Selection of a Rose Queen, tours of rose gardens and green houses, art exhibits, industrial displays, floral arrangements, photography contest.   Country music, square dancing, and belly dancing.   Spiritual groups, ethnic exhibits, parades, antique shows, historical tours, and tournaments.

★ 114 ★
Rockville - PARKE COUNTY MAPLE FAIR.   Late February-early March, 2 weekends, 4-H Fairgrounds and Billie Creek Village.   Contact: Executive Secretary, Billie Creek Village, Incorporated, Box 165, Rockville, Indiana 47872.

INDIANA (Continued)

Bus tours to sugar camps, painting demonstrations, pancake-sausage-maple syrup meal, demonstrations of pioneer crafts and activities: hog-butchering, and pioneer style syrup gathering. Billie Creek is a restored village.

★ 115 ★
Rockville - STEAM HARVEST DAYS. July, 3 days, Billie Creek Village. Contact: Michael J. Allen, Post Office Box 165, Rockville, Indiana 47872.

Fiddlers convention and bluegrass music, turn-of-century harvest methods exhibited, cooking, and arts and crafts.

★ 116 ★
Rushville - PIONEER ENGINEERS CLUB REUNION. Early August, annual, 3 days, Rosh County Conservation Grounds. Contact: President, Pioneer Engineers Club of Indiana, Incorporated, 133 Hillenbrand Avenue, Batesville, Indiana 47006.

An exhibition of steam, gas, and animal-powered machines, including vennering machines, lumber saws, threshers, and popcorn machines. In addition, there are flea markets, antique stands, and a fiddler's contest.

★ 117 ★
Salem - FODDER FESTIVAL. Early October, annual, 2 days. Contact: Don H. Martin, WSLM, Radio Ridge, Salem, Indiana 47167.

Displays of fodder shocks, pumpkins, bittersweet, and persimmons. Carnival rides, flea markets, antique stands, parade, carnival-fiesta, home-baked foods, and sidewalk sale. Begun around 1958.

★ 118 ★
Tipton - TIPTON COUNTY PORK FESTIVAL. Early September, 3 days. Contact: General Chairman, Tipton County Pork Festival, c/o Tipton Daily Tribune, 110 West Madison Street, Tipton, Indiana 46072.

A barbeque of 6 tons of pork. Arts, crafts, antique show, carnival events, free entertainment, two parades, beauty pageant, dances, and top-name entertainment.

★ 119 ★
Troy - PERRY COUNTY DOGWOOD FESTIVAL. Late April, 2 days. Contact: Cecil M. Lasher, Citizens National Bank, 529 Main Street, Tell City, Indiana 47586.

Three driving tour routes cover the entire county and feature in addition to the spring blossoms, several stops along the way which offer homemade and handmade items.

IOWA

★ 120 ★
Cedar Rapids - ALL IOWA FAIR. Late June-early July, annual, 10 days, Hawkeye Downs. Contact: Cedar Rapids Chamber of Commerce, 127 Third Street, Northeast, Cedar Rapids, Iowa 52401.

Large fair featuring arts and crafts, agricultural, horticultural and a variety of other displays. Includes a horse show.

★ 121 ★
Cresco - FARM FEST (AG FEST). Early September, 1 day, Main Street. Contact: Cresco Chamber of Commerce, Post Office Box 93, Cresco, Iowa 52136.

A traditional festival emphasizing the importance of farming in the area. Exhibits and displays of farm methods, equipment and crops.

★ 122 ★
Des Moines - CORN HARVEST FESTIVAL. Early October (around the 1st), annual, 2 days, Living History Farms. Contact: Program Director, Living History Farms, Rural Route 1, Des Moines, Iowa 50322.

The Farms is an action museum of farming methods dating back to the 1840's. For this festival corn pickers are allotted a certain amount of time and the winner is determined according to the weight of the corn. During the festival there are tours of the 1840 Pioneer Farm, the 1900 Horse Farm, and the museum.

★ 123 ★
Des Moines - FARMING OF THE FUTURE. Late August, 3 days, Living History Farms. Contact: Program Director, Living History Farms, Rural Route 1, Des Moines, Iowa 50322.

Demonstrations, displays, and exhibits of advanced agricultural methods and equipment.

★ 124 ★
Des Moines - GRAIN HARVEST FESTIVAL. Late July, annual, Living History Farms. Contact: Program Director, Living History Farms, Rural Route 1,

Agriculture

IOWA (Continued)

Des Moines, Iowa 50322.

The Farms is an action museum of farming methods dating back to the 1840's where old time methods of threshing and grain cradling and flailing are demonstrated for this festival. An old fiddlers' contest is held. Tours of the 1840 Pioneer Farm, the 1900 Horse Farm and the museum.

★ 125 ★

Des Moines - 1900 FARM DAYS. Late June, 3 days, Living History Farms. Contact: Program Director, Living History Farms, Rural Route 1, Des Moines, Iowa 50322.

Displays and demonstration of traditional farm techniques of an earlier era.

★ 126 ★

Elkader - SWEET CORN DAYS. Early August, annual, 3 days, Elkader Recreation Park. Contact: Chamber of Commerce, Box 599, Elkader, Iowa 52043.

Activities include annual Canoe Races; water show including a newspaper race (contestants must read paper aloud while swimming across the pool), a watermelon race (sort of an aquatic football), diving show; a variety show with local talent; rope pull (tug-o-war between teams from different communities); a parade with floats, costumes, marching and equestrian units and celebrities. The main attraction is the give away of tons of buttered sweet corn. Also features a tractor pull and a carnival. Sponsored by the Jaycees. Started in 1963.

★ 127 ★

Gladbrook - CORN CARNIVAL. Late July-early August, 3 days. Contact: Chamber of Commerce, Gladbrook, Iowa 50635.

A community celebration in honor of the corn crop.

★ 128 ★

Humeston - WATERMELON DAYS. Mid July, 1 day. Contact: Chamber of Commerce, Humeston, Iowa 50123.

A community celebration in honor of the watermelon, an important local crop.

★ 129 ★

Long Grove - STRAWBERRY FESTIVAL. Early June (2nd Sunday), annual, 1 day, Long Grove Civic Center. Contact: Long Grove Civic League, Dan Nagle, Box 75, Long Grove, Iowa 52756.

Events include a children's costume parade, senior citizens sing-a-long, women's early dress contest, beard contest, kid's contest, antique displays, musket shoot, and dancing in the evening. Refreshments are available, including strawberry shortcake and ice cream. Started in 1960.

★ 130 ★

Mount Pleasant - MIDWEST OLD SETTLERS AND THRESHERS REUNION. Early September (Labor Day weekend), annual, 4 days. Contact: Herbert Hult, c/o Old Settlers Reunion, Mount Pleasant, Indiana 52641.

One of the largest action exhibits of steam engines, steam powered machines and miniatures in the country. Threshing, sorghum making, baling and other jobs done "the way grandpa used to do them". There is a steam-powered merry-go-round. Old steam-powered trains and vintage trolleys provide transportation of visitors on the grounds. There is a grand collection and showing of antique autos. Quilting, broom-making and other early-American crafts are demonstrated. Fiddlers' convention. Begun around 1950.

★ 131 ★

Orange City - TULIP FESTIVAL. Mid May (2nd weekend), annual. Contact: Orange City Chamber of Commerce, 125 Central Avenue, Southeast, Orange City, Iowa 51041.

In preparation, the citizens follow an old world custom and scrub the streets before the dignitaries arrive. The scrubbers frequently get wet as well. In honor of their Dutch heritage, the celebrants dress in Dutch costumes and do wooden shoe dances in the streets. Tulips and marching bands, wooden shoe making, flower shows, tulip exhibit, coronation ceremonies, and drill demonstrations are featured. Parade includes floats. Started in 1936.

★ 132 ★

Pella - TULIP TIME FESTIVAL. Mid May (2nd weekend), annual, 2-3 days, City-wide. Contact: Pella Chamber of Commerce, Box 145, Pella, Iowa 50219 or for art fair; Dennis Steenhock, 507 Franklin, Pella, Iowa 50219.

In honor of Dutch heritage citizens wear Dutch costumes and scrub the streets (an old custom

IOWA (Continued)

preparatory to a visit by dignitaries). Tulip exhibitions, stage productions, music, folk dancing, foods, a parade with Dutch Street Organ, coronation of queen, and folk games are featured. There are conducted tours, visits to Pella Historical Village and Tulip Toren--a tower honoring the founding fathers, whom the festival also honors. Other events include a display of antiques and historic items, square dancing, Volks Parade, massed bands, and Parade of Provinces. There is also a Pella Tulip Time Festival Art Fair (3 days) in the Pella Historical Village. Started in 1936.

★ 133 ★
Pierson - WATERMELON DAY. Late July, annual, 1 day. Contact: Chamber of Commerce, Pierson, Iowa 51048.

A traditional community festival honoring an important (and delicious) local crop.

★ 134 ★
Sheldon - SOYBEAN DAYS. Late June, annual, 3 days. Contact: Chamber of Commerce, 416 Ninth Street, Sheldon, Iowa 51201.

A traditional community celebration honoring an important local crop.

★ 135 ★
Spencer - OLD TIME THRESHING BEE. Early August, 2 days, The oat field of A.M. "Stub" Johnson of Stub's Ranch Kitchen. Contact: Stub Johnson, Stub's Ranch Kitchen, Spencer, Iowa 51301.

The 40-acre field is harvested entirely by authentic antique horse and steam powered equipment, including binders, racks, threshers, and a grain elevator and baler. In addition, there are demonstrations of horses plowing, and a steam engine which drives a buzz saw and a corn sheller. Bundle pitchers and straw stackers are invited to participate in this colorful and nostalgic activity.

★ 136 ★
Stanhope - WATERMELON DAY. Early August (1st Tuesday), annual, 1 day, Stanhope Park. Contact: Orlo Bibler, Stanhope, Iowa 50246; or Chamber of Commerce, Stanhope, Iowa 50246.

A parade and other traditional festivities including the eating of watermelon.

★ 137 ★
State Center - ROSE FESTIVAL. Late June (3rd weekend), annual, 3 days, Rose Garden. Contact: Mrs. Alan Hilleman, Secretary, Rose Festival Board, State Center, Iowa 50247.

Begins with the crowning of the Rose Queen. Includes a parade and various festival activities. State Center is officially and formally dedicated as the Rose Capitol of Iowa (since June 27, 1959). Begun around 1960.

★ 138 ★
Strawberry Point - STRAWBERRY DAYS. Early June, annual, 3 days. Contact: Thomas R. Munter, Secretary, Chamber of Commerce, Strawberry Point, Iowa 52076.

The celebration is "just the town's way of saying 'Strawberry Point is a town as good as its name'". The highlight of the event is the serving of free strawberries and ice cream; other activities include a parade and a carnival. Sponsored by the Chamber of Commerce. Started in 1965.

KANSAS

★ 139 ★
Topeka - MID AMERICA FAIR. Mid September (2nd week), annual, 5 days, Fairgrounds. Contact: The Greater Topeka Chamber of Commerce, 722 Kansas Avenue, Topeka, Kansas 66603.

One of the largest expositions in the southwest, much like the state fairs, but rather a combined celebration.

KENTUCKY

★ 140 ★
Cynthiana - IRIS FESTIVAL. Mid March, 1 day. Contact: Cynthiana-Harrison County Chamber of Commerce, Post Office Box 262, Cynthiana, Kentucky 41031.

A festival, parade, and tour highlight the events in celebration of the blooming of the iris - the beginning of spring.

★ 141 ★
Louisville - AUDUBON FESTIVAL OF THE DOGWOODS. Mid April, 6 days, Audubon Park. Contact: Mrs. E. A. Gudridge, 1145 Dove Road, Louisville, Kentucky 40213.

An outdoor arts and crafts festival is included in the

Agriculture

events honoring the spring season and the blooming of the dogwood trees.

★ 142 ★

Pineville - MOUNTAIN LAUREL FESTIVAL. Late May (last weekend), annual, 4 days, National Amphitheatre in Pine Mountain State Resort Park. Contact: Charles Bishop, General Chairman, Post Office Box 151, Pineville, Kentucky 40977.

Celebrates the blooming of the mountain laurel. Each college sends a respresentative to a queen pageant. Winner is customarily crowned by the governor of Kentucky. Art exhibits, band concert, receptions, fireworks, a parade, coronation, grand ball, queens breakfast, style show, and mountain crafts exhibit are featured. Started 1931.

★ 143 ★

Stanford - LINCOLN COUNTY JUNE DAIRY DAY FESTIVAL. Mid June, 1 day. Contact: Lincoln County Extension Office, Courthouse, Box 326, Stanford, Kentucky 40484.

A salute to the dairy industry with a parade featuring colorful floats in the afternoon and top the day off with the crowning of a Dairy Day Princess.

LOUISIANA

★ 144 ★

Abbeville - LOUISIANA DAIRY FESTIVAL. Late October, 2-4 days. Contact: Louis J. DeBlanc, 404 South Louisiana Avenue, Abbeville, Louisiana 70510.

Community fun including a fair, street dances, blessing of the dairy products, dairy cattle show; butter churning contest, horse shows, parades and fireworks, rodeo, and performance by French singers. A queen coronation and queen's parade and ball. Started in 1949.

★ 145 ★

Basile - LOUISIANA SWINE FESTIVAL. Early November, 2 days. Contact: Shirley F. Ledoux, Post Office Box 457, Basile, Louisiana 70515.

King Porky and Queen Petunia pageant and coronation, talent show, greasy pig contest, boudin eating contest, swine show and judging, arts and crafts show, parade, and a carnival highlight the events.

★ 146 ★

Bastrop - NORTH LOUISIANA COTTON FESTIVAL AND FAIR. Late September, 5-6 days, Fairgrounds. Contact: Ron Simmons, Post Office Box 1175, Bastrop, Louisiana 71220.

Events include a carnival, country music, gospel singing, Cotton Prince and Princess Pageant Parade, entertainment acts, arena activities, commercial exhibits, and livestock exhibits. Started in 1949.

★ 147 ★

Baton Rouge - LSU JUNIOR DIVISION LIVESTOCK SHOW AND CHAMPIONSHIP RODEO. Late February-early March, 5 days. Contact: Louisiana Tourist Commission, Post Office Box 44291, Baton Rouge, Louisiana 70804; or C. W. Kennedy, Post Office Drawer H, University Station, Baton Rouge, Louisiana 70803.

Livestock exhibits, contests, etc., created by and featuring youngsters.

★ 148 ★

Bogalusa - DOGWOOD FESTIVAL. Late March, 2 days. Contact: Executive Director, Louisiana Tourist Commission, Post Office Box 44291, Baton Rouge, Louisiana 70804.

Crowning of Dogwood Queen and presentation of the court, Creative Craze Carnival of local arts and crafts, display of the Cassidy Collection of rare duck decoys and hand made canes, and tour of local residences.

★ 149 ★

Colfax - LOUISIANA PECAN FESTIVAL. Early November, annual, 2-3 days. Contact: Pecan Festival, c/o Colfax Chamber of Commerce, Colfax, Louisiana 70401.

A festival to promote the pecan industry. Activities include a street carnival, trail ride, cook out, country store, costume contests, beard-growing contest, cooking contests, fox hound bench show, old time fiddlers' contest, turkey shoot, donkey basketball game, pet parade for children, and a Queen's Ball. Begun around 1970.

★ 150 ★

Crowley - INTERNATIONAL RICE FESTIVAL. Early October, 2 days. Contact: Crowley Chamber of Commerce, Post Office Box 1444, Crowley, Louisiana 70526.

LOUISIANA (Continued)

Features a rice eating contest, rice farmer of the year award, and a creole cooking contest. Also includes a grand parade, frog jumping derby, livestock show, street dances, contests and races, and a carnival.

★ 151 ★
Farmerville - LOUISIANA WATERMELON FESTIVAL. Late July, 3 days. Contact: John M. Muckleroy, Sr., 505 North Main, Farmerville, Louisiana 71241.

A community celebration in honor of an important local crop.

★ 152 ★
Fort Jackson - ORANGE FESTIVAL. Early December, 2 days. Contact: Louisiana Tourist Commission, Post Office Box 44291, Baton Rouge, Louisiana 70804.

The events include carnival rides, games, walking tour of the fort, music, races, and dances. Contests include fish skinning, duck and goose calling, shrimp and oyster shucking. Featured food includes: orange juice, orange wine, oysters, gumbo, and oyster loaves.

★ 153 ★
Gonzales - STRAWBERRY FESTIVAL. April, 2 days. Contact: A. B. Sheets, 730 East Rome Street, Gonzales, Louisiana 70737.

Traditional festivities in honor of the local crop of strawberries.

★ 154 ★
Hammond - SOUTHEAST LOUISIANA DAIRY FESTIVAL AND LIVESTOCK SHOW. Mid April. Contact: E. E. Puls, 300 Louisiana Avenue, Hammond, Louisiana 70401.

Livestock show, commercial exhibits, flower show, food, handicrafts, and strawberry exhibits are featured. Begun around 1946.

★ 155 ★
Jonesville - LOUISIANA SOYBEAN FESTIVAL. Late July, 3 days. Contact: Jo Schumann, Post Office Box 597, Jonesville, Louisiana 71343.

Featuring exhibits of the uses of soybeans and includes livestock, hobby, and handcraft displays, and a Queen's Pageant and Ball.

★ 156 ★
Leesville - WEST LOUISIANA FORESTRY FESTIVAL. Late September. Contact: A. J. Stevens, Box 559, Leesville, Louisiana 71446.

Coupled with a fair, this celebration offers contests, exhibits, and other activities, focusing on the recreational and industrial gifts of the forest.

★ 157 ★
Minden - FAIR AND FOREST FESTIVAL. Early October, 5 days. Contact: Stephen R. Burk, Post Office Box 819, Minden, Louisiana 71055.

Events include contests, exhibits, and other activities starring the recreational and industrial gifts of the forest.

★ 158 ★
New Iberia - LOUISIANA SUGAR CANE FESTIVAL. Late September, 4 days. Contact: Mrs. Eve P. Oubre, Star Route A, Box 54, New Iberia, Louisiana 70560.

Events include blessing of the cane fields, parades, concerts, coronations, exhibits and displays, square dancing, art show, livestock auction, fireman's waterfight, sports events, and pageants. Started in 1938.

★ 159 ★
Opelousas - LOUISIANA YAMBILEE FESTIVAL. Late October, annual, 3 days. Contact: Mrs. Yvonne Bruner, Post Office Box 444, Opelousas, Louisiana 70570.

Celebrates the yam with the crowning of King WillYam and Queen Marigold. Other festivities include a flower show, yam judging, cooking contest, parades, yam auction, fashion show, arts and crafts show, sports events, sweet potato show, diaper derby, blessing of the sweet potatoes, horticultural exhibit, and giant fireworks display. Started in 1945.

★ 160 ★
Ponchatoula - STRAWBERRY FESTIVAL. Early April, annual, 2 days. Contact: Richard Stilley, Post Office Box 446, Ponchatoula, Louisiana 70454.

A community celebration in honor of the beautiful delicious strawberry - traditional festivities. Begun around 1972.

★ 161 ★
Ruston - PEACH FESTIVAL. Mid June, annual,

Agriculture

LOUISIANA (Continued)

7 days. Contact: Dr. Robert M. Caruthers, 430 Forest Circle, Ruston, Louisiana 71270.

Focuses on Lincoln Parish's major industry, resulting from the peach crop. Events include a peach cookery contest, peach growers exhibit, and Miss Princess Peach contest. There is also a dog and pet parade, bread baking contest, flower show, bicycle race, street dance, sidewalk sale, antique show, and sports events. Begun around 1951.

★ 162 ★

Ville Platte - LOUISIANA COTTON FESTIVAL. Mid October, 4 days. Contact: Cotton Festival, c/o Ville Platte Chamber of Commerce, Ville Platte, Louisiana 70586.

Features a Tournoi (a medieval jousting tournament), Cajun music, cotton exhibit, street dances, country store, livestock show, cotton fashion show, and Grand Parade of Cotton. The Tournoi pits horse and rider against the enemies of cotton, such as the boll weevil, and is an exacting test of horsemanship. The festival begins with an Acadian Music Festival and Old Folks Dance which presents one of the distinctive aspects of Acadian culture. Coronation of Queen Cotton, Princess luncheon and tea, flower show and carnival.

★ 163 ★

Vivian - REDBUD FESTIVAL. March, 20 days, National Guard Armory, North Caddo High School Auditorium, etc. Contact: Mrs. Verlon Graves, 311 West Mary Street, Vivian, Louisiana 71082.

Spring style show, Little Miss North Caddo Parish contest, Redbud Queen's Pageant, parade, art display and sale, horseriding show, fiddler's contest, and street dance. Pierian art and craft display, bicycle races, open bass tournament, Rhythm Masters Jamboree, hayride, golf, bowling, bridge tournament, flower shows, and concerts.

★ 164 ★

West Monroe - OUACHITA VALLEY FAIR. Late September, Fairgrounds. Contact: West Monroe Chamber of Commerce, 1613 North Seventh Street, Post Office Box 427, West Monroe, Louisiana 71291

Events include 4-H and livestock shows, arts and crafts, dried flower show, canning and baking show, home demonstration booths, clothing exhibits, free acts and carnival. Started in 1931.

MAINE

★ 165 ★

Belfast - BROILER FESTIVAL. Mid July, annual, 6-8 days, Belfast City Park. Contact: Belfast Chamber of Commerce, Belfast, Maine 04915.

Celebrates the chicken industry. Giant chicken barbeque on Boiler Day with more than 4,000 meals being served. Other events include poultry exhibits, beauty pageant, professional entertainment, sheep shearing, and wool spinning. Started in 1948.

★ 166 ★

Fort Fairfield - POTATO BLOSSOM FESTIVAL. Mid July, annual, 4 days. Contact: Chamber of Commerce, 208 Main Street, Post Office Box 607, Fort Fairfield, Maine 04742.

Celebrates the potato fields coming into bloom and includes the following events: Potato Blossom Queen Pageant, giant parade, karate tournament, horseshoe pitching contest, motorcycle hill climbing, horse show, street dancing, swimming meets, tennis tourney, golf tournament, blueberry pie eating contest, sky diving, art and farm machinery displays, Potato Blossom Festival Ball, and dinner. Began in 1935.

★ 167 ★

Fryeburg - FRYEBURG FAIR. Late September-early October, annual, 7 days, Fairgrounds. Contact: Chamber of Commerce, Fryeburg, Maine 04037.

Features the Saco Valley Woodsmen Field Day, livestock parade, exhibition, vaudeville entertainment, international 4-H competition, and baby beef auction. Area's autumn foliage is another attraction.

★ 168 ★

Fryeburg - SACO VALLEY WOODSMEN'S FIELD DAY. Late September, annual, 1 day. Contact: Chamber of Commerce, Fryeburg, Maine 04037.

A salute to the lumber industry. Competition in traditional lumberjack activities such as log rolling, tree cutting, and chain sawing. Held in conjunction with the Fryeburg Fair, the Monday of the fair.

★ 169 ★

Madison - CORN FESTIVAL. Late August, annual, 2 days. Contact: Chamber of Commerce, Madison, Maine 04950.

Held in conjunction with the Indian celebration, marking the anniversary of the Abenaki Massacre, the

MAINE (Continued)

event features an all corn menu including fresh cor-on-the-cob, parade and other activities.

★ 170 ★
Oxford - BEANHOLE BEAN FESTIVAL. Late July, annual, New Oxford County Fairgrounds. Contact: Chamber of Commerce, Oxford, Maine 04270.

Beanhole beans feast and special entertainment high-light this community festival.

★ 171 ★
Pittsfield - CENTRAL MAINE EGG FESTIVAL. Late July, 1 day, Manson Park. Contact: Chamber of Commerce, Pittsfield, Maine 04967.

World's largest (possibly only) gold plated egg contest. Also an egg feast--giant pan cooks up to five dozen eggs at one time. Activities include country-western music, fireworks shaped like a giant chicken, golf tournament, beauty pageant, special events, and entertainment. Begun around 1973.

★ 172 ★
Union - MAINE BLUEBERRY FESTIVAL. Mid August, annual, 1 day, Fairgrounds. Contact: Chamber of Commerce, Union, Maine 04862.

Held in conjunction with the Union Fair, features Blueberry Queen Pageant, pie-eating contest, sale of fresh and frozen blueberries and blueberry products, and free blueberry pies.

MARYLAND

★ 173 ★
Chevy Chase - NATURAL GARDENING FOR WILDLIFE BENEFIT FAIR. April (3rd or 4th weekend), annual, 2 days, Audubon's Estate, Woodend. Contact: Natural Gardens for Wildlife Benefit Fair, Audubon Naturalist Society, 8940 Jones Mill Road, Chevy Chase, Maryland 20015.

Demonstrations of how to plant a garden that is hospitable to wildlife, sale of materials for organic gardening, exhibition of Audubon Society gardens, information about indoor gardens, terrariums, sale of wildlife crafts, food, sale of indoor plants, bird houses, and bird baths. Nature walks. Begun in 1975.

★ 174 ★
College Park - FARM VISITATION DAY. Late June,

annual, 1 day. Contact: Special Agent, Symons Hall, University of Maryland, College Park, Maryland 20742.

Sponsored by the University of Maryland, Agricultural Division, Maryland farms throughout the state are open to public visitation. Begun around 1967.

★ 175 ★
Easton - DELMARVA CHICKEN FESTIVAL. May or June, annual, 2 days, Location varies. Contact: Delmarva Poultry Industry, Incorporated, Route 2, Box 47, Georgetown, Delaware 19947.

This festival, held each year, somewhere on the Delmarva Peninsula features a giant chicken barbeque and fry in the "giant chicken frypan and the Chicken Capers - competition between specially trained chickens in the olympics of the chicken world. Other events include a chicken cooking contest, band concerts, antique flea market, princess pageant, antique car show, a parade, and country and western music. Begun around 1949.

★ 176 ★
Ellicott City - FLOWER FESTIVAL. Early May, annual, 1 day, Main Street. Contact: Ellicott City Business Association, Post Office Box 51, Ellicott City, Maryland 21043.

Features displays of flowers and plants, with related crafts also exhibited. Begun around 1972.

★ 177 ★
Federalsburg - WHEAT THRESHING STEAM AND GAS ENGINE SHOW. Early August, annual, 3 days. Contact: James L. Layton, Route 2, Box 266, Federalsburg, Maryland 21632.

Demonstrations of steam engines, threshers, antique tractors, and gas engines. Miniature steam train rides, ox team, shingle sawing, sawmill, black-smithing, flea market, crafts, and entertainment. Begun around 1961.

★ 178 ★
Thurmont - MAPLE SYRUP DEMONSTRATIONS. March, annual, 3 weekends, Cunningham Falls State Park. Contact: Cunningham Falls State Park, Route 1, Thurmont, Maryland 21788.

Park Rangers demonstrate tree tapping and sap boiling and explain the process of maple syrup production. Begun around 1972.

Agriculture

MARYLAND (Continued)

★ 179 ★
Westminster - CORN ROAST.   Early August, annual,
1 day, Union Mills Homestead and Mill.   Contact:
Chamber of Commerce, Westminster, Maryland 21157.

A corn roast over a wood fire with the corn still in
the husk.   Other foods are also offered.   There is
a country store.

★ 180 ★
Westminster - FALL HARVEST DAY.   Mid October
(2nd Saturday), annual, 1 day, Carroll County Farm
Museum.   Contact: Carroll County Farm Museum,
Route 6, Box 412, Westminster, Maryland 21157.

A variety of colorful nineteenth century farming demonstrations.   Crafts on display in museum: quilting,
spinning, weaving, blacksmithing, tin smithing, candle
making, pottery, and broom making.   Also to see,
taste, or enjoy: apple butter, bread, butter, butchering,
chair-caning, dried apple dolls, steam calliope, horse
and wagon rides, and pumpkin contest.   Begun around
1966.

★ 181 ★
Westminster - STEAM UP AND MILITIA DAYS
(STEAM SHOW DAYS).   Mid September, annual,
4 days, Carroll County Farm Museum.   Contact:
Carroll County Farm Museum, Route 6, Box 412,
Westminster, Maryland 21157.

Steam operated equipment used in shingle sawing,
threshing, etc.   There is also a parade and a flea
market.

MASSACHUSETTS

★ 182 ★
Cummington - CUMMINGTON FAIR.   Late August,
annual, 3 days, Cummington Fairgrounds.   Contact:
Pioneer Valley Association, Incorporated, 333 Prospect
Street, Northampton, Massachusetts 01060.

Features agricultural exhibits, horse draws and a midway.   Nearly 100 years old.

★ 183 ★
Falmouth - STRAWBERRY FESTIVAL.   Mid June,
annual, 1 day, Village Green.   Contact: Falmouth
Chamber of Commerce, Falmouth, Massachusetts 02540.

Culinary delights in honor of the strawberry include
jams, jellies, and shortcakes.   Participants may amuse
themselves with games, rides and browsing at craft
tables.

★ 184 ★
Florida - TURNIP FESTIVAL.   Late September-early
October, annual.   Contact: The Mohawk Trail
Association, Incorporated, Charlemont, Massachusetts
01339.

The festival celebrates the harvest of turnips which
are said to have a unique flavor here.

★ 185 ★
South Carver - CRANBERRY FESTIVAL.   Late
September, annual, 2 days.   Contact: Plymouth
County Development Council, Incorporated, Post
Office Box 1620, Pembroke, Massachusetts 02359.

The celebration features old-fashioned fun with carnival
booths, pie-eating contest, special rides and entertainment, elephant rides, corn roast, cranberry games,
magic shows, and 4-H club exhibits.

★ 186 ★
West Springfield - EASTERN STATES EXPOSITION
(THE BIG E).   Mid September, annual, 10 days.
Contact: Eastern States Exposition, 1305 Memorial
Avenue, West Springfield, Massachusetts 01089.

Features agricultural, industrial, and educational
shows.   Famous name performers and championship
horse show.   Has 50 permanent buildings, Coliseum,
Better Living Center and Storrowton Tavern restaurant.

MICHIGAN

★ 187 ★
Caro - SAGINAW VALLEY LIVE STEAM ASSOCIATION.
Mid August.   Contact: Chamber of Commerce, 119
South State Street, Caro, Michigan 48723.

Exhibits of antique equipment and demonstrations of
the equipment in operation.

★ 188 ★
Coloma - GLADIOLUS FESTIVAL.   Early August
(1st weekend), annual, 3 days.   Contact: Coloma-
Watervliet-Paw Paw Lake Area Chamber of Commerce,
Post Office Box 428, Coloma, Michigan 49038.

A community celebration honoring the beauty of the
gladiolus flowers.

MICHIGAN (Continued)

★ 189 ★
Hart - NATIONAL ASPARAGUS FESTIVAL. Mid
June, 3 days. Contact: Chamber of Commerce, 127
State Street, Box 106, Hart, Michigan 49420; or
Shelby Area Chamber of Commerce, 195 North
Michigan Avenue, Shelby, Michigan 49455.

A celebration honoring an important local crop -
asparagus. Also held in two other nearby towns -
New Era and Shelby.

★ 190 ★
Holland - TULIP TIME. Mid May, annual, 4 days.
Contact: Holland Tulip Festival, 150 West Eighth
Street, Holland, Michigan 49423.

There are tours of tulip fields and flower shows (the
city is a center for tulips), Dutch costumes and Dutch
dances. Entertainment events include a parade
(Volksparade), a musicale, organ recital, band concert, barbershop quartet, square dancing, and contests.
Begun around 1928.

★ 191 ★
Manistee - NATIONAL STRAWBERRY FESTIVAL.
Early July (4th of July weekend), 4 days. Contact:
West Michigan Tourist Association, Hospitality House,
136 Fulton East, Grand Rapids, Michigan 49502.

The entertainment includes a carnival and a parade,
dancing, and a water ski show. In addition, there
is a huge ox roast.

★ 192 ★
Niles - FOUR FLAGS AREA APPLE FESTIVAL. Late
September-early October, annual, 9 days. Contact:
Four Flags Area Apple Festival, Post Office Box 672,
Niles, Michigan 49120.

Activities include a grand parade, arts and crafts
fair, dances, historical tours, boat races, carnivals,
puppet shows, showboat play and competitive games
such as the "Apple Seed Popping Contest". Started
in 1973.

★ 193 ★
Saint Joseph - BLOSSOMTIME FESTIVAL. May,
annual, 1 week. Contact: Blossomtime, Incorporated,
311 Colfas Avenue, Benton Harbor, Michigan 49022.

Salutes the opening of the agricultural growing season.
Events include the selection of Miss Blossomtime, the
annual Blossomtime Sport Fishing Derby, art show,

blessing of the blossoms, tours of the cities, Blossomtime Fashion Show, lottery drawing, youth parade,
concert, youth dance, Grand Floral Parade, square
dance, and Grand Floral Ball. Also held in Benton
Harbor.

★ 194 ★
South Haven - NATIONAL BLUEBERRY FESTIVAL.
July, annual. Contact: Chamber of Commerce,
South Haven, Michigan 49090.

A celebration of the Michigan blueberry growing
industry, which is centered in the South Haven area.
The celebration features "food-fun-fellowship" in the
form of athletic events, a parade, contests, and a
variety of entertainments. Started in 1965.

★ 195 ★
Traverse City - NATIONAL CHERRY FESTIVAL.
Early July (1st full week after July 4), annual, 6
days, Grand Traverse Bay area. Contact: National
Cherry Festival, Mrs. Dorothy L. Walkmeyer, Executive Manager, Box 141, Traverse City, Michigan
49684.

To promote the cherry industry and celebrate the
cherry harvest. The festival is preceded by a
National Cherry Queen pageant. Other events
include a music camp and concert, educational
exhibits, entertainment, cherry products, souvenirs,
rides, concessions, cherry-pie eating contests, cherry
orchard tours, concerts, bingo, blessing of the harvest,
frog-jumping contest, turtle races, tennis tournament,
cooking contests, regatta, art exhibit, parade, dances,
open house at Coast Guard Air Station, air-sea rescue
demonstration, foot race, Bavarian Night, bike race,
and polka night. Begun around 1927.

MINNESOTA

★ 196 ★
Bovey - FARMER'S DAY. Early September, 1 day.
Contact: Editor, Scenic Range News, Bovey,
Minnesota 55709.

Display of produce with premiums, parade, barbeque,
athletic events, carnival, rides, and entertainment
highlight this community festival.

★ 197 ★
Dalton - LAKE REGION PIONEER THRESHERMEN'S
ASSOCIATION SHOW. Early-mid September, 3
days. Contact: Chamber of Commerce, Dalton,
Minnesota 56324.

Agriculture

MINNESOTA (Continued)

Antique machinery includes gas tractors, threshers, and saw mill. There is a parade, a variety show, and an agricultural museum. Begun around 1954.

★ 198 ★
Ellsworth - NOBLES COUNTY DAIRY DAYS. Mid June, 3 days. Contact: Mrs. Fabian Deutsch, Optimist Club, Ellsworth, Minnesota 56129.

Events include Dairy Day Banquet, princess contest, dairy cattle show, parade, carnival, plays, craft display and judging.

★ 199 ★
Frazee - TURKEY DAYS. Early August, 3 days. Contact: Chamber of Commerce, Frazee, Minnesota 56544.

A queen coronation, carnival, parade, and, of course, turkey dinners highlight the festivities.

★ 200 ★
Golden Valley - LILAC FESTIVAL. Mid May, 7 days. Contact: Chamber of Commerce, Post Office Box 27106, Golden Valley, Minnesota 55427.

A Lilac Ball and lilac displays, in addition to a queen contest and a flea market.

★ 201 ★
Hopkins - RASPBERRY FESTIVAL. Late July (3rd week), annual, 7 days. Contact: Jaycees; Hopkins, Minnesota 55343; or West Suburban Hopkins Chamber of Commerce, 1593 Highway #7, Hopkins, Minnesota 55343.

Festival events include parades, contests, music, raspberry pancake breakfasts, barbeque contest, frog-jumping contests, wrestling matches, a carnival, and a queen contest. Started in 1935.

★ 202 ★
Kelliher - WILD RICE FESTIVAL. Mid July, annual, 1 day. Contact: Bemidji Area Chamber of Commerce, Post Office Box 806, Bemidji, Minnesota 56601.

A community festival honoring an important local crop. Begun around 1973.

★ 203 ★
Kellogg - WATERMELON FESTIVAL. Early September,

2 days. Contact: Chamber of Commerce, Kellogg, Minnesota 55945.

Carnivals, parades, queen contest, and watermelons for all.

★ 204 ★
La Crescent - APPLE FESTIVAL. Late September, 3 days. Contact: Chamber of Commerce, La Crescent, Minnesota 55947.

King Apple Parade, queen coronation, queen's ball, contests, banquet, carnival, kiddies parade, horsepull contest, soapbox derby, and pancake breakfast highlight the festival events.

★ 205 ★
Lakefield - PORK DAY. Mid July, annual, 1 day. Contact: Chamber of Commerce, Lakefield, Minnesota 56150.

Free barbequed pork sandwiches, and a parade highlight this festival honoring an important local industry.

★ 206 ★
Mantorville - MARIGOLD DAYS. Early September, 2 days. Contact: Chamber of Commerce, Mantorville, Minnesota 55955.

The festival events include an arts and crafts show, parades, queen coronation, music, flea market, flower show, tennis tournaments, pioneer feed, and dance.

★ 207 ★
Rollag - STEAM THRESHERS REUNION. Late August-early September, 4 days, Thresherman's Hill. Contact: Bob Brekken, Route 3, Hawley, Minnesota 56549.

One of the biggest threshing festivals, the events include antique machinery in running order, and displays of local crafts such as spinning and weaving, lathe and shingle making, cider making, blacksmithing, and rug-making. Also, home talent entertainment, parades, and meals.

★ 208 ★
Sanborn - WATERMELON DAYS. Late July, 2 days. Contact: Chamber of Commerce, Sanborn, Minnesota 56083.

Festival events include carnival, parades, queen coronation, baseball, flower show, and, of course, melon eating and melon seed spitting contest.

★ 209 ★
Thief River Falls - NORTHWEST DAIRY DAYS. Mid June, annual, 1 day, Fairgrounds. Contact: Chamber of Commerce, Post Office Box 514, Thief River Falls, Minnesota 56701.

MINNESOTA (Continued)

A dairy calf show and a Dairy Princess contest highlight the events.

★ 210 ★
Waskish - WILD RICE FESTIVAL. Mid July, 1 day. Contact: Bemidji Area Chamber of Commerce, Post Office Box 806, Bemidji, Minnesota 56601.

A community festival honoring an important local crop. Begun around 1973.

★ 211 ★
Worthington - KING TURKEY DAY. Mid September, 1 day. Contact: Chamber of Commerce, Worthington, Minnesota 56187.

Great Gobbler Gallop, square dancing, fireworks, horse show, football dance, parade, and carnival. Begun around 1941.

MISSISSIPPI

★ 212 ★
Greenwood - DELTA COTTON WIVES COTTON FAIR. October, annual, 1 day. Contact: Delta Council, Stoneville, Mississippi 38776.

Pays tribute to the many attributes and uses of cotton through the media of a craft show and sale; modeling; demonstration of weaving and needlework; relevant displays. Held in a private home.

★ 213 ★
Kosciusko - CENTRAL MISSISSIPPI FAIR, RODEO AND STATE DAIRY SHOW. September, annual, 5 days, Central Mississippi Fairgrounds. Contact: Travel/Tourism Department, Mississippi Agricultural and Industrial Board, Post Office Box 849, Jackson, Mississippi 39205.

Dairy show with awards of trophies and premiums, and a rodeo. Other traditional fair activities included.

★ 214 ★
Lucedale - WATERMELON FESTIVAL. Early July, 1 day, Intersection of U.S. 98 and Highway 613. Contact: Travel/Tourism Department, Mississippi Agricultural and Industrial Board, Post Office Box 849, Jackson, Mississippi 39205.

In honor of the important area fruit, the townspeople have feasts of watermelon and contests in melon-eating,

seed-spitting and seed-thumping.

★ 215 ★
McComb - LIGHTED AZALEA FESTIVAL AND TRAIL. March, 10 days. Contact: Travel Department, Mississippi Agricultural and Industrial Board, Post Office Box 849, Jackson, Mississippi 39205.

The highlight of the festival is a tour of McComb to view the azaleas, which are spotlighted for evening viewing. In addition, there are band concerts, garden club open houses, square dancing and the selection and crowning of the McComb Azalea Queen.

★ 216 ★
Meridian - MISSISSIPPI-ALABAMA FAIR. Early October, annual, 6 days, Meridian Fairgrounds (I-20 and I-59 intersection). Contact: Mississippi Economic Development Agency, 2000 Walter Sillers Building, Post Office Box 849, Jackson, Mississippi 39205.

Agricultural exhibits, cattle show, and a carnival highlight the events of this two state festival.

★ 217 ★
Osyka - DAY LILY FESTIVAL. Late May-June (begins Saturday nearest Memorial Day), annual, 1 month. Contact: Travel/Tourism Department, Mississippi Agricultural and Industrial Board, Post Office Box 849, Jackson, Mississippi 39205.

The festival kicks off with a one day tour of the gardens in which thousands of varieties of day lilies are on exhibit during the month of June.

MISSOURI

★ 218 ★
Camdentown - DOGWOOD FESTIVAL. Mid April, annual, 3 days. Contact: Camdentown Chamber of Commerce, Highway 54 East, Camdentown, Missouri 65020; or Larry Risner, Chairman, c/o Dogwood Festival, Camdentown, Missouri 65020.

Arts and crafts displays, a parade, and tours over three trails to see the dogwoods (Missouri's state tree) in bloom. A fiddle contest, and square dance. Begun around 1953.

★ 219 ★
Kansas City - AMERICAN ROYAL LIVESTOCK AND HORSE SHOW. Mid October or November, annual, 8-9 days, Kemper Arena. Contact: Convention and

Agriculture

MISSOURI (Continued)

Visitors Bureau of Greater Kansas City, 1221 Baltimore, Kansas City, Missouri 64105.

Commemorates the important role of both city and state in the American livestock industry. Largest combined livestock and horseshow, and largest quarter horse show in the country. Includes a queen coronation, coronation ball, grand parade through downtown Kansas city, and nationally known entertainers. Begun around 1900.

★ 220 ★
Sikeston COTTON CARNIVAL. Late September, 6 days. Contact: Chamber of Commerce, 301 North New Madrid, Sikeston, Missouri 63801.

The festival spotlights the importance of cotton to southeast Missouri economy. Features include live entertainment, a parade, displays, and beauty contests.

★ 221 ★
Springfield - OZARK EMPIRE FAIR. Early August, annual, 10 days. Contact: Director, Ozark Empire Fair, Box 630, Springfield, Missouri 65801.

More than 10,000 exhibits, the second largest fair in the state. Agricultural exhibits, a craft show, midway, and livestock show. Grandstand entertainment includes auto races and well-known professional entertainment, individuals and groups.

★ 222 ★
West Plains - HEART OF THE OZARKS FAIR. Mid June, annual, 4 days, Fairgrounds. Contact: Chamber of Commerce, 220 West Main Plaza, West Plains, Missouri 65775.

A stock show, home economics displays, 4-H and FFA exhibits are featured at this traditional agricultural festival. Begun around 1947.

MONTANA

★ 223 ★
Bozeman - MONTANA WINTER FAIR. Late January-early February, annual, 8 days. Contact: Montana Winter Fair, Box 117, Bozeman, Montanta 59715.

The events include judging of sheep, swine, cows including heifers, herefords, shorthorns, charolais and angus, and horses including appaloosa, paint horses, arabians and quarter horses. There are also horse shows,

Needlework Award and Style Show, lamb shearing contest, food and cooking contests, and banquets for many community organizations and breeders associations. A special event is the Montana Championship Draft Horse Pulling Contest. Begun around 1947.

★ 224 ★
Polson - CHERRY BLOSSOM FESTIVAL. Early May (Mother's Day), annual, Flathead Lake. Contact: Polson Chamber of Commerce, Post Office Box 677, Polson, Montana 59860.

A Montana girl is selected as queen of the event. There is a parade and other gala events in celebration of the blooming of the cherry blossoms. Begun around 1968.

NEBRASKA

★ 225 ★
Nebraska City - ARBOR DAY CELEBRATION. Late April. Contact: Nebraska City Chamber of Commerce, Post Office Box 1221, 117 North Eighth Street, Nebraska City, Nebraska 68410.

Events include a parade honoring the trees of America and a National Awards Banquet.

★ 226 ★
Niobrara - NORTHEAST NEBRASKA THRESHERS REUNION. September, annual. Contact: Community Club, Incorporated, Niobrara, Nebraska 68760.

Demonstrations of steam engine powered and horse powered threshers and tractors. The strength and power of the machines is exhibited and tested.

NEW JERSEY

★ 227 ★
Atlantic City - HYDRANGEA FESTIVAL. July, annual, all month. Contact: Greater Atlantic City Chamber of Commerce, 10 Central Pier, Atlantic City, New Jersey 08401.

Honors the city's official flower with tours of flower trails, processions, queen selection and coronation. Started in 1942.

NEW MEXICO

★ 228 ★
Eagle Nest - ASPEN FESTIVAL AND PAUL BUNYAN DAY. Late September, annual, 1 day. Contact:

NEW MEXICO (Continued)

Tourist Division, New Mexico Department of Development, 113 Washington Avenue, Santa Fe, New Mexico 87503.

Log rolling, log jousting, axe throwing, chopping, pole climbing, and barbeque. Begun in 1975.

★ 229 ★
Farmington - APPLEBLOSSOM FESTIVAL. Late April, annual, 1 week, San Juan College. Contact: San Juan College, Farmington, New Mexico 87401.

A gala festival at the time of and in honor of the apple blossoms, featuring arts and crafts, drama, horse show, track and sports events.

★ 230 ★
Portales - PEANUT VALLEY FESTIVAL. Early October, annual, Eastern New Mexico University. Contact: Eastern New Mexico University, Portales, New Mexico 88130.

Peanut food fair, sports events, music, and an arts and crafts fair which started in 1969. This festival was first held in 1974.

★ 231 ★
Truth or Consequences - SIERRA COUNTY FARM BUREAU COTTON EXTRAVAGANZA. Early July, annual, 1 day. Contact: County Agent, Sierra County Farm Bureau, Truth or Consequences, New Mexico 87901.

Cotton exhibits highlight the festival events.

★ 232 ★
Tularosa - ROSE FESTIVAL. Early May, annual, 4 days. Contact: Chamber of Commerce, 301 Central, Post Office Box 1026, Tularosa, New Mexico 88352.

Events include a rose parade featuring floral floats, garden tours, banquets, and dances. Begun around 1959.

NEW YORK

★ 233 ★
Albany - TULIP FESTIVAL. Mid May, annual, 4 days, Washington Park. Contact: Chamber of Commerce, 510 Broadway, Albany, New York 12201.

Display of tulips in the park, flower-filled parade, crowning of the Tulip Queen, street scrubbing, pageant, children's carnival, Dutch costumes, and concerts.

★ 234 ★
Bath - STEUBEN COUNTY DAIRY FESTIVAL. Early June, annual, 1 day, Fairgrounds. Contact: Finger Lakes Association, Incorporated, 309 Lake Street, Penn Yan, New York 14527.

A parade with a dairyland theme, a banquet, and round and square dancing highlight the festival events. Begun around 1958.

★ 235 ★
Bethpage - LONG ISLAND AGRICULTURAL FAIR. Mid October, annual, Old Bethpage Village Restoration. Contact: Travel Bureau, New York State Department of Commerce, 99 Washington Avenue, Albany, New York 12210.

Honors farming in the spirit of the 1800's. Exhibitors dressed like nineteenth century farm people. Exhibits include vegetables, cattle, jams, honemake pickles, honey cakes, homemade bread, and square dance music. Started in 1841.

★ 236 ★
Dansville - DOGWOOD FESTIVAL. Mid May, annual, 7 days. Contact: Finger Lakes Association, Incorporated, 309 Lake Street, Penn Yan, New York 14527.

Little Miss Dogwood contest, art exhibits, historic exhibits, antique exhibits, and a carnival highlight the festival events. Begun around 1967.

★ 237 ★
Marathon - NEW YORK STATE MAPLE SYRUP FESTIVAL. Early April, 2 days. Contact: Finger Lakes Association, Incorporated, 309 Lake Street, Penn Yan, New York 14527.

Booths and demonstrations in the "Sugar House" of maple syrup and maple candy being made.

★ 238 ★
Penn Yan - GRAPE FESTIVAL. Late September, 3 days. Contact: Mr. Amos Hammond, Yates County Extension Service, Finger Lakes Association, Incorporated, 309 Lake Street, Penn Yan, New York 14527.

Agriculture

NEW YORK (Continued)

The festive events are in honor of the grape and the products therefrom. Started in 1976.

★ 239 ★
Pultneyville - APPLE BLOSSOM FESTIVAL. Mid May, 1 week, Forman Park. Contact: Finger Lakes Association, Incorporated, 309 Lake Street, Penn Yan, New York 14527.

Festival events include parades, races, craft markets, contests, and a carnival. Also held in Williamson.

★ 240 ★
Rochester - LILAC TIME FESTIVAL. Mid May (3rd weekend), annual, Highland Park Botanic Gardens. Contact: Finger Lakes Association, Incorporated, 309 Lake Street, Penn Yan, New York 14527.

Displays of over 535 different varieties of lilacs, coronation of a Lilac Queen, and band concerts highlight the festival activities.

★ 241 ★
Williamson - APPLE BLOSSOM FESTIVAL. Mid May, Forman Park. Contact: Finger Lakes Association, Incorporated, 309 Lake Street, Penn Yan, New York 14527.

Festival events include parades, races, craft markets, contests and a carnival. Also held in Pultneyville.

NORTH CAROLINA

★ 242 ★
Angier - CREPE MYRTLE FESTIVAL. Early July (around the 4th), annual, 1 day, most events at Angier High School. Contact: Angier Chamber of Commerce, Box 47, Angier, North Carolina 27501.

The event is named in honor of the flowering shrub which blooms throughout the town. The festival is preceded by a parade, and includes a horse show and fireworks display. Started in 1974.

★ 243 ★
Cary - GOURD FESTIVAL. Mid September (2nd weekend), annual, 2 days, Jordan Hall Community Center. Contact: Mr. Marvin Johnson, President, Post Office Box 666, Fuquay-Varina, North Carolina 27526.

The Cary Gourd Club exhibits gourds and gourd crafts including domestic utensils, objets d'art, play pretties, and gourd whimsies. The crafts are also demonstrated. Begun around 1941.

★ 244 ★
Chadbourn - STRAWBERRY FESTIVAL. Late April-early May, 9 days. Contact: Greater Chadbourn Chamber of Commerce, 208-A Brown Street, Chadbourn, North Carolina 28431.

Strawberries are honored with a parade, a queen's ball, a strawberry cooking contest, and an art exhibit. There are tournaments for tennis players and golfers.

★ 245 ★
Clarkton - TOBACCO FESTIVAL. Early October, annual. Contact: Norwood Meggs, Clarkton, North Carolina 28433.

Clarkton honors the tobacco crop with a beauty pageant, parade, a golf tournament, dances, and a Field Day in the Park.

★ 246 ★
Clayton - NORTH CAROLINA SOYBEAN FESTIVAL. September (1st or 2nd week), annual, 3 days, most activities on Main Street. Contact: Office of the Executive Secretary, Clayton Chamber of Commerce, Post Office Box 246, Clayton, North Carolina 27520.

Activities of the festival include tours of the Research Station, bingo games, a fish fry, sidewalk sales, arts and crafts show, youth games, a drawing for approximately 50 country hams, karate demonstrations, and the coronation of the North Carolina Soybean Festival Queen. Started in 1972.

★ 247 ★
Fairmont - FARMER'S FESTIVAL. Late September, 9 days. Contact: Lenwood Rich, President, Fairmont Chamber of Commerce, Post Office Box 27, Fairmont, North Carolina 28340.

The event includes a beauty pageant and a parade. Arts and crafts are displayed; there are shows of flowers and farm equipment. Additional activities include street square dancing and a golf tournament.

★ 248 ★
Hendersonville - NORTH CAROLINA APPLE FESTIVAL. Late August-early September, annual, 16 days. Contact: General Manager, Greater Hendersonville Chamber of Commerce, 330 North King Street, Post Office Box 1302, Hendersonville, North Carolina 28739.

NORTH CAROLINA (Continued)

The festival features a variety of events including beauty contests, parades, a sidewalk sale, square dancing, orchard tours, a folk dance jamboree and a gospel sing. Mountain music jamboree and hoedown to entertain.

★ 249 ★
Rose Hill - NORTH CAROLINA POULTRY JUBILEE. Late September. Contact: W. H. Suanders, Rose Hill, North Carolina 28458.

The jubilee claims the "world's largest frying pan", from which they serve chicken to the festival participants. There is also a beauty pageant, a parade, and a carnival.

★ 250 ★
Wilmington - NORTH CAROLINA AZALEA FESTIVAL. Mid April, annual, 4 days. Contact: T. H. Salade, Star Newspapers, Post Office Box 840, Wilmington, North Carolina 28401.

Celebrates the blooming of the azalea bushes with garden tours, concerts, horse shows, a parade, the coronation of the queen, air shows and art exhibits. In addition, there is a sailing regatta and a variety show. Started in 1948.

NORTH DAKOTA

★ 251 ★
Edgeley - THRESHING BEE. Mid September, annual. Contact: North Dakota State Highway Department, Capitol Grounds, Bismarck, North Dakota 58505.

Collections of antique farm implements are fired up and put to use. Various harvest skills are demonstrated, along with rope making and display of antique cars and trucks.

★ 252 ★
Lansford - STEAM THRESHING SHOW. Late September-early October, annual. Contact: North Dakota State Highway Department, Capitol Grounds, Bismarck, North Dakota 58505.

Collections of antique farm implements are fired up and put to use. Various harvest skills are demonstrated.

★ 253 ★
Makoti - STEAM THRESHING SHOW. Late September-early October, annual. Contact: North Dakota State Highway Department, Capitol Grounds, Bismarck, North Dakota 58505.

Collections of antique farm implements are fired up and put to use. Demonstrations of various harvest skills are given. Display of crafts by women, entertainment, and meals round out the event.

★ 254 ★
New Rockford - STEAM THRESHING SHOW. Late September-early October, annual. Contact: North Dakota State Highway Department, Capitol Grounds, Bismarck, North Dakota 58505.

Collections of antique farm implements are fired up and put to use. Various harvest skills are demonstrated.

★ 255 ★
Oakes - IRRIGATION DAYS. Early June, annual, 3 days. Contact: North Dakota State Highway Department, Capitol Grounds, Bismarck, North Dakota 58505.

This community celebration features a display of agricultural products and machines, and arts and crafts. There is also a parade, entertainment, dancing, and food.

OHIO

★ 256 ★
Barberton - CHERRY BLOSSOM FESTIVAL. Mid May, 5 days, High School-Akron Area. Contact: Brad Porcella, Barberton Jaycees, 1316 Wooster Road, West Barberton, Ohio 44203.

Among the events and exhibits are a parade, country-western show, fireworks, and polka shows.

★ 257 ★
Burton - APPLE BUTTER FESTIVAL. Mid October, annual, 2 days, Village Green. Contact: Chamber of Commerce, Burton, Ohio 44021.

Delicacies such as apple butter cooked over an open fire, apple fritters, and fresh baked bread are served in the atmosphere created by pioneer homes, a country store, a one-room school, steam engines, and horse drawn carriages.

Agriculture

OHIO (Continued)

★ 258 ★

Chardon - MAPLE FESTIVAL.   April, annual, 3
days.   Contact: Geauga County Maple Festival,
Post Office Box 124, Chardon, Ohio 44024.

Demonstrations of maple syrup processing and samples
of the products.   Contests of pancake eating and
rooster crowing, and antique show.   Entertainment
includes rides, concessions, and parades.

★ 259 ★

Circleville - PUMPKIN SHOW.   Late October
(starting 3rd Wednesday), annual, 4 days.   Contact:
Circleville Pumpkin Show, Incorporated, Post Office
Box 228, Circleville, Ohio 43113.

This harvest festival was begun to give the area farmers
a chance to display their harvest, and to bring the
citizens of Circleville together with the rural population.   Billed as the "Greatest Free Show on Earth",
it features seven parades, contests for Miss and Little
Miss Pumpkin Queen, prettiest baby, hog-calling,
egg throwing, pumpkin pie eating, photography and
pets, entertainment and rides.   On display are
pumpkins and other vegetables, home crafts, art work,
and flowers.   Pumpkin delicacies abound.   Started
in 1903.

★ 260 ★

Columbus - OHIO STATE FARM SCIENCE REVIEW.
Late September, annual, 3 days.   Contact: Chamber
of Commerce, Huntington Bank Building, 17 South
High, Room 820, Columbus, Ohio 43215.

A tribute to the technology of farming, more then
250 exhibits offer displays and demonstrations of farm
equipment.   Members of the Ohio State University
College of Agriculture and Home Economics use field
tests and exhibits to present new developments in
improved living and farming.

★ 261 ★

Defiance - JOHNNY APPLESEED FESTIVAL.   Late
September (last weekend), annual, Au Glaize Village.
Contact: Defiance County Historical Society, Box
801, Defiance, Ohio 43512.

The festival honors Johnny Appleseed (John Chapman),
who lived in the area between 1811 and 1828, during
which time he planted several apple orchards.   Held
in a restored village depicting Defiance County life
between 1860 and 1920, activities include the pressing
of apple cider on the village cider press, the making
of apple butter over an open fire, and other pioneer
activities such as spinning, weaving, bread baking in

a dutch oven, wheat threshing, and the making of
sorghum molasses.   Started in 1966.

★ 262 ★

Geneva - GRAPE JAMBOREE.   Late September,
annual, 2 days.   Contact: Chamber of Commerce,
Geneva, Ohio 44041.

The newly harvested crop turns into an abundance of
grape juice, jellies, jams, and pies.   Grape pickers
dress in colorful costumes.   There are bus tours of
the grape vineyards and nearby historic and scenic
sites.   For entertainment, there are folk dancers,
parades, and games.

★ 263 ★

Hueston Woods State Park - MAPLE SYRUP WEEKENDS.
Late February-mid March, 6 days (3 weekends).
Contact: Bill Loebick, Division of Parks and Recrea-
tion, Fountain Square, Columbus, Ohio 43224.

Visitors to the park are invited to watch the processing
of maple sap, from the tapping of the trees to the
production of maple syrup and sugar.

★ 264 ★

Jackson - APPLE FESTIVAL.   Late September, annual,
4 days.   Contact: Chamber of Commerce, 210 Main
Street, Jackson, Ohio 45640.

Apples, apple cider and other apple based foods are
highlighted by displays, parades, and a street fair.

★ 265 ★

Lebanon - HONEY FESTIVAL.   Mid September,
annual, 3 days.   Contact: Judy Williamson, Ohio
Festivals and Events, Post Office Box 6, 213 South
Quarry, Bainbridge, Ohio 45512.

Honey and its many by-products are offered for sale
amidst educational displays and cooking demonstrations.
Entertainment is offered in the form of parades, stage
entertainment, rides, queen coronation, band and
float contests, square dancing, and an art exhibit.
Begun around 1968.

★ 266 ★

Lisbon - JOHNNY APPLESEED FESTIVAL.   Mid
September, annual, 3 days, Village Green.   Contact:
Chamber of Commerce, Village Hall, Lisbon, Ohio
44432.

This apple-producing region recalls the days of the
legendary Johnny Appleseed.   Apples, apple cider,

OHIO (Continued)

and other apple foods and by-products. Costumes, window displays and historic artifacts set the scene for demonstrations of old arts and crafts.

★ 267 ★
Middlefield - SWISS CHEESE FESTIVAL. Mid June, annual, 2 days. Contact: Wilton Town, Middlefield Festival, Post Office Box 455, Middlefield, Ohio 44062.

The event offers guided tours of Amish farm areas and the cheese plant. Good food is offered, including Amish homemade bread, trail bologna, cheese, barbequed chicken, and a cake display and demonstration. There is a flea market, flower show, rides, entertainment, a parade, and square and street dancing. Begun around 1959.

★ 268 ★
Milan - MELON FESTIVAL. Late August-early September, annual, 3 days, Village Square. Contact: Chamber of Commerce, Lockwood Road, Milan, Ohio 44846.

Milan's melons are lauded with an unusual parade and a street fair. There are plenty of the melons on hand for the enjoyment of the festival-goers.

★ 269 ★
Millersport - SWEET CORN FESTIVAL. Late August-early September, annual, 4 days. Contact: Millersport Lions Club, State Route 204, Buckeye Lake, Ohio 43008.

The star attraction is sweet corn, with corn-eating contests and roasted corn-on-the-cob fresh from the field. There are flea markets and pot-luck dinners. Entertainment is provided by band concerts, professional and amateur entertainers, and a parade.

★ 270 ★
Mount Gilead - OLD FASHIONED DAYS. Mid October, annual, 2 days, Morrow County Fairgrounds. Contact: Draft Horses Association, Mr. David W. Smith, Route 3, Cardington, Ohio 43315.

The festival conjures an older era with contests and activities of the past. Horses and their handlers demonstrate and compete with the walking plow, the sulky plow and the gang plow, as well as light and heavy weight log skiding, team horsemanship, and a team hitch class. Antique farm machinery and gas engines are on display. There are demonstrations of

steam thrashing, apple butter making, sorghum molasses making, spinning, oxen working, and quilting. There is a hobby show, flea market and square dancing. Started in 1973.

★ 271 ★
Reynoldsburg - TOMATO FESTIVAL. Mid September, annual, 5 days. Contact: Chamber of Commerce, Reynoldsburg, Ohio 43068.

The festival celebrates the development of the area's tomato industry. There are exhibits of tomatoes, free tomato juice, rides, entertainment, and a parade.

★ 272 ★
Rio Grande - BOB EVANS FARM FESTIVAL. Mid October, annual, 3 days, Bob Evans Farm, U.S. Route 35. Contact: Lee Durieux, Public Relations, 66 South Sixth Street, Columbus, Ohio 43215.

The festival includes a vast array of exhibits of arts and crafts, including such things as bobbin lace, slate painting and corn husk dolls. Costumed participants demonstrate some of the chores and activities of early farm life including churning, bow and arrow shooting, and moonshine distilling. Sheepshearers and border collies demonstrate in the field. The outdoor theater hosts square and folk dancing, bluegrass, ballads, and country music. The unique International Chicken Flying meet is flown. Begun in 1971.

★ 273 ★
Tipp City - MUM FESTIVAL. Early October (2nd Saturday), annual, 1 day. Contact: Tipp City Mum Festival, Box 1, Tipp City, Ohio 45371.

The actual festival is preceded by related events, including flower shows and the selection of the Mum Queen. There is a parade with floats and marching bands, a flea market, antique car display, float and flower show award presentations, and a band show. A theme is selected each year for the event. Begun around 1959.

★ 274 ★
Urbana - PIONEER DAYS AND STEAM THRESHERS FESTIVAL. Mid July, 4 days. Contact: Urbana Area Chamber of Commerce, 300 North Main Street, Four Gables Building, Urbana, Ohio 43078.

Demonstration of working antique equipment: tractors, threshers, etc.; models on display.

Agriculture

OKLAHOMA

★ 275 ★
Muskogee - AZALEA FESTIVAL.   April, annual,
22 days.   Contact: Oklahoma Tourism and Recreation Department, 500 Will Rogers Building, Oklahoma City, Oklahoma 73105.

Events include tours of public and private gardens, concerts, parades, the Azalea Ball, and a lighting contest.   Begun around 1968.

★ 276 ★
Porter - PEACH FESTIVAL.   Early August, annual, 1 day.   Contact: Oklahoma Tourism and Recreation Department, 500 Will Rogers Building, Oklahoma City, Oklahoma 73105.

The activities include a frog-jumping contest.   There is also an ice-cream giveaway.

OREGON

★ 277 ★
Albany - WORLD CHAMPIONSHIP TIMBER CARNIVAL.   Early July, annual, 4 days.   Contact: Timber Carnival Association, Post Office Box 38, Albany, Oregon 97321.

International competition among loggers for trophies in such events as tree climbing, tree topping, chopping, sawing, axe throwing, and birling (log rolling). Giant fireworks display on the Fourth.

★ 278 ★
Brookings - AZALEA FESTIVAL.   Late May, annual, 4 days, Azalea State Park.   Contact: Brookings Chamber of Commerce, Brookings, Oregon 97415.

Azaleas, which grow profusely throughout this area, are the focal point for this annual festival.   A parade and selection of a queen and court are among activities.

★ 279 ★
Brooks - ANTIQUE POWERLAND FARM FAIR.   Early August, annual, 2 days.   Contact: Antique Powerland, 3995 Brooklake Road, Northeast, Salem, Oregon 97305.

Fair features exhibits of antique, steam-powered farm equipment and demonstrations of old farming methods. Formerly called the Great Oregon Steam-Up.

★ 280 ★
Florence - RHODODENDRON FESTIVAL.   Mid May, annual, 3 days.   Contact: Florence Chamber of Commerce, Florence, Oregon 97439.

A festival honoring the rhododendron which grows profusely throughout the area.

★ 281 ★
Lebanon - STRAWBERRY FESTIVAL.   Early June, annual, 5 days.   Contact: Lebanon Chamber of Commerce, Lebanon, Oregon 97355.

A festival honoring the strawberry, a major agricultural crop of the area.   The festival includes a queen and court, dances, parades, a variety of exhibits and features the World's Largest Strawberry Shortcake-- more than 6,000 pounds of it.

★ 282 ★
McMinnville - TURKEY-RAMA.   Early July, annual, 2 days.   Contact: McMinnville Chamber of Commerce, McMinnville, Oregon 97128.

Festival honoring the turkey industry in the Willamette Valley.   A feature of the festivities is a turkey race with civic and political leaders coaxing an entry along.

★ 283 ★
Portland - ROSE FESTIVAL.   Early June, annual, 10 days.   Contact: Portland Rose Festival Associations, Hilton Hotel, Portland, Oregon 97204.

Includes a queen and princesses, several parades, including a Grand Floral Parade with flower floats, bands and marching units, rose show, stage events, Indian pow wow, river carnival, ski meet, auto race, figure skating championships, and milk carton boat races.   Started in 1907, grew out of a rose show started in 1889.

★ 284 ★
Rogue River - NATIONAL ROOSTER CROWING CONTEST.   Late June, annual, 1 day.   Contact: Grants Pass Chamber of Commerce, Grants Pass, Oregon 97526.

Roosters from across the nation are entered in this contest to see which can crow the most times in 30 minutes.   The record is 109 times set in 1953 by "Beetle Baum".

OREGON (Continued)

★ 285 ★
Springfield - OREGON BROILER FESTIVAL.   Early
July, annual, 2 days, Willamalane Park.   Contact:
Springfield Chamber of Commerce, Springfield,
Oregon 97477.

An outdoor barbeque chicken dinner is a feature of
this festival honoring the chicken industry in the area.

★ 286 ★
Stayton - SANTIAM BEAN FESTIVAL.   Late July,
annual, 2 days.   Contact: Stayton Chamber of
Commerce, Stayton, Oregon 97383.

A community festival honoring the vast fields of
Santiam beans that grow in this area.

★ 287 ★
Warm Springs - HUCKLEBERRY FEAST.   Mid August
(2nd week), annual, Hee Hee Long House, Warm
Springs Reservation.   Contact: Portland Area Office,
Bureau of Indian Affairs, U.S. Department of the
Interior, 1425 Irving Street, Northeast, Box 3785,
Portland, Oregon 97208.

A celebration held when the huckleberries become
ripe.

PENNSYLVANIA

★ 288 ★
Amity Hall - AGRICULTURAL AMERICANA FOLK
FESTIVAL.   Late July-early August, annual, 1
week, Intersection of Routes 11, 15, 322.   Contact:
Department of Commerce, Bureau of Travel Development, 431 South Office Building, Harrisburg, Pennsylvania 17120.

Large collection of early American farm equipment
and Rube Goldberg type contraptions on display and
demonstrated.   Steam show, thrashing, horse-plowing
contests, old fashioned picnic basket auction, square
dancing, and arts and crafts demonstrations.

★ 289 ★
Bangor - PLAINFIELD FARMERS FAIR.   Late July,
annual, 4 days, Route 191, 5 miles south of Bangor.
Contact: Mr. Ray Mack, Rural Delivery 1, Box 237,
Pen Argyl, Pennsylvania 18072.

Garden and tractor pull, nightly entertainment, pie
and watermelon eating contests, exhibits, cattle and
land judging, entries of home economics, etc.

★ 290 ★
Brookville - WEST PENN LAUREL FESTIVAL.   Mid
June, annual, 1 week (8 days).   Contact: Western
Pennsylvania Laurel Festival, Incorporated, Post
Office Box 142, Brookville, Pennsylvania 15825.

Events include antiques show, concerts, country-western
choral, queen coronation, bowling tournament, art and
photo show, hobby show, swim meet, parades, soap
box derby, golf classic, sidewalk sales, drum and
bugle tournament, gun show, and archery shoot.

★ 291 ★
Centre Hall - STEAM ENGINE DAYS.   Mid September, annual, 3 days, Penn's Cave Grounds.   Contact:
Russell Mark, Nittany Antique Machinery Association
for Central Pennsylvania, Centre Hall, Pennsylvania
16828.

Parade of power equipment, threshing, baling, and
shingle sawing.   Making of apple butter, cider,
and ice cream.   Displays of steam and gas engines,
shingle mill, threshing machines, antique fire engines,
corn meal grinder and roaster.   Cavern tours, antique
flea market, and Conestoga rides.

★ 292 ★
Coudersport - POTTER-TIOGA MAPLE FESTIVAL.
Early May, annual, 2 days.   Contact: Potter County
Recreation, Incorporated, Post Office Box 245,
Coudersport, Pennsylvania 16915.

Festival features parades and queen contest. Maple
products on display and served as refreshments.

★ 293 ★
Coudersport - WOODMEN'S CARNIVAL.   Early
August, annual, 2 days, Cherry Springs State Park
(Route 44 south of Route 6, Potter County).   Con-
tact: Potter County Recreation, Incorporated, Post
Office Box 245, Coudersport, Pennsylvania 16915.

Logging contest--top professional lumberjacks.   Log
rolling, tree felling, log chopping, cross-cut and
horse pulling contests.   Displays and demonstrations
of the latest logging equipment.

★ 294 ★
Gallitzin - HUCKLEBERRY FAIR.   Mid July, annual,
2 days.   Contact: Cambria County Association,
Box 247, Edensburg, Pennsylvania 15931.

Huckleberry Finn and Becky chosen to reign over
event which features a huckleberry picking contest,
parade, games and blueberry goodies.

Agriculture

PENNSYLVANIA (Continued)

★ 295 ★
Gettysburg - APPLE BLOSSOM FESTIVAL. May
(2nd weekend), annual, 1 day, South Mountain Fairgrounds. Contact: Gettysburg Travel Council, 35
Carlisle Street, Gettysburg, Pennsylvania 17325.

Crowning of the Apple Blossom Queen who reigns
over the celebration. During festival time, Gettysburg National Military Park is a panorama of beauty
when the pink, red and white dogwood and redbud
blossoms transform the fields and surrounding hills
of the historic area. There are band concerts,
exhibits, and free apple juice.

★ 296 ★
Gettysburg - APPLE HARVEST FESTIVAL. Mid
October, annual, 2 days, South Mountain Fairgrounds.
Contact: Executive Director of Tourism, Gettysburg
Travel Council, 35 Carlisle Street, Gettysburg,
Pennsylvania 17325.

The visitor may sample the fruits of the harvest in
nearby Boyer Orchards where all are free to picnic
under the trees and enjoy free cider and an apple.
Quantities of fruit may also be bought at bargain
rates. Back at the fairgrounds, more than 50 exhibitors display their artwork, crafts, antiques, and
favorite recipes for apples. There are free rides in
a wagon drawn by an antique steam tractor.

★ 297 ★
Kecksburg - DOWN ON THE FARM. Mid September,
annual, 3 days, William Howard Farm. Contact:
Mr. William Howard, Rural Delivery 5, Mount
Pleasant, Pennsylvania 15666.

Dedicated to portraying life as it lived "down on the
farm" long ago. Works, crafts and arts acted out.
Apple-butter making, sauerkraut cutting, threshing,
bailing, log skidding, and pole climbing are demonstrated. Antique farm equipment displayed.

★ 298 ★
Lancaster - HARVEST DAYS. Early October, annual,
2 days, Pennsylvania Farm Museum of Landis Valley.
Contact: Pennsylvania Farm Museum of Landis Valley,
2451 Kissel Hill Road, Lancaster, Pennsylvania 17601.

Demonstrations of traditional crafts, skills, and other
activities associated with harvest time in rural
Pennsylvania.

★ 299 ★
Liverpool - APPLE BUTTER BOILING. Early October,
annual, 1 day, Barner's Church Grove (3 miles northwest of Liverpool). Contact: Mr. Robert Gelnett,
Rural Delivery 1, Liverpool, Pennsylvania 17045.

Apple butter and cider sold (bring own container).
Hundreds of gallons of apple butter boiled down in
copper kettles over an open wood fire as in colonial
days. Enjoy delicious Dutch dinner, served family
style.

★ 300 ★
Meyersdale - PENNSYLVANIA MAPLE FESTIVAL.
Late March, 3 days, Festival Park. Contact:
Chamber of Commerce, Route 3, Box 223, Meyers-
dale, Pennsylvania 15552.

Demonstrations of the making of maple syrup and
maple products, parade of antique automobiles, arts
and crafts displays, carnival, and horse-pulling contest.

★ 301 ★
Philadelphia - AZALEA FESTIVAL. Early May,
annual, 1 day, East River Drive. Contact: Department of Commerce, Bureau of Travel Development,
431 South Office Building, Harrisburg, Pennsylvania
17120.

Over 2,000 azaleas are in bloom at the Azalea
Gardens behind the Art Museum. Music and entertainment available.

★ 302 ★
Schaefferstown - CHERRY FAIR. Mid June, annual,
1 day. Contact: Mr. John Hickernell, Schaefferstown, Pennsylvania 17088.

Tours of farm museum, arts and crafts demonstrated
and on display. Refreshments of cherry fritters,
cherry pies, and cherry ice cream.

★ 303 ★
Schaefferstown - HARVEST FAIR. Late September,
annual, 2 days, Historic Shaefferstown. Contact:
Historic Schaefferstown Festival Committee, Box 307,
Schaefferstown, Pennsylvania 17088.

The fair centers on traditional harvest time activities
such as apple butter making, threshing, grinding corn
meal, cider making and demonstrations of other crafts
and skills. Gospel singing, entertainment, and displays of agricultural products complete the event.
Begun around 1966.

PENNSYLVANIA (Continued)

★ 304 ★
Soudersburg - FALL HARVEST CRAFT DAYS. Late
October, annual, 3 days, Mill Bridge Craft Village.
Contact: Mr. Donald Delinger, Mill Bridge Craft
Village, Soudersburg, Pennsylvania 17577.

Features high wheel bike races, apple butter making,
cider making, wood turning, spinning, broom making,
and corn husking bee.

★ 305 ★
Wellsboro - PENNSYLVANIA STATE LAUREL
FESTIVAL. Mid June, annual, 4-6 days. Contact:
Wellsboro Chamber of Commerce, Post Office Box
733, Wellsboro, Pennsylvania 16901.

Features pagan ritual honoring the mountain laurel -
the state flower. Over 70 beautiful young ladies
compete for the title of Pennsylvania State Laurel
Queen during the blooming period of the state flower.
Craft fair, amusement rides, nightly concerts, art
exhibits, plays, dances, flea market, etc. Gas-lit
main street. Gala parade several hours long. Visits
to Pennsylvania's Grand Canyon and other outlooks
during laurel-time.

★ 306 ★
Whitehall - OX PULL FESTIVAL. Late September,
annual, 3 days, Routes 145 and 22. Contact:
Department of Commerce, Bureau of Travel Development, 431 South Office Building, Harrisburg, Pennsylvania 17120.

Teams from as far away as Maine and Nova Scotia
compete in events, beginning with a parade. Community wide ox roast, and international ox pull.

★ 307 ★
Wilkes-Barre - CHERRY BLOSSOM FESTIVAL. May,
annual, 3 days, River Common. Contact: Department of Commerce, Bureau of Travel Development,
431 South Office Building, Harrisburg, Pennsylvania
17120.

Art exhibits, open house, raft races, parades, concert, special events, and much more in celebration of
the blooming of the cherry blossoms.

★ 308 ★
York - INTER-STATE FAIR. Mid September, annual,
9 days. Contact: Ms. Catherine O. Morgart, 334
Carlisle Avenue, York, Pennsylvania 17404.

Exhibits of livestock, farm and home products, art,
flowers, 4-H, FFA-FHA, school and youth exhibits.
Harness racing. Flower show. Star attractions on
all weather covered stage.

RHODE ISLAND

★ 309 ★
Bristol - HARVEST FAIR. Mid October, annual,
2 days, Coggeshall Farm, Colt State Park. Contact:
Rhode Island Department of Economic Development,
Tourist Promotion Division, One Weybosset Hill,
Providence, Rhode Island 02903.

Activities include carriage rides, craft demonstration,
puppet shows, and haystack sliding. Jonnycakes
are served.

★ 310 ★
East Greenwich - ROCKY HILL STATE FAIR. Late
August, 6 days, Fairgrounds. Contact: Mr. Richard
Hamilton, 1408 Division Road, East Greenwich, Rhode
Island 02818.

Mainly an agricultural event, but includes an arts
and crafts exhibit.

SOUTH CAROLINA

★ 311 ★
Charleston - COASTAL CAROLINA FAIR. Late
October-early November, annual, 9 days. Contact:
Senator R. B. Scarborough, Post Office Box 855,
Charleston, South Carolina 29402.

In addition to midway rides and shows, the fair includes cattle and poultry exhibits, art photography
and crafts exhibits, cooking shows and commercial
exhibits.

★ 312 ★
Charleston - EXPERIMENTAL FARMING FESTIVAL.
Early June, annual, Charles Towne Landing. Contact: Lucia H. Jaycocks, Charles Towne Landing,
1500 Old Towne Road, Charleston, South Carolina
29407.

A celebration of the achievements of experimental
farming from 1670 to the present. Demonstrations
include rice-beating, cotton ginning, and indigo dye
making, as well as modern techniques and exhibits.

★ 313 ★
Dillon - INTERNATIONAL STEAM AND HOBBY
REUNION. Early April, annual, 3 days, Farm

Agriculture

SOUTH CAROLINA (Continued)

Museum.   Contact: Robert Rogers, Farm Museum, Interstate 95 and Highway 9, Dillon, South Carolina 29536.

Displays include machinery run by every conceivable source of power--steam, gas, kerosene, man, mule, air, dog, and water.   Thousands of flowers are also on display.

★ 314 ★
Estill - HAMPTON COUNTY WATERMELON FESTIVAL.   Late June, annual, 1 day.   Contact: President, Estill Jaycees, Rural Free Delivery, Estill, South Carolina 29918.

Events include a parade, speeches by politicians and guests of honor, watermelon contests, street dance, and the crowning of Miss Coastal Empire. One of South Carolina's oldest festivals. (Held in Hampton, South Carolina, in even numbered years.)

★ 315 ★
Gilbert - LEXINGTON COUNTY PEACH FESTIVAL. Early July, annual, 1 day.   Contact: Raymond L. Boozer, Box 124, Gilbert, South Carolina 29407.

A full day of activities is planned specifically honoring the peach with peach fruit contest, hundreds of peach products, and the selection of the Peach Queen. Entertainment throughout the day includes noted guest speakers, street dancing, and a golf tournament.

★ 316 ★
Greenville - UPPER SOUTH CAROLINA STATE FAIR. Late August-early September, annual, 10 days. Contact: A. H. Blackwell, 725 Parkins Mill Road, Greenville, South Carolina 29607.

The fair includes agricultural exhibits and livestock shows for junior beef, dairy animals, and swine. There are booth exhibits and individual exhibits of scale models of planes and cars, needlework, ceramics, baking, crafts, and photography.   In addition to free grand stand entertainment, there are fireworks, midway rides, and stock car races.

★ 317 ★
Greenwood - SOUTH CAROLINA FESTIVAL OF FLOWERS.   Late July, annual, 4 days.   Contact: South Carolina Festival of Flowers, Post Office Box 980, Greenwood, South Carolina 29646.

The festival includes garden tours, a highlight of which is an open house and field day at the Park Seed Company with its nine acres of trial gardens. Other activities include the South Carolina Princess of Flowers Pageant, an art show and contest, hobbies and crafts show, photo exhibit and contest, cultural performances, and a street dance.

★ 318 ★
Hampton - HAMPTON COUNTY WATERMELON FESTIVAL.   Late June, annual, 1 day.   Contact: President, Estill Jaycees, Rural Free Delivery, Estill, South Carolina 29918.

Events include a parade, speeches by politicians and guests of honor, watermelon contests, street dance, and the crowning of Miss Coastal Empire.   One of South Carolina's oldest festivals.   (Held in Estill, South Carolina, in odd numbered years.)

★ 319 ★
Orangeburg - SOUTH CAROLINA FESTIVAL OF ROSES.   Early May, annual, 3 days, Edisto Gardens.   Contact: Greater Orangeburg Chamber of Commerce, Post Office Drawer 328, Orangeburg, South Carolina 29115.

Around the beauty of thousands of roses center a variety of activities, including the Rose Festival Beauty Pageant, parade with over 100 units, flower show, art show, canoe races, turtle races, puppet show, concert, rodeo, community church services, and tours.

★ 320 ★
Pageland - PAGELAND WATERMELON FESTIVAL. Mid July, annual, 2 days.   Contact: Mrs. Boyd Hayes, Box 121, Pageland, South Carolina 29728; or Chamber of Commerce, Box 6, Pageland, South Carolina 29728.

Activities include a parade and square dancing, the crowning of a festival queen, and the festival ball.

★ 321 ★
Spartanburg - PIEDMONT INTERSTATE FAIR.   Mid October, annual, 6 days.   Contact: Paul Black, Montgomery Building, Spartanburg, South Carolina 29301.

Agricultural fair, cattle show, flower show, arts and crafts, band concerts, auto racing, and fireworks.

SOUTH CAROLINA (Continued)

★ 322 ★
Sumter - IRIS FESTIVAL. Mid-late May, annual, 7 days. Contact: Mrs. Margaret M. Harris, Harris Funeral Home, 501 Bultman Drive, Sumter, South Carolina 29150.

The flowering of the iris is honored with a series of more than 30 events. There is a parade, and a lavish Neptune's Daughter Pageant. The entertainment includes a sidewalk art show, a flower show, and a Little Theater Production. Other activities include a golf tournament, bike races, street dancing, model airplane fly-in, and a "diaper derby".

★ 323 ★
Trenton - TRENTON RIDGE PEACH FESTIVAL. Mid-late June, annual, 1 day. Contact: J. Frotz Huiett, Peach Festival Chairman, Trenton Post Office, Trenton, South Carolina 29847.

This full day of activities includes such events as a beauty pageant, parade, concession stands, flea markets, contests and games for all ages, concerts in the park, a barbeque, and home churned peach ice cream. The festival ends with a dance in the gym.

★ 324 ★
Westminster - APPLE FESTIVAL. Early September, annual, 2-3 days. Contact: South Carolina Division of Tourism, Post Office Box 1358-E, Columbia, South Carolina 29202.

The festival honors the "apple-grower of the year" with an award. Other activities include a barbeque, wagon train, square dances, beauty pageant, and a golf tournament.

★ 325 ★
Woodruff - GOLDEN MUSCADINE FESTIVAL. Late September-early October, annual, 1 day, Woodruff and Oakview Farms. Contact: R. L. Leizear, Route 3, Woodruff, South Carolina 29388.

Features such activities as mechanical picking of vineyards, processing of grapes, wine-tasting and a grape stomp. Also included are an antique flea market, beauty pageant, antique autos, bike races, street dance, music, contests, and an arts and crafts show. Begun in 1972.

SOUTH DAKOTA

★ 326 ★
Canton - CORN CARNIVAL. Late August, annual, 2 days. Contact: Division of Tourism Development, State Office Building 2, Pierre, South Dakota 57501.

The town celebrates its harvest with a carnival and parade. Entertainment includes rides, dances for teens and adults, a band concert, a barbeque, a tractor pull, and fire department water fights. Begun around 1971.

★ 327 ★
Groton - SUNFLOWER DAZE. Late September, 1 day. Contact: Division of Tourism Development, State Office Building 2, Pierre, South Dakota 57501.

The "sunflower capitol" celebrates the flower with a barbeque and prizes.

★ 328 ★
Leola - RHUBARB FESTIVAL. Early-mid June, annual, 2 days. Contact: Vera Kohlhoff, Leola, South Dakota 57456.

An old fashioned festival celebrating one of the town's main crops. There is a cooking contest, and rows and rows of booths selling rhubarb products such as homemade desserts, breads, jams, jellies and sauces. Other activities include two parades, a horse show, dances, golfing, horse shoe tournament, and a queen contest.

★ 329 ★
Madison - STEAM THRESHING JAMBOREE. Late August, annual, 3 days, Prairie Village. Contact: Prairie Village, Madison, South Dakota 57042.

Taking place in a reconstructed pioneer town, this festival brings the older times alive. There are demonstrations of the machines used by the pioneers in threshing their crops, a recreation of an early school, the opening of the land office, and a religious service.

★ 330 ★
Mitchell - CORN PALACE FESTIVAL. September, annual, 7 days. Contact: Tone La Breche, Mitchell Chamber of Commerce, Mitchell, South Dakota 57301.

The Corn Palace has outside panels decorated each year with bushels of grain. Inside are exhibits of the grains of the area, corn delicacies, corn products,

SOUTH DAKOTA (Continued)

and top performing artists and entertainers. Parades and carnivals complete the entertainment.

★ 331 ★
Phillip - TRI-COUNTY FESTIVAL AND FAIR. Late July-early August, annual, 3 days. Contact: Division of Tourism Development, State Office Building 2, Pierre, South Dakota 57501.

The celebration includes 4-H achievement days, parades, and other summer events.

★ 332 ★
Rapid City - CENTRAL STATES FAIR. Mid August, annual, 6 days. Contact: Chamber of Commerce, 428 1/2 Saint Joe, Post Office Box 747, Rapid City, South Dakota 57701.

The fair includes a horse show, cattle show, and many open exhibits. There are rodeos, stars and many other attractions. Held at the same time as the Fine Arts Festival.

★ 333 ★
Salem - HARVEST FESTIVAL. Early August, annual, 3 days, National Guard Armory. Contact: Division of Tourism Development, State Office Building 2, Pierre, South Dakota 57501.

The community celebrates harvest time with carnival and parades. There are 4-H achievement days, a chicken barbeque, and games for all, including a demo derby, street sports and a tractor pull.

TENNESSEE

★ 334 ★
Cosby - RAMP FESTIVAL. Late April, annual. Contact: Tennessee Department of Economic and Community Development, 1007 Andrew Jackson State Office Building, Nashville, Tennessee 37219.

The Cosby Ruritan club sponsors a tribute to the "sweetest tasting and vilest smelling plant that grows", the ramp. The festival serves as a homecoming and reunion for former residents of the area. Ample food, speeches, and mountain music are on hand.

★ 335 ★
Elizabethton - RHODODENDRON FESTIVAL. June, annual, 2 days, Roan Mountain. Contact: Elizabethton,

Chamber of Commerce, Post Office Box 190, Elizabethton, Tennessee 37643.

The town and its visitors celebrate the beauty of the 600 acres of wild rhododendron growing on Roan Mountain with a pageant, parade, and parties.

★ 336 ★
Memphis - COTTON CARNIVAL. Late April-early May, annual, 8-9 days. Contact: Memphis Convention and Visitors Bureau, Post Office Box 224, Memphis, Tennessee 38101; or Cotton Carnival Association, 547 North Main Street, Memphis, Tennessee 38101.

The court of the king and queen of the festival is carried in a parade of floats down the Mississippi. Other activities include a beauty contest, jazz concerts, carnival, regatta, balls, tours of homes, dancing on the royal barge, and exhibits. Started in 1931.

★ 337 ★
South Fulton - INTERNATIONAL BANANA FESTIVAL. Mid August, annual, 5 days. Contact: Mrs. Robert A. Batts, Executive Secretary, Post Office Box 428, Fulton, Kentucky 42041.

Located in the twin cities of Fulton, Kentucky and South Fulton, Tennessee, the Banana Festival brings together the peoples of the Americas and joins them in an atmosphere of friendship and understanding. There are arts and crafts exhibits, nationally known personages from the entertainment world, dancing to the Marimba Band from Guatemala, banana bake-off, parades and other exciting events, topped off by the one-ton banana pudding, made in a vat bigger than a bathtub.

TEXAS

★ 338 ★
Abilene - IRIS FESTIVAL AND TRAIL. April, annual. Contact: Abilene Convention and Visitors Bureau, Box 2281, Abilene, Tecas 79604.

Colorful gardens with thousands of iris in bloom highlight this festival.

★ 339 ★
Abilene - WEST TEXAS FAIR. September, annual, 6 days. Contact: Chamber of Commerce, Post Office Box 2281, Abilene, Texas 79604.

Features exhibits and amusements reflecting early days of Abilene, plus modern attractions of West Texas.

TEXAS (Continued)

★ 340 ★
Athens - BLACK-EYED PEA JAMBOREE.   August,
annual.   Contact: Athens Chamber of Commerce,
502 South Palestine, Post Office Box 608, Athens,
Texas 75751.

Features fun, games, and championship pea cooking
competition.   Further entertainment is provided by
a beauty pageant and musical events.   Begun around
1971.

★ 341 ★
Atlanta - FOREST FESTIVAL.   September or October,
annual, 3 days.   Contact: Chamber of Commerce,
Post Office Drawer 29, Atlanta, Texas 75551.

Dedicated to area forests and forest products.   Name
entertainment, parade, arts and crafts show, skill
contests, pageants, and product displays are among
highlights.

★ 342 ★
Bay City - RICE FESTIVAL.   Late September-early
October, annual, 3 days.   Contact: Mr. Jim
Sumpter, 2420 Seventh Street, Post Office Box 768,
Bay City, Texas 77414.

Reflects importance of this harvest in area economy
with gala festivities, including a parade, pageant,
and carnival.

★ 343 ★
Beaumont - SOUTH TEXAS STATE FAIR.   October,
annual, 10 days.   Contact: Mr. Whayne R. Moore,
San Jacinto Building, Fourth Floor, Post Office Box
3150, Beaumont, Texas 77704.

Traditional exhibits, displays and festivities draw
thousands each year.

★ 344 ★
Brownfield - HARVEST FESTIVAL.   October, annual,
1 day.   Contact: Mr. Gordon Hoopman, Chamber
of Commerce, 221 Lubbock Road, Post Office Box
152, Brownfield, Texas 79316.

Pays tribute to the agricultural bounty of the area
with gala festivities.

★ 345 ★
Brownsville - COTTON CARNIVAL.   September,
annual, 3 days.   Contact: Chamber of Commerce,

1600 East Elizabeth Street, Post Office Box 752,
Brownsville, Texas 78520.

Visitors are often surprised at major cotton production
in Border Tropics which the festivities celebrate.

★ 346 ★
Cleveland - CLEVELAND DAIRY DAYS.   April,
annual, 3 days.   Contact: Chamber of Commerce,
709 South Washington, Post Office Drawer HH,
Cleveland, Texas 77327.

Features displays of poultry, beef, hogs, and dairy
products.   Highlights of the show held in Stancil
Memorial Park include Dairy Day parade and coronation of Dairy Queen.

★ 347 ★
Corpus Christi - FESTIVAL OF FLOWERS.   April,
annual, 2 days.   Contact: Chamber of Commerce,
1201 North Shoreline Boulevard, Post Office Box 640,
Corpus Chrisit, Texas 78403.

Features more than 4,000 floral designs and other
festive activities and events.

★ 348 ★
Dalhart - INTER-STATE FAIR.   Late September,
annual, 3 days.   Contact: Gene C. Allen, Chamber
of Commerce, Box 967, Dalhart, Texas 79022.

Features traditional agricultural and livestock exhibits,
competition, and old-fashioned fun.

★ 349 ★
De Leon - PEACH AND MELON FESTIVAL.   Early
August, annual, 6 days, Fairgrounds.   Contact:
State Department of Highways and Public Transportation,
Travel and Information Division, Post Office Box 5064,
Austin, Texas 78763; or Betty Terri, Box 44, De
Leon, Texas 76444.

Features coronation of Peach and Melon Queen, old-
time fiddlers' contest, commercial and community
exhibits.   Parade kicks off the event which is a
popular homecoming occasion for a host of former
residents.

★ 350 ★
Falfurrias - WATERMELON FESTIVAL.   Early June
(1st Saturday), annual, 1 day.   Contact: State
Department of Highways and Public Transportation,
Travel and Information Division, Post Office Box 5064,
Austin, Texas 78763; or Chamber of Commerce, Box
476, Falfurrias, Texas 78355.

Agriculture

TEXAS (Continued)

Tribute to agricultural economy in general, succulent melons in particular. Events include a parade, barbeque, and a coronation.

★ 351 ★
Floresville - FLORESVILLE PEANUT FESTIVAL.
October, annual, 2 days. Contact: Chamber of Commerce, Box 220, Floresville, Texas 78114.

Highlights include coronation, parade, fiddlers' contest, art show, street dances and rodeo, all in honor of the important local crop.

★ 352 ★
Fort Worth - SOUTHWEST HARDWARE AND IMPLEMENT ASSOCIATION CHAMPIONSHIP TRACTOR PULL. Early March, annual, 5 days, Tarrant County Convention Center. Contact: Tarrant County Convention and Visitors Bureau, 700 Throckmorton Street, Fort Worth, Texas 76102.

Competition between different types of tractors to see which tractor can pull the heaviest weights.

★ 353 ★
Friona - MAIZE DAYS FESTIVAL. September-October, annual, 3 days. Contact: Ms. Peggy Bryant, Chamber of Commerce, Box 905, Friona, Texas 79035.

Tribute to the fertile soil and immense grain production of the area at this harvest time. Events include a queen contest, parade, carnival, and barbeque.

★ 354 ★
Gilmer - EAST TEXAS YAMBOREE. Late October, annual, 3 days. Contact: Upshur County Chamber of Commerce, Box 854, Gilmer, Texas 75644.

Held in honor of the yam, the star of the festival is featured in yam, corn and yam pie contests. A festival queen is coronated. Other activities include parades and a pageant, street and barn dances, crafts, hobby, and art shows, livestock shows; and many other activities. There are marching bands and fiddlers' contests as part of the program of continuous musical entertainment. Begun around 1938.

★ 355 ★
Houston - HOUSTON LIVESTOCK SHOW AND RODEO. Late February-early March, annual,

12 days, Astrodome. Contact: Leroy Schafer, Houston Livestock Show and Rodeo, Post Office Box 20070, Houston, Texas 77025.

The largest livestock exhibition in the state, this event attracts the finest livestock and top cowboys for steer-roping, bull-riding and barrel-jumping competitions. Leading entertainers are on hand to perform.

★ 356 ★
Luling - WATERMELON THUMP AND QUEEN CORONATION. Late June, annual. Contact: Chamber of Commerce, Post Office Box 710, Luling, Texas 78648.

Pays tribute to a major crop of the area. Beauty queen selection, arts and crafts exhibits, golf tournament, parade and dance are attractions, highlighted by Grand Champion Melon Auction. ($625.00 record price for the Grand Champion Melon.) Additional events include a car rally, a carnival, a seed-spitting contest, melon eating contest, farmer's auction, and fiddle contest.

★ 357 ★
Marshall - FARM-CITY WEEK. Late April, annual, 1 week. Contact: Chamber of Commerce, 301 East Austin, Box 520, Marshall, Texas 75670.

Shows lavish variety of agricultural exhibits, national entrants in Yorkshire Breeders Association, all-breed bull show, and Young Farmer's Rodeo.

★ 358 ★
Mission - TEXAS CITRUS FIESTA. January, annual Contact: Chamber of Commerce, Post Office Box 431, Mission, Texas 78572; or Texas Citrus Fiesta, Post Office Box 407, Mission, Texas 78572.

Salute to Texas Ruby Red grapefruit. Highlight of week-long event is style show in which all garments are made of Valley products. Queen Citriana and King Citrus reign over festivities. Golfers participate in Golden Grapefruit Golf Tournament.

★ 359 ★
Monahans - PECAN PERFECTION DAY. Late November (last week), annual, 1 week. Contact: Mr. Joe B. Cozby, Chamber of Commerce, 401 South Dwight, Post Office Box 1058, Monahans, Texas 79756.

Area growers compete for prizes for best nut specimens, and luscious variety of pecan dishes and pastries receive culinary attention.

TEXAS (Continued)

★ 360 ★
Mount Vernon - FRANKLIN COUNTY HAY SHOW.
September, annual.   Contact: Chamber of Commerce,
Box 554, Mount Vernon, Texas 75457.

Combines a festival atmosphere with agricultural displays on the town square.

★ 361 ★
Munday - KNOX COUNTY VEGETABLE FESTIVAL.
Late June, annual, 2 days.   Contact: Chamber of
Commerce, Post Office Drawer L, Munday, Texas
76371.

Honors irrigated farmland.   Citywide celebration
with prize agricultural displays, beauty contests, arts
and crafts shows, and variety of entertainment.

★ 362 ★
Pharr - ALL-VALLEY WINTER VEGETABLE SHOW.
Early December, annual.   Contact: Chamber of
Commerce, Post Office Drawer X, Pharr, Texas
78577.

Teaches 4-H and FFA students how to grow, exhibit
and judge vegetables.   Around 1,200 students
participate for thousands of dollars in prizes.

★ 363 ★
Plainview - HIGH PLAINS COTTON FESTIVAL.
October, annual, 3 days.   Contact: Jim Ferrell,
Chamber of Commerce, Post Office Box 340, Plain-
view, Texas 79072.

Pays tribute to the important cotton crop of the area.

★ 364 ★
Poteet - STRAWBERRY FESTIVAL.   April.   Contact:
Chamber of Commerce, Box 158, Quanah, Texas 79252.

The "Strawberry Capitol of Texas" offers activities
including a queen coronation, a strawberry auction,
and a fiddlers' contest.

★ 365 ★
Quitman - DOGWOOD FIESTA.   March-early April,
annual.   Contact: State Department of Highways and
Public Transportation, Travel and Information Division,
Post Office Box 5064, Austin, Texas 78763.

Features marked trail through the most striking beauty
spots of the area.   Activities include horse shows,

trail rides, arts, crafts and antique shows, and queen
coronation.

★ 366 ★
Stockdale - WATERMELON JUBILEE.   June.   Contact: Pauline Humphries, Box 271, Stockdale, Texas
78160.

The festival is centered around the watermelon crop.
Activities include a queen coronation, rodeo, dance,
carnival, and parade.

★ 367 ★
Stonewall - PEACH JAMBOREE.   June, annual,
2 days.   Contact: Chamber of Commerce, Box 225,
Stonewall, Texas 78671.

Queen's pageant and coronation, rodeo parade, barbeque, peach displays and eating contests, and fresh
peach ice cream!

★ 368 ★
Sulphur Springs - HOPKINS COUNTY DAIRY
FESTIVAL.   May, annual, 2 days.   Contact: Mr.
Larry E. Gee, Chamber of Commerce, Post Office
Box 347, Sulphur Springs, Texas 75482.

Parade, coronation of festival queen, talent and livestock shows, contests and exhibits highlight the events.

★ 369 ★
Tyler - AZALEA TRAILS AND SPRING FLOWER
SHOW.   Late March-early April, annual, 10 days.
Contact: Chamber of Commerce, CCE, 407 North
Broadway, Post Office Box 390, Tyler, Texas 75701.

Heralds the arrival of spring.   Some 75 home gardens
are open to the public; visitors see showcases of
azaleas ranging from crimson to purple to white.
Redbud, dogwood, wisteria and other blooms add to
the color.   Hoop-skirted young ladies are hosts at
art shows and historical exhibits.

★ 370 ★
Tyler - EAST TEXAS FAIR.   Late September, annual,
6 days.   Contact: Chamber of Commerce, CCE, 407
North Broadway, Post Office Box 390, Tyler, Texas
75701.

Outstanding livestock event in East Texas.   Large
variety of breeds exhibited include all popular beef
and dairy cattle plus Shetland ponies, swine, sheep
and industrial displays.   Exhibits and midway
attraction draw some 100,000 visitors.

Agriculture

TEXAS (Continued)

★ 371 ★
Tyler - TEXAS ROSE FESTIVAL.   October, annual,
5 days. Contact: Chamber of Commerce, CCE,
407 North Broadway, Post Office Box 390, Tyler,
Texas 75701.

Tribute to harvest of Tyler rosebushes.   One of the
state's greatest floral pageants, event features coronation of Rose Queen, parade of floats, tours of rose
gardens, and a rose show where hundreds of thousands
of blooms are arranged in magnificent displays. Attendance reaches 150,000.

★ 372 ★
Waco - HEART O' TEXAS FAIR.   Early October,
annual, 5 days. Contact: Chamber of Commerce,
108 West Denison, Waco, Texas 76706; or Chamber
of Commerce, Drawer 1220, Waco, Texas 76703.

Among the state's largest fairs; traditional livestock,
farm, and home exhibits plus a feature rodeo and
fun-filled midway.

★ 373 ★
Weatherford - PARKER COUNTY FRONTIER DAYS
RODEO AND LIVESTOCK SHOW.   Late July (last
week), annual, 1 week. Contact: Mr. Lloyd
Gilley, 119 North Main Street, Weatherford, Texas
76086.

A week of Western excitement, sponsored by Parker
County Sherriff's Possee.

★ 374 ★
Winnie - TEXAS RICE FESTIVAL.   Early October
(1st Saturday), annual, 1 day. Contact: Winnie
Area Chamber of Commerce, Post Office Box 147,
Winnie, Texas 77665.

Honors the crop with the crowning of the Rice Queen,
parades, art shows, contests, exhibits, carnivals, and
a horse show.

★ 375 ★
Woodville - TYLER COUNTY DOGWOOD FESTIVAL.
Late March-early April, annual. Contact: Chamber
of Commerce, 118 West Pavillion Street, Woodville,
Texas 75979.

Relives area history in pageant, story and song as
landscape is dotted with beautiful white blooms.
First event is Western Weekend with trail rides and
horsemanship competition followed by dancing. The

second weekend features an historical pageant and
coronation of Festival Queen.

UTAH

★ 376 ★
Bear Lake - RASPBERRY FESTIVAL.   Late July,
annual, 1 day, Sweetwater Park and surrounding
areas. Contact: Utah Travel Council, Council
Hall, Capitol Hill, Salt Lake City, Utah 84114.

To honor the raspberry harvest, Bear Lake holds
sports events, games, and contests.

★ 377 ★
Brigham City - PEACH DAYS CELEBRATION.   Early
September (1st weekend after Labor Day), annual,
2 days. Contact: Utah Travel Council, Council
Hill, Capitol Hill, Salt Lake City, Utah 84114.

Events include a parade, a queen contest, and a
flower show.   Entertainment includes a carnival and
other events.   Associated with the Peach Days Art
Festival.   Begun around 1905.

★ 378 ★
Cache Valley - CACHE VALLEY DAIRY FESTIVAL.
Late May, annual, 1 week. Contact: Utah Travel
Council, Council Hall, Capitol Hill, Salt Lake City,
Utah 84114.

A celebration honoring the dairy industry, an important one in this area.

★ 379 ★
Fountain Green City - LAMB DAY CELEBRATION.
July, annual. Contact: Utah Travel Council,
Council Hall, Capitol Hill, Salt Lake City, Utah
84114.

Events include a parade, contest activities, a program, and barbequed lamb.

★ 380 ★
Garland - WHEAT AND BEET DAYS.   Early August,
annual, 2 days. Contact: Utah Travel Council,
Council Hall, Capitol Hill, Salt Lake City, Utah
84114.

A parade and other events highlight the festivities
honoring two local crops.

UTAH (Continued)

★ 381 ★
Hooper - TOMATO DAYS.   Late August, annual,
2 days.   Contact: Utah Travel Council, Council
Hall, Capitol Hill, Salt Lake City, Utah 84114.

A community celebration in honor of an important
local product.

VERMONT

★ 382 ★
Brownsville - MAPLE SUGAR FESTIVAL.   Mid April,
annual, 2 days.   Contact: Events Editor, State of
Vermont Agency of Development and Community
Affairs, 61 Elm Street, Montpelier, Vermont 05602.

Band concerts, movies, dances, and a pancake meal
highlight the festival events.   The festival originated
in 1940.

★ 383 ★
Enosburg Falls - VERMONT STATE DAIRY FESTIVAL
(JUNE DAIRY FESTIVAL).   Early June, annual, 2
days.   Contact: State of Vermont, Agency of De-
velopment and Community Affairs, Montpelier,
Vermont 05602.

An old-fashioned festival with livestock demonstrations
and displays of the local products.   Also features a
parade.

★ 384 ★
Saint Albans - VERMONT STATE MAPLE FESTIVAL.
Early April, 3 days.   Contact: Director, Vermont
Maple Festival, Chamber of Commerce, Box 109,
Saint Albans, Vermont 05478.

Maple syrup is consumed in the form of maple candy
mixed with cream and in "Sugar on Snow" parties.
Musical events include a square dance, fiddlers'
contest and ladies' barbership music concert.   In
addition, there is an ice review and show, flea markets and craft shows, dances, and demonstrations of
how maple syrup is processed.   Begun in 1968.

VIRGINIA

★ 385 ★
Charlottesville - DOGWOOD FESTIVAL.   April,
annual, 11 days. Contact: Darden Towe, 416 East
Main Street, Charlottesville, Virginia 22901.

The blooming of the dogwoods is honored with the

selection of a queen, parades, historic tours, pageants,
and sports events.   The entertainment continues with
a fashion show, games, a carnival, bands, art shows,
celebrated entertainers and aerobatics.   Begun around
1950.

★ 386 ★
Emporia - PEANUT FESTIVAL.   Late September,
annual, 1 day.   Contact: Chamber of Commerce,
312 South Main Street, Emporia, Virginia 23847.

As a salute to the staple crop of the area, Emporia
hosts a parade, a beauty pageant and the coronation
of a queen.

★ 387 ★
Great Falls - LOGGING AND CUTTING CONTESTS.
January, annual, Colvin Run Mill Park.   Contact:
Colvin Run Mill Park, 10017 Colvin Run Road, Great
Falls, Virginia 22066.

Features typical lumber competitions.

★ 388 ★
Harrisonburg - VIRGINIA POULTRY FESTIVAL.   Mid
May, annual, 4-5 days.   Contact: Jerry H. Gass,
Virginia Poultry Federation, Post Office Box 1036,
Harrisonburg, Virginia 22801.

Attractions include parade, tennis, antique show, art
exhibit, go-kart races, music, and food.   The
Virginia Poultry Festival's Friends of Feather's Golf
Tournament is held at Ingleside Inn, Staunton.   Begun around 1970.

★ 389 ★
Monterey - HIGHLAND COUNTY MAPLE SUGAR
FESTIVAL.   Late March (last 2 weekends), annual,
4 days.   Contact: Chairman, Maple Sugar Festival,
Monterey, Virginia 24465.

The festival is reminiscent of the days when tree sugar
and molasses production was a part of every spring.
This, the southern most molasses festival, includes
tours, demonstrations of the sugaring process, arts and
crafts displays, square dancing and a hoedown.   Begun around 1959.

★ 390 ★
Norfolk - INTERNATIONAL AZALEA FESTIVAL.
April (usually around the last weekend), annual, 8
days, Garden-by-the-Sea.   Contact: Chamber of
Commerce, 475 Saint Paul's Boulevard, Norfolk,
Virginia 23510; or Guy P. Bordelon, Jr., Executive

Agriculture

VIRGINIA (Continued)

Director, 475 Saint Paul's Boulevard, Norfolk,
Virginia 23510.

The town honors NATO Atlantic Headquarters which
is located here. A different country is honored
each year. The Azalea Queen and her court of
Princesses represent each of the member nations, and
are selected by the embassies. The events include
band concerts, parades, a coronation ceremony, games,
military demonstrations, a civic ballet, fireworks,
balls, and scenic and historic tours. Begun in 1954.

★ 391 ★
Richmond - NATIONAL TOBACCO FESTIVAL. Late
September-early October, annual, 8 days. Contact:
Carlton Duffus, 13 East Franklin Street, Richmond,
Virginia 23219.

In tribute to the broadleafed plant, the "Tobacco
Capital of the World", crowns the Queen of Tobacco-
land, stages a grand ball and hostess coronation,
concerts, exhibits, and an illuminated parade. Also
featured are the Tobacco Bowl football games. Other
activities may include fashion shows, lunches and
receptions and tours of tobacco factories and plantations. Begun in 1949.

★ 392 ★
Vinton - DOGWOOD FESTIVAL. April, annual,
8 days. Contact: Dogwood Festival of Vinton,
Incorporated, Post Office Box 384, Vinton, Virginia
24179.

In honor of the flowering tree, Vinton holds a parade,
dances, and crowns a queen. Other entertainment
includes art and antique car shows, band and choir
concerts, celebrities, and a talent show.

★ 393 ★
Virginia Beach - LOTUS FESTIVAL WEEK. Late
July, annual, 1 week, Lotus Garden and the Taber-
nacle United Methodist Church. Contact: Mrs.
Cecil Reed, Cape Henry Women's Club, 5524 War
Admiral Road, Virginia Beach, Virginia 23462.

The festival celebrates the blooming of the rare
American lotus. The public is invited to view the
gardens. Special events include a special service
at the church, a luncheon served by church women,
and a bazaar featuring such items as handwork, decorated flower pots, white elephant sale, beaded and
zodiac necklaces, ceramic ducks, clothespin dolls,
aprons and decoupage. There may also be lectures
or other programs about the lotus. Picnic sites are

available at the garden. Sponsored by the Cape
Henry Women's Club, which has adopted the flower
and strives to prevent its extinction, and the Department of Conservation and Economic Development.
Started in 1955.

★ 394 ★
Winchester - SHENANDOAH APPLE BLOSSOM
FESTIVAL. Late April-early May, annual, 3 days.
Contact: Shenandoah Apple Blossom Festival, Post
Office Box 699, Winchester, Virginia 22601.

The festival celebrates the arrival of spring and the
apple industry of "Apple Blossom Land". Included
in the events is the crowning of Queen Shenandoah
and Miss Shenandoah Apple Blossom. Parades include the Fireman's Parade, the largest display of
firefighters and their equipment in the country, and
the elaborate Grand Feature Parade, marshaled by a
celebrity. There is plenty of music with roaming
barbershop quartets, concerts, square and folk dancing
exhibitions, concert band and marching band competitions. Other events include horse shows, arts
and crafts, luncheons, historical pageants, antique
cars, a midway and rides, and an apple baking contest. Apple blossom tour maps are available. Begun in 1924.

WASHINGTON

★ 395 ★
Granger - CHERRY FESTIVAL. May (1st weekend)
annual. Contact: Forrest Miller, c/o Granger
Lions Club, Granger, Washington 98932.

Events include a parade, a carnival, a jeep rodeo,
and obstacle course. Begun around 1953.

★ 396 ★
Marysville - STRAWBERRY FESTIVAL. June (third
week), annual, 5 days. Contact: Marysville
Chamber of Commerce, 1060 State Street, Marysville,
Washington 98270.

The strawberry harvest is celebrated by the strawberry
shortcake offerings of the many concession booths.
In addition, there is a parade, carnival, talent show,
and ASA sanctioned softball tournament. A grand
prix of kiddie tricycles for contestants 21 years of
age or older includes three beer guzzling pit stops
as part of the obstacle course. Begun around 1956.

★ 397 ★
Morton - LOGGERS JUBILEE. August (2nd weekend),
annual, 2 days. Contact: Gary Coleman, Box 456,
Morton, Washington 98356.

WASHINGTON (Continued)

Inspired by one of Washington's chief industries, events include tree topping, tree climbing, log rolling, and a loggers breakfast and show. There is all night street dancing and a rock and gem show. Begun around 1945.

★ 398 ★
Port Townsend - RHODODENDRON FESTIVAL. May (3rd weekend), annual, 2 days. Contact: Richard Spindor, Chairman, Post Office Box 766, Port Townsend, Washington 98368.

In honor of the flowering bush, the town hosts a rhododendron show, and a parade and crowns a queen. Further entertainment is provided by a carnival, arts and crafts show, and an antique show.

★ 399 ★
Puyallup - PUYALLUP VALLEY DAFFODIL FESTIVAL. Late March-early April, annual, 9 days. Contact: Public Relations, Puyallup Valley Daffodil Festival, Post Office Box 1933, Tacoma, Washington 98401.

Hundreds of varieties of daffodils are displayed at an immense flower show. A floral parade visits each of the participating cities. Aquatic events include a regatta, a marine parade, and drag-boat races. Queen pageant, coronation, and grand ball; musical performances, art and crafts exhibitions and demonstrations, tours of the daffodil fields, sales of daffodil flowers and bulbs, plus other special events for a total of nearly 70 festival-related activities. Started in 1934. Also held in Sumner and Tacoma.

★ 400 ★
Sedro Woolley - LOGGERODEO. June or July, annual, 2-3 days. Contact: Chamber of Commerce, 714 Metcalf Street, Sedro Woolley, Washington 98284.

In honor of one of Oregon's foremost industries. Logging events include tree climbing, log sawing, bucking, splicing, timber falling, etc. Other attractions include a grand parade, a kiddie parade, a queen contest, carnival and a rodeo.

★ 401 ★
Sequim - IRRIGATION FESTIVAL. May (2nd weekend), annual, 3 days. Contact: H. S. Fleisher, Post Office Box 114, Carlsborg, Washington 98324; or Chamber of Commerce, c/o Salley Sue Barney, Sequim, Washington 98382.

The oldest festival in the state, the events offer a queen's pageant, parade, demolition derby, horse show, arts and crafts, and a barbeque.

★ 402 ★
Shelton - MASON COUNTY FOREST FESTIVAL. May (4th weekend), annual, 5 days. Contact: Darryl R. Cleveland, Post Office Box 252, Shelton, Washington 98584.

The forest theme is carried out with a Paul Bunyan parade, old time and modern logging demonstrations. Further entertainment includes a queen coronation, banquet, musical, art shows, and displays. Begun around 1946.

★ 403 ★
Spokane - INTERSTATE FAIR. September (1st Saturday after Labor day), annual, 10 days. Contact: Interstate Fair Grounds, Post Office Box 143, Park Water Station, Spokane, Washington 99211.

All the states and Canada are invited to display at this agriculture and rural living fair. Outstanding FFA and 4-H exhibits supplemented by demonstrations of sewing, baking and home canning. Unique to this fair is the glass walled milk processing plant and the kiddie barnyard where children touch and hold domestic baby farm animals. Home arts include a large photo hobbyist display and paintings in both amateur and professional classes. Begun around 1954.

★ 404 ★
Spokane - SPOKANE LILAC FESTIVAL. Mid May, annual, 9 days. Contact: Spokane Lilac Festival, Post Office Box 802, Spokane, Washington 99210.

In honor of the flowers, the festival includes the crowning of a lilac queen, a lilac flower show, and several parades, including the junior parade, the armed forces day parade and the lilac festival torch-light parade. Other activities include River Cleanup Day, luncheons, a carnival, open house at Fairchild Air Force Base, and a band concert. There are competitions in many sports, including bike races, a wet suit river race, archery, softball, and logging events. There is special entertainment and crafts for youth. Begun in 1938.

★ 405 ★
Sumner - PUYALLUP VALLEY DAFFODIL FESTIVAL. Late March-early April, annual, 9 days. Contact: Public Relations, Puyallup Valley Daffodil Festival, Post Office Box 1933, Tacoma, Washington 98401.

Agriculture

WASHINGTON (Continued)

Hundreds of varieties of daffodils are displayed at an immense flower show. A floral parade visits each of the participating cities. Aquatic events include a regatta, a marine parade, and drag-boat races. Queen pageant, coronation, and grand ball; musical performances, arts and crafts exhibitions and demonstrations, tours of the daffodil fields, sales of daffodil flowers and bulbs, plus other special events for a total of nearly 70 festival related activities. Started in 1934. Also held in Puyallup and Tacoma.

★ 406 ★
Tacoma - GARDENERS' PARADISE DAYS. May (lst weekend), annual, Point Defiance Park. Contact: Chief Horticulturist of the Metropolitan Park District, 10 Idaho Street, Tacoma, Washington 98409.

Education in horticulture of flowers, shrubs and trees with displays and information booths. Begun around 1960.

★ 407 ★
Tacoma - PUYALLUP VALLEY DAFFODIL FESTIVAL. Late March-early April, annual, 9 days. Contact: Public Relations, Puyallup Valley Daffodil Festival, Post Office Box 1933, Tacoma, Washington 98401.

Hundreds of varieties of daffodils are displayed at an immense flower show. A floral parade visits each of the participating cities. Aquatic events include a regatta, a marine parade, and drag-boat races. Queen pageant, coronation, and grand ball, musical performances, art and crafts exhibitions and demonstrations, tours of the daffodil fields, sales of daffodil flowers and bulbs, plus other special events for a total of nearly 70 festival-related activities. Started in 1934. Also held in Puyallup and Sumner.

★ 408 ★
Wenatchee - WASHINGTON STATE APPLE BLOSSOM FESTIVAL. Late April-early May, annual, 17 days. Contact: Festival Administrator, Post Office Box 850, Wenatchee, Washington 98801.

There is a festival queen and princesses who represent various communities in Washington and Canada. Activities include a parade, youth and music theaters, a state art exhibition, a carnival, a horse show, Ginkgo gem and mineral show, band competition, antique autorama, outdoor pancake breakfast, motorcycle hill climb, hydroplane races, drill team conclave, Canadian tattoo, coronation, and a ball. Started in 1920.

WEST VIRGINIA

★ 409 ★
Berkeley Springs - APPLE BUTTER FESTIVAL. Mid October, annual, 2 days. Contact: Berkeley Springs-Morgan County Chamber of Commerce, Berkeley Springs, West Virginia 25411.

Activities include demonstrations of crafts and apple butter making. In addition, there is an antique car caravan and display, a beard contest, and a bake sale.

★ 410 ★
Buckhannon - STRAWBERRY FESTIVAL. Early June, annual, 5 days. Contact: H. Gene Starr, Post Office Box 117, Buckhannon, West Virginia 26201.

An arts and crafts display and sale is included in the festival celebrating the strawberry crop.

★ 411 ★
Elkins - MOUNTAIN STATE FOREST FESTIVAL. October (lst week), annual, 8 days. Contact: Mountain State Forest Festival, Box 369, Elkins, West Virginia 26241.

Presided over by Maid Sylvia, the festival places an emphasis on the conservation and preservation of the state's natural resources. Events include the crowning of Queen Sylvia by the governor of West Virginia, public square dances, tours of Davis and Elkins College, the Coronation Ball, the Mountain State Horse show, the running of the Cass Railroad, Fine Arts Preview, and various exhibits. The Knights of South Branch Riding Tournament, the West Virginia Open Fiddler Championship, the little league football game and archery competition are only a few of the many games and competitions going on. There is an antique car parade, a Fireman's Parade and a number of concerts. Begun in 1930.

★ 412 ★
Grafton - APPLE FESTIVAL. Mid September, annual, 6 days. Contact: John Wilson, Department of Employment Security, East Main Street, Grafton, West Virginia 26354.

Features apples, with events including an art show and crafts, carnival, and a horse show.

★ 413 ★
Hendricks - HICK FESTIVAL. Late August-early September (2 days prior to Labor Day), annual, 3 days. Contact: Delton Mullenax, Parsons, West Virginia 26287.

WEST VIRGINIA (Continued)

Most events are connected with the lumbering industry, including wood chopping, crosscut sawing, chain sawing, horse pulling, live raccoon chasing on the water and up trees. Each year a queen is chosen. Chicken barbeques, cake walks, barn dance, fiddlers' contest, tug-of-war, horse show and archery contest are part of the festivities. "Hick" domes from "wood-hick" - oldtime nickname for timber workers.

★ 414 ★
Huntington - DOGWOOD FESTIVAL. Early May, 5 days. Contact: Jim Robinson, 25 South Queens Court, Huntington, West Virginia 25705; or West Virginia Department of Commerce, Arts and Crafts Division, Building 6, 1900 Washington Street, East, Charleston, West Virginia 25305.

Arts and crafts are featured at this festival in this celebration of the beauty of the dogwood blossoms.

★ 415 ★
Kingwood - PRESTON COUNTY BUCKWHEAT FESTIVAL. September (last weekend), annual, 4 days. Contact: Buckwheat Festival, Kingwood, West Virginia 26537.

In honor of the grain, Queen Ceres and King Buckwheat are crowned and every day buckwheat cake and sausage dinners are served. Other activities include square dancing, parades, an arts and crafts show, baby beef show and sale, a flower show, antique car show and a pet show. Also among the festivities are the queen's ball and banquet. Special days are set aside to honor the firemen, the school community, the farmers and the senior citizens. Begun in 1938.

★ 416 ★
Mathias - WEST VIRGINIA TURKEY FESTIVAL. October (4th Saturday), annual, 1 day. Contact: Lacy E. Cochran, Mathias Ruritan Club, Mathias, West Virginia 26812.

The festival features a shooting match, turkey dinner and the selection of "Miss West Virginia Turkey Queen". Other entertainment is on hand. The event is sponsored by the Ruritan club. Begun in 1954.

WISCONSIN

★ 417 ★
Bayfield - APPLE FESTIVAL. Early October, 2 days. Contact: Bayfield Chamber of Commerce, Box 138, Bayfield, Wisconsin 54814.

Concession stands offer apple pies, apple baked goods, apple cider, caramel apples, and plain apples. The Volunteer Fire Department holds a fish boil, and there is a Venetian lighted boat parade, sponsored by the Bayfield Trollers Association, and followed by fireworks.

★ 418 ★
Hayward - LUMBERJACK WORLD CHAMPIONSHIPS. Late July. Contact: Hayward Chamber of Commerce, Post Office Box 404, Hayward, Wisconsin 54843.

Events include log-rolling, chopping, sawing, tree topping and speed climbing.

★ 419 ★
Warrens - CRANBERRY FESTIVAL. Early October, annual, 3 days. Contact: Chamber of Commerce, Warrens, Wisconsin 54666; or Director, Vacation and Travel Development, Department of Natural Resources, Wisconsin State Division of Tourism, Post Office Box 450, Madison, Wisconsin 25305.

In honor of the timely fruit, the festival features tours of cranberry bogs and canning plants and booths of cranberry products. Other activities include a parade, carnival, horse show, dancing, tent gospel singing, a bike-a-rama and firemen water fights. The visitor may also browse; antique, hobby, arts and crafts shows. Begun around 1973.

CANADA - BRITISH COLUMBIA

★ 420 ★
Creston - CRESTON VALLEY BLOSSOM FESTIVAL. May, annual, 4 days, Recreation Centre. Contact: Tourist Information, 1627 Canyon Street, Creston, British Columbia, Canada.

Festival events include a queen pageant with a dance, a midway, a Jaycee speakeasy, a children's day parade, and a fiddlers' contest. Arts and crafts are on display. There is a golf tourney and beer barrel water fight.

★ 421 ★
Nanaimo - VANCOUVER ISLAND EXHIBITION.

Agriculture

CANADA - BRITISH COLUMBIA (Continued)

Mid August, annual, 3 days, Beban Park, Bowen Road. Contact: Tourist Information, 100 Cameron Road, Nanaimo, British Columbia, Canada.

The event features class "B" agricultural exhibits, with outstanding livestock, 4-H, domestic science, arts and crafts, and a hobby show. In addition, there are various displays and stage entertainment.

★ 422 ★
Penticton - HARVEST AND GRAPE FIESTA. August or September, 2 days, Peach Bowl. Contact: Tourist Information, Jubilee Pavilion, Lakeshore Drive, Penticton, British Columbia, Canada.

The event features over 3,000 agricultural exhibits, 4-H displays, a kiddies parade, and pet show.

★ 423 ★
Penticton - PEACH FESTIVAL. August (1st week), annual, 4 days, Peach Bowl. Contact: The Department of Travel Industry, Travel Information Services, Parliament Buildings, Victoria, British Columbia, Canada.

A celebration in honor of a local crop.

CANADA - MANITOBA

★ 424 ★
Austin - THRESHERMEN'S REUNION. July, annual, Manitoba Agricultural Museum and Home-steaders' Village. Contact: Mr. W. Moncur, Threshermen's Reunion, Box 10, Austin, Manitoba R0H 0C0, Canada.

Agricultural fair featuring old-time steam and gas farm machinery, agricultural exhibits, demonstrations and contests in old farming skills such as tying, stooking, and threshing.

★ 425 ★
Brandon - PROVINCIAL EXHIBITION OF MANITOBA. Early August, Fairgrounds. Contact: Mr. G. MacArthur, Manitoba Provincial Exhibition, Royal Manitoba Winter Fair, Box 977, Brandon, Manitoba R7A 5Z9, Canada.

Industrial and livestock shows, rodeos, stage show entertainment, and carnival attractions are held. Largest agricultural fair in the province.

★ 426 ★
Brandon - ROYAL MANITOBA WINTER FAIR. Early April, annual, 1 week, Keystone Centre and Fairgrounds. Contact: Mr. G. MacArthur, Royal Manitoba Winter Fair, Manitoba Provincial Exhibition, Box 977, Brandon, Manitoba R7A 5Z9, Canada.

One of the largest indoor agricultural shows in western Canada. Includes livestock judging and sales, light and heavy horse shows, exhibits, baby animal farm, poultry show, and 4-H club competition.

★ 427 ★
Morden - APPLE BLOSSOM TIME. May, Agricultural Research Station. Contact: Manitoba Government Travel, 200 Vaughn Street, Winnipeg, Manitoba R3C OP8, Canada.

Timed to coincide with the blooming of many fruit trees, including peach, pear, crab apple, cherry and many more.

★ 428 ★
Morden - CORN AND APPLE FESTIVAL. Late August, annual, 2 days. Contact: Mr. W. J. Breakey, Corn and Apple Festival, Box 455, Morden, Manitoba R0G 1J0, Canada.

This festival draws together residents of the community and their visitors for a corn roast, free apple cider, and an apple tree draw. Also features a barbeque, fiddling contest, golf tournament, and stage show.

★ 429 ★
Russell - BEEF AND BARLEY FESTIVAL. Mid October, annual, 5 days. Contact: Director, Department of Tourism, Recreation and Cultural Affairs, Tourist Branch, 801 Mall Centre, 491 Portage Avenue, Winnipeg, Manitoba R3B 2E7, Canada.

This harvest festival honors the importance of both beef and barley to the rural community. Theme of festival is carried out with a steak barbeque, steer raffle and cattlemen's round-up, a "Barley Barrel" and a Western Canada homemade beer competition.

CANADA - NEW BRUNSWICK

★ 430 ★
Grand Falls - POTATO FESTIVAL. Late June-early July, annual, 7 days. Contact: Special Events Co-ordinator, Tourism New Brunswick, Post Office Box 12345, Fredericton, New Brunswick, Canada.

A community festival in honor of an important local crop.

CANADA - NEW BRUNSWICK (Continued)

★ 431 ★
Hartland - POTATO FESTIVAL.   Mid July, annual,
4 days.   Contact: Special Events Co-ordinator,
Tourism New Brunswick, Post Office Box 12345,
Fredericton, New Brunswick, Canada.

A community festival in honor of an important local
crop.

★ 432 ★
Saint Jacques - CORN FESTIVAL.   Late July, 3
days.   Contact: Special Events Co-ordinator,
Tourism New Brunswick, Post Office Box 12345,
Fredericton, New Brunswick, Canada.

A community get-together in honor of corn - an
important local crop.

CANADA - NEWFOUNDLAND

★ 433 ★
Saint John's - LIONS TRADE FAIR.   May, annual,
Memorial Stadium.   Contact: Lions Trade Fair,
Newtown Road, Saint John's, Newfoundland, Canada.

The event is primarily an agricultural exhibition.

CANADA - NOVA SCOTIA

★ 434 ★
Amherst - BLUEBERRY HARVEST FESTIVAL.   Early
September, annual, 2 weeks.   Contact: Travel
Division, Department of Tourism, Post Office Box
130, Halifax, Nova Scotia B3J 2M7, Canada.

The fruit is honored with a berry raking contest, in
addition to parades and other entertainments.

★ 435 ★
Annapolis Valley - APPLE BLOSSOM FESTIVAL.
Early June, annual, 4 days.   Contact: Nova Scotia
Department of Tourism, Travel Division, Post Office,
Box 130, Halifax, Nova Scotia B3J 2M7, Canada.

Festival features dances, entertainment, sports events,
and a parade with millions of lovely and fragrant
apple blossoms.

★ 436 ★
Bridgewater - SOUTH SHORE EXHIBITION.   Late
July-early August, annual, 6 days.   Contact: Nova
Scotia Department of Tourism, Travel Division, Post

Office Box 130, Hailfax, Nova Scotia B3J 2M7,
Canada.

A provincial exhibition with agricultural exhibits and
competitions, livestock shows, international ox and
horse pulls, entertainment and a mammoth parade.

★ 437 ★
Truro - NOVA SCOTIA SHEEP FAIR.   Early
September, annual, 3 days, Nova Scotia Agricultural
College.   Contact: Nova Scotia Department of
Tourism, Travel Division, Post Office Box 130,
Halifax, Nova Scotia B3J 2M7, Canada.

Fair features wool craft displays and demonstrations,
such as spinning and knitting, breeding stock sale,
shearing competitions, dog trials, tanning, soap and
candle-making, workshops, and a lamb barbeque.

★ 438 ★
Yarmouth - WESTERN NOVA SCOTIA EXHIBITION.
Mid August, 6 days.   Contact: Nova Scotia De-
partment of Tourism, Travel Division, Post Office
Box 130, Halifax, Nova Scotia B3J 2M7, Canada.

Includes animal judging, equestrian events, agricultural
displays, craft demonstrations and exhibits, a midway,
and entertainment.

CANADA - ONTARIO

★ 439 ★
Elmira - ELMIRA MAPLE SUGAR FESTIVAL.   Early
April, annual, 1 day.   Contact: The Ministry of
Industry and Tourism, Parliament Buildings, Toronto,
Ontario M7A 2E5, Canada.

Tours of maple bush and the surrounding countryside,
plus an old fashioned sugaring off and a maple syrup
and pancake meal in the town mall.

★ 440 ★
Ottawa - CANADIAN TULIP FESTIVAL.   Mid May,
annual, 11 days.   Contact: The Ministry of Industry
and Tourism, Parliament Buildings, Toronto, Ontario
M7A 2E5, Canada.

Held in honor of the millions of tulip blossoms with
which the nation's capital welcomes spring.   Includes
parades, regattas and fireworks among its activities.

CANADA - QUEBEC (Continued)

★ 441 ★

Plessisville - MAPLE FESTIVAL. April-May. Contact: Maple Festival, B^d des Sucreries, Post Office Box 361, Plessisville, Quebec, Canada.

Various activities for sugaring off time such as taffy-pulling, French Canadian suppers, and evenings at the sugar shack.

Antiques

CALIFORNIA

★ 442 ★

Sonoma - ANTIQUE SHOW. June, annual, 3 days, Community Center, 276 East Napa Street. Contact: Visitors Information Center, Redwood Empire Association, 476 Post Street, San Francisco, California 94102.

Homemade food and antiques are on display and available for purchase.

CONNECTICUT

★ 443 ★

Coventry - NATHAN HALE ANTIQUES FESTIVAL. Late July, annual, 1 day, Hale Homestead. Contact: Connecticut Department of Commerce, 210 Washington Street, Hartford, Connecticut 06106.

A display and sale of antiques in the historic and beautiful Hale Homestead. Begun around 1968.

★ 444 ★

New Haven - FALL NEW HAVEN ANTIQUES SHOW. Mid September, annual, 3 days, Veterans Memorial Coliseum. Contact: Connecticut Department of Commerce, 210 Washington Street, Hartford, Connecticut 06106.

Antiques of quality from a priceless heritage. Begun around 1938.

★ 445 ★

New London - NEW LONDON ANTIQUES FESTIVAL. Late August, annual, 1 day, Connecticut College Campus. Contact: Connecticut Department of Commerce, 210 Washington Street, Hartford, Connecticut 06106.

Quality antique show and sale on the campus of Connecticut College.

★ 446 ★

Riverton - COUNTRY ANTIQUES FESTIVAL. Early July, annual, 3 days, Fairgrounds Buildings. Contact: Russell Carrell, Route 44, Salisbury, Connecticut 06068.

Quality collector's items from a priceless heritage.

★ 447 ★

Salisbury - SALISBURY ANTIQUES FAIR AND FALL FESTIVAL. Early October, 3 days, Town Hall. Contact: Connecticut Department of Commerce, 210 Washington Street, Hartford, Connecticut 06106.

A celebration of the beauty of the season with a showing of antiques.

INDIANA

★ 448 ★

Madison - HISTORIC HOOSIER HILLS FALL ANTIQUE SHOW. Late September, 3 days, Court House Square. Contact: Helen Gourley, Chairman, Historic Hoosier Hills Guild, 2242 Cragmont Street, Madison, Indiana 47250.

Artists, craftsmen and antique dealers from several states display and sell their works and wares. Home-baked goods and old-fashioned confections.

IOWA

★ 449 ★

Algona - SIDEWALK ANTIQUE FAIR. Late August, annual, 1 day. Contact: William F. Steele, 114 North Noore, Post Office Box 500, Algona, Iowa 50511.

Over 60 exhibitors from Iowa, Minnesota and South Dakota display and sell quality antiques.

LOUISIANA

★ 450 ★

Lafayette - ACADIANA ANTIQUE SHOW AND SALE. Mid October, annual, 3 days, Lafayette Municipal Auditorium. Contact: Louisiana Tourist Commission, Post Office Box 44291, Baton Rouge, Louisiana 70804.

There are collections from over two dozen dealers from Alabama, Florida, Georgia, Louisiana, New Jersey,

LOUISIANA (Continued)

Oklahoma, Tennessee and Texas on display and available for purchase. The show benefits local worthwhile causes. Begun around 1969.

MARYLAND

★ 451 ★
Gaithersburg - ANTIQUES FAIR. Mid June (and Thanksgiving weekend), semi-annual, 3 days, Gaithersburg Fairgrounds. Contact: Bellman Promotions, Incorporated, Route 7, Bradshaw, Maryland 21021.

Exhibits of antiques, all for sale, in three exhibit halls. Begun around 1970.

MASSACHUSETTS

★ 452 ★
Brimfield - ANTIQUE SHOW AND FLEA MARKET. May (day before Mother's Day), July (around the 4th), September (near the 15th), 1 day (each time). Contact: Pioneer Valley Association, Incorporated, 333 Prospect Street, Northampton, Massachusetts 01060.

The largest such event in New England, these shows and markets bring dealers from across the nation to display their pieces.

★ 453 ★
Hyannis - HYANNIS ANTIQUES FAIR. Mid July, annual, 5 days, National Guard Amory. Contact: Nattall-Bostick-Wendy Management, Five Harbor Lane, Rye, New York 10580; or Cape Cod Chamber of Commerce, Hyannis 200, Massachusetts 02601.

A large collection of quality antiques of beauty and with heritage.

★ 454 ★
Northampton - PIONEER VALLEY ANTIQUE DEALERS ASSOCIATION EXHIBIT AND SALE. Mid April, annual, 2 days, Smith's School arena. Contact: Pioneer Valley Association, 333 Prospect Street, Northampton, Massachusetts 01060.

One of the largest shows in New England, the event is an exhibit and sale of quality antiques.

★ 455 ★
Orleans - CAPE COD ANTIQUES EXPOSITION. Early August, 3 days, Nauset Reg. School. Contact:

Cape Cod Chamber of Commerce, Hyannis 200, Massachusetts 02601.

An indoor show with over 50 dealers displaying and selling their stock.

★ 456 ★
South Yarmouth - OLDE YARMOUTH ANTIQUES FAIR. Late July, 1 day, Dennis-Yarmouth Field. Contact: Cape Cod Chamber of Commerce, Hyannis 200, Massachusetts 02602.

An outdoor show with over 100 dealers displaying and selling their collections.

MICHIGAN

★ 457 ★
Dearborn - OLD CAR FESTIVAL. Early September, annual, 2 days, Greenfield Village. Contact: Greenfield Village, Dearborn, Michigan 48121.

A recapturing of America's early automobile days. Cars vintage 1896-1925 compete for prizes and ribbons. Other features are highwheel bicycles, Dixieland Music, and flapper-hostesses.

NEW JERSEY

★ 458 ★
Morristown - ANTIQUES FAIR AND SALE. Mid April, National Guard Armory. Contact: Westchester Enterprises, Incorporated, Five Harbor Lane, Rye, New York 10580.

A show and sale of quality antiques from many areas and dealers.

NEW YORK

★ 459 ★
Hempstead - LONG ISLAND ANTIQUES FAIR AND SALE. Early February, 3 days, Holiday Inn. Contact: Westchester Enterprises, Incorporated, Five Harbor Lane, Rye, New York 10580.

A benefit for the Garden City League for I.H.B.

★ 460 ★
Seneca Falls - ANTIQUE FESTIVAL. Mid June, annual, 2 days, Eisenhower College Campus. Contact: Finger Lakes Association, Incorporated, 309 Lake Street, Penn Yan, New York 14527.

A large show and sale of quality antiques for the benefit of the Taylor Brown Memorial Hospital. Begun around 1968.

Antiques

NEW YORK (Continued)

★ 461 ★
White Plains - EASTERN STATES ANTIQUE FAIR
AND SALE.   Late April-early May, annual, 6 days,
Westchester County Center.   Contact: Westchester
Enterprises, Incorporated, Five Harbor Lane, Rye,
New York 10580.

An old and very well-known fair featuring quality
antiques. A similar event is held in the fall.

★ 462 ★
White Plains - EASTERN STATES ANTIQUES FAIR AND
SALE.   November, Westchester County Center.   Con-
tact: Westchester Enterprises, Incorporated, Five
Harbor Lane, Rye, New York 10580.

A large showing and sale of quality antiques.   A
similar event is held in the spring.

NORTH CAROLINA

★ 463 ★
Asheville - ANTIQUES FAIR.   Early-mid August,
annual, 4 days, Asheville Civic Center.   Contact:
Asheville Chamber of Commerce, Post Office Box
1011, Asheville, North Carolina 28802.

Antique dealers bring their wares for display and sale
at the area's oldest antique fair.   Sponsored by the
Vetust Study Club of Asheville.

OHIO

★ 464 ★
Lancaster - OLD CAR CLUB SPRING FESTIVAL.
Early June, 2 days, Fairfield County Fairgrounds.
Contact: Edson Devore, Lancaster Old Car Club,
Incorporated, Box 322, Lancaster, Ohio 43130.

One of Ohio's largest antique car shows, with a related flea market, and an antique car auction.

★ 465 ★
Millersburg - HOLMES COUNTY ANTIQUE FESTIVAL.
Mid October, annual, 2 days. Contact: Millers-
burg Area Chamber of Commerce, Hotel Millersburg,
Millersburg, Ohio 44654.

For a week prior to the festival, stores along the main
street of the town display antiques in their windows.
The festival offers an antique mart, displays and demonstrations of arts and crafts, parades, a fiddler's contest,
and a horse shoe pitch.

RHODE ISLAND

★ 466 ★
Providence - ANTIQUE SHOW AND SALE.   Early
October, annual, 2 days, Central Baptist Church.
Contact: Central Baptist Church, Lloyd and Wayland
Avenue, Providence, Rhode Island 02906.

Attractions include a boutique and a talent corner,
in addition to the large display of quality antiques.

TEXAS

★ 467 ★
Alto - SHOWING OF PAST TREASURES.   October,
annual, 1 weekend.   Contact: State Department
of Highways and Public Transportation, Travel and
Information Division, Post Office Box 5064, Austin,
Texas 78763.

Features antiques at one of several historic sites such
as Forest Hill Plantation, built in 1847.

★ 468 ★
Chappell Hill - BLUEBONNET ANTIQUE SHOW.
April, annual, 2 days.   Contact: State Department
of Highways and Public Transportation, Travel and
Information Division, Post Office Box 5064, Austin,
Texas 78763.

Attracts collectors and dealers.   Staged in conjunction with Bluebonnet Trails at Brenham; trails are
charted where blossoms are most profuse.

★ 469 ★
Dallas - ANTIQUES FAIR.   Late November-early
December, annual, 4 days.   Contact: Dallas
Chamber of Commerce, Fidelity Union Tower at Akard
and 1507 Pacific Avenue, Dallas, Texas 75201.

Popular event for a quarter-century showcasing arts
and crafts of bygone years.

★ 470 ★
Fort Worth - WORLD-WIDE ANTIQUE SHOW.
February, annual, 3 days.   Contact: Mr. Bill R.
Shelton, 700 Throckmorton Street, Fort Worth, Texas
76102.

Exhibits of historical treasures and miscellanea;
buying, selling, and trading.

VIRGINIA

★ 471 ★

Richmond - ANTIQUES SHOW AND SALE. Mid March, annual, 3 days, Hotel Jefferson. Contact: Women's Auxiliary, Richmond Academy of Medicine, 205 Oxford Circle East, Richmond, Virginia 23221.

Well-known antique and art dealers exhibit at the show, which is highlighted by special exhibits and lectures.

The Arts

(Includes festivals which cluster several forms of artistic expression)

See also: ARTS AND CRAFTS; DANCE; FILM; MUSIC; THEATER AND DRAMA

ALABAMA

★ 472 ★

Birmingham - FESTIVAL OF ARTS. Mid-late April, annual, 10-16 days. Contact: Birmingham Festival of Arts, Suite 1004, Woodward Building, 1927 First Avenue, North, Birmingham, Alabama 35203.

Each year the festival honors the arts, crafts, and foods of a different country. Music, theater, dance, visual arts, lectures, films, arts and crafts, and trade shows are featured. Artists from the selected country perform throughout the festival. A traditional dinner honors the ambassador from the designated country. CAMM (crafts, arts, music and movies of youth 13-30) is another feature. Book and Author Luncheon follows the reading of winning poems and stories of the national Hackney Literary Awards. The annual Alabama Arts Hall of Fame presentation is made. Begun around 1951.

★ 473 ★

Mobile - METROPOLITAN MOBILE ALLIED ARTS FESTIVAL. March. Contact: Mobile Area Chamber of Commerce, Post Office Box 2187, Mobile, Alabama 36601.

A series of cultural events from opera and symphonic performances to sidewalk art show.

★ 474 ★

Montgomery - FESTIVAL IN THE PARK. September, annual, 1-2 days, Oak Park. Contact: Montgomery Area Chamber of Commerce, 41 Commerce Street, Post Office Box 79, Montgomery, Alabama 36101.

Exhibits of various types including arts, crafts, handiwork, etc. with demonstrations given by some craftsmen. Drama groups, dance classes, macrame, sewing, weaving, oil painting, entertainment, including bands, clowns, and puppets. Begun around 1973.

★ 475 ★

Talladega - ARTS FESTIVAL. Early-mid April, annual, 1 week, Talladega College Campus. Contact: Dr. Roland Braithwaite, Dean of the College, Talladega College, Talladega, Alabama 35160.

Concerts, recitals, exhibitions of art, dramatic and dance presentations, and lectures.

ALASKA

★ 476 ★

Anchorage - ALASKA NATIVE ARTS FESTIVAL. June, annual. Contact: Alaska Festival of Music, Box 325, Anchorage, Alaska 99501; or Alaska Division of Tourism, Pouch E, Juneau, Alaska 99801.

Held within the framework of the Alaska Festival of Music, the event features exhibitions of native arts, crafts and games, with concerts of Eskimo music and dance performances.

ARIZONA

★ 477 ★

Flagstaff - FLAGSTAFF SUMMER FESTIVAL. June-August, annual, over 7 weeks, Northern Arizona University. Contact: Flagstaff Summer Festival, Incorporated, Post Office Box 1607, Flagstaff, Arizona 86001.

Dance, instrumental music, vocal music, theater, and festival. Purpose: "To produce and offer the finest professional arts festival in the region in the summer months". Also includes a series of film classics, exhibits by a variety of artists, chamber music, orchestras, jazz bands, recitals, different plays, ballet companies, children's theater, and crafts. Begun around 1966.

★ 478 ★

Phoenix - GREATER PHOENIX SUMMER FESTIVAL. June-August, annual. Contact: Phoenix Chamber of Commerce, 805 North Second Street, Phoenix, Arizona 85004.

Concerts, ballet, theater, and art exhibits are featured events.

The Arts

★ 479 ★
Tubac - FESTIVAL OF THE ARTS. February, annual,
9 days. Contact: Chamber of Commerce, Tubac,
Arizona 85640.

A celebration of the arts with various forms on display or in performance.

★ 480 ★
Yuma - GARCES CELEBRATION OF THE ARTS.
Early May. Contact: Garces Celebration of the
Arts, 248 Madison Avenue, Yuma, Arizona 85364.

Concerts (orchestral, choral, chamber), dance, drama,
fine arts exhibits, and art sale.

ARKANSAS

★ 481 ★
Bella Vista - BELLA VISTA FINE ARTS CENTER
FESTIVAL. June-August (summer). Contact: Bella
Vista Fine Arts Center, Bella Vista, Arkansas 72712.

Concerts, art exhibits, and symposiums highlight this
cultural celebration.

★ 482 ★
Siloam Springs - SIMON SAGER CABIN DEDICATION,
MUSIC AND ART FESTIVAL. Late April, 8 days.
Contact: Siloam Springs Chamber of Commerce,
Siloam Springs, Arkansas 72761.

Ceremony, festival of arts, and performances of
music highlight the events.

★ 483 ★
Stuttgart - GRAND PRAIRIE FESTIVAL OF ARTS.
Mid September, annual, 4 days, Grand Prairie War
Memorial Auditorium. Contact: Chamber of Com-
merce, Post Office Box 932, Stuttgart, Arkansas
72160.

The goal of the festival, sponsored by the Grand
Prairie Arts Council, is to encourage cultural development and work towards the establishment of an
Arts Center. There are performances and exhibitions
of the graphic, musical, and literary arts. Begun
around 1957.

CALIFORNIA

★ 484 ★
Carlsbad - CARLSBAD BOOK FAIR. Mid May,
annual, 1 day, Holiday Park. Contact: San Diego
Convention and Visitors Bureau, 1200 Third Avenue,
Suite 824, San Diego, California 92101.

"Old Fashioned Sunday in the Park" - books, records,
art prints and crafts for sale. Begun around 1962.

★ 485 ★
Fullerton - FULLERTON ART FAIR. Early October,
2 days, Fullerton College. Contact: Southern
California Visitors Council, 705 West Seventh Street,
Los Angeles, California 90017.

Events include visual and performing art exhibits and
demonstrations, folk dancing, band concerts, films,
and children's activities.

★ 486 ★
Georgetown - GEORGETOWN PERFORMING ARTS
CENTER FESTIVAL. July-August, Balsar Opera
House. Contact: Georgetown Performing Arts Center
Festival, Post Office Box 411, Georgetown, California
95634.

A series of concerts and operas by different composers;
dance, instrumental music, vocal music, and theater.

★ 487 ★
Hayward - FESTIVAL OF THE ARTS. May (3rd
weekend), annual, 3 days, Sun Gallery. Contact:
Hayward Area Festival of the Arts, Incorporated,
Post Office 656, Hayward, California 94543.

Arts and crafts. High school show, junior high
show, commercial booths, and silent auction. A
constant performing arts show including mime, bands,
poetry reading, belly dancing, etc. Begun around
1961.

★ 488 ★
Hollywood - LOS ANGELES PERFORMING ARTS
FESTIVAL. July, annual, 3 weeks, Barnsdall Park.
Contact: Chamber of Commerce, 6520 Sunset Boule-
vard, Hollywood, California 90028; or Southern
California Visitors Council, 705 West Seventh Street,
Los Angeles, California 90017.

More than 400 events including symposia and exhibits,
center around the arts. Begun around 1973.

CALIFORNIA (Continued)

★ 489 ★
La Mirada - FIESTA DE ARTES.   Late June, 10
days.   Contact: La Mirada Fiesta de Artes, Post
Office 232, La Mirada, California 90638.

Arts and crafts, demonstrations, dancing, instrumental
music, vocal music, and theater.

★ 490 ★
Laguna Beach - FESTIVAL OF THE ARTS AND
PAGEANT OF THE MASTERS.   Mid July-late August,
annual, 1 1/2 months, Irvine Bowl.   Contact:
Festival of the Arts, Pageant of the Masters, 1455
Terrace Way, Laguna Beach, California 92651.

Display of all forms of art and special demonstrations
by artists.   Nightly performances of music and
puppet shows.   In the Pageant of the Masters, people
from the community impersonate scenes from master-
works of art.   Begun around 1936.

★ 491 ★
Mendocino - THANKSGIVING FESTIVAL.   November,
2 days, Mendicino Art Center.   Contact: Redwood
Empire Association, Visitors Information Center, 476
Post Street, San Francisco, California 94102.

California artists exhibit and sell jewelry, ceramics,
macrame, weaving, woodwork, toys, and other gift
items.   The gallery's display includes paintings,
prints, and photographs for rent or sale.   Drama,
music by local musicians, puppet show, poetry reading,
wreath and green sale.

★ 492 ★
San Diego - FESTIVAL OF THE ARTS.   August or
September, annual, 11 days, Balboa Park.   Contact:
Mrs. Bea Evenson, 340 San Gorgonio, San Diego,
California 92106.

Sponsored by the Committee of 100, the free outdoor
entertainment includes everything in the way of arts
from mimes to jazz ensembles.   Usually associated
with the America's Finest City Week.   Begun around
1974.

★ 493 ★
San Francisco - INTERNATIONAL ANTIQUARIUM
BOOK FAIR.   September, biennial, 3 days, Fair-
mount Hotel.   Contact: R. E. Lewis, Post Office
Box 72, Nicaseo, California 94946.

Dealers come from all over the United States and

Europe to exhibit and sell old books, maps, prints,
autographs, etc.   The treasures are brought from
London, Bonn, Amsterdam, Massachusetts, New Jersey,
and California.   The Fair takes place on the West
Coast on alternate (even) years.   It takes place on
the East Coast in odd years.   (See New York, March).

★ 494 ★
Santa Maria - ARTI GRAS.   September or October
(Fall), annual, Santa Maria High School.   Contact:
Santa Maria Arts Council, Post Office Box 5, Santa
Maria, California 93454.

Artist exhibits, and performances.   First offered in
1968.

★ 495 ★
Santa Monica - SANTA MONICA SPORTS AND
ARTS FESTIVAL.   Late August-early September, 10
days.   Contact: California Chamber of Commerce,
455 Capitol Mall, Sacramento, California 95814;
or Southern California Visitors Council, 705 West
Seventh Street, Los Angeles, California 90017.

More than 40 events including dory races, outdoor
dance, music festival, art show and aquacade.

★ 496 ★
Stanford - STANFORD SUMMER FESTIVALS OF THE
ARTS.   Mid-June to mid-August, annual, Campus
of Stanford University.   Contact: Stanford Summer
Festivals of the Arts, c/o Stanford Summer Festivals,
Post Office Box 3006, Stanford, California 94305.

The festival incorporates a wide variety of art forms
in addition to music.   Performances are by jazz
groups and soloists, symphony orchestra, chamber
music ensembles, opera companies, ballet and dance
groups, and repertory theater companies.   Lectures,
exhibitions, seminars, concerts, demonstrations, and
audience briefings.   First festival held in 1964.

★ 497 ★
Torrance - INTER ARTS FESTIVAL.   Mid October,
9 days.   Contact: Southern California Visitors
Council, 705 West Seventh Street, Los Angeles,
California 90017.

Festival events include a symphony concert, art show,
and a play.

★ 498 ★
Valencia - CAL ARTS SPRING FAIR.   May, annual,
2 days, California Institute of Arts.   Contact: Spring

The Arts

CALIFORNIA (Continued)

Fair Co-ordinator, California Institute of the Arts, Valencia, California 91355.

Painting and sculpture exhibits, modern dance performances, graphic, photography, product and environmental design exhibits and sales. Student and faculty films, traditional, contemporary, and ethnic music performances. Plays, clowns, street theater, and special events for children. Handicrafts for sale, and international foods.

COLORADO

★ 499 ★
Central City - CENTRAL CITY OPERA AND DRAMA FESTIVAL. June-July, annual, 16 days, Opera House. Contact: Central City Festival, c/o Central City Opera House Association, 910 16th Street, Suite 636, Denver, Colorado 80202.

The festival produces opera production, plays and other theatrical productions featuring well-known stars of Hollywood, the stage, and television. Other programs include chamber music and. Gilbert and Sullivan operettas.

★ 500 ★
Denver - ROCKY MOUNTAIN BOOK FESTIVAL. Late April-early May, 3 days, Denver Auditorium Arena. Contact: Duncan M. Luke, Festival Director, Box 20188, Denver, Colorado 80220.

Publishers' exhibits, author-speakers appearing every hour, book-related movies, story hours for children and "rap" sessions for teenagers with authors, and autographing parties. Begun in 1968.

★ 501 ★
Snow-Mass-at-Aspen - COLORADO CRAFT-IN. Early August, 8 days. Contact: Elise McGuire, Pinebrook Hills, Boulder, Colorado 80302.

An exciting week of demonstration and displays of arts and crafts, appearances by famous musicians and actors, and other cultural events designed for the enjoyment of all age groups. Special entertainment includes Hawaiian hula dancers, a Mime Theatre, an old-time melodrama and an Ute Indian Theatre.

★ 502 ★
Steamboat Springs - STEAMBOAT SUMMER ARTS FESTIVAL. July-August, annual, 31 days. Contact: Steamboat Springs Council of the Arts and Humanities,

Post Office Box 1913, Steamboat Springs, Colorado 80477.

Performances of dance, drama, music; showing of films, workshops (approximately 50) on both novice and master level in a wide variety of arts and crafts, and a show and sale of visual arts. Sponsored by several state, county and civic groups. Begun in 1973.

CONNECTICUT

★ 503 ★
Hartford - GREATER HARTFORD CIVIC AND ARTS FESTIVAL. Early June, annual, 9-10 days, Constitution Plaza. Contact: Catherine Wysmuller, Director, 250 Constitution Plaza, Hartford, Connecticut 06103.

Paintings, sculpture, decorative items and handicrafts. Student and professional ensembles perform twentieth century chamber music, new and experimental music, jazz, popular music, and choral music in a week of free public concerts.

★ 504 ★
New Haven - NEW HAVEN FESTIVAL OF ARTS. May, annual, 1 week. Contact: New Haven Festival of Arts, c/o Box 104, New Haven, Connecticut 06513.

The community-oriented festival consists of concerts, dance performances, plays, films, and exhibits of books, architecture, photography, and crafts. Prizes for winning works, daily sessions called "Art in Action" (live demonstrations of techniques by artists), exhibitions by invited artists and teenage artists are all important aspects of the festival. Concerts take place in the open air on New Haven Green.

★ 505 ★
Norwich - NORWICH ROSE-ARTS FESTIVAL. Late June to early July, annual, 1 week, Tent erected on Norwich's Chelsea Parade. Contact: Norwich Rose-Arts Festival, One Constitution Plaza, Norwich, Connecticut 06360.

The festival is a community-oriented annual event offering mainly popular arts, entertainment, and sports. Operas for children, pop concerts, the variety show, drum corps competition, band concerts, and plays are featured. Popular music performers engaged are well-known bands, folk groups, and vocalists. Flower bedecked floats and garden displays. Founded 1964.

CONNECTICUT (Continued)

★ 506 ★
Torrington - TORRINGTON ARTS FESTIVAL. Early August, annual, 1 day, Coe Memorial Park. Contact: Marie N. Wetelinck, Northwest Connecticut Chamber of Commerce, 40 Main Street, Torrington, Connecticut 06790.

Includes concerts and art exhibits in all media. Begun around 1963.

DISTRICT OF COLUMBIA

★ 507 ★
Washington, D.C. - ART NOW FESTIVAL. Late April-early June, annual, 6 weeks, Kennedy Center. Contact: Art Now Festival, John F. Kennedy Center for the Performing Arts, 2700 F Street, Northwest, Washington, D.C. 20037.

Each year the festival honors some aspect of art with exhibits surveying its history, demonstrations, panel discussions, and films.

FLORIDA

★ 508 ★
Gainesville - SPRING ARTS FESTIVAL. Mid May, annual, 4 days, Santa Fe Community College. Contact: Barbara Kirkpatrick, Santa Fe Community College, Gainesville, Florida 32601.

Arts and crafts exhibit and sale. International buffet, and a French pastry shop. Live dramatic and musical entertainment, full-length movies, and a petting zoo. An author lecture is presented in conjunction with the festival.

★ 509 ★
Hollywood - SEVEN LIVELY ARTS FESTIVAL. Mid April, 9 days, Young Circle Park. Contact: Mrs. Jane Rose, Lively Arts Festival, Incorporated, 2030 Polk Street, Hollywood, Florida 33200.

Event pays tribute to all the arts: music, dance, drama, photography, painting, and poetry. Special activities are planned in each category; contests are conducted in art, poetry, and photography.

★ 510 ★
Niceville - OWJC AMERICAN ARTS FESTIVAL. Mid June, 3 days, Okaloosa-Walton Junior College. Contact: R. Hotes, Okaloosa-Walton Junior College, Information Offices, Niceville, Florida 32578.

A cross-section in miniature of Americana. Outstanding national and international figures are featured. Entertainment is provided by well-known performers as well as area bands, barbershop quartets and choral groups. Arts and crafts demonstrations include spinning, weaving, net-tying, metal sculpture, jewelry design, batik, macrame, and use of the potter's wheel. Symposia of artistic techniques are conducted by noted specialists.

★ 511 ★
Pensacola - FESTIVAL FEVER DAYS. September, 2 days, Municipal Auditorium. Contact: Bill Mathers, Pensacola-Escambia Development Commission, 803 North Palafox, Pensacola, Florida 32501.

A marriage of the arts, this celebration includes drama, dance, art, sculpture, photography, music, and crafts. Other scheduled activities include Shakespeare and country skits, symphony jazz, bluegrass hoedowns, and artists and craftsmen styling their creations before the public. Highlight of the festival is the Discovery Tent where children may wander through a wonderland of culture without parental guidance.

★ 512 ★
Tallahassee - FSU FINE ARTS FESTIVAL. February, Florida State University. Contact: Bill Edwards, Florida State University, 321 Physical Science Administration Building, Tallahassee, Florida 32306.

A series of musical, dramatic and artistic events.

★ 513 ★
Tampa - FESTIVAL OF THE HILL. Early November, annual, 2 days, Crescent Hill, behind University Center. Contact: Fran Lala, Program Director, University Center Program Office, University of South Florida, Tampa, Florida 33620.

Arts and crafts fair, and performing artists. Local, campus and national continuing entertainment: music dance, poetry, bands, circus, slide show, theater, and gospel choir. First held in 1974.

★ 514 ★
Winter Park - SIDEWALK ART FESTIVAL. Mid March, 3 days, Park Avenue, Central Park. Contact: I.S.K. Reeves V, Art Festival Commission, Post Office Box 1210, Winter Park, Florida 32789.

Cash prizes awarded in all arts and crafts categories. Concerts, plays and ballet in the park, and strolling musicians. Exhibits are for sale.

The Arts

GEORGIA

★ 515 ★
Atlanta - ARTS FESTIVAL OF ATLANTA.   Mid
March, annual, 8 days, Phipps Plaza, Piedmont
Park.   Contact: Art Festival of Atlanta, Incorporated,
800 Peachtree Street, Northeast, Room 616, Atlanta,
Georgia 30308.

Events include art auction, wine and cheese preview
party for artists and festival members, bluegrass and
folk music festival, singers, plays, ballet, puppet-
making class, puppet shows, rock music, musical
plays, previews of Atlanta Film Festival, jazz groups,
contemporary dance, unicyclists, and mime company.

★ 516 ★
Atlanta - MIDSUMMER ARTS CARNIVAL.   Summer,
Allison Art Acres Gallery School of Art.   Contact:
Director, Allison Art Acres Gallery School of Art,
3940 North Peachtree Road, Chamblee, Atlanta,
Georgia 30341.

Indoor-outdoor show in all media, with craftsmen and
performing artists as well.

★ 517 ★
Roswell - FINE ARTS AND MUSICAL FESTIVAL.
Early-mid April, 9 days, Bulloch Hall.   Contact:
Georgia Department of Community Development,
Tourist Division, Post Office Box 38097, Atlanta,
Georgia 30334.

A display and sale of arts and performances by
musical groups to entertain.

★ 518 ★
Saint Simons Island - GOLDEN ISLES ARTS
FESTIVAL.   October, annual, 1 week.   Contact:
Mrs. William C. Hendrix, Director, Glynn Art
Association, Post Office Box 673, Saint Simons
Island, Georgia 31522.

Open air art show with cash awards, all media.
Also features twentieth century chamber music and
jazz played by student and professional ensembles.

★ 519 ★
Savannah - SAVANNAH ARTS FESTIVAL.   Early May
(lst weekend), 3 days, Emmett Park.   Contact:
Savanna Art Association, Savanna Area Chamber of
Commerce, Post Office Box 530, Savannah, Georgia
31402.

Savannah Youth Orchestra, Windsor Forest High School

Band, piano concerts, jazz bands, theater groups,
dancing exhibitions, bluegrass music, choruses,
barbershop quartets, painting and crafts, and
Parisian cafe.   Begun around 1961.

★ 520 ★
Vidalia - VIDALIA FESTIVAL OF THE ARTS.   Early
April, 2 days, Georgia Tobacco Warehouse.   Con-
tact: Georgia Department of Community Development,
Tourist Division, Post Office Box 38097, Atlanta,
Georgia 30334.

A variety of visual and performing arts.

HAWAII

★ 521 ★
Honolulu - FESTIVAL OF THE ARTS OF THIS
CENTURY.   Late June, annual.   Contact: Festival
of the Arts of This Century, c/o Music Department,
University of Hawaii, Honolulu, Hawaii 96822.

Through music, dance, drama, films, art exhibitions,
and lectures, the festival focuses on contemporary
Asian and Western arts.   Guest composers, artists,
and dancers perform at evening events.   The programs
are replete with world or Hawaii premiere performances
with a concomitant emphasis on the composer and his
music rather than on performers or ensembles.   The
performers are generally those of the faculty or students
of the University of Hawaii; the concerts of electronic
music, solo and ensemble music, the music of young
composers, and orchestra concerts.   Founded in 1957.

★ 522 ★
Waikiki - GREAT HAWAIIAN JUBILEE.   Early April,
annual, 2 days, Kapiolani Park.   Contact: The State
Foundation on Culture and the Arts, 250 South King
Street, Room 310, Honolulu, Hawaii 96813.

Festival for cross-cultural sharing.   Activities include
traditional hula; Samoan entertainment, crafts, kava
ceremony, and food; other events and performing
arts activities.

ILLINOIS

★ 523 ★
Bloomington - FINE ARTS FESTIVAL.   March, 13
days, Alice Miller Center for Fine Arts, Illinois
Wesleyan University.   Contact: Illinois Wesleyan
University, 210 East University, Bloomington, Illinois
61701.

A celebration of the fine arts - visual and performing.

ILLINOIS (Continued)

★ 524 ★
DeKalb - FESTIVAL OF THE ARTS. Late March-
early April, annual, 7 days, Northern Illinois University. Contact: Assistant Dean, College of Visual
and Performing Arts, Visual Arts Building, Northern
Illinois University, DeKalb, Illinois 60115.

Dance performances, plays, programs of music, lectures and discussions on the arts, workshops, oral
interpretations, jazz bands, slide presentations,
orchestra concerts, quartets, and sculpture exhibits
are included in the activities available.

★ 525 ★
DeKalb - WOMEN'S WEEK FESTIVAL. Late February
(last week), annual, 7 days, Northern Illinois University. Contact: Women Studies Center, 535-3
Lucinda, DeKalb, Illinois 60115.

Feminist activities including speakers, films, workshops
and performances.

★ 526 ★
East Peoria - ICC FINE ARTS FESTIVAL. April-May
(last week - lst week), annual, 7-12 days, Illinois
Central College. Contact: Illinois Central College,
2129 High View Road, East Peoria, Illinois 61611.

Theatrical performances, orchestra concerts, jazz concerts, musical recitals, plays, readings, ballet, and
movies. Art: murals, jewelry, sketching, sculpture,
ceramics, painting, etc. Many of the works are
for sale. Coffee house, dance, demonstrations of
crafts and handiwork such as candle dipping, blacksmithing, and weaving. Begun in 1973.

★ 527 ★
Normal - EWING ART AND PLEASURE FESTIVAL.
April (26th), annual, 1 day, Ewing Museum of
Nations. Contact: Stephanie Amster, Art Depart-
ment CVA 119, Illinois State University, Normal,
Illinois 61761.

Events include an art auction, art booths (invited
artists), children's area with art and activities for
children, demonstrations (e.g. glass-blowing, spinning), puppet shows, foods (both homemade and such
as hotdogs), wandering minstrels, planned musical
performances (madrigals, medieval quintet, recorder
music, etc), mime troupe, court jesters and clowns,
Society of Creative Anachronism (troupe of medieval
players in full armor), and special areas (make your
own art, thieves market-students sell own work, and
dingbell-test of strength). Fair began in 1971.

★ 528 ★
Peoria - SPRING ARTS FESTIVAL. April, annual,
2 days, Bradley University. Contact: Bradley
University, 1501 West Bradley Avenue, Peoria, Illinois
61606.

All academic performing arts and art areas are represented by students, faculty and alumni only (Speech
and Theater, English, Art, Music, Crafts, Physical
Education). Continuous displays of art, readings
and interpretations, vocal and instrumental music selections, karate exhibitions, dramatic presentations, mime,
movies and panel discussions thereof, gymnastic demonstrations, and dancing.

★ 529 ★
Rockford - ARTS FESTIVAL. June-July, 4-1-day
festivals, Seventh Street; Levings Park; Talcott-Page
Park; Beattie Park. Contact: Rockford Art Association, 737 North Main Street, Rockford, Illinois 61103.

Street theater, jazz, cinema, concert band, fruit
stand, square dance, and barbershop singing are included in this celebration of the arts.

★ 530 ★
Urbana - FESTIVAL OF CONTEMPORARY ARTS.
Late February to early April, biennial. Contact:
Festival of Contemporary Arts, University of Illinois,
110 Architecture Building, Urbana, Illinois 61801.

The festival features musical events, exhibitions,
lectures, dance concerts and the like. The contemporary arts encompassed by the festival theme include
music, dance, visual arts, drama, film, architecture,
landscape architecture, literature, radio and television,
and such categories as "design for communication" and
home economics. Concerts include full-length operas
and all varieties of ensemble and recital performances.
Electronic music concerts in whole or in part are not
uncommon. Formed in 1948.

★ 531 ★
Waukegan - ARTS FESTIVAL AND CONCERT. Mid
August, 2 days, Bowen Park. Contact: The Division
of Tourism, Illinois Department of Business and Economic Development, 222 South College Street, Springfield, Illinois 62706.

A display and sale of a variety of arts and crafts and
musical entertainment.

The Arts

INDIANA

★ 532 ★
Evansville – OHIO RIVER ARTS FESTIVAL.   Late
April–early May, 17 days.   Contact: Executive
Director, Evansville Arts Council, 10600 Old State
Road, Evansville, Indiana 47711.

Each day offers a different assortment of entertainment:
puppets, musicians, dancers, craftsmen, etc., sponsored
by the Evansville Arts and Education Council.

★ 533 ★
Fort Wayne – FORT WAYNE FINE ARTS FESTIVAL.
July and August, annual, 5–6 days, Franke Park.
Contact: Fort Wayne Fine Arts Festival, c/o Fort
Wayne Fine Arts Foundation, 232 1/2 West Wayne
Street, Fort Wayne, Indiana 46802.

Some of the programs include concerts by the Fort
Wayne Philharmonic and performances of opera and
ballet.   Other events are exhibits of art and architecture, theater-in-the-round, historical exhibits,
puppetry, public art classes and workshops, and jazz
concerts.   Established in 1958.

★ 534 ★
Gary – JAZZ AND BOURBON STREET ART FAIR.
Late June, 1 day.   Contact: Gary Artist League,
400 South Lake Street, Gary, Indiana 46401.

New Orleans jazz, displays and sales of arts and
crafts.   Sponsored by the Gary Artist League.

★ 535 ★
Gas City – ART IN THE PARK.   Mid June, 6 days,
Gas City Community Park.   Contact: Peg Seeler,
Executive Director, Mississinewa Arts Council, 2400.
South Washington, Marion, Indiana 46952.

Workshops include jewelry making, crafts, drama, art,
music, and dance.   Evening entertainment in Matter
Park.   Also held in Marion.

★ 536 ★
Kokomo – CREATIVE ARTS FESTIVAL.   Late April-
early May.   Contact: Mrs. Dwight Callaway, 2510
Elaine Court, Kokomo, Indiana 46901.

Visual and performing arts: photography, crafts
exhibits and demonstrations, concerts, dance, and
theater programs.

★ 537 ★
Marion – ART IN THE PARK.   Mid June, 6 days,
Matter Park.   Contact: Peg Seeler, Executive
Director, Mississinewa Arts Council, 2400 South
Washington, Marion, Indiana 46952.

Workshops include jewelry making, crafts, drama,
art, music, and dance.   Evening entertainment in
Matter Park.   Also held in Gas City.

★ 538 ★
Nappanee – PLETCHER VILLAGE ART FESTIVAL.
Early August, 4 days, Amish Acres.   Contact:
Richard Pletcher, 1600 West Market Street, Nappanee,
Indiana 46550.

Arts and crafts, flea market where paintings, ceramics,
sculpture, jewelry, leather, and weaving are displayed.
Amish farmstead, horseshoeing, quilting, and threshing.
Playhouse reviews, and Punch and Judy puppets.

★ 539 ★
Notre Dame – SOPHOMORE LITERARY FESTIVAL.
March (Spring), annual, 1 week, University of Notre
Dame campus.   Contact: University of Notre Dame,
Department of Information Services, Notre Dame,
Indiana 46556.

Brings to campus for classroom and public discussions
eight to ten major authors, poets, screenwriters or
playwrights who discuss in great detail their thoughts
on writing, and experiences that might be helpful to
the students, etc.

★ 540 ★
Valpraiso – VALPRAISO ART FESTIVAL.   Early June,
2 days, Lincoln Square.   Contact: Marti Dierking,
Secretary, Porter County Art Commission, 452 Chestnut
Street, Valpraiso, Indiana 46383.

Serious artists in the fields of drama, music, sculpture,
painting and crafts hold a forum.   Many works are
for sale and skills are demonstrated.

★ 541 ★
West Lafayette – DAWN (DISCOVER THE ART WORLD
NOW).   Dates uncertain, in a state of change,
Purdue University, various buildings.   Contact:
Purdue Convocations, Graduate House East, Purdue
University, West Lafayette, Indiana 47907.

The events include concerts (classical, jazz, folk
music, and dance), craft fairs, poetry readings, multi-
media presentations, films of various kinds (classic
feature films, unusual techniques, documentaries,

INDIANA (Continued)

film-making), craft demonstrations, and art exhibits. All of these are free and meant to give the students and local community an introduction to many and varied art forms. Originally it was an annual festival held in April for a week to a week and a half. In 1975, a week in February was added. It is now in flux with plans to convert it to a series of year long events. Started in 1972.

★ 542 ★

West Lafayette - PURDUE FESTIVAL SERIES. Late March-early April, 3 days, 1 week apart, Elliott Hall of Music. Contact: Convocations and Lectures, Graduate House East, Purdue University, West Lafayette, Indiana 47907.

Events have included a pantomime circus, musical adaptation of Shakespearean play, and vocal concerts.

IOWA

★ 543 ★

Cedar Rapids - FALL FINE ARTS FESTIVAL. Late October to mid-November, annual. Contact: Fall Fine Arts Festival, c/o Coe College, Cedar Rapids, Iowa 52402.

In addition to music, there are lectures, poetry readings, dance concerts, dramatic plays, and exhibits. Soloists, in recital or concert, and chamber ensembles are generally the featured performers. The Cedar Rapids Symphony Orchestra is used to accompany soloists in concert. Founded in 1952.

★ 544 ★

Des Moines - OUTDOOR ART FAIR. Early June (1st weekend), annual, 1 day, Art Center. Contact: Des Moines Art Center, Edmundson Art Foundation, Incorporated, Greenwood Park, Des Moines, Iowa 50312.

The fair takes a theme each year, such as Renaissance, English, Greek, Mexican, and American. The fair offers the wares of many artists (by invitation only), including painters, sculptors, potters, weavers, and jewelers. Performing arts are represented by the Des Moines Symphony, the Des Moines Civic Ballet, magicians, story tellers, mimists, and others. Food relating to the theme is also sold.

★ 545 ★

Iowa City - FESTIVAL OF CHILDREN'S BOOKS. Early November, annual, 1 day, Iowa Memorial Union.

Contact: School of Library Science, 3087 Library, Iowa City, Iowa 52242.

Sponsored by the University of Iowa School of Library Science, this is a thematic festival which concerns itself with children and their books. Begun in 1969.

★ 546 ★

Keokuk - ART IN THE PARK. Early June, 1 day, Rand Park (Cardinal Stritch High School in the event of rain). Contact: Mrs. Darrell Rodger, 1801 Park Lane, Keokuk, Iowa 52632.

Performing arts, art exhibits, demonstrations, and sales.

★ 547 ★

Marshalltown - ART FAIR. Mid May, annual, 2 days, Fischer Community Center. Contact: Carol Quam, 1601 Norris Place, Marshalltown, Iowa 50158.

In addition to the art display, there is a barbeque (BYO), and a performing "happening" at Log Cabin Riverview Park; also canoe races, sailboat races; music and drama. Sponsored by the Central Iowa Art Association. Begun around 1951.

KANSAS

★ 548 ★

Lawrence - UNIVERSITY OF KANSAS FESTIVAL OF THE ARTS. March, annual, 1 week, Hoch Auditorium on campus. Contact: University of Kansas Festival of the Arts, c/o Student Union Activities, Kansas Union, University of Kansas, Lawrence, Kansas 66044.

The purpose of the festival is to present a week's artistic events--such as films, poetry readings, music-- and exchanges of ideas about the creative arts in the form of lectures, exhibitions, and discussions. The emphasis is on contemporary American creators and performers in music. This translates interestingly and logically enough into jazz and other associative pop music. Conceived in 1966.

LOUISIANA

★ 549 ★

Baton Rouge - SUMMER FESTIVAL OF ARTS. June-July, annual, Louisiana State University campus. Contact: Louisiana State University, Office of Information Services, Thomas Boyd Hall, Baton Rouge, Louisiana 70803.

A series of programs, free and open to the public.

LOUISIANA (Continued)

Campus departments which sponsor performers and speakers for the festival include speech, health, physical and recreational education, fine arts, music, and landscape architecture. Events may include satirical drama, classical ballet, opera, and lectures on industrial design and landscape architecture. In addition to performances, there may be lectures or workshops in the arts.

★ 550 ★
Lafayette - LE FESTIVAL WILLIS F. DUCREST DES ARTS ACADIENS ET FRANCAIS. Mid October-early November, 10 days, University of Southwestern Louisiana. Contact: Director, School of Music, University of Southwestern Louisiana, Lafayette, Louisiana 70501.

Concerts, dramatic presentations, dances, vocalists, exhibits, and demonstrations by artisans, all oriented towards French or Acadian cultures. Music includes chamber music, vocal, impressionistic, spiritual, etc. Begun around 1973.

★ 551 ★
Lafayette - FOREIGN LANGUAGE FESTIVAL. Mid April, annual, 1 day, University of Southwestern Louisiana. Contact: Dr. Gerard L. St. Martin, Professor of French, University of Southwestern Louisiana, Lafayette, Louisiana 70501.

A competition among high schools intended to encourage the study of foreign languages and reward hard working students and teachers. The school may enter a student in each of the four levels in prose and poetry recitation, one student in extemporaneous conversation, and four one-act plays. An award is offered for the school which does best overall in French, German, Latin, Spanish, plus a grand prize for the best overall in languages.

★ 552 ★
Napoleonville - MADEWOOD ARTS FESTIVAL. Mid April, annual, 3-4 days, Madewood Plantation. Contact: Executive Director, Louisiana Tourist Commission, Post Office Box 44291, Baton Rouge, Louisiana 70804.

A vast array of cultural events in the home and on the grounds of this famous plantation. Exhibits of regional arts and crafts for public viewing, and seminars by visiting artists. Literary discussions initiated by several of Louisiana's outstanding writers. Musical programs include concerts of songs and arias, bands and orchestras, ballet, and a symphony orchestra

concert. There is also an Acadian fair.

★ 553 ★
Shreveport - SPAR YOUTH ART FESTIVAL. January, 10 days, Barnwell Art and Garden Center. Contact: Shreveport-Bossier Convention and Tourist Bureau, Post Office Box 1761, Shreveport, Louisiana 71166.

A display of the artwork of public school students. Prizes are awarded by grades. The event is sponsored by the Shreveport Parks and Recreation Department. Started in 1973.

MAINE

★ 554 ★
Bar Harbor - BAR HARBOR ARTS FESTIVAL. August, annual, 2 weeks. Contact: Bar Harbor Arts Festival, c/o Bar Harbor Festival Corporation, Bar Harbor, Maine 04609.

Programs, some offered free, consist of concerts, films, lectures, and exhibits of painting, sculpture, and photography, orchestral concerts and dance programs. The leading ensemble is the Bar Harbor Festival Orchestra. Founded in 1964.

MARYLAND

★ 555 ★
Annapolis - ANNAPOLIS ARTS FESTIVAL. Mid June, annual, 3 days, Annapolis City Dock. Contact: Annapolis Fine Arts Foundation, 18 West Street, Annapolis, Maryland 21401.

A wide variety of arts and crafts are displayed and sold; there are demonstrations in macrame, glass-blowing, weaving, pottery, wood-carving, and jewelry making. Sound and light show, singing and dancing sessions for the children, playground facilities for the children, magic show, child care center, dancers, folk singers, rock bands, and concerts by high school bands. The crafts are in a large tent. There is an open air stage, where, in addition to aforementioned activities, there is mime, choral singing, hand bell ringing, and folk dancing. There is also the Youth Symphony Orchestra Workshop for musically talented young people, walking tours of the city including the United States Naval Academy and museums, and a sightseeing tour of Annapolis harbor. Begun around 1963.

★ 556 ★
Baltimore - BALTIMORE-WASHINGTON BOOK FAIR. October, annual, 1 day. Contact: Ms. B. S.

MARYLAND (Continued)

Braunstein, UMBC Library, 5401 Wilkens Avenue, Baltimore, Maryland 21228; or Mrs. L. S. Pita, Provident Hospital Library, 2600 Liberty Heights Avenue, Baltimore, Maryland 21215.

The Baltimore Chapter of the Special Libraries Association sponsors this fair which is designed to inform all sectors of the public and the library community of the book-buying resources available to them in the Baltimore-Washington area. Book buying and browsing is welcome at this one-stop walking tour of a diverse spectrum of area booksellers. The fair features multi-faceted booksellers' exhibits.

★ 557 ★
Baltimore - 3400 ON STAGE. Late April (usually last weekend), annual, 3 days, Johns Hopkins University, Homewood Campus. Contact: Assistant Director, Special Events, Shriver Hall, Johns Hopkins University, Baltimore, Maryland 21218.

Sponsored by the Student Council, an outdoor festival of arts, crafts, theater and music. There are arts and crafts exhibitors, "moving plays", movies, antique car exhibits, and concerts of all kinds - classical, popular, and choral.

★ 558 ★
Bowie - FESTIVAL OF FINE ARTS. Early May, annual, 7 days, Bowie State College. Contact: Bowie State College Humanities Division, Bowie, Maryland 20715.

Events include dramatic productions, choral presentations, banquets, speakers, gallery tours, student exhibits, demonstrations of arts, films, slides, musical selections by Bowie State College Jazz Band, dance routine, poetry reading and awards, gymanstic demonstrations, writers contest, essay contest, cultural exhibits, sports activities, banquet, concert by Bowie State College Chorale and Instrumental Ensemble.

★ 559 ★
Ellicott City - A SHOW OF HANDS. August (2nd weekend), annual, Main Street. Contact: Owl and the Pussycat, 8126 Main Street, Ellicott City, Maryland 21043.

A big, open party featuring music - bluegrass, rock, etc. - and crafts - weavers, potters, jewelers, toymakers, candlemakers, leatherworkers, and other quality craftspeople in the area. Other entertainment includes puppet shows, story tellers, etc.

★ 560 ★
Hagerstown - HAGERSTOWN PARK ARTS FESTIVAL. Late June, annual, 2 days, City Park. Contact: Washington County Tourism Division, 40 Summit Avenue, Hagerstown, Maryland 21740.

Artists and craftsmen demonstrate and sell their creations. A variety of entertainment including well known individuals and groups from the musical world - guitarists, bands, choral groups, jazz groups, theater groups, ethnic dancers, ballet, mime, bluegrass, etc. For Children Only where 12 and under can create, browse, or buy. Begun around 1969.

★ 561 ★
Towson - TOWSONTOWNE COURTHOUSE ARTS FESTIVAL. Early June, annual, 1 day, Courthouse Square. Contact: Martha Dearman, Department of Parks and Recreation, 401 Washington Avenue, Baltimore, Maryland 21202.

Displays and sale of paintings, sculpture, photography, and crafts. Musical, dramatic, and dance performances. Refreshments offered. Begun around 1952.

MASSACHUSETTS

★ 562 ★
Boston - BOSTON GLOBE BOOK FESTIVAL. October or November, annual, 2 days. Contact: The Boston Globe, 135 Morrissey Boulevard, Boston, Massachusetts 02107.

The festival features films, lectures, and demonstrations, the latter two generally given by visiting authors. There is also an exhibition hall, where publishers and libraries demonstrate their products and services. Retailers are on hand (in addition to the general public), offering the visiting authors' books.

★ 563 ★
Boston - FESTIVAL OF ARTS. Mid June to mid-July, annual, Public Garden behind the Common. Contact: Greater Boston Chamber of Commerce, 125 High Street, Boston, Massachusetts 02110.

Exhibitions of the visual and performing arts. Concerts, opera, jazz, ballet, plays, poetry readings, and art exhibits.

★ 564 ★
Boston - SUMMERTHING. July-August, annual, 8 weeks, City Parks. Contact: Summerthing, 603 City Hall Annex, 23 Court Street, Boston, Massachusetts 02108.

MASSACHUSETTS (Continued)

Dubbed "Boston's Neighborhood Festival", the plan of Summerthing is to bring to each of Boston's distinct neighborhood communities free cultural entertainment in many categories; workshops for art, music, drama, dance, photography, and film making. Performances of popular music, jazz, square or folk dancing, and band competitions presented in neighborhood parks and playgrounds. Offered in five major city parks.

★ 565 ★
Cohasset - SOUTH SHORE ARTS FESTIVAL. Early July (4th), annual, 1 day, Cohasset Village - Saint Stephen's Church. Contact: Massachusetts Department of Commerce and Development, Division of Tourism, Box 1775, Boston, Massachusetts 02105.

Weekly carillon concerts are included in the events.

★ 566 ★
North Dartmouth - EISTEDDFOD. September, annual, 3 days, Southeastern Massachusetts University. Contact: Cultural Affairs Committee, Southeastern Massachusetts University, North Dartmouth, Massachusetts 02747.

Traditional British and American music concerts and workshops. There is also storytelling, country dancing, and crafts.

★ 567 ★
Worcester - ESTHER FORBES WEEK. Mid April, annual, 1 week. Contact: Massachusetts Department of Commerce and Development, Division of Tourism, Box 1775, Boston, Massachusetts 02105.

Honors the late biographer of Paul Revere and Johnny Tremaine. Exhibits and lecture.

MICHIGAN

★ 568 ★
Detroit - CHILDREN'S BOOK FAIR. Late October-early November, annual, 14 days, Wayne State University Community Arts Building. Contact: Detroit Adventure, c/o Wayne State University, Detroit, Michigan 48202.

Storytellers, authors, touring theater, puppeteer, and browsing days highlight this book fair.

★ 569 ★
Grand Haven - UP IN CENTRAL PARK MUSIC,

ART, FLOWER FESTIVAL. Mid July (3rd week), annual, 2-3 days, art and music in Central Park; flowers in Community Center. Contact: North West Ottawa County Chamber of Commerce, One Washington Avenue, Grand Haven, Michigan 49417.

Intended to promote the arts in the area and to offer a desirable summer activity for residents and visitors. Artists display and sell their works. They may also do portrait work. Flower show entrants present horicultural specimens and flower arrangements. There is a concert on Friday night. Used books and periodicals are also on sale at the Paris Book Stall. Started in 1955.

★ 570 ★
Grand Rapids - FESTIVAL OF ARTS. Early June (lst weekend), annual, 3 days, Vandenburg Center. Contact: Arts Council of Greater Grand Rapids, 126 College, Southeast, Grand Rapids, Michigan 49502.

Many kinds of music including jazz, country and bluegrass, gospel, rock and roll, folk, swing band, concert band, wooden music, electronic, polka, etc. Includes both vocal and instrumental, bands, soloists, trios, etc. and is played on a wide variety of instruments. In addition, events include films, puppet shows, theater, poetry readings, ballet, various types of dance, story tellers, arts and crafts exhibits and demonstrations, exhibits by organizations and institutions which make up the cultural life of the city, and food booths. Started in 1970.

MINNESOTA

★ 571 ★
Lutsen - NORTH SHORE ART FAIR. Mid July, annual, 2 days. Contact: North Shore Arts Association, Box 57, Lutsen, Minnesota 55612.

A juried art show, crafts display, sculpture, cultural entertainment, jazz, rock, and Shakespeare. Begun around 1969.

★ 572 ★
Minneapolis - TWIN CITIES SCIENCE FICTION FESTIVAL. Mid October, 2 days. Contact: LaRae H. Wales, Minneapolis Public Library, Minneapolis, Minnesota. 55402.

Brings together fans, science fiction scholars, and writers. Workshops on writing and teaching science fiction are held.

MINNESOTA (Continued)

★ 573 ★
Rochester - ROCHESTER ART FESTIVAL.   Mid June,
annual, 1 day, Rochester Art Center.   Contact:
Art Festival Committee, 320 East Center Street,
Rochester, Minnesota 55901.

Art works displayed, live music and performances,
food, children's games, and activities.   Begun
around 1949.

MISSISSIPPI

★ 574 ★
Cleveland - CROSSTIE FESTIVAL.   April, annual,
1 day, Cleveland Courthouse Square.   Contact:
Malcom Norwood, Delta State University, Cleveland,
Mississippi 38732.

An arts festival complete with sidewalk artists, puppet
shows, musicians, craftsmen, and various types of
entertainment.

★ 575 ★
Greenwood - ARTS FESTIVAL.   May, annual, 5-7
days.   Contact: Greenwood-Leflore County Chamber
of Commerce, Post Office Box 848, Highway 49-82
Bypass, Greenwood, Mississippi 38930.

The Greater Greenwood Foundation of Arts sponsors
visiting performers, seminars, plays, and exhibitions
in a tribute to the arts.

★ 576 ★
Jackson - MISSISSIPPI ARTS FESTIVAL.   Late April-
early May, annual, 6-9 days. Contact: Mississippi
Arts Festival, Post Office Box 4584, Jackson, Mississippi 39216.

Performances by the Jackson Symphony Orchestra as
well as ballet, theater, arts and crafts exhibits, and
competitions in literature and music.

★ 577 ★
Meridian - LIVELY ARTS FESTIVAL.   Early-mid April,
annual, 10 days, Meridian Museum of Art, Village
Fair Mall, Temple Theatre.   Contact: Lively Arts
Festival, c/o Greater Meridian Chamber of Commerce,
Post Office Box 790, Meridian, Mississippi 39301.

Events include exhibits of artwork, both professional
and student, square dancing exhibition, children's
programs, films, concerts by the Meridian High School
band, bluegrass and marching military bands, and

nationally known and local instrumentalists and
vocalists.

★ 578 ★
Senatobia - SYCAMORE ARTS FESTIVAL.   Early
April, 7 days, Northwest Junior College.   Contact:
Northwest Mississippi Junior College, Senatobia,
Mississippi 38668.

Musical performances for both adults and children,
bluegrass music, screenings of classic films, flea
market, and pottery exhibition.

★ 579 ★
Tupelo - GUM TREE ARTS FESTIVAL.   Mid May,
2-3 days, Lee County Courthouse Lawn.   Contact:
Travel Department, Mississippi Agricultural and Industrial Board, Post Office Box 849, Jackson, Mississippi 39205.

Outdoor juried art show, film festival, and old fashioned picnic.   Supported by the Cultural Enrichment
Committee of the Community Development Foundation
and local individuals and businesses, awards and prizes
are offered.

★ 580 ★
Yazoo City - DELTA ARTS AND CRAFTS FESTIVAL.
Early May, 1 day.   Contact: Travel Department,
Mississippi Agricultural and Industrial Board, Post
Office Box 849, Jackson, Mississippi 39205.

Seminars, plays, exhibitions, and visiting performers
are included in the events featured in this festival
of arts.

MISSOURI

★ 581 ★
Kansas City - CHAUTAUQUA (A Combined Arts
Program).   April, 3 days.   Contact: Greater
Kansas City Chamber of Commerce, 920 Main Street,
Kansas City, Missouri 64105.

A parade, festival, and performance highlight this
festival of the arts.

★ 582 ★
Kansas City - MULTI MEDIA FESTIVAL.   Late
October, 1 day, Jewish Community Center.   Contact:
Convention and Visitors Bureau of Greater Kansas
City, 1221 Baltimore, Kansas City, Missouri 64105.

Poetry, music, dance and films are featured in this
cultural arts festival.

MISSOURI (Continued)

★ 583 ★
Rolla - ROLLA ARTS FESTIVAL.   Mid April to early
May, annual, 2 weeks.   Contact: Rolla Arts Festival,
University of Missouri, Rolla, Missouri 65401.

Festival of community organizations relating to all the
arts at the University of Missouri, Rolla.

MONTANA

★ 584 ★
Missoula - FESTIVAL OF THE ARTS.   April-May,
City-wide.   Contact: Missoula Area Chamber of
Commerce, 207 East Main, Post Office Box 1518,
Missoula, Montana 59801.

Art exhibits and demonstrations; workshops of painting,
sculpture, pottery, weaving, jewelry making, photography, and dancing.   A major literary symposium.

NEW HAMPSHIRE

★ 585 ★
Andover - ARTS AND CRAFTS FESTIVAL.   Early
July, annual, 3 days, Field House, Proctor Academy.
Contact: Arts and Crafts Festival, Proctor Academy,
Andover, New Hampshire 03216.

Demonstrations in arts, crafts, dance, drama, and
music.   Begun around 1962.

★ 586 ★
Franconia - WHITE MOUNTAINS FESTIVAL OF
CHILDREN'S LITERATURE.   Late July-early August,
annual, 1 week, Franconia College.   Contact:
White Mountains Festival of Children's Literature,
Franconia College, Franconia, New Hampshire 03580.

Designed to permit the participants to explore the
world of children's literature.   Activities include
seminars, panel discussions, lectures, and workshops
for teachers, librarians, writers, artists, and anyone
interested in children's literature and in reading.
There are special programs for children including
crafts, storytelling, films, and nature activities.
Started in 1974.

★ 587 ★
Hanover - CONGREGATION OF THE ARTS.   Late
June to mid August, annual.   Contact: Congregation
of the Arts, Hopkins Center, Dartmouth College, Hanover, New Hampshire 03755.

Symphony and chamber ensemble concerts, including

world premieres; open rehearsals.   Plays, art shows,
films, and exhibitions.

★ 588 ★
Newport - LIBRARY FESTIVAL.   Late August, annual,
3 days, Richards Library.   Contact: Library Festival,
58 North Main Street, Newport, New Hampshire 03773.

Events include lectures, awarding of Sarah Josepha
Hale Award, book sales, art prints and stationery
sale, and food sale.   Begun around 1954.

★ 589 ★
Pike - WHITE MOUNTAINS FESTIVAL OF THE
SEVEN ARTS.   July and August, annual, held on
the 5,500 acre White Mountain resort of Lake Tarleton
Club.   Contact: White Mountains Festival of the
Seven Arts, Pike, New Hampshire 03780.

The essence of the festival is the outdoor discussion
forum involving not only people in the performing,
graphic, and literary arts, but also those well-known
in politics, journalism, radio and television, and
sciences.   Musical performances have featured singers,
solo instrumentalists, and folk singers and popular
music vocalists, and dancers.   Founded in 1948.

NEW JERSEY

★ 590 ★
Hackensack - BERGEN COUNTY FESTIVAL.   Mid
March-mid April.   Contact: Bergen County Festival,
144 Main Street, Hackensack, New Jersey 07601.

Music, dance, films, drama, jazz, and children's
events.   Sponsored by New Jersey Cultural Council
and Bergen Community College.

NEW MEXICO

★ 591 ★
Farmington - ARTS FESTIVAL.   October, annual,
all month.   Contact: Chamber of Commerce, Post
Office Box 267, Farmington, New Mexico 87401.

In conjunction with art month;   features art and
theater.

★ 592 ★
Socorro - ARTS FIESTA.   Mid April, annual, 3 days,
New Mexico Institute of Mining and Technology.
Contact: Chamber of Commerce, Post Office Box 743,
Socorro, New Mexico 87801.

NEW MEXICO (Continued)

Various forms of the arts for the public to enjoy. Begun in 1974.

★ 593 ★

Taos - FESTIVAL OF ARTS. Early October, annual, 5 days. Contact: Chamber of Commerce, Post Office Drawer 1, Taos, New Mexico 87571.

A true festival of the arts encompassing many: poetry readings, seminars, arts and crafts, film, musical and dance performances, and dramatic presentations. The exhibits are spread throughout the town in hundreds of galleries and shops. The crafts include Indian and others. The art includes paintings, drawings, sculpture, photography, etc. Started in 1975.

NEW YORK

★ 594 ★

Bronx - HOSTOS ARTS FESTIVAL. May, annual, 3 days, site varies. Contact: Hostos Community College of The City University of New York, 475 Grand Concourse, Bronx, New York 10451.

Directed by the Visual and Performing Arts Department and the Student Activities Department, the festival is part of the "Bronx Week" celebration. The participants are members of the college and South Bronx community. Their talents are displayed in exhibits of photography and art, performances of music, song and dance, and dramatic presentations including operas and original works by students. In order to promote better understanding of the many ethnic heritages of the college, there are performances of ethnic songs and dances, as well as exhibits of such items as Haitian rugs and other examples of weaving, carving, etc. Begun around 1973.

★ 595 ★

Ithaca - SPRING FESTIVAL. Late April-early May, annual, 4 days, Risley College, Cornell University. Contact: Cornell University, Office of Public Information, Day Hall, Ithaca, New York 14850.

Called Primavera in '75 and Medieval Fair in '74, both generally a Spring celebration with different themes. Past events have included plays; music such as jazz, medieval, chamber, operas, bag-piping, etc.; film festival; dancers, including folk, belly, and modern; poetry readings; art show; puppet show; lectures, and tournaments. In general, dedicated to the arts.

★ 596 ★

New York - AVANT GARDE FESTIVAL. Late September, annual, 1 day, Floyd Bennett Field. Contact: Floyd Bennett Field Association, 225 Varick, New York, New York 10013.

A showing of over 500 artists and their avant garde creations and media, including music, video, holograms, and art created from almost every material imaginable. Begun around 1964.

★ 597 ★

New York - COLUMBIA UNIVERSITY SCHOOL OF THE ARTS SPRING FESTIVAL: ARTS DROP-IN. April, annual, 3-5 days, Columbia University Campus. Contact: School of The Arts, 617 Dodge, Columbia University, New York, New York 10027.

Includes special events and showings of graduate students' original work in film, music, poetry, prose, theater, painting and sculpture. Several colloquia are held featuring well-known artists and critics. "Events for Children" includes readings, songs, poetry and mime for children. There are also informal coffee hours for students, guest artists and administrators.

★ 598 ★

New York - CULTURAL FESTIVAL. April (Spring), annual, Pace University Campus. Contact: Pace University, New York Campus, Pace Plaza, New York, New York 10038.

Sponsored by the Black, Chinese, African, Puerto Rican and Caribbean Student Organizations, the festival is a potpourri of performing arts, a display of artifacts and works of arts, sampling of ethnic foods, motion pictures, and fashion show all presenting the cultures of the sponsoring organizations. Started around 1972.

★ 599 ★

New York - FESTIVAL OF THE ARTS. October-May, annual, 8 month season, New York City Community College - Klitgord Center. Contact: Festival of the Arts, New York City Community College of the City University of New York, 300 Jay Street, Brooklyn, New York 11201.

The program includes a film series, a Wednesday Afternoon Concert Series for Adults at Leisure, another Concert Series which includes such events as musicals, dance troupes, singers, operas, and musicians, Children's Theater, and art exhibits. Begun around 1965.

The Arts

NEW YORK (Continued)

★ 600 ★
New York - FLOATING BOOK FAIR.   Late May,
annual, 3 days, ferryboat: "The Floating Book Fair"
(formerly the John F. Kennedy).   Contact: Susan
Strausberg or Ruth Randall, Women's Guide to Books,
655 Madison Avenue, New York, New York 10021.

Sponsored by the International Women's Arts Festival
Literature Committee and the Women's Guide to Books,
the fair features 500 books by and about women.
Activities include panel discussions, readings, and
art exhibits.   Authors are on hand to talk and sign
autographs.

★ 601 ★
New York - INTERNATIONAL ANTIQUARIAN BOOK
FAIR.   Late March or April, biennial, 3-4 days,
Plaza Hotel.   Contact: Antiquarian Booksellers
Association, 630 Fifth Avenue, Concourse Shop 2,
New York, New York 10020; or New York Con-
vention and Visitors Bureau, Incorporated, 90 East
42nd Street, New York, New York 10017.

Dealers come from all over the United States and
Europe to exhibit and sell old books, maps, prints,
autographs, etc.   The treasures are brought from
London, Bonn, Amsterdam, Massachusetts, New Jersey,
and California.   The Fair takes place in New York
on alternate (odd) years, in which event it is sponsored
by the Middle Atlantic Chapter of the Antiquarian
Booksellers Association of America.   It takes place
on the West Coast in even years. (See San Francisco,
September).

★ 602 ★
New York - INTERNATIONAL COMPUTER ART
FESTIVAL.   June, annual, City University of New·
York.   Contact: International Computer Art Festival,
City University of New York, Graduate School and
University Center, 33 West 42nd Street, New York,
New York 10019.

Computer music is performed as a featured event.

★ 603 ★
New York - SPRING FESTIVAL.   Late April,
annual, 1 day, Barnard College Campus.   Contact:
Millicent McIntosh Center, Office of College Activi-
ties, Barnard College, Columbia University, New York,
New York 10027.

Events include displays of club activities, films, food
tasting, art exhibits, palm readings, photography
exhibit, antique miniature car display, pottery co-op

sale, dramatic presentations, medieval sword and
sheild fighting, puppet show, dances, bowling tournament, and music.

★ 604 ★
New York - WINTER FESTIVAL.   Mid February,
annual, Barnard College Campus.   Contact: Milli-
cent McIntosh Center, Office of College Activities,
Barnard College, Columbia University, New York,
New York 10027.

Dedicated to the performing arts, many art forms
are presented.   Started in 1969.

★ 605 ★
Petersburg - FOX HOLLOW FAMILY FESTIVAL OF
TRADITIONAL MUSIC AND ARTS.   Early August,
annual, 4 days.   Contact: Evelyne Burnstine, Fox
Hollow Festival, Route 2, Petersburg, New York
12138.

Events include participation bands-fiddle and concertina,
workshops for hammered and plucked dulcimer, autoharp, fiddle, concertina, traditional music and arts.
Begun around 1966.

★ 606 ★
Potsdam - SPRING FESTIVAL OF THE ARTS.   March-
May, annual.   Contact: Spring Festival of the
Arts, State University College at Potsdam, Potsdam,
New York 13676.

In addition to music, the festival includes drama,
dance, films, poetry readings, photography and
graphic arts.   Resident performing groups, along
with well-known guest artists.   Established in 1931.

★ 607 ★
Roslyn - JUNE ARTS FESTIVAL.   June, annual.
Contact: County of Nassau Office of Cultural De-
velopment, June Arts Festival, Northern Boulevard,
Post Office Box D, Roslyn, New York 12280.

Professional ensembles perform chamber and orchestral
music in a series of public concerts.   Art exhibits
are also featured.   Sponsored by the County of
Nassau Office of Cultural Development.

★ 608 ★
Syracuse - SYRACUSE FESTIVAL OF THE ARTS.
Late April-early May, annual, Syracuse University.
Contact: Syracuse Festival of the Arts, Syracuse
University, Syracuse, New York 13210.

Music (several concerts), dance, drama, art, poetry, films, lectures, etc. are featured.

★ 609 ★
Utica - UTICA ARTS FESTIVAL. Mid July, annual, 10 days, Munson-Williams-Proctor Institute. Contact: Public Relations Manager, Munson-Williams-Proctor Institute, 310 Genesee Street, Utica, New York 13502.

Free professional and community performing arts events including drama, music, and dance, as well as a sidewalk art show. Sponsored by the Institute.

NORTH CAROLINA

★ 610 ★
Albemarle - STANLY COUNTY ARTS FESTIVAL. September, 5 days. Contact: Stanly County Arts Council, Post Office Box 909, Albemarle, North Carolina 28001.

Events include chorus concerts, performances by clog and square dance teams, films, performances by marching band and drill teams, bluegrass music, visits by the Artrain - a traveling art show, and street dancing.

★ 611 ★
Banner Elk - AVERY COUNTY CRAFTS FAIR AND ARTS FESTIVAL. Early July, 1 day. Contact: Boone Area Chamber of Commerce, 827 Blowing Rock Road, Boone, North Carolina 28607.

Event features exhibitions and concerts in the fine arts, the performing arts, native and folk crafts.

★ 612 ★
Boone - WATAUGA COUNTY ARTS FESTIVAL. Late June, 1 day. Contact: Boone Area Chamber of Commerce, 827 Blowing Rock Road, Boone, North Carolina 28607.

The festival features displays and performances in the fine arts, the performing arts and native folk arts.

★ 613 ★
Boone - WATAUGA COUNTY SPRING FESTIVAL. Late April, 1 day, Appalachian State University. Contact: Boone Area Chamber of Commerce, 827 Blowing Rock Road, Boone, North Carolina 28607.

Features the arts, both visual and performing. There are displays and demonstrations of arts and crafts, enlivened by performances of mountain music and dancing.

★ 614 ★
Charlotte - FESTIVAL IN THE PARK. September, annual, 6 days, Freedom Park. Contact: Charlotte Chamber of Commerce, Public Relations Department, 222 South Church Street, Charlotte, North Carolina 28202.

Six stages provide continuous entertainment simultaneously. One stage has big name entertainers and bands, one has dramatic presentations, one has clowns, one has magicians, one has children's theater, one has opera. In addition, there are craft exhibits, displays of painting and photography. The entire event is free and is sponsored by the Charlotte Chamber of Commerce. Started in 1964.

★ 615 ★
Davidson - SPRING CELEBRATION. April, annual, 1 day, Davidson College. Contact: Director of Communications, Davidson College, Davidson, North Carolina 28036.

Davidson hails spring with piano and organ recitals, choral concerts, an exhibition of the works from the Davidson National Print and Drawing Competition, plays and a humorous debate. Started in 1974.

★ 616 ★
Durham - DOWNTOWN STREET ART CELEBRATION. Early September, annual. Contact: Durham Arts Council, 810 West Proctor Street, Durham, North Carolina 27707.

The festival presents displays of arts, crafts, screening of films, and the performance of music, dancing, and shows. Begun around 1974.

★ 617 ★
Durham - TRIANGLE FESTIVAL OF CRAFTS. Late April-early May, 3 days, Durham Civic Center. Contact: Durham Arts Council, 810 West Proctor Street, Durham, North Carolina 27707.

The festival features displays of crafts, music and dance performances, and the screening of films.

★ 618 ★
Elizabeth City - FINE ARTS FESTIVAL. Mid-late March, 7 days, Elizabeth City State University.

NORTH CAROLINA (Continued)

Contact: Chamber of Commerce, 100 East Main Street, Elizabeth City, North Carolina 27909.

A festival of fine arts on display and in performance on the campus of Elizabeth City State University.

★ 619 ★
Franklin - MOUNTAINEER BOOK FAIR.   Early July, 3 days, Macon County Fairgrounds.   Contact: Adelaide Key, Chairman, Post Office Box 108, Franklin, North Carolina 28734.

A literary event with additional festivities for all ages.

★ 620 ★
West Jefferson - ASHE COUNTY ARTS FESTIVAL. Early May, 1 day.   Contact: Boone Area Chamber of Commerce, 827 Blowing Rock Road, Boone, North Carolina 28607.

The fine arts, the performing arts, and native folk arts are all represented in a series of concerts, displays, exhibits and performances.

★ 621 ★
Wilson - FESTIVAL OF CONTEMPORARY ARTS. Mid February to mid March, annual, Atlantic Christian College.   Contact: Festival of Contemporary Arts, Atlantic Christian College, Wilson, North Carolina 27893.

A musical concert series by guest groups and solo artists on campus is part of the Arts Festival.   Other arts are also represented.

★ 622 ★
Winston-Salem - FINE ARTS FESTIVAL.   Mid March, 8 days, Winston-Salem State University.   Contact: Harry E. Pickard, Winston-Salem State University, Columbia Heights, Winston-Salem, North Carolina 27107.

A festival of fine arts on display and in performance at Winston-Salem State University.

★ 623 ★
Winston-Salem - NORTH CAROLINA SUMMER FESTIVAL.   June-August, annual, 5 weeks, North Carolina School of the Arts.   Contact: North Carolina School of the Arts, Post Office Box 4657, Winston-Salem, North Carolina 27107.

The festival presents a variety of performing arts events.   There are films, performances of popular musicals, and productions by the North Carolina Dance Theatre, the Festival Orchestra, and the Piedmont Chamber Players.

NORTH DAKOTA

★ 624 ★
Dunseith - INTERNATIONAL FESTIVAL OF THE ARTS. June-July, annual, International Peace Garden Amphitheater.   Contact: Assistant Travel Director, North Dakota State Highway Department, Capitol Grounds, Bismarck, North Dakota 58505.

A series of cultural events, musical presentations, dance, dramas, and art exhibits, staged in an outdoor amphitheater on the border between North Dakota and Manitoba, Canada.

OHIO

★ 625 ★
Cleveland - CLEVELAND SUMMER ARTS FESTIVAL. Mid June to late August, annual.   Contact: Cleveland Summer Arts Festival, 11125 Magnolia Drive, Cleveland, Ohio 44106.

Attempt by a major city to provide free widespread entertainment and participation activities in the arts for both the young and adults.   Workshops for art, drama, dance and music; opera drama; performances by the Cleveland Ballet Guild and Ballet Russe of Cleveland; and a host of popular music programs featuring leading musicians and ensembles.   Established in 1967.

★ 626 ★
Dayton - WESTMINSTER FESTIVAL OF RELIGIOUS ARTS.   May, annual, Westminster Presbyterian Church.   Contact: Westminster Festival of Religious Arts, Westminster Presbyterian Church, First Street and Perry, Dayton, Ohio 45402.

Fine arts and performing arts are featured.

★ 627 ★
Toledo - TOLEDO FESTIVAL OF THE ARTS.   Late June, 2 days, Crosby Gardens.   Contact: Travel and Tourist Bureau, Ohio Department of Economic and Community Development, Box 1001, Columbus, Ohio 43216.

An outdoor, juried show of music, arts, crafts, dance, and drama.   Open to exhibitors throughout the United States.

OHIO (Continued)

★ 628 ★
Willoughby - OUTDOOR ART FESTIVAL.   Late July,
annual, 3 days, by the Lake.   Contact: Ms. Reita
Hutson, School of Fine Arts, 38660 Mentor Avenue,
Willoughby, Ohio 44094.

The festival includes the display of the works of
artists and craftpersons from Ohio and the surrounding
states, plus dramas, comic operas, puppet shows and
recitals.   Begun around 1973.

OKLAHOMA

★ 629 ★
Oklahoma City - FESTIVAL OF THE ARTS.   April
(Spring), annual, Civic Center Mall.   Contact:
Arts Council of Oklahoma City, 1426 North East
Expressway, Oklahoma City, Oklahoma 73111.

The mall is covered with tents full of paintings,
pottery, weavings, watercolors, photographs, leather
goods, leaded glass, metal sculpture and all of the
other products of artists selected from many states.
The Creative Education area gives children the
opportunity to try their hand.   Singers, bands,
symphonies and theatrical performances complete
the homage to the arts.

★ 630 ★
Oklahoma City - MUSKOGEE ARTS FESTIVAL.
Late April, annual, J.H.S. and Fine Arts Auditoriums.
Contact: Muskogee Arts Festival, Civic Center Music
Hall, Oklahoma City, Oklahoma 73102.

Concerts featuring the Oklahoma City Symphony and
other events related to the arts.

★ 631 ★
Stillwater - AUTUMN FESTIVAL OF THE ARTS.
October (Autumn), annual, Oklahoma State University.
Contact: Autumn Festival of the Arts, Oklahoma
State University, Stillwater, Oklahoma 74074.

The theaters, auditoriums, and other buildings on
campus serve as the locations of the musical events,
which are only part of a larger festival program of
drama, lectures, films, poetry readings, exhibits, and
other events familiar to academic arts festivals.
Guest artists.   Established in 1944.

★ 632 ★
Stillwater - SPRING FESTIVAL OF THE ARTS.   April
(Spring), annual, Oklahoma State University.   Contact:

Spring Festival of the Arts, Oklahoma State University,
Stillwater, Oklahoma 74074.

The theaters, auditoriums, and other buildings on
campus serve as the locations of the musical events,
which are only part of a larger festival program of
drama, lectures, films, poetry readings, exhibits, and
other events familiar to academic arts festivals.
Guest artists.   Established in 1944.

OREGON

★ 633 ★
Jacksonville - PETER BRITT GARDENS MUSIC AND
ARTS FESTIVAL.   August, annual, 2 weeks.   Con-
tact: Peter Britt Gardens Music and Art Festival,
Box 669, Jacksonville, Oregon 97530.

Rich and varied in musical programming, orchestral
and chamber works.   Although works by the great
composers played include the familiar, there is a good
representation of the lesser-known works.   The outdoor pavilion located in the gardens is the site for
the orchestral concerts, youth concerts, and open
rehearsals.   The Festival Orchestra is a "pick-up"
orchestra of about 50 musicians, primarily from the
Western states.   Founded in 1963.

★ 634 ★
Lake Oswego - FESTIVAL OF THE ARTS.   Late June,
annual, 4 days.   Contact: Lake Oswego Chamber
of Commerce, Lake Oswego, Oregon 97034.

A community-wide event including art exhibitions, concerts, dance exhibitions, art auction, garden show and
parade.

★ 635 ★
Monmouth - OCE SUMMER ARTS FESTIVAL.   June-
July (Summer), annual, 2 weeks, Oregon College of
Education.   Contact: Director, Summer Arts Festival,
Oregon College of Education, Monmouth, Oregon
97361.

Features a musical, an invitational art exhibit, faculty
and guest recitals, a multi-media show, festival films
and other events.   Started in 1967.

PENNSYLVANIA

★ 636 ★
Bethlehem - ART FESTIVAL WEEK.   April, annual,
6 days, Moravian Academy Upper School.   Contact:
Chairperson, Fine Arts Department, Moravian Academy,
4313 Green Pond Road, Bethlehem, Pennsylvania 18017.

PENNSYLVANIA (Continued)

A different event is featured each day, exploring the arts through films, concerts, ensemble, and soloist performances.   Started in 1972.

★ 637 ★
Erie - SPRING ARTS FESTIVAL.   Late April, annual, 10 days, Gannon Auditorium.   Contact: Department of Commerce, Bureau of Travel Development, 431 South Office Building, Harrisburg, Pennsylvania 17120.

Festival features collection of arts, music, painting, sculpture, and handicrafts.

★ 638 ★
Lewisburg - ARTS FESTIVAL.   Early May, 9 days. Contact: Department of Commerce, Travel Development Bureau, Room 431, South Office Building, Harrisburg, Pennsylvania 17120.

Exhibits of arts and crafts from the penitentiary, country music concerts, tours of historic and interesting houses highlight the festival events.

★ 639 ★
Philadelphia - PHILADELPHIA FESTIVAL.   April (Spring), annual, 1 month, throughout the city. Contact: The Philadelphia Convention and Visitors Bureau, 1525 John F. Kennedy Boulevard, Philadelphia, Pennsylvania 19102.

The event is a vast fair in honor of America's cultural heritage and the vitality of the arts and humanities, sponsored by the institutions of the Greater Philadelphia Cultural Alliance.   There are recitals and concerts featuring music and musicians from all over the world and from classical to jazz.   Live theater presentations include a wide range: Broadway, professional children's theater, and comedies.   The Philadelphia Philm Festival is also part of the events.   Dance companies perform in a variety of styles.   Noted artists and local art students alike contribute to the displays of visual art including such exotic media as banner and sky-writing design competitions.   Local institutions such as the Philadelphia Zoo and the Franklin Institute plan special exhibits and activities.

★ 640 ★
Philadelphia - PHILADELPHIA FLING.   Mid June-September, annual.   Contact: Philadelphia Convention and Tourist Bureau, 1525 John F. Kennedy Boulevard, Philadelphia, Pennsylvania 19102.

Free fun and entertainment.   Summer Evenings at Rittenhouse Square--nights of dance, music, theater, ballet, and choral groups.   Mummers String Band Concerts--Kennedy Plaza. Concerts at the Art Museum--steps of the Museum, music, ethnic groups perform.   "A Nation is Born"--sound and light show at Independence Hall;   patriotic, exciting story of Fight for Liberty.   At Kennedy Plaza, music, dance, unusual acts and entertainment, stars, sports, and celebrities.

★ 641 ★
Pittsburgh - WOMEN'S CULTURAL FESTIVAL. January, annual, 4 days, Schenley Hall, Student Union.   Contact: Undergraduate Women's Union, University of Pittsburgh, Pittsburgh, Pennsylvania 15213.

The Undergraduate Women's Union coordinates the festival for the purpose of providing a forum where feminists can gather for serious feminist thought, discussion, and entertainment.   To this end they have speakers, panel discussions, workshops, films, theatrical work, concerts, and a coffeehouse. Started in 1971.

★ 642 ★
Quakertown - ARTS FESTIVAL.   Mid September, annual, 3 days, Broad and Main Streets.   Contact: Quakertown Historical Society, 44 South Main Street, Quakertown, Pennsylvania 18951.

Authentic country store, horse drawn carriage rides, music and entertainment, crafts, flea market, bake sale, and food.

★ 643 ★
Rose Tree - SUMMER FESTIVAL.   Early June to early September, annual, 3 months.   Contact: Delaware County Commission, Toal Building, Second and Orange Streets, Media, Pennsylvania 19063.

Events include programs of music, drama, children's theater, historical pageant dealing with period of the Revolution, and ethnic festivities.

★ 644 ★
Scranton - LACKAWANNA ARTS FESTIVAL.   Mid September, annual, 4 days, Court House Square. Contact: Department of Commerce, Bureau of Travel Development, 431 South Office Building, Harrisburg, Pennsylvania 17120.

Exhibits, concerts, exotic foods, and musical variety shows highlight the fun-filled activities.

PENNSYLVANIA (Continued)

★ 645 ★
Slippery Rock - BUTLER COUNTY MUSIC AND ARTS
FESTIVAL.   Mid July, annual, 2 days, Armco Park.
Contact: Department of Commerce, Bureau of Travel
Development, 431 South Office Building, Harrisburg,
Pennsylvania 17120.

Craft making skills of candle making, ceramics, and
metal sculpturing are demonstrated.   Art show, plus
visual and performing arts program open to the public,
free of charge.

★ 646 ★
State College - CENTRAL PENNSYLVANIA FESTIVAL
OF THE ARTS. Mid July, annual, 4 days, Pennsyl-
vania State University.   Contact: Department of
Commerce, Bureau of Travel Development, 431 South
Office Building, Harrisburg, Pennsylvania 17120.

One of the largest exhibits of art in the East.
Festival includes performing arts, sidewalk art and
craft sales, artists in action, and a demonstration
of colonial crafts and skills.   Free parking available
on campus with shuttle bus service every 15 minutes
to festival site.

★ 647 ★
Tamiment - TAMIMENT FESTIVAL OF MUSIC AND
ART.   July, annual, Concert Hall.   Contact:
Tamiment Festival of Music and Art, Concert Hall,
Tamiment, Pennsylvania 18371.

Chamber music and art exhibits highlight the festival
activities.

★ 648 ★
University Park - NITTANY MOUNTAIN SUMMER.
July-August, annual, 3 weeks, Pennsylvania State
University.   Contact: Nittany Mountain Summer,
University Arts Services, The Pennsylvania State
University, 111 Arts Building, University Park,
Pennsylvania 16802.

A celebration of the visual and performing arts,
featuring accomplished professional artists.   Works
ranging from classical to modern are presented by
the Pennsylvania Ballet, the Pennsylvania Orchestra's
Shirt-Sleeve Concerts, and the University's Museum
of Art.   Special guest artists also appear.   With
talks, tours and demonstrations, the festival attempts
to foster informal contacts between artists and visitors.
The Festival of American Theatre is held concurrently.

★ 649 ★
Upper Black Eddy - SUNDANCE FESTIVAL.   July
and August, annual, Sundance Theatre.   Contact:
Sundance Festival, Upper Black Eddy, Pennsylvania
18972.

The festival events include chamber music, theater,
dance, and a film at Sundance Theatre.

★ 650 ★
Wilkes-Barre - FINE ARTS FIESTA.   May, annual,
3 days, Public Square.   Contact: Goldberg Ad
Agency, IBE Building, Suite 1117, Wilkes-Barre,
Pennsylvania 18701.

Painting exhibits by accomplished artists, poetry reading, fashion show of locally manufactured clothing,
craft demonstrations, and special children's programs.
Philharmonic Orchestra, barbershop quartets, musical
comedy, choruses, folk singers, drama, puppet shows,
and folk dancing.

★ 651 ★
Williamsport - ARTS FESTIVAL.   Mid April, annual,
2 weeks.   Contact: Department of Commerce, Bureau
of Travel Development, 431 South Office Building,
Harrisburg, Pennsylvania 17120.

A festival celebrating the arts - visual, fine, and
performing.   A variety of activities and events to
please all who join in the celebration.

SOUTH CAROLINA

★ 652 ★
Charleston - COLLEGE OF CHARLESTON FINE
ARTS FESTIVAL.   Late March, annual, 2 days,
College of Charleston.   Contact: College Relations,
College of Charleston, Charleston, South Carolina
29401.

Activities include a Founders Day ceremony and
panel discussions.

★ 653 ★
Charleston - FESTIVAL OF TWO WORLDS.   Late
May-early June, 10 days.   Contact: Charleston
Trident, Post Office Box 975, Charleston, South
Carolina 29402.

An American counterpart of the Spoleto (Italy)
Festival, since 1958 one of Europe's most creative and
comprehensive performing arts festivals.   Will begin
in Charleston in 1977.

The Arts

SOUTH CAROLINA (Continued)

★ 654 ★
Clinton - FESTIVAL OF ARTS.   May, annual.
Contact: Festival of Arts, Presbyterian College,
Clinton, South Carolina 29325.

Visual arts, theater, and music events highlight the
festival.

★ 655 ★
Columbia - FIESTA.   Mid April, annual, 3 days.
Contact: Greater Columbia Chamber of Commerce,
Post Office Box 1306, Columbia, South Carolina
29202.

This city's spring festival includes a huge arts and
crafts display and sale with participation crafts for
young and old.   Performing groups from the
Columbia area participate in the festival with music,
dance and drama.

★ 656 ★
Greenville - GREENVILLE ARTS FESTIVAL.   Mid
May, annual, 4 days, Fine Arts Center.   Contact:
Mrs. Harold C. Clark, Jr., 109 Byrd Boulevard,
Greenville, South Carolina 29605.

Exhibitions of visual arts created by artists ranging
from school children to professionals.   Performing
arts, including the Greenville Symphony, Civic
Ballet, plus salon and cafe performances, are also
featured.   There is also a creative writing contest
with monetary prizes.   Artwork may be purchased.

SOUTH DAKOTA

★ 657 ★
Springfield - FINE ARTS FESTIVAL.   Late April,
annual, 8 days, University of South Dakota, Springfield.   Contact: Division of Tourism, State Office
Building 2, Pierre, South Dakota 57501.

The University hosts a festival of the fine arts.

★ 658 ★
Vermilion - FESTIVAL OF THE ARTS.   April, 1
month, University of South Dakota.   Contact:
Division of Tourism Development, State Office
Building 2, Pierre, South Dakota 57501.

The events include plays, concerts, and symposiums
on arts.

TENNESSEE

★ 659 ★
Jonesboro - STORYTELLING FESTIVAL.   October,
annual, 2 days.   Contact: Jimmy Neil Smith,
Parson's Table, Jonesboro, Tennessee 37659.

Folklorists librarians, teachers, children and other
interested people meet to discuss, perfect, and enjoy
the art of storytelling.

★ 660 ★
Knoxville - DOGWOOD ARTS FESTIVAL.   April,
annual, 10 days, Market Square Mall, and other
places about town.   Contact: Knoxville Dogwood
Arts Festival, 705 Gay Street, Southwest, Knoxville,
Tennessee 37902.

There are numerous arts and crafts fairs, exhibits,
and shows scattered throughout the city offering a
variety of amateur and professional pieces.   Many
artisans give demonstrations.   There are tours of
historic sites, bird walks, and tours of the dogwood
trails.   Entertainment is provided by top-name performers, as well as high school band concerts, local
vocalists, USAF Band, a bluegrass concert, and
dance performances and demonstrations.   Other
activities include a turtle derby, theatrical performances, boat and bicycle races, sports events, etc.
Begun in 1961.

TEXAS

★ 661 ★
Abilene - FESTIVAL OF ARTS.   April, annual, 2
weeks.   Contact: Chamber of Commerce, Post
Office Box 2281, Abilene, Texas 79604.

Offers art, drama, music, and entertainment.

★ 662 ★
Austin - FINE ARTS FESTIVAL.   November, annual,
3 weeks.   Contact: Fine Arts Festival, University
of Texas, College of Fine Arts, Post Office Box 7547,
University Station, Austin, Texas 78712.

The festival is considered one of the important
academic arts festivals in the Southwest.   Embraces
fine arts, drama, music, and architecture.   Besides
concerts there are lectures, art exhibitions, and performances of dramatic productions.   Founded in 1942.

★ 663 ★
Fort Worth - FINE ARTS FESTIVAL.   Mid April to
mid May, annual, 3 weeks, Ed Landreth Auditorium

TEXAS (Continued)

and the University Theatre, Texas Christian University. Contact: Fine Arts Festival, School of Fine Arts, Texas Christian University, Fort Worth, Texas 76129.

The festival includes performances by the University Symphony Orchestra and University Chorus; faculty piano, organ, or voice recitals; chamber music programs; and often the staging of an opera. In general, the music programs are based on some unifying theme. Art exhibitions and dramatic plays are also part of the festival. Begun about 1940.

★ 664 ★
Galveston - FESTIVAL USA ON THE STRAND. August. Contact: Executive Director, Galveston County Cultural Arts Council, Box 1105, Galveston, Texas 75550.

The festival focuses on the arts - music, dance, drama, sculpture, painting, and films, and searches for American cultural roots from diverse heritages.

★ 665 ★
Houston - MAIN STREET. Mid October, annual, 2 days, Main Street at Montrose. Contact: Houston Chamber of Commerce, Cultural Affairs Committee, Post Office Box 53600, Houston, Texas 77052.

Houston's largest festival, sponsored by the Chamber of Commerce Cultural Affairs Committee, is a comprehensive salute to the arts. There is a wide range of musical experiences available: classical, jazz, country, barbershop, etc., as performed by symphonies, orchestras, chorales and other groups. Ballet folkloric and Indian dancers perform. Blocks upon blocks of booths where artists and craftsmen demonstrate, exhibit, and sell their works. There are light shows, video presentations, balloon art, street painting and other artistic endeavors. Special programs for children are provided. Begun around 1971.

★ 666 ★
Houston - OCTOBER HOUSTON ARTS FESTIVAL. October, annual, 1 month. Contact: October Houston Arts Festival, Houston Chamber of Commerce, Post Office Box 53600, Houston, Texas 77052.

The festival covers all areas of the fine arts and performing arts. Symphonic concerts, outstanding musical performers, string quartets, chamber orchestras, etc. The nonmusical aspects of the October Festival include dramatic plays, some lectures, but a particularly strong emphasis on gallery exhibitions of works of art. Founded in 1966.

★ 667 ★
Odessa - FINE ARTS FESTIVAL. April, annual, all month. Contact: Mr. Gene Garrison, Chamber of Commerce, 412 North Lincoln, Box 3626, Odessa, Texas 79760.

A citywide celebration of the arts with shows, performances, etc.

VERMONT

★ 668 ★
Manchester - FESTIVAL OF THE ARTS. June-October, annual, 4 months, Southern Vermont Art Center. Contact: Director, Festival of the Arts, Southern Vermont Art Center, Manchester, Vermont 05254.

The festival honors a variety of the arts. The galleries and pavilions house exhibitions of sculpture, paintings, photographs, drawings, serigraphs, watercolors, brass rubbings, batiks, etc. Concerts are given by choral groups, instrumental groups, and soloists, including pops concerts and a special children's concert. Dancers also perform. There is an International Film Festival as well. Begun around 1929.

★ 669 ★
Stratton Mountain - STRATTON ARTS FESTIVAL. Early September-mid October, annual, Stratton Mountain Base Lodge. Contact: Stratton Arts Festival, Stratton Mountain Base Lodge, Stratton Mountain, Vermont 05155.

Concerts, art, sculpture, crafts, and photography are included in the things to see and enjoy at this festival of the arts.

VIRGINIA

★ 670 ★
Bristol - BRISTOL SPRING ARTS FESTIVAL. Early April, annual. Contact: Bristol Spring Arts Festival, Bristol Chamber of Commerce, Box 1039, Bristol, Virginia 24201.

Concerts, ballet, theater, and art exhibits highlight the festival events.

★ 671 ★
Norfolk - NORFOLK ARTS FESTIVAL. Late June-July, annual, 4 weeks. Contact: The Matthews Agency, Incorporated, 610 West 25th Street, Norfolk, Virginia 23517.

The Arts

VIRGINIA (Continued)

Daily events of music, art shows, plays, and dance--all offered free to the public. Local or state talent, performances of the military service bands. Founded in 1961.

★ 672 ★

Richmond - FESTIVAL OF ARTS. Mid June to early August, annual, 7 weeks, Dogwood Dell in Richmond's Byrd Park. Contact: Festival of Arts, Department of Recreation and Parks, 900 East Broad Street, Richmond, Virginia 23219.

Performing organizations such as the Richmond Symphony, Richmond Ballet, Richmond Civic Opera Association, Richmond Choral Society, and others. Children's plays, plays by Shakespeare, carillon concerts, ballet, and poetry readings compose the programs. The series opens with a "Picture Carnival", a juried open exhibit for amateur artists and photographers and features a summer-long display of art and exhibits by member groups of the Federated Arts Council. Begun in 1957.

★ 673 ★

Roanoke - FESTIVAL IN THE PARK. Early June, annual, 3 days, Elmwood Park. Contact: Downtown Roanoke, Incorporated, 410 First Street, Southwest, Roanoke, Virginia 24011; or (For the Art Show) Roanoke Fine Arts Center, 301 23rd Street, Roanoke, Virginia 24014.

The festival is billed as a "fun-filled weekend of art, music and entertainment." Included is the sidewalk art show, an open show of paintings, sculpture, graphics and photography. Cash awards are given and most of the work is for sale; this is one of the East's largest open shows. There is big band, rock, country, bluegrass and pop music. The Kiddie Korral offers fun, games and crafts for children over three years of age. The Big Stick-up offers a creative workshop in dimensional media. There are also marionette shows, musical dramas, historical and crafts exhibits, and other entertainment. Begun around 1970.

★ 674 ★

Vienna - INTERNATIONAL CHILDREN'S FESTIVAL. Mid September, annual, 4 days, Wolf Trap Farm Park. Contact: Miss Carol V. Harford, Assistant to the Chairman, Wolf Trap Foundation, 1624 Trap Road, Vienna, Virginia 22180.

Included in the program are puppet shows, plays, dance performances, musical interludes, mimes, and craft demonstrations. The children can wander around, walking in and out of performances on many stages. Performers come not only from the Maryland-Virginia area; exhibitions are contributed by numerous foreign embassies. Begun in 1971.

★ 675 ★

Vienna - WOLF TRAP FARM PARK FOR THE PERFORMING ARTS. June to September, annual, Filene Center Auditorium and other places at Wolf Trap Farm Park. Contact: Wolf Trap Farm Park, Post Office Box 12, Vienna, Virginia 22180; or Wolf Trap Foundation, 801 19th Street, Northwest, Washington, D.C. 20006.

Wide-ranging summer concert season of symphonic music, opera, ballet, pops concerts, jazz, folk, musical theater, and special events. Outstanding guest orchestras, companies, groups, classical and popular artists perform at the new Filene Center auditorium; grass seating in the natural bowl about the structure. Other events include band concerts, Summer Academy concerts, National Folk Festival, International Children's Day, and art exhibits. Picnic areas. Started in 1971.

★ 676 ★

Williamsburg - AN OCCASION FOR THE ARTS. Early October, annual, 1 day. Contact: An Occasion for the Arts, Post Office Box 363, Williamsburg, Virginia 23185.

Celebration in honor of crafts, arts, theater, music and the performing arts.

WASHINGTON

★ 677 ★

Burien - BURIEN ARTS FESTIVAL. June (3rd weekend), annual, 3 days. Contact: Mrs. Paul G. Harper, 1626 Southwest 156th, Seattle, Washington 98166.

The festival is a celebration of music, drama, dance, sculpture, painting, pottery and fabrics. Begun around 1967.

★ 678 ★

Edmonds - EDMONDS ART FESTIVAL. June (4th weekend), annual, 3 days, Edmonds Civic Center. Contact: J. Ward Phillips, President, Post Office Box 9344, Seattle, Washington 98109.

Events include live drama, arts and crafts, and artists in action. Begun around 1959.

WASHINGTON (Continued)

★ 679 ★
Olympia - OUTDOOR ART FESTIVAL.   July (2nd weekend), annual.   Contact: Eula Benefiel, 520 Eskridge Way, Olympia, Washington 98501.

Artists in action working with crafts, sculpture, wood carvings, candles and macrame.   Performing events include music, folk dances and ballet.   Begun around 1970.

★ 680 ★
Port Angeles - ANGELES ARTS IN ACTION.   July (3rd weekend), annual, 3 days.   Contact: V. Earlen Harrison, 130 Oakcrest Way, Port Angeles, Washington 98362.

More than 50 artists and craftsmen demonstrate painting, sculpture and ceramics.   There is also a junior exhibit and a clothesline sale of paintings.   Drama by community players and live music round out the events.   Begun around 1969.

WEST VIRGINIA

★ 681 ★
Lewisburg - GREENBRIER VALLEY ARTS AND HUMANITIES FESTIVAL.   Late April-early May, 2 weeks.   Contact: Greenbrier College of Ostepathic Medicine, Jane Front, Route 2, Box 306A, Lewisburg, West Virginia 24901.

A festival of the arts - visual and performing.

WISCONSIN

★ 682 ★
LaCrosse - COULEE REGION FESTIVAL OF ARTS.
August, annual, Myrick Park.   Contact: Coulee Region Festival of Arts, Viterbo College Fine Arts Center, LaCrosse, Wisconsin 54601.

"Great River Symphony" and guest soloists--orchestral concerts, chamber music, and ballet.   Art exhibits are also a part of the festival.

★ 683 ★
Milwaukee - WISCONSIN FESTIVAL OF ART.
Early November, 2 days, State Fair Park.   Contact: Convention and Visitors Bureau, 828 North Broadway, Milwaukee, Wisconsin 53202.

A variety of arts - visual and performing - for the enjoyment of young and old.

★ 684 ★
Wausau - FESTIVAL OF THE ARTS.   Early September, annual, Yawkey Park.   Contact: Festival of the Arts, Marathon County Historical Society, 403 McIndoe Street, Wausau, Wisconsin 54401.

The festival offers exhibitions of paintings, works of sculpture, and the crafts.   Prizes are offered exhibiting artists whose works are also offered for sale. Other events have been added to the festival with a view to attracting more interest: poetry recitation, Indian dances, jazz, barbershop singing, brief musical concerts such as a performance by a concert band, an opera scene, etc.   Founded in 1965.

CANADA - ALBERTA

★ 685 ★
Banff - BANFF FESTIVAL OF THE ARTS.   August, annual, approximately 19 days.   Contact: Banff Festival of the Arts, Banff School of Fine Arts, Banff, Alberta, Canada.

Orchestral and chamber concerts, drama, musical theater, and ballet at the mountain campus of the Banff School of Fine Arts.   Performances each evening; afternoon lectures, workshops, films, and gallery tours.

CANADA - MANITOBA

★ 686 ★
Boissevain - INTERNATIONAL FESTIVAL OF THE ARTS.   June and July, annual, International Peace Garden Amphitheater.   Contact: Manitoba Government Travel, 200 Vaughn Street, Winnipeg, Manitoba R3C 0P8, Canada.

A series of cultural events, musical presentations, dance, dramas, and art exhibits staged in an outdoor amphitheater on the border between North Dakota and Manitoba, Canada.

★ 687 ★
Gimli - CREATIVE ARTS WEEK.   Late August, 10 days.   Contact: Manitoba Government Travel, 200 Vaughn Street, Winnipeg, Manitoba R3C 0P8, Canada.

Includes a one-day festival amidst a week-long celebration of the creative arts.

★ 688 ★
Neepawa - HOLIDAY FESTIVAL OF THE ARTS.
Early July (lst 2 weeks) 2 weeks.   Contact: Ms. Marlene Siatecki, Holiday Festival of Arts, Box 147, Neepawa, Manitoba R0J 1H0, Canada.

CANADA - MANITOBA (Continued)

Workshops and instructions for the whole family in various art forms such as painting, music, drama, dance, sculpture, ceramics, etc.

CANADA - NEWFOUNDLAND

★ 689 ★
Saint John's - SUMMER FESTIVAL OF THE ARTS. July, annual, 1 month, Arts and Culture Centre. Contact: Newfoundland Department of Tourism, Confederation Building, Saint John's, Newfoundland, Canada.

This extensive festival allows local talents a chance to display their particular entertaining skill. Various imported entertainers also appear.

CANADA - NOVA SCOTIA

★ 690 ★
Halifax/Dartmouth metropolitan area - NOVA SCOTIA FESTIVAL OF THE ARTS. August, annual, 1 week, Dalhousie University. Contact: Co-ordinator and General Administrator, Dalhousie Art Centre, 6101 University Avenue, Halifax, Nova Scotia, Canada.

Handcrafts are displayed and sold, there are art gallery exhibitions, a flea market, and flower shows. Headline entertainers perform each evening in addition to opera society performances and theatrical presentations including films, puppet shows, magicians, Scottish pipers, dancers and singers, outdoor concerts, military band concerts and beer gardens. Begun around 1956.

CANADA - ONTARIO

★ 691 ★
Guelph - GUELPH SPRING FESTIVAL. Late April-mid May, annual, 16 days. Contact: The Ministry of Industry and Tourism, Parliament Buildings, Toronto, Ontario M7A 2E5, Canada.

Brings together an international group of noted artists. Features operas, concerts, symphonies, musical comedies, films, and an art exhibition.

CANADA - QUEBEC

★ 692 ★
Montreal - MONTREAL INTERNATIONAL BOOK FAIR. Mid May, annual, 5 days, Place Bonaventure. Contact: The Tourist Information Division, 150 Boulevard Saint Cyrille East, Quebec, Quebec G1R 4Y3, Canada.

The festival is for nations and individual publishers from all over the world. It is intended to give publishers a chance to either sell the rights to their works or introduce them to publishers, libraries, the public and other persons in North America interested in the book trade. Started in 1975.

Arts and Crafts
(Includes Decorative Arts, Fine Arts, Folk Crafts, Photography)
See also: THE ARTS

ALABAMA

★ 693 ★
Anniston - ANNISTON ARTS AND CRAFTS FESTIVAL. Mid April. Contact: Mrs. Charles O. Stephens, Route 10, Box 123, Anniston, Alabama 36201.

Antique car show, tour of homes, school art exhibits, Night of Music, Little Theater presentation, opera, craft sales in park, and hymn festival.

★ 694 ★
Birmingham - BLUFF PARK ARTS AND CRAFTS SHOW. Early October, annual, 1 day. Contact: Mrs. James Haggard, 2211 Southwood Road, Birmingham, Alabama 35216.

Arts and crafts exhibited and for sale, barbeque. Begun around 1964.

★ 695 ★
Birmingham - HANDS AT WORK CRAFTSMEN'S FAIR. Early November, annual, 2 days, Birmingham Botanical Gardens Center Building. Contact: Bureau of Publicity, State of Alabama, Montgomery, Alabama 36130.

See, learn, and buy from craftspeople who demonstrate and display their crafts. Begun around 1973.

★ 696 ★
Dothan - HOUSTON ARTS AND CRAFTS FESTIVAL. Mid April, annual, 1 week, Houston Memorial Library. Contact: Stan Herrin, Houston Memorial Library, Post Office Box 1369, Dothan, Alabama 36301.

Week long exhibits of arts and crafts with nightly demonstrations. Begun around 1971.

ALABAMA (Continued)

★ 697 ★
Fairhope - ARTS AND CRAFTS WEEK.   Mid-late
March, 1 week.   Contact: Mobile Area Chamber
of Commerce, Post Office Box 2187, Mobile, Alabama
36601; or Eastern Shore Chamber of Commerce, Post
Office Box 507, Fairhope, Alabama 36532.

A week-long arts exhibit, theater and dance programs,
arts and crafts demonstrations, folk singing and dancing in costume, pine needle crafts, ceramics, net-
making, pottery-on-wheel, polishing rocks and
semi-precious stones, and shell craft, crowning of
the Dogwood Queen, home and garden tour, horse-
man's show, and a play, antique cars, flea markets,
strolling musicians, choral groups, ethnic programs,
fish fries, barbeques and bake sales.   Begun around
1953.

★ 698 ★
Fairhope - WORKING CRAFTSMEN'S FAIR.   August,
3 days.   Contact: Bureau of Publicity, State of
Alabama, Montgomery, Alabama 36104.

Glassblowers, silversmiths, stone cutters, stone carving,
faceting in gem stones; demonstrations and objects
for sale.   Sponsored by the Adult Recreation Club.

★ 699 ★
Foley - OUTDOOR ART SHOW.   Mid June, annual,
2 days.   Contact: Chairman, Center for the Performing Arts, Box 295, Foley, Alabama 36535.

A local outdoor art show with various medium represented.   Begun around 1973.

★ 700 ★
Fort Deposit - CALICO FORT ARTS AND CRAFTS
FAIR.   Mid April.   Contact: Mrs. W. H. Lee,
Box 310, Fort Deposit, Alabama 36032.

Arts and crafts exhibition, Indian dancers, children's
theater, storytellers, demonstrations and illustrations.

★ 701 ★
Fort Payne - ARTS AND CRAFTS SHOW.   Early
September, annual, 1 day, Manitou Cave.   Contact:
Bureau of Publicity, State of Alabama, Montgomery,
Alabama 36104.

Exhibition and sale of art and craft items.   Begun
around 1963.

★ 702 ★
Gadsden - MID-SUMMER ARTS AND CRAFTS
FESTIVAL.   August, annual, 1 week, Convention
Hall.   Contact: Mrs. Margaret Hand, Downtown
Motor Hotel Building, Gadsden, Alabama 35901.

Large collection of art and craft items for sale or
just for viewing.

★ 703 ★
Huntsville - ARTS-IN-THE-PARK OUTDOOR
FESTIVAL.   Early June, annual, 1 day, Big Spring
Park.   Contact: Arts Council, Incorporated, Rison
School Building, 509 Oak Avenue, Huntsville,
Alabama 35811.

Band concert, ballet, vocalists, folk music, classical
guitar, and barbershop singing, photography, and arts
and crafts exhibits.   Begun around 1972.

★ 704 ★
Millbrook - 17 SPRINGS ART, CRAFT AND HOBBY
FAIR.   Late April, Camp Grandview.   Contact:
Mrs. Jay Leavell, Director, Box 134, Montgomery,
Alabama 36101.

Exhibits and demonstrations by artisans, home-cooked
food, puppet show, guitar and banjo picking, and
donkey rides.

★ 705 ★
Mobile - OUTDOOR ART AND CRAFTS FAIR.   Late
September, annual, 2 days, Mobile Art Gallery
Grounds in Langan Park.   Contact: Mrs. Martina
Roser, Mobile Art Gallery, Langan Park, Mobile,
Alabama 36608.

Prizes given for arts and crafts.   Music, food, and
games for children.   Begun around 1965.

★ 706 ★
Montgomery - DIXIE ANNUAL.   March, annual,
Montgomery Museum of Fine Arts.   Contact:
Registrar, Montgomery Museum of Fine Arts, 440
South McDonough Street, Montgomery, Alabama
36104.

Drawings, prints, watercolors, and gouaches.   Juried
prizes and museum purchases.   Open to artists of
Alabama, Arkansas, Florida, Georgia, Kentucky,
Louisiana, Mississippi, Missouri, North Carolina, South
Carolina, Tennessee, Texas, and Virginia.

Arts and Crafts

ALABAMA (Continued)

★ 707 ★
Northport - KENTUCK ARTS AND CRAFT FESTIVAL.
Early September, annual, 2 days, Kentuck Park.
Contact: Mr. and Mrs. Al Knight, 20-U Northwood
Lake, Northport, Alabama 35476.

Artists and craftsmen from throughout Alabama, with
many giving demonstrations. Street dancing. Begun around 1972.

★ 708 ★
Opelika - ARTS FESTIVAL. Mid April, annual,
Municipal Park. Contact: Mrs. Charles A. Jones
III, Publicity Chairman, 610 Terracewood Drive,
Opelika, Alabama 36801.

Arts, crafts, handwork, flowers, pottery, antiques,
entertainment and southern style food. Begun around
1969.

★ 709 ★
Prattville - FOUNTAIN CITY FESTIVAL OF ARTS
AND CRAFTS. Late October, 1 day, Pratt Park.
Contact: Mr. Everett Barnes, 116 Cedar Drive,
Prattville, Alabama 36067.

Arts, crafts, music, dancing, boat rides, and food.

★ 710 ★
Troy - ARTS AND CRAFTS FESTIVAL. October,
2 days, Pike County Museum. Contact: Bureau
of Publicity, State of Alabama, Montgomery, Alabama
36104.

Artists and craftspeople display and sell their products.
Sponsored by the local Chamber of Commerce.

★ 711 ★
Tuscumbia - TENNESSEE VALLEY ART ASSOCIATION'S
ANNUAL ART SHOW. Early June, annual, 1 day,
on lawn of "Ivy Green" (birthplace of Helen Keller).
Contact: Mrs. Nelle Bigbee, 303 East Sixth Street,
Tuscumbia, Alabama 35674.

Art show at lovely, historic home.

★ 712 ★
Wetumpka - RUMBLING WATERS ARTS AND CRAFTS
SHOW. October, 1 day, Community Center. Con-
tact: Mrs. Gail Bass, Wetumpka, Alabama 36092.

Exhibition and sales of a variety of arts and crafts.

Begun around 1971.

ALASKA

★ 713 ★
Anchorage - ARTS FAIR. September, annual, 1 day,
Anchorage Community College. Contact: ACC
Arts Affiliates Office, 2533 Providence Avenue,
Anchorage, Alaska 99507.

Coffeehouse, different ethnic foods, bingo, flea
market, movies, music and dancing, craft activities:
puppet-making, weaving, macrame, printmaking, etc.
Ballet performances, ethnic and square dancing,
flower-arranging, art demonstrations, wild-flower and
herb drying, and ceramics.

★ 714 ★
Mount Edgecumbe - NATIVE STUDENTS ART SHOW.
Early April (1st week), Sitka Centennial Building.
Contact: Juneau Area Office, Bureau of Indian
Affairs, U.S. Department of the Interior, Federal
Building, Box 3-8000, Juneau, Alaska 99801.

Students display their artwork in many media including
ceramics, block paintings, charcoal, oil, water colors,
sculpture, soapstone, wood carving, ivory, silk screening, copper tooling, leather work, collages, and
macrame.

ARIZONA

★ 715 ★
Douglas - TWO FLAGS ART FESTIVAL. October,
annual. Contact: Douglas Art Association, Box
256, Douglas, Arizona 85607.

Outdoor and medallion shows. Juried, all media.
Sponsored by the Douglas Art Association. Open
to all artists in the United States and Mexico. Cash
awards, purchase awards, and prizes.

★ 716 ★
Flagstaff - NAVAJO CRAFTSMEN SHOW. Late
July-early August, 7-8 days, Museum of North
Arizona. Contact: Chamber of Commerce, Post
Office Box 1150, Beaver and Santa Fe, Flagstaff,
Arizona 86001.

An exhibition of Navajo crafts.

★ 717 ★
Tucson - TUCSON FESTIVAL EXHIBITION. April-
May, biennial. Contact: Executive Director, Tucson

ARIZONA (Continued)

Art Center, 325 West Franklin, Tucson, Arizona 85705.

All craft media, open to all residents of Arizona.

ARKANSAS

★ 718 ★
Eureka Springs - SIDEWALK ART AND CRAFTS FESTIVAL. Late May, annual, 3 days. Contact: Chamber of Commerce, Five North Main Street, Eureka Springs, Arkansas 72632.

Quality arts and crafts on display and for sale in an outdoor setting.

★ 719 ★
Fort Smith - FORT SMITH ART CENTER ANNUAL COMPETITION. March, annual. Contact: Registrar, Fort Smith Art Center, 423 North Sixth Street, Fort Smith, Arkansas 72901.

Painting, watercolor, and drawing. Juried with prizes and purchase awards given. The show is open to arts of Arkansas, Kansas, Louisiana, Missouri, Oklahoma, Tennessee and Texas.

★ 720 ★
Greenwood - GREENWOOD ARTS AND CRAFTS FAIR. June, 4 days. Contact: Chamber of Commerce, Greenwood, Arkansas 72936; or Department of Parks and Tourism, 149 State Capitol, Little Rock, Arkansas 72201.

A display and sale of a variety of arts and crafts.

★ 721 ★
Hindsville - OZARK ARTS AND CRAFTS SHOW. Mid October, annual, War Eagle Mills. Contact: Mrs. Blanche Elliot, War Eagle Mills Farm, Hindsville, Arkansas 72738.

A display of a wide variety of traditional and contemporary crafts and artwork produced by artisans of the Ozark region including wood carvings, oil paintings, pottery, toys, handwoven fabrics, jewelry, sculpture and needlework.

★ 722 ★
Hot Springs - HOMEMAKERS ARTS AND CRAFTS FAIR. Early October, annual, 3 days, Fairgrounds. Contact: Mrs. Don Wayman, 1101 Higdon Road, Hot Springs, Arkansas 71901.

A display and sale of arts and crafts created by those who are full-time homemakers. Begun around 1969.

★ 723 ★
Little Rock - DELTA ART EXHIBIT. October-November, annual, Arkansas Art Center. Contact: Director, The Arkansas Arts Center, MacArthur Park, Little Rock, Arkansas 72203.

A display of the works of artists born or residing in the states of Arkansas, Louisiana, Mississippi, Missouri, Oklahoma, Tennessee or Texas. All paintings and sculptures (under 500 pounds) are eligible. Both cash awards and purchase awards are given.

★ 724 ★
Little Rock - PRINTS, DRAWINGS AND CRAFTS EXHIBITION. May-June, annual, Arkansas Arts Center. Contact: Little Rock Chamber of Commerce, Continental Building, Suite 500, Little Rock, Arkansas 72201.

This exhibition is open to artists who were born in or reside in Arkansas, Louisiana, Mississippi, Missouri, Oklahoma, Tennessee, or Texas. Eligible prints and drawings in any media; the crafts are clay, glass, metal, plastics, textiles, wood or a combination of media; photographs in color or monochrome. Prizes include cash and purchase awards.

★ 725 ★
Malvern - ARTS AND CRAFTS FAIR. April, 3 days. Contact: Chamber of Commerce, Malvern, Arkansas 72104; or Department of Parks and Tourism, 149 State Capitol, Little Rock, Arkansas 72201.

A display and sale of a variety of arts and crafts.

★ 726 ★
Monticello - PIONEER DAYS ARTS AND CRAFTS FESTIVAL. April, 1 week. Contact: Chamber of Commerce, Monticello, Arkansas 71655; or Department of Parks and Tourism, 149 State Capitol, Little Rock, Arkansas 72201.

A display and sale of arts and crafts in the pioneer tradition.

★ 727 ★
Mount Gaylor - OZARK NATIVE CRAFTS FAIR. June. Contact: Chamber of Commerce, Mount Gaylor, Arkansas; or Department of Parks and Tourism, 149 State Capitol, Little Rock, Arkansas 72201.

Arts and Crafts

ARKANSAS (Continued)

Native crafts of the Ozark Mountains are demonstrated and on sale.

★ 728 ★
Mountain View - OZARK FOLK CENTER HARVEST FESTIVAL. Late October, 3 weeks, Ozark Folk Center. Contact: Ozark Folk Festival, Post Office Box 68, Mountain View, Arkansas 72560.

Festival includes craft demonstrations related to pioneer preparation of necessities for winter--soap and hominy making, sorghum and cornmeal milling, quilting, candle dipping, etc. Celebration of the harvest.

★ 729 ★
Newport - SUGGIN FOLK LIFE ART SHOW. April, annual, 11 days. Contact: Chamber of Commerce, Newport, Arkansas 72112; or Department of Parks and Tourism, 149 State Capitol, Little Rock, Arkansas 72201.

Arts and crafts are displayed and for sale, particularly those representative of the local heritage.

★ 730 ★
Rison - PIONEER CRAFT FESTIVAL. Late March, 3 days. Contact: Chamber of Commerce, Rison, Arkansas 71665.

Fair and parade highlight this display and exhibition of a variety of crafts.

★ 731 ★
Russellville - ARTS AND CRAFTS FAIR. Early November, 2 days. Contact: Chamber of Commerce, Russellville, Arkansas 72801; or Department of Parks and Tourism, 149 State Capitol, Little Rock, Arkansas 72201.

A display and sale of a variety of arts and crafts.

CALIFORNIA

★ 732 ★
Borrego Springs - DESERT ART FESTIVAL. April. Contact: San Diego Convention and Visitors Bureau, 1200 Third Avenue, Suite 824, San Diego, California 92101.

Southern California artists display works in this beautiful desert spot.

★ 733 ★
Catalina - FESTIVAL OF ART. Mid September, annual, 2 days, Avalon. Contact: Southern California Visitors Council, 705 West Seventh Street, Catalina, California 90017.

Amateur and professional artists exhibit paintings, crafts, photographs, and compete for cash awards. Events include a festival dinner dance. Begun around 1959.

★ 734 ★
Chula Vista - CHULA VISTA SUMMER ART FESTIVAL. Mid July, annual, 4 days, Chula Vista Shopping Center. Contact: Chula Vista Art Guild, Box 1213, Chula Vista, California 92012.

Open to all San Diego County artists. Prizes for oils, watercolors and mixed media. Features "Westways Collection of Original Art" from Automobile Club of Southern California. Begun around 1968.

★ 735 ★
Concord - ALL WEST CRAFTS FAIR. Early August, 2 days. Contact: California Chamber of Commerce, 455 Capitol Mall, Sacramento, California 95814.

Arts and crafts are demonstrated and displayed by artists from the West Coast area.

★ 736 ★
Crescent City - CRESCENT CITY ART FESTIVAL. July, 2 days, Cultural and Convention Center. Contact: Redwood Empire Association, Visitors Information Center, 476 Post Street, San Francisco, California 94102.

A show and sale of a variety of art forms.

★ 737 ★
Ferndale - FERNDALE ARTS FESTIVAL. Early May, 8 days. Contact: Information Officer, State of California Department of Commerce, 1400 Tenth Avenue, Sacramento, California 95814; or Chamber of Commerce, Ferndale, California 95536.

A kinetic art contest as well as more traditional art forms.

★ 738 ★
Fillmore - FESTIVAL OF ARTS AND CRAFTS. Late September, annual, 2 days, Veteran's Memorial Building. Contact: Chamber of Commerce, Fillmore, California 93015.

CALIFORNIA (Continued)

Exhibits of paintings, watercolors, and photographs. Craft demonstrations of potting and weaving. Begun around 1969.

★ 739 ★
Fortuna - FORTUNA ART FESTIVAL. Early October, 2 days, Rohner Park. Contact: Redwood Empire Association, Visitors Information Center, 467 Post Street, San Francisco, California 94102.

Arts and crafts in an outdoor setting. Begun around 1968.

★ 740 ★
Hermosa Beach - ARTS 'N CRAFTS BY THE SEA. Early September, 2 days, Pier Avenue. Contact: California Chamber of Commerce, 455 Capitol Mall, Sacramento, California 95814.

Nearly 300 artists exhibit, display and sell many craft forms including gold and silver jewelry, pottery, macrame, planters, wood-working, candles, and leatherworks.

★ 741 ★
Hermosa Beach - FIESTA DEL ARTES. Late May, 2 days, Pier Avenue. Contact: Southern California Visitors Bureau, 705 West Seventh Street, Los Angeles, California 90017; or Chamber of Commerce, 1035 Valley Drive, Post Office Box 404, Hermosa Beach, California 90254.

Exhibit of the crafts of more than 200 artists. Included are gold and silver jewelry, pottery, macrame and stained glass.

★ 742 ★
Julian - WEED SHOW AND ART MART. Mid August-early September, annual, 23 days, Julian Community Hall. Contact: San Diego Conventions and Visitors Bureau, 1200 Third Avenue, Suite 824, San Diego, California 92101.

Display of weeds, wood and stone in unusual arrangements. Arrangements and arts and crafts for sale. Begun around 1963.

★ 743 ★
Kernville - SIERRA ART FAIR. Mid October, annual, 3 days, Kernville Circle Park. Contact: Chamber of Commerce, Box 397, Kernville, California 93238.

Arts and crafts in the park. Begun around 1965.

★ 744 ★
Laguna Beach - ALL CALIFORNIA SHOW. July-August, annual. Contact: Laguna Beach Museum of Art, 307 Cliff Drive, Laguna Beach, California 92651.

An exhibition of graphics, paintings and sculptures which is open to residents of California, or members of the museum. Both cash and purchase prizes are awarded.

★ 745 ★
Laguna Beach - ART-A-FAIR. Mid July-late August, 1 1/2 months. Contact: Chamber of Commerce, 357 Glenneyre, Post Office Box 396, Laguna Beach, California 92652.

An outdoor exhibit of the work of more than 100 artists, featuring traditional painting and sculpture.

★ 746 ★
Laguna Beach - LAGUNA CRAFT GUILD STREET SHOW. November (Thanksgiving), annual, Thanksgiving day-Sunday, Forest Avenue. Contact: Orange County Chamber of Commerce, 401 Bank of America Tower, The City, One City Boulevard, West, Orange, California 92668.

Over 140 exhibits of weaving, jewelry, sculpture, woodcarving, and leathercraft.

★ 747 ★
Laguna Beach - SAWDUST ART AND CRAFT FESTIVAL. Mid July-late August, 1 1/2 months, in a eucalyptus grove. Contact: Chamber of Commerce, 357 Glenneyre, Post Office Box 396, Laguna Beach, California 92652.

Artists display their artwork and crafts, including sculpture and jewelry. More than 160 exhibitors.

★ 748 ★
Loma Linda - FINE ARTS FESTIVAL. March (Spring), annual, Loma Linda University Campus. Contact: Loma Linda University Student Affairs Office, Loma Linda University, Loma Linda, California 92354.

An event placing emphasis on the fine arts. Students, faculty, employees, and public are invited to display their own art. Guest artists are invited to give demonstrations. Begun in 1974.

★ 749 ★
Long Beach - ART FESTIVAL. Early July, 2 days,

Arts and Crafts

CALIFORNIA (Continued)

Civic Center.   Contact: Chamber of Commerce,
121 Linden Avenue, Long Beach, California 90802.

The festival features the display of a variety of art
and craft work, including paintings, sculpture, and
pottery.

★ 750 ★
Los Angeles - FLOWER DAY AND CAMERA DAY.
Late June, 1 day, El Pueblo de Los Angeles State
Historic Park, Olvera Street.   Contact: Southern
California Visitors Council, 705 West Seventh Street,
Los Angeles, California 90017.

Young children, pretty senoritas and caballeros
dressed in Spanish costumes pose for pictures by professional and amateur photographers.   Free advice
on proper use of film, lenses, etc.

★ 751 ★
Los Angeles - INDUSTRIAL GRAPHICS INTERNATIONAL
FESTIVAL.   September, annual.   Contact: O. L.
Hopper, Industrial Graphics International, 6515 Wil-
shire Boulevard, Suite 7, Los Angeles, California
90048.

Open to any illustrator, designer, painter or photographer in any media.   Awards consist of prizes and
ribbons.

★ 752 ★
Los Angeles - WESTWOOD FALL SIDEWALK ART
AND CRAFTS SHOW.   Late September, annual, 2
days, Westwood Village.   Contact: Westwood
Chamber of Commerce, 1145 Glendon Avenue, Los
Angeles, California 90024.

Arts and crafts, puppet shows, mime theater, and
musical groups are featured in this colorful outdoor
festival on the sidewalks of Westwood Village.

★ 753 ★
Los Angeles - WESTWOOD SIDEWALK ART AND
CRAFTS SHOW.   Early May, 2 days, Westwood
Village.   Contact: Southern California Visitors
Council, 705 West Seventh Street, Los Angeles,
California 90017; or Westwood Chamber of Com-
merce, 1145 Glendon Avenue, Los Angeles, California
90024.

Over 500 artists and crafts persons display their creations on the sidewalks of 27 blocks of Westwood
Village.

★ 754 ★
Millbrae - ART AND WINE FESTIVAL.   Mid
September, 2 days.   Contact: California Chamber
of Commerce, 455 Capitol Mall, Sacramento, California 95814.

A celebration with arts and crafts and wine.

★ 755 ★
Mission Bay - MISSION BAY PHOTO FESTIVAL.
September or October, annual, Vacation Village
Hotel, Mission Bay Park.   Contact: San Diego
Convention and Visitors Bureau, 1200 Third Avenue,
Suite 824, San Diego, California 92101.

More than 100 models pose for photographers; photos
are eligible for contest by Mission Bay Associates
and Western Photographer Magazine.

★ 756 ★
Mountain View - FIESTA DE LIERRA VISTA ARTS
AND WINE FESTIVAL.   Early September, 2 days.
Contact: California Chamber of Commerce, 455
Capitol Mall, Sacramento, California 95814.

Arts and crafts and wine tasting are the highlights
of this celebration.

★ 757 ★
Norwalk - ART FESTIVAL.   Late September, annual,
3 days.   Contact: California Chamber of Commerce,
455 Capitol Mall, Sacramento, California 95814.

Arts and crafts are demonstrated and displayed for
sale.   Begun around 1961.

★ 758 ★
Pacific Palisades - PALISADES VILLAGE FIESTA.
Mid April, 3 days.   Contact: Southern California
Visitors Council, 705 West Seventh Street, Los
Angeles, California 90017.

Sidewalk arts and crafts show with more than 100
exhibitors.

★ 759 ★
Point Reyes - CRAFT FESTIVAL.   December, annual,
Point Reyes Station - Dance Palace.   Contact: Redwood Empire Association, Visitors Information Center,
476 Post Street, San Francisco, California 94102.

Quality crafts are demonstrated, displayed, and on
sale.

CALIFORNIA (Continued)

★ 760 ★
Rancho Bernardo - PHOENIX FINE ARTS FESTIVAL.
Late October, 2 days, The Mercado.   Contact:
Southern California Visitors Council, 705 West
Seventh Street, Los Angeles, California 90017.

Professional art on display and for sale.

★ 761 ★
Richmond - BAZAAR.   Early December (1st Sunday),
annual, 1 day, Richmond Art Center facilities and
exhibition galleries.   Contact: Director and Chairman, Richmond Art Center, Civic Center Plaza,
Richmond, California 94804.

Members of the Art Center and students present the
festival.   There is a display and sale of student
arts and crafts, such as ceramics, jewelry, lapidary,
textiles and accessories, as well as demonstrations
of craft techniques.   There are booths of refreshments, a white elephant-junque booth, and a live
and silent auction of items solicted from Bay Area
artists.

★ 762 ★
Richmond - RICHMOND ART CENTER FESTIVAL.
December-May (dates change), biennial, Richmond
Art Center.   Contact: Richmond Art Center, Civic
Center Plaza, Richmond, California 94804.

Open to all artists--jury awards.   Painting alternating
with sculpture.

★ 763 ★
Sacramento - SACRAMENTO WEAVERS GUILD
OPEN HOUSE.   Late January, annual, 2 days.
Contact: Mrs. Jane Swenson, 4600 Briarwood Drive,
Sacramento, California 95821.

A demonstration and display of the craft of weaving
and the products thereof.

★ 764 ★
San Diego - OLD SAN DIEGO ART FIESTA (OLD
TOWN ART FIESTA).   Late June, annual, 2 days,
Old Town Plaza.   Contact: Mrs. Arlene Kesler,
Kesler Art Gallery, 2481 Congress Street, San Diego,
California 92110.

Artists exhibit and demonstrate oils, watercolors,
marquetry, ceramics, sandcasting, and sculpture.
Drawings for merchandise, mariachi music.   Begun
around 1952.

★ 765 ★
San Diego - PHOENIX FINE ART FESTIVAL.   Mid
April, 2 days, The Mercado Ranch, Bernardo.   Con-
tact: Southern California Visitors Council, 705 West
Seventh Street, Los Angeles, California 90017.

Art exhibit featuring many southern California professional artists.

★ 766 ★
San Diego - SAN DIEGO ART INSTITUTE ART
EXHIBITION.   August, annual, 30 days.   Contact:
House of Charm, 1449 El Prado, Balboa Park, San
Diego, California 92101.

Juried exhibition, all art works for sale.   Begun
around 1954.

★ 767 ★
San Diego - WOODCARVER'S JAMBOREE.   Mid
July, 3 days, The Mercado at Rancho Bernardo.
Contact: San Diego Convention and Visitors Bureau,
Department WD, 1200 Third Avenue, San Diego,
California 92101.

Juried show of woodcarvings by artists from throughout
California and some parts of Arizona.

★ 768 ★
San Francisco - GRANT AVENUE STREET FAIR.
Mid June, 2 days.   Contact: Redwood Empire
Association, Visitors Information Center, 476 Post
Street, San Francisco, California 94102.

Arts and crafts are demonstrated and sold on Grant
Street.

★ 769 ★
San Francisco - OUTDOOR ART FESTIVAL.   Septem-
ber, 4-5 days, Civic Center Plaza.   Contact:
Information Officer, State of California Department
of Commerce, 1400 Tenth Street, Sacramento,
California 95814.

Arts and crafts displayed and on sale in an outdoor
setting.

★ 770 ★
San Rafael - SAN QUENTIN ART SHOW AND SALE.
Late September, annual, 1 day, Prison gates.   Con-
tact: California Chamber of Commerce, 455 Capitol
Mall, Sacramento, California 95814.

The arts and crafts of the prisoners are on display
and on sale.

CALIFORNIA (Continued)

★ 771 ★
Santa Barbara - OLD MISSION HAND CRAFTS FAIR.
July, annual, 1 day, Mission Santa Barbara.   Con-
tact: Southern California Visitors Council, 705 West
Seventh Street, Los Angeles, California 90017.

Quality crafts are demonstrated and displayed in the
historic mission.   Begun around 1967.

★ 772 ★
Santa Rosa - STATEWIDE OUTDOOR ART SHOW.
Late August-early September, annual, 5 days, Fre-
mont Park.   Contact: Information Officer, State
of California Department of Commerce, 1400 Tenth
Street, Sacramento, California 95814.

Fremont Park is the setting for this outdoor exhibit
and sale of art.

★ 773 ★
Sausalito - ART FESTIVAL.   Late August-September,
annual, 3-4 days, Nevada School.   Contact: Redwood Empire Association, Visitors Information Center,
476 Post Street, San Francisco, Californi   94102.

Arts and crafts displayed and for sale in this pictur-
esque seaside town.

★ 774 ★
Ventura - ART-BY-THE-SEA.   Mid June, 2 days.
Contact: Southern California Visitors Council, 705
West Seventh Street, Los Angeles, California 90017.

Special exhibits by professionals, amateurs, and
children.

★ 775 ★
Willits - WILLITS ARTS FESTIVAL.   Mid June,
annual, 1 day, Willits Recreation Grove.   Contact:
Redwood Empire Association, Visitor Information
Center, 476 Post Street, San Francisco, California
94102.

All varieties of arts are displayed and demonstrated.
Begun around 1972.

COLORADO

★ 776 ★
Carbondale - COLORADO MOUNTAIN FAIR. July
(weekend of the 4th), annual, Town Park.   Contact:
Community Chamber of Commerce, Box 427, Carbondale, Colorado 81623.

The Carbondale Arts and Humanities Council sponsors
a display of the works of local artists and craftsmen.
Begun in 1972.

★ 777 ★
Central City - ALL DAY SIDEWALK ART FESTIVAL.
Late June, 1 day.   Contact: Jack Hidahl, Public
Relations Coordinator, Central City, Colorado 80427.

The festival is open to all artists for display and sale
of their works.   Awards are offered in all categories.

★ 778 ★
Colorado Springs - PIKES PEAK ARTISTS ASSOCIATION
ANNUAL AND INTERNATIONAL ART SHOW.
September-October (Fall), annual.   Contact: Pikes
Peak Artists Association, Garden Valley Motel, 2860
South Circle Drive, Colorado Springs, Colorado
80906.

All media are on display;   cash awards are given.

★ 779 ★
Crested Butte - ARTS AND CRAFTS FAIR.   Mid
August, annual, 3 days.   Contact: Chamber of
Commerce, Crested Butte, Colorado 81224.

A showing and sale of arts and crafts in a variety of
media.   Begun around 1971.

★ 780 ★
Dillon - ARTS AND CRAFTS FESTIVAL.   Early
August, 3 days.   Contact: Lake Dillon Area
Chamber of Commerce, Box 446, Dillon, Colorado
80435.

A demonstration and display of arts and crafts.

★ 781 ★
Fort Collins - CONTEMPORARY CRAFTS OF THE
AMERICAS: (YEAR) EXHIBITION.   Mid-late May,
20 days, Colorado State University.   Contact: Professor Nilda Fernandez Getty, Contemporary Crafts
of the Americas, Department of Art, Colorado State
University, Fort Collins, Colorado 80523.

An extraordinary display of quality crafts.

★ 782 ★
Golden - COLORADO ART FESTIVAL.   Late May,
4 days.   Contact: Chamber of Commerce, Golden,
Colorado 80401.

A colorful display of all types of works of art.

COLORADO (Continued)

★ 783 ★
Grand Junction - 8 WEST.   July, biennial (even years), Western Colorado Center for the Arts.   Contact: Western Colorado Center for the Arts, 1803 North Seventh Street, Grand Junction, Colorado 81501.

Juried show with cash awards; categories include painting, drawing and printmaking.   Competitors are drawn from the eight western states of Arizona, Colorado, New Mexico, Oklahoma, Kansas, Nebraska, Wyoming and Utah.   Started in 1970.

★ 784 ★
Grand Junction - OBJECTS.   July, biennial (odd years), Western Colorado Center for the Arts.   Contact: Western Colorado Center for the Arts, 1803 North Seventh Street, Grand Junction, Colorado 81501.

A juried show with cash awards for competing craftspersons from throughout the United States.   Consideration is being given to limiting the show to persons from Arizona, Colorado, New Mexico, Oklahoma, Kansas, Nebraska, Wyoming and Utah.

★ 785 ★
Ouray - ARTISTS ALPINE HOLIDAY AND FESTIVAL.   Late August, 9 days.   Contact: Chamber of Commerce, Ouray, Colorado 81427.

Competition in all media and a national exhibit.

CONNECTICUT

★ 786 ★
Bethlehem - ARTISTS AND WRITERS OF CONNECTICUT ANNUAL ARTS AND CRAFTS STREET FAIR.   Mid August, annual, 1 day, Bethlehem Green.   Contact: Connecticut Department of Commerce, 210 Washington Street, Hartford, Connecticut 06106.

A day of street festivities featuring quality arts and crafts on display and for sale.

★ 787 ★
East Haddam - CONNECTICUT RIVER ARTS AND CRAFTS FESTIVAL.   May, 1-2 days, Goodspeed Landing.   Contact: Nancy Cornwall, Ray Hill Road, East Haddam, Connecticut 06423.

Crafts are displayed and for sale.   Eligibility is by invitation.

★ 788 ★
East Haddam - PAINT AND PUTTER ARTS AND CRAFTS SHOW.   June-August (Summer), annual.   Contact: Reverend McWaid, First Church of Christ, Town Street, East Haddam, Connecticut 06423.

A display and sale of quality arts and crafts.

★ 789 ★
Farmington - CRAFTS EXPO.   Early June, annual, 3 days, Farmington Polo Grounds.   Contact: Ruby Kowalczyk, Post Office Box 274, Farmington, Connecticut 06032.

All media represented in this show and sale of quality craft items.   Begun around 1972.

★ 790 ★
Glastonbury - OUTDOOR ART SHOW AND SALE (ON THE GREEN ART SHOW AND SALE).   Early September, annual, 2 days, on the green.   Contact: Katharine G. Duggan, Director, Box 304, Glastonbury, Connecticut 06033.

An outdoor showing and competition with cash awards. Begun around 1963.

★ 791 ★
Hartford - ARTS AND CRAFTS FAIR.   Late March, annual, 1 day, McGovern Hall, Saint Joseph College.   Contact: Miss Virginia Miller, 54 Wilson Street, Hartford, Connecticut 06106.

Quality arts and crafts demonstrated and displayed. Begun around 1968.

★ 792 ★
Mystic - MYSTIC OUTDOOR ARTS FESTIVAL.   Early August, annual, 2 days.   Contact: Mystic Art Association Building, Water Street, Mystic, Connecticut 06355.

One of the most widely attended events in the state. A sidewalk art show, with awards, that is open to professional and amateurs alike.   The artists are permitted to dispose of their works, if they choose, in any fashion--selling, bartering, etc.   Begun around 1958.

★ 793 ★
New London - CAPTAIN'S WALK CRAFT FESTIVAL.   Mid July, annual, 2 days, Captain's Walk Mall.   Contact: Robert B. Norris, Post Office Box 94, Storrs, Connecticut 06268.

Arts and Crafts

CONNECTICUT (Continued)

Quality crafts on display and for sale - works of members.   Begun in 1974.

★ 794 ★
Newington - JAYCEE JUNE FESTIVAL.   Mid June, 6 days, Town Green.   Contact: Herb Toback, 15 Arrowhead Drive, Newington, Connecticut 06111.

All media of arts and crafts are on display and for sale.

★ 795 ★
Norwich - ART SHOW.   April, annual, Slater Memorial Museum.   Contact: The Slater Memorial Museum, 108 Crescent Street, Norwich, Connecticut 06360.

Juried show with prizes, open to all Connecticut residents.   All media including sculpture.

★ 796 ★
Prospect - ARTS FESTIVAL.   Early June, annual, 1 day, The Green.   Contact: Mr. and Mrs. John Garrity, Route 69, Prospect, Connecticut 06712.

All media are on display and for sale.   Begun around 1974.

★ 797 ★
Shelton - ART AND CRAFT FESTIVAL.   Early June, annual, 1 day, Huntington Green.   Contact: Lee Munch, 76 Capitol Drive, Shelton, Connecticut 06484.

All media represented in this show and sale of arts and crafts.   Begun around 1965.

★ 798 ★
Shelton - OSBORNEDALE ARTS FESTIVAL.   Mid August, 1 day, Osbornedale State Park.   Contact: Robert Katz, 56 Wakelee Avenue, Shelton, Connecticut 06484.

All media on display and for sale in an outdoor setting.

★ 799 ★
Southington - SOUTHINGTON ARTS AND CRAFTS APPLE HARVEST ART SHOW.   Early October, annual.   Contact: Southington Arts and Crafts Apple Harvest Art Show, 230 High Tower Road,

Southington, Connecticut 06489.

An exhibition of all media of arts and crafts in conjunction with the community's Apple Harvest Festival.

★ 800 ★
Stratford - ART FESTIVAL.   Mid June, 2 days, Main Street.   Contact: Connecticut Department of Commerce, 210 Washington Street, Hartford, Connecticut 06106.

Main Street is adorned with many types of arts and crafts on display and for sale.

★ 801 ★
Westbrook - ARTS AND CRAFTS FESTIVAL.   Mid July, annual, 1 day, Town Hall.   Contact: Mrs. Guy Chamberlain, Spencer Plains Road, Westbrook, Connecticut 06498.

Painting, drawing, graphics, crafts, and photography are featured.   Begun around 1972.

★ 802 ★
Westport - FALL ART FESTIVAL.   Early November, 3 days, Nature Center.   Contact: Mrs. Robert J. Amirault, Eight Brenner Lane, Norwalk, Connecticut 06851.

Invited artists display paintings and sculptures.

★ 803 ★
Westport - HANDCRAFTS FAIR.   Early June, annual, 2 days.   Contact: Connecticut Department of Commerce, 210 Washington Street, Hartford, Connecticut 06106.

A demonstration and display of quality crafts.   Begun around 1967.

★ 804 ★
Wethersfield - WETHERSFIELD SPRING ARTS FESTIVAL.   Mid May, 4 days.   Contact: Mrs. John R. Sweeney, 425 Church Street, Wethersfield, Connecticut 06109.

Artists and craftsmen living and/or working around Wethersfield display their works.   All media.

DELAWARE

★ 805 ★
Wilmington - BRANDYWINE ARTS FESTIVAL.   Mid September, annual, 2 days, North Brandywine Park.

DELAWARE (Continued)

Contact: Division of Economic Development, Delaware State Visitors Service, 45 The Green, Dover, Delaware 19901.

Oil paintings, sculpture, and crafts by Delaware Valley artists. All work is shown on the banks of the historical Brandywine and is for sale or put on auction.

DISTRICT OF COLUMBIA

★ 806 ★
Washington, D.C. - OUTDOOR ART FAIR. Late May-mid June, annual, 16 days, President's Park. Contact: D.C. Department of Recreation, 3149 16th Street, Northwest, Washington, D.C. 20010, Attention: Arts and Crafts.

Sponsored by the District of Columbia Department of Recreation and Sears, Roebuck and Company in co-operation with the National Park Service, National Capital Area. Juried show open to all media and artists and craftsmen. Some participants have come from as far as California. Visitors stroll in the park across from the White House to view the displayed arts and crafts. Begun around 1940.

FLORIDA

★ 807 ★
Cape Coral - CAPE CORAL ART LEAGUE ANNUAL NATIONAL ART SHOW (CAPE CORAL NATIONAL). January, annual. Contact: Cape Coral Art League, Box 425, Cape Coral, Florida 33904.

Juried show of paintings with cash awards. Open to all United States artists.

★ 808 ★
Cedar Key - SIDEWALK ARTS AND CRAFTS FESTIVAL. Mid April (Saturday and Sunday following Easter), annual, 2 days. Contact: Mrs. Rheta Wilson, Cedar Key, Florida 32625.

Outdoor show and sale featuring visiting and local artists.

★ 809 ★
Cocoa Beach - SPACE COAST ART FESTIVAL. Late November (3 days after Thanksgiving), annual, 7 days. Contact: Mrs. Allan Brush, Post Office Box 135, Cocoa Beach, Florida 32931.

Prize money awarded in seven categories: paintings, watercolors, graphics and drawing, photography, sculpture, ceramics and other crafts.

★ 810 ★
DeLand - SIDEWALK ART FESTIVAL. Mid March, annual, 2 days. Contact: Mrs. Virginia Clausen, 1642 South Boulevard, DeLand, Florida 32720.

Paintings and sculptures in various categories are displayed for viewing and sale in this annual show.

★ 811 ★
Hallandale - HALLANDALE FALL ART FESTIVAL. Late November, 2 days, Gulfstream Park Race Track. Contact: Division of Tourism, Department of Commerce, 107 West Gaines, Tallahassee, Florida 32304.

A display and sale of arts and crafts in beautiful Gulfstream Park Race Track.

★ 812 ★
Hollywood - SEVEN LIVELY ARTS WINTER ART SHOW. December, Young Circle Park. Contact: Greater Hollywood Chamber of Commerce, Postal Service Number 2345, Hollywood, Florida 33022.

Artists and craftsmen from many parts of the country display their works. Entertainment provided.

★ 813 ★
Indiatlantic - FLORIDA SEASIDE ART SHOW. Late April, (3rd weekend), annual, 3 days. Contact: Bernice T. Ammerman, Indiatlantic Improvement Association, Post Office Box 3157, Indiatlantic, Florida 32903.

Artists from throughout the nation and Canada exhibit original artworks in this sidewalk art show. Cash prizes are awarded, with competition including: Florida landscape, wildlife, nude, nautical, medical, oriental, farm/rural, Florida seascape, sport, portrait and abstract. The works are for sale.

★ 814 ★
Jensen Beach - OUTDOOR ART FESTIVAL. Early March (weekend closest to March 1st), annual, 2 days. Contact: Ernest Baker, Jensen Beach Chamber of Commerce, 51 Commercial Street, Jensen Beach, Florida 33457.

Exhibitors come from throughout Florida. Festival has a country-fair atmosphere.

Arts and Crafts

FLORIDA (Continued)

★ 815 ★
Kissimmee - OSCEOLA ARTS FESTIVAL.   October
(3rd weekend), annual, 2 days.   Contact: Pete
Hadley, Osceola County Art Association, Post Office
Box 1303, Kissimmee, Florida 32741.

Arts and crafts show with merit awards in five
categories: oils, watercolors, graphics, sculpture,
and crafts.

★ 816 ★
Miami - CERAMICS FAIR.   Late November-early
December, 2 days, Museum of Science.   Contact:
Greater Miami Chamber of Commerce, 1200 Biscayne
Boulevard, Miami, Florida 33132.

A show and sale of quality ceramic items done by
craftspeople, sponsored by the Ceramic League of
Miami.

★ 817 ★
Miami - COCONUT GROVE ART FESTIVAL.   Mid
February, annual, 3 days, Coconut Grove.   Contact:
Maysie Beller, Coconut Grove Association, Incorpo-
rated, Post Office Box 757, Coconut Grove, Miami,
Florida 33133.

Exhibits of paintings, jewelry, ceramics, metal-welded
sculptures and other art forms.   Prizes awarded.

★ 818 ★
Miami - JAYELL ART FESTIVAL.   September or
October (Fall).   Contact: Jack H. Lann, 19108-10
West Dixie Highway, Miami, Florida 33160.

Paintings, sculpture and crafts are featured.   Cash
and purchase awards.

★ 819 ★
Orlando - COLLEGE PARK SIDEWALK ART FESTIVAL.
Early May, annual, 2 days.   Contact: Hugh C.
Waters, Post Office Box 7605, Orlando, Florida
32804.

More than 250 artists in an open competition show including painting, sculpture, arts and crafts, photography, and graphics.   Paintings, etc. are for sale.

★ 820 ★
Ormond Beach - HALIFAX AREA ART FESTIVAL.
Early November, 3 days, Ormond Beach Hotel.
Contact: Halifax Area Art Festival, Post Office

Box 504, Ormond Beach, Florida 32074.

Art show and sale.

★ 821 ★
Palm Beach - EXHIBITION OF CONTEMPORARY
AMERICAN PAINTINGS (THE SOCIETY OF THE
FOUR ARTS).   December, annual, Four Arts Plaza.
Contact: The Society of the Four Arts, Four Arts
Plaza, Palm Beach, Florida 33480.

An exhibit of the work of artists residing in the United
States including drawings, flat collages, mixed media
works, oil paintings and watercolors.   Cash prizes
are awarded.

★ 822 ★
Pensacola - FALL ART FESTIVAL.   October, Seville
Square.   Contact: Bill Mathers, Pensacola-
Escambia Development Commission, 803 North Palafox,
Pensacola, Florida 32506.

Competition in six categories and special exhibits of
art presented at the Art Center in conjunction with
the festival.   Art works are for sale.

★ 823 ★
Saint Augustine - SAINT AUGUSTINE ARTS AND
CRAFTS FESTIVAL.   Mid April (Palm Sunday week-
end), annual, 3 days, Downtown Plaza.   Contact:
Dan Holiday, Post Office Box 547, Saint Augustine,
Florida 32084.

More than 100 artists and craftsmen from the southeast
exhibit for judging and sale.

★ 824 ★
Saint Cloud - SAINT CLOUD ART FESTIVAL.   Early
March, annual, 2 days, Veteran's Memorial Park.
Contact: Mrs. Ruth Smith, Post Office Box 5, Saint
Cloud, Florida 32769.

Art festival and exhibition which draws artists from
throughout the nation and Canada.   Six categories
of judging with prizes awarded.

★ 825 ★
Winter Park - WINTER PARK MALL ART FESTIVAL.
Early October, 2 days, Winter Park Mall.   Contact:
Division of Tourism, Department of Commerce, 107
West Gaines, Tallahassee, Florida 32304.

A display and sale of arts and crafts in many media.

GEORGIA

★ 826 ★
Blakely - ARTS AND CRAFTS FESTIVAL. Early October, 1 day, Courthouse Square. Contact: Georgia Department of Community Development, Tourist Division, Post Office Box 38097, Atlanta, Georgia 30334.

Quality arts and crafts on display and for sale.

★ 827 ★
Cartersville - CROWE SPRINGS CRAFTSMEN FAIR. Mid September, 2 days. Contact: Georgia Department of Community Development, Tourist Division, Post Office Box 38097, Atlanta, Georgia 30334.

See and learn from craftspeople of all ages who display, demonstrate, and sell their wares.

★ 828 ★
Cochran - FINE ARTS FESTIVAL. Early May, 10 days, Middle Georgia College. Contact: Georgia Department of Community Development, Tourist Division, Post Office Box 38097, Atlanta, Georgia 30334.

A showing of the arts in many media.

★ 829 ★
Marietta - ART FESTIVAL IN THE PARK. Mid July, 2 days, City Square. Contact: Georgia Department of Community Development, Tourist Division, Post Office Box 38097, Atlanta, Georgia 30334.

A show and sale of art works in an outdoor setting.

★ 830 ★
Newnan - POWERS CROSSROADS HERITAGE ARTS AND CRAFTS FESTIVAL. Late May, 2 days. Contact: Georgia Department of Community Development, Tourist Division, Post Office Box 38097, Atlanta, Georgia 30334.

A show and sale of quality arts and crafts.

★ 831 ★
Power's Crossroads - POWERS CROSSROADS COUNTRY FAIR AND ARTS FESTIVAL. Early September, 3 days. Contact: Country Fair and Arts Festival, c/o Powers Crossroads Chamber of Commerce, Powers Crossroads, Georgia.

The event is set outdoors in a natural woodland. The exhibits include sculpture, pottery, painting, leatherwork, antiques, and horticulture, for a total of more than 1,500 exhibitors.

★ 832 ★
Saint Simons Island - ART FESTIVAL AND CRAFTS. Early October, annual, 2 days, Neptune Park. Contact: Georgia Department of Community Development, Tourist Division, Post Office Box 38097, Atlanta, Georgia 30334.

A display and sale of a variety of arts and crafts in the beautiful park setting.

★ 833 ★
Soperton - MILLION PINES ARTS AND CRAFTS FESTIVAL. Early November, 2 days, Iva Park. Contact: Georgia Department of Community Development, Tourist Division, Post Office Box 38097, Atlanta, Georgia 30334.

Quality arts and crafts in many media on display and for sale.

★ 834 ★
Thomasville - DEEP SOUTH ARTS AND CRAFTS FESTIVAL. Mid May, annual, 2 days, Deep South Fairgrounds. Contact: Georgia Department of Community Development, Tourist Division, Post Office Box 38097, Atlanta, Georgia 30334.

A display, sale, and demonstration of arts and crafts in many media. Begun around 1972.

★ 835 ★
Waycross - ARTS FAIR. Late April, 2 days, Memorial Stadium. Contact: Georgia Department of Community Development, Tourist Division, Post Office Box 38097, Atlanta, Georgia 30334.

A large display and sale of all media of arts and crafts.

HAWAII

★ 836 ★
Honolulu - ARTISTS OF HAWAII (Part I). (Part II in March). December, annual. Contact: Assistant Director, Honolulu Academy of Arts, 900 South Beretania Street, Honolulu, Hawaii 96814.

Open to all artists in Hawaii, all media. Works of art intended to be viewed mainly from the front (i.e. as opposed to art in the round).

Arts and Crafts

HAWAII (Continued)

★ 837 ★
Honolulu – ARTISTS OF HAWAII (Part II). March, annual. Contact: Assistant Director, Honolulu Academy of Arts, 900 South Beretania Street, Honolulu, Hawaii 96814.

A juried show for artists residing in Hawaii. All media. Works intended to be viewed in the round.

IDAHO

★ 838 ★
Boise – ART FESTIVAL. March, annual, Boise Gallery of Art. Contact: Director, Boise Gallery of Art, Post Office Box 1505, Boise, Idaho 83701.

Open to current residents of Idaho, all media including sculpture. Juried with purchase awards.

★ 839 ★
Coeur d'Alene – ARTS AND CRAFTS OUTDOOR FESTIVAL. August (1st weekend), annual, 3 days, North Idaho College campus. Contact: Citizens Council for the Arts, Post Office Box 901, Coeur d'Alene, Idaho 83814.

Performances are given by dancers and musicians, including folksinging, guitar, recorder and fiddle playing. There are also exhibitions of batik, weaving, quilting, glass, pottery, silk screening, painting, metalwork, jewelry, candles, sculpture, dried flowers, macrame, photography and furniture. Begun around 1969.

★ 840 ★
Sun Valley – SUN VALLEY ARTS AND CRAFTS FAIR. Early August, annual, 1 day, Sun Valley Mall. Contact: James W. Ball, Manager, Ketchum-Sun Valley Chamber of Commerce, Box 465, Ketchum, Idaho 83340.

Artists are present by invitation only. Displays of arts and crafts from the entire state. The items are for sale and are of high quality.

ILLINOIS

★ 841 ★
Chicago – FELICIAN COLLEGE ARTS AND CRAFTS FESTIVAL. July (second Sunday), 1 day, Felician College campus. Contact: Chairman, Felician College Arts and Crafts Festival, Felician College Library, 3800 Peterson Avenue, Chicago, Illinois 60659.

Work displayed and sold by professional artists. Admission is free to the public. Entertainment and refreshments are provided. The variety of art work exhibited includes paintings in oils, watercolor, acrylics, Japanese brush, sculpture in bronze, sand, decoupage, tole, macrame, leatherwork, candles, dolls, portrait painting and sketching, pillows, glass, jewelry, and wood carvings. A purchase award is presented to the college.

★ 842 ★
Chicago – 57TH STREET ART FAIR. Early June, annual, 2 days. Contact: The Division of Tourism, Illinois Department of Business and Economic Development, 222 South College Street, Springfield, Illinois 62706.

One of the oldest arts fairs in the country.

★ 843 ★
Chicago – GOLD COAST ART FAIR. Mid August, annual, 3 days, between Chicago Avenue and Cedar Street on the banks of Lake Michigan. Contact: Chairman, Gold Coast Art Fair, 26 East Huron Street, Chicago, Illinois 60611.

One of the country's largest outdoor art shows. Hundreds of artists, not only from the immediate area, but from the other states and even other countries enter their works. Begun around 1959.

★ 844 ★
Chicago – NEW HORIZONS IN ART. June, annual. Contact: North Shore Art League, 620 Lincoln Avenue, Winnetka, Illinois 61103.

A display of graphics, paintings, photographs and sculpture of Illinois artists. Cash prizes, ribbons and purchases awards are given. Sponsored by the North Shore Art League.

★ 845 ★
Chicago – OLD ORCHARD ART FESTIVAL. September, annual. Contact: North Shore Art League, 620 Lincoln Avenue, Winnetka, Illinois 60093.

An art exhibit for all media.

★ 846 ★
Chicago – OLD TOWN ART FAIR. Early June, annual, 2 days, Old Town. Contact: Chairman, Old Town Art Fair, 1818 North Wells Street, Chicago, Illinois 60614.

ILLINOIS (Continued)

One of three major art fairs in Illinois. Features mediums from sculpture to painting and traditional chicken teriaki dinner.

★ 847 ★

Evanston - SENIOR CITIZENS ARTS AND CRAFTS SHOW. Late September, annual, 3 days, Indoor Shopping Mall, Levy Center. Contact: The Division of Tourism, Illinois Department of Business and Economic Development, 222 South College Street, Springfield, Illinois 62706.

Handmade articles of all types and in all materials, made by the local senior citizens, are on display and for sale.

★ 848 ★

Galena - ARTS AND CRAFTS FESTIVAL. June, annual, 2 days, Grant Park. Contact: The Division of Tourism, Illinois Department of Business and Economic Development, 222 South College Street, Springfield, Illinois 62706.

Quality arts and crafts on display and for sale.

★ 849 ★

Ithaca - ARTS AND CRAFTS FAIR. Mid August, annual, 1 day, Village Green, along banks of Spring Brook Creek. Contact: The Division of Tourism, Illinois Department of Business and Economic Development, 222 South College Street, Springfield, Illinois 62706.

A display and sale of quality arts and crafts in an outdoor setting.

★ 850 ★

Monticello - ARTS AND CRAFTS FESTIVAL. Early April, 2 days, Pioneer Heritage Center. Contact: Division of Tourism, Department of Business and Economic Development, 222 South College Street, Springfield, Illinois 62706.

A quality showing of many forms of arts and crafts.

★ 851 ★

Nauvoo - ARTS, CRAFTS AND ANTIQUE FAIR. Mid June, annual, 2 days, City Park. Contact: J. Marvin Crozier, Nauvoo Fair, Box 192, Nauvoo, Illinois 62354.

Artists display, demonstrate, and sell their works.

There is also a juried show.

★ 852 ★

Peoria Heights - FINE ARTS FAIR. Mid June, annual, 2 days, Tower Park. Contact: The Division of Tourism, Illinois Department of Business and Economic Development, 222 South College Street, Springfield, Illinois 62706.

Seven states participate in this art display and sale.

★ 853 ★

Petersburg - LAND OF LINCOLN CRAFTS FESTIVAL. October or September, annual, 2 days, New Salem Carriage Museum. Contact: The Division of Tourism, Illinois Department of Business and Economic Development, 222 South College Street, Springfield, Illinois 62706.

Festival and flea market. More than 60 crafts are demonstrated in old-time fashion.

★ 854 ★

Quincy - ART SHOW. November, annual, 22 days, Art Center. Contact: The Division of Tourism, Illinois Department of Business and Economic Development, 222 South College Street, Springfield, Illinois 62706.

Juried art show of quality artists. Begun around 1950.

★ 855 ★

Springfield - OLD CAPITOL ART FAIR. Mid May, annual, 2 days, Old State Capitol Plaza. Contact: The Division of Tourism, Illinois Department of Business and Economic Development, 222 South College Street, Springfield, Illinois 62706.

Approximately 200 exhibitors who work in mediums including oils, watercolors, acrylics, macrame, sculpture, and jewelry. All items are juried before being accepted into the fair.

INDIANA

★ 856 ★

Anderson - FINE ARTS FALL FESTIVAL. Mid September, annual, 1 day, Fine Arts Center. Contact: Mrs. George Johnston, 806 Oakdale Drive, Anderson, Indiana 46011.

Professional and non-professional artwork, carnival atmosphere. Ice cream social, boutique booths, art auction, and flea market.

Arts and Crafts

INDIANA (Continued)

★ 857 ★
Battle Ground - SUMMER ART FAIR.   Early August,
2 days.   Contact: Director, Battle Ground Historical
Corporation, Box 225, Battle Ground, Indiana 47920.

Turn of the century theme: barbershop quartets,
dixieland music, ice cream, lemonade, and cotton
candy.   Artists and artisans display and sell their
works.

★ 858 ★
Centerville - ARTS AND CRAFTS FESTIVAL.   Late
August, 2 days, Main Street.   Contact: Financial
Vice President, Centerville Jaycees, 209 McMinn
Road, Centerville, Indiana 47330.

Artists exhibit leatherwork, pottery, jewelry and
other handmade crafts.   Many antique shops are
in the town all the time.   Chicken and corn
barbeque.

★ 859 ★
Chesterton - CHESTERTON ARTS AND CRAFTS.
Early August, annual, 2 days, Saint Patrick's School.
Contact: Art Fair Committee,   Association of Artists
and Craftsmen of Porter County, Gilbert Gallery,
Post Office Box 143, Chesterton, Indiana 46304.

Displays include paintings, leatherwork, pottery,
glass, needlework and carvings.   Pony rides and
food available.   Begun around 1959.

★ 860 ★
Dunlapsville - HOOSIER HERITAGE HANDICRAFT
FESTIVAL.   Early July, 3 days, Treaty-Line Museum.
Contact: Executive Director, Treaty-Line Museum,
Incorporated, Dunlapsville Trail, Rural Route 4,
Liberty, Indiana 47353.

Butter churning, fresh baked bread, blacksmithing,
needlecraft, candle dipping and molding, woodworking,
rag-rug making, spinning, weaving, chair-caning,
broom-making, pottery and silhouette art.   For
children there are animals to pet, haylofts to play in
and animated puppets.   Three log cabins on the
grounds around which most of the demonstrations take
place.

★ 861 ★
Elkhart - BOULEVARD OF COLOR.   Late June, 4
days, Concord Mall.   Contact: Ken Owens, 3701
South Main, Elkhart, Indiana 46514.

Art works in various media including oil, watercolor,
and sculpture.

★ 862 ★
English - ARTS AND CRAFTS STREET FAIR.   Early
June, 2 days.   Contact: Mrs. Beatrice W. Farris,
President, Crawford County Lincoln Hills Arts and
Crafts Association, Nine Chandler Avenue, Evansville,
Indiana 47713.

Crafts from the past from weaving and broom-making
to quilting and wood carving.   Cooking: ham and
beans, homemade bread, and barbeque.   Old-time
fiddlers' dance.

★ 863 ★
Evansville - ART AND CRAFT SHOW.   Mid Novem-
ber, 2 days.   Contact: Pattie Davis, Washington
Square Mall, 5011 Green River Road, Evansville,
Indiana 47715.

Arts and crafts show and sale.

★ 864 ★
Fort Wayne - BOULEVARD OF COLOR.   Late May-
early June, 4 days, Mall of Glenbrook Center.
Contact: William A. Schneider, Promotion Director,
Glanbrook Center, 4201 Coldwater Road, Fort Wayne,
Indiana 46805.

Sponsored by the Fort Wayne Artists Guild, this is an
art show where painters, sculptors, metal-workers and
others display and sell their wares.   Demonstrations
are also featured.

★ 865 ★
Homer - HOMER FESTIVAL OF ARTS AND CRAFTS.
June (Fathers' Day weekend), 2 days.   Contact:
Bob Waggener, Post Office Box 2, Homer, Indiana
46146.

Cabinet-making, sculpting, and other crafts are demonstrated.   Antiques, flea market, theater, and
puppet shows.   A German band, folk music and
instruments.

★ 866 ★
Indianapolis - TALBOTT STREET ART FAIR.   Early-
mid June, annual, 2 days, 2100 block of North
Talbott.   Contact: Ms. Barta Monro, Chairman,
Talbot Street Art Fair, 6841 South Tibbs, Indianapolis,
Indiana 46217.

Several hundred artists display and sell their wares

INDIANA (Continued)

amid strolling musicians and art demonstrations.
Club entertainment is offered at the Galley Seafood
Theatre. Displays include painting, ceramics,
sculpture, enameling, and woodworking.

★ 867 ★
Jeffersonville - RIVERFRONT ARTS AND CRAFTS
FESTIVAL. Early September, 2 days, Ohio River-
front. Contact: Johnny Maupin, Chairman,
J.U.M.P. Committee, 2002 Ruck Lane, Jeffersonville,
Indiana 47130.

Displays and sales by artists and craftsmen working in
a variety of media. Sidewalk painting for children
and musical performances.

★ 868 ★
Lowell - ARTS AND CRAFTS FESTIVAL. Early July
1 day, Town Square. Contact: Director, Lowell's
Arts and Crafts Festival, 123 South Union Street,
Lowell, Indiana 46356.

Homemade lunches served amidst more than 50 displays
by artists and craftsmen.

★ 869 ★
Madison - HISTORIC HOOSIER HILLS ANTIQUE AND
CRAFT SPRING FESTIVAL. Late May, 4 days,
Court House Square. Contact: Mrs. Helen Gourley,
2242 Cragmont, Madison, Indiana 47250.

Antique dealers and craftsmen from many states demonstrate, display and sell their works. Home-baked
goods and other foods.

★ 870 ★
Madison - MADISON CHAUTAQUA OF THE ARTS.
Late September, 2 days, Main Street. Contact:
Dixie McDonough, Green Hills Pottery, 601 West
Main Street, Madison, Indiana 47250.

Working artists and craftsmen compete in awards
competition. Sale of works.

★ 871 ★
Mishawaka - ARTS AND CRAFTS FESTIVAL. Mid
July, 2 days, 100 Center Complex (restored Kamm's
Brewery). Contact: William Strong, Director, 100
Center Complex, Box 806, Mishawaka, Indiana 46544.

Artists exhibits, bluegrass bands, and a sausage roast
are included in the events.

★ 872 ★
Muncie - BALL STATE UNIVERSITY DRAWING AND
SMALL SCULPTURE SHOW. March (Spring), annual,
Art Gallery, Ball State University. Contact:
Director, Art Gallery, Ball State University, Muncie,
Indiana 47306.

Juried show open to all artists. Media include
drawings and small sculptures.

★ 873 ★
New Albany - ARTS FESTIVAL. July, annual, 1
day. Contact: New Albany Jaycees, Incorporated,
Post Office Box 204, New Albany, Indiana 47150.

Amateurs and professionals compete for ribbons, cash
prizes, and guaranteed purchases.

★ 874 ★
Noblesville - PIONEER CRAFT DAYS. Early June,
2 days, Conner Prairie. Contact: Public Relations
Manager, Conner Prairie Pioneer Settlement, 30
Conner Lane, Noblesville, Indiana 46060.

Pioneer crafts including candle dipping, quilting,
corn huskery, caning, basketry, rug pulling, spinning,
dying, weaving (both wool and flax) shingle making,
and muzzle-loading rifle shoots. Tours of simple
log and frame houses in the village, pioneer foods
and country music.

★ 875 ★
Ramsey - LINCOLN HILLS ARTS AND CRAFTS SHOW.
Early October, 2 days. Contact: Violet Wendell,
Ramsey, Indiana 47166.

Local artists display, demonstrate and sell materials
made from various media including clay, wood, corn
husks, and various types of needle work.

★ 876 ★
Rockport - SPENCER COUNTY ARTS AND CRAFTS
SHOW. Late November, 2 days, Chrisney Youth
and Community Center. Contact: Brother Kim
Malloy, Saint Meinrad Archabbey, Saint Meinrad,
Indiana 47577.

Demonstrations of the pioneer crafts: spinning,
pottery-making, patchwork, woodcarving, needlework,
and painting. Many are for sale.

★ 877 ★
Shelbyville - BLUE RIVER VALLEY PIONEER CRAFT
FAIR. Early October, 2 days, Shelby County

INDIANA (Continued)

Fairgrounds. Contact: Jack W. Warble, Post Office Box 74, Shelbyville, Indiana 46176.

Demonstrations of pioneer work such as cobbling, soap making, and an apple cider press. Early artistry is represented by corn husk dolls, dulcimers, and samplers. Pioneer cooking. Many crafts are for sale. Displays of antique tools, steam and gas engines, muzzle-loading rifleshoot, and folk music entertainment.

★ 878 ★
South Bend - LEEPER PARK ART FAIR. Mid June, annual, 2 days, Leeper Park on the Saint Joseph River. Contact: Lynn L. Edison, Chairman, Leeper Park Art Fair, 60341 Saint Joseph Street, South Bend, Indiana 46614.

Artists from Indiana and neighboring states display and sell original paintings, pottery and sculpture. Many stage demonstrations. A string quartet provides entertainment.

IOWA

★ 879 ★
Algona - ALGONA SIDEWALK ART SHOW. Early June, annual, 1 day, downtown sidewalks. Contact: William Steele, Algona Chamber of Commerce, 114 North Moore, Algona, Iowa 50501.

The show offers classifications for both adults and students, with "Best of Show" awards and ribbons.

★ 880 ★
Anamosa - GRANT WOOD ART FESTIVAL. Mid June, 2 or 3 days, Main Street. Contact: Don B. Goodman, 804 East First, Anamosa, Iowa 52205; or Mrs. Glen Russell, 200 East First Street, Anamosa, Iowa 52205.

Arts and crafts are exhibited and for sale.

★ 881 ★
Bentonsport - SUMMER ARTS FESTIVAL. Late June, annual, 2 days. Contact: Van Buren County Development Association, Post Office Box 9, Keosauqua, Iowa 52565.

Arts and crafts show and sale. Begun around 1970.

★ 882 ★
Burlington - SNAKE ALLEY ART FAIR. Late June, annual, 1 day, Snake Alley. Contact: Art Guild of Burlington, c/o Chamber of Commerce, Hotel Burlington, Burlington, Iowa 52601.

A display of the works of artists from all over the country. There are generally around 90 exhibitors. The paintings are displayed on snow fences set up along both sides of the winding street. Cash prizes are awarded. Usually associated with Steamboat Days. Begun around 1968.

★ 883 ★
Carroll - SIDEWALK ART FAIR. Late April, 1 day, downtown. Contact: M. J. 'Mike' Arts, 223 West Fifth Street, Box 307, Carroll, Iowa 51401.

The show is for amateur Iowa artists. There are two divisions, one for adults and one for students under 18. Media divisions include oils, prints, batik and sketches, acrylic and watercolor, pottery and ceramics, three dimensional. Ribbons are awarded for each division, ribbon and cash for the best-in-show. Sponsored by the Chamber of Commerce.

★ 884 ★
Centerville - CRAFTS FESTIVAL. Mid June, annual, 1 day, in the square. Contact: Tom Kappes, 316 North 12th Street, Centerville, Iowa 52544.

A demonstration, display, and sale of a variety of arts and crafts in an outdoor setting.

★ 885 ★
Clinton - ART-IN-THE-PARK. Mid May, annual, 2 days, Lyons Four Square Park. Contact: William R. Ross, 530 Fourth Avenue, North, Clinton, Iowa 52732.

Artists bring their own equipment to arrange their works; all pieces are for sale. Open to all media for amateur and professional artists alike. All work must be original in design and execution. Sponsored by the Lyons merchants and the Clinton Art Association. Begun around 1970.

★ 886 ★
Cresco - ARTS AND CRAFTS SHOW. Early August, annual, 1 day, Beadle Park. Contact: Cresco Chamber of Commerce, Box 403, Cresco, Iowa 52136.

Ribbons awarded to category winners. Arts and crafts on display and on sale. Begun around 1962.

IOWA (Continued)

★ 887 ★
Des Moines - CRAFT FESTIVAL. Mid May, 2 days,
Living History Farms. Contact: Program Director,
Living History Farms, Rural Route 1, Des Moines,
Iowa 50322.

A quality show of arts and crafts of a priceless
heritage.

★ 888 ★
Hampton - TAM AND SMOCK ART FAIR. Early
August, 4 days, Franklin County Fairgrounds. Con-
tact: Mrs. Irene Korth, 321 First Avenue, Northwest,
Hampton, Iowa 50441.

A display and sale of a variety of arts and crafts.

★ 889 ★
Lake City - ARTS AND CRAFTS SHOW. Early
July, 1 day, City Square. Contact: Mrs. Paul
Mack, 101 East Main Street, Lake City, Iowa
51449.

All artwork is welcome, prizes are awarded to the
two best pieces in each class. Sponsored by the
Chamber of Commerce and handled by the senior
Girl Scouts.

★ 890 ★
Livermore - ARTS AND CRAFTS FESTIVAL. Early
June, 8 days. Contact: Mrs. Robert Wilson,
Festival Chairman, Box 64, Livermore, Iowa 50558.

Demonstrations, exhibitions and sales of arts and
crafts such as straw-weaving, woodcarving, and
quilting. Scheren schnitte, parades, street acts, and
music including bluegrass and jazz. Rodeo, demonstrations of gymnastics, kung fu, karate, magicina,
puppet show, and square dancing are part of the
entertainment.

★ 891 ★
Marion - COUNTRY FAIR DAYS ART SHOW. Mid
July, 2 days, City Square Park. Contact: Mr.
Charles A. Beahm, 760 11th Street, Marion, Iowa
52302.

The show is in conjunction with "Country Fair Days",
and is limited to 75 artists, and to oils, acrylics,
watercolors and pastels. Sculpture and handicrafts
are not included. The show is a display and sale,
not a competition.

★ 892 ★
Ottumwa - OTTUMWA HEIGHTS FAMILY OUTDOOR
ART FESTIVAL. Early August, annual, 1 day, on
the Ottumwa Heights College campus. Contact:
Jerry G. Solloway, President, Ottumwa Heights
College, Ottumwa, Iowa 52501; or Mr. Steven
Stoltz, Steffen and Stoltz Architects, 125 1/2 East
Second, Ottumwa, Iowa 52501.

Each year the Ottumwa Heights Art Board, sponsors
of the event, select a theme for that year's event.
The park is a wooded, five acre area, and the
sponsors look forward to sharing down-home Iowa
hospitality. There is entertainment. First held
in 1973.

★ 893 ★
Rock Rapids - TRI-STATE ART SHOW. Late March-
early April (week after Easter), annual, 8 days,
Lyon County State Bank. Contact: Mrs. Donald
Calkins, Chairman, 1008 South Tama, Rock Rapids,
Iowa 51246.

A display of original works by junior and senior
high school students: paintings in various media,
drawings, sculpture, free form ceramics, photography
and jewelry. Senior high artists are judged. Begun around 1964.

★ 894 ★
Sheffield - ART FAIR. Mid June, 1 day. Con-
tact: Mrs. Marian Atkinson, 288 South Fourth,
Sheffield, Iowa 50475.

A demonstration and display of a variety of arts and
crafts.

★ 895 ★
Sioux Center - CELEBRATION OF OUR HERITAGE.
Early May, 2 days, Community Center. Contact:
Mrs. Dale Den Herder, 236 Eighth Street, Northeast,
Sioux Center, Iowa 51250.

Featured crafts include rug braiding, woodcarving,
spinning, cornhusk dolls, tatting, hairpin lace,
quilting and more.

★ 896 ★
Sioux City - NEW DOWNTOWN ART FAIR. Late
June, 2 days, New Downtown Mall. Contact: Mr.
David Spatola, 312 Fourth Street, Sioux City, Iowa
51106.

Arts and crafts on display and on sale.

Arts and Crafts

IOWA (Continued)

★ 897 ★
Sioux City - SIOUX CITY ART CENTER FALL SHOW.
September-October, annual.   Contact: Director,
Sioux City Art Center, 513 Nebraska Street, Sioux
City, Iowa 51101.

One-man jury awarding cash and purchase prizes.
All works on display and most are for sale.

★ 898 ★
Spencer - FESTIVAL OF PHOTOGRAPHY.   Mid
October, 8 days. Contact: Spencer Chamber of
Commerce, 603 South Grand, Spencer, Iowa 51301.

Amateur photographer's contest, with ribbons awarded,
professional displays, and "old-time" displays.

★ 899 ★
Spencer - ON-THE-AVENUE FESTIVAL OF ART.
Late May or early June (Saturday), annual, 1 day,
Grand Avenue and East Fourth Street.   Contact:
Spencer Chamber of Commerce, 603 South Grand,
Spencer, Iowa 51301.

Held outdoors and features artists from all over the
midwest.   Paintings are displayed and sold; cash
prizes are offered.   Begun around 1967.

★ 900 ★
West Des Moines - VALLEY ARTS FESTIVAL.   Late
September, 1 day, 200 block Fifth Street.   Contact:
Secretary, Chamber of Commerce of West Des Moines,
221 Fifth Street, West Des Moines, Iowa 50265.

An all juried show of quality works of art.

★ 901 ★
Winterset - WINTERSET ART CENTER STREET FAIR.
Mid June, 1 day, alley off the square.   Contact:
Ralph E. Cline, 609 East Jefferson Street, Winterset,
Iowa 50273.

A traditional community festival with arts and crafts,
food, and fun for all.

KANSAS

★ 902 ★
Hillsboro - ARTS AND CRAFTS FAIR.   Late Septem-
ber, 1 day.   Contact: Publications Division, Kansas
Department of Economic Development, State Office
Building, Room 122S, Topeka, Kansas 66612.

A display and sale of all media and forms of arts
and crafts.

★ 903 ★
Lindsborg - ARTS AND CRAFTS FAIR.   Mid October,
1 day.   Contact: Publications Division, Kansas
Department of Economic Development, State Office
Building, Room 112S, Topeka, Kansas 66612.

Quality arts and crafts, all varieties, displayed and
on sale.

★ 904 ★
Mission - OKTOBERFEST ART FESTIVAL.   Early
October, 3 days.   Contact: Publications Division,
Kansas Department of Economic Development, State
Office Building, Room 122S, Topeka, Kansas 66612.

An art festival, show, and sale along with traditional
fall festivities.

★ 905 ★
Topeka - OKTOBERFEST - TOPEKA ARTS FESTIVAL.
October, 1 month.   Contact: Publications Division,
Kansas Department of Economic Development, State
Office Building, Room 122S, Topeka, Kansas 66612.

A celebration of the fall harvest season with an arts
festival in conjunction.

KENTUCKY

★ 906 ★
Berea - KENTUCKY GUILD OF ARTISTS AND
CRAFTSMEN FAIR.   Mid May, 4 days, Indian Fort
Theatre.   Contact: Garry Barker, Kentucky Guild
of Artists and Craftsmen, Box 291, Berea, Kentucky
40403.

Artists and craftsmen demonstrate and sell their works.
Features folk music, puppets, and a special exhibition
of both contemporary and traditional items, including
pottery and decorative wood items.   Begun around
1967.

LOUISIANA

★ 907 ★
Lafayette - ACADIAN CERAMIC SHOW.   Early
October, annual, 2 days, Lafayette Municipal
Auditorium.   Contact: Louisiana Tourist Commission,
Post Office Box 44291, Baton Rouge, Louisiana
70804.

LOUISIANA (Continued)

The show is presented by the Acadian Ceramic Club. Prizes include awards for first, second, third and honorable mention, as well as a prize for the individual receiving the highest number of points over all. Classes include best of the division, best hobbyist, best teenager, best professional, best of children's class, best of tiny tots, best senior citizen and best club. Begun around 1969.

★ 908 ★
Lafayette – LOUISIANA NATIVE CRAFT FESTIVAL. Late October, 3 days, Lafayette Natural History Museum and Planetarium. Contact: Greater Lafayette Chamber of Commerce, 804 East Street, Post Office Box 51352, Lafayette, Louisisan 70501.

A display of a variety of crafts of and by local craftspeople.

★ 909 ★
Monroe – FINE ARTS FESTIVAL. Mid March, 8 days, Northeast Louisiana University. Contact: Northeast Louisiana University, 700 University Avenue, Monroe, Louisiana 71201.

An exhibit of various types of works of art.

MAINE

★ 910 ★
Cumberland – UNITED MAINE CRAFTSMEN'S FAIR. Early August, annual, 3 days. Contact: Maine Chamber of Commerce, 477 Congress Street, Portland, Maine 04111.

More than 200 craftspeople come to display, demonstrate and sell their work. Event includes an old-fashioned country store, snack bar, and a restaurant. Begun around 1970.

MARYLAND

★ 911 ★
Baltimore – WINTER MARKET/BALTIMORE. February, annual, 2 days trade only, 2 days public, Baltimore Civic Center. Contact: Northeast Craft Fair, Limited, 12 North Chestnut Street, New Paltz, New York 12561.

Sponsored by the Northeast Craft Fair, Limited, 400 craftsmen exhibit and sell their works. This fair is planned to be held for the first time in 1977.

★ 912 ★
Bethesda – CRAFT FAIR. Late May, annual, 2 days, Georgetown Square Shopping Center, KB Theater. Contact: Craft Fair, Georgetown Square Shopping Center, Old Georgetown Road and Democracy Boulevard, Bethesda, Maryland 20034.

Appalachia craftsmen demonstrating and selling pottery, weaving, dollmaking, knife making, bell making, chair making, bird carving (with a chainsaw), and cement mushrooms. Begun in 1975.

★ 913 ★
Big Pool – FORT FREDERICK CRAFT DAYS. Mid August, 2 days, Fort Frederick State Park. Contact: Hagerstown Chamber of Commerce, c/o James W. Stone, 92 West Washington Street, Hagerstown, Maryland 21740.

A weekend of displays and demonstrations of colonial crafts.

★ 914 ★
Centreville – QUEEN ANNE'S COUNTY CRAFTS FESTIVAL. Mid May, annual, 2 days, 4-H Park. Contact: John Miller, Rural Delivery 3, Box 74, Centreville, Maryland 21617.

A demonstration and exhibits of crafts including candlemaking, antique restoring, crochet, decoy sculpture, and gunsmithing. Begun around 1973.

★ 915 ★
Charlestown – COLONIAL CHARLESTOWN FAIR. Mid May, annual, 2 days. Contact: Michael Miklas, Box 27, Charlestown, Maryland 21914.

Imitates a 1744 fair with colonial crafts demonstrated and sold and performances by the third Maryland Regiment of Revolution. Modern handicrafts are also exhibited and sold.

★ 916 ★
College Park – UNIVERSITY OF MARYLAND ARTS AND CRAFTS FESTIVAL. October, annual, 2 days, Undergraduate Library Mall. Contact: University Relations, Special Events, College Park, Maryland 20742.

Students and other artists, craftsmen, photographers, etc., display and sell their works. Usually held during Homecoming Weekend.

Arts and Crafts

MARYLAND (Continued)

★ 917 ★
Frederick - ART IN THE PARK. Early June, annual, 1 day, Memorial Park. Contact: Frederick County Chamber of Commerce, Division of Tourism, Frederick, Maryland 21701.

Competition, exhibit and sale for both professional and amateur artists. Other activities include raffles, folk dancing, and singing. Strolling musicians are on hand. Begun around 1967.

★ 918 ★
Frederick - FREDERICK CRAFT FAIR. Early June, annual, 3 days, Frederick Fairgrounds. Contact: Director, Frederick Craft Fair, Gapland, Maryland 21736.

Craftsmen from throughout the nation compete to participate in this show. Familiar and obscure crafts on exhibit include potters, quilters, carvers, metal workers, toy makers, printers, book binders, bagpipe and oboe makers, wooden pitchfork carvers, weavers, and many more. Nationally known musicians perform. Begun in 1975.

★ 919 ★
Hagerstown - JONATHAN HAGER FRONTIER CRAFTS DAY. July and August, annual, 1 day each month, Hager House, Hagerstown City Park. Contact: Washington County Tourism Division, 40 Summit Avenue, Hagerstown, Maryland 21740.

Frontier crafts are demonstrated on the lawn of the 1739 frontier house of the founder of Hagerstown: blacksmithing, woodcarving, broom-making, gun-smithing, chair caning, candle-dipping, and country music. Begun around 1971.

★ 920 ★
Havre de Grace - HAVRE DE GRACE ART SHOW. Mid August, annual, 1 day, Millard E. Tydings Memorial Park. Contact: Dr. G. Hirsch, 131 South Union Avenue, Havre de Grace, Maryland 21078.

Outdoor exhibition featuring arts and crafts, sculptive photography, and other arts. Begun around 1964.

★ 921 ★
Salisbury - OUTDOOR ART SHOW. Mid September, annual, 1 day, Salisbury City Park. Contact: Wicomico Art League, Post Office Box 193, Salisbury, Maryland 21801.

Arts and crafts, band music, flea market, refreshments to entertain the assembled. Begun around 1967.

★ 922 ★
Street - OLD TIME ARTS AND CRAFTS DAY. Early June, annual, 2 days, Steppingstone Museum. Contact: J. Edmund Bull, Street, Maryland 21154.

Exhibits of artifacts and equipment from the turn of the century, plus demonstrations of over 40 crafts. Begun around 1971.

★ 923 ★
Westminster - SHEEP AND WOOL CRAFTS FESTIVAL. early May, annual, 2 days, Carroll County Agricultural Center. Contact: Janet Sorrels, Agricultural Center, Westminster, Maryland 21157.

All types of demonstrations and exhibits - shearing, dyeing, spinning, weaving, tanning, crafts - with antique equipment and as it is done today. Fashion show, working sheep dogs, music, and square dancing.

★ 924 ★
Woodlawn - YE OLDE WOODLAWN CRAFTS FESTIVAL. Late June (lst weekend after Baltimore County schools close), annual, 2 days, Woodlawn Senior High School. Contact: Woodlawn Recreation and Parks Council, 2131 Woodlawn Drive, Baltimore, Maryland 21207.

In perpetration of the old, featured are woodworking, glass blowing, pottery making, chair caning, weaving and other crafts. All are demonstrated and unique. Maryland foods are available. Entertainment includes haystack for jumping, square dancing, barber-shop quartet, and children's entertainment.

MASSACHUSETTS

★ 925 ★
Attleboro - ART IN THE PARK. Mid June, annual, 1 day, Capron Park. Contact: Bristol County Development Council, Incorporated, 154 North Main Street, Fall River, Massachusetts 02722.

Outdoor art show, various arts and crafts shown and for sale.

★ 926 ★
Brewster - CRAFTSMEN'S FAIR. Mid August, annual, 2 days, Brewster Elementary School. Contact: Cape Cod Chamber of Commerce, Hyannis 200, Massachusetts 02602.

MASSACHUSETTS (Continued)

A display and sale of quality crafts in many media. Sponsored by the Society of Cape Cod Craftsmen. Begun around 1953.

★ 927 ★
Brockton - POPS-IN-THE-PARK CRAFTS FAIR. Mid-late June, 1 day, Brockton Art Center. Contact: Plymouth County Development Council, Incorporated, Post Office Box 1620, Pembroke, Massachusetts 02359.

An arts and crafts display and sale with musical entertainment.

★ 928 ★
Cummington - CRAFTSPRODUCERS CRAFT FAIR. Mid July, annual, 3 days, Cummington Farm Village. Contact: Craftsproducers, Incorporated, Box 92, Readsboro, Vermont 05350.

A juried show open to any active craftsman or woman. Offers both indoor and outdoor displays. Begun in 1976.

★ 929 ★
Fall River - NATIONAL SHOW. Mid-late May, annual, 22 days. Contact: Greater Fall River Art Association, 80 Belmont Street, Fall River, Massachusetts 02722.

Paintings, graphics, sculpture, pottery, blown glass, and textiles are included in the show. Begun around 1959.

★ 930 ★
Great Barrington - BERKSHIRE CRAFTS FAIR. Mid August, 3 days, Monument Mountain Regional High School. Contact: Berkshire Hills Conference, Incorporated, 107 South Street, Pittsfield, Massachusetts 01201.

One hundred exhibits from throughout the Northeast are at this juried fair. Crafts include glassblowing, pottery, leather, pewter, jewelry, batik, weaving, quiltmaking, woodworking, enameling and others. The best of the works are in a Special Recognition Room.

★ 931 ★
New Bedford - CRAFTS FAIR. Mid August, annual, 2 days. Contact: Bristol County Development Council, Incorporated, 154 North Main Street, Fall River, Massachusetts 02722.

Outdoor craft fair in the historic waterfront district of New Bedford.

★ 932 ★
Pembroke - ARTS FESTIVAL. Mid August, annual, 3 days. Contact: Pembroke Arts Festival, Box 1973, Pembroke, Massachusetts 02359.

Juried competition with cash awards, open to New England artists.

★ 933 ★
Plymouth - OUTDOOR ART SHOW. Mid September, annual, 9 days. Contact: Plymouth Chamber of Commerce, 85 Samoset Street, Plymouth, Massachusetts 02360.

A juried show for amateur and professional artists, held in the open air.

★ 934 ★
Stoughton - ARTS FESTIVAL. Mid April, annual, 1 day. Contact: Massachusetts Department of Commerce and Development, Division of Tourism, Box 1775, Boston, Massachusetts 02105.

Arts festival opens series of events to celebrate the anniversary of the town.

★ 935 ★
Vineyard Haven - TISBURY STREET FAIR. Early July, annual, 1 day. Contact: Massachusetts Department of Commerce and Development, Division of Tourism, Box 1775, Boston, Massachusetts 02105.

Local crafts for sale, many varieties and media.

MICHIGAN

★ 936 ★
Ann Arbor - STREET ART FAIR. Mid July, 4 days. Contact: Southeast Michigan Travel and Tourist Association, Executive Plaza, 1200 Sixth Avenue, Detroit, Michigan 48226.

A large array of arts and crafts in an outdoor setting.

★ 937 ★
Charlevoix - WATERFRONT ART FAIR. Mid August, annual, 1 day. Contact: Chamber of Commerce, 408 Bridge Street, Post Office Box 217, Charlevoix, Michigan 49720.

Arts and Crafts

MICHIGAN (Continued)

Various types of arts and crafts are displayed and on sale along the waterfront.   Begun around 1959.

★ 938 ★
Fremont - ART FAIR.   Early August (1st Saturday), annual, 1 day, City Park.   Contact: Old State Bank of Fremont, Box 70, Fremont, Michigan 49412.

Participants in the fair include artists and craftsmen from all over the state.   Music concerts are provided in the afternoon by the Blue Lake Fine Arts Camp.   Started in 1965.

★ 939 ★
Grand Haven - WATERFRONT ART FAIR.   Late July (4th weekend), annual, 3 days, Waterfront Park and downtown.   Contact: North West Ottawa County Chamber of Commerce, One Washington Avenue, Grand Haven, Michigan 49417.

Art festival for artists exhibiting only their own creations.   Categories of exhibits include sculptures in metal, clay, wood, stone and plastic; hand-weaving; macrame; handthrown and slab pottery; sand-mold and hand-dipped candles; hand-blown glass; tooled leather and jewelry made entirely by the artist.   Started in 1974.

★ 940 ★
New Buffalo - ART AND CRAFTS FAIR.   Mid July, 3 days.   Contact: Chamber of Commerce, 41 North Whittaker Street, New Buffalo, Michigan 49117.

Quality arts and crafts in various media on display and for sale.

★ 941 ★
Spring Lake - ARTS AND CRAFTS FESTIVAL.   Late June (last weekend), annual, 2 days, downtown. Contact: Ms. Mary Streeting, 117 West Savidge Street, Spring Lake, Michigan 49456.

Artists and craftsmen display and sell paintings, crafts and other art work.   Portraits are done during the show.   Refreshments are available.   First held in 1970.

MINNESOTA

★ 942 ★
Bemidji - ART IN THE PARK.   Late July, 1 day. Contact: Bemidji Area Chamber of Commerce, Post

Office Box 806, Bemidji, Minnesota 56601.

All forms of original art including painting, ceramics, photography, metal sculpture, woodcarvings, weaving, violin making, etc.   Musical performances in the bandstand.

MISSISSIPPI

★ 943 ★
Batesville - ART MART.   Late June, annual, 1 day. Contact: South Panola Area Chamber of Commerce, Highway 51 North, Post Office Box 528, Batesville, Mississippi 38606.

The outdoor show is open to all who wish to exhibit or sell their crafts or antiques.   It is held in a pecan grove.   Begun in 1967.

★ 944 ★
Biloxi - OUTDOOR FESTIVAL.   Late April, 3 days, Broadwater Beach Marina.   Contact: Travel Department, Mississippi Agricultural and Industrial Board, Post Office Box 849, Jackson, Mississippi 39205.

Arts and crafts of local artisans are displayed outdoors.

★ 945 ★
Carthage - ARTS AND CRAFTS FESTIVAL.   Late March, annual, 2 days, Carthage Coliseum.   Contact: Travel Tourism Department, Mississippi Agricultural and Industrial Board, Post Office Box 849, Jackson, Mississippi 39205.

Over 125 artists and craftsmen come to display and some to demonstrate their needlework, Choctaw basket weaving, woodcrafts, paintings, and antiques.

★ 946 ★
Clinton - ARTS AND CRAFTS FAIR.   Mid April (2nd Saturday), annual, 1 day, Mississippi College Quadrangle.   Contact: Arts and Crafts Fair, Post Office Box 473, Clinton, Mississippi 39056.

Features paintings and handcrafted items; commercially produced objects or antiques are not allowed.   Members of the League sell homemade items at the Sweet Shoppe including candies, cakes, candles, cookies, and pies.   Entertainment is provided throughout the day by musicians and vocalists.   Food and drink is offered at a hospitality booth.   Sponsored by the Junior Civic League.   Begun around 1972.

MISSISSIPPI (Continued)

★ 947 ★
Greenville - MAINSTREAM ARTS AND CRAFTS
FESTIVAL.   Mid May (2nd Saturday), annual, 1 day,
Washington County Courthouse Square.   Contact:
Chamber of Commerce, Post Office Drawer 933,
Greenville, Mississippi 38701.

Exhibitors from neighboring states sell and display their
art and craft works.

★ 948 ★
Hattiesburg - HATTIESBURG FLEA MARKET.   March,
Hattiesburg Community Center.   Contact: Travel
and Tourism Department, Mississippi Agricultural and
Industrial Board, Post Office Box 849, Jackson,
Mississippi 39205.

A display and sale of arts, crafts, and antiques
sponsored by the South Mississippi Art Association.

★ 949 ★
Inverness - INVERNESS ARTS FESTIVAL.   May,
annual, Inverness Library.   Contact: Chamber of
Commerce, Inverness, Mississippi 38753; or
Inverness Library, Inverness, Mississippi 38753.

Displays of paintings, sculpture, and handicrafts
highlight this festival of arts.

★ 950 ★
Kilmichael - ARTS AND CRAFTS FESTIVAL.   Mid
April, 1 day.   Contact: Travel Department,
Mississippi Agricultural and Industrial Board, Post
Office Box 849, Jackson, Mississippi 39205.

Old-time gathering with refreshments, folk entertainment, and a crafts display and sale.

★ 951 ★
Morton - BARTER DAY.   Mid June, annual, 1 day,
Roosevelt State Park.   Contact: Morton Chamber
of Commerce, Morton, Mississippi 39117.

A festival of arts and crafts to which all desiring
to display or sell arts, crafts or other items of general
interest are welcome.   No exhibit fees.

★ 952 ★
Natchez - GREAT RIVER ROADS CRAFT FESTIVAL.
Mid October, annual, 3 days, Natchez Civic Center.
Contact: National Folk Festival Association, In-
corporated, 1345 Connecticut Avenue, Northwest,

Washington, D.C. 20036; or Natchez-Adams
Chamber of Commerce, Post Office Box 725, Natchez,
Mississippi 39120.

Features folk music and ballet, handicraft demonstration and exhibit, tours of historic buildings, and
creole gumbo dinner.   Begun in 1973.

★ 953 ★
Ruleville - SIDEWALK SALE FIESTA.   Early August,
(1st Saturday), annual, 1 day, downtown.   Contact:
Chamber of Commerce, Ruleville, Mississippi 38771.

Arts and crafts show and sale with a variety of other
forms of entertainment available.

MISSOURI

★ 954 ★
Forsyth - WHITE RIVER ARTS AND CRAFTS FAIR.
Mid August, annual, 3 days.   Contact: Chamber
of Commerce, Box 777, Forsyth, Missouri 65653.

A display and sale of arts and crafts in many media.

★ 955 ★
Gainesville - HOOTIN' AN' HOLLERIN'.   Early
October, annual, 3 days.   Contact: Chamber of
Commerce, c/o the Bank of Gainesville, Gaines-
ville, Missouri 65655.

Ozarks arts and crafts festival with displays, sales,
and fun for all.

★ 956 ★
Kansas City - PLAZA ART FAIR.   Late September,
annual, 3 days, Country Club Plaza.   Contact:
Convention and Visitors Bureau of Greater Kansas
City, 1221 Baltimore, Kansas City, Missouri 64105.

Artists from throughout the Midwest display and sell
art work including oils, watercolors, drawings, prints,
sculpture, woodcarvings, pottery and glasswork.   Begun around 1932.

★ 957 ★
Silver Dollar City - NATIONAL CRAFTS FESTIVAL.
Late September-mid October (3rd Saturday-2nd Sun-
day), annual, 17 days, throughout the city.   Con-
tact: Chamber of Commerce, Silver Dollar City,
Missouri 65616; or Ms. Jeanne Nichols, Festivals
Coordinator, Silver Dollar City, Missouri 65616.

Craftsmen demonstrate five dozen rare and historic

Arts and Crafts

MISSOURI (Continued)

skills, plus Silver Dollars' 24 resident crafts. Demonstrations include doll making from corn cobs, glass blowing, soapmaking, rope making, quilting, chair set weaving from corn husks, log hewing, basket weaving, pottery, and spinning. Largest exhibition of its kind. Started in 1963.

★ 958 ★
Springfield - WATERCOLOR U.S.A. April-June, annual. Contact: Director, Springfield Art Museum, 1111 East Brookside Drive, Springfield, Missouri 65804.

A juried show of watercolors by artists from throughout the United States. Cash and purchase prizes awarded.

MONTANA

★ 959 ★
Billings - ART FESTIVAL. Mid July, 2 days. Contact: Chamber of Commerce, Box 2519, Billings, Montana 59103.

A two day show and sale of arts and crafts.

NEBRASKA

★ 960 ★
Omaha - JOSLYN ART MUSEUM MIDWEST BIENNIAL. March. Contact: Director/Curator, Joslyn Art Museum, 2200 Dodge Street, Omaha, Nebraska 68102.

Painting, sculpture and graphics (prints and drawings). Open to residents of Nebraska, Arkansas, Colorado, Illinois, Iowa, Kansas, Louisiana, Minnesota, Missouri, South Dakota, Montana, New Mexico, North Dakota, Texas, Oklahoma and Wyoming.

NEVADA

★ 961 ★
Las Vegas - NATIONAL ART ROUND-UP. Early April-early May, annual, 1 month. Contact: Las Vegas Art League, 3333-6 West Washington, Las Vegas, Nevada 89107.

The display and sale of works in all media, including ceramics, graphics, jewelry, painting, sculpture and textiles. Awards include cash, purchase, and ribbons. All artists are eligible.

NEW HAMPSHIRE

★ 962 ★
Canaan - REGIONAL CRAFTSMEN'S FAIR. Late July, annual, 2 days, Methodist vestry and yard. Contact: Chamber of Commerce, Canaan, New Hampshire 03741.

Craftsmen of the area demonstrate, display, and sell various items they have produced. Begun around 1971.

★ 963 ★
Gilford - LAKES REGION CRAFTSMEN SHOW. Mid July, 2 days, Gunstock Recreational Area. Contact: Lakes Region Chamber of Commerce, Nine Veterans Square, Laconia, New Hampshire 03246.

A variety of arts and crafts are displayed and for sale.

★ 964 ★
Kingston - ROCKINGHAM CRAFTSMEN'S FALL FAIR. Early November, 1 day, Town Hall and Church by Lake. Contact: Secretary, Rockingham Craftsmen's Fall Fair, Kingston, New Hampshire 03848.

A demonstration, display, and sale of quality craft items of many categories.

★ 965 ★
Newbury - CRAFTSMEN'S FAIR. Early August, annual, 6 days, Mount Sunapee State Park. Contact: League of New Hampshire Craftsmen Director, 205 North Main Street, Concord, New Hampshire 03301.

Products on display range from small items to furniture; and include silverware, hooked rugs, jewelry, hand woven and/or dyed and printed fabrics. All pieces for sale are judged as to excellence of technique and design. Other events include children's theater and puppetry, regular theater, and folk music. Begun around 1932.

NEW JERSEY

★ 966 ★
Cape May - ARTS AND CRAFTS FESTIVAL. Mid June, 2 days, Convention Hall on the Boardwalk. Contact: Mr. Kenneth Evanson, Post Office Box 102, Green Creek, New Jersey 08219.

A large assortment of arts and crafts are on display and for sale.

NEW JERSEY (Continued)

★ 967 ★
Long Branch - FESTIVAL OF FINE ARTS.   Mid
April-early May, annual, 3 weeks, Monmouth College,
Wilson Hall.   Contact: Art Department, Monmouth
College, Long Branch, New Jersey 07740.

Mixed media exhibit sponsored by the college and
the Monmouth County Arts Council.   Started in 1961.

★ 968 ★
Long Branch - MAURICE PODELL MEMORIAL
OUTDOOR SUMMER ART FESTIVAL.   July or August,
annual, 4 days, Long Branch Historical Museum.
Contact: Long Branch Chamber of Commerce, 494
Broadway, Long Branch, New Jersey 07740.

A display of original works by both professional and
amateur artists in all media including oils, watercolor,
graphics, etchings, prints, sculpture, ceramics, and
photography.   Also present are crafts, ceramics,
jewelry and sketch artists.   Begun around 1962.

★ 969 ★
Ocean City - BOARDWALK ART SHOW.   August,
annual, 1 day.   Contact: Ocean City Cultural
Arts Center, 409 Wesley Avenue, Ocean City, New
Jersey 08226.

An art and craft show including all media, professional
and amateur artists, cash awards.

★ 970 ★
West Long Branch - SHOWCASE __ (name includes
number of festival).   Early May, annual, 2 days,
Monmouth College campus.   Contact: Community
Relations Office, Monmouth College, West Long
Branch, New Jersey 07764.

Countywide festival of the arts sponsored by the
Monmouth County Arts Council and Monmouth college.
Started in 1972.

★ 971 ★
West Long Branch - TEEN ARTS FESTIVAL.   Early
April, 2 days, Wilson Hall, Monmouth College
campus.   Contact: Community Relations Office,
Monmouth College, West Long Branch, New Jersey
07764.

Countywide teen arts festival sponsored by the college
and a variety of community groups.   Begun in 1974.

★ 972 ★
West Orange - ART SHOW.   November, annual.
Contact: Mrs. Patricia Sprouls, 188 Kaywin Drive,
Paramus, New Jersey 07652.

Open to all realistic artists working in the media:
oil, watercolor, and mixed graphics.   Cash awards.
Sponsored by the New Jersey Chapter of the American
Artists Professional League.

★ 973 ★
Willingboro - FESTIVAL OF ART.   July, annual.
Contact: President, Willingboro Art Alliance, Box
613, Willingboro, New Jersey 08046.

An open exhibition of quality art work sponsored by
the Willingboro Art Alliance.

NEW MEXICO

★ 974 ★
Albuquerque - BLACK HERITAGE WEEK ARTS AND
CRAFTS FESTIVAL.   Mid February, annual, 2 days,
University of New Mexico.   Contact: Afro-American
Studies Center, University of New Mexico, Uni-
versity Hill Northeast, Albuquerque, New Mexico
87106.

Contemporary works of black artists throughout New
Mexico are on display.   Sponsored by the Alpha
Kappa Alpha Sorority.   Begun around 1973.

★ 975 ★
Albuquerque - CHURCH STREET FAIR.   Mid June,
annual, 3 days, Old Town Plaza.   Contact: The
New Mexico Art League, 400 Romero Northwest,
Albuquerque, New Mexico 87140.

Original arts and crafts only.   Sale of paintings,
sculpture, pottery, jewelry, etc.   Sponsored by the
Professional Artists' Association: New Mexico Art
League Gallery.

★ 976 ★
Albuquerque - CRAFTS 6.   Mid April-mid June,
biennial, 2 months, Museum of Albuquerque.   Contact: Museum Office, Museum of Albuquerque,
Albuquerque, New Mexico.

Juried exhibit of contemporary New Mexico crafts.

★ 977 ★
Albuquerque - NATIONAL SMALL PAINTINGS SHOW.
February, annual, all month, New Mexico Art League

NEW MEXICO (Continued)

Gallery.   Contact: New Mexico Art League, Old Town Gallery, 400 Romero Street, Northwest, Albuquerque, New Mexico 87108.

A juried show, awarding prizes.   Open to all artists and media. Sponsored by the New Mexico Art League. Begun around 1970.

★ 978 ★
Albuquerque - NEW MEXICO ARTS AND CRAFTS FAIR.   Late June (last weekend), annual, 3 days, Fairgrounds.   Contact: New Mexico Arts and Crafts Fair, Post Office Box 8801, Albuquerque, New Mexico 87108.

An outdoor display of both traditional and contemporary crafts - the largest in the state.   On display are handmade items including rugs, jewelry and clothes, done in Spanish and Indian styles.   Other categories are painting, graphic arts, photography, ceramics, woods and metals, and leather.   The fair is open for participation to New Mexico residents only and works are subject to a jury of standards.   Begun in 1962.

★ 979 ★
Albuquerque - NIZHONI DAYS.   April, annual. Contact: Native American Studies Center, University of New Mexico, 1812 Las Lomas Northeast, Albuquerque, New Mexico 87106.

This event features crafts produced by Native American students at the University of New Mexico; only these students are allowed to exhibit.

★ 980 ★
Albuquerque - SOUTHWEST ARTS AND CRAFTS FESTIVAL.   Early November (1st weekend), annual, 3 days, Fairgrounds.   Contact: Southwest Arts and Crafts Fair, Post Office Box 25351, Albuquerque, New Mexico 87125.

A major contemporary arts and crafts show.   The fair is completely invitational and only residents of New Mexico may exhibit.   Begun around 1973.

★ 981 ★
Albuquerque - STARVING ARTISTS ARTS AND CRAFTS FAIR.   March, annual. Contact: Women's Association of Allied Beverage Industries, 1724 Washington Northeast, Albuquerque, New Mexico 87110.

A variety of arts and crafts on display and for sale.

★ 982 ★
Grants - VALENCIA COUNTY ARTS AND CRAFTS FAIR.   Late November, annual, 3 days.   Contact: Grants and West Valencia County Chamber of Commerce, 500 West Santa Fe Avenue, Post Office Box 297, Grants, New Mexico 87020.

A county-wide show and sale of a variety of arts and crafts.

★ 983 ★
Los Alamos - BANDELIER INDIAN ARTS AND CRAFTS SHOW.   Mid June, annual, 2 days, Bandelier National Monument.   Contact: Superintendent John Hunter, Bandelier National Monument, Los Alamos, New Mexico 87544.

Works of craftsmen from nearby pueblos which may be connected with the prehistoric peoples who lived in the Bandelier ruins.   Begun around 1972.

★ 984 ★
Los Alamos - NORTHERN NEW MEXICO ARTS AND CRAFTS FAIR.   Mid May, biannual, 1 day. Contact: Betty Lilienthal, Los Alamos Arts Council, Los Alamos, New Mexico 87544.

Contemporary southwest arts from throughout the region are on display and for sale.

★ 985 ★
Roswell - PIONEER DAYS ARTS AND CRAFTS FAIR. Early May, 2 days, New Mexico State Fairgrounds. Contact: Chamber of Development and Commerce, 131 West Second Street, Post Office Drawer 70, Roswell, New Mexico 88201.

Sponsored by the Roswell Jaycees, this juried fair features the efforts of 100 participants from New Mexico.

★ 986 ★
Ruidoso - ARTS AND CRAFTS FAIR.   Mid August, annual, 3 days.   Contact: Chamber of Commerce, Ruidoso, New Mexico 88345.

An outdoor showing and sale of local arts and crafts. Begun around 1972.

★ 987 ★
Sante Fe - SOUTHWEST FINE ARTS BIENNIAL. April-May, biennial.   Contact: Director, Museum of New Mexico, Box 2087, Santa Fe, New Mexico 87501.

NEW MEXICO (Continued)

A juried show giving awards and selecting works for a traveling show. Open to artists from the south-southwest; all painting and sculpture media.

★ 988 ★
Santa Fe - SOUTHWESTERN CRAFTS BIENNIAL. Early June-early September, biennial, 3 days, Museum of International Folk Art. Contact: Museum Office, Museum of International Folk Art, Santa Fe, New Mexico 87501.

A juried show of contemporary folk art by southwestern artists.

★ 989 ★
Santa Fe - SPANISH MARKET. Late July, annual, 2 days, Santa Fe Plaza. Contact: Folk Art Museum, Museum of New Mexico, Santa Fe, New Mexico 87501; or Spanish Colonial Arts Society, Santa Fe, New Mexico 87501.

Traditional southwest Spanish crafts including colcha embroidery, weaving, woodcarving, and filigree jewelry.

NEW YORK

★ 990 ★
Chautauqua - CHAUTAUQUA EXHIBITION OF AMERICAN ART. July, annual. Contact: Chautauqua Gallery of Art, Wyth Avenue, Chautauqua, New York 14722.

A juried exhibition open to all residents of the United States and its territories. Media include casein, mixed media, oil, tempura and watercolor. Cash prizes.

★ 991 ★
Greenville - CRAFT DAY. Late July, 1 day, Greenville Central Junior-Senior High School. Contact: Ms. Chris McDonald, Publicity Chairman, Box 123, Rural Delivery 1, Greenville, New York 12083.

A variety of crafts on display and for sale. Sponsored by the Catskill Valley Historical Society.

★ 992 ★
Hammondsport - ART SHOW. Early August, annual, 2 days, Hammondsport Village Square. Contact: Finger Lakes Association, Incorporated, 309 Lake Street, Penn Yan, New York 14527.

A display and sale of artwork. Refreshments offered. Begun around 1967.

★ 993 ★
Ithaca - CRAFTSMEN FAIR. Early August, annual, 1 week. Contact: Finger Lake Association, Incorporated, 309 Lake Street, Penn Yan, New York 14527.

Sponsored by the York State Craftsmen's Association, the fair features an art display and crafts exhibition and demonstrations. The sponsors emphasize the educational nature of the fair, and workshops are held for various crafts. Seminars are also given, and there is a sale of crafts. Begun around 1959.

★ 994 ★
Lockport - 100 AMERICAN CRAFTSMEN. Early June, annual, 3 days, Kenan Arena. Contact: Ms. Jeanne Gunby, 433 Locust Street, Post Office Box 296, Lockport, New York 14094.

Crafts of all varieties are demonstrated, displayed, and for sale.

★ 995 ★
New York - CRAFTS REVISITED EXHIBITION. Late June-early July, World Trade Center. Contact: New York City Bicentennial Corporation, Post Office Box 1976, FDR Station, New York, New York 10022.

Exhibition of arts and crafts of America-past and present.

★ 996 ★
New York - NATIONAL ARTS AND ANTIQUES. Mid October. Contact: New York Convention and Visitors Bureau, 90 East 42nd Street, New York, New York 10017.

A huge collection of paintings, furniture, and decorative items on display and for sale.

★ 997 ★
New York - WASHINGTON SQUARE OUTDOOR ART SHOW. Late May and early June, 17 days, Greenwich Village. Contact: New York Convention and Visitors Bureau, Incorporated, 90 East 42nd Street, New York, New York 10017; or Chamber of Commerce and Industry, 65 Liberty Street, New York, New York 10005.

Arts and Crafts

NEW YORK (Continued)

All through the Village and especially in Washington Square, artists and craftsmen display and sell their wares.

★ 998 ★
Oceanside - ARTS AND CRAFTS FAIR. Early May, annual, 2 days, First United Methodist Church. Contact: Arts and Crafts Fair Director, First United Methodist Church, Atlantic Avenue and Davidson Street, Oceanside, New York 11572.

A display and sale of a variety of arts and crafts. Begun in 1974.

★ 999 ★
Rhinebeck - NORTHEAST CRAFT FAIR. Late June (last week), annual, 5 days, Dutchess County Fair-grounds. Contact: The Director, Northeast Craft Fair Limited, 12 North Chestnut Street, New Paltz, New York 12561.

Craftsmen demonstrate, exhibit and sell their crea-tions, and also hold workshops to teach crafts to children. In addition to three days that the event is open to the public, it is open two days to the trade only. There is exhibition space for 500 craftsmen. Started in 1965.

★ 1000 ★
Rochester - CURBSTONE ART FESTIVAL. Late July, annual, downtown business and shopping area. Contact: Retail Merchants Council, Rochester Chamber of Commerce, 55 Saint Paul Street, Rochester, New York 14604.

Local artists and art clubs display their paintings.

★ 1001 ★
Rochester - MID-TOWN PLAZA CRAFT SHOW. Late February-early March, annual, 3 days, Mid-Town Plaza. Contact: Finger Lakes Association, 309 Lake Street, Penn Yan, New York 14527.

Clay, fiber, metals, wood, enamel and glass are the media for the works on display and for sale. Begun in 1974.

★ 1002 ★
Setauket - GALLERY NORTH OUTDOOR ART SHOW. Mid July, annual. Contact: Gallery North Out-door Art Show, Box 1145, North Country Road, Setauket, New York 11733.

A competitive show for all media, held out-of-doors.

NORTH CAROLINA

★ 1003 ★
Asheville - SOUTHERN HIGHLANDS CRAFTSMEN'S FAIR. Mid July, annual, 5 days, Civic Center. Contact: Mr. Robert Gray, Director, Southern Highland Handicraft Guild, Post Office Box 9145, Asheville, North Carolina 28805.

Traditional and contemporary craftsmen display and demonstrate their work: enameling, woodcarving, instrument making, weaving, spinning, knotting, fringing, stain glass, leather work, pottery, stained glass, jewelry, smithing, and printing. In addition, traditional dancing and music are presented. Dem-onstrations and sales of Indian crafts. Sponsored by the Southern Highlands Handicrafts Guild. Begun in 1948.

★ 1004 ★
Asheville - VILLAGE ARTS AND CRAFTS FAIR. Early August, annual, 2 days, All Souls Church. Contact: Asheville Area Chamber of Commerce, Post Office Box 1011, Asheville, North Carolina 28802.

Exhibitions and sale of native crafts, held concurrently with the Mountain Dance and Folk Festival in Ashe-ville. Sponsored by the New Morning Art Gallery.

★ 1005 ★
Boone - BOONE CRAFTS FESTIVAL. Early August, 5 days, Holiday Inn Conference Center. Contact: Blue Ridge Hearthside Crafts Association, Post Office Box 128, Sugar Grove, North Carolina 28679.

More than 75 mountain craftspeople sell their craft work and give demonstrations of their techniques. In addition, there is mountain-style entertainment with banjo and dulcimer, etc.

★ 1006 ★
Brevard - SIDEWALK ART SHOW AND SALE. Early August, annual, 1 day, Courthouse Lawn. Contact: Mrs. Harold Matthews, Transylvania Art Guild, 113 Park Avenue, Brevard, North Carolina 28712.

Display and sale of various art works on the lawn of the courthouse.

★ 1007 ★
Elizabeth City - ALBEMARLE CRAFTSMAN'S FAIR.

NORTH CAROLINA (Continued)

Late September (last Wednesday-Sunday), annual, 5 days, Knobbs Creek Community Center. Contact: Elizabeth City Area Chamber of Commerce, Post Office Box 426, Elizabeth City, North Carolina 27909.

Craftsmen exhibit, demonstrate and sell such crafts as wood-working, egg shell craft, Swedish embroidery, crocheting, copper tooling, chair caning, pine needle crafts, dolls, stool bottoming, etc. Begun around 1959.

★ 1008 ★
Fontana Dam - MOUNTAIN ARTS AND CRAFTS FAIR. Late August, annual, 2 days, Fontana Village Resort. Contact: Fontana Village Resort, Fontana Dam, North Carolina 28733.

Exhibition of artwork and crafts pieces, many reflecting traditionals of folk art in the Smoky Mountains. Begun around 1973.

★ 1009 ★
Franklin - MACON COUNTY ARTS AND CRAFTS SHOW. Late June (3rd weekend), annual, 4 days, Macon County Fairgrounds. Contact: Miss Eva Thaller, Route 1, Franklin, North Carolina 28734.

A demonstration, display and sale of a variety of arts and crafts. Special exhibits and entertainment are included. Begun in 1975.

★ 1010 ★
Greensboro - SOUTHEASTERN ART AUCTION AND SALE. October, annual. Contact: Greensboro Artists' League, Incorporated, 404-B Fisher Park Circle, Greensboro, North Carolina 27401.

The sale is a fund-raiser for the C. L. Phillips Memorial Arts Scholarship which provides assistance to art students at the five nearby colleges. It is open to artists throughout the southeastern United States; all works must be for sale. The works include collages, drawings, paintings, pastels and prints.

★ 1011 ★
Lake Waccamaw - ARTS AND CRAFTS FESTIVAL OF SOUTHEASTERN NORTH CAROLINA. Late April, 2 days, Boy's Home campus. Contact: Ann A. Hood, Route 2, Box 211, Elizabethtown, North Carolina 28337.

Exhibitions of arts, crafts and the performing arts, and presentations of history and literature. Begun around 1969.

★ 1012 ★
Maggie Valley - ARTS AND CRAFTS SHOW. Mid September, 3 days, Stallard Plaza. Contact: North Carolina Travel Development Section, Division of Economic Development, Department of Natural and Economic Resources, Raleigh, North Carolina 27611.

The show features a display of arts and crafts, with square dancing, round dancing, mountain clog dancing and mountain music to enliven the event.

★ 1013 ★
Mocksville - DAVIE CRAFT CORNER. Late November (Friday and Saturday before Thanksgiving), annual, 2 days, National Guard Armory. Contact: Davie Craft Association, c/o Mrs. Nancy Hartmen, Post Office Box 812, Mocksville, North Carolina 27028.

A show and sale of items produced by the Davie Craft Association, with an emphasis on the promotion of high-quality country crafts. Started in 1970.

★ 1014 ★
Morehead City - ARTS AND CRAFTS SHOW AND SALE. Late January, 1 day. Contact: Morehead City Festival Committee, 112 Taylor Street, Morehead City, North Carolina 28557.

A display and sale of quality arts and crafts.

★ 1015 ★
Morgantown - FALL FESTIVAL. Mid October, annual, Old Burke County Courthouse Square. Contact: Chamber of Commerce, Post Office Box 751, Morgantown, North Carolina 28655.

Local craftspeople display and sell their handcrafts.

★ 1016 ★
Murphy - SMOKY MOUNTAIN ART AND CRAFT SHOW. Early July (around July 4th), annual, 4 days, Old Rock Gym. Contact: Murphy Rotary Club, John Bolin, Box 493, Murphy, North Carolina 28906.

Artists and craftspeople from throughout the southern Appalachian Mountains are drawn to this, the largest area show. Begun around 1970.

Arts and Crafts

NORTH CAROLINA (Continued)

★ 1017 ★
Raleigh - CRAFTS FESTIVAL. Late April-early May,
4 days. Contact: Blue Ridge Hearthside Crafts
Association, Incorporated, Post Office Box 128,
Sugar Grove, North Carolina 28679.

Demonstration and displays by craftsmen from eight
states, over 100 in all.

★ 1018 ★
Wilmington - ARTS AND CRAFTS FESTIVAL. Late
May, 2 days, Greenfield Park. Contact: Lower
Cape Fear Council for the Arts, Post Office Box 212,
Wilmington, North Carolina 28401.

A colonial theme runs through the exhibits, arts and
crafts display, food and band concerts of this event.

★ 1019 ★
Wilson - SUNDAY IN THE PARK FESTIVAL OF
ARTS AND CRAFTS. Early May, 1 day, city park.
Contact: Chamber of Commerce, 220 Broad Street,
Post Office Box 979, Wilson, North Carolina 27893.

An outdoor show and sale of a variety of arts and
crafts.

★ 1020 ★
Winston-Salem - ARTS FESTIVAL. Late March, 2
days. Contact: Greater Winston-Salem Chamber
of Commerce, Post Office Box 1408, Winston-Salem,
North Carolina 27102.

The North Carolina Women's Club sponsors this event
featuring show and sale of arts and crafts.

★ 1021 ★
Winston-Salem - PIEDMONT CRAFTS FAIR. Early
November (1st weekend), annual, 2 days, Winston-
Salem Memorial Coliseum. Contact: Piedmont
Craftsmen, Incorporated, 936 West Fourth Street,
Winston-Salem, North Carolina 27101.

Exhibit, demonstrations and sale of crafts by craftsmen
from all over the eastern United States. Items include both traditional crafts and contemporary adapta-
tions.

NORTH DAKOTA

★ 1022 ★
Fort Ransom - SHEYENNE VALLEY ARTS AND CRAFTS

FESTIVAL. Late September, annual. Contact:
North Dakota State Highway Department, Capitol
Grounds, Bismarck, North Dakota 58505.

The festival includes amateur arts and crafts shows
with historical exhibits as well. There is a turkey
barbeque.

★ 1023 ★
Grand Forks - NORTH DAKOTA PRINT AND
DRAWING EXHIBITION. April, annual. Contact:
North Dakota Annual Print and Drawing Exhibition,
Art Department, University of North Dakota, Grand
Forks, North Dakota 58201.

An exhibition of prints and drawings, open to all
United States artists. Juried; monetary prizes are
awarded.

OHIO

★ 1024 ★
Akron - WONDERFUL WORLD OF OHIO MART.
Late September-early October, annual, 4 days, Stan
Hywet Hall. Contact: Akron Area Chamber of
Commerce, 137 South Main, Akron, Ohio 44308.

The event features the display and sale of some of
the special products of Ohio, including the original,
handmade work of artists and craftspeople. There
is continuous entertainment, and the demonstration of
many skills, such as weaving, etching, spinning, etc.

★ 1025 ★
Cambridge - SALT FORK ARTS AND CRAFTS
FESTIVAL. Mid August, 3 days. Contact: Grant
Hafley, Ohio Arts and Crafts Foundation, Cambridge,
Ohio 43725.

Housed in tents and pavilions in a local park, artists
from many disciplines exhibit and demonstrate. All
have been previously matched against the standards
of the Ohio Arts and Crafts Guild. Artists and
craftspersons display, demonstrate and sell their work.
Musicians, dancers, and actors perform. Home
cooked foods are served. Awards are given in the
art shows.

★ 1026 ★
Crooksville - POTTERY FESTIVAL. Mid June,
annual, 3 days. Contact: Mrs. Gladys Rider,
3372 Linn Drive, Zanesville, Ohio 43701.

Calling their area the "Pottery Center of the World",
these two towns (also held in Roseville) offer tours

OHIO (Continued)

of potteries, demonstrations of arts and crafts, and bargains in the sale of pottery. The Ohio Ceramic Museum is open, and there is a special display of antique pottery. Other activities include a parade, music, dramatic presentations, and a queen contest.

★ 1027 ★
East Liverpool - TRI-STATE POTTERY FESTIVAL. Mid June, annual, 3 days. Contact: Tri-State Pottery Festival Association, Incorporated, c/o The Evening Review, East Liverpool, Ohio 43920.

The event includes tours of pottery plants, a great variety of displays of pottery and a "pottery olympics". In addition, there is a parade, a rose show, and an antique show.

★ 1028 ★
Mansfield - OHIO CRAFTSMAN'S FESTIVAL. April, annual. Contact: Mansfield Art Center, 700 Marion Avenue, Mansfield, Ohio 44906.

A showing and sale of a variety of crafts.

★ 1029 ★
Mansfield - OHIO CRAFTSMAN'S FESTIVAL. Late September, 3 days, Art Center. Contact: Mansfield Area Chamber of Commerce, 33 Park Avenue, West, Mansfield, Ohio 44902.

A showing and sale of a variety of craft items.

★ 1030 ★
Marietta - MAINSTREAMS. Early April-mid May, annual, 6 weeks, Grover M. Herman Fine Arts Center. Contact: William Gerhold, Marietta College, Marietta, Ohio 45750.

The Marietta College International Exhibit of Painting and Sculpture. Purchases prizes are awarded by a jury of nationally recognized experts on the basis of a slide competition. Begun around 1966.

★ 1031 ★
Massillon - OHIO ARTISTS AND CRAFTSMEN SHOW. July-August, biennial (even numbered years), The Massillon Museum. Contact: Miss Mary Merwin, The Massillon Museum, 212 Lincoln Way East, Massillon, Ohio 44646.

The show is open to all past and present residents of Ohio exhibiting crafts, drawings, photographs, prints

and sculpture. Prizes and purchase awards.

★ 1032 ★
Roseville - POTTERY FESTIVAL. Mid June, annual, 3 days. Contact: Mrs. Gladys Rider, 3372 Linn Drive, Zanesville, Ohio 43701.

Calling their area the "Pottery Center of the World", these two towns (also held in Crooksville) offer tours of potteries, demonstrations of arts and crafts, and bargains in the sale of pottery. The Ohio Ceramic Museum is open, and there is a special display of antique pottery. Other activities include a parade, music, dramatic presentations, and a queen contest.

★ 1033 ★
Sylvania - OUTDOOR ART FESTIVAL. Early September, annual, 1 day, Main and Monroe Streets. Contact: Toledo Area Chamber of Commerce, 218 Huron Street, Toledo, Ohio 43604.

The festival is open to everyone and features the work of artists from the region and surrounding states. Refreshments are also offered.

★ 1034 ★
Toledo - OUTDOOR JUBILEE. Late August, Toledo Artists Club. Contact: Toledo Area Chamber of Commerce, 218 Huron Street, Toledo, Ohio 43604.

Artists from across the country display their works. Music, entertainment and refreshments round out the festival. Begun around 1945.

★ 1035 ★
Toledo - TOLEDO AREA ARTISTS' EXHIBITION. Late May-mid June, annual, 3 weeks, Museum of Art. Contact: Roger Mandle, Federation of Arts, 2445 Monroe Street, Toledo, Ohio 43620.

A juried exhibit featuring crafts, drawings, paintings, prints, and sculpture created by artists from the Toledo area. Begun around 1919.

★ 1036 ★
Youngstown - OHIO CERAMIC AND SCULPTURE SHOW. January-February, annual. Contact: Secretary, Butler Institute of American Art, 534 Wick Avenue, Youngstown, Ohio 44502.

Purchase awards for past and present residents of Ohio for their work in ceramics, enamel, and sculpture. Jury.

Arts and Crafts

OKLAHOMA

★ 1037 ★
Poteau - DOGWOOD ART FESTIVAL. April-May (Easter-Mothers Day), annual. Contact: President, Green Country Art Association, 1307 South Main, Tulsa, Oklahoma 74119.

The festival features the paintings and sculpture of artists from Arkansas, Kansas, Missouri, Oklahoma and Texas. The event is juried, and sponsored by the Green County Art Association.

★ 1038 ★
Tulsa - FESTIVAL '(YEAR). Late May, annual, 3 days. Contact: Festival '(year), Downtown Tulsa Unlimited, 324 Main Mall, Tulsa, Oklahoma 74103.

An arts and crafts fair with a large variety of creations to look at and to buy.

★ 1039 ★
Tulsa - GREEN COUNTRY ART ASSOCIATION PLUS 65 SHOW. March, annual. Contact: President, Green Country Art Association, 1307 South Main, Tulsa, Oklahoma 74119.

Exhibit and sale of the painting and sculpture of artists from Arkansas, Kansas, Missouri, Oklahoma and Texas. Artists over 65 are not required to pay fees.

★ 1040 ★
Tulsa - PHILBROOK ART CENTER OKLAHOMA ANNUAL. April, annual. Contact: Director, Philbrook Art Center, 2727 South Rockford Road, Tulsa, Oklahoma 74114.

The event features graphics, painting and sculpture, and is open to all past and present residents of Oklahoma (of at least one year's residency). There is a jury and prizes are awarded.

OREGON

★ 1041 ★
North Portland - CERAMIC AND CRAFTS SHOW. Late March, annual, 3 days, Multnormah County Exposition Center. Contact: Show Director, 918 North East 191st Avenue, Portland, Oregon 97230.

A quality showing and sale of crafts with ceramics as a focal point.

PENNSYLVANIA

★ 1042 ★
Allentown - COLONIAL CRAFTS DAY. Mid June, annual, 3 days, Hamilton Mall. Contact: Allentown Center City Association, 462 Walnut Street, Allentown, Pennsylvania 18105.

Craft demonstrations of the colonial period highlight the events of the three day festival.

★ 1043 ★
Allentown - SIDEWALK ARTS AND CRAFTS SHOW. Mid August, annual, 1 day, Hamilton Mall. Contact: Allentown Center City Association, 462 Walnut Street, Allentown, Pennsylvania 18105.

Prize money for painting, drawing, sculpture, photography, and graphics; student work (17 years and younger). Begun around 1970.

★ 1044 ★
Bedford - NORTH APPALACHIAN CRAFTS FESTIVAL. Late May, annual, 5 days (2 weekends), Bedford Fairgrounds. Contact: Mrs. Wendy Cox, Bedford Heritage Commission, Bedford, Pennsylvania 15522.

Fireman's parade, concert, third annual "Great Bed Race", crafts, and exhibits.

★ 1045 ★
Brownsville - ARTS AND CRAFTS FESTIVAL. Early July, annual, 2 days, Nemacolin Castle. Contact: Brownsville Historical Society, Front Street, Brownsville, Pennsylvania 15417.

Crafts demonstrations and also food, games, entertainment, and guided tours of the castle.

★ 1046 ★
Coudersport - PALMA CRAFT FESTIVAL AND BIRLING CONTEST. Early July, annual, 2 days, between Galeton and Coudersport, Route 6. Contact: Potter County Recreation, Incorporated, Post Office Box 245, Coudersport, Pennsylvania 16915.

Crafts by artisans demonstrated, displayed and sold. Prizes to amateurs in the birling contest, a log rolling event on the sawmill pond.

★ 1047 ★
Erwinna - TINICUM ART FESTIVAL. Early July, annual, 1 day, Tinicum Park. Contact: Tinicum Civic Association, Incorporated, Stover Mills, Erwinna, Pennsylvania 18920.

PENNSYLVANIA   (Continued)

Festival offers displays, exhibits, crafts, art show, food and entertainment.

★ 1048 ★
Gettysburg - STATE CRAFT FAIR.   Late July, annual, 2 days, Hauser Fieldhouse, Gettysburg College.   Contact: Executive Director, Pennsylvania Guild of Craftsmen, 227 West Beaver Avenue, State College, Pennsylvania 16801.

More than 200 guild craftsmen from all over Pennsylvania gather here for unusual mixture of traditional and contemporary crafts.   Craftsmen can talk with visitors while making and selling their crafts.   Crafts-books and supplies available for purchase.   Sponsored by the Pennsylvania Guild of Craftsmen.

★ 1049 ★
Johnstown - ARTS FESTIVAL.   Mid September, annual, 1 day, Community Arts Center.   Contact: Community Arts Center, 1217 Menoher Boulevard, Johnstown, Pennsylvania 15905.

Food, fun and entertainment.   About 60 artists and craftsmen demonstrate, display and sell their work. "Center" Gallery Exhibit and Children's Creative Arts Colony are special features.

★ 1050 ★
Lancaster - CRAFT DAYS.   Mid June, annual, 2 days, Pennsylvania Farm Museum of Landis Valley, Contact: Pennsylvania Farm Museum of Landis Valley, 2451 Kissel Hill Road, Lancaster, Pennsylvania 17601.

Approximately 50 traditional crafts and skills of rural people of Pennsylvania are demonstrated including open hearth cooking, spinning, weaving, gunsmithing, pottery, tinsmithing and many other activities.

★ 1051 ★
Lancaster - PENNSYLVANIA GUILD OF CRAFTSMEN STATE FAIR.   Early August, annual, 3 days, Franklin and Marshall College.   Contact: Executive Director, Pennsylvania Guild of Craftsmen, 227 West Beaver Avenue, State College, Pennsylvania 16801.

Demonstrations by craftsmen.   Wares sold.   Seminars for craftsmen.

★ 1052 ★
Middletown - EARLY AMERICAN ARTS AND CRAFTS FAIR.   Mid June, annual, 3 days, Hoffer Park.

Contact: Mr. Daniel Tunnel, 29 Woodmere, Middle-town, Pennsylvania 17057.

Craftsmen demonstrating and selling handcrafts of the colonial through 1876 era.   Early American food, minstrels, German band, puppeteer, bill ringer choir, and theater.

★ 1053 ★
Mill Run - PIONEER CRAFTS FESTIVAL.   Mid July, 5 days.   Contact: Pioneer Crafts Council, Box 110, Mill Run, Pennsylvania 15464.

The festival features demonstrations, exhibitions, and sales of traditional Pennsylvania crafts, including quilting, leather-crafting, glass blowing, potting, macrame, batik-printing, spinning, dyeing, rug hooking, print-making from nature, backstrap-weaving, flax scutching, creation of corn husk dolls, wood-carving, shingle-making, blacksmithing, candle-making and jewelry-making.

★ 1054 ★
Philadelphia - EMBROIDERY EXHIBIT AND DEMONSTRATION.   May, 26 days, Art Alliance Museum.   Contact: The Embroiderers' Guild of America, 120 East 56th Street, Room 228, New York, New York 10022.

Given by the Delaware Valley Chapter of the Embroiderers' Guild of America, an unusual display of quality work.

★ 1055 ★
Philadelphia - HEAD HOUSE SQUARE ARTS AND CRAFTS FAIR.   June-August, annual, weekends all summer, Society Hill.   Contact: The Phila-delphia Convention and Visitors Bureau, 1525 John F. Kennedy Boulevard, Philadelphia, Pennsylvania 19102.

Takes place in an eighteenth century colonial market and offers all description of crafts, antiques, bric-a-brac, plants, and food delicacies from around the world.   Special entertainment is on hand.

★ 1056 ★
Pittsburgh - THREE RIVERS ART FESTIVAL.   Late May-early June, 10 days, Gateway Center.   Con-tact: Department of Commerce, Travel Development Bureau, Room 431, South Office Building, Harrisburg, Pennsylvania 17120.

Brings together artists and craftsmen of the surrounding area to display and demonstrate their works of painting,

Arts and Crafts

PENNSYLVANIA (Continued)

photography, sculpture, and crafts. There is a special Children's Creative Center. The events are enlivened by daily concerts.

★ 1057 ★
Shirleysburg - HUNTINGDON COUNTY ARTS FESTIVAL. Mid June, annual, 3 days. Contact: Huntingdon County Arts Council, Huntingdon, Pennsylvania 16652.

Juried art show with prizes, performing arts, all day outdoor displays of crafts and folk art.

★ 1058 ★
Somerset - MOUNTAIN CRAFT FESTIVAL. Mid September, annual, 2 days, Historical and Genealogy Society Center (old Route 219). Contact: Historical and Genealogy Society, Somerset, Pennsylvania 15501.

Exhibits showing life of pioneers and the crafts of the time.

★ 1059 ★
Spring City - CRAFT FAIR. May, annual, 2 days, Main Street. Contact: Department of Commerce, Bureau of Travel Development, 431 South Office Building, Harrisburg, Pennsylvania 17120.

A block party with a large variety of crafts displayed and for sale.

★ 1060 ★
Washington - WASHINGTON AND JEFFERSON COLLEGE NATIONAL PAINTING SHOW. March-April, annual, Washington and Jefferson College. Contact: Art Department, Washington and Jefferson College, Washington, Pennsylvania 15301.

A national exhibition of paintings with the initial jurying being done by slides. The paintings are sold, and there are cash awards and purchase awards. All United States artists 18 or over are eligible.

RHODE ISLAND

★ 1061 ★
Charlestown - OUTDOOR CRAFTS SHOW. Mid August, annual, 1 day, Kimball Wildlife Refuge, Watchaug Pond. Contact: Eloise Saunders, 145 Post Road, Westerly, Rhode Island 02891.

A variety of crafts shown and for sale in a lovely outdoor setting.

★ 1062 ★
Charlestown - RHODE ISLAND ASSOCIATION OF CRAFTSMEN SHOW. Late July-mid August, annual, 17 days, Windswept Farm. Contact: Mrs. Bruce Glenn, Windswept Farm, Route 1, Charlestown, Rhode Island 02813.

A scenic setting and a variety of crafts demonstrated, displayed, and for sale.

★ 1063 ★
Coventry - INTERNATIONAL CERAMIC FAIR. Early August, 4 days, Jack and Jill Exposition grounds. Contact: Rhode Island Department of Economic Development, Tourist Promotion Division, One Weybosset Hill, Providence, Rhode Island 02903.

A showing and sale of a large number and variety of ceramics.

★ 1064 ★
Harrisville - BURRILLVILLE ARTS AND CRAFTS FAIR. Early August, annual, 2 days, Assembly grounds. Contact: Rhode Island Department of Economic Development, Tourist Promotion Division, One Weybosset Hill, Providence, Rhode Island 02903.

Arts and crafts of many varieties on display and for sale in an outdoor setting. Begun around 1965.

★ 1065 ★
Newport - OUTDOOR ART FESTIVAL. Late July-early August, annual, 4 days, Touro and Eisenhower Parks, Long Wharf Mall. Contact: Rhode Island Department of Economic Development, Tourist Promotion Division, One Weybosset Hill, Providence, Rhode Island 02903.

A variety of arts and crafts displayed in an outdoor setting. Begun around 1962.

★ 1066 ★
North Scituate - SCITUATE ART FESTIVAL. October (2nd Monday), annual, 3 days, Village Green. Contact: Scituate Art Festival on the Village Green, Route 116, North Scituate, Rhode Island 02857.

The celebration is on the Rhode Island Columbus Day. The show is put on by a committee of local citizens to support local projects. There is a limit of 160 on the number of artists and craftsmen who may participate; all types of crafts and paintings are on exhibition. Begun around 1966.

RHODE ISLAND (Continued)

★ 1067 ★
Portsmouth - OUTDOOR ART FESTIVAL.   Late July,
3 days, East Main Road.   Contact: Newport County
Chamber of Commerce, 93 Thames Street, Newport,
Rhode Island 02840.

A variety of arts and crafts on display and for sale
in an outdoor setting.

★ 1068 ★
Providence - PROVIDENCE ART CLUB CRAFTS SHOW.
May, annual.   Contact: Providence Art Club, 11
Thomas Street, Providence, Rhode Island 02903.

Open to New England artists and craftsmen – a
quality show in a variety of media.

★ 1069 ★
Providence - PROVIDENCE ART CLUB PAINTING
SHOW.   March, annual.   Contact: Providence
Art Club, 11 Thomas Street, Providence, Rhode
Island 02903.

The show is open to New England artists.   Monetary prizes are awarded.

★ 1070 ★
Providence - RENAISSANCE CRAFTS AND ART
SHOW.   Mid May, 2 days, Rhode Island College
campus.   Contact: Stephen Carlomuste, 41
Shirley Boulevard, Cranston, Rhode Island 02910.

A show and sale of a variety of arts and crafts during
a festival in the mood of the Renaissance era.

★ 1071 ★
Wakefield - SNUG HARBOR ART FESTIVAL.   Mid
August, 2 days, Marina Park.   Contact: John A.
DelSesto, Westcote Drive, Wakefield, Rhode Island
02879.

The park and the harbor area are the setting for the
variety of arts and crafts displayed and for sale.

★ 1072 ★
Warwick - ALL RHODE ISLAND ART SHOW.   May,
annual, 3 days, Warwick Mall.   Contact: General
Manager, Warwick Mall, Warwick, Rhode Island
02886; or East Greenwich Art Club, Box 189,
East Greenwich, Rhode Island 02818.

A display of the work of Rhode Island artists.   Open

to all Rhode Island artists.   Begun in 1972.

★ 1073 ★
Westerly - WESTERLY ART FESTIVAL.   Mid July,
annual, 4 days, Wilcox Park.   Contact: Art
Festival, The Greater Westerly-Pawcatuck Area
Chamber of Commerce, 159 Main Street, Westerly,
Rhode Island 02891.

An outdoor exhibition of graphics, sculpture, paintings and applied arts.   For the fine arts, there is
snow fencing for works to be exhibited on, or the
artists may choose to bring his own racks.   The
works are judged and ribbons or monetary prizes
awarded.   There is a special exhibit area for
students still in school (elementary-high school).
Begun around 1967.

★ 1074 ★
Wickford - WICKFORD ART FESTIVAL.   Mid July,
annual, 3 days.   Contact: Wickford Art Association Art Festival, c/o Mrs. Sarah McGrury, 22 West
Main Street, North Kingdom, Rhode Island 02852;
or Bristol County Development Council, Incorporated,
154 North Main Street, Fall River, Massachusetts
02818.

Displays of artwork on the sidewalks of the town.
Begun around 1962.

SOUTH CAROLINA

★ 1075 ★
Aiken - SPRING ARTS FESTIVAL.   Early May,
annual, 2 days, in the Parkway on Park Avenue.
Contact: City Recreation Department, Post Office
Box 1177, Aiken, South Carolina 29801.

Various exhibits of arts and crafts of many varieties.

★ 1076 ★
Camden - KERSHAW COUNTY CRAFTS FESTIVAL.
Early June, annual, 2 days, Historic Camden.
Contact: Greater Kershaw County Chamber of Com-
merce, Post Office Box 605, Camden, South Carolina
29020.

Show and sales of arts and crafts, plus bazaar booths,
a country store, pony rides, tours of Historic Camden
and other family-type entertainment.   Begun in 1973.

★ 1077 ★
Charleston - CHARLES TOWNE LANDING CRAFTS
FAIR.   Early December, annual, 3 days, Charles

Arts and Crafts

Towne Landing. Contact: E. Pat Joyce, Charles Towne Landing, 1500 Olde Towne Road, Charleston, South Carolina 29407.

A gathering and exhibition of the finest in countless fields of craftsmenship. Many exhibitors demonstrate as well as sell their wares. Begun in 1973.

★ 1078 ★
Charleston - CHARLESTON ARTIST GUILD SIDEWALK SHOW. Mid April, annual, 2 days, Church Street. Contact: Charles Parnelle, 833 Darwin Street, Charleston, South Carolina 29412.

Displays of the work of local artists - a wide variety of arts and crafts.

★ 1079 ★
Clemson - FESTIVAL OF ARTS, HOBBIES, AND HANDCRAFTS. Early February, 1 day, Clemson House. Contact: Ross Cornwall, Trustee House, Clemson University, Clemson, South Carolina 29631.

Sponsored by the Clemson University Women's Club, this festival offers a display of various art forms and unusual hobbies.

★ 1080 ★
Columbia - FESTIVAL OF TALENTS. Mid May, annual, 8 days, Columbia Museums of Art and Science. Contact: Mrs. Ally Cahill, Columbia Museum of Art, 1112 Senate Street, Columbia, South Carolina 29201.

Students of the Richland Art School exhibit their work.

★ 1081 ★
Easley - FOOTHILLS FESTIVAL. Mid August, annual, 2 days, Old Market Square. Contact: George Vadney, Chairman, Foothills Festival, Post Office Box 1042, Clemson, South Carolina 29631.

Sponsored by area art councils and craft guilds, the festival features workshops and special emphasis on pioneer crafts.

★ 1082 ★
Murrells Inlet - MURRELLS INLET OUTDOOR ARTS AND CRAFTS FESTIVAL. Late April, annual, 3 days. Contact: Wilma D. Martin, Box 231, Murrells Inlet, South Carolina 29576; or Greater Myrtle Beach Chamber of Commerce, Post Office Box 1326,

Myrtle Beach, South Carolina 29577.

Many artists from South Carolina and other states exhibit under the ancient Spanish-moss hung oaks. Planned entertainment focuses on the performing arts.

★ 1083 ★
Pendleton - SOUTH CAROLINA ARTS AND CRAFTS FESTIVAL. Mid August, annual, 2 days. Contact: Foothills Arts and Crafts Guild, Post Office Box 365, Pendleton, South Carolina 29670.

Exhibits and booths of artists working in various media. Craft demonstrations. Begun around 1970.

★ 1084 ★
Spartanburg - SIDEWALK ART EXHIBIT AND FESTIVAL. Early May, annual, 1 day, sidewalks around Converse College. Contact: Spartanburg County Art Association, 151 North Fairview, Spartanburg, South Carolina 29302.

Professional and amateur artists display their arts and crafts. Many crafts are demonstrated and items are for sale.

★ 1085 ★
Spartanburg - SPARTANBURG JUNIOR WOMEN'S CLUB ARTS AND CRAFTS SHOW. Early October, annual, 3 days, Spartanburg Memorial Auditorium. Contact: Mrs. Henry E. Mitchell, Jr., 420 Ransdell Drive, Spartanburg, South Carolina 29302.

Features craftsmen from several states displaying, selling and demonstrating their crafts, such as glass blowing, pottery, Penobscot Indian beads and jewelry, metal work, lapidary, and macrame. Begun around 1969.

★ 1086 ★
Summerville - LOW COUNTRY ARTS AND CRAFTS FESTIVAL. Early August, annual, 3 days. Contact: Frances Stogner or Susan Droste, Post Office Box 1042, Clemson, South Carolina 29631.

Over 30 artists and craftsmen exhibit their talents in such areas as weaving, spinning, leather and metal working, pottery, and basketweaving. Other attractions include food, music, dance, and fun for all ages.

SOUTH DAKOTA

★ 1087 ★
Pine Ridge - RED CLOUD ART SHOW. Early June-early August, 2 months. Contact: Aberdeen Area Office, Bureau of Indian Affairs, U.S. Department of the Interior, 820 South Main Street, Aberdeen, South Dakota 57401.

A competitive exhibition for Indian artists who display their paintings; one of the tops in the country.

★ 1088 ★
Rapid City - FINE ARTS FESTIVAL. Mid August, annual, 6 days. Contact: Chamber of Commerce, 428 1/2 Saint Joe, Post Office Box 747, Rapid City, South Dakota 57701.

The events include displays of arts and booths filled with various South Dakota products, special children's productions, and sales of crafts. Held at the same time as the Central States Fair.

TENNESSEE

★ 1089 ★
Gatlinburg - CRAFTMAN'S FAIR. Late October (3rd week), annual, 5 days. Contact: Eastern Area Office, Bureau of Indian Affairs, U.S. Department of the Interior, Washington, D.C. 20245.

Craftman display their creations, including Indian crafts, baskets, spinning, brooms, iron and vegetable dyes, glass-blowing, wood-working, amidst craft demonstrations and the music and dancing of the area. Sponsored by the Southern Highlands Handicraft Guild. Started in 1948.

★ 1090 ★
Memphis - MISSISSIPPI RIVER CRAFT SHOW. October-November, annual. Contact: Mississippi River Craft Show, Brooks Memorial Art Gallery, Overton Park, Memphis, Tennessee 38112.

The show is open to craftsmen who reside in states bordering on the Mississippi river; a large variety of crafts are on display and for sale.

TEXAS

★ 1091 ★
Amarillo - ARTS IN ACTION. Late November, annual, 2 days, Amarillo Civic Center. Contact: Amarillo Chamber of Commerce, 301 South Polk, Amarillo Building, Amarillo, Texas 79102.

Over 150 artists exhibit their work at this judged competition. Some of the pieces are given away as door prizes in drawings held throughout the show. Performing groups take the stage at various intervals. Begun in 1972.

★ 1092 ★
Amarillo - CORONADO ARTS AND CRAFTS SHOW. Mid August, annual, 3 days, Quality Inn. Contact: Naomi Nelson, Quality Inn, Post Office Box 4205, Amarillo, Texas 79104.

A display and sale of arts and crafts.

★ 1093 ★
Austin - LAGUNA GLORIA ART FIESTA. May, annual, 2 days. Contact: Chamber of Commerce, Post Office Box 1967, Austin, Texas 78767; or Laguna Gloria Museum, 3809 West 35th Street, Austin, Texas 78703.

A great variety of art originals and crafts in atmosphere of gala outdoor fair.

★ 1094 ★
Beaumont - KALEIDOSCOPE. Mid May (2nd weekend), annual, 1 weekend, Beaumont Art Center. Contact: Mr. Whayne R. Moore, San Jacinto Building, Fourth Floor, Post Office Box 3150, Beaumont, Texas 77704.

Creative arts and crafts festival, international foods and auction held on the grounds of Beaumont Art Center.

★ 1095 ★
Blanco - BLANCO ART SHOW. Late August, annual. Contact: Chamber of Commerce, Box 625, Blanco, Texas 78606.

Showcases fascinating local arts and crafts, on display and for sale.

★ 1096 ★
Breckenridge - FINE ARTS FESTIVAL. April, annual, 3 days. Contact: Chamber of Commerce, 112 West Walker, Box 1466, Breckenridge, Texas 76024.

Offers local-regional arts and handicrafts - on display and for sale.

Arts and Crafts

TEXAS (Continued)

★ 1097 ★
Buchanan Dam - ARTS AND CRAFTS FESTIVAL.
October, annual, 9 days.   Contact: Chamber of
Commerce, Route 1, Box 34, Buchanan Dam, Texas
78609.

Held in conjunction with other Highland Lakes communities, a variety of arts and crafts are shown and
sold.

★ 1098 ★
Burnet - HIGHLAND LAKES ARTS AND CRAFTS
FESTIVAL.   October, annual, 2 weekends.   Contact: Chamber of Commerce, Box 27, Burnet, Texas
78611.

Festival held with neighboring towns to display and
sell the arts and crafts of area artists.

★ 1099 ★
Carrizo Springs - ARTS AND CRAFTS SHOW.   May,
annual, 1 day.   Contact: Chamber of Commerce,
307 North Fifth Street, Carrizo Springs, Texas
78834.

Show features exhibits and displays by area residents
in a variety of media.

★ 1100 ★
Corpus Christi - DEL MAR COLLEGE DRAWING
AND SMALL SCULPTURE SHOW.   May, annual,
Del Mar College. Contact: Chairman, Department
of Art, Del Mar College, Corpus Christi, Texas
78404.

A juried show open to all paintings and sculptures
of American artists.   Prizes and purchase awards
are given.

★ 1101 ★
Daingerfield - MORRIS COUNTY ARTS AND CRAFTS
SHOWS.   April and September, annual, 3 days.
Contact: Chamber of Commerce, 110 Coffey Street,
Daingerfield, Texas 75638.

Held on a farm at Rocky Branch Community in center
of the county about five miles north of Daingerfield,
arts and crafts are on display and for sale.

★ 1102 ★
El Paso - SUN CARNIVAL ART EXHIBITION.   December, annual, El Paso Museum of Art.   Contact: El

Paso Museum of Art, 1211 Montana Avenue, El
Paso, Texas   79902.

The art festival is open to United States citizens
residing in the United States or its territories.   Purchase awards are given;   there is a jury.

★ 1103 ★
Fort Worth - TARRANT COUNTY ART SHOW.
April, annual, almost all month.   Contact: Mr.
Bill R. Shelton, 700 Throckmorton Street, Fort Worth,
Texas 76102.

Outstanding exhibits of southwestern arts and crafts.

★ 1104 ★
Freeport - OUTDOOR ART FAIR.   Late May-early
June, annual.   Contact: State Department of High-
ways and Public Transportation, Travel and Information
Division, Post Office Box 5064, Austin, Texas 78763.

Lake Jackson hosts works by local and nationally
known artists.

★ 1105 ★
Hillsboro - BOND'S ALLEY ARTS AND CRAFTS
SHOW.   June, annual, 2nd Fridays and Saturdays,
Historic Bond's Alley.   Contact: J. A. Attebery,
Manager, Chamber of Commerce, Box 358, Hillsboro,
Texas 76645.

An open air show and sale for area artists, with other
events such as a jazz concert and book stall.   Begun
in 1965.

★ 1106 ★
Hondo - MEDINA MUSEUM DAY CELEBRATION.
May.   Contact: Frank Graff, Bandera Road, Hondo,
Texas 78861.

Arts and crafts fair with other exhibits as well.
Events also include a chili cookoff and an antique
auction.

★ 1107 ★
Houston - OLD MARKET SQUARE SIDEWALK ART
SHOW AND FESTIVAL.   May.   Contact: Conven-
tion and Visitors Council, 1006 Main, Houston,
Texas 77002.

Artists display in Houston's revitalized oldest district.

TEXAS (Continued)

★ 1108 ★
Houston - SPRING ARTS FESTIVAL.   March and
April, annual, 3-4 weeks, Houston Museum of Fine
Arts.   Contact: Mr. Louie Welch, Post Office Box
53600, Houston, Texas 77052.

A fine arts fair held at the museum with a showing
of various media.

★ 1109 ★
Ingram - APRIL ARTS FESTIVAL.   April, Hill
Country Arts Foundation.   Contact: Gene Ball.
Box 176, Ingram, Texas 78025.

Arts exhibit at the famed Foundation.

★ 1110 ★
Kemp - ARTS AND CRAFTS SHOW.   April, 2 days,
the main street.   Contact: Chamber of Commerce,
Box 276, Kemp, Texas 75143.

An arts and crafts exhibit along the town's main
street.

★ 1111 ★
Kerrville - ARTS AND CRAFTS FAIR.   Late May-
early June, annual, 3-4 days, Schreiner College
campus.   Contact: Texas Arts and Crafts Foundation,
Post Office Box 1589, Kerrville, Texas 78028; or
Chamber of Commerce, 1200 Sidney Baker Street,
Post Office Box 790, Kerrville, Texas 78028.

Over 200 artists and craftspeople offer a wide variety
of handcrafted creations and artworks.   Many are
demonstrated on the spot.   In addition there are
demonstrations of things from bygone days, including
a steam engine, a blacksmith, soap making, pioneer
cooking, and the entire process of making textiles from
the shearing of the sheep to the weaving.   Musical
events include an old time fiddlers' contest and the
Kerrville folk festival which includes folk-rock and
country-folk music by noted performers.

★ 1112 ★
Killeen - ARTS AND CRAFTS FESTIVAL.   April,
annual.   Contact: Chamber of Commerce, Box 75,
Killeen, Texas 76541.

A celebration of arts and crafts that has brought
thousands of visitors to the town.   Begun in 1965.

★ 1113 ★
Kingsland - BLUEBONNET TRAIL ARTS AND CRAFTS
SHOW.   March-April.   Contact: Mrs. Sandra Hall,
Route 1, Box 112-P, Kingsland, Texas 78639.

In connection with the famous spring flower trail,
the town presents an arts and crafts show and boat
races in the Texas Highland Lakes country.

★ 1114 ★
Longview - SPRING ARTS FESTIVAL.   April.   Con-
tact: Museum and Arts Center, 200 North Green,
Longview, Texas 75601.

A citation show for the East Texas Fine Arts Association, this event features a collectors show and a
photography show.

★ 1115 ★
Marble Falls - HIGHLAND LAKES BLUEBONNET
ART SHOW.   March-April.   Contact: Highland
Arts and Crafts Guild, Box 92, Marble Falls, Texas
78654.

Attractions include the display and sale of works by
Hill Country artists and magnificent wild flower
displays.

★ 1116 ★
Meridian - BOSQUE ARTS AND CRAFTS SHOW.
September.   Contact: Chamber of Commerce,
Meridian, Texas 76665.

An arts and crafts show with the added attractions of
a barbeque and street square dance.

★ 1117 ★
Port Arthur - ARTS AND CRAFTS FESTIVAL.   October.   Contact: Greater Port Arthur Chamber of
Commerce, Post Office Box 460, Port Arthur, Texas
77640.

A show and sale of a variety of arts and crafts.

★ 1118 ★
Salado - SALADO ART FAIR.   Early August, annual,
1 weekend.   Contact: Chamber of Commerce, Box
81, Salado, Texas 76571.

Year's feature event.   Thousands attend exhibits,
auction, and sales booths offering works of more than
150 artists.

Arts and Crafts

TEXAS (Continued)

★ 1119 ★
San Antonio - RIVER ART SHOW.   Early October,
annual, 1 weekend.   Contact: Chamber of Commerce, Post Office Box 1628, San Antonio, Texas
78296.

Lavish displays of arts and crafts by local and regional artists.

★ 1120 ★
San Antonio - STARVING ARTISTS SHOW.   March
(Easter), annual.   Contact: Chamber of Commerce,
Post Office Box 1628, San Antonio, Texas 78296.

Hundreds of artists display their work at La Villita
along the River Walk; nothing priced over $10.

UTAH

★ 1121 ★
Brigham City - PEACH DAYS ART FESTIVAL.
September, annual, 30 days, Brigham City Museum-
Gallery.   Contact: Utah Travel Council, Council
Hall, Capitol Hill, Salt Lake City, Utah 84114.

Features the work of Brigham City artists.   Associated with the Peach Days Celebration.

★ 1122 ★
Cedar City - THE WORKS.   Late May, annual, 4
days, Southern Utah State College.   Contact: "The
Works", Art Department, Southern Utah State College,
Cedar City, Utah 84720.

All intermountain artists and craftspeople are invited
to display, demonstrate, and sell their works.   The
show is juried, and prospective exhibitors must submit
four slides of their work with their application.   All
material is original work.   Begun in 1976.

★ 1123 ★
Logan - GREAT WEST FAIR.   Late July-early August,
annual, 9 days, Utah State University.   Contact:
The Festival of the American West, Old Main Building
116, UMC 14, Utah State University, Logan, Utah
84322.

Part of the Festival of the American West, the fair
assembles the top craftsmen of the Rocky Mountain
region to present a variety of western crafts, including those of both the American pioneers and the
Indians.   Visitors may buy and they may watch
demonstrations or ask questions of potters, weavers,

woodcarvers, sandpainters, quilters, crocheters, dyers,
etc.   The event takes place under outdoor canopies.
Begun in 1973.

★ 1124 ★
Park City - ARTS FESTIVAL.   Mid August, annual,
2 days, Main Street.   Contact: Park City Chamber
of Commerce, Post Office Box 758, Park City, Utah
84060.

Main Street is closed to all but foot traffic for the
event.   Individual artists are invited to display their
work amidst Park City's unique atmosphere in a spirit
of friendliness which has become a tradition.   The
acceptable categories of crafts are limited and have
included paintings, ceramics, sculpture, and stained
glass; for the current year the Chamber of Commerce
issues a list.   All artists must have their works judged
before they are accepted as exhibitors.   Begun in
1969.

VERMONT

★ 1125 ★
Montpelier - FALL FESTIVAL OF VERMONT CRAFTS.
Early October, annual.   Contact: Central Vermont
Chamber of Commerce, City Hall, Montpelier,
Vermont 05602.

A display and sale of a variety of local crafts.

★ 1126 ★
Mount Snow - CRAFTSPRODUCERS CRAFT FAIR AT
MOUNT SNOW.   Early August (1st week), annual,
Mount Snow Base Lodge.   Contact: Craftsproducers,
Incorporated, Box 92, Readsboro, Vermont 05350.

One hundred fine craftspeople sell and demonstrate
their works, both in and out of doors.   The juried
show includes such diverse media as clay, wood,
pottery, graphics, leather, fiber, pastel works,
weaving, jewelry, glass, metal, macrame, etc.   In
addition, there are invitational musical and theatrical
events.   Begun in 1974.

★ 1127 ★
Mount Snow - CRAFTPRODUCERS FOLIAGE FESTIVAL.
Mid October, annual, 3 days, Mount Snow Base
Lodge.   Contact: Craftsproducers, Incorporated,
Box 92, Readsboro, Vermont 05350.

An indoor juried show, limited to 50 invited craftspeople; any working craftsman or woman may apply.
Begun in 1976.

VIRGINIA

★ 1128 ★
Abingdon - SPRING SAMPLER.   Late May (Memorial Day weekend), annual, 4 days, Cave House.   Contact: Holston Mountain Arts and Crafts, 279 East Main Street, Abingdon, Virginia 24210.

Art and handcrafts are on display with demonstrations, music, and other events, all offered by the Holston Mountain Arts and Crafts Co-operative.   Begun around 1972.

★ 1129 ★
Accomac - ART AND CRAFT SHOW ON OLD COURTHOUSE GREEN.   Late April, annual, 2 days, Old Courthouse Green.   Contact: Eastern Shore of Virginia Chamber of Commerce, Accomac, Virginia 23301.

Sponsored by the Chamber of Commerce and the Art and Craft Guild of the Eastern Shore, the event features local artists working and displaying their work of duck carving, wood sculpture, paintings in acrylics, oil, and water colors, macrame, leather crafts and others.

★ 1130 ★
Accomac - ART AND CRAFT SHOW ON OLD COURTHOUSE GREEN.   Mid October, annual, 1 day, Old Courthouse Green.   Contact: Eastern Shore of Virginia Chamber of Commerce, Accomac, Virginia 23301.

Sponsored by the Chamber of Commerce and the Art and Craft Guild of the Eastern Shore, the event features local artists working and displaying their work of duck carving, wood sculpture, paintings in acrylic, oil, and water colors, macrame, leather crafts and others.

★ 1131 ★
Alexandria - JURIED SHOW.   September-October, annual, 1 month, Scope Gallery in the Torpedo Factory.   Contact: Isabel Lee, 8701 Clydesdale Road, Springfield, Virginia 22151.

Work by members of the Kiln Club of Washington is judged by a noted potter, and put on exhibit.   This is primarily a display, although works may also be for sale.   Begun around 1946.

★ 1132 ★
Big Stone Gap - LONESOME PINE ARTS AND CRAFTS FESTIVAL.   Early May, annual, 2 days, National

Guard Armory and June Toliver House.   Contact: June Toliver House, Big Stone Gap, Virginia 24219.

Area craftsmen demonstrate, exhibit, and sell their works.

★ 1133 ★
Bristol - ARTS AND CRAFTS FAIR.   Mid May (3rd weekend), annual, Reynolds Arcade Building.   Contact: Greater Bristol Area Chamber of Commerce, Reynolds Arcade Building, Post Office Box 1039, Bristol, Virginia 24201.

Includes amateur and professional works on display and for sale.

★ 1134 ★
Colonial Beach - BOARDWALK ART AND CRAFT FESTIVAL.   Mid August, annual, 2 days.   Contact: James D. Karn, Secretary, Colonial Beach Chamber of Commerce, Two Boundary Street, Colonial Beach, Virginia 22443.

An outdoor exhibit of art, ceramics, and handcrafts by people whose lives are closely tied to the famous Potomac River.   Exhibitors welcome.   Begun around 1967.

★ 1135 ★
Danville - ART SHOW.   April (1st week), annual, Ballou Park.   Contact: Chamber of Commerce, 635 Main Street, Post Office Box 1538, Danville, Virginia 24541.

Sponsored by a number of community organizations, this is an outdoor show with a variety of arts and crafts for sale.

★ 1136 ★
Fincastle - HISTORIC FINCASTLE ANNUAL ARTS AND CRAFTS FESTIVAL.   Mid August, annual, 2 days.   Contact: Mrs. Page Ware, Box 143, Fincastle, Virginia 24090.

All artists and craftspeople are invited to join in craft exhibits and displays and an art show.   Museums and old churches are open.   There are quilt and afghan shows, folk dance exhibitions, square dancing, and a country store to recall the past.   A barbeque chicken dinner is offered, and home-baked desserts are on sale.

★ 1137 ★
Gloucester - ART ON THE GREEN.   Late April,

Arts and Crafts

VIRGINIA (Continued)

annual, Court House Green. Contact: Travel Development Department, Virginia State Chamber of Commerce, 611 East Franklin Street, Richmond, Virginia 23219.

This outdoor show corresponds with the opening of Gloucester County Homes for Historic Garden Week in Virginia, and is sponsored by the Gloucester Chapter of the Virginia Museum of Fine Arts.

★ 1138 ★
Hampton - BUCKROE BEACH BOARDWALK ART SHOW. Mid August, annual, 3 days. Contact: Herbert Goldstein, 120 West Queen Street, Hampton, Virginia 23669.

An outstanding boardwalk display of paintings, graphics, ceramics, sculpture, and crafts. Begun around 1966.

★ 1139 ★
Lorton - GUNSTON HALL ARTS AND CRAFTS SHOW. Late July, annual, 2 days, Gunston Hall Plantation. Contact: Gunston Hall Plantation, Lorton, Virginia 22079.

Arts and crafts of the eighteenth, nineteenth and twentieth centuries are demonstrated by appropriately costumed craftsmen and women.

★ 1140 ★
Manassas - VIRGINIA CRAFTS COUNCIL CRAFT FAIR. Late April, annual, 3 days, National Guard Armory. Contact: Harriette Anderson, Virginia Crafts Council, 6449 West Langley Lane, McLean, Virginia 22101.

Craftsmen of Virginia display, demonstrate, and sell their crafts. Media include hand-built and thrown pottery, batik, leather, screen printing, kiln-fired glass, enameling, stichery, etc.

★ 1141 ★
New Market - NEW MARKET ARTS AND CRAFTS SHOW. September, annual, Henkel House. Contact: New Market Area Chamber of Commerce, New Market, Virginia 22844.

Artisans and artists demonstrate their skills and exhibit their work, some of which is for sale.

★ 1142 ★
Portsmouth - NATIONAL SEAWALL ART SHOW. May, annual. Contact: Recreation Department, One High Street, Portsmouth, Virginia 23704.

The event is open to all artists working in acrylic, crafts, graphics, oil, photography, sculpture, and watercolor. Awards include cash, prizes, purchase awards, and ribbons.

★ 1143 ★
Richmond - CITY-WIDE ART AND CRAFTS SHOW. Late March, annual, 1 week, the Carillon in Byrd Park. Contact: City of Richmond Department of Recreation and Parks, 900 East Broad Street, Richmond, Virginia 23219.

Sponsored by the Department of Recreation, this juried show features work done by members of the many adult arts and crafts classes and groups throughout Richmond. Begun around 1947.

★ 1144 ★
Richmond - FALL CRAFT FAIR. Mid October (2nd weekend), annual, 2 days, Hand Work-Shop gardens. Contact: Hand Work-Shop, 316 North 24th Street, Richmond, Virginia 23223.

Virginia and Maryland craftsmen sell and demonstrate their work, including weaving, pottery, raku firing, metal sculpture, enameling, stained glass, and jewelry. Approximately 40 craftpeople participate. Begun around 1964.

★ 1145 ★
Richmond - VIRGINIA ARTISTS. May-June, biennial (odd years), Virginia Museum of Fine Arts. Contact: Virginia Museum of Fine Arts, Boulevard and Grove Avenues, Richmond, Virginia 23221.

The juried show includes collages, drawings, graphics, paintings, sculptures and watercolors. Awards are distributed. Residents of Virginia are eligible.

★ 1146 ★
Richmond - VIRGINIA CRAFTSMEN. March-April, biennial (even years), Virginia Museum for Fine Arts. Contact: Virginia Museum of Fine Arts, Boulevard and Grove Avenues, Richmond, Virginia 23221.

Natives and residents of Virginia (and former residents of at least five years) exhibit original works in ceramics, metal, textiles, leather and wood. The show is juried and awards are distributed.

VIRGINIA (Continued)

★ 1147 ★
Richmond - VIRGINIA DESIGNERS. January-February, biennial, Virginia Museum of Fine Arts. Contact: Virginia Museum of Fine Arts, Boulevard and Grove Avenues, Richmond, Virginia 23221.

This juried exhibition is open to natives and residents of Virginia or former residents who lived in the state at least five years. Entries include brochures, cataloges, folders, posters, programs, newspaper and magazine advertisements, and other examples of designing.

★ 1148 ★
Richmond - VIRGINIA PHOTOGRAPHERS. October-November, biennial, Virginia Museum of Fine Arts. Contact: Virginia Museum of Fine Arts, Boulevard and Grove Avenues, Richmond, Virginia 23221.

A display of monochromes, and color prints and transparencies created by natives and residents or former residents (for at least five years) of Virginia. The show is juried and awards are given.

★ 1149 ★
Staunton - SHENANDOAH VALLEY CRAFT SHOW. Late August, annual, 1-2 days. Contact: Staunton-Augusta County Chamber of Commerce, Post Office Box 389, Staunton, Virginia 24401.

A juried show with demonstrations and exhibits of Appalchian and surrounding craftspeople. Items for sale include thrown pottery, hand decorated jewelry, silver and gold jewelry, lapidary, wood carvings, tooled leather, wrought iron, creative stichery and other. Begun in 1973.

★ 1150 ★
Virginia Beach - VIRGINIA BEACH BOARDWALK ART SHOW. Late June, annual, 5 days. Contact: Virginia Beach Boardwalk Art Show, Box 913, 5306 Atlantic Avenue, Virginia Beach, Virginia 23451.

An outdoor show for all media. Monetary awards are given. Visitors stroll the boardwalk in Virginia Beach and view the arts and crafts on display and for sale.

★ 1151 ★
Warm Springs - CRAFT SHOW. Late September, annual, 1 day, Gristmill Square. Contact: Gristmill Square, Warm Springs, Virginia 24484.

The lovely courtyard forms a backdrop for an outdoor exhibit of arts and crafts by area artists and crafts people.

★ 1152 ★
Warm Springs - OUTDOOR ART SHOW. Mid-late October, annual, 1 day, Gristmill Square. Contact: Gristmill Square, Warm Springs, Virginia 24482.

The show presents the talents of Virginia and West Virginia artists during the height of the fall foliage season.

★ 1153 ★
Winchester - APPLE HARVEST ARTS AND CRAFTS FESTIVAL. Late September, annual, 2 days, Winchester Recreation Park. Contact: Winchester Chamber of Commerce, 29 South Cameron Street, Box 667, Winchester, Virginia 22601.

Artists and craftspeople from the entire East Coast present a cross section of high quality native crafts. Concerts of bluegrass music are presented. Fresh local apples are on sale in the park. Sponsored by the Winchester Rotary Club. Begun in 1975.

WASHINGTON

★ 1154 ★
Anacortes - ARTS AND CRAFTS FESTIVAL. August (1st weekend), annual, 2 days, downtown Anacortes. Contact: Chairman, Anacortes Arts and Crafts Festival, Post Office Box 6, Anacortes, Washington 98221.

A sidewalk arts and crafts festival with professional and amateur competition. Artists demonstrate and sell their works. Begun around 1963.

★ 1155 ★
Bellevue - BELLEVUE VILLAGE MALL FESTIVAL. June (2nd weekend), annual, 4 days. Contact: Mrs. Melvin Love, 10431 South East 23rd. Bellevue, Washington 98004.

Leading artists and craftsmen of the Pacific Northwest display their works at this festival. Begun around 1970.

★ 1156 ★
Bellevue - PACIFIC NORTHWEST ARTS AND CRAFTS FAIR. July (last full weekend), annual, 3 days. Contact: Mrs. R. M. Connell, 5648 118th Southeast,

Arts and Crafts

WASHINGTON (Continued)

Bellevue, Washington 98006.

Reputed to be the largest outdoor arts and crafts fair in the United States, more than 800 artists and crafts-people are represented. Artist in action, craft booths, sculpture, film festival, prints and drawings and a junior show make up the events. Begun around 1951.

★ 1157 ★
Longview - LOWER COLUMBIA ARTS AND CRAFTS FESTIVAL. June (3rd weekend), annual, 3 days, Lower Columbia College. Contact: R. Henderson, Three Treetop Road, Longview, Washington 98632.

The program includes the judging of adult and children's art exhibits. Oregon and Washington artists offer their works for sale. Other entertainment is provided by strolling musicians, singing groups, puppet shows, and craft booths. Begun around 1971.

★ 1158 ★
Ocean City and Ocean Shores - NORTH BEACH ART FESTIVAL. August (2nd weekend), annual, Hogan's Junction. Contact: Spindrift Arts, Ocean City, Washington 98569.

Open air festival where 100 local artists compete for prize money in art, crafts, sculpture and wood carving. Works are both displayed and sold. Begun around 1972.

★ 1159 ★
Renton - RENTON ART SHOW. August (1st weekend), annual, Renton Shopping Center. Contact: Mrs. Rudolph Cumberbatch, 11607 137th Avenue, Southeast, Renton, Washington 98055.

A juried show of paintings and an invitational show of crafts. Begun around 1963.

★ 1160 ★
Seattle - ART FAIR. May, annual, 1 week, Odegaard Undergraduate Library and Student Union Building, University of Washington. Contact: Art Fair Coordinator, ASUW, University of Washington, FK-10, Seattle, Washington 98195.

The variety of activities center around a core of graphic and performing arts exhibits and competitions. Other imaginative events, varying from year to year, have included belly dancing, handwriting analysis, a

geodesic dome, astrology, a kite flying contest, etc. Begun in 1972.

★ 1161 ★
Wapato - SPEELYI-MI INDIAN ARTS AND CRAFTS CLUB TRADE FAIR. March (2nd weekend), annual. Contact: Portland Area Office Bureau of Indian Affairs, U.S. Department of the Interior, 1425 Irving Street, Northeast, Box 3785, Portland, Oregon 97208.

Arts and crafts exhibitions and dancing exhibitions are included in the events. Begun around 1969.

WEST VIRGINIA

★ 1162 ★
Beckley - APPALACHIAN ARTS AND CRAFTS FESTIVAL. August (3rd weekend), annual, 3 days, Raleigh County Armory-Civic Center. Contact: Beckley-Raleigh County Chamber of Commerce, Box 1798, 106 McCreery Street, Beckley, West Virginia 25801.

The festival honors the traditional Appalachian Mountain arts and crafts. The largest art show in the state, it includes exhibits by many of the area's finest artists working in leather, quilting, pottery, crocheting, coal craft, and other media. The quilt show offers some of the most beautiful and artistic handmade articles in existence. Musical entertainment, continuing throughout the entire festival, features such instruments as banjos, mandolins and the traditional fiddle. Begun around 1964.

★ 1163 ★
Bluefield - ARTS AND CRAFTS FESTIVAL. June (1st weekend), annual, 2 days, East River Mountain Craft Shop, Skyland. Contact: Bob Connor, Skyland, Incorporated, Post Office Box 1178, Bluefield, West Virginia 24701; or West Virginia Department of Commerce, Arts and Crafts Division, Building 6, 1900 Washington Street East, Charleston, West Virginia 25305.

The event consist of demonstrating craftspeople such as potters, blacksmiths, glass "weavers", basket makers and so forth, as well as a wide selection of original art in different media, including metal sculpture. The craftspeople set up outside, on the balcony, in the lobby and other places around the shop. Highland folkdancers perform Scottish dances.

★ 1164 ★
Bluefield - ARTS AND CRAFTS FESTIVAL. October (2nd weekend), annual, 2 days, East River Mountain

WEST VIRGINIA (Continued)

Craft Shop, Skyland. Contact: Bob Connor, Skyland, Incorporated, Post Office Box 1178, Bluefield, West Virginia 24701.

The event consists of demonstrating craftspeople such as potters, blacksmiths, glass "weavers", basket makers, and so forth, as well as a wide selection of original art in different media, including metal sculpture. The craftspeople set up outside, on the balcony, in the lobby, and other places around the shop. Highland folk dancers perform Scottish dances.

★ 1165 ★
Charleston - CAPITAL CITY ART AND CRAFT FESTIVAL. Mid November, 3 days. Contact: Bill Lanyi, 3820 North Crede Drive, Charleston, West Virginia 25304; or West Virginia Department of Commerce, Arts and Crafts Division, Building 6, 1900 Washington Street East, Charleston, West Virginia 25305.

A West Virginia craft event with demonstrations, displays, and sales.

★ 1166 ★
Charleston - RHODODENDRON OUTDOOR ART AND CRAFTS FESTIVAL. May (3rd Sunday), annual, 1 day, State Capitol Grounds. Contact: Mrs. Eleanor Chandler, Director, 3804 Noyes Avenue, Southeast, Charleston, West Virginia 25304.

Original art works, designed and executed by the exhibitor, in all media, including painting, drawing, prints, sculpture, crafts, and photography, are exhibited and judged. Prizes and purchase awards are given in a number of categories including sculpture, primitive, oil realism and abstract, etc. A special award is given for a work pertaining especially to West Virginia. Begun in 1967.

★ 1167 ★
Chloe - UPPER WEST FORK ART AND CRAFT FAIR. Late July-early August, 3 days. Contact: Upper West Fork, Box 26, Chloe, West Virginia; or West Virginia Department of Commerce, Arts and Crafts Division, Building 6, 1900 Washington Street East, Charleston, West Virginia 25305.

Arts and crafts of the mountain heritage displayed and for sale.

★ 1168 ★
Fairmont - MONONGAHELA ART AND CRAFT FAIR.

Late October, 2 days. Contact: Mrs. Wallace Peirce, 108 Oakwood Estates, Winfield, West Virginia 25560; or West Virginia Department of Commerce, Arts and Crafts Division, Building 6, 1900 Washington Street East, Charleston, West Virginia 25305.

Arts and crafts demonstrated, displayed and for sale.

★ 1169 ★
Fairmont - NORTH CENTRAL WEST VIRGINIA ART AND CRAFT FESTIVAL. Late May, 2 days, National Guard Armory. Contact: Henry Stern, 310 Tenth Street, Fairmont, West Virginia 26554; or West Virginia Department of Commerce, Arts and Crafts Division, Building 6, 1900 Washington Street East, Charleston, West Virginia 25305.

A wide array of arts and crafts on display and for sale.

★ 1170 ★
Gassaway - BRAXTON COUNTY ART AND CRAFT SHOW. April, annual, 2 days, Braxton County Armory. Contact: Mrs. George Hoylman, 940 Riverside Drive, Gassaway, West Virginia 26624; or West Virginia Department of Commerce, Arts and Crafts Division, Building 6, 1900 Washington Street East, Charleston, West Virginia 25305.

Arts and crafts of local heritage. Many are demonstrated, all are on display.

★ 1171 ★
Grantsville - WOOD FESTIVAL. Early June, annual, 3 days, Grantsville Courthouse Square. Contact: Clifford Byers, Post Office Box 313, Grantsville, West Virginia 26147.

Exhibits and sales of wood furniture, carvings, whittling, handicrafts, logs and antiques.

★ 1172 ★
Harpers Ferry - HARPERS FERRY ART FESTIVAL. Mid June, annual, 2 days. Contact: West Virginia Department of Commerce, Arts and Crafts Division, Building 6, 1900 Washington Street East, Charleston, West Virginia 25305.

Arts and crafts of this mountain community and the environs are demonstrated, displayed, and for sale.

★ 1173 ★
Harpers Ferry - MOUNTAIN HERITAGE ARTS AND

Arts and Crafts

CRAFTS FESTIVAL. Mid June, annual, 3 days, Harpers Ferry Cavern grounds. Contact: Director of Public Relations, West Virginia Arts and Crafts Festival, Box 430, Charles Town, West Virginia 25414; or Jefferson County Chamber of Commerce, Post Office Box 430, Charles Town, West Virginia 25414.

Quality arts and crafts demonstrated, displayed and for sale.

★ 1174 ★
Harpers Ferry - MOUNTAIN HERITAGE ARTS AND CRAFTS FESTIVAL. Mid October, 4 days. Contact: Jefferson County Chamber of Commerce, Post Office Box 430, Charles Town, West Virginia 25414; or West Virginia Department of Commerce, Arts and Crafts Division, Building 6, 1900 Washington Street East, Charleston, West Virginia 25305.

A demonstration, show, and sale of a variety of arts and crafts, particularly those indigenous to the mountain people.

★ 1175 ★
Lewisburg - GREENBRIER VALLEY ARTISANS/ CRAFTSMENS FAIR. Early December, 3 days. Contact: West Virginia Department of Commerce, Arts and Crafts Division, Building 6, 1900 Washington Street East, Charleston, West Virginia 25305.

A West Virginia craft event featuring demonstrations, displays, and sales of quality arts and crafts.

★ 1176 ★
Milton - MILTON GARDEN CLUB ART AND CRAFT SHOW. Early October, 2 days. Contact: Mrs. Jonathan Y. Lowe, 1066 Hillview Drive, Milton, West Virginia 25541; or West Virginia Department of Commerce, Arts and Crafts Division, Building 6, 1900 Washington Street East, Charleston, West Virginia 25305.

A quality show of arts and crafts.

★ 1177 ★
Morgantown - MORGANTOWN COURT HOUSE ART/ CRAFT SHOW. Late June, annual, Court House Square. Contact: Mrs. Jan Shafer, Post Office Box 658, Morgantown, West Virginia 26505; or West Virginia Department of Commerce, Arts and Crafts Division, Building 6, 1900 Washington Street East, Charleston, West Virginia 25305.

Arts and crafts demonstrated, displayed and for sale at Court House Square.

★ 1178 ★
Morgantown - MOUNTAINEER ART AND CRAFT FESTIVAL. Mid November, West Virginia University. Contact: West Virginia Department of Commerce, Arts and Crafts Division, Building 6, 1900 Washington Street East, Charleston, West Virginia 25305.

A part of Morgantown's Mountaineer Week, this is a juried event with displays, demonstrations, and sales.

★ 1179 ★
Mullens - MULLENS ART AND CRAFT FESTIVAL. Mid November, 3 days. Contact: Mrs. Gerald W. Snyder, 627 Church Street, Mullens, West Virginia 25882; or West Virginia Department of Commerce, Arts and Crafts Division, Building 6, 1900 Washington Street East, Charleston, West Virginia 25305.

Quality arts and crafts demonstrated, displayed, and for sale.

★ 1180 ★
North Charleston - FAIR SPRINGTIME CELEBRATION OF ARTS AND CRAFTS. Late April-early May, 3 days. Contact: Arts and Crafts Director, North Charleston Community Center, 2009 Seventh Avenue, Charleston, West Virginia 25330.

A display and sale of quality arts and crafts.

★ 1181 ★
Parkersburg - HARVEST MOON FESTIVAL OF ARTS AND CRAFTS. Mid September, 2 days. Contact: Fine Arts Council, Dr. Gary Ogilvie, President, City Park, Parkersburg, West Virginia 26101; or West Virginia Department of Commerce, Arts and Crafts Division, Building 6, 1900 Washington Street East, Charleston, West Virginia 25305.

Quality arts and crafts are demonstrated and displayed at this festival which also celebrates the fall season.

★ 1182 ★
Petersburg - POTOMAC HIGHLANDS CRAFTS SHOW. Early April, 2 days. Contact: Laura Dasher, 23 1/2 Virginia Avenue, Petersburg, West Virginia 26847.

A quality show of a variety of crafts.

WEST VIRGINIA (Continued)

★ 1183 ★
Philippi – ALDERSON-BROADDUS COLLEGE ART/
CRAFT FESTIVAL.   Early October, 1 day, Alderson-
Broaddus College.   Contact: Carl Hatfield, Director,
Student Activities, A-B College, Box 1397, Philippi,
West Virginia 26416;   or West Virginia Department
of Commerce, Arts and Crafts Division, Building 6,
1900 Washington Street, East, Charleston, West
Virginia 25305.

Quality arts and crafts on display and for sale.

★ 1184 ★
Princeton – QUILT FAIR.   Late September, 2 days,
Brushfork Armory.   Contact: Margaret M. Meador,
Home Demonstration, Post Office Box 591, Prince-
ton, West Virginia 24740;   or West Virginia Depart-
ment of Commerce, Arts and Crafts Division, Building
6, 1900 Washington Street East, Charleston, West
Virginia 25305.

A show and sale of beautiful handmade quilts.

★ 1185 ★
Ripley – CRAFTS CENTER WORKSHOPS.   Late
April-mid May;   early August, annual, 4 weeks,
Cedar Lakes.   Contact: Crafts Center, Cedar
Lakes Conference Center, Ripley, West Virginia
25271.

Spring and summer crafts workshops, some oriented to
help the craftsperson perfect quality and design, others
to introduce the beginner to the fundamental skills.
The workshops last for a weekend or a week for an
in-depth experience.   Included are rug braiding,
beginning basketry, frame loom weaving, the elements
of design, wood sculpture, spinning, folk art design
painting and more.   Begun in 1975.

★ 1186 ★
Ripley – MOUNTAIN STATE ART AND CRAFT FAIR.
July (weekend of the 4th), annual, 5 days, Cedar
Lakes.   Contact: Mountain State Art and Craft
Fair, Cedar Lakes Conference Center, Ripley, West
Virginia 25271.

In celebration of the hill country heritage, the fair
presents the traditional foods, music and crafts.
Nearly 200 arts and crafts people demonstrate and
display their work.   Fiddles, guitars, banjo, and
dulcimers are used to perform the mountain music.
Heritage foods such as kettle-cooked apple butter,
sassafras tea, buckwheat cakes and more are available.
Educational lectures and square dancing complete the
events.

★ 1187 ★
Salem – SALEM COLLEGE HERITAGE ARTS FESTIVAL.
Late April, annual, 3 days.   Contact: Heritage
Arts Festival Committee, c/o Salem College, Salem,
West Virginia 26426.

Arts and crafts of this local heritage are on display
and for sale.

★ 1188 ★
Weirton – WEIRTON ART AND CRAFT FESTIVAL.
Early November, 1 day.   Contact: Mrs. Robert
Hesse, General Chairman, 3804 Collins Way, Weirton,
West Virginia 26062;   or West Virginia Department
of Commerce, Arts and Crafts Division, Building 6,
1900 Washington Street East, Charleston, West
Virginia 25305.

Arts and crafts displayed and for sale.

★ 1189 ★
Wheeling – OGLEBAY INSTITUTE ART AND CRAFT
FAIR.   June–July, annual, 2 days, The White
Palace, Wheeling Park.   Contact: Mary E. Fisher,
Director, Creative Arts Department, 316 Washington
Avenue, Wheeling, West Virginia 26003.

Begun as a hobby show, the event has evolved into
an opportunity for the display, demonstration and
sale of original art and crafts work by local, regional
and national artists and craftsmen.   Sponsored by the
Oglebay Institute.   Begun in 1950.

★ 1190 ★
Winfield – WINFIELD ART AND CRAFT FESTIVAL.
Late October, 2-3 days.   Contact: Mrs. Wallace
Peirce, 108 Oakwood Estates, Winfield, West
Virginia 25560;   or West Virginia Department of
Commerce, Arts and Crafts Division, Building 6,
1900 Washington Street East, Charleston, West
Virginia 25305.

Quality arts and crafts on display and for sale.

WISCONSIN

★ 1191 ★
Madison – CLAY-O-RAMA CERAMIC SHOW.   Mid-
late October, annual, 2 days, Dane County Exposition
Center.   Contact: Chamber of Commerce, 615 East
Washington Avenue, Madison, Wisconsin 53703.

A show and sale of a variety of hand-crafted ceramics.
Begun around 1970.

Arts and Crafts

★ 1192 ★
Milwaukee - LAKEFRONT FESTIVAL OF ARTS.
Late June, annual, 3 days, Lakefront adjacent to
the Milwaukee Art Center.   Contact: Barbara
Coffman, Lakefront Festival Coordinator, Milwaukee
Art Center, 750 North Lincoln Drive, Milwaukee,
Wisconsin 53202.

A festival featuring the original work of American
artists.   Outstanding artists from previous shows are
invited to attend, others may submit slides for selection by jury.   The displaying artists work in many
media, including painting, sculpture, graphics, photography and crafts in fibers, clay and metal.   All
works are for sale.   There are prizes awarded, with
a special competition for the design of the awards to
be given for that year.   Many artists demonstrate,
and the public has the opportunity to learn different
art forms.   Entertainment includes strolling musicians,
dance troupes, improvisational actors, mimists, etc.
Begun around 1963.

★ 1193 ★
Milwaukee - WINTER ART FAIR.   Early November,
3 days, Brookfield Shopping Center.   Contact:
Convention and Visitors Bureau, 828 North Broadway,
Milwaukee, Wisconsin 53202.

An arts and crafts show at the shopping center.

★ 1194 ★
Milwaukee - WISCONSIN PAINTERS AND
SCULPTORS.   March-April, biennial (odd years).
Contact: Wisconsin Exhibitions, Milwaukee Art
Center, 750 North Lincoln Memorial Drive, Milwaukee,
Wisconsin 53202.

A juried show for Wisconsin artists at least 21 years
of age.   Media include oil, pastel, and watercolor
paintings (no drawings or prints), and sculpture.

★ 1195 ★
Stevens Point - WISCONSIN ANNUAL.   September
or October (Fall), annual.   Contact: Wisconsin
Annual, c/o Mrs. James Delzell, Stevens Point,
Wisconsin 54481.

For Wisconsin residents;   awards are given in various
categories.

★ 1196 ★
Whitewater - FESTIVAL OF THE ARTS.   October,
annual.   Contact: Festival of the Arts, University

of Wisconsin, College of the Arts, Whitewater,
Wisconsin 53545.

Both professionals and students display their creations
in various media.

CANADA - BRITISH COLUMBIA

★ 1197 ★
Langley - CHILDREN AND THE ARTS.   Early May-
late June, annual, 7 weeks, Langley Mall.   Con-
tact: The Department of Recreation and Travel
Industry, 1019 Wharf Street, Victoria, British Columbia
V8W 2Z2, Canada.

All of the schools in the district participate in a
display of arts and crafts.

CANADA - NEW BRUNSWICK

★ 1198 ★
Mactaquac - MACTAQUAC HANDCRAFT FESTIVAL.
Early September, 2 days.   Contact: Special Events
Co-ordinator, Tourism New Brunswick, Post Office
Box 12345, Fredericton, New Brunswick, Canada.

A demonstration, display, and sale of handcrafted
items.

★ 1199 ★
Oromocto - OROMOCTO ARTS AND CRAFTS
FESTIVAL.   Late May, 1 day.   Contact: Special
Events Co-ordinator, Tourism New Brunswick, Post
Office Box 12345, Fredericton, New Brunswick,
Canada.

A show and sale of quality arts and crafts.

★ 1200 ★
Saint John - FUNDY CRAFT FESTIVAL.   Late
July-early August, annual, 2 days, Rockwood Park.
Contact: Special Events Co-ordinator, Tourism New
Brunswick, Post Office Box 12345, Fredericton, New
Brunswick, Canada.

An outdoor show and sale of quality crafts.

CANADA - NOVA SCOTIA

★ 1201 ★
Bridgetown - ARTISAN' (year).   Late May, 2 days.
Contact: Nova Scotia Department of Tourism,
Travel Division, Post Office Box 130, Halifax, Nova
Scotia B3J 2M7, Canada.

CANADA - NOVA SCOTIA (Continued)

Arts and crafts festival, featuring handicrafts demonstrations, displays and sales.

★ 1202 ★
Bridgetown - WESTERN NOVA SCOTIA HANDCRAFT DEMONSTRATION. Late July, 2 days. Contact: Nova Scotia Department of Tourism, Travel Division, Post Office Box 130, Halifax, Nova Scotia B3J 2M7, Canada.

The crafts that are demonstrated at this event include weaving, woodcarving, wood turning, silver jewelry, rug-hooking, pottery, leather work, candle making and batik. There are special attractions for children as well as a nursery service.

★ 1203 ★
Bridgewater - SPRING FLING FAIR. Early June, 1 day. Contact: Nova Scotia Department of Tourism, Division of Travel, Post Office Box 130, Halifax, Nova Scotia B3J 2M7, Canada.

Handicrafts festival featuring art displays, exhibits, sales and auctions, in addition to boutiques and children's games.

CANADA - ONTARIO

★ 1204 ★
Toronto - ORT FESTIVAL OF CRAFTS. Early March, 2 days, Four Seasons Sheraton Hotel. Contact: Convention and Tourist Bureau of Metropolitan Toronto, 85 Richmond Street, West, Suite 300, Toronto, Ontario M5H 1H9, Canada.

Macrame wall hangings, jewelry, pottery, hand-blown glass, and other hand crafts are on display and for sale.

★ 1205 ★
Windsor - SOUTHWEST 33. February, annual, Art Gallery of Windsor. Contact: Art Gallery of Windsor, Willistead Park, Windsor 15, Ontario, Canada.

A juried, all media show for artists of the southwestern Ontario region. Prizes are awarded.

Book Fairs
See: THE ARTS

Community
See also: STATE FAIRS

ALABAMA

★ 1206 ★
Alexander City - WIND CREEK ROCK SWAP. June, annual, 4 days, Wind Creek State Park on Lake Martin. Contact: Franky Tyson, Route 3, Alexander City, Alabama 35010.

Interested persons swap or sell gems, minerals, fossils, specimens, and lapidary equipment. Co-sponsored by the Alabama Mineral and Lapidary Society, Incorporated and Lake Martin Rock and Gem Club. Begun around 1963.

★ 1207 ★
Birmingham - COUNTRY FAIR. September, 1 day, Arlington Antebellum Home. Contact: Bureau of Publicity, State of Alabama, Montgomery, Alabama 36104.

Flea market, outdoor art show, country store, emporium, attic treasures and white elephant sales. Sponsored by the Arlington Historical Association.

★ 1208 ★
Decatur - SPIRIT OF AMERICA FESTIVAL. July (4th), annual, 1 day, Point Mallard Park. Contact: Frank J. Shepherd, Executive Director, Point Mallard Park, Post Office Box 1865, Decatur, Alabama 35601.

Set in eighteenth century and features anvil shoots, fireworks, pickin' & singin', watermelon slicings and outdoor barbeque. Also, rock'n roll bands, barbershop harmony, greased pole contests, exhibits, concerts, and statewide Miss Independence beauty pageant.

★ 1209 ★
Mobile - GREATER GULF STATE FAIR. Mid October, annual, Hartwell Field. Contact: Mobile Area Chamber of Commerce, Post Office Box 2187, Mobile, Alabama 36601.

Exhibits include commercial, art, hobby, cultural, military, professional, and agricultural. Grandstand show and motorized midway.

Community

ALABAMA (Continued)

★ 1210 ★
Mobile Bay Area - MARDI GRAS.   March (prior
to Ash Wednesday), annual, 10 days.   Contact:
Mobile Area Chamber of Commerce, Post Office
Box 2187, Mobile, Alabama 36601.

Festival originated in Mobile 200 years ago (before
New Orleans festival).   Bands, floats, gaily-colored
costumes, minstrels, mummers, marching units, parades
and balls, and Krew de Bienville Ball for visitors.
Mardi Gras day, Tuesday before Ash Wednesday–all
day and night.

★ 1211 ★
Scottsboro - FIRST MONDAY.   All year, the first
Monday of each month, Courthouse Square.   Con-
tact: Bureau of Publicity, State of Alabama,
Montgomery, Alabama 36104.

Natives from surrounding mountains come down for a
barter day: dogs, antiques and junk are swapped
and sold.   Banjo playing.

★ 1212 ★
Stockton - LIVE OAKS RIVERFRONT MARKET AND
COUNTY FAIR.   April, 3 days.   Contact: Stockton Chamber of Commerce, Stockton, Alabama
36579.

Festival and fair with many good things on display
and for sale.   Entertainment.

★ 1213 ★
Tuscaloosa - HERITAGE CELEBRATION
(TUSCALOOSA HERITAGE WEEK).   Early-mid April,
2 weeks, Tuscaloosa and the University of Alabama.
Contact: Tuscaloosa County Preservation Society,
Post Office Box 3155, Tuscaloosa, Alabama 35401.

Parade, art show, pilgrimage of homes, antiques
show, theater, sports events, and flower show, all
celebrating the history of the city.

ALASKA

★ 1214 ★
Soldotna - SOLDOTNA DAYS.   July, annual, 3
days.   Contact: Alaska Division of Tourism, Pouch
E, Juneau, Alaska 99801.

Rodeo with Brahman bulls, hoedown western dance,
Bowhunter's Rendezvous, motorcycle races, fly-in
breakfast and air show, King and Queen contest for

tourists, arts and crafts show, etc.   Begun around
1963.

ARIZONA

★ 1215 ★
Scottsdale - PARADA DEL SOL AND RODEO.
Late January-early February, annual, 5 days.   Con-
tact: Scottsdale Chamber of Commerce, Post Office
Box 129, Scottsdale, Arizona 85252.

A sun worshipping event with horsemanship exhibitions,
parties, and parades.

ARKANSAS

★ 1216 ★
Harrison - DOGPATCH DAYS.   May.   Contact:
Chamber of Commerce, Harrison, Arkansas 72601;
or Department of Parks and Tourism, 149 State
Capitol, Little Rock, Arkansas 72201.

Special events and fun for local folk and visitors.

★ 1217 ★
Heber Springs - OZARK FRONTIER TRAIL FESTIVAL
AND CRAFT SHOW.   Mid October-early November,
annual, 3 days.   Contact: Chamber of Commerce,
Heber Springs, Arkansas 72543; or Department of
Parks and Tourism, 149 State Capitol, Little Rock,
Arkansas 72201.

Begins with an antique show and the presentation of
a play.   A craft show opens; musical program includes a bagpiper group.

CALIFORNIA

★ 1218 ★
Alpine - VIEJAS DAYS.   Mid September, 8 days,
McCall's Ranch.   Contact: Information Officer,
State of California Department of Commerce, 1400
Tenth Street, Sacramento, California 95814.

A parade, horse show, barbeque, and street dance
highlight this community celebration.   Begun around
1962.

★ 1219 ★
Anaheim - HALLOWEEN FESTIVAL AND PARADE.
Late October-early November, annual, 3 days.
Contact: Chamber of Commerce, Post Office Box
969, 130 South Lemon Street, Anaheim, California
92805.

CALIFORNIA (Continued)

Events include masquerades, games, costume judging, kids parade, kids day at a recreation amusement park, a show window decorating contest, annual pumpkin bowl football game, teen dance, arts and crafts fair, and ice melting contest. Begun around 1924.

★ 1220 ★
Angels Camp - CALEVERAS COUNTY FAIR AND JUMPING FROG JUBILEE. Mid May, annual, 4 days. Contact: Chamber of Commerce, Angels Camp, California 95222.

Features the internationally renowned frog jumping contest inspired by the Mark Twain tale. Communities and individuals from throughout the world groom their finest frogs for the honor of competing in this event. There is also a general fair and exhibits.

★ 1221 ★
Apple Valley - APPLE VALLEY POW WOW DAYS. Late July, 3 days, Community Center. Contact: Southern California Visitors Council, 705 West Seventh Street, Los Angeles, California 90017.

Events include beard growing, beautiful legs and knobby knees contests for men, Indian dances and a barbeque.

★ 1222 ★
Azusa - GOLDEN DAYS. Early October, annual, 9 days. Contact: Southern California Visitors Council, 705 West Seventh Street, Los Angeles, California 90017.

Features a variety of activities, including a parade, crafts show, street dances, and a pancake breakfast. There are competitions in beard growing, arm wrestling and a golf tournament.

★ 1223 ★
Bakersfield - MUSEUM HERITAGE DAYS. Late April, 2 days, Kern County Museum and Pioneer Village. Contact: Kern County Museum, 3801 Chester Avenue, Bakersfield, California 93301.

A parade, mock trials, can-can dancing, flea market, white elephant sale, epitaph contest, folk dancing, fashion show, and a Model A car show.

★ 1224 ★
Barstow - CALICO DAYS. Mid October, annual, 3 days, Calico Ghost Town. Contact: California Chamber of Commerce, 455 Capitol Mall, Sacramento, California 95814.

1880 Boom Town celebration with gunfight skits, Poker Trail ride, old prospectors' burro run, western parade, and square dancing. Begun around 1968.

★ 1225 ★
Big Bear Lake - OLD MINER'S DAYS. Early-mid August, 5 days - 1 week. Contact: Chamber of Commerce, Box 2860, Big Bear Lake, California 92315.

Burro derby, parade, beard growing contest, quick draw competition, and entertainment highlight this celebration of early days in Big Bear Lake.

★ 1226 ★
Bishop - HOMECOMING AND LABOR DAY CELEBRATION. Early September, annual, 4 days. Contact: Southern California Visitors Council, 705 West Seventh Street, Los Angeles, California 90017.

Special events include a street dance, rodeo, and Old Timer's Picnic. Begun around 1934.

★ 1227 ★
Bishop - HUCK FINN RIVER DAY FESTIVAL. Mid August, 1 day, Owens River. Contact: Southern California Visitors Council, 705 West Seventh Street, Los Angeles, California 90017.

Events include inner tube race on four and a half mile course, tube decoration contest, barbeque, and horse shoe pitching contest.

★ 1228 ★
Bishop - MULE DAYS CELEBRATION. Late May, annual, 3 days, Tri County Fairgrounds. Contact: Southern California Visitors Council, 705 West Seventh Street, Los Angeles, California 90017; or Bishop (Crowley Lake), Route 3, Box 189 ZC, Bishop, California 93514.

Area is "Mule Capitol of the World". Events include mule shows and sale, mule shoeing contest, and naming of "World Champion Mule". There is also a dance and an animal parade. Begun around 1970.

CALIFORNIA (Continued)

★ 1229 ★
Boonville - BUCKAROO DAYS. Mid June, 2 days.
Contact: Redwood Empire Association, Visitors Infor-
mation Center, 476 Post Street, San Francisco,
California 94102.

A junior rodeo and a barbeque highlight this western
celebration in Boonville.

★ 1230 ★
Boonville - MENDOCINO COUNTY FAIR AND
APPLE SHOW. Late September, 3 days. Contact:
Information Officer, State of California Department
of Commerce, 1400 Tenth Street, Sacramento,
California 95814; or Chamber of Commerce, Boon-
ville, California 95437.

A carnival, horse show, open rodeo, dance, and
parade in this community celebration reflecting the
importance of the apple crop.

★ 1231 ★
Boron - 20-MULE TEAM DAYS. September, 3 days,
Boron Community Park. Contact: Boron Chamber
of Commerce, Box 281, Boron, California 93516.

A community celebration commemorating mule-hauling
days. Special events include booths, parade,
carnival, dances, whiskerino contest, honorary mayor
contest, Mrs. 20-Mule Team and junior king and
queen contests, and gymkhana. Trophies awarded.

★ 1232 ★
Brisbane - BRISBANE WESTERN DAYS. Early June,
4 days. Contact: California Chamber of Commerce,
455 Capitol Mall, Sacramento, California 95814.

A carnival, dancing, a barbeque, booths, and a
parade are part of this celebration of western heritage
for the community and visitors.

★ 1233 ★
Cambria - PINEDORO. Early September, annual,
2 days. Contact: California Chamber of Commerce,
455 Capitol Mall, Sacramento, California 95814.

Parade, arts and crafts, and a barbeque. Begun
around 1948.

★ 1234 ★
Chatsworth - PUMPKIN FESTIVAL. October, 2
days every weekend. Contact: Southern California

Visitors Council, 705 West Seventh Street, Los
Angeles, California 90017.

The entertainment includes a circus, music, games,
booths of arts and crafts, and food.

★ 1235 ★
Chico - PIONEER WEEK. Late April-early May,
6 days. Contact: California Chamber of Commerce,
455 Capitol Mall, Sacramento, California 95814.

A parade and an open rodeo. Ghost Town celebration.

★ 1236 ★
Chico - SILVER DOLLAR FAIR. Late May-early
June, 6 days. Contact: California Chamber of
Commerce, 455 Capitol Mall, Sacramento, California
95814.

Open rodeo, horse show, arts and crafts, carnival,
and livestock exhibitions highlight this celebration.

★ 1237 ★
Chula Vista - FIESTA DE LA LUNA. September-
October, 16 days. Contact: Chula Vista Jaycees,
Post Office Box 404, Chula Vista, California 92012.

Events include a carnival, parade, square dance,
arts and crafts, art mart, flower show, band concerts,
beauty contest, kid's day parade, and Spanish-
Western parade. Begun around 1934.

★ 1238 ★
Clear Lake Highlands, Lakeport - LAKE COUNTY
AIR FAIR. Early June, 2 days, Pearce Field;
Lampson's Field. Contact: Redwood Empire Associa-
tion, Visitor Information Center, 476 Post Street,
San Francisco, California 94102.

Two days of exhibits and entertainment for flying
fans and others.

★ 1239 ★
Concord - TODOS SANTOS FIESTA. Early
September, 2 days. Contact: California Chamber
of Commerce, 455 Capitol Mall, Sacramento,
California 95814.

Contests and other festivities for the residents and
visitors in Concord.

CALIFORNIA (Continued)

★ 1240 ★
Corcoran - COTTON FESTIVAL.   Early October,
1 day.   Contact: California Chamber of Commerce,
455 Capitol Mall, Sacramento, California 95814.

Parade, barbeque, contests, and a carnival are included in this celebration of a local crop.

★ 1241 ★
Costa Mesa - FIESTA DE COSTA MESA.   October,
3 days, downtown City Park.   Contact: Orange
County Chamber of Commerce, 401 Bank of America
Tower, The City, One City Boulevard, West, Orange,
California 92668.

A traditional festival reflecting the Mexican heritage
of the community.

★ 1242 ★
Crestline - CRESTLINE MOUNTAINEER DAYS.
Early July, 4 days.   Contact: Southern California
Visitors Council, 705 West Seventh Street, Los
Angeles, California 90017.

Festival activities include a parade, fireworks, a
puppet show, and contests in beard growing and
fishing.

★ 1243 ★
Del Mar - JUMPING FROG JAMBOREE.   Late
April, annual, 1 day, Del Mar Fairgrounds.   Con-
tact: Ken Morrison, 1663 Olmeda Street, Encinitas,
California 92024.

Prize for the best dressed frog, jumping frog contest,
clown acts, dog show, and judo exhibition.   Also
prizes for longest, smallest, and best jumping frog.
Frogs may be rented, or you can bring your own.
Claims to be the only official West Coast preliminary
to the Frog Olympics at Calvaras County.   Begun
around 1954.

★ 1244 ★
Del Mar - SOUTHERN CALIFORNIA EXPOSITION.
June-July (usually ends July 4th), annual, 2 weeks,
Del Mar Fairgrounds.   Contact: Ralph Trembley,
Del Mar Fairgrounds, Del Mar, California 92014.

Grandstand shows, all-servicemen's rodeo, world's
largest performing horse show, flower and garden show,
livestock show, art and photo shows, fun zone, home
arts, hobby show, gem and minerals competition,
agricultural, industrial, commercial and military exhibits,

and continuous entertainment.   Begun around 1889.

★ 1245 ★
Delano - DELANO WINE AND HARVEST FESTIVAL.
Early October, 4 days, Delano Memorial Park.   Con-
tact: Delano Wine and Harvest Festival, Incorporated,
Post Office Box 427, Delano, California 93215.

Barbeque, carnival, open rodeo, livestock exhibitions,
parade, old timers' picnic, junior queen, junior livestock sale, and a kiddie parade are included in the
festival events.

★ 1246 ★
Elk Grove - WESTERN FESTIVAL.   Early May, 2
days.   Contact: Chamber of Commerce, Elk Grove,
California 95624;   or California Chamber of Commerce, 455 Capitol Mall, Sacramento, California
95814.

A parade, a pancake breakfast, dancing, a carnival,
and a gymkhana show highlight this celebration of the
West and its traditions.

★ 1247 ★
Fallbrook - PIONEER DAYS.   September, Fallbrook
Riders' Field.   Contact: San Diego Convention
and Visitors Bureau, 1200 Third Avenue, Suite 824,
San Diego, California 92101.

IRA rodeo, Fallbrook Riders parade, pancake breakfast,
carnival booths, and a country western dance in
celebration of earlier days in Fallbrook.

★ 1248 ★
Fort Bragg - PAUL BUNYAN DAYS.   Late August-
early September (Labor Day weekend), annual, 4
days.   Contact: Chamber of Commerce, Fort Bragg,
California 95437;   or Information Officer, State of
California Department of Commerce, 1400 Tenth
Street, Sacramento, California 95814.

Dancing, a carnival, a parade, and contests for fun
and prizes are included in this celebration of a
mythical folk hero.

★ 1249 ★
Frazier Park - FRAZIER MOUNTAIN PARK FIESTA
DAZE.   Mid July, 2 days, Frazier Mountain Park.
Contact: Mountain Memories Association, Post Office
Box 334, Frazier Park, California 93225.

Parade, teen queen contest, honorary mayor contest,
barbeque, old timers' contest, best costume, and
whiskerino contest highlight the events.

Community

CALIFORNIA (Continued)

★ 1250 ★
Guerneville - STUMPTOWN DAYS.   June, 2 days.
Contact: Visitors Information Center, Redwood
Empire Associates, 476 Post Street, San Francisco,
California 94102.

A parade, a rodeo, and a barbeque highlight this
celebration and frolic.

★ 1251 ★
Hesperia - HESPERIA DAYS.   Late June, annual,
3 days.   Contact: California Chamber of Commerce,
455 Capitol Mall, Sacramento, California 95814.

Dancing, a barbeque, a rodeo, and a parade are
featured in this community celebration.

★ 1252 ★
Joshua Tree - TURTLE DAYS.   Early May.   Con-
tact: Southern California Visitors Council, 705 West
Seventh Street, Los Angeles, California 90017; or
Chamber of Commerce, 61731 Twenty-nine Palms High-
way, Joshua Tree, California 92252.

Events include dancing, a parade, contests, booths,
and mechanical turtle races.

★ 1253 ★
Julian - SANTA YSABEL MISSION FIESTA AND PIT
BARBEQUE.   Mid June, 1 day, Santa Ysabel
Mission near Julian.   Contact: Southern California
Visitors Council, 705 West Seventh Street, Los
Angeles, California 90017.

Entertainment features caballeros, mariachis, and
Indian dances.

★ 1254 ★
Laguna Beach - WINTER FESTIVAL.   Mid February-
March.   Contact: Chamber of Commerce, Box 396,
Laguna Beach, California 92652.

The festival extends a welcome to the winter visitors
to the town and features arts and crafts, parade,
sports contests, craftsmen's fair, art exhibits, films,
tennis tournament, and Hobie Cat regatta.

★ 1255 ★
Lone Pine - WILD WEST DAYS.   Mid October, 3
days.   Contact: California Chamber of Commerce,
455 Capitol Mall, Sacramento, California 95814.

Arts and crafts, barbeque, dancing, and livestock
shows are featured in this celebration with a western
flavor.

★ 1256 ★
Long Beach - INTERNATIONAL FESTIVAL OF KITES.
Early April, annual, 1 day.   Contact: Southern
California Visitors Council, 705 West Seventh Street,
Los Angeles, California 90017.

Children display and fly the kites that they themselves built.   Special division for kites which were
built by adults, or entered from another country.
Begun around 1927.

★ 1257 ★
Long Beach - LONG BEACH HERITAGE WEEK.
Early May, 8 days.   Contact: Chamber of Commerce,
121 Linden Avenue, Long Beach, California 90802.

In its honor, the community of Long Beach stages a
number of festivities including musical presentations,
dramatic presentations, and a fair.

★ 1258 ★
Los Angeles - CALIFORNIA SCIENCE FAIR.   Late
April-mid May, 2 weeks, California State Museum
of Science and Industry.   Contact: Southern
California Visitors Council, 705 West Seventh Street,
Los Angeles, California 90017.

Top student science projects on display.

★ 1259 ★
Los Angeles - FESTIVAL OF FRIENDSHIP.   Late
May-early June, annual, 3 days.   Contact:
California Chamber of Commerce, 455 Capitol Mall,
Sacramento, California 95814.

A pancake breakfast, a carnival, booths, games,
contests, and other traditional fair festivities celebrating the community and its visitors.

★ 1260 ★
Los Angeles - PACIFIC 21.   Late June-late
September, 2 months, Century City area.   Contact:
Southern California Visitors Council, 705 West Seventh
Street, Los Angeles, California 90017.

Festival and international exhibition focusing on the
business and economic activity culture, art and industry of more than 35 Pacific-basin nations.   Theme
is unity through diversity and it is to promote new
cooperative efforts between nations of the Pacific in

CALIFORNIA (Continued)

business, trade and other economic activity.

★ 1261 ★
Malibu - MALIBU FESTIVAL.   Late July, 2 days.
Contact: California Chamber of Commerce, 455
Capitol Mall, Sacramento, California 95814.

Pancake breakfast, horse show, arts and crafts,
classic cars, and water sports.

★ 1262 ★
Miracle Hot Springs - HOBO DAZE.   Mid May,
2 days.   Contact: Southern California Visitors
Council, 705 West Seventh Street, Los Angeles,
California 90017.

Events include a dance, a hayride, and a hobo stew
dinner.   A prize is awarded for the best hobo
costume.

★ 1263 ★
Montebello - MONTEBELLO FUN FESTIVAL.   Early
September, annual, 4 days.   Contact: California
Chamber of Commerce, 455 Capitol Mall, Sacramento,
California 95814.

A carnival, a pageant, and a parade highlight this
community celebration.

★ 1264 ★
Mountain Ranch - EL DORADO DAYS.   Mid August,
2 days.   Contact: Information Officer, State of
California Department of Commerce, 1400 Tenth
Street, Sacramento, California 95814.

Dancing, contests, and a flea market highlight this
community celebration.

★ 1265 ★
Novato - NOVATO'S PIONEER DAYS.   Late May-
early June, 4 days, Atherton and Bugeia Roads.
Contact: Information Officer, State of California
Department of Commerce, 1400 Tenth Street,
Sacramento, California 95814.

Contests, parades, barbeque, hayrides, buck-a-roo
breakfast, and a carnival in honor of early days of
Novato.

★ 1266 ★
Novato - OLD TOWN FESTIVAL AND OUTDOOR

SHOW.   Late September, 2 days.   Contact:
California Chamber of Commerce, 455 Capitol Mall,
Sacramento, California 95814.

Arts and crafts are featured in this community celebration.

★ 1267 ★
Ocean Beach - KITE FESTIVAL.   March (usually a
Saturday), annual, 1 day, Ocean Beach Recreation
Center and Ocean Beach Elementary School.   Contact: Don Hodo, Ocean Beach Recreation Center,
4726 Santa Monica Boulevard, San Diego, California
92107.

A kite flying contest for all ages.   Thousands of
youngsters parade through the streets with kites in
hand as they head for the competition.   Prizes
awarded in several categories.   Elementary school
children are judged for the originality of their kite
design.   Sponsored by the Kiwanis and the Recreation and Parks Department.   Begun around 1952.

★ 1268 ★
Paradise - JOHNNY APPLESEED FESTIVAL.   Early
October, 1 day.   Contact: California Chamber of
Commerce, 455 Capitol Mall, Sacramento, California
95814.

Pancake breakfast, games, music, and dancing highlight this community festival.

★ 1269 ★
Poway - POWAY POW WOW DAYS.   Mid October,
annual, 8 days, Old Poway Village.   Contact:
Poway Chamber of Commerce, Post Office Box 34,
Poway, California 92064.

Contests, carnival, barbeque, art shows, dog shows,
swim show, street dance, parade, and rodeo.   Poway
posse shoot-out, pearl pureheart contest, Indian
dancers, horse show, and historical exhibits.   Begun
around 1963.

★ 1270 ★
Ramona - COUNTRY FAIR.   Early September,
annual, 3 days.   Contact: Southern California
Visitors Council, 705 West Seventh Street, Los
Angeles, California 90017.

Events include a livestock show, horse show, food
and game booths, parade, and barbeque.   Begun
around 1971.

Community

CALIFORNIA (Continued)

★ 1271 ★
Reedly - INTERNATIONAL FESTIVAL.   October
(3rd weekend), annual, 3 days.   Contact: Tourist
Information Center, 1270 West Belmont, Fresno,
California 93728.

A pageant, a barbeque, and a parade are included
in the festivities honoring the various ethnic groups.

★ 1272 ★
San Diego - AMERICA'S FINEST CITY WEEK.
August or September, annual, 9 days.   Contact:
Public Information Office, City Administration
Building, 202 C Street, San Diego, California
92101.

City wide celebration with special events by local
groups, started by mayoral proclamation when the
Republican National Convention decided to go elsewhere.   Events include the finest city cup bathtub
race, San Diego lifeguard relays, sidewalk decorating,
etc.   Usually the Festival of the Arts is associated
with this event.   Begun in 1971.

★ 1273 ★
San Diego - FIESTA DEL VERANO.   Late August, 3
days, Old Town State Park.   Contact: Charylon
Cummings, 4895-B Collwood Boulevard, San Diego,
California 92115.

Arts and crafts exhibits, mariachis, country/western
music, Mexican and Indian dances, cookery demonstrations, pinata breaking, and traditional Mexican
food served.

★ 1274 ★
San Diego - GOD BLESS AMERICA WEEK.   June-
July (ties in with July 4th), annual, 1 week.
Contact: Ralph Stewart, God Bless America Week,
Incorporated, Post Office Box 670, San Diego,
California 92112.

Various patriotic activities including essay contest
for high school students, scholarships awarded and
Heritage Breakfast.

★ 1275 ★
San Diego - GREATER SAN DIEGO SCIENCE AND
ENGINEERING FAIR.   Mid April, annual, 4 days,
Federal Building, Balboa Park.   Contact: Clifford
T. Frederickson, Education Center, San Diego,
California 92101.

Students from San Diego and Imperial Counties'
public, private and parochial schools, grades 7-12,
enter science projects for judging.   Begun around
1956.

★ 1276 ★
San Diego - OLD TOWN BIRTHDAY FIESTA.   Mid
July, 3 days, Old Town State Park.   Contact:
Charylon Cummings, 4895-B Collwood Boulevard, San
Diego, California 92115.

Mexican and Indian dances, mariachis, country/
western music, 150 arts and crafts and sidewalk
exhibits.   Cutting of birthday cake.   Reconstruction
of Father Serra's journey to found first mission in San
Diego.

★ 1277 ★
San Fernando - SAN FERNANDO FIESTA DAYS.
Late May, 5 days.   Contact: Southern California
Visitors Council, 705 West Seventh Street, Los
Angeles, California 90017.

Events include entertainment, a parade, a beauty
pageant, and a tortilla contest.

★ 1278 ★
San Luis Obispo - LA FIESTA DE SAN LUIS OBISPO.
May (3rd weekend), 4 days, Mission San Luis Obispo.
Contact: Southern California Visitors Council, 705
West Seventh Street, Los Angeles, California 90017;
or Chamber of Commerce, 1039 Chorro Street, San
Luis Obispo, California 93401.

Events of the celebration include a parade, music,
western dancing, carnival, Spanish marketplace, and
rodeo.

★ 1279 ★
San Rafael - MARIN COUNTY FAIR AND NATIONAL
FILM COMPETITION.   Late August-September, 5
days, Marin Veteran's Memorial Auditorium and
Civic Center Fairgrounds.   Contact: Information
Officer, State California Department of Commerce,
1400 Tenth Street, Sacramento, California 95814.

Crafts, boats, rides, carnival, and a photography
exhibit highlight this festive event.

★ 1280 ★
Santa Barbara - COMMUNITY FAIR AND CARNIVAL.
Early June, annual, 4 days, Earl Warren Showgrounds.
Contact: Southern California Visitors Council, 705
West Seventh Street, Los Angeles, California 90017.

CALIFORNIA (Continued)

Trade and community fair with carnival and novelty booths. Begun around 1950.

★ 1281 ★
Santa Barbara - GOOD HEALTH FAIR. Mid April, 1 day, La Cumbre Plaza. Contact: Southern California Visitors Council, 705 West Seventh Street, Los Angeles, California 90017.

Exhibits by 14 different groups concerning good health and disease prevention.

★ 1282 ★
Santa Margarita - DAYS OF THE DONS. Early September, annual, 3 days. Contact: California Chamber of Commerce, 455 Capitol Mall, Sacramento, California 95814.

In celebration of the Spanish heritage of this community.

★ 1283 ★
Selma - SELMA FUN FAIR. Early September, 4 days. Contact: California Chamber of Commerce, 455 Capitol Mall, Sacramento, California 95814.

A carnival, a queen contest, entertainment, and games highlight this community festival of fun.

★ 1284 ★
Signal Hill - SIGNAL HILL FIESTA. Mid June, 1 day. Contact: California Chamber of Commerce, 455 Capitol Mall, Sacramento, California 95814.

A carnival, barbeque, square dance, and Model T parade are featured in this community festival.

★ 1285 ★
Sutter Creek - SOURDOUGH DAYS. Early September, 2 days. Contact: California Chamber of Commerce, 455 Capitol Mall, Sacramento, California 95814.

Arts and crafts, tours, gold panning, and entertainment highlight this early West festival.

★ 1286 ★
Tehachapi - TEHACHAPI MOUNTAIN FESTIVAL. Mid August, 2 days. Contact: Tehachapi Chamber of Commerce, Post Office Box 401, Tehachapi, California 93561.

Parade, rodeo, arts and crafts, barbeque, dance, art fair, and Miss Tehachapi contest.

★ 1287 ★
Thousand Oaks - CONEJO VALLEY DAYS. Late April-early May, 9 days. Contact: Southern California Visitors Council, 705 West Seventh Street, Los Angeles, California 90017.

Beauty pageant, carnival, tent exhibits, entertainment, barbeque, rodeo, parade, sports events, and a children's parade are included in the festive events.

★ 1288 ★
Twenty-nine Palms - PIONEER DAYS CELEBRATION. Mid October, annual, 5 days. Contact: California Chamber of Commerce, 455 Capitol Mall, Sacramento, California 95814.

A rodeo, carnival, parade, game booths, horse show, and honorary races for mayor and sheriff.

★ 1289 ★
Valley Center - WESTERN DAYS. Early June, annual, 7 days, Valley Center Community Hall. Contact: Eleanor Ratner, San Diego Convention and Visitors Bureau, 1200 Third Avenue, Suite 824, San Diego, California 92101.

Gymkhana shows, square dancing, arts and crafts, a barbeque, a parade, and carnival booths highlight this western style celebration.

★ 1290 ★
Ventura - INVENTORS WORKSHOP EXPO. Mid May, 4 days, County Fairgrounds. Contact: Southern California Visitors Council, 705 West Seventh Street, Los Angeles, California 90017; or Greater Ventura Chamber of Commerce, 785 South Seaward Avenue, Ventura, California 93003.

A "creative idea/product/invention" contest, open to college and university students throughout the nation. Begun around 1974.

★ 1291 ★
Visalia - WESTERN DAYS AND MOOSE RODEO. Late September, annual, 3 days. Contact: California Chamber of Commerce, 455 Capitol Mall, Sacramento, California 95814.

A rodeo and a parade highlight this celebration of the Old West.

Community

CALIFORNIA (Continued)

★ 1292 ★
Walnut Creek - WALNUT FESTIVAL. Late September, annual, 4 days. Contact: California Chamber of Commerce, 455 Capitol Mall, Sacramento, California 95814.

Events include a queen contest, marathon race, songfest, fashion show, contest for children, parade, folk dancing, band concerts, carnival, rodeo, and miscellaneous races. Begun in 1911.

★ 1293 ★
Willits - FRONTIER DAYS CELEBRATION. July, annual, 3 days. Contact: Information Officer, State of California Department of Commerce, 1400 Tenth Avenue, Sacramento, California 95814.

Parade, barbeque, rodeo, cowboy breakfast, and entertainment. Begun around 1927.

★ 1294 ★
Wofford Heights - EARLY CALIFORNIA DAYS. Mid October, 2 days, Wofford Heights Community Park. Contact: Wofford Heights Improvement Group, Post Office Box 65, Wofford Heights, California 93285.

Events include a barbeque, contests, parade, special entertainment, "Game Night", costume parade, old timers' picnic, and a marshall contest.

★ 1295 ★
Yorba Linda - FIESTA DAY. October, 1 day. Contact: Orange County Chamber of Commerce, 401 Bank of America Tower, The City, One City Boulevard, West, Orange, California 92668.

A parade and carnival style booths are part of this community celebration.

COLORADO

★ 1296 ★
Breckenridge - PACK BURRO RACES AND FESTIVAL. Late July-early August, annual, 3 days, Hoosier Pass between Breckenridge and Fairplay. Contact: Chamber of Commerce, Box 312, Fairplay, Colorado 80440.

The celebration begins with western music and dancing. The main event is a race to see who can ride, push, or pull their burro, carrying all of the equipment miners used to use, over the icy 13,000 foot pass.

★ 1297 ★
Canon City - BLOSSOM AND MUSIC FESTIVAL. Early May, 2 days. Contact: Chamber of Commerce, 816 River Street, Canon City, Colorado 81212.

Pop music, a carnival, bands, and a parade highlight this community celebration.

★ 1298 ★
Durango - NAVAJO TRAILS FIESTA. Early August, annual, 3 days. Contact: Chamber of Commerce, Durango, Colorado 81301.

Square dancing, rodeo roping and riding events, horse racing, parade, food, and tribal dances performed by Indians in native dress.

★ 1299 ★
Fairplay - PACK BURRO RACES AND FESTIVAL. Late July-early August, annual, 3 days, Hoosier Pass between Breckenridge and Fairplay. Contact: Chamber of Commerce, Box 312, Fairplay, Colorado 80440.

The celebration begins with western music and dancing. The main event is a race to see who can ride, push, or pull their burro, carrying all of the equipment miners used to use, over the icy 13,000 foot pass.

★ 1300 ★
Grand Junction - PEACH FESTIVAL. Late August. Contact: Chamber of Commerce, 127 North Fourth Street, Post Office Box 1330, Grand Junction, Colorado 81501.

A square dance festival is featured in this community celebration.

★ 1301 ★
Grand Lake - WESTERN WEEK. Mid June, 1 week. Contact: Grand Lake Area Chamber of Commerce, Post Office Box 57, Grand Lake, Colorado 80447.

Traditional community celebration honoring the Old West.

★ 1302 ★
Greeley - MAY DAYS. Mid May, annual, 1-2 days, University of Northern Colorado. Contact: Eric Lundberg, Director, University News Service, University of Northern Colorado, Greeley, Colorado 80639.

COLORADO (Continued)

One to two day weekender a la Woodstock (beer, pretzels, music, thunderstorm) held on campus, sponsored by the student government. First held in 1970 as a celebration of University status.

★ 1303 ★
Leadville - PACK BURRO RACES AND FESTIVAL. Late July-early August, annual, 3 days, Hoosier Pass between Breckenridge and Fairplay. Contact: Chamber of Commerce, Box 312, Fairplay, Colorado 80440.

The celebration begins with western music and dancing. The main event is a race to see who can ride, push, or pull their burro, carrying all of the equipment miners used to use, over the icy 13,000 foot pass.

★ 1304 ★
Rocky Ford - ARKANSAS VALLEY FAIR AND WATERMELON DAY. August (last week), annual, 7 days. Contact: Chamber of Commerce, Rocky Ford, Colorado 81067.

Started by Senator George W. Swink, founder of Rocky Ford and originator of Watermelon Day in 1878. Governor of Colorado presents a melon to the oldest surviving member of Swink's family. Watermelons are given to fair visitors - all they can eat. Colorado's oldest fair.

CONNECTICUT

★ 1305 ★
Bridgeport - BARNUM FESTIVAL. Late June-early July (around July 5th, Barnum's birthday), annual, 4 days. Contact: The Barnum Festival Society, Incorporated, 804 Main Street, Bridgeport, Connecticut 06604.

King and queen coronation, Las Vegas night, flea market, luncheons, parade, wing ding, speed boat races, festival beer garden, Wonderland of Ice, fireworks, and Miss Jenny Lind (both a Swedish and an American) contest - winners appear in concert. Tom Thumb and Lavinia Warren contest (children chosen on the basis of essays to represent the two famous midgets who toured with P.T. Barnum). Clowns, antique auto show, ringmasters ball, mayor's reception, square dance, spul night, polka night, armed forces bands, drill teams, aerial shows, circus, drum corps competition and arts and crafts show. Begun in 1949.

★ 1306 ★
New Milford - VILLAGE FAIR DAYS. Late July, 2 days, New Milford Village Green. Contact: Richard Newberg, New Milford Chamber of Commerce, 38 Danbury Road, New Milford, Connecticut 06776.

Paintings, photography, and crafts are featured in this community festival.

★ 1307 ★
Storrs - CAMPUS COMMUNITY CARNIVAL. Early April, annual, several weeks, University of Connecticut, ROTC Hangar. Contact: Mr. Don McCullough, Student Activities Office, University of Connecticut, Storrs, Connecticut 06268.

Carnival-type midway featuring various types of fun and games for the benefit of a pool of charities. Preliminary types of fund-raising gimmicks and stunts extend several weeks ahead of the carnival climax date. Sponsored by various campus organizations. Begun around 1950.

DELAWARE

★ 1308 ★
Lewes - GREAT DELAWARE KITE FESTIVAL. March or April (around Easter), annual, 1 day, parade grounds, Cape Henlopen State Park. Contact: Mary Ellsworth, Secretary, Delaware Kite Flying Society, 308 Savannah Road, Lewes, Delaware 19958.

A large assortment of kites of many sizes, shapes, and categories compete for prizes.

★ 1309 ★
Milton - BIG THURSDAY. Mid August, 1 day. Contact: Division of Economic Development, State Visitors Service, 45 The Green, Dover, Delaware 19901.

A Gay 90's festival - fun and frolic for young and old.

DISTRICT OF COLUMBIA

★ 1310 ★
Washington, D.C. - CITY CELEBRATION. June, 1 day, on the Ellipse. Contact: Regina Saxton, 777 14th Street Northwest, Washington, D.C. 20005.

This is a street festival with dancing, craft demonstrations, food and drink, and music and stage productions.

Community

DISTRICT OF COLUMBIA (Continued)

★ 1311 ★
Washington, D.C. - FAMILY RECREATION DAY.
Late August, annual, 1 day, Fort Circle Park.
Contact: Everett Scott, 3149 16th Street, Northwest,
Washington, D.C. 20010.

Includes puppet shows, craftmobile and showmobile
revue, games, rides, activities for children, youth,
and senior citizens. Community groups contribute
activities and demonstrations. Sponsored by the
D.C. Department of Recreation. Begun in 1974.

★ 1312 ★
Washington, D.C. - PAGEANT OF PEACE. Mid
December-January 1st, annual. Contact: National
Park Service, 1100 Ohio Drive, Southwest, Washing-
ton, D.C. 20242.

Events include the lighting of the National Christmas
Tree by the President and nightly singing by choir
groups from across the country.

FLORIDA

★ 1313 ★
Cape Coral - MARDI GRAS CARNIVAL. Early
February, annual, 2 Saturdays. Contact: Jack
FitzMaurice, 5246 Tower Drive, Cape Coral,
Florida 33904.

Sponsored by German-American Social Club and
patterned after European festivals, people dress in
costumes; Prince Carnival and his Princess rule over
Carnivalia; Prince Carnival reads a proclamation
committing his subjects to unrestricted gaity, dancing
and revelry.

★ 1314 ★
Clearwater - FUN 'N SUN FESTIVAL. Late March,
10 days. Contact: Sergeant Bob Kennedy, 120 North
Osceola Avenue, Clearwater, Florida 33515.

State pram regatta, national records power boat race,
pancake festival, state baton twirling contest, beach
day, art festival, beauty pageant, golf, state shuffleboard and lawn bowling tournaments, and fish fry.
Climax is the two and a half hour Fun 'n Sun night
parade.

★ 1315 ★
Davie - ORANGE FESTIVAL AND RODEO. Early
March, 2 days. Contact: Ed Brockman, 4185
Southwest 64th Avenue, Davie, Florida 33314.

The west comes to this town as residents and visitors
don ten-gallon hats and high-heeled boots. There
is a parade, western breakfast, barbeque, old-fashioned
carnival and rodeo performances.

★ 1316 ★
Daytona Beach - DIXIE FROLICS. Early July
(around the 4th), annual, 4 days. Contact: Mrs.
Lyn Jordan, Daytona Beach Jaycees, Chamber of
Commerce Building, Daytona Beach, Florida 32015.

A Miss Daytona Beach pageant and fireworks on the
beach are part of this community celebration.

★ 1317 ★
Delray Beach - DELRAY AFFAIR. Late April,
annual, 2 days, Atlantic Avenue. Contact: Ken
Ellingsworth, 64 Southeast Avenue, Delray Beach,
Florida 33444.

Arts, crafts, flowers and produce are displayed throughout the festival. Artists and craftsmen throughout
the state participate.

★ 1318 ★
Fort Myers - EDISON PAGEANT OF LIGHT. Early-
mid February, 10 days. Contact: Chamber of
Commerce, Fort Myers-Lee County, 1365 Hendry
Street, Post Office Box CC, Fort Myers, Florida
33902.

Competitions include tennis tournaments and sailboat
races. Additional activities include flower shows,
parties, parades, strolling flower show, and antique
car show. The climax of the entire event is the
night-time Parade of Light.

★ 1319 ★
Fort Myers Beach - FAMILY FUN FESTIVAL. Mid
August, 4 days. Contact: D.L. Botorff, Fort
Myers-Lee County Chamber of Commerce, Post Office
Box CC, Fort Myers, Florida 33902.

Sandcastle contest, two-day fishing tournament for
children, sail and power boat races, Mr. and Mrs.
Suntan Contest, family-style barbeque, and entertainment.

★ 1320 ★
Fort Pierce - SANDY SHOES FESTIVAL. Late
January (third week), annual, 10 days. Contact:
Mrs. Joanne Parrish, Post Office Box 3326, Fort
Pierce, Florida 33450.

FLORIDA (Continued)

Taking its name from the theory that once visitors get sand in their shoes while in Florida, they will be compelled to re-visit the state. Events include shoot-outs, art shows, rodeo, turkey shoot, archery contests, band-o-rama, and water ski show. Cattlemen's Day parade, western and pioneer costumes.

★ 1321 ★
Fort Walton Beach - BILLY BOWLEGS FESTIVAL. Early June (first full week), annual, 9 days. Contact: Mrs. Iris Baughman, Greater Fort Walton Beach Chamber of Commerce, 34 Miracle Strip Parkway, Southeast, Fort Walton Beach, Florida 32548.

Legendary pirate Billy Bowlegs and his riotous crew steal in from the sea. Boat parade during the pirates' landing, street parades, "sacking" of the city, treasure hunts, pirate markets, art show, sand sculpture contest, ski show and tournament.

★ 1322 ★
La Belle - SWAMP CABBAGE FESTIVAL. Late February, annual, 3 days. Contact: T. A. Smith, La Belle, Florida 33935.

Florida's state tree, the Sabal Palm, commonly known as the Cabbage Palm is honored in a homecoming weekend, parade with floats decorated with the palm, a swamp cabbage queen, and "Heart of the palm" or swamp cabbage, is featured at a barbeque and on menus of local restaurants. Centennial clothes are worn. Rodeo and dances.

★ 1323 ★
Lake Worth - PIONEER DAYS. Late March, 7 days. Contact: George Parker, Greater Lake Worth Chamber of Commerce, Post Office Box 1422, Lake Worth, Florida 33460.

Antique auto show, parade, sidewalk art show and sale, square dancing, and barbeque.

★ 1324 ★
Miami - ORANGE BOWL FESTIVAL. Late December, annual, 12 days, downtown Miami. Contact: Orange Bowl Committee, Post Office Box 748, Miami, Florida 33135.

The festival centers around the Orange Bowl game on New Year's night. Included in the events is the King Orange Jamboree Parade, plus luncheons, breakfasts, and other sports tournaments. Begun in 1933.

★ 1325 ★
Pensacola - FIESTA OF THE FIVE FLAGS. June and September, semiannual, 8 days, 3 days. Contact: Fiesta of Five Flags, Executive Director, 2121 West Intendencia Street, Post Office Box 1943, Pensacola, Florida 32589.

A reenactment of the landing of Don Tristan de Luna and his Spanish colonists in 1559. Celebration commemorates the city's turbulent history under the flags of five different nations. Each year the festival celebrates one of the nations. More than 60 recreational, sports, cultural and educational activities are planned. Events include a series of parades, pageantry, regatta, art exhibits, concerts, street fair, international fishing rodeo, and a treasure hunt.

★ 1326 ★
Safety Harbor - COUNT PHILLIPPI FESTIVAL AND HOBBY SHOW. Early April, 6 days. Contact: Safety Harbor Chamber of Commerce, 200 Main Street, Safety Harbor, Florida 33572.

Indoor hobby show, parade, and festival. To bid farewell to the tourists.

★ 1327 ★
Saint Augustine - EASTER WEEK FESTIVAL. Mid April (Easter week), 8 days. Contact: Thomas King, Saint Augustine Chamber of Commerce, Ten Castillo Drive, Saint Augustine, Florida 32084.

Starting with an Easter sunrise service atop the Castillo de San Marcos, the city observes both religious and historic events. The Parade de Los Caballos y Coches, (horses wearing easter bonnets) consists of elaborately decorated carts filled with costumed residents and drawn by horses. Reigning over the festivities are members of the royal family, descendents of the early San Augustine families. Traditional activities include a Minorcan Day celebration, an alfresco art show on the plaza, and tours of old buildings and gardens. On Low Sunday, the festival ends with a religious procession and benediction at the Shrine Nombre de Dios.

★ 1328 ★
Saint Cloud - WINTER FRIENDS FESTIVAL. Mid December (2nd week), annual, 7 days. Contact: M. L. Whitacre, 1422 Carolina Avenue, Saint Cloud, Florida 32769.

In appreciation of winter visitors. Christmas theme used in decorations, parade, Christmas tree lighting ceremony, and selection and coronation of a festival queen.

Community

FLORIDA (Continued)

★ 1329 ★
Saint Petersburg - FESTIVAL OF STATES. Late March-early April, annual, 13 days. Contact: Herbert Melleney, Festival of the States Association, Post Office Box 1731, Saint Petersburg, Florida 33731.

Visiting high school bands from around the country participate in a national band marching competition and out-of-state field show competition for the mayor's trophy. Series of concerts, youth parade, champions on parade, parade of states, and national flag pageant featuring authentic full-sized reproductions of historically interesting flags, each born by a youth in an appropriate costume. Sports tournaments, fireworks display, and coronation of Mr. Sun and the Sungoddess. First held in 1917, started on a regular basis in 1922.

★ 1330 ★
Sarasota - INTERNATIONAL SANDCASTLE CONTEST. Early May, annual, 1 day. Contact: Siesta Key Chamber of Commerce, 5481 Riverbluff Circle, Post Office Box 5188, Sarasota, Florida 33579.

Sand sculpting for fun and for prizes. Begun around 1967.

★ 1331 ★
Tampa (Ybor City) - BACK TO YBOR CITY DAY. Late October, 1 day. Contact: Ybor City Chamber of Commerce, Post Office Box 5287, Tampa, Florida 33605.

Glimpses of yesteryear, honoring Ybor City natives, especially those born in the nineteenth century. Events include entertainment by strolling musicians, adult and children's games, domino tournament, bocce (Italian bowling) and a sidewalk art show.

★ 1332 ★
Venice - VENETIAN SUN FESTIVAL. Late October, 4 days. Contact: Mr. Bill McFarland, Venice Area Chamber of Commerce, Post Office Box 937, Venice, Florida 33595.

Animals from the Ringling Brothers-Barnum and Bailey Circus, parades and fireworks, beauty contests, displays of new and antique cars and planes, boats and recreational vehicles, air show, and boat and balloon races.

GEORGIA

★ 1333 ★
Athens - GEORGIA STATE SCIENCE AND ENGINEERING FAIR. April, annual, University of Georgia Coliseum. Contact: University of Georgia, Office of. Public Relations, 117 Terrell Hall, Athens, Georgia 30602.

Competitive event in which students in junior and senior high schools prepare exhibits and demonstrations on research conducted in one of the physical and biological sciences. Through a series of semifinals, the winners may work their way up to the International Science and Engineering Fair.

★ 1334 ★
Atlanta - DOOLEY'S FROLICS. Early May, annual, several days, Emory University Campus. Contact: Interfraternity Council, c/o Dean for Men's Office, Emory University, Atlanta, Georgia 30322.

Starts when Dooley, an apochryphal campus figure, arrives by helicopter on the upper athletic field. This starts off a series of festivities including dances, athletic competitions, competition between fraternities which put on elaborate skits, elaborate decorations, corn roasts, and bluegrass music. Dooley is permitted to cancel classes. Started by the Emory Press Club in 1941.

★ 1335 ★
Fitzgerald - YANK/REB FESTIVAL. Mid August, annual, 3 days. Contact: Georgia Department of Community Development, Tourist Division, Post Office Box 38097, Atlanta, Georgia 30334.

Traditional festivities honoring the time of the Civil War. Begun in 1973.

★ 1336 ★
Folkston - OKEFENOKEE FESTIVAL. Early July, annual, 7 days. Contact: Georgia Department of Community Development, Tourist Division, Post Office Box 38097, Atlanta, Georgia 30334.

A traditional community festival. Begun around 1972.

★ 1337 ★
Savannah - HISTORIC SAVANNAH FOUNDATION FAIR AND FESTIVAL. Mid February, 2 days, Emmet Park. Contact: Savannah Visitors Center, Savannah Area Chamber of Commerce, Post Office Box 530, Savannah, Georgia 31402.

GEORGIA (Continued)

Part of Georgia Week. Booths of crafts, food, arts, bands, puppet shows, colonial dance groups, and children's costume parade.

★ 1338 ★
Savannah - WATERFRONT FESTIVAL. February-June, 1 day/month, River Street, Contact: Savannah Visitors Center, Savannah Area Chamber of Commerce, Post Office Box 530, Savannah, Georgia 31402.

A community celebration with traditional festive activities and events.

HAWAII

★ 1339 ★
Hilo - MERRY MONARCH FESTIVAL. Mid April, 4 days. Contact: Hawaii Island Chamber of Commerce, 180 Kinooki Street, Hilo, Hawaii 96720.

Named for the last ruling king of Hawaii, David Kalakaua. Music, international pageant, parade, queen coronation, dancing, feasting, Grog Shoppe, a Miss Aloha hula competition, traditional and rock music, arts and crafts show, and cultural exhibits. Begun around 1964.

★ 1340 ★
Honolulu - FESTIVAL OF TREES. Early December, 6 days. Contact: Hawaii Visitors Bureau, Suite 801, Waikiki Business Plaza, 2270 Kalakaua Avenue, Honolulu, Hawaii 96815.

Imaginative exhibits of decorated trees, wreaths and yule items. Sale for the benefit of Queen's Hospital. Traditional and Hawaiian Christmas carols are performed by choral groups.

★ 1341 ★
Honolulu - LEI DAY. May (1st), annual, 1 day, Wakiki State Park. Contact: Hawaii Visitors Bureau, Suite 801, Waikiki Business Plaza, 2270 Kalakaua Avenue, Honolulu, Hawaii 96815.

Festival in honor of the lei. The leis are exhibited statewide, there are competitions for the best. A Lei-Day Queen and court are chosen. There is a hula pageant with singing, dancing, and chanting at the Wakiki Shell.

★ 1342 ★
Honolulu - SUNSHINE FESTIVAL. Early January,

1 day, Diamond Head Crater. Contact: Hawaii Visitors Bureau, Special Events Department, Honolulu, Hawaii 96815.

Folk, rock, and Hawaiian music. Food and crafts booths.

IDAHO

★ 1343 ★
Bonners Ferry - HUCKLEBERRY FESTIVAL. Mid July, 2 days. Contact: Chamber of Commerce, Post Office Box 375, Bonners Ferry, Idaho 83805.

A parade and other traditional festivities.

★ 1344 ★
Buhl - SAGEBRUSH DAYS. Early July, 2 days. Contact: President, Buhl Chamber of Commerce, Post Office Box 28, Buhl, Idaho 83116.

Free barbeque, parade, fireworks, dancing, rodeo, and a sidewalk bazaar are included in the festivities.

★ 1345 ★
Cascade - THUNDER MOUNTAIN DAYS. Early July, 2 days. Contact: Chamber of Commerce, Post Office Box 26, Cascade, Idaho 83226.

A parade, barbeque, horse races, and children's races are included in this western style celebration.

★ 1346 ★
Coeur d'Alene - LAKE COEUR D' ALENE DAYS. Early May, 2 days. Contact: Division of Tourism and Industrial Development, Room 108, Capitol Building, Boise, Idaho 83720.

Festival, parade, air show, cruises, logger's contest, sidewalk sales, and car and boat show.

★ 1347 ★
Grangeville - BORDER DAYS. Early July, 3 days. Contact: Chamber of Commerce, 221 West Main, Grangeville, Idaho 83530.

Amateur rodeo, parade, fireworks, barbeque, street games, square dancing, trap shooting, cowboy breakfast, museum display and art show. Begun around 1913.

★ 1348 ★
Hailey - DAYS OF THE OLD WEST. July, annual,

Community

IDAHO (Continued)

3 days, City Park.   Contact: Chamber of Commerce, Box 100, Hailey, Idaho 83333.

Rodeo, parade, beef and lamb barbeque, art show of "Days of the Old West" art, kiddie parade, street fair, fireworks, and "shoot out" races.

★ 1349 ★
Idaho Falls - PIONEER DAYS STAMPEDE.   Late July, 3 days.   Contact: Karl T. Homer, Chairman, Pioneer Days, Box 2107, Idaho Falls, Idaho 83401.

A chuck wagon and chariot races are featured in this western style community celebration.

★ 1350 ★
Kooskia - KOOSKIA DAY.   Late July.   Contact: Chamber of Commerce, Kooskia, Idaho 83539.

A parade, street sports, old-time fiddlers' jamboree, raft races, horse show, rock and artifacts display are included in the festival events.

★ 1351 ★
Nampa - SNAKE RIVER STAMPEDE.   July (3rd week), annual, 5 days, Stampede Grounds.   Contact: Snake River Stampede, Post Office Box 231, Nampa, Idaho 83651.

Contest events include bareback bronc riding, saddle bronc riding, steer wrestling, calf roping and brahma bull riding.   In addition, there are special acts such as trained horses and bullfighting.   The contest for next year's queen takes place over the five nights of the event.   Each night also features a parade.   Begun in 1915.

★ 1352 ★
Nordman - FRONTIER DAYS.   Early July.   Contact: Chamber of Commerce, Nordman, Idaho 83848.

A carnival, lumberjack competition, and horseshoe pitching are among the events celebrating early days in this western city.

★ 1353 ★
Orofino - LUMBERJACK DAYS AND CLEARWATER COUNTY FAIR.   Mid September, annual, 1 weekend.   Contact: Orofino Celebrations, Incorporated, Post Office Box 543, Orofino, Idaho 83544.

Carnival, kiddie's parade, auction of logs, lumber, and commercial products.   4-H livestock auction and stage-show with nationally known stars.   Logging events including birling, sawing, chopping, axe throwing, and speed climbing.   Teen dance, truck driving contest and horse-pulling contest.   Associated with the three day Clearwater County Fair which has typical fair exhibits.   Lumberjack Days started in 1947.

★ 1354 ★
Payette - APPLE BLOSSOM FESTIVAL AND BOOMERANG DAYS (BOOMERANG DAYS BLOSSOM FESTIVAL).   May (2nd Sunday), City Park.   Contact: Idaho Department of Commerce and Development, Room 108, Capitol Building, Boise, Idaho 83707.

A parade, barbeque, carnival, rodeo, and other events honoring the western heritage and the apple blossoms of Payette.

★ 1355 ★
Plummer - INDIAN DAYS AND PLUMMER FESTIVAL (PLUMMER DAYS).   Late July or early August.   Contact: Chamber of Commerce, Plummer, Idaho 83851.

Coeur d'Alene pow-wow and festival with parade are held in conjunction with Plummer Days celebration. Street games are included in the events.

★ 1356 ★
Priest River - PRIEST RIVER LOGGERS CELEBRATION. Mid July, annual, 2 days.   Contact: Chamber of Commerce, Priest River, Idaho 83856.

Lumberjack competition, parade, auctions, luncheons, Jaycee raft race, horse show, horseshoe pitching, dancing, local music, fireworks, carnival, Idaho-style auction, wood-crafts, and children's events.

★ 1357 ★
Saint Maries - PAUL BUNYAN DAYS.   Early September, 3 days.   Contact: Chamber of Commerce, 724 Main, Saint Maries, Idaho 83861.

Events include lumberjack competition, musket and archery shoots, blue ox watering trough.   In conjunction with the Benewah County fair.   Parades, dances, games, pancake breakfast, barbeque, and street dancing.

IDAHO (Continued)

★ 1358 ★
Salmon - SALMON RIVER DAYS.   Early July.
Contact: Chamber of Commerce, Post Office Box
1227, Salmon, Idaho 83467.

A parade, motorcycle races, demolition derby, free
breakfast, competitive trail ride, water-can contest,
dances, fireworks, and old-time car show.

★ 1359 ★
Smelterville - SMELTERVILLE LIONS FRONTIER
DAYS.   Late June, annual, 3 days.   Contact:
Ron Maden, Lions Club, Smelterville, Idaho 83868.

Fiddlers' convention, mining and log sawing contests,
and fiddlers' contest.   Begun around 1964.

★ 1360 ★
Winchester - WINCHESTER DAYS.   Early July, 1
day.   Contact: Chamber of Commerce, Winchester,
Idaho 83555.

A parade and a fiddlers' contest highlight this community celebration.

ILLINOIS

★ 1361 ★
Belvidere - GREEN FESTIVAL.   Late May-early
June, 4 days.   Contact: The Division of Tourism,
Illinois Department of Business and Economic Develop-
ment, 222 South College Street, Springfield, Illinois
62706.

A parade, drum and bugle corps competition, and a
queen contest highlight this community festival.

★ 1362 ★
Cave-In-Rock - FRONTIER DAYS.   Mid July, 3
days, State Park and riverfront.   Contact: The
Division of Tourism, Illinois Department of Business
and Economic Development, 222 South College Street,
Springfield, Illinois 62706.

Three days of midsummer fun and frolic in celebration
of earlier days.

★ 1363 ★
Decautur - YESTERYEAR FAIR.   Late August, 3 days,
North Fork Museum.   Contact: The Division of
Tourism, Illinois Department of Business and Economic
Development, 222 South College Street, Springfield,

Illinois 62706.

A traditional fair atmosphere in celebration of earlier
days.

★ 1364 ★
Freeport - DAIRY DAYS IN FREEPORT.   Mid June,
4 days.   Contact: Stephenson County Extension
Office, Highland Community College, Freeport,
Illinois 61032.

Window displays, museum exhibits, square dance,
store displays, dairy bake-off, queen reception, pork
barbeque, contests, entertainment, dairy lunch stands,
floats in a parade, and a marching band contest are
featured events of the festival.

★ 1365 ★
Goreville - COUNTRY DAYS (SOUTHERN ILLINOIS
COUNTRY DAYS).   Late April, 2 days, Ferne
Clyffe State Park.   Contact: Division of Tourism,
Illinois Department of Business and Economic Develop-
ment, 222 South College Street, Springfield, Illinois
62706.

Events highlight the cultural heritage of southern
Illinois during a weekend of nature tours, bluegrass
music, games, and arts and crafts demonstrations.

★ 1366 ★
Lincoln - ABRAHAM LINCOLN NATIONAL
RAILSPLITTING CONTEST AND CRAFTS FESTIVAL.
Mid September, annual, 2 days, Fairgrounds.   Con-
tact: The Division of Tourism, Illinois Department
of Business and Economic Development, 222 South
College Street, Springfield, Illinois 62706.

Amateur and junior class railsplitters, as well as a
professional class to determine the national champion.
Food concessions and crafts displays, and a gala
parade.

★ 1367 ★
Park Forest - EARTHWEEK.   Mid April, 7 days.
Contact: Division of Tourism, Illinois Department
of Business and Economic Development, 222 South
College Street, Springfield, Illinois 62706.

A junk sculpture contest and film festival are included in the events calling attention to our earth
and its environment.

★ 1368 ★
Rockford - PATRIOTIC DAYS.   Early July, 4 days.

Community

ILLINOIS (Continued)

Contact: The Division of Tourism, Illinois Department of Business and Economic Development, 222 South College Street, Springfield, Illinois 62706.

Art festival, centennial tea party, and drum and bugle corps are included in this salute to earlier times.

★ 1369 ★
Ruma - STRAWBERRY ICE CREAM FESTIVAL. Mid June, 1 day, Saint Patrick's Church. Contact: The Division of Tourism, Illinois Department of Business and Economic Development, 222 South College Street, Springfield, Illinois 62706.

Homemade ice cream is served in a festive atmosphere.

INDIANA

★ 1370 ★
Alexandria - SIDEWALK DAYS FESTIVAL. Mid July, 2 days, Harrison Street. Contact: Manager, Alexandria Chamber of Commerce, 122 West Church Street, Alexandria, Indiana 46001.

Dunking booth, square dance, barbeque, music, clowns, children's events, and merchants' booths.

★ 1371 ★
Aurora - HOOSIER MINI FESTIVAL. Late July, 2 days, Aurora City Park. Contact: President, Hoosier Mini Festival Association, 205 Hillview Drive, Aurora, Indiana 47001.

Local home demonstration clubs present a handicraft display and sale. Performances by the Cincinnati Ballet Company, the Cincinnati Symphony Orchestra, and vocalists.

★ 1372 ★
Bedford - BEDFORD LIMESTONE FESTIVAL. Late June, annual, 11 days, 16th Street Shopping Plaza and Bedford High School. Contact: Glen Vergon, Chairman, Bedford Limestone Festival, 1109 O Street, Bedford, Indiana 47421.

Contests, tournaments, talent show, queen contest, carnival, square dancing, parade, wrestling match, boat race, fish fry, six-mile foot race, and chess tourney. Honors Bedford's famous industry.

★ 1373 ★
Bluffton - BLUFFTON FREE STREET FAIR. Mid September, annual, 5 days. Contact: President, Bluffton Free Street Fair Association, 420 East Silver Street, Bluffton, Indiana 46714.

Many parades, bands, free entertainment, art, needlework, agricultural displays, contest with state-wide competition, carnival, and industrial displays.

★ 1374 ★
Bremen - FIREMEN'S FESTIVAL. Early July, 6 days, Sunnyside Park. Contact: Bob Widmar, 1403 West Dewey Street, Bremen, Indiana 46506.

Country-western shows, rides, concessions, industrial and commercial exhibits, and parade.

★ 1375 ★
Cambridge City - WHITEWATER CANAL DAYS. Late September, annual, 2 days. Contact: Vern Clingenpeel, People's State Bank, Cambridge City, Indiana 47327.

Crafts such as chair caning and apple butter-making. Sky-jumping, kiddie rides, flea markets, arts and crafts shows, doll show, gospel sing, pet show, and parade.

★ 1376 ★
Cannelton - CANORAMA. Late June, 8 days, Main Street and Riverfront Park. Contact: William Garrett, Pleasant Valley, Cannelton, Indiana 47520.

Events include rides, music, and refreshment stands.

★ 1377 ★.
Cayuga - PIONEER DAYS FESTIVAL. Late May-early June, 2 days. Contact: Mr. Otto Albright, Fifth Street, Cayuga, Indiana 47928.

A king, a queen and a belle reign over the festivities. Events include a horse show, bean dinners, art displays, a Sunday pancake and sausage breakfast at the firehouse, horseshoe pitching, and a flea market. Historic places of interest include the Grondyke House, a 102 year old covered bridge, and the Eugene Methodist church bilt in 1859. Also takes place in Eugene.

★ 1378 ★
Dunkirk - GLASS DAYS FESTIVAL. Late July, 4 days, Kerr Glass facilities, Indiana Glass Plant, Main Street. Contact: Chairman, Glass Days Committee, 121 East Washington Street, Dunkirk, Indiana 47336.

INDIANA (Continued)

Tours of glass factories where products are being produced, Queen of Glass, amusement rides, refreshments, and glass blowing demonstrations.

★ 1379 ★
Elwood - ELWOOD GLASS FESTIVAL. Mid July-early August, 4-5 days. Contact: Executive Secretary, Greater Elwood Progress Association, 1301 Main Street, Elwood, Indiana 46036.

Antique glass displays in downtown stores, and tours of modern glassworks. Championship wrestling in junior high gym, sidewalk days, fish fry, fashion show, flea market, pet and bike parade, art show, golf tournament, talent shows and cooking schools.

★ 1380 ★
Eugene - PIONEER DAYS FESTIVAL. Late May-early June, 2 days. Contact: Mr. Otto Albright, Fifth Street, Cayuga, Indiana 47928.

A king, a queen and a belle reign over the festivities. Events include a horse show, bean dinners, art displays, a Sunday pancake and sausage breakfast at the firehouse, horseshoe pitching and a flea market. Historic places of interest include the Grondyke House, a 102 year old covered bridge, and the Eugene Methodist church built in 1859. Also takes place in Cayuga.

★ 1381 ★
Evansville - FREEDOM FESTIVAL. June-July, annual. Contact: Executive Director, Freedom Festival Foundation of Evansville, Incorporated, c/o Executive Inn, 600 Walnut Street, Evansville, Indiana 47708.

Events include lighting of the freedom torch, horse show, chess tournament, drum and bugle corps drill, beauty pageants, boat races, Banquet of the Golden Plate, giant parade, nation's largest display of fireworks (July 4th), golf, rugby, and tennis tournaments, Heiken puppet show, autocross sport car rally, bands, concerts, religious ceremonies, championship midget airplane races, the Press Club Bierstube, and pageants.

★ 1382 ★
Garrett - GARRETT DAYS. Early August, 2 days, Main Street. Contact: Secretary, Garrett Merchants Association, 617 South Randolph Street, Garrett, Indiana 46738.

Bikes, floats, and pets parade down Main Street.

Street sale, talent show, queen crowning, free pancake breakfast are additional highlights.

★ 1383 ★
Geneva - WABASH VALLEY FESTIVAL. Mid July, 3 days. Contact: Beverly Smith, Post Office Box 325, Geneva, Indiana 46740.

Antiques, arts and crafts, flower show, and a gas and steam engine show highlight this community festival.

★ 1384 ★
Hammond - SCIENCE FAIR. Early April, 2 days, Hammond Civic Center. Contact: Michael Bicanic, Hammond Civic Center, 5825 Sohl Avenue, Hammond, Indiana 46320.

Sponsored by Purdue University's Calumet campus to show outstanding science experiments and projects.

★ 1385 ★
Greenfield - JAMES WHITCOMB RILEY FESTIVAL. Early October, 3 days. Contact: Greenfield Chamber of Commerce, 110 South State, Greenfield, Indiana 46140.

Parade of flowers, homemade cooking, antique cars, old fiddlers' contest, go-cart races, queen contest, and country and western music. Dedication of the "Old Swimmin' Hole" near Riley's home. Riley Day parade. Free entertainment, special Riley exhibits, antique auto show, art and crafts fair, and flea market, all in honor of the life and times of the poet.

★ 1386 ★
Greentown - GREENTOWN GLASS FESTIVAL. Early June, annual, 3 days, Greentown Glass Museum. Contact: Vice President, Greentown Glass Festival, 833 Holiday Drive, Greentown, Indiana 46936.

Events include a carnival, street fair sales, antique show, parade, art show, and a chicken barbeque. Begun around 1970.

★ 1387 ★
Hope - HERITAGE DAY. Late September, 1 day, Town Square. Contact: Secretary, Heritage of Hope, Incorporated, Post Office Box 52, Hope, Indiana 47246.

Demonstrations of early crafts, window decorations, costume judgings, antiques displayed and for sale, and a parade.

Community

INDIANA (Continued)

★ 1388 ★
Indianapolis - 500 FESTIVAL. May, annual, 1
month. Contact: Executive Director, 500 Festival
Associates, Incorporated, One Indiana Square, Suite
2260, Indianapolis, Indiana 46204.

The festival precedes the running of the Indianapolis
500. It opens with the mayor's breakfast. The
events of the month include a Festival of Arts, gin
rummy tournament, golf tournament, mid-west radio
controlled car race, a large parade, classic car displays, banquets, including the mechanics banquet, the
victory dinner, the Queen's Ball, bridge tournament,
children's activities, and memorial service.

★ 1389 ★
Liberty - LIBERTY FESTIVAL. Early July, 2 days,
Town Square. Contact: Ted J. Montgomery, Post
Office Box 217, Liberty, Indiana 47353.

Special events for children, old fashioned flea market and antique show, chicken barbeque, and fireworks display.

★ 1390 ★
Marion - DOWNTOWN FESTIVAL. Mid July, 3
days, downtown area. Contact: Secretary, Marion
Area Chamber of Commerce, 325 South Adams,
Marion, Indiana 46952.

Sidewalk sales, arts and crafts booths, senior citizen
contest, and a rocking chair contest are included in
the events.

★ 1391 ★
Martinsville - AMERICAN DONKEY AND MULE
SOCIETY JUBILEE FESTIVAL. Mid July, 2 days,
Morgan County 4-H Fairgrounds. Contact: Office
Manager and Secretary, Chamber of Commerce, 233
East Washington Street, Martinsville, Indiana 46151.

Held in conjunction with the National Show of the
American Donkey and Mule Society. Square dancing,
ox roast, parade, exhibits, and country music.

★ 1392 ★
Metamora - CANAL DAYS-TRADERS RENDEZVOUS.
Early October, 2 days, Whitewater Canal. Contact:
Bert Wittenbaum, 7301 Garden Road, Cincinnati,
Ohio 45236.

Recreation of a nineteenth century shipping village
market with arts, crafts, and antiques. Canal boat

rides, flea market, crafts demonstrations, Indian
village, and Indian fighters with muzzle-loading
rifles.

★ 1393 ★
Mooreland - MOORELAND FREE FAIR. Mid August,
7 days. Contact: Mrs. Michael Modjeski, Rural
Route 1, Moreland, Indiana 47360.

Set up in tents: antiques, art and hobby exhibits,
merchants' wares, food, special programs and bingo.

★ 1394 ★
New Carlisle - WILDERNESS OLD TIMES FESTIVAL.
Mid July, annual, 1-2 days, Bendix Woods county
park. Contact: Program Director, Saint Joseph
County Park and Recreation Department, Rural Route
2, Box 72 A, New Carlisle, Indiana 46552.

Demonstrations of log-rolling, tobacco spitting,
mountaineering, canoe and kayak running, orienteering,
archery shooting, and old time crafts. Cross country
run, contests in fishing, horseshoe and log-rolling,
wilderness safety programs, and cross country skiing
demonstrations.

★ 1395 ★
New Harmony - RAINTREE HEY DAYS FESTIVAL.
Mid June, 4 days, downtown. Contact: Mrs.
Irvin C. Reynolds, 630 South Street, New Harmony,
Indiana 47631.

Beer garden, band music, dances, rides, parades,
tours of the historic district, contests, turtle and
sack races, arts and crafts show, and prince and
princess contests highlight the festival events.

★ 1396 ★
North Manchester - FUN FEST. Mid August,
annual, 10 days, throughout the town. Contact:
Chairman, Fun Fest, 114 West Main Street, North
Manchester, Indiana 46962.

Square dance, parade, Manchester antique show,
historic home and exhibits, tractor pulls, and marching band show. Begun around 1971.

★ 1397 ★
North Webster - MERMAID FESTIVAL. Late June,
9 days. Contact: Secretary, North Webster Lions
Club, Post Office Box 301, North Webster, Indiana
46555.

Mermaid Ball, horseshoe pitch, chicken barbeque,

INDIANA (Continued)

waterball, cutie parade, basketball tourney, tournament of knights, ski show, beauty pageant, coronation of the King of Sports, and a parade highlight the festival events.

★ 1398 ★
Pendleton - JUNE JAMBOREE. Mid June, 4 days, Falls Park. Contact: Lloyd Kelley, President, Pendelton Lions Club, Rural Route 4, Pendleton, Indiana 46064.

Exhibits, rides, crafts, games, contests, bands and song, and homemade church dinners.

★ 1399 ★
Peru - CIRCUS CITY FESTIVAL. Mid July, annual, 4-6 days. Contact: President, Circus City Festival, Incorporated, 154 North Broadway, Post Office Box 482, Peru, Indiana 46970.

Peru was once the winter headquarters of seven top circuses. Amateur jugglers, acrobats, tumblers, trapeze artists, high-wire artists, etc., entertain at this gathering.

★ 1400 ★
Plainfield - CELEBRITY FESTIVAL. Early October, 4 days, Swinford Park, Plainfield Elementary School, high school auditorium. Contact: Chairman, Plainfield Celebrity Festival, Post Office Box 115, Plainfield, Indiana 46168.

Bazaar, antique show, antique car display, and a vareity show are included in the festivities.

★ 1401 ★
Sheridan - BUTTONWOOD SWAMP FESTIVAL. Early August, 2 days, Main Street. Contact: Barbara Rodgers, Rodgers Finishing Tools, 508 East Sixth Street, Sheridan, Indiana 46069.

Folk singing and exhibits by artists and craftsmen highlight this community celebration.

★ 1402 ★
Terre Haute - BANKS OF THE WABASH FESTIVAL. Late May-early June, annual, 9 days, Fairbanks Park. Contact: Director, Banks of the Wabash Festival, Terre Haute House, Room 304, Terre Haute, Indiana 47807.

The purpose is to promote the area with a weeklong

'fun festival' telling the Terra Haute story. Farmers' day, fiddle contest, canoe and raft racing, log-rolling, bicycle tours, bike races, dramatic productions, golf, tennis, parade, ethnic displays, arts and crafts, and film festival. Industrial displays, beauty pageant, dances, recitals, ball, dinners, cooking contests, concerts (various types of music), circus, displays of books in the library, speakers, historical displays, and horse show. Begun around 1974.

★ 1403 ★
Vallonia - FORT VALLONIA DAYS. Mid-late October, 2 days, Fort Vallonia. Contact: President, Fort Vallonia Days, Incorporated, Vallonia, Indiana 47281.

Flea markets, crafts demonstrations, free street entertainment, antique machinery in operation, judged trail ride, muzzle-loading rifle shoot, parade, teen dance, a square dance, horseshoe pitching, pumpkin pie and yeast bread contests, and brothers-of-the-brush beard competition.

★ 1404 ★
Van Buren - POP CORN FESTIVAL. Mid August, annual, 3 days. Contact: Bob Hemmick, Post Office Box 434, Van Buren, Indiana 46991.

The world's largest popcorn industry provides the basis of the festival featuring a parade, queen contest, dance, flea market, waterball fight, tractor pull, parachute jump, and assorted contests.

★ 1405 ★
Veedersburg - YEDDO OLD SETTLERS REUNION. Mid August, annual, 3 days, Hub Park. Contact: Vern French, 117 East Second Street, Veedersburg, Indiana 47987.

The old settlers are honored with prizes for the oldest participants, those coming the longest distance, and the couple married the longest. Carnival rides, a fish fry, talent shows, a baby show, tractor pull, and horseshoe pitch complete the events. Begun around 1879.

★ 1406 ★
Wabash - WABASH CANAL DAYS. Late July, 2 days, downtown. Contact: Executive Secretary, Wabash Chamber of Commerce, Post Office Box 371, Wabash, Indiana 46992.

A parade and sidewalk sales of arts, crafts, and other items, including refreshments, highlight this community celebration.

Community

INDIANA (Continued)

★ 1407 ★
Whitestown - PIONEER DAYS. Late September, annual, 2 days. Contact: Mrs. Mary Frances Hardin, Route 1, Box 23, Whitestown, Indiana 46075.

Parade, horse pull, husband calling contest, hog calling contest, rooster crowing contest, bike and trike decorating contest, sack race, street dance, senior citizens beauty contest, horse show, carnival rides, clowns, antique and historical displays, art show and game booths.

★ 1408 ★
Winchester - WINCHESTER SPEEDWAY OLDTIMERS FESTIVAL. Late July, 3 days, Winchester Speedway. Contact: Roger W. Holdeman, Rural Route 1, Winchester, Indiana 47394.

Gathering of famous racing personalities of yesteryear with old restored racing and street cars on parade, running of the restored race cars, and running of USAC sprint cars.

IOWA

★ 1409 ★
Ames - VEISHEA CELEBRATION. Early May (1st weekend, usually), annual, 3 days, campus of the Iowa State University of Science and Technology. Contact: Iowa State University of Science and Technology, Information Service, Morrill Hall, Ames, Iowa 50010.

The name Veishea is derived from the first letters of the five divisions of what was then the Iowa State College in 1922. Centers on open houses in the departments of the five colleges within the university. These are educational in nature and manned, designed and built by students. Questions are answered about curricula, and scholarships are awarded. Other events include canoe races on Lake LaVerne with competitors from the Greek system, residence houses and independent organizations. Veishea concert offers nationally known musicians and groups. "Stars over Veishea" is a theatrical production. Sports events include the spring football game and the Big Eight Conference baseball. Parade with 40-50 floats, 25-30 high school bands, and a famous person as the parade marshall. Produced by students with a faculty-advisor corps.

★ 1410 ★
Bellevue - HERITAGE DAYS. Early July, annual,

2-3 days, Cole Park. Contact: Bellevue Chamber of Commerce, Mr. Tim Gallagher, Chairman, Bellevue, Iowa 52031.

A traditional community festival celebrating earlier days.

★ 1411 ★
Britt- HOBO CONVENTION. Early August, annual, 1-2 days. Contact: Britt Chamber of Commerce, James C. Bennett, Secretary, Britt, Iowa 50423.

A carnival, competition for the titles of king and queen of the hobos, and a parade. "Mulligan Stew" is distributed free to the public. Hobos come from across the country to participate. Hobo Day art show and talent show. First held in 1900, began with regularity in 1933.

★ 1412 ★
Burlington - STEAMBOAT DAYS AND DIXIELAND JAZZ FESTIVAL. Late June (3rd week), annual, 1 week, downtown riverfront (most events). Contact: Steamboat Days, Incorporated, Chamber of Commerce, Burlington Plaza, Burlington, Iowa 52601.

Top-name musicians ranging from jazz to rock to folk and country and western entertain. There is a carnival, parade, waterfront excursions, steamboat races, Miss Burlington pageant, beer garden, players' workshop, canoe races, helicopter rides, river rides, steamboat ball, square dancing, antique and muzzle loading firearms demonstration, water ski races, marionettes, magicians, boat parade, fireworks, crafts exhibits and demonstrations, and sales. The Des Moines County Historical Society also presents programs in conjunction including special displays at museums, tours, trolley rides, antique and used items sale. A separate event, the Snake Alley Art Fair, is usually held on the last day of Steamboat Days. Begun around 1963.

★ 1413 ★
Drakesville - OLD SOLDIERS AND SETTLERS REUNION. Late July (last Thursday, Friday, and Saturday), annual, 3 days. Contact: Bill D. Bassett, Post Office Box 1, Drakesville, Iowa 52501.

Events include a tractor pull contest with classes for all sizes of tractors, the selection of a Davis County Conservation Queen, a baby contest, childrens' contest, presentation of the chair to the oldest soldier resident in Davis county in attendance at the reunion, a muzzle shoot, a parade, a concert by the Davis County High School Band, a horse show, sheep dog

IOWA (Continued)

trials, presentation of chair to oldest settler of the county, mini bike and cycle show, barbershop quartet, and round and square dancing. Begun over 100 years ago.

★ 1414 ★
Fort Dodge - FRONTIER DAYS. Early June, annual, 7 or 8 days. Contact: Chamber of Commerce, Post Office Box T, Fort Dodge, Iowa 50501.

Events include a parade of floats, bands and marching units. In addition, there are concerts and music shows by bands, glee clubs, and other local and professional talent, including the Karl King Fort Dodge Band and the Fort Dodge Glee Club. The Re-Generation, a musical group of college-age performers has appeared. Started in 1975.

★ 1415 ★
Glenwood - PIONEER DAYS. Mid June, 3 days. Contact: Chamber of Commerce, Glenwood, Iowa 51534.

A community festival celebrating an earlier era.

★ 1416 ★
Keokuk - WORLD'S LARGEST STREET FAIR. Mid June, annual, 6 days. Contact: Keokuk Chamber of Commerce, Eppers Hotel, Keokuk, Iowa 52632.

Large fair featuring arts and crafts, agricultural, horticultural and a variety of other displays.

★ 1417 ★
Manning - CHILDREN'S DAY. Early June (1st Monday), annual, 1 day. Contact: Manning Chamber of Commerce, Manning, Iowa 51455.

The day begins with a parade led by the reigning king and queen. About 1,700 children participate in the parade, including the Manning high, junior high and grade school bands. A basketball free throw contest for boys and girls up to the age of 15 is held; prizes are awarded to the winners. The new king and queen are crowned. Rides for children of all ages, concession stands, and a dance provide entertainment. Originally called Kinderfest Celebration. Started in 1881.

★ 1418 ★
Manning - GOOD OLD DAYS. Early August, annual, 1 day, old athletic field and city park.

Contact: Manning Chamber of Commerce, Manning, Iowa 51455.

Activities include a horseshoe pitching contest, wood-sawing contest, egg throwing, barrel roll race, three-legged race and a sack race. There are demonstrations of threshing, old time straw baling, and old time rope making. There is a dunking stand, bingo, and a lunch stand. Festival ends with a dance in city park and a drawing for prizes. Started in 1973.

KANSAS

★ 1419 ★
Baldwin City - MAPLE LEAF FESTIVAL. Mid October, annual, 2-3 days. Contact: Mrs. Bettie Metsker, Route 5, Lawrence, Kansas 66044.

In 1958 the citizens of the city began a long term project of planting maple trees to beautify the city. The festival stems from this. It includes historical and musical dramas, tours to spots of historical interest, arts and craft displays, a carnival, prairie breakfast, parades, antique quilt shows, hobby shows, pony pulls, a Quayle Bible display, etc.

★ 1420 ★
Independence - NEEWOLLAH CELEBRATION. Late October, annual, 4 days. Contact: Chamber of Commerce, 108 West Myrtle, Independence, Kansas 67301.

Features a grand parade, a children's Halloween parade, carnival, free street acts, stage shows, football games, the coronation of Queen Neelah, dances, and country and western bands.

★ 1421 ★
Lawrence - SPRING ON THE HILL. Mid April, annual, 3 days, the campus of University of Kansas. Contact: University Relations, 135 Carruth-O'Leary, The University of Kansas, Lawrence, Kansas 66045.

All-university open house. The various departments welcome the visitors with varying degrees of formality. They may have them in open classes and/or labs, exhibits of their fields of endeavor; e.g. the art department may have an art exhibit, the microbiology department may have slides of disease-causing microorganisms, etc. They may also have movies, lectures, displays, theatrical productions, panel discussions, receptions, tours, recitals, concerts, etc.

Community

KENTUCKY

★ 1422 ★
Grayson - GRAYSON MEMORY DAYS. Late May, annual, 7 days. Contact: Mrs. Christian McGlone, Route 3, Grayson, Kentucky 41143.

People in old-fashioned dress, antique displays, arts and crafts displays, parades, country music, trade day, horse show and an outdoor prayer meeting. Begun around 1971.

★ 1423 ★
Hitchins - DAVY'S RUN HOMECOMING FESTIVAL. Late July, annual, 1 day. Contact: Hubert L. Rogers, Route 2, Box 180, Grayson, Kentucky 41143.

Basket dinner at noon followed by an afternoon of fellowship and folk/country music concerts. Begun around 1965.

★ 1424 ★
Lexington - LITTLE KENTUCKY DERBY. Early April (lst or 2nd week), annual, 1 week, University of Kentucky. Contact: LKD Committee, Student Center Activities Board, University of Kentucky, Lexington, Kentucky 40506.

Parties honoring favorite members of the faculty "apple polishing", special concerts, eating contests, "goofy games", a queen contest, and turtle races are scheduled throughout the week. Men team up for bike races; the women team up for scooter races.

★ 1425 ★
Louisville - KENTUCKY DERBY FESTIVAL. Late April-early May, annual, 10 days. Contact: Kentucky Derby Festival, 621 West Main Street, Louisville, Kentucky 41143.

Celebration leads up to the running of the Kentucky Derby horse race. Pegasus Parade (Pegasus is the symbol of the festival), pop concert with name entertainment, Kentucky Colonels banquet, Derby Festival Coronation ball, banquets and dinners, balloon race, bicycle race, mini-marathon, basketball classic, fireworks, great steamboat race, Festival of Stars, kiting off the Clark Memorial bridge, square dance exhibition, water spectacular, fashion fair, dance cruise, Schlitz 40-horse hitch, musical entertainments, parties, art shows, tours of historic Louisville, and a three boat steamboat competition highlight the events. Started in 1956.

★ 1426 ★
Owingsville - MAY DAY FESTIVAL. Early May, 1 day. Contact: Darvin Estes, Ridgeway Estates, Owingsville, Kentucky 40360; or Owingsville Lions Club, Owingsville, Kentucky 40360.

Parades, marching bands, and antique cars grace the streets of Owingsville during their salute to the month of May. The new Miss Bath County is chosen during the evening to reign over the next year festivities.

★ 1427 ★
Prestonburg - MOUNTAIN DEW FESTIVAL. Mid April, annual, 3 days, Prestonburg Community College. Contact: Coordinator of Student Affairs, Prestonburg Community College, Prestonburg, Kentucky 41653.

Athletic competition among junior and community college students from Kentucky, Ohio and West Virginia. A parade, dance, and outdoor concert, and talent and queens contests also are held during the festival.

★ 1428 ★
Washington - WASHINGTON HAYSEED FESTIVAL. Mid June, 2 days. Contact: Gerald Bramel, Route 2, Box 161, Maysville, Kentucky 41056; or Robert Suite, Post Office Box 44, Washington, Kentucky 41096.

An old time festival with a little bit of something for everyone: beauty pageants, parade, street dance, frog derby, hay rides, amusement rides, games, food and various kinds of displays and contests.

★ 1429 ★
West Liberty - SORGHUM FESTIVAL. Mid October, annual, 3 days. Contact: Mrs. James R. Perry, Keeton Heights, West Liberty, Kentucky° 41472.

To encourage preservation of old hand crafts that are slowly going out of existence and to promote the cane production of Morgan County. Craft booths, sorghum by the gallon or jug, old time food production, country store, parade, and country/folk music.

LOUISIANA

★ 1430 ★
Acadiana (district including Mamou, Church Point, Ville Platte and Eunice) - MARDI GRAS. February (on Shrove Tuesday), annual, 1 day. Contact:

LOUISIANA (Continued)

Louisiana Tourist Commission, Post Office Box 44291, Baton Rouge, Louisiana 70804.

A band of grotesquely masked and garbed horsemen start out in the dawn hours and ride into the country-side under the leadership of "Le Capitaine", who rides a richly decked horse. The leader blows a cow horn at each farmhouse and inquires if anyone is in mourning. If yes, they ride on, if not the men (if welcomed) sing folk songs and cavort for the entertainment of the household. They then seek a gift to be used in making gumbo. The farmer may hand them rice, or let loose a chicken which they must catch. After they have been to all the farms, the booty is taken back to town and cooked by the women. The whole town feasts, after which there is revelry, music, dancing, and libations.

★ 1431 ★
Baton Rouge - STATE SOCIAL STUDIES FAIR. Mid April, annual, 3 days, Louisiana State University. Contact: Supervisor of Social Studies, Louisiana State Department of Education, Post Office Box 44064, Baton Rouge, Louisiana 70804.

Thirteen regional fairs precede this statewide one and the winners from the regions compete here. The students display projects in one of six social science disciplines: Anthropology, Economics, Geography, History, Political Science, or Sociology. Started in 1967.

★ 1432 ★
Chauvin - LAGNIAPPE ON THE BAYOU. Mid October, 3 days. Contact: Louisiana Tourist Commission, Post Office Box 44291, Baton Rouge, Louisiana 70804.

An old-fashioned festival including a country store, seafood, games and street dances. There is a saloon with live entertainment, a replica of a shrimp drying platform, rides and country booths where the townspeople sell the items which they have been making for the past year. Cajun food such as pecan gralle and sweet-dough pie are served. The festival is an expression of Acadian culture.

★ 1433 ★
DeRidder - BEAUREGARD PIONEER FESTIVAL. Mid September, 1 day. Contact: Louisiana Tourist Commission, Post Office Box 44291, Baton Rouge, Louisiana 70804.

Civic, religious and social organizations in the parish

gather gifts of merchandise to be sold at a gigantic flea market. Artifacts of the pioneer days are assembled to place on exhibit. In addition, there are buggy rides, a quilting bee, a square dance, a battle of the bands, tours of the Beauregard Museum and contests including pioneer costumes, beard grow-ing, fiddling, log sawing, pet judging, etc. Guest entertainers from Fort Polk.

★ 1434 ★
Galliano - CAJUN FESTIVAL. Mid June, annual, 3 days, South Lafourche High School. Contact: Dale Guidry, Post Office Drawer A, Galliano, Louisiana 70354.

Rides and games, formal opening and dedication ceremonies, Cajun street dance, potato dance con-test, a waltzing contest, Cajun dress contest, displays, food, Cajun piroque race, air show, continuous Cajun music, auction, beauty contest, choir, airplane rides, beard contest, Cajun play, Cajun foods, bike race, quilting, and commercial exhibits.

★ 1435 ★
Greenwood - PIONEER DAYS. Late August, 2-3 days. Contact: Executive Director, Louisiana Tourist Commission, Post Office Box 44291, Baton Rouge, Louisiana 70804.

Pioneer Days is a birthday party for the city of Greenwood. The activities associated with the event include a parade, a free watermelon supper, a square dance exhibition, a pie-eating contest, terrapin races, a fine arts and antique show, a barbeque, fiddler's contest, country and western dance, horse show, crafts fair and flea market, and historic homes and gardens tour. Also featured is a tug of war between the city fathers of Greenwood and Shreveport symbolizing an old quarrel over the location of the parish seat of government.

★ 1436 ★
Lafayette - LOUISIANA INDUSTRIAL ARTS STUDENTS FAIR (STUDENT CRAFTSMAN FAIR). March, annual, 1 day, Student Union Complex, University of South-western Louisiana. Contact: Mr. Joseph Pons, Assistant Professor, Industrial and Technical Education, University of Southwestern Louisiana, Lafayette, Louisiana 70501.

The state is divided into four areas, each area is sponsored by a university. All elementary, junior high and senior high school students are invited to participate in the fair. There are categories for the various phases of industrial arts, e.g. drafting, wood-working, metal work, electrical work, etc. These

Community

LOUISIANA (Continued)

are further subdivided by the grade level of the student. The student enters the project or display along with plans and/or a description of research and/or processes involved in construction. These displays and/or projects are displayed and are judged on 100 points. First, second and third place winners participate in the statewide fair. Started in 1967.

★ 1437 ★
Lafayette - SCIENCE FAIR (REGION VI). Early March (1st Saturday), annual, 1 day, University of Southwestern Louisiana. Contact: Mrs. Grace Eyster, Instructor of Biology, University of Southwestern Louisiana, Lafayette, Louisiana 70501.

Students from grades 7-12 compete at the county level. The three top winners from each category are thus able to participate at the Region VI Fair. Each student displays a project which he has completed within a year's period related to the physical, biological, or behavioral sciences. Walking tours of the campus are provided; various departments demonstrate special equipment or procedures. Begun in 1947.

★ 1438 ★
Lafayette - SOCIAL STUDIES FAIR (REGION VI). March, annual, University of Southwestern Louisiana campus. Contact: Mr. Louis J. Nicolosi, Supervisor of Social Studies, Louisiana State Department of Education, Post Office Box 44064, Baton Rouge, Louisiana 70804; or Director, Region VI Social Studies Fair, Office of Community and School Services, Post Office Box 4548, USL Station, Lafayette, Louisiana 70501.

Students from 4 to 12 prepare display projects in one of the six social science disciplines: Anthropology, Economics, Geography, History, Political Science or Sociology. After a pre-selection process in the local schools, participants advance to the regional fairs. Winners from the regional fairs in turn, compete in the statewide social science fair held in Baton Rouge. Projects may be done individually or by a group; individual and group projects compete separately in each age-group division and discipline. Projects are judged by faculty members from the University of Southwestern Louisiana and by other interested and qualified persons. Begun around 1967.

★ 1439 ★
Lake Charles - CONTRABAND DAYS. Early May (1st weekend), annual, 4 days, Civic Center, downtown. Contact: Executive Director, Louisiana Tourist

Commission, Post Office Box 44291, Baton Rouge, Louisiana 70804.

The official start of the festival is the capture of the town by a group of residents disguised as pirates and waving swords. Miss Contraband is crowned. There is a band festival featuring high school bands from several states, all of which participate in a parade. Southern regional gymnastics meet. Cajun Days, featuring nine hours of Cajun music. Other events include a bathtub race, fireworks display, sailboat race, powerboat race, etc. Celebrates the opening of the watersports season and the exploits of Jean Laffite.

★ 1440 ★
Logansport - FRONTIER DAYS CELEBRATION. Mid February, 1 day. Contact: Louisiana Tourist Commission, Post Office Box 44291, Baton Rouge, Louisiana 70804.

Contests and entertainment with a western theme highlight this community celebration.

★ 1441 ★
Monroe - SCIENCE FAIR (REGION III). Late March, 2 days, Northeast Louisiana University, Ewing Coliseum. Contact: Northeast Louisiana University, 700 University Avenue, Monroe, Louisiana 71201.

Students compete in various categories, projects are displayed and often demonstrated. Winners participate in further competition.

★ 1442 ★
Morgan City - GOOD TIMES ON THE BAYOU. Late April, 8 days. Contact: Executive Director, Louisiana Tourist Commission, Post Office Box 44291, Baton Rouge, Louisiana 70804.

Art show, high school tennis tourney, Mad Hatter's Luncheon, talent show, parade, Cajun dance, style show, tours, stage show, a teen dance, and the Bayou Ball highlight this community celebration.

★ 1443 ★
Morgan City - LOUISIANA SHRIMP AND PETROLEUM FESTIVAL. Late August, annual, 4 days. Contact: Mr. Joseph R. Joy, Jr., 117 Everett, Morgan City, Louisiana 70380.

Giant feast of boiled shrimp, and a regatta, blessing of the fleet, kites, arts and crafts exhibits, water parade, coronation court show, children's day, $20,000 bass tournament, football jamboree, and fireworks. Started in 1935.

LOUISIANA (Continued)

★ 1444 ★
New Orleans - MARDI GRAS. February (12th Night-Shrove Tuesday), annual, 2 weeks. Contact: Louisiana Tourist Commission, Post Office Box 44291, Baton Rouge, Louisiana 70804.

In this, perhaps the most famous of all the Mardi Gras festivals, revelers wear costumes, and mummers stroll through the streets throwing doubloons and trinkets. Parties and balls (at least five dozen private masked balls in the Municipal Auditorium) are frequent and lavish. Marching bands, animated paper mache figures and displays, and elaborate floats in the parades through the streets. Observers become participants, and the fun is infectious.

★ 1445 ★
New Roads - LE FESTIVAL DE POINTE COUPEE. Mid October, 2 days, National Guard Armory. Contact: New Roads Jaycees, Post Office Box 34, New Roads, Louisiana 70760.

Arts and crafts including paintings, leathercraft, pottery, and woodcraft. Contests including duck calling, costume making, whittling, hunting and shooting skills. Music, including Cajun, bluegrass, rock, soul, country and western, folk and blues music is played continuously. There are also tours of antebellum plantations, and a unique event, a liars convocation. Started in 1975.

★ 1446 ★
Rayne - FROG FESTIVAL. September, 2 days, festival grounds in North Rayne. Contact: Hilda Haure, Post Office Box 383, Rayne, Louisiana 70578.

Rayne, known as the frog capital of the world, celebrates the bullfrog and the commercial frog business. The events include the selection of Little Miss Rayne and the Frog Festival Queen. The latter is followed by a queen's ball. Activities include the diaper derby, the frog derby (in which the Frog Derby Queen is chosen to be the girl who can make her frog jump the furthest), the frog eating contest (just the legs), the frog art contest, and the grand parade which includes floats and dignitaries from the Cajun country. Booths on the festival grounds sell handmade articles, souvenirs, Cajun food, etc. Begun around 1973.

★ 1447 ★
Shreveport - HOLIDAY IN DIXIE. April, annual, 10 days, Louisiana State Fairgrounds, Barksdale Air Force Base in Bossier City. Contact: Jim Leslie and Associates, 804 Mid South Drive, Shreveport,

Louisiana 71101.

Murphy Brothers Exposition open daily, air show by the Thunderbirds and other flying groups, and a display of military aircraft, equipment and space exhibits at the base. Beauty pageant--Queen Holiday in Dixie, parade, water show, plus boxing, bicycle racing, bowling, badmitton, handball, raquetball, roller skating, powerlifting, gymnatics, yachting, piroque racing, golf and drill team and rifle competitions. Performances by barbershop quartets, jazz and high school bands. Flower shows and tours of local gardens. Art, gun, hobby, auto and style shows. Square dancing and pipe-smoking contests. Arts and crafts sale. Commemorates the signing of the Louisiana Purchase Agreement. Started in 1949.

★ 1448 ★
Walker - LOUISIANA PINE TREE FESTIVAL. Early May, 3 days, Old South Jamboree and Walker High School. Contact: Velma A. Cockerham, Route 1, Box 266 C, Walker, Louisiana 70785.

Band concert, gospel show, beauty contest for young people aged 1-16, street dance, crowning of the Pine Tree King (takes place at a guest luncheon), amateur talent contest, selection of a Pine Tree Queen, serving of jambalaya, giant country and western show.

MARYLAND

★ 1449 ★
Baltimore - BALTIMORE CITY FAIR. Late September, annual, 3 days, Inner Harbor. Contact: Baltimore City Fair, 222 East Saratoga Street, Baltimore, Maryland 21202.

Baltimore's communities join together to present an array of foods, exhibits, ethnic and cultural demonstrations in one of the best attended fairs in the country. The neighborhood exhibits display what is unique about each neighborhood. An international village features booths, food, and ethnic dances. There is a large amusement area and entertainment thru out - big name bands, a symphony orchestra, and high school chorus. Begun around 1970.

★ 1450 ★
Baltimore - FEDERAL HILL CELEBRATION. Mid May, annual, 1 day, Federal Hill. Contact: Mary Frances Garland, 1407 William Street, Baltimore, Maryland 21230.

A community festival featuring music and an art show. Begun around 1969.

Community

★ 1451 ★

Baltimore - FELLS POINT FUN FESTIVAL. Early October, annual, 2 days, Wolf Street, Bond Street, Fleet Street to the water. Contact: Ed Potocki, 327 South Ann, Baltimore, Maryland 21231; or Society for the Preservation of Federal Hill, Montgomery Street and Fells Point, 804 South Broadway, Baltimore, Maryland 21231.

Events include arts and crafts, entertainment, tours of historic Fells Point and other sites in Baltimore, rides, music (bluegrass, jazz, Polish, pops concert, sea chanteys), paddle boats, maritime display, super seafood supper, flea market, and the Green Scene (houseplants).

★ 1452 ★

Baltimore - MARYLAND KITE FESTIVAL. April (last Saturday), annual, 1 day, Campfield School grounds. Contact: The Maryland Kite Society, 7106 Campfield Road, Baltimore, Maryland 21207.

Kite flyers of all ages compete with mostly "homemade" kites. Grand prize for best-scoring kite judged on design, ingenuity, craftsmanship, beauty and flight performance. Many other prizes for age classes. There are also special prizes for family groups, most beautiful kite, wittiest kite, best advertising kite, largest kite, youngest entrant, oldest entrant, etc. Championship kite dueling for $500,000 in Monopoly money. Band music. In 1976 a world kite competition was added to follow the Maryland kite competition. Begun in 1967.

★ 1453 ★

Baltimore - PREAKNESS FESTIVAL WEEK. Mid May (week preceding Preakness-3rd Saturday), annual, 10 days, city wide. Contact: Baltimore Promotion Council, 22 Light Street, Baltimore, Maryland 21202.

More than 200 events throughout the city including Fine Arts Festival in Hopkins Plaza, concerts, one of the nation's largest parades, hot-air balloon race across the Chesapeake, a sailboat regatta, and art shows. All leads up to the running of the Preakness. Begun around 1969.

★ 1454 ★

Baltimore - SCIENCE FAIR. Late March, annual, 2 days, Johns Hopkins University Gymnasium. Contact: Joseph Dowling, 3331 Ravenwood Avenue, Baltimore, Maryland 21213.

Participants from many areas in Maryland compete in categories within biology and the physical sciences. Winners are sent to the International Science Fair. The event is co-sponsored by the Towson and Baltimore Kiwanis Clubs and Johns Hopkins University. Begun around 1956.

★ 1455 ★

Baltimore - U.S.A. DAY FESTIVAL. Mid June, annual, 1 day, Union Square. Contact: Ardebella Dean, 1504 Hollins Street, Baltimore, Maryland 21223.

Music, arts and crafts exhibits, kiddie rides and clowns highlight this community, patriotic festival. Begun around 1968.

★ 1456 ★

Boonsboro - BOONESBOROUGH DAYS. September, annual, 2 days, Shafer Park. Contact: Washington County Tourism Division, 40 Summit Avenue, Hagerstown, Maryland 21740.

Civil war momentoes, vintage automobiles, talented craftsmen and their wares, antiques, costume parade, and a variety of country food. Crafts include hooked rugs, weaving, toleware and china painting, macrame, etc. The festival seeks to recreate every aspect of life as it has been since 1780. Activities include square dancing, jousting tournament, musketry demonstration, and display of vintage automobiles. Memorabilia from the past is exhibited. There is also a county auction. A Grand Ball in which everyone is to wear costumes from the past 200 years is held. Begun around 1971.

★ 1457 ★

Brunswick - BRUNSWICK-POTOMAC RIVER FESTIVAL. Early August (2nd weekend), annual, 3 days, in the vicinity of the Museum. Contact: Brunswick-Potomac Foundation, 40 West Potomac Street, Brunswick, Maryland 21716.

This small Maryland town displays life on the C & O Canal and the Potomac. Special exhibits in town museum, musical programs, crafts demonstrated and sold, athletic events, film festival of railroading, railroad bus tour, display of rolling stock, antique sale and flea market, and U.S. Park Service displays. First held in 1969.

★ 1458 ★

California - BENEFIT AIR FAIR. Mid June, annual, 2 days, Saint Mary's County Airport. Contact: Saint Mary's County Air Fair Association, Post Office Box AF, California, Maryland 20619.

MARYLAND (Continued)

Air show, sky diving, air rides, K-9 demonstration by the State Police, beauty contest, dance bands, a variety of exhibits, and entertainment are included in the festival events.

★ 1459 ★
Cambridge - CAMBRIDGE OUTDOOR SHOW. Mid February, annual, 3 days, Cambridge High School. Contact: Chamber of Commerce, Cambridge, Maryland 21613.

Miss Outdoors beauty pageant, national muskrat skinning championship, country and western music and talent show, goose and duck calling contests, and log sawing competition highlight the events of this winter celebration. Begun around 1946.

★ 1460 ★
College Park - AVIATION HERITAGE DAYS. August, 2 days, College Park Airport. Contact: Prince Georges County Chamber of Commerce, Peoples National Bank Building, Kenilworth Avenue and Greenbelt Road, Greenbelt, Maryland 20770.

The history of the nation's oldest airport is commemorated with displays of antique and experimental airplanes, helicopters, hot air balloon, and airplane rides, and a mini-museum depicting the history of the airport.

★ 1461 ★
College Park - STAR TREK FESTIVAL. Early August (1st weekend), annual, 3 days, University of Maryland Student Union Building and Denton Hall. Contact: University of Maryland, Office of University Relations, College Park, Maryland 20742.

Movies all night on Friday and all day Saturday. Talks, discussions, memorabilia, huckster hall, original Star Trek art show and sale, trivia contest, show episodes, scientific lectures relating to space, displays of Star Trek costumes, and demonstrations of sewing of uniforms. Speakers include well-known authors and scientists. Has also been called The August Party.

★ 1462 ★
Cumberland - HOSPITALITY DAYS. September or August, annual, 3-4 days, downtown. Contact: Division of Tourism, 2425 Riva Road, Annapolis, Maryland 21401; or Ruth V.T. Hammel, Fort Cumberland Hotel, Cumberland, Maryland 21502.

Sidewalk vendors, crafts, antiques, arts, coin and stamp show, and antique and classic cars. Begun in 1974.

★ 1463 ★
Denton - SEPTEMBER FESTIVAL. Mid September, annual, 3 days, Caroline County 4-H Park. Contact: Denton Jaycees, Post Office Box 125, Denton, Maryland 21629.

Fire company stages water battle and Pelican Sky Divers stage air show. Other events include horseshoe and volleyball tournaments, games, arts and crafts, carnival booths, crab feast, and chicken barbeque. Begun around 1974.

★ 1464 ★
Oxford - DAY IN OXFORD. Mid April, annual, 1 day. Contact: Mrs. Robert T. Valliant, Jr., Box 188, Oxford, Maryland 21654.

A tour of the quaint town on Maryland's eastern shore. a plant sale and other events of a hospitable nature. Begun around 1959.

★ 1465 ★
Pocomoke City - POCOMOKE CYPRESS FESTIVAL. Mid July, 3 days. Contact: Chamber of Commerce, Box 356, Pocomoke City, Maryland 21851.

Events include a parade, a raft race, children's games, a horse show, tours of a Coast Guard cutter, craft sales and rides. There are several concerts including handbell, gospel, rock and country music. Refreshments are available.

★ 1466 ★
Saint Michaels - SAINT MICHAELS DAYS. Late September (3rd full weekend), annual, 2 days. Contact: The Banner, Easton, Maryland 21601.

House tours and open house at Saint Mary's Square Museum, Jim Leitch's workshop, the Masonic Temple, and the fire department. There are workboat races and log canoe races, a Tidewater Fisheries demonstration, and cruises aboard the Patriot. Also included in the events are art and craft demonstrations and displays, an antique show, a horse show, an auction, and various types of musical entertainment. Begun around 1972.

★ 1467 ★
Takoma Park - BEN FRANKLIN KITE FLYING CONTEST. Late March, 1 day. Contact:

Community

MARYLAND (Continued)

Montgomery County Chamber of Commerce, Rockville, Maryland 20850.

A competition and festival with all sorts of kites and kite-flyers participating.

★ 1468 ★
Towson - GOUCHER COUNTRY FAIR. Mid May, annual, 1 day, Dorm areas and College Center of Goucher College campus. Contact: Office of Public Relations, Goucher College, Towson, Maryland 21204.

Sponsored by the Alumnae Association. Games and rides for children, handcrafts, gifts, plants, flea market, auction, book sale for adults, and entertainment for all ages.

★ 1469 ★
Towson - INTELLECTUAL COUNTRY FAIR. Late October (last Saturday), annual, 1 day, College Center and surrounding campus, Goucher College. Contact: Public Relations Office, Goucher College, Towson, Maryland 21204.

In each time sequence (one hour) up to five different lectures, workshops, demonstrations, and musical events (music, art, history) are offered. Participants choose what appeals to them from each hour. Speakers are faculty, staff, emeriti faculty and staff, and occasional invited speakers. Started in 1959 in celebration of the seventy-fifth anniversary of the college.

★ 1470 ★
Westminster - MAY DAY CARNIVAL. Early May (1st weekend), annual, 1 day, Western Maryland College. Contact: Western Maryland College, Office of Publicity, Westminster, Maryland 21157.

Art show and contest (student and faculty art); booths by various campus organizations: food, games, crafts, and sponge throws. Activities such as greased pig contest, car smash, and pony rides. Book sale in the library of discarded books. Dancing (exhibition and/or participation): square dancing, and ethnic dancing. Started in 1972.

★ 1471 ★
Woodbine - APPLE BUTTER FESTIVAL. October, annual, 1 day, Morgan Chapel Church. Contact: Apple Butter Festival, Woodbine, Maryland 21797.

Old-time apple butter making, costumes, demonstrations, and food in the old country atmosphere. Begun around 1971.

MASSACHUSETTS

★ 1472 ★
Beverly - HOMECOMING WEEK. Mid August, annual, 1 week. Contact: Beverly Chamber of Commerce, 275 Cabot Street, Beverly, Massachusetts 01915.

Begins with pancake breakfast then continues with a six-mile road race, tour of historic homes, lobster festival, Old Timers' Day, arts and crafts exhibits and sales. Open house and sightseeing rides at Beverly Airport. Concludes with exhibits and concert, square dancing, and band concert.

★ 1473 ★
Conway - FESTIVAL OF THE HILLS. October (1st weekend), annual, 1 weekend. Contact: Michael Gery, Publicity Chairman, Reeds Bridge Road, Conway, Massachusetts 01341.

To celebrate and show off the delights of their town, the residents invite visitors for a round of activities including a horse drawing, crafts show, home-cooked meals, etc.

★ 1474 ★
Dalton - OLD HOME WEEK. Mid-late June, annual, 1 week. Contact: Massachusetts Department of Commerce and Development, Division of Tourism, Box 1775, Boston, Massachusetts 02105.

Rural games in this Berkshire Hills town - greased pole climbing, stilt-walking, double header of Old Timers' soft ball, and nightly square dancing. Other features include a colonial fair, huskin', spelling and sewing bees, old fashioned bonfire, parade, and barbeque get-together.

★ 1475 ★
Gloucester - FIESTA. Late June, annual, 3 days. Contact: Massachusetts Department of Commerce and Development, Division of Tourism, Box 1775, Boston, Massachusetts 02105.

Block dances, concerts, games and dory races. Concludes with solemn mass and blessing of fishing fleet.

★ 1476 ★
Goshen - GALA FUN WEEKEND. July (3rd weekend),

MASSACHUSETTS (Continued)

annual, 2 days. Contact: Pioneer Valley Association, Incorporated, 333 Prospect Street, Northampton, Massachusetts 01060.

The Goshen Recreation Association sponsors the meriment with a flea market, a block dance, a chicken barbeque, and special activities for children.

★ 1477 ★
Great Barrington - BARRINGTON FAIR. Mid September, annual, 11 days. Contact: Berkshire Hills Conference, Incorporated, 107 South Street, Pittsfield, Massachusetts 01201; or President and General Manager, Barrington Fair, Barrington, Massachusetts 01230.

The fair is generally acknowledged to be the oldest, continuously running such event in the country. Attractions include horse races and all types of exhibits. Begun around 1841.

★ 1478 ★
Ipswich - YANKEE HOMECOMING. August, annual, 1 week. Contact: Chamber of Commerce, Ipswich, Massachusetts 01938.

A traditional community celebration honoring past residents and guests with activities for remembering and just for fun.

★ 1479 ★
Lancaster - OLD HOME WEEK. Early-mid July, annual, 8 days. Contact: Massachusetts Department of Commerce and Development, Division of Tourism, Box 1775, Boston, Massachusetts 02105.

Square dancing on the green. Parade, puppet show, exhibits of local artists and a bicentennial ball are highlights of the week.

★ 1480 ★
Marshfield - MARSHFIELD FAIR. Mid-late August, annual, 10 days, Fairgrounds. Contact: Plymouth County Development Council, Incorporated, Post Office Box 1620, Pembroke, Massachusetts 02359.

Featuring contests, rides and exhibits, the event harkens back to the days when the annual fair was leading event in small-town life.

★ 1481 ★
Nantucket - MAIN STREET FAIR. Early August,

annual, 1 day. Contact: Massachusetts Department of Commerce and Development, Division of Tourism, Box 1775, Boston, Massachusetts 02105.

Crafts, antiques, and entertainment to benefit historical society.

★ 1482 ★
Newburyport - YANKEE HOMECOMING. Mid August, annual, 1 week. Contact: Greater Newburyport Chamber of Commerce, 21 Pleasant Street, Newburyport, Massachusetts 01950.

The festival offers boatrides around the harbor, and tours of local historic homes. Onlookers can enjoy an auction and a ten-mile road race.

★ 1483 ★
Rowe - OLD HOME DAYS. Mid July, annual, 3 days. Contact: Massachusetts Department of Commerce and Development, Division of Tourism, Box 1775, Boston, Massachusetts 02105.

Colonial costume ball, followed by parade, crafts fair, dinner and fireworks with music by fife and drum corps. Dedication of Fort Pelham and recently restored colonial tool factory as a creative arts and crafts center.

★ 1484 ★
Salem - CHESTNUT STREET DAYS. Mid June, annual, 2 days. Contact: Massachusetts Department of Commerce and Development, Division of Tourism, Box 1775, Boston, Massachusetts 02105.

Charm of yore with horse drawn trolleys, costumed participants, tour of mansions, and a band concert.

★ 1485 ★
Salem - HERITAGE DAYS. Mid August, annual, 8 days. Contact: Massachusetts Department of Commerce and Development, Division of Tourism, Box 1775, Boston, Massachusetts 02105.

Weeklong series of events includes circus acts, boat regatta, New England supper on town common, and a giant parade.

★ 1486 ★
Salem - MARKET DAYS. Mid September, annual, 2 days, Derby Square. Contact: Massachusetts Department of Commerce and Development, Division of Tourism, Box 1775, Boston, Massachusetts 02105.

Community

MASSACHUSETTS (Continued)

Foods, crafts and entertainment in this community festivity.

★ 1487 ★
Salem - SPRING MARKET DAYS.   Late May,
annual, 2 days, Derby Square.   Contact: Massachusetts Department of Commerce and Development,
Division of Tourism, Box 1775, Boston, Massachusetts
02105.

Gathering of greengrocers, skilled craftsmen, and
talented musicians for a colorful interchange.

★ 1488 ★
South Carver - CHRISTMAS FESTIVAL OF LIGHTS.
Mid November-early January, annual, 1 1/2 months.
Contact: Bristol County Development Council, In-
corporated, 154 North Main Street, Fall River,
Massachusetts 02722.

Christmas exhibits and attractions along train route,
daily except for Thanksgiving and Christmas days.

★ 1489 ★
South Carver - RAIL-FANS DAY.   Mid June, annual,
1 day.   Contact: Bristol County Development
Council, Incorporated, 154 North Main Street, Fall
River, Massachusetts 02722.

Trains--double header, mixed, and diesel.   Other
special activities.

★ 1490 ★
Southwick - HOMECOMING WEEK.   Mid-late
June, annual, 9 days.   Contact: Massachusetts
Department of Commerce and Development, Division
of Tourism, Box 1775, Boston, Massachusetts 02105.

Festivities include a horse pull, antique auto rally,
and arts and craft show.   Performance by a chorale.
Parade.

★ 1491 ★
Woods Hole - WOODS HOLE DAY.   Late May, 1
day.   Contact: Falmouth Chamber of Commerce,
Falmouth, Massachusetts 02540.

The villagers hold a festival with displays and games,
crafts and food sales.

MICHIGAN

★ 1492 ★
Bellaire - AVIATION FESTIVAL.   October, annual,
4 days.   Contact: West Michigan Tourist Association,
136 Fulton East, Hospitality House, Grand Rapids,
Michigan 49502.

Sometimes held in conjunction with the Autumn
Festival or Color Time in Bellaire, the emphasis here
is on airplanes and other flying devices.

★ 1493 ★
Cedar Springs - RED FLANNEL FESTIVAL.   Early
October (1st Saturday), annual, 9 days.   Contact:
Chamber of Commerce, Cedar Springs, Michigan
49319.

The festival celebrates the town's red flannel industry and the lumberjacks of the past.   Events
begin with the selection of the Red Flannel Queen.
There is also a lumberjack supper, amusement rides,
a musical melodrama, tours of the red flannel factory,
a golf tourney.   On the second Saturday, Red Flannel Day, the citizenry dress in red flannel, keystone
cops patrol in an antique fire engine, there is a large
parade, and a variety of games and contests.   There
is also a band festival, an arts and crafts show, and
a chicken barbeque.   Started in 1939.

★ 1494 ★
Centreville - COVERED BRIDGE FESTIVAL.   Early
July (4th of July weekend), annual, 3 days, through-
out the town.   Contact: Centreville Chamber of
Commerce, Centreville, Michigan 49032.

Events include sidewalk sales, arts and crafts shows
and demonstrations, doll show, obedience and leader
dog training exhibition, minstrels, puppet show,
square dance, cake walk, band concert, ice cream
social, barbershop chorus, antique tractor show,
farmer's market, book sale, carnival, canoe races,
karate demonstration, horse show, street dance, games,
contests, and concerts.   Begun around 1972.

★ 1495 ★
Charlevoix - VENETIAN FESTIVAL.   Late July,
annual, 3 days.   Contact: Chamber of Commerce,
408 Bridge Street, Post Office Box 217, Charlevoix,
Michigan 49720.

Regional foods, fireworks, boat parade on Round Lake
and a street parade highlight this celebration.   Begun around 1931.

MICHIGAN (Continued)

★ 1496 ★
Detroit - INTERNATIONAL FREEDOM FESTIVAL.
Late June-July, annual. Contact: Department of
Public Information, City-County Building, Detroit,
Michigan 48226.

A joint celebration by Detroit and Windsor (Canada)
groups of Dominion Day (Canada, July 1) and Independence Day (United States, July 4). Events
include Miss Freedom Festival contest, competitive
art exhibit, pleasure craft water parade, concerts,
baton-twirling contests, puppet shows, kite-flying
contests, sky-diving, foreign folk festivities, square
dancing, water polo, hootenany, a horse show,
international gold cup powerboat race, and fireworks.
Started in 1959.

★ 1497 ★
Fremont - OLD FASHIONED DAYS. Mid July (3rd
weekend), annual, 3 days, Main Street. Contact:
Fremont Chamber of Commerce, 101 East Main Street,
Fremont, Michigan 49412.

The celebration includes a carnival, window displays,
and old fashioned costumes. There are two parades,
one for children and an Old Fashioned Parade with
floats, bands, and antique automobiles. Additional
activities include a shuffleboard contest, a flower
show, a pie-eating contest, and a water battle.
Entertainment is provided by street musicians, clowns,
magic shows, concerts, exhibition dancers, professional
stage shows and an old fashioned gospel sing. In
addition, there are bike and foot races, and sidewalk
sales. A king and queen are crowned; contestants
must have celebrated their fiftieth wedding anniversary.
Begun around 1951.

★ 1498 ★
Port Huron - BLUE WATER FESTIVAL. Mid July,
8-9 days. Contact: Greater Port Huron-Marysville
Chamber of Commerce, 920 Pine Grove Avenue, Port
Huron, Michigan 48060.

Festival events include a carnival, contests, live
entertainment, food, parade, and fireworks.

★ 1499 ★
Romeo - PEACH FESTIVAL. Late August-early
September, annual, 3 days. Contact: Chamber of
Commerce, Romeo, Michigan 48065.

A large floral parade with floats and marching bands.
Also a carnival, Bierstube, pancake breakfast, and
coronation ball.

★ 1500 ★
Vermontville - MAPLE SYRUP FESTIVAL. Late
April (last Saturday), annual, 1 day. Contact:
State of Michigan Tourist Council, Division of
Department of Natural Resources, Commerce Center
Building, 300 South Capitol Avenue, Lansing,
Michigan 48926.

The evening before the festival there is a talent
contest. The festival includes a children's parade,
presentation of the Maple Queen and her court,
grand parade, pony pulling contest, pancake derby,
wood-chopping contest, square dancing exhibition,
round and square dancing, entertainment on stage,
band concerts, movies, and food offered by various
community groups. Maple syrup and maple syrup
products on sale all through the event; the products
are also displayed and judged. Started in 1940.

MINNESOTA

★ 1501 ★
Big Lake - SPUD FEST DAYS. Late June, 3 days.
Contact: Civic and Commercial Club, Big Lake,
Minnesota 55309.

A typical community festival featuring a baseball
tournament, horse show, bingo, beer garden, and
carnival.

★ 1502 ★
Brooklyn Park - TATER DAZE. Mid June, 5 days.
Contact: Brooklyn Park Jaycees, 4600 75th Avenue
North, Brooklyn Park, Minnesota 55443.

Parades, a carnival, softball and horseshoe tournaments, bands, and fireworks are included in the
festivities.

★ 1503 ★
Buffalo - BUFFALO DAYS. Mid June, 7 days.
Contact: Junior Chamber of Commerce, Buffalo,
Minnesota 55313.

Events include a parade, barbeque, games, water show,
queen coronation, and a bike riding contest.

★ 1504 ★
Buffalo Lake - HARVEST FESTIVAL. Early August,
3 days. Contact: Chamber of Commerce, Buffalo
Lake, Minnesota 55314.

Athletic events, parade, queen pageant and coronation, queen's ball, and a picnic highlight the festive
events.

Community

MINNESOTA (Continued)

★ 1505 ★
Cosmos - COSMOS SPACE FESTIVAL. Late July, 2 days. Contact: Chamber of Commerce, Cosmos, Minnesota 56228.

A model rocket contest and a space science display highlight the events.

★ 1506 ★
Crookston - PIONEER DAYS. Early July, 6 days. Contact: Chamber of Commerce, 109 South Main, Crookston, Minnesota 56716.

Contests, plays, a carnival, class reunions, a parade, a pageant, a banquet, pioneer couple selected and honored are highlights of this community festival.

★ 1507 ★
Hastings - HASTINGS FUN FEST. Mid July, 2 days. Contact: Hastings Area Chamber of Commerce, Box 352, Hastings, Minnesota 55033.

Events include parades, water show, archery competition, river boat rides, art show, old time car displays, and carnival.

★ 1508 ★
Henning - HARVEST FESTIVAL. Early July, 3 days. Contact: Henning Commercial Club, Henning, Minnesota 56551.

Events include a parade, coronation of Harvest Festival Queen, midway, and a carnival.

★ 1509 ★
Lakeville - PANORAMA OF PROGRESS (PAN-O-PROG). Mid July, 5 days. Contact: Millie Brandl, 20028 Kenwood Trail West, Lakeville, Minnesota 55044.

Events include queen coronation, horse show, parades, dances, softball, soap box derby, treasure hunt, and pet show.

★ 1510 ★
Lindstrom - KARL OSKAR DAYS. Late June, 3 days. Contact: Lindstrom Commercial Club, Lindstrom, Minnesota 55045.

A typical community festival honoring its heritage with fun events including a carnival, queen contest, sailing regatta, parade, golf and softball tournaments.

★ 1511 ★
Litchfield - INTERNATIONAL PEANUT BUTTER AND MILK FESTIVAL. Mid February, annual, 3-4 days. Contact: Litchfield Area Chamber of Commerce, 126 North Marshall Avenue, Litchfield, Minnesota 55355.

Snowdeo, softball-on-ice, banquet, and guest from sister city of Hartford, Alabama. Tours of surrounding farms and agricultural industries. Begun around 1972.

★ 1512 ★
Minneapolis - AQUATENNIAL. July, annual, 10 days, downtown Nicollet Mall. Contact: Program Director, Minneapolis Aquatennial, 15 South Fifth Street, Minneapolis, Minnesota 55402.

Each year has a theme (e.g. 40's Flashback). Over 240 events, including two parades, classic cars, judo, gymnastics, ice cream social, softball tourney, water ski tourney, Senior Citizens' Day, tennis tourney, pontoon boat rides, midwest square dance festival, horse show, fashion shows, chorus, folk festival, art fair, milk carton boat race, polo match, beach party, fireworks, Queen of the Lakes drum and bugle pageant, crafts market, children's day at the mall, Schweigert's Band competition, Showboat on the Mississippi, and world's largest fish fry.

★ 1513 ★
Minnesota Lake - FESTAG. Late July, 2 days. Contact: Minnesota Lake Chamber of Commerce, Minnesota Lake, Minnesota 56068.

A livestock show, display and sale of arts and crafts, crop and food fair, queen contest, and a parade highlight the events.

★ 1514 ★
Mound - MOUND CITY DAYS. Late June, 2 days. Contact: Chamber of Commerce, Mound, Minnesota 55364.

Events include a parade, water ball fight, canoe races, Westonka Queen coronation, free turkey burgers, and steak fry.

★ 1515 ★
Nicollet - FRIENDSHIP DAYS. Late July, 3 days, City Park. Contact: Chamber of Commerce, Nicollet, Minnesota 56074.

Festival events include water fights, queen and band contests, parade, and old time beer garden.

MINNESOTA (Continued)

★ 1516 ★
Onamia - ONAMIA DAYS. Mid June, 3 days.
Contact: Onamia Area Civic Association, Onamia,
Minnesota 56359.

Events include a fishing contest, carnival, parade,
fireworks, music, dancing, flea market, queen
pageant and coronation.

★ 1517 ★
Paynesville - TOWN AND COUNTRY DAYS. Mid
June, 3 days. Contact: Chamber of Commerce,
Paynesville, Minnesota 56362.

Miss Paynesville coronation, parades, carnival, street
games, Art in the Park, races, softball, and free
ice cream are highlight events of this community
festival.

★ 1518 ★
Perham - PIONEER FESTIVAL. Mid August, Pioneer
Village. Contact: Historical Society, Perham,
Minnesota 56573.

Old time threshing, log sawing, horse show, flea
market, contests, pancake breakfast, dance, sawmill
and threshing demonstrations, and games highlight
the events.

★ 1519 ★
Remer - HARVEST FESTIVAL. Early August, 2 days.
Contact: Chamber of Commerce, Remer, Minnesota
56672.

Festival events include a trap shoot, games, horseshoe contest, parade, turkey barbeque, dance, displays and prizes.

★ 1520 ★
Sauk Centre - SINCLAIR LEWIS DAYS FESTIVAL.
Mid July, 3 days. Contact: Chamber of Commerce,
405 1/2 Sinclair Lewis Avenue, Sauk Centre, Minnesota 56378.

A dance, parades, band concert, water fight, concessions, entertainment, carnival rides, crowning of
Miss Main Street, ball, and an outdoor show highlight
the festive events.

★ 1521 ★
Stillwater - LUMBERJACK DAYS. Late July, 4 days.
Contact: Saint Croix Valley Area Chamber of

Commerce, 408 East Chestnut Street, Stillwater,
Minnesota 55082.

The festival events include log-rolling, parade, Miss
Stillwater contest, horse show, boat races, sky divers,
fireworks, and drum and bugle contest featuring the
top drum and bugle corps and marching units in the
nation.

★ 1522 ★
Tamarack - TAMARACK HEY DAY. Early August,
annual, 1 day. Contact: Chamber of Commerce,
Tamarack, Minnesota 55787.

A parade, dance, games, rides, smorgasbord, prizes,
and a carnival highlight the festive events.

★ 1523 ★
Tracy - BOX CAR DAYS. Early September, 1 day.
Contact: Chamber of Commerce, Tracy, Minnesota
56175.

Box cars are honored with festive events including a
horse show, parades, carnival, queen coronation, and
a softball tournament. The festival was inaugurated
in 1927 when box cars were the chief means of transport across the nation.

★ 1524 ★
Underwood - HARVEST FESTIVAL. Late August,
2 days. Contact: Chamber of Commerce, Underwood, Minnesota 56586.

Sports events, parade, dance, and queen coronation
highlight the festive events.

★ 1525 ★
Waterville - BULLHEAD DAYS. Mid June, 3 days.
Contact: Waterville Commercial Club, Waterville,
Minnesota 56096.

Miss Waterville pageant, children's fishing contest,
water show, parade, fireworks, and a carnival are
featured events of the festivities.

★ 1526 ★
White Bear Lake - MANITOU DAYS. Late July-
early August, 9 days. Contact: Chamber of Commerce, 613 Fourth Street, White Bear Lake, Minnesota 55110.

Festival events include softball, tennis, Sweet Adelines concert, flea market, Lake Shore Art Fair, water
ski show, boat parade, and golf tournament.

Community

MINNESOTA (Continued)

★ 1527 ★
Winona - WINONA STEAMBOAT DAYS.   Early
July, 7 days.   Contact: Jaycees, Winona, Minne-
sota   55987.

Events include Miss Winona scholarship pageant,
carnival, parade, power boat races, water ski show,
drum and bugle corps competition.   Queen Style
Show and Luncheon, teen dance, fireworks, and
handball and softball tournaments.

★ 1528 ★
Wright - WRONG DAYS IN WRIGHT.   Mid July,
2 days.   Contact: Chamber of Commerce, Wright,
Minnesota   55798.

Festival events include dance, parade, ballgame,
prizes, concessions, and smorgasbord.

MISSISSIPPI

★ 1529 ★
Biloxi - MARDI GRAS.   March (day prior to Ash
Wednesday), annual, 1 day.   Contact: Travel/
Tourism Department, Mississippi Agricultural and
Industrial Board, Post Office Box 849, Jackson,
Mississippi   39205.

In continuation of the ancient French and Creole
tradition, Biloxi celebrates Fat Tuesday with evening
and afternoon parades and pageantry including lavish
floats, costumed celebrants, carnival favors, and
special balls.

★ 1530 ★
Brookhaven - TOWN AND COUNTRY FESTIVAL.
Late October.   Contact: Travel/Tourism Depart-
ment, Mississippi Agricultural and Industrial Board,
Post Office Box 849, Jackson, Mississippi   39205.

Coinciding with an antique show, activities include
a fair, exhibits, bicycle races, folk art show, children's zoo and moto-cross racing.

★ 1531 ★
Carthage - LEAKE COUNTY SPORTSMAN DAY.
Early July (4th), annual, 1 day.   Contact: Leake
County Chamber of Commerce, Post Office Box 209,
Carthage, Mississippi   39051.

Activities include turkey shoots, fishing, turkey and
duck calling, horseshoe pitching, greased pole climbing, with door prizes and trophies awarded for the

winners of competitive events.   Sky-divers and
entertainment are on hand.

★ 1532 ★
French Camp - HARVEST FESTIVAL.   Mid October,
1 day, French Camp Academy campus.   Contact:
National Folk Festival Association, 1346 Connecticut
Avenue, Washington, D.C. 20036; or French Camp
Academy, French Camp, Mississippi   39745.

A display of Indian artifacts, special children's
activities, and auction of handmade items.   A
dinner is offered consisting of contributions from the
townspeople and is served on a 100-foot suspended
table.

★ 1533 ★
Greenville - MAINSTREAM FESTIVAL.   Late June-
early July, 7 days, Lake Ferguson.   Contact:
Travel Department, Mississippi Agricultural and In-
dustrial Board, Post Office Box 849, Jackson,
Mississippi   39205.

Nationally famous entertainers, fireworks, and other
festive activities are featured in this community
festival.

★ 1534 ★
Jackson - ARTS, CRAFTS AND FLOWER FESTIVAL.
Mid March, 3 days.   Contact: Chamber of Commerce, Post Office Box 22548, Jackson, Mississippi
39205.

Arts and crafts on exhibit and for sale, tours of
flower areas, and festival entertainment.

★ 1535 ★
Kosciusko - NATCHEZ TRACE FESTIVAL.   Mid
April (2nd Saturday), 1 day, Attala County Court-
house Square.   Contact: Kosciusko-Attala Chamber
of Commerce and Industrial Development Corporation,
Post Office Box 696, Kosciusko, Mississippi   39090.

In the style of an old-fashioned village festival.
Displays by local artists and craftsmen, antique car
parade, folk music, and homemade bread.

★ 1536 ★
Moorhead - YELLOW DOG FESTIVAL.   Late April,
1 day.   Contact: Travel Department, Mississippi
Agricultural and Industrial Board, Post Office Box 849,
Jackson, Mississippi   39205.

A flea market, art sale, country store, and live band

MISSISSIPPI (Continued)

music are the featured events in this community celebration.

★ 1537 ★
Raleigh - TOBACCO SPITTING CHAMPIONSHIP.
July, annual, 1 day, Billy John Crumpton's Pond.
Contact: Travel/Tourism Department, Mississippi
Agricultural and Industrial Board, Post Office Box
849, Jackson, Mississippi 39205.

The pageantry surrounding the world championship
competition for tobacco spitters includes political
speakers, mule racing, music, good food, and bird
calling contests. Begun around 1957.

★ 1538 ★
Ripley - FIRST MONDAY. January (1st Monday),
monthly, 1 day each month, Ripley Fairgrounds.
Contact: Chamber of Commerce, Post Office Box
115, Ripley, Mississippi 38663.

One of the largest "Trading Days" offered in Mississippi,
the first Monday of each month brings in a vast variety
of items to be sold or swapped. Over 100 years old.

MISSOURI

★ 1539 ★
Branson - KEWPIESTA. Mid April, annual, 3 days.
Contact: Chamber of Commerce, Post Office Box
220, Branson, Missouri 65616.

In honor of Rose O'Neill, the Ozark artist, sculptor,
author, illustrator, and creator of the Kewpie doll.

★ 1540 ★
Florissant - VALLEY OF FLOWERS FESTIVAL. Early
May, 3 days. Contact: Florissant Chamber of
Commerce, 100 Saint Francois Street, Florissant,
Missouri 63031.

Features tours of historic homes, a large parade, art
show, antique auction, book fair, and an old
fashioned homemade ice cream social.

★ 1541 ★
Hannibal - TOM SAWYER DAY FESTIVAL AND
NATIONAL FENCE PAINTING CONTEST. Early
July, annual, 1 week. Contact: Chamber of Commerce, 623 Broadway, Hannibal, Missouri 63401.

Modern-day Tom Sawyers, representing the ten states

that border on the Mississippi, compete in the contest based on the episode in Twain's book. Other
related events include frog jumping, raft racing, and
a fireworks display launched from a barge moored in
the river. The painting contest takes place at
Mark Twain's boyhood home.

★ 1542 ★
Kansas City - BLUEGRASS COUNTRY FAIR. Late
June, 1 day, Rodeway Inn South. Contact: Convention and Visitors Bureau of Greater Kansas City,
1221 Baltimore, Kansas City, Missouri 64105.

Booths featuring crafts, food, and exhibits. Fiddling contest is the highlight of the festival.

★ 1543 ★
Kirkwood - GREEN TREE FESTIVAL. Early September, 10 days, various locations in Kirkwood, Missouri.
Contact: Convention and Visitors Bureau of Greater
Saint Louis, 500 Broadway Building, Saint Louis,
Missouri 63102.

Events include antiques, horse show, dancing, concerts, crafts, art, races, food, and an Old Time
Fiddlers Contest.

★ 1544 ★
Rockaway Beach - BRUSH ARBOR DAYS. Mid
October, annual, 10 days. Contact: Chamber of
Commerce, Box 117, Rockaway Beach, Missouri
65740.

The festival features tours, displays, shows, contests,
and live entertainment.

★ 1545 ★
Saint Louis - CARONDELET DAYS. Early July,
2 days, Carondelet Park. Contact: Convention
and Visitors Bureau of Greater Saint Louis, 500
Broadway Building, Saint Louis, Missouri 63102.

Events include bus tours of historic points, fashion
shows, fishing clinics, large parade, tree-shaded
midway of hundreds of carnival rides, food, continuous entertainment, and sports events.

★ 1546 ★
Saint Louis - FAIR SAINT LOUIS. Mid May,
annual, 3 days, Forest Park. Contact: Convention
and Visitors Bureau of Greater Saint Louis, 500
Broadway Building, Saint Louis, Missouri 63102.

Community

MISSOURI (Continued)

Events include bands, sky diving, sailboat regattas, archery, bait casting, golf, canoe races with special awards, dancing, exotic and American cuisine, and an arts and crafts show.

★ 1547 ★
Saint Louis - GO FAIR.   Early October, 1 day, McDonald Park (Grand Oak Hill).   Contact: Convention and Visitors Bureau of Greater Saint Louis, 500 Broadway Building, Saint Louis, Missouri 63102.

Flea market with an international flavor.   Many different types of foods served.   Old fashioned ice cream social and three parades.   Arts and crafts including needlework are on display.   Souvenirs, beer gardens, and continuous entertainment.

★ 1548 ★
Saint Louis - MUSTARD SEED FESTIVAL.   Mid June, 1 day, Maryland Plaza.   Contact: Convention and Visitors Bureau of Greater Saint Louis, 500 Broadway Building, Saint Louis, Missouri 63102.

Activities include arts, crafts, food, drinks, films, live theater, bluegrass and magic shows, continuous entertainment, dancing, and the Saint Louis Symphony orchestra performs.

★ 1549 ★
Silver Dollar City - ROOT DIGGIN' DAYS.   May (all weekends).   Contact: Chamber of Commerce, Silver Dollar City, Missouri 65616.

This festival celebrates and relives the Ozark tradition that families search for their year's supply of medicinal roots and herbs in the spring.   Events range from pitchfork pitching and Civil War cannon firing to donkey-powered merry-go-round rides, a steam engine tug-of-war and red flannel underwear "getting-out-of" contests.

MONTANA

★ 1550 ★
Billings - WESTERN DAYS.   Mid July, 2 days. Contact: Chamber of Commerce, Box 2519, Billings, Montana 59103.

Traditional wild west activities highlight this community festival.

★ 1551 ★
Bridger - JIM BRIDGER DAYS.   Late July (next to last weekend), annual, 3 days, City Park.   Contact: Bridger Lions Club, Bridger, Montana 59014.

Honors Jim Bridger, a famous mountaineer, trapper and scout of Montana's territorial days.   The celebrations include a barbeque and picnic; family and individual type sports such as horseshoe pitching, softball, jack pot rodeo, races, and parades.   Begun around 1937.

★ 1552 ★
Dillon - BANNACK DAYS FESTIVAL.   Mid August, 2 days, restored townsite of Bannack.   Contact: Thomas Dooling, Post Office Box 1776, Dillon, Montana 59725.

Square dance exhibitions and public dancing, tours of the restored buildings of Bannack, kangaroo courts, concessions, historical costumes, historical exhibits, and a drama.   First held on the occasion of Bannack's centennial in 1962.

★ 1553 ★
Glendive - BADLANDS APPRECIATION FESTIVAL. Mid September, 2 days, West Park.   Contact: Chamber of Commerce, Box 930, Glendive, Montana 59330.

Traditional community festival events and featuring a fiddlers' contest.

★ 1554 ★
Libby - LOGGER DAYS.   Mid July, 3 days. Contact: Chamber of Commerce, 808 Mineral Avenue, Libby, Montana 59923.

Traditional western and logging events, contests and fun.

★ 1555 ★
Miles City - BUCKING HORSE SALE.   May. Contact: Jim Parker, Miles City Jaycees, 808 South Montana, Miles City, Montana 59301.

Events include wild horse races, a rodeo and western celebrations.

★ 1556 ★
Shelby - MARIAS FAIR.   Mid July (3rd week), annual, 4 days.   Contact: Chamber of Commerce, Box 488, Shelby, Montana 59474.

MONTANA (Continued)

The fair is operated by the Toole County Fair Board
and serves the counties of Toole, Ponders, Glacier
and Liberty.   Events include four days of parimutual
horse racing, and three days of rodeo.   In addition,
there are exhibits, open class and 4-H; a carnival,
night shows and free acts.   Begun around 1940.

★ 1557 ★
Wolf Point - WILD HORSE STAMPEDE.   July, annual,
3 days.   Contact: Wolf Point Chamber of Commerce
and Agriculture, Box 237, Wolf Point, Montana
59201.

The celebration is designed to keep in tune with the
customs and traditions of the heyday of the cowboys
and the cattle ranchers. It is the oldest annual
rodeo in the state.   Top rodeo performers compete
in the events; in addition, there is a western parade,
Indian dancers, and a carnival.   Begun in the
1920's.

NEBRASKA

★ 1558 ★
North Platte - NEBRASKA LAND DAYS.   Mid June,
annual, 8 days. Contact: Chamber of Commerce,
512 North Bailey Avenue, Post Office Box 968,
North Platte, Nebraska 69101.

The festival commemorates the first United States
rodeo with cowboy stunts and skills, pageants, a
recreation of a shootout, parade, and revues.

★ 1559 ★
Ponca - DAYS OF '56 RODEO AND CELEBRATION.
Late June.   Contact: Ponca Commercial Club,
Ponca, Nebraska 68770.

Events include three days of rodeo competitions, a
carnival, parades, and historical programs.

NEVADA

★ 1560 ★
Las Vegas - HELLDORADO.   Early May.   Contact:
Las Vegas Convention and Visitors Authority, Con-
vention Center, Post Office Box 14006, Las Vegas,
Nevada 89114.

Events include a leading rodeo and a parade.

NEW HAMPSHIRE

★ 1561 ★
Canterbury - CANTERBURY FAIR AND AUCTION.
Late July, annual, 1 day, Canterbury Center.   Con-
tact: Secretary, Canterbury Fair and Auction,
Canterbury, New Hampshire 03224.

Festival events include an antique market, chicken
barbeque, auction, table sales of handicrafts, food,
children's activities, arts, crafts, photography exhibit, craft demonstrations, and country store.

★ 1562 ★
Concord - TRI-STATE COLLECTORS EXHIBITION.
Mid October, 2 days, Concord Community Center.
Contact: Concord Community Center, 39 Green
Street, Concord, New Hampshire 03301.

Coins, stamps, dolls, buttons, guns, and bottles are
on exhibition.

★ 1563 ★
Conway - HANG GLIDING FESTIVAL.   Mid
October, 2 days, Mount Cranmore.   Contact:
Chamber of Commerce, Post Office Box 385, Conway,
New Hampshire 03818.

A gathering of participants and observers of the
thrilling sport of hang gliding.

★ 1564 ★
Greenfield - CHOWDER PARTY AND SLEIGH RIDE.
Late January, 1 day.   Contact: Chamber of Com-
merce, Greenfield, New Hampshire 03047.

A gala festival with hot homemade chowders and
cool rides through the snow on old fashioned sleighs.

★ 1565 ★
Hooksett - STREET FAIR.   Mid July, annual, 1
day, Congregational Church.   Contact: Secretary,
Annual Hooksett Street Fair, Hooksett, New Hampshire 03106.

An auction, handicraft booths, food sales, and
chicken supper highlight this community festival.

★ 1566 ★
Jackson - HANG GLIDING FESTIVAL.   Mid August
(2nd weekend), Wild Cat Mountain.   Contact:
Chamber of Commerce, Post Office Box 385, Conway,
New Hampshire 03818.

Community

NEW HAMPSHIRE (Continued)

A gathering of those who enjoy soaring through the air and those who enjoy watching.

★ 1567 ★
New Ipswich - CHILDREN'S FAIR. Mid August, annual, 1 day, Congregational Church and Town Hall. Contact: Children's Fair Chairman, Main Street, New Ipswich, New Hampshire 03071.

Events include games, rides, entertainment, kid food, auction, barbeque, puppet theater, pie-eating contest, concert, and film show. Begun around 1860.

★ 1568 ★
Newmarket - FIREMAN'S MUSTER. Early August, 1 day. Contact: Secretary, Fireman's Muster, Newmarket, New Hampshire 03857.

Hand engines (1824-1884) come from as far away as Maine, Connecticut, and New York. There is a parade and pumping demonstration.

★ 1569 ★
Newmarket - SIDEWALK FAIR. Late May, 1 day, Route 108. Contact: Secretary, Newmarket Sidewalk Fair, Newmarket, New Hampshire 03857.

The festive events include rides, games, crafts, food, displays, concert, magician, Indian dancers, supper, and dance.

★ 1570 ★
Pelham Center - OLD HOME DAY. Early September, 1 day, First Congregational Church. Contact: Chamber of Commerce, Pelham Center, New Hampshire 03076.

Booths, food, crafts, games, rides, parade, supper, square and block dancing highlight the festive events.

★ 1571 ★
Portsmouth - JUBILEE WEEK. Mid August, 8 days. Contact: Secretary, Jubilee Week, Portsmouth, New Hampshire 03801.

Dances, parade, fireworks, tugboat rides, beauty contests, and a tug-o-war are included in the festival events.

★ 1572 ★
Sunapee - NEW HAMPSHIRE GEM AND MINERAL

FESTIVAL. Mid August, annual, 2 days, Mount Sunapee State Park. Contact: Secretary, New Hampshire Gem and Mineral Festival, Sunapee, New Hampshire 03782.

Gathering of professional and amateur collectors and a grand display of items in the gem and mineral families. Begun around 1964.

★ 1573 ★
Tamworth - SWAP, TALK AND BRAG DAY AND MICROMOUNTERS ROUNDUP Mid September, 1 day, Kenneth A. Brett School. Contact: Saco Valley Gem and Mineral Club, Incorporated, Box 263, Conway, New Hampshire 03818.

Festivities for mineral collectors, lapidarists, micromounters, and hobbyists. Includes Micromounters Roundup, mineral auction, and swapping bee.

NEW JERSEY

★ 1574 ★
Paterson - GREAT FALLS FESTIVAL OF PATERSON. Early September (Labor Day weekend), 4 days, Great Falls Park. Contact: Greater Paterson Chamber of Commerce, 100 Hamilton Plaza, Paterson, New Jersey 07505.

The objective is to provide an enjoyable and inexpensive diversion for area residents. Heavy emphasis on ethnic foods and dance, constant activities and attractions ranging from antique car shows to daredevil acts performed over the Great Falls Chasm. Organized by the Chamber of Commerce with participation by the Development Corporation and the city of Paterson.

NEW MEXICO

★ 1575 ★
Alamogordo - COWBOY OCTOBERFEST. October, annual, all month, two counties, seven towns. Contact: Chamber of Commerce, 1301 White Sands Boulevard, Box 518, Alamogordo, New Mexico 88310.

Takes place also in other cities spread over two counties. Activities include ghost town tours, arts and crafts shows, food shows, barbeque, historical pageants, tours of Trinity, site of the first atomic bomb explosion at the White Sands Missile Range, sports tournament and races, chuck wagon dinners, dances, aspencades, and fiddler's contests. Begun in 1973.

NEW MEXICO (Continued)

★ 1576 ★
Albuquerque - INTERNATIONAL BALLOON FIESTA
AND WORLD HOT AIR BALLOON CHAMPIONSHIPS.
Mid October, annual. Contact: Greater Albuquerque Chamber of Commerce, 401 2nd Street, Northwest,
Albuquerque, New Mexico 87102.

Includes competition for world champion in hot air
balloons. The fiesta was first held in 1972 and the
championship competition began in 1974.

★ 1577 ★
Albuquerque - REDISCOVER NEW MEXICO. Late
April-early May, 6 days, Winrock Shopping Center.
Contact: Bill Roller, Post Office Box 30065, Albuquerque, New Mexico 87110.

Exhibit of New Mexico's tourist attractions. Begun
in 1974.

★ 1578 ★
Albuquerque - SAN FELIPE DE NERI FIESTA. Early
June, annual, 3 days, Old Town Plaza. Contact:
Church Office, San Felipe de Neri Church, Albuquerque, New Mexico 87104.

Honors the patron saint of the San Felipe de Neri
Church, first in Albuquerque, built in 1710, and one
of the oldest in New Mexico.

★ 1579 ★
Aztec - AZTEC FIESTA DAYS. Mid July, annual,
4 days. Contact: Chamber of Commerce, 125
North Main, Aztec, New Mexico 87410.

Traditional festive activities in a community environment. Begun around 1961.

★ 1580 ★
Carrizozo - COWBOY OCTOBERFEST. October,
annual, all month, two counties, seven towns. Contact: Chamber of Commerce, Carrizozo, New Mexico
88301.

Takes place also in other cities spread over two
counties. Activities include ghost town tours, arts
and crafts shows, food shows, barbeques, historical
pageants, tours of Trinity—site of the first atomic
bomb explosion at the White Sands Missile Range,
sports tournaments and races, chuck wagon dinners,
dances, aspencades and fiddler's contests. Begun in
1973.

★ 1581 ★
Cimarron - CIMARRON DAYS. Late September,
annual, 1 weekend, Old Aztec Mill. Contact:
Chamber of Commerce, Cimarron, New Mexico
87714.

A parade and a street fair highlight the festivities.
Begun in 1974.

★ 1582 ★
Cloudcroft - COWBOY OCTOBERFEST. October,
annual, all month, two counties, seven towns.
Contact: Chamber of Commerce, Box 125, Cloudcroft, New Mexico 88317.

Takes place also in other cities spread over two
counties. Activities include ghost town tours, arts
and crafts shows, food shows, barbeque, historical
pageants, tours of Trinity—site of the first atomic
bomb explosion at the White Sands Missile Range,
sports tournaments and races, chuck wagon dinners,
dances, aspencades, and fiddler's contests. Begun
in 1973.

★ 1583 ★
Deming - BUTTERFIELD TRAIL DAYS. May-June,
annual, 3 days. Contact: Deming-Luna County
Chamber of Commerce, 109 East Pine, Post Office
Box 8, Deming, New Mexico 88030.

Events include a parade, barbeques, donkey baseball,
and an air show.

★ 1584 ★
Deming - KLOBASE (Bohemian Sausage) FESTIVAL.
Mid October, annual, 1 day. Contact: Deming-Luna County Chamber of Commerce, 109 East Pine,
Post Office Box 8, Deming, New Mexico 88030.

A community festival featuring the klobase with
various entertaining events.

★ 1585 ★
Dulce - LITTLE BEAVER ROUNDUP. Late July,
annual, 5 days. Contact: Post Office Box 122,
Dulce, New Mexico 87528.

The highlight of the season in Jicarilla County.
Like a county fair with even more attractions including rodeos, western dance, parade, Indian dances,
arts and crafts show - the Jicarillas do excellent
basketwork and beautiful beadwork, fine paintings
too.

Community

NEW MEXICO (Continued)

★ 1586 ★
Eagle Nest - MORENO VALLEY FISH FRY AND
SQUARE DANCE FESTIVAL.   Late May, annual,
2 days.   Contact: Tourist Division, New Mexico
Department of Development, 113 Washington Avenue,
Santa Fe, New Mexico 87503.

A festive community gathering for food and dancing.

★ 1587 ★
La Luz - COWBOY OCTOBERFEST.   October,
annual, all month, two counties, seven towns.
Contact: Chamber of Commerce, La Luz, New Mexico
88337.

Takes place also in other cities spread over two
counties.   Activities include ghost town tours, arts
and crafts shows, food shows, barbeque, historical
pageants, tours of Trinity - site of the first atomic
bomb explosion at the White Sands Missile Range,
sports tournaments and races, chuck wagon dinners,
dances, aspencades, and fiddler's contests.   Begun
in 1973.

★ 1588 ★
Las Cruces - FIESTA DE MUJERES (CELEBRATION
OF WOMEN).   Late August, annual, 2 days.
Contact: Tourist Division, New Mexico Department
of Development, 113 Washington Avenue, Santa Fe,
New Mexico 87503.

Seminars, exhibits, entertainment, rodeo, tennis,
softball and golf tournaments.   Begun in 1975.

★ 1589 ★
Las Vegas - FOURTH OF JULY FIESTA.   Early
July (tied to the 4th), annual, 3 days.   Contact:
Las Vegas-San Miguel Chamber of Commerce, Post
Office Box 148, Las Vegas, New Mexico 87701.

In commemoration of the history of Las Vegas.

★ 1590 ★
Los Chavez - FIESTA DE SAN JUAN.   Late June,
1 day.   Contact: Greater Belen Chamber of Commerce, Post Office Box 818, Belen, New Mexico
87002.

The occasion is honored with a mass and a procession,
plus games, a barbeque and dancing.

★ 1591 ★
Lincoln - COWBOY OCTOBERFEST.   October,
annual, all month, two counties, seven towns.
Contact: Chamber of Commerce, Lincoln, New
Mexico 88338.

Takes place also in other cities spread over two
counties.   Activities include ghost town tours, arts
and crafts shows, food shows, barbeque, historical
pageants, tours of Trinity - site of the first atomic
bomb explosion at the White Sands Missile Range,
sports tournaments and races, chuck wagon dinners,
dances, aspencades, and fiddler's contest.   Begun
in 1973.

★ 1592 ★
Magdelena - OLD TIMERS FAIR AND RODEO.
Mid July, annual, 3 days.   Contact: Chamber of
Commerce, Magdalena, New Mexico 87825.

A celebration for homecoming and for local residents
as well as tourists who wish to join in the fun.   Begun around 1972.

★ 1593 ★
Portales - LA FIESTA DE PORTALES.   July, annual,
3 days.   Contact: Chamber of Commerce, Post
Office Box 488, Portales, New Mexico 88130.

A traditional community celebration.   Begun around
1970.

★ 1594 ★
Red River - ASPENCADE AND SQUARE DANCE
FESTIVAL.   Late September, annual, 3 days.
Contact: Chamber of Commerce, Red River, New
Mexico 87558.

A square dance festival, arts and crafts show, jeep
tours to view aspens, chairlift rides, and horseback
rides.

★ 1595 ★
Red River - COMMUNITY HOUSE SQUARE DANCE
FESTIVAL AND PIONEER REUNION.   Mid June,
3 days.   Contact: Chamber of Commerce, Red
River, New Mexico 87558.

The event honors the original inhabitants of Red
River.

★ 1596 ★
Red River - RED RIVER VALLEY FAIR.   Late May-
early June, annual, 2 days.   Contact: Chamber

NEW MEXICO (Continued)

of Commerce, Red River, New Mexico 87558.

Square dance festival, bicycle races, hot air balloons, old time contests and events highlight the festival activities.

★ 1597 ★
Ruidoso - COWBOY OCTOBERFEST.   October, annual, all month, two counties, seven towns. Contact: Chamber of Commerce, Ruidoso, New Mexico 88345.

Takes place also in other cities spread over two counties.   Activities include ghost town tours, arts and crafts shows, food shows, barbeque, historical pageants, tours of Trinity – site of the first atomic bomb explosion at the White Sands Missile Range, sports tournament and races, chuck wagon dinners, dances, aspencades, and fiddler's contests.   Begun in 1973.

★ 1598 ★
Santa Rosa - SANTA ROSA DAY AND COMMUNITY PICNIC.   Late May, annual, 1 day.   Contact: Chamber of Commerce, 486 Parker Avenue, Santa Rosa, New Mexico 88435.

A community get-together with festive events to please locals and visitors to the area.

★ 1599 ★
Silver City - INDEPENDENCE DAY/FRONTIER DAYS.   Early July (around the 4th), annual, 1 day. Contact: Chamber of Commerce, 925 North Hudson, Silver City, New Mexico 88061.

A rodeo, air show, and fireworks highlight the events. Other activities include art shows, cowboy breakfast, barbeque, and a parade.

★ 1600 ★
Socorro - SAN MIGUEL FIESTA.   Late September, annual, 3 days, San Miguel Church.   Contact: Socorro County Chamber of Commerce, Post Office Box 743, Socorro, New Mexico 87801.

The festival honors the city's patron saint.   The sponsor, San Miguel Church, is one of the oldest still in use.

★ 1601 ★
Socorro - STATE SCIENCE FAIR.   Mid April, annual, 2 days, New Mexico Institute of Mining and Tech-

nology.   Contact: Chamber of Commerce, Post Office Box 743, Socorro, New Mexico 87801.

The final state competition of school science projects. Projects are on display to the public.

★ 1602 ★
Taos - FIESTA.   Late July, annual, 2 days.   Contact: Chamber of Commerce, Drawer I, Taos, New Mexico 87571.

A celebration honoring the feasts of Santa Ana and Santiago.   A festival queen is crowned in the plaza with great ceremony.   Bailes or dances are held throughout the town.   Also a barbeque, booths, and a parade.

★ 1603 ★
Taos Pueblo - SAN YSIDRO FEAST DAY (BLESSING OF THE FIELDS).   Mid May, annual, 2 days. Contact: Pueblo Office, Taos Pueblo, New Mexico 87571; or Albuquerque Area Office, Bureau of Indian Affairs, U.S. Department of the Interior, 5301 Central Avenue, Post Office Box 8327, Albuquerque, New Mexico 87108.

A blessing of fields and a candlelight procession highlight this community festival.

★ 1604 ★
Truth or Consequences - RALPH EDWARDS FIESTA. Late April or early May, annual, 4 days.   Contact: Chamber of Commerce, Truth or Consequences, New Mexico 87901.

Many celebrities entertain and there is a rodeo in honor of the TV star and his show.

★ 1605 ★
Tucumcari - PINATA FESTIVAL AND QUAY COUNTY FAIR.   Early September, annual, 4 days.   Contact: Chamber of Commerce, 404 West Tucumcari Boulevard, Tucumcari, New Mexico 88401.

Festival events include a parade, dances, pageant, roping, and motorcycle races.

★ 1606 ★
Tularosa - COWBOY OCTOBERFEST.   October, annual, all month, two counties, seven towns. Contact: Chamber of Commerce, 301 Central, Post Office Box 1026, Tularosa, New Mexico 88352.

Takes place also in other cities spread over two

Community

NEW MEXICO (Continued)

counties.   Activities include tours of ghost towns,
arts and crafts shows, food shows, barbeque, historical pageants, tours of Trinity – site of the first
atomic bomb explosion at the White Sands Missile
Range, sports tournament and races, chuck wagon
dinners, dances, aspencades, and fiddler's contests.
Begun in 1973.

NEW YORK

★ 1607 ★
Big Flats - COMMUNITY DAYS.   Late June,
annual, 3 days, Big Flats Community Center.   Contact: Finger Lakes Association, Incorporated, 309
Lake Street, Penn Yan, New York 14527.

A parade, kiddies korner, rides, games, food, and
drink are featured among the festive events.

★ 1608 ★
Bronxville - SARAH LAWRENCE COLLEGE
CHILDREN'S FAIR.   Early May, annual, 1 day,
Sarah Lawrence College campus.   Contact: Sarah
Lawrence College News Office, Director, Bronxville,
New York 10708.

Traditionally run by the freshman class for the benefit
of the College Scholarship fund, the festival has had
the theme "The Circus" for the last two years.
Clowns and circus performers walk on stilts, play
with the children, ride unicycles, paint faces, sell
balloons, peanuts, popcorn and candied apples.
Games include shave the balloon, pin the tail on
the giraffe, apple bobbing, and sponge throwing.
Other events include craft sales, tractor rides, book
sales and other booths, plus children' concerts and
theater performances.   In addition, there is a
children's theater workshop.   Begun around 1960.

★ 1609 ★
Elbridge - GERRY DAYS.   Late June, 3 days,
elementary school.   Contact: Finger Lakes Association, Incorporated, 309 Lake Street, Penn Yan, New
York 14527.

Children's parade, grand parade, flea market, games,
entertainment, field days, and a chicken barbeque
are the featured festival events.

★ 1610 ★
Nunda - FUN DAYS.   Late May, annual, 3 days.
Contact: Finger Lakes Association, Incorporated, 309
Lake Street, Penn Yan, New York 14527.

An art show, selection and coronation of Miss Nunda,
photography contests, parades, pageants, auctions,
and dinners are featured in this community festival
of fun.   Begun around 1965.

★ 1611 ★
Painted Post - COLONIAL DAYS.   Early June,
annual, 3 days.   Contact: Finger Lakes Association,
309 Lake Street, Penn Yan, New York 14527.

Festival events include sidewalk sale, crowning of the
Colonial Days Queen, costume contest, merchants
prizes, and a block dance.   Sponsored by the Board
of Trade.

★ 1612 ★
Palmyra - CANAL TOWN DAYS.   Mid September,
annual, 3 days.   Contact: Finger Lakes Association,
Incorporated, 309 Lake Street, Penn Yan, New York
14527.

Events. include house tours, fashion show, concert,
antique show and sale, historical craft display, canal
boat rides, Civil War muster, art show and sale, and
flea market.

★ 1613 ★
Petersburg - MIDSUMMER FAIRE.   Mid July, 3
days, Fox Hollow.   Contact: Midsummer Faire,
Fox Hollow, Petersburg, New York 12138.

Participants are urged to come in costume, dressed
like a merchant, peasant, beggar, musician or gypsy.
The event offers music and dancing.   Bring your
instrument.

★ 1614 ★
Phelps - SAUERKRAUT FESTIVAL.   Early August,
annual, 4 days.   Contact: Finger Lakes Association,
Incorporated, 309 Lake Street, Penn Yan, New York
14527.

An arts and crafts show, flea market, chicken barbeque,
sanctioned marathon race, midway, and parade highlight the festival events.   Begun around 1967.

★ 1615 ★
Troy - COMMUNITY CARNIVAL.   Early October,
annual, 1 day, Russell Sage College campus.   Contact: Director, Intercultural Center, Russell Sage
College, Troy, New York 12180.

The festival is sponsored by the Intercultural Studies
Center and the SGA of Russell Sage College.

NEW YORK (Continued)

Features displays by student organizations and community services including such things as Big Brother, Big Sister, Transcendental Meditation, Black Students Alliance, etc. Started in 1972.

NORTH CAROLINA

★ 1616 ★
Aulander – AULANDER DAY. May, 1 day. Contact: North Carolina Travel Development Section, Division of Economic Development, Department of Natural and Economic Resources, Raleigh, North Carolina 27611.

The festival is an old fashioned homecoming with athletic events, concerts and a picnic.

★ 1617 ★
Benson – MULE DAY CELEBRATION. Late September, annual. Contact: Travel and Promotion Division, State of North Carolina, Post Office Box 27687, Raleigh, North Carolina 27611.

Events include mule pulling, beauty contests, a parade, a street dance, and the Governor's Mule Race.

★ 1618 ★
Black Mountain – FAIR. Late June, annual. Contact: Black Mountain-Swannanoa Chamber of Commerce, 411 West State Street, Black Mountain, North Carolina 28711.

The festival features entertainment, mountain crafts, and food.

★ 1619 ★
Blowing Rock – OLD TIME RAILROADERS DAY AT TWEETSIE RAILROAD. Late June, 1 day. Contact: Boone Area Chamber of Commerce, 827 Blowing Rock Road, Boone, North Carolina 28607.

The celebration is in honor of the former employees of Tweetsie (East Tennessee and Western North Caroline) Railroad.

★ 1620 ★
Brevard – FESTIVAL OF THE ARTS. July, annual, 1 week. Contact: Chamber of Commerce, 28 East Main Street, Post Office Box 589, Brevard, North Carolina 28712.

The diversity of events includes a country fair, pet shows, crafts shows, flower shows and mineral shows. Musical events include a gospel sing and square dancing in the street. There are hikes and tours of the forests.

★ 1621 ★
Center – CENTER FAIR. Mid September (2nd Saturday), annual, 2 days, Center Community. Contact: Center Community Development Association, c/o Mr. Larry Harpe, Route 1, Mocksville, North Carolina 27028.

Exhibits and competitions in fine arts and crafts for both children and adults. On display are field crops, horticulture, canning, household furnishings, crafts and hobbies, plants and flowers, pantry and dairy, and clothing. Refreshments are served. In the evening there is entertainment under the century-old Center Arbor. First held in 1960.

★ 1622 ★
Chapel Hill – APPLE CHILL FAIR. Early-mid April, 7 days, downtown. Contact: Shirley Harper, Chapel Hill Recreation Department, Chapel Hill, North Carolina 27514.

Sidewalk sales and displays, street decorations, band concerts, and dancing are featured events during the festival days.

★ 1623 ★
Erwin – DENIM FUN DAYS. Late September-early October, 3 days. Contact: North Carolina Travel Development Section, Division of Economic Development, Department of Natural and Economic Resources, Raleigh, North Carolina 27611.

Erwin calls itself the "World Denim Capitol" and celebrates the fabric with this festival.

★ 1624 ★
Franklin – MACON COUNTY GEMBOREE. Late July (4th weekend), annual, 4 days, Macon County Fairgrounds. Contact: Franklin Area Chamber of Commerce, Post Office Box 504, Franklin, North Carolina 28734.

Sale and show of gems and minerals from all over the world. A nationally known show, with both swap shops and retail sales. There are special exhibits. Begun around 1966.

Community

NORTH CAROLINA (Continued)

★ 1625 ★
Grifton - SHAD FESTIVAL.   Mid April, 3 days.
Contact: Mrs. Janet Haseley, Box 147, Grifton,
North Carolina 28530.

Events of the festival include the crowning of the
Shad Queen, a parade, and a display of arts and
crafts.   There is competition in horseshoe pitching,
canoe racing, golf and a horse show.   Square
dancing and a fish fry round out the events.

★ 1626 ★
Manteo - DARE DAYS.   Early June, 2 days.
Contact: Outer Banks Chamber of Commerce, Kitty
Hawk, North Carolina 27949.

The festival features exhibitions, craft displays and
entertainment.

★ 1627 ★
Morehead City - OLD QUAWK'S DAY.   Mid March,
2 days, City Park.   Contact: Carteret County
Chamber of Commerce, Post Office Drawer B,
Morehead City, North Carolina 28557.

Celebration and fun inspired by the legend of a ship-
wrecked mariner.

★ 1628 ★
Saluda - COON DOG DAY.   Early July, 1 day.
Contact: Mayor E.B. Hall, Box 248, Saluda, North
Carolina 28773.

Coon dogs trials and show are surrounded by such
diverse activities as an arts and crafts show, a
parade, flea market, and the crowning of the Coon
Dog Queen.

★ 1629 ★
Spivey's Corner - NATIONAL HOLLERIN' CONTEST.
Mid June, annual, 1 day, intersection of U.S. 421
and U.S. 13.   Contact: National Hollerin' Con-
test, Post Office Box 332, Spivey's Corner, North
Carolina 28334.

The main event is a contest in hollerin', the farmers'
traditional means of communication and self-expression.
In addition, there are special events for children.
Begun around 1969.

NORTH DAKOTA

★ 1630 ★
Dickinson - ROUGHRIDER DAYS.   Early July
(around the 4th), annual, 3 days.   Contact: North
Dakota State Highway Department, Capitol Grounds,
Bismarck, North Dakota 58505.

A cowboy-style event with an RCA rodeo, parades
and street dancing.   Arts and crafts are on display.
Meals and entertainment are provided.

★ 1631 ★
Mandan - RODEO FEST.   Early July (around the
4th), annual, 3 days.   Contact: North Dakota
State Highway Department, Capitol Grounds, Bismarck, North Dakota 58505.

The largest rodeo in North Dakota includes among
its activities a parade, an arts and crafts display,
a barbeque and entertainment.

OHIO

★ 1632 ★
Bellevue - CHERRY FESTIVAL.   Late June, 4 days.
Contact: Ms. Val Schmidt, Post Office Box 222,
Bellevue, Ohio 44811.

The largest blacktop festival in Ohio, the event includes contests such as a golf tournament, a pie
baking contest, and a pony pull.   There is a queen's
pageant and dance, a parade, and square dancing.
On display are antique cars, arts and crafts, historical railroad exhibits.   In addition, there is an
auction, games, midway rides, a helicopter show,
rides, and a raffle.

★ 1633 ★
Canton - PRO FOOTBALL HALL OF FAME FESTIVAL.
Early August, annual, 2 days, downtown Canton,
Canton Park, Pro Football Hall of Fame.   Contact:
Greater Canton Chamber of Commerce, 229 Wells
Avenue, Northwest, Canton, Ohio 44703.

The festival begins with the mayor's breakfast.   In
addition, there is a style show luncheon, featuring
the lastest in women's fashion, a banquet in honor
of the persons to be enrolled in the Hall of Fame
and other notables in the world of football.   There
is a large parade with floats, bands, and special
attractions, followed by enshrinement ceremony for
the new additions to the Hall of Fame.   The climax
of the event is the Hall of Fame Program.   Begun
around 1963.

OHIO (Continued)

★ 1634 ★
Celina - CELINA LAKE FESTIVAL.   Late July, 3
days.   Contact: Celina Area Chamber of Commerce,
106 South Main Street, Celina, Ohio 45822.

The lake becomes a raceway for boats, as Celina
celebrates with a grand parade, fireworks, rides and
contests.   Browsers are welcome to an antique auto
show and sidewalk sales.

★ 1635 ★
Hamilton County Park District - PARK DISTRICT'S
ANNUAL KITE CONTEST.   Mid March, annual,
1 day, Sharon Woods.   Contact: Park District
Naturalist, 10245 Winton Road, Cincinnati, Ohio
45231.

The contest is held to encourage kite flying as a
form of outdoor recreation which is both creative and
non-polluting.   Awards are given in several categories: the largest kite, smallest kite, most original
kite, and the highest flying kite.

★ 1636 ★
Massillon - MASSILLON MERCHANTS SIDEWALK
FESTIVAL.   Mid July, annual, 3 days, downtown
Massillon.   Contact: Jon Arnold, Engelhardt's
Music Center, Massillon, Ohio 44646; or Sarita
Cunningham, Quickprint Centers, Massillon, Ohio
44646.

The festival features a Miss Massillon Merchant beauty
contest, sales in downtown stores, amusement rides,
concerts, concession and craft booths.

★ 1637 ★
Nelsonville - PARADE OF THE HILLS.   Mid August,
annual, 7 days.   Contact: Bob Pierce, Parade of
the Hills Committee, Nelsonville, Ohio 45764.

Several towns in the Ohio hill country sponsor this
event.   Opened by an old timer's baseball game,
the festival activities include contests such as egg-
pitching and fireman's water hosing, a carnival, and
an athletic day.   Entertainment is provided by the
annual Paul Bunyan Show at Hocking Technical College, the coronation of the festival queen, parades,
displays, and the Hocking Valley Scenic Railway.

★ 1638 ★
Orrville - JELLY JAM-BOREE.   Late September (3rd
weekend), annual, 3 days, Orr Park, West High
Street.   Contact: Orrville Festival Association,

Orrville Chamber of Commerce, Incorporated, 132
South Main Street, Orrville, Ohio 44667.

Visitors may view arts and crafts displays and industrial exhibits or browse through a flea market.
There is a contest to select the "Sweetest Queen in
Ohio", and a parade.   Good food is prepared by
local service organizations, and there is a wide
variety of entertainment including kiddie rides, square
dancing, band concerts, barbership, gospel, and pop
music, helicopter rides, water barrel fights, and other
activities.   Started in 1973.

★ 1639 ★
Piqua - CHAUTAUQUA FESTIVAL.   Late July-early
August, 3 days.   Contact: Pat Brest, Box 43, Piqua,
Ohio 45356.

Closed to traffic, the main thoroughfare of the town
is lined with booths housing exhibits and demonstrations
of arts and crafts and concessions.   There is square
dancing and an antique show, karate demonstrations,
and a tent theater to entertain the visitor.

★ 1640 ★
Seven Hills - SEVEN HILLS HOME DAY.   Mid
July, 1 day.   Contact: Ms. Kathleen Raleigh,
Seven Hills Home Day Committee, Seven Hills,
Ohio 44131.

The town strives for an old fashioned flavor with a
parade, a water fight, a queen's contest, a band concert and an exhibition of the Clydesdale horses.

★ 1641 ★
Toledo - CITY RECREATION FESTIVAL.   Mid
August, 1 week, various parks in Toledo.   Contact:
Toledo Area Chamber of Commerce, 218 Huron Street,
Toledo, Ohio 43604.

The festival is the climax of the parks' recreation
programs.   Beginning with a parade, the events
include tennis tournaments, a fishing rodeo, arts
and crafts exhibit, swim meets, softball tournament,
golf tournament and table tennis competition.

★ 1642 ★
Uhrichsville - NATIONAL CLAY WEEK FESTIVAL.
Mid June, annual, 8 days.   Contact: National
Clay Festival, Post Office Box 49, Uhrichsville,
Ohio 44685.

The area celebrates the clay which it exports to the
world.   Activities include a large parade, midway
rides, games and food, a flea market, square dancing,

Community

OHIO (Continued)

boxing, a horse and pony pull, and an antique car show. Begun around 1950.

★ 1643 ★
Utica - OLD FASHIONED ICE CREAM FESTIVAL.
Late May, annual, 2 days, Ye Olde Mill (Route 62).
Contact: R.O. Lewis, Box 303, Utica, Ohio 43080.

Arts and crafts are exhibited and demonstrated, along with displays of antique cars and gas engines. There are contests, singing, square dancing, an ice cream parlor, and tours of the mill. Begun in 1975.

OKLAHOMA

★ 1644 ★
Beaver - CIMARRON TERRITORY CELEBRATION.
Mid April, 7 days. Contact: Chamber of Commerce, Box 878, Beaver, Oklahoma 73932.

This homesteaders celebration features the National Cow Chip Throwing Contest. Among the participants, the most proficient of all - politicians. Other events include a talent show, rodeo, and a horseshoe throwing contest.

★ 1645 ★
Tulsa - RIVER PARKS FESTIVAL. Early July, 4 days. Contact: River Parks Festival, Post Office Box 52268, Tulsa, Oklahoma 74152.

A river festival and craft show.

OREGON

★ 1646 ★
Brownsville - LINN COUNTY PIONEER PICNIC.
Mid June, annual, 3 days. Contact: Linn County Pioneer Picnic Association, Brownsville, Oregon 97327.

For nearly 80 years, Oregon pioneers and their descendents have gathered for an old fashioned picnic and observance of their heritages.

★ 1647 ★
Canyonville - PIONEER DAYS. August, annual, 4 days. Contact: Harry Clemons, Pioneer Days Committee, Post Office Box 204, Canyonville, Oregon 97417.

Traditional American music, arts and crafts, western

dance, barbeque, children's events, and a fiddler's contest. Begun around 1967.

★ 1648 ★
Cottage Grove - BOHEMIA MINING DAYS. Mid July, annual, 4 days. Contact: Cottage Grove Chamber of Commerce, Cottage Grove, Oregon 97424.

A festival honoring the historic Bohemia gold strikes. Train rides to the Bohemia mining district in the Cascade Mountains are among the activities, along with a rodeo.

★ 1649 ★
Joseph - CHIEF JOSEPH DAYS. Late July, annual, 1 week. Contact: Joseph Chamber of Commerce, Joseph, Oregon 97846.

The festival features two parades and an evening Indian dance pageant in addition to the usual rodeo fare. The event honors famed Indian Chief Joseph, who lived in this area. The festival began around 1947.

★ 1650 ★
Newport - LOYALTY DAYS FESTIVAL. Late April-early May, annual, 3 days. Contact: Newport Chamber of Commerce, Newport, Oregon 97365.

A celebration dedicated to loyalty to America, featuring a parade, queen and court, sports car races, Navy ships in port, art exhibit, air show and fly-in, agate show and other special activities.

★ 1651 ★
Nyssa - THUNDEREGG DAYS. Early August, annual, 4 days. Contact: Thunderegg Days, Post Office Box 335, Nyssa, Oregon 97913.

A celebration in honor of the Oregon State Rock, the thunderegg, which is found in considerable quantity in this area. It includes a rock and hobby show, barbeque and tours of "rockhounding" areas.

★ 1652 ★
Pendleton - PENDLETON ROUND-UP. Mid September, annual, 4 days. Contact: Round-Up Association, Post Office Box 609, Pendelton, Oregon 97801.

Festival is held to celebrate the end of harvest. Features pony express, Indian, cowgirl and baton races, and wild horse races - a total of 18 events per day. Also parade, street shows, crafts and night shows reliving the past.

OREGON (Continued)

★ 1653 ★
Prineville - CROOKED RIVER ROUNDUP. Early
July, annual, 2 days. Contact: Prineville Chamber
of Commerce, Prineville, Oregon 97754.

One of Oregon's larger rodeos also featuring a parade
and parimutal horse racing.

★ 1654 ★
Prineville - ROCKHOUNDS POW WOW. Late
June-early July, annual, 1 week. Contact: All
Rockhounds Incorporated, Prineville, Oregon 97754.

Several thousand rock collectors gather to hunt
agates, thundereggs, petrified wood and other rocks
in nearby areas and to swap rocks and tales.

★ 1655 ★
Sweet Home - SPORTMAN'S HOLIDAY. Early
August, annual, 4 days. Contact: Sweet Home
Chamber of Commerce, Sweet Home, Oregon 97386.

This festival includes the Western Oregon Logging
Championships, variety show, and other events relating to outdoor living.

PENNSYLVANIA

★ 1656 ★
Allentown - FOREFATHERS' DAY. Mid May, annual,
1 day. Contact: Mrs. Marilyn Klein, 462 Walnut
Street, Allentown, Pennsylvania 18105.

Celebration of ethnic contributions to American life
and spirit of brotherhood. Events include food,
games, music, dance, and crafts.

★ 1657 ★
Athens - STEPHEN FOSTER ICE CREAM SOCIAL AND
MUSIC FESTIVAL. Late July, annual, 1 day, Tioga
Point Museum. Contact: Tioga Point Museum, Box
143, Athens, Pennsylvania 18810.

Arts and crafts exhibits, old fashioned clothes, antique
cars and band concerts highlight the festival events.

★ 1658 ★
Avella - NATURE DAY. May, annual, 1 day,
Meadowcroft Village (3 miles west of Avella, Wash-
ington County). Contact: Meadowcroft Village,
Rural Delivery 1, Avella, Pennsylvania 15321.

Outdoor festival in dispersed restored rural community,
Meadowcroft Village.

★ 1659 ★
Beavertown - FOLK FROLIC DAYS. Mid July,
annual, 1 week. Contact: Department of Commerce,
Bureau of Travel Development, 431 South Office
Building, Harrisburg, Pennsylvania 17120.

Picnic, walking tours, parade, heritage show, religious services, baseball game, and time vault
ceremony highlight the festival events.

★ 1660 ★
Bethlehem - FESTIVAL. Mid July, annual, 6 days.
Contact: Mrs. Ann McGready, Bethlehem City Hall,
Bethlehem, Pennsylvania.

Over 100,000 people, more than 70 booths, ethnic
groups, colonial craft show and exhibits presented at
the festival.

★ 1661 ★
Boalsburg - OLE TOWN DAYS. Late May, annual,
1 week (8 days). Contact: Department of Commerce,
Bureau of Travel Development, 431 South Office
Building, Harrisburg, Pennsylvania 17120.

Tours through Pennsylvania Military Museum. "Home
town activities", children's concerts, organ recital,
and high school class reunions. A Day in Towne
with special activities for the children, old time
craft demonstrations, tours, food, souvenirs, open
churches, museums, a Center County shoofly pie
contest, and baking of a ten-foot in diameter shoofly
pie from the winning recipe. Fireman's parade and
carnival. Church service, picnic, and historical
pageant planned.

★ 1662 ★
Bradys Run Country Park - CAMPFEST. Mid Septem-
ber, annual, 3 days. Contact: Department of
Commerce, Bureau of Travel Development, 431 South
Office Building, Harrisburg, Pennsylvania 17120.

Festival features entertainment, exhibits, displays,
and family camping. Usually 800 units participate.

★ 1663 ★
Brownsville - NATIONAL PIKE FESTIVAL. Mid
May, annual, 2 days, along the Pike. Contact:
Washington-Greene County Tourist Promotion Agency,
The Meadowlands Hilton Inn, Rural Delivery 1, Race
Track Road, Washington, Pennsylvania 15301.

Community

PENNSYLVANIA (Continued)

The dogwood festival includes spelling bee, revival meeting, barn dance, art show in the toll houses, antiques, rail splitting and stone breaking contests. Displays of antique tools and equipment like wagons and stone breaking tools used in making the pike. Entertainment with fiddlers and banjos; refreshments featuring pork roasted on a spit, mutton and funnel cakes. The festival is held from Brownsville to the West Virginia line, along the pike at such towns as Chalk Hill, Turkey Foot, Egg Nog Hill, and Coon Island.

★ 1664 ★
Coudersport - SIDEWALK FESTIVAL DAYS. Early July, annual, 3 days. Contact: Potter County Recreation, Incorporated, Post Office Box 245, Coudersport, Pennsylvania 16915.

Baby and pet parades, and chicken barbeques highlight the events of this community festival.

★ 1665 ★
East Smithfield - OLD TIMERS DAY. Mid August, annual, 3 days. Contact: Bono Van Noy, Rural Delivery 3, Troy, Pennsylvania 16947.

Antique steam and gas equipment in operation; also antique exhibits, crafts, flea market, and free rides.

★ 1666 ★
Easton - FESTIVAL. Late May, annual, 1 day, Meuser Park. Contact: Northampton County Commission, 61 North Third Street, Easton, Pennsylvania 18042.

Includes Little Folks Song Festival, and beginning of walking tours of the Easton historic area.

★ 1667 ★
Elysburg - ALL HOME DAYS. Late August-early September, annual, 5 days, Ralpho Community Park. Contact: Mr. Bob Lee, Ralpho Community Park, Elysburg, Pennsylvania 17824.

Features parades and carnivals, ethnic attractions, queen contest, flower show, crafts exhibits, and tractor pulling contest.

★ 1668 ★
Greensburg - FESTIVAL DAYS. Late May-early June, annual, 6 days, Madison Borough. Contact: Westmoreland County Association, Courthouse,

Greensburg, Pennsylvania 15601.

Country crafts, food, entertainment and a Heritage Parade highlight the celebration.

★ 1669 ★
Harmony - DANKFEST. Late August, annual, 2 days, Harmonist Historic and Memorial Association. Contact: Department of Commerce, Bureau of Travel Development, 431 South Office Building, Harrisburg, Pennsylvania 17120.

Craft demonstrations, exhibits, etc. on the Old Harmony Museum grounds.

★ 1670 ★
Hidden Valley - OLD VILLAGES OF YESTERYEAR DAY. Mid July, annual, 1 day, Forest Hill Campgrounds (Route 192, Union County). Contact: Mr. David Reed, Rural Delivery 2, Mifflinburg, Pennsylvania 17844.

Square dancing, cake walk, antique show and flea market, barbeque, overnight camping facilities, arts and crafts.

★ 1671 ★
Huntingdon - OLD-FASHIONED FAIR. Mid August, annual, 5 days, Fairgrounds Road off Route 22. Contact: Mr. John W. McCracken, 1325 Mount Vernon Avenue, Huntingdon, Pennsylvania 16652.

Exhibits of animals, fruits, vegetables, flowers and domestic arts. Displays of farm machinery, automotive equipment, appliances, house trailers and campers, 4-H, and FFA exhibits. Harness horse racing, horse show, demolition derby, thrill shows, animal show, and variety show.

★ 1672 ★
Lansdale - FESTIVAL SUNDAY. Mid June, annual, 1 day. Contact: Department of Commerce, Bureau of Travel Development, 431 South Office Building, Harrisburg, Pennsylvania 17120.

Band concert, celebrities, "Fly-in", continental army demonstrations, baseball game, clothesline art show, teen and square dancing, banana and pie eating contest, archery contest, food and refreshments, flower show, flea market, dog show, antique car show, baby parade, midway, etc., are all parts of the events taking place all over town.

PENNSYLVANIA (Continued)

★ 1673 ★
Lewisburg - FESTIVAL. Mid June, annual, 1 day,
throughout Union County. Contact: Union County
Commission, Court House, Lewisburg, Pennsylvania
17837.

Includes day-long house tour, crafts show, demonstrations, food, and fun.

★ 1674 ★
Lititz - SERENDIPITY SATURDAY. Mid June,
annual, 1 day, Linda Hall campus. Contact:
Department of Commerce, Bureau of Travel Develop-
ment, 431 South Office Building, Harrisburg,
Pennsylvania 17120.

Requires costumes ranging from Indian and pioneer
period to 1900 for admittance. Horse show, puppet
show, mini-plays, band concert, dance demonstration,
baby parade, barbershop quartet, strawberry festival
and dance band.

★ 1675 ★
Lobachsville - JOHNNY APPLESEED FESTIVAL.
Late October, annual, 2 days, Keim Homestead.
Contact: Department of Commerce, Bureau of
Travel Development, 431 South Office Building,
Harrisburg, Pennsylvania 17120.

Cider-making, schnitzing contest, folk music, butter
and ice cream churning, seminars, applebutter and
homemade bread, and hoe downing.

★ 1676 ★
McClure - MCCLURE BEAN SOUP FESTIVAL.
September or October, annual, 4 days, McClure
Community Park. Contact: Kirby Bubb, McClure
Community Park, Route 522, McClure, Pennsylvania
17841.

Civil War reunion featuring humble bean (internationally famous soup served), food, entertainment,
and rides. Political dignitaries are there.

★ 1677 ★
Millersville - CELEBRATION. Mid June, 8 days.
Contact: H.R. Hershey, 424 Manor Avenue, Millers-
ville, Pennsylvania 17551.

The activities include a historical pageant and
Village Green Day. On display is a show of
sixteenth-nineteenth century arts and crafts. Some
events are held at Millersville State College.

★ 1678 ★
Millerton - MILLERTON FESTIVAL. Early July,
annual, 3 days. Contact: Mrs. Catherine Ayres,
Rural Delivery 2, Millerton, Pennsylvania 16936.

Festivities include softball, parade, and barbeque.

★ 1679 ★
Morris - OLD HOME DAY. Late August-early
September, annual. Contact: Morris Volunteer
Fire Company, Route 287, Morris, Pennsylvania
16938.

Features ox roast, ball games, parades, rides, food,
and amateur talent contest.

★ 1680 ★
Norristown - FREEDOM VALLEY FESTIVAL FAIR.
May, annual, 1 day, Valley Forge State Park.
Contact: Montgomery County Convention and
Visitors Bureau, One Montgomery Plaza, Suite 207,
Norristown, Pennsylvania 19401.

Games, contests and colonial crafts are included in
the festival events and activities.

★ 1681 ★
Ohiopyle - OHIOPYLE AREA FESTIVAL. July,
annual. Contact: Department of Commerce, Bureau
of Travel Development, 431 South Office Building,
Harrisburg, Pennsylvania 17120.

The events of the Ohiopyle Area Festival include
story-telling, tomahawk throwing, log-sawing, town
square dance, shingle making, and rail splitting.

★ 1682 ★
Perryopolis - PIONEER DAYS. Late September-
early October, annual, 3-4 days. Contact: Perryopolis Area Historical Society, Incorporated, Post
Office Box 238, Perryopolis, Pennsylvania 15473.

Festivities include band concerts, crowning of queen,
exhibits, polka dancing, crafts demonstrations, wagon
tours, chicken barbeque, smorgasbord, teenage dancing,
colonial shoot, auction, antique show, parade, and
country store.

★ 1683 ★
Philadelphia - ELFRETH'S ALLEY DAY. Early
June, annual, 1 day, Elfreth's Alley. Contact:
Elfreth's Alley Association, 126 Elfreth Alley,
Philadelphia, Pennsylvania 19106; or The Phila-
delphia Convention and Visitors Bureau, 1525 John

Community

PENNSYLVANIA (Continued)

J. F. Kennedy Boulevard, Philadelphia, Pennsylvania 19102.

The costumed inhabitants of the nation's oldest street still in residential use hold an open house with refreshments and a tour. Fife and drum corps perform.

★ 1684 ★
Philadelphia - FAIRMOUNT FALL FESTIVAL. Late September-early October, annual, 2 weeks, Fairmount Park. Contact: The Philadelphia Convention and Visitors Bureau, 1525 John F. Kennedy Boulevard, Philadelphia, Pennsylvania 19102.

The activities are designed to focus attention on what the largest metropolitan park in the world has to offer the area residents. Providing fun and recreation for all are art exhibits, special tours of the park's historical and cultural facilities including colonial mansions, bike races, crew matches and other special recreational activities.

★ 1685 ★
Philadelphia - FESTIVAL OF FOUNTAINS. June or July, 1 day, Benjamin Franklin Parkway. Contact: The Philadelphia Convention and Visitors Bureau, 1525 John F. Kennedy Boulevard, Philadelphia, Pennsylvania 19102.

A gigantic parade of Mummers String Bands, floats, celebrities, marching units, plus colored fountain and dancing waters and a huge fireworks display.

★ 1686 ★
Philadelphia - PHILADELPHIA FLEA MARKET. May-September, Independence Mall. Contact: The Philadelphia Convention and Visitors Bureau, 1525 John F. Kennedy Boulevard, Philadelphia, Pennsylvania 19102.

Over 100 booths offer arts, crafts, antiques, music, entertainment, a cafe and other unusual events and happenings at the "nation's largest urban outdoor flea market". Held every Sunday mid May-June, selected Sundays July-September.

★ 1687 ★
Philadelphia - SUPER SUNDAY. Early October, annual, 1 day, Benjamin Franklin Parkway at Logan Circle to the Art Museum. Contact: The Philadelphia Convention and Visitors Bureau, 1525 John F. Kennedy Boulevard, Philadelphia, Pennsylvania 19102.

Sponsored by the many cultural institutions which line the Parkway, the "giant block party" includes a midway of booths with all kinds of antiques, games, entertainment, music, and refreshments. There is a super swap where visitors may trade small items, the New People Game, a sundae made with thousands of pounds of ice cream, and special exhibits. An international bazaar features a world-wide variety of foods. The Medical Mile offers free tests. There are special events for children, and guest personalities are on hand.

★ 1688 ★
Pittsburgh - GREEK WEEK. March, annual, 1 week, University of Pittsburgh. Contact: University of Pittsburgh, Pittsburgh, Pennsylvania 15213.

A fun-filled week which includes activities and events to raise funds for the Western Pennsylvania Heart Fund. Sponsored by 38 Pitt fraternities and sororities.

★ 1689 ★
Port Royal - OLD HOME DAYS. Late July-early August, annual, 3-4 days. Contact: Port Royal Old Home Days, Rural Delivery 2, Port Royal, Pennsylvania 17082.

Parades, fireworks, contests such as rolling-pin throwing, pie eating, and community tug of war. Displays of arts and crafts with techniques demonstrated including woodcarving, quilting, potting and more. Pageant depicting massacre of the early settlers by Tuscarora Indians highlight the events.

★ 1690 ★
Pottstown - MINI-FESTIVAL. Mid July, annual, 1 day, Sanatoga Park. Contact: Department of Commerce, Bureau of Travel Development, 431 South Office Building, Harrisburg, Pennsylvania 17120.

Community picnic, family reunion, pageant, demonstrations of colonial arts and crafts, band concert, square and folk dancing, colonial sports and games, and supper.

★ 1691 ★
Pottsville - DOWNTOWN FAIR DAYS. Mid May, annual. Contact: Schuylkill County Committee, Rural Delivery 2, Hometown, Tamaqua, Pennsylvania 18252.

Ethnic groups present their crafts, foods, costumes, etc. A great variety of arts and crafts on display and for sale.

PENNSYLVANIA (Continued)

★ 1692 ★
Roseville - OLD HOME DAY.   Early August,
annual, 1 day, Route 549 off U.S. 6.   Contact:
Roseville Home Day Committee, Rural Delivery 2,
Mansfield, Pennsylvania 16933.

Morning parade, queen contest, band concert, barbeque, food stands, round and square dancing.

★ 1693 ★
Schaefferstown - KUCH FESCHT.   Mid September,
annual, 1 day.   Contact: Historic Schaefferstown
Festival Committee, Box 307, Schaefferstown, Pennsylvania 17088.

Features cooking festival and plowing contest.

★ 1694 ★
Scranton - NEIGHBORHOOD SUMMER FESTIVALS.
May-July, annual.   Contact: Department of Com-
merce, Bureau of Travel Development, 431 South
Office Building, Harrisburg, Pennsylvania 17120.

Ethnic food, carnivals and shows emphasizing community pride, held at various times.

★ 1695 ★
Shirleysburg - FORT SHIRLEY CELEBRATION.   Mid
May, annual, 6 days.   Contact: Huntingdon
County Tourist Promotion Agency, Box 601, Hunting-
don, Pennsylvania 16652.

Carnival, exhibits, rides and family fun nightly
highlight the festival events.

★ 1696 ★
Sweet Valley - SWEET VALLEY DAYS.   Late May,
annual, 3 days.   Contact: Sweet Valley Volunteer
Fire Company, Sweet Valley, Pennsylvania 18656.

Rural celebration featuring parade, county fair, and
various other events.

★ 1697 ★
Tioga - OLD HOME DAY. Mid August, annual,
3 days, U.S. Route 15.   Contact: Mr. Francis
Murphy, Box 374, Tioga, Pennsylvania 16946.

A historical pageant, evening parade, fireworks,
and local concessions highlight the festival events.

★ 1698 ★
Tower City - CELEBRATION.   Mid June, annual,
1 week.   Contact: Mr. Lemar Myers, 526 East
Grand Avenue, Tower City, Pennsylvania 17980.

Colonial baking contest, colonial olympics, arts
and crafts displays, parades, pageant and a week
long fair highlight the activities and events of the
festival.

★ 1699 ★
Warminster Heights - SPINNING WHEELS DAY.
Late July, annual, 1 day.   Contact: Book-Bike,
Incorporated, Post Office Box 6, Doylestown,
Pennsylvania 18901.

Parade for all ages with anything on wheels without
an engine to promote "Book-Bike".   Begun around
1973.

★ 1700 ★
Waterford - HERITAGE DAYS.   Mid July, annual,
3 days.   Town Square.   Contact: Mrs. Virginia
Bullman, 151 West First Street, Waterford, Pennsylvania
16441.

Non-motorized parade, a six hour long Bluegrass
Jamboree, the "Skirmish of LeBoeuf Creek" (over
100 participating Indians and soldiers from a six
state area), several concerts in the Victorian Bandstand in Town Square, ice cream socials, street
dances, old fashioned games, art exhibits, colonial
craftsmen (chair caning, weaving, spinning, blacksmithing, hand rifling a musket barrell, thrashing),
oxen, horses, and unicycles.   Home cooking.

★ 1701 ★
Waynesburg - COVERED BRIDGE FESTIVAL.   Mid
September, annual, 2 days, throughout Greene
County.   Contact: Greene County Historical
Museum, Waynesburg, Pennsylvania 15370.

"Sparkin" bridges are the scene of arts and crafts
exhibits and demonstrations.

★ 1702 ★
West Chester - CHESTER COUNTY DAY.   Early
October, annual, 1 day.   Contact: Chester County
Tourist Promotion Bureau, 406 North Wing, Court
House, West Chester, Pennsylvania 19380.

See old homes and mansions dating back to pre-
Revolutionary War days, historic landmarks throughout
the county.   Antiques, arts, and fine country food
are on display and on sale.

Community

PENNSYLVANIA (Continued)

★ 1703 ★
West Newton - OLD HOME WEEK.   Early August,
annual, 1 week.   Contact: Department of Commerce, Bureau of Travel Development, 431 South
Office Building, Harrisburg, Pennsylvania 17120.

Budd Car Excursion, water battle and tug-of-war,
old time movies, pageant and parade.

RHODE ISLAND

★ 1704 ★
Charlestown - CHARLESTOWN HISTORICAL SOCIETY
COUNTRY FAIR.   Mid July, 1 day, Sarah Browning
Strawberry Hill Estate.   Contact: Rhode Island
Department of Economic Development, Tourist Promotion
Division, One Weybosset Hill, Providence, Rhode
Island 02903.

Traditional country fair atmosphere and events with
a historical flavor.

★ 1705 ★
Coventry - COVENTRY OLD HOME DAYS.   Mid
July, 5 days, Rice Field, Knotty Oak Road.   Con-
tact: Rhode Island Department of Economic Develop-
ment, Tourist Promotion Division, One Weybosset
Hill, Providence, Rhode Island 02903.

Some of the nights have their own individual theme,
e.g. German, Polish, Italian, etc., with appropriate
activities including parades, musters, fireworks, a
clambake, car and bike races.

★ 1706 ★
Cranston - FIREWORKS IN FEBRUARY.   February,
annual, 1 day.   Contact: Greater Cranston
Chamber of Commerce, 900 Park Avenue, Cranston,
Rhode Island 02910.

Day of winter activities on Washington's birthday.

★ 1707 ★
East Greenwich - COLONIAL FAIR.   Mid May,
annual, 1 day, Rocky Hill School.   Contact: Rhode
Island Department of Economic Development, Tourist
Promotion Division, One Weybosset Hill, Providence,
Rhode Island 02903.

Activities include rides on antique fire engines and
helicopters.

★ 1708 ★
Naragansett - BLESSING OF THE FLEET FESTIVAL.
Early August, 2 days.   Contact: Rhode Island
Department of Economic Development, Tourist Pro-
motion Division, One Weybosset Hill, Providence,
Rhode Island 02903.

Activities include a ten mile foot race, a Blessing
of the Fleet ceremony, a battle of bands, and other
special events.   Entertainment is provided by a
German band and country and western musicians.

★ 1709 ★
Newport - CHRISTMAS IN NEWPORT.   December,
annual, 30 days.   Contact: Bristol County Development Council, Incorporated, 154 North Main Street,
Fall River, Massachusetts 02722.

Observance throughout the city.   Colonial decorations
and lighting, varied seasonal activities - exhibits,
concerts, candlelight tours of eighteenth and nineteenth century houses, special church services, flower
shows, craft fairs, and a skating party.   Begun around
1971.

★ 1710 ★
North Scituate - ASTRONOMY DAY.   Early June-
late October, 2 days (1 each month), Seagrave
Memorial Observatory.   Contact: Rhode Island
Department of Economic Development, Tourist Pro-
motion Division, One Weybosset Hill, Providence,
Rhode Island 02903.

Sponsored by Skyscrapers, Incorporated, the events
include films, displays, astronomical entertainment,
and beginners level instruction.

★ 1711 ★
Usquepaug - JOHNNYCAKE FESTIVAL.   October,
annual.   Contact: Paul Drum, 11 Elam Street,
Wickford, Rhode Island 02819.

Events include feasting on johnnycakes, a tour of the
historic mill, Indian dancing, and local craft work.

★ 1712 ★
Wakefield - SOUTH COUNTY HERITAGE FESTIVAL.
July (weekend of the 4th), annual, 3 days, Marina
Park.   Contact: Jim Norman, Publicity Director,
11 Whitehorn Drive, Kingston, Rhode Island 02881.

The festival features booths, a flea market and a
la carte seafood dinners.   There are competitive
events for children, and the Point Judith Yacht Club
Heritage Festival Sailboat Regatta.   Entertainment

RHODE ISLAND (Continued)

includes German bands, Sweet Adeline country-western music, strolling musicians, a sing-a-long, clowns, a beer fest, and an antique car parade. Other activities include pony rides, paddleboats and other rides for children.   Sponsored by the Lions Club, there is no admission charge.   Associated with Colonial Week.   Begun in 1970.

SOUTH CAROLINA

★ 1713 ★
Charleston - BROAD STREET JUBILEE.   Early April; 2 days.   Contact: Charleston Trident, Post Office Box 975, Charleston, South Carolina 29402.

A performance and other festival events highlight the gala activities.

★ 1714 ★
Charleston - CHARLES TOWNE LANDING LABOR DAY CELEBRATION.   Early September, annual, 1 day, Charles Towne Landing.   Contact: E. Pat Joyce, Charles Towne Landing, 1500 Old Towne Road, Charleston, South Carolina 29407.

This last fling at summer includes special exhibits, entertainment, bike rides, cart tours, kayaks on the lagoon, and lots of good food.   The topper of the day is a gigantic fireworks display at dark.

★ 1715 ★
Charleston - FESTIVAL OF HOUSES.   Mid-late March-mid April, annual, 25 days.   Contact: Mrs. Alicia Rudolf, Tour Director, Historic Charleston Foundation, 41 Meeting Street, Charleston, South Carolina 29401.

Seven different afternoon and evening candlelight walking tours are offered, each tour including eight or more sites, among them many of Charleston's private homes and walled gardens.   Reservations recommended.

★ 1716 ★
Georgetown - PLANTATION TOUR FESTIVAL.   Mid April, annual, 2 days.   Contact: Mrs. W.D. Bourne, 530 Prince Street, Georgetown, South Carolina 29440.

A series of activities timed to coincide with the Annual Georgetown Tours of historic sites.   Included are art exhibits, golf, fishing, free movies, etc.

★ 1717 ★
Harleyville - SEE SAW DAZE.   Late April, annual, 3 days.   Contact: David Spivey, Harleyville, South Carolina 29448.

This festival gives tribute to the saw mill industries of the 1870's and the cement industries of the 1970's. The weekend is filled with such events as a beauty contest, parade, novelty concessions, guided tours, pancake breakfast, barbeque and chicken suppers, street dances, contests for all ages, and flea markets.

★ 1718 ★
Jamestown - HELL HOLE SWAMP FESTIVAL.   Early May, annual, 3 days.   Contact: Cecil B. Guerry, Post Office Box 125, Jamestown, South Carolina 29453; or Santee-Cooper Counties Promotion Commission, Post Office Box 12, Santee, South Carolina 29142.

One of South Carolina's most colorful rural festivals includes such activities as moonshine-making, a "Tall Tales of Hell Hole Swamp" contest, talent contest, lancing tournament, and crowning of Miss Hell Hole Swamp.   Other events include dancing, historic tours, field day activities, a spiritual concert, and other fun activities for all ages.

★ 1719 ★
Kershaw County - KERSHAW COUNTY HERITAGE DAYS.   Mid November, annual, 9 days.   Contact: Greater Kershaw County Chamber of Commerce, Post Office Box 605, Camden, South Carolina 29020.

Planned activities include historical driving tours, South Carolina Annual Breakfast Meeting, airplane rides, rock and mineral displays, bazaar, luncheon, and children's circus with special activities in Liberty and Bethune.   Begun around 1972.

★ 1720 ★
Mountain Rest - HILLBILLY DAY.   Early July, annual, 1 day.   Contact: Mrs. Miriam Dawson, Mountain Rest, South Carolina 29664.

The tiny mountain community comes alive with the pageantry of city slickers come country with square dancing, clogging, greased pig chases, and a hootenany.   The twang of real hillbilly music sets the stage for mountain victuals.

★ 1721 ★
Myrtle Beach - HOLIDAY FIESTA.   Late November-late December, annual, 1 month.   Contact: Greater Myrtle Beach Chamber of Commerce, Post Office Box 1326, Myrtle Beach, South Carolina 29577.

Community

SOUTH CAROLINA (Continued)

Special holiday activities include turkey shoots, community worship services, golf tournaments, Christmas observances, community caroling, Christmas concert, home tours, film festival, art exhibits, and package plans at motels and hotels.

★ 1722 ★
Ridgeland – SERGEANT JASPER FESTIVAL. Early October, annual, 3 days. Contact: Jasper County Chamber of Commerce, Post Office Box 483, Ridgeland, South Carolina 29936.

This colorful low-country festival features a parade, country fair, crafts displays, field events, boat and ski races, fireworks, and catfish stew. The events are between Ridgland and Hardeeville.

★ 1723 ★
Springfield – GOVERNOR'S FROG JUMPING CONTEST. Late March, annual, 1 day, Main Street. Contact: Lila G. Williams, Box 113, Springfield, South Carolina 29146; or Mayor Oswald K. Furtick, Railroad Avenue, Springfield, South Carolina 29146.

The finest frogs in the state compete in this dramatic contest. Judging is done by state dignitaries, and the winning frog is sent to Calaveras County, California, for the national frog jumping competition. Other activities include a horseshoe contest, parade, barbeque, square dancing and country music. Begun around 1968.

★ 1724 ★
Springfield – INTERNATIONAL EGG STRIKING CONTEST. Late March, annual, 1 day. Contact: Lila G. Williams, Box 113, Springfield, South Carolina 29146; or Mayor Oswald K. Furtick, Railroad Avenue, Springfield, South Carolina 29146.

The hardest boiled eggs that can be found are paired in striking duels. Excitement builds with every strike of the rock-like eggs in this colorful folk custom. Other events include Easter egg hunts and free Easter eggs for children.

★ 1725 ★
Summerville – FLOWER TOWN FESTIVAL. Early April, annual, 3 days. Contact: Frances Stogner, Post Office Box 843, Summerville, South Carolina 29483.

Activities at the festival, sponsored by the Y.W.C.O.,

include an art show, pet show, and historical tours. There is a parade, band concert, and other entertainment. Low-country foods are offered.

★ 1726 ★
Wagener – WAGONS TO WAGENER. Early May, annual, 3 days. Contact: Paul C. Hunt, 116 North Main Street, Wagener, South Carolina 29164.

Events include a beauty pageant, dance, a parade, a flea market, barbeque, and various contests.

SOUTH DAKOTA

★ 1727 ★
Belle Fourche – BLACK HILLS ROUNDUP. Early July, annual, 2 days. Contact: U.A. Jarvi, President, Tri-State Fair and Sales Association, Belle Fourche, South Dakota 57717.

Billed as the upper midwest's oldest and finest rodeo, this event includes top rodeo competition, western street parades and carnival rides. The rodeo retains all the old time western flavor and "ride-em-cowboy" spirit that everyone loves. Includes the Miss South Dakota Rodeo Queen contest. Begun around 1922.

★ 1728 ★
DeSmet – OLD SETTLERS DAYS. Mid June, annual, 2 days. Contact: Division of Tourism Development, State Office Building, Pierre, South Dakota 57501.

This is the day when all of DeSmet's old timers return to the town or come to town to celebrate their favorite place to live. The days are filled with parades, the crowning of a queen, a dance, tractor pulling contests and tours through the Laura Ingalls Wilder memorials. (Laura Ingalls Wilder based several of her famous children's books on her life in DeSmet, the little town on the prairie.)

★ 1729 ★
Dupree – PIONEER DAYS. Mid June, annual, 2 days. Contact: Division of Tourism, State Office Building 2, Pierre, South Dakota 57501.

The celebration usually includes a parade through the downtown, with a rodeo each afternoon, and ends with a fireworks display.

★ 1730 ★
Elkton – HARVEST FESTIVAL. Late June, annual, 2 days. Contact: Division of Tourism Development, State Office Building 2, Pierre, South Dakota 57501.

SOUTH DAKOTA (Continued)

The celebration includes parades, queens, and amusements for children.   Well attended by surrounding communities.

★ 1731 ★
Gary - OLD SETTLERS PICNIC AND RODEO.
Early July (the 4th), annual, 2 days.   Contact: Division of Tourism Development, State Office Building 2, Pierre, South Dakota 57501.

Celebrates Independence Day with a gathering of oldsters and youngsters, for two days of games, a picnic, and a parade.

★ 1732 ★
Highmore - OLD SETTLERS DAY.   Mid June, annual, 1 day.   Contact: Division of Tourism Development, State Office Building 2, Pierre, South Dakota 57501.

Celebration honoring the old timers of the area with class reunions, parade, demolition derby, rodeo, dance, and the crowning of royalty selected from the old settlers.

★ 1733 ★
Hill City - HEART OF THE HILLS DAYS.   Mid July, annual, 3 days.   Contact: Division of Tourism Development, State Office Building 2, Pierre, South Dakota 57501.

The city celebrates its heritage and location with logging demonstrations, timber shows, square dances, parades, horse shows and special homemade barbeques.

★ 1734 ★
Mobridge - SITTING BULL STAMPEDE.   Early July (the 4th), annual, 3 days.   Contact: Mobridge Chamber of Commerce, Mobridge, South Dakota 57601.

Cowboys from across the nation participate in one of the largest rodeos and parades.   Includes top RCA cowboys, with the finest stock available, including National Rodeo Finals Animals.   Begun around 1946.

★ 1735 ★
Parkston - JUNE FESTIVAL.   Late June, annual, 2 days.   Contact: Division of Tourism Development, State Office Building 2, Pierre, South Dakota 57501.

Combines contests, games, and sports for the entire

community, for kids and adults, with a main street carnival.

★ 1736 ★
Pierre - OAHE DAYS.   Mid August, annual, 5 days.
Contact: Division of Tourism Development, State Office Building 2, Pierre, South Dakota 57501.

South Dakota's capital city becomes a town of summer activity during this festival.   The celebration includes a fishing contest, stock car races, parades, children's games, contests and rodeos with name entertainers.   It also includes the North American Finals for the Buffalo Chip Flipping Contest that could be held only where the buffalo roam.

★ 1737 ★
Sioux Falls - NORDLAND FEST.   Mid June, annual, 3 days.   Contact: Division of Tourism Development, State Office Building 2, Pierre, South Dakota 57501.

Events include exhibits, arts and crafts demonstrations, cooking demonstrations, tours of the town and surrounding areas, a theater production, and food galore.

★ 1738 ★
Valley Springs - BOOSTER DAYS.   Mid July, annual, 2 days.   Contact: Division of Tourism Development, State Office Building 2, Pierre, South Dakota 57501.

Celebration features horse show, carnival, races, band concert and a parade.   Sponsored by the Optimist Club of Valley Springs.

★ 1739 ★
White River - WHITE RIVER FRONTIER DAYS.   Mid August, annual, 2 days, city of White River and White River Rodeo grounds.   Contact: Daniel R. Petrik, Secretary, White River Lions Club, White River, South Dakota 57579.

Events include a parade, a rodeo, and a carnival. There are many exhibits, including buffalo riding. There is a big dance in the evening of one of the days.   Sponsored by the Legion Club and the Lions Club.   Begun in early 1920's.

★ 1740 ★
Whitewood - WHITEWOOD DAYS CELEBRATION.
Late July, 2 days.   Contact: Division of Tourism Development, State Office Building 2, Pierre, South Dakota 57501.

Community

SOUTH DAKOTA (Continued)

Barbeque, businessmen's roping, street dance and games highlight the activities.

TENNESSEE

★ 1741 ★
Memphis – MID SOUTH FAIR. Mid September. Contact: Memphis Area Chamber of Commerce, 42 South Second Street, Post Office Box 324, Memphis, Tennessee 38103.

A traditional community fair emphasizing the agricultural achievements, homemaking, animal shows and contests, and entertainment for all.

TEXAS

★ 1742 ★
Alvarado – JOHN COUNTY PIONEERS AND OLD SETTLERS REUNION. August, annual, 6 days. Contact: A. L. Creswell, Reunion President, Box 301, Alvarado, Texas 76009.

The celebration features a fiddlers' contest and carnival. Fiddle music, gospel songs and western music are performed, and there is dancing. Begun around 1893.

★ 1743 ★
Amarillo – TRI-STATE FAIR. September, annual, 6 days. Contact: Mr. Donald L. Hileman, Chamber of Commerce, 301 South Polk, Amarillo Building, Amarillo, Texas 79102.

Thousands of visitors from the vast Panhandle Plains area and neighboring states come to see the exhibits, demonstrations, shows, etc.

★ 1744 ★
Bandera – FUN-TIER CELEBRATION. May, annual. Contact: Bob Miller, Box 638, Bandera, Texas 78003.

Chili cookoff, arts and crafts show, barbeque, western parade, dances, and a river float highlight the activities in this city of dude ranches.

★ 1745 ★
Bastrop – HOMECOMING AND RODEO. Late July or early August, annual, 3 days. Contact: Chamber of Commerce, Box 681, Bastrop, Texas 78602.

Brings hosts of visitors and former residents. Parades and pageantry highlight the events.

★ 1746 ★
Beaumont – NECHES RIVER FESTIVAL. April, annual, 5 days. Contact: Whayne R. Moore, San Jacinto Building, Fourth Floor, Post Office Box 3150, Beaumont, Texas 77704; or Otho Plummer, 245 Bowie, Beaumont, Texas 77701.

Parades, dances, water sports, pageantry and coronations, plus contests and art exhibits highlight the festival events.

★ 1747 ★
Beeville – WESTERN WEEK. Late October-early November, annual, 1 week. Contact: Mr. Wilson I. Clark, Chamber of Commerce, Post Office Box 99, Beeville, Texas 78102.

Held for more than third of a century, the event features a huge parade, first class rodeo, and South Texas Hereford Association show/sale.

★ 1748 ★
Brackettville – FRONTIER FAIR. May. Contact: Chamber of Commerce, Box 386, Brackettville, Texas 78832.

The event is opened with a parade. There is an arts and crafts show, a flea market, and live entertainment for the visitor.

★ 1749 ★
Brady – JULY JUBILEE. Early July (around the 4th), annual, 3 days. Contact: Mr. Boyd Hunt, 101 East First Street, Brady, Texas 76825.

Parade, dances, beauty pageants, and Quarter Horse Futurity are highlights.

★ 1750 ★
Brownwood – RATTLESNAKE ROUNDUP AND ANTIQUE SHOW. March, annual, 3 days. Contact: Chamber of Commerce, 521 East Baker, Box 880, Brownwood, Texas 76801.

Provides entertainment at opposite ends of recreational spectrum. Rattlesnake hunters "bring 'em back alive", and both dealers and individuals show prize antiques.

TEXT AS (Continued)

★ 1751 ★
Camp Wood - OLD SETTLERS REUNION.   Mid
August, annual.   Contact: Chamber of Commerce,
Camp Wood, Texas 78833.

Brings together old timers from Neuces Canyon country.
Fiddlers compete, and there is a style show and huge
barbeque.

★ 1752 ★
Canton - FIRST MONDAYS.   All year, first Monday
of each month.   Contact: Mrs. Baker Cox, 143
North Buffalo Street, Canton, Texas 75103.

Long traditional swap day in rural Texas; regular
tradition with current emphasis on trading of hunting
dogs (day often referred to as "Dog Monday").   At
the "Jockey Grounds", where bartering goes on,
lively rivalry as vendors, auctioneers and salesmen
vie for attention of visitors.

★ 1753 ★
Carthage - PANOLA COUNTY WESTERN WEEK AND
RODEO.   July-August, annual, 3 days.   Contact:
Chamber of Commerce, 316 West Panola Street, Box
207, Carthage, Texas 75633.

Festivities feature parades and top cowboys in arena
excitement.   Other western style entertainment and
contests.

★ 1754 ★
Childress - CHILDRESS COUNTY OLD SETTLERS
REUNION.   July, annual, 3 days.   Contact:
Chamber of Commerce, Post Office Box 28, Childress,
Texas 79201; or President, Greenbelt Town and
Country, Childress, Texas 79201.

Features nightly rodeo along with other reunion
events including a parade, fiddlers' contest, and
a dance.   Held for more than 80 years.

★ 1755 ★
Coleman - RATTLESNAKE HUNT AND ANTIQUE
SHOW.   March, annual.   Contact: Chamber of
Commerce, Post Office Box 796, Coleman, Texas
76834.

Amateur snake hunters bring in live rattlers by
hundreds; collectors and dealers trade, sell and
display antiques.

★ 1756 ★
Columbus - MAGNOLIA HOMES TOUR.   May,
annual, 2 days.   Contact: Chamber of Commerce,
Post Office Box 343, Columbus, Texas 78934.

Includes antique show and sale, and sidewalk art
show, melodrama under marquee, and tour of early
Texas homes.   Visitors dine at sidewalk cafes,
view antique car parade and watch continuous entertainment under magnolia trees on courthouse square.

★ 1757 ★
Crosbyton - WEST TEXAS PIONEERS AND OLD
SETTLERS REUNION.   August, annual.   Contact:
Mrs. Charlie Wheeler, Crosbyton, Texas 79322.

Events include parade, basket lunch, a horse show,
and square dancing.   Further entertainment is provided by a parade of styles, fiddlers' contest and
singing.

★ 1758 ★
Cuero - TURKEYFEST AND JAMBOREE.   September.
Contact: Quero Fair and Turkey Trot Association,
118 West Main, Cuero, Texas 77954.

Events include a beauty pageant, turkey races,
fiddlers' contest and dancing.   Begun in 1912.

★ 1759 ★
Dalhart - XIT RODEO AND REUNION.   Early
August, annual, 3 days.   Contact: Chamber of
Commerce, Box 967, Dalhart, Texas 79022.

World's largest ranch under fence in the 1880's,
some three million acres.   Sold into smaller farms
and ranches until now there is less than two per
cent of the original acreage.   Old XIT hands
gather to reminisce and enjoy events including
parades, antique car exhibit, coin and gun shows,
pony express races, dances, free watermelon and
barbeque, plus the rodeo.

★ 1760 ★
Decatur - WISE COUNTY OLD SETTLERS REUNION.
Late July-early August, annual, 5 days.   Contact:
Mrs. Rosalie Gregg, Box 474, Decatur, Texas
76234.

Originally a Confederate Reunion, now attracts
families who camp out and visit old friends.

★ 1761 ★
Denver City - OLD SETTLERS REUNION.   October.

Community

TEXAS (Continued)

Contact: Chamber of Commerce, 104 West Third, Denver City, Texas 79323.

Country-western and gospel music, old fiddlers' contest, queen contest and other events highlight the activities.

★ 1762 ★
Dimmit – CASTRO COUNTY ROUND-UP WEEK. August, annual, 1 week. Contact: Ms. Dorothy Magness, Chamber of Commerce, 201 East Jones, Box 924, Dimmit, Texas 79027.

Begins with "Miss Grain Sorghum of the Nation" beauty pageant. Includes air show, rodeo, parade, barbeque, and an old settlers' reunion.

★ 1763 ★
Dumas – DOGIE DAYS. June, annual, 3 days. Contact: Gerald Van Zanten, Chamber of Commerce, Post Office Box 735, Dumas, Texas 79029.

Began as a tribute to early settlers, has grown to a major festival: nearly 10,000 persons served at an annual barbeque. Activities include a new car given each year, rodeo, parade, and carnival.

★ 1764 ★
Eagle Pass – NATIONAL FAIR. August, annual. Contact: Ing. Elias Sergio Trevino, Mayor, Piedras Negras, Coahuila, Mexico.

More than 100,000 people gather for the border's largest festival event.

★ 1765 ★
Edinburg – FIESTA HIDALGO. March. Contact: Chamber of Commerce, Box 85, Edinburg, Texas 78539.

Events include a parade, a carnival, an art show, farm exposition, and a barbeque. Bicycle races, dancing, a trail ride, antique car races and kite tournament are also among the activities.

★ 1766 ★
Edna – TEXANA DAYS. Late June (last week), annual, 1 week. Contact: Chamber of Commerce, Post Office Box 788, Edna, Texas 77957.

Countywide festival in remembrance of the ghost town of Texans; major events daily: horse shows, trail ride, street dances, river race, drama, a rodeo, and gospel singing.

★ 1767 ★
El Paso – SOUTHWESTERN SUN CARNIVAL. Late December–January, annual, 13 days. Contact: El Paso Chamber of Commerce, Ten Civic Center Plaza, El Paso, Texas 79944; or Executive Director, Southwestern Sun Carnival, Post Office Box 95, El Paso, Texas 79941.

El Paso swings with beauty contests and balls; swim, golf, tennis, and polo meets; sports car races; rodeo events, and the annual Sun Bowl football game. January 1 winds it up with the glittering Sun Carnival Parade.

★ 1768 ★
Ellinger – CHAMBER OF COMMERCE FESTIVAL AND PARADE. May, annual. Contact: Chamber of Commerce, Route 1, Ellinger, Texas 78938.

An annual event for approximately 40 years, the events include a parade, dinner-dance, and a carnival.

★ 1769 ★
Fairfield – FREESTONE COUNTY FAIR AND HOMECOMING. August, annual, 3 days. Contact: Chamber of Commerce, Post Office Box 956, Fairfield, Texas 75840.

Draws 10,000 visitors. Outgrowth of former Confederate Reunions. Festival calendar includes parade, livestock show, rodeo, and lots of country music.

★ 1770 ★
Floydada – OLD SETTLERS REUNION. Late May, annual. Contact: Mr. William E. Flynt, Chamber of Commerce, 206 West California, Floydada, Texas 79235.

Honors area pioneers in a western style festival.

★ 1771 ★
Fort Stockton – PONY EXPRESS DAY. August, annual. Contact: Chamber of Commerce, Drawer C, Fort Stockton, Texas 79735.

Pony Express riders, western games and exhibitions, and a barbeque highlight the festival events.

TEXAS (Continued)

★ 1772 ★
Freer - OIL-O-RAMA AND RATTLESNAKE ROUNDUP.
April. Contact: Chamber of Commerce, Box 717,
Freer, Texas 78357.

A highlight of the event is a snake show and hunt.
There is also a parade, queen contest, barbeques,
an arts and crafts show and a carnival.

★ 1773 ★
Georgetown - WESTERN WEEK. Late June, annual,
3 days. Contact: Chamber of Commerce, 804 Main,
Box 346, Georgetown, Texas 78626.

Festivities and rodeo competition attract nearly
20,000 attendance.

★ 1774 ★
Glen Rose - OLD SETTLERS REUNION. Early
August, annual, 2 days. Contact: Carroll Gann,
Post Office Box 121, Glen Rose, Texas 76043.

A time for picnics and visiting old friends. There
is bluegrass music and fiddling, with contests for
both, as well as dancing. Begun around 1890.

★ 1775 ★
Glen Rose - ROLLIN' ROCK ROUNDUP. May,
annual, 2 days. Contact: Carroll Gann, Post
Office Box 121, Glen Rose, Texas 76043.

Features gem and mineral exhibits.

★ 1776 ★
Glen Rose - ROUNDUP DAYS. Early July (around
the 4th), annual, 3 days. Contact: Carroll Gann,
Post Office Box 121, Glen Rose, Texas 76043.

Parades, dances, junior rodeo, fiddler's contest and
tours to dinosaur tracks.

★ 1771 ★
Hallettsville - DOMINO TOURNEY. January,
annual, 1 day. Contact: Mr. Henry Joe Henke,
Jr., Post Office Box 313, Hallettsville, Texas 77964.

State championship draws young and old players to
day-long event.

★ 1778 ★
Helotes - CORNYVAL AND ART SHOW. May,

annual. Contact: Mrs. J.S. Rogers, 6367 Mondean,
San Antonio, Texas 78213.

A celebration of the city's founding and an outdoor
art show.

★ 1779 ★
Henrietta - CLAY COUNTY PIONEER REUNION,
RODEO AND HORSE SHOW. September, annual,
3 days. Contact: Chamber of Commerce, 116
South Bridge Street, Post Office Box 75, Henrietta,
Texas 76365.

Noted event for nearly four decades. Among features
is huge free barbeque that attracts more than 10,000
people.

★ 1780 ★
Hondo - HOLY CROSS HOMECOMING. August.
Contact: Reverend Victor Schmidzinsky, Box 426,
D'Hannia, Texas 78850.

Features exhibits, rides, a barbeque, and Alsatian
food.

★ 1781 ★
Houston - INTERNATIONAL FESTIVAL AND SIDEWALK
ART SHOW. October, annual, 1 weekend. Con-
tact: Mr. Louie Welch, Chamber of Commerce, Post
Office Box 53600, Houston, Texas 77052.

Presented at Old Market Square, arts and crafts as
well as food and entertainment from various ethnic
backgrounds.

★ 1782 ★
Hurst - FIESTA WEEK. July. Contact: Bart
Burnett, H.E.B. Chamber of Commerce, 1206 West
Euless Boulevard, Euless, Texas 76039.

A three-town fiesta celebration with parades and
balls.

★ 1783 ★
Junction - RACE MEET AND BILLY SALE. August.
Contact: Hill Country Fair Association, Dr. Ted
Holekamp, 810 Main, Junction, Texas 76849.

The activities include three racing days, the world's
largest billy sale, a mammoth street parade, and
dances.

Community

TEXAS (Continued)

★ 1784 ★
League City - VILLAGE FAIR. May. Contact:
Jack Rowe, 1600 East Main, League City, Texas
77573.

Civic organizations and businesses participate in an
all-community fair.

★ 1785 ★
Lockhart - FUN-TIER FESTIVAL. June, annual,
1 week. Contact: Chamber of Commerce, 201
South Main Street, Lockhart, Texas 78644.

Parade, rodeo, hobby and art show, and beauty revue
for selection of festival queen are highlights of this
fun festival.

★ 1786 ★
Madisonville - SIDEWALK CATTLEMAN'S
CELEBRATION. June. Contact: Winn Crossly,
MSCA President, 110 South Elm, Madisonville,
Texas 77864.

Events include a trail ride, a parade, a rodeo,
western dance, barbeque dinner, calf show and sale.

★ 1787 ★
Marble Falls - HOWDY-ROO FESTIVAL. June.
Contact: Clyde Griffin, Drawer 430, Marble Falls,
Texas 78654.

Events include a chili cookoff, water sports, arts
and crafts displays, a beauty pageant, and a flea
market.

★ 1788 ★
Marshall - CITIZENS BAND RADIO JAMBOREE.
Late June, annual, 1 weekend. Contact: Chamber
of Commerce, 301 East Austin, Box 520, Marshall,
Texas 75670.

Attracts some 1,500 ham radio operators who come
together to exchange information and have fun.

★ 1789 ★
Matador - MOTLEY-DICKENS COUNTIES OLD
SETTLERS REUNION. Late August, annual, 3 days.
Contact: State Department of Highways and Public
Transportation, Travel and Information Division, Post
Office Box 5064, Austin, Texas 78763.

Nearly half a century old, reunion recaptures pioneer

history with a variety of activities and displays.

★ 1790 ★
Miami - NATIONAL COW-CALLING CONTEST AND
PIONEER ROUNDUP. Late May-early June, annual,
2 days. Contact: Charles Bailey, Chamber of
Commerce, Box 66, Miami, Texas 79059.

The cow-calling contest, which reflects city's
western heritage, attracts national attention.

★ 1791 ★
Olney - PIONEER DAYS CELEBRATION. June,
annual, 3-6 days. Contact: Chamber of Commerce,
Post Office Box 338, Olney, Texas 76374.

Antique exhibits, antique auto show, parades, rodeo,
cutting horse competition, dances, baking contest,
and a prize for the most impressive beard are included
in the festive events.

★ 1792 ★
Plainview - PIONEER ROUND-UP. May, annual.
Contact: Jim Ferrell, Chamber of Commerce, Post
Office Box 340, Plainview, Texas 79072.

This community festival sees local citizens and former
residents join in friendly festivities.

★ 1793 ★
Pleasanton - COWBOY HOMECOMING CELEBRATION.
August. Contact: President, Cowboy Association,
107 West Hunt Street, Pleasanton, Texas 78064.

Celebration includes rodeo, dances, barbeque, and
an arts and crafts fair.

★ 1794 ★
Port Arthur - CAVOILCADE. October, annual,
3 days. Contact: Chamber of Commerce, Post
Office Box 460, Port Arthur, Texas 77640.

City's annual salute to petroleum industry. Festivities
include queen coronation, downtown street parade,
musical events and competition, contests, banquets,
regattas and fishing rodeo on Pleasure Island.

★ 1795 ★
Quanah - PIONEER CELEBRATION AND RODEO.
August. Contact: Chamber of Commerce, Box 158,
Quanah, Texas 79252.

Activities include a parade, horse show, art show,

TEXAS (Continued)

barbeque, and old fiddler's contest.

★ 1796 ★
Quitman - WOOD COUNTY OLD SETTLERS REUNION AND FIDDLERS CONTEST. Mid August, annual, 4 days, Governor Hogg State Park. Contact: State Department of Highways and Public Transportation, Travel and Information Division, Post Office Box 5064, Austin, Texas 78763; or Harold Galloway, Quitman, Texas 75783.

Held on the grounds of Governor Hogg State Park, events include prominent speakers, band concerts, carnival, gospel singing, old fiddlers' contest and dancing.

★ 1797 ★
Round Rock - FRONTIER DAYS. July, annual, 2 days. Contact: Chamber of Commerce, Box 356, Round Rock, Texas 78664.

Prior to Old Settlers Day, features pageantry, dances and parades, Sam Bass Shoot-Out, trail ride and cookout.

★ 1798 ★
Round Rock - OLD SETTLERS DAYS. July, annual, 8 days. Contact: Chamber of Commerce, Box 356, Round Rock, Texas 78664.

Festivities include old fiddlers' contest, square dances, concerts, gospel singing, and memorial programs. Staged since turn of the century.

★ 1799 ★
San Antonio - FIESTA SAN ANTONIO. Mid-late April, annual, 9 days. Contact: Chamber of Commerce, Post Office Box 1628, San Antonio, Texas 78296; or Fiesta Commission, Box 1628, San Antonio, Texas 78296.

The feature fiesta in a fiesta-loving city; innumerable associate events: art exhibitions, coronation of King Antonio, Pilgrimage to the Alamo, concerts, band festivals, Battle of Flowers Parade, King's River Parade, Fiesta Flambeau (night) Parade, championship rifle and skeet shoots, flower and fashion shows, musical productions, balls and street dancing, fireworks, and the fabulous series of "Nights in Old San Antonio". Festivities are centered around La Villita, a re-created Mexican Village of a century ago, in the heart of San Antonio.

★ 1800 ★
San Benito - TOURIST FESTIVAL AND SHUFFLEBOARD TOURNEY. January, annual, 3 days. Contact: Chamber of Commerce, 210 East Heywood, Post Office Drawer 1623, San Benito, Texas 78586.

Festival draws winter visitors for the event.

★ 1801 ★
San Juan - SPORT SHIRT FESTIVAL. Late February (Washington's Birthday), annual, 1 day. Contact: State Department of Highways and Public Transportation, Travel and Information Division, Post Office Box 5064, Austin, Texas 78763.

Visitors from nearby and tourists converge for carefree festival - prizes are awarded for important and humorous reasons. Events include picnic lunch, shuffleboard contest, and other competitions.

★ 1802 ★
San Patricio - WORLD CHAMPIONSHIP RATTLESNAKE RACES AND SAINT PATRICK DAY CELEBRATION. Mid March (17th), annual. Contact: Lonnie Glasscock, Route 2, Box 45, Mathis, Texas 78368.

Unusual celebration includes rattlesnake races, fair events, barbeque and old fashioned races. In honor of Saint Patrick, green beer is served.

★ 1803 ★
Shamrock - TOURIST DAY. Early September (on or around Labor Day), annual, 1 day. Contact: Ray White, Chamber of Commerce, Post Office Box 588, Shamrock, Texas 79079.

Tons of watermelons are served free to tourists as part of the festivities.

★ 1804 ★
Stamford - TEXAS COWBOY REUNION. Early July (around the 4th), annual, 3 days. Contact: Chamber of Commerce, Box 1206, Stamford, Texas 79553.

Dedicated to the Old West. Nonprofit community enterprise, the unchallenged greatest amateur rodeo in the world. Population of city more than triples when 500-plus rodeo contestants converge - drawn by prizes of handmade saddles and cash. Food served from chuck wagons. Western art show, rodeo grounds pavillion. Started in 1930.

Community

TEXAS (Continued)

★ 1805 ★
Stanton - OLD SETTLERS REUNION.   Mid July,
annual, 1 day.   Contact: Chamber of Commerce,
Post Office Box 615, Stanton, Texas 79782.

Held for nearly 40 years; event features parade,
barbeque, and community homecoming.

★ 1806 ★
Stratford - STRATFORD JAMBOREE AND SHERMAN
COUNTY FAIR.   Mid September, annual, 3 days.
Contact: Mr. Bill McMinn, Chamber of Commerce,
303 North Main, Box 570, Stratford, Texas 79084.

Features a parade, free barbeque, dances, and old-
time county fair exhibits and midway.

★ 1807 ★
Sweetwater - RATTLESNAKE ROUNDUP.   March,
Coliseum. Contact: Chamber of Commerce, Box
1148, Sweetwater, Texas 79556.

The events range from a Miss Snake Charmer Contest
to an arts and crafts show, but the highlight is the
thousands of live rattlesnakes brought in and displayed
in the coliseum's arena.

★ 1808 ★
Taft - BOLL WEEVIL FESTIVAL.   December. Contact: Chamber of Commerce, Box 65, Taft, Texas
78390.

When others are thinking of Santa Claus, Taft residents
are thinking of Boll Weevils!   Festivities include
arts and crafts how, flea market, food booths, fair,
and entertainment.

★ 1809 ★
Teague - WESTERN DAYS CELEBRATION.   Early
July (around the 4th), annual, 3 days.   Contact:
Chamber of Commerce, Box 187, Teague, Texas
75860.

Events include a rodeo, parade, entertainment at
Golden Garter Saloon and Olde Opry House.

★ 1810 ★
Temple - PIONEER DAY CELEBRATION.   Late June,
annual, 1 day.   Contact: Chamber of Commerce,
Two North Fifth, Post Office Box 158, Temple, Texas
76501.

Recalls the frontier heritage of the town and its
people with gala festivities.

★ 1811 ★
Texarkana - FOUR STATES FAIR AND RODEO.   Mid
September, annual, 6 days.   Contact: Chamber of
Commerce, Box 1468, Texarkana, Texas 75501; or
Executive Director, Four States Fairgrounds, Post
Office Box 1915, Texarkana, Texas 75501.

Opens with colorful parade; top national cowboys
compete in the rodeo, and the prettiest cowgirls vie
for "Queen of the Fair" title.   The fair calendar
includes Appaloosa and Quarter Horse Shows, livestock and agricultural exhibits and arts and crafts of
the area.

★ 1812 ★
Throckmorton - THROCKMORTON COUNTY PIONEER
DAY CELEBRATION AND RODEO.   Mid June,
annual, 3 days.   Contact: Chamber of Commerce,
Box 711, Throckmorton, Texas 76083.

Events include parades (one features vehicles and
costumes of the early west), tours, costume and old
fiddler's contests.

★ 1813 ★
Trinity - TRINITY COMMUNITY FAIR.   Late
September, annual, 3 days.   Contact: Chamber of
Commerce, Post Office Box 549, Trinity, Texas
75862.

A feature for more than two decades.   Queen's
coronation begins events which include All Trophy
Open Youth Horse Show, auction, arts and crafts
exhibit, parade, and carnival midway.

★ 1814 ★
Van Horn - FRONTIER DAY CELEBRATION.   June,
annual, 3 days.   Contact: Chamber of Commerce,
Box 762, Van Horn, Texas 79855.

Events include a junior rodeo, parade, barbeque,
and dance.

★ 1815 ★
Victoria - ARMADILLO CONFAB AND EXPOSITION.
May, annual. Contact: Chamber of Commerce, Box
2465, Victoria, Texas 77901.

Zany celebration includes beer can smash, body
painting contest, great mud pie pat, and, of course,
armadillo races.   Miss, Little Miss and Mr. Vacant
Lot are chosen.

TEXAS (Continued)

★ 1816 ★
Waco - BEAR DOWNS WEEK.   Mid April, annual,
9 days, Baylor University campus.   Contact: News
and Information Service, Baylor University, Post Office
Box 6337, Baylor Station, Waco, Texas 76706.

The Baylor Student Foundation sponsors a series of
sports events to raise money for student scholarships.
The highlight of the activities is the 50-mile Bear
Downs bicycle race.   Other contests include men's
and women's golf tournaments (not open to students),
tennis tournaments, a football game, a bik-a-thon,
and the Baylor Invitational Track Meet.   Aquatic
events include men's and women's canoe races, a
coed paddle race, a sailboat race and an innertube
race.   Begun in 1971.

★ 1817 ★
Waco - DIADELOSO.   Mid April, annual, 1 day,
Baylor University campus.   Contact: News and
Information Service, Baylor University, Post Office
Box 6337, Baylor Station, Waco, Texas 76706.

The name means the Day of the Bear and provides for
the Baylor community a chance to leave the classroom
for carnival-like activities.   Activities include football games, puppet shows, hayrides, movies and a
rodeo complete with cattle roping contest, greased
goats and coed barrel racing.   Campus clubs and
organizations set up booths and sell food items.   The
Diaseloso Queen and her princesses are presented.
School elections are also held on this day.   Music
is provided during the event by Waco and Austin
bands.   Sponsored by the Baylor Chamber of Commerce.
Begun around 1941.

★ 1818 ★
Yoakum - TOM TOM RODEO AND CELEBRATION.
June, annual, 3 days.   Contact: Mr. Dan Autrey,
Chamber of Commerce, Post Office Box 591, Yoakum,
Texas 77995.

Names related to tomatoes (not Indians) and event
began some 40 years ago when Yoakum was a large
tomato producing center.   Tomato crop not as important now, but rodeo, parades, beauty pageant and
other festivities draw visitors from over state.

UTAH

★ 1819 ★
Parowan - IRON COUNTY FAIR.   Early September
(Labor Day weekend), annual.   Contact: Karma
Huler, General Delivery, Parowan, Utah 84761.

Events include fireworks, horse races, dances, and
a rodeo.   In addition, participants may watch a
parade or view the fair's exhibits and displays.   Begun in 1863.

★ 1820 ★
Payson - GOLDEN ONION DAYS AND
HOMECOMING.   Early September (Labor Day
weekend), annual.   Contact: Utah Travel Council,
Council Hall, Capitol Hill, Salt Lake City, Utah
84114.

Events include horse racing, parade, art shows,
flower shows, and fireworks.

★ 1821 ★
Price - PIONEER DAYS.   Late July, annual, 1
day.   Contact: Utah Travel Council, Council Hall,
Capitol Hill, Salt Lake City, Utah 84114.

This community celebration includes a parade, a rodeo,
and other festive events in the park.

★ 1822 ★
Provo - FREEDOM FESTIVAL.   Early July, annual,
5 days.   Contact: Utah Travel Council, Council
Hall, Capitol Hill, Salt Lake City, Utah 84114.

Events include parades, carnivals, bazaars, and a
variety of other activities.

★ 1823 ★
Riverside - RIVERSIDE CELEBRATION.   Early July
(around the 4th), annual, 1 day.   Contact: Utah
Travel Council, Council Hall, Capitol Hill, Salt
Lake City, Utah 84114.

Events include a breakfast and a parade.

★ 1824 ★
Saint George - AMERICANISM WEEK.   Late April,
annual, 1 week, Dixie College.   Contact: Utah
Travel Council, Council Hall, Capitol Hill, Salt
Lake City, Utah 84114.

A week of activities stressing the patriotism and
heritage of our country.

VIRGINIA

★ 1825 ★
Alexandria - ALEXANDRIA DAYS.   Late August,
annual, 3 days, Market Square, King and Royal Streets,

VIRGINIA (Continued)

Old Town. Contact: Board of Trade, 400 South Washington Street, Post Office Box 359, Alexandria, Virginia 22313.

Included among the events are a variety of musical and dance performances: Scottish and Nordic dancing, pipes and drums, puppet theater, military orchestra, and more.

★ 1826 ★
Bealeton - BALLOON FESTIVAL. Late August (last weekend), annual, 2 days, Flying Circus Aerodome. Contact: The Flying Circus Aerodome, Bealeton, Virginia 22712.

The festival features a balloon competition and an airshow, with skydivers, vintage aircrafts, wingwalkers, dog fights and colorful comedy flying. Rides in open cockpit biplanes and balloons are offered. Begun in 1974.

★ 1827 ★
Bluemont - BLUEMONT FAIR. September-October, annual, 2 days. Contact: Donna Miner, Post Office Box 235, Bluemont, Virginia 22012.

Events include museum and historical slide show at old Snickerville general store, gospel singing, military marches, games for children, art show, craft show, country crafted goods for sale, children's events, cooking, bluegrass and traditional American music. Begun around 1969.

★ 1828 ★
Covington - RAILFAN STEAM WEEKEND. Mid May, 3 days. Contact: State Travel Service, 906. 17th Street, Northwest, Washington, D.C. 20006.

Scenic tours of the Virginia/West Virginia mountains in steam trains leaving from Covington and Cass, West Virginia.

★ 1829 ★
Fredericksburg - MARKET SQUARE FAIR. Mid May, annual, 1 day, City Square. Contact: Fredericksburg Area Chamber of Commerce, 806 Princess Anne Street, Fredericksburg, Virginia 22401.

Sponsored by the Historic Fredericksburg Foundation, Incorporated, the fair has the dual purposes of calling attention to the city square, and participating in National Historic Preservation Week. Craftsmen from all over Virginia appear at the festival. Photo-

graphers offer the chance to be photographed in eighteenth century clothing. Lebanese food is offered for eating. First held in 1738.

★ 1830 ★
Great Falls - NOVEMBER FESTIVAL. November, annual, Colvin Run Mill Park. Contact: Colvin Run Mill Park, 10017 Colvin Run Road, Great Falls, Virginia 22066.

Offers food delicacies such as split pea soup, home-baked bread, with flour ground at the mill. There are also exhibitions of crafts.

★ 1831 ★
Hampton - HAMPTON FAIR DAY. Mid September, annual, 1 day, Gosnold's Hope Park. Contact: Walter F. Ponzar, City Hall, Hampton, Virginia 23669.

A full day of entertainment featuring games, music, skydiving, police and fireman demonstrations, arts and crafts, horse show and fireworks.

★ 1832 ★
Lorton - KITE FESTIVAL. Mid March, annual, 1 day, Gunston Hall Plantation. Contact: Gunston Hall Plantation, Lorton, Virginia 22079.

Children, accompanied by an adult, up to the age of 16 are admitted free of charge to fly their kites on the fields. In addition, there are tours of the mansion and its gardens.

★ 1833 ★
Lovingston - NELSON COUNTY DAY. May (2nd Saturday), annual, 1 day, Nelson County High School. Contact: Bernard L. McGinnis, Shipman, Virginia 22971.

Events include a parade, dances, country music and band concerts, and the crowning of a queen. Additional entertainment includes rides, arts and crafts, antique cars, and food. Begun around 1941.

★ 1834 ★
Reston - RESTON COMMUNITY ASSOCIATION BIRTHDAY FESTIVAL. Early June (1st weekend), annual. Contact: Reston Community Association Birthday Festival, c/o Joan Bronsword, 2341 Paddock Lane, Reston, Virginia 22091.

An indoor and outdoor festival featuring parades, exhibits, arts and crafts shows, and entertainment by musical and theatrical groups.

VIRGINIA (Continued)

★ 1835 ★
Virginia Beach - VIRGINIA BEACH NEPTUNE FESTIVAL. Late September-early October, annual, 10 days, throughout the city. Contact: Virginia Beach Neptune Festival, Post Office Box 390, Virginia Beach, Virginia 23458.

A wide variety of events held all over the city for people of all ages. Some of the activities are a parade, a boardwalk seafood feast, sporting events, a sand-castle building contest, Youth Day with a milk carton regatta, balls, and a concert.

WASHINGTON

★ 1836 ★
Blaine - PEACE ARCH CELEBRATION. June (2nd Sunday), annual, 1 day, Peace Arch Park. Contact: Donald E. Snow, 2471 Birchbay Lynden Road, Custer, Washington 98240.

Events include a parade, a flag raising and a veterans ceremony - flowers for peace. There are two youth speakers and entertainers on hand. Begun around 1950.

★ 1837 ★
Burlington - BERRY-DAIRY DAYS. June (4th weekend), annual, 4 days. Contact: Doug Powell, Post Office Box 527, Burlington, Washington 98233.

Northwest artists display and sell their works. Other attractions include a carnival, sales and booths, and children's games with prizes. Begun around 1965.

★ 1838 ★
Coupeville - FESTIVAL DAYS. August (2nd weekend), annual, 2 days. Contact: Central Whidbey Island Chamber of Commerce, Post Office Box 152, North 17 Front Street, Coupeville, Washington 98239.

Events include an arts and crafts show with hobby and crafts displays on the street. There is also a salmon barbeque. Begun around 1965.

★ 1839 ★
Ephrata - U.S.A. FREEDOM FESTIVAL. June (4th weekend), annual, 3 days. Contact: Sandra Kulick, Post Office Box 275, Ephrata, Washington 98823.

An old fashioned American festival with flags, a parade, family games and events.

★ 1840 ★
Everett - ROTARY INTERNATIONAL AIR FAIR. July (3rd weekend), annual, 3 days, Paine Field. Contact: Air Fair Office, Terminal Building, Paine Field, Everett, Washington 98204.

Largest air show west of the Mississippi with industrial displays and demonstrations. Experimental, home built, antique, World War I and World War II airplanes from everywhere. World famous stunt pilots perform for hours, including the barn storming, wing walking act. Also included are Canadian and United States jet precision flying teams, England's vertical take off jet demonstration, sky diving, and the Goodyear blimp.

★ 1841 ★
Ferndale - OLD SETTLERS DAYS. July (last full weekend), annual, 3 days. Contact: Hal Reimer, Chamber of Commerce, Old National Bank, Ferndale, Washington 98248.

Activities include a rodeo, carnival, grand parade, queen's pageant, picnic and dance. Begun around 1901.

★ 1842 ★
Leavenworth - CHELAN COUNTY OLD TIMERS DAY. August (3rd Sunday), annual, 1 day. Contact: Mrs. Myna McGauhey, Post Office Box 53, Leavenworth, Washington 98826.

Picnic lunch, old time orchestra, antique cars, and miniature train rides highlight the festival events. Begun around 1960.

★ 1843 ★
Omak - STAMPEDE AND SUICIDE RACE. August (2nd weekend), annual, 3 days. Contact: Jud Lockwood, Executive Secretary, Post Office Box 916, Omak, Washington 98841.

Features are a colorful Indian village of more than 100 teepees, authentic Indian dances, and a wild west rodeo. Each days' performance is climaxed by the "suicide race", a swirling mass of horses and riders plunging down a steep hill, crossing a river, and racing to the arena finish line. Begun around 1935.

★ 1844 ★
Soap Lake - SUDS AND SUN. July (last full weekend), annual, 4 days. Contact: Soap Lake Chamber of Commerce, Post Office Box 433, Soap Lake, Washington 98851.

Community

WASHINGTON (Continued)

Events include a parade, carnival, dances, contests and Indian crafts. Begun around 1965.

★ 1845 ★
Tekoa - SLIPPERY GULCH. July (weekend of the 4th), annual, 1 day. Contact: Bill McCombs, Box 77, Tekoa, Washington 99033.

A day of activities designed for the entire family include semi-professional performances including a musical tour of the United States of America plus a western barbeque, a parade, a demolition derby, and fireworks. Begun around 1950.

★ 1846 ★
Yakima - SUNFAIR. September (last weekend), annual, 3 days. Contact: Yakima Chamber of Commerce, 410 East Yakima Avenue, Yakima, Washington 98901.

300 days of sunshine each year is the reason for this festival. An elite contingent of hosts called the "Sundusters" welcome you to Yakima. Activities include a grand parade, the Mount Adams climb, contests, dances, and a river raft race. The Central Washington Fair runs concurrently. Begun around 1969.

★ 1847 ★
Yelm - YELM PRAIRIE DAYS. July (4th week), annual, 8 days. Contact: Tom Ledington, Post Office Box 281, Yelm, Washington 98597.

Coronation of queen, carnival pet parade, food, music, and various events each evening. Begun around 1943.

WEST VIRGINIA

★ 1848 ★
Beckley - U.S. COAL FESTIVAL. Late August-early September, annual, 8 days. Contact: Mountainaire Travel Council, 1613 North Walker Street, Princeton, West Virginia 24740.

This important natural resource of West Virginia is the focus for mining and manufacturing exhibits and a variety of activities, including sports tournaments, bike races, and a parade.

★ 1849 ★
Beverly - COMMUNITY WEEK. Late July-early

August, 4 days. Contact: Mrs. Richard L. Plant, Post Office Box 271, Beverly, West Virginia 26253.

An arts and crafts show and sale is included in this community celebration.

★ 1850 ★
Cass - RAILFAN STEAM WEEKEND. Mid May, 3 days. Contact: Travel Division, West Virginia Department of Commerce, 1900 Washington Street, East, Charleston, West Virginia 25305.

Scenic tours of the mountains around the Virginia and West Virginia border aboard steam-driven trains. Also leave from Covington, Virginia.

★ 1851 ★
Charleston - JOHN HENRY FESTIVAL. Late August, 3 days, Camp Virgil Tate. Contact: Edward J. Cabbell, Director, John Henry Memorial Foundation, Incorporated, Post Office Box 135, 419 Mercer Street, Princeton, West Virginia 24740; or West Virginia Department of Commerce, Arts and Crafts Division, Building 6, 1900 Washington Street East, Charleston, West Virginia 25305.

A craft show is included in this community celebration.

★ 1852 ★
Charleston - STERNWHEEL REGATTA. Late August-early September, annual, Kanawha River. Contact: Bill Kenny, Post Office Box 2749, Charleston, West Virginia 25314.

Activities include a river boat race, a 15-mile distance run, parades, and concerts.

★ 1853 ★
Franklin - SPELUNKERS REUNION. Late August-early September, annual, 2 days. Contact: Municipality of Franklin, West Virginia 26807.

Features tours of limestone grottos and exhibits of interest to those who are fascinated by caves and caverns.

★ 1854 ★
Franklin - TREASURE MOUNTAIN FESTIVAL. September (3rd weekend), annual, 3-4 days. Contact: Eston Teter, President, Treasure Mountain Festival Association, Franklin, West Virginia 26807.

The festival features a parade, music, several square dances and a teen dance along with concerts of

WEST VIRGINIA (Continued)

mountain and gospel music. Films of the area are shown and the Fort Seybert massacre is portrayed in a drama. There are dinners, barbeques and a pancake breakfast. Contests include a beard and mustache event, muzzleloading rifle shoots, tomahawk throwing and other events. Logging demonstrations include a steam sawmill and a cross-saw demonstration and contest. Other demonstrations, exhibits and displays include archery, a horse show, a wildlife exhibit, arts and crafts and many more.

★ 1855 ★
Harpers Ferry - WEST VIRGINIA COUNTRY FLING. Early May, 3 days. Contact: Inez Daniel, Box 416, Harpers Ferry, West Virginia 25425; or West Virginia Department of Commerce, Arts and Crafts Division, Building 6, 1900 Washington Street, East, Charleston, West Virginia 25305.

Arts and crafts are an important part of this festival.

★ 1856 ★
Hedgesville - HEDGESVILLE HERITAGE FESTIVAL. Mid September, 1 day. Contact: Virginia L. Hessler, Route 3, Box 138A, Hedgesville, West Virginia 25427; or West Virigina Department of Commerce, Arts and Crafts Division, Building 6, 1900 Washington Street East, Charleston, West Virginia 25305.

A crafts show and sale is featured at this community celebration.

★ 1857 ★
Huntington - OLD GUYANDOTTE DAYS. Early July, 2 days. Contact: Mrs. Ruth Sullivan, GIAP, 101 Richmond Street, Huntington, West Virginia 25702.

An arts and crafts show and sale is included in this community celebration.

★ 1858 ★
Hurricane - HURRICANE HERITAGE DAYS. Late May, 3 days. Contact: West Virginia Department of Commerce, Arts and Crafts Division, Building 6, 1900 Washington Street East, Charleston, West Virginia 25305.

Crafts, displayed and on sale, are a featured part of this festival.

★ 1859 ★
Independence - HOMECOMING-WATERMELON DAYS. August (1st weekend), annual, 2 days. Contact: Independence Community Association, Independence, West Virginia 26374.

The festival begins with a traditional parade, following which free watermelon is distributed to all the participants. A Watermelon Queen and her court are chosen; the ceremony is followed by an old-fashioned square dance. A program of local entertainment with music and other talents is given on the lawn of the grade school. One of the West Virginia senators is the guest speaker. More watermelon is distributed to everyone. Other typical activities include antique displays, old-fashioned entertainment, arts and crafts, and performances by muzzleloader associations. Food and refreshments are available. Begun in 1892.

★ 1860 ★
Moorefield - HERITAGE WEEKEND. Late September, annual, 3 days. Contact: J. Holmes Spence, Mayor, Wardensville, West Virginia 26851.

Many historic homes and churches are open to the public. In addition there are exhibits of antique quilts, old china and glass, and crafts demonstrations including spinning, weaving, and pottery making. Activities include an old-time rifle shoot and a jousting tournament.

★ 1861 ★
Morgantown - MOUNTAINEER WEEK. Late October-November, annual, West Virginia University. Contact: Booker T. Walton, Jr., Program Advisor, 105 Martin Hall, Morgantown, West Virginia 26506.

Honoring the traditions and heritage of West Virginia, the festival includes a variety of activities. Musical events include mountain music such as dulcimer playing and a bluegrass concert. Guest speakers lecture on the folklore of the state. A country store and log cabin are on display, with the sale of mugs, corn cob pipes, hillbilly hats, and T-shirts. There is a mountain heritage fashion show. Other events include a mountain climb, football games, including a girls' Powder-Puff Flag event. Also included in the celebration is the Mountain Arts and Crafts festival, a juried event with displays, demonstrations and sales. Begun in 1972.

★ 1862 ★
New Martinsville - TOWN AND COUNTRY DAYS. Mid August, 5 days, Wetzel County 4-H Camp. Contact: Robert Leasure, 241 Virginia Street, New

Community

WEST VIRGINIA (Continued)

Martinsville, West Virginia 26155.

Events include yodeling, arm wrestling, motorcycle contest, tobacco chewing and spitting competitions.

★ 1863 ★
Oak Hill - WEST VIRGINIA SPORTS FESTIVAL. Late August, annual, 8 days. Contact: Fred Neudek, 120 Lively Avenue, Oak Hill, West Virginia 25901.

The festival offers a variety of sports and activities including an autocross, horse shoe pitching, bowling tournament, football, softball, and dancing. A festival queen is crowned. There are various receptions and concerts of gospel and country and western music. Crafts demonstrations are held along with an art show, a bazaar, plant show and sale, bake and sidewalk sales. There are fireworks and a parade.

★ 1864 ★
Parkersburg - PARKERSBURG COLLEGE HERITAGE DAYS. Late April-early May, 3 days, Parkersburg Community College. Contact: Nancy Pansing, Route 5, Box 167, Parkersburg, West Virginia 26101.

Arts and crafts are on display and for sale as part of this heritage festival.

★ 1865 ★
Ravenswood - OHIO RIVER FESTIVAL. July or August, 3-7 days, Riverfront Park. Contact: Greater Ravenswood Chamber of Commerce, 240 Washington, Post Office Box 121, Ravenswood, West Virginia 26164.

Boat racing, music, a parade, and arts and crafts are featured at this community celebration.

★ 1866 ★
Richwood - AMERICAN HERITAGE WEEK FESTIVAL. Early July, 5 days. Contact: Dorothy Morris, Nine Hill, Richwood, West Virginia 26261.

Includes arts and crafts as a part of this community heritage celebration.

★ 1867 ★
Richwood - CHERRY RIVER FESTIVAL. Mid August, 5 days. Contact: Richard M. White, II, Box 103, Richwood, West Virginia 26261.

An arts and crafts show and sale is featured at this community celebration.

★ 1868 ★
Rupert - RUPERT COUNTRY FLING. Mid June, 3 days. Contact: Jeanne Brenneman, Route 2, Box 36A, Rupert, West Virginia 25984; or West Virginia Department of Commerce, Arts and Crafts Division, Building 6, 1900 Washington Street East, Charleston, West Virginia 25305.

Crafts of all varieties are displayed and for sale as an important aspect of this festival.

★ 1869 ★
Saint George - SAINT GEORGE DAYS. June (3rd weekend), annual, 2 days. Contact: Saint George Days Committee, Saint George, West Virginia 26290.

The Order of Saint George is presented to outstanding citizens. Other events include arts and crafts exhibits, a talent show, and country and gospel music concerts. Old homes are open for tours. There is square dancing and a picnic.

★ 1870 ★
Sistersville - WEST VIRGINIA OIL AND GAS FESTIVAL. Mid September, annual, 4 days. Contact: Stewart Bradfield, Post Office Box 25, Sisterville, West Virginia 26175; or Susan L. Boyles, 133 Walnut Street, Sisterville, West Virginia 26175.

Fun, entertainment and learning about the state's oil and gas history. Contests include paddlewheel boat race, old fashioned water battles, and art and craft awards.

★ 1871 ★
South Charleston - FRONTIER DAYS. Late August, annual, 5 days. Contact: Oscar Fudge, 411 1/2 D Street, South Charleston, West Virginia 25303.

People in West Virginia display and sell arts and crafts. There are also amusement rides.

★ 1872 ★
Spencer - BLACK WALNUT FESTIVAL. Mid October, 3 days. Contact: Evelyn L. Zinn, 421 Center Street, Spencer, West Virginia 25276; or West Virginia Department of Commerce, Arts and Crafts Division, Building 6, 1900 Washington Street East, Charleston, West Virginia 25305.

WEST VIRGINIA (Continued)

Craft events are included in this festival celebrating the black walnuts which grow in the area.

★ 1873 ★
Thomas - MOUNTAINEER DAYS.   July (around the 4th), annual, 4 days, on the sidewalks of Thomas.   Contact: Mary Stilley, Box 9, Davis, West Virginia 26260.

The festivities include a pageant, a queen's ball, a baby contest and "Little Miss Mountaineer Days". Other events include a parade, pet show, beer drinking contest, fire department water battles, a pie eating contest, and gospel singing.   The sidewalks are filled with many different and interesting booths: flea markets, special craft stands, and refreshment and eating areas.   New additions are made every year, and it is a family affair with fun for everyone.

★ 1874 ★
Weston - STONEWALL JACKSON HERITAGE ARTS AND CRAFTS JUBILEE.   Early September (Labor Day weekend), annual, 4 days, Jackson's Mill. Contact: Stonewall Jackson Jubilee, Incorporated, Post Office Box 956, Weston, West Virginia 26452.

The Jubilee celebrates the craftsmanship, artistry, and heritage of the Appalachian people.   The festival features crafts exhibitions including china dolls, candles, sculpture, toys, quilts, etc.   Mountain music and dancing are performed.   Other special attractions include an old engine exhibit, wagon rides, hot air balloons, and more.   The event is held at the boyhood home of "Stonewall" Jackson, general C.S.A.   Begun in 1974.

★ 1875 ★
Wheeling - TRUCKERS JAMBOREE.   Late August-early September, annual, 1 day, Capitol Music Hall and Wheeling Downs.   Contact: C. Gurley, 1015 Main Street, Wheeling, West Virginia 26003.

Attractions include western music and trucking exhibits.

★ 1876 ★
Williamson - KING COAL FESTIVAL.   Late June-early July, 5 days.   Contact: Dimple Scott, c/o Chamber of Commerce, Williamson, West Virginia 25561; or West Virginia Department of Commerce, Arts and Crafts Division, Building 6, 1900 Washington Street East, Charleston, West Virginia 25305.

A celebration of the local industry and a display of crafts.

WISCONSIN

★ 1877 ★
Appleton - APPLEFEST.   Mid October, annual, 9 days, Goodland Field, Appleton East High School, Appleton YMCA, Appleton West High School.   Contact: Appleton Area Chamber of Commerce, 100 East Washington Street, Post Office Box 955, Appleton, Wisconsin 54911.

The festival includes numerous musical events: barbershop quartets, country western shows, rock groups, orchestras, polka bands, etc.   There is a home talent show, a square dancing jamboree, and an arts and crafts show.   Other attractions include a carnival, parade, and the Miss Appleton-Applefest Pageant. Begun around 1973.

★ 1878 ★
Lake Geneva - INDIAN SUMMER FESTIVAL.   Mid October, annual, 3 days, Flat Iron Park.   Contact: Greater Lake Geneva Area Association of Commerce and Industry, 100 Lake Street, Post Office Box 66, Lake Geneva, Wisconsin 53147.

Entertainment includes a balloon race, drum and bugle corps competition, a nationally known auto race, sidewalk sales, carnival rides, and a pig and bratwurst roast.   Visitors may tour Geneva Lake by boat.

★ 1879 ★
Milwaukee - OLD MILWAUKEE DAYS.   Late June-July, 7 days.   Contact: Milwaukee Convention and Visitors Bureau, 828 North Broadway, Milwaukee, Wisconsin 53202.

Events include fireworks, band concerts, beer, food, and a July 4th parade featuring old-time circus wagons and calliope music.

★ 1880 ★
Oshkosh - SAWDUST DAZE FESTIVAL.   Mid July, annual, 3 days.   Contact: Oshkosh Chamber of Commerce, 27A Washington Avenue, Oshkosh, Wisconsin 54901.

In the last century, Oshkosh was known as Sawdust City.   At least fifty wood processing mills were supplied by the trees cut from the northwoods and floated down the Fox River.   In honor of this heritage, the city holds this festival.

Community

WYOMING

★ 1881 ★
Buffalo - BUCKSKIN RENDEZVOUS.   Late July,
2 days.   Contact: Wyoming Travel Commission, 2320
Capitol Avenue, Cheyenne, Wyoming 82002.

Events include muzzle loading contests, firing demonstrations, and wild game dinners.

★ 1882 ★
Casper - CENTRAL WYOMING FAIR AND RODEO.
Early August, 7 days, Central Wyoming Fairgrounds.
Contact: Manager, Central Wyoming Fair and Rodeo,
1700 Fairgrounds Road, Casper, Wyoming 82601.

Events include a rodeo, carnival, parade and demolition derby.   Troopers, clowns and well known
entertainers appear.   There is a petting zoo for
children.

★ 1883 ★
Cheyenne - FRONTIER DAYS.   Late July, annual,
9 days, Frontier Park.   Contact: Jack Miller,
Cheyenne Frontier Days, Box 2385, Cheyenne,
Wyoming 82001.

A nationally known event with a total of nine rodeos
featuring more than one thousand cowboys competing
at bareback, saddle and bull-riding, and wild horse
races.   There are four parades featuring the world's
largest collection of horse-drawn vehicles, square
dancing, concessions, rides, and a free public pancake breakfast.   Also nightly melodrama and historic
tours of Cheyenne and the F.E. Warren Air Force
Base.   The Oglala Indians demonstrate the authentic
lifestyle of the Plains Indians and perform ritual
dances.   Nightly shows feature chuck wagon races
and country-western shows by well known singers.
Nicknamed "The Daddy of 'em all".

★ 1884 ★
Encampment - WOODCHOPPERS JAMBOREE.   June
(3rd weekend), annual, 2 days, school grounds.   Contact: Encampment-Riverside Lions Club, Encampment,
Wyoming 82325.

The event is a Paul Bunyan celebration sponsored by
the Encampment-Riverside Lions Club.   Woodsman
events include a tree climbing exhibition and competitions in tree felling, handsawing, power saw log-
bucking, axe chopping, and choker setting.   There is
a rodeo featuring bareback riding, calf roping, bull
riding and other events.   Additional activities include
chicken catching, a hobby show, dunk board, tug-o-war
and children's events.   There are also booths, exhibits,

a barbeque and a dance.   Begun in 1963.

★ 1885 ★
Evanston - COWBOY DAYS.   Early September
(Labor Day weekend), annual, 3 days.   Contact:
Evanston Chamber of Commerce, Post Office Box
265, Evanston, Wyoming 82930.

A homecoming celebration with a western flair.

★ 1886 ★
Fort Bridger - MOUNTAIN MEN RENDEZVOUS.
Early September (Labor Day weekend), annual, 3
days.   Contact: Evanston Chamber of Commerce,
Post Office Box 365, Evanston, Wyoming 82930.

A community get-together with a western flair.

★ 1887 ★
Lander - LANDER PIONEER DAYS.   Early July,
3 days.   Contact: Lander Chamber of Commerce,
160 North First Street, Lander, Wyoming 82520.

Events include a parade, three rodeo performances,
antique auto show, art show, fireworks, band performance, demolition derby, Rockcrushers Ball, and
a carnival.

★ 1888 ★
Laramie - JUBILEE DAYS.   Mid July, 5 days,
county fairgrounds.   Contact: Pete Burns, 1270
North Third Street, Laramie, Wyoming 82070.

Events include a carnival, rodeo, steer roping, horse
show, barbeque, parades, and nightly entertainment.

★ 1889 ★
Lovell - MUSTANG DAYS.   July (full week fol-
lowing July 4th week), annual, 5 days, rodeo grounds,
theater, area in and around Lovell.   Contact: Lovell
Chamber of Commerce, 836 Nevada Avenue, Lovell,
Wyoming 82431.

The events include a historical parade, a rodeo, a
dance and the fun-filled "Mustang Day Follies".
There is an art exhibit, bazaar, carnival and community
barbeque.   A Mustang Days Rose Queen is crowned.
The event is the outgrowth of pioneer days, begun in 1915.

★ 1890 ★
Rawlins - RAWLINS RENEGADE ROUNDUP DAYS.
Early July, annual, 4 days, Carbon County Fairgrounds,
Rodeo and Spruce Streets.   Contact: Mrs. Lois J.
Higley, 511 West Spruce, Rawlins, Wyoming 82301.

WYOMING (Continued)

Events include a Little Britches Rodeo, barbeque, fireworks and a parade.

CANADA - ALBERTA

★ 1891 ★
Calgary - CALGARY STAMPEDE. Mid July, annual, 10 days. Contact: Calgary Exhibition and Stampede, Box 1060, Calgary T29 2K8, Canada.

Celebration includes world championship rodeo, agricultural exhibits, starlit stage shows, chuckwagon races, a parade, dancing, marching bands, a frontier casino, and a new midway. Free flapjack breakfasts are served. The stampede is one of the few events outside the borders of the United States that was designated an official American Revolution Bicentennial Program in 1976. Special family attractions and days include Senior Citizens Day, Children's Day, Teen Day, Commercial Exhibits, Arts Alive Exhibit, an International Bazaar and an Indian village.

★ 1892 ★
Fairview - FRONTIER DAYS. Late July, 2 days. Contact: Travel Alberta, 10255-104 Street, Edmonton, Alberta T5J 1B1, Canada.

A community celebration in honor of earlier times.

★ 1893 ★
Hanna - PIONEER DAYS. Late May, 2 days. Contact: Travel Alberta, 10255-104 Street, Edmonton, Alberta T5J 1B1, Canada.

A community festival with memories of yesteryear.

★ 1894 ★
Jasper - KOBASA KAPERS. Late April, 3 days. Contact: Travel Alberta, 10255-104 Street, Edmonton, Alberta T5J 1B1, Canada.

A fun weekend featuring crazy ski races, a goofy golf tournament, and town dances.

CANADA - BRITISH COLUMBIA

★ 1895 ★
Atlin - ATLIN FESTIVAL. Early July, 1 day. Contact: Tourist Information, Atlin Historical Museum, Atlin, British Columbia, Canada.

The event features a princess contest, a parade, and a beer garden, with activities such as races, games and a dance.

★ 1896 ★
Fruitvale - BEAVER VALLEY DAYS CELEBRATION. Late May, annual, 2 days. Contact: The Department of Recreation and Travel Industry, 1019 Wharf Street, Victoria, British Columbia V8W 2Z2, Canada.

The festival includes a ball tournament, children's races, bingo, a barbeque and a Beverage Garden.

★ 1897 ★
Ladner - FESTIVAL BICYCLE RACES. Mid July, 5 days. Contact: Delta Chamber of Commerce, Box 8, Ladner, British Columbia, Canada.

Features a variety of sporting events and community activities.

★ 1898 ★
Ladysmith - DOGWOOD DAYS. Late July-early August, 3 days, Transfer Beach Park. Contact: The Department of Recreation and Travel Industry, 1019 Wharf Street, Victoria, British Columbia V8W 2Z2, Canada.

Events include a parade, races, logging sports, water sports, and other competitions.

★ 1899 ★
Nanaimo - EMPIRE DAY CELEBRATIONS. Late May, annual, 4 days, Beban Park, Georgia Park, and other locations in the city. Contact: Tourist Information, 100 Cameron Road, Nanaimo, British Columbia, Canada.

Features the crowning of the May Queen and a torch-light parade at dusk. There are public dances, band concerts, and displays by band and drill teams. Further entertainment includes logger sports, an Empire Day parade, a seafood barbeque, and fireworks.

★ 1900 ★
Port McNeill - PORT MCNEILL DAYS. Late May, annual, 4 days, Community Hall. Contact: Port McNeill Chamber of Commerce, Port McNeill, British Columbia, Canada.

The event features rides, games, live entertainment, a dance, and a special children's day.

Community

CANADA - BRITISH COLUMBIA (Continued)

★ 1901 ★
Vancouver - ROCK, GEM AND MINERAL SHOW.
Early May, annual, 2 days, 3096 East Hastings Street.
Contact: Tourist Information, 650 Burrard Street,
Vancouver, British Columbia, Canada.

Features handcrafted jewelry and silversmithing,
silver lost wax casting, and working with opal.

★ 1902 ★
Williams Lake - WILLIAMS LAKE STAMPEDE.   Late
June-early July.   Contact: The Department of
Travel Industry, Travel Information Services, Parlia-
ment Buildings, Victoria, British Columbia, Canada.

Largest such event in the province, it includes horse
racing, square dancing and outdoor breakfasts.

CANADA - MANITOBA

★ 1903 ★
Boissevain - CANADIAN TURTLE DERBY.   Mid
August, annual.   Contact: Mr. Ray Zelowsky,
Canadian Turtle Derby, Box 272, Boissevain, Manitoba
R0K 0E0, Canada.

Turtle races are featured.   Other events include
horseshoe tournaments, trapshooting, mixed summer
curling bonspiel, fishing derby, farmer's markets, and
sweepstakes drawing.

★ 1904 ★
Gimli - ICELANDIC FESTIVAL.   Early August,
annual, 4 days.   Contact: Ted Arnason, Gimli
Icelandic Festival, Box 1499, Gimli, Manitoba
R0C 1B0, Canada.

Features traditional foods, toasts, speeches and dress,
entertainment, water sport events, races, fine arts
demonstrations, and creative arts.

★ 1905 ★
Minnedosa - MINNEDOSA FUN FESTIVAL.   Mid
July, annual.   Contact: Mr. Gascoigne, Minnedosa
Fun Festival, c/o Minnedosa Tribune, Minnedosa,
Manitoba R0J IE0, Canada.

Based on the contributions of the railroad to prairie
life, this festival features the best of a traditional
country carnival.   Events include farmers' smorgasbord, canoe races, midway, dances, steam train rides
and Railroaders' Day.

★ 1906 ★
The Pas - NORTHERN MANITOBA TRAPPERS FESTIVAL.
February, annual.   Contact: Mrs. Sandra Handley,
Northern Manitoba Trappers' Festival, Incorporated,
Box 475, The Pas, Manitoba R9A 1K6, Canada.

One of the major events in Manitoba.   The main
feature is a 150-mile dog sled race.   Other activities
include rat skinning, trap setting, ice fishing, bannock
baking, tea boiling, flour packing, tree felling, log
sawing, moccasin dancing, jigging, moose calling,
snowshoe racing, and canoe portaging, all based on
traditional trappers' activities.   There is also competition for the best pelts of beaver and lynx.   The
Handicraft Exhibition displays beaded buckskin articles
by Indians of Metis (mixed bloods of either French-
Canadian Indian, or English-Scottish Indian ancestry).

★ 1907 ★
Saint Pierre - FROG FOLLIES.   August.   Contact:
Mr. Lennox Harris, Frog Follies, Saint Pierre,
Manitoba R0A 2A0, Canada

The Canadian Frog Jumping Championship is a key
event at this festival.

★ 1908 ★
Swan River - NORTHWEST ROUND-UP.   Late July,
annual.   Contact: Northwest Round-up Exhibition
and Agricultural Fair, Ninth Avenue North, Swan
River, Manitoba R0L 1Z0, Canada.

The round-up features rodeo events, horse shows,
chuckwagon races, barrel racing and other competition,
midway, and exhibits.

★ 1909 ★
Thompson - NICKEL DAYS.   July, annual.   Con-
tact: Mr. Morry Brown, Thompson Nickel Days
Corporation, Box 567, Thompson, Manitoba R8N 1N4,
Canada.

Miners from the surrounding community gather to make
fun of what is otherwise everyday work for them.
One of Manitoba's biggest events.   Competition in
drilling, hauling, etc. for the title of King Miner.

★ 1910 ★
Winnipeg - CANADA DAY.   Early July (1st day),
annual, 1 day, Legislative Grounds.   Contact:
Director, Department of Tourism, Recreation and
Cultural Affairs, Tourist Branch, 801 Mall Centre,
491 Portage Avenue, Winnipeg, Manitoba R3B 2E7,
Canada.

CANADA - MANITOBA (Continued)

Celebrates Dominion Day. Features ethnic entertainment in addition to bands giving concerts.

★ 1911 ★
Winnipeg - FESTIVAL OF GEMS. Mid July, 4 days. Contact: Mrs. A. Bailey, Gem and Mineral Exhibition, Rock and Mineral Club, 191 Douglas Park Road, Winnipeg, Manitoba R3J 1Z3, Canada.

Exhibition features demonstrations, rock swapping, films and guest speakers as well as gold panning and a pancake breakfast.

★ 1912 ★
Winnipeg - FESTIVAL OF LIFE AND LEARNING. Early-mid February, annual, 3-4 days, Fort Garry campus of the University of Manitoba. Contact: Assistant University Relations and Information Officer, The University of Manitoba, Winnipeg, Manitoba R3T 2N2 Canada.

Although of primary interest to the university community, the festival is also an event open to the public at large. Events include a variety of speakers from within and outside Canada, panel discussions on various themes of current interest, films of all types, demonstrations and displays, pancake breakfasts, tricycle races, monopoly tournaments, etc. Also includes the Canadian Film Symposium, which brings together directors, producers, distributors, government policy makers and interested critics and viewers, for three days of talking and film viewing. Begun around 1968.

★ 1913 ★
Winnipeg - RED RIVER EXHIBITION. Late June, annual. Contact: Director, Department of Tourism, Recreation and Cultural Affairs, Tourist Branch, 801 Mall Centre, 491 Portage Avenue, Winnipeg, Manitoba R3B 2E7, Canada.

Industrial showcase, carnival attractions and stage shows featuring entertainment from home and abroad. This is the city's biggest carnival.

CANADA - NEW BRUNSWICK

★ 1914 ★
Chatham - PIONEER DAYS AND MIRAMACHI AGRICULTURAL EXHIBITION. Early-mid August, annual, 7 days. Contact: Special Events Co-ordinator, Tourism New Brunswick, Post Office Box 12345, Fredericton, New Brunswick, Canada; or Charles

McCoombs, Secretary Manager, Miramachi Exhibition, Chatham, New Brunswick, Canada.

Sometimes called Old Home Week and Pioneer Days, this community celebration includes reunions and agricultural exhibits, displays, contests, etc.

★ 1915 ★
Cocagne - COCAGNE ACADIAN BAZAAR AND INTERNATIONAL HYDROPLANE REGATTA. August, annual, 10 days. Contact: Special Events Co-ordinator, Tourism New Brunswick, Post Office Box 12345, Fredericton, New Brunswick, Canada.

Included among the events is a regional folk fair in which the descendents of the first French settlers in North America recreate older times with Breton costumes and ancient folk songs. The celebration coincides with the opening of the lobster season, so this fishing village appropriately offers lobster dinners, along with clam-bakes, deepsea fishing, and saltwater swimming. There is a parade and a special feature, the Hydroplane Regatta, the world's fastest hydroplane races. A lobsterboat race may also be included. Begun in 1974.

★ 1916 ★
Fredericton - GOOD NEIGHBOR DAYS. Late June or early July, annual, 3 days. Contact: Special Events Co-ordinator, Tourism New Brunswick, Post Office Box 12345, Fredericton, New Brunswick, Canada.

A community-style celebration and homecoming event.

★ 1917 ★
Saint George - FAMILY FUN DAYS. Mid July, 6 days. Contact: Special Events Co-ordinator, Tourism New Brunswick, Post Office Box 12345, Fredericton, New Brunswick, Canada.

A community celebration with family-style fun, food, entertainment.

CANADA - NORTHWEST TERRITORIES

★ 1918 ★
Hay River - DOMINION DAY CELEBRATIONS. Early July, 1 day. Contact: President, Hay River Chamber of Commerce, Box 1278, Hay River, Northwest Territories, Canada.

Includes children's games, raft races, and a men's softball tournament. Associated with the South MacKenzie Fair.

Community

CANADA - NORTHWEST TERRITORIES (Continued)

★ 1919 ★
Inuvik - DELTA DAZE.   September (1st weekend).
Contact: Travel Arctic, Yellowknife, Northwest
Territories X1A 2L9, Canada.

A local celebration with a gambling casino, musical
entertainment, a barbeque, queen contest, and
dances.   Sponsored by the Lions Club.

CANADA - NOVA SCOTIA

★ 1920 ★
Aylesford - FAIR DAYS.   Early August, annual,
2 days.   Contact: Nova Scotia Department of
Tourism, Travel Division, Post Office Box 130,
Halifax, Nova Scotia B3J 2M7, Canada.

Offers sports events including tug-o-war, a midway,
Scottish concert, parade, and home-cooked food.
Sometimes called Aylesford Days.

★ 1921 ★
Bear River - CHERRY CARNIVAL.   Late July, annual,
1 day.   Contact: Nova Scotia Department of Tourism,
Travel Division, Post Office Box 130, Halifax, Nova
Scotia B3J 2M7, Canada.

Offers a variety of land and aquatic sports, bingo, a
parade, amusement show, afternoon auction, and home-
cooked meals.

★ 1922 ★
Dalhousie - FAIR.   Mid September, 1 day.   Con-
tact: Nova Scotia Department of Tourism, Travel
Division, Post Office Box 130, Halifax, Nova Scotia
B3J 2M7, Canada.

Features horse and ox pulls, 4-H club displays and
judging, games of chance, a parade, old-style
dancing, and home-cooked meals.

★ 1923 ★
Dartmouth - NATAL DAY.   Early August, annual,
1 day.   Contact: Nova Scotia Department of Tourism, Travel Division, Post Office Box 130, Halifax,
Nova Scotia B3J 2M7, Canada.

Events include a water ski display, a regatta, road
and swimming races, a midway, parade, band concert,
variety show, fireworks, and dances.

★ 1924 ★
Guysborough - COME HOME WEEK.   Late July,
4 days.   Contact: Nova Scotia Department of
Tourism, Travel Division, Post Office Box 130,
Halifax, Nova Scotia B3J 2M7, Canada.

Event includes yacht and canoe races, golf and baseball tournaments, dances, dinners and a Scottish
variety show.

★ 1925 ★
Halifax - ATLANTIC WINTER FAIR.   Mid October,
annual, 8 days.   Contact: Nova Scotia Department
of Tourism, Travel Division, Post Office Box 130,
Halifax, Nova Scotia B3J 2M7, Canada.

This festival, one of the biggest in the Atlantic Provinces, features livestock displays and judging, daily
horse shows, stage shows, arts, crafts, displays of
flowers, a midway, casino, commercial exhibits, and
Grand Prix Horse Jumping.

★ 1926 ★
Halifax - KERMESSE.   Late May, 1 day, Saint
Mary's University.   Contact: Saint Mary's University,
Halifax, Nova Scotia, Canada.

Bazaar with sale of handcrafts and homemade foods,
puppet shows, flea market, flower boutiques, and
rides.

★ 1927 ★
Halifax - NATAL DAY.   Late July, annual, 1
day.   Contact: Nova Scotia Department of Tourism,
Travel Division, Post Office Box 130, Halifax, Nova
Scotia B3J 2M7, Canada.

Features sports events, including a six-mile race.
There are rock concerts, band concerts, a rock dance,
children's program, parade, fireworks and a barbeque.

★ 1928 ★
Halifax/Dartmouth - JOSEPH HOWE FESTIVAL.
Early October, annual, 10 days.   Contact: Nova
Scotia Department of Tourism, Travel Division,
Post Office Box 130, Halifax, Nova Scotia B3J
2M7, Canada.

Festival honors Joseph Howe, Nova Scotia's most
famous statesman.   Major event is the oratorical
contest, the winners of which become "Mr. and Mrs.
Joe Howe".   They preside over the other events,
which include pony express ride, pancake breakfasts,
open air and craft markets, kite flying contests, dances,
concerts, beer fests, parades (including a costume

CANADA - NOVA SCOTIA (Continued)

parade), boat races, sporting events, a bazaar and
a multi-cultural concert.

★ 1929 ★
Hantsport - DOMINION DAY CELEBRATIONS.
Early July (1st day), 1 day.   Contact: Nova Scotia
Department of Tourism, Travel Division, Post Office
Box 130, Halifax, Nova Scotia B3J 2M7, Canada.

Includes a children's parade, road race (six miles),
horseshoe tournament, a regular parade, midway,
chicken barbeque, dance, and finally a tug-of-war.

★ 1930 ★
Iona - HIGHLAND VILLAGE DAY.   Early August,
annual, 1 day.   Contact: Nova Scotia Department
of Tourism, Travel Division, Post Office Box 130,
Halifax, Nova Scotia B3J 2M7, Canada.

Highland dancing and competitions, a concert, and
a dance are featured events in this community festival.

★ 1931 ★
Musquodoboit Harbour - MUSQUODOBOIT HARBOUR
FAIR AND EXHIBITION.   Mid July, 2 days.   Con-
tact: Nova Scotia Department of Tourism, Travel
Division, Post Office Box 130, Halifax, Nova Scotia
B3J 2M7, Canada.

The fair includes arts and crafts exhibitions and sales,
a parade, carnival, displays, and suppers.

★ 1932 ★
North Sydney - BAR 90 + 1 DAYS.   Late August,
3 days.   Contact: Nova Scotia Department of
Tourism, Travel Division, Post Office Box 130,
Halifax, Nova Scotia B3J 2M7, Canada.

This event is the celebration of the town's birthday.
Featured events include a steer barbeque, fishing
derby, fireworks and a parade.

★ 1933 ★
Parrsboro - ROCKHOUND ROUNDUP.   Mid August,
annual, 3 days.   Contact: Nova Scotia Department
of Tourism, Travel Division, Post Office Box 130,
Halifax, Nova Scotia B3J 2M7, Canada.

Features displays and demonstrations related to rocks
and semi-precious stones.   Demonstrations include
polishing, cutting, tumbling, and faceting.   Trips
are made to fossil fields.   Also lectures, art show,

entertainment, demonstration and sale of handicrafts,
and home-cooked meals.

★ 1934 ★
Port Hawkesbury - FESTIVAL OF THE STRAIT.   Early
July, annual, 3-4 days.   Contact: Nova Scotia
Department of Tourism, Travel Division, Post Office
Box 130, Halifax, Nova Scotia B3J 2M7, Canada.

This multi-cultural festival features a talent show,
parade, dances, sporting events, bazaar, hydroplane
and boat races, dinners and barbeques, and an exhibition of local art and handicrafts.

★ 1935 ★
Thorburn - EAST PICTOU FAIR.   July-early August,
annual, 3 days.   Contact: Nova Scotia Department
of Tourism, Travel Division, Post Office Box 130,
Halifax, Nova Scotia B3J 2M7, Canada.

Among the activities are track and field events, a
ladies rolling-pin contest, games, dances, and a
barbeque.   Pipe band concerts, a beer garden,
handcraft displays, a parade and a midway provide
entertainment for the visitors.

★ 1936 ★
Windsor - SAM SLICK DAYS AND REGATTA.   Late
July, 3 days.   Contact: Nova Scotia Department
of Tourism, Travel Division, Post Office Box 130,
Halifax, Nova Scotia B3J 2M7, Canada.

Includes a children's parade, fireworks, dances,
band concerts, aquatic events, a midway, and a street
carnival.   There are games and sports, including a
car rally and a soap box derby.   Food is on sale.

CANADA - ONTARIO

★ 1937 ★
Cambridge (Hespeler) - TEXTILE FESTIVAL.   Mid
September, annual, 2 days.   Contact: The Ministry
of Industry and Tourism, Parliament Buildings, Toronto,
Ontario M7A 2E5, Canada.

Includes factory tours, textile trade fair, parade,
sewing competitions and fashion show.

★ 1938 ★
Windsor - WINDSOR-DETROIT INTERNATIONAL
FREEDOM FESTIVAL.   Late June-early July, annual,
8 days.   Contact: The Ministry of Industry and
Tourism, Parliament Buildings, Toronto, Ontario
M7A 2E5, Canada.

Dance

CANADA - ONTARIO (Continued)

A joint celebration of the national holidays of the United States and Canada - Canada's Dominion Day (July 1) and the United States' Independence Day (July 4). Dignitaries from both countries attend. There is a parade, an air show, a horse show, concetts, dancing, and many sports events such as boat racing. There is also an art show and the largest fireworks display in North America. Begun in 1959.

CANADA - QUEBEC

★ 1939 ★
Quebec - SAINT-JEAN-BAPTISTE DAY. June (around 24th), annual, 1 day, banks of the Saint Lawrence River. Contact: The Tourist Information Division, 150 Boulevard Saint-Cyrille East, Quebec, Quebec G1R 4Y3, Canada.

Quebec's national day, with religious processions, fireworks, ceremonies, and bonfires. The celebration is held throughout the province of Quebec.

★ 1940 ★
Saint-Tite - WESTERN FESTIVAL. Mid September, annual, 10 days. Contact: Festival Western Annuel, Post Office Box 95, Saint-Tite (Champlain), Canada.

A parade, horse show, rodeo, and other forms of entertainment highlight this festival with a western flair.

★ 1941 ★
Sherbrooke - FESTIVAL DES CANTONS. Late May-early June, 10 days, six streets in mid-town Sherbrooke. Contact: Permante Secretariate, 220 Marchant, Sherbrooke J1H 5G1, Canada.

Festival with a genuine Quebec atmosphere - dancing, music, songs, handicrafts, sports, theater, food, movies, and antiques. About 300 artists and crafts workers participate. Six streets in mid-town are closed to vehicular traffic and festival activities take place there. Several Canadian championships are decided such as horse-pulling, tug-of-war, and wrist-pulling. There is also a "French-Canadian" evening (soiree) as well as a provincial Golden Age Festival, a provincial semi-marathon, band concerts, "Quebecois" shows (singers, music, comedy, theater), camp-fires, and fireworks displays. Special children's activities according to age (plastic arts, marionnettes, shows), and gourmets can savour the "Quebecois" cuisine at the terrace cafe or at the Grande Tablee.

CANADA - SASKATCHEWAN

★ 1942 ★
North Battleford - THOSE WERE THE DAYS: ANTIQUE SHOW AND FESTIVAL. Late July, 2 days. Contact: Travel Information, Department of Tourism and Renewable Resources, Post Office Box 7105, Regina, Saskatchewan S4P 0B5, Canada.

A celebration of earlier times with fun events and antiques for sale.

★ 1943 ★
Regina - BUFFALO DAYS. Late July-early August, annual, 6 days. Contact: Travel Information, Department of Tourism and Renewable Resources, Post Office Box 7105, Regina, Saskatchewan S4P 0B5, Canada.

The townspeople and their visitors dress up in western outfits (party-poopers are thrown into the Buffalo Days mobile jail). Activities include parades, street dances, stage shows, rodeo events, pancake breakfasts, and cookouts.

★ 1944 ★
Saskatoon - PIONEER DAYS. Mid July, annual, 6 days. Contact: Travel Information, Department of Tourism and Renewable Resources, Post Office Box 7105, Regina, Saskatchewan S4P 0B5, Canada.

The festival offers old-fashioned fun with a parade, a costume ball, stage show, and livestock show. There are also some unique events, including the World-Holopchi Eating Championship and a relay race in which the participants alternately run, ride horses, and paddle canoes. There are pancake breakfasts and barbeques.

Crafts
See: ARTS AND CRAFTS

Dance
See also: THE ARTS

ALABAMA

★ 1945 ★
Birmingham - ALABAMA JUBILEE. Early April, annual, Birmingham City Auditorium. Contact: Jim Harper, Executive Secretary, Post Office Box 1085. Birmingham, Alabama 35201.

ALABAMA (Continued)

Sponsored by the Birmingham Square Dance Association.   Begun around 1954.

★ 1946 ★
Gadsden - SQUARE DANCE FESTIVAL.   Mid July, annual, 3 days, Convention Hall.   Contact: Gadsden Chamber of Commerce, Corner Fourth and Walnut, Post Office Box 185, Gadsden, Alabama 35902.

Square dancers from many areas convene for the fun of the dance, colorful costumes, and lively music. Sponsored by the Gadsden Whirl-A-Ways.   Begun around 1968.

ALASKA

★ 1947 ★
Anchorage - ALASKA SQUARE/ROUND DANCE FESTIVAL.   July, annual, 3 days.   Contact: Alaska Division of Tourism, Pouch E, Juneau, Alaska 99801.

National callers and round dancing taught.   Begun around 1967.

★ 1948 ★
Anchorage - SPRING FLING FOLK DANCE FESTIVAL. May, annual, 1 day.   Contact: Alaska Division of Tourism, Pouch E, Juneau, Alaska 99801.

The local folk gather to dance and celebrate the arrival of spring.   Begun around 1971.

ARIZONA

★ 1949 ★
Globe - BUSTLE AND BOOTS SQUARE DANCE FESTIVAL.   October, 2 days.   Contact: Chamber of Commerce, Globe, Arizona 85501.

Square dancers in colorful costumes gather to dance and entertain.

CALIFORNIA

★ 1950 ★
Anaheim - NATIONAL SQUARE DANCE CONVENTION.   Late June, annual, 3 days. Contact: G. Ken Parker, 427 Phillips Way, Vista, California 92083.

A convocation of square dancing groups.   In addition

to dancing, activities include a style show, pageant, and educational panels.   Begun around 1952.

★ 1951 ★
Fresno - OBAN FESTIVAL.   July (2nd Saturday), annual, 1 day.   Contact: Tourist Information Center, 1270 West Belmont, Fresno, California 93728.

Japanese dancing - Oban-dori dancing in full costume to authentic music.

★ 1952 ★
San Diego - AMERICAN DANCE FESTIVAL.   Late May, 3 days.   Contact: Southern California Visitors Council, 705 West Seventh Street, Los Angeles, California 90017;   or San Diego Chamber of Commerce, 233 A Street, Suite 300, San Diego, California 92101.

Demonstrations and explanations of the origin of all forms of dancing.

★ 1953 ★
San Diego - FIESTA DE LA CUADRILLA.   November (1st weekend), annual, 3 days, Balboa Park.   Contact: San Diego Parks and Recreation Department, Conference Building, Balboa Park, San Diego, California 92101.

Square dance festival, workshops and demonstrations, and colorful costumes highlight the festival activities. Sponsored by the Recreation and Parks Department and the San Diego Square Dance Association.   Begun around 1950.

★ 1954 ★
San Diego - MAY TIME FROLIC.   Mid May, annual, 1 day.   Contact: San Diego Convention and Visitors Bureau, 1200 Third Avenue, Suite 824, San Diego, California 92101.

Square dancing and round dancing are the highlights of this gala day in San Diego.   Begun around 1974.

★ 1955 ★
San Diego - SAN DIEGO ROUND DANCE FESTIVAL. Late March, annual, 3 days, Balboa Park Club. Contact: San Diego Parks and Recreation Department, San Diego Convention and Visitors Bureau, 1200 Third Avenue, Suite 824, San Diego, California 92101.

Workshops and dance sessions for participation or

Dance

CALIFORNIA (Continued)

observation.   Begun around 1967.

★ 1956 ★
Stockton - SQUARE DANCE FESTIVAL.   Late
September, 2 days.   Contact: California Chamber
of Commerce, 455 Capitol Mall, Sacramento,
California 95814.

A gathering of those who like to perform or watch
the square dancing.

CONNECTICUT

★ 1957 ★
New London - AMERICAN DANCE FESTIVAL.
Late June-August, annual, Palmer Auditorium of Con-
necticut College.   Contact: American Dance Festival,
Connecticut College, 270 Mohegan Avenue, New
London, Connecticut 06320.

An outgrowth of the Bennington Dance Festival, this
concentrates mainly on modern dance, giving students
and visitors a chance to see works as performed by
the creators.   Students come from foreign countries,
as well as from across the United States.   The festival has outreach programs to take the dance to
neighboring communities and institutions.   Begun in
1948.

FLORIDA

★ 1958 ★
Panama City - SQUARE DANCE FESTIVAL.   Late
January, 2 days.   Contact: George Bowie, 1059
Bay Circle Drive, Panama City, Florida 32401.

Visitors watch and participate as the American heritage of this folk dance is reenacted by dancers in
western costumes.

HAWAII

★ 1959 ★
Waikiki - HULA FESTIVAL.   Early August, 8 days,
Kapiolani Park Bandstand.   Contact: Hawaii Visitors
Bureau, Special Events Department, Honolulu, Hawaii
96815.

Student dancers of all ages are taught traditional
Hawaiian dances by the Department of Parks and
Recreation.   Students from professional schools and
individuals perform ancient and modern versions of
the dance.

IDAHO

★ 1960 ★
McCall - IDAHO STATE SQUARE AND ROUND
DANCE FESTIVAL.   Mid July, 4 days.   Contact:
Chamber of Commerce, Box D, McCall, Idaho
83638.

Square dance exhibitions, outdoor breakfast, workshop, fashion show, and street dancing with national
caller.   This festival may be held elsewhere within
the state each year.

IOWA

★ 1961 ★
Durant - POLKA FEST.   Early September (1st weekend after Labor Day), annual, 2 days.   Contact:
Mr. Ron Alpen, Chairman-Polka Fest, Durant, Iowa
52747.

A large number of bands, German food such as
bratworst, German potato salad, sauerkraut, and
beer.   There is bingo and dancing in the streets.
Began in 1973.

MASSACHUSETTS

★ 1962 ★
Lee - JACOB'S PILLOW DANCE FESTIVAL.   July
and August, annual, Ted Shawn Theatre.   Contact:
Jacob's Pillow Dance Festival, Incorporated, Box 287,
Lee, Massachusetts 01238.

The festival features ballet, modern dance, ethnic
dance, and other related studies; a series of lecture-
demonstrations, film-slide studies, and discussions.
The dance programs are of the highest calibre, offering guest soloists and companies in premieres of new
works and works in the repertory.   Mimes and dance
satirists are often featured.   Formed in 1941.

MINNESOTA

★ 1963 ★
Princeton - POLKA FESTIVAL.   Early June, 1 day.
Contact: Chamber of Commerce, Princeton, Minne-
sota 55371.

A parade, polka bands, and a polka dance contest
highlight the festive events.

MONTANA

★ 1964 ★
Missoula - SQUARE DANCE FESTIVAL.   Mid May, 2 days.   Contact: Missoula Area Chamber of Commerce, 207 East Main, Post Office Box 1518, Missoula, Montana   59801.

Fun for dancers and observers alike as devotees of square dancing gather in colorful costumes and dance, dance, dance.

NEBRASKA

★ 1965 ★
Lincoln - SQUARE DANCE FESTIVAL.   May. Contact: Nebraska Association of Commerce and Industry, Post Office Box 81556, Lincoln, Nebraska 68501.

Square dance enthusiasts gather for the fun of the dance and to learn new dances from others.   Colorful costumes.   Begun in 1941.

NEW HAMPSHIRE

★ 1966 ★
Troy - FOLK DANCE WEEKEND.   Early May, 3 days, Inn at East Hill Farm.   Contact: Ralph Page, 117 Washington Street, Keene, New Hampshire 03431.

American square and conra dancing, and international folk dancing are featured during the festivities.

★ 1967 ★
Troy - SQUARE DANCE WEEKEND.   Early November, 3 days, Inn at East Hill Farm.   Contact: Ralph Page, 117 Washington Street, Keene, New Hampshire 03431.

A gala gathering of participants to enjoy good country music and square dancing.

NEW MEXICO

★ 1968 ★
Albuquerque - STATE SQUARE DANCE FESTIVAL AND WORKSHOP.   Early May, 2 days, Convention Center.   Contact: Greater Albuquerque Chamber of Commerce, 401 Second Street, Northwest, Albuquerque, New Mexico   87102.

Dancers and spectators come to dance, observe, and learn.

★ 1969 ★
Red River - SQUARE DANCE FESTIVAL.   Early September (Labor Day weekend), annual, 2 days. Contact: Chamber of Commerce, Red River, New Mexico   87558.

A gathering of dancers and country music fans and musicians in a colorful festival of square dances.

NEW YORK

★ 1970 ★
New York - NEW YORK DANCE FESTIVAL. Early September, annual, Delacorte Theater in Central Park.   Contact: New York Convention and Visitors Bureau, Incorporated, 90 East 42nd Street, New York, New York   10017.

Companies, ensembles and soloists offer every style of dance from classical ballet to modern rock.

NORTH CAROLINA

★ 1971 ★
Cullowhee - INVITATIONAL MOUNTAIN DANCE FESTIVAL.   Early May, 1 day, Western Carolina University.   Contact: Office of Public Information, Western Carolina University, Cullowhee, North Carolina   28723.

Invited dancers participate in various types of mountain dancing, including smooth and precision clogging. There is also public square dancing.   Started in 1976.

★ 1972 ★
Fontana Dam - ACCENT ON ROUNDS WITH SQUARES FESTIVAL.   Mid-late May and mid September, semi-annual, 8 days, Fontana Village Resort.   Contact: Fontana Village Resort, Fontana Dam, North Carolina   28733.

The festival offers callers and teachers for both western style square dancing and round dancing. There are 'swaps' of calls and dances, workshops, parties, and special events.   Started in 1967.

★ 1973 ★
Fontana Dam - FONTANA FALL JUBILEE FESTIVAL. Early-mid October, annual, 8 days, Fontana Village Resort.   Contact: Fontana Village Resort, Fontana Dam, North Carolina   28733.

The festival offers callers and teachers for both western style square dancing and round dancing. There are 'swaps' of calls and dances, workshops,

Dance

NORTH CAROLINA (Continued)

parties, and special events.   Started in 1972.

★ 1974 ★
Fontana Dam - FONTANA SPRING FLING.   Late
April, annual, 4 days, Fontana Village Resort.
Contact: Fontana Village Resort, Fontana Dam,
North Carolina 28733.

One of the best square dance vacations in America,
the festival offers callers and teachers for both
western style square dancing and round dancing.
There are 'swaps' of calls and dances, workshops,
parties and special events.   Started in 1976.

★ 1975 ★
Fontana Dam - FUN FEST.   Late May and early-
mid September, semi-annual, 8-9 days, Fontana
Village Resort.   Contact: Fontana Village Resort,
Fontana Dam, North Carolina 28733.

The festival features callers and teachers for both
western style square dancing and round dancing.
There are 'swaps' of calls and dances, workshops,
parties and special events.   Started in 1959.

★ 1976 ★
Fontana Dam - REBEL ROUNDUP FESTIVAL. Mid
May and late September, semi-annual, 8 days,
Fontana Village Resort. Contact: Fontana Village
Resort, Fontana Dam, North Carolina 28733.

The festival offers callers and teachers for both
western style square dancing and round dancing.
There are 'swaps' of calls and dances, workshops,
parties and special events.   Started in 1964.

★ 1977 ★
Fontana Dam - SWAP SHOP FESTIVAL.   Late
April-early May and late September-early October,
semi-annual, 8-9 days, Fontana Village Resort.
Contact: Fontana Village Resort, Fontana Dam,
North Carolina 28733.

One of the best square dance vacations in the United
States, the festival offers callers and teachers for
both western style square dancing and round dancing.
There are 'swaps' of calls and dances, workshops,
and special events.   Started in 1953.

PENNSYLVANIA

★ 1978 ★
Erie - POLKA FESTIVAL.   Late August, annual, 3

days, Waldameer Park.   Contact: Department of
Commerce, Bureau of Travel Development, 431 South
Office Building, Harrisburg, Pennsylvania 17120.

Twenty-two bands play for the dancers and observers
of the festive scene.   Begun around 1966.

★ 1979 ★
Gettysburg - SQUARE DANCE ROUND-UP.   Mid
May, annual, 1 day, Gettysburg College.   Contact:
Clair Hikes, Gardners, Pennsylvania 17324.

Nationally known callers in annual event which
celebrates the fun and tradition of the colorful
square dance.

★ 1980 ★
Norristown - WORLDDANCE FESTIVAL.   Mid June
- early August, 8 weeks, Temple Music Fair, Ambler
Campus, Montgomery County.   Contact: Montgomery
County Convention and Visitors Bureau, One Montgomery Plaza, Suite 207, Norristown, Pennsylvania•
19401.

Dance companies from all over the world perform in
an eight week series.   Music Fair grounds transformed
into an ethnic village.

★ 1981 ★
Pittsburgh - SQUARE DANCE FESTIVAL.   Mid
November, annual, 1 day, Pittsburgh Area Square
and Round Dance Federation.   Contact: Rudy or
Marlene Valente, 2123 Chalfant Street, Pittsburgh,
Pennsylvania 15221.

Features Nelson Watkins, La Mesa, California, and
Melton Luttrell, Fort Worth, Texas, as callers and
rounds by Chuck and Marge Carter, Columbus, Ohio.

RHODE ISLAND

★ 1982 ★
Newport - AMERICAN DANCE FESTIVAL/NEWPORT.
Late August, 6 days, Rogers High School.   Contact:
The American Dance Festival, Swanhurst, Bellevue
Avenue, Newport, Rhode Island 02840.

The festival brings dynamic and innovative dance
companies together to demonstrate the variety and
vitality of dancing in America.

SOUTH CAROLINA

★ 1983 ★
Myrtle Beach - MYRTLE BEACH SQUARE DANCE
FESTIVAL.   Mid March, annual, 1 day.   Contact:
Artie Banker, 1125 Echo Glen Road, Charlotte,
North Carolina 28213.

Western style square dancing is the featured event.

★ 1984 ★
Myrtle Beach - SQUARE DANCE FESTIVAL.   Mid
September, annual, 3 days, Myrtle Beach Convention
Center.   Contact: Greater Myrtle Beach Chamber
of Commerce, Box 1326, Myrtle Beach, South
Carolina 29577.

Lively entertainment for everyone with western style
square dancing.   Begun around 1970.

TEXAS

★ 1985 ★
Odessa - SQUARE DANCE FESTIVAL.   February,
annual, 2 days.   Contact: Mr. Gene Garrison,
412 North Lincoln, Box 3626, Odessa, Texas
79760.

Leading callers and 100 squares at Ector County
Coliseum.

VERMONT

★ 1986 ★
Burlington - MAPLE SUGAR SQUARE DANCE
FESTIVAL.   Mid March, annual.   Contact:
Burlington-Lake Champlain Chamber of Commerce,
131 Main Street, Park Centre, Box 453, Burlington,
Vermont 05401.

The dancers perform to the country and fiddle music
and the maple sugar is harvested.

★ 1987 ★
Montpelier - FALL FOLIAGE SQUARE DANCE
FESTIVAL.   Early October, annual.   Contact:
Central Vermont Chamber of Commerce, City Hall,
Montpelier, Vermont 05602.

A square dancing festival to celebrate the beauty of
the season in Vermont.

WEST VIRGINIA

★ 1988 ★
Cairo - SQUARE DANCE FESTIVAL.   Late August,
2 days, North Bend State Park.   Contact: Bob
Rogers, North Bend State Park, Cairo, West Virginia
26337;   or West Virginia Department of Commerce,
Arts and Crafts Division, Building 6, 1900 Washington
Street East, Charleston, West Virginia 25305.

A get-together for square dancers.   A craft show is
included.

CANADA - NEW BRUNSWICK

★ 1989 ★
Fredericton - SPRING SQUARE DANCE FESTIVAL.
Early May, annual, 1 day.   Contact: Special
Events Co-ordinator, Tourism New Brunswick, Post
Office Box 12345, Fredericton, New Brunswick,
Canada.

A gathering of square dancers and musicians and
those who like to watch and listen.

·CANADA - NORTHWEST TERRITORIES

★ 1990 ★
Fort Smith - SQUARE AND ROUND DANCE
JAMBOREE.   Late May, annual, 4 days.   Con-
tact: President, Frosty Squares Square Dance Club,
Box 65, Fort Smith, Northwest Territories, Canada.

A weekend of square and round dancing.   Begun
in 1968.

★ 1991 ★
Kakisa Village - TRAVELLING SQUARES CAMPOREE.
Late July-early August, 4 days, Lady Evelyn Falls
Territorial Park.   Contact: Northwest Territories
Square and Round Dance Association, Box 323, Pine
Point, Northwest Territories, Canada.

Participants camp out in their own tents, campers and
trailers.   In addition to the dancing, there are
games, races, and fishing contests.   Begun in 1973.

Drama
See: THEATER AND DRAMA

Ethnic Events

See also: FOLK

ALABAMA

★ 1992 ★
Birmingham - JAPANESE TEA CEREMONY.   June,
1 day, Japanese Gardens, Botanical Gardens. Contact: Bureau of Publicity, State of Alabama, Montgomery, Alabama 36104.

Authentic tea ceremony and colorful Japanese costumes.

★ 1993 ★
Montgomery - GERMAN FOLK FESTIVAL.   Mid
July, 2 days, Jasmine Hill. Contact: Jim T.
Inscoe, Jasmine Hill, Post Office Box 6001, Mont-
gomery, Alabama 36106.

Authentic German foods and outdoor performance by
German folk dancers and musicians.   A part of the
Smithsonian Institution's "Old Ways in a New World".

ALASKA

★ 1994 ★
Fairbanks - MIDNIGHT SUN HIGHLAND GAMES.
June, annual, 2 days. Contact: Alaska Travel
Division, Pouch E, Juneau, Alaska 99801.

This event includes traditional Scottish competitions
in throwing the caber, tossing the sheaf, and the
shot put, as well as highland and country dancing.
The Alaska State Pipeband championship competition
also takes place, and a Scottish Tattoo.   Begun in
1974.

★ 1995 ★
Fairbanks - OKTOBERFEST.   Late September,
annual, 2 days, Gold Dome at Alaskaland.   Contact: Alaska Division of Tourism, Pouch E, Juneau,
Alaska 99801.

A traditional Old World celebration, includes dancing,
beer-drinking contests, and German food.

★ 1996 ★
Petersburg - LITTLE NORWAY FESTIVAL.   Mid May,
annual, 3 days. Contact: Division of Tourism,
Pouch E, Juneau, Alaska 99801.

Festival celebrating Norwegian Independence Day,
Armed Forces Day, and the first halibut landing.
A festival pageant features a reenactment of Norway's
Declaration of Independence, Norwegian folk dancers
and singers.   A huge smorgasbord, pancake breakfasts, Norwegian coffee shop, fish-o-rama, and
salmon bake offer a wide range of culinary delights.
Dancing, a "mellerdrama", and an art show are part
of the entertainment.

ARIZONA

★ 1997 ★
Nogales - FIESTA DE MAYO.   Early May (1st
week), annual.   Contact: Chamber of Commerce,
Nogales, Arizona 85621.

A joint celebration with the sister city of Nogales
across the Mexican border. Features mariachi bands,
a bullfight in Mexican Nogales, dances, parades,
and special Mexican foods.

★ 1998 ★
Tucson - LA FIESTA DE LA PLACITA.   Early April,
annual, Tucson's Old Square.   Contact: Tucson
Festival Society, Eight West Paseo Redondo, Tucson,
Arizona 85705.

All the lively sights and sounds of a traditional
Mexican fiesta with good refreshment, bright paper
flowers, games, and continuous entertainment.   A
highlight is the presentation of the Fiesta Queen.

★ 1999 ★
Tucson - SAN XAVIER FIESTA.   Early April,
annual, San Xavier del Bac Mission.   Contact:
Chamber of Commerce, 420 West Congress Street,
Tucson, Arizona 85701.

American Indians, Mexicans, and other groups perform a colorful and interesting pageant.   Celebrated
with bonfires and fireworks.

★ 2000 ★
Tucson - TUCSON FESTIVAL.   April, annual,
variety of locations around Tucson area.   Contact:
Tucson Festival Society, Incorporated, 2720 East
Broadway, Tucson, Arizona 85716.

Fiestas, fairs, special events; promoting and preserving the cultural heritage of the southwest and its
regional arts and crafts.   Festival of folklore, history,
music and dance, with Spanish, Mexican, Indian, and
pioneer themes.   Begun around 1951.

CALIFORNIA

★ 2001 ★
Auburn - OCTOBERFEST.   Early October, 1 day.
Contact: California Chamber of Commerce, 455
Capitol Mall, Sacramento, California 95814.

Traditional Octoberfest activities including beer
drinking contests, German food and music.

★ 2002 ★
Bakersfield - MEXICAN FIESTA.   Early May, annual,
1 day, Kern County Fairgrounds.   Contact: Comision
Honarific Mexican, 910 20th Street, Bakersfield,
California 93301.

A festival celebrating the area's Mexican heritage.
Features mariachi bands, special food booths, and
dances.   A queen is chosen to reign over the fair.

★ 2003 ★
Big Bear Lake - OKTOBERFEST.   Early October,
3 days, Gold Mine Ski Area.   Contact: California
Chamber of Commerce, 455 Capitol Mall, Sacramento,
California 95814.

Tyrolian dancers, bands, contests (including pretzel
eating and beer drinking), German and Bavarian food,
dancing and music.

★ 2004 ★
Borrego Springs - DESERT FESTIVAL.   Mid October,
annual, 3 days.   Contact: Chamber of Commerce,
Post Office Box 66, Borrego Springs, California
92004; or Borrego Springs Desert Festival, Post Office
Box 127, Borrego Springs, California 92004.

Commemorates the state's Mexican and Spanish heritage.   The celebration of the "Days of the Dons"
includes a big parade, dance performances, strolling
mariachi players, a crafts and art show, and campfire programs.   Mexican foods, a barbeque, and
pancake breakfast are other features.   Begun around
1966.

★ 2005 ★
Camarillo - CAMARILLO FIESTA.   Late October
(last weekend), annual, 2 days.   Contact: Ed
Genhart, 2175 Wilcox Avenue, Camarillo, California
93010.

Features a parade, a Fiesta Ball and crowning of Miss
Camarillo, continuous outdoor entertainment, and
booths offering a variety of articles for sale.   After
the parade the traditional blessing of the animals takes

place.   Dons and Donas, chosen by the Historical
Society each year, are honored in the festival.
Begun around 1965.

★ 2006 ★
Delano - CINCO DE MAYO CELEBRATION.   Early
May.   Contact: Southern California Visitors Council,
705 West Seventh Street, Los Angeles, California
90017; or Delano District Chamber of Commerce,
931 High Street, Post Office Box 1210, Delano,
California 93215.

A parade, a carnival, and other happy events celebrating the commemoration of May 5th, Mexican
Independence Day.

★ 2007 ★
Desert Hot Springs - CANADIAN DAY.   Early
February, annual, 1 day.   Contact: Southern
California Visitors Council, 705 West Seventh Street,
Los Angeles, California 90017; or Chamber of
Commerce, Desert Hot Springs, California 92240.

A salute to the Canadians, with events including a
golf tournament and a picnic, games, and celebrations.

★ 2008 ★
Kingsburg - KINGSBURG SWEDISH FESTIVAL.   Mid
May, annual, 1 day.   Contact: Tourist Information
Center, 1270 West Belmont, Fresno, California 93728;
or California Chamber of Commerce, 455 Capitol Mall,
Sacramento, California 95814.

A parade and a pancake breakfast are featured in
this celebration honoring the Swedish population.

★ 2009 ★
Lakewood - PAN AMERICAN FESTIVAL.   April,
annual, 8 days.   Contact: Southern California
Visitors Council, 705 West Seventh Street, Los
Angeles, California 90017.

Parade, carnival, flag exchange ceremonies, luncheons, dinners, dances, a fiesta, art and cultural
exhibits, Latin American entertainment, Latin foods,
and sports contests are featured.

★ 2010 ★
Lompoc - LA PURISIMA MISSION FESTIVAL
(MISSION FIESTA DAY).   Mid May (3rd Sunday),
annual, 1 day.   Contact: Lompoc Valley Chamber
of Commerce, 199 East Cypress Avenue, Lompoc,
California 93436.

Ethnic Events

CALICA (Continued)
CALIFORNIA (Continued)

Commemorates California's most completely restored mission. A bean and tortilla lunch is served. Live historical demonstrations include candle making, adobe brick making, and Indian weaving.

★ 2011 ★
Long Beach - INTERNATIONAL FESTIVAL. Mid May, 1 day, Recreation Park. Contact: Southern California Visitors Council, 705 West Seventh Street, Los Angeles, California 90017; or Long Beach Chamber of Commerce, 121 Linden Avenue, Long Beach, California 90802.

A multi-ethnic celebration featuring a "Parade of Nations", and the art, dances, music and food of many nations.

★ 2012 ★
Los Angeles - FESTIVAL DE CINCO DE MAYO. May (around the 5th), 1 day, Music Center and Olvera Street. Contact: Southern California Visitors Council, 705 West Seventh Street, Los Angeles, California 90017.

All day celebration with mariachis, singers, dancers, arts and crafts show, and booths - in honor of Mexican Independence Day.

★ 2013 ★
Los Angeles - HUNGARIAN PRESS DAY FESTIVAL. Late September, annual, 1 day, Croatian American Center. Contact: Southern California Visitors Council, 705 West Seventh Street, Los Angeles, California 90017.

Special events include Hungarian Dance Festival, gypsy music, and open-fire goulash.

★ 2014 ★
Los Angeles - INTERNATIONAL HERITAGE FAIR. Late May, 2 days, Los Angeles Mall. Contact: Southern California Visitors Council, 705 West Seventh Street, Los Angeles, California 90017; or Los Angeles Area Chamber of Commerce, 404 South Bixel Street, Los Angeles, California 90051.

The events celebrate the heritage and contributions of the diverse ethnic groups that have made up the history and population of Los Angeles.

★ 2015 ★
Los Angeles - MEXICAN FIESTA DAYS. Early

September, Los Angeles Zoo. Contact: Southern California Visitors Council, 705 West Seventh Avenue, Los Angeles, California 90017.

Free admission for anyone wearing Latin costumes. Special events include Mexican dancing groups, mariachi music, and Mexican food.

★ 2016 ★
Los Angeles - NISEI WEEK. August (3rd week), annual, 9 days, Little Tokyo. Contact: Southern California Visitors Council, 705 West Seventh Street, Los Angeles, California 90017.

Cultural exhibits, demonstrations of karate and judo, sword tournaments, flower arrangements, Cha-No-Yu tea ceremony, and Ondo parade of kimono clad dancing girls and serpentine dancers with a portable shrine (Mikoshi) on their shoulders. Art and photo show at the Koyasan Buddhist Temple. Begun around 1941.

★ 2017 ★
Los Angeles - OKTOBERFEST. Late September-early October, 15 days, Busch Gardens. Contact: Southern California Visitors Council, 705 West Seventh Street, Los Angeles, California 90017.

Features German bands, dancers, entertainment, and foods of Bavaria. The park is decorated like Oktoberfest in Munich.

★ 2018 ★
Martinez - MEXICAN INDEPENDENCE PARADE AND FIESTA. Mid September, 1 day. Contact: California Chamber of Commerce, 455 Capitol Mall, Sacramento, California 95814.

Parade, arts and crafts, music, and food in celebration of Mexican Independence Day.

★ 2019 ★
Marysville - BOK KAI FESTIVAL (BOMB DAY FESTIVAL). Late February or early March, 2 days. Contact: Greater Yuba City-Marysville Chamber of Commerce, 429 Tenth Street, Post Office Box 1429, Marysville, California 95901.

The unique feature of this festival is the firing of "lucky bombs". Other activities include the traditional lion dance, a parade, street entertainment, and Chinese opera.

CALIFORNIA (Continued)

★ 2020 ★
Oceanside - SAN LUIS REY FIESTA AND BARBECUE.
Late July, annual, 2 days, Mission San Luis Rey.
Contact: San Diego Convention and Visitors Bureau,
1200 Third Avenue, Suite 824, San Diego, California
92101; or Brother Howard Casey, Old Missions, 133
Golden Gate, San Francisco, California 94102.

Festivities begin when gaily decorated pets and other
animals are brought to the mission steps for an Old
World "Blessing of the Animals". Activity moves to
a midway of food and arts and crafts booths. Mexican and Spanish dancers, musicians, and actors provide
continuous entertainment. Visitors participate in
games, rides, and street dancing. Second day, an
outdoor mass is performed by a 100-voice choir. A
deep-pit Mexican style barbeque is served. Los
Caballeros del Camino Real, 100 trek riders in authentic costume, arrive after an overnight campout for a
traditional ceremony. Started in 1951.

★ 2021 ★
Ojai - MEXICAN FIESTA. Mid September, annual,
1 day. Contact: California Chamber of Commerce,
455 Capitol Mall, Sacramento, California 95814.

A traditional Mexican celebration in honor of Mexican
Independence Day. Begun around 1967.

★ 2022 ★
Palmdale - HACIENDA FIESTA. Early October,
annual, 3 days, McAdam Park. Contact: Southern
California Visitors Council, 705 West Seventh Street,
Los Angeles, California 90017.

Salute to sister city of Poncitlan, Jalisco, Mexico.
Events include a parade and mariachi bands.

★ 2023 ★
Rancho Bernardo - OCTOBERFEST. Mid October,
2 days, The Mercado. Contact: Southern California
Visitors Council, 705 West Seventh Street, Los
Angeles, California 90017.

Entertainment includes the music of German bands
and dancing.

★ 2024 ★
San Diego - AKITA KANTO FESTIVAL. Early October, 1 day. Contact: Southern California Visitors
Council, 705 West Seventh Street, Los Angeles, California 90017.

Japanese lantern festival.

★ 2025 ★
San Diego - CABRILLO FESTIVAL. Late September-
October, annual, 1 week, Cabrillo National Monu-
ment. Contact: Cabrillo Festival, Incorporated,
Post Office Box 6366, San Diego, California 92106.

A reenactment of the discovery of the United States'
West Coast by the Portuguese explorer, Juan Rodriguez
Cabrillo in 1542 highlights the festival. Authentic
costumes, Portuguese folk dancing and singing, banquets and dances commemorate the Portuguese heritage,
as well as historical seminars, children's art shows,
and solemn ceremonies. Started in 1965.

★ 2026 ★
San Diego - FESTIVAL OF THE BELLS. Late July,
annual, Mission San Diego de Alcala. Contact:
San Diego Convention and Visitors Bureau, 1200
Third Avenue, Suite 824, San Diego, California
92101; or Mission San Diego de Alcala, 10818
San Diego Mission Road, San Diego, California
92108.

Commemorates the founding of the mission. Starts
with the blessing of the bells and ringing of the
Angelus. Features games, shows, mariachi bands,
Spanish and Indian dancers, Mexican food, booths,
and children's rides. Sunday mass is celebrated,
the blessing of the animals takes place, and a grand
prize is awarded. Started in 1963.

★ 2027 ★
San Diego - FIESTA DE LA PRIMAVERA. Mid May,
4 days, Old Town State Park. Contact: Southern
California Visitors Council, 705 West Seventh Street,
Los Angeles, California 90017; or Chamber of Commerce, 233 A Street, Suite 300, San Diego, California 92101.

In a re-creation of the Spanish era in California's
history, the fiesta features an art show, historical
exhibits, mariachis and a buffalo barbeque.

★ 2028 ★
San Diego - SCOTTISH HIGHLAND GAMES. Septem-
ber or October, annual, 1 day, Balboa Stadium.
Contact: Alex Sandie, Highland Games Chieftain,
Post Office Box 20754, San Diego, California 92120.

Bagpipe bands, dancers, and athletes from the United
States, Canada, and Scotland compete in individual
and group events. Massed bagpipe bands, highland
dancing, and traditional Scottish athletics enliven the

Ethnic Events

CALIFORNIA (Continued)

festivities. Spectators watch the ancient tossing of the caber, hammer throw, stone put, tug-of-war, sheaf toss, soccer and rugby matches, and track events. Scottish foods and handicrafts are offered. Begun around 1974.

★ 2029 ★
San Francisco - AKI MATSURI (FALL FESTIVAL). Late September, annual, 3 days, Japan Center. Contact: Greater San Francisco Chamber of Commerce, 465 California Street, San Francisco, California 94104.

Japanese harvest festival with cultural events such as tea ceremonies, traditional songs, music and dancing, bonsai demonstrations, judo and karate demonstrations, Japanese cooking, flower shows, movies, and art exhibits.

★ 2030 ★
San Francisco - BRITISH WEEK FESTIVAL. Early October, 9 days. Contact: Redwood Empire Association, Visitors Information Bureau, 476 Post Street, San Francisco, California 94102.

Highlights British imports, art, history, and music. A "Pub" is set up in Union Square.

★ 2031 ★
San Francisco - CHERRY BLOSSOM FESTIVAL (NIHONMACHI CHERRY BLOSSOM FESTIVAL). April, 2 weekends, Japan Town, Japan Center. Contact: Information Officer, State of California, Department of Commerce, 1400 Tenth Street, Sacramento, California 95814.

Classical theater, Bonsai displays, Japanese entertainment, tea ceremonies, parade, haiku contest, and sports events including Japanese professional baseball teams. Minyo (mass folk song and dance fest), suwa taiko (beating of barrel-shaped drums), demonstrations of kendo, judo, aikido and karate. Special children's programs, ikebana (flower arranging), chanoyu (tea ceremony), calligraphy, poetry chanting, Japanese doll making, caricature drawing, paintings and films, and show of Akita dogs. Queen's competition and coronation.

★ 2032 ★
San Francisco - CHINESE NEW YEAR CELEBRATION. February (lunar new year), annual, 9 days, Chinatown. Contact: Chinese Chamber of Commerce, 730 Sacramento Street, San Francisco, California 94108; or San Francisco Convention and Visitors

Bureau, Fox Plaza, San Francisco, California 94102.

Activities include parades; lion dancers; fireworks; Miss Chinatown coronation; displays of martial arts such as judo, jujitsu and kung fu; Chinese dramas and operas; cultural exhibits; coronation ball; tours of Chinatown; a carnival; fashion show; folk dancing and ceremonial dancing; and music. The festivities climax in a parade with dragons, lions, Oriental deities, floats with mythical animals, the festival queen and her court, and troupes of costumed musicians and lantern bearers.

★ 2033 ★
San Francisco - IRISH FESTIVAL. Late September-mid October, Irish Center. Contact: John Whooley, c/o Irish Center, Incorporated, 2123 Market Street, San Francisco, California 94114.

Exposition of heritage, culture, traditions, and food of the Irish. Dramatic events, folk dancing, music, art shows, concerts, contests, and coronation of Miss Ireland.

★ 2034 ★
San Francisco - LATIN-AMERICAN FIESTA. Early May, annual, 1 weekend, Mission District. Contact: San Francisco Convention and Visitors Bureau, Fox Plaza, San Francisco, California 94102.

A spectacular parade with floats, drill corps, mounted units, bands, and novelty entries highlights the ethnic celebration. A coronation ball features Latin-American musicians and dancers. Sponsored by the Spanish-Speaking Citizens Foundation. Started in 1966.

★ 2035 ★
San Francisco - SAINT PATRICK'S FROLIC. Mid March (17th), annual, 1 day. Contact: San Francisco Convention and Visitors Bureau, Fox Plaza, San Francisco, California 94102.

The events include a parade with floats, dignitaries, dancers, musicians, drill corps, and equestrians. There is a Saint Patrick's Dance with special Irish entertainment and a Green and Gold Ball at which "Miss Shamrock" is crowned. There is a snake race in Zellerbach Plaza, entertainment by Irish bands, dancers and pipers. Ireland's top football and hurling teams compete at Balboa Stadium.

★ 2036 ★
San Juan Bautista - FESTIVAL OF OUR LADY OF GUADALUPE. Mid December (14th), annual, Mission Grounds. Contact: Chamber of Commerce,

CALIFORNIA (Continued)

San Juan Bautista, California 95045.

Honors the patron saint of the Mexican people with candlelight services, a parade, Mexican music, games, and food.

★ 2037 ★
San Ysidro - FIESTA PATREIAS. Mid September, 3 days, Old Town. Contact: Southern California Visitors Bureau, 705 West Seventh Street, Los Angeles, California 90017.

Celebration of Mexican Independence Day. Events include a parade and a carnival. The Mexican consul ends the celebration with the shout "El Grito" that led Mexico in rebellion against Spain.

★ 2038 ★
Santa Barbara - OLD SPANISH DAYS FIESTA. Mid August (during the full moon), annual, 5 days. Contact: Chamber of Commerce, Santa Barbara, California 92702.

Celebrates the city's Spanish heritage with a fiesta and pageantry depicting the history of Santa Barbara. Festivities include arts and crafts show, Mexican marketplace, rodeo, promenade, parade, and music. Begun around 1924.

★ 2039 ★
Sante Fe Springs - MEXICAN FIESTA. Early August, 1 day, Town Center Hall. Contact: Southern California Visitors Council, 705 West Seventh Street, Los Angeles, California 90017.

Entertainment includes a live mariachi band, Spanish dancers, Mexican food and breaking of the pinata.

★ 2040 ★
Santa Monica - SCOTTISH GATHERING AND GAMES. Late June, annual, 1 day, Consair Field, Santa Monica City College. Contact: Chamber of Commerce, Santa Monica, California 95006; or Southern California Visitors Council, 705 West Seventh Street, Los Angeles, California 90017.

Bagpipe bands and highland dancers perform at this annual gathering of Scottish groups. Caber toss and many other Scottish sports competitions enliven this event. Scottish souvenir and gift booths offer items for sale.

★ 2041 ★
Santa Rosa - OKTOBERFEST. October, annual, Sonoma County Fairgrounds. Contact: Santa Rosa Jaycees, Post Office Box 1025, Santa Rosa, California 95402.

Traditional German entertainment, food, and beer.

★ 2042 ★
Solvang - DANISH DAYS. Late September, 2-3 days, Copenhagen Square. Contact: Chamber of Commerce, 515 Fourth Place, Post Office Box 465, Solvang, California 93463.

This celebration ties into Danish Independence Day. Danish singers, dancers and musicians. Danish food such as meatballs or an aebleskive breakfast are served. Parade (sometime torchlight), Danish costumes, and Hans Christian Anderson story hour.

★ 2043 ★
Squaw Valley - SIERRA SCHWINGFEST. Late August, annual, 2 days, Olympic Village. Contact: Placid Fuchslin, Post Office Box 4097, South Lake Tahoe, California 95705.

A festival featuring Swiss wrestling competitions, which are entirely different from American wrestling. Dancing and yodeling, accordion selections, and alphorn blowing enliven the festival. Swiss foods are served. Visitors can participate in various sports, such as horseback riding, tennis, swimming, ice skating, etc. Sponsored by the Sierra Swiss Club.

★ 2044 ★
Stockton - GREEK FOOD FESTIVAL. Mid October, annual, 2 days. Contact: California Chamber of Commerce, 455 Capitol Mall, Sacramento, California 95814.

Dance, songs, displays, and of course, all varieties of Greek foods.

★ 2045 ★
Stockton - MEXICAN INDEPENDENCE DAY CELEBRATION. Mid September, annual, 2 days, Civic Auditorium. Contact: Greater Stockton Chamber of Commerce, 1105 North El Dorado, Stockton, California 95202.

Opens with the coronation of a queen of festivities, performances by a mariachi band, the Folklorico dancers and singers, and the introduction of a drum and bugle corps sponsored by Comision Honorifica Mexicana. A Queen's Ball takes place the next

Ethnic Events

CALIFORNIA (Continued)

night at the auditorium. The celebration ends with the salute of Mexican and American flags and a dance at the Comision Honorifica Mexicana.

★ 2046 ★
Torrance - GERMAN DAY. Early September, 1 day, Alpine Village. Contact: Southern California Visitors Council, 705 West Seventh Street, Los Angeles, California 90017.

Entertainment features a German brass band, Bavarian dance band, singing and dancing.

★ 2047 ★
Torrance - GERMAN FESTIVAL. May, each Sunday, Alpine Village. Contact: Southern California Visitors Council, 705 West Seventh Street, Los Angeles, California 90017; or Torrance Area Chamber of Commerce, 1510 Cravens Avenue, Torrance, California 90501.

The celebrations feature German culinary specialties, drinks, German dancing and bands.

★ 2048 ★
Torrance - GREEK FESTIVAL. October (first weekend), annual, Torrance Recreation Center. Contact: Saint Katharine's Greek Orthodox Church, 722 Knob Hill Avenue, Redondo Beach, California 90277.

The Hellenic heritage is recreated by dance groups, continuous live music and entertainment, and authentic preparation of Greece's exotic pastries and cuisine. Greek exhibits and demonstrations are set up. There are also children's booths.

★ 2049 ★
Torrance - OKTOBERFEST. Late September-late October, 29 days, Alpine Village. Contact: Southern California Visitors Council, 705 West Seventh Street, Los Angeles, California 90017.

Events include beer drinking, yodeling, wood chopping, pretzel eating, beer stein carrying contests, and entertainment by a twelve man brass band from Bavaria.

★ 2050 ★
Torrance - TYROLEAN FESTIVAL. Mid July-late August, 1 1/2 months, Alpine Village. Contact: Torrance Area Chamber of Commerce, 1510 Cravens Avenue, Torrance, California 90501.

A German and Austrian ethnic festival with German food and entertainment and Austrian singing, dancing and music.

★ 2051 ★
Torrance - WURST FESTIVAL. June, Alpine Village. Contact: Southern California Visitors Council, 705 West Seventh Street, Los Angeles, California 90017.

Sausage from the continent on sale. Entertainment includes brass band from Germany.

★ 2052 ★
Valencia - MEXICAN INDEPENDENCE DAY CELEBRATION. Early September, 2 days, Magic Mountain. Contact: Southern California Visitors Council, 705 West Seventh Street, Los Angeles, California 90017.

Celebration throughout the park featuring top Mexican entertainment in honor of Mexican Independence Day.

COLORADO

★ 2053 ★
Central City - ETHNIC FESTIVAL. Early August, 1 day. Contact: Jack Hidahl, Public Relations Coordinator, Central City, Colorado 80427.

The music, dancing and cuisine of all Colorado ethnic groups throughout the day in the streets and various establishments. Show of historic Colorado fashions in the Opera House.

★ 2054 ★
Central City - PAT CASEY DAY. Early October, 1 day. Contact: Jack Hidahl, Public Relations Coordinator, Central City, Colorado 80427.

Honors the Irish of the old mining camp. Public procession headed by bagpipes marches along Casey's route. An Irish stew dinner is held at the Belvidere, with an exhibition of Irish folk dances.

★ 2055 ★
Central City - TOMMY KNAWKER DAY. Mid September, 1 day. Contact: Jack Hidahl, Public Relations Coordinator, Central City, Colorado 80427.

Salute to the Welsh and Cornish contributions to the mining camp. 100 year old traditions: rock drilling contest, hose cart race, pastie dinner, Welsh choir, etc.

COLORADO (Continued)

★ 2056 ★
Colorado Springs - BLACK ARTS FESTIVAL. Early
April, 1 day. Contact: Chamber of Commerce,
Post Office Drawer B, Colorado Springs, Colorado
80901.

Festival sponsored by U.S. Air Force honoring the
artistic endeavors of Black Americans.

★ 2057 ★
Georgetown - FASCHING. Mid February, 9 days.
Contact: The Chamber of Commerce, Post Office
Box 655, Georgetown, Colorado 80444.

A German celebration with specially prepared delicacies, singing, dancing, and Gemeutlichkeit (good
fellowship).

CONNECTICUT

★ 2058 ★
Bridgeport - HARAMBEE FIESTA. Early April, 1
day. Contact: Bridgeport Chamber of Commerce,
Chapel Street, Bridgeport, Connecticut 06603.

Black and Puerto Rican cultures are expressed in
this one day festival.

★ 2059 ★
Storrs - INTERNATIONAL FAIR. Early April,
annual, 1 day, University of Connecticut, ROTC
Hangar. Contact: Mr. Don McCullough, Student
Activities Office, The University of Connecticut,
Storrs, Connecticut 06268.

Information booths, sale of native foods and crafts,
music, dancing and vocal groups illustrate the culture
of the various national and ethnic groups in the
student body and surrounding community. Begun
around 1967.

DELAWARE

★ 2060 ★
New Castle - A DAY IN OLD NEW CASTLE. Mid
May (3rd Saturday), annual, 1 day. Contact: New
Castle Chamber of Commerce, New Castle, Delaware
19720; or Division of Economic Development, Dela-
ware State Visitors Service, 45 the Green, Dover,
Delaware 19901.

Celebrates the culture of the Dutch, Swedes, Finns,
and English. Community draws on its wealth of

well-tended colonial homes, antiques, heirloom silver,
and boxwood gardens. Often period dances are performed on the village green. Public buildings and
homes are open. Oldest town in Delaware.

★ 2061 ★
Wilmington - SWEDISH COLONIAL DAY. March
(9th), annual. Contact: Chamber of Commerce,
Wilmington, Delaware 19899.

Celebrates the Swedish heritage of the region with a
ceremony commemorating the landing of the Swedes
in Delaware.

DISTRICT OF COLUMBIA

★ 2062 ★
Washington, D.C. - FOLK FESTIVAL. September,
annual, 1 weekend, Saints Constantine and Helen
Greek Orthodox Church. Contact: Saints Constan-
tine and Helen Greek Orthodox Church, 4115 16th
Street Northwest, Washington, D.C. 20011.

Events include clowns, pony rides, Greek dance
group performances with audience participation, native
food, arts and crafts booths, and white elephant sale.

★ 2063 ★
Washington, D.C. - SPANISH HERITAGE WEEK.
Late July, annual, 1 week. Contact: Spanish
Heritage Week, 1470 Irving Street, Northwest,
Washington, D.C. 20010.

Celebrating the people of Spanish heritage in the
D.C. area. There is a Sports Day with a soccer
game; a Senior Citizens Day featuring a breakfast
and arts and crafts exhibition; Education Day with
workshops and discussions pertinent to issues of importance to local Latins; Childrens Day with a picnic,
field trip, games, etc.; Cultural Day including films
and workshops on historical and contemporary issues;
Womens Day; Youth Day; Parade Day; and other
events such as dances, theater (in Spanish and in
English), piano recitals, etc. Begun around 1972.

FLORIDA

★ 2064 ★
Bradenton - DE SOTO CELEBRATION. Mid March,
annual, 1 week, de Soto National Memorial Park.
Contact: Chamber of Commerce, Bradenton, Florida
33870; or De Soto Celebration, Mrs. C. Dowell,
Executive Secretary, 809 14th Street, West, Bradenton,
Florida 33505.

Ethnic Events

FLORIDA (Continued)

Conquistadores in authentic sixteenth century battle dress come ashore at de Soto National Memorial Park to reenact de Soto's conquest of the country in the name of Spain in 1539. Festivities include street dances, concerts, sports tournaments, and selection of a queen. Ends with a spectacular parade and fireworks show.

★ 2065 ★
Cape Coral - OKTOBERFEST.   October (1st and 3rd Saturdays), annual, 2 days.   Contact: Jack FitzMaurice, German-American Social Club, Post Office Box 902, Cape Coral, Florida 33904.

Event features traditional costumes of the old and new worlds, food, dancing, German-American music, and beer. Sponsored by the German American Social Club, it is a counterpart to the Munich Beer Festival and strives to promote a feeling of Gemuetlichkeit, or good fellowship.

★ 2066 ★
Daytona Beach Shores - CANADIAN WEEKEND.
Late January (last weekend).   Contact: Reverend Wallace Pomplun, Drive-in Christian Church, 3812 Emilia Drive, Daytona Beach, Florida 32019.

The theme of the festival is "Hands of Friendship across the Border". The celebration honors Canadian visitors to the area. Special guests fly in by jet. Various activities, including a joint worship service via special telephone hookup between the Carmen United Church in Toronto and the Drive-in Christian Church in Daytona Beach Shores.

★ 2067 ★
Dunedin - HIGHLAND GAMES AND FESTIVAL.
Late March, annual, 3 days.   Contact: Robert Longstreet, 1137 Bass Boulevard, Dunedin, Florida 33528.

In a salute to its Scottish heritage, Dunedin stages a celebration with music, dances, and games of skill reminiscent of Scotland. Events include the Ceilidh (piping, dancing, and singing highland tunes); individual competition in drumming, dancing, and piping; and sports events such as tossing the caber, tossing the sheaf, hammer throwing, and Scottish wrestling. The grand finale is a parade of massed bands and presentation of awards.

★ 2068 ★
Jensen Beach - LIEF ERIKSEN DAY PAGEANT.

Early October (Sunday closest to October 9), annual, 1 day.   Contact: Richard Campbell, Post Office Box 787, Jensen Beach, Florida 33457.

Features a reenactment of Lief Eriksen and his band of Vikings landing on the shores of this community. The festivities include Viking boat races in 100-year-old seperings from Norway; performances by the famed Leikar Dancers; Norwegian folk dances and public dancing to Norwegian music. Pageantry and colorful costumes abound at the full day of festivities.

★ 2069 ★
Lake Buena Vista - FIESTA SALUDOS AMIGOS.
Late May, annual, 2 weeks, Walt Disney World. Contact: Walt Disney World, Post Office Box 40, Lake Buena Vista, Florida 32830.

The "Magic Kingdom" offers a salute to Mexico, Puerto Rico, and other Spanish-speaking countries of Central and South America. Special parades, theme decorations, and concerts greet friends from south of the border. Special entertainment groups perform.

★ 2070 ★
Lake Buena Vista - WALT DISNEY WORLD CANADIAN FESTIVAL.   January, 7 days, Walt Disney World.   Contact: Publicity Office, Post Office Box 40, Lake Buena Vista, Florida 32830.

Honors Canada with special concerts, ceremonies, parades, decorations and guest Canadian entertainers.

★ 2071 ★
Masaryktown - CZECHOSLOVAKIAN INDEPENDENCE DAY CELEBRATION.   October (Sunday nearest 28), annual, 1 day.   Contact: Vera Buchton, Route 1, Box 242, Masaryktown, Florida 33512.

This town was settled in the mid-1920's by Czechs, and each year they celebrate their heritage and old world traditions. Included in the festivities are a dinner, dancing, and performances by the Beseda Dancers, who wear traditional Czech costumes and do national dances.

★ 2072 ★
Miami - AROUND THE WORLD FAIR.   Mid March, 2 days.   Contact: Tish Fryer, Patrons, Museum of Science, 3280 South Miami Avenue, Miami, Florida 33129.

All-encompassing international fair stresses foods of other nations, Left Bank artists, international

FLORIDA (Continued)

entertainment groups, bargain and boutique booths. Trips and exotic items are raffled off at the climax.

★ 2073 ★
Miami - GRAN ROMERIA HISPANO-AMERICANA. Mid March, 1 day, Police Benevolent Association Park. Contact: Greater Miami Chamber of Commerce, 1200 Biscayne Boulevard, Miami, Florida 33132.

Spanish-American open air festival.

★ 2074 ★
Miami, Miami Beach - INTER-AMERICAN FESTIVAL. October, annual, 1 month. Contact: Dr. Avelina Soriano, 130 Northeast Second Street, Miami, Florida 33132.

A county-wide festival held as a special salute to Latin American countries. Scheduled activities include street festivals and folklore extravaganzas, art shows, sports events, university seminars, and a children's carousel.

★ 2075 ★
Miami, Miami Beach - LATIN AMERICAN FESTIVAL. July, annual, streets surrounding the Miami Beach Convention Center. Contact: Hal Cohen, Miami Beach Tourist Development Authority, 555 17th Street, Miami Beach, Florida 33139.

A colorful Old World festival patterned after the famous fiesta celebration in Rio de Janeiro. The streets are jammed with merrymakers reveling in music, dancing, and gay costumes.

★ 2076 ★
Saint Augustine - DAYS IN SPAIN FIESTA. Mid August, annual, 4 days, Saint George Street. Contact: Thomas King, Saint Augustine Chamber of Commerce, Ten Costillo Drive, Saint Augustine, Florida 32084.

A colorful fiesta commemorates the city's founding in 1565. The street is festooned with gay banners and baskets of flowers. Booths where Spanish handicrafts and foods are sold line the street, and residents are dressed in Spanish attire. Periodic bouts of sword fighting break out from balconies and along the street as Jaycees, costumed as conquistadores, engage in duels. An amusement area features rides for children.

★ 2077 ★
Tampa - LATIN AMERICA FIESTA. Early March, annual, 1 week. Contact: Greater Tampa Chamber of Commerce, Post Office Box 420, Tampa, Florida 33601.

Presents Old World color, music, dancing, and gay costumes. At Election Ball a Fiesta Queen and her court are chosen. Fiesta Week ends with a gala Coronation Ball celebrated in the Latin American mood. Started in the 1920's.

★ 2078 ★
Tampa (Ybor City) - YBOR CITY PIRATE FIESTA DAYS. Early February, annual. Contact: Chamber of Commerce, Post Office Box 5287, Tampa, Florida 33605.

The Latin Quarter of Tampa has its own fiesta related to the Gasparilla Pirate Invasion celebration. Costumed pirates, armed with loaves of Cuban bread and accompanied by senoritas, attack a Federal ship in the harbor. At the Spanish Bean Soup Festival free soup, Cuban coffee, and bread are served. Ends with a gala Torchlight Parade.

★ 2079 ★
Tarpon Springs - GREEK CROSS DAY. Early January, annual, 1-2 days. Contact: Father Elias Kalariotes, Post Office Box 248, Tarpon Springs, Florida 33589.

On January 5th, the sponge fleet is blessed, and there is a Greek dinner dance. On the 6th, Epiphany, there are observances commemorating the baptism of Christ. Among these is the ceremony of "diving for the cross", in which divers attempt to retrieve a cross blessed and cast into the water by the priest. It is believed to confer good fortune upon the finder. A Greek festival follows.

★ 2080 ★
Tavares - TAVARES FIESTA. Early March (9th weekend of the year), annual, 3 days. Contact: Mrs. Wilma Taylor, Tavares Chamber of Commerce, Post Office Box 697, Tavares, Florida 32778.

Activities in a Spanish setting - all ages, annual dinner and treasure hunt.

GEORGIA

★ 2081 ★
Atlanta - ATLANTA GREEK FESTIVAL. Early October, Greek Orthodox Cathedral. Contact:

Ethnic Events

GEORGIA (Continued)

Georgia Department of Community Development, Post Office Box 38097, Atlanta, Georgia 30334.

Celebrates Grecian culture with authentic Greek cooking, music, dancers, handicrafts and artwork, records and tapes, posters, jewelry, and clothing. There is a Grecian wine cellar and continuous films on Greece.

★ 2082 ★
Atlanta - BLACK CULTURAL FESTIVAL (Atlanta Black Artists Association).   July-October, once a month, 2 days each month, Gun Club Park, Branham, Grant Park, Washington Park.   Contact: Chamber of Commerce, 1101 Commerce Building, Atlanta, Georgia 30303.

"To share the special strength and vitality of Black culture", events include city showmobile, Atlanta Dance Theatre, the Life Force, the New Cosmos Cultural Theatre, the Al Murphy Quintet, the People's Art Ensemble, the Soundsations, the Atlanta Federation of Musician's Jazz Big Band, art exhibit, crafts, and refreshments.

★ 2083 ★
Atlanta - SCOTTISH FESTIVAL AND HIGHLAND GAMES.   Mid October, annual, Stone Mountain Park.   Contact: Stone Mountain Park, 1090 Lanier Boulevard, Atlanta, Georgia 30306.

Events include competitions in piping, highland dancing, drumming, drum majors, and the Eastern U.S. Pipe Band championships.   The highland games display skill in caber toss, sheaf toss, stone toss, and tug o' war.   A parade and massed bands, Scottish costumes, booths with Scottish woolens and other goods, including Scottish foods, add to the festivities.

★ 2084 ★
Dublin - SAINT PATRICK'S FESTIVAL.   March (17th), annual.   Contact: Chamber of Commerce, 400 Bellevue Avenue, Dublin, Georgia 31021.

The Irish flavor festivities include a parade, barbeques, a boat show, leprechaun contest, bowling and billiards tournaments, children's games, a beauty pageant, and golf tournaments, including the Shamrock International. Begun in 1966.

★ 2085 ★
Helen - BAVARIAN OKTOBERFEST.   September-October, 5 (2-day) celebrations, recreated Bavarian Village.   Contact: Oktoberfest, Helen Chamber of Commerce, Helen, Georgia 30545.

Starts the first weekend in September and is held each weekend through the first weekend in October. Music, dancing, food and drinks.   Yodeling contests and summer stock theater.

★ 2086 ★
Stone Mountain - SCOTTISH FESTIVAL AND HIGHLAND GAMES.   Late October, annual, 1 day, Stone Mountain Park.   Contact: Stone Mountain Park, 1090 Lanier Boulevard, Atlanta, Georgia 30306.

Events include competition in piping, highland dancing, drumming, pipe band, highland games, caber toss, sheaf toss, stone toss, and tug o' war.   Parades and bands provide additional entertainment.

HAWAII

★ 2087 ★
Hilo - INTERNATIONAL FESTIVAL OF THE PACIFIC. Mid-late July, 7 days.   Contact: Hawaii Visitors Bureau, Special Events Department, Honolulu, Hawaii 96815.

A view of Polynesian culture and lifestyles, opens with a lantern-lit parade, ethnic dancing and music at a lavish international pageant.

★ 2088 ★
Honolulu - CHERRY BLOSSOM FESTIVAL.   February, March, and April, annual.   Contact: Hawaii Visitors Bureau, Special Events Department, Honolulu, Hawaii 96815.

Artificial cherry blossoms are fashioned because cherry trees do not prosper in Hawaii's climate.   Floats in a parade are decorated with lanterns and flowers and peopled with costumed Japanese fairy tale characters. A Shinto Shrine is carried by men in kimonos, children carry lanterns, Bon dances, traditional Buddist folk rites to honor ancestoral spirits, operettas, Lion Dance, fashion show, queen contest, popular entertainment, coronation ball, cultural show at which elaborate formal and informal kimona and kokeshi dolls are displayed, demonstrations of Japanese cooking, tea ceremonies, bonsai, bonseki, and flower arrangements. Begun around 1953.

★ 2089 ★
Honolulu - FIESTA FILIPINA.   May-June, 1 month. Contact: United Filipino Council, 1834 Nweana

HAWAII (Continued)

Avenue, Honolulu, Hawaii 96817; or Jose Sanidad, Aveco Travel, 1160 Nuuanu Avenue, Honolulu, Hawaii 96817.

Music, food, dancing, and pageantries of the Philippines. Queen pageant and coronation contests, games, songs, and dramas portraying the Philippino revolt against the Spanish. Terno Ball (terno is a Philippine dress), cooking and food show, Concert of the Stars, fashion show of Philippine fashions, Barrio Fiesta, and Santa Cruzan musical play. Begun around 1959.

★ 2090 ★
Honolulu - KOREAN HERITAGE FESTIVAL. June, annual. Contact: The State Foundation on Culture and the Arts, 250 South King Street, Room 310, Honolulu, Hawaii 96813.

Korean music, dance, art, martial art, architecture, lectures, and demonstrations.

★ 2091 ★
Honolulu - NARCISSUS FESTIVAL. Mid January-mid February (associated with dates of Chinese New Year), annual. Contact: Hawaii Visitors Bureau, Special Events Department, Honolulu, Hawaii 96815.

"A night in Chinatown" with dancing in the streets, firework display, queen contest, and coronation ball. Rampaging lion, dances, dinners, art, fashion, garden shows and traditional tea ceremony, historical pageant, floral display, and demonstration of Chinese cooking. The first three days are traditionally dedicated to family reunions and visits to friends. The third day - prayers are offered to the God of Wealth, then for the next ten days the birthdays of different animals and grains are celebrated. A parade with the beating of gongs and cymbals and a Chinese Village Fair.

★ 2092 ★
Honolulu - SAMPAGUITA FESTIVAL. Mid June. Contact: The State Foundation on Culture and the Arts, 250 South King Street, Room 310, Honolulu, Hawaii 96813.

Music, dance, drama, art, and other Filipino ethno-cultural traditions. Part of the Filipino Fiesta.

★ 2093 ★
Kamuela - WAIMEA HIGHLAND GAMES. October, Hawaii Preparatory Academy. Contact: Pacific Area

Travel Association, 228 Grant Avenue, San Francisco, California 94108.

Blend of Scottish and Hawaiian sports and pageantry, dancing, and exhibits.

★ 2094 ★
Maui - NA MELE O MAUI. Mid September, 4-5 days. Contact: Na Mele O Maui, Post Office Box 778, Wailukee, Hawaii 96793.

A glimpse of Hawaiian lifestyles: plants and flowers, arts and crafts, dances and music, fashion show, and luau.

IDAHO

★ 2095 ★
Coeur d'Alene - SCOTTISH HIGHLAND FESTIVAL AND TATTOO. Late July, annual, 2-3 days, banks of Lake Coeur d'Alene. Contact: Chamber of Commerce, Post Office Box 850, Coeur d'Alene, Idaho 83814.

The banks of the lake provide an ideal atmosphere for the "skirling" of bagpipes. Besides the bagpipe competition, visitors can enjoy the Tattoo where Scottish descendants perform precision drills dressed in their colorful clan plaids. A scottish picnic completes the festivities.

★ 2096 ★
Sun Valley - BASQUE FESTIVAL. Mid July, annual, weekend, Trail Creek Cabin, Sun Valley Village. Contact: James W. Ball, Manager, Ketchum-Sun Valley Chamber of Commerce, Box 465, Ketchum, Idaho 83340; or Jack Brown, Sun Valley, Idaho 83353.

Lamb barbeque, typical Basque dinner. The Oinkari dancers perform in typical costumes. There are Basque games, strength contests such as weight lifting and carrying, and wood-chopping. In general, Basque folklife. There is also a live sheep auction, raffle, and prizes. Sponsored by the Ketchum-Sun Valley Chamber of Commerce and the Hemingway Park.

ILLINOIS

★ 2097 ★
Belleville - DEUTSCHFEST. Late June, 2 days, Moose Park. Contact: The Division of Tourism, Illinois Department of Business and Economic Development, 222 South College Street, Springfield, Illinois 62706.

Ethnic Events

ILLINOIS (Continued)

Octoberfest with German atmosphere, bands, food, dancing, rides, and recreational events.

★ 2098 ★
Bishop Hill - JORDBRUKDAGARNA. Early October, annual, 2 days. Contact: Swedish Festival, Bishop Hill Chamber of Commerce, Bishop Hill, Illinois 61419.

Recreates the Swedish communal life style of the 1840's at Bishop Hill, a commune built by Swedish immigrants in the mid-nineteenth century. Agrarian and cultural demonstrations offer a chance of participation to the visitor.

★ 2099 ★
Brimfield - JUBILEE COLLEGE OLD ENGLISH FAIRE. Late June, 2 days, Jubilee College State Park. Contact: Illinois Department of Conservation, Division of Parks and Memorial, Program Services Section, Springfield, Illinois 62706.

Jubilee College was responsible for bringing some of the British culture into mid-Illinois. A great deal of the original Gothic architecture remains at the school. Strolling troubadours, colorful pageants, traditional English plays are featured events, and hot air ballooning.

★ 2100 ★
DeKalb - BLACK ARTS FESTIVAL. February, annual, 1 month, Northern Illinois University. Contact: Minority Students, Northern Illinois University, 535-1 Lucinda, DeKalb, Illinois 60115.

Speakers, films and concerts are presented in honor of Black History Month. Begun in 1970.

★ 2101 ★
DeKalb - BLACK ARTS FESTIVAL. April, annual, 1 week, Northern Illinois University. Contact: Minority Students, 535-1 Lucinda, Northern Illinois University, DeKalb, Illinois 60115.

Speakers and concerts pay tribute to the Black woman. Begun in 1970.

★ 2102 ★
DeKalb - BLACK ARTS FESTIVAL. June, annual, Northern Illinois University. Contact: Minority Students, 535-1 Lucinda, Northern Illinois University, DeKalb, Illinois 60115.

Titled "Interdisciplinary Perspectives" there are conferences on African, Afro-American, or Caribbean studies. Begun in 1970.

★ 2103 ★
East Moline - GREEK FESTIVAL. Mid August, 1 day, U.A.W. Hall. Contact: The Division of Tourism, Illinois Department of Business and Economic Development, 222 South College Street, Springfield, Illinois 62706.

Ethnic music and dances highlight this one day celebration of Greek heritage.

★ 2104 ★
Geneva - SWEDISH FESTIVAL. Mid June, annual, 1 week. Contact: Chamber of Commerce, Geneva, Illinois 60134.

Celebrated with parades, street dances, Swedish costumes, carnivals, fireworks, and delicious homecooked Swedish foods.

★ 2105 ★
Prairie du Rocher - FORT DE CHARTRES RENDEZVOUS. Early June, annual, 2 days, Fort de Chartres State Park. Contact: Special Events, Illinois Department of Conservation, 605 State Office Building, Springfield, Illinois 62706.

Revives Illinois' early French frontier period. Period music and costumes, greased pole contest, contests in flintlock shooting, tomahawk, a voyageur-frontiersman tug-o-war, birch bark canoe races, musket firing, flintlock pistol firing, and Seneca run. Demonstrations in breadmaking, candlemaking, canon firing, herb display, tanning, woodcarving, blacksmith, carpentry, coppersmith, silversmith, soap-making, canoe display, weaving, and cooking, all using authentic tools of the period. Also ox-cart rides, martial demonstrations, roving minstrel singers, trading session (no money allowed), dancers, and fife and drum corps. The fort is partially reconstructed. Begun around 1970.

INDIANA

★ 2106 ★
Batesville - OKTOBERFEST. Late September, 1 day, Liberty Park. Contact: Dennis M. Harmeyer, Rural Route 3, Batesville, Indiana 47006.

German singing, sauerkraut and sausage, dancing and beer in celebration of the area's German heritage.

INDIANA (Continued)

★ 2107 ★
Clinton - LITTLE ITALY FESTIVAL.   August-September, annual, 4 days, Little Italy Town.   Contact: Publicity Chairman, Little Italy Festival, 849 North Street, Clinton, Indiana 47842.

Grape stomping, strolling musicians, Italian singers, Italian food, gondola rides, costumes, "Mostache" contest, spagetti and pizza eating contests, tour of coal mines, celebrity auction, food and craft booths, parade, street dancing, wine tasting, and state bocce ball championships.

★ 2108 ★
Indianapolis - INDIANA BLACK EXPO.   Early July, annual, 2 days, Exposition-Convention Center. Contact: President, Indiana Black Expo, 1241 North New Jersey Street, Indianapolis, Indiana 46202.

Historical exhibits, commercial booth displays from national and local businesses, Miss Black Expo beauty pageant, amateur golf tournament, black cultural exhibits, continuous free entertainment from local musicians, gospel program, variety shows, and Independence Day celebration.

★ 2109 ★
Lafayette - FIESTA.   Early August, 1 day, Lafayette Art Center.   Contact: Chairman, Fiesta, Lafayette Art Center, 101 South Ninth Street, Lafayette, Indiana 47905.

Somberros, pininatias and paper flowers are on sale to the rhythm of Mexican songs, dances and mariachis. Demonstrations include batiking, weaving, pottery making and other crafts, with Mexican and American food available.

★ 2110 ★
Newburgh - OKTOBERFEST.   Late September, 3 days.   Contact: Newburgh Council of Clubs, Newburgh, Indiana 47630.

The festival features a beer hall with traditional German foods, music and dancing, reminiscent of Bavaria.   There is also a parade with floats.

★ 2111 ★
Saint Henry - HEINRICHSDORF FEST.   Late May, 2 days.   Contact: Dennis L. Durcholtz, Rural Route 1, Box 42-A, Ferdinand, Indiana 47532.

A Germanic festival with beer gardens serving country

sausage and Saint Henry style barbeque ribs and chicken, while oom-pah-pah music plays.

★ 2112 ★
Seymour - OKTOBERFEST.   Early October, 3 days, downtown.   Contact: Larry Krukewitt, 224 South Chestnut, Post Office Box 312, Seymour, Indiana 47274.

Booths offering folk objects and special foods line the downtown streets to celebrate town's German heritage.   Bands, biergartens, crafts, antiques, carnival and parades.

★ 2113 ★
South Bend - ETHNIC FESTIVAL; TIPPECANOE PLACE ANTIQUE SHOW AND TOUR.   Early July, 3 days, Clement Studebaker Mansion, Tippecanoe Place.   Contact: Executive Director, Southhold Restorations, Incorporated, 228 West Colfax, South Bend, Indiana 46601.

Tours of the mansion, antique dealers, ethnic festival in River Bend Plaza.

★ 2114 ★
Tell City - SCHWEIZER FEST.   Early August, annual, 4 days, City Park.   Contact: Theodore H. Hickerson, 1117 Blum Street, Tell City, Michigan 47586.

A musik halle, biergarten, and general spirit of gemuetlichkeit highlight the Swiss festival.   Bank concerts, arts and crafts, amusement rides, flea market, teen scene, kiddies street car parade, food and drink contribute to the festivities.

★ 2115 ★
Terre Haute - OKTOBERFEST.   Late September, 2 days, Wabash Valley Fairgrounds.   Contact: Lee Phifer, General Chairman, Terre Haute German Oberlandler Club, Incorporated, 1937 Clay Avenue, Terre Haute, Indiana 47805.

Biergarten, Bavarian bands, German food and costumes, amusement rides, muzzle-loading rifle shoot, and helicopter ride.   Demonstrations of German folk-dancing provide more entertainment.

★ 2116 ★
Vevay - SWISS WINE FESTIVAL.   Mid August, annual, 4 days.   Contact: Swiss Wine Festival, Incorporated, Post Office Box 164, Vevay, Michigan 47043.

INDIANA (Continued)

Each year visitors enjoy polka dancing and music, wine gardens, grape stomping, and steintossen (stone tossing). A street fair features arts and crafts, special food concessions, flea market, and carnival. A parade, square dancing, teen dances, a Princess Contest, and horsedrawn carriage tours of the town are scheduled.

IOWA

★ 2117 ★
Amana - OKTOBERFEST. Early October (1st Saturday), annual, 1-2 days, Amana Colonies. Contact: Amana Colonies Travel Council, Amana, Iowa 52203; or Oktoberfest, South Amana, Iowa 52334.

Celebrates the Colonies' strong German heritage. Authentic German costumes, German beers, music and dance, food and wines. Places of interest to visit include the wineries, Amana refrigeration plant, woolen mills, cloak factory, and furniture factory.

★ 2118 ★
Decorah - NORDIC FEST FOLK WEEK. Late July (last weekend), annual, 3 days, downtown district. Contact: Nordic Fest, Post Office Box 364, Decorah, Iowa 52101.

Celebrations by Norwegian-Americans of their ethnic heritage. The festival is non-commercial, with an emphasis on authenticity. Included in the events is the Norwegian-American Folk Music Festival; arts and crafts displays including demonstrations of blacksmithing, carving kubbestol (Norse chairs), weaving, stitchery and rosemaling; ethnic costumes, dancing and cooking. Other activities include sports, puppet shows, tug-o-war, planetarium show, pony rides, concerts, antique show and sale, fairy tales and folk songs portrayed by dolls, drum and bugle corps and a Sutr (Norse fire god) celebration.

★ 2119 ★
Emmetsburg - SAINT PATRICK'S DAY CELEBRATION. Mid March, annual. Contact: Saint Patrick's Association, Emmetsburg, Iowa 50536.

Named for an Irishman, the city is a sister-city to Dublin, and the guests of honor at the celebration are dignitaries from the Irish capitol. Activities include a Miss Saint Patrick pageant, a parade, contests and other thematic events.

★ 2120 ★
Story City - SCANDINAVIAN DAYS. Early June, annual, 2 days, various places in town-churches, Main Street, horse show arena. Contact: Scandinavian Days Committee, Story City, Iowa 50248.

The purpose is to celebrate the Scandinavian heritage of the residents. Events include a kiddie parade and a festival parade. Scandinavian dinners, with Scandinavian delicacies offered throughout the festival. Music includes marching bands, jazz concerts, polka band, square dancing, Sweet Adelines, mass choir, and the Norseman Quartet. Antiques displays, craft demonstrations including chair caning, rosemaling, wood lathe, bobbin lace, rug making, glass blowing, klostersen, quilting, sweater knitting, junk art, etc. Carnival rides, concessions, sports including baseball and golf. Fireman's water fight, horse show, sky divers, and model airplanes. Begun around 1966.

KANSAS

★ 2121 ★
Lindsborg - SVENSK HYLLINGFEST. October, biennial (odd number years). Contact: Leland Olson, Post Office Box 191, Lindsborg, Kansas 67456.

Lindsborg has often been called "Little Sweden". The fest is a tribute to the spirit and accomplishments of the early Swedish settlers. Old World traditions: Swedish folklife, arts and crafts, cooking, folk dancing, games, costumes, dances, and smorgasbord. Held in conjunction with the Bethany College Homecoming. Started in 1941.

★ 2122 ★
Wichita - BLACK ARTS AND HERITAGE FESTIVAL. Early July, annual, 1 month. Contact: Mr. Leonard Garrett, Heritage Center, 2412 East 13th Wichita, Kansas 67214; or Mr. Henry Nathan, Director of Community Arts, Century II - 225 West Douglas, Wichita, Kansas 67202.

Touring groups from West African nations and the Caribbean participate in this celebration of the accomplishments of the Blacks.

★ 2123 ★
Wilson - AFTER HARVEST CZECH FESTIVAL. Late July, annual, 2 days. Contact: Chamber of Commerce, Box 328, Wilson, Kansas 67490.

Czechoslavakian food, dancers, a parade with floats, musical attractions, arts and crafts exhibits, horseshoe pitching contests, and tractor pulls. Kolaches

KANSAS (Continued)

(pastries) and jaternize (sausages) are sold.

KENTUCKY

★ 2124 ★
Fulton - INTERNATIONAL BANANA FESTIVAL. Mid
August, annual, 5 days. Contact: Mrs. Robert A.
Batts, Executive Secretary, Post Office Box 428,
Fulton, Kentucky 42041.

Located in the twin cities of Fulton, Kentucky and
South Fulton, Tennessee. The Banana Festival brings
together the peoples of the Americas and joins them
in an atmosphere of friendship and understanding.
There are arts and crafts exhibits, nationally famous
personages from the entertainment world, dancing to
the Marimba Band from Guatemala, banana bake-off,
parades and other exciting events, topped off by the
one-ton banana pudding, made in a vat bigger than a
bathtub.

LOUISIANA

★ 2125 ★
Albany - HUNGARIAN HARVEST DANCE. Novem-
ber, annual, 1 day (or more), Saint Margaret Catholic
Church. Contact: Louisiana Tourist Commission,
Post Office Box 44291, Baton Rouge, Louisiana
70804.

Albany is America's only rural Hungarian settlement.
The dance celebrates both their traditional culture
and the harvest. The festival begins with costumed
dancers performing traditional Hungarian dances.
Fruit decorates the ceiling of the hall; after the
dance, everyone is expected to join in grabbing the
fruit. Those with fruit are chased by the dancers
and must pay a small 'fine' if they are caught.
Everyone is welcome to join into the dancing later.
Both Hungarian and contemporary American music is
played.

★ 2126 ★
Independence - LITTLE ITALY FESTIVAL. Late April,
1 day, Catholic school grounds. Contact: John M.
Masaracchia, Post Office Box 826, Independence,
Louisiana 70443.

Italian music, food and refreshments, parade, dancing exhibitions, and street dancing are featured in
this community celebration.

★ 2127 ★
New Orleans - FRANCE LOUISIANA FESTIVAL.
Early July (4-14), annual, 11 days. Contact:
France-Louisiana Festival, New Orleans Bicentennial
Commission, 545 Saint Charles Avenue, New Orleans,
Louisiana 70130.

The festival commemorates the special association
of Louisiana and France through joint commemoration
of France's Bastille Day and America's Independence
Day. Included in this festival is the New Orleans
Food Festival. Events include special art displays
and exhibits, Louisiana craft exhibits and demonstrations, etc. In addition there are concerts, ballets,
children's chorale, films, jazz and gospel evening,
comic opera, singers from Quebec, and fireworks display.

★ 2128 ★
Plaquemine - INTERNATIONAL ACADIAN FESTIVAL.
Late October, annual, 1 week. Contact: Plaque-
mine Chamber of Commerce, Post Office Box 248,
Plaquemine, Louisiana 70454.

Celebrates the Acadian culture and story of Evangeline
with street dances, Cajun costumes, and costume contests, horse shows, rodeo, boat parade, street parade
and a re-enactment of Evangeline's journey. Also
includes fireworks, Acadian art and photography show,
sports, contests, games, rides, food and drink, shows,
arts and crafts, handicraft and commercial exhibits.

MAINE

★ 2129 ★
Waterville - OKTOBERFEST. Early October, annual,
1 day. Contact: Waterville Area Chamber of Commerce, 82 Common Street, Waterville, Maine 04901.

A German-style dance with German music, pretzels,
beer, German dinners, and German costumes.
Sponsored by the Waterville Area Chamber of Commerce.

MARYLAND

★ 2130 ★
Baltimore - OKTOBERFEST. Mid October, annual,
3 days. Contact: Kurt Kuenzel, 1215 Hillside Road,
Pasadena, Maryland 21122.

The German community celebrates its cooking, culture
and folk art and shares it with their visitors. Brass
bands, dancing, and German-American entertainment.
Started in 1968.

Ethnic Events

MARYLAND (Continued)

★ 2131 ★
Baltimore - POLISH FESTIVAL. Late July, annual,
2 days, War Memorial Plaza. Contact: Baltimore
Promotion Council, Incorporated, 102 Saint Paul
Street, Baltimore, Maryland 21202.

A festival celebrating the Polish heritage with traditional music and folk dances, piano and accordion
concerts, magic show, civic and religious ceremonies,
and a polka contest. Many different music and
dance groups perform. A cultural display of original
Polish art is exhibited, and feature films with English
subtitles are shown throughout the festival. Held in
conjunction with the Baltimore Promotion Council's
"Showcase of Nations."

★ 2132 ★
Bowie - OKTOBERFEST. Late October, annual,
1 day, Bowie Race Course. Contact: Recreation
and Arts Office, Bowie, Maryland 20715.

Presents Bavarian cultural and folk life in the manner
of the Munich original. Various organizations
present German entertainment, food (beer, sauekraut
and sausage), rides, exhibition dancers, and bands.
Continuous entertainment on both inside and outside
stages. Begun around 1968.

★ 2133 ★
Fairhill - SCOTTISH GAMES (COLONIAL HIGHLAND
GATHERING). Early June (1st Saturday), annual,
1 day. Contact: Scottish Games Association of
Delaware, Incorporated, Post Office Box 4717,
Newark, Delaware 19711.

This gathering is held in Maryland, just across the
Delaware border. Feature attractions are the Eastern
U.S. Pipe Band Championship and the International
Open Sheepdog Trials. Other activities include
highland dancing, Scottish country dancing, tossing
the caber, tossing the sheaf, piping and drumming.
Scottish exhibits, antique car exhibits and massed
pipe bands add interest to the festivities. Started
in 1962.

★ 2134 ★
Grantsville - SPRINGS FOLK FESTIVAL. Early
October, annual, 2 days. Contact: Dr. Alta E.
Shrock, Penn Alps, Incorporated, Grantsville, Mary-
land 21536.

"Pioneer Days", crafts, farm demonstrations and area
tours of Amish and Mennonite settlements. Ladies
quilt, dip candles, bake bread and make spotza.

Men and women press apples into cider and make
apple butter. Shingles and axe handles are shaved
on a "schnitzelbank". Dutch style meals are served.
Co-sponsored by the Penn Alps, Incorporated and
Springs, Pennsylvania Historical Society. Begun
around 1960.

★ 2135 ★
Rockville - NATIONAL CAPITOL AREA SCOTTISH
FESTIVAL. Early May (1st Saturday), annual, 1
day, Robert E. Peary High School. Contact:
Robert Clarke, Robert E. Peary High School, 13300
Artic Avenue, Rockville, Maryland 20853.

Events include bagpipe bands performing drumming,
Scottish country dancing exhibitions, highland dancing exhibitions, and Scottish vocalists. Begun
around 1966.

★ 2136 ★
Rockville - PURIM CELEBRATION. Early March
or late February, annual, Jewish Community Center
of Greater Washington. Contact: Jewish Community Center of Greater Washington, 6125 Montrose
Road, Rockville, Maryland 20852.

A celebration in honor of Queen Esther's rescue of
the Jews from Haman's plotting. Features a children's
play, magic shows, a carnival, belly dancing as in
the court of King Ahasuerus, and the story of Esther
retold with rock music accompaniment. Glittery
costumes, earsplitting noise-makers called groggers,
and special triangular tarts called hamantaschen add
to the merrymaking. Demonstrations show how to
make groggers, masks, and hamantaschen.

★ 2137 ★
Silver Spring - INTERNATIONAL FOLK FESTIVAL.
Mid April, 1 day, White Oak Amory (East Randolph
and Route 29). Contact: Montgomery County
Chamber of Commerce, Rockville, Maryland 20850;

International food, crafts and entertainers including
Hawaiian, Nordic, Israeli, Polish, Russian, Bavarian,
Irish, Scottish, and Hungarian. International folk
dancers and a karate demonstration. Door prizes,
wine raffle, and food and craft booths.

MASSACHUSETTS

★ 2138 ★
Boston - CHINESE NEW YEAR. Late January-mid
February, Chinatown. Contact: Greater Boston
Chamber of Commerce, 125 High Street, Boston,
Massachusetts 02110.

MASSACHUSETTS   (Continued)

The celebration includes Chinese folk songs, classical dancing, opera and drama (in English), traditional costumes, Chinese foods, and dragon dancing.

★ 2139 ★
Bridgewater - CROWN FESTIVAL.   Late June, annual, 2 days, Portuguese Holy Ghost Society, Broad Street.   Contact: Massachusetts Department of Commerce and Development, Division of Tourism, Box 1775, Boston, Massachusetts   02105.

Portuguese ceremonies, concert and dancing.   Parade followed by traditional dinner.   Auction dance and concerts.

★ 2140 ★
Fall River - PORTUGUESE SPRING FESTIVAL.   Late May, 3 days, Bristol Community College campus.   Contact: Greater Fall River Area Chamber of Commerce, Post Office Box 1871, 101 Rock Street, Fall River, Massachusetts 02722.

In honor of the heritage of Portugal, events include wine tasting, and Portuguese cafes.   There is a competition in folk dancing, as well as a band concert, fado singing, a parade and other forms of entertainment.   On exhibit is artwork, handicrafts, films, slides and Portuguese food.

★ 2141 ★
New Bedford - FEAST OF THE BLESSED SACRAMENT.   Early August, annual, 2 days.   Contact: Massachusetts Department of Commerce and Development, Division of Tourism, Box 1775, Boston, Massachusetts 02105.

Tribute to a group of Portuguese who arrived safely from Madeiras in a small boat.   Portuguese singing, dancing and cooking.   Held in Madeira Field and New Bedford.

★ 2142 ★
Northampton - BEERFEST.   Mid June, annual, 1 day, Tri County Fairgrounds.   Contact: Massachusetts Department of Commerce and Development, Division of Tourism, Box 1775, Boston, Massachusetts 02105.

Beerfest goes Polish - four bands for polkas and mazurkas, home cooked ethnic delicacies, and many surprises.

★ 2143 ★
Sagamore - ITALIAN FIESTA.   Early September, annual, 2 days, Keith Memorial Field.   Contact: Massachusetts Department of Commerce and Development, Division of Tourism, Box 1775, Boston, Massachusetts   02105.

Games and contests are included in the events celebrating the town's Italian heritage.

★ 2144 ★
Springfield - ETHNIC FESTIVAL.   Mid October, annual, 2 days.   Contact: Massachusetts Department of Commerce and Development, Division of Tourism, Box 1775, Boston, Massachusetts   02105.

Columbus Day parade and a music festival in Symphony Hall highlight the events commemorating the discoverers of the United States.

MICHIGAN

★ 2145 ★
Alma - HIGHLAND FESTIVAL.   Late May, annual.   Contact: Alma Chamber of Commerce, Post Office Box 506, Alma, Michigan 48801.

Highland dancing, piping, and drumming, and athletic games and contests take place at festival time in Alma, also called "Scotland, U.S.A."   A festival parade with massed bands highlights the event, along with the U.S. Open Pipe Band Championship.   The Alma Highland Festival Art Show and Ceilidh-Scottish Pub and Dance are other attractions.

★ 2146 ★
Bronson - POLISH FESTIVAL DAYS.   Early August, annual, 3 days.   Contact: Bronson Chamber of Commerce, 206 North Walker Street, Bronson, Michigan 49028.

Features Polish dinners, polka dance contests and bands, a festival parade, street dancing, and a Polish mock wedding.   Activities include various contests, such as tractor pulling, horseshoe pitching, tennis, drag racing, and pony pulling.   Carnival rides, handicraft booths, baked goods, and art exhibits add to the festivities.

★ 2147 ★
Detroit - ETHNIC FESTIVALS.   Late May (Memorial Day weekend) to late September, annual, 4 months.   Contact: City of Detroit, Public Information Department, 1008 City-County Building, Detroit, Michigan 48226.

Ethnic Events

MICHIGAN (Continued)

There is a different festival each weekend honoring different ethnic groups. There are ethnic style musicians, dancers, singers, comedians, exhibitions and dramatic productions. There are booths decorated with original ethnic artwork which display and sell ethnic food, drink, and other items. There is also a display booth outlining the heritage of each group with its costumes, history, artifacts and handicraft demonstrations. Ethnic groups which have participated include Greek, Irish, Slovak, German, Italian, American, French, Far Eastern, Afro-American, Indian, Ukranian, Polish, Scandinavian, Armenian, Mexican, Arab and Latin American. Most are held on the Detroit River behind Cobo Hall; the French one is on the Kern Block; the Greek celebration is in Greektown.

★ 2148 ★
Detroit - OKTOBERFEST. September, 10 days, German-American Cultural Center. Contact: German-American Cultural Center, 5251 East Outer Drive, Detroit, Michigan 48234.

Traditional German fall festival with music, food, crafts, etc.

★ 2149 ★
Frankenmuth - BAVARIAN FESTIVAL. Mid June (2nd week), annual, 1 week, Heritage Park Festival Grounds. Contact: William Clinger, Chamber of Commerce, 635 South Main Street, Frankenmuth, Michigan 48734.

Music by authentically costumed German bands; Bavarian folk songs; townspeople in costumes; Bavarian foods such as bratwurst, knockwurst, metwurst, and beer; parades; Bavarian princesses; marching bands; craftsmen; clowns; childrens' events; battle of the polka bands and polka dancing; drum and bugle competition. Started in 1959.

★ 2150 ★
Greenville - DANISH FESTIVAL. Mid August (3rd weekend), annual, 3 days. Contact: Danish Festival, Incorporated, 302 South Lafayette Street, Greenville, Michigan 48838.

Danish folk music, dancing, costumes, and food (smorgasbords) are featured. Danish souvenirs are available in addition to antiques, and flea market items and arts and crafts for sale at street stands. Entertainment includes a parade, a dance, air fair, auto show, bands, concerts, and amusement rides. Begun in 1965.

MINNESOTA

★ 2151 ★
Askov - RUTABAGA FESTIVAL AND DANISH DAYS. Late August, 2 days. Contact: Chamber of Commerce, Askov, Minnesota 55704.

Festival events include a parade, folk dancing, exhibits, talent show for the locals, entertainment by the inmates from Sandstone prison, aebleskivers (Danish pancake delicacy), sports and rides.

★ 2152 ★
Berne - SWISS FEST. Mid August, annual, 1 day. Contact: Zwingli United Church of Christ, West Concord, Minnesota 55985.

Activities include yodeling, Swiss folk dancing, alphorn blowing, Swiss wrestling and stone throwing. Traditional Swiss delicacies are offered: white sugar cookies, Big Nothings (a cookie called kuechlis), pear bread (berrebrot), and rabbit ears (musli).

★ 2153 ★
Cambridge - SWEDISH FESTIVAL. Mid June, annual, 3 days. Contact: Chamber of Commerce, Cambridge, Minnesota 55008.

The Swedish Institute Dancers perform and gourmands can eat their fill of the famous Swedish meatballs at the festival. A beauty pageant, parade, rope pulling contest, and canoe races across the Rum River, are part of the celebration.

★ 2154 ★
Chisago City - KI CHI SAGO DAY. Mid September (14), annual, 1 day. Contact: Vernon Shoquist, Chisago City, Minnesota 55013.

The town of Chisago City celebrates Ki Chi Sago Day with an Old World Market, parade, and dance. The participants in the Old World Market sell antiques, food, and craftwork and wear native Swedish dress in their booths.

★ 2155 ★
Edgerton - DUTCH FESTIVAL. Mid July, annual, 2 days. Contact: Edgerton Dutch Festival, Chamber of Commerce, Edgerton, Minnesota 56128.

Traditional Dutch costumes and special entertainments as well as ball games, midway, parades, and bands to entertain. Begun around 1950.

MINNESOTA (Continued)

★ 2156 ★
Elbow Lake - SISTER CITY CELEBRATION.   Mid
June, annual, 1 day.   Contact: Jon Stafsholt,
Elbow Lake, Minnesota 56531; or Chamber of
Commerce, Elbow Lake, Minnesota 56531.

A celebration is held to honor Elbow Lake's sister
city of Flekkefjord, Norway.   Features Norwegian
music and cultural activities, including a choir from
Norway.

★ 2157 ★
Eveleth - ALL-SLAV-DAY.   Late July, annual, 1
day.   Contact: Eveleth Civic Association, Post
Office Box 657, Eveleth, Minnesota 55734.

A celebration held in various towns of the Iron Range
including Ely, the first settlement of Slavs in Minnesota, and Eveleth.   Slovanian performers provide
singing and dancing.   Refreshments include locally
made sausage.   Begun around 1950.

★ 2158 ★
Ghent - BELGIAN AMERICAN DAY.   Mid August,
annual, 1 day.   Contact: Department of Economic
Development, 480 Cedar Street, Saint Paul, Minnesota 55101.

Featuring prysbolling (Belgian national sport), Belgian
cookies and waffles, a parade and a queen coronation.

★ 2159 ★
Ivanhoe - POLSKA KIELBASA DAYS.   Mid August,
annual, 2 days.   Contact: Department of Economic
Development, 480 Cedar Street, Saint Paul, Minnesota 55101.

The town, settled by the Poles around 1900, serves
free Polska kielbasa (Polish sausage) during its festivities.   Polish American dancers perform.   Wycinanki
(Polish paper cutting) is taught and demonstrated.

★ 2160 ★
Mapleton - ROBERT BURNS CELEBRATION.   Late
January, annual, 1 day.   Contact: Chamber of
Commerce, Mapleton, Minnesota 56065.

Features Scottish music, dancing, singing, gathering
of the clans, and crowning of Miss Bonnie Lass.
Curling trophies are awarded.   Haggis, a special
Scottish dish made from oatmeal, suet, and spices,
is available.   The festival commemorates the birth

of Scottish poet Robert Burns.

★ 2161 ★
Mapleton - SCOTTISH HIGHLAND GAMES.   Early
June, annual, 2 days.   Contact: John Lake,
Mapleton, Minnesota 56065.

Athletic events include the hammer throw, weight
and stone toss, and caber pole toss.   Highland
dancing competitions take place along with music
from massed bagpipe and drum bands.

★ 2162 ★
Minneapolis - DANISH DAY AT MINEHAHA PARK.
Early June (9th, Danish Constitution Day), 1 day,
Minehaha Park.   Contact: Greater Minneapolis
Chamber of Commerce, 15 South Fifth Street,
Minneapolis, Minnesota 55402.

Events include folk music and dancing, smorgesbord
lunch, clowns, gymnastics, and an outdoor church
service.

★ 2163 ★
Minneapolis - NORWAY DAY.   Mid July, annual,
1 day, Minnehaha Park.   Contact: Reverend Iver
B. Olson, 3311 14th Avenue, South, Minneapolis,
Minnesota 55407.

People of Norwegian descent gather for a morning
church service in Norwegian followed by speeches,
folk dancing, and singing.

★ 2164 ★
Minneapolis - SNOOSE BOULEVARD FESTIVAL.
May, annual, 3 days, Cedar-Riverside Area.   Con-
tact: Maury Bernstein, Post Office Box 14171,
University Station, Minnesota 55414.

Focuses on the entertainment heritage of Scandinavian-
Americans in days gone by through reconstructing the
Scandinavian entertainment of the Cedar-Riverside area,
where dance halls like Dania Hall once thrived.   Features folk singing, parades, dancing for schottische
enthusiasts, fiddlers, and accordionists.   Scandinavian foods are sold and the old time entertainment
culture revived.

★ 2165 ★
Minneapolis - SVENSKARNAS DAG.   Late June,
annual, 1 day, Minnehaha Park.   Contact: Iver
Johnson, 1605 Louisiana Avenue, South, Minneapolis,
Minnesota 55426.

Ethnic Events

MINNESOTA (Continued)

This festival follows the Swedish tradition of having a celebration in mid-summer and promotes traditional Swedish culture. A church service in the morning is followed by a band concert, folk dancing and singing, and coronation of a mid-summer queen. There are awards, prizes, and food.

★ 2166 ★
Montevideo - INTERNATIONAL FIESTA DAYS.
June , 3 days. Contact: Dr. Larry Lambert, 105 North Fourth Street, Montevideo, Minnesota 56265.

Dignitaries from South America and Washington, D.C. participate in this festive event. A parade highlights the activities.

★ 2167 ★
Montgomery - KOLACKY DAY. Early September, 1 day. Contact: Chamber of Commerce, Montgomery, Minnesota 56069.

In honor of the Kolacky (a Bohemian bun). Events include a parade, slow pitch softball tournament, midway, king and queen coronation. King chosen on the basis of how many Kolackies he can eat. Also polka bands and street dancing. Begun around 1935.

★ 2168 ★
Mora - DALA DAYS. Mid June, 3 days. Contact: Jaycees or the Mora Commercial Club, Mora, Minnesota 55051.

The name comes from Dalsland, the area where Mora, Sweden, is located and where the Dala horse was once worshipped. Festival events include canoe races and a street dance.

★ 2169 ★
Mora - VASALOPPET CROSS COUNTY SKI RACE.
February, annual. Contact: Department of Economic Development, 480 Cedar Street, Saint Paul, Minnesota 55101.

A ski race patterned after one in the sister city of Mora, Sweden. About 10,000 competitors begin the race in a "mass start" instead of staggered groupings or heats. Blueberry soup shipped from Sweden is served at the festival.

★ 2170 ★
Saint Paul - MEXICAN INDEPENDENCE CELEBRATION.

Mid October (Friday and Saturday before October 16), 2 days, downtown area. Contact: New Mexican Celebration Committee, 825 Stickney, Saint Paul, Minnesota 55107.

A parade, dances, and other traditional festivities highlight the events of the celebration.

★ 2171 ★
Saint Paul - SCOTTISH COUNTRY FAIR. Late April, 1 day, Macalester College. Contact: Scottish Country Fair, Macalester College, Saint Paul, Minnesota 55105.

Highland games, pipe bands, and a craft fair are included in the festive events.

★ 2172 ★
Spring Grove - SYTTENDE MAI FEST. Mid May (around May 17, Norwegian Independence Day), 3 days. Contact: Don Ellestad, Box 213, Spring Grove, Minnesota 55974.

This Norwegian National Holiday festival features the coronation of a Queen and King of the Trolls, Olympic runners, a parade, smorgasbord, fiddlers' bee, and a drawing for a trip to Norway. Norwegian music, dancing, arts and crafts are other attractions.

★ 2173 ★
Tyler - AEBLESKIVER DAYS. Mid June, 2 days. Contact: Department of Economic Development, 480 Cedar Street, Saint Paul, Minnesota 55101.

Aebleskivers (Danish pancakes) are served throughout the festival. Other events include a barbeque, queen contest, regional dairy days for local 4-H clubs, and a parade.

★ 2174 ★
Willmar - KAFFE FEST. Late June, 3 days. Contact: Chamber of Commerce, Marv Beach, Willmar, Minnesota 56201.

The town is known for its afternoon coffee tradition, derived from a coffee drinking club founded many years ago. During the Scandinavian festival free coffee and cookies are served. Other events include a carnival, parades, and queen coronation.

★ 2175 ★
Young America - STIFTUNGFEST. Late August, annual, 3 days. Contact: Chamber of Commerce, Young America, Minnesota 55397.

MINNESOTA (Continued)

Begun as a German songfest, this festival now includes such events as open pit barbeque, carnival,
dances, softball, musical entertainment, beer garden,
and polka dancing.   Begun around 1862.

MISSOURI

★ 2176 ★
Hermann - MAIFEST.   Mid May, 2 days.   Con-
tact: Chamber of Commerce, 312 Schiller Street,
Hermann, Missouri 65041.

Events include tours of historic homes; visit to a
local winery; German costumes, food, music, beer,
biergarten; arts and crafts; children's events;
dancing; tours of museum; church suppers; and
parade.   The purpose of the festival is to preserve
German arts and culture brought over by the early
settlers, and to encourage the restoration and preservation of old buildings.   Begun around 1951.

★ 2177 ★
Kansas City - FIESTA FILIPINA.   Mid July, 2
days, Crown Center Square.   Contact: Convention
and Visitors Bureau of Greater Kansas City, 1221
Baltimore, Kansas City, Missouri 64105.

The festival features music, dance, food, and entertainment from the Philippine Islands.

★ 2178 ★
Kansas City - GREEK PLAKA.   Late June, annual,
3 days, Crown Center Square.   Contact: Convention
and Visitors Bureau of Greater Kansas City, 1221
Baltimore, Kansas City, Missouri 64105.

Greek food, music and dancing highlight this gala
festival.   Begun around 1973.

★ 2179 ★
Kansas City - ITALIAN FESTIVAL.   Mid August,
3 days, Crown Center Square.   Contact: Convention and Visitors Bureau of Greater Kansas City,
1221 Baltimore, Kansas City, Missouri 64105.

This old world festival features food, music, dance,
and entertainment in the Italian atmosphere.

★ 2180 ★
Rolla - SAINT PAT'S CELEBRATION.   Mid March,
annual, 2 days, University of Missouri, Rolla.
Contact: Public Information Office, University of

Missouri at Rolla, Rolla, Missouri 65401.

Honors Saint Patrick, patron saint of engineers.
"Saint Pat" arrives in town by handcar, dressed in
green, as are the members of his court.   A parade
begins with the painting of Main Street green.   In
a more solemn ceremony, Saint Pat dubs members of
the graduating class knights in the "Order of Saint
Patrick".   Visiting dignitaries are made honorary
knights.   Due reverence is paid the Blarney Stone.
Other events include beard judging and shillelagh
judging.   Started in 1907.

★ 2181 ★
Saint Louis - BADENFEST.   Early September, 1 day,
8200 North Broadway (Baden area).   Contact:
Saint Louis Regional Commerce and Growth Association, Ten Broadway, Saint Louis, Missouri 63102.

German foods, music, and dancing are featured.
There are displays of German heritage and culture
along with a children's area complete with rides and
games.   Dining rooms for dinners of sauerbraten,
bratwurst, etc., wine gardens, beer gardens and
handmade souvenirs.

★ 2182 ★
Saint Louis - BEVO DAY.   Mid September, 1 day,
Bevo Mill area.   Contact: Convention and Visitors
Bureau of Greater Saint Louis, 500 Broadway Building,
Saint Louis, Missouri 63102.

Four stages to provide continuous entertainment including German bands and dancing.   There are
games and rides for young and old.   Authentic
German food including dinners and sandwiches.
Cultural activities, art show, crafts, and musical
concert.

★ 2183 ★
Saint Louis - DUTCHTOWN OKTOBERFEST.   Early
October, 1 day, Marquette Park.   Contact: Convention and Visitors Bureau of Greater Saint Louis,
500 Broadway Building, Saint Louis, Missouri 63102.

Festival emphasizes the German-Slavic heritage of
the area.   Entertainment includes tamburitza, German
brass band, drinking, dining, dancing (mainly polkas),
a giant beer tent, arts, crafts and games.

★ 2184 ★
Saint Louis - FETE DE NORMANDIE.   Late September,
2 days, Pasadena Mall.   Contact: Convention and
Visitors Bureau of Greater Saint Louis, 500 Broadway
Building, Saint Louis, Missouri 63102.

Ethnic Events

MISSOURI (Continued)

French flavor prevails in the events including a parade, entertainment, arts, crafts, booths, carnival games, food, and refreshments.

★ 2185 ★
Saint Louis - HILL DAY. Mid August, 1 day, city's "Hill" region (around Saint Ambrose Church). Contact: Convention and Visitors Bureau of Greater Saint Louis, 500 Broadway Building, Saint Louis, Missouri 63102.

Ethnic celebration honors Saint Louisans of Italian descent. Street dancing, arts, crafts, Italian food, and grape stomping contest. All artcrafts and foods are prepared by area residents.

★ 2186 ★
Saint Louis - SOULARD SUNDAY. Mid July, 1 day, Soulard Market. Contact: Convention and Visitors Bureau of Greater Saint Louis, 500 Broadway Building, Saint Louis, Missouri 63102.

This festival seeks to capture the French and pioneer spirit of the city's founders. Market dates back to 1779 French cuisine, international music, international dancing, tours of the area and refreshments.

★ 2187 ★
Saint Louis - STRASSENFEST. Mid July, 3 days, 12th Street, 15th Street, Market Street, Olive Street, Memorial Plaza. Contact: Convention and Visitors Bureau of Greater Saint Louis, 500 Broadway Building, Saint Louis, Missouri 63102.

Authentic German street festival featuring German dress, food, folk songs, exhibits of crafts, cultural events, family entertainment, games, street dancing, and rides.

★ 2188 ★
Sainte Genevieve - JOUR DE FETE. Early August, 2 days. Contact: Sainte Genevieve Chamber of Commerce, Box 166, Sainte Genevieve, Missouri 63670.

Honors the town's French heritage and its founding in 1735 as the first permanent settlement west of the Mississippi. Tours of several homes, dating back to 1770, which have been restored and preserved. Events include folk dancing, a pageant, parades, arts and crafts displays, international cuisine, French costumes and a King's Ball.

MONTANA

★ 2189 ★
Laurel - HERBSTFEST. Late September (last week), 5 days. Contact: Chamber of Commerce, Box 395, Laurel, Montana 59044.

A harvest festival with a German theme. Participants frequently wear costumes identical to those traditional in the region of Germany from which their ancestors came. The activities include parades and pageants. Started in 1973.

★ 2190 ★
Red Lodge - FESTIVAL OF NATIONS. Early August, annual, 9 days, evening program in Civic Center, exhibits next door in school. Contact: Chamber of Commerce, Post Office Box 998, Red Lodge, Montana 59068.

Each day and evening a different ethnic group is celebrated with folk dance, exhibitions, singing, food and parades. The international craft and art exhibit features a fine display of paintings, sculpture and ornamental objects. Free food and evening programs. Flags representing the various nations are on display in the auditorium, along with some state flags. In connection with the festival, there is a flower show and a show for professional and amateur Montana artists. Active crafts, such as spinning, weaving, violin making, pottery, wood carving, lace making, enameling, etc., are displayed every day in the windows of the business establishments along the main street.

NEBRASKA

★ 2191 ★
Loup City - POLISH FESTIVAL. Late June, annual. Contact: Chamber of Commerce, Loup City, Nebraska 68853.

Features a polka contest, platefuls of Polish food, singing and dancing by local talent, a parade, and crafts show. Carnival rides provide thrills for young and old.

★ 2192 ★
McCook - GERMAN HERITAGE DAYS. Early May, 2 days. Contact: Lester Harsh, Chairman, German Heritage Committee, 2205 Norris, McCook, Nebraska 69001.

A celebration of the German heritage dating back to McCook's early settlers. Ethnic items include arts and crafts, food, folk dancing, music, and children's

NEBRASKA (Continued)

events. There is also a parade. Begun around 1970.

★ 2193 ★
Minden - DANISH DAYS CELEBRATION. Mid June, annual, 2-3 days. Contact: Chamber of Commerce, Box 375, Minden, Nebraska 68959.

Descendents of Danish settlers present ethnic cooking, folk dancing, a parade, and an exhibit of Danish handicrafts.

★ 2194 ★
O'Neill - SAINT PATRICK'S DAY CELEBRATION. March (17), annual, 1 day. Contact: O'Neill Area Chamber of Commerce, 430 East Douglas, Box 407, O'Neill, Nebraska 68763.

The citizens of O'Neill celebrate their Irish heritage with a grand parade, costumed dancers, Irish food with green beer, and a celebration dance.

★ 2195 ★
Scottsbluff - MEXICAN-AMERICAN FESTIVAL. Mid September, annual. Contact: Scottsbluff-Gering United Chamber of Commerce, 1419 Broadway, Box 167, Scottsbluff, Nebraska 69361.

Descendants of original Mexican settlers celebrate their heritage. Features a fine display of Mexican folk dancing and a large exhibit of ornate and beautiful Mexican crafts. Crispy tacos, bowls of spicy chili con carne, and other ethnic dishes are served in abundance.

★ 2196 ★
Stromberg - SWEDISH FESTIVAL. Late June, annual. Contact: Commercial Club, Box 453, Stromberg, Nebraska 68666.

Features a lavish parade with marching bands and bright-colored floats, the crowning of a king and queen, ethnic dancing, and singing exhibitions. A splendid Swedish smorgasbord adds to the festivities.

★ 2197 ★
Verdigre - KOLACH DAYS. Early June, 2 days. Contact: Improvement Club, Verdigre, Nebraska 68783.

In honor of the fruit-filled Czechoslovakian pastries. Events include the crowning of the Kolach queen,

exhibition dancing of national dances, and dancing by the spectators (the dance troup gives the visitor a chance to try dancing the traditional dances), and a parade.

★ 2198 ★
Wilber - CZECH FESTIVAL. Early August, annual, 2 days. Contact: Milo T. Jelinek, President, Nebraska Czechs of Wilber, Incorporated, Wilber, Nebraska 68465.

Celebration of the town's Czechoslavakian heritage featuring folk dances, songs and music, and ethnic cooking. Arts and crafts displays and demonstrations, accordion contest, and a parade are also featured. Begun around 1960.

NEVADA

★ 2199 ★
Elko - NATIONAL BASQUE FESTIVAL. Early July (1st weekend), annual, 2 days. Contact: Elko Euzkaldunak Club, Post Office Box 1321, Elko, Nevada 89801.

Celebrates the ancient heritage of the Basques with feasting, dancing, music, costumes, handicrafts and basque games. Contests including sheepherding, log throwing, sheep shearing, and mountaineering skills. Also a parade.

NEW HAMPSHIRE

★ 2200 ★
Manchester - OCTOBERFEST. Mid October, 3 days. Contact: New Hampshire Division of Economic Development, Concord, New Hampshire 03301.

German music, food, and minstrels highlight the events of this traditional fall gathering.

★ 2201 ★
Waterville - SWISS INDEPENDENCE DAY. Early August (Saturday closest to August 3), annual, 1 day. Contact: Waterville Valley, Incorporated, Waterville, New Hampshire 03223.

Swiss Independence Day is celebrated in Waterville with Swiss food, music, songs, and folk dancing.

Ethnic Events

NEW JERSEY

★ 2202 ★
Freehold - IRISH FEIS AND SCOTTISH GAMES
FESTIVAL.   Mid July, 1 day, Freehold Raceway.
Contact: Freehold Raceway, Freehold, New Jersey
07728.

The celebration includes the singing of ballads, step
dancing, Irish and Scottish band music, and pipeband competition.   There are both Irish and Scottish
field sports, including Gaelic football and soccer.

★ 2203 ★
Holmdel - BLACK HERITAGE FESTIVAL.   Mid July,
annual, 1 day, Garden State Arts Center, Telegraph Hill Park.   Contact: Black Heritage Festival,
New Jersey Highway Authority, Garden State Parkway, Woodbridge, New Jersey 07095.

Salutes Black heritage.   Features Expo on the Arts,
gospel singers, jazz ensembles, rock groups, dancers
(including, if not exclusively, African dance), solo
vocalists, and instrumentalists.   Begun around 1973.

★ 2204 ★
Holmdel - GERMAN-AMERICAN FESTIVAL.   Sep-
tember, annual, 1 day, Garden State Arts Center,
Telegraph Hill Park.   Contact: German-American
Festival, New Jersey Highway Authority, Garden
State Parkway, Woodbridge, New Jersey 07095.

A demonstration of the treasured traditions of Germans
in America and their meaning to the American way
of life.   The various German-American societies
show what they are doing.   There are singers,
turners, Bavarian and Burgenlaender folkdancers,
children from the German language schools, German
folk theater, soccer games, presentation of banners,
mass chorus, bands, German food and souvenirs.
Begun in 1974.

★ 2205 ★
Holmdel - GRECIAN ARTS FESTIVAL.   Late Septem-
ber, annual, 1 day, Garden State Arts Center,
Telegraph Hill Park.   Contact: Grecian Arts Festival,
New Jersey Highway Authority, Garden State Parkway,
Woodbridge, New Jersey 07095.

Greek culture, ancient and modern.   Greek food,
singers, musicians, and dancers, art exhibits, Greek
drama, and chorales.   Greek foods and other refreshments are available.   Begun in 1974.

★ 2206 ★
Holmdel - HUNGARIAN FESTIVAL.   Mid September,
annual, 1 day, Garden State Arts Center, Telegraph
Hill Park.   Contact: Hungarian Festival Committee,
American Hungarian Studies Foundation, Post Office
Box 1084, New Brunswick, New Jersey 08903.

On display throughout the day are Hungarian folk arts
including embroidery, ceramics, tapestries, and woodcarving.   The works of New Jersey artists are also
on display.   In addition, the folk festivities include
exhibits by churches and organizations, a csardas
contest, Hungarian folk dancers, solo vocalists,
orchestras, and choirs performing Hungarian music.
Also Hungarian folk costumes and sports events.

★ 2207 ★
Holmdel - IRISH FESTIVAL.   Late June, annual,
1 day, Garden State Arts Center, Telegraph Hill
Park.   Contact: Irish Festival, New Jersey Highway
Authority, Garden State Parkway, Woodbridge, New
Jersey 07095.

A salute to Irish heritage: Irish Pipe Band competition,
Irish singers, musicians and celebrities, and folk
dancers, Irish harpists, and step dancing.   Begun
around 1971.

★ 2208 ★
Holmdel - ITALIAN FESTIVAL.   Late June, annual,
1 day, Garden State Arts Center.   Contact: Italian
Festival, New Jersey Highway Authority, Garden
State Parkway, Woodbridge, New Jersey 07095.

Festival is to honor the many manifestations of
Italian culture, stage, screen and television stars.
Events include performances by stage, screen and
television artists, talented Italian American teenagers,
Metropolitan Opera stars, and choral groups.   Fashion
show of clothing by Italian American designers, ex-
hibit and sale of arts and crafts (Italian), Piazza
Stati D'Giardino (a typical Italian street scene).
Begun around 1971.

★ 2209 ★
Holmdel - JEWISH FESTIVAL OF THE ARTS.   Mid
June, annual, 1 day, Garden State Arts Center.
Contact: Jewish Festival of the Arts, New Jersey
Highway Authority, Garden State Parkway, Wood-
bridge, New Jersey 07095.

The festival is intended as a salute to Jewish culture
and as a mark of pride in being New Jersey residents.
Features a program of Jewish concert singers, violinist,
comedian, Cantorial music, and Israeli folk dancers.
Started in 1973.

NEW JERSEY (Continued)

★ 2210 ★
Holmdel - POLISH FESTIVAL.   Early June, annual,
Garden State Arts Center.   Contact: Polish Festival,
New Jersey Highway Authority, Garden State Park-
way, Woodbridge, New Jersey 07095.

Features Polish singers, folk dance groups, pianists,
and the Polish Championship String Band.   A Polish-
American art exhibit and sale takes place at the
Plaza and Mall.   Started in 1972.

★ 2211 ★
Holmdel - PUERTO RICAN HERITAGE FESTIVAL.
September, annual, 1 day, Garden State Arts
Center.   Contact: Puerto Rican Heritage Festival,
New Jersey Highway Authority, Garden State Park-
way, Woodbridge, New Jersey 07095.

In celebration of Puerto Rican culture, including
traditional dances, music, arts and crafts, foods,
etc.

★ 2212 ★
Holmdel - SCOTTISH HERITAGE FESTIVAL.   Mid
September, annual, 1 day, Garden State Arts Center.
Contact: Scottish Heritage Festival, New Jersey
Highway Authority, Garden State Parkway, Wood-
bridge, New Jersey 07095.

A colorful morning program includes highland dancing,
country dancing, mini tattoo pipes and drums, tossing
the caber, and exhibits of Scottish crafts.   A formal
afternoon program on stage presents Scottish concert
singers and entertainers.   Started in 1973.

★ 2213 ★
Holmdel - UKRAINIAN FESTIVAL.   Early June,
annual, Garden State Arts Center.   Contact:
Ukrainian Festival, New Jersey Highway Authority,
Garden State Parkway, Woodbridge, New Jersey
07095.

Offers Ukrainian folk singing and dancing, ballet,
and Ukrainian solists of the opera and concert stage.
Displays Ukrainian art, including embroidery, ceramics,
tapestry, and wood-carving.   Sponsored by the New
Jersey Branch of the Ukrainian Congress Committee
of America, which includes all major Ukrainian
American organizations in the state.

★ 2214 ★
Waterville - OKTOBERFEST.   Early October (1st
Saturday), annual, 1 day.   Contact: Waterville

Valley Incorporated, Waterville, New Jersey 03223.

The festival offers not only German beer, but German
cuisine, music and dance.   In addition, the visitor
can revel in the beauty of the fall foliage.

NEW MEXICO

★ 2215 ★
Bernalillo - LA FIESTA DE SAN LORENZO.   Mid
August, annual.   Contact: Tourist Department of
Greater Albuquerque Chamber of Commerce, 400 Elm
Street, Northeast, Albuquerque, New Mexico 87102.

Features Los Matchines dances brought to the New
World by Spanish missionaries and colonists.   Nine
ancient folk tunes are used in the dances.   Los
Abuelos (the clowns) provide comic relief, and music
is furnished by a violinist and a guitarist.   The costumes are carefully homemade.   Festivities begin
with La Entrada de Coronado, commemorating the
arrival of the Coronado Expedition in 1540.   A
fiesta queen is crowned, and Indians from several
pueblos present ceremonial dances.

★ 2216 ★
Isleta Pueblo - SAN AUGUSTIN FIESTA.   Late
August, annual, 1-2 days.   Contact: Albuquerque
Area Office, Bureau of Indian Affairs, U.S. Depart-
ment of the Interior, 5301 Central Avenue, Northeast,
Post Office Box 8327, Albuquerque, New Mexico
87108.

A carnival and street dancing, Spanish fiesta style.
(No Indian dancing.)

★ 2217 ★
Las Cruces - MINI-WORLD.   Late April, annual,
2 days, New Mexico State University.   Contact:
University Information Service, New Mexico State
University, Box 3072, Las Cruces, New Mexico
88003.

The students international bazaar featuring the flavor
of other countries in entertainment and exhibits.

★ 2218 ★
Sante Fe - FIESTA DE SANTA FE.   Late August
or early September, annual, 4 days.   Contact:
Chamber of Commerce, La Fonda Hotel, Post Office
Box 1928, Santa Fe, New Mexico 87501.

Oldest non-Indian celebration in the United States.
Commemorates the peaceful reconquest of New Mexico
in 1692 by Don Diego de Vargas.   Begins with the

Ethnic Events

NEW MEXICO (Continued)

burning of Zozobra (Old Man Gloom). Events include parades, mariachi concerts, style show, historical pageant, melodrama (local political satire), arts and crafts, folkloric and Indian dances, on the 365 year old plaza. Started in 1713.

NEW YORK

★ 2219 ★
Canandaigua - OKTOBERFEST. Mid October, 2 days, Bristol Mountain Ski Lodge. Contact: Finger Lakes Association, Incorporated, 309 Lake Street, Penn Yan, New York 14527.

A German buffet, dance and campout with an ox roast and a German band. Entertainment includes a bicycle race and chair lift rides.

★ 2220 ★
Cape Vincent - FRENCH FESTIVAL. Mid July (weekend before Bastille Day), annual, 1 day. Contact: Annual French Festival, Cape Vincent, New York 13618.

Events include the coronation of a festival queen and a parade featuring floats, bands and marching units, with special performances being given by the bands. Meanwhile, the streets are lined with carts selling foods and souvenirs, and with exhibits of historical and cultural interest including an art show, films, etc. A French mass is offered, and there is a concert of popular music and a fireworks display. Bands, buffet dinner, and dancers complete the events. Begun around 1969.

★ 2221 ★
Jamaica - FOREIGN LANGUAGE FESTIVAL. Mid May, annual, 1 day, Rufus King Park. Contact: York College, 150-14 Jamaica Avenue, Jamaica, New York 11432.

Sponsored by the Foreign Language Department of York College, the theme for the festival is expressed through representations of various nationalities. Events include music, dancing, art and fashion displays, open cafes and booths, while a display of relevant artifacts are exhibited in the York College Library before and during the event. New York City high schools and community groups join in the festivities. Begun around 1968.

★ 2222 ★
New York - CHINESE NEW YEAR. Late January-mid February, annual. Contact: New York Convention and Visitors Bureau, Incorporated, 90 East 42nd Street, New York, New York 10017.

The celebration includes a parade with many floats and colorful costumes, lion dances, fireworks, feasting and music.

★ 2223 ★
New York - DELPHIC FESTIVAL. Year-round, 40 weeks, One Sheridan Square (old Cafe Society). Contact: Greek Art Theater, Incorporated, One Sheridan Square, New York, New York 10014.

Presented by the Greek Art Theater, the festival is a presentation in English of ancient and modern Greek plays and other ethnic cultural activities such as concerts and national dancers. The theater also plans to serve as a training studio and library.

★ 2224 ★
New York - FEAST OF SAN GENARRO. September, annual, 10 days, Little Italy. Contact: New York Convention and Visitors Bureau, Incorporated, 90 East 42nd Street, New York, New York 10017.

The streets are decorated with lights and lined with booths selling souvenirs and southern Italian (especially Neopolitan) food. Italian singers aboard floats serenade the spectators. Both Italian and American music is played during the festival. The statue of San Genarro is carried in procession. Started in 1925.

★ 2225 ★
New York - FESTIVAL AT GATEWAY EAST. Early-mid August, Floyd Bennett Field, Jamaica Bay Unit of Gateway National Recreation Area. Contact: National Folk Festival Association, Incorporated, 1346 Connecticut Avenue, Northwest, Washington, D.C. 20036.

Four of New York's many ethnic groups hold festivals similar to the sort of effort that they would put on in their own communities. In addition, there is a continuous series of performances by local artists.

★ 2226 ★
New York - FOLKLORE FIESTA. Late August, annual, 1 day, Central Park. Contact: New York Convention and Visitors Bureau, Incorporated, 90 East 42nd Street, New York, New York 10017.

Picnics; hispanic music of all sorts: religious, dance, popular; dance groups including the Ballet Hispanico. Begun around 1966.

NEW YORK (Continued)

★ 2227 ★
New York - HISPANIC ARTS FESTIVAL.   Mid July,
annual, 1 day, Lincoln Center Plaza.   Contact:
New York Convention and Visitors Bureau, Incorporated, 90 East 42nd Street, New York, New York 10017.

The Association of Hispanic Arts sponsors a program of
Spanish music and drama, including the dancers of the
Ballet Hispanico de New York.   Begun in 1976.

★ 2228 ★
New York - NINTH AVENUE INTERNATIONAL
FESTIVAL.   Mid May, annual, 2 days, Ninth Avenue
(36th - 54th Street).   Contact: Chamber of Com-
merce and Industry, 65 Liberty Street, New York,
New York 10005; or New York Convention and
Visitors Bureau, Incorporated, 90 East 42nd Street,
New York, New York 10017.

The festival features cooking demonstrations and
offerings of the delicacies of 22 countries including
China, Santo Domingo, Peru, Argentina, India,
Central Africa, Cuba and the Philippines.   There
are also guided tours, a children's parade, entertainment, wine lectures, special bargains in shops
and restaurants, and presentation of civic awards.
Begun in 1974.

★ 2229 ★
New York - ONE WORLD FESTIVAL.   Mid September, annual, 2 days, Saint Vartan Armenian Cathedral.   Contact: Saint Vartan Armenian Cathedral,
620 Second Avenue between 34th and 35th Streets,
New York, New York 10016.

Choral and dance groups give performances of traditional songs and dances including Lithuanian, Spanish,
Polish, Philippine, Italian, Armenian, and Chinese.
In addition, there are booths offering displays and
sales of traditional foods and crafts.   Special
children's activities are offered, and there is an art
show.   Begun in 1973.

★ 2230 ★
Purlington - GERMAN ALPS FESTIVAL.   Mid August,
annual, 9 days, Bavarian Manor.   Contact: Director,
German Alps Festival, 329 East Fifth Street, New
York, New York 10003.

An old-fashioned festival with a German beer garden
and wine cellar, German food and singing waiters,
German bands and folk dancing.

★ 2331 ★
Rochester - OKTOBERFEST.   Late September, 1 day.

East Avenue to Genesee River area.   Contact:
Finger Lakes Association, Incorporated, 309 Lake
Street, Penn Yan, New York 14527.

German food and entertainment, farmers market,
bicycle race, parade, art and crafts sale, and a
flea market highlight the festival events.

★ 2232 ★
Syracuse - CENTRAL NEW YORK SCOTTISH GAMES.
Mid August (2nd Saturday), annual, 1 day, Griffin
Field.   Contact: Earl Marshall, 143 Minerva Street,
Syracuse, New York 13203.

Massed band parades celebrate the gathering of the
clans.   Individual pipe bands compete in march,
strathspey, and reel contests.   Athletic contests
test skill in tossing the caber and pitching the sheaf.
Prizes are awarded for dancing the highland fling,
sword dance, Seann Triubhas, Irish jig, and sailors
hornpipe.   Drumming, individual piping, and drum
major contests are other events of the day.   Started
in 1940.

★ 2233 ★
Utica - CELEBRATION OF NATIONS.   Mid May,
annual, 2 days.   Contact: Central New York
Community Arts Council, Incorporated, 800 Park
Avenue, Utica, New York 13501.

The celebration is an ethnic arts festival and presents
the food, customs, arts, crafts, music, and dance of
15 nations.   The nations vary every year.

NORTH CAROLINA

★ 2234 ★
Charlotte - CHARLOTTE INTERNATIONAL FOLK
FESTIVAL.   Early November, annual, 3 days,
Charlotte Civic Center.   Contact: Paul Buck,
Managing Director, Auditorium-Coliseum-Civic
Center, 2700 East Independence Boulevard, Charlotte,
North Carolina 28205.

Diverse ethnic groups are honored and represented
by displays, entertainment, and their distinctive
food, music and dancing.

★ 2235 ★
Linville - GRANDFATHER MOUNTAIN HIGHLAND
GAMES.   Mid July, annual, 2 days, Grandfather
Mountain (MacRae Meadows).   Contact: Grand-
father Mountain Highland Games, Incorporated,
Linville, North Carolina 28646.

NORTH CAROLINA (Continued)

Quick-footed dancers dressed in colorful kilts perform the highland fling, sword dance, reel, and jig. Bagpipers and drummers compete. Visitors can watch fast-moving track and field events, such as the two-mile run and pole vaulting. They can observe highland wrestling, tossing the sheaf, and other Scottish games.

NORTH DAKOTA

★ 2236 ★
Edgeley - POLKA DAY. Late August, annual, Main Street. Contact: North Dakota State Highway Department, Capitol Grounds, Bismarck, North Dakota 58505.

Polka bands play along Main Street as the merry makers drink beer, dance, and enjoy German food. A variety of other activities may include such events as turtle races, or other specialties for the year.

★ 2237 ★
Lidgerwood - KOLACHE DAY. Early April, annual. Contact: North Dakota Highway Department, Highway Building, Capitol Grounds, Bismarck, North Dakota 58505.

Features Polish handicrafts and antiques on exhibit, free kolaches, and dancing.

★ 2238 ★
New Leipzig - OKTOBERFEST. Late September-early October, annual. Contact: North Dakota State Highway Department, Capitol Grounds, Bismarck, North Dakota 58505.

Festival activities include polka music and dancing, and feasting on traditional German cuisine.

★ 2239 ★
Tioga - SYTTENDE MAI. Mid May (17th), annual, 1 day. Contact: North Dakota State Highway Department, Capitol Grounds, Bismarck, North Dakota 58505.

To commemorate Norway's Independence Day, the town decorates its Main Street with Norse motifs. Ethnic displays and entertainment complete the event.

★ 2240 ★
Wishek - SAUERKRAUT DAY. Mid October, annual, 1 day. Contact: North Dakota Highway Department, Capitol Grounds, Bismarck, North Dakota 58505.

Area residents recall their German heritage with music, folk dancing, and food, notably honoring the sauerkraut.

OHIO

★ 2241 ★
Akron - ENGLISH FAIRE. Late February, 2 days, Stan Hywet Hall. Contact: Director of Public Relations, Stan Hywet Hall Foundation, 714 North Portage Path, Akron, Ohio 44303.

Visitors are invited to join the revelry in costume and enter into a traditional English village celebration. A village is set up in Manor Auditorium with a pub wine cellar, tea room and craft shops. The Carriage House offers games: skittles, darts, dunk-the-wench, fortune-telling and apple bobbing.

★ 2242 ★
Bucyrus - BRATWURST FESTIVAL. Mid August, 3 days. Contact: Mike Halms, Bratwurst Festival, Incorporated, 1545 Hopley Avenue, Bucyrus, Ohio 44820.

The celebration of the German delicacy includes a parade with floats, band and drill teams; a festival queen is selected; there are exhibits of crafts and photographs; free entertainment; rides; games; and hundreds of thousands of bratwurst links.

★ 2243 ★
Cadiz - INTERNATIONAL MINING AND MANUFACTURING FESTIVAL. Late September, annual, 4 days. Contact: President, International Mining and Manufacturing Festival, Rural Free Delivery 3, Cadiz, Ohio 43907.

The area's ethnics get together in traditional costumes for music and dancing in the streets. Six stages provide continuous entertainment. Exhibits on a wide variety of themes and food from all over the world are offered.

★ 2244 ★
Columbus - HAUS UND GARTEN TOUR. Late June (last Sunday), annual, 1 day, German Village. Contact: The German Village Society, 624 South Third Street, Columbus, Ohio 43216.

Visitors tour the restored village's houses, shops, and gardens. German foods are available from restaurants and booths. Entertainment is provided

OHIO (Continued)

by costumed dancers (The Whetstone Dancers) and a German band, the Harmonaires. The Lederhouse Five stroll through the village playing German airs. In addition, there are art and publication exhibitions. Started in 1960.

★ 2245 ★
Columbus - OKTOBERFEST. Early October, 4 days, German Village, Ohio State Fairgrounds. Contact: Chamber of Commerce, 50 West Broad Street, Post Office Box 1527, Columbus, Ohio 43216.

The visitor can savor German beer and cooking, watch a parade, visit a craftshow, or enjoy the special entertainment at the fairgrounds.

★ 2246 ★
Dayton - A WORLD A'FAIR. Early June, annual, 3 days, Convention Center. Contact: International Festival, Dayton Council on World Affairs, 40 South Main Street, Room 520, Dayton, Ohio 45402.

Almost 40 nationalities present the best of their culture with displays of foods and crafts, dances, costumes and songs. Begun around 1974.

★ 2247 ★
Maumee - GERMAN-AMERICAN FESTIVAL. Late August, 3 days, Lucas Recreation Center. Contact: Lee Weber, Publicity Chairman, Seven Clubs of Toledo, 2614 Chestnut Street, Toledo, Ohio 43608.

The celebration is patterned after the Munich Octoberfest, with polka dancing, German music, gymnasts, German food, and exhibits of German crafts and handiwork.

★ 2248 ★
Sugarcreek - OHIO SWISS FESTIVAL. Late September or early October, annual, 2 days. Contact: Chamber of Commerce, Sugarcreek, Ohio 44681.

Offers a symphony of Swiss music, yodeling, dancing, and bright costumes. Features a parade, free entertainment, street dancing, and Swiss games such as steintossen (stone tossing) and schwingfest (wrestling). Tons of Swiss cheese from more than 20 plants and numerous other gourmet items may be purchased.

★ 2249 ★
Toledo - GREEK-AMERICAN FAMILY FESTIVAL. Early September, Church of the Holy Trinity. Con-

tact: Church of the Holy Trinity, 740 Superior Street, Toledo, Ohio 43604.

Authentic Greek dishes such as strudel, shishkebab and mousakas are prepared by the women of the church. Bread, olives and cheese are offered at the dakaliko, or gourmet shop, and gifts are sold at the agora or marketplace. Three orchestras provide live entertainment. Those wishing to learn the Greek dances can receive instruction. There is also a wine garden and game booths for the children.

★ 2250 ★
Toledo - HUNGARIAN WINE FESTIVAL. Early September (1st or 2nd weekend), annual, Saint Stephen's Church Hall. Contact: Jim Szegti, 209 Cherry Street, Toledo, Ohio 43608.

The festival is held by the Hungarian Club of Toledo and timed to coincide with a similar one in Hungary, celebrating the country's wine production (second only to France). Hungarian food and wine is offered to the visitors, including 25 different types of pastries. Gypsy music fills the air.

★ 2251 ★
Toledo - INDEPENDENCE DAY OF MEXICO. Mid September (around the 16th), annual, downtown Toledo. Contact: Guadalupi Center, 436 Segue Avenue, Toledo, Ohio 43609.

The festivities, sponsored by the Mexican-American Patriotic Committee, begin with a parade. Local dance groups play during the day, and cultural and folkloric dances traditionally performed in Mexico are illustrated. There are games and dances for children. Mexican foods, such as tacos and enchilladas, are featured. In the evening a band plays for dancing, and a queen is selected.

★ 2252 ★
Toledo - INTERNATIONAL FESTIVAL. Mid May, annual, 3 days, Toledo Sports Arena. Contact: International Festival, c/o International Institute, 2040 Scottwood Avenue, Toledo, Ohio 43620.

A celebration of diverse ethnic groups through traditional costumes, crafts, foods, songs, dances, and dramas. Centering on the theme, "A Mixture Called America", each community celebrates the role of their ethnic heritage in the development of the United States. Begun around 1959.

★ 2253 ★
Toledo - SYRIAN-LEBANESE-AMERICAN FAMILY

Ethnic Events

OHIO (Continued)

FESTIVAL. Late September, annual. Contact: Saint Elias Orthodox Church, 1312 Huron Street, Toledo, Ohio 43604.

In addition to the usual ethnic fare - food, music, booths - a huge folk dance or "hafli" climaxes each evening's festivities. Guests can sample Syrian bread, grape leaves, shishkebab, and pastries, and then purchase the recipes compiled in a cookbook. To show the Arab way of life, a Toledo artist paints scenes of the Middle Eastern culture. An array of imports such as Syrian drums, water pipes, guitars, and "worry beads", are available for purchase. The top prize in a raffle is a free trip to one of five destinations, including Lebanon and Syria, of course.

★ 2254 ★
Waynesville - OHIO SAUERKRAUT FESTIVAL. Mid October, annual, 2 days. Contact: Chamber of Commerce, 581 North Street, Post Office Box 588, Waynesville, Ohio 45068.

A German folk-festival with German delicacies, including of course, sauerkraut. There is continuous entertainment, folk music and dancing. Craftsmen display and demonstrate, and the village is full of antique shops to browse in. There is a large antique car display.

OKLAHOMA

★ 2255 ★
McAlester - ITALIAN FESTIVAL. Late September, annual, 1 day. Contact: Chamber of Commerce, Post Office Box 759, McAlester, Oklahoma 74501.

Italian-Americans, many of them descendents of the coal miners who migrated to this region in the 1880's, celebrate their heritage. The events include Italian cooking, folk music, dances, and costumes.

★ 2256 ★
Prague - KOLACHE FESTIVAL. Early May, annual, 1 day. Contact: Chamber of Commerce, Post Office Box 223, Prague, Oklahoma 74864.

In honor of the kolache roll, the inhabitants of the town put on Czech costumes and perform Czech dances, hold a parade, a rodeo, and a beauty contest.

★ 2257 ★
Yukon - CZECH FESTIVAL. Early October, annual, 1 day. Contact: Director, Czech Festival, Route 2,

Box 106, El Reno, Oklahoma 73036.

Events include strolling polka bands, traditional Czech dances. Ethnic delicacies including kolaches and kholbasy are served. There are also parades and a beauty contest.

OREGON

★ 2258 ★
Junction City - SCANDINAVIAN FESTIVAL. Early August, annual, 4 days. Contact: Scandinavian Festival Association, Post Office Box 5, Junction City, Oregon 97448.

Dancing, singing, feasting, and games celebrate the Scandinavian ancestry of many of the early settlers in the area. One day each honors the Swedish, Norwegian, Finnish, and Danish nationalities. Colorful pennants decorate the community, and street booths offer Scandinavian foods and wares. A viking ship on wheels navigates the streets.

★ 2259 ★
Mount Angel - OKTOBERFEST. Mid-late September, annual, 4 days. Contact: Oktoberfest Association, Mount Angel, Oregon 97362.

This festival combines a biergarten and German food with harvest displays, street dancing, art shows and a parade.

PENNSYLVANIA

★ 2260 ★
Ambridge - KUNSTFEST. Early June, annual, 2 days, Old Economy Village. Contact: Harmonic Associates, Incorporated, Court House, Beaver Falls, Pennsylvania 15009.

The village is a restoration of the original built by the German religious society, the Harmonists, believers in prayer and hard work. The festival features their day-to-day crafts: weaving, spinning, sewing, lace-making, shoemaking, cabinet making, doughnut baking, candle-making, and so forth.

★ 2261 ★
Ambridge - NATIONALITY DAYS. Mid May, annual, 3 days. Contact: Greater Ambridge Area Chamber of Commerce, 292 Fifth Street, Ambridge, Pennsylvania 15003.

Ethnic groups provide a variety of entertainment, food and exhibits. There is a large parade.

PENNSYLVANIA (Continued)

★ 2262 ★
Barnesville - BAVARIAN SUMMER FESTIVAL. Late
June-July, 17 days, Lakewood Park. Contact:
Kermit A. Deitrich, Rural Delivery 2, Kempton,
Pennsylvania 19529.

A variety of German bands provide continuous music
with exhibition dancing by the Schuhplattlers. Further entertainment is provided by bell-ringers and
Alpine horn blowers. German food and beer abundant.
Other activities include arts and crafts exhibitions
and demonstrations, horse pulling, soccer games,
animal nursery land, marionette shows, and water
skiing shows. For added authenticity and merriment,
the grounds are gaily decorated with maypoles, flower
boxes, heraldic shields and flags.

★ 2263 ★
Devon - DELCO SCOTTISH GAMES. Mid-June,
annual, Devon Horse Show Grounds. Contact:
Chamber of Commerce, Devon, Pennsylvania 19333.

Features bagpipe bands and competition in Scottish
sports such as tossing the caber, throwing the weight,
tossing the stone, and throwing the hammer.

★ 2264 ★
Doylestown - POLISH FESTIVAL. September, annual,
5-7 days (around 2 weekends), National Shrine of Our
Lady of Czestochowa, Iron Hill and Ferry Road.
Contact: Society of Shrine Volunteers, National
Shrine of Our Lady of Czestochowa, Iron Hill and
Ferry Road, Doylestown, Pennsylvania 18901.

Folk dances, foods and delicacies, cultural exhibits,
games, rides, and polka bands, all contributing to
the flavor of the festival and county fair.

★ 2265 ★
East Greenville - GOSCHENHOPPEN FOLK FESTIVAL.
Mid August, annual, 3 days. Contact: Montgomery
County Convention and Visitors Bureau, One
Montgomery Plaza, Suite 207, Norristown, Pennsyl-
vania 19401.

Crafts, foods, and presentations depicting the lifestyle
of the Pennsylvania Dutch.

★ 2266 ★
Evanstown - SLOVENIAN DAYS. Early September,
annual, 3 days, Westmoreland County Federation
Park. Contact: Westmoreland County Bicentennial
Association, Incorporated, Court House, Greensburg,

Pennsylvania 15601.

Banquet, talent show, coronation of a queen, picnic,
and ethnic activities highlight the festival events.

★ 2267 ★
Hershey - PENNSYLVANIA DUTCH DAYS. Late
July, annual, 6 days, Hershey Park Arena. Contact:
Roger Connor, Hershey Estates, Hershey, Pennsylvania
17033.

Lectures and demonstrations of the arts, crafts, costumes and folklore of the Pennsylvania Dutch farmers
who settled the area. Displays of handstitched items.
Entertainment includes programs in both English and
dialect, folk dancers and singers, plowing contests,
pony show, auction sale, and demonstrations of farming equipment. Samples of Pennsylvania Dutch
cooking are on hand.

★ 2268 ★
Hollidaysburg - ETHNIC DAYS. Mid June, annual,
6 days, throughout Blair County. Contact: Blair
County Commission, Court House Annex Two, Hollidaysburg, Pennsylvania 16648.

Various ethnic groups provide dancers, musicians,
and singers to be rotated over the county.

★ 2269 ★
Kempton - PENNSYLVANIA DUTCH FARM FESTIVAL.
Early September, annual, 2 days, Farm Museum.
Contact: Don Conover, 329 East Fifth Street, New
York, New York 10003.

Demonstrations by the Amish and Mennonites of their
traditional farm crafts, including the exhibition of
old, rare farm tools still in working order. The
savory home cooked foods for which they are famous
are served, including funnel cakes, scrapple, etc.
Children can take a ride on an old fashioned hay
wagon. Begun around 1965.

★ 2270 ★
Kutztown - PENNSYLVANIA DUTCH KUTZTOWN
FOLK FESTIVAL. Late June-early July, annual,
8 days. Contact: Peg Zecher, 717 Swarthmore
Avenue, Swarthmore, Pennsylvania 17081.

The purpose of the festival is to display and demonstrate the culture of the Pennsylvania Dutch. There
are abundant displays of their arts and crafts, both
exhibits and demonstrations, including quilting, tatting,
hex sign painting, sheep shearing, food preserving,
etc. Amish style cooking is served. Further

PENNSYLVANIA (Continued)

insights are gained through movies, an Amish pageant, a barn raising, a 'plain-Dutch wedding', wagon rides, and a hanging. In addition, there are hoedowning contests, balloon ascensions, children's games, animals, a country auction, and various other activities. Begun in 1950.

★ 2271 ★
Lancaster - DUTCH FAMILY FESTIVAL. Late June-late August, 2 months, Route 30, 6 miles east of Lancaster. Contact: Chamber of Commerce, 300 West Orange Street, Lancaster, Pennsylvania 17604.

Exhibitions and demonstrations offered by Amish and Mennonite craftspeople. The people offer a Plain People Pageant.

★ 2272 ★
Lenhart - PENNSYLVANIA DUTCH FOLK FESTIVAL. Late July (3rd weekend), annual, 1 weekend. Contact: Chamber of Commerce, Hamburg, Pennsylvania 19526.

The celebration includes bands, folksongs, costumes, arts and crafts demonstrations and exhibitions, and Pennsylvania Dutch foods.

★ 2273 ★
Ligonier - LIGONIER HIGHLAND GAMES. Mid September, annual, 1 day, Idlewild Park (U.S. 30). Contact: Ligonier Highland Games, 1208 24th Avenue, Altoona, Pennsylvania 16601.

Present day Scots and Scottish descendants meet in a colorful pageant of dancing. Flipping of a massive log the Scots call the caber; others team up in five-man tug of war. Demonstrations of sheep dogs uncanny ability to move and control Highland sheep. Pipe bands parade twice. Awards ceremony.

★ 2274 ★
Macungie - DAS AWKSCHT FESCHT. August or October, annual, 2 days, Macungie Memorial Park. Contact: Allentown-Lehigh County Chamber of Commerce, Fifth and Walnut Streets, Allentown, Pennsylvania 18105.

A rural festival celebrating the arts, crafts, customs and foods which date as far back as 200 years. In addition, there are antique, classic and sport car shows; a horse show; and an antique car flea market. Comedy and musical entertainment are scheduled for the outdoor theater. Begun in 1964.

★ 2275 ★
Media - GREEK FESTIVAL. Late July, annual, 2 days, Rose Tree County Park. Contact: Delaware County Commission, Toal Building, Second and Orange Streets, Media, Pennsylvania 19063.

Greek festival with food, dancing, games and festivities.

★ 2276 ★
Nanticoke - AMERICAN-UKRAINIAN FESTIVAL. Late August or early September, annual, 3 days, Holy Transfiguration Church. Contact: Holy Transfiguration Church, 240 Center Street, Nanticoke, Pennsylvania 18634.

Entertainment by Ukrainian and polka bands, open air concerts of traditional Ukrainian folk songs, and Kolomezka performed by groups in authentic costumes of Eastern Europe. Offers bazaar games, prizes, and exhibits of Ukrainian arts and crafts, such as pysanka (colored eggs) and vyshyzanka (shawls). Features a variety of Ukrainian foods: karpopelanee platsky (potato pancakes), pyrohy, strutzla (Ukrainian twist bread), and also American type food.

★ 2277 ★
Philadelphia - CHINESE NEW YEAR. Late January-mid February, annual, Chinatown. Contact: Philadelphia Convention and Visitors Bureau, 1525 John F. Kennedy Boulevard, Philadelphia, Pennsylvania 19102.

The event features special programs including parades, fireworks, and fire dragons.

★ 2278 ★
Philadelphia - OLD SWEDE'S CHURCH FAIR. Early June, annual. Contact: Philadelphia Convention and Visitors Bureau, 1525 John F. Kennedy Boulevard, Philadelphia, Pennsylvania 19102.

Commemorates the Swedish settlements in the area. Held at the oldest church in the city. Features folk dances, Swedish foods, and pageantry.

★ 2279 ★
Pittsburgh - BLACK WEEK FESTIVAL. November, annual, 7 days, University of Pittsburgh. Contact: Black Action Society, University of Pittsburgh, Pittsburgh, Pennsylvania 15213.

Black Week is the largest educational, political and social event sponsored by the Black Action society, including input from the community as well as the

PENNSYLVANIA (Continued)

black organizations and departments on campus. The events include lectures, dramatic presentations, and performances by dance ensembles. Black Market Day features booths of jewelry, handicrafts, and food. There are also fashion shows, African storytellers, and an African Charity Ball with African attire. Begun in 1969.

★ 2280 ★
Reading - FESTIVAL OF NATIONS. Mid November, annual, 3 days, YMCA. Contact: Department of Commerce, Bureau of Travel Development, 431 South Office Building, Harrisburg, Pennsylvania 17120.

"Americans All". Foods and exhibits of all nations.

★ 2281 ★
Richfield - DUTCH DAYS FESTIVAL. Mid July, annual, 4 days. Contact: Russell Kratzer, Richfield, Pennsylvania 17086.

Country store, crafts, Penn-Dutch cooking, chicken barbeque, nightly entertainment, games, and parades.

★ 2282 ★
Somerset - POLISH DAYS. Late June, 1 day. Contact: Department of Commerce, Bureau of Travel Development, 431 South Office Building, Harrisburg, Pennsylvania 17120.

Ethnic celebration including Polish foods, costumes, and folk dances.

★ 2283 ★
Uniontown - POLISH FESTIVAL DAYS. Mid August, annual, 2 days, Penn State, Fayette Campus. Contact: Department of Commerce, Bureau of Travel Development, 431 South Office Building, Harrisburg, Pennsylvania 17120.

A celebration of the Polish heritage with food, entertainment, crafts, etc.

RHODE ISLAND

★ 2284 ★
Cranston - MIDSUMMER FESTIVAL (MIDSOMMAR FEST). Mid June (3rd Saturday), annual, 1 day, Scandinavian Home for the Aged. Contact: Board of Directors and Auxiliary, Scandinavian Home for the Aged, 1811 Broad Street, Cranston, Rhode Island 02910.

The area is decorated with Swedish motifs. The midsummer pole is raised amidst Swedish folk dancing, music and song. Begun in early 1930's.

★ 2285 ★
Jamestown - OKTOBERFEST. Mid October, 1 day, Fort Getty. Contact: Rhode Island Department of Economic Development, Tourist Promotion Division, One Weybosset Hill, Providence, Rhode Island 02903.

German bands and dancing are included in the festive events.

★ 2286 ★
Pawtucket - MID-EAST FESTIVAL. Early August, annual, 2 days, Narragansett Park. Contact: Rhode Island Department of Economic Development, Tourist Promotion Division, One Weybosset Hill, Providence, Rhode Island 02903.

An Arabic theme is carried out in the festival through the music, dancing and food.

★ 2287 ★
Providence - INTERNATIONAL FAIR. April-May, annual, 2 days, Meehan Auditorium. Contact: International House of Rhode Island, Incorporated, Eight Stimson Avenue, Providence, Rhode Island 02906.

Volunteers from the International House (an organization dedicated to "bringing together the international community and Americans in a spirit of cooperation and goodwill") build and run booths housing the cuisine and artifacts of many lands. The volunteers wear national costumes and present demonstrations representative of the culture of the country. Continuous international entertainment is provided by different ethnic groups, such as Scottish bagpipers, Korean chorale groups, African dance troupes, Portuguese folk singers, and German bands. Begun around 1971.

SOUTH CAROLINA

★ 2288 ★
Charleston - BLACK EMPHASIS FESTIVAL. January-February (date may vary), 1 month. Contact: Mr. James B. Bagwell, Jr., 313 Pitt Street, Mount Pleasant, South Carolina 29464.

Part of Founders' Festivals, a continuing series of month-long festivals centering on the ethnic groups which were instrumental in the founding and growth of Charleston. Special exhibits in the Gibbes Art Gallery and Charleston Museum, special ethnic foods

Ethnic Events

SOUTH CAROLINA (Continued)

offered in local restaurants, and two or three major events.

★ 2289 ★
Charleston - ENGLISH EMPHASIS FESTIVAL. November, annual, 1 month. Contact: Mr. James B. Bagwell, Jr., 313 Pitt Street, Mount Pleasant, South Carolina 29464.

Part of the Founders' Festivals, a continuing series of month-long festivals centering on the ethnic groups which were instrumental in the founding and growth of Charleston. Special exhibits in the Gibbes Art Gallery and Charleston Museum, special ethnic foods in local restaurants, and two or three major events. (Date may vary.)

★ 2290 ★
Charleston - FOUNDERS' FESTIVAL. January-November, annual. Contact: Mr. James B. Bagwell, Jr., 313 Pitt Street, Mount Pleasant, South Carolina 29464.

This is a continuing series of month-long festivals centering on the ethnic groups which were instrumental in the founding and growth of Charleston: Black Emphasis Festival, French Emphasis Festival, Irish Emphasis Festival, Jewish Emphasis Festival, Greek Emphasis Festival, Scottish Emphasis Festival, German Emphasis Festival, and English Emphasis Festival.

★ 2291 ★
Charleston - FRENCH EMPHASIS FESTIVAL. February-March, 1 month. Contact: Mr. James B. Bagwell, Jr., 313 Pitt Street, Mount Pleasant, South Carolina 29464.

Part of Founders' Festivals, a continuing series of month-long festivals centering on the ethnic groups which were instrumental in the founding and growth of Charleston. Special exhibits in the Gibbes Art Gallery and Charleston Museum, special ethnic foods offered in local restaurants, and two or three major events. (Date may vary.)

★ 2292 ★
Charleston - GERMAN EMPHASIS FESTIVAL (GERMAN HERITAGE FESTIVAL). October, annual, 1 month. Contact: Mr. James B. Bagwell, Jr., 313 Pitt Street, Mount Pleasant, South Carolina 29464.

Part of the Founders' Festivals, a continuing series of month-long festivals centering on the ethnic groups

which were instrumental in the founding and growth of Charleston. Special exhibits in the Gibbes Art Gallery and Charleston Museum, special ethnic food in local restaurants and two or three major events. (Date may vary.)

★ 2293 ★
Charleston - GREEK EMPHASIS FESTIVAL (GREEK HERITAGE FESTIVAL). May, 1 month. Contact: Mr. James B. Bagwell, Jr., 313 Pitt Street, Mount Pleasant, South Carolina 29464.

Part of Founders' Festivals, a continuing series of month-long festivals centering on the ethnic groups which were instrumental in the founding and growth of Charleston. Special exhibits in the Gibbes Art Gallery and Charleston Museum, special ethnic foods offered in local restaurants, and two or three major events.

★ 2294 ★
Charleston - GREEK SPRING FESTIVAL. May, 1 day, Middleton Place. Contact: Alan Powell, Middleton Place Gardens and Plantation Stableyards, Route 4, Charleston, South Carolina 29407.

The Greek community welcomes spring, first with a Greek Orthodox church service, and then with bazoukia music and folk dancing for both experts and novices. Greek specialties such as baklava, feta cheese and stuffed grape leaves are on hand for enjoyment.

★ 2295 ★
Charleston - IRISH EMPHASIS FESTIVAL. March-April, 1 month. Contact: Mr. James B. Bagwell, Jr., 313 Pitt Street, Mount Pleasant, South Carolina 29464.

Part of the Founders' Festivals, a continuing series of month-long festivals centering on the ethnic groups which were instrumental in the founding and growth of Charleston. Special exhibits in the Gibbes Art Gallery and Charleston Museum, special ethnic foods offered in local restaurants, and two or three major events. (Date may vary.)

★ 2296 ★
Charleston - JEWISH EMPHASIS FESTIVAL. April, 1 month. Contact: Mr. James B. Bagwell, Jr., 313 Pitt Street, Mount Pleasant, South Carolina 29464.

Part of the Founders' Festivals, a continuing series of month-long festivals centering on ethnic groups which were instrumental in the founding and growth of Charleston. Special exhibits in the Gibbes Art

SOUTH CAROLINA (Continued)

Gallery and Charleston Museum, special ethnic foods offered in local restaurants, and two or three major events. (Date can vary.)

★ 2297 ★
Charleston - SCOTTISH EMPHASIS FESTIVAL (SCOTTISH HERITAGE FESTIVAL). September, annual, 1 month. Contact: Mr. James B. Bagwell, Jr., 313 Pitt Street, Mount Pleasant, South Carolina 29464.

Part of Founders' Festivals, a continuing series of month-long festivals centering on the ethnic groups which were instrumental in the founding and growth of Charleston. Special exhibits in the Gibbes Art Gallery and Charleston Museum, special ethnic foods in local restaurants, and two or three major events. (Date may vary.)

★ 2298 ★
Charleston - SCOTTISH GAMES AND HIGHLAND GATHERING. Late September, annual, Middleton Place. Contact: Alan Powell, Middleton Place, Route 4, Charleston, South Carolina 29407.

Medieval games of strength and agility highlight Scotland's day at Middleton Place. Features kilted bagpipers, highland dancing, and fair booths with tartans and kilts, meat pies and shortbread.

★ 2299 ★
Myrtle Beach - CANADIAN-AMERICAN DAYS. Mid March, annual, 9 days. Contact: Greater Myrtle Beach Chamber of Commerce, Post Office Box 1326, Myrtle Beach, South Carolina 29577.

Honors Canadian visitors with square dances, parades, tours of historic sites, sand-castle building contests, fishing tourney, receptions, amusement parks, kids' day, and golfing. At roughly the same time, there is a Canadian-American Folk Festival in Myrtle Beach. This consists of concerts, workshops, lore, and arts and crafts displays by Canadian and American artists. It lasts for 1 day. Started in 1962.

SOUTH DAKOTA

★ 2300 ★
Corsica - DUTCH SMORGASBORD AN KLOMPEN DANCE. May (22nd). Contact: Mrs. Margaret Mulder, Corsica, South Dakota 57328.

Events include a bountiful homecooked meal served in smorgasbord style and Klompen (wooden shoe) dances.

★ 2301 ★
Freeman - SCHMECKFEST. March or April, annual, 3 days, Freeman Junior College. Contact: Schmeckfest, Freeman, South Dakota 57029.

Features the cooking of the Mennonites, the Hutterites, and the Low Germans. There is also a series of demonstrations of pioneer life, including sausage making, noodle-making, basket weaving, rug braiding, quilting, etc. There is a student theater production. Begun around 1962.

★ 2302 ★
Tabor - CZECH DAYS FESTIVAL. Mid June, annual, 2 days. Contact: Czech Days, Box 128, Tabor, South Dakota 57063.

A gala celebration in honor of the town's Czecho-slavakian heritage. Features singing, dancing, oom-pa-pa bands, parades, colorful costumes and good food. Spontaneous street dancing, yummy kolaches (fruit filled pastries), and a queen contest add to the festivities. Begun around 1949.

★ 2303 ★
Viborg - DANISH DAYS CELEBRATION. Early June (5th), annual, 2 days. Contact: Division of Tourism, State Office Building 2, Pierre, South Dakota 57501.

Celebration of Denmark's Independence Day and the Danish heritage of the local people. Events include ethnic singing, dancing and food.

TENNESSEE

★ 2304 ★
Erin - WEARIN' O' THE GREEN. Mid March, (weekend closest to March 17), annual, City Hall. Contact: City Hall, Post Office Box 270, Erin, Tennessee 37061.

Celebrates the predominantly Irish-American heritage of the region. The festivities include beauty contests, parades, bicycle rodeo, and an Irish Ball.

TEXAS

★ 2305 ★
Andrews - SPANISH FIESTA. May, annual, 1 day. Contact: Mr. Lloyd L. Longley, Jr., Chamber of

Ethnic Events

TEXAS (Continued)

Commerce, 204 North East First Street, Andrews, Texas 79714.

A citywide celebration with a Spanish influence.

★ 2306 ★
Bay City - NEGRO LIFE AND ACHIEVEMENT WEEK. Late February, 7 days. Contact: Chamber of Commerce, Post Office Box 768, Bay City, Texas 77414.

Historical and biographical exhibits are the highlights of this festival. There is entertainment.

★ 2307 ★
Boerne - BERGES FEST. Mid June, annual, 2 days. Contact: Chamber of Commerce, Post Office Box 429, Boerne, Texas 78006.

This "Feast of the Hills" celebrates the German heritage of Boerne, dating back to the original settlers. Activities include German costumes, bands, and foods; a queen coronation; a jumping frog contest; turtle races; games and a parade.

★ 2308 ★
Brenham - MAIFEST. Mid May, annual, 2 days. Contact: Chamber of Commerce, Post Office Box 810, Brenham, Texas 77833.

Traditional German Volksfest. Entire town joins in festivities; dances, feasts, and parades. Dates from 1874.

★ 2309 ★
Brownsville - CHARRO DAYS. March, annual, 4 days (beginning Thursday, preceding Ash Wednesday). Contact: Chamber of Commerce, 1600 East Elizabeth Street, Post Office Box 752, Brownsville, Texas 78520.

Costume fiesta, held for nearly third of a century, combines charm and culture of this two-nation area. Swirling glittering skirts of China Poblanas (national costume of Mexico) contrast with dashing mustachioed Mexican riders or "charros". Fiesta attracts some 350,000 visitors.

★ 2310 ★
Castroville - SAINT LOUIS DAY CELEBRATION. August, annual, Koenig Park on the banks of Medina River. Contact: Castroville Chamber of Commerce, Post Office Box 572, Castroville, Texas 78009; or Father Larry Steubben, Castroville, Texas 78009.

Descendants of Alsatian pioneers gather for annual homecoming. The festival atmosphere is brightened by traditional Alsace-style costumes, dances and rich foods of European heritage. A dance and tours of pioneer homes are other features. There is continuous entertainment throughout the day. Begun in 1889.

★ 2311 ★
Corpus Christi - DIEZ Y SEIS CELEBRATION. Mid September, annual. Contact: Chamber of Commerce, 1201 North Shoreline Boulevard, Post Office Box 640, Corpus Christi, Texas 78403.

Observance of Mexican Independence Day with festival events.

★ 2312 ★
Del Rio - FIESTA DE AMISTAD. October, annual, 5 days. Contact: Chamber of Commerce, 405 East Gibbs, Post Office Box 1388, Del Rio, Texas 78840.

When Del Rio and Ciudad Acuna, two border cities, combine to celebrate international friendship (amistad). Features are Miss Amistad beauty pageant, Abrazo (clasp of friendship) on International Bridge, huge Good Neighbor parade (Gran Desfile del Buen Vicino), fly-in breakfast, golf and bowling tournaments, fireworks, dances and chariade (rodeo) in Ciudad Acuna bull ring.

★ 2313 ★
Eagle Pass - GEORGE WASHINGTON INTERNATIONAL FIESTA (INTERNATIONAL FRIENDSHIP FESTIVAL). February or March, annual, 3 days. Contact: Chamber of Commerce, 400 Garrison Street, Post Office Box 1188, Eagle Pass, Texas 78852.

Piedras Negras, Mexico, joins with Eagle Pass for Latin-accented balls, pagenatry and parades. The queen coronation highlights the festival atmosphere.

★ 2314 ★
El Paso - BORDER FOLK FESTIVAL (FIESTA CHAMIZAL). Early October, annual, 3-6 days, Chamizal National Memorial. Contact: Carlos Chavez, Chamizal National Memorial, 620 Southwest National Bank Building, El Paso, Texas 79901.

The programs are "Dedicated to the peaceful coexistence and cultural exchange of the Mexican and American people". Featured are the best traditional performers of the cultures of the area including Apache, Cajun, Mexican, and Texas. Music includes jazz, country-western, blues, marimba, etc. Workshops, concerts, and informal sessions; all programs are introduced in

TEXAS (Continued)

both Spanish and English.   Crafts and children's shows.   Begun in 1973.

★ 2315 ★
El Paso - FIESTA DE LAS FLORES.   Late August or early September (Saturday and Sunday preceding Labor Day), annual, 2 days, Washington Park.   Contact: El Paso Chamber of Commerce, Ten Civic Center Plaza, El Paso, Texas 79944; or Carlos Villesca, Box 1469, El Paso, Texas 79948.

Promotes friendship and understanding between El Paso and Mexico.   Opens with a parade through downtown El Paso.   The Kermess Fair treats visitors to regional Mexican dances, singing, and mariachi music.   Booths offer Mexican cuisine, games, handcrafts, and other attractions.   Started more than a decade ago.

★ 2316 ★
Ennis - NATIONAL POLKA FESTIVAL.   Early May, annual, 1 weekend.   Contact: Jack McKay, 109 North Main, Post Office Box 159, Ennis, Texas 75119.

Dedicated to enjoyment of polka music, rich food, and colorful Czech traditions.   Dozen or more bands provide polkas, local cooks privide country style klobase, dumplings and sauerkraut, barbeque, apple strudel and kolache.   Visitors come from throughout the nation.

★ 2317 ★
Fredericksburg - A NIGHT IN OLD FREDERICKSBURG.   Late July, annual, 1 weekend.   Contact: Chamber of Commerce, Post Office Box 506, Fredericksburg, Texas 78624.

Features old world traditions with music, food, and colorful costumes.

★ 2318 ★
Goliad - FIESTA ZARAGOZA.   May, annual. Contact: Lurlene Urban, Post Office Box 606, Goliad, Texas 77963.

Honors the Mexican hero, General Ignacio Zaragoza, born in Goliad.   His defeat of the French army is celebrated throughout Mexico and on several Texas border cities.   Features the Charreada Rodeo, street dances, live entertainment, and an arts and crafts show.

★ 2319 ★
Houston - FIESTAS PATRIAS.   September, annual, week-long.   Contact: Johnny Mata, 3326 Canal, Houston, Texas 77003.

A Mexican-American festival featuring a beauty pageant, parade, ball, and other special events.

★ 2320 ★
Houston - GREEK FESTIVAL.   Mid October, annual, Greek Orthodox Cathedral (3511 Yoakum Boulevard).   Contact: S. Paul Voinis, Post Office Box 13089, Houston, Texas 77019.

The festival features authentic Greek foods and pastries.   An agora or marketplace offers displays of imported foods and wines.   In addition, there are novelties, antique brass and copperware, jewelry, records, books, and pottery.   Greek dances and music are performed, travel films and literature are offered, and icons are on display.   Tours of the church are given.   Begun in 1967.

★ 2321 ★
Houston - SCANDINAVIAN CLUB OF HOUSTON'S SPRING FESTIVAL.   Late April, annual.   Contact: Einar Beckman, 2353 Firnat, Houston, Texas 77016.

Features Scandinavian food, dances, music, and products to promote the culture and traditions of Scandinavia.

★ 2322 ★
Laredo - GEORGE WASHINGTON'S BIRTHDAY CELEBRATION.   February, annual, 1 day.   Contact: Laredo Chamber of Commerce, Laredo, Texas 78040.

The festival is held in conjunction with Nueva Laredo, Mexico, to honor the United States' first president and to invoke Mexican-American friendship.   Events include an international fiesta, stock shows, bull fights, sports events, dances and a spectacular show featuring Mexico's top entertainers.

★ 2323 ★
Nederland - HERITAGE FESTIVAL.   March, annual, 5 days.   Contact: Chamber of Commerce, Post Office Box 891, Nederland, Texas 77627.

A salute to the Dutch heritage of the community with a queen contest, carnival, flea market, arts and crafts exhibit.

Ethnic Events

TEXAS (Continued)

★ 2324 ★
New Braunfels - CZECH FEST.   Early June,
annual, 2 days.   Contact: Chamber of Commerce,
390 South Sequin, Post Office Box 180, New
Braunfels, Texas 78130.

The celebration includes ethnic costumes, folk dancing, Czech cuisine, and horse racing.

★ 2325 ★
New Braunfels - WURSTFEST (SAUSAGE FESTIVAL).
Early November, annual, 10 days.   Contact:
Chamber of Commerce, 390 South Sequin, Post Office
Box 180, New Braunfels, Texas 78130.

Rich in German heritage accented with plenty of
polka music and gemuetlichkeit (good fellowship).
Features singing societies, traditional German bands,
dancing groups, and sausages of every description.
Sausage king and queen are crowned; a "sausage"
dog show with dachshunds; a sausage golf tourney;
and oom-pah music, all in honor of the sausage,
for which the town is known.

★ 2326 ★
Port Arthur - MEXICAN INDEPENDENCE DAY
(DIEZ Y SEIS).   September, annual.   Contact:
Greater Port Arthur Chamber of Commerce, Post
Office Box 460, Port Arthur, Texas 77640.

In honor of the Mexican Independence Day, the
fiesta includes dancers and street dancing, mariachi
groups, a Children's Parade of Costumes, "Little
Bullfights" and Mexican food.

★ 2327 ★
Port Arthur - TEXAS-LOUISIANA CAJUN FESTIVAL.
May, annual.   Contact: Greater Port Arthur
Chamber of Commerce, Post Office Box 460, Port
Arthur, Texas 77640.

An ethnic celebration including the Monsieur and
Madam Cajun contest, with a king and queen coronation.   A cooking contest featuring the renowned
creole cooking and French and rock music.   Additional activities include a dune buggy parade, accordion contest, and baseball tournaments.

★ 2328 ★
Salado - GATHERING OF SCOTTISH CLANS OF
TEXAS.   Early November (around the 11th), annual,
1 weekend.   Contact: Chamber of Commerce, Box
81, Salado, Texas 76571.

Attracts some 2,000 people; accented by skirl of
bagpipes and colorful tartan banners.

★ 2329 ★
San Antonio - FIESTA NOCHE DEL RIO.   Early
June to late August, annual, every Tuesday, Friday,
and Saturday evening, Arneson River Theater at La
Villita.   Contact: Chamber of Commerce, Post
Office Box 1628, San Antonio, Texas 78296.

Colorful two-hour shows of authentic Spanish and
Mexican dances, music and songs.   The Arneson
River Theater is open air.

★ 2330 ★
San Antonio - GREEK FUNSTIVAL.   October.
Contact: Saint Sophia Greek Orthodox Church,
2504 South Saint Mary's Street, San Antonio, Texas
78210.

The festival salutes the heritage of the Greeks.

★ 2331 ★
San Antonio - MEXICAN-AMERICAN FRIENDSHIP
WEEK.   Mid September (around the 16th), annual.
Contact: Chamber of Commerce, Post Office Box
1628, San Antonio, Texas 78296.

In honor of Mexican Independence Day.   Includes
Diez y Seis Fiesta and Parade.

★ 2332 ★
San Elizario - FIESTA OF SAN ISIDRO.   Mid May,
annual.   Contact: San Elizario Community Association and the Church Council, San Elizario, Texas
79849.

The San Isidro procession through the community
follows a solemn high mass celebrated in the San
Elizario Mission.   This colorful El Paso County
festival features Spanish music, food and drink,
booths, and games.   The Billy the Kid Pageant,
telling of the Kid's escape from jail, is staged.

★ 2333 ★
Schulenberg - FESTIVAL.   August, annual.   Contact: Bill Klesel, Schulenberg, Tedas 78956.

In honor of their German heritage, local residents
hold a parade, barbeque, horse show, biergarten
and art show.

TEXAS (Continued)

★ 2334 ★
Shamrock - SAINT PATRICKS CELEBRATION. March, annual. Contact: Chamber of Commerce, Post Office Box 588, Shamrock, Texas 79079.

The celebration includes a competition for the title of "Miss Irish Rose" and floats decorated with real shamrocks.

★ 2335 ★
West - SAINT MARY'S ANNUAL HOMECOMING FESTIVAL. June. Contact: Reverend George Doskocil, Church of the Assumption, West, Texas 76691.

A church festival which celebrates the Czech tradition with ethnic foods, arts and crafts, auction, and games.

UTAH

★ 2336 ★
Price - INTERNATIONAL DAYS. Early July, annual, 1 day. Contact: Carbon County Chamber of Commerce, Municipal Building, Box 764, Price, Utah 84501.

An ethnic festival featuring arts, crafts, and foods.

★ 2337 ★
Salt Lake City - OBON FESTIVAL. Mid July, annual. Contact: Buddhist Church, 211 West First Street South, Salt Lake City, Utah 84101.

Events include street dancing and Japanese folk dances.

★ 2338 ★
Snowbird - OKTOBERFEST. Early September (Labor Day weekend), annual, Snowbird Plaza. Contact: Utah Travel Council, Council Hall, Capitol Hill, Salt Lake City, Utah 84114.

The event features German specialties and entertainment. Begun in 1974.

VIRGINIA

★ 2339 ★
Alexandria - SCOTTISH CHRISTMAS WALK IN HISTORIC ALEXANDRIA. Early December, annual, 3 days. Contact: YWCA, 602 Cameron Street, Alexandria, Virginia 22314.

Celebrated with a parade of bagpipe bands, Scottish dances, costumes, and food specialities.

★ 2340 ★
Alexandria - VIRGINIA SCOTTISH GAMES AND GATHERING OF THE CLANS. Late July, annual, 1 day, Episcopal High School stadium and fields. Contact: Alexandria Tourist Council, 221 King Street, Alexandria, Virginia 22314.

Offers competitive events for athletes, bagpipers, highland dancers and Scottish fiddlers from the United States and Canada. Events include a band parade and awards ceremony. Begun in 1974.

★ 2341 ★
Charlottesville - MERRIE OLD ENGLAND CHRISTMAS CELEBRATION. Late December (Christmas week), annual. Contact: Boar's Head Inn, Ednam Forest, Charlottesville, Virginia 22903.

A medieval celebration featuring costumed performers, ancient carols and madrigals, musical tumblers, jugglers, a conjurer, court dancers, mummers, musicians with medieval instruments, fireworks, and a bonfire.

★ 2342 ★
Reston - RESTON BLACK ARTS FESTIVAL. Early September (Labor Day weekend), annual, Hunters Woods Village Center Atrium. Contact: Reston Black Focus, Incorporated, Post Office Box 793, Reston, Virginia 22091.

This festival is sponsored by the Reston Black Focus as an opportunity to show Black life styles and Black culture as part of the Reston community. It features arts and crafts, an auction, and entertainment by musical and theater groups. Begun in 1969.

WASHINGTON

★ 2343 ★
Gig Harbor - MIDSOMMERFEST. June (3rd Sunday), annual, 1 day, Scandia Gaard. Contact: Harold M. Anderson, Route 3, Box 3060, Gig Harbor, Washington 98335; or Gordon E. Tracie, Post Office Box 5657, University Station, Seattle, Washington 98105.

An authentic Scandinavian celebration in old country style. Norwegian, Swedish, Finnish, and Danish descendants perform novelty dances, hear fiddlers play sprightly ethnic tunes, and watch the raising of the traditional fir pole decked with greens. Nordic food specialties abound. Begun around 1959.

Ethnic Events

WASHINGTON (Continued)

★ 2344 ★
Kelso - HILANDER SUMMER FESTIVAL.   Early July
(2nd weekend), annual, 2 days.   Contact: Kelso
Chamber of Commerce, Post Office Box 58, 1407
Allen Street, Kelso, Washington 98626.

A festival honoring the sister city of Kelso, Scotland.
Activities include a parade, a jeep play day of various
racing events, and the Kon Tiki raft race down the
Cowlitz River.   The Tartan Ball is held Saturday
night.   Sunday events include hydroboat racing and
water ski flying.   Started in 1972.

★ 2345 ★
Leavenworth - CHRISTMAS LIGHTING CEREMONY.
December (1st weekend), annual, Bavarian style
village.   Contact: Chamber of Commerce, Leavenworth, Washington 98826.

A Bavarian style village is decorated and lighted for
Christmas.   The Edelweiss Dancers give performances,
as do several choirs and choruses.   There are snowmobile rides and dog sled demonstrations.   Started
in 1969.

★ 2346 ★
Odessa - DEUTSCHES FEST.   September (3rd weekend), annual.   Contact: Odessa Chamber of Commerce, Nine East First Avenue, Odessa, Washington
99159.

German food and beer is sold in booths, there are
German bands, dancing, and entertainment, and
the participants wear German costumes.   In addition,
there is a German church service, a football game,
and German movies.

★ 2347 ★
Poulsbo - VIKING FEST.   May (weekend closest
to the 17th).   Contact: Jim Hoke, Post Office
Box 56, Poulsbo, Washington 98370.

A Norwegian Independence Day celebration (Syttende
Mai) featuring folk dancing and a smorgasbord.   A
regional arts and crafts show is held.

★ 2348 ★
Seattle - CHRISTMAS AROUND THE WORLD.
December.   Contact: Seattle Chamber of Commerce,
215 Columbia Street, Seattle, Washington 98104.

The festival was begun by the Museum of History and
Industry in Seattle to provide for foreign students

living in the area a holiday celebration.   Now
over eighteen separate groups participate in the event,
each one decorating a Christmas tree according to the
customs of his country.   Native costumes are worn
and ethnic food is served.

WISCONSIN

★ 2349 ★
LaCrosse - OKTOBERFEST U.S.A.   Early October.
Contact: Greater LaCrosse Chamber of Commerce,
710 Main Street, Post Office Box 842, LaCrosse,
Wisconsin 54601; or Managing Director, 224 South
Seventh Street, Box 1063, LaCrosse, Wisconsin 54601.

The festivities include a Festmasters Ball which opens
the celebration.   At this time the Festmaster is
chosen.   In addition, there is a contest for Miss
Oktoberfest, Mrs. Oktoberfest, a costume contest,
German bands, a Maple Leaf parade and a Torchlight
parade.

★ 2350 ★
Milwaukee - FOLK FAIR.   Late November, annual,
3 days, Exhibits and Convention Center, Arena,
Auditorium.   Contact: Milwaukee Convention and
Visitors Bureau, 828 North Broadway, Milwaukee,
Wisconsin 53202.

Sponsored by the International Institute and the Pabst
Brewing Company, the fair pays tribute to the ethnic
heritages of the city.   Included are displays of
handcrafts, ethnic cooking, costumes, songs and
dances.   Begun in 1944.

★ 2351 ★
New Glarus - WILHELM TELL FESTIVAL AND
DRAMA.   Early September (Labor Day weekend),
annual, 3 days.   Contact: Director, Vacation and
Travel Development, Department of Natural Resources,
Wisconsin State Division of Tourism, Post Office Box
450, Madison, Wisconsin 53701.

Schiller's classic play about William Tell shooting
the apple from his son's head is performed on three
consecutive nights.   The Sunday evening performance
is in German.   Post-show entertainment features Swiss
folk dancers, yodelers, flag-throwers, and Alpine
horn blowers.   Begun around 1938.

★ 2352 ★
Stoughton - SYTTENDE MAI CELEBRATION.   Mid
May, annual.   Contact: Stoughton Chamber of
Commerce, 143 West Main Street, Stoughton,
Wisconsin 53589.

WISCONSIN (Continued)

A celebration of the independence of Norway, observed here because of the large number of Norwegian settlers who founded Stoughton.

WYOMING

★ 2353 ★
Evanston - CELEBRATION IN EVANSTON'S CHINATOWN.   Late January, 6 days.   Contact: Evanston Chamber of Commerce, Box 365, Evanston, Wyoming 82930.

Events include a tour, festival, exhibit, fair, ceremony, parade, and performance.

★ 2354 ★
Worland - OKTOBERFEST.   Late September, annual. Contact: Wyoming Travel Commission, 2320 Capitol Avenue, Cheyenne, Wyoming 82002; or Walt Jorgenson, 824 South 14th, Worland, Wyoming 82401.

In the Munich tradition, Worland celebrates with a parade with color guards, horse patrols, and marching units; at the Festhall, the participants sport Bavarian costumes and elaborate wagons are drawn by draft horses.   German food and beer are served to the accompaniment of bands.

CANADA - BRITISH COLUMBIA

★ 2355 ★
Nanaimo - SCOTTISH HIGHLAND GAMES.   Mid July, 1 day, Caledonia Park.   Contact: Tourist Information, 100 Cameron Road, Nanaimo, British Columbia, Canada.

Features highland competitions for field events and piping.   There is a special portion for children.

★ 2356 ★
Trail - TRAIL INTERNATIONAL FESTIVAL.   Mid May, 10 days, Pedestrian Mall and Memorial Center. Contact: Tourist Information, Trail Memorial Centre, Trail, British Columbia, Canada.

Entertainment and functions with an international flavor.

★ 2357 ★
Vernon - MULTI-CULTURAL FESTIVAL.   Mid May, 3 days.   Contact: The Department of Travel Industry, Travel Information Services, Parliament

Buildings, Victoria, British Columbia, Canada.

A gathering of various ethnic groups to celebrate their heritage.

CANADA - MANITOBA

★ 2358 ★
Dauphin - CANADA'S NATIONAL UKRAINIAN FESTIVAL.   Late July, annual, 4 days.   Contact: Mrs. Marion Warnock (Acting President), Canada's National Ukrainian Festival, Nine - Third Avenue Northwest, Dauphin, Manitoba R7N 1H7, Canada.

Colorful event features traditional food, customs, and culture of Canada's Ukrainian population.   Ukrainian entertainment, crafts, historical presentations, and music.   Also handicrafts demonstrations.

★ 2359 ★
La Broquerie - FETE FRANCO-MANITOBAINE. Late June, annual, 2 days.   Contact: M. Marcel Marin, Fete Franco-Manitobain, La Broquerie, Manitoba R0A 0W0, Canada.

Celebration of Saint John the Baptist Day.   Features French music, folk singing, fiddling contests, games, traditional foods such as tortiere and pea soup, and a fire dance.

★ 2360 ★
Selkirk - HIGHLAND GATHERING.   Early July, annual.   Contact: Mr. S. Davidson, President, Selkirk Highland Gatherings, Incorporated, Box 9600, Selkirk, Manitoba R1A 2B1, Canada.

Scottish celebration featuring highland dancing, piping, drumming and caber toss contests.   A highpoint is the mass concert at the end of the celebration when all the bands and dance groups gather together for a grand finale.

★ 2361 ★
Steinbach - PIONEER DAYS.   Early August, annual, 3-4 days, Mennonite Village Museum.   Contact: Steinbach Pioneer Days, Mennonite Village Museum, Steinbach, Manitoba R0A 2A0, Canada.

Celebrates the founding of the Mennonite settlement in 1874.   Features Mennonite pioneer skills and crafts: rope making, weaving, spinning, churning, bread making, etc.   Traditional Mennonite food is served.

Ethnic Events

CANADA - MANITOBA (Continued)

★ 2362 ★
Winnipeg - FESTIVAL DU VOYAGEUR. Mid
February, annual, 1 week, Saint Boniface (French
speaking community). Contact: M. Gerry Turenne,
Festival du Voyageur, 219 Provencher Boulevard,
Winnipeg, Manitoba R2H 3B5, Canada.

Features all the "joie de vivre" of the early voyageurs
with dances, entertainment, and special foods. The
Voyageur presides in period costume. There is free
pea soup, moccasin dances, casinos, a costume ball,
and a parade.

★ 2363 ★
Winnipeg - FESTIVAL OF NATIONS. July (Summer).
Contact: Director, Department of Tourism, Recreation
and Cultural Affairs, Tourist Branch, 801 Mall Centre,
491 Portage Avenue, Winnipeg, Manitoba R3B 2E7,
Canada.

Festival has representatives from several countries in
a cultural exchange of music, dance and fun.

★ 2364 ★
Winnipeg - OKTOBERFEST. Mid October, annual,
Winnipeg Arena. Contact: Director, Department
of Tourism, Recreation and Cultural Affairs, Tourist
Branch, 801 Mall Centre, 491 Portage Avenue,
Winnipeg, Manitoba R3B 2E7, Canada.

Bavarian beer festival featuring German bands, food,
and dancing for the general public.

CANADA - NEW BRUNSWICK

★ 2365 ★
Caraquet - ACADIAN FESTIVAL (FESTIVAL ACADIAN
DE CARAQUET). Early August, annual, 10 days.
Contact: Special Events Co-ordinator, Tourism New
Brunswick, Post Office Box 12345, Fredericton,
New Brunswick, Canada.

The festival has a strong Acadian flavor. A boy
and a girl are chosen to represent the legendary
Gabriel and Evangeline, figures from the Dispersion,
and are honored throughout the festival. At the
Evangeline and Gabriel Ball, hundreds of dancers
appear in traditional Acadian costumes. Acadian
singers perform. The Blessing of the Fleet, dating
back to at least 1757, is performed, and a wreath
is thrown into the water to honor the memory of the
fishermen who have died at sea. There is entertainment on the wharf and a Fishermen's Ball. Other
events include a horse-hauling contest, a horseshoe

tournament, automobile rally, and tuna fishing contest. Begun in 1963.

CANADA - NORTHWEST TERRITORIES

★ 2366 ★
Tuktoyaktuk - BELUGA JAMBOREE. April (3rd
week), annual. Contact: Travel Arctic, Yellowknife, Northwest Territories X1A 2L9, Canada.

Features traditional Eskimo games and contests of
skill such as harpoon throwing, ice hole digging and
dog team races.

CANADA - NOVA SCOTIA

★ 2367 ★
Antigonish - HIGHLAND GAMES. Mid July, 3
days. Contact: Nova Scotia Department of Tourism,
Travel Division, Post Office Box 130, Halifax, Nova
Scotia B3J 2M7, Canada.

These games include track and field events such as
the caber toss and hammer throw. Also features
highland dancing and piping competitions, concerts,
parades, and a pipe band tattoo.

★ 2368 ★
L'Ardoise - ACADIAN DAY FESTIVAL. Late July-
early August, 3 days. Contact: Nova Scotia
Department of Tourism, Travel Division, Post Office
Box 130, Halifax, Nova Scotia B3J 2M7, Canada.

Events include a children's parade, a parade of
floats, concert. Of further interest, there are
exhibits, games, pipe and brass bands, home cooked
meals, and dancing.

★ 2369 ★
Meteghan River - ACADIAN FESTIVAL OF CLARE.
Mid July, 3 days. Contact: Nova Scotia Department of Tourism, Travel Division, Post Office Box
130, Halifax, Nova Scotia B3J 2M7, Canada.

Festival includes square dancing, sea cruises, demonstrations, fishing, arts and crafts exhibitions and
sales, a parade and a bazaar. Special events and
days include Senior Citizens' Day, Children's Day
(featuring a parade), Women's Day, Lumberjack and
Sports Day, and Farmers' Day.

★ 2370 ★
New Glasgow - FESTIVAL OF THE TARTANS.
Early August, annual, 4 days. Contact: Nova

CANADA - NOVA SCOTIA (Continued)

Scotia Department of Tourism, Travel Division, Post Office Box 130, Halifax, Nova Scotia B3J 2M7, Canada.

A highland festival with track and field events, highland competitions, a parade, barbeque, beer garden, and band concerts.

★ 2371 ★
Pugwash - GATHERING OF THE CLANS. Early July (1st day), 1 day. Contact: Nova Scotia Department of Tourism, Travel Division, Post Office Box 130, Halifax, Nova Scotia B3J 2M7, Canada.

Gathering features highland dancing and piping competitions, parade, water displays, boat races, ox pulls, lobster dinners, a midway, and band concerts.

★ 2372 ★
Saint Ann's - GAELIC MOD. Early August, annual, 6 days. Contact: Nova Scotia Department of Tourism, Travel Division, Post Office Box 130, Halifax, Nova Scotia B3J 2M7, Canada.

Scottish-style events such as highland dancing and piping and drumming competitions, with evening Scottish concerts, all in an attractive highland setting.

★ 2373 ★
Sydney - HIGHLAND GAMES. Early July, 2 days. Contact: Nova Scotia Department of Tourism, Travel Division, Post Office Box 130, Halifax, Nova Scotia B3J 2M7, Canada.

Features dancing, piping and chanter competitions, and a track and field meet. An extra attraction is the Centennial Garden.

CANADA - ONTARIO

★ 2374 ★
Kingston - AMITY 300. February, 8 days, International Centre and Grant Hall, Queen's University. Contact: News Department, Queen's University, Kingston, Ontario, Canada.

The various nationalities of students at Queen's University present demonstrations of their cultures, including food, dancing, art, etc.

★ 2375 ★
Saint Catharines - FOLK ARTS FESTIVAL. Late May-early June, annual. Contact: The Ministry of Industry and Tourism, Parliament Buildings, Toronto, Ontario M7A 2E5, Canada.

Honors a variety of ethnic groups with concerts, singing, dancing and cooking. There is a parade and an exhibition of arts and crafts.

Fall
See: SEASONS

Film
See also: THE ARTS

ALABAMA

★ 2376 ★
Birmingham - BIRMINGHAM INTERNATIONAL EDUCATIONAL FILM FESTIVAL. March, 4-5 days. Contact: Birmingham International Educational Film Festival, Box 2641, Birmingham, Alabama 35291.

A competitive event for 16mm films awarding statuettes, plaques and cash scholarships. The subject of the films may include safety, teacher education, performing arts, applied arts, social studies, mathematics, sciences, physical education, human relations, ethnic studies, early childhood, energy and ecology, language arts student productions, and the American Bicentennial. Started in 1973.

★ 2377 ★
Mobile - SPRING HILL COLLEGE FILM FESTIVAL. March, annual. Contact: Spring Hill College Film Festival, Spring Hill College, Mobile, Alabama 36608.

The festival is held to show the public the works of selected film artists, including high school and college students, faculty and community members. There are monetary awards. Started in 1970.

CALIFORNIA

★ 2378 ★
Hollywood - HOLLYWOOD FESTIVAL OF WORLD TELEVISION. October, annual. Contact: Hollywood Festival of World Television, Post Office Box 2430, Hollywood, California 90028.

The festival gives creative members of the Hollywood

Film

CALIFORNIA (Continued)

entertainment center an opportunity to see the best television made outside of the United States for the world's television screens; and to screen the world's most honest television programs on a competitive basis. Started in 1964.

★ 2379 ★
Hollywood - INTERNATIONAL BROADCASTING AWARDS FESTIVAL. March, annual. Contact: International Broadcasting Awards, 1717 North Highland Avenue, Hollywood, California 90028.

The festival seeks to encourage and upgrade television and radio advertising through the awarding of trophies to the best commercials submitted to the event. Commercials include live action, animation, humorous, public service, station identification, and other categories. Started in 1959.

★ 2380 ★
Inglewood - PSA-MPD INTERNATIONAL AMATEUR FILM FESTIVAL. August, annual. Contact: PSA-MPD International Amateur Film Festival, 810 Edgewood Street, Suite 204, Inglewood, California 90302.

The festival seeks to recognize the best of non-professional films, open to all non-commercial films. "Gold Scissors" awarded for best-editing. Started in 1930.

★ 2381 ★
Los Altos - INDEPENDENT FILM-MAKERS FESTIVAL. May, annual. Contact: Independent Film-Makers Festival, Foothill Junior College, 12345 El Monte Road, Los Altos, California 94022.

The festival seeks to encourage individual expression and experimentation in the visual, technical and esthetic aspects of filmmaking, through a monetary award for cartoon and animation, documentary, abstract and faction and/or fantasy, nature-process, about children, protest and criticism, and synacategormatic. The term "independent" according to the sponsors, connotes a quality of mind, rather than the financial state of the filmmaker. Started in 1962.

★ 2382 ★
Los Angeles - HOLLYWOOD INTERNATIONAL FILM FESTIVAL. October, annual. Contact: Hollywood International Film Festival, Los Angeles, California 90048.

The festival recognizes outstanding films through screening of features and shorts open to the general public. This is awarded with either a "Gold Leaf" or a "Silver Leaf". Started in 1969.

★ 2383 ★
Monterey - MONTEREY INDEPENDENT FILM-MAKERS FESTIVAL. August, annual. Contact: Monterey Independent Film-Makers Festival, Community Services Office, Monterey Peninsula College, 980 Fremont, Monterey, California 93940.

The festival seeks to provide unrestricted focus for the exhibition of short movies, live action, animated, etc., made as an expression of individual creative effort outside the theatrical and sponsored film market. A monetary award is presented. Started in 1968.

★ 2384 ★
Saint Mary's - SAINT MARY'S COLLEGE 8MM FILM FESTIVAL. April, annual. Contact: Saint Mary's College 8mm Film Festival, Saint Mary's College of California, Saint Mary's, California 94575.

The festival seeks to upgrade filmmaking by providing a film forum where filmmakers may compare their work and also inform the audience as to the latest in 8mm techniques. This filmmaking does not include commercials and educational films. Started in 1968.

★ 2385 ★
San Francisco - INTERNATIONAL EROTIC FILM FESTIVAL. December, annual. Contact: International Erotic Film Festival, 369 Sutter Street, San Francisco, California 94108.

The festival encourages independent filmmakers to make sensually exciting films and provides a setting where the whole range of human expression, including sexuality, can be realistically presented on the screen. Started in 1970.

★ 2386 ★
San Francisco - SAN FRANCISCO INTERNATIONAL FILM FESTIVAL. October, annual, 12 days, Palace of Fine Arts. Contact: Information Officer, State of California Department of Commerce, 1400 Tenth Street, Sacramento, California 95814.

First United States film festival of true international status. Films from various nations are shown. "It has as its purpose to demonstrate through the exhibition of the finest in motion pictures, the development of cinematic art in different countries, to contribute to knowledge of the film history, and to reveal styles and trends in film making". The jury was abolished

CALIFORNIA (Continued)

in 1965, as it was felt that it would be more of a cultural event without the contest.   Begun in 1957.

★ 2387 ★
San Jose - SURVIVAL FAIRE FESTIVAL.   March (Spring), annual.   Contact: Survival Faire, San Jose State College, Humanities 160, ASB College Union, San Jose, California 95114.

The festival seeks to present the problems of environmental survival, creating general awareness of ecology, and to stimulate an active role in preserving communities.   Films are on subjects such as pollution, waste, city, and transportation problems.   Started in 1970.

CONNECTICUT

★ 2388 ★
New Haven - YALE FILM FESTIVAL.   October, annual.   Contact: Yale Film Festival, c/o Audio-Visual Center, 59 High Street, New Haven, Connecticut 06520.

The festival seeks to promote and encourage film as an art form and to award outstanding experimental films.   Started in 1968.

FLORIDA

★ 2389 ★
Pensacola - UNIVERSITY OF WEST FLORIDA FILM FESTIVAL.   October, annual.   Contact: University of West Florida Film Festival, Pensacola, Florida 32504.

The festival encourages artistic achievement films by bringing to the campus films outstanding for artistic merit.   These films are awarded the "Golden Chambered Nautilus", "Silver Chambered Nautilus" and an "Enameled Nautilus", each with a monetary award. Started in 1968.

★ 2390 ★
Tampa - UNIVERSITY OF SOUTH FLORIDA FILM FESTIVAL.   April, annual.   Contact: University of South Florida Film Festival, Tampa, Florida 33620.

The festival is a platform for filmmakers, unrestricted in category.   Monetary awards are presented. Started in 1970.

GEORGIA

★ 2391 ★
Atlanta - INTERNATIONAL FILM FESTIVAL.   Mid August, 10 days, Memorial Arts Center.   Contact: Director, Atlanta International Film Festival, Drawer 13258, Atlanta, Georgia 30324.

Films are shown, both contemporary and old classics. Children's films are also shown.   Areas of competition include television, film strips, and super 8mm films.   Prominent personalities associated with the film industry appear.

ILLINOIS

★ 2392 ★
Bellwood - U.S. INDUSTRIAL FILM FESTIVAL. April (last Thursday), annual, 1 day, Downtown hotel-subject to change each year.   Contact: J. W. Anderson, U.S. Industrial Film Festival, 1008 Bellwood Avenue, Bellwood, Illinois 60104.

The festival was created to honor the achievements of the industrial film producer.   In order to give recognition to producers with varying facilities and budgets, the entries are divided into four separate groups for judging: commercially produced;   in-plant produced;   university produced;   and government produced.   The festival is devoted to 16mm industrial films, 35mm slide programs, 35mm film strips, and 3/4" video tape.   It is the best known industrial film festival internationally, and is the largest United States festival devoted exclusively to the predominant forms of industrial film formats.   Awards include the Gold Camera Award, Silver Screen Award, and certificates of creative excellence.   Started in 1967.

★ 2393 ★
Bellwood - U.S. TELEVISION COMMERCIALS FESTIVAL.   November (2nd from last Thursday), annual, 1 day, Downtown hotel-subject to change each year.   Contact: J. W. Anderson, U.S. Television Commercials Festival, 1008 Bellwood Avenue, Bellwood, Illinois 60104.

Honors the outstanding television commercials of the United States and Canada.   The entries are presented either on 16mm film or 3/4" video cassette.   Judges are selected from a cross section of ad agency personnel, television sponsors, and television commercial producers.   Entries are eligible for competition in 14 different subject areas, and eight different technique areas.   Begun in 1970.

Film

ILLINOIS (Continued)

★ 2394 ★
Chicago - CHICAGO INTERNATIONAL FILM
FESTIVAL.   Early November, annual, 2 weeks.
Contact: J. Jenkins, Chicago Film Board, 415
North Dearborn Street, Chicago, Illinois 60610.

Feature film, short subject, documentary film, educational film, student film, entertainment film for
children, television productions, television commercials,
business and industrial, training, health, medicine and
safety, and multi-media presentation.   Amateurs and
professionals, independent or commercial.   Awards
given.   Started in 1964.

INDIANA

★ 2395 ★
Bloomington - ARGO-INDIANA UNIVERSITY STUDENT
EXPERIMENTAL FILM FESTIVAL.   April, annual.
Contact: Argo-Indiana University Student Experi-
mental Film Festival, Indiana Memorial Union, Board
of Directors, Bloomington, Indiana 47401.

The festival promotes and provides a showcase for
local, national and international student filmmakers
in documentary and experimental categories.   Started
in 1970.

MARYLAND

★ 2396 ★
Baltimore - BALTIMORE AMATEUR FILM FESTIVAL.
April, annual.   Contact: Baltimore Amateur Film
Festival, University of Baltimore, Maryland Avenue
and Olive Street, Baltimore, Maryland 21201.

The festival seeks to provide entertainment and circu-
lation of amateur films.   It is non-competitive.
Started in 1970.

★ 2397 ★
Baltimore - BALTIMORE FILM FESTIVAL.   Mid
March-mid April, 1 month.   Contact: Baltimore
Film Festival, Box 7186, Waverly Station, Baltimore,
Maryland 21218.

The categories for entries into the festival include
movies by and for women or children; documentaries;
animated films;   or films about liberty in 35mm or
16mm.   Cash awards are given.

★ 2398 ★
College Park - WASHINGTON NATIONAL STUDENT

FILM FESTIVAL.   December, annual, 1 day, Uni-
versity of Maryland campus.   Contact: Washington
National Student Film Festival, Radio-TV-Film
Division, University of Maryland, College Park,
Maryland 20742.

The festival was created for the purpose of allowing
student filmmakers to see what their fellow students
were doing around the country with their cameras.
The several hundred entries include documentaries,
narratives, and animations.   Awards and cash
prizes are given by a team of judges.   Begun in
1971.

★ 2399 ★
Wheaton - WORLD RAILWAY FILM FESTIVAL.   Mid
February-mid March, annual, 5 Sundays, National
Capitol Trolley Museum.   Contact: Robert H.
Flack, 1909 Forest Dale Drive, Silver Spring, Mary-
land 20903.

Shows, a different one each day, to educate and
amuse, on the subject of railways.   Begun around
1972.

MASSACHUSETTS

★ 2400 ★
Cambridge - NEW ENGLAND STUDENT FILM
FESTIVAL.   April.   Contact: New England Stu-
dent Film Festival, University Film Study Center,
Box 275, Cambridge, Massachusetts 02138.

Open to the documentaries, dramas, animation and
experimental films of students in New England, both
graduate and undergraduate.   Winners join in a
festival touring package.

MICHIGAN

★ 2401 ★
Ann Arbor - ANN ARBOR FILM FESTIVAL.   March,
annual.   Contact: Ann Arbor Film Festival, Post
Office Box 283, Ann Arbor, Michigan 48107.

The festival encourages independent filmmakers.
Monetary awards are presented.   Started in 1963.

NEW YORK

★ 2402 ★
Hempstead - LONG ISLAND INTERNATIONAL FILM
FESTIVAL.   Late September, annual, 5 days, Calderone
Theatre.   Contact: Chamber of Commerce, 1776
Nichols Court, Hempstead, New York 11550.

NEW YORK (Continued)

Features the winners of the Golden Image Award, the best of the entries as judged by a panel of professional filmmakers.

★ 2403 ★
New York - AMERICAN FILM FESTIVAL. May, annual. Contact: American Film Festival, 17 West 60th Street, New York, New York 10023.

Real users and buyers of films see the very best available materials for their special needs in films on education and information, art and culture, business, industry, etc. Television commercials are not available. Started in 1958.

★ 2404 ★
New York - AMERICAN RADIO COMMERCIALS FESTIVAL. June, annual. Contact: American Television and Radio Commercials Festival, 30 East 60th Street, New York, New York 10022.

The festival awards special recognition of outstanding local, regional, and international advertising on radio. Started in 1967.

★ 2405 ★
New York - AMERICAN TELEVISION COMMERCIALS FESTIVAL. May, annual. Contact: American Television and Radio Commercials Festival, 30 East 60th Street, New York, New York 10022.

The festival awards special recognition of outstanding local, regional, and international advertising from television. Started in 1960.

★ 2406 ★
New York - DANCE FILMS FESTIVAL. Late June. Contact: Dance Films Festival, Dance Films Association, Incorporated, 250 West 57th Street, New York, New York 10019.

Open to film producers and distributors, the festival features 16mm and 8mm films on all forms of dance, including modern, jazz, ballet, folk or ethnic dancing, and therapeutic dancing.

★ 2407 ★
New York - INTERNATIONAL ANIMATION FESTIVAL. Late September-early October, International Affairs Auditorium, Columbia University. Contact: Office of Public Information, Columbia University, 116th Street and Broadway, New York, New York 10027.

A showing of animated films from 20 countries, including both new and old works. Over 200 films in all. Begun around 1973.

★ 2408 ★
New York - INTERNATIONAL FILM AND TV FESTIVAL OF NEW YORK. October, annual. Contact: International Film and TV Festival of New York, 121 West 45th Street, New York, New York 10036.

Festival seeks to honor individuals and companies which produce filmstrips, industrial films, television and cinema commercials, introductions, lead-in/titles, public service television programs, featurettes and multi-media presentations, and promotional films and newsfilms, through the awarding of trophies for those contributing to the greatness of the industry with their outstanding creations. A seminar is held during the festival to provide a showcase for new developments, new ideas and techniques. Started in 1956.

★ 2409 ★
New York - INTERNATIONAL FILM AND VIDEO FESTIVAL: CITIES, SUBURBS AND SMALL TOWNS. Early November, 12 days, Columbia University Graduate School of Architecture and Planning. Contact: Columbia University Graduate School of Architecture and Planning, Francois Confino, Room 410H, Avery Hall, Columbia University, New York, New York 10027.

A film festival in this specialized field of study. Begun in 1974.

★ 2410 ★
New York - INTERNATIONAL PSYCHIC FILM FESTIVAL. September-October. Contact: International Psychic Film Festival, 35 East 84th Street, Suite 3B, New York, New York 10028.

Short and feature length movies are shown in first-run theaters, with those adjudged to be the best receiving prizes and wide-range distribution. The definition of what constitutes a psychic film is left to the discretion of the entrant. The festival is held simultaneously in London. Started in 1975.

★ 2411 ★
New York - NATIONAL STUDENT FILM FESTIVAL. October, annual. Contact: National Student Film Festival, 537 La Guardia Place, New York, New York 10012.

The festival encourages creative filmmaking among

NEW YORK (Continued)

American college and university students through awards of money and also for two American Film Institute-Schlitz Fellowships.   Started in 1965.

★ 2412 ★
New York - NEW YORK FILM FESTIVAL.   Late September-early October, annual, Lincoln Center. Contact: Administrator of the Film Society of Lincoln Center, 1865 Broadway, New York, New York 10023.

A non-competitive event with both short and feature length films in all categories.   The films are a selection of significant films from throughout the world.   In addition to the current films, there are retrospectives of films rarely seen in the United States.

★ 2413 ★
New York - PRSA FILM FESTIVAL.   November, annual, 1 day.   Contact: PRSA Annual Film Festival, Public Relations Society of America, 845 Third Avenue, New York, New York 10022.

Features 16mm films sponsored by members of the Public Relations Society of America on the subject of public relations.

★ 2414 ★
Rochester - MOVIES ON A SHOESTRING INTER-NATIONAL AMATEUR FILM FESTIVAL.   May, annual.   Contact: Movies on a Shoestring International Amateur Film Festival, Post Office Box 7604, Rochester, New York 14622.

The festival seeks to provide to an appreciative audience the fine quality of non-theatrical films. Started in 1957.

★ 2415 ★
Rochester - ROCHESTER INTERNATIONAL FILM FESTIVAL.   October, annual.   Contact: Rochester International Film Festival, 904 Midtown Tower, Rochester, New York 14604.

The festival presents a selection of the world's finest films, both short and feature length; also animated cartoons, which are imaginative in treatment and which contribute to the vital growth of contemporary cinema of all countries.   Started in 1970.

OHIO

★ 2416 ★
Columbus - COLUMBUS INTERNATIONAL FILM FESTIVAL.   October, annual.   Contact: Columbus International Film Festival, Columbus Film Council, Kresge Building, 83 South High Street, Room 408, Columbus, Ohio 43215.

The festival seeks to create a greater understanding and usage of 16mm motion pictures, slides, and filmstrips in business and industry, etc.   Categories included are films on business and industry, information and education, health, mental health, medicine and safety.   Also filmstrips, graphic and cultural arts, religion and ethics, and world travel.   Started in 1942.

OREGON

★ 2417 ★
Portland - LEWIS AND CLARK COLLEGE QUASI-WIDE-OPEN FILM FESTIVAL.   May, annual. Contact: Lewis and Clark College Quasi-Wide-Open Film Festival, Box 197, Lewis and Clark College, Portland, Oregon 97219.

The festival hopes to promote and encourage amateur filmmaking.   Monetary awards are presented. Started in 1968.

PENNSYLVANIA

★ 2418 ★
Philadelphia - INTERNATIONAL FESTIVAL OF SHORT FILMS.   October, annual.   Contact: International Festival of Short Films, Philadelphia Museum of Art, Parkway at 26th Street, Philadelphia, Pennsylvania 19130.

The festival hopes to expose to the audience the finest work now being done in short films throughout the world and to exhibit the diversity, vitality and originality of the most talented artists working in motion pictures today.   Started in 1967.

★ 2419 ★
Philadelphia - PHILADELPHIA PHILM FESTIVAL. Spring, annual, 6 days, Walnut Street Theatre. Contact: The Philadelphia Convention and Visitors Bureau, 1525 John F. Kennedy Boulevard, Philadelphia, Pennsylvania 19102.

The festival specializes in important new or rarely seen works· produced by major filmmakers from around the world.   Usually takes place under the umbrella of the Philadelphia Festival.

TENNESSEE

★ 2420 ★
Greeneville - SINKING CREEK FILM CELEBRATION.
April.   Contact: Sinking Creek Film Celebration,
Tusculum College, Greeneville, Tennessee 37743.

Festival provides most inventive non-professional
United States filmmaker a new showcase for his best
works and acknowledges his artistry with awards.
Films which appeal to educable mentally retarded,
elementary or intermediate school age and high school
age children, also films appealing to adults are included.

TEXAS

★ 2421 ★
Dallas - U.S.A. FILM FESTIVAL.   March, annual,
1 week, Bob Hope Theater, Southern Methodist
University.   Contact: U.S.A. Film Festival, South-
ern Methodist University, Mockingbird Lane and
Hillcrest, Dallas, Texas 75275.

The festival devotes itself to American filmmakers.
Each year one veteran director is honored by a
retrospective look at his career.   The films shown
include mainstream works, offbeat, and short films.
People associated with some of the films are on hand
to give talks.   Begun around 1971.

WASHINGTON

★ 2422 ★
Bellevue - BELLEVUE FILM FESTIVAL.   July, annual.
Contact: Bellevue Film Festival, 376 Bellevue Square,
Bellevue, Washington 98004.

The festival seeks to show the important and original
contributions being made by the independent filmmakers to contemporary art and cinema.   Monetary
awards are presented.   Started in 1967.

★ 2423 ★
Pullman - INDEPENDENT FILM FESTIVAL
COMPETITION.   October, annual.   Contact: In-
dependent Film Festival Competition, Washington
State University, Pullman, Washington 99163.

The festival's purpose is to encourage the respectful
consideration for all types of films from amateurs and
students, as well as experienced professionals and
experimental filmmakers.   The monetary award includes revenues from the tour which includes schools
and theaters in California, Idaho and New York.
Started in 1965.

★ 2424 ★
Seattle - NORTHWEST FILMMAKER'S FESTIVAL.
June, annual.   Contact: Northwest Filmmaker's
Festival, Post Office Box 15440, Seattle, Washington
98115.

The festival seeks to recognize and give unrestricted
exposure to films produced by independent filmmakers
in the Northwest.   Started in 1969.

★ 2425 ★
Seattle - TEN BEST OF THE WEST FESTIVAL.
October, annual.   Contact: Ten Best of the West,
4541 California Avenue, Southwest, Seattle, Washington 98116.

The festival seeks through the awarding of certificates to encourage unrestricted quality and expert
craftsmanship in filmmaking by the amateur filmmakers living in 11 western states of the United
States and in Canada, Alaska, and Hawaii.   Started
in 1956.

CANADA - MANITOBA

★ 2426 ★
Brandon - BRANDON FILM FESTIVAL.   Mid March,
4 days.   Contact: Director, Department of Tourism,
Recreation and Cultural Affairs, Tourist Branch, 801
Mall Centre, 491 Portage Avenue, Winnipeg, Manitoba
R3B 2E7, Canada.

A competition and showing of films.

CANADA - NORTHWEST TERRITORIES

★ 2427 ★
Yellowknife - NORTHWEST TERRITORIES NORTHERN
FILM FESTIVAL.   Late November, annual, 2 days.
Contact: Travel Arctic, Yellowknife, Northwest
Territories X1A 2L9, Canada.

The festival is open to exhibitors from all over the
world, but the films must be on the subject of the
Canadian territories north of 60.   Both amateurs and
professionals may participate.   Begun in 1975.

Flowers
See: AGRICULTURE

Folk
See also: ETHNIC EVENTS

ALABAMA

★ 2428 ★
Hodges - FOLKLORE FROLIC.   June-November, monthly, 1 day each month, Rock Bridge Canyon. Contact: Bureau of Publicity, State of Alabama, Montgomery, Alabama 36104.

Folk music and singing, folk crafts, antiques, and souvenirs.   Sponsored by the Rock Bridge Folklore Society.

★ 2429 ★
Steele - FOLK FESTIVAL.   October, annual, 2 days, Horse Pens 40.   Contact: Warren Musgrove, Horse Pens 40, Route 1, Box 379, Steele, Alabama 35987.

Appalachian folk music, dance, drama, arts and crafts, performances, demonstrations, and displays. Begun around 1962.

ARIZONA

★ 2430 ★
Tucson - TUCSON MEET YOURSELF.   Early October, annual, 3 days, Presidio Park.   Contact: Jim Griffith, Route 11, Box 624, Tucson, Arizona 85706.

A wide variety of musical talent including blues, cowboy, gospel, Amerindian and ethnic performers. In addition, there are booths of ethnic food and ethnic dancing.   Begun around 1974.

ARKANSAS

★ 2431 ★
Eureka Springs - OZARK FOLK FESTIVAL.   October, annual, 4 days.   Contact: Eureka Springs Chamber of Commerce, Five North Main Street, Eureka Springs, Arkansas 72632; or Ozark Folk Festival, c/o Ozark Festival, Incorporated, Eureka Springs, Arkansas 72632.

Celebrates the 1890's in a resort which retains the architecture and feeling of the turn of the century. There is an 1890's revue, floats depicting 1890's theme, a barefoot ball, and variety shows with the music, dance, and folklore of the Ozarks.   The

festival is claimed to be one of the oldest of its kind in the nation.   Founded in 1947.

★ 2432 ★
Fayetteville - ARKANSAS FOLKLORE SOCIETY MEETING AND FOLK FESTIVAL.   June-August (Summer), annual, University of Arkansas at Fayetteville.   Contact: Arkansas Folklife Society, University of Arkansas, Fayetteville, Arkansas 72701.

The festival features both scholarly research and traditional performances of traditional music, including singing, banjos, zithers and fiddles.   Begun in 1947.

★ 2433 ★
Fayetteville - ARKANSAS ONION FOLK FESTIVAL. April (generally last Sunday), annual, 1 day, lawn in front of Old Main.   Contact: Arkansas Union, Room 511, University of Arkansas, Fayetteville, Arkansas 72701.

Primarily music, with some arts and crafts for display and sale.   Has been in the past a bluegrass and a Delta blues festival, but was a folk festival for past two years and very likely will remain so in the future. Sponsored by Arkansas Union-Union Programs Office. Started in 1972.

★ 2434 ★
Mountain View - ARKANSAS FOLK FESTIVAL. Mid April, annual, 3 weekends, Ozark Folk Center. Contact: Ozark Folk Center, Mountain View, Arkansas 72560.

Native Ozark craftsmen demonstrate and sell works: furniture making, hominy making, blacksmithing, etc. Rackensack Folklore Society plays traditional folk music on guitar, 5-string banjo, bow, autoharp, mountain dulcimer, ancient Irish and Scottish ballads sung.   Parades and rodeo.   Purpose is to introduce visitors to traditional Ozark music.   Traditional old time fiddlers play, amateurs permitted to participate if approved by Rackensack.   Begun around 1963.

CALIFORNIA

★ 2435 ★
Los Angeles - UCLA FOLK FESTIVAL.   Mid April, 3 days, Royce Hall.   Contact: Public Information Office, UCLA, 405 Hilgard Avenue, Los Angeles, California 90024.

Concerts performed by important figures in folk music.

CALIFORNIA (Continued)

★ 2436 ★
San Diego - SAN DIEGO STATE UNIVERSITY FOLK
FESTIVAL. Mid April, 5 days, San Diego State
University. Contact: Louis F. Curtis, c/o Folk
Arts, 3743 Fifth Avenue, San Diego, California
92103.

Workshops, concerts, and other traditional activities,
demonstrations, etc. are included in the festival
events.

★ 2437 ★
San Francisco - WESTERN FOLK FESTIVAL. Mid
October, annual, 3 days, Golden Gate Recreation
Area. Contact: National Folk Festival Association,
1346 Connecticut Avenue, Northwest, Washington,
D.C. 20036.

The festival represents the cultural richness of California's multi-ethnic heritage with music, dancing,
singing, food and crafts. Represented groups include Oriental, Mexican, Afro, Russian and native
American tribes such as the Yurok, Karok, Tolawa
and Hoopa. Performances and workshops. Begun
in 1975.

COLORADO

★ 2438 ★
Denver - WESTERN FOLKLORE FESTIVAL. June-
August (Summer), annual. Contact: Adams County
Chamber of Commerce, 5911 North Washington Street,
Denver, Colorado 80216.

Held in conjunction with the Western Folklore Conference, the festival offers a mixture of scholarly
discussion and the performance of traditional music
and dancing. Started in 1941.

CONNECTICUT

★ 2439 ★
Hartford - CONNECTICUT FAMILY FOLK FESTIVAL.
Mid August, 2 days, Elizabeth Park. Contact:
Len Domler, 290 Middletown Avenue, Wethersfield,
Connecticut 06109.

Music, crafts, food, etc. - fun for the whole family.

DISTRICT OF COLUMBIA

★ 2440 ★
Washington, D.C. - FESTIVAL OF AMERICAN

FOLKLIFE. July, annual, 5 days, On the Mall.
Contact: Division of Performing Arts, Smithsonian
Institution, Washington, D.C. 20560.

Dedicated to the conservation of the United States
national folk culture heritage. Many outstanding
folk artists and groups in a variety of concerts; music,
dance, and folk arts. Wide variety of crafts demonstrated and performances by various ethnic groups.
Foods of many cultures. In 1976, in honor of the
United States bicentennial, this festival was held all
through the summer, but it is normally only five days.
Begun around 1959.

FLORIDA

★ 2441 ★
Dade City - HEART OF FLORIDA FOLK FESTIVAL.
Late February-early March, 6 days. Contact: L. L.
Rozar, Jr., Post Office Box 248, Dade City, Florida
33525.

Presented in conjunction with the Pasco County Fair.
Features traditional folklore. Program of dances,
songs, and pioneer crafts. Participants include
both local and visiting performers. Included in the
past have been Scottish bagpipers, bluegrass singers,
and authentically attired dancers representing various
countries. Demonstrations include spinning, weaving,
and use of the potters wheel.

★ 2442 ★
Miami - INTERNATIONAL FOLK FESTIVAL. Late
May-June, 4 days. Contact: Morty Freedman,
2539 South Bayshore Drive, Miami, Florida 33132.

Pageantry and customs of the city's various ethnic
groups, including Latin, Oriental, Hungarian, Italian
and Afro cultures. Parade, arts and crafts exhibit,
and international food festival. Parade of Nations,
international bazaar, international soccer tournament,
and international travel film show.

★ 2443 ★
White Springs - ALL-FLORIDA FOLK FESTIVAL.
May, annual, 3 days, Stephen Foster Memorial.
Contact: Chamber of Commerce, Post Office Box
334, White Springs, Florida 32096.

Presents traditional British, native American, and
ethnic singing, dancing and music, square dancing,
fiddle-playing, games, story-telling, spirituals, etc.

★ 2444 ★·
White Springs - FLORIDA FOLK FESTIVAL. Early

FLORIDA (Continued)

September (Friday, Saturday, Sunday before Labor Day), annual, 3 days, Stephen Foster Memorial. Contact: Annual Florida Folk Festival, White Springs, Florida 32096.

Entertainment combined with a little instruction in the folk activity offered by communities, rural areas and schools. "Organized to keep alive the passing ways of the old South". Includes Czech, English, French, Indian, Irish, Minorcan, Negro, Scottish, and Spanish. Children's rhymes and the customs and folklore of cowboys, farmers, lumber camps, and railroads are emphasized, as are indigenous ghost and witch stories, legends and superstitions. Wood carving, whittling, palmetto products, quilting, weaving, and pottery are displayed, along with traditional ethnic foods, and music saw playing. Inaugurated in 1953.

GEORGIA

★ 2445 ★
Hiawasee - GEORGIA MOUNTAIN FAIR. Mid August, 7 days. Contact: Georgia Mountain Fair, Hiawasee Chamber of Commerce, Hiawasee, Georgia 30546.

The festival features country-western, bluegrass, and mountain clogging music. Old-time mountain crafts including soap-making, wood-carving, and needle-crafts are demonstrated and displayed. Antique cars and buggies are paraded.

IDAHO

★ 2446 ★
Idaho Falls - FOLK FESTIVAL OF THE SMOKIES. March, 1 day. Contact: Folk Festival of the Smokies, Box 8, Cosby, Tennessee 37722.

A traditional folk festival with entertainment, arts and crafts, etc.

ILLINOIS

★ 2447 ★
Clayville - FALL FESTIVAL. Mid October, annual, 2 days. Contact: The Division of Tourism, Illinois Department of Business and Economic Development, 222 South College Street, Springfield, Illinois 62706.

Folk arts and crafts displays and demonstrations. Country kitchen featuring pioneer cooking. Sewing bee, folk life seminar. The museum is an 1800's vintage inn. The festival is the climax of an entire summer of folk events. Begun around 1965.

★ 2448 ★
DuQuoin - SOUTH ILLINOIS FOLK FESTIVAL. Early October, annual, 3 days, DuQuoin State Fairgrounds. Contact: Mrs. Mike Prusacki, Box 303, DuQuoin, Illinois 62832.

Winemaking, carving, tomahawk throwing, hog-calling, quilting, cornhusk dolls, apple-butter making, taffy pull, and bread making are demonstrated. Early pioneer games, country store, Punch and Judy show, art show, old-fashioned meals, and flea market for entertainment. Begun around 1972.

INDIANA

★ 2449 ★
South Bend - FOLK LIFE FESTIVAL. Early April, 7 days, Indiana University at South Bend. Contact: Continuing Education Office, Indiana University at South Bend, 1825 Northside Boulevard, South Bend, Indiana 46615.

Crafts fairs, folk singing, and a bazaar are included in the events of this folk festival.

IOWA

★ 2450 ★
Bettendorf - INTERNATIONAL FOLK FESTIVAL. Mid June (2nd full weekend), annual, 2 days, Bettendorf Middle School, 18th Street and Middle Road. Contact: Festival Director, International Folk Festival, Box 686, Bettendorf, Iowa 52722.

The culture, music, dress, dance, crafts and food of more than 20 nationalities are displayed and demonstrated. There are two performances of "International Showtime" daily and the International Cafe is open throughout the festival. The program is intended to be both educational and entertaining. Representatives of the various nationality groups compete for the title of Festival Queen. International fashion show, rugby game, and community bands. There is an essay contest prior to the festival. The theme of the festival is "Span of Nations" to symbolize a desire to promote international friendship. There is a place to purchase souvenirs of all of the countries represented (20-30). There is currently a plan to extend the festival to three days, later to a week. Begun around 1967.

KANSAS

★ 2451 ★
North Newton - BETHEL COLLEGE FALL AND FOLK
FESTIVAL.   Early October, 2 days.   Contact:
Publications Division, Kansas Department of Economic
Development, State Office Building, Room 122S,
Topeka, Kansas 66612.

Folk music, crafts, arts, etc. in conjunction with
traditional fall festivities.

KENTUCKY

★ 2452 ★
Berea - MOUNTAIN FOLK FESTIVAL.   Mid April,
annual, 1 day, Berea College.   Contact: John M.
Ramsay, Director of Recreation Extension, Post Office
Box 287, Berea, Kentucky 40403.

Brings together young people of high school and
college age for three days of sharing folk songs and
dances.   Traditional American music and singing
games.   The dancing includes Danish, English and
traditional American.   A final program is prepared
for the public with a processional and lively music.
Started in 1935.

★ 2453 ★
Grayson - MOUNTAIN HERITAGE FOLK FESTIVAL.
Late May, 3 days, Grayson Lake State Park.   Con-
tact: Nancy McClellan, 2637 Alonquin Avenue,
Ashland, Kentucky 41101.

Traditional American music, both instrumental and
vocal, as done by mountain performers.   Workshops
and arts and crafts.   Begun around 1970.

★ 2454 ★
Irvine - FOOTHILLS FOLK FESTIVAL.   Early July,
3 days, Fairgrounds.   Contact: Jim Gaskin, WIRV
Radio, Irvine, Kentucky 40336.

Traditional American music and dance, fiddle convention, bluegrass, arts and crafts, children's events,
and gospel sing.   Begun in 1973.

★ 2455 ★
London - MOUNTAIN FOLK FESTIVAL.   Late
September, annual, Levi Jackson State Park.   Contact: John M. Ramsay, Director or Recreation Extension, Post Office Box 287, Berea, Kentucky 40403.

An adult version of the festival held at Berea College
in April - singing, dancing, and lively music.

★ 2456 ★
Olive Hill - AMERICAN FOLKSONG FESTIVAL.
Early June (1st weekend), annual, 3 days, Carter
Caves State Park, Cascade Area.   Contact: Ameri-
can Folksong Festival, c/o 3201 Cogan Street,
Ashland, Kentucky 41101.

The festival is an attempt to preserve and promote
a lyric Anglo-Saxon culture which has its roots in
the Elizabethan ballads brought to the hills by the
earliest settlers.   Participants in the festival are of
all ages and come with their homemade skills mani-
est: homespun .costumes, musical instruments, and
songs.   Folk arts and crafts and dancing, singing
and playing of music.   All the music is performed
in natural surroundings on an open wooden stage set
up before a log cabin.   Performers play such traditional instruments as the 3- or 54-string dulcimer,
Irish harp, fiddle, recorder, paw-paw whistle, sixteenth century lute, mouth harp, and cornstalk fiddler.
Founded in 1930.

★ 2457 ★
Prestonburg - KENTUCKY HIGHLANDS FOLK
FESTIVAL.   Late August, annual, 3 days, Jenny
Wiley State Resort Park Amphitheatre.   Contact:
Edith James, Program Director, Kentucky Highlands
Folk Festival, Prestonburg, Kentucky 41653.

Dongers, dancers, tale-tellers, poets, musicians
and artists gather to share the lore of the southern
mountains and to preserve and encourage the continued use of the traditional expressions of our people.
Begun in 1966.

LOUISIANA

★ 2458 ★
Columbia - ART AND FOLK FESTIVAL.   Mid October, 2 days.   Contact: Louisiana Tourist Commission,
Post Office Box 44291, Baton Rouge, Louisiana
70804.

Lye soap making, chicken 'pickin', cornbread and
bisquit making, coffee roasting, straight razor shaving,
quilting and log splitting and other early American
crafts and skills are featured.   There is also a flower
show, a program of music and singing, home baked and
canned goods for sale, and other forms of entertainment.
The theme of the festival is "Discover America".

MASSACHUSETTS

★ 2459 ★
Amherst - FIVE COLLEGE FOLK FESTIVAL.   Late
April-early May, Hampshire College, Mount Holyoke

Folk

MASSACHUSETTS (Continued)

College. Contact: Five College Folk Festival, Box 1C16, Hampshire College, Amherst, Massachusetts 01002.

Performances by professional folk singers and other events highlight this folk festival.

★ 2460 ★
Attleboro - HILLSIDE FOLK FESTIVAL. Late May, annual, 1 day, LaSalette Shrine. Contact: Bristol County Development Council, Incorporated, 154 North Main Street, Fall River, Massachusetts 02722.

Outdoor mass followed by folk singing till early evening.

★ 2461 ★
Natick - NEW ENGLAND FOLK FESTIVAL. Mid April, annual, 3 days, Natick High School. Contact: Northeast Folk Festival Association, Incorporated, Director, 57 Roseland Street, Somerville, Massachusetts 02143.

The purpose of the event is to preserve New England traditions. There are demonstrations of folk arts and skills, ethnic folklife, children's events, workshops, jams, exhibits, and dances.

MICHIGAN

★ 2462 ★
Hastings - FOLK LIFE FESTIVAL. Mid September, annual, 2 days, Charlton Park Village and Museum. Contact: West Michigan Tourist Association, Hospitality House, 136 Fulton East, Grand Rapids, Michigan 49502.

Pioneer crafts are demonstrated.

MINNESOTA

★ 2463 ★
Duluth - FOLK FESTIVAL. Early August, 1 day, Leif Erickson Park. Contact: Duluth Area Chamber of Commerce, 220 Medical Arts Building, Duluth, Minnesota 55802.

Events include an arts and crafts fair, program of ethnic music, songs and dances.

MISSISSIPPI

★ 2464 ★
Biloxi - GREATER GULF COAST ARTS COUNCIL FOLKLIFE FESTIVAL. Mid April, 3 days, Edgewater Mall. Contact: Travel Department, Mississippi Agricultural and Industrial Board, Post Office Box 849, Jackson, Mississippi 39205.

Displays from throughout the state as well as in Biloxi in celebration of the folk heritage of the area and this country.

★ 2465 ★
Decatur - MISSISSIPPI FOLKLORE SOCIETY FESTIVAL. April, annual, One of the state universities. Contact: The Mississippi Folklore Society, Ovid S. Vickers, Secretary-Treasurer, Department of English, East Central Junior College, Decatur, Mississippi 39327.

Papers are given, folk dances are danced, songs are sung, crafts including wood carving, quilting, etc. Started in 1967. Location varies from year to year.

★ 2466 ★
Tishomingo - FOLKLORE FROLIC. Early June, annual, 1 day, Tishomingo State Park. Contact: Mr. Olin Burcham, Northwest Alabama Junior College, Phil Campbell, Alabama 35581.

The purpose of this festival is to keep pioneer arts and crafts alive. The event is non-competitive. There is fiddling and other music also. Begun around 1973.

MISSOURI

★ 2467 ★
West Plains - FOLK MUSIC AND CRAFT FAIR. Early September, annual, 1 day, Fairgrounds. Contact: Council on Arts of West Plains, Linda Shortridge, President, 1008 West Eighth Avenue, West Plains, Missouri 65775.

Demonstrations and exhibits of a wide variety of native crafts, about 40 exhibits in all. Begun around 1974.

NEW JERSEY

★ 2468 ★
Middletown - JUNE FOLK FESTIVAL (MIDDLETOWN FOLK FESTIVAL). Late June, annual, 2 days, Bodman Park. Contact: Dick Levine, 11 Carnegie

NEW JERSEY (Continued)

Court, Middletown, New Jersey 07748.

Events include arts and crafts, traditional American music, children's events. There are several concerts featuring instrumental and vocal music, such as bluegrass, folk and gospel, and ethnic dancers. In addition, there are music and dancing workshops; a puppet theater; storytelling; singalongs, and craft shows and demonstrations. Begun around 1967.

★ 2469 ★
Trenton - ASSUNPINK CREEK FOLK FESTIVAL. Mid October, annual, 1 day, Mercer County Community College. Contact: Festival Co-ordinator, c/o Princeton Folk Music Society, Incorporated, Post Office Box 461, Princeton, New Jersey 08540.

Includes an afternoon of workshops on American and British song and dances, mini-concert, square dance, and a larger evening concert. Begun in 1975.

★ 2470 ★
West Orange - JUNE DAYS FOLK FESTIVAL. Mid June, 2 days, Eagle Rock Reservation. Contact: Folk Music Society of Northern New Jersey, Post Office Box 649, Maplecrest Station, Maplewood, New Jersey 07040.

Contemporary folk music, traditional folk music, arts and crafts exhibits, concerts, workshops, and children's events are featured in this folk festival.

NEW YORK

★ 2471 ★
Petersburg - FOLK AND FOLK SONG FESTIVALS. Early August, annual, 4 days, Fox Hollow. Contact: Beers Family, Route 2, Petersburg, New York 12138.

The Beers Family Festival of Traditional Music and Arts (Petersburg). Folk song concerts, sing-a-long groups, dancing, exhibits, folk crafts, music, and instrument making.

★ 2472 ★
Petersburg - GOTTAGEGON. Late May, annual. Contact: Pick'n 'n Sing'n Gather'n', c/o Spence, Rural Delivery 1, Wormer Road, Vorheesville, New York 12186.

A folk and folk song festival with audience participation.

★ 2473 ★
Tarrytown - HUDSON VALLEY FOLK FESTIVAL. Early June, annual, 1 day, Lyndhurst Estate. Contact: Lyndhurst Estate, Route 9, Tarrytown, New York 10591.

Top names in folk, blues, ragtime, rock, and bluegrass music appear along with clowns, dancers, jump-ropers and story-tellers. A special children's concert is featured. The activities are rounded out by a picnic, a craft show and square dancing. Begun around 1967.

NORTH CAROLINA

★ 2474 ★
Angier - ANGIER FESTIVAL. Mid July, annual, 3 days, Dixie Campgrounds. Contact: National Folk Festival Association, Incorporated, 1346 Connecticut Avenue, Northwest, Washington, D.C. 20036.

Also called the Eastern North Carolina Bluegrass and Folk Festival, the featured events are folk music and craft shows. Begun around 1973.

★ 2475 ★
Black Mountain - BLUEGRASS AND OLD TIME MOUNTAIN FESTIVAL. Early September (Labor Day weekend), annual, Monte Vista Farm. Contact: Asheville Area Chamber of Commerce, Post Office Box 1011, Asheville, North Carolina 28802.

Lively mountain music and dancing. In addition, there are displays of mountain arts and crafts for sale.

★ 2476 ★
Franklin - MACON COUNTY FOLK FESTIVAL. Early-mid August, annual, 3 days, Franklin High School. Contact: Franklin Area Chamber of Commerce, Post Office Box 504, Franklin, North Carolina 28734; or Bob Hendrix, Riverbend Estates, Franklin, North Carolina 28734.

Local fiddlers and bands perform mountain music. Dancers compete at square dancing, clog and buck dancing.

★ 2477 ★
Hendersonville - FESTIVAL OF FOLK ARTS AND CRAFTS. Late July, annual, 4 days, Blue Ridge Technical Institute; Mountain Folkways Centers; local churches. Contact: Harold McLaughlin, Blue Ridge Technical Institute, Hendersonville, North Carolina 28739.

Folk

NORTH CAROLINA (Continued)

A wide variety of crafts including woodcarving, pottery, glass-blowing, leatherwork, etc., are displayed and demonstrated at a variety of churches, all within walking distance of each other (the Walking Fair). In addition, there are concerts of mountain music by local performers and singing and dancing. Started in 1975.

★ 2478 ★
Mars Hill - BASCOM LAMAR LUNSFORD MOUNTAIN MUSIC AND DANCE FESTIVAL. Early October (1st weekend), annual, 3 days, Mars Hill College campus. Contact: Donald N. Anderson, Director, Southern Appalachian Center, Mars Hill College, Mars Hill, North Carolina 28754.

Honors Bascom Lamar Lunsford, the "Minstrel of the Appalachias", who dedicated his life to preserving and promoting the traditions of his native mountains, and was co-founder of the festival. Events include smooth, mountain clog, and back dancing; workshops, concerts, and jam sessions of mountain music played on banjos, guitars, fiddles and dulcimers; and displays and demonstrations of such crafts as whittling, spinning, quilting, weaving and woodworking. Started in 1968.

★ 2479 ★
Waynesville - SMOKY MOUNTAIN FOLK FESTIVAL. Late July, annual, 3 days, Waynesville Junior High School. Contact: Joe Sam Queen, 449 South Main Street, Waynesville, North Carolina 28786.

From Georgia, the Carolinas, and Tennessee come craftsmen, dancers, and musicians to participate in concerts, workshops, square dancing, a fiddle convention, and an arts and crafts exhibit. Begun around 1972.

OHIO

★ 2480 ★
Quaker City - OHIO HILLS FOLK FESTIVAL. Mid July, annual, 2-5 days. Contact: George Osborn, 125 Pike Street, Quaker City, Ohio 43773.

The festival offers a wide choice in traditional and old time music: dulcimers, fiddles, calliope, revival hymns, banjos, bands, guitar, Gay 90's music and minstrels. The visitor may watch competition in a muzzle-loading rifle shoot, a horse show, or fiddle and banjo contests; or browse a country store, flea market, Farm Museum, art show or craft hall. Further entertainment is provided by rides, concessions,

square dancing and a parade. Begun in the early 1900's.

PENNSYLVANIA

★ 2481 ★
Chester - NEW LIFE FOLK FESTIVAL. Early November, annual, 2 days, Widner College. Contact: Public Information Office, Widner College, 14th and Chestnut Street, Chester, Pennsylvania 19013.

The event features music workshops in the afternoon, and concerts at night with a variety of different artists performing.

★ 2482 ★
Kittanning - FORT ARMSTRONG FOLK FESTIVAL. Early August, annual, 4 days, Waterfront Park. Contact: Mr. William E. Martin, 325 Market Street, Kittanning, Pennsylvania 16201.

Colonial crafts: coppersmithing, glass blowing, soap making, and various methods of that era's homemaking demonstrated.

★ 2483 ★
McConnellsburg - FULTON FALL FOLK FESTIVAL. Mid October, annual, 3 days, throughout Fulton County. Contact: Fulton County TPA, Box 141, McConnellsburg, Pennsylvania 17233.

Country music show, talent contest, apple butter boil-Harrisonville, antique farm equipment display, buggy and horse rides, house tour, barbeque chicken dinner, muzzle loader meet, ox roast at the fire hall, and square dancing. Tours of Grist Mill, flea market, craft fair, buckwheat pancake eating (from Fulton County grown and ground buckwheat), and more.

★ 2484 ★
Oley - COLONIAL AMERICAN CHERRY FAIR. Late May, 3 days, Lobachsville. Contact: American Folklife Society, Rural Delivery 2, Oley, Pennsylvania 19547.

A recreation of the early days of the hamlet, founded around 1745. The women prepare colonial dishes over the open hearth. Craftsmen weave coverlets, dig the clay to make colonial bricks and roof tiles. Conestoga wagons bring in produce, and balladeers sing traditional songs. Lobachsville is located between Oley and Boyertown.

PENNSYLVANIA (Continued)

★ 2485 ★
Philadelphia - PHILADELPHIA FOLK FAIR.   Late
April, annual, 3 days, Philadelphia Civic Center.
Contact: Folk Fair, Nationalities Service Center,
1300 Spruce Street, Philadelphia, Pennsylvania 19107.

The fair explores the cultures of over 50 different
ethnic groups.   Traditionally costumed performers
do folk songs and dances such as the Thai Peacock
dance, the Mozambique Kitoto dance, and traditional
Estonian, Bulgarian, Israeli and other national dances.
Authentic crafts are exhibited and demonstrated including, for example, Ghanian drum signaling, ceramics from Holland or the art of egg painting.
Ethnics foods are also on hand.   Begun around 1955.

★ 2486 ★
Pittsburgh - PITTSBURGH FOLK FESTIVAL.   May or
June, 3 days, Civic Arena.   Contact: Director,
Pittsburgh Folk Festival, 575 Sixth Avenue, Pittsburgh,
Pennsylvania 15219.

Performers from more than two dozen countries present
live music and folk dancing in authentic native
costumes.   Display booths feature artifacts and handicrafts while ethnic foods are served.

★ 2487 ★
Schaefferstown - FOLK FESTIVAL.   Late July,
annual, 2 days.   Contact: Historic Schaefferstown
Festival Committee, Box 307, Schaefferstown, Pennsylvania 17088.

Festival offers demonstration of cooking, crafts,
gardening, decoration of eggs.   Tour of eighteenth
century farmhouse and wagon rides are available.
Display of old fashioned farm tools, entertainment,
gospel singing, and flea market.

★ 2488 ★
Schwenksville - PHILADELPHIA FOLK FESTIVAL.
Late August, annual, 3 days, Old Pool's Farm.
Contact: Howard Yanks, Chairman, Philadelphia
Folk Festival, c/o The Philadelphia Folksong Society,
7113 Emlen Street, Philadelphia, Pennsylvania 19119.

Presents mainly folk music, dancing and crafts. Musicians include boogie woogie and blues piano players,
fiddlers, American Indian music, Latin bands, bluegrass and symphony, playing in both evening and daytime concerts.   There is clog dancing, traditional
British dancers, Afro-American Dance Ensemble, and
Eastern European dancers.   There are also craft exhibits, workshops and campfire sings.   Called one of

the most important events of its kind in the United
States.   Begun around 1962.

★ 2489 ★
Springs - DUTCH MOUNTAIN FOLK FESTIVAL.
Early October, annual, 2 days, Between Salisbury,
Pennsylvania (U.S. 219) and Grantsville, Maryland
(U.S. 40 on Pennsylvania 669).   Contact: Springs
Folk Festival, Springs, Pennsylvania 15562; or
Alta E. Schrock, Penn Alps, Grantville, Maryland
21536.

Early days in historic, scenic Casselman Valley are
relived.   Men hollow out wooden troughs with an
adze; shave shingles; thresh grain with hand flails;
operate two-horse ·tread power cleaning grain with
old "wind-mill"; demonstrate boring of wooden water
pipes; blacksmithing and horse-shoeing.   Women
weave and spin, make rugs, do quilting, candlemaking,
etc.   Demonstrations of handicraft are in large crafts
tent, which include quilting, wool processing, and
rugmaking.

★ 2490 ★
West Hazelton - FOLK FESTIVAL.   Mid June,
annual, 2 days, Village of Eckley.   Contact: Department of Commerce, Bureau of Travel Development,
431 South Office Building, Harrisburg, Pennsylvania
17120.

Country, bluegrass, polka music; workshops; crafts
demonstrations; and exhibits highlight the festival
events and activities.

★ 2491 ★
White Haven - POCONO'S BLUEGRASS FOLK
FESTIVAL.   Mid July, annual, 3 days, Ski Lodge
and Campgrounds.   Contact: National Folk Festival
Association, Suite 1118, 1346 Connecticut Avenue,
Northwest, Washington, D.C. 20036.

Bluegrass music and folk arts and crafts highlight
this festival in the beautiful setting of the Pocono
Mountains.

RHODE ISLAND

★ 2492 ★
Newport - NEWPORT FOLK FESTIVAL.   Mid July,
annual, 1 weekend.   Contact: Newport Folk Festival,
Newport, Rhode Island 02840.

Leading folk-music singers, along with performers from
the ranks of commercial country and western music,
rhythm and blues, and folk-inspired rock music.
Founded in 1959.

Folk

SOUTH CAROLINA

★ 2493 ★
Darlington - DARLINGTON FOLK FESTIVAL. Late November, annual, 2 days. Contact: Chamber of Commerce, 102 Orange Street, Box 274, Darlington, South Carolina 29532.

Features a concert with groups from all over the country, and sometimes Canada, plus a coffee house. Begun around 1967.

TENNESSEE

★ 2494 ★
Cosby - FOLK FESTIVAL OF THE SMOKIES. Mid September, 3 days. Contact: Jean and Lee Schilling, Post Office Box 8, Cosby, Tennessee 37722.

Traditional musicians play the folk music of the Appalachians. In addition, there is story telling, workshops, and a hymn sing. Begun in 1970.

TEXAS

★ 2495 ★
Kerrville - KERRVILLE FOLK FESTIVAL. Late May (Memorial Day weekend), annual, 4 days, Quiet Valley Ranch. Contact: Kerrville Festivals, Box 1466, Kerrville, Texas 78028.

A 50 booth craft village is set up. Musical events include workshops and afternoon and evening concerts of contemporary Texas folksongs, plus a Sunday folk mass and the National Yodeling contest. Also featured is the Texas Hot Air Balloon Race. Begun in 1972.

★ 2496 ★
Livingston - FOLK LIFE FESTIVAL. August. Contact: Polk County Chamber of Commerce, Box 1267, Livingston, Texas 77351.

Activities include a square dance and photo contest, or the visitor may seek entertainment at the art show, antique show, or melodrama.

★ 2497 ★
San Antonio - TEXAS FOLKLIFE FESTIVAL. Early August, annual, 4 days, Institute of Texas Cultures, HemisFair Plaza. Contact: Texas Folklife Festival, U.T. Institute of Texas Cultures, Post Office Box 1226, San Antonio, Texas 78294; or Chamber of Commerce, Post Office Box 1628, San Antonio, Texas 78296.

Celebrates the ethnic groups that have contributed to the history of Texas, featuring their costumes, arts, crafts, food, dances and music. There are many contests such as roping, arm wrestling, watermelon seed spitting, caber and sheaf tossing, and Cajun crawfish races. Many crafts are demonstrated, along with many of the activities of pioneer life such as house raising or rail splitting. Begun in 1972.

★ 2498 ★
Seagraves - HOLIDAY FOLK FESTIVAL. November. Contact: Seagraves Chamber of Commerce, Box 1316, Seagraves, Texas 79359.

Activities include fiddlers' contest, folk dancing, crafts demonstrations, $50 penny sandpile for kids, and booths with homemade food.

VERMONT

★ 2499 ★
Lyndon Center - FIDDLE CONTEST AND CRAFT FAIR. April, 1 day, Lyndon State College. Contact: Lyndon State College, Lyndon Center, Vermont 05850.

A folksy affair with fiddlers' fiddling and display and sale of a variety of local crafts.

VIRGINIA

★ 2500 ★
Abingdon - FOLK AND FOLK SONG FESTIVALS. July and August, annual. Contact: Folk and Folk Song Festivals, Washington County Chamber of Commerce, 127 West Main Street, Abingdon, Virginia 24210.

Singing and dancing in the local folk style; rustic handicraft exhibits, and plays. Sponsored by the Virginia Highlands Festival of Arts and Crafts.

★ 2501 ★
Abingdon - HIGHLAND ARTS AND CRAFTS FESTIVAL. August, annual, 15 days. Contact: Abingdon Chamber of Commerce, 127 West Main Street, Post Office Box 738, Abingdon, Virginia 24210.

A celebration of the traditional life in the Blue Ridge Mountains. Crafts are exhibited and demonstrated, and folk singing and dancing are performed. In addition there are lectures, seminars, and art classes. Plays are presented and tours given.

VIRGINIA (Continued)

★ 2502 ★
Arlington - NORTHERN VIRGINIA FOLK FESTIVAL
AND BAZAAR. Early May, annual, 3 days,
Thomas Jefferson Community Center. Contact:
Arlington County Recreation Division, 300 North Park
Drive, Arlington, Virginia 22203.

General activities including displays of historic interest,
and demonstrations of crafts such as glass-blowing.
On the C & O Canal, a flatbottomed boat and a
rope make an improvised ferry. Begun around 1970.

★ 2503 ★
Ferrum - BLUE RIDGE FOLKLIFE FESTIVAL. Late
October, 2 days, Ferrum College. Contact: Blue
Ridge Institute, Ferrum College, Ferrum, Virginia
24088.

Traditional American music with more than 100 participating musicians. Special musical workshops,
and square dancing. Traditional regional foods are
offered. More than 100 craftsmen demonstrate quilting, soap-making, and other traditional crafts. Begun in 1974.

★ 2504 ★
Norfolk - OLD DOMINION UNIVERSITY FOLK
FESTIVAL. Mid October, annual, 3 days, Old
Dominion University. Contact: Songmakers of
Virginia, 4318 Hampton Boulevard, Norfolk, Virginia
23518; or Bob Zentz, 4318 Hampton Boulevard,
Norfolk, Virginia 23508.

The festival offers traditional and contemporary music.
Events include concerts, dancing, mini-concerts, and
workshops in a wide variety. Children's concerts
are also offered. Many different performing artists
are present.

★ 2505 ★
Vienna - NATIONAL FOLK FESTIVAL. July or
August, annual, 3 days, Wolf Trap Farm Park.
Contact: National Folk Festival Association, Suite
1118, 1346 Connecticut Avenue, Northwest, Washing-
ton, D.C. 20036.

Traditional music and dancing presented by such groups
as the Basques, the Cajuns, Mexican-Americans, West
Indians, British, Amerindians, Ozark Mountaineers,
etc. Noted musicians demonstrate a variety of styles.
Workshops are held in instrument and musical style.
Instrument-makers demonstrate, teach and sell their
work. Folk dancing is not only demonstrated, but
taught. Each year, a featured craft is demonstrated

and exhibited. There are dance parties and special
children's activities.

WASHINGTON

★ 2506 ★
Seattle - NORTHWEST REGIONAL FOLKLIFE
FESTIVAL. May, annual, 4 days, Seattle Center.
Contact: C.D. Hughbanks, Seattle Center Depart-
ment, 305 Harrison Street, Seattle, Washington 98109.

Traditional American and Indian music and dance, arts
and crafts, bluegrass, blues, and fiddlers' contest.
Begun around 1972.

WEST VIRGINIA

★ 2507 ★
Charleston - APPALACHIAN FESTIVAL. Early April,
annual, 3 days, Morris Harvey College. Contact:
Department of Commerce, State of West Virginia,
Capitol Building, Charleston, West Virginia 25305.

The purpose of the festival always has been to examine
and celebrate the living heritage of southern Appalachia, as it is expressed by distinguished practitioners
in the fields of humanities, social science, and performing arts. Consequently, the festival has not
explored in depth the folklife traditions of the regions.
Events include films, forums, seminars, workshops,
concerts, and the display and sale of mountain crafts
by traditional craftsmen. Begun around 1969.

★ 2508 ★
Glenville - WEST VIRGINIA STATE FOLK FESTIVAL.
Mid June, annual, 4 days, Glenville College Auditorium. Contact: Fern Rollyson, Box 127, Glenville, West Virginia 26351.

Events include drama, folk music, square dancing,
exhibits, a spelling bee, a fiddlers' contest, a
country auction, old-time hymns, concerts, arts and
crafts, and over 50 different contests. Begun around
1950.

★ 2509 ★
Keyser - MOUNTAIN HERITAGE FESTIVAL. April,
annual, 4 days, Potomac State College. Contact:
Lowell Markey, Mountain Heritage Committee, Potomac
State College, Keyser, West Virginia 26726.

Events include fiddling and banjo contests, arts and
crafts, square dance, and cooking. Begun around
1972.

WEST VIRGINIA (Continued)

★ 2510 ★
Pipestem - PIPESTEM FOLK MUSIC FESTIVAL.
August, 2-3 days, Appalachian South Folklife Center.
Contact: Don West, Post Office Box 5, Pipestem,
West Virginia 25979.

Appalachian folklife, music, arts and crafts, workshops, and concerts - very traditional.

WISCONSIN

★ 2511 ★
Milwaukee - SUMMERFEST.   Mid July, annual,
10 days.   Contact: Convention and Visitors Bureau,
828 North Broadway, Milwaukee, Wisconsin 53202.

Music concerts including jazz and country-western
multi-national folk festival.

CANADA - MANITOBA

★ 2512 ★
Winnipeg - FOLKLORAMA.   Mid August, annual,
1 week.   Contact: Mr. Vic Krens, Public Relations, Folklorama, 807-294 Portage Avenue, Winnipeg, Manitoba R3C 0B9, Canada.

Popular international festival displays the colorful
ethnic mosaic of the city in a variety of settings,
with more than 50 different local ethnic groups in
pavillions located around the city.   Entertainment
is provided in the form of traditional music, dance,
song, culture, crafts, costumes, and food.

★ 2513 ★
Winnipeg - WINNIPEG FOLK FESTIVAL.   July,
annual, 3 days (1 weekend).   Contact: The Winnipeg Folk Festival, 107 Osborne Street, Winnipeg,
Manitoba R3L 1Y4, Canada.

Features top folk artists from across the continent.
Designed for all ages and musical tastes, workshops
and entertainment are provided.   The variety of
Canadian folk-styles includes Scottish, English,
Prairie, Acadian, and Maritime.   There is also some
United States folk music.

CANADA - ONTARIO

★ 2514 ★
Toronto - MARIPOSA FOLK FESTIVAL.   Late June,
annual, 3 days, Toronto Islands.   Contact: Mariposa
Folk Festival, 329 Saint George Street, Toronto,

Ontario M5R 2R2, Canada.

An international folk festival featuring ethnic exhibits, demonstrations, and dancing; a variety of
musical entertainment, workshops, and crafts.

Food and Drink
(Includes Wine)

ALASKA

★ 2515 ★
Anchorage - NATIVE FOODS DAY.   February.
Contact: Juneau Area Office, Bureau of Indian
Affairs, U.S. Department of the Interior, Federal
Building, Box 3-8000, Juneau, Alaska 99801.

A selection of the foods of the native Eskimos:
muktuk, wild berries, seal oil and liver, Sitka deer,
reindeer, caribou shee fish, white fish, seaweed and
Eskimo ice cream.

CALIFORNIA

★ 2516 ★
Gilroy - BONANZA DAYS WINE FESTIVAL.   Late
September, 4 days, 2 each, 1 week apart.   Contact:
California Chamber of Commerce, 455 Capitol Mall,
Sacramento, California 95814.

A parade, barbeque, games, and, of course, wine
tasting and displays.

★ 2517 ★
Healdsburg - RUSSIAN RIVER WINE FEST.   Mid
May, 1 day, Healdsburg Plaza.   Contact: Information Officer, State of California Department of Commerce, 1400 Tenth Street, Sacramento, California
95814.

Tasting of local Sonoma wines, food, entertainment,
a barbeque, and a dance.

★ 2518 ★
Lodi - LODI GRAPE FESTIVAL AND NATIONAL
WINE SHOW.   Mid September, 3 days, Festival
Grounds.   Contact: Chamber of Commerce, Lodi,
California 95240.

Entertainment, parades, exhibits, events in stadium,
dancing, songs, and "wine, wine, wine".

★ 2519 ★
Los Angeles - WINE FESTIVAL.   October, annual,

CALIFORNIA (Continued)

all month (on weekends), San Antonio Winery. Contact: Southern California Visitors Council, 705 West Seventh Street, Los Angeles, California 90017.

Music, wine tasting, and winery tours celebrating over 58 years of operation. Begun around 1970.

★ 2520 ★
Napa - GRECIAN WINE FESTIVAL. Mid September, 1 day. Contact: California Chamber of Commerce, 455 Capitol Mall, Sacramento, California 95814.

A wine fest in this area of grape and wine production.

★ 2521 ★
Sonoma - VALLEY OF THE MOON VINTAGE FESTIVAL (VALLEY OF THE MOON FOLK DANCE FESTIVAL). September, 1-2 days, Sonoma Plaza. Contact: Redwood Empire Association, 476 Post Street, San Francisco, California 94102; or Chamber of Commerce, Sonoma, California 95437.

A wine festival including wine-tasting, folk dances, parades, arts and crafts, games, music, and entertainment. Commemorates the colorful history of California and the viticulture of the environ. Historic vignettes and an auction.

ILLINOIS

★ 2522 ★
Nauvoo - GRAPE FESTIVAL. August-September (Labor Day weekend), banks of the Mississippi. Contact: The Division of Tourism, Illinois Department of Business and Economic Development, 222 South College Street, Springfield, Illinois 62706.

Re-enactment of an old French rite, Wedding of the Wine and Cheese, symbolic of the idea that the two are best when taken together. Festival honors early Mormon and French settlers.

LOUISIANA

★ 2523 ★
Bridge City - GUMBO FESTIVAL. Mid October, annual, 2-3 days. Contact: Mrs. Elaine Boatwright, 515 Oak Avenue, Bridge City, Louisiana 70094.

An enormous gumbo pot with gumbo cooking and eating contests, art exhibition, continuous Cajun entertainment, fireworks, regional food, parade, sky divers, coronation of King Creole Gumbo, Coro-

nation Ball, and beautiful child contest. Started in 1973.

★ 2524 ★
Chackbay - GUMBO FESTIVAL. Mid August, annual, 2 days, Schneider Park. Contact: Louisiana Tourist Commission, Post Office Box 44291, Baton Rouge, Louisiana 70804.

The festival offers many varieties of Cajun food, including, of course, gumbo, and seafood, chicken, sausage, seafood with okra, andouille varieties. Activities include "fais-do-do" (street dancing); a street fair with booths and carnival rides; Cajun, country and rock bands; auction; and Gumbo Parade with a festival king and queen. Begun around 1972.

★ 2525 ★
Delcambre - SHRIMP FESTIVAL. Mid August, annual, 5 days. Contact: Corey Bourgue, Post Office Box 288, Delcambre, Louisiana 70528.

Shrimp galore! Festivities include dances, bingo, street dancing, water fights, and bicycle races.

★ 2526 ★
Gonzales - JAMBALAYA FESTIVAL. Early June, annual, 2 days. Contact: Elsie B. Walker, 432 East McArthur, Gonzales, Louisiana 70737.

Honors the Creole-Cajun dish, jambalaya. There is a cooking contest, at which the new World Champion Jambalaya Cook is crowned by the Jambalaya Queen. Jambalaya eating contest, Jambalaya Handicaps race for quarter horses, and Jambalaya Golf Tournament. In addition, there is an Open House Show, a fair with all types of booths, a large art and ceramics show, presentation of the Jamabalaya Queen, and bands playing for street dancing, archery contest, skydiving and a baseball game. Begun around 1967.

★ 2527 ★
LaPlace - ANDOUILLE FESTIVAL. Late October, 3 days, LaPlace Dragway on Airline Highway. Contact: Louisiana Tourist Commission, Post Office Box 44291, Baton Rouge, Louisiana 70804.

The festival centers around the smoked pork sausage known as andouille which is served along with other delicacies. Continuous entertainment is provided by local bands, exhibits, and shows of all types. Cooking and eating contests.

Food and Drink

LOUISIANA

★ 2528 ★
New Orleans - FOOD FESTIVAL. Early July, 2-3
days, Rivergate, International Hotel. Contact:
Louisiana Restaurant Association, 2000 International
Trade Mart, New Orleans, Louisiana 70130; or
Ms. Gayle Burchfield, 334 Royal Street, New Orleans,
Louisiana 70130.

The festival opens with the ceremonial breaking of a
loaf of French bread. World renowned chefs compete in culinary art displays, shown at Rivergate.
In addition, there is a food tasting event. In the
International Hotel, there is a banquet, Gourmet
Dinner de l'Art Culinaire International. The dinner
is preceded by cocktails and consists of many courses
of New Orleans' famous cuisine. Started in 1969.

★ 2529 ★
Raceland - SAUCE PIQUANTE FESTIVAL AND
PIROQUE RACE. Early October, annual, 1 day,
Bayou Lafourche-Saint Mary Nativity Church. Con-
tact: Louisiana Tourist Commission, Post Office Box
44291, Baton Rouge, Louisiana 70804.

The evening before the festival, Queen Sauce Piquante and her King are crowned at the Central
Lafourche High School auditorium. The food attractions include sauce piquante, chicken, and other
delicacies. Also included are tours of local plantations, art exhibits, an auction, hay ride, entertainment and piroque (a boat used in the bayou) races.
Begun around 1970.

MICHIGAN

★ 2530 ★
Paw Paw - GRAPE AND WINE FESTIVAL. Late
September. Contact: Chamber of Commerce, Box
3, Paw Paw, Michigan 49079.

The grape is honored with wine tasting, winery tours,
an exhibition of a mechanical grape picker, and a
grape stomping contest. There are games and competitions, including a pony pull, bingo, a waterball
contest and turtle derby. Entertaining the participants are dramatic performances, a magic show,
parades, a carnival, folk dancers, choral groups,
an art show, window displays and an ice cream
social. Begun around 1968.

NEW YORK

★ 2531 ★
New York - INTERNATIONAL WINE AND CHEESE

TASTING FESTIVAL. Mid October, 9 days, New
York Coliseum. Contact: New York Convention
and Visitors Bureau, Incorporated, 90 East 42nd
Street, New York, New York 10017.

"A festival of fun, learning and good taste". The
festival features a selection of wines and cheeses from
around the world. All of the exhibits are meant to
be sampled and savored.

OKLAHOMA

★ 2532 ★
Stillwater - CHEESE FESTIVAL. Late October-early
November, annual, 2 days, Stillwater National Bank
Parking Garage. Contact: Department of Animal
Sciences and Industry, Oklahoma State University,
Stillwater, Oklahoma 74074; or Chamber of Com-
merce, 502 South Main Street, Stillwater, Oklahoma
74074.

The most famous feature of the event is the sampling
of cheese and sausage offered free of charge by exhibiting companies. Student clubs also sell food and
cider in booths at the fair. Special exhibits and
foods are also prepared. Sausage and cheese recipes
are judged and prizes awarded. The Oklahoma State
Dairy princess appears at the festival. Co-sponsored
by the Oklahoma State University and the Stillwater
Chamber of Commerce. Begun in 1950.

PENNSYLVANIA

★ 2533 ★
Barnesville - INTERNATIONAL WINE AND CHEESE
FESTIVAL. Late July-early August, annual, 3 days,
Lakewood Park. Contact: Department of Commerce,
Bureau of Travel Development, 431 South Office
Building, Harrisburg, Pennsylvania 17120.

Wine and cheese from all over the world. Craftsmen,
and wine-making demonstrations, music, and entertainment.

TEXAS

★ 2534 ★
Crane - FREEZE OFF. August. Contact: Chamber of Commerce, 409 South Gaston, Crane, Texas
79731.

Centers around the judging and selling of homemake
ice cream. Festival also includes carnival-midway
and beauty pageant.

TEXAS (Continued)

★ 2535 ★
San Marcos - REPUBLIC OF TEXAS CHILYMPIAD.
September, annual, 3 days, Hay's County Civic
Center. Contact: Chamber of Commerce, Box
2310, San Marcos, Texas 78666.

This is the State Chili Cooking Contest. Chile chefs
concoct their firery brews for a panel of judges from
the Chili Appreciation Society, International. Other
attractions include an old fiddlers' contest, western
music and dancing, and an arts and crafts display.
Begun around 1970.

★ 2536 ★
Terlingua - WORLD'S CHAMPIONSHIP CHILI
COOK-OFF. Early November, annual. Contact:
Texas Tourist Development Agency, Box 12008,
Capitol Station, Austin, Texas 78711.

Annual cook-off decides the champion chili cooker.
Up to 5,000 contestants, hecklers and spectators converge on downtown Terlingua for the unpredictable
event. Dirt airstrip hosts planes from throughout the
nation, and since there are no accommodations in
Terlingua, campers and makeshift facilities are much
in evidence. Texas is represented by winner of
earlier state chili cook-off; other contestants include
individuals and representatives from world-wide chapters
of Chili Appreciation Society International. Event
is controlled by CASI and members of Terlingua
"city council", composed of columnists, writers and
humorists - all non-residents. Every contest sees
heated debate, charges of fraud and skulduggery, and
occasional masked "outlaws" stealing or switching
ballot boxes.

★ 2537 ★
Victoria - INTERNATIONAL FOOD FAIR. Late
August, annual, 1 day, Victoria Community Center.
Contact: Food Fair, HEAR Foundation, Rowland
School, Victoria, Texas 77901.

Sponsored by the Board of the HEAR Foundation, the
event offers a variety of interesting foods and an
evening of continuous entertainment. Begun around
1969.

VIRGINIA

★ 2538 ★
Great Falls - FLAPJACK FESTIVAL. Late August,
annual, 1 day, Colvin Run Mill Park. Contact:
Colvin Run Mill Park, 10017 Colvin Run Road, Great
Falls, Virginia 22066.

In addition to a flapjack eating contest, and cider
and biscuits, there are tours of the grist mill and the
miller's house, craft exhibitions, live bluegrass music,
entertainment, games, contests, and crafts exhibitions.
Begun in 1976.

CANADA - ONTARIO

★ 2539 ★
Saint Catharines - NIAGARA GRAPE AND WINE
FESTIVAL. Late September, annual, 10 days.
Contact: Niagara Grape and Wine Festival, c/o
Brian Leyden, Ontario Editorial Bureau, 215 Ontario
Street, Post Office Box 745, Saint Catharine's,
Ontario L2R 6Y3, Canada.

A celebration of the grape harvest with wine-tasting
parties, and barbeques. King and queen coronation,
bands, street dancing, parades, including the Pied
Piper parade, and ethnic events complete the activities.

History

ALABAMA

★ 2540 ★
Birmingham - BIRMINGHAM GENEALOGICAL
SOCIETY FESTIVAL. October, 1 day, Art Gallery
of Birmingham Public Library. Contact: Mrs. Thomas
Seay, Post Office Box 2432, Birmingham, Alabama 35201.

Exhibits of family history and genealogy by members
of the society.

ALASKA

★ 2541 ★
Fairbanks - GOLDEN DAYS CELEBRATION. Late
July (around the 22nd), annual, 1 week. Contact:
Alaska Division of Tourism, Pouch E, Juneau, Alaska
99801.

Celebrates discovery of gold at Fairbanks by Felix Pedro,
July 22, 1902. Largest summer event in Alaska.
Parades, gold panning, street dancing and "Golden"
girls 'arrest' anyone not wearing pioneer outfits.

★ 2542 ★
Kodiak - CRY OF THE WILD RAM. Early August,
annual, 9 days, Monashka Bay's Amphitheatre. Contact:
Margaret Childs, Kodiak-Baranoff Productions, Incorporated, Post Office Box 1792, Kodiak, Alaska 99615.

This historical drama is part of the Russian festival.

ALASKA   (Continued)

★ 2543 ★
Sitka - ALASKA DAYS FESTIVAL.   Mid October,
annual, 3 days.   Contact: Alaska Travel Division,
Pouch E, Juneau, Alaska 99801.

Features a reenactment of the ceremony of transfer
of Alaska from Russia to the United States.   Other
highlights are a parade, Tlingit dances, and the
Baranof Ball.

ARIZONA

★ 2544 ★
Glendale - FIESTA DE INDEPENDENCIA DE MEXICO.
September (15th and 16th), annual, 2 days, Rose
Land Park or City Park.   Contact: Glendale Cham-
ber of Commerce, 7125 North 58th Drive, Glendale,
Arizona 85301.

Grito de Dolores - the cry of independence by Father
Dolores Hidalgo.   Coronation of the fiesta queen--
symbol of the kind of government ruling Mexico.
Sponsored by the Junta Patriotica Mexicana de Glendale.   Started in 1932.

★ 2545 ★
Wickenburg - GOLD RUSH DAYS.   Early February,
3 days.   Contact: Round-Up Club, Incorporated,
Post Office Drawer CC, Wickenburg, Arizona 85358.

Celebrates the 'wild west' with panning for gold
(finders keepers), parades, pony express races, shoot-
outs, simulated massacre, and a rodeo.

CALIFORNIA

★ 2546 ★
Agoura - RENAISSANCE PLEASURE FAIRE AND
SPRINGTIME MARKET.   Late April-late May,
annual, 6 weekends, Old Paramount Ranch.   Con-
tact: Chamber of Commerce, Post Office Box 208,
Agoura, California 91301.

Recreation of an English country fair featuring entertainment, crafts, music, foods, games and pageantry
of Elizabethan England in Drake's era.   Begun
around 1962.

★ 2547 ★
Angels Camp - RENAISSANCE FAIR.   Mid June,
1 day.   Contact: California Chamber of Commerce,
455 Capitol Mall, Sacramento, California 95814.

Arts and crafts, entertainment, and other activities
to recall earlier times.

★ 2548 ★
Bodfish - EARLY VALLEY DAYS.   July, 4 days,
Silver City Ghost Town.   Contact: Dave Mills,
Ghost Town, Post Office Box 187, Bodfish, Cali-
fornia 93205.

To attract farmers and hobbyists of old trucks, tractors,
steam or gas engines, hay bailers and threshing machines in working order.   Costumes of the 1800's.
Trophies and prizes.   Visitors invited to come as you
are for a real chuckwagon breakfast and dinner from
the original Larson 1800 Chuck Wagon.   Homemade
bread and pies from old woodburning range.   Begun
around 1974.

★ 2549 ★
Brea - BONANZA DAYS.   Late April-early May,
5 days.   Contact: Southern California Visitors
Council, 705 West Seventh Street, Los Angeles,
California 90017.

Events include a beard growing contest, baking and
pigtail contests, and a parade.

★ 2550 ★
Coloma - GOLD DISCOVERY DAYS.   Late January,
2 days.   Contact: Chamber of Commerce, Coloma,
California 95613; or California Chamber of Commerce, 455 Capitol Mall, Sacramento, California
95814.

Dancing, parade, fiddler contest, and other events
in this celebration of the days when gold was dis-
covered in California.

★ 2551 ★
Fillmore - EARLY CALIFORNIA DAYS FESTIVAL.
May, 3 days.   Contact: California Chamber of
Commerce, 455 Capitol Mall, Sacramento, Cali-
fornia 95814.

A parade, a carnival, and food and games booths
highlight this celebration of earlier times in California.

★ 2552 ★
Fullerton - MEDIEVAL FESTIVAL.   Late April-early
May, annual, 5 days, California State University,
Fullerton "quad".   Contact: Charmaine Coker,
Medieval Festival Coordinator, University Activities
Center, California State University, Fullerton,
California 92634.

CALIFORNIA (Continued)

The festival is an attempt to look at history by bringing an era to life stressing the literature, culture, food and dress. Major events include English and foreign plays, poetry readings, musicians, chants, fencing, films, chess tournaments, art, plant and food booths. Displays of brass rubbings and manuscripts are located in several areas of the campus.

★ 2553 ★
Kernville - WHISKEY FLATS DAYS. Mid February, 3-5 days. Contact: Kernville Chamber of Commerce, Box 397, Kernville, California 93238.

Reliving of the gold rush days when the town was known as Whiskey Flats. Tours of old mining camps, beard growing, fiddlers, frog jumping, greased pig contest, old-time fiddlers' contest, mule races, pet parade, Boot Hill epitaph writing contest, and an authentic 1860's costume competition.

★ 2554 ★
Lake Elsinore - FRONTIER DAYS. May, 3 days, State Park. Contact: Southern California Visitors Bureau, 705 West Seventh Street, Los Angeles, California 90017.

This celebration of early days in frontier California includes a parade and a rodeo.

★ 2555 ★
Laytonville - RENAISSANCE FAIR. Late May, 3 days. Contact: Chamber of Commerce, Laytonville, California 95454; or California Chamber of Commerce, 455 Capitol Mall, Sacramento, California 95814.

Arts and crafts, wandering minstrels, and period costumes all to transport those in attendance back to an earlier time.

★ 2556 ★
Los Angeles - RENAISSANCE PLEASURE FAIRE. Mid April, 3 days, California State Museum of Science and Industry. Contact: Southern California Visitors Council, 705 West Seventh Street, Los Angeles, California 90017.

Exhibition of cottage industry filled with folk history, giant figures, costumes and crafts.

★ 2557 ★
Petaluma - OLD ADOBE DAYS FIESTA. Mid August,

annual, 1-2 days, Petaluma Adobe or Petaluma Old Adobe State Park. Contact: Redwood Empire Association, Visitor Information Center, 476 Post Street, San Francisco, California 94102.

Parades, games, crafts, demonstrations in a re-creation of the life of the Adobe Indians in the·1840's.

★ 2558 ★
Placentia - HERITAGE DAY FESTIVAL. October, 10 days. Contact: Orange County Chamber of Commerce, 401 Bank of America Tower, The City, One City Boulevard, West, Orange, California 92668.

Gala events in celebration of earlier times in Placentia.

★ 2559 ★
Sacramento - PONY EXPRESS ANNIVERSARY CELEBRATION. April, annual, 2 days. Contact: R. M. Stone, 1029 Second Street, Sacramento, California 95814.

Ceremony and festival including concerts and historic displays, related to the pony-express service, of which Sacramento was the western-most terminus.

★ 2560 ★
San Diego - OLD TOWN FIESTA DE LA PRIMAVERA. Mid May, annual, 4 days, Old Town State park. Contact: Dick Yale, San Diego Union Museum, 2626 San Diego Avenue, San Diego, California 92110.

An art show, historical exhibits, mariachis, fiddlers and banjo contests, a buffalo barbeque, Spanish dancers and Indian exhibits invoke the "Day of the Dons". Begun around 1970.

★ 2561 ★
San Diego - RAMONA FESTIVAL. Mid November, annual, 2 days, Old Town San Diego, 2400 Block San Diego Avenue. Contact: San Diego Convention and Visitors Bureau, 1200 Third Avenue, Suite 824, San Diego, California 92101.

Recreation of an Indian village with authentic teepees and demonstrations of Indian crafts such as jewelry making and the making of Indian fry bread. Indian and Mexican dancers and mariachis entertain, and there is a tour of the adobe chapel (supposed site of the marriage of Ramona and Alessandro) by costumed guides. Arts and crafts show and demonstration. Mexican cantina, and pancake sale. Sponsored by San Diego Historical Days Association.

History

CALIFORNIA (Continued)

★ 2562 ★
San Diego - TREK TO THE CROSS. July, annual,
2 days, Old Town Plaza to Presidio Park Cross (near
Serra Museum). Contact: Old San Diego Chamber
of Commerce, 3966 Mason Street, San Diego, California 92110.

The Trek is a historical costume parade recreating
the journey of Padre Junipero Serra. Additional
festivities include mariachis, arts and crafts exhibits,
and night street dancing. Begun around 1956.

★ 2563 ★
San Francisco - COLUMBUS DAY CELEBRATION.
October (around Columbus Day), 9 days, Telegraph
Hill, Ghirardelli Square, Aquatic Park, Washington
Square. Contact: San Francisco Convention and
Visitors Bureau, News Bureau, 1390 Market Street,
San Francisco, California 94102.

Large parade with floats and bands. Re-enactment
of the Columbus landing. A "You Are There" inter-
view with Queen Isabella and her court. Jugglers,
jesters, actors, acrobats, swordsmen, "surprise guests".
Also in the parade, equestrians, state, county and
city officials, drill corps, baton twirlers, clowns,
puppeteers, a calliope, antique vehicles and numerous
novelty units. Golf tournament, softball tournament,
bocce ball tournament, and soccer match. Carnival,
blessing of the fishing fleet, aquatic pageant, ceremonies at the statue of Columbus on Telegraph Hill,
beauty pageant to choose Queen Isabella.

★ 2564 ★
San Francisco - GREAT DICKENS CHRISTMAS FAIR
AND PICKWICK COMIC. Late November-late
December, annual, 6 weekends, next to the San
Francisco Produce Market. Contact: Theme Events
Enterprises, Post Office Box 18104, San Francisco,
California 94118.

Five stages feature continuous entertainment in the
Victorian style including a Christmas pantomime, a
music hall, acrobats, comic recitation, magicians
and bands. In addition, there are Victorian shops,
an ale house, the passing of the Wassail Bowl, and
Fezziwig's Dance Party. Participants are urged to
wear Victorian costumes. Begun around 1970.

★ 2565 ★
San Pedro - SAN PEDRO CABRILLO FESTIVAL.
Early October, 1 day, Cabrillo Beach. Contact:
Southern California Visitors Council, 705 West
Seventh Street, Los Angeles, California 90017.

Includes a re-enactment of the historic landing of
the Portuguese navigator Juan Rodriguez Cabrillo.
Other special events are model ship building, mural
painting, sand construction contest, outdoor dinner,
and folk dancing.

★ 2566 ★
San Rafael - RENAISSANCE PLEASURE FAIRE.
Late August-September, annual, 6 weekends, Oak
Forest (Novato). Contact: Renaissance Faire, Post
Office Box 18104, San Francisco, California 94118.

Re-creation of an Elizabethan fair with giants, jugglers, fire-eaters, jesters, music, mummery, pageants,
plays, puppet shows, ale and wine gardens, variety
of gourmet foods, and hand-crafted wares. Opportunity to try crafts and games such as pitch-the-hay and
tug-o-war. Begun around 1963.

★ 2567 ★
Santa Barbara - WELCOME OF THE DE ANZA TREK.
Late February, 3 days, Fairgrounds. Contact:
Southern California Visitors Council, 705 West
Seventh Street, Los Angeles, California 90017.

The festival is a re-enactment of the 1775-1776
expedition from Mexico to San Francisco led by Juan
Bautista. The families who took part in the expedition are represented in the traveling party by persons
in Spanish costumes. Also takes place in Ventura.

★ 2568 ★
Santa Ynez - TORTILLA DAY. Early June, annual,
2 days. Contact: Southern California Visitors
Council, 705 West Seventh Street, Los Angeles,
California 90017.

Commemorates the anniversary of the founding of
Santa Ynez. Parade, booths, entertainment, competition in pie-eating contest, hog calling contest,
and tobacco spitting contest. Begun around 1964.

★ 2569 ★
Ventura - WELCOME OF THE DE ANZA TREK.
Late February, 3 days, Fairgrounds. Contact:
Southern California Visitors Council, 705 West
Seventh Street, Los Angeles, California 90017.

The festival is a re-enactment of the 1775-1776
expedition from Mexico to San Francisco led by Juan
Bautista. The families who took part in the expedition are represented in the traveling party by persons
in Spanish costumes. Also takes place in Santa
Barbara.

CALIFORNIA (Continued)

★ 2570 ★
Yucca Valley – GRUBSTAKE DAYS.   Late May,
4 days.   Contact: Southern California Visitors
Council, 705 West Seventh Street, Los Angeles,
California 90017.

Special events include a parade, a burro race and
rides, a beard contest, a greased pole contest, and
a pie eating contest.

COLORADO

★ 2571 ★
Central City – COLORADO DAY.   Early August
(1st), 1 day.   Contact: Jack Hidahl, Public Relations Coordinator, Central City, Colorado 80427.

The celebration described is in honor of Colorado's
statehood.   The celebration begins with a parade
of bands and floats with ethnic and historic themes.
Later in the day there is a City Hall restoration
ceremony, with a Colorado Day dinner at the Teller
House.

★ 2572 ★
Central City – GREGORY DAY.   Early May, 1
day, Gregory Monument.   Contact: Jack Hidahl,
Public Relations Coordinator, Central City, Colorado
80427.

Celebration of John Gregory's discovery in 1859 of
the first lode gold in Colorado.   Parade of bands
and floats with historic and ethnic themes.   The
Gilpin County Historical Society Annual Dinner is
held in the evening, followed by the Miner's Ball.
Celebrants are urged to wear appropriate costumes.

★ 2573 ★
Central City – LOU BUNCH DAY.   Late August,
1 day.   Contact: Jack Hidahl, Public Relations
Coordinator, Central City, Colorado 80427.

Salute to the madams and girls of Colorado's first
century.   Bed race on Main Street with award for
winning team.   Madams and Miners Ball in the
Teller House Ballroom with a Grand March to select
and present trophies to Madam of the Year and
Sporting House Girl of the Year.   Participants are
urged to wear costumes.

DELAWARE

★ 2574 ★
Dover – OLD DOVER DAYS.   Early May (1st week-
end), annual, 2 days.   Contact: Friends of Old
Dover, Box 44, Dover, Delaware 19901.

A public tour of some of the gardens and historic
buildings of Dover plus a few buildings of interest
located nearby.   Activities besides the tour include
little school children dance, horse and carriage
promenade, proclamation, maypole, minute men drill,
historical playlet, concerts and receptions.   Begun
in 1934.

★ 2575 ★
Newark – HERITAGE FAIR.   Mid July, annual,
White Clay Creek Park.   Contact: Greater Newark
Chamber of Commerce, 250 East Main Street, Newark,
Delaware 19711.

Medieval fair with jousting, archery, entertainment,
crafts, and food.

FLORIDA

★ 2576 ★
Miami – GRAN ROMERIA PONCE DE LEON.   Early
March, 1 day, Police Benevolent Association Park.
Contact: Greater Miami Chamber of Commerce, 1200
Biscayne Boulevard, Miami, Florida 33132.

An open air festival honoring Ponce de Leon.

★ 2577 ★
Punta Gorda – CHARLOTTE COUNTY HISTORICAL
FESTIVAL.   Mid March, 4 days.   Contact: Mrs.
Vasco Peeples, 3105 South Tamiami Trail, Punta
Gorda, Florida 33950.

Replay of Ponce de Leon's landing in Punta Gorda,
air show, boat races, parade and luncheon.

★ 2578 ★
Tampa – GASPARILLA PIRATE INVASION.   Mid
February, annual.   Contact: Ybor City Chamber
of Commerce, Post Office Box 5287, Tampa, Florida
33605.

A pirate crew sails into Tampa harbor to capture the
city and kidnap the mayor.   Victorious pirates swagger
through the streets during a parade of spectacular
floats and marching bands.   Pirates again appear in
a Torchlight Parade through Ybor City following an
afternoon Spanish Bean Soup Festival.   Free bean

FLORIDA (Continued)

soup, Cuban coffee, and bread are served to visitors as Spanish musicians and dancers entertain. Based on exploits of Jose Gaspar, the notorious pirate who once ravaged the Florida coast. Begun in 1904.

GEORGIA

★ 2579 ★
Savannah - GEORGIA WEEK CELEBRATION. Mid February, 8 days. Contact: Savannah Area Chamber of Commerce, 301 West Broad Street, Post Office Box 530, Savannah, Georgia 31402.

The celebration has a colonial theme. The parade includes youngsters in colonial costumes, demonstrations of spinning, the making and tasting of the coastal area's rolled sweet wafers, a slide presentation of colonial activities, country fair, and an historical pageant.

★ 2580 ★
Westville - FAIR OF 1850. Early November, annual, 10 days. Contact: 1850 Fair, c/o Westville Chamber of Commerce, Westville, Georgia.

Visitors to the re-created museum village are taken back to the life of 1850 with old time herbal medicines, mid nineteenth century needlework, ancient rifles, and other exhibits.

HAWAII

★ 2581 ★
Honolulu - ALOHA WEEK. Late October (around 3rd week), annual. Contact: Aloha Week Headquarters, 680 Ala Moana Boulevard, Room 402, Honolulu, Hawaii 96813.

The celebration is based on an ancient custom in Hawaii when the chief of Hawaii accepted taxes on the Name of Lono and the islanders then engaged in a week long festival of thanksgiving to the god for the gifts of the land. Celebrated on all the Hawaiian Islands this pageantry includes street dances, luaus, royal ball (Oahu), parade, canoe race, (Aloha Week Molokai-Oahu Canoe Race), floral floats in parade, and a songfest. There are exhibitions of poi-pounding, tapa-making, lei-stringing, and hala-weaving at a grass-thatched village in Ala Moana Park. Aloha Week king and queen (state wide) are selected. Begun around 1948.

★ 2582 ★
Honolulu - KING KAMEHAMEHA FESTIVITIES. Early June, annual, 5 days. Contact: Kamehameha Day Celebration, Post Office Box 119, Honolulu, Hawaii 96810.

June 11th is Kamehameha Day, honoring the king who was the first to rule over all of the islands. Festivities cover several days preceding and take place on various islands. There are parades, the statue of the King is draped with leis, canoe regattas, races, flower shows, marching bands, princesses to represent the various islands, balls, songs, dances, water sports, and hula pageants.

★ 2583 ★
Kauai Island - PRINCE KUHIO FESTIVAL. Early March, 9 days. Contact: Hawaii Visitors Bureau, 444 Rice Street, Lihue, Kauai, Hawaii 96766.

Honors Prince Junah Kuhio Kalanianaole, first Hawaiian delegate to Congress. Pageantry with songs and dances from that era. Ethnic programs, youth activities, sporting events, parade and elaborate royal ball, canoe races, and memorial services.

IDAHO

★ 2584 ★
Pierce - 1860 DAYS. August (1st weekend), 3 days. Contact: Carla Province, Pierce Celebrations, Incorporated, Pierce, Idaho 83546.

Fiddlers' contest, traditional American music, children's events, longhorn barbeque, lumberjack competition, Wheeley contest, horseshoe pitching, motorcycle and mini-bike races. Begun around 1969.

ILLINOIS

★ 2585 ★
Clayton - TURN-OF-THE-CENTURY CELEBRATION. Mid September, 2 days, Siloam State Park. Contact: Director, Division of Parks and Memorials, Program Services Section, 605 State Office Building, Springfield, Illinois 62706.

1880's-1920's era celebrated in music, theater, games, contests, and cultural demonstrations of the era, as well as a hot-air balloon ascent.

★ 2586 ★
Galena - U.S. GRANT CIVIL WAR CANTONMENT. Mid May, annual, 3 days. Contact: The Division

ILLINOIS (Continued)

of Tourism, Illinois Department of Business and Economic Development, 222 South College Street, Springfield, Illinois 62706.

Civil War re-enactment. Parade, Military Ball, demonstrations of musket, pistol and cannon firing, tomahawk and knife-throwing contests are featured events.

INDIANA

★ 2587 ★
Battle Ground - RALLY FOR OLD TIPPECANOE. Late May-early June, annual, 2 days, Tippecanoe battlefield. Contact: Program Director, Battleground Historical Corporation, Box 225, Battleground, Indiana 47920.

Celebration of "Tippecanoe and Tyler too" military drill, calvary and band units, fife and drum corps in period costumes, barbeque and buffalo stew, frontier drafts, horse-drawn vehicle parade, traditional arts and crafts, and early American music.

★ 2588 ★
Brookville - EARLY AMERICANA FESTIVAL. Mid June, 2 days, Franklin County Fairgrounds. Contact: Bill Culley, Moonlite Motel, Rural Route 1, Versailles, Indiana 47042.

Skills from an earlier era: log splitting and log-sawing contests, canoe and raft races, antique car and farm equipment contests, square dancing and fiddlers' contest plus early American arts and crafts, flea market and Civil War skirmish in full uniform.

★ 2589 ★
Columbus - MAY FAIRE. Late May-early June, 4 days, Mill Race Park, Columbus Commons. Contact: Director, Visitors Center, 506 Fifth Street, Columbus, Indiana 47201.

A Renaissance theme. Games and crafts (marathon games of chess, checkers, monopoly, etc.), demonstrations and sale of crafts products, Renaissance music, athletic events, jousting and gymnastics, parade, and all-community dance featuring everything from ballroom dancing to square dancing.

★ 2590 ★
Fort Wayne - THREE RIVERS FESTIVAL. Early July, 9 days, The Landing. Contact: Executive Director, Three Rivers Festival, 309 Central Building, Fort

Wayne, Indiana 46802.

Centers around Fort Wayne's historical background and ethnic diversity. International village, international pageants, arts and crafts, flower shows, athletic competitions, bazaars, bike tours, and special entertainment. Boat rides, a raft race, art and hobby shows, rugby, tennis, fast-pitch tournaments, Kekionga long rifles, a bed race, tractor pull, marathon, soap box derby, slow pitch games, dance-athon, and historical re-enactments.

★ 2591 ★
Friendship - SPRING MUZZLE-LOADING RIFLE SHOOTS. Mid May and mid August. Contact: Indiana Division of Tourism, 336 State House, Indianapolis, Indiana 46204.

Pioneer skills are demonstrated, including the shooting of muzzle-loading rifles, knife and tomahawk throws. There are deerskin costumes, and crafts and antiques are on display.

★ 2592 ★
Muncie - DELAWARE COUNTY HISTORICAL FESTIVAL. Late June, 2 days, Court House Square and McCulloch Park. Contact: Ern Parkison, Chairman, 1304 Greenbriar, Muncie, Indiana 47305.

Historical displays, flea markets, parade, art show, and cow-milking contest. 1890's men vs women baseball game. Rocker-thon and Calico Fancy Dress Ball. Horseshoe pitching, hay ride, games, music concert, Indian village, and historical pageants.

★ 2593 ★
New Carlisle - HISTORICAL DAYS. Late July, 3 days. Contact: Chairman, New Carlisle Historical Days, 123 East Michigan, New Carlisle, Indiana 46552.

Home tours, antique cars, horse show, staged bank hold-up and gunfight, arts and crafts, a flea market, antique airplanes and parachuting, old fashioned vocal and instrumental music, period costume contest, visits to vineyards and wine cellars, threshing, saw-milling, horse-pulling, antique car parade, and folk-dancing.

★ 2594 ★
Osgood - ROARING TWENTIES FESTIVAL. Late May-early June, 3 days, downtown area. Contact: Howard Bloss, Rural Route 3, Osgood, Indiana 47037.

Arts and crafts, flea markets, parade, antique car

INDIANA (Continued)

shows, "Roaring Twenties" fashion show, old-time movies, Miss Roaring Twenties contest, teen and adult dances, contests and booths, old time "Medicine Minstrel Show", street cakewalk, and gold-fish eating contest.

★ 2595 ★
Rockville - PARKE COUNTY COVERED BRIDGE FESTIVAL. Mid October, 10 days, Billie Creek Village. Contact: Executive Secretary, Parke County, Incorporated, Box 165, Rockville, Indiana 47872.

Re-creates the atmosphere of the last century with period costumes, farmers market and bazaar. Driving tours of the surrounding countryside. Activities relating to pioneer days. Montezuma, Mecca, Bridgeton and Rosedale also offer special displays and programs.

★ 2596 ★
West Lafayette - FEAST OF THE HUNTER'S MOON. Mid-late October, annual, 2 days, Fort Ouiatenon. Contact: Director, Tippecanoe County Historical Society, Tenth and South Streets, Lafayette, Indiana 47901.

Canoes race up the Wabash. French traders and Indians gather to celebrate a bountiful harvest. Pioneer clad craftsmen revive the arts of spinning, candle-dipping, and blacksmithing. Music provided by fiddlers, fifes and drums. Buffalo stew, home-baked bread and fresh churned butter are provided. French folk music and dancing plus an eighteenth century French play. Fort is a reconstruction of the original eighteenth century structures.

IOWA

★ 2597 ★
Winterset - COVERED BRIDGE FESTIVAL. Mid October (2nd weekend), annual, 2 days, Courthouse Square (booths), Fairgrounds (antique displays), stores (displays). Contact: Madison County Covered Bridge Festival, Winterset, Iowa 50273.

Devoted to the nostalgic past before the turn of the century. Townspeople wear costumes, local senior citizens are crowned as king and queen to reign over the festivities. There is a spelling bee on the courthouse steps with prizes and trophies. Also included are demonstrations of some of the old crafts needed for life in the old days, tours of the seven covered bridges in the area, and displays of antiques,

some of which are for sale. In addition there are scarecrow contest, muzzle-loading contest, marble shoot, Marathon Championship, melodramas, and house tours. Music is provided every day and includes barbershop harmony, hymn sings, home-grown talent, and marching bands. Started in 1970.

KANSAS

★ 2598 ★
Liberal - INTERNATIONAL PANCAKE DAY RACE. Mid February (Shrove Tuesday), annual, 1-2 days. Contact: Rod Wilson, Chamber of Commerce, Box 676, Liberal, Kansas 67901.

Housewives in Olney, England and Liberal, Kansas, compete simultaneously in running a half-mile with a pancake in a skillet and tossing it twice while running. Started in Liberal in 1950 after the Jaycee president saw a picture of the pancake race in Olney. The winner gets the traditional "Kiss of Peace". Pancake racing began around 500 years ago when the story goes it was customary to use up accumulated cooking grease by making pancakes. One housewife was so engrossed as to forget the time. When the church bells rang, she ran to church still in her apron and carrying the pancakes in her skillet. In the course of the Liberal celebration, there are also pancake eating contests, beauty pageants, parades, children's races, and musical performances.

KENTUCKY

★ 2599 ★
Barbourville - DANIEL BOONE FESTIVAL. Early October, 6 days. Contact: Universal Auto Parts, Barbourville, Kentucky 40221.

Celebrates the signing of the cane treaty between the Cherokee nation and the people of Barbourville with a huge barbeque. Members of the Cherokee nation invade Barbourville to demonstrate their skills in archery and dancing.

★ 2600 ★
Lexington - INTERNATIONAL FESTIVAL. Early October, 3 days, Memorial Coliseum. Contact: Mrs. Harriett Van Meter, 17 Mentelle Park, Lexington, Kentucky 40502.

The festival has honored some 30 countries of the world with special exhibits, foods, and entertainment. The festival theme centers around Kentucky's 200-year historical involvement in the world. The horse, the tobacco, and the bourbon industry, and the numerous

KENTUCKY (Continued)

world personalities who are normally attracted to an institution such as the University of Kentucky are highlighted throughout the three-day festival. Begun in 1974.

★ 2601 ★
Richmond - WHITEHALL N-SSA SKIRMISH AND FLEA MARKET. Late August-early September, annual, 3 days. Contact: Bucky Walters, Whitehall State Shrine, Rural Route 7, Richmond, Kentucky 40475.

Target competition for black powder and musket. A dress parade and drill competition, ladies dress competition, black powder ham shoot, arts and crafts, flea market, and guided tours of the Whitehall State Shrine.

★ 2602 ★
South Union - SHAKER FESTIVAL. Mid July, annual, 10 days, Shakertown. Contact: Miss Julia Neal, Publicity Chairman, Shakertown, South Union, Kentucky 42283.

Features nightly outdoor drama "Shakertown Revisited" which tells the history of the South Union Shaker Society from 1807-1922 by means of dialogue, songs and dances. Shaker Museum is open during this time.

MAINE

★ 2603 ★
Bath - HERITAGE DAYS. Early July, annual. Contact: Bath Area Chamber of Commerce, 45 Front Street, Bath, Maine 04530.

Features New England Fireman's Muster, Fourth of July celebration, parade, art show, and crafts fair. The muster began around 1850.

★ 2604 ★
Hallowell - OLD HALLOWELL DAYS. Mid July, annual. Contact: Chamber of Commerce, Hallowell, Maine 04347.

Pageant by the townspeople of this historic river town on the Kenebec, famed for its granite quarries, old homes, and antique and crafts shops.

MARYLAND

★ 2605 ★
Annapolis - HERITAGE WEEKEND. Late September, annual, 3 days. Contact: Historic Annapolis, 18 Pinkney Street, Annapolis, Maryland 21401.

Events include historic exhibits; tours of historic homes, including some not normally open to the public; candlelight ceremonies; waterfront tours; plantation dinner and hunt breakfast. Begun around 1955.

★ 2606 ★
Annapolis - RATIFICATION DAY. Mid January (around the 14th), annual, 1 day. Contact: Maryland Division of Tourist Development, 2525 Riva Road, Annapolis, Maryland 21401.

The event is in celebration of the ratification of the Treaty of Paris, which established the United States as a separate nation.

★ 2607 ★
Chestertown - TEA PARTY FESTIVAL. Late May, annual, 2 days. Contact: Jack Shroeder, Tea Party Festival, Box 1774, Chestertown, Maryland 21620.

Celebration and re-enactment of 1774 tea party. Militia demonstrations, sound and light show of Chestertown history, tours of historic homes, contests, and Eastern Shore delicacies.

★ 2608 ★
Cumberland - HERITAGE DAYS. Mid June, annual, 2 days, Washington Street. Contact: Allegany County Tourism, Baltimore at Green Street, Cumberland, Maryland 21502.

Pageant and tour of Washington's headquarters and other sites. Festival of the arts, crafts, and history of western Maryland. Exhibits of sculpture, prints, photography, jewelry, macrame, and pottery. Food and novelty stands, antique autos, a historical play "Legacy", and continuous entertainment. Begun around 1969.

★ 2609 ★
Frederick - BELL AND HISTORY DAYS. Mid June, annual, 3 days. Contact: Frederick County Chamber of Commerce, Division of Tourism, Frederick, Maryland 21701.

Tours of Frederick's historic homes, street dancing, outdoor concerts, historical pageantry, flea market,

MARYLAND (Continued)

crafts, antique cars and carriages.

★ 2610 ★
Indian Head - REVOLUTIONARY WAR DAYS.
Early May (1st weekend), annual, 2 days, Small-
wood's Retreat, Smallwood State Park.   Contact:
Tri-County for Southern Maryland, Post Office Box
301, Waldorf, Maryland 20601.

This festival commemorates Maryland's contribution to
America's battle for independence and gives visitors
a chance to learn about the customs and attitudes
that prevailed during the Revolutionary period.   The
First Maryland Regiment supplies music and marching
demonstrations.   Craft demonstrations,   puppet shows,
square dancing, band concerts, colonial songs and
exhibits.   Begun in 1968.

★ 2611 ★
Prince Frederick - CAVALIER DAYS.   Late May
(date may vary), annual, 3 days, Calvert County
Fairgrounds.   Contact: Southern Maryland Art
and Craft Center, Incorporated, Barstow, Maryland
20610.

Celebrates the 1600's in southern Maryland.   Parade;
demonstration of life in a seventeenth century Pis-
cataway Indian village; a pageant of the Arrival of
Robert Brooke; demonstrations of colonial life including cabin raising, dancing, flintlock firing,
games and music of the era; food; crafts; etc.
Festival participants wear colonial costumes.   Visitors are permitted to participate in the games.
Jousting,   bagpipe band, and tobacco auction.   Indian archeology displays and working foxhounds.
Includes the Thomas Tasker Turtlement.   Begun around
1971.

★ 2612 ★
Princess Anne - OLDE PRINCESS ANNE DAYS.
Mid October, annual, 2 days.   Contact: Olde
Princess Anne Days, Incorporated, Princess Anne,
Maryland 21853.

Candlelight reception in Teakle Mansion, tours of
historic homes, gardens, and churches.   Begun
around 1958.

★ 2613 ★
Saint Mary's City - MARYLAND DAYS CELEBRATION.
Late March (around the 25th), annual, 1 day.   Con-
tact: Tri-County Council for Southern Maryland,
Post Office Box 301, Waldorf, Maryland 20601.

Pomp and pageantry, symbolic legislative meeting
in the State House of 1676.

★ 2614 ★
Westminster - STEAM-UP AND MILITIA DAYS.
Late May (Memorial Day weekend), annual, 3 days,
Carroll County Farm Museum.   Contact: Carroll
County Farm Museum, Westminster, Maryland 21157.

Civil War re-enactments, American Revolutionary
War music, musketry demonstrations, fife and drum
corps, crafts demonstrations and exhibitions, old
steam engines and equipment, and country food.
Begun around 1963.

MASSACHUSETTS

★ 2615 ★
Acton - CROWN RESISTANCE DAY.   Late September, annual, 1 day.   Contact: Massachusetts Department of Commerce and Development, Division
of Tourism, Box 1775, Boston, Massachusetts 02105.

Colonial militia units in full regalia and a parade,
foods, crafts, and colonial fair highlight the events
commemorating an historic event.

★ 2616 ★
Northampton - PIONEER VALLEY COLONIAL
MUSTER DAYS.   Early October, annual, 3 days,
Tri-County Fairgrounds.   Contact: Massachusetts
Department of Commerce and Development, Division
of Tourism, Box 1775, Boston, Massachusetts 02105.

Farmers market, demonstrations, and a mock battle
highlight the events commemorating earlier days.

★ 2617 ★
Plymouth - THANKSGIVING DAY CELEBRATION.
Late November, annual, 1 day.   Contact: Massa-
chusetts Department of Commerce and Development,
Division of Tourism, Box 1775, Boston, Massachusetts
02105.

Held where first Thanksgiving was celebrated in 1621.
Historic houses open, many serve cider and doughnuts
to visitors.   At nearby Plimoth Plantation, replica
of settlement as it looked in 1627, costumed attendants
take you on tour of Pilgrim houses and shops.   Most
restaurants feature special dinners of turkey, cran-
berries, and Indian pudding.   Costumed re-enactment
of Pilgrim's church processing.

MASSACHUSETTS (Continued)

★ 2618 ★
Vineyard Haven - MARTHA'S VINEYARD
RENAISSANCE FAIR.   Early July, annual, 4 days.
Contact: Massachusetts Department of Commerce and
Development, Division of Tourism, Box 1775, Boston,
Massachusetts 02105.

Costumed troubadors, plays and concerts.   Colorful
sale of superb handcrafts of Artworker's Guild.

★ 2619 ★
Wilbraham - TOWN FAIR.   Mid May, annual, 1
day, Wilbraham-Monson Academy.   Contact: Massachusetts Department of Commerce and Development,
Division of Tourism, Box 1775, Boston, Massachusetts
02105.

Revitalized Yankee crafts demonstrated and sold.
Homemade ethnic and colonial foods.   Tour of historic homes and farmhouses, many built before the
town was incorporated in 1763.

MICHIGAN

★ 2620 ★
Dearborn - COUNTRY FAIR OF YESTERYEAR.   Mid
May, annual, 4 days, Greenfield Village.   Contact:
Greenfield Village, Dearborn, Michigan 48121.

Re-creation of the rural fairs of the last century and
earlier with a parade, marching bands, farm animals,
a children's midway, demonstration of crafts, etc.

★ 2621 ★
Dearborn - MUZZLE LOADERS FESTIVAL.   Late
June, annual, 2 days, Greenfield Village.   Con-
tact: Greenfield Village, Dearborn, Michigan 48121.

Costumed participants (including uniformed scouts and
soldiers of frontier and Civil War days) with muzzle
loading weapons.   Civil War cannon firing demonstrations, marching bands, special displays, and
muskets.

★ 2622 ★
Dearborn - OLD TIME SUMMER FESTIVAL.   Late
June-early September, 9 weeks, Greenfield Village.
Contact: Greenfield Village, Dearborn, Michigan
48121.

The Greenfield Village Players present a series of
summer diversions recalling the entertainment of yesteryear: strolling minstrels, a musical revue, and a

puppet show, medicine show from the back of a gaily
painted wagon, stories drawing from the writings of
Mark Twain, a dialogue with Benjamin Franklin, and
a re-enactment of the famous debates between Stephen
Douglas and Abraham Lincoln.   Started in 1974.

MINNESOTA

★ 2623 ★
Chaska - RENAISSANCE FESTIVAL.   August-Septem-
ber, annual, 4 weekends, Wooded area on State
Highway 169.   Contact: Renaissance Festivals, In-
corporated, Route 1, Post Office Box 125, Chaska,
Minnesota 55318.

A sixteenth century fair including music, dancers,
actors, mime artists, gourmet menus, engineering
competition, gypsy dance caravan, jousting, horse
races, contests, parades, arts and crafts festival,
period costuming, jugglers, players of ancient instruments, magicians, jesters, puppeteers, and tumblers all reminiscent of Elizabethan England.   Begun
in 1971.

★ 2624 ★
Northfield - DEFEAT OF JESSE JAMES DAY.   Early
September, 4 days.   Contact: Northfield Area
Chamber of Commerce, 415 1/2 Division Street,
Box 198, Northfield, Minnesota 55057.

Festival events include a bank raid re-enactment,
parade, and Arts Guild Fair.

MISSOURI

★ 2625 ★
Harrisonville - CASS COUNTY LOG CABIN
FESTIVAL.   Early October (1st weekend), annual,
3 days.   Contact: Harrisonville Chamber of Commerce, 400 East Mechanic, Harrisonville, Missouri
64701.

Activities based upon pioneer life, including contests,
music, parades, arts and crafts displays.   Sponsored
by the Cass County Historical Society, Bicentennial
Commission, Cass County Court, Agricultural Bicentennial Committee and the Harrisonville Chamber
of Commerce.   Started in 1975.

★ 2626 ★
Independence - SANTA-CALI-GON.   Early September (Labor Day weekend), annual, 4 days, Independence Square.   Contact: Director, Public Relations,
Independence Chamber of Commerce, Post Office Box
147, 213 South Main Street, Independence, Missouri
64051.

History

MISSOURI (Continued)

Centers around pioneer life with booths and demonstrations of crafts, arts and activities. The name comes from the time when the Sante Fe, California, and Oregon Trails started in Independence during the days of covered wagons. Children's theater, carnival, drama and melodrama, kangaroo court, log cabin and pioneer wagon exhibits, Gay 90's Review, Indian dance, teenage talent contest, shootout, fire department demonstration, eating contest, costume contest, grandstand entertainment, parade, antique car show, film festival, band concert, battle of the bands (rock and country western), and bus tours of historical areas. First held in 1940, then again in 1947, started as an annual in 1974.

NEW HAMPSHIRE

★ 2627 ★
Charlestown - OLD MUSTER DAY. Mid July, annual, 1 day, Old Fort #4. Contact: Secretary, Annual Old Muster Day, Charlestown, New Hampshire 03603.

The firing of an antique cannon and a costume parade of the early militia.

★ 2628 ★
New Castle - FORT CONSTITUTION. Mid October, annual, 1 day. Contact: Joseph Copley, New Castle, New Hampshire 03854

Celebration in honor of the raid on the fort by patriots in December 1774. Drills, demonstrations by colonial militia units, exhibits, crafts, small parade, etc.

★ 2629 ★
New London - MUSTER DAY. Mid June, 1 day. Contact: Secretary, New London Muster Day, New London, New Hampshire 03257.

Events of skill and daring between colonial regiments, parade, sham battle, drill, and barbeque.

NEW MEXICO

★ 2630 ★
Espanola - FIESTA DE ONATE. Mid July, annual, 3 days. Contact: Chamber of Commerce, Espanola, New Mexico 87532.

Commemorates the founding in 1598 of the first European settlement in North America by Don Juan de Onate. Events include entrada de Juan de Onate,

historical parade, children's parade, grandstand entertainment, horse races, and fireworks. All of the activities are colorful with costumes of traditional Spanish dress of the Onate period. Mariachi music throughout.

★ 2631 ★
Lincoln - OLD LINCOLN DAYS. Early August, annual, 3 days. Contact: Bill R. Ward, Old Wortley Hotel, Lincoln, New Mexico 88338.

Historical pageant about Billy the Kid, and the Lincoln County War of the 1880's. Other events include pony express race, ghost town tours, fiddler's contest, and a parade.

★ 2632 ★
Ranchos de Taos - FIESTA OF SAINT FRANCIS. Early October, 2 days, Saint Francis of Assisi Church. Contact: Church Office, Saint Francis of Assisi Church, Ranchos de Taos, New Mexico 87557.

Events include a procession to the historic church (built in 1710) and a fiesta.

★ 2633 ★
Santa Fe - HARVEST FESTIVAL. Early October (1st weekend), annual, 2 days, Rancho de las Golondrinas in Upper Cienega, Cienega Village Museum. Contact: Colonial New Mexico Historical Foundation, 135 Camino Escondido, Santa Fe, New Mexico 87501.

The mills, blacksmith and wheel wright shops are open. Carding, spinning, weaving, soap making, threshing and other harvest tasks are performed in the old way. Spanish colonial dancers perform; there is a Spanish colonial crafts market with traditional crafts, as well as a country store selling chili, posole, chicos and other similar foods.

★ 2634 ★
Tularosa - SAINT FRANCIS DE PAULA FIESTA. Early May, annual, 3 days. Contact: Chamber of Commerce, 301 Central, Post Office Box 1026, Tularosa, New Mexico 88352.

Commemorates the 1868 battle of Round Mountain which resulted in the founding of the historic Francisian mission. The festival is over 105 years old.

NORTH CAROLINA

★ 2635 ★
Asheville - PIONEER LIVING DAY. Mid-late
September, 1 day, Zebulon Vance Birthplace State
Historic Site. Contact: North Carolina Travel
Development Section, Division of Economic Develop-
ment, Department of Natural and Economic Resources,
Raleigh, North Carolina 27611.

A re-creation of a typical pioneer day, with costumes,
outdoor cooking and tours of log cabins.

★ 2636 ★
Asheville - PIONEER SUNDAY. Mid April, 1
day, Zebulon Vance Birthplace State Historic Site.
Contact: North Carolina Travel Development Section,
Division of Economic Development, Department of
Natural and Economic Resources, Raleigh, North
Carolina 27611.

Celebrates the pioneering days with a re-creation of
the times. There is a log cabin and sheds, pioneer
costumes, and outdoor cooking.

★ 2637 ★
Cherokee - UNTO THESE HILLS. Late June-late
August, annual, 2 months, Cherokee Reservation.
Contact: Chamber of Commerce, Box 465, Cherokee,
North Carolina 28719.

The drama tells the story of the Cherokee, from the
arrival of DeSoto, to the forcible removal of most of
the people to Oklahoma, including the stubborn resistance of the few who managed to remain in their
ancestral home, and whose descendents live on the
reservation.

★ 2638 ★
Greensboro - COMMEMORATION OF BATTLE AT
GUILFORD COURTHOUSE. Mid March, annual,
3 days, Guilford Courthouse National Military Park.
Contact: W. W. Danielson, Superintendent, Post
Office Box 9334, Greensboro, North Carolina 27408.

Garbed in the military costumes of the era, troops
drill and fire an eighteenth century cannon. There
is a ceremony featuring speeches and a gala festival.

★ 2639 ★
Winston-Salem - CHRISTMAS IN OLD SALEM. Mid
December (2nd week), annual. Contact: Director
of Information, Old Salem December, Incorporated,
Drawer F, Salem Station, Winston-Salem, North
Carolina 27108.

A return to the original Moravian town of the eighteenth to early nineteenth century. In the restored
buildings, visitors have the opportunity to observe the
work of the era: pottery, gunsmithing, baking,
needlework, woodwork, tinsmithing and coffee roasting.
A night watchman announces the hour with a conch
shell and chants. Costumed townspeople ride by
on their horses, and children play eighteenth century
games. Bands, choruses, and other instrumentalists
and vocalists perform period pieces.

NORTH DAKOTA

★ 2640 ★
West Fargo - BONANZAVILLE DAYS (PIONEER
DAYS). Late August-early September (weekend prior
to Labor Day), annual, 2 days, Bonanzaville. Con-
tact: North Dakota State Highway Department,
Capitol Grounds, Bismarck, North Dakota 58501.

A reconstructed pioneer town is the site of demonstrations of the skills, arts, and pastimes of the
frontier, demonstrated by costumed experts, many of
whom used the skills in their youth. There are
German and Norwegian language church services,
milking and threshing contests, traditional foods and
buggy rides.

OHIO

★ 2641 ★
Berlin - PIONEER DAYS. Late July, 2 days.
Contact: Mrs. Delmer Hecker, Box 90, Millersburg,
Ohio 44654.

The town recalls earlier days with tours of Amish
homes and displays of antiques. Activities include
buggy rides and demonstration of such historic crafts
and chores as chaircaning, carpet weaving, and
spinning. Old fashioned food is on hand. There
is also a parade and free home talent entertainment.

★ 2642 ★
Canal Fulton - CANAL DAYS. Mid July, annual,
3 days. Contact: James F. McCabe, Closter
5712, Canal Fulton, Ohio 44614.

The festival evokes the canal boat era of the 1800's.
Participants are urged to wear period costumes as they
ride on the canal boats, tour historic homes, view
the exhibit of crafts from the era and watch a muzzle-
loading shoot. Other events include several parades,
a fiddle and banjo contest, games, rides, stage productions, square dancing and sidewalk bands.

History

OHIO (Continued)

★ 2643 ★
Greenville - ANNIE OAKLEY DAYS.   Late July,
4 days.   Contact: Chamber of Commerce, 813 East
Main Street, Greenville, Ohio 45331.

The western heroine is honored with appropriate
activities, including, of course, a shooting contest,
a fast draw contest, a parade, and a pilgrimage.
Entertainment includes an old-time melodrama, vocal
acts, western square dancing, a horse and pony show
and an ice cream social.   Visitors may also browse
an arts and crafts show, an old book sale and a flea
market.   A chicken barbeque is provided.

★ 2644 ★
Piketon - HISTORIC DOGWOOD FESTIVAL.   Late
April, annual, 3 days.   Contact: Forest Litterst,
Coordinator, Historic Dogwood, Incorporated, Box
335, Piketon, Ohio 45661.

The history of Ohio figures prominently in this event
with tours of area and historic buildings, demonstrations of early crafts such as stonecarving and
quilting.   Participants may watch a parade, wander
through an antique car show or a flea market or art
display.   There is a Civil War re-enactment, a
long rifle shoot, horseshoe-trucshooting and musical
events.

★ 2645 ★
Zanesville - ZANE'S TRACE COMMEMORATION.
Mid June, 3 days.   Contact: James I. Dally,
Zanesville Chamber of Commerce, Zanesville, Ohio
43701.

In 1797, Ebenezer Zane (grandfather of novelist Zane
Grey) laid out the first trail through the Ohio frontier, Zane's Trace.   His accomplishment is honored
with a giant parade, a fine arts show, a hobby craft
show, boat rides, and a boat parade on the Musk-
ingum River.

OREGON

★ 2646 ★
Forest Grove - GAY 90'S FESTIVAL.   February-
March, annual, 3 days.   Contact: Gay 90's
Festival, 1933 21st Avenue, Forest Grove, Oregon
97116.

The city is decorated with the decor of the Gay 90's.
The theme is carried out with a Gay 90's revue, with
a parade, and the Original All-Northwest Barber Shop
Ballad Contest.   The visitor may choose to browse the
gem and mineral show, or watch the Old-Time Fiddlers' Contest and other entertainment.

★ 2647 ★
Sheridan – PHIL SHERIDAN DAYS.   Late June, 3
days.   Contact: Sheridan Chamber of Commerce,
Sheridan, Oregon 97378.

A rodeo and celebration honoring General Phil
Sheridan, Civil War hero, and a soldier in this area
just prior to the Civil War.

PENNSYLVANIA

★ 2648 ★
Baumstown - PATRIOT DAYS.   Mid June, annual,
3 days, Daniel Boone Homestead.   Contact: Department of Commerce, Bureau of Travel Development,
431 South Office Building, Harrisburg, Pennsylvania
17120.

Features arts and crafts, scout encampments, and
colonial demonstrations by brigades of American
Revolution, from as far away as Maine.

★ 2649 ★
Boyertown - DURYEA DAY.   Late August, annual,
1 day, Boyertown Museum of Historic Vehicles.
Contact: Boyertown Museum of Historic Vehicles,
Boyertown, Pennsylvania 19512.

Features past of horseless carriage era.   Antique
auto show and meet, competition in several divisions,
according to age of the car.

★ 2650 ★
Delmont - BYE-GONE DAYS.   Mid July, annual,
2 days, Pennsylvania 66 and U.S. 22.   Contact:
Salem Crossroads Historical Society, Post Office Box,
Delmont, Pennsylvania 15626.

The history of the area is celebrated with festival
events.

★ 2651 ★
Fallsington - COLONIAL FAIR.   Early October,
annual, 1 day.   Contact: Mrs. Clare Nelson,
Historic Fallsington, Incorporated, Four Yardley
Avenue, Fallsington, Pennsylvania 19054.

Parade with fife and drum corps.   Ballad singer and
eighteenth century dancing.   Open houses and kitch-
en featuring specialties.   Handcraft exhibits and
demonstrations.   Home baked goods.

PENNSYLVANIA (Continued)

★ 2652 ★
Greensburg - COLONIAL FESTIVAL. Mid July,
annual, 1 day, Welty Street School. Contact:
Department of Commerce, Bureau of Travel Development, 431 South Office Building, Harrisburg, Pennsylvania 17120.

Demonstrations of candle making, leather making,
corn husking, pottery, and band music to entertain.

★ 2653 ★
Hopewell - ESTABLISHMENT DAY. Early August,
annual, 1 day, Hopewell Village National Historic
Site. Contact: Department of Commerce, Bureau
of Travel Development, 431 South Office Building,
Harrisburg, Pennsylvania 17120.

Early American industrial and household trades and
crafts performed by employees dressed in period costumes. A noted feature is the pouring of aluminum
in sand-cast moulds.

★ 2654 ★
Kreamer - PIONEER DAYS. Late July, annual,
4-7 days. Contact: Department of Commerce,
Bureau of Travel Development, 431 South Office
Building, Harrisburg, Pennsylvania 17120.

Tours of Schoch Blockhouse used between 1770 and
1785 by settlers as a place of refuge and defense in
case of Indian uprising. Re-creation of Stock Massacre which occurred in 1781, pony pulling contests,
musket shoot, tomahawk and knife throws, parade,
nightly entertainment, rides, buffalo roast, etc.

★ 2655 ★
Ligonier - FORT LIGONIER DAYS. October, annual,
3 days, Route 30 and 71, 60 miles east of Pittsburgh.
Contact: Department of Commerce, Bureau of Travel
Development, 431 South Office Building, Harrisburg,
Pennsylvania 17120.

Celebrating the anniversary of Battle of Ligonier, key
engagement of the French and Indian Wars. Continuous activity including a community parade, a
re-enactment of the battle, sidewalk sales, outdoor
entertainment, antique displays, and demonstrations
of pioneer crafts and skills.

★ 2656 ★
Manheim - RED ROSE FESTIVAL. Mid June, annual,
1 day, Zion Lutheran Church. Contact: Manheim
Chamber of Commerce, 32 North Main Street,

Manheim, Pennsylvania 17545.

Event to pay red rose for rental of land to descendant
of Henry Stiegel, founder of Manheim.

★ 2657 ★
Shartlesville - BADOLIA DAYS. Early August,
annual, 3-4 days. Contact: Department of Commerce, Bureau of Travel and Development, 431 South
Office Building, Harrisburg, Pennsylvania 17120.

Badolia is the Pennsylvania Dutch word for battalion.
Celebration features periodic inspection of arms and
drills by the Fifth Battalion of Shartlesville Militia
which played a part in the Revolutionary War. Also
features Pennsylvania Dutch food, music and crafts.

★ 2658 ★
Stahlstown - FLAX SCUTCHING FESTIVAL. Mid
September, annual, 1 day. Contact: Flax Scutch-
ing Festival, Box 77, Stahlstown, Pennsylvania 15687.

The fete demonstrates how flax from the field is processed and was made into early American home spun
clothing. In addition there is a mock Indian raid
and music and square dancing for entertainment.
Buckwheat cakes and sausage are on hand for eating.
Begun around 1910.

★ 2659 ★
Ulysses - HARVEST FAIR. Mid November, annual,
1 day, Fire Hall. Contact: Potter County Recreation,
Incorporated, Post Office Box 245, Coudersport,
Pennsylvania 16915.

Demonstrations of old-fashioned home arts; crafts,
food displays and sales; old time games: apple
bobs, and spelling bees. Old-fashioned fashion
show and square dancing.

★ 2660 ★
Valley Forge - CHERRIES JUBILEE. Mid February,
annual, 4 days, Valley Forge State Park. Contact:
Ms. Bettina C. McGarvey, Montgomery County
Convention and Visitors Bureau, Court House, Norris-
town, Pennsylvania 19404.

Uniformed military musters, costumes, enactments,
and living history demonstrations of Revolutionary-era
baking, candle-dipping and other crafts. Film
dramatizing the Continental Army's stay at Valley
Forge. Costumed ladies bake and dispense wine-and-
brandy soaked slices of authentic Martha Washington's
Great Cake. Accommodations and meal packages
available.

PENNSYLVANIA (Continued)

★ 2661 ★
Wellsboro - TIOGA COUNTY EARLY DAYS. Mid July, annual, 4 days, Midway between Mansfield and Wellsboro, off Route 6, Whitneyville. Contact: Mrs. Nancy A. Costley, Rural Delivery 5, Box 205, Wellsboro, Pennsylvania 16901.

Steam and gas engines, tractors, and antique farm machinery on display. Saw mill, drag saw, shingle making, stone crushing, horse sweep, tread mill, blacksmithing, flour and meal grinding demonstrations. Making of brooms, candle dipping, wool dyeing, spinning, and quilting. See how to make maple syrup. Displays of household items and small tools.

RHODE ISLAND

★ 2662 ★
Newport - RHODE ISLAND INDEPENDENCE CELEBRATION. Early May, 1 day. Contact: Rhode Island Department of Economic Development, Tourist Promotion Division, One Weybosset Hill, Providence, Rhode Island 02903.

The reading of the Independence Proclamation by the governor, (Rhode Island declared its independence May 4, 1776), is followed by a parade and tours of Revolutionary War fortifications and battle sites.

★ 2663 ★
Pawtuxet - GASPEE DAYS. Early June, annual, 10 days. Contact: Gaspee Day Committee, Box 1772, Pilgrim Station, Warwick, Rhode Island 02888.

The festival celebrates the "First Blow for Freedom" which occured when a group of Rhode Islanders burned the "Gaspee", a British ship which has been harassing shipping in an attempt to enforce the stamp act. There are re-enactments of the burning, colonial costume balls and contests, fireworks, a parade and the mustering of the fife and drum corps. Other events include the Miss Gaspee pageant, the Pawtuxet Village Arts and Crafts Festival, a clambake and band concerts. There are a variety of sports events, including canoe races, a sailboat regatta, footraces, softball games, and bicycle races.

★ 2664 ★
South Kingstown - COLONIAL WEEK. Late June-early July, annual, 9 days. Contact: South Kingstown Chamber of Commerce, Box 289, Wakefield, Rhode Island 02880.

The colonial era is celebrated with open houses at historic buildings, fireworks, picnics and a parade. The Narragansett Tribe of Indians sponsors a pow wow. Musical offerings include concerts by the Sweet Adelines and the Narragansett Bay Chorister, rock and band concerts, and the drum and bugle corps invitational. There are canoe races, gymnastic exhibitions, a bowling tournament, a golf tournament, a softball game, bicycle races, baseball, moonlight sails, and square dancing. There are parties, picnics and a fashion show-luncheon. Additional events include the Heads and Hands Art Festival, and the South County Heritage Festival. Begun in 1973.

SOUTH CAROLINA

★ 2665 ★
Branchville - RAYLRODE DAZE FESTIVAL. Late September, annual, 3 days, Main Street. Contact: Mrs. T.R. McCracken, Festival Chairman, Post Office Box 111, Branchville, South Carolina 29432.

Branchville's Main Street is the location of the oldest railroad junction in the world. Everyone participates by dressing up in colonial and railroad costumes. One of the highlights of the festival is a visit to the Railroad Shrine and Museum to view the dining room where three Presidents of the United States have eaten. Other attractions in the festival include a beauty contest, street dance, parade, tour of homes, horse show, antique displays and sales, arts and crafts show and sales, and plenty of good food and free entertainment.

★ 2666 ★
Myrtle Beach - GEORGE WASHINGTON DAYS. Mid February, annual, 5 days. Contact: Greater Myrtle Beach Chamber of Commerce, Post Office Box 1326, Myrtle Beach, South Carolina 29577.

The festival includes George Washington Trail Tours and tours of historic homes and gardens in the area. Golf tournaments are planned. Hotels and motels offer special package plans, and local merchants hold sales. Begun in 1972.

SOUTH DAKOTA

★ 2667 ★
Bonesteel - POWDER RIVER DAYS. Mid November, annual, 1 day. Contact: Division of Tourism Development, State Office Building 2, Pierre, South Dakota 57501.

Melodrama, and a dance. Participants are encouraged to wear old time outfits.

SOUTH DAKOTA (Continued)

★ 2668 ★
Custer - GOLD DISCOVERY DAYS. Late July-
early August, annual, 3 days. Contact: Custer
Chamber of Commerce, Custer, South Dakota 57730.

Commemorates the discovery of gold in the area by
one of General Custer's men over 100 years ago.
Includes parades, pageants, rodeos, Indian raids, and
a carnival.

★ 2669 ★
Deadwood - DAYS OF '76. Early August (1st weekend), annual, 3 days. Contact: Deadwood Chamber
of Commerce, Deadwood, South Dakota 57732.

Probably the wildest festival in the state, as the town
and its visitors celebrate the days of gold-panning and
lusty living. Included in the events is an RCA rodeo
with all the latest specialty acts and the slatiest
rodeo stock. Sioux Indians perform authentic ceremonial dances. Parades with colorful costumes de-
pict Deadwood's history. There is a re-enactment
of the trial of Jack McCall (who shot Wild Bill
Hickok here), beginning with a shootout on Main
Street. Begun around 1923.

TENNESSEE

★ 2670 ★
Germantown - RIVER CITY RENAISSANCE FAIR.
Mid September, 2 days. Contact: Ms. Brenda
Burgess, Knudson Leather and Silver Shop, 722
South Highland Street, Memphis, Tennessee 38111.

Arts and crafts demonstrations, displays, and sales
are part of the festivities.

TEXAS

★ 2671 ★
Anderson - ANDERSON TEXAS TREK. Early May,
annual, 1 day. Contact: State Department of
Highways and Public Transportation, Travel and Information Division, Post Office Box 5064, Austin,
Texas 78763; or Mrs. Emory Bay, Anderson, Texas
77830.

Based on tours of notable historic homes, many over
a century old. Hosts are dressed in costumes of
bygone years; there is an antique show, and a
parade featuring horse drawn vehicles of the nineteenth century.

★ 2672 ★
Corpus Christi - BUCCANEER DAYS CELEBRATION.
Late April or early May, annual, 11 days. Contact:
Chamber of Commerce, 1201 North Shoreline Boule-
vard, Post Office Box 640, Corpus Christi, Texas
78403; or The Buccaneer Commission, Post Office
Box 1200, Corpus Christi, Texas 78403.

Outstanding attraction of the year; citywide festival
includes pageantry, coronation ball, night parade,
fireworks, statewide music festival, and sporting events.
Buccaneer Days recalls legendary early days of Corpus
Christi. Pirates invade the city, setting off a reign
of fun. Begun in 1938.

★ 2673 ★
Fort Worth - PIONEER DAYS FIESTA. May, annual,
4 days. Contact: Mr. Bill R. Shelton, 700 Throckmorton Street, Fort Worth, Texas 76102.

A rousing salute to the frontier heritage of Fort
Worth, with fun for all the visitors and local people.

★ 2674 ★
Gonzales - COME AND TAKE IT. October, annual,
3 days. Contact: Preston Van Hanken, Chamber of
Commerce, Post Office Box 134, Gonzales, Texas
78629.

Celebration observes famed battle cry of opening con-
flict for Texas independence. Highlights are parade,
rodeo, art exhibit, antique show, and historical pilgrimage.

★ 2675 ★
Harlingen - REBEL DAYS. October, annual, 3
days. Contact: Chamber of Commerce, Box 189,
Harlingen, Texas 78550.

Event honors the Confederate Air Force in Harlingen
with carnival rides, athletic events and an air show
by the Confederate Air Force.

★ 2676 ★
Houston - TEXAS INDEPENDENCE DAY OBSERVANCE.
Late April (21st), annual, 1 day. Contact: Mr.
Louie Welch, Chamber of Commerce, Post Office
Box 53600, Houston, Texas 77052.

Independence Day Observance and review of Texas
Navy, at San Jacinto Battleground State Park.

★ 2677 ★
Jefferson - JEFFERSON HISTORICAL PILGRIMAGE.

History

TEXAS (Continued)

Early May, annual, 1 weekend.   Contact: Chamber of Commerce, 108 East Lafayette, Jefferson, Texas 75657; or Jessie Allen Wise Garden Club, Excelsior Hotel, Jefferson, Texas 75657.

With all traditional flavor of the Old South, hoop-skirted belles usher guests through gracious and historic old homes, collections of antiques, and gardens at the height of spring bloom.   Highlights include a parade and re-enactment of the Diamond Bessie Murder Trial, a notorious scandal of the 1870's.

★ 2678 ★
Marshall - STAGECOACH DAYS.   May. Contact: Mrs. James Abney, Post Office Box 92, Marshall, Texas 75670.

With historic homes tour, and stage coach rides, the town commemorates history as a hub of transportation since stagecoach days.   Other events include a crafts fair and art shows.

★ 2679 ★
Montgomery - MONTGOMERY COUNTY TEXAS TREK.   Mid April, annual, 1 day.   Contact: State Department of Highways and Public Transportation, Travel and Information Bureau, Post Office Box 5064, Austin, Texas 78763;   or Mrs. Smith Owen, Route 2, Montgomery, Texas 77356.

Based on tours of notable historic homes, many over a century old.   Hosts are dressed in costumes of bygone years, and an ox wagon provides rides to church services.   Lavish display of antiques and pioneer artifacts.

★ 2680 ★
San Antonio - EL DIA DE LAS MISIONES (THE DAY OF THE MISSIONS).   Early August (around the 6th), annual, 1 day.   Contact: Chamber of Commerce, Post Office Box 1628, San Antonio, Texas 78296.

A salute to the five historic missions of San Antonio with festive events.

★ 2681 ★
Waco - BRAZOS RIVER FESTIVAL AND PILGRIMAGE, COTTON PALACE PAGEANT.   Late April, annual, 1 weekend. Contact: Chamber of Commerce, 108 West Denison, Waco, Texas 76706.

Pilgrimage visits five historic houses, museums from Waco's early days, plus other historic sites;   features outdoor art shows, food booths, children's center, "Thieves' Market", and an old-fashioned melodrama. Cotton Palace Pageant depicts early Waco and Texas history, plus coronation of Cotton Palace royalty.

UTAH

★ 2682 ★
Logan - FESTIVAL OF THE AMERICAN WEST.   Late July-early August, annual, 9 days, Utah State University.   Contact: The Festival of the American West, Old Main Room 116, UMC 14, Utah State University, Logan, Utah 84322.

The festival is kicked off by the Old West Cookout and the Old West Parade.   The latter includes hundreds of participants in costume.   There is a historical pageant performed nightly: "The West: America's Odyssey", which uses music, traditional songs, slides and dances to present a multi-media recounting of episodes in the settling of the West by the American pioneers.   The costumes reflect changing fads and fancies of the West.   Nearby, is the Ronald V. Jensen Living Historical Farm, which offers tours and demonstrations illustrative of pioneer life.   Also included are the Great West Fair and Windows West.   Begun in 1973.

★ 2683 ★
Logan - WINDOWS WEST.   Late July-early August, annual, 9 days, Utah State University.   Contact: The Festival of the American West, Old Main Room 116, UMC 14, Utah State University, Logan, Utah 84322.

Part of the Festival of the American West, the event is a pictoral record of life in the frontier West. Featured are photographs and paintings of all aspects of the era and the people who lived it: pioneers, railroaders, cowboys, lawmen, outlaws, Indians and homesteaders.   Begun in 1972.

★ 2684 ★
Ogden - DAYS OF '47 CELEBRATION (PIONEER DAYS PARADE AND RODEO).   Late July, annual, 1 day.   Contact: Utah Travel Council, Council Hall, Capitol Hill, Salt Lake City, Utah 84114.

Frontier days are recalled with a parade, chuck wagon breakfast, rodeo, and the mock hanging of Billy the Kid.

★ 2685 ★
Promontory - GOLDEN SPIKE CEREMONY.   Early-mid May, annual, 1 day.   Contact: Golden Spike

UTAH (Continued)

National Historic Site, Promontary Star Route, Corinne, Utah 84307.

The event includes a re-enactment of the driving of the "Golden Spike" to commemorate the linking up of the tracks of the Union Pacific Railroad and the Central Pacific Railroad to create the first continental railroad in the United States. The program also includes displays, movies and slide presentations.

★ 2686 ★
Salt Lake City - DAYS OF '47. July, annual, throughout the town. Contact: Utah Travel Council, Council Hall, Capitol Hill, Salt Lake City, Utah 84114.

It was in 1847 that the Mormons, led by Brigham Young, settled in Utah. There is a wide diversity of events associated with the city's celebration of the pioneer era, occuring at different times throughout the month. There are old fashioned celebrations and street shows. Entertainment includes a pops concert, selection of queens, a horse parade, a youth parade, a rodeo and other activities.

★ 2687 ★
Salt Lake City - NATIONAL HISTORIC PRESERVATION WEEK. May, annual. Contact: Utah Heritage Foundation, 603 East South Temple, Salt Lake City, Utah 84102.

Takes place over four Utah counties. The week is highlighted by guided tours of Utah's historic buildings.

VIRGINIA

★ 2688 ★
Cape Henry - CAPE HENRY DAY. Late April, annual, 1 day, Fort Story. Contact: Mr. Fairfax M. Berkley, President, The Order of Cape Henry 1607, 708 Baldwin Place, Norfolk, Virginia 23517.

The Order of Cape Henry 1607 celebrates the anniversary of the landing of the first English speaking settlers to found a permanent colony in America (April 26, 1607). The ceremonies are of a religious nature.

★ 2689 ★
Great Falls - SAMPLE DAYS. February, annual, Colvin Run Mill. Contact: Colvin Run Mill Park, 10017 Colvin Run Road, Great Falls, Virginia 22066.

Features different products made from the meal ground at the mill.

★ 2690 ★
Jamestown - JAMESTOWN DAY. Mid May (2nd Sunday), annual, 1 day. Contact: Superintendent, Colonial National Historical Park, Yorktown, Virginia 23690.

The ceremonies commemorate the arrival of the colonists of the first permanent English settlement in America on May 13, 1607, at Jamestown.

★ 2691 ★
Richmond - MASSING OF THE FLAGS. Early June, annual, 1 day, Jefferson Davis Monument. Contact: Metropolitan Richmond Chamber of Commerce, 201 East Franklin, Richmond, Virginia 23219.

A memorial program in honor of Jefferson Davis. Begun around 1966.

★ 2692 ★
Yorktown - YORKTOWN DAY. Mid October (19th), annual, 1 day, Colonial National Historical Park. Contact: Superintendent, Colonial National Historical Park, Yorktown, Virginia 23690.

Observance of the day the Revolutionary War ended with the surrender by Lord Cornwallis to General Washington on the battlefield at Yorktown, October 19, 1781.

WASHINGTON

★ 2693 ★
Fall City - FALLSHIRE RENAISSANCE FAIRE. August-early September, 4 weekends, Snoqualmie Falls Forest Theater. Contact: Snoqualmie Falls Forest Theater, Executive Director, 14240 Southeast Allen Road, Bellevue, Washington 98006.

A re-creation of a medieval country fair. Mummers, troubadors, magicians, dancers, musicians, and actors perform in the costumes of the era. Displays of jewelry, woodcrafts, pots, woven fabrics, clothes, candles and batik wares, pottery, etc. Fencing and jousting tournaments. Put on by members of the Society for Creative Anachronism.

★ 2694 ★
Mount Vernon - GEORGE WASHINGTON BIRTHDAY RIVER CROSSING. February (22nd), annual, 1 day. Contact: Chamber of Commerce, 310 Pine Street,

WASHINGTON (Continued)

Mount Vernon, Washington 98273.

A festival, ceremony, and parade highlight the events of this celebration of a moment in history.

WEST VIRGINIA

★ 2695 ★
Marlinton - POCOHONTAS COUNTY PIONEER DAYS. July (2nd weekend), annual, 3 days. Contact: Mr. Doug Dunbrack, 218 Eighth Street, Marlinton, West Virginia 24954; or Mrs. Alfred McNeil, Hillsboro, West Virginia 24946.

Yesteryear activities, including crafts events. Begun in 1967.

WISCONSIN

★ 2696 ★
Fort Atkinson - PIE FESTIVAL. Early October, annual, 1 day, Eli May House. Contact: Chamber of Commerce, Eight South Water Street East, Fort Atkinson, Wisconsin 53538.

The members of the Council for Wisconsin Writers, who are restoring the May house to be used as a Hall of Honor for Wisconsin writers, furnish home made pies served with ice cream or a piece of Wisconsin cheese. In cooperation with the Fort Atkinson Historical Society, a program of tours is offered, including museums and restored homes. A pageant is performed, and the honorees for the Writers Hall of Honor are announced.

WYOMING

★ 2697 ★
Fort Bridger - MUZZLE LOADING RENDEZVOUS. Late August, 3 days. Contact: Wyoming Travel Commission, 2320 Capitol Avenue, Cheyenne, Wyoming 82001.

Events include shooting challenges, bullwhip fights, knife and tomahawk throwing, flint and steel fire-building races, and eye-gouging and ear-biting contests

★ 2698 ★
Pinedale - GREEN RIVER RENDEZVOUS. July (2nd Sunday), annual, 1 day. Contact: Sublette County Historical Society, Incorporated, Post Office Box 666, Pinedale, Wyoming 82941.

The Rendezvous, in the early 1800's, was a fixed meeting place where mountain men and pioneers came to do business in the fur trade annually. The program, sponsored by the Sublette County Historical Society, brings the impact of the historical significance of the Rendezvous to life. In a permanent fort-like building (Fort Bonneville), an Indian encampment and a trapper's camp, local people play the part of trappers, Indians, wagon drivers, and other historical characters. The event is followed by a barbeque. Begun in 1936.

★ 2699 ★
Thermopolis - GIFT OF THE WATERS. August, annual. Contact: Wyoming Travel Commission, 2320 Capitol Avenue, Cheyenne, Wyoming 82002.

A historical pageant recalling events which shaped Wyoming.

CANADA - ALBERTA

★ 2700 ★
Edmonton - KLONDIKE DAYS. Mid July, annual, 2 weeks, Klondike Days Exposition Grounds. Contact: Edmonton Visitors Bureau, 5068 103 Street, Edmonton, Alberta T6H 4N6, Canada.

Celebration is based on traditional activities and events of the old-time goldrush days. Activities include a Sunday Promenade, free entertainment on every street corner, dressing up in Klondike clothes, watching marching bands from all over North America, panning for real gold nuggets, dancing, horse races, river raft races, tray races and live melodramas each evening at the Citadel Theatre.

CANADA - BRITISH COLUMBIA

★ 2701 ★
New Westminster - HYACK FESTIVAL. May (last full week), annual, 10 days, throughout the city. Contact: Royal City Society, 610 Clarkson Street, New Westminster, British Columbia V3M 1C8, Canada.

A unique highlight of the event is the 21-gun salute (without gun), fired by the Hyack Anvil Battery, using two anvils. The ceremony honors the memory of Queen Victoria. The wide variety of other events includes river cruises, art exhibits, a parade, gymnastics, concerts, flea market, dances, theatrical events, and much more. There are many sporting activities, such as auto races, swim meets, bowling, lacrosse, canoe marathons, weight-lifting, etc. The anvil firing dates back to 1870; it is the official opening of the festival.

CANADA - BRITISH COLUMBIA (Continued)

★ 2702 ★
Victoria - VICTORIAN DAYS.   Late May, 1 week.
Contact: The Department of Travel Industry, Travel
Information Services, Parliament Buildings, Victoria,
British Columbia, Canada.

A flashback to the days of bustles and bows, top
hats and walrus mustaches, with the entire community
taking part.   A feast of nostalgia.

CANADA - MANITOBA

★ 2703 ★
Winnipeg - FORT GARRY FRONTIER DAYS.   Mid
June, 3 days, Fort Garry.   Contact: Mr. Les
Robinson, Fort Garry Froniter Days, 87 Farwell Bay,
Winnipeg, Manitoba R3T 0S6, Canada.

A celebration remembering an earlier era.

CANADA - NEW BRUNSWICK

★ 2704 ★
Saint John - LOYALIST DAYS.   Late July-early
August, annual, 5 days.   Contact: Special Events
Co-ordinator, Tourism New Brunswick, Post Office
Box 12345, Fredericton, New Brunswick, Canada.

The festival sets aside a time for the city's residents
to re-live the early years of their area and share
their culture with visitors.   Activities include a re-
enactment of the landing of the United Empire Loyal-
ists in 1783, costumes, parades, and a doll carriage
parade in which the participants and dolls are dressed
in period costume.   Other events include an open
golf tournament, an aquatic event, a beauty pageant,
and concerts by top entertainers from across the country.   Begun in 1971.

CANADA - NEWFOUNDLAND

★ 2705 ★
Saint John's - SIGNAL HILL MILITARY TATTOO.
Late July, annual, 2-4 days.   Contact: Newfound-
land Department of Tourism, Confederation Building,
Saint John's, Newfoundland, Canada.

The event is an authentic enactment of the drills
performed here by British soldiers in the 1700's
while defending Signal Hill.

CANADA - YUKON

★ 2706 ★
Dawson City - DISCOVERY DAY.   August (weekend
nearest the 17th), annual, 3 days.   Contact: Klondike Visitors Association, Box 335, Dawson City,
Yukon Territory, Canada.

On August 17th, 1896, George Carmack found gold
in Bonanza stream and started the most fantastic gold
rush ever known.   Dawson City was the transfer point
and government headquarters for the thousands who
poured into the Klondike.   The Yukon order of Pioneers marks the anniversary of the discovery with a
celebration that includes a parade, a ball, sports
events which include a raft race on the Klondike
River, and a horticultural display.   Indian dances
are performed, and the clock is turned back to the
frantic days of the gold rush.

Indians

ALASKA

★ 2707 ★
Fairbanks - WORLD ESKIMO AND INDIAN OLYMPIC
GAMES.   July, annual, 3 days.   Contact: Alaska
Division of Tourism, Pouch E, Juneau, Alaska 99801.

Various tribes of Eskimos and Indians compete in games
focusing in strength and endurance to pain.   Games
include ear weight, ear pulling, knuckle hop (walking
on toes and knuckles), one- and two- footed high
kick, body weight carrying, seal-skinning, dance
competition by tribal categories, muktuk eating
(whale blubber with skin attached), Indian-stick pull,
women's parky contest, baby contest, Native Queen
contest (winner enters Miss American Indian Contest),
and native women vs. caucasian men tug o'war contest.   Currently includes Indians from Alaska and
Canada, hoping to expand to include United States,
Greenland, Lapland and Siberia.   Started in
1961.

★ 2708 ★
Kotzebue - INDIAN FESTIVAL.   July (4th), 1 day.
Contact: Juneau Area Office, Bureau of Indian
Affairs, U.S. Department of the Interior, Federal
Building, Box 3-8000, Juneau, Alaska 99801.

Arctic Baby and Miss Arctic Beauty contests, prizes
for the biggest Baluga whale brought in by a Eskimo
hunter since the winter break-up, kayak races,
motorboat races, Eskimo dancing, Eskimo high-kick
contest, and blanket toss.

Indians

ALASKA (Continued)

★ 2709 ★
Tanana - INDIAN CELEBRATION. June. Contact: Juneau Area Office, Bureau of Indian Affairs, U.S. Department of the Interior, Federal Building, Box 3-8000, Juneau, Alaska 99801.

Competitive Indian dancing, canoe races across the Yukon, archery competition, greased pole walking contest, cross-country foot races, and Indian arm wrestling.

ARIZONA

★ 2710 ★
Casa Grande - INDIAN POW WOW. Mid February, 3 days. Contact: Casa Grande Chamber of Commerce, 201 East Fourth Street, Casa Grande, Arizona 85222.

The rodeo draws American Indian horsemen from tribes throughout the southwest. In addition, Indian crafts are exhibited, dancers perform authentic rituals, and native foods are prepared.

★ 2711 ★
Cedar Creek - WHITE MOUNTAIN ALL-INDIAN POW WOW. Early June, annual, 1 weekend. Contact: Arizona Visitor Development Section, 1645 West Jefferson, Cedar Creek, Arizona 85007.

Apache Indians compete in a rodeo. There are performances of the ritual Sunrise Dance and Crown Dance, and exhibitions of arts and crafts.

★ 2712 ★
Flagstaff - FLAGSTAFF INDIAN POW WOW (ALL INDIAN POW WOW OR SOUTHWEST INDIAN POW WOW). Late June-early July, annual, 1 week, City Park. Contact: Chamber of Commerce, Post Office Box 1150, Beaver and Santa Fe, Flagstaff, Arizona 86001.

The Pow Wow is staged as a civic event by Indian, civic and business groups. Activities include a parade with equestrians, bands and dancers representing Indian tribes from throughout the United States, Mexico, and Canada. In addition, there is a rodeo, ceremonial dancing, and a bazaar. All of the activities' participants are Indians; non-Indians are welcome as spectators. In addition, there are picnics and barbeques. Indian games include such traditionals as dance contests, teepee pitching contests, spear throwing contests, foot races, tug of war, etc. Over 100 years old.

★ 2713 ★
Hopi Indian Reservation - CEREMONIAL DANCES. August, annual. Contact: Winslow Chamber of Commerce, Post Office Box 621, Winslow, Arizona 86047.

A religious festival, the Snake Dance, done with live rattlesnakes, and a prayer for rain.

★ 2714 ★
Laveen - SAINT JOHN'S INDIAN MISSION FESTIVAL. Early March, 1 day. Contact: Chamber of Commerce, Laveen, Arizona 85339.

Gila River Indian dances and food, arts and crafts exhibits.

★ 2715 ★
Peach Springs - AMERICAN INDIAN DAY. Late September (last Friday). Contact: Phoenix Area Office, Bureau of Indian Affairs, U.S. Department of the Interior, 124 West Thomas Road, Box 7007, Phoenix, Arizona 85011.

A parade and tribal activities to honor the leaders and people of the American Indians.

★ 2716 ★
Peach Springs - HUALAPAI TRIBAL POW-WOW AND RODEO. Late August (4th weekend). Contact: Hualapai Tribal Council, Post Office Box 168, Peach Springs, Arizona 86434.

Indian singing, dancing, and a rodeo.

★ 2717 ★
Phoenix - INDIAN FAIR OR HEARD MUSEUM INDIAN FAIR. April, annual, 2 days, Heard Museum. Contact: Patrick T. Haulihan, Museum Director, Heard Museum Guild, 22 East Monte Vista Road, Phoenix, Arizona 85004.

Dances, arts and crafts, and foods of the Indians. Indian crafts-men and women demonstrate such things as pottery of different tribes, silver-working, basketry, beadwork, cradle board making, etc. Performances are given by Indian dancers. There are children's crafts and Indian singers. Begun around 1958.

★ 2718 ★
Phoenix - YAQUI HOLY WEEK CEREMONIALS. March (the week before Easter), annual, 7 days. Contact: Phoenix Area Office, Bureau of Indian

ARIZONA (Continued)

Affairs, U.S. Department of the Interior, 124 West Thomas Road, Box 7007, Phoenix, Arizona 85011.

A combination of Christian and ancient traditional Yaqui rituals. Pageantry includes Easter ceremonies and the Deer Dance.

★ 2719 ★
Salt River Indian Community - AMERICAN INDIAN DAY. Late September (last Friday). Contact: Phoenix Area Office, Bureau of Indian Affairs, U.S. Department of the Interior, 124 West Thomas Road, Box 7007, Phoenix, Arizona 85011.

The Indian peoples and their leaders are honored with dancing, entertainment and a food bazaar.

★ 2720 ★
Salt River Indian Community - SALT RIVER NATIONAL INDIAN TRADE FAIR. March (last week), annual. Contact: Phoenix Area Office, Bureau of Indian Affairs, U.S. Department of the Interior, 124 West Thomas Road, Box 7007, Phoenix, Arizona 85011.

Events include a rodeo, Miss Indian Arizona contest, and exhibition of Indian trades and crafts.

★ 2721 ★
Sells - PAPAGO ALL INDIAN FAIR. Late November, annual, 6 days, Papago Reservation. Contact: Papago, Post Office Box 837, Sells, Arizona 85634.

Events include the display and demonstration of hand-crafted pottery, jewelry, and woven rugs. There are also Indian games and a rodeo.

★ 2722 ★
Supai - HAVASUPAI TRIBAL PEACH FESTIVAL. Late August (weekend prior to children returning to boarding school). Contact: Havasupai Tourist Enterprise, Supai, Arizona 86435.

An Indian festival and dancing.

★ 2723 ★
Tucson - YAQUI HOLY WEEK CEREMONIALS. March (the week before Easter), annual, 7 days. Contact: Phoenix Area Office, Bureau of Indian Affairs, U.S. Department of the Interior, 124 West Thomas Road, Box 7007, Phoenix, Arizona 85011.

A combination of Christian and ancient traditional Yaqui rituals. Pageantry includes Easter ceremonies and the Deer dance.

★ 2724 ★
Whiteriver - WHITE MOUNTAIN APACHE TRIBAL FAIR AND RODEO. Late August-early September (Labor Day weekend), 3 days. Contact: Phoenix Area Office, Bureau of Indian Affairs, U.S. Department of the Interior, 124 West Thomas Road, Box 7007, Phoenix, Arizona 85011.

Includes Crown dances and other ceremonies, night performances, and a rodeo.

★ 2725 ★
Window Rock - NAVAJO NATION FAIR. Late August-early September, 4 days. Contact: Navajo Area Office, Bureau of Indian Affairs, U.S. Department of the Interior, Box 1060, Window Rock, Arizona 86515.

Parades, rodeo, Indian dances, "fry-bread" contests, and an arts and crafts exhibit. More than 30 tribes are represented.

★ 2726 ★
Yuma - AMERICAN INDIAN DAY. Late September (last Friday). Contact: Phoenix Area Office, Bureau of Indian Affairs, U.S. Department of the Interior, 124 West Thomas Road, Box 7007, Phoenix, Arizona 85011.

The Quechan tribe perform Indian dances and play Indian games. A barbeque is served.

CALIFORNIA

★ 2727 ★
Banning - MALKI INDIAN FIESTA AND BARBEQUE. Late May, annual, 1 day, Malki Museum. Contact: Chamber of Commerce, 78 North Murray, Banning, California 92220.

Ceremonials, barbeque, and dance. Indians sell their wares in arts and crafts. Indian food is also available. Begun around 1967.

★ 2728 ★
Bishop - BISHOP INDIAN RODEO AND POW WOW. Early August, 2 days. Contact: Southern California Visitors Council, 705 West Seventh Street, Los Angeles, California 90017.

Indians

CALIFORNIA (Continued)

Indian dance and hand games performed by Paiute and Shoshone Indians.

★ 2729 ★
Burbank - BUFFALO FEAST AND POW WOW. Early June, 1 day, annual, Buena Vista Park. Contact: Southern California Visitors Council, 705 West Seventh Street, Los Angeles, California 90017.

Special events include buffalo barbeque, Indian dances, and demonstrations of Indian rug-making, silver work, and beading. Begun around 1972.

★ 2730 ★
Crescent City - NATIONAL INDIAN OBSERVANCE DAY. Late September, annual, 2 days. Contact: Del Norte Chamber of Commerce, Box 246, Crescent City, California 95531.

Rodeo, dancing, ceremonial dancing, marathon race, Indian village, speeches by visiting Indian dignitaries, salmon feed and barbeque.

★ 2731 ★
Guerneville - PAGEANT OF FIRE MOUNTAIN.
Early September, annual, 2 days, Russian River, Johnson Beach. Contact: Information Officer, State of California, Department of Commerce, 1400 Tenth Street, Sacramento, California 95814.

Indian pageant and Indian dances are performed. Mountain of Fire. Retelling of an Indian love-legend, as well as other legendary pageants. Begun around 1947.

★ 2732 ★
Pala - CORPUS CHRISTI FIESTA. May or June (Sunday after the Corpus Christi Feast Day), annual, 1 day, Mission San Antonio de Pala. Contact: Brother Howard Casey, Old Missions, 133 Golden Gate, San Francisco, California 94102.

Holy feast of obligation in the Roman Catholic Church, occuring 60 or 63 days after Easter. High Mass, after which young Indian girls wearing white dresses lead a procession, scattering flowers as they go. Three times the procession stops at altars made of flowers, fronds, and ferns. Afterwards there is a barbeque, Indian games, and other activities and dances. Begun around 1816.

★ 2733 ★
Pala - PALA MISSION CHILDREN'S FESTIVAL.
October (5th), annual, 1 day, Mission San Antonio de Pala. Contact: Brother Howard Casey, Old Missions, 133 Golden Gate, San Francisco, California 94102.

Celebration of the Feast Day of Saint Francis, patron of the Cupeno Indians. Indian games and contests and tribal dances in colorful costumes. Procession. Sponsored by the Old Missions of California.

★ 2734 ★
Santa Monica - INDIAN CEREMONIAL AND POW WOW. Early June, 3 days, Civic Auditorium. Contact: Southern California Visitors Council, 705 West Seventh Street, Los Angeles, California 90017.

Indian jewelry, baskets, pottery, rugs, paintings, and sculptures on display and for sale. Entertainment includes ceremonial Indian dances.

★ 2735 ★
Tuolumne - MI-WUK INDIAN ACORN FESTIVAL.
Mid September, 2 days, Tuolumne Rancheria. Contact: California Chamber of Commerce, 455 Capitol Mall, Sacramento, California 95814.

A traditional Indian festival with dancing in honor of the acorn.

COLORADO

★ 2736 ★
Colorado Springs - NATIONAL CHIN-QUA-PIN DAYS (NATIONAL NATIVE AMERICAN INDIAN FESTIVAL). Late June, 3 days. Contact: Chamber of Commerce, Post Office Box B, Colorado Springs, Colorado 80901.

A traditional Indian festival with entertainment and Indian crafts.

★ 2737 ★
Ignacio - SOUTHERN UTE SUN DANCE. July (usually 1st week), annual. Contact: Albuquerque Area Office, Bureau of Indian Affairs, U.S. Department of the Interior, 5301 Central Avenue, Northeast, Post Office Box 8327, Albuquerque, New Mexico 87108.

A traditional Indian celebration with dancing and colorful costumes.

FLORIDA

★ 2738 ★
Hollywood - SEMINOLE TRIBAL FAIR.   Mid February, annual, Seminole Okalee Indian Village.   Contact: Fred Smith, Seminole Tribe of Florida, 6073 Sterling Road, Hollywood, Florida 33024.

Indian pow-wow, native dancing, costume contests, and selection of the Seminole princess.   Arts and crafts displayed by the Miccosukee Tribe and some western tribes.   Rodeo performances.

GEORGIA

★ 2739 ★
Cairo - MUSCOGEE-CREEK INDIAN POW WOW. July (4th), annual, 1 day.   Contact: Georgia Department of Community Development, Tourist Division, Post Office Box 38097, Atlanta, Georgia 30334.

A traditional Indian celebration with arts and crafts, dancing, etc.   Begun around 1973.

IDAHO

★ 2740 ★
Craigmont - TALMAKA CAMP MEETING.   Late June-early July, annual, 12 days.   Contact: Craigmont Chamber of Commerce, Craigmont, Idaho 83523.

The Nez Perce Indians gather for this festival to which the public is invited.   Unusual handcrafts are displayed and sold, made from such unusual materials as deerskin and cornhusks.   In addition, there are dances and good food.

★ 2741 ★
Fort Hall - SHOSHONE-BANNOCK INDIAN DAYS. Late September, 3 days.   Contact: Portland Area Office, Bureau of Indian Affairs, U.S. Department of the Interior, 1425 Irving Street, Northeast, Box 3785, Portland, Oregon 97208.

Indian games and dancing, all-Indian rodeo.

★ 2742 ★
Fort Hall - SHOSHONE-BANNOCK INDIAN FESTIVAL.   August, annual, 4 days.   Contact: U.S. Department of the Interior, Bureau of Indian Affairs, Fort Hall Indian Reservation 83203, c/o Hiram E. Olney, Superintendent.

At each festival a young woman, at least one-fourth Shoshone-Bannock, Bannock or both, is chosen to be Miss Shoshone-Bannock.   Other events at the festival include children's parade, games and field activities, an Indian mounted costume class, war and social dances, all Indian pageant; little britches all-Indian rodeo, little princess contest, and war dance contest.

★ 2743 ★
Fort Hall - SUN DANCES.   Mid July, Putnam Lodge.   Contact: Portland Area Office, Bureau of Indian Affairs, U.S. Department of the Interior, 1425 Irving Street, Northeast, Post Office Box 3785, Portland, Oregon 97208.

Religious Indian observance and buffalo feast.   Public welcome to observe the war dances and Indian games.

★ 2744 ★
Lapwai - E-PAH-TES WAR DANCE CHAMPIONSHIP. Early March (1st week).   Contact: Portland Area Office, Bureau of Indian Affairs, U.S. Department of the Interior, Federal Office Building, 2800 Cottage Way, Sacramento, California 95825.

Members of the Nez Perce tribe compete in Indian games and war dance contests.

★ 2745 ★
Lapwai - PI-NEE-WAUS DAYS.   August (3rd week). Contact: Portland Area Office, Bureau of Indian Affairs, U.S. Department of the Interior, 1425 Irving Street, Northeast, Box 3785, Portland, Oregon 97208.

Nez Perce soul music, war dancing, friendship feast barbeque, parade, races, baseball, exhibits, Indian games and music.

INDIANA

★ 2746 ★
Attica - POTAWATOMI INDIAN FESTIVAL.   Mid-late October, 3 days.   Contact: Ben Day, Community Investments, 401 East Monroe Street, Attica, Indiana 47918.

A large parade is the highlight of a weekend festival celebrating the state's Indian heritage.   Includes barbeque, square dance, flea market, arts and crafts displays, farmer's market, tour of historic homes, tomahawk throw, muzzle rifle shoot, antique show and sale, archery shoot, boat rides on the Wabash, and pancake-sausage breakfast.

INDIANA (Continued)

★ 2747 ★
Battle Ground – TECUMSEH LODGE INDIAN POW
WOW.   Late August, 2 days, Tippecanoe Battlefield.
Contact: Program Director, Battle Ground Historical
Corporation, Box 225, Battle Ground, Indiana 47920.

Tribal dances, rare costumes, traditional foods, and
sales of a wide assortment of handmade jewelry and
leatherwork highlight the festival events.

IOWA

★ 2748 ★
Tama – MESQUAKI INDIAN POW WOW (TAMA
POW WOW).   Mid August (2nd week), annual, 4
days, Mesquaki Indian Settlement.   Contact:
Donald W. Wanatee, Route 2, Box 55, Tama, Iowa
52339.

The Mesquaki are the only tribe living in Iowa and
they own their land.   They are sometimes called
the Sac and the Fox.   Festivities include Indian
dancing and music, arts and crafts displayed and
demonstrated, cooking, folklife, and games and contests including the Midwest Indian Dancing Championship.   Sponsored by the Mesquaki Indian Pow Wow
Association/Sac and Fox Tribe.   Begun around 1916.

★ 2749 ★
Titonka – INDIAN DAYS.   Late June, 2 days.
Contact: Chamber of Commerce, Titonka, Iowa
50480.

A traditional celebration of Indian heritage – dancing,
arts and crafts, etc.

KANSAS

★ 2750 ★
Wichita – MID AMERICA ALL-INDIAN POW WOW.
Early August, annual, 3 days, Mid-America All
Indian Center.   Contact: Jay R. Hunter, 1650
East Central, Wichita, Kansas 67214.

Indian music and dancing, arts and crafts.   Dance
contests for all ages.   Recreation typical of the
Plains Indians.   Begun in 1967.

LOUISIANA

★ 2751 ★
Baton Rouge – SOUTHEASTERN INDIAN FESTIVAL.
Mid May, annual, 1 day, John M. Parker Agri-

cultural Center.   Contact: Executive Director,
Louisiana Tourist Commission, Post Office Box 44291,
Baton Rouge, Louisiana 70804.

A competition between Indian dance teams of the
Order of the Arrow Lodges of the Boy Scouts of
America from throughout the United States.   There
is also a display of Indian arts, crafts, and cultural
artifacts.   Begun around 1970.

MAINE

★ 2752 ★
Old Town – INDIAN PAGEANT.   Late July, annual,
Indian Island.   Contact: Chamber of Commerce,
Old Town, Maine 04468.

Indian ceremonial dances, canoe races, and a tour
of historic sites highlight this Indian festival.

MARYLAND

★ 2753 ★
Gaithersburg – INDIAN FAIR.   Late April, annual,
3 days, Fairgrounds.   Contact: Chamber of Commerce, Post Office Box 652, Gaithersburg, Maryland
20760.

Sale of Indian jewelry and crafts; performances of
Indian dances and singing.

★ 2754 ★
Gaithersburg – INDIAN FAIR.   September, annual,
3 days, Fairgrounds.   Contact: Chamber of Commerce, Post Office Box 652, Gaithersburg, Maryland
20760.

Sale of Indian jewelry and arts and crafts; performances of Indian dances and singing.

MASSACHUSETTS

★ 2755 ★
Mashpee – WAMPANOAG INDIAN FESTIVAL.
Early July, 3 days, Attaquin Park.   Contact: Falmouth Chamber of Commerce, Falmouth, Massachusetts
02540.

A full range of activities and displays centered
around the outdoor Indian exhibit in Attaquin Park.

MICHIGAN

★ 2756 ★
Hastings - INDIAN POW WOW. August, annual,
2 days, Charlton Park Village and Museum. Contact: West Michigan Tourist Association, Hospitality
House, 136 Fulton East, Grand Rapids, Michigan
49502.

A traditional Indian celebration with dancing, crafts,
and food.

★ 2757 ★
Marquette - INDIAN AWARENESS PROGRAM.
October, annual, 1 week, Northern Michigan
University. Contact: University News Bureau,
Northern Michigan University, Marquette, Michigan
49855.

Designed to highlight American Indian culture and
to help the student body and general public become
more aware of the role of Indian culture in American
society. Sponsored by the Organization of North
American Indian Students (ONAIS) and first started
in 1971.

MISSISSIPPI

★ 2758 ★
Philadelphia - CHOCTAW INDIAN FAIR. Mid
July, annual, 4 days, Choctaw High School. Con-
tact: Philadelphia Chamber of Commerce, Post
Office Box 51, Philadelphia, Mississippi 39350.

Each of the seven Choctaw Indian reservation communities is represented in exhibits, sports competition
and cultural activities. Many Choctaw wear traditional costumes. Events include ceremonial dances;
Choctaw stickball game between opposing communities; blow gun, drum beating, and princess contests;
community and individual exhibits of Indian arts and
crafts including beadwork, dolls, native dress, wood
carving, caning, stone jewelry, artifacts, and agricultural produce. Such things as paintings, woven
baskets, and other hand-made trinkets are usually
offered for sale. Poultry and livestock are exhibited
and there is a carnival. A wide selection of contemporary American Indian paintings is available for
purchase. Nightly drama performance. Sponsored
by the Mississippi band of Choctaw Indians. Started
in 1949.

MONTANA

★ 2759 ★
Browning - NORTH AMERICAN INDIAN DAYS. Mid

July (2nd or 3rd week), annual, 3-4 days, Blackfeet
Indian Reservation. Contact: Chamber of Commerce,
Box 608, Browning, Montana 59417; or Blackfeet
Tribal Council, Browning, Montana 59417.

Sponsored by the Blackfeet Indians, the festival includes a pageant of the history of the Blackfeet
tribe, Indian dances, ceremonials, games and parades.
The participants wear tribal costumes. Other activities include Indian singing and a rodeo.

★ 2760 ★
Crow Agency - CUSTER RE-ENACTMENT. Late
June, annual, 1 day, near the site of Custer's last
stand, on the Cherokee reservation. Contact:
Billings Area Office, Bureau of Indian Affairs, U.S.
Department of the Interior, 316 North 26th Street,
Billings, Montana 59101.

A cast composed mainly of Crow Indians re-enacts
the famous battle.

★ 2761 ★
Hardin - CROW INDIAN FAIR. Mid August (3rd
weekend), annual, 5 days, Crow Agency. Contact:
Chamber of Commerce, Crow Agency, Hardin,
Montana 59022.

Features a costume parade every morning, with prizes
awarded. In the afternoon there are races and an
all-Indian rodeo. In the evening there are dances
and ceremonials in traditional Crow clothing. There
is a large arts and crafts area with items on display
and for sale.

★ 2762 ★
Wolf Point - OPETA-YE-TECA INDIAN CELEBRATION.
Late July, 3 days. Contact: Chamber of Commerce,
Box 237, Wolf Point, Montana 59201.

Traditional Indian dancing, ceremonies, crafts, etc.,
are featured in this festival.

NEVADA

★ 2763 ★
Nixon - INDIAN NEVADA DAY. Late October
(31st), annual, 1 day. Contact: Phoenix Area
Office, Bureau of Indian Affairs, U.S. Department
of the Interior, 124 West Thomas Road, Box 7007,
Phoenix, Arizona 85011.

Rodeo, dancing, hand games, and a barbeque are
the highlights of this annual celebration.

Indians

NEW MEXICO

★ 2764 ★
Acoma Pueblo - GOVERNOR'S FIESTA. Late
January or early February, annual. Contact:
Pueblo Office, Acoma Pueblo, New Mexico;
or Albuquerque Area Office, Bureau of Indian
Affairs, U.S. Department of the Interior, 5301
Central Avenue, Northeast, Post Office Box 8327,
Albuquerque, New Mexico 87108.

Various Indian dances are performed during the festival.

★ 2765 ★
Acoma Pueblo - SAN ESTEVAN (SAINT STEPHEN)
FEAST DAY. Early September (2nd), annual, 1
day. Contact: Albuquerque Area Office, Bureau
of Indian Affairs, U.S. Department of the Interior,
5301 Central Avenue, Northeast, Post Office Box
8327, Albuquerque, New Mexico 87108.

The harvest dance is performed by costumed Indians.

★ 2766 ★
Acoma Pueblo - SAN LORENZO (SAINT LAWRENCE)
FEAST DAY. Early August (10th), annual, 1 day,
Acomita. Contact: Albuquerque Area Office,
Bureau of Indian Affairs, U.S. Department of the
Interior, 5301 Central Avenue, Northeast, Post
Office Box 8327, Albuquerque, New Mexico 87108.

The corn dance is performed by the Indians in traditional costume.

★ 2767 ★
Acoma Pueblo - SAN PEDRO FEAST DAY. June
(29th), annual, 1 day. Contact: Albuquerque
Area Office, Bureau of Indian Affairs, U.S. Department of the Interior, 5301 Central Avenue, Northeast,
Post Office Box 8327, Albuquerque, New Mexico
87108.

A fiesta, including a rooster pull and other traditional
events and dances. Also held at Santa Ana, San
Felipe, Santo Domingo, Cochiti and Isleta Pueblos.

★ 2768 ★
Albuquerque - AMERICAN INDIAN ARTS FESTIVAL.
Early May, annual, 3 days, State Fairgrounds. Con-
tact: Rio Grande Indian Festival, c/o Clyde Duncum,
Bonnie Gems Indian Arts, 110 Romero, Northwest,
Albuquerque, New Mexico 87104.

A variety of Indian arts and crafts, dancing, food,

etc. Begun around 1973.

★ 2769 ★
Albuquerque - INTER-TRIBAL POW WOW. Mid
June, annual, 3 days, Indian School. Contact:
University of New Mexico, Native American Studies
Center, University Hill Northeast, Albuquerque,
New Mexico 87106.

Most of the Southwestern tribes are represented as
they perform their tribal dances in hand-crafted
costumes and headdresses, in one of the largest Indian
dance shows. Begun around 1968.

★ 2770 ★
Albuquerque - RIO GRANDE INDIAN FESTIVAL.
Early May, annual, 3 days, Convention Center.
Contact: Clyde Duncum, Rio Grande Arts and Crafts
Association, 110 Romero, Northwest, Albuquerque,
New Mexico 87104.

A major Indian arts and crafts show.

★ 2771 ★
Cochiti - CANDELERIA (CANDLEMAS) DAY. Early
February (Candlemas), annual, 1 day. Contact:
Pueblo Office, Cochiti Pueblo, New Mexico 87041.

The Indians of the pueblo perform ceremonial dances.

★ 2772 ★
Cochiti Pueblo - COMING OF THE RIVERMEN.
Early May, annual, 1 day. Contact: Pueblo
Office, Cochiti Pueblo, New Mexico 87041; or
Albuquerque Area Office, Bureau of Indian Affairs,
U.S. Department of the Interior, 5301 Central Avenue
Northeast, Post Office Box 8327, Albuquerque, New
Mexico 87108.

Green corn dance is performed.

★ 2773 ★
Cochiti Pueblo - SAINT BUENAVENTURA FEAST
DAY. Mid July (14th), annual, 1 day. Contact:
Albuquerque Area Office, Bureau of Indian Affairs,
U.S. Department of the Interior, 5301 Central
Avenue, Northeast, Post Office Box 8327, Albuquer-
que, New Mexico 87108.

The Indians dance the corn dance and celebrate with
a grand fiesta.

★ 2774 ★
Cochiti Pueblo - SAN PEDRO FEAST DAY. June

Indians

NEW MEXICO (Continued)

(29th), annual, 1 day.   Contact: Albuquerque
Area Office, Bureau of Indian Affairs, U.S. Department of the Interior, 5301 Central Avenue, Northeast,
Post Office Box 8327, Albuquerque, New Mexico
87180.

A fiesta, including a rooster pull and other traditional
events and dances.   Also held at Isleta, Acoma,
Santa Ana, San Felipe and Santo Domingo Pueblos.

★ 2775 ★
Gallup - INTER-TRIBAL INDIAN CEREMONIAL.
Mid August, annual, 3-5 days, Red Rock State Park.
Contact: Albuquerque Area Office, Bureau of Indian
Affairs, U.S. Department of the Interior, 5301
Central Avenue, Northeast, Post Office Box 8327,
Albuquerque, New Mexico 87108.

One of the oldest and largest Indian expositions,
open to all tribes (United States, Mexico, and
Canada).   Large display and sale of Indian handicrafts, large rodeo, dances, exhibitions, and competitions.

★ 2776 ★
Isleta Pueblo - SAN AUGUSTINE'S DAY.   Early
September (3rd-4th), annual, 1-2 days.   Contact:
Albuquerque Area Office, Bureau of Indian Affairs,
U.S. Department of the Interior, 5301 Central
Avenue, Northeast, Post Office Box 8327, Albuquer-
que, New Mexico 87108.

The corn dance and the harvest dance are performed
and there is a gala carnival.

★ 2777 ★
Isleta Pueblo - SAN PEDRO FEAST DAY.   June
(19th), annual, 1 day.   Contact: Albuquerque
Area Office, Bureau of Indian Affairs, U.S. Department of the Interior, 5301 Central Avenue, Northeast,
Post Office Box 8327, Albuquerque, New Mexico
87108.

A fiesta, including a rooster pull and other traditional
events.   Also held at Acoma, Santa Ana, San
Felipe, Santo Domingo and Cochiti Pueblos.

★ 2778 ★
Jemez Pueblo - FEAST DAY.   Mid November (12th),
annual, 1 day.   Contact: Albuquerque Area Office,
Bureau of Indian Affairs, U.S. Department of the
Interior, 5301 Central Avenue, Northeast, Post Office
Box 8327, Albuquerque, New Mexico 87108.

In honor of the Pueblo's patron saint, San Diego,
the participants hold a fiesta and perform the harvest
and corn dances.

★ 2779 ★
Jemez Pueblo - OLD PECOS BULL CELEBRATION.
Early August (2nd), annual, 1 day.   Contact:
Albuquerque Area Office, Bureau of Indian Affairs,
U.S. Department of the Interior, 5301 Central Avenue,
Northeast, Post Office Box 8327, Albuquerque, New
Mexico 87108.

A celebration to honor the people who come from
the Pecos Pueblo in 1838 to join the Jemez Pueblo.
Includes the former Pecos Pueblo Celebration.

★ 2780 ★
Laguna Pueblo - SAINT ANTHONY FEAST DAY AND
CARNIVAL.   Mid August (15th), annual, 1 day,
Mesita Village.   Contact: Albuquerque Area Office,
Bureau of Indian Affairs, U.S. Department of the
Interior, 5301 Central Avenue, Northeast, Post Office
Box 8327, Albuquerque, New Mexico 87108.

Harvest and social dances are performed in traditional
costume.

★ 2781 ★
Laguna Pueblo - SAINT ELIZABETH FEAST DAY.
Late September (25th), annual, 1 day.   Contact:
Albuquerque Area Office, Bureau of Indian Affairs,
U.S. Department of the Interior, 5301 Central Avenue,
Northeast, Post Office Box 8327, Albuquerque, New
Mexico 87108.

Social and harvest dances are performed as part of
the festival activities.

★ 2782 ★
Laguna Pueblo - SAINT JOSEPH FEAST DAY.   Mid
March (around the 19th), annual, 1 day.   Contact:
Pueblo Office, Laguna Pueblo, New Mexico 87026;
or Albuquerque Area Office, Bureau of Indian Affairs,
U.S. Department of the Interior, 5301 Central Avenue,
Northeast, Post Office Box 8327, Albuquerque, New
Mexico 87108.

Harvest and social dances are featured at this Indian
festival.

★ 2783 ★
Laguna Pueblo - SAINT JOSEPH FEAST DAY.   Mid
September (around the 19th), annual, 1 day, Old
Laguna Village.   Contact: Albuquerque Area Office,

301

Indians

NEW MEXICO (Continued)

Bureau of Indian Affairs, U.S. Department of the Interior, 5301 Central Avenue, Northeast, Post Office Box 8327, Albuquerque, New Mexico 87108.

Harvest dance, other dances, and sporting events. A great fair attended by other Indians from other pueblos as well.

★ 2784 ★
Laguna Pueblo - SAN LORENZO FEAST DAY GRAB DAY.   Early August (10th), annual, 1 day.   Contact: Albuquerque Area Office, Bureau of Indian Affairs, U.S. Department of the Interior, 5301 Central Avenue, Northeast, Post Office Box 8327, Albuquerque, New Mexico 87108.

Persons named after the saint throw food and gifts from the rooftops.

★ 2785 ★
Mescalero - MESCALERO APACHE GAHAN CEREMONIAL.   Early July, 3 days, Mescalero Apache Reservation.   Contact: Albuquerque Area Office, Bureau of Indian Affairs, U.S. Department of the Interior, 5301 Central Avenue, Northeast, Post Office Box 8327, Albuquerque, New Mexico 87108.

The Apaches perform their Gahan (also called mountain spirit or devil) dance and hold a rodeo.

★ 2786 ★
Mescalero - RUIDOSO-MESCALERO APACHE INDIAN CELEBRATION.   June, annual, 3 days. Contact: Albuquerque Area Office, Bureau of Indian Affairs, U.S. Department of the Interior, 5301 Central Avenue, Northeast, Post Office Box 8327, Albuquerque, New Mexico 87108.

"World's richest Indian dances". $10,000 in prize money.   Also held in Ruidoso.

★ 2787 ★
Nambe Pueblo - SAN FRANCISCO FEAST DAY. Early October (4th), annual, 1 day.   Contact: Albuquerque Area Office, Bureau of Indian Affairs, U.S. Department of the Interior, 5301 Central Avenue, Northeast, Post Office Box 8327, Albuquerque, New Mexico 87108.

The Indians perform a number of dances, including the elk dance.   There is a fiesta.

★ 2788 ★
Picuris Pueblo - SAN LORENZO (SAINT LAWRENCE) FEAST DAY.   Early August, annual, 2 days.   Contact: Albuquerque Area Office, Bureau of Indian Affairs, U.S. Department of the Interior, 5301 Central Avenue, Northeast, Albuquerque, New Mexico 87108.

The summer corn dance and sunset dance are performed and there are feast day celebrations, foot races, other dances, and a pole climb.

★ 2789 ★
Ruidoso - RUIDOSO-MESCALERO APACHE INDIAN CELEBRATION.   June, annual, 3 days.   Contact: Albuquerque Area Office, Bureau of Indian Affairs, U.S. Department of the Interior, 5301 Central Avenue, Northeast, Post Office Box 8327, Albuquerque, New Mexico 87108.

"World's richest Indian dances". $10,000 in prize money.   Also held in Mescalero.

★ 2790 ★
San Felipe Pueblo - CANDELERIA (CANDLEMAS) DAY.   Early February (Candlemas), annual, 1 day. Contact: Pueblo Office, San Felipe Pueblo, New Mexico 87001.

Indians of the pueblo perform ceremonial dances, among them, the buffalo dance.

★ 2791 ★
San Felipe Pueblo - FEAST DAY (FIESTA).   Early May (1st), annual, 1 day.   Contact: Pueblo Office, San Felipe Pueblo, New Mexico 87001; or Albuquerque Area Office, Bureau of Indian Affairs, U.S. Department of the Interior, 5301 Central Avenue, Northeast, Post Office Box 8327, Albuquerque, New Mexico 87108.

Green corn dance is featured at this Indian festival.

★ 2792 ★
San Felipe Pueblo - SAINT ANNE DAY GRAB DAYS.   Late July (around the 25th), 2 days. Contact: Albuquerque Area Office, Bureau of Indian Affairs, U.S. Department of the Interior, 5301 Central Avenue, Northeast, Post Office Box 8327, Albuquerque, New Mexico 87108.

Persons named after the patron saint throw food and gifts from housetops.

NEW MEXICO (Continued)

★ 2793 ★
San Felipe Pueblo - SAN PEDRO FEAST DAY.
June (29th), annual, 1 day. Contact: Albuquerque
Area Office, Bureau of Indian Affairs, U.S. Depart-
ment of the Interior, 5301 Central Avenue, North-
east, Post Office Box 8327, Albuquerque, New
Mexico 87108.

A fiesta including a rooster pull and other traditional
events and dances. Also held at Santo Domingo,
Cochiti, Isleta, Acoma and Santa Ana Pueblos.

★ 2794 ★
San Ildefonso Pueblo - SAN ANTONIO FEAST DAY.
June (13th), annual, 1 day. Contact: Albuquerque
Area Office, Bureau of Indian Affairs, U.S. Depart-
ment of the Interior, 5301 Central Avenue, Northeast,
Post Office Box 8327, Albuquerque, New Mexico
87108.

Various dances, including corn and buffalo.

★ 2795 ★
San Ildefonso Pueblo - SAN ILDEFONSO FEAST
DAY. Late January (23rd), annual, 1 day. Con-
tact: Albuquerque Area Office, Bureau of Indian
Affairs, U.S. Department of the Interior, 5301
Central Avenue, Northeast, Post Office Box 8327,
Albuquerque, New Mexico 87108.

Buffalo and Comanche dances - hunting dance.

★ 2796 ★
San Juan Pueblo - SAN ANTONIO FEAST DAY.
June (13th), annual, 1 day. Contact: Albuquerque
Area Office, Bureau of Indian Affairs, U.S. Depart-
ment of the Interior, 5301 Central Avenue, Northeast,
Post Office Box 8327, Albuquerque, New Mexico
87108.

Various dances, including corn and buffalo.

★ 2797 ★
San Juan Pueblo - SAN JUAN FEAST DAY. Late
June, annual, 1-2 days. Contact: Albuquerque
Area Office, Bureau of Indian Affairs, U.S. Depart-
ment of the Interior, 5301 Central Avenue, Northeast,
Post Office Box 8327, Albuquerque, New Mexico
87108.

An annual feast in honor of the parton saint, Saint
John the Baptist. Performances of the buffalo dance,

war dances, and foot races. The dance groups at
San Juan are beautifully costumed.

★ 2798 ★
Sandia Pueblo - FEAST DAY. June (13th), annual,
1 day. Contact: Albuquerque Area Office, Bureau
of Indian Affairs, U.S. Department of the Interior,
5301 Central Avenue, Northeast, Post Office Box
8327, Albuquerque, New Mexico 87108.

The corn dance is performed.

★ 2799 ★
Santa Ana Pueblo - SAINT ANNE FEAST DAY
(SANTIAGO'S AND SAINT ANNE'S DAY). Late
July (26th), annual, 2 days. Contact: Albuquerque
Area Office, Bureau of Indian Affairs, U.S. Depart-
ment of the Interior, 5301 Central Avenue, North-
east, Post Office Box 8327, Albuquerque, New Mexico
87108.

Buffalo and corn dances are performed as a highlight
of the festivities.

★ 2800 ★
Santa Ana Pueblo - SAN PEDRO FEAST DAY.
June (29th), annual, 1 day. Contact: Albuquerque
Area Chamber of Commerce, Bureau of Indian Affairs,
U.S. Department of the Interior, 5301 Central Avenue,
Northeast, Post Office Box 8327, Albuquerque, New
Mexico 87108.

A fiesta, including a rooster pull and other traditional
events and dances. Also held at San Felipe, Santo
Domingo, Cochiti, Isleta and Acoma Pueblos.

★ 2801 ★
Santa Clara Pueblo - PUYE CLIFF CEREMONIAL.
Late July, annual, 2 days, Puye Cliff Ruins. Con-
tact: Albuquerque Area Office, Bureau of Indian
Affairs, U.S. Department of the Interior, 5301
Central Avenue, Northeast, Albuquerque, New Mexico
87108.

Tours of ruins (ancestral home to the people of the
Santa Clara Pueblo) built of stone or adobe. Dances
are performed by members of several pueblos. Major
Indian arts and crafts show, and food sales.

★ 2802 ★
Santa Clara Pueblo - SAN ANTONIO FEAST DAY.
June (13th), annual, 1 day. Contact: Albuquerque
Area Office, Bureau of Indian Affairs, U.S.

Indians

NEW MEXICO (Continued)

Department of the Interior, 5301 Central Avenue, Northeast, Post Office Box 8327, Albuquerque, New Mexico 87108.

Various dances, including corn and buffalo.

★ 2803 ★
Santa Clara Pueblo – SANTA CLARA FEAST DAY. Mid August (12th), annual, 1 day. Contact: Albuquerque Area Office, Bureau of Indian Affairs, U.S. Department of the Interior, 5301 Central Avenue, Northeast, Post Office Box 8327, Albuquerque, New Mexico 87108.

Corn, harvest and social dances are performed in ceremonial costumes.

★ 2804 ★
Santa Fe – SANTA FE INDIAN MARKET. Mid August, annual, 2 days. Contact: Chamber of Commerce, La Fonda Hotel, Post Office Box 1928, Santa Fe, New Mexico 87501.

Major display of Indian arts and crafts. In Hopi villages, the snake dance is performed. Begun around 1922.

★ 2805 ★
Santo Domingo Pueblo – CANDELERIA (CANDLEMAS) DAY. Early February (Candlemas), annual, 1 day. Contact: Pueblo Office, Santo Domingo Pueblo, New Mexico 87052.

The Indians of the pueblo perform ceremonial dances.

★ 2806 ★
Santo Domingo Pueblo – SAN PEDRO FEAST DAY. June (29th), annual, 1 day. Contact: Albuquerque Area Chamber of Commerce, Bureau of Indian Affairs, U.S. Department of the Interior, 5301 Central Avenue, Northeast, Post Office Box 8327, Albuquerque, New Mexico 87108.

A fiesta, including rooster pull and other traditional events and dances. Also held at Cochiti, Isleta, Acoma, Santa Ana and San Felipe Pueblos.

★ 2807 ★
Santo Domingo Pueblo – SANTO DOMINGO FEAST DAY. Early August (4th), annual, 1 day. Contact: Albuquerque Area Office, Bureau of Indian Affairs, U.S. Department of the Interior, 5301 Central

Avenue, Post Office Box 8327, Albuquerque, New Mexico 87108.

Summer corn dance and fiesta. With over 500 clowns, dancers and singers, it is the largest of the pueblo dances.

★ 2808 ★
Shiprock – NAVAJO FAIR (NORTHERN NAVAJO FAIR AND RODEO). Early October, annual, 3-4 days. Contact: Navajo Area Office, Bureau of Indian Affairs, U.S. Department of the Interior, Box 1060, Window Rock, Arizona 86515.

Traditional Indian dances and a rodeo are featured at this Indian festival.

★ 2809 ★
Stone Lake – STONE LAKE FIESTA. Mid September, annual, 2 days. Contact: Tourist Division, New Mexico Department of Development, 113 Washington Avenue, Santa Fe, New Mexico 87503.

Jicarilla Apache campout, rodeo, dances, and foot races.

★ 2810 ★
Taos Pueblo – FEAST DAY. Late June, annual, 1-2 days. Contact: Albuquerque Area Office, Bureau of Indian Affairs, U.S. Department of the Interior, 5301 Central Avenue, Northeast, Post Office Box 8327, Albuquerque, New Mexico 87108.

Saint John the Baptist feast day. Corn dance and rabbit hunt.

★ 2811 ★
Taos Pueblo – SAINT JAMES AND SAINT ANNE'S DAY CELEBRATION. Late July (26th), annual, 2 days. Contact: Albuquerque Area Office, Bureau of Indian Affairs, U.S. Department of the Interior, 5301 Central Avenue, Northeast, Post Office Box 8327, Albuquerque, New Mexico 87108.

Buffalo and green corn dances and a rabbit hunt highlight the festive events.

★ 2812 ★
Taos Pueblo – SAN ANTONIO FEAST DAY. June (13th), annual, 1 day. Contact: Albuquerque Area Office, Bureau of Indian Affairs, U.S. Department of the Interior, 5301 Central Avenue, Northeast, Post Office Box 8327, Albuquerque, New Mexico 87108.

NEW MEXICO (Continued)

Various dances, including corn and buffalo.

★ 2813 ★
Taos Pueblo - SAN GERONIMO FEAST DAY.   Late
September (29th-30th), annual, 2 days.   Contact:
Albuquerque Area Office, Bureau of Indian Affairs,
U.S. Department of the Interior, 5301 Central
Avenue, Northeast, Post Office Box 8327, Albuquer-
que, New Mexico 87108.

The dances include the sundown dance and war
dances.   Other events are pole climbing, foot
races, clown antics, and fiesta.

★ 2814 ★
Taos Pueblo - SANTA CRUZ FEAST DAY.   Early
May (3rd), annual, 1 day.   Contact: Albuquerque
Area Office, Bureau of Indian Affairs, U.S. Depart-
ment of the Interior, 5301 Central Avenue, North-
east, Post Office Box 8327, Albuquerque, New
Mexico 87108.

Green corn dance, children's race, foot races, and
other dances are featured events in this Indian festival.

★ 2815 ★
Tesuque Pueblo - CORN OR FLAG DANCES.   Late
May-early June, annual, 7 days.   Contact: Albu-
querque Area Office, Bureau of Indian Affairs, U.S.
Department of the Interior, 5301 Central Avenue,
Northeast, Post Office Box 8327, Albuquerque, New
Mexico 87108.

Indians perform the corn and flag dances in a blessing
of the fields.

★ 2816 ★
Tesuque Pueblo - FEAST OF SAN DIEGO.   Mid
November (12th), annual, 1 day.   Contact:
Albuquerque Area Office, Bureau of Indian Affairs,
U.S. Department of the Interior, 5301 Central
Avenue, Northeast, Post Office Box 8327, Albuquer-
que, New Mexico 87108.

Flag, deer or buffalo dances performed during the
fiesta.

★ 2817 ★
Zia Pueblo - ASSUMPTION FEAST DAY.   Mid

August (15th), annual, 1 day.   Contact: Albuquer-
que Area Office, Bureau of Indian Affairs, U.S.
Department of the Interior, 5301 Central Avenue,
Northeast, Post Office Box 8327, Albuquerque, New
Mexico 87108.

The green corn dance is performed by the Indians in
ceremonial costumes.

NEW YORK

★ 2818 ★
Canandaigua - FESTIVAL OF LIGHTS.   Late August
or September (Saturday before Labor Day), annual,
1 day, Keuka, Canandaigua, Lamoka, and Waneta
Lakes.   Contact: Executive Vice President, Chamber of Commerce, 3210 Eastern Boulevard, Canandaigua,
New York 14424; or Finger Lakes Association, Incorporated, 309 Lake Street, Penn Yan, New York
14527.

A re-creation of an ancient Indian ritual of Thanksgiving.   A ring of fire around the Lakes.

NORTH CAROLINA

★ 2819 ★
Cherokee - CHEROKEE INDIAN FALL FESTIVAL.
Late September-early October, annual, 5 days,
Historical Festival Grounds on the Cherokee Indian
Reservation.   Contact: Cherokee Indian Reservation,
Cherokee, North Carolina 28719.

Features dances, archery and blow gun contests,
Cherokee Indian stickball games, craft exhibits,
singing and thanksgiving for the past year and the
harvest.

NORTH DAKOTA

★ 2820 ★
Bismarck - UNITED TRIBES POW WOW.   Early
September (weekend after Labor Day), annual.
Contact: North Dakota State Highway Department,
Capitol Grounds, Bismarck, North Dakota 58505.

An outdoor event with an all-Indian rodeo and the
national Indian singing and dancing finals.

★ 2821 ★
Fort Totten - FORT TOTTEN DAYS.   Late July,
3 days.   Contact: Aberdeen Area Office, Bureau
of Indian Affairs, U.S. Department of the Interior,
820 South Main Street, Aberdeen, South Dakota
57401.

Indians

NORTH DAKOTA (Continued)

Indian dancing, rodeo, parade, races, arts and crafts, and Indian ceremonials highlight the events.

★ 2822 ★
Fort Yates - CHAMPIONSHIP ALL-AMERICAN INDIAN POW-WOW AND RODEO FINALS. Early August (1st weekend), annual, Standing Rock Reservation. Contact: Aberdeen Area Office, Bureau of Indian Affairs, U.S. Department of the Interior, 820 South Main Street, Aberdeen, South Dakota 57401.

Traditional Indian dances and ceremonials as well as western-style contests and rodeo.

★ 2823 ★
New Town - FALL INDIAN FESTIVAL AND FORT BERTHOLD ARTS AND CRAFTS FAIR. August. Contact: Aberdeen Area Office, Bureau of Indian Affairs, U.S. Department of the Interior, 820 South Main Street, Aberdeen, South Dakota 57401.

Traditional Indian dances and ceremonials along with a showing and sale of arts and crafts.

OHIO

★ 2824 ★
Coshocton - INDIAN LORE DAY. Mid June, 1 day, Roscoe Village. Contact: Mrs. Pat Brown, 381 Hill Street, Coshocton, Ohio 43812.

The celebration honors the Delaware Indians who lived in this area with Indian dancing, cooking, crafts, exhibits and games.

★ 2825 ★
Whitehouse - INDIAN CRAFTS AND CULTURE POW-WOW. Early July, 3 days. Contact: Gary Buerk, Ohio Indian Crafts and Culture Association, 7200 Jeffers Road, Whitehouse, Ohio 43571.

Members of the Ohio Indian Crafts and Culture Association and other interested persons take this opportunity to exchange their ideas, knowledge, skills and craft items relating to the cultures of the American Indians. There are performances of Indian songs and dances, plus a contest for and sales of crafts.

OKLAHOMA

★ 2826 ★
Anadarko - AMERICAN INDIAN EXPOSITION. Mid August, annual, 6 days. Contact: Chamber of Commerce, Box 366, Anadarko, Oklahoma 73005.

Tribes from many parts of the country gather to celebrate their heritage. Parades, pageants, ceremonial and war dancing, exhibits of arts and crafts, cultural displays, horse-racing, and demonstrations of skill. Most of the participants wear native Indian clothing. Begun in 1932.

★ 2827 ★
Anadarko - PLAINS INDIAN CEREMONIALS AND DANCES. July, annual, Saturday nights. Contact: Anadarko Area Office, Bureau of Indian Affairs, U.S. Department of the Interior, Federal Building, Box 368, Anadarko, Oklahoma 73005.

Ancient dances and ceremonials performed in traditional costumes.

★ 2828 ★
Tahlequah - TRAIL OF TEARS. Late June-late August, 2 months, Tsa-La-Gi Cherokee Village. Contact: Director, Tsa-La-Gi, Box 515, Tahlequah, Oklahoma 74464.

A drama re-enacting the tragedy of the removal of the Cherokee to Oklahoma and the struggles of the people to survive.

★ 2829 ★
Tulsa - TULSA INDIAN POW WOW. Mid July, annual, 4 days. Contact: Tulsa Chamber of Commerce, 616 South Boston, Tulsa, Oklahoma 74119.

The largest Indian festival in the country with ceremonial dances and a variety of crafts.

OREGON

★ 2830 ★
LaGrande - INDIAN FESTIVAL OF THE ARTS. Late August. Contact: Mrs. Gladys Price, Indian Festival of Arts, Post Office Box 193, LaGrande, Oregon 97850.

American Indians concentrate on the arts of their past and their achievements of today, ranging from traditional dances and beadwork to modern music.

OREGON (Continued)

★ 2831 ★
Pendleton - ROOT FESTIVAL.   Late April or early
May, annual, Umatilla Reservation.   Contact:
Portland Area Office, Bureau of Indian Affairs,
U.S. Department of the Interior, 1425 Irving Street,
Northeast, Box 3785, Portland, Oregon 97208.

The festival is held when the first roots are ready
for harvesting.

★ 2832 ★
Warm Springs - PI-YUM-SHA.   Late June, 3 days.
Contact: Portland Area Office, Bureau of Indian
Affairs, U.S. Department of the Interior, 1425 Irving
Street, Northeast, Box 3785, Portland, Oregon
97208.

Indians hold a Pow Wow with dance competitions
and a rodeo.

PENNSYLVANIA

★ 2833 ★
Everett - AMERICAN INDIAN REVISITED.   August,
annual, 3 weeks.   Contact: Everett Bicentennial
Office, Borough Office, Everett, Pennsylvania
15537.

Events include Indian dancing and ceremonials, and
a parade.

★ 2834 ★
Media - INDIAN HERITAGE DAYS.   Mid July,
annual, 3 days, Rose Tree County Park.   Contact:
Department of Commerce, Bureau of Travel Depart-
ment, 431 South Office Building, Harrisburg,
Pennsylvania 17120.

Native dances, crafts, etc., featuring representatives
from 12 mid-Atlantic Indian nations, in commemoration of first land treaty with the Lenape.

RHODE ISLAND

★ 2835 ★
Charlestown - NARRAGANSETT INDIAN TRIBE
AUGUST MEETING, INDIAN DAY AND POW WOW.
Mid August, annual, 2 days, Indian Church.   Con-
tact: Rhode Island Department of Economic Develop-
ment, Tourist Promotion Division, One Weybosset
Hill, Providence, Rhode Island 02903.

A meeting, get-together, and celebration with tradi-

tional Indian dances, ceremonials, foods, crafts,
etc.

★ 2836 ★
Lafayette - AMERICAN INDIAN FEDERATION POW
WOW.   Late July-early August, annual, 2 days,
Indian Hall.   Contact: Rhode Island Department
of Economic Development, Tourist Promotion Division,
One Weybosset Hill, Providence, Rhode Island
02993.

A traditional Indian celebration with ceremonial
dancing, crafts, foods, etc.

★ 2837 ★
Lincoln - AMERICAN INDIAN POW WOW.   Mid
June, annual, 2 days, North Gate, Route 246.
Contact: Rhode Island Department of Economic
Development, Tourist Promotion Division, One
Weybosset Hill, Providence, Rhode Island 02903.

An overnight campout of American Indians and Boy
Scouts.   Sponsored by the Blackstone Valley Historical Society.   Begun around 1972.

★ 2838 ★
Newport - INDIAN FESTIVAL OF SONGS AND
DANCES.   Early July, 1 day, Ochre Court, Salve
Regina College.   Contact: Rhode Island Depart-
ment of Economic Development, Tourist Promotion
Division, One Weybosset Hill, Providence, Rhode
Island 02903.

A one day Indian celebration with traditional ceremonials, dances, songs, and costumes.

SOUTH DAKOTA

★ 2839 ★
Eagle Butte - MYSTIC CALF PIPE AND SUNDANCE
CEREMONIES.   Mid August, annual, 3 days.
Contact: Aberdeen Area Office, Bureau of Indian
Affairs, U.S. Department of the Interior, 820 South
Main Street, Aberdeen, South Dakota 57401.

Indian events, ceremonials, dances, costumes, etc.

★ 2840 ★
Lower Brule - LAKOTA NATION TRADE FAIR
(POW WOW).   Mid August, annual, 2 days, Lower
Brule Sioux Reservation.   Contact: Lower Brule
Sioux Tribe, Lower Brule Sioux Reservation, Lower
Brule, South Dakota 57548.

Indians

SOUTH DAKOTA (Continued)

Activities include a rodeo, a pow wow, and a trade fair.

★ 2841 ★
Rosebud - ROSEBUD SIOUX FAIR, POW WOW AND RODEO. Late August, annual, 3 days, Rosebud Sioux Indian Reservation. Contact: Director, Rosebud Indian Reservation, Rosebud, South Dakota 57570.

Includes dances and a ceremonial buffalo dinner. Arts and crafts are on exhibit. A rodeo is included in the events.

TEXAS

★ 2842 ★
El Paso - FIESTA OF SAN ANTONIO. Mid June, annual, 1 day, Our Lady of Mount Carmel (Nuestra Senora del Carmen). Contact: Tigua Indian Reservation, Post Office Box 17579, Ysleta Station, El Paso, Texas 79917.

One of the oldest religious ceremonies in the nation, the celebration is held by the Tigua Indians. Events include a field mass, Indian ceremonial dancing, and the serving of Indian food. The tribal officials also take office on this day, but the ceremony is private. Begun in 1620.

★ 2843 ★
Livingston - ALL INDIAN POWWOW. May-June, Alabama-Coushatta Indian Reservation. Contact: Walter Broemer, Route 3, Box 170, Livingston, Texas 77351.

Competition in Indian dances for all age groups. Gathered for the event are representatives from some 80 Indian tribes.

UTAH

★ 2844 ★
Fort Duchesne - NORTHERN UTE POW WOW. Early July, annual, 3 days. Contact: Ute Indian Tribe, Fort Duchesne, Utah 84026.

This gathering of the members of the Ute Indian tribes includes dance contests for men, women, and children. Many of the dances are never performed publicly outside of this pow wow. Other events include a queen contest, fireworks, a parade, hand games, and a bear dance exhibition.

★ 2845 ★
Whiterocks - UTE TRIBAL BEAR DANCE. Late March or April, annual. Contact: Utah Travel Council, Council Hall, Capitol Hill, Salt Lake City, Utah 84114.

An ancient and traditional Indian ceremonial, lasting an entire night. Also held at Ouray and Randlett.

★ 2846 ★
Whiterocks - UTE TRIBAL SUN DANCES. July-August, annual. Contact: Aberdeen Area Office, Bureau of Indian Affairs, U.S. Department of the Interior, 820 South Main Street, Aberdeen, South Dakota 57401.

The Sun Dance is one of the most sacred rituals of the Plains Indians.

WASHINGTON

★ 2847 ★
La Conner - SWINOMISH FESTIVAL. Late May (Memorial Day), Swinomish Reservation. Contact: Portland Area Office, Bureau of Indian Affairs, U.S. Department of the Interior, 1425 Irving Street, Northeast, Box 3785, Portland, Oregon 97208.

Swinomish Reservation hosts baseball games, Indian stick games, dances, and a salmon bake.

★ 2848 ★
La Conner - SWINOMISH TRIBAL COMMUNITY CELEBRATION. July (weekend of the 4th), annual. Contact: Paul Thompson, Post Office Box 446, La Conner, Washington 98257.

The celebration includes sports and games: a baseball tournament, bone games and war canoe races. A big Indian chinook salmon barbeque is held. Begun around 1950.

★ 2849 ★
Marietta - LUMMI STOMISH WATER CARNIVAL. June, (1st two weeks), annual, 2 weeks, Lummi Reservation. Contact: Portland Area Office, Bureau of Indian Affairs, U.S. Department of the Interior, 1425 Irving Street, Northeast, Box 3785, Portland, Oregon 97208.

Events include canoe races, International War Canoe Races, games, salmon barbeque, and Indian dances.

WASHINGTON (Continued)

★ 2850 ★
Marysville - TULALIP TRIBE'S TREATY DAYS.
January (weekend including or near the 22nd),
Tulalip Reservation.   Contact: Portland Area Office,
Bureau of Indian Affairs, U.S. Department of the
Interior, 1425 Irving Street, Northeast, Box 3785,
Portland, Oregon 97208.

The tribe celebrates the signing of the Point Elliot
treaty with ceremonial dances and a smoked salmon
feast.   Non-Indians are permitted to attend by invitation only.

★ 2851 ★
Neah Bay - MAKAH DAYS.   August (weekend
closest to the 26th), Makah Reservation.   Contact:
Portland Area Office, Bureau of Indian Affairs,
U.S. Department of the Interior, 1425 Irving Street,
Northeast, Box 3785, Portland, Oregon 97208.

The Makah Indians celebrate the acquisition of
United States citizenship with ceremonial dances,
Indian games, and feasts of traditional foods.

★ 2852 ★
Spokane - SMOO-KEE-SHIN POW-WOW.   Mid
May, 2 days, Spokane Indian Community Center.
Contact: Portland Area Office, Bureau of Indian
Affairs, U.S. Department of the Interior, 1425
Irving Street, Northeast, Box 3785, Portland, Oregon
97208.

Indian games and war dance contests are featured
events.

★ 2853 ★
Suquamish - CHIEF SEATTLE DAYS.   August (last
weekend), 2 days.   Contact: Portland Area Office,
Bureau of Indian Affairs, U.S. Department of the
Interior, 1425 Irving Street, Northeast, Box 3785,
Portland, Oregon 97208.

Events include a pageant of the history of the Indians
of the area, including the lives of Chief Seattle and
Chief Kitsap.   Canoe races, baked salmon, and a
clambake are also featured.

★ 2854 ★
Taholah - QUINAULT DERBY DAYS.   Late May
(Memorial Day), Quinault River, Quinault Lake,
Quinault Reservation.   Contact: Portland Area
Office, Bureau of Indian Affairs, U.S. Department
of the Interior, 1425 Irving Street, Northeast, Box

3785, Portland, Oregon 97208.

Events include a race up the river with motored
dug-out canoes, a salmon barbeque, a trout derby
on the lake, and a Volunteer Fireman's Ball.

★ 2855 ★
White Swan - ALL-INDIAN ENCAMPMENT.   Early
June, annual, 2 days, White Swan Rodeo Grounds,
Yakima Reservation.   Contact: Portland Area Office,
Bureau of Indian Affairs, U.S. Department of the
Interior, 1425 Irving Street, Northeast, Box 3785,
Portland, Oregon 97208.

Indian encampment, games, rodeo, cowboy dance,
and a salmon bake highlight the events.

WEST VIRGINIA

★ 2856 ★
Charleston - AMERICAN INDIAN FALL FESTIVAL.
Late October, 1 day, Sunrise.   Contact: Curator,
Children's Museum and Planetarium, Sunrise, In-
corporated, 755 Myrtle Road, Charleston, West
Virginia 25314.

The events feature different cultural aspects from
different tribes.   Held first in 1976.   Might not
be held again, museum is moving toward different
activities for each year.

WISCONSIN

★ 2857 ★
Hayward - GATHERING OF THE TRIBES.   Early
July, 3 days, reconstructed Chippewa Village.
Contact: Director, Vacation and Travel Develop-
ment, Department of Natural Resources, Wisconsin
State Division of Tourism, Post Office Box 450,
Madison, Wisconsin 53701.

An Indian pow wow with traditional ceremonials,
dancing and singing, and Indian crafts.

WYOMING

★ 2858 ★
Ethete - ARAPAHO SUN DANCE.   July (2nd week).
Contact: Billings Area Office, Bureau of Indian
Affairs, U.S. Department of the Interior, 316 North
26th Street, Billings, Montana 59101.

The Sun Dance is one of the holiest religious ceremonies of the Plains Indians and the performance of
it is a moving and entertaining experience.

WYOMING (Continued)

★ 2859 ★
Fort Washakie - SHOSHONE SUN DANCE. July (last week), annual. Contact: Billings Area Office, Bureau of Indian Affairs, U.S. Department of the Interior, 316 North 26th Street, Billings, Montana 59101.

The Sun Dance is one of the holiest religious ceremonies of the Plains Indians and is both moving and entertaining.

★ 2860 ★
Sheridan - ALL-AMERICAN INDIAN DAYS AND MISS INDIAN AMERICA PAGEANT. Late July, annual, 3 days. Contact: All American Indian Days, Mark Badgett, 165 West Montana, Sheridan, Wyoming 82801.

Includes Indian games (archery, lance-throwing, races), dances, contests, arts and crafts, a parade, buffalo barbeque, and Miss Indian America pageant. The Indians keep alive their own proud culture and attempt to create better understanding between Indians and non-Indians. Begun around 1955.

CANADA - ALBERTA

★ 2861 ★
Banff - INDIAN DAYS. Late July, annual, 3-4 days. Contact: Tourist Committee, Banff-Lake Louise Chamber of Commerce, Box 1298, Banff, Alberta T0L 0C0, Canada.

Indian games, dances (Chicken and Owl Dance), Indian costumes, parades, and a rodeo are the featured events. Believed to have started in 1889.

★ 2862 ★
Kinuso - SPRUCE POINT INDIAN DAYS. Late August, 2 days. Contact: Travel Alberta, 10255-104 Street, Edmonton, Alberta T5J 1B1, Canada.

Traditional Indian dances, costumes, and arts and crafts.

CANADA - MANITOBA

★ 2863 ★
The Pas - OPASQUIA INDIAN DAYS. August, annual. Contact: Mr. Joe Ross, Opasquia Indian Days, Box 297, The Pas, Manitoba R9A 1K4, Canada.

This celebration takes place in The Pas and is organized by Opasquia Indians from the reserve near The Pas. Features Canadian Indian events such as native woodland games, traditional foods, crafts, and canoe races.

CANADA - NOVA SCOTIA

★ 2864 ★
Chapel Island - INDIAN MISSION. Late July-early August, 3 days. Contact: Nova Scotia Department of Tourism, Travel Division, Post Office Box 130, Halifax, Nova Scotia B3J 2M7, Canada.

Includes colorful religious ceremonies, re-enactments of historical events, and sports events, including canoe races.

Mardi Gras
See: COMMUNITY

Marine

ALABAMA

★ 2865 ★
Bayou La Batre - ALABAMA SEAFOOD FESTIVAL. Late June, annual, 3 days. Contact: William E. Powell, 800 Downtowner Boulevard, Suite 104, Mobile, Alabama 36609.

Miss Seafood pageant, arts and crafts exhibit, historical exhibit, seafood "tasting bee" and fish fry, golf tournament, flea market and auction, fish expo, Shriners parade, street dance, and fiddler's jamboree. Begun around 1975.

★ 2866 ★
Bayou la Batre - BLESSING OF THE SHRIMP FLEET. July (last Sunday), annual, 1 day. Contact: Bureau of Publicity, State of Alabama, Montgomery, Alabama 36104; or Mobile Area Chamber of Commerce, Post Office Box 2187, Mobile, Alabama 36601.

Shrimp fleets from Bayou la Batre, Coden and Dauphin Islands parade down the bayou before the boats are blessed as they go to sea. Ancient custom, very colorful.

ALABAMA (Continued)

★ 2867 ★
Eufaula - LAKE EUFAULA FESTIVAL. Late August
(last weekend), annual, 3 days, Lake Eufaula.
Contact: Bureau of Publicity, State of Alabama,
Montgomery, Alabama 36104.

National championship races of the American Power
Boat Association, beauty pageant, other events including professional art displays, western square
dancing, and a barbeque. Begun around 1964.

★ 2868 ★
Mobile - ALABAMA SHRIMP FESTIVAL. October,
annual, 2 days, Gulf Shores. Contact: Bureau
of Publicity, State of Alabama, Montgomery, Alabama
36104; or Mobile Area Chamber of Commerce, Post
Office Box 2187, Mobile, Alabama 36601.

Midway, arts and crafts exhibit, beauty pageant
"Miss Sunny", street dance, shrimp boat parade,
blessing of the fleet, contests, seafood delicacies,
boat racing at Lake Shelby, seafood cooking contest,
and fireworks display. Begun around 1971.

ALASKA

★ 2869 ★
Kodiak - KING CRAB FESTIVAL. Early May (1st
week), annual, 3 days. Contact: Alaska Division
of Tourism, Pouch E, Juneau, Alaska 99801.

Parade, world's championship seal-skinning contest,
crowning of Festival Queen, crab races, carnival
rides, midway booths and exhibits, crab feed, crab
recipe contest, judging of crabs for weight and size,
street tug-o-war, parachute jump, deep sea and
scuba diving, arts and crafts exhibits, and boat tours.

ARKANSAS

★ 2870 ★
Batesville - WHITE RIVER CARNIVAL. Early
August, annual, 2 days. Contact: Mr. Fay Lindsey,
Batesville Chamber of Commerce, 409 Vine Street,
Batesville, Arkansas 72501.

Included are a grand parade, dances, a Queen White
River Beauty pageant, an arts and crafts show, a
catfish picnic, fireworks, and a canoe race. A
lively and fun event. Begun around 1938.

CALIFORNIA

★ 2871 ★
Arcata - SALMON FESTIVAL. Early August,
annual, 1 day. Contact: California Chamber of
Commerce, 455 Capitol Mall, Sacramento, California
95814.

A celebration in honor of the salmon fishing in this
area.

★ 2872 ★
Bodega Bay - FISHERMAN'S FESTIVAL. Early
April, 2 days. Contact: Redwood Empire Associa-
tion, Visitors Information Center, 476 Post Street,
San Francisco, California 94102.

A boat parade, a display and sale of arts and crafts,
and a festive carnival highlight this local celebration.

★ 2873 ★
Imperial Beach - SUN 'N SEA FESTIVAL. July,
annual, 4 days, Marina Vista Park, Imperial Beach
Pier. Contact: San Diego Convention and Visitors
Bureau, Department WD, 1200 Third Avenue, San
Diego, California 92101; or Imperial Beach Chamber
of Commerce, 825 Coronado Avenue, Imperial Beach,
California 92032.

Sports events include rough water swim, paddleboard
races, and yacht races. Other activities include a
parade, All-states Picnic, international dinner, flower
and art shows, military rodeo, and a craft fair.

★ 2874 ★
Klamath - SALMON FESTIVAL. June (last Sunday),
annual, 1 day. Contact: Information Officer,
State of California Department of Commerce, 1400
Tenth Avenue, Sacramento, California 95814.

Included in this celebration of the salmon are Indian
dance performances, salmon barbeque, logging contests, and Indian games.

★ 2875 ★
Long Beach - CALIFORNIA INTERNATIONAL SEA
FESTIVAL. Early August, annual, 17 days. Con-
tact: Southern California Visitors Council, 705 West
Seventh Street, Los Angeles, California 90017.

Festival events include sailboat and dory races, paddle-
craft, speed skiing, swimming competition, sculpture
contest and lifeguard championships as well as a
parade, costume ball, concerts, fishing derby, open
house aboard Navy ships, aquatic festival, and

Marine

CALIFORNIA (Continued)

Henessy Cup Power Boat races.   Begun around 1966.

★ 2876 ★
Oceanside - OCEANSIDE HARBOR DAYS.   October, annual, 3 days, Oceanside Small Craft Harbor. Contact: Oceanside Jaycees, Post Office Box 306, Oceanside, California 92054.

Full variety of harbor activities including bathtub races, boat and model boat shows, catamaran rides, Navy ships on display, theater entertainment, carnival rides, and booths.   Begun in 1961.

★ 2877 ★
Pismo Beach - CLAM FESTIVAL.   Late February or early March, annual, 2-3 days.   Contact: Chamber of Commerce, Pismo Beach, California 93449.

Claim chowder is the specialty, along with a parade, fishing and clamming contest, flower and art shows, a horse show, sports car races, a statewide surfing contest.   Other events include crafts exhibits, sack races, hang gliding, and horse race sprints.   Begun around 1946.

COLORADO

★ 2878 ★
Grand Lake - YACHT CLUB REGATTA AND WATER SPORTS FESTIVAL.   August, annual.   Contact: Grand Lake Area Chamber of Commerce, Post Office Box 57, Grand Lake, Colorado 80447.

Events include the Yacht Club Regatta, the Lipton Cup race, and other aquatic sports.

FLORIDA

★ 2879 ★
Apalachicola - SEAFOOD FESTIVAL.   Early November, annual, 1 day.   Contact: Jimmie Nichols, Post Office Drawer 78, Apalachicola, Florida 32320.

Tribute to the seafood industry.   Noon luncheon features seafood, art and antique shows, crab races, and a parade of decorated boats with a prize awarded to the best.   Tours of historic homes and seafood factories.   Fireworks.

★ 2880 ★
Fort Myers Beach - ISLAND SHRIMP FESTIVAL. Late February (last full week in February), annual,

1 week.   Contact: Bill Wotring, 137 Cutlass Drive, Fort Myers Beach, Florida 33931.

Honors the shrimp industry.   Booths along the beach offer the shrimp in a variety of ways. Blessing of the Fleet ceremony, bowling and shuffleboard tournaments, street parade, art and flower show, arts and crafts bazaar, shell exhibits and judging, and coronation of a festival queen.

★ 2881 ★
Grant - SEAFOOD FESTIVAL.   Mid February (3rd weekend), annual, 2 days.   Contact: William Boscovich, Route 2, Box 260, Grant, Florida 32901.

In recognition of the seafood industries in the Grant-Sebastian area.   Seafood from the Indian River is featured; entertainment is provided.

★ 2882 ★
Key West - OLD ISLAND DAYS.   Late January or early February-April or March, annual, about 40 days.   Contact: Key West Chamber of Commerce, 402 Wall Street, Key West, Florida 33040.

Islanders celebrate the sea with delicacies such as the Shrimp and Sauce Sampler, and a tribute to the conch in the form of Conch Flavours Day and a conch shell blowing contest.   In addition, there is a Blessing of the Fleet, a street parade and art show, dance, and Cafe Havana-Madrid Nights.

★ 2883 ★
Sanibel - SANIBEL ISLAND SHELL FAIR.   Early March, annual, 3 days, Community House.   Contact: Victor Hagerstrom, Sanibel Community Association, Post Office Box 90, Sanibel, Florida 33957.

Amateur and professional collectors display fine rare shells from the local area and around the world. Best-of-Show is awarded the duPont Trophy of the Delaware Museum of Natural History.   Live exhibit featuring exotic shells and animals.   Works of local artists and photographs of island birds are shown by Sanibel-Captiva Audubon Society.   Begun in 1928.

★ 2884 ★
Sarasota - KING NEPTUNE FROLICS.   Late March, 8 days.   Contact: J.B. Townsend, Post Office Box 1752, Sarasota, California 33578.

The ruler of the sea comes ashore and proclaims a week of merry-making.   Events include the landing of King Neptune and Queen Athena and Ye Mystic Krewe, a fish fry, water ski show, sports car rally,

FLORIDA (Continued)

and children's parade.   Festivities end with the Grand Night Parade.

HAWAII

★ 2885 ★
Makaha - DUKE KAHANAMOKU SURFING CLASSIC AND AQUATIC FESTIVAL.   November (scheduled according to best wave conditions).   Contact: Pacific Area Travel Association, 228 Grant Avenue, San Francisco, California 94108.

Surfing championship and body-surfing exhibition highlight this marine festival.

★ 2886 ★
Oahu (Haleiwa-Waialua area) - HALEIWA SEA SPREE.   February, 4 days.   Contact: Hawaii Visitors Bureau, 2270 Kalalaua Avenue, Suite 801, Honolulu, Hawaii 96815.

Celebration of the days of Queen Liliokalani with surfing competition, canoe races, torchlight pageant, and a carnival.

IDAHO

★ 2887 ★
Weiser - WATER CARNIVAL AND SWIM FESTIVAL. August, annual.   Contact: Chamber of Commerce, 16 East Idaho Street, Weiser, Idaho 83672.

A celebration of summer activities.

ILLINOIS

★ 2888 ★
Chicago - LAKEFRONT FESTIVAL.   Mid August, annual, 1 week-10 days, Lake Michigan Waterfront. Contact: Director, Chicago Convention and Tourism Bureau, 332 South Michigan, Chicago, Illinois 60604.

The crowning of Miss Chicago, arrival of Neptune, swimming races, a regatta, music in Soldier Field, pipe bands, drum and bugle corps championships, air and water show, Venetian nights (a parade of lighted and decorated boats), and ethnic dance festival.

★ 2889 ★
Peoria - STEAM BOAT DAYS.   Early August, annual, 3 days, foot of Main Street along the banks of the

Illinois River.   Contact: The Division of Tourism, Illinois Department of Business and Economic Development, 222 South College Street, Springfield, Illinois 62706.

Celebrates the days of the steam riverboat.   The climax of the festival is a race between the Delta Queen and the Julia Belle Swain (steam boats). The Julia Belle Swain is from Peoria and the Delta Queen is from Cincinnati.

INDIANA

★ 2890 ★
Brookville - WHITEWATER VALLEY CANOE RACES AND FESTIVAL.   Late September, 2 days.   Contact: David Cook, Post Office Box 211, 481 Main Street, Brookville, Indiana 47012.

Canoeists compete in a series of U.S.C.A. sanctioned races.   Flea market, arts and crafts displays, home-cooked foods, games, queen contest and a parade.

IOWA

★ 2891 ★
Clinton - RIVERBOAT DAYS.   Early July, annual, 3 days, Showboat Rhododendron.   Contact: Clinton Chamber of Commerce, 333 Fourth Avenue, South, Clinton, Iowa 52732.

Many water-oriented activities plus theatrical productions by the Rhododendron Players aboard the Showboat Rhododendron, a moored river museum. Fireworks display, carnival, main event with some special talent.   Began in 1962.

★ 2892 ★
Muscatine - GREAT RIVER DAYS.   Late August, 4 days, riverfront, downtown Muscatine.   Contact: Muscatine Chamber of Commerce, 319 East Second Street, Muscatine, Iowa 52761.

Mississippi catfish and Muscatine melons served on the riverfront.   Carnival, children's fishing contest, beer garden, square dancing, teen dancing, river cruise, and canoe races.

KANSAS

★ 2893 ★
Wichita - WICHITA RIVER FESTIVAL.   May, annual, 9 days.   Contact: Wichita Festivals, Incorporated, 350 West Douglas, Wichita, Kansas 67202; or Wichita Area Chamber of Commerce, 350 North

KANSAS (Continued)

Douglas, Wichita, Kansas 67202.

Primarily to celebrate the good life that Wichita has to offer, events include antique bathtub races; a cowtown pageant based on the legend of Windwagon Smith; ethnic group folk dances; various water activities such as crew races and canoe races. All climaxed by an outdoor concert given by the Wichita Symphony playing the 1812 overture.

LOUISIANA

★ 2894 ★
Breaux Bridge - CRAYFISH FESTIVAL. Early May (1st weekend), biennial (even number years), 2 days. Contact: Patricia B. Green, Post Office Box 25, Breaux Bridge, Louisiana 70517; or Robert K. Irwin, President, 802 Saint Charles, Breaux Bridge, Louisiana 70517.

French-Acadian folk music, songs and dances, trips to farms where crayfish are served, and other culinary delights. Fais-do-do (street dance), crayfish races, crayfish eating and peeling contests, Queen's Parade on the Bayou, and fireworks display.

★ 2895 ★
Galliano - LOUISIANA OYSTER FESTIVAL. Mid July, 3 days, South LaFourche High School. Contact: Mrs. Helen Cheramie, Post Office Box 372, Galliano, Louisiana 70354.

Events include a king and queen coronation ball, bayou boat parade, oyster eating contest, oyster shucking contest, and cooking contest. Begun in 1969.

★ 2896 ★
Pearl River - CATFISH FESTIVAL. Mid June, 1 day. Contact: Robert Harper, Mayor, Slidell, Louisiana 70452.

Exhibit booths featuring arts and crafts and fine food. Events include pole peeling, greased pig contests, rod and reel skill throw, raffles, bingos, tobacco spitting contest, story teller, bands, Little Miss and Mr. Catfish contest.

MAINE

★ 2897 ★
Boothbay Harbor - SHRIMP FESTIVAL. Mid March, annual, 2 days. Contact: Boothbay Harbor Region

Chamber of Commerce, Boothbay Harbor, Maine 04538.

Festival features excursion boat rides to watch the shrimp fleet in action, tour of fish processing plants, picking-shucking-filleting contest, marine exhibits, shrimp and fish dinners, Miss Shrimp pageant, and fishermen's dance.

★ 2898 ★
Boothbay Harbor - WINDJAMMER DAYS. Early July, annual, 3 days. Contact: Boothbay Harbor Region Chamber of Commerce, Meadow Road, Boothbay, Maine 04538.

Celebrates the return of the windjammers to harbor. Street parades, beauty pageant, band concerts, church suppers, seafood suppers, boat parade, and entry of old sailing vessels into port highlight the activities.

★ 2899 ★
Camden - SCHOONER DAYS. Late June, annual, 3 days. Contact: Rockport-Camden-Lincolnville Chamber of Commerce, Public Landing, Post Office Box 246, Camden, Maine 04843.

Camden was home port for many old time sailing vessels and now is active in the vacation cruise trade. Open house on old time schooners provides fun and knowledge to the guests.

★ 2900 ★
Rangeley - WATER CARNIVAL. Mid July, annual, 2 days, Rangeley Town Park. Contact: Rangeley Lakes Region, Chamber of Commerce, Box 317, Rangeley, Maine 04970.

Events include boat parade, swim races, canoe races, ice cake races, rowboat races, sailboat regatta, canoe tilting, water skiing, log rolling, hang gliding, water polo, golf putting contest, bathtub races, swim marathon, cookout, and a dance.

★ 2901 ★
Rockland - MAINE SEAFOODS FESTIVAL. Late July-early August, annual, 4 days, Fishermen's Memorial Pier. Contact: Rockland Festival Corporation, Mrs. Ivy W. Dodds, One Park Drive, Rockland, Maine 04841.

To promote Maine seafoods and entertain summer visitors. Festivities are opened by King Neptune and his court as they arise up out of the water. Events include shrimp fry, pancake breakfast, floats

MAINE (Continued)

parade, arts and crafts, lobster and shrimp and clam
dinner, carnival marine parade, crowning of the
Maine Sea Goddess, midway, square dancing, and
fireworks. Festival boasts the World's Largest
Lobster Boiler", with a capacity for 5,000 pounds
of lobster. Sponsored by the Maine Department
of Sea and Shore Fisheries, and various local industries and clubs. Started in 1947.

★ 2902 ★
Winter Harbor - LOBSTER FESTIVAL AND LOBSTER-
BOAT RACES. Early August, annual, 1 day,
Frazier Point, Acadia National Park. Contact:
Chamber of Commerce, Winter Harbor, Maine 04693.

A lobster feast and boat races highlight this festival
honoring a local industry.

★ 2903 ★
Yarmouth - CLAM FESTIVAL. Mid July, annual,
3 days. Contact: Chamber of Commerce, 40 Main
Street, Yarmouth, Maine 04096.

Features Maine soft-shell clams cooked in a variety
of ways, and other seafood delicacies. Beauty
pageant, parade, giant clambake, church bazaars,
baked bean supper, auctions, arts and crafts, symphony orchestra, pole climbing contest, wood chopping contest, square dancing, diaper derby, clam
shucking contest, and a giant midway are additional
activities.

MARYLAND

★ 2904 ★
Annapolis - CHESAPEAKE APPRECIATION DAY.
Late October-early November (Saturday closest to
November 1st), annual, 1-2 days, Sandy Point State
Park. Contact: Annapolis Chamber of Commerce,
171 Conduit Street, Annapolis, Maryland 21401.

Celebration of the opening of the Chesapeake Bay
oyster dredging season. Highlight is the race of
the Chesapeake Bay skipjacks, the last working sailing fleet in North America. Also features nautical
exhibits, boating safety demonstrations, demonstrations
of equipment used by Chesapeake Bay watermen, and
Maryland seafood. Tours of the local area and the
Eastern shore are tied into the celebration. Begun
around 1965.

★ 2905 ★
Annapolis - MARYLAND CLAM FESTIVAL. Early

August (1st full weekend), annual, 3 days, City
Dock. Contact: Chamber of Commerce of Greater
Annapolis, 171 Conduit Street, Annapolis, Maryland
21401.

Festival offers clams cooked in a variety of ways;
crowning of the Maryland Clam Queen, who officially
represents the state as a goodwill ambassador; International Invitational Clam Shell Pitching Contest
offering politicians an opportunity to demonstrate their
pitching prowess before television and newspaper
cameras; antique boat parade, musical entertainment
including Dixieland, rock, barbershop, soul, and
bluegrass; blessing of the clam fleet; and Chesapeake Bay cruises. Begun around 1966.

★ 2906 ★
Baltimore - HISTORIC HARBOR RENDEZVOUS AND
CLASSIC YACHT PARADE. June, annual, 2 days,
Inner Harbor Basin, Federal Hill and Fells Point.
Contact: James Holechek, 204 North Liberty Street,
Baltimore, Maryland 21202.

Historic celebration including antique yacht parade,
concert, and walking tours of Federal Hill and Fells
Point homes.

★ 2907 ★
Cambridge - BAY COUNTRY FESTIVAL. Early
August, 2 days, Long Wharf. Contact: Cambridge
Jaycees, Post Office Box 124, Cambridge, Maryland
21613.

Fishing competitions, work boat races, National
Crab Picking Championship, Princess Neptune pageant,
canoe jousting, games, food, rides, talent show,
musical entertainment, pie and watermelon eating
contests.

★ 2908 ★
Crisfield - NATIONAL HARD CRAB DERBY AND
FAIR. Early September (Labor Day weekend), annual,
3 days. Contact: Mrs. Shirley Ennis, 206 Laird
Avenue, Crisfield, Maryland 21817.

A crab race with entries from all 50 states (Governor's Cup). A crab feed, fishing contests, beauty
pageant, and Maryland seafood delicacies. The
oyster-dredging skipjacks, North America's only
fleet of working sailboats, run a race from Deal
Island to Tangier Sound. Street and boat parades,
entertainment (nationally-known), music show, and
fireworks. Begun in 1948.

Marine

MARYLAND (Continued)

★ 2909 ★
Cumberland - GREATER CUMBERLAND SEAFOOD FESTIVAL. Mid September, 2 days, Cumberland Fairgrounds. Contact: Tourism Director, Greater Cumberland Jaycees, Cumberland, Maryland 21502.

Chesapeake Bay seafood is celebrated and enjoyed: fried clams, crab cakes, fresh oysters, hard shelled crabs, fresh corn and draft beer. Events include bands, demonstrations, arts and crafts, Queen City Antique Auto Rally, continuous entertainment, and gasoline model airplanes.

★ 2910 ★
Frederick - FREDERICK SEAFOOD FESTIVAL. Late August, annual, 1 day, Monocacy Pinecliff Park. Contact: Frederick County Chamber of Commerce, Division of Tourism, Frederick, Maryland 21701.

Seafood served up in a wide variety of ways, entertainment, and crab races. Begun around 1971.

★ 2911 ★
Hagerstown - SEAFOOD FESTIVAL. Mid September, annual, 2 days, Hagerstown Fairgrounds. Contact: Washington County Tourism, 40 Summit Avenue, Hagerstown, Maryland 21740.

A seafood dinner includes typical Maryland delicacies such as fried clams, crab cakes, fried oysters, filet of fish, hardshell crabs, french fries and coleslaw. Wares at the flea market and craft show include handpainted porcelain miniatures, patchwork, crocheted items, wood working, broom-making, chaircaning and antiques. Begun around 1971.

★ 2912 ★
Leonardtown - SAINT MARY'S OYSTER FESTIVAL. Mid October (2nd weekend), annual, 2 days, Saint Mary's County Fairgrounds. Contact: Saint Mary's County Office of Economic Development, Leonardtown, Maryland 20650; or Saint Mary's County Chamber of Commerce, Leonardtown, Maryland 20650.

Includes the National Oyster Shucking Championship for men and women. Local watermen demonstrate shucking and harvesting methods; tools and crafts are on display. Special classes in oyster-shucking are offered each day. Additional attractions include a colonial farm museum, square dancing exhibitions, films, music, flea market, a bakery and a plant bazaar. There is an oyster feast, with oysters prepared in a wide variety of styles; other types of food are also available. Begun around 1967.

★ 2913 ★
North East - WATER FESTIVAL. June or July, annual, 3 days. Contact: Robert Boyd, Rural Delivery 1, Box 3, North East, Maryland 21901.

Water-oriented events include boat parades, canoe jousting, and state sculling championships. Also a queen contest, band concerts, tours, and a fish fry. Begun around 1969.

★ 2914 ★
Ocean City - SEAFOOD FESTIVAL. Mid July, annual, 1 day, Ocean City Convention Hall. Contact: Paul F. Brown, Post Office Box 172, Ocean City, Maryland 21842.

A Maryland seafood smorgasbord including a raw bar, seafood platter, and cole slaw. Entertainment includes a military band, vocal talent, and country/western music. Begun around 1970.

★ 2915 ★
Stevensville - CHESAPEAKE BAY FISHING FAIR. Mid August, annual, 2 days, Matapeake Park. Contact: Bill Perry, Post Office Box 1925, Annapolis, Maryland 21401.

Fishing fun for everyone with prizes in many categories. Entertainment and food. Begun around 1936.

MASSACHUSETTS

★ 2916 ★
Buzzards Bay - BOURNE BAY SCALLOP FESTIVAL. Mid October, annual, 3 days, Playland Field. Contact: Bristol County Development Council, Incorporated, 154 North Main Street, Fall River, Massachusetts 02722.

Scallop cooking and eating and other entertaining events. Begun around 1970.

MICHIGAN

★ 2917 ★
Grand Haven - COAST GUARD FESTIVAL. Late July-early August (week preceding the 1st weekend in August), annual, 9 days, throughout the city. Contact: Northwest Ottawa County Chamber of Commerce, One Washington Avenue, Grand Haven, Michigan 49417.

The festival, which was established to honor the men of United States Coast Guard, includes an open house

MICHIGAN (Continued)

aboard Coast Guard Ships, where visitors are permitted to witness the equipment and procedures. In addition, there is a parade, air show, sporting events, carnival, big name entertainment, fireworks display, festival of bands, pistol matches, water thrill show and concert. On the final weekend, there is an outdoor crafts fair sale and display, and Coast Guard Festival Crafts Fair, sponsored by the Chamber of Commerce and held in Central Park. Started in 1936.

★ 2918 ★
Grand Haven - VENETIAN PARADE FESTIVAL. Late August (4th weekend), annual, 1 day, on Grand River. Contact: North West Ottawa County Chamber of Commerce, One Washington Avenue, Grand Haven, Michigan 49417.

The purpose of the festival is to promote boating in North West Ottawa County. Decorated boats parade for the public in the late evening. Started in 1972.

★ 2919 ★
Kalkaska - NATIONAL TROUT FESTIVAL. Late April, annual, 3 days. Contact: Kalkaska County Chamber of Commerce, 328 South Cedar Street, Kalkaska, Michigan 49646.

Opening of the trout season. Parades, fishing contests, canoe race, children's fishing derby, midway, horse race, parade, king and queen contests, and speeches.

★ 2920 ★
New Baltimore - BAYRAMA FESTIVAL. Late July, 6 days. Contact: Southeast Michigan Travel and Tourist Association, Executive Plaza, 1200 Sixth Avenue at Howard, Detroit, Michigan 48226.

Water events include swimming races and marathons. There is also a carnival, baking contest, and handicraft shows.

MINNESOTA

★ 2921 ★
Detroit Lakes - NW WATER CARNIVAL. July, annual, 7 days. Contact: Chamber of Commerce, 700 Washington Avenue, Detroit Lakes, Minnesota 56501.

A pageant, boat races, water ski shows, midway, parade, sailboat regattas, softball, and bands highlight the festive events.

★ 2922 ★
Fairmont - FESTIVAL OF LAKES. Early July, 3 days. Contact: Fairmont Area Chamber of Commerce, 101 South North Avenue, Box 826, Fairmont, Minnesota 56031.

A boat parade, boat races, and other competitive events highlight this community festival.

★ 2923 ★
Glenwood - WATERAMA. Late July, annual, 3 days. Contact: Chamber of Commerce, 130 East Minnesota Avenue, Glenwood, Minnesota 56334.

Water skiing competition, canoe racing, water thrill show, sailboat races, parades, art show, button dance, queen coronation, and queen ball highlight the festive events. Begun around 1955.

★ 2924 ★
Lake City - WATER SKI DAYS. Late June, 3 days. Contact: Chamber of Commerce, 120 South Washington Avenue, Lake City, Minnesota 55041.

A summer festival with fun-filled events including a carnival, craft fair, parade, water show, dance with a live band, Senior Citizen King and Queen crowned, art show, and parachutists.

★ 2925 ★
Litchfield - WATERCADE. Early July, annual, 3 days, Lake Ripley and downtown. Contact: Litchfield Area Chamber of Commerce, 126 North Marshall Avenue, Litchfield, Minnesota 55355.

A watershow, fireworks, softball, parade, queen pageant, carnival, and canoe race highlight the events. Begun around 1967.

★ 2926 ★
Nevis - MUSKIE DAYS. Early July, 2 days. Contact: Nevis Civic and Commerce Association, Nevis, Minnesota 56467.

A water show on Lake Belle Taine, parades, street dance, stage show, fishing contest, queen coronation, band concert, and prizes are included in the festive events.

Marine

MINNESOTA (Continued)

★ 2927 ★
New London - WATER SHOW AND FUN DAYS.
Mid June, 3 days.   Contact: Chamber of Commerce,
New London, Minnesota 56273.

Events include a water show, parades, fireworks, and
a carnival.

★ 2928 ★
Windom - RIVER DAYS.   Mid June, 2 days.   Con-
tact: Chamber of Commerce, 222 Tenth Street,
Windom, Minnesota 56101.

River racing in canoes and a parade, softball tournament, and fishing contests.

MISSISSIPPI

★ 2929 ★
Biloxi - SHRIMP FESTIVAL AND BLESSING OF THE
SHRIMP FLEET.   Early June (1st weekend), annual,
3 days.   Contact: Travel/Tourism Department,
Mississippi Agricultural and Industrial Board, Post
Office Box 849, Jackson, Mississippi 39205.

In accordance with ancient European tradition,
hundreds of colorfully decorated boats sail past the
priest from Saint Michael's Catholic Church to receive his blessing.   Other activities, presided over
by the king and queen, include a parade, street
dancing, and a seafood jamboree.

★ 2930 ★
Gulfport - DEEP SEA FISHING RODEO.   Late
June-early July, annual, 3 days, Gulfport Small
Craft Harbor.   Contact: Travel/Tourism Department,
Mississippi Agricultural and Industrial Board, Post
Office Box 849, Jackson, Mississippi 39205.

Claiming to be the world's largest rodeo of its kind,
the event offers fireworks, a beauty pageant, carnival and other entertainments to augment the spear
fishing, fresh water fishing and deep sea fishing.
Started in 1947.

NEW YORK

★ 2931 ★
Moravia - FILLMORE FROLIC CANOE RACE.   Early
May, annual, Owasco Inlet.   Contact: Finger Lakes
Association, Incorporated, 309 Lake Street, Penn Yan,
New York 14527.

A raffle for a canoe, the race, and a chicken
barbeque highlight the festive and fun events.   Begun around 1973.

NORTH CAROLINA

★ 2932 ★
Morehead City - MARLIN FESTIVAL.   Early-mid
June, 9 days.   Contact: Carteret County Chamber
of Commerce, Morehead City, North Carolina 28557.

Celebrates the marlin with a marlin tournament, boat
parade, street dance and sidewalk art show.

★ 2933 ★
Morehead City - NORTH CAROLINA CRAB DERBY.
Mid August, 1 day.   Contact: Carteret Carolina
Development Corporation, Post Office Box 730,
Morehead City, North Carolina 28557.

In honor of the crab, the festival includes crab
races, a crab picking contest, crab stew, a fish
fileting contest, kite flying and other games.

★ 2934 ★
Swansboro - MULLET FESTIVAL.   Early-mid October,
1 day.   Contact: North Carolina Travel Develop-
ment Section, Division of Economic Development,
Department of Natural and Economic Resources,
Raleigh, North Carolina 27611; or American
Business Women's Association, Swansboro, North
Carolina 28584.

Fun events include fishing contests and a parade.

OHIO

★ 2935 ★
Coshocton - COSHOCTON CANAL FESTIVAL.   Mid
August, annual, 3 days, Roscoe Village.   Contact:
Mrs. Pat Brown, Roscoe Village, 381 Hill Street,
Coshocton, Ohio 43812.

Art exhibits, demonstrations of traditional crafts,
old-fashioned clothing, music concerts, dancing,
and food commemorate the arrival of the first boat
on the canal from Cleveland in 1830 on August 21st.
An authentic replica of the boat is featured in the
festival, presented by the Coshocton Chamber of Commerce and the Roscoe Village Restoration.   Contests,
including frog jumping and wood chopping, are among
the activities.

OHIO (Continued)

★ 2936 ★
Huron - WATER FESTIVAL.   Mid July, annual, 3-4
days, downtown.   Contact: Chamber of Commerce,
202 Cleveland Road, West, Post Office Box 43,
Huron, Ohio 44839.

The citizenry takes advantage of the proximity of
Lake Erie to stage a variety of aquatic events including power boat races, and a water ski show;
the fun continues on shore with fireworks, a parade,
summer theater musicals, and arts and crafts exhibits.

★ 2937 ★
Pomeroy - BIG BEND REGATTA.   Mid-late June,
annual, 3 days.   Contact: Ms. Katie Crew, Public
Relations, Daily Sentinal, Pomeroy, Ohio 45769.

The festival features power boat races of national
prominence.   Attractions from the amphibian world
include an International Frog Jumping Contest and
the Frog Derby (run on racetrack with jockeys).
In addition, there are helicopter rides, carnival
rides, flower show and a parade.

★ 2938 ★
Portsmouth - RIVER DAYS FESTIVAL.   Late August-
early September, annual, 6 days.   Contact: Portsmouth Area Chamber of Commerce, 740 Second Street,
Post Office Box 509, Portsmouth, Ohio 45662.

The Ohio river is the scene of national championship
boat races.   On the shore, there is a carnival on
the river bank while Portsmouth's business district is
the site of a parade and other entertainment.

★ 2939 ★
Vermilion - FESTIVAL OF THE FISH.   Mid June,
4 days.   Contact: Vermilion Chamber of Commerce,
Post Office Box 145, Vermilion, Ohio 44089.

Aquatic events include boat rides, a sailboat race,
a model boat show and a parade of boats.   Meanwhile, on the land, there is an antique car parade,
a grand parade, and an arts and crafts show.

OKLAHOMA

★ 2940 ★
Madill - NATIONAL SAND BASS FESTIVAL.   Late
June, annual.   Contact: Madill Chamber of Com-
merce, Box 542, Madill, Oklahoma 73446.

Events include fishing contests, a parade, boat races,

dances, a rodeo, terrapin races, and a gigantic
fish fry.

OREGON

★ 2941 ★
Astoria - ASTORIA REGATTA.   Late July, annual,
4 days.   Contact: Astoria Chamber of Commerce,
Astoria, Oregon 97103.

A festival honoring the fishing industry, shipping
industry and recreational boating of the Columbia
River and the Pacific Ocean.

★ 2942 ★
Depoe Bay - INDIAN STYLE SALMON BAKE.   Mid
September, annual, 1 day.   Contact: Depoe Bay
Chamber of Commerce, Box 21, Depoe Bay, Oregon
97341.

Fresh ocean-caught salmon cooked Indian-style before an open fire at Fogarty Creek State Park is
served with all the trimmings buffet style alongside
the sea.

PENNSYLVANIA

★ 2943 ★
Connellsville - YOUGHIOGHENY RIVER FESTIVAL.
Late June to early July, annual, 1 week (8 days).
Contact: Department of Commerce, Bureau of Travel
Development, 431 South Office Building, Harrisburg,
Pennsylvania 17120.

Features boat races, fishing derby, and two day stop-
over of Appalachian Wagon Train.   Folk festival
with local participation and national recording artist.

★ 2944 ★
Easton - WATER CARNIVAL.   Late August, annual,
2 days, Riverfront.   Contact: Department of Commerce, Bureau of Travel Development, 431 South
Office Building, Harrisburg, Pennsylvania 17120.

Floats, canoes, and powerboat races, awards, and
fireworks from the river.

★ 2945 ★
Essington (Boro of) - SEAFARING DAYS.   Mid
August, annual, 2 days, next to Philadelphia Inter-
national Airport.   Contact: Department of Commerce,
Bureau of Travel Development, 431 South Office
Building, Harrisburg, Pennsylvania 17120.

Marine

PENNSYLVANIA (Continued)

Delaware County's contributions to the maritime heritage of the nation are celebrated in Essington. Sea chanty songfest featured at Rose Tree Park, Media.

★ 2946 ★
Monongahela - RIVER FESTIVAL. Late July, annual, 3 days, Aquatorium. Contact: Washington County Commission, 400 West Main Street, Monongahela, Pennsylvania 15063; or Department of Commerce, Bureau of Travel Development, 431 South Office Building, Harrisburg, Pennsylvania 17120.

Events include barbeque and dance, and boat parade with colonial motif.

RHODE ISLAND

★ 2947 ★
Gaililee - BLESSING OF THE FLEET. August. Contact: Walter Brine, 179 Oak Hill Road, Narragansett, Rhode Island 02882.

Events include a ten mile road race, a German beer fest, and the blessing of the fleet.

SOUTH CAROLINA

★ 2948 ★
Beaufort - BEAUFORT WATER FESTIVAL. Mid July, annual, 7 days. Contact: Beaufort County Chamber of Commerce, Post Office Box 910, Beaufort, South Carolina 29902.

Activities include the selection and coronation of the Queen of the Sea Islands who presides over a glamorous ball. There is a parade, street dances, air show, golf tournament, shrimp boat parade, Blessing of the Fleet, motor boat race, band concerts, and a barbeque. Contests include washtub races, wheel-barrow races, ice-sitting contests, pie-eating contests, tug-a-war, etc.

★ 2949 ★
Eutawville - DERBY AWARDS NIGHT FESTIVAL. Mid-late June, annual, 1 day. Contact: Santee-Cooper Counties Promotion Commission, Post Office Box 12, Santee, South Carolina 29142.

This celebration is held at the conclusion of the World's Championship Landlocked Striped Bass Fishing Derby on the Santee-Cooper Lakes. Activities include presentation of awards, country music show,

square dancing, beauty queens, refreshments, and a fishing clinic.

TENNESSEE

★ 2950 ★
Paris - PARIS FISH FRY (WORLD'S BIGGEST FISH FRY). Late April, annual, 6 days. Contact: Greater Paris-Henry County Chamber of Commerce, Post Office Box 82, Paris, Tennessee 38242; or World's Biggest Fish Fry, Post Office Box 867, Paris, Tennessee 38242.

Catfish is served with hush puppies in the town square. Other activities include a parade, beauty contest, Tennessee style hootenanny, and square dancing. Considered to be the world's largest fish fry and fishing rodeo.

TEXAS

★ 2951 ★
Aransas Pass - SHRIMPOREE. July, annual. Contact: Chamber of Commerce, 452 Cleveland, Aransas Pass, Texas 78336.

Salutes the shrimp industry with a giant shrimp boil luncheon, beauty contests, rodeo, fishing derby, and the colorful blessing of the shrimp fleet.

★ 2952 ★
Austin - AQUA FESTIVAL. August, annual, 10 days. Contact: Austin Aqua Festival, Executive Director, Post Office Box 1967, Austin, Texas 78767.

Parades, pageants and water-related contests centered around Town Lake in the city, with other events scheduled on the chain of Highland Lakes northwest of Austin. Boating events range from open canoe race to power boat races in all classes with some of the fastest boats in the nation. A lighted night water parade and fireworks extravaganza are other features. Begun in 1962.

★ 2953 ★
Borger - LAKE MEREDITH FESTIVAL. June, annual, 3 days. Contact: Mr. Oran Back, Chamber of Commerce, 600 North Deahl, Box 911, Borger, Texas 79007.

Includes the "world's largest fish fry", Miss Lake Meredith contest, boat and dog shows, a fishing "rodeo", water sports and entertainment.

TEXAS (Continued)

★ 2954 ★
Brazosport - FISHING FIESTA AND SHRIMP FESTIVAL.
July, annual, 5 days.   Contact: Chamber of Com-
merce, Box 2470, Brazosport, Texas 77541.

Texas Gulf Coast residents celebrate coastal fishing
and shrimp industries with boat races, fireworks and
other activities.

★ 2955 ★
Corpus Christi - NAVY RELIEF FESTIVAL.   June,
annual, 2 days.   Contact: Chamber of Commerce,
1201 North Shoreline Boulevard, Post Office Box
640, Corpus Christi, Texas 78403.

One of the largest festivals at any Navy installation.
Event features aerial shows and static displays.

★ 2956 ★
Denison - NATIONAL SAND BASS FESTIVAL.
June, annual, 8 days, Lake Texoma.   Contact:
James S. Hardy, 315 West Woodward, Denison,
Texas 75020.

On Lake Texoma, draws hundreds of anglers from
throughout the nation.

★ 2957 ★
Freeport - FISHIN' FIESTA AND SHRIMP FESTIVAL.
Early July (around the 4th), annual, 4 days.   Con-
tact: State Department of Highways and Public
Transportation, Travel and Information Division, Post
Office Box 5064, Austin, Texas 78763.

In addition to fishing competition ranging from deepsea to scuba, activities include a golf tournament,
beauty contest, fish fry, shrimp boil, crab crawl,
boat races, ski shows and dances.

★ 2958 ★
Freeport - SHRIMP BOIL.   Early May, annual.
Contact: State Department of Highways and Public
Transportation, Travel and Information Division, Post
Office Box 5064, Austin, Texas 78763.

Features bushels of delicious Gulf shrimp, followed
by an auction of sports equipment at nearby Lake
Jackson.

★ 2959 ★
Galveston - SHRIMP FESTIVAL AND BLESSING OF
THE FLEET.   Late April, annual, 1-2 weeks.   Con-

tact: Douglas S. Drown, Chamber of Commerce,
315 Tremont, Galveston, Texas 77550.

Features week of activities in honor of the shrimp
boats and their catch at this major port city. Events
include the Blessing of the Fleet, a parade, and the
crowning of the Shrimp Queen.   Cash prizes are
awarded in sand castle and sand sculpture building
contests.

★ 2960 ★
Port Lavaca - JAYCEE FISHING FESTIVAL.   Early
September (around Labor Day), annual, 3 days.
Contact: Mr. James T. Wilson, Chamber of Com-
merce, Post Office Box 528, Port Lavaca, Texas
77979.

Prize for biggest and most among several saltwater
species of fish.

★ 2961 ★
Port Lavaca - TEXAS WATER SAFARI.   June,
annual, 1 week.   Contact: Mr. James T. Wilson,
Chamber of Commerce, Post Office Box 528, Port
Lavaca, Texas 77979.

Begins in San Marcos (Ranch and Hill Country Section), ends at Seadrift.   One of world's toughest
canoe races; teams must carry all supplies during
several hundred miles of river and bay paddling.

★ 2962 ★
Seymour - FISHIN' DAY.   Early May (1st Monday),
annual, 1 day.   Contact: Chamber of Commerce,
301 1/2 North Washington, Box 1329, Seymour,
Texas 76380.

Entire town closes down and everybody "goes fishin"
on Lake Kemp.   Festivities include beauty pageant,
boat and motorcycle races, and skiing contests.
Tagged fish are good for prizes until next "Fishin'
Day".

★ 2963 ★
Texas City - TACKLE TIME FESTIVAL.   Mid June
to July 4th, annual, several weeks.   Contact:
Leslie H. Box, Chamber of Commerce, 625 Eighth
Avenue North, Texas City, Texas 77590.

Citywide festival featuring boat races, water ski
shows, musical review, beauty contests, golf tournament, giant shrimp boil, barbeque feast, festival ball,
and fishing contests.

VIRGINIA

★ 2964 ★
Chincoteague Island - OYSTER FESTIVAL. Mid
October (Columbus Day), annual, 1 day, Safari
Camp Ground. Contact: Chincoteague Chamber
of Commerce, Post Office Box 258, Chincoteague
Island, Virginia 23336.

The event offers "all you can eat" from a menu of
cole slaw, potato salad, hush puppies and, of
course, oysters - raw, steamed, fried or as fritters.
Hamburgers and hotdogs are also available. Begun
in 1974.

★ 2965 ★
Chincoteague Island - SEAFOOD FESTIVAL. Early
May, annual, 1 day, Tom's Cove Park. Contact:
Chamber of Commerce, Accomac, Virginia 23301.

Local cooks prepare local foods such as oysters,
clams, crabs, eels, sea squab, fish, cole slaw,
french fried sweet potatoes, hush puppies, and
beverages for an all-you-can-eat feast. Begun
around 1969.

★ 2966 ★
Urbanna - OYSTER FESTIVAL. November, annual.
Contact: Secretary, Urbanna Chamber of Commerce,
Urbanna, Virginia 23175.

A parade, antique car show, beauty pageant, and
grand ball all mark another season for the harvest
of the Virginia oyster. Begun around 1949.

WASHINGTON

★ 2967 ★
Des Moines - WATERLAND FESTIVAL. August
(1st weekend), annual, 2 days. Contact: Victor
H. Lebel, Festival President, Post Office Box 98866,
Des Moines, Washington 98188.

Attractions include a float parade, queen pageant,
carnival, exhibits, and shows. Begun around 1963.

★ 2968 ★
Everett - SALTY SEA DAYS. June (1st weekend),
annual, 1 day. Contact: Dennis A. Wintch,
1712 Pacific, Everett, Washington 98201.

Events include a parade, contest, carnival and other
local events. A stern wheeler and naval ships are
on display. Begun around 1972.

★ 2969 ★
Gig Harbor - HARBOR HOLIDAYS. June (1st or
2nd weekend depending on tides), annual. Contact:
Harbor Holidays, Post Office Box 321, Gig Harbor,
Washington 98335.

The quaint harbor is the site of the unique and
amusing leaky tiki race, pitting a 12 foot barrel
against a 12 foot model of fake teeth and dozens
of other creative entries. The propulsion systems
are no less imaginative. Other events include a
water ski show, a sky diving show, free cruises on
national guard landing boats, local talent side shows
and arts and crafts displays. Begun around 1972.

★ 2970 ★
Issaquah - ISSAQUAH SALMON FESTIVAL. October
(1st weekend), annual. Contact: Mrs. Fern Ronnell,
Secretary, Post Office Box 430, Issaquah, Washington 98027.

Not a fishing derby, but an educational tour of the
salmon hatchery and explanation of the mysteries of
this fish. Included is a salmon barbeque. Side-
lights include a sidewalk art display, a parade, carnival and dance. Begun in 1972.

★ 2971 ★
Olympia - CAPITAL LAKEFAIR. July (2nd weekend),
annual, 3 days. Contact: Dale Hume, Olympia
Chamber of Commerce, Post Office Box 1427, Olympia,
Washington 98507.

The festival is highlighted by aquatic events including
visiting naval ships, dragboat races, hydroplane races,
sailboat races, bathtub races and water ski kite flying. Other activities include skydiving, teen dances,
musical concerts, a golf tournament, parade, and a
queen coronation. On display are antique cars,
an art festival, a bazaar, and fireworks. Begun
around 1958.

2972 ★
Port Angeles - SALMON DERBY DAYS. August-
September (Labor Day weekend), annual. Contact:
Dorothy Munkeby, 1217 East First Street, Port
Angeles, Washington 98362.

Activities include a children's day parade and plank
car derby, salmon bake, drum and bugle corp, youth
dance, and water ski race both ways across the
Strait of Juan de Fuca between Port Angeles and
Victoria, British Columbia. Begun around 1969.

WASHINGTON (Continued)

★ 2973 ★
Port Orchard - FATHOMS O' FUN.   July (weekend of the 4th), annual, 3 days.   Contact: Fathoms O' Fun, 742 Bay Street, Port Orchard, Washington 98366.

The famous Dinghy Derby Race highlights this festival and provides enough laughs to last all year.   Sailboat race, frog jumping contest, a snake race, fireworks display, 4-wheeler jamboree, and carnival complete the fun.

★ 2974 ★
Seattle - BALLARD HALIBUT FEED.   July (last weekend), annual, Ballard District.   Contact: Ballard Chamber of Commerce, 2431 Northwest Market, Seattle, Washington 98107.

A halibut barbeque as a part of Seafair.   Pirates, clowns, and music.   Begun around 1967.

★ 2975 ★
Seattle - SEAFAIR.   July (last week)-August (1st week), annual, 10 days.   Contact: Seafair, 1618 Fourth Avenue, Seattle, Washington 98101.

Events include the International Milk Carton Boat Race, National Championship Boat Races, the Seafair Grand Parade and Torchlight Parade, the World Championship Unlimited Hydroplane Races, and the National Canoe and Kayak Races.   Other events include the queen coronation, the Seafair and the Salmon Fishing Derby.   Not all events are within the above time span, but the main concentration is during that time.   There is some event almost every weekend from mid-July to mid-September.

★ 2976 ★
Tri Cities - TRI CITY WATER FOLLIES.   July (3rd weekend), annual, 10 days.   Contact: Water Follies Association, Post Office Box 2051, Tri Cities, Washington 99302.

Qualifying heats and Atomic Cup finals provide hydroplane thrills for this weekend.   The miles of viewing space on each side of the river provide ample space for this two way pylon turn, five mile race of the world's fastest boats.   Sky-diving entertainment between races.   Begun around 1968.

WEST VIRGINIA

★ 2977 ★
Hinton - WATER FESTIVAL.   Late August-early September, annual, 5 days, Bluestone Dam Resevoir (Lake Bluestone).   Contact: Mountainaire Travel Council, 1613 North Walker Street, Princeton, West Virginia 24740.

Activities include hydroplane, powerboat and canoe races, plus log-rolling, and arts and crafts.

★ 2978 ★
Petersburg - WHITE WATER WEEKEND.   March (last weekend)-April (1st weekend), annual, 6 days (2 weekends), North Fork of the South Branch of the Potomac River.   Contact: Petersburg White Water Weekend, Box 666, Petersburg, West Virginia 26847.

Included in the whitewater events are canoe and kayak races, Middle States Wildwater and Slalom Races, the Potomac Highland Wildwater Championship and the April Fools Race, open to anything that floats (except a boat).   Additional activities include a craft show, white water movies, square dancing, a fish fry, muzzle loading rifle match, a chicken barbeque and more.   Started in 1963.

CANADA - BRITISH COLUMBIA

★ 2979 ★
Denman Island - OYSTER FESTIVAL.   Late May, 1 day.   Contact: The Department of Recreation and Travel Industry, 1019 Wharf Street, Victoria, British Columbia V8W 2Z2, Canada.

Includes the World Oyster Shucking Championships and other events centered around the oyster.

★ 2980 ★
Richmond - SALMON CARNIVAL AND PARADE.   Early July, annual, 1 day, Steveston Park.   Contact: Tourist Information, Richmond Square Mall, Suite 302-641, Buswell Road, Richmond, British Columbia, Canada.

Thousands of pounds of salmon are barbequed in an open pit.   In addition, there is authentic Japanese food.   Flowers and vegetables are shown, and there is a hobby display.   Begun around 1945.

★ 2981 ★
White Rock - SEA FESTIVAL.   Early July, 4 days, Semiahmoo Park.   Contact: Tourist Information,

CANADA - BRITISH COLUMBIA (Continued)

Marine Drive, White Rock, British Columbia, Canada.

The festival features aquatic games, sports and events. There is a grand parade, a grand ball, barbeque, and bingo.

CANADA - MANITOBA

★ 2982 ★
Flin Flon - FLIN FLON TROUT FESTIVAL. Early July, annual, 3 days. Contact: Mrs. Del Baird, Treasurer, Executive Committee, Flin Flon Trout Festival, Box 751, Flin Flon, Manitoba R8A 1N6, Canada.

Three-day canoe race to determine which angler brings in the biggest trout. Big prizes are given for both the largest lake trout and the biggest northern pike. Visitors to the festival can participate in an amateur canoe race, the Gold Rush Canoe Derby for professionals, water skiing, diving and boat races. Indians stage wrestling matches and pack flour in feats of strength.

★ 2983 ★
Norway House - YORK BOAT DAYS. August, annual, 3 days. Contact: Mr. K. O. Albert, Co-ordinator, York Boat Days, Norway House Indian Band, Box 218, Norway House, Manitoba R0B 1B0, Canada.

Features a three-day York Boat Race. The boats are built by residents of the community.

CANADA - NEW BRUNSWICK

★ 2984 ★
Richibucto - SCALLOP FESTIVAL. Late June-early July, annual, 5 days. Contact: Special Events Coordinator, Tourism New Brunswick, Post Office Box 12345, Fredericton, New Brunswick, Canada.

Takes place in the area surrounding Richibucto, in celebration of the harvesting of scallops from the sea.

★ 2985 ★
Shediac - SHEDIAC LOBSTER FESTIVAL. Mid July, annual, 4 days. Contact: Department of Tourism, Post Office Box 1030, Fredericton, New Brunswick, E3B 5C3, Canada.

Parties and feasts of lobster and other regional delicacies.

CANADA - NORTHWEST TERRITORIES

★ 2986 ★
Fort Providence - MACKENZIE RIVER RAFT DAYS. Late July-early August, annual, 4 days. Contact: Travel Arctic, Yellowknife, Northwest Territories X1A 2L9, Canada.

The highlight of the festival is the raft races down the Mackenzie River. In addition, there is a parade, and other sports events.

CANADA - NOVA SCOTIA

★ 2987 ★
Lunenburg - NOVA SCOTIA FISHERIES EXHIBITION. Mid September, annual, 5 days. Contact: Nova Scotia Department of Tourism, Travel Division, Post Office Box 130, Halifax, Nova Scotia B3J 2M7, Canada.

Features displays on fisheries, model ships, international dory races and schooner races, scallop shucking and fish fileting contests, grand parade, water sports, art demonstrations, stage and talent shows, children's parade and midway.

★ 2988 ★
Pictou - LOBSTER CARNIVAL. Mid July, 3 days. Contact: Nova Scotia Department of Tourism, Travel Division, Post Office Box 130, Halifax, Nova Scotia B3J 2M7, Canada.

The festival includes lobster boat races, a harbour swim, soap-box derby, parades, pipe band concerts, band concerts, stage shows, dancing in the streets, and a lobster and beer garden.

Music
See also: THE ARTS

ALABAMA

★ 2989 ★
Athens - TENNESSEE VALLEY OLD-TIME FIDDLERS CONVENTION. Early October (1st Saturday), annual, 2 days, Athens College Gym. Contact: Miss Emilil Lawson, Director of Public Relations, Athens College, Athens, Alabama 35611.

Competition in old-time fiddling, banjo, old-time string bands, guitar, buck dancing, etc. Begun around 1967.

ALABAMA (Continued)

★ 2990 ★
Gadsden - MID-SOUTH MARCHING BAND FESTIVAL
AND PARADE.   Late September, annual, 1 day,
Murphree Stadium.   Contact: Bert Mitchell, Post
Office Box 92, Gadsden, Alabama 35902.

Over 50 bands from eight states in competition.
Parade - downtown Gadsden, and field competition.

★ 2991 ★
Mobile - MOBILE JAZZ FESTIVAL.   June, annual,
3 days, Mobile Municipal Theatre.   Contact:
Mobile Jazz Festival, Incorporated, Jack Maples,
Director, Mobile Municipal Theatre, 401 Auditorium,
Mobile, Alabama 36602.

The festival features both professional and the best
collegiate jazz musicians and vocalists.   Includes
competitive events and prizes.   Begun in 1966.

★ 2992 ★
Mobile - MOBILE JAZZ FESTIVAL PRESENTS THE
ALL-AMERICAN HIGH SCHOOL STAGE BAND
FESTIVAL.   June, annual, 3 days, Municipal
Theatre.   Contact: Director, Mobile Municipal
Theatre, 401 Auditorium Drive, Mobile, Alabama
36602; or Mobile Area Chamber of Commerce, Post
Office Box 2187, Mobile, Alabama 36601.

Participants are winners from eight regional festivals
held throughout the country.   Includes collegiate
jazz-musicians and vocalists and professional ensembles.   First held in 1966.

★ 2993 ★
Steele - ALABAMA STATE CHAMPIONSHIP SLING-
SHOT CONTEST AND BLUEGRASS DAY.   Early
July (4th), annual, 1 day.   Contact: Warren Mus-
grove, Horse Pens 40, Route 1, Box 379, Steele,
Alabama 35987.

Open slingshot contest and bluegrass concerts.   Begun around 1972.

★ 2994 ★
Steele - FALL BLUEGRASS MUSIC FESTIVAL.
October, annual, 3 days, Horse Pens 40.   Contact:
Warren Musgrove, Horse Pens 40, Route 1, Box 379,
Steele, Alabama 35987.

Also a spring (May) and mid-summer festival (July-
August) of popular bluegrass music.   Begun around
1973.

★ 2995 ★
Steele - SPRING BLUEGRASS MUSIC FESTIVAL.
Mid May, annual, 3 days.   Contact: Warren
Musgrove, Route 1, Box 379, Steele, Alabama
35987.

An outdoor festival with bluegrass music concerts
and arts and crafts exhibits.

★ 2996 ★
Steele - VACATION FLAT-TOP SUMMIT AND
BLUEGRASS FESTIVAL (HORSE PENS MIDSUMMER
BLUEGRASS FESTIVAL).   Late July-August, 4
days, Outside Theater, Horse Pens 40.   Contact:
Warren Musgrove, Route 1, Box 379, Steele,
Alabama 35987.

Bluegrass, flat-top guitar contest, workshops for
guitar, fiddle, banjo, and bands.

ALASKA

★ 2997 ★
Anchorage - ALASKA FESTIVAL OF MUSIC.   June,
annual, 2 weeks, Anchorage West High School and
other locations.   Contact: Alaska Festival of
Music, Box 325, Anchorage, Alaska 99501.

The festival is sponsored by the Anchorage Symphony,
the Anchorage Community Chorus, and the Anchorage
Community College of the University of Alaska.   In
addition to musical performances, there are lectures
and exhibitions.   Also within the framework of the
festival is the Alaska Native Arts Festival, consisting
of exhibitions of native arts, crafts, games, and
Eskimo music and dance.   Founded in 1956.

★ 2998 ★
Sitka - SITKA SUMMER MUSIC FESTIVAL.   June,
annual, 17 days.   Contact: Paul Rosenthal, Music
Director, Post Office Box 907, Sitka, Alaska
99835.

A festival of chamber music sponsored by Sheldon
Jackson College and Sitka Concert Association.

ARIZONA

★ 2999 ★
Payson - COUNTRY MUSIC FESTIVAL (OLD-TIME
COUNTRY MUSIC FESTIVAL).   June, 2 days, Payson
Rodeo Arena.   Contact: Chamber of Commerce,
Drawer A, Payson, Arizona 85541.

Old-time country music contest, gospel singers, and

Music

ARIZONA (Continued)

folk dancers highlight the festival events.

★ 3000 ★

Payson - OLD-TIME GOSPEL MUSIC FESTIVAL.
May, annual, 2 days, Payson Rodeo Arena.   Con-
tact: Payson Chamber of Commerce, Drawer A,
Payson, Arizona 85541.

Aimed at the preservation of gospel music as an integral part of our American heritage.   Gospel
singing, fiddling, jazz-stage band, variety entertainment, and patriotic medley by a quartet.

ARKANSAS

★ 3001 ★

Eureka Springs - INSPIRATION POINT FINE ARTS
COLONY FESTIVAL.   Late July, annual, 2 weeks.
Contact: Inspiration Point Fine Arts Colony Festival,
Route 62, Eureka Springs, Arkansas 72632.

The festival performs operas presented by students,
both singers and instrumentalists, who study at the
colony's opera and orchestra workshops.   Four or
five operas are performed along with concerts of
orchestral and choral music.

★ 3002 ★

Fort Smith - ARKANSAS BLUEGRASS AND COUNTRY
FESTIVAL.   June, 3 days, Kay Rogers Park.   Con-
tact: Walt Barden, Grand Ole Opry, Box 2138,
Nashville, Tennessee 37214.

A traditional country-style festival with the emphasis
on bluegrass music.

★ 3003 ★

Herber Springs - ARKANSAS BLUEGRASS FESTIVAL.
May, 3 days.   Contact: Chamber of Commerce,
Heber Springs, Arkansas 72543; or Department
of Parks and Tourism, 149 State Capitol, Little Rock,
Arkansas 72201.

Festival of bluegrass music, fiddlers, etc.

CALIFORNIA

★ 3004 ★

Aptos - CABRILLO MUSIC FESTIVAL.   Mid August,
annual, 10 days, Cabrillo College Theater.   Contact: Cabrillo Music Festival, 6500 Soquel Drive,
Aptos, California 95003.

The festival consists of concerts, evening and afternoon performances of orchestral music, concertos,
works for dance and orchestra, staged opera, choral
music, chamber music and solo recitals.   Non-musical
events are the free art exhibits open before and after
the concerts.   A significant amount of new music is
played, as well as rarely performed old works including United States and world premieres.   Founded in
1963.

★ 3005 ★

Barstow - CALICO SPRING FESTIVAL.   May,
annual, 2-3 days, Calico Ghost Town.   Contact:
Don V. Tucker, 825 East Third Street, San Bernardino,
California 92415.

Traditional American music and dance, fiddlers' convention, bluegrass music, children's events, amateur
and professional contests, concert, barbershop singing,
square dancing, and fiddle playing.   Contests for
the fiddle, banjo, and guitar.   Street melodramas.
Begun around 1973.

★ 3006 ★

Berkeley - JUNIOR BACH FESTIVAL.   April, annual,
4 days.   Contact: Junior Bach Festival, Box 590,
Junior Bach Festival Association, Berkeley, California
94701.

The festival comprises four days of performances exclusively of the music of Johann Sebastian Bach by
musicians under the age of 21.   The performers are
selected by a series of auditions.   Every category of
Bach's music is offered.   Choral and instrumental
groups are from secondary schools in the Berkeley
area.   Founded in 1953.

★ 3007 ★

Burbank - STARLIGHT BOWL.   Mid June to mid
September, annual.   Contact: Starlight Bowl, c/o
Burbank Park and Recreation Department, 275 East
Olive Avenue, Burbank, California 91503.

The festival program content includes light opera,
variety shows, ballet, pops concerts, and ice shows.
Performing ensembles are the Burbank Symphony
Orchestra, Burbank Choral Club, and the Civic Light
Opera Chorus and Orchestra.

★ 3008 ★

Carmel - CARMEL BACH FESTIVAL.   Mid July,
annual, 10 days.   Contact: Carmel Bach Festival,
Box 503, Carmel, California 93921.

Although the festival focuses on the music of J.S.

CALIFORNIA (Continued)

Bach, his major choral works, cantatas, chamber music, organ works, and concertos, the music of other seventeenth and eighteenth century composers is an important aspect of the programming. Thus the music of Haydn, Mozart, Purcell, Monteverdi, J.S. Bach, and Beethoven is also performed. In addition to the concerts, there are lectures and occasional symposiums. Founded in 1935.

★ 3009 ★
Carmel - MUSIC FROM BEAR VALLEY FESTIVAL. August. Contact: Music from Bear Valley Festival, 'Post Office Box 3056, Carmel, California 93921.

Scheduled and impromptu concerts; special children's concerts, and guest artists. Concerta and rehearsals are open to the public and free of charge.

★ 3010 ★
Claremont - CLAREMONT MUSIC FESTIVAL. Mid June through early August, annual, Campus of Pomona College. Contact: Claremont Music Festival, Pomona College, Claremont, California 91711.

Chamber concerts, instrumental and vocal ensembles; informal recitals. Festival Institute offers summer study program, workshops, and master classes. Begun around 1969.

★ 3011 ★
Claremont - MUSIC HERE AND NOW FESTIVAL. May–June, annual. Contact: Director, Scripps College, Music Department, Claremont, California 91711.

Twentieth century chamber music and new and experimental music is performed by student and professional ensembles at Scripps College.

★ 3012 ★
Concord - CONCORD SUMMER FESTIVAL. Late July-early August, annual, 2 weekends. Contact: Director, Concord Pavilion, 1950 Parkside Drive, Concord, California 94519.

Professional and amateur musical groups play chamber, jazz and orchestral music.

★ 3013 ★
Dominguez Hills - FESTIVAL OF AMERICAN MUSIC. March (Spring), annual. Contact: Director, California State College, Music Department, Dominguez Hills, California 90747.

Both student and professional ensembles participate in a series concerning itself with the works of American composers. Concerts and lectures are presented.

★ 3014 ★
Fresno - CALIFORNIA STATE UNIVERSITY SPRING FESTIVAL OF MUSIC. March (Spring). Contact: Peter Gena, Director, Recital Hall, Fresno, California 93740.

Student ensembles perform chamber music, new, experimental, and multi-media music.

★ 3015 ★
Idyllwild - ISOMATA MUSIC FESTIVAL. Mid August to early September, annual. Contact: Isomata Music Festival, Idyllwild Arts Foundation, Box 38, Idyllwild School of Music and the Arts (ISOMATA), Idyllwild, California 92349.

The festival is held in conjunction with the Idyllwild School, a summer school founded in 1950 and owned and operated by the University of Southern California since 1964. Choral, orchestral, and chamber music is performed Friday and Saturday evenings and Sunday afternoons. Founded in 1962.

★ 3016 ★
Inverness - INVERNESS MUSIC FESTIVAL. June-July, 24 days. Contact: Redwood Empire Association, 476 Post Street, San Francisco, California 94102.

Concerts of opera, chamber music, and jazz.

★ 3017 ★
Los Angeles - GREEK THEATRE FESTIVAL. July (Summer). Contact: Greek Theatre Festival, 2700 North Vermont Avenue, Los Angeles, California 90027.

Concerts, ballet, opera, musical comedy, operetta, and popular soloists. Picnic areas nearby.

★ 3018 ★
Los Angeles - HOLLYWOOD BOWL SUMMER FESTIVAL. July through early September. Contact: Hollywood Bowl Association, 135 North Grand Avenue, Los Angeles, California 90012.

Outdoor symphonic, operatic, choral, and pops

Music

CALIFORNIA (Continued)

concerts; outstanding guest conductors and guest artists. Picnic box dinners; picnic areas.

★ 3019 ★
Los Angeles - LOS ANGELES BACH FESTIVAL.
November, annual, First Congregational Church in Wilshire District of Los Angeles. Contact: Los Angeles Bach Festival, First Congregational Church, 540 South Commonwealth at Sixth Street, Los Angeles, California 90020.

Soloists, ensembles, and chorus perform the music of Bach.

★ 3020 ★
Los Angeles - UCLA CONTEMPORARY MUSIC FESTIVAL. January, University of California at Los Angeles. Contact: UCLA Contemporary Music Festival, c/o Music Department, University of California at Los Angeles, Los Angeles, California 90024.

The festival includes concerts, panel discussion, and lectures about contemporary music. First festival held in 1968.

★ 3021 ★
Monterey - MONTEREY JAZZ FESTIVAL. Late September, annual, 3 days, Monterey County Fairgrounds. Contact: Jazz Festival, Box JAZZ, Monterey, California 93940.

Concerts, impromptu jam sessions, and many jazz professionals. Usually five concerts in the three days. Begun in 1958.

★ 3022 ★
National City - MAYTIME BAND REVIEW. May (1st Saturday), 1 day. Contact: San Diego Convention and Visitors Bureau, 1200 Third Avenue, Suite 824, San Diego, California 92101.

A parade, a musical competition, and an awards ceremony in Kimball Park.

★ 3023 ★
Norco - GOLDEN WEST BLUEGRASS FESTIVAL.
Late October, 2 days, Silver Lake. Contact: Dick Tyner, 830 South Melrose Drive, Vista, California 92083.

Events include banjo and fiddle contests. More than 17 groups perform.

★ 3024 ★
Northridge - PERCUSSIVE ARTS SOCIETY FESTIVAL.
March (Spring), annual. Contact: President, Percussive Arts Society, California Chapter, Post Office Box 34, Northridge, California 91324

Twentieth century chamber music, new and experimental music, and jazz performed before enthusiastic audiences.

★ 3025 ★
Oakville - NAPA VALLEY SUMMER MUSIC FESTIVAL.
Late June-early July, 1 day/week, 5 weeks, Robert Mondavi Winery. Contact: Redwood Empire Association, 476 Post Street, San Francisco, California 94102.

Open air jazz concerts and guest performers. Wine and cheese at intermissions.

★ 3026 ★
Ojai - OJAI FESTIVAL. May or June, annual, 3 days, Ojai Festival Bowl in Civic Center Park. Contact: Ojai Festival, c/o Ojai Festivals, Limited, Post Office Box 185, Ojai, California 93023.

The festival includes performances in the morning, afternoon, and evening programs. Contemporary music has always remained an important part of the programs. There are well known guest performers. Founded in 1947.

★ 3027 ★
Ojai - OJAI FOLK DANCE FESTIVAL. Late March, 2 days. Contact: California Chamber of Commerce, 455 Capitol Mall, Sacramento, California 95814.

Exhibition of dancing and native songs.

★ 3028 ★
Redlands - REDLANDS BOWL SUMMER MUSIC FESTIVAL. June through August, annual, Redlands Bowl. Contact: Redlands Bowl Summer Music Festival, c/o Redlands Bowl, Post Office Box 466, Redlands, California 92373.

The festival is held in an outdoor amphitheater, with programs similar to many outdoor bowl concerts. Concerts, recitals, opera, and ballet in Redland Bowl in Smiley Park. Founded in 1924.

★ 3029 ★
Riverside - CONTEMPORARY MUSIC FESTIVAL.

CALIFORNIA (Continued)

March, annual, 3 days, University of California, Riverside. Contact: University of California, Riverside, Contemporary Music Festival, Music Department, Riverside, California 92502.

Student and professional ensembles perform twentieth century chamber music and new and experimental music.

★ 3030 ★
Rohnert Park - REDWOOD EMPIRE STAGE BAND FESTIVAL. November, annual. Contact: Director, Redwood Empire Stage Band Festival, California State University, Sonoma, Ives Hall of Music, Rohnert Park, California 94928.

Jazz is performed by student ensembles.

★ 3031 ★
Ross - NEW ORLEANS JAZZ FESTIVAL. Mid September, 1 day. Contact: California Chamber of Commerce, 455 Capitol Mall, Sacramento, California 95814.

Jazz, New Orleans style, is performed and enjoyed.

★ 3032 ★
San Anselmo - INVERNESS MUSIC FESTIVAL. June-July, 24 days. Contact: Redwood Empire Association, 476 Post Street, San Francisco, California 94102.

Concerts of opera, chamber music, and jazz. Also held in Inverness, San Rafael and Stinson Beach.

★ 3033 ★
San Diego - SAN DIEGO KOOL JAZZ FESTIVAL. Mid June, annual, 2 days, San Diego Stadium. Contact: Southern California Visitors Council, 705 West Seventh Street, Los Angeles, California 90017.

Nationally known professional musicians as well as local talent entertain. Begun in 1975.

★ 3034 ★
San Diego - PIANO FESTIVAL. Mid September (about 3rd Sunday), annual, 1 day, Balboa Park Bowl. Contact: Thearles Music Company, Mission Valley Center, San Diego, California 92120.

A mass piano recital in which pianists play simultaneously. 1,000 young pianists, ages 7-17, from throughout the county perform at 101 pianos at a time. Sponsored by the Thearle Music Company, San Diego Branch of the Music Teacher's Association, and the National Guild of Piano Teachers. Begun around 1948.

★ 3035 ★
San Francisco - MUNICIPAL POPS FESTIVAL. July, annual, 1 month, Civic Auditorium. Contact: Art Commission, 165 Grove Street, San Francisco, California 94102.

A series of concerts sponsored by the city of San Francisco and organized by the Art Commission. The Pops Orchestra is drawn from the San Francisco Symphony. Main floor seats are arranged around tables where refreshments are served.

★ 3036 ★
San Francisco - STERN GROVE FESTIVAL. Mid June to late August, annual, 11 successive Sunday afternoons. Contact: Stern Grove Festival, c/o Stern Grove Festival Association, 2100 Pacific Avenue, San Francisco, California 94115.

The setting is famed for its natural beauty and acoustics and comprises some 63 acres. The festival is meant to be enjoyed by individuals, groups, and families. All of the festival programs are offered free on 11 successive Sunday afternoons and consist of orchestral performances, ballet, musical theater, productions of entire operas, and jazz. Most of the groups appearing at the festival are from the Bay area. First established in 1938.

★ 3037 ★
San Rafael - INVERNESS MUSIC FESTIVAL. June-July, 24 days. Contact: Redwood Empire Association, 476 Post Street, San Francisco, California 94102.

Concerts of opera, chamber music, and jazz. Also held at Inverness, San Anselmo and Stinson Beach.

★ 3038 ★
Santa Barbara - OLD-TIME FIDDLE CONVENTION. Mid October, annual, 1 day, University of California. Contact: Southern California Visitors Council, 705 West Seventh Street, Los Angeles, California 90017.

Features folk music, country fiddle style, and string bands. Begun around 1972.

Music

CALIFORNIA (Continued)

★ 3039 ★
Santa Barbara - SUMMER FESTIVAL SERIES (MUSIC ACADEMY OF THE WEST). July-August, annual, Lobero Theatre. Contact: Summer Festival Series, Music Academy of the West, 1070 Fairway Road, Santa Barbara, California 93103.

The festival includes performances of a special series of recitals, concerts, and opera given by the faculty and students attending the summer sessions of the Academy. Opera productions usually limited to one opera sung in English. Began in 1947.

★ 3040 ★
Saratoga - MONTALVO SUMMER MUSIC FESTIVAL. June-July, annual, Carriage House Theater and Amphitheater. Contact: Montalvo Summer Music Festival, Post Office Box 158, Villa Montalvo, Saratoga, California 95070.

Performances of chamber music, opera, general classical pieces, and recitals.

★ 3041 ★
Saratoga - MUSIC AT THE VINEYARDS. June to August, annual, 3 weekends. Contact: Music at the Vineyards, Post Office Box 97, Saratoga, California 93306.

The location of the festival is at the historic Paul Masson Mountain Winery on Pierce Road in Saratoga. The program contest emphasizes music that is infrequently performed. Each concert features one performing group or solo artist. Founded in 1958.

★ 3042 ★
Sausalito - OLD TIME CAMP MEETING AND REVIVAL. Late May (Memorial Day weekend), annual, Kirby Cove State Park. Contact: San Francisco Folk Music Club, 885 Clayton, San Francisco, California 94117.

This event is mainly for members of the San Francisco Folk Music Club, but members of the general public do attend. The events include workshops for guitars, dulcimers, mandolins and other instruments; various types of folk dancing; special singing styles; crafts, such as macrame, quilting, whittling, etc.; song swaps; and other special activities such as yoga, Tai Chi, and juggling. Begun around 1965.

★ 3043 ★
Stinson Beach - INVERNESS MUSIC FESTIVAL.

June-July, 24 days. Contact: Redwood Empire Association, 476 Post Street, San Francisco, California 94102.

Concerts of opera, chamber music and jazz. Also held in Inverness, San Anselmo and San Rafael.

★ 3044 ★
Topanga - TOPANGA FOLK FESTIVAL. June, annual, 1 day, Topanga Canyon Women's Club, 1440 North Topanga Boulevard. Contact: Dorian Keyser, 5922 Corbin Avenue, Tarzana, California 91356.

Styles of fiddling workshop, jam sessions, plus other instrumental, folk song, and clog dance workshops. Traditional American music plus bluegrass.

★ 3045 ★
Valencia - '50'S FESTIVAL OF ROCK N' ROLL. March, annual, 2 days, Magic Mountain. Contact: Southern California Visitors Council, 705 West Seventh Street, Los Angeles, California 90017.

Dick Clark and Chubby Checker and/or other rock personalities star in a Rock 'n' Roll show. Begun around 1973.

COLORADO

★ 3046 ★
Aspen - ASPEN MUSIC FESTIVAL. Late June to late August, annual, 9 weeks. Contact: Aspen Music Festival, Post Office Box AA, Aspen, Colorado 81611.

The spectacular setting of the festival and the reputation of the summer music school and its faculty combine to make the Aspen Festival one of America's most attractive summer musical events. Included are lectures, master classes, and private lessons conducted by the artist-faculty, who teach as well as perform publicly in the large tent-amphitheater. Festival performances run the gamut of orchestral concerts, chamber, solo, vocal, and instrumental recitals. Founded in 1949.

★ 3047 ★
Colorado Springs - COLORADO OPERA FESTIVAL. June-July, Colorado College. Contact: Chamber of Commerce, Holly Sugar Building, Colorado Springs, Colorado 80902.

Innovative performances in English of both familiar and rarely performed operas.

COLORADO (Continued)

★ 3048 ★

Colorado Springs - PAPPY DAVE STONE COUNTRY MUSIC FESTIVAL. Mid June, annual, 2 days, 1 week apart, Radio Station KPIK. Contact: Radio Station KPIK, Mayfair Hotel, 120 East Platte Avenue, Colorado Springs, Colorado 80902.

A nationwide hunt for new talent is a part of this celebration of the country music scene.

★ 3049 ★

Denver - COLORADO COUNTRY MUSIC FESTIVAL. June, annual, 6 days, Denver Merchandise Mart; Howard Johnson Motor Lodge. Contact: Country Music Federation of Colorado, Post Office Box 19435, Denver, Colorado 80219.

Gospel groups and fiddlers are included in the groups which entertain in the country music style. Begun around 1963.

★ 3050 ★

Denver - RED ROCKS MUSIC AND DRAMA FESTIVAL. June-August, annual. Contact: Colorado Visitors Bureau, 225 West Colfax Avenue, Denver, Colorado 80202.

Includes concerts and performances by noted artists in a natural amphitheater.

★ 3051 ★

Estes Park - MUSIC IN THE MOUNTAINS. July and August. Contact: Rocky Ridge Music Center, Estes Park, Colorado 80517.

Concerts; chamber music with resident string quartet.

★ 3052 ★

Evergreen - COLORADO PHILHARMONIC FESTIVAL. July-August, annual, 6 weeks. Contact: Colorado Philharmonic Festival, Box 975, Evergreen, Colorado 80439.

The festival is a series of public performances of works prepared during a period of intensive rehearsals and practice. Nearly one-half of the works performed are infrequently or hardly ever heard in the typical concert hall anywhere in the nation. Four children's concerts are performed. Founded in 1966.

★ 3053 ★

Henderson - ROCKY MOUNTAIN BLUEGRASS

FESTIVAL. August (3rd weekend), annual, 3 days, Adams County Fairgrounds. Contact: C.K. Webb, 6255 West 78th Place, Arvada, Colorado 80003; or Colorado Bluegrass Music Society, 1040 Cedar Street, Broomfield, Colorado 80020.

Bluegrass-style fiddling, arts and crafts, concerts and contests. Both local and nationally famous bands entertain. Jam sessions and gospel music are also featured. Contests include banjo picking, flat-top guitar picking, fiddling, and bluegrass band performing. Food concessions. Begun around 1973.

★ 3054 ★

Loveland - GREAT ROCKY MOUNTAIN NATIONAL BLUEGRASS FESTIVAL. Late July, 3 days, Riverside Campground. Contact: Clif Callahan, Route 1, Bridgeport, Illinois 62417.

Bluegrass music concerts with appearances by famous name groups and soloists. Competitive events for fiddle and banjo.

CONNECTICUT

★ 3055 ★

Bridgeport - FESTIVAL OF CONTEMPORARY MUSIC. March, annual, 3 days, University of Bridgeport. Contact: Festival of Contemporary Music, Dr. Harris R. Valante, Director, University of Bridgeport, Mertens Theater, Bridgeport, Connecticut 06602.

Student and professional ensembles perform twentieth century chamber music, orchestral music, and choral music. The festival honors a different composer each year.

★ 3056 ★

Danbury - TWENTIETH CENTURY ARTS FESTIVAL. April-May (Spring), annual, Western Connecticut State College. Contact: Howard Tuvelle, Director, Twentieth Century Arts Festival, Western Connecticut State College, Ives Concert Hall, Danbury, Connecticut 06810.

Professional ensembles perform twentieth century chamber music and new and experimental music.

★ 3057 ★

Falls Village - FALL FOLK MUSIC WEEKEND. Mid October, 4 days, Camp Freedman. Contact: Wayne Hollingsworth or Alan Friend or Adele Harris, Country Dance and Song Society of America, New York Pinewoods Folk Music Club, 35-41 72nd Street, Jackson Heights, New York 11372.

Music

CONNECTICUT (Continued)

The event includes informal workshops in various instruments and vocal music, as well as classes, concerts, informal singing and song swaps. There is also a class in instrument construction (dulcimer in 1975).

★ 3058 ★
Falls Village - MUSIC MOUNTAIN CONCERTS. Early July to early September, annual, Concert Hall atop Music Mountain. Contact: Music Mountain Concerts, Falls Village, Connecticut 06031.

The concerts at Music Mountain are among the oldest chamber music series in America. Programs feature the Berkshire Quartet on ten successive Saturday afternoons from early July to early September. Guest artists perform with the quartet. Classical and contemporary works are programmed along with occasional premiere performances. Begun around 1931.

★ 3059 ★
Falls Village - SPRING FOLK MUSIC WEEKEND. Late April-early May, 3 days, Camp Freedman. Contact: Country Dance and Song Society of America, New York Pinewoods Folk Music Club, 35-41 72nd Street, Jackson Heights, New York 11372.

The weekend consists of a series of informal workshops and classes in a variety of musical endeavors, including dulcimer, banjo, fiddle, vocal styles and vocal production. In addition there are unscheduled jam sessions and singing. Featured performers give a concert on Saturday night.

★ 3060 ★
Hamden - STARLIGHT FESTIVAL OF CHAMBER MUSIC. Late June-July, annual, Yale University's Law School Courtyard. Contact: The Starlight Festival of Chamber Music, Post Office Box 6065, Hamden, Connecticut 06514.

The concerts (Tuesdays) feature the Festival Quartet and the Festival Orchestra in performances of chamber music varying widely in style, dimension, and the number of musicians. Guest performers. Founded in 1955.

★ 3061 ★
Hartford - HARTFORD FESTIVAL OF MUSIC. July (4 Wednesdays), annual, Auditorium of Hartford Tower. Contact: Hartford Festival of Music, Incorporated, 834 Asylum Avenue, Hartford, Connecticut 06105.

The festival features a series of four Wednesday concerts of music for chamber orchestra. Performing ensembles are the Hartford Festival Orchestra and the Festival Chorus. Guest performers. Founded in 1957.

★ 3062 ★
New Canaan - SILVERMINE CHAMBER MUSIC FESTIVAL. July and August, annual, Gifford Auditorium. Contact: Silvermine Chamber Music Festival, c/o Silvermine Guild Chamber Music Center, Silvermine Avenue, New Canaan, Connecticut 06840.

The festival was originally organized around a series of performances by the Silvermine String Quartet. The festival now also includes performances by the 15-member Silvermine String Orchestra. The festival maintains a distinctive level of sophistication in programming seldom-heard works by masters of the past and first performances of works by both American and European contemporary composers. Guest performers. Begun in 1959.

★ 3063 ★
New London - MACDOWELL FESTIVAL OF AMERICAN MUSIC. July, Mitchell College. Contact: MacDowell Festival of American Music, Box 391, Mitchell College, New London, Connecticut 06320.

Festival for performance and promotion of American music.

★ 3064 ★
Norfolk - NORFOLK CONCERTS. Late June-late August, annual, Music Shed. Contact: Norfolk Concerts, c/o Yale Summer School of Music and Art, Norfolk, Connecticut 06058.

Performances by the resident faculty as soloists and in ensemble. Recitals by students. Choral sings. Great musicians are linked with the history of music at Norfolk. Founded in 1899.

★ 3065 ★
West Hartford - HARTT COLLEGE SUMMER CHAMBER MUSIC FESTIVAL. July, Millard Auditorium at the University of Hartford. Contact: Hartt College of Music, 200 Bloomfield Avenue, West Hartford, Connecticut 06117.

Chamber music concert series presented by the Hartt

CONNECTICUT (Continued)

College of Music.   Founded in 1964.

★ 3066 ★
West Hartford - INTERNATIONAL HARP FESTIVAL.
June, annual, 1 week.   Contact: International
Harp Festival, c/o Hartt College of Music, University
of Hartford, 200 Bloomfield Avenue, West Hartford,
Connecticut 06117.

Along with performances in the evening there are
films, lectures, and the master classes themselves,
which, although intended for harpists, are also open
to observers for a fee.   Well-known harpists are
usually invited to participate in the master classes
and the festival.   Founded in 1964.

★ 3067 ★
Woodstock - WOODSTOCK ACADEMY MUSIC
FESTIVAL.   July, annual, Bowen Building, Wood-
stock Academy.   Contact: Woodstock Academy
Music Festival, Bowen Building, Woodstock Academy,
Woodstock, Connecticut 06281.

Weekly chamber music concerts and recitals.

DELAWARE

★ 3068 ★
Glasgow - OLD TIME BLUEGRASS FESTIVAL
(DELAWARE BLUEGRASS FESTIVAL).   Early September
(Labor Day weekend), annual, 3 days, Gloryland
Park.   Contact: Carl Goldstein, Box 3504, Green-
ville, Delaware 19807.

Band contest, outdoor concerts, craft shows, instrument displays, and concessions.   Begun around
1972.

DISTRICT OF COLUMBIA

★ 3069 ★
Washington, D.C. - AMERICAN MUSIC.   April
(Spring), annual, 1 week, Kennedy Center.   Con-
tact: American Music Festival, John F. Kennedy
Center for the Performing Arts, 2700 F Street, North-
west, Washington, D.C. 20037.

The festival is a series of free, informal concerts
featuring a variety of styles of American music, tri-
butes to composers, and noted guest artists.

★ 3070 ★
Washington, D.C. - FESTIVAL OF AMERICAN MUSIC.
June, annual, East Garden Court of the National
Gallery of Art.   Contact: Festival of American
Music, c/o National Gallery of Art, Washington,
D.C. 20565.

Last four concerts of National Gallery Orchestra's
free Sunday evening series.   Begun in 1944.

★ 3071 ★
Washington, D.C. - FESTIVAL OF CHAMBER MUSIC.
Late October-early November, irregular, 3 days,
Library of Congress.   Contact: Festival of Chamber
Music, Library of Congress, First Street between
East Capital Street and Independence Avenue, South-
east, Washington, D.C. 20540.

The festival features evening and afternoon concerts
of chamber music at the Library of Congress, sponsored
by the Elizabeth Sprague Collidge Foundation; the Serge
Koussevitsky Music Foundation, and the McKim Fund.
Outstanding ensembles and vocalists, instrumentalists
and chamber music of all periods is featured.   Mrs.
Elizabeth Sprague Coolidge initiated the concerts with
the establishment of a foundation in 1925.   Special
exhibits related to the concert may also be on display.
Always scheduled around Mrs. Coolidge's birthday.
Begun around 1961.

★ 3072 ★
Washington, D.C. - INTER-AMERICAN MUSIC
FESTIVAL.   April-May, triennial, selected audi-
toriums in Washington, D.C.   Contact: Inter-
American Music Festival of Washington, Organization
of American States, Washington, D.C. 20006.

The festival is sponsored by the Organization of
American States and the Inter-American Music Council
and features composers from the Americas.   Professional ensembles perform twentieth century chamber
music, new and experimental music, and contemporary
orchestral music, with soloists from the United States,
Canada, and Latin America.   Founded in 1958.

★ 3073 ★
Washington, D.C. - WASHINGTON KOOL JAZZ
FESTIVAL.   Late July, annual, 2 days, Robert F.
Kennedy Stadium.   Contact: Washington Area Con-
vention and Visitors Bureau, 1129 20th Street, North-
west, Washington, D.C. 20036.

The festival features live performances by well-known
musicians and vocalists.   Begun in Washington, D.C.
in 1976.

Music

FLORIDA

★ 3074 ★

Daytona Beach - FLORIDA INTERNATIONAL MUSIC FESTIVAL. Mid July to early August, Peabody Auditorium. Contact: Florida International Music Festival, Post Office Box 1733, Daytona Beach, Florida 32015.

Symphony, chamber music concerts, and recitals. Orchestra rehearsals open to public Thursday mornings. Institute for advanced music students.

★ 3075 ★

Jacksonville - DELIUS FESTIVAL. Late January-early February, annual, 5 days. Contact: Delius Association of Florida, Incorporated, Delius House, Jacksonville University, Jacksonville, Florida 32211; or Delius Association, 3305 Saint John's Avenue, Jacksonville, Florida 32202.

Features music of Frederick Delius who lived in Jacksonville from 1884 to 1886. Symphonic and choral music by other composers also included. There is a special exhibit on Delius in the library. The festival precedes and follows January 29, Delius' birthday.

★ 3076 ★

Saint Petersburg - FLORIDA TOURNAMENT OF BANDS. Mid December, 1 day, Bayfront Center, Northeast Senior High School. Contact: Florida Tournament of Bands, Bayfront Hilton Hotel, 333 First Street South, Post Office Box 1731, Saint Petersburg, Florida 33701.

Units of high school bands are inspected and judged, both standing still and parading. The parade of bands covers a five block distance. There is also a field show competition. The inspection of the band is on the basis of posture, uniforms, instruments, personal appearance and the general appearance of the group.

★ 3077 ★

Sarasota - NEW COLLEGE SUMMER MUSIC FESTIVAL. June, annual, 2 weeks, Van Wezel Performing Arts Hall. Contact: New College Summer Music Festival, Post Office Box 1898, Sarasota, Florida 33578.

The festival concerts include a series of performances played by the guest artist-faculty, who conduct a series of master classes at New College for about two weeks. The stress is on chamber music, and various-sized groups are formed from the ten or more faculty members. Activities during rhe festival period con-

sist of master classes, ensemble sessions, open rehearsals of faculty performances, and orchestra rehearsals. Among the works performed are usually one or two new works commissioned for the festival. Founded in 1965.

★ 3078 ★

Winter Park - BACH FESTIVAL OF WINTER PARK. March, annual, 2 days, Knowles Memorial Chapel on the campus of Rollins College. Contact: Bach Festival of Winter Park, Box 160, Rollins College, Winter Park, Florida 32789.

The festival is devoted mainly to the music of Johann Sebastian Bach but sometimes presents the large choral masterpieces of such composers as Beethoven, Haydn, Brahms, and others. All concerts are held in Knowles Memorial Chapel on the campus of Rollins College. The performing ensembles are the Bach Festival Choir and the Bach Festival Orchestra consisting of instrumentalists drawn from the Florida Symphony Orchestra of Orlando. Well-known vocal soloists. Program events include afternoon and evening concerts and a morning lecture. Founded in 1936.

GEORGIA

★ 3079 ★

Atlanta - GRAND OPERA AT THE PARK. August. Contact: Municipal Theater, Incorporated, 710 Peachtree Street, Northeast, Atlanta, Georgia 30308.

Grand opera in an open amphitheater.

★ 3080 ★

Hiawassee - FALL COUNTRY MUSIC FESTIVAL. Late October, 3 days, Towns County High School Grounds. Contact: Robert L. Anderson, Post Office Box 444, Hiawassee, Georgia 30546.

American music and gospel singing are featured with other styles of country music.

★ 3081 ★

Hiawassee - SPRING COUNTRY MUSIC FESTIVAL. Late May-early June, 3 days. Contact: Robert L. Anderson, Post Office Box 444, Hiawassee, Georgia 30546.

Traditional American music, gospel singing, and various other country style musical talents entertain.

GEORGIA (Continued)

★ 3082 ★
Lumpkin - WESTVILLE HISTORICAL MUSIC DAY.
September, annual, 1 day, Westville. Contact:
Fred Fussell, Post Office Box 1850, Lumpkin,
Georgia 31815.

Purpose is to enjoy and preserve early American
music of all types indigenous to the southeastern
United States. Begun around 1971.

★ 3083 ★
Macon - COUNTRY MUSIC FESTIVAL. April,
annual, 1 day, Coliseum. Contact: Georgia
Department of Community Development, Tourist
Division, Post Office Box 38097, Atlanta, Georgia
30334.

Country music groups and individuals perform for
enthusiastic audiences. Begun around 1970.

★ 3084 ★
Statesboro - NEW MUSIC CONCERT FESTIVAL.
May, annual, 1 day, Georgia Southern College.
Contact: Director, New Music Concert Festival,
Georgia Southern College, Foy Fine Arts Building,
Statesboro, Georgia 30458.

Students and professionals perform new and experimental music.

HAWAII

★ 3085 ★
Honolulu - HAWAIIAN MUSIC FESTIVAL. April and
July (Spring and Summer), 2 periods of 8 days, Waikiki
Shell. Contact: Hawaii Visitors Bureau, Suite 801,
Waikiki Business Plaza, 2270 Kalakaua Avenue, Hon-
olulu, Hawaii 96815.

Over 1,500 high school and college musicians perform in band and choral competition. Classical,
semi-classical, folk, and pop music.

★ 3086 ★
Honolulu - HAWAIIAN SONG FESTIVAL AND
SONG COMPOSING CONTEST. Mid March,
Kapiolani Park Bandstand. Contact: Hawaii Visitors
Brueau, Suite 801, Waikiki Business Plaza, 2270
Kalakaua Avenue, Honolulu, Hawaii 96815.

Beautiful singing, original and traditional songs.

IDAHO

★ 3087 ★
Weiser - NATIONAL OLD-TIME FIDDLERS CONTEST
AND FESTIVAL. June (3rd week), annual, 6 days,
Weiser High School Gymnasium. Contact: Margaret
Whittington, Chamber of Commerce, 16 East Idaho
Street, Weiser, Idaho 83672.

Fiddle competition for cash and trophies: area champions, women's champion, winners of junior, senior
and trick-fiddling contests. Also includes parades,
jam sessions, street dances, melodrama, vigilantes,
old-time fashion show, and square dancing. Nearby
is a museum with a Fiddlers Hall of Fame. Started
in 1953.

ILLINOIS

★ 3088 ★
Aledo - BLUEGRASS MUSIC WEEKEND. Late July-
early August, annual, 3 days, Mercer County Fairgrounds. Contact: Jim Barnes, Viola, Illinois
61486.

Brings together bluegrass bands for evening concerts
and gospel singing. Begun around 1973.

★ 3089 ★
Alton - BLUEGRASS FESTIVAL. Mid June, annual,
3 days, Delhi Farms Campground. Contact: Missouri
Area Bluegrass Committee, Frank and Betty Wurtz,
11650 Holly Springs Drive, Saint Louis, Missouri
63141.

A bluegrass music festival with concerts by well-known
groups, a fiddle contest, and a wide variety of displays
of arts, crafts, and music. Family type entertainment.
Begun in 1972.

★ 3090 ★
Ashland - BLUEGRASS FESTIVAL. Early June,
annual, 3 days, Crazy Horse Big Indian Campground.
Contact: Missouri Area Bluegrass Committee, Frank
and Betty Wurtz, 11650 Holly Springs Drive, Saint
Louis, Missouri 63141.

Features top midwestern bluegrass bands to delight
the assembled crowds. Begun around 1974.

★ 3091 ★
Carlyle - LAKESIDE BLUEGRASS FESTIVAL. Mid
June, 3 days, The Pampered Camper. Contact:
Clif Callahan, Route 1, Bridgeport, Illinois 62417.

Music

ILLINOIS (Continued)

Bluegrass music concerts with appearances by famous name groups and soloists. Competition in fiddle and banjo.

★ 3092 ★
Carlyle - SOUTHERN ILLINOIS BLUEGRASS FESTIVAL. Early August, annual, 3 days. Contact: Clif Callahan, 233 East Chestnut Street, Olney, Illinois 62450.

Band concerts and competition for bands, banjo, and fiddle players. Begun in 1975.

★ 3093 ★
Carmi - MID-STATES BLUEGRASS FESTIVAL. Late August, 3 days, White County Fairground. Contact: Clif Callahan, Route 1, Bridgeport, Illinois 62417.

Bluegrass music concerts with appearances by famous name groups and soloists. Competitive events for fiddle and banjo. Begun in 1975.

★ 3094 ★
Champaign - CENTRAL ILLINOIS BLUEGRASS FESTIVAL. Early September, 3 days, Tincups Campgrounds. Contact: Clif Callahan, Route 1, Bridgeport, Illinois 62417.

Bluegrass music concerts with appearances by famous name groups and soloists. Competitive events for fiddle and banjo.

★ 3095 ★
Chicago - GRANT PARK CONCERTS. Late June to late August, annual, 9 weeks, Grant Park Music Shell, Grant Park on Lake Michigan. Contact: Grant Park Concerts, Chicago Park District, 425 East 14th Boulevard, Chicago, Illinois 60605.

The Grant Park Symphony, an orchestra first organized in 1944, is the featured ensemble, playing symphonic, operatic, and ballet music under a succession of well-known guest conductors. Not only works in the classic, romantic, and contemporary symphonic and concerto repertories, concert versions of Mozart and Verdi operas, large-scale choral works, but also music infrequently programmed within the framework of the usual free outdoor concerts. A Pops Concert Series includes gospel, rock, folk music, blues, and jazz and features known pop musicians and groups. Begun in 1935.

★ 3096 ★
Chicago - RAVINIA FESTIVAL. Late June-September, annual, 13 weeks, Ravinia Pavillion, Ravinia Park. Contact: Ravinia Festival, 22 West Monroe Street, Chicago, Illinois 60603.

A major American summer festival, it is cast in the large proportions of festivals organized around ranking orchestral ensembles - in this case the Chicago Symphony Orchestra. Musical concerts, dance programs, or special programs such as mime or puppet theater. Symphonic programs, opera in concert version, and a few recitals. Jazz, rock, folk, blues, and other pop music categories. Dance programs. Theatrical productions. First established in 1936.

★ 3097 ★
DeKalb - COLLEGE CHORAL FESTIVAL. Mid February, 1 day, New Music Building, Northern Illinois University. Contact: Northern Illinois University, University Programming and Activities, DeKalb, Illinois 60115.

Choral groups gather to make beautiful music.

★ 3098 ★
Edwardsville - MISSISSIPPI RIVER FESTIVAL. July and August, annual, 6 weeks, campus of Southern Illinois University. Contact: Mississippi River Festival, 718 North Grand Boulevard, Saint Louis, Missouri 63103.

The Saint Louis Symphony Orchestra is the permanent ensemble around which the festival is organized. Festival presents the orchestra in six concerts with standard format featuring orchestral works and works for soloists and orchestra. There is also an arts and crafts festival. Guest performers. Pops series. The festival is held in Edwardsville across the Mississippi River from Saint Louis. First held in 1969.

★ 3099 ★
Goodfield - BIG TIMBER BLUEGRASS FESTIVAL. Early July, 3 days, Timberline Campground. Contact: Clif Callahan, Route 1, Bridgeport, Illinois 62417.

Bluegrass music concerts with appearances by famous name groups and soloists. Competitive events for fiddle and banjo.

★ 3100 ★
Ina - SHADEY FOREST BLUEGRASS FESTIVAL. Late

ILLINOIS (Continued)

July-early August, 3 days, Sherwood Campground. Contact: Clif Callahan, Route 1, Bridgeport, Illinois 62417.

Bluegrass music concerts with appearances by famous name groups and soloists. Competitive events for fiddle and banjo.

★ 3101 ★
Jacksonville - BLUEGRASS MUSIC FESTIVAL. May-June, annual, 2 days, Crazy Horse Campground. Contact: The Division of Tourism, Illinois Department of Business and Economic Development, 222 South College Street, Springfield, Illinois 62706.

The singing and playing of bluegrass music in an outdoor setting.

★ 3102 ★
Knoxville - KNOXVILLE BLUEGRASS FESTIVAL. Late May, annual, 3 days, Knox County Fairgrounds. Contact: James Oliver Smith, Rural Route 1, Gilson, Illinois 61436.

Bluegrass music, a fiddle contest, and gospel singing are featured in this musical festival. Begun around 1971.

★ 3103 ★
Springfield - INTERNATIONAL CARILLON FESTIVAL. Late June, annual, 8 days, Washington Park, Rees Memorial Carillon. Contact: The Division of Tourism, Illinois Department of Business and Economic Development, 222 South College Street, Springfield, Illinois 62706.

Concerts and other events associated with bells played manually on a keyboard. Carilloneurs from the Netherlands, Germany, New Zealand, Canada and the United States are featured.

★ 3104 ★
Yorkville - NATIONAL CHICAGOLAND AND NORTHERN ILLINOIS BLUEGRASS FESTIVAL. Late August, 3 days, Hideaway Lakes. Contact: Clif Callahan, Route 1, Bridgeport, Illinois 62417.

Bluegrass music concerts with appearances by famous name groups and soloists. Competitive events for fiddle and banjo.

INDIANA

★ 3105 ★
Battle Ground - FIDDLERS GATHERING. Mid July, annual, 3 days, Tippecanoe Battlefield. Contact:

Director, Battle Ground Historical Corporation, Box 225, Battle Ground, Indiana 47920.

Fiddlers, banjoists, guitarists, autoharp and dulcimer players from all over the country participate in jam sessions, workshops, and lectures around the clock. Craft and food booths.

★ 3106 ★
Battle Ground - TIPPECANOE AND BLUEGRASS TOO. Late September, 2 days. Contact: Director, Battle Ground Historical Corporation, Box 225, Battle Ground, Indiana 47920.

Traditional American bluegrass music. Food and musical crafts offered.

★ 3107 ★
Beanblossom - BLUEGRASS MUSIC FESTIVAL. Mid June, 5 days, Brown County Jamboree Barn. Contact: Birch Monroe, 829 South Colfax Street, Martinsville, Indiana 46151; or Indiana Division of Tourism, 336 State House, Indianapolis, Indiana 46204.

Banjo players from around the nation. Gospel sings, hoedowns and competitions. Begun around 1967.

★ 3108 ★
Bloomington - SUMMER OPERA FESTIVAL. July and August, annual, Outdoor amphitheater at Indiana University School of Music. Contact: Summer Opera Festival, Indiana University School of Music, Bloomington, Indiana 47401.

Opera performances in an outdoor setting.

★ 3109 ★
Boswell - BLUEGRASS REUNION. Mid August, annual, 2 days, 4-H Fairgrounds. Contact: George and Georgia Colclasure, Box 272, Cissna Park, Illinois 60924.

Fiddle contest, bluegrass music, and concerts are included in the musical entertainment.

★ 3110 ★
Brookville - LARRY SPARKS BLUEGRASS FESTIVAL. Late August, 3 days, Bluebird Hill Park. Contact: Don Short, Route 3, Box 93, Brookville, Indiana 47012.

Bluegrass and gospel are featured at this get-together of music lovers.

Music

INDIANA (Continued)

★ 3111 ★
Evansville - MADRIGAL DINNERS.   Early December,
Forum Room, Indiana State University.   Contact:
Indiana State University, 8600 University Boulevard,
Evansville, Indiana 47712.

The festivities begin with the fanfare of trumpets and
the arrival of strolling minstrels, court jesters and a
bowl of steaming wassail.   The feast is celebrated
in the tradition of a sixteenth century English manor.
The Mid-America Singers costumed in authentic and
elegant brocades and laces perform a round of madrigals.   A flaming pudding is served.

★ 3112 ★
Greencastle - FESTIVAL OF CONTEMPORARY MUSIC.
April, annual, 3 days, De Pauw Performing Arts
Center, DePauw University.   Contact: Annual Festi-
val of Contemporary Music, School of Music, DePauw
University, Greencastle, Indiana 46135.

Each festival is centered around a guest composer or
conductor, with the former usually engaged to conduct
or perform his own works and to lecture and lead informal discussions of his music or modern music in
general.   The music of other composers is always
included on the programs.   Begun in 1963.

★ 3113 ★
Indianapolis - BAROQUE FESTIVAL.   June-July,
3 a week for 6 weeks, Concert Terrace and Showalter
Theatre of the Indianapolis Museum of Art.   Contact:
Festival Music Society of Indiana, Incorporated, Suite
422, Board of Trade Building, 143 North Meridian
Street, Indianapolis, Indiana 46204.

A series of concerts of baroque music staged by such
groups as the Cologne Chamber Orchestra from Germany, the Butler Summer Ballet and the All-City
Chorus.   Numerous soloists also appear.

★ 3114 ★
Indianapolis - ROMANTIC FESTIVAL.   April-May,
annual, 1 week, Clowes Memorial Hall.   Contact:
Romantic Festival, Jordan College of Music, Butler
University, Indianapolis, Indiana 46208.

Orchestral, chamber, choral concerts and ballet.
Festival orchestra, guest orchestras, conductors, and
soloists present music of known and little-known
Romantic composers in a musical rediscovery.   Founded
in 1968.

★ 3115 ★
Muncie - FESTIVAL OF NEW MUSIC.   January,
annual, 6 days, Ball State University.   Contact:
Director, Festival of New Music, Ball State University,
University Hall, Muncie, Indiana 47306.

Student and professional ensembles perform concerts of
twentieth century chamber music, new and experimental music.

★ 3116 ★
Notre Dame - COLLEGIATE JAZZ FESTIVAL.   March,
annual, campus of the University of Notre Dame.
Contact: Collegiate Jazz Festival, Box 115, Notre
Dame, Indiana 46556.

Campus and big bands from across the nation compete
for prizes.   Run by students with the assistance of
a faculty advisor and the partial sponsorship of the
University of Notre Dame Student Union.   The
emphasis of the festival is on the educational aspects
of jazz and on providing the opportunity to college
jazz soloists and groups to perform before those who
are capable of rendering meaningful critical judgment
regarding the fine points of jazz performance.   Begun in 1959.

IOWA

★ 3117 ★
Algona - BAND FESTIVAL.   Early October (1st
Saturday), annual, 1 day, downtown.   Contact:
Chamber of Commerce, Post Office Box 500, Algona,
Iowa 50511.

Parade with 25 bands, band queens, and floats is
followed by luncheons for the participants.   In the
afternoon, there is a program of high school and
college jazz bands, followed by the crowning of
the new Festival Queen.   Begun around 1950.

★ 3118 ★
Burlington - BAND FESTIVAL.   Early October
(1st or 2nd Saturday), annual, 1 day, downtown and
Bracewell Stadium.   Contact: Burlington Chamber
of Commerce, Hotel Burlington, Burlington, Iowa
52601.

The event involves high school bands within a radius
of 50 miles.   There is a parade, a judging of high
school queens, and a massed band concert in Bracewell Stadium at night, at which the Band Festival
Queen is crowned.   Begun in 1953.

IOWA (Continued)

★ 3119 ★

Centerville - SOUTHERN IOWA BLUEGRASS MUSIC FESTIVAL. Late July, annual, 3 days, Appanoose County Fairgrounds. Contact: Dan Exline, 606 West State, Centerville, Iowa 52544.

Acoustical music on stage each afternoon and evening, with gospel music in addition on Sunday morning. Begun in 1976.

★ 3120 ★

Central City - CENTRAL CITY BLUEGRASS FESTIVAL. Early September, annual, 3 days, Linn County Fairgrounds. Contact: Chet Steetz, 54-21st Avenue, Southwest, Cedar Rapids, Iowa 52404.

Many musicians and music lovers gather for the playing of and listening to bluegrass music.

★ 3121 ★

Cherokee - NORTHWEST IOWA CHORAL FESTIVAL. Late January, 1 day, Washington High School. Contact: Chamber of Commerce, 227 West Maple, Cherokee, Iowa 51012.

A large number of schools participate in the event. The singing is enjoyed by the participants and the audiences.

★ 3122 ★

Cincinnati - BLUEGRASS AND COUNTRY MUSIC FESTIVAL. Late August-early September, 4 days, City Park. Contact: Dan Exline, 606 West State, Centerville, Iowa 52544.

Events include a fiddle contest, banjo contest, and bluegrass band concert. All interested musicians are allowed to perform. Bluegrass music on stage each day, Nashville stage show on one day and a parade on one day. Sponsored by the Cincinnati Labor Day committee. Started in 1975.

★ 3123 ★

Council Bluffs - OLD TIME COUNTRY MUSIC CONTEST AND PIONEER EXPOSITION. Early September, annual, 3 days. Contact: Iowa Old Time Country Music Contest and Pioneer Exposition, Room 301, First Federal Bank Building, Broadway and Main, Council Bluffs, Iowa 51501.

A festival of music contests, arts and crafts. Prize money and trophies awarded for arts and crafts, bluegrass bands, country combos, country singers, fiddlers,

folk singers, square dance callers, and more.

★ 3124 ★

Des Moines - FOLK MUSIC FESTIVAL. Mid June, 2 days, Living History Farms. Contact: Program Director, Living History Farms, Rural Route 1, Des Moines, Iowa 50322.

Two days filled with folk music, singing, fiddling, etc. at Living History Farms.

★ 3125 ★

Drakesville - COUNTRY AND OLD TIME MUSIC FESTIVAL. Mid September (3rd weekend), 2-3 days, Drakesville City Park. Contact: Bill Wignall, Country Cousin, 320-N Birch, Ottumwa, Iowa 52501; or Bill D. Bassett, Post Office Box 1, Drakesville, Iowa 52501.

Put on by Country Cousins, a country/western musical group, and the community of Drakesville, the purpose of the event is to give people a chance to relax and enjoy themselves eating, sleeping, picking and visiting. The music is mostly country-western and bluegrass, although there are no restrictions of type. The groups and individuals perform on stage and then hold jam sessions on the grounds. Also includes square dancing and gospel music. Begun around 1972.

★ 3126 ★

Dubuque - PIANO FESTIVAL. Mid April, 2 days, Clarke College. Contact: Dubuque Area Chamber of Commerce, 607 Fischer Building, Dubuque, Iowa 52001.

A festival of piano music on the campus of Clarke College.

★ 3127 ★

Mason City - NORTH IOWA BAND FESTIVAL. Early June, annual, various places, grand finale at Roosevelt Field. Contact: Mason City Area Chamber of Commerce, 122 North Federal, Mason City, Iowa 50401.

More than 100 high school bands converge on Mason City (home of Meredith Wilson, author of Music Man). There is a grand parade of all the bands and a band competition. Also in the parade are queens and floats. There are concerts in the afternoon, and a mass concert by all the bands in the evening. Also included are twirling champions, drum and bugle corps, and dignitaries from the music world. The queens are introduced and concerts are given in various

Music

IOWA (Continued)

parts of the city. In addition to the high school bands there are service bands, e.g. Navy, Army. Begun around 1939.

★ 3128 ★
Mount Vernon - CORNELL COLLEGE MUSIC FESTIVAL. April or May, annual, 3 days, King Chapel on campus. Contact: Cornell College Music Festival, c/o Cornell College, Mount Vernon, Iowa 52314.

Known as the "oldest music festival west of the Mississippi River", the festival regularly features a major symphony orchestra, a chamber ensemble, and a soloist appearing on three successive evenings. The Chicago Symphony Orchestra has been the orchestra most frequently engaged for the festival. Founded in 1899.

KANSAS

★ 3129 ★
Emporia - FESTIVAL OF 20TH CENTURY MUSIC. April, annual, 2 days, Emporia Kansas State College. Contact: Director, Festival of 20th Century Music, Emporia Kansas State College, Beach Hall, Emporia, Kansas 66801.

Student and faculty ensembles drawn from various college campuses throughout Kansas perform pieces written for them by resident composers. This is part of the Kansas Cooperative College Composers Project. Other twentieth century works are also performed.

★ 3130 ★
Lindsborg - MESSIAH FESTIVAL. March (Easter week), annual, 1 week, Presser Hall. Contact: Chamber of Commerce, 120 East Lincoln, Lindsborg, Kansas 67456; or Messiah Festival, Bethany College, Lindsborg, Kansas 67456.

Rendering of religious and choral music by Bethany College students and local townspeople. Started in 1881 by Dr. and Mrs. Swenton, who had heard the Messiah by Handel in London and were impressed by it. The decided to organize a performance by their community. Also includes the Midwest Art Exhibit, the Midwest Music Auditions, concerts and recitals by Bethany students, faculty members, campus organizations, and guest soloists.

★ 3131 ★
Manhattan - CENTRAL STATES JAZZ FESTIVAL. Mid February, 3 days. Contact: Chamber of Commerce,

414 Poyntz Avenue, Box 988, Manhattan, Kansas 66502.

Three days of jazz performances to delight music lovers.

★ 3132 ★
Paola - BLUEGRASS MUSIC FESTIVAL. Mid June, annual, 3 days, Wallace City Park. Contact: Dick Miller, 605 South Grant, Olathe, Kansas 66061.

Bluegrass music, fiddle convention, gospel music, fiddle contest and workshops. Begun around 1973.

★ 3133 ★
Wichita - A WEEK OF JAZZ. Early July, annual, 1 week, Duerkson Fine Arts Center, Wichita State University. Contact: Wichita Jazz Festival, Post Office Box 18371, Wichita, Kansas 67218.

Noted artists in the field of jazz are brought together to instruct students in arranging and theory, ear training, and other aspects of jazz. There is a clinic for both combos and big bands. The staff also gives performances and there are panel discussions. Begun in 1975.

★ 3134 ★
Wichita - WICHITA JAZZ FESTIVAL. April, annual, 3 days, Duerkson Fine Arts Center at Wichita State University and Century II (civic auditorium). Contact: Maxcene Adams, Executive Director, Wichita Jazz Festival Incorporated and All That, 1736 South Mission Road, Wichita, Kansas 67207.

The purpose of the festival is to promote community spirit and educational growth in jazz as an art form. Some of the events include dance, instrumental music, and vocal music. There is a full day of competition for college bands and combos. Adjudicators are well known jazz educators and stars. An all-star band is also chosen from all the bands. There is a day for high school bands. Clinics and workshops are conducted by the adjudicators. There is a 12 hour show of continuous jazz on the last day. Usually there are five big names appearing in 45 minute segments. Begun in 1972.

★ 3135 ★
Winfield - NATIONAL GUITAR FLAT-PICKING CHAMPIONSHIP; BLUEGRASS MUSIC, FOLK ARTS AND CRAFTS FESTIVAL. Mid-late September, annual, 3 days, Fairgrounds. Contact: Walnut Valley Bluegrass Festival, Box 245, Winfield, Kansas 61756.

KANSAS (Continued)

Traditional American music and bluegrass music. Also several contests including Walnut Valley Flat Pick Guitar Championship, Walnut Valley Bluegrass Band Championship, Walnut Valley Bluegrass Fiddle Championship, and Walnut Valley Bluegrass Banjo Championship. Judges certified by the SPBGMA (Society for the Preservation of Bluegrass Music of America). Also, a large craft fair for traditional crafts, a folk-music workshop, and a fiddlers' convention. Begun in 1972.

KENTUCKY

★ 3136 ★
Benton - BIG SINGING DAY. Late May, annual, 1 day, Marshall County Court House. Contact: Mrs. Nina Joyce, Route 6, Box 282, Benton, Kentucky 42025.

Presents the unique singing of Southern Harmony using the original 1835 fasola tunebook by William Walker. The music dates from the Elizabethan period. Uses shape-note music, a four-note system designed to simplify music readings. Begun around 1884.

★ 3137 ★
Grayson - KENTUCKY FOLK SONG FESTIVAL. Early June, 3 days, Cascade Cave area of Carter Caves State Resort Park. Contact: Hubert L. Rogers, Route 2, Box 180, Grayson, Kentucky 41143.

Authentic mountain music of the past, bluegrass, square dancing, and arts and crafts are featured during the festival.

★ 3138 ★
Louisville - BLUEGRASS MUSIC FESTIVAL OF THE U.S.A. Late May-early June, 3 days, River City Mall and Riverfront Plaza. Contact: Ms. Mary Louise Dean, Promotion Manager, Louisville Central Area Incorporated, 2305 Citizens Plaza, Louisville, Kentucky 40202.

Bluegrass musicians from across the United States present the "only free festival of bluegrass in an urban area". Begun around 1973.

★ 3139 ★
Olive Hill - FRALEY FAMILY MOUNTAIN MUSIC FESTIVAL. Early August, 3 days, Cascades State Park, Cascade Caves area. Contact: J.P. and Annadeene Fraley, Box 1, Rush, Kentucky 41168.

Traditional American music, old time fiddlers, square

dance, and concerts. Begun around 1971.

★ 3140 ★
Owensboro - GREAT WESTERN KENTUCKY BLUEGRASS FESTIVAL. Late May, 3 days, Windy Hollow Campgrounds. Contact: Clif Callahan, Route 1, Bridgeport, Illinois 62417.

Bluegrass music concerts with appearances by famous name groups and soloists. Competitive events for fiddle and banjo.

LOUISIANA

★ 3141 ★
Abbeville - FRENCH ACADIAN MUSIC FESTIVAL. Late April, annual, 1 day, Comeaux Recreation Center. Contact: Robert P. Prejean, 209 North Bailey Avenue, Abbeville, Louisiana 70510; or Louisiana Tourist Commission, Post Office Box 44291, Baton Rouge, Louisiana 70804.

The festival commemorates the coming of the Acadians to Louisiana and is also intended to further the preservation of French customs and traditions. The program includes contests in singing, playing French folksongs, French skits, short stories and poems. This is followed by dance performances and contests, including the mazurka, polka, two-step, and the Lancer Dance, an ancient French dance. Acadian handicrafts are on sale. Begun around 1971.

★ 3142 ★
Baton Rouge - LOUISIANA STATE UNIVERSITY FESTIVAL OF CONTEMPORARY MUSIC. March or April, annual, University or Union Theaters, Louisiana State University campus. Contact: Louisiana State University Festival of Contemporary Music, c/o School of Music, Louisiana State University, Baton Rouge, Louisiana 70803.

Believed to be the oldest festival of its kind in the United States. The music performed is contemporary music with a special emphasis on music of quite recent origin. The programs will alternately feature works for chamber groups, choral ensembles, symphonic band, symphony orchestra, and solo performers. Each year a noted contemporary composer, generally from the Americas, is honored at the festival and visits the campus to lecture on his music and perhaps conduct a concert of his works. The works of well-known composers are always included, but a special effort is made to perform works by newer - even student - American composers. Founded in 1944.

Music

LOUISIANA (Continued)

★ 3143 ★
Lafayette - EVA MOUTON KEYBOARD FESTIVAL.
Late March, annual, 2-3 days, University of South-
western Louisiana. Contact: Eva Marie Mouton
Keyboard Festival, University of Southwestern Louisi-
ana School of Music, Drawer 1207, Lafayette,
Louisiana 70501; or Director, School of Music,
University of Southwestern Louisiana, Lafayette,
Louisiana 70501.

A piano festival and an organ festival. Each is a
competition in that students receive a written criticism of their work, a rating, and in the case of a
superior rating, a certificate and medal. The
festivals include various levels.

★ 3144 ★
Lafayette - JAMES DICK INTERNATIONAL FESTIVAL-
INSTITUTE. Mid July, 3 days, University of South-
western Louisiana. Contact: Director, School of
Music, University of Southwestern Louisiana, Lafayette,
Louisiana 70501.

Recitals and concerts including student and professional
artists.

★ 3145 ★
New Orleans - JAZZ AND HERITAGE FESTIVAL.
Mid April, annual, 5 days, Louisiana Superdome,
New Orleans Fairgrounds, the Admiral (steamboat).
Contact: Allison Miner, Post Office Box 2530, New
Orleans, Louisiana 70176; or Executive Director,
Louisiana Tourist Commission, Post Office Box 44291,
Baton Rouge, Louisiana 70804.

Three music-filled Mississippi cruises on the steamboat
Admiral: the Steamboat Stomp, the Rhythm and
Blues Cruise, the Contemporary Jazz Cruise. Musical performers play almost around the clock at the
Superdome and the Fairgrounds. At the Heritage
fair portion of the celebration, types of music includes bluegrass, blues, Cajun, Dixieland, folk,
ragtime, rhythm-and-blues, country-western and
gospel. Also a wide variety of Louisiana cuisines
are assembled. Arts and crafts displayed and sold.
Started in 1970.

★ 3146 ★
New Orleans - NEW ORLEANS SUMMER POPS.
Late June through early August, annual, 7 weeks,
Municipal Auditorium. Contact: New Orleans
Summer Pops, c/o New Orleans Summer Pops, In-
corporated, 203 Gallier Hall, 545 Saint Charles
Avenue, New Orleans, Louisiana 70130.

The festival provides tables and chairs for groups of
four and the serving of refreshments. A 55-piece
orchestra performs the usual pops concert fare of
light classics and popular music. Founded in 1953.

MAINE

★ 3147 ★
Blue Hill - BLUE HILL MUSIC FESTIVAL. July and
August, annual, biweekly. Contact: Blue Hill
Music Festival, Kneisel Hall, Blue Hill, Maine
04614.

Concerts of chamber music, sponsored by the Kneisel
Hall Summer School for String and Ensemble playing.
Members of the faculty perform with prominent assisting
artists.

★ 3148 ★
Boothbay - BLUEGRASS MUSIC FESTIVAL. Late
August, annual, 2 days, Railway Museum, Route 27.
Contact: Jimmy Cox, Four Garden Lane, Topsham,
Maine 04086.

Two days of fiddling, singing, playing, etc. in the
bluegrass tradition.

★ 3149 ★
Brunswick - BOWDOIN COLLEGE SUMMER MUSIC
SERIES. July and August, annual, Smith Auditorium
in Sills Hall. Contact: Bowdoin College Summer
Music Series, Bowdoin College, Brunswick, Maine
04011.

The summer series features the Aeolian Chamber
Players and well-known guest artists. A combination of piano, strings, and winds. Begun in 1959.

★ 3150 ★
Brunswick - CONTEMPORARY MUSIC FESTIVAL.
July and August, annual, 2 or 3 days, Wentworth
Hall in Senior Center. Contact: Contemporary
Music Festival, Bowdoin College, Brunswick, Maine
04011.

The concerts feature works commissioned by Bowdoin
and receiving their first performances, works established in the modern music repertory, and lesser known
or unknown pieces. Begun in 1965.

★ 3151 ★
Hancock - MONTEUX MEMORIAL FESTIVAL. August,
annual. Contact: Monteux Memorial Festival, c/o
Forest Studio 555, Hancock, Maine 04640.

MAINE (Continued)

The festival invites musicians to play in training sessions and concerts. Festival consists of some four or five Sunday orchestral concerts and many chamber music performances. Begun in 1965.

★ 3152 ★
Waterville - COLBY COLLEGE SUMMER FESTIVAL. July and August, annual. Contact: Colby College Summer Festival, Colby College, Waterville, Maine 04901.

Symphonic and chamber music concerts.

MARYLAND

★ 3153 ★
Callaway - BLUEGRASS FESTIVAL. June, annual, 3 days, Take-It-Easy Ranch. Contact: Tri-County Council for Southern Maryland, Post Office Box 301, Waldorf, Maryland 20601.

This festival features well-known performers and traditional American mountain music. Camping is available. Begun around 1972.

★ 3154 ★
College Park - INTERNATIONAL PIANO FESTIVAL AND COMPETITION. Early August, annual, 7 days, Tawes Fines Arts Center, University of Maryland. Contact: Dr. Stewart Gordon, Department of Music, University of Maryland, College Park, Maryland 20742.

Professional pianists, teachers and students are invited to attend a series of workshops, master-classes, and lecture-recitals. Evening concerts are given by internationally known artists. Students compete in a world-wide competition. Grew out of the American Matthay Festival, which began in 1965. The current festival began in 1971.

★ 3155 ★
Cumberland - ALLEGANY BLUEGRASS FESTIVAL. Late September or early October, annual, 2 days, Allegany Community College. Contact: Director of Student and Public Relations, Allegany Community College, Post Office Box 870, Cumberland, Maryland 21502.

In addition to the bluegrass music by a variety of groups, there is competition in woodsmen's skills including dot split, pulp toss for distance, bolt split, tobacco spit, archery, axe and hatchet throw, log roll, cross-cut, chain saw, speed chop, and tug-of-war. There is also a best beard contest for men and a best Appalachian costume competition for women. Also included is an Appalchian Arts and Crafts exhibit. Begun around 1973.

★ 3156 ★
Largo - DIMENSION IN MUSIC. May or June, annual, 2 days, Prince George's Community College. Contact: Maryland National Capital Park and Planning Commission, 6600 Kenilworth Avenue, Riverdale, Maryland 20840.

There are jazz bands, opera companies, symphony orchestra, string band, choruses, and others performing jazz, opera, classical, rock, folk, barbershop, etc. Craft demonstrations include weaving, leatherwork, spinning, hooking, jewelry making, enameling, macrame, pottery, etc. There are children's concerts and a craft "drop-in" for the youngsters.

MASSACHUSETTS

★ 3157 ★
Boston - BOSTON POPS CONCERTS. April-June, annual, 9 weeks. Contact: Boston Pops Concerts, Symphony Hall, Boston, Massachusetts 02115.

The orchestra and the special kind of music programing it excels in are archetypical of the pops idea adapted in recent years by so many major and community symphonic organizations in the United States. 90 players from the Boston Symphony Orchestra perform. Light refreshments and a musical fare that is characteristically mixed: movements from symphonic works, light classics, current popular songs and medleys in arrangements, and a solo performer. The Pops concerts are Boston's first "festival" following the close of the regular symphony season. First founded in 1885.

★ 3158 ★
Boston - ESPLANADE CONCERTS. Late June, annual, 2 weeks, Hatch Memorial Shell on the Charles River Esplanade. Contact: Esplanade Concerts, 251 Hunnington Avenue, Boston, Massachusetts 02115.

The Esplanade Orchestra, conducted out-of-doors, is made up of members of the Boston Symphony Orchestra. Performed at the Hatch Memorial Shell on the Charles River Esplanade. Founded in 1929.

★ 3159 ★
Cummington - BLUEGRASS JAMBOREE. Mid August,

Music

MASSACHUSETTS (Continued)

annual, 2 days, Cummington Farm Village.   Contact: Pioneer Valley Association, Incorporated, 333 Prospect Street, Northampton, Massachusetts 01060.

A gathering of folk who enjoy the sounds of bluegrass music and those who provide it.

★ 3160 ★
Great Barrington - NEW MARLBOBO MUSIC CENTER. Mid July to August, annual.   Contact: New Marlboro Music Center, Red Fox Music Camp, Star Route 70, Box 140, Great Barrington, Massachusetts 01230.

The music center is organized as part of the activities of the Red Fox Music Camp.   The New Marlboro Chamber Players, the resident group, are 14 professional musicans who offer seven Saturday evening concerts of varied chamber music.   Formed in 1958.

★ 3161 ★
Ipswich - CASTLE HILL FESTIVAL.   Late June-mid August, annual.   Contact: Castle Hill Festival, c/o New England Conservatory of Music, Castle Hill Festival Series, Box 519, Ipswich, Massachusetts 01938.

The festival is among a number in the United States whose most striking primary feature is its location - in this instance, a Georgian-style Great House built in 1927.   Castle Hill and Great House dominate the coast line just above Crane Beach, just east of Ipswich, 25 miles northeast of Boston.   The festival presents a variety of musical programs such as solo instrument and song recitals, choral programs, chamber music, jazz and folk music concerts, and staged operas. Established in 1950.

★ 3162 ★
Lenox - BERKSHIRE MUSIC FESTIVAL.   Early July-late August, annual, 8 weeks.   Contact: Berkshire Music Festival, Tanglewood, Lenox, Massachusetts 01240.

Amont the most esteemed of the world's summertime musical events.   Activities and musical offerings are multifaceted: 24 concerts featuring the Boston Symphony Orchestra under the direction of some of the best-known conductors, concerts by the Boston Pops Orchestra, "Gala" called "Tanglewood-on-Parade" and contemporary "nonclassical" music. Founded in 1934.

★ 3163 ★
Lenox - FESTIVAL OF CONTEMPORARY MUSIC. Mid August, annual, Theater at Tanglewood.   Contact: Festival of Contemporary Music, Theater at Tanglewood, Lenox, Massachusetts 01240.

The Berkshire Music Center Orchestra in a series of five concerts of contemporary music, including first performances of new works commissioned by the Center.

★ 3164 ★
North Dartmouth - SOUTHEASTERN MASSACHUSETTS UNIVERSITY INSTITUTE FESTIVAL.   June and July, annual.   Contact: Southeastern Massachusetts University, North Dartmouth, Massachusetts 02747.

Chamber music, orchestral music, music education workshops, and operatic music are featured at this festival.

★ 3165 ★
Orange - NEW ENGLAND MUSIC FESTIVAL. August, annual, First Universalist Church.   Contact: New England Music Festival, First Universalist Church, Orange, Massachusetts 01364.

Chamber concerts, New England Festival Ensemble.

★ 3166 ★
Pittsfield - SOUTH MOUNTAIN CONCERTS.   Mid July to mid October, annual.   Contact: South Mountain Concerts, Box 23, Pittsfield, Massachusetts 01201.

Provides "Young Audiences Concerts" for about 20,000 children in the Berkshire region, the Temple of Music.   Chamber music and opera performances comprise the programs, which are scheduled on Saturday and Sunday afternoons.   Established in 1918 as the Berkshire Festival of Chamber Music and maintained, since 1935, by South Mountain Association.

★ 3167 ★
Whitman - CRANBERRY FESTIVAL DRUM AND BUGLE CORPS.   Late July, annual, 1 day, Whitman-Hanson Regional High School.   Contact: Plymouth County Development Council, Incorporated, Post Office Box 1620, Pembroke, Massachusetts 02359.

More than 20 bands from throughout the state participate in a contest of martial music.

MASSACHUSETTS (Continued)

★ 3168 ★

Worcester - WORCESTER MUSIC FESTIVAL.   October, annual, 5 days.   Contact: Worcester Music Festival, Memorial Auditorium, Worcester, Massachusetts 01608.

The featured orchestral ensemble in the past has been the Philadelphia Orchestra;   more recently, the Detroit Symphony has made regular appearances.   Works performed make use of solo instrumentalists and singers, as well as the chorus and orchestra.   Concertos, oratorios and other large-scale choral works, operatic arias and songs, and symphonic works.   Founded in 1858.

MICHIGAN

★ 3169 ★

Ann Arbor - ANN ARBOR BLUES AND JAZZ FESTIVAL.
Early September, annual, 3 days.   Contact: Ann Arbor Blues and Jazz Festival, Box 381, Ann Arbor, Michigan 48107.

Features blues and jazz by top name performers.
Once was held in Windsor, Ontario at Saint Clair College.

★ 3170 ★

Ann Arbor - MAY FESTIVAL.   April-May, annual, 4 days, Hill Auditorium.   Contact: Ann Arbor May Festival, c/o University Musical Society, Burton Tower, University of Michigan, Ann Arbor, Michigan 48104.

Music for orchestra shared with solo voice or instrument, and two choral programs also with orchestra. Philadelphia Orchestra, well-known singers, pianists and violinists perform at this traditional highlight of the University of Michigan spring music season. Founded in 1894.

★ 3171 ★

Grosse Pointe Woods - DETROIT CONCERT BAND SUMMER SERIES.   Early June, annual, 8 weeks. Contact: Detroit Concert Band Summer Series, 20962 Mack Avenue, Grosse Pointe Woods, Michigan 48236.

All concerts are free.   The band's repertory is unusually large and consists of works of symphonic nature, marches, waltzes, a multitude of transcriptions, and arrangements of both popular and classical music, and works for solo instruments.   Established in 1946.

★ 3172 ★

Interlochen - INTERLOCHEN SUMMER FESTIVAL.
July and August, annual, Sunday afternoons and nightly except Mondays.   Contact: Interlochen Summer Festival, National Music Camp/Interlochen Arts Academy, Interlochen, Michigan 49643.

Concerts, plays, ballet, and other performances, in connection with the famous Interlochen Music Camp.

★ 3173 ★

Kalamazoo - BACH FEST.   March (usually 1st 2 weeks), annual, 2 weeks, Stetson Chapel, Kalamazoo College.   Contact: The Kalamazoo Bach Festival Society, Incorporated, Kalamazoo College, Kalamazoo, Michigan 49007.

Includes the Young Artists' Auditions and Concerts. These were introduced in 1965 as a means of interesting young artists in baroque music in general and in the music of the Bach in particular.   After a screening of tapes, the finalist play in front of three adjudicators.   There is also a chamber music concert and a performance of a major work by Bach.   Nationally and internationally known artists have appeared at the festival.   First took place in 1947.

★ 3174 ★

Rochester - MEADOW BROOK MUSIC FESTIVAL.
Late June to August, annual, 8 weeks.   Contact: Meadow Brook Music Festival, Oakland University, Rochester, Michigan 48063.

The Detroit Symphony Orchestra is the central musical organization.   Orchestra plays some 34 major concerts in Baldwin Memorial Pavilion on the University campus.   Superior acoustics;   ballet.   Founded in 1964.

MINNESOTA

★ 3175 ★

Duluth - HEAD OF THE LAKES JAZZ FESTIVAL.
Mid April, annual, 2 days, University of Minnesota at Duluth.   Contact: Director, Head of the Lakes Jazz Festival, Marshall Performing Arts Center, Duluth, Minnesota 55812.

A non-competitive festival for high school jazz bands. Each band has one-half hour to play any jazz music that it chooses.   Three guest artists are present to judge the performances.   They may, if they choose, award a NAJE outstanding band award to any bands which they feel are particulary good.   There is a mid-day clinic, presided over by the judges, and evening performances by the UMD Jazz Ensemble,

Music

MINNESOTA (Continued)

at which the guest artists solo.   Started in 1975.

★ 3176 ★
Grand Rapids - MISS MELODY FESTIVAL
(MISSISSIPPI MELODY FESTIVAL).   July, 3 week-
ends, on the banks of the Mississippi River.   Con-
tact: Mississippi Showboat, Incorporated, Grand
Rapids, Minnesota 55744.

A showboat goes up and down the river putting on
an old-fashioned show.

★ 3177 ★
Luverne - TRI-STATE BAND FESTIVAL.   Late
September, 1 day.   Contact: Chamber of Commerce,
Luverne, Minnesota 56156.

A parade and band competition highlight the festival
events.

★ 3178 ★
Minneapolis - MOZART/HAYDN FESTIVAL.   Mid-
late August, 4 days, Orchestra Hall.   Contact:
Greater Minneapolis Area Chamber of Commerce, 15
South Fifth Street, Minneapolis, Minnesota 55402.

Features noted conductors leading the Minnesota
Orchestra in programs featuring the music of Mozart
and Haydn.

★ 3179 ★
Northfield - CARLETON SUMMER MUSIC FESTIVAL.
Mid June, annual, 5-6 days, Carleton College.
Contact: Carleton College, Department of Music,
Music Hall, Northfield, Minnesota 55057.

Events include a candlelight concert, piano workshop,
voice workshop, master classes, recitals, and concerts.   The concerts include medieval to modern
music played and performed by orchestras, soloists,
chorales, quartets, trios, etc.   Each year there are
featured guest artists.

★ 3180 ★
Saint Joseph - MINNESOTA FESTIVAL OF MUSIC
AND ARTS.   August, annual.   Contact: Minnesota
Festival of Music and Arts, College of Saint Benedict,
Saint Joseph, Minnesota 56374.

Summer Music Center; orchestral (Saint Paul Chamber
Orchestra) and choral concerts; other events.

MISSISSIPPI

★ 3181 ★
Jackson - FESTIVAL OF HARMONY.   Late May,
1 day, Jackson Municipal Auditorium.   Contact:
Travel/Tourism Department, Mississippi Agricultural
and Industrial Board, Post Office Box 849, Jackson,
Mississippi 39205.

A charity performance of barbership quartet music
sponsored by the SPEBSQSA, Magnolia Chapter.

★ 3182 ★
Jackson - GOSPEL EXTRAVAGANZA.   April
(Spring), 1 day, Jackson State College Auditorium.
Contact: Travel/Tourism Department, Mississippi
Agricultural and Industrial Board, Post Office Box
849, Jackson, Mississippi 39205.

Sponsored by the SGA, the event features invited
soloists and choirs of gospel singers.

★ 3183 ★
Jackson - OPERA/SOUTH.   April (Spring-and again
in the Fall), annual, Jackson Auditorium.   Contact:
Travel/Tourism Department, Mississippi Agricultural
and Industrial Board, Post Office Box 849, Jackson,
Mississippi 39205.

Sponsored by Jackson State, Tougaloo, and Utica
Junior College, the events include a contemporary
opera by a black composer, performed in the fall,
and a grand opera in the spring.   Founded in 1971.

★ 3184 ★
Meridian - JIMMIE RODGERS FESTIVAL.   May,
3-5 days, Ray Stadium, Temple Theatre.   Contact:
Greater Meridian Chamber of Commerce, 2000
Ninth Street, Post Office Box 790, Meridian,
Mississippi 39301.

Music is performed by top country singers.   Activities
include films, cookouts, a dance, and special ceremonies.

★ 3185 ★
Monticello - BLUEGRASS FESTIVAL.   Mid June,
2 days.   Contact: Travel Department, Mississippi
Agricultural and Industrial Board, Post Office Box
849, Jackson, Mississippi 39205.

Outdoor event featuring nationally known performers.
Other activities include canoe races, a fishing rodeo,
a tennis tournament and a flea market.

MISSOURI

★ 3186 ★
Arnold - SUMMERTIME (SUMMER BLUEGRASS FESTIVAL). Mid August, annual, 3 days, Spring Valley Ranch. Contact: Missouri Area Bluegrass Committee, Ms. Fran Greco, 1046 Kuhlman Lane, Webster Groves, Missouri 63119.

Top bluegrass groups and soloists, bluegrass band contest, concerts, gospel sing, and church service. Begun around 1969.

★ 3187 ★
Bismarck - BLUEGRASS JAMBOREE. Mid July, annual, 3 days, Sundale Park. Contact: Kenneth W. Moyers, Rural Route 1, Box 102, Caledonia, Missouri 63631.

Sponsored by the V.F.W. of Bismarck, a gathering of jamboree fans. Begun in 1973.

★ 3188 ★
Dixon - BLUEGRASS PICKIN TIME. Early September (Labor Day weekend), annual, 3 days, Fairview Community Center. Contact: Fairview Community Center, Dixon, Missouri 65459.

The festival includes stage performances and jam sessions, featuring traditional bluegrass and gospel music. The festival's purpose is for the participants to enjoy playing and listening to bluegrass. Begun around 1969.

★ 3189 ★
Eminence - OZARK MOUNTAIN BLUEGRASS FESTIVAL. Early July, annual, 4 days, Cross-country Trailrides Park. Contact: Ozark Mountain Bluegrass Festival, Box 118, Eminence, Missouri 65466.

Bluegrass, traditional American music, and square dance. Concerts, workshops and contests for fiddle, banjo, and guitar. Begun around 1970.

★ 3190 ★
Farmington - BLUEGRASS FESTIVAL (MABC FALL FESTIVAL). Mid-late July, 3 days, Campfire Campgrounds. Contact: Missouri Area Bluegrass Committee, Frank and Betty Wurtz, 11650 Holly Springs Drive, Saint Louis, Missouri 63141.

Events include a band contest for amateur bands, and concerts by noted bluegrass groups with the winners of the contest participating in one concert.

★ 3191 ★
Farmington - SPRING BLUEGRASS FESTIVAL. Mid May, annual, 3 days. Contact: Missouri Area Bluegrass Committee, 7403 Haywood Drive, Saint Louis, Missouri 63133.

Music by a wide variety of bluegrass bands. A banjo contest with cash awards. Usually held in an outdoor setting, often a campground. Sponsored by the Missouri Area Bluegrass Committee. Begun around 1969.

★ 3192 ★
Fort Leonard Wood - PINEY RIVER BLUEGRASS MUSIC FESTIVAL. Mid May, annual, 3 days, N.S.T.R. Base Camp. Contact: SPBGMA, Box 94, Lake Ozark, Missouri 65049.

Concerts of bluegrass music performed by award-winning bands and musicians. Started in 1976.

★ 3193 ★
Glenwood - INVITATIONAL COUNTRY-BLUEGRASS-OLD TIME MUSIC FESTIVAL. Early June, annual, 3 days, City Park. Contact: Bob and Oma Corder, Kirksville, Missouri 63501.

Sponsored by the Glenwood Reunion Committee. Started in 1976.

★ 3194 ★
Grassy - BLUEGRASS FESTIVAL. Mid June, bi-ennial, 7 days, Arrowhead Hills Campground. Contact: Don Brown, 213 Chambers Road, Saint Louis, Missouri 63137; or Chamber of Commerce, Grassy, Missouri 63753.

Presented by Don Brown and the Ozark Mountain Trio, the festival features bluegrass and gospel music. Concerts are performed by well-known groups. Other activities are available at the campgrounds, including swimming, fishing and miniature golf.

★ 3195 ★
Grassy - BLUEGRASS FESTIVAL. Early September, biennial, 3 days, Arrowhead Hills. Contact: Don Brown, 213 Chambers Road, Saint Louis, Missouri 63137.

Bluegrass: fiddle contest, gospel, workshops, and a band contest highlight the events. Beginning in 1977, festival will be week-long and in June.

Music

MISSOURI (Continued)

★ 3196 ★
Hillsboro – DUB CROUCH'S BLUEGRASS FESTIVAL.
Late June, 3 days, Hillsboro Fairgrounds.   Contact:
Dub Crouch, 4515 Bellewood Drive, Saint Louis,
Missouri 63125.

Three days of fiddling and other bluegrass music and
friendly folk.

★ 3197 ★
Holt – BLUEGRASS FESTIVAL.   Late August, annual,
3 days.   Contact: Missouri Area Bluegrass Committee,
Ms. Fran Greco, 1046 Kuhlman Lane, Webster Groves,
Missouri 63119.

Sponsored by Jim Perry, this festival features bluegrass
performers in traditional style music.   Begun around
1972.

★ 3198 ★
Kahoka – BLUEGRASS FESTIVAL.   Mid August,
annual, 3 days, Clark County Fairgrounds.   Contact:
Delbert Spray, Rural Route 1, Kahoka, Missouri
63445.

A fiddle convention, bluegrass, arts and crafts,
gospel, and concerts.   Fiddles, mandolins, banjos,
flat-top guitars, bass fiddles, and dobro guitar are
among the instruments played.   Begun around 1973.

★ 3199 ★
Kansas City – BLUEGRASS AMERICA.   Mid October,
3 days, American Royal Center.   Contact: Chuck
Stearman, SPBGMA, Box 95, Lake Ozark, Missouri
65049.

Big Forty Bluegrass Band Showcase, bluegrass, exhibits, gospel sing, and Old Time Fiddlers Contest.

★ 3200 ★
Kansas City – JAZZ FESTIVAL.   July (date may
vary), 2 days, Municipal Auditorium or Royals
Stadium.   Contact: Convention and Visitors Bureau
of Greater Kansas City, 1221 Baltimore, Kansas City,
Missouri 64105.

Intended to re-establish Kansas City as a jazz center,
as well as to honor its past as a birthplace of jazz.
Features a broad range of American jazz classics
and many national and local stars.

★ 3201 ★
Knob Noster – HERB SMITH'S BLUEGRASS MUSIC
FESTIVAL.   Mid July, annual, 3 days, Herman
Smith's Jamboree Park.   Contact: Herman C. Smith,
811 North Broadway, Knob Noster, Missouri 65336.

Bluegrass concerts by well-known bands, with a band
contest also scheduled.   Jam sessions follow the show.
Arts and crafts are welcomed for display.   Begun in
1971.

★ 3202 ★
Lake Ozark – SPBGMA BLUEGRASS MUSICIAN
CONVENTION AND AWARDS BANQUET, BLUEGRASS
FESTIVAL.   Early December, annual, 2 days, Lodge
of the Four Seasons.   Contact: SPBGMA, Box 95,
Lake Ozark, Missouri 65049.

The awards competition is for amateur and semi-
professional musicians throughout the mid-west.   In
addition, the festival includes a variety of bluegrass
groups, gospel singing, and jam sessions.   Also
called Winter Bluegrass Festival and Awards or Bluegrass Festival and Awards.   Begun around 1973.

★ 3203 ★
Mexico – LITTLE DIXIE BLUEGRASS FESTIVAL.   Early
September, 3 days, Blackmore Lake.   Contact: Les
Tate, Route 2, Mexico, Missouri 65265.

Traditional bluegrass music in an outdoor setting.
Begun around 1973.

★ 3204 ★
Mine LaMott – MISSOURI BLUEGRASS FESTIVAL.
Early August, annual, 4 days.   Contact: Missouri
Area Bluegrass Committee, Frank and Betty Wurtz,
11650 Holly Springs Drive, Saint Louis, Missouri
63141.

The festival features noted bluegrass musicians and
band concerts.   Begun in 1976.

★ 3205 ★
Perryville – BLUEGRASS FESTIVAL.   Mid July,
annual, 3 days, KOA Kampground.   Contact: Don
Brown, 213 Chambers Road, Saint Louis, Missouri
63137; or Bob Ray, Post Office Box 430, Route 5,
Perryville, Missouri 63775.

Includes top bluegrass musicians and musical groups.
There are Sunday morning church services and gospel
sings.   The campgrounds include or ajoin facilities
for fishing, miniature golf, concessions, and playground.   Begun in 1976.

MISSOURI (Continued)

★ 3206 ★
Rocheport - CENTRAL MISSOURI BLUEGRASS MUSIC
FESTIVAL.   Early June, annual, 3 days, Safari
Campgrounds.   Contact: SPBGMA, Box 95, Lake
Ozark, Missouri 65049.

The event features concerts by professional bluegrass
bands, gospel singing, and a fiddle contest.

★ 3207 ★
Saint Charles - BLUEGRASS FESTIVAL.   Early July,
annual, 1 day, Blanchette Park.   Contact: Jim
Dustin, c/o Post Office Box 125, Saint Charles,
Missouri 63301.

The Saint Charles Jaycees sponsor contests for old
time fiddlers and banjo pickers.   Cash prizes are
awarded.   Begun in 1972.

★ 3208 ★
Saint Joseph - OLD TIME FIDDLERS FESTIVAL.   Mid
September, annual, 3 days, East Hills Shopping
Center.   Contact: Vern Popp, East Hills Shopping
Center, Belt Highway and Frederick Avenue, Saint
Joseph, Missouri 64506.

Traditional American music, fiddle convention and
competition.   Begun around 1970.

★ 3209 ★
Saint Louis - O'FALLON JAMBOREE.   Late August,
2 days, O'Fallon Park around lake, 4500 West
Florissant.   Contact: Convention and Visitors
Bureau of Greater Saint Louis, 500 North Broadway,
Saint Louis, Missouri 63102.

An outdoor festival/jamboree in a beautiful setting.

★ 3210 ★
Saint Louis - RAGTIME FESTIVAL.   June or July,
annual, 5-6 days, Goldenrod Showboat on the
Mississippi River near Gateway Arch.   Contact:
Convention and Visitors Bureau of Greater Saint
Louis, 500 Broadway Building, Saint Louis, Missouri
63102.

Nationally prominent Dixieland and ragtime bands
and individual artists perform.   Begun around 1965.

★ 3211 ★
Saint Louis - SAINT LOUIS MUNICIPAL OPERA.
July-August, annual.   Contact: Saint Louis

Municipal Opera, Municipal Theatre, Forest Park,
Saint Louis, Missouri 63112.

The opera provides a summer season of "packaged"
productions of popular music-entertainment shows and
musical plays.   Stars of Hollywood, Broadway, and
television are often engaged for leading roles in the
musical plays.   Founded in 1919.

★ 3212 ★
Silver Dollar City - FESTIVAL OF MOUNTAIN
FOLKS' MUSIC.   Mid June, annual, 9 days.
Contact: Chamber of Commerce, Box 76, Silver
Dollar City, Missouri 65616.

Traditional American music - in particular, mountain
music.   Over 100 mountain musicians play native
instruments including dulcimers, autoharps, jawbones,
jew's harps, flutes, and guitars.   There is also vocal
music.

★ 3213 ★
Van Buren - BLUEGRASS FESTIVAL.   September,
annual, 3 days, KOA Kampground.   Contact: Don
Brown, 213 Chambers Road, Saint Louis, Missouri
63137.

Band contests, fiddlers, and music galore fills the
three days with fine bluegrass music and fellowship.

★ 3214 ★
Warrensburg - CENTRAL MISSOURI STATE
UNIVERSITY JAZZ FESTIVAL.   February, annual,
Hendricks Hall and Utt Music Building.   Contact:
Central Missouri State University Jazz Festival,
Robert M. Gifford, Director, Hendricks Hall and Utt
Music Building, Warrensburg, Missouri 64093.

Student and professional ensembles participate.   The
festival permits college and high school students to
come in contact with professional jazz musicians.
Events include clinics, concerts, and jazz band
composition contests.   Started in 1975.

MONTANA

★ 3215 ★
Bozeman - CONTEMPORARY MUSIC FESTIVAL.
April, annual, Montana State University campus.
Contact: Annual Contemporary Music Festival,
Montana State University, Music Building, Recital
Hall, Bozeman, Montana 59715.

Student and professional ensembles perform twentieth
century chamber music and new and experimental

Music

MONTANA (Continued)

music.   Started in 1975.

★ 3216 ★
Bozeman - JAZZ FESTIVAL.   January, annual,
Music Building, Recital Hall, Montana State University campus.   Contact: Annual Jazz Festival, Montana
State University, Music Building, Recital Hall, Bozeman, Montana 59715.

A jazz concert performed by student ensembles with
guest faculty artists.

★ 3217 ★
Red Lodge - RED LODGE MUSIC FESTIVAL
(STUDENT MUSIC FESTIVAL).   Mid June, 9 days.
Contact: Chamber of Commerce, Box 998, Red Lodge,
Montana 59068.

The festival permits student musicians to practice and
play with professional musicians.

NEVADA

★ 3218 ★
Las Vegas - CONTEMPORARY MUSIC FESTIVAL.
January and February, annual, approximately 10
days, Judy Bayley Theatre.   Contact: Annual Contemporary Music Festival, University of Nevada,
Judy Bayley Theatre, Las Vegas, Nevada 89154.

Guest professional ensembles and soloists perform seven
concerts and seven lecture-demonstrations.   Features
twentieth century chamber music, new and experimental music, operatic music and electronic music.

★ 3219 ★
Las Vegas - UNIVERSITY OF NEVADA, LAS VEGAS,
JAZZ FESTIVAL.   March, annual, 3 days.   Contact: Chairman, University of Nevada, Department
of Music, 4505 Maryland Parkway, Las Vegas,
Nevada 89154.

Professional jazz musicians who live and work around
Las Vegas perform.

★ 3220 ★
Reno - INTERNATIONAL JAZZ FESTIVAL.   March
or April, annual, 4 days, Pioneer Theatre Auditorium.
Contact: Director, Reno International Jazz Festival,
Pioneer Theatre Auditorium, Reno, Nevada 89502.

Student and professional ensembles perform new and

experimental music and jazz.

NEW HAMPSHIRE

★ 3221 ★
Center Harbor - NEW HAMPSHIRE MUSIC FESTIVAL.
July-August, annual, 6 weeks.   Contact: New
Hampshire Music Festival, Post Office Box 147,
Center Harbor, New Hampshire 03226.

The festival presents a series of tour concerts located
in various communities in New Hampshire's Lake
Region; special children concerts, Festival of New
Music, choral concerts, and others directed towards
special audiences.   Program content is remarkably
varied and balanced.   Founded in 1953.

★ 3222 ★
Jaffrey - MONADNOCK MUSIC.   Late July-early
September, annual, Jaffrey Center Meeting House and
various churches in Nelson, Peterborough, Keene,
and other locations.

Chamber orchestra presents free chamber concerts.

★ 3223 ★
Portsmouth - STRAWBERY BANKE CHAMBER MUSIC
FESTIVAL.   June-August, annual.   Contact:
Director, Strawbery Banke Chamber Music Festival,
Post Office Box 300, Portsmouth, New Hampshire
03801.

Chamber music, new and experimental music, and
operatic music are featured.

NEW JERSEY

★ 3224 ★
Holmdel - GARDEN STATE ARTS CENTER GALA.
Early June to early September, annual, Garden
State Arts Center.   Contact: Garden State Arts
Center Gala, Box 116, Holmdel, New Jersey 07733.

The music programs are grouped into two series:
"popular" subscription series and "classical" subscription series.   Created in 1968.

★ 3225 ★
Martinsville - PEE WEE RUSSELL MEMORIAL STOMP.
Mid February (2nd Sunday), annual, 1-2 days,
Martinsville Inn.   Contact: New Jersey Jazz Society,
c/o Jack Stein, Colonial Liquors, Pluckemin, New
Jersey 07978.

NEW JERSEY (Continued)

Professional ensembles play jazz music to raise funds for a jazz scholarship at Rutgers University. Usually about eight different bands play. Started in 1963.

★ 3226 ★
Stanhope - WATERLOO VILLAGE MUSIC FESTIVAL. Late June through August. Contact: New Jersey Department of Economic Development, Post Office Box 2766, Trenton, New Jersey 08625.

New Jersey Symphony Orchestra with guest performers; held in a 2,000 seat tent theater with additional outdoor seating.

NEW MEXICO

★ 3227 ★
Las Cruces - ALL-STATE MUSIC FESTIVAL. Early January, annual, 3 days, New Mexico State University, Pan American Center. Contact: Campus Activities Office, New Mexico State University, Box 3072, Las Cruces, New Mexico 88003.

High school band, orchestra, and vocal competitions of musical students from throughout the state.

★ 3228 ★
Las Cruces - JAZZ FESTIVAL. Late March, annual, 2 days, New Mexico State University. Contact: Campus Activities Office, New Mexico State University, Box 3072, Las Cruces, New Mexico 88003.

A festival of jazz music sponsored by the New Mexico State University and held on campus.

★ 3229 ★
Santa Fe - CHAMBER MUSIC FESTIVAL. Late June-early August, annual, 6 weeks. Contact: Chamber Music Festival, Post Office Box 853, Santa Fe, New Mexico 87501.

Internationally known chamber music players and soloists give concerts and talk about music, about their instruments — discussion and reharsal sessions are very much a part of the format. Included are the Spanish-American, Indian, and Anglo contingents that make up New Mexico's cultural mix. Concerts are given in various sites throughout the state - some quite unorthodox and memorable.

★ 3230 ★
Santa Fe - FEBRUARY FESTIVAL FOR THE ARTS.

Early February, Saint Francis Auditorium. Contact: Tourist Division, New Mexico Department of Development, 113 Washington Avenue, Santa Fe, New Mexico 87503.

The Orchestra of Santa Fe's Concert of American Music performs works of American, perferably local (state) composers.

★ 3231 ★
Santa Fe - SANTA FE OPERA FESTIVAL. Early July to late August, annual, Opera Theatre. Contact: Santa Fe Opera Festival, Post Office Box 2408, Santa Fe, New Mexico 87501.

The festival consists of six or seven works totaling about 26 performances; internationally known stage directors, set and costumer designers, and guest conductors. Each season features important premieres and new productions. Half of the operas performed during any given season are works of this century. Founded in 1957.

★ 3232 ★
Taos - TAOS SCHOOL OF MUSIC SUMMER CHAMBER MUSIC CONCERTS. June-July, annual, 6 weeks, Taos Community Auditorium and Hotel Saint Bernard. Contact: Director, Taos School of Music, Box 1879, Taos, New Mexico 87571.

A six week school session is held for students of strings and piano in study of and performance of chamber music. Faculty give four concerts; students give four concerts. There are esteemed artists and groups in residence.

NEW YORK

★ 3233 ★
Chautauqua - CHAUTAUQUA SUMMER MUSIC FESTIVAL. Late June-August, annual, 8 weeks, Norton Memorial Hall. Contact: Chautauqua Summer Music Programs, Chautauqua Institution, Chautauqua, New York 14722.

Program of lectures, seminars, classes, religious services, theatrical and dance productions, and music concerts. The concerts offer a broad range of programs with occasional instrumental and vocal soloists. The repertory includes light opera, operettas, and Broadway musical shows, as well as works from the standard repertory. Foreign folk ensembles, United States service bands, and dance ensembles round out the typical season.

Music

NEW YORK (Continued)

★ 3234 ★
Cornwall - STORM KING CHAMBER MUSIC SERIES.
July and August, annual, Storm King Art Center.
Contact: Storm King Chamber Music Series, Box 99,
Cornwall, New York 12518.

Concerts are played in the drawing room of the Center
with sound amplification for those seated in the garden. The works featured in the programs represent
a wide stylistic literature. Established in 1959.

★ 3235 ★
Forest Hills - FOREST HILLS MUSIC FESTIVAL.
July and August, annual, Forest Hills Tennis Stadium.
Contact: Forest Hills Music Festival, 11 Station
Square, Forest Hills, New York 11375.

Jazz, folk, rock, and other popular music; guest
performers.

★ 3236 ★
Fort Ann - SMOKEY GREENE'S BLUEGRASS FESTIVAL.
Mid August, annual, 4 days, Country Music Park.
Contact: Smoky Greene, Box 71, Schuylerville,
New York 12871.

Bluegrass music including fiddle and bluegrass bands
in contests and concerts. Begun around 1973.

★ 3237 ★
Glen Cove - MORGAN PARK SUMMER MUSIC
FESTIVAL. July and August, annual, Glen Cove.
Contact: Morgan Park Summer Music Festival, Eight
Southfield Road, Glen Cove, New York 11542.

A series of summer musical events in the park.

★ 3238 ★
Glen Falls - LAKE GEORGE OPERA FESTIVAL. July
to late August, annual, Festival Auditorium, Queens-
bury School. Contact: Lake George Opera Festival,
Box 471, Glen Falls, New York 12801.

The festival performances are of operas from the
standard and modern repertory sung in English.
Founded in 1962.

★ 3239 ★
Hempstead - HOFSTRA UNIVERSITY JAZZ CLINIC
AND FESTIVAL. March, annual. Contact: Hofstra
University Annual Jazz Clinic and Festival, John
Cranford Adams Playhouse, 1000 Fulton Street, Hemp-

stead, New York 11550.

Student and professional ensembles perform jazz, new
and experimental music.

★ 3240 ★
Huntington - FOLK MUSIC FESTIVAL. Mid July
(usually 2nd Saturday), annual, 1 day, Heckscher
Park, bandstand. Contact: Mr. and Mrs. Harvey
Hellering, 517 Ann Lane, Wantagh, New York
11793.

A folk music concert, often accompanied by a group
of ballet or folk dancers. Sponsored by the Folk
Music Society of Huntington. Started in 1969.

★ 3241 ★
Ithaca - CORNELL FESTIVAL OF CONTEMPORARY
MUSIC. November, annual. Contact: Cornell
Festival of Contemporary Music, Cornell University
Music Department, Ithaca, New York 14850.

Wide spectrum of twentieth century music in a variety
of media - chamber, choral, orchestral concerts;
solo recitals.

★ 3242 ★
Katonah - CARAMOOR FESTIVAL. Mid June to
August, annual, 2 months. Contact: Caramoor
Festival, Katonah, New York 10536.

Located northeast of New York City in Westchester
County, Caramoor, with its Spanish Courtyard and
outdoor Venetian Theater surrounded by wooded grounds,
presents music in one of the most attractive settings
in the East. Wednesday afternoon lectures on music
can be credited with a number of distinct musical
achievements. In addition to operatic works, there
are orchestral concerts, chamber music, and recitals.
Soloists are invariable drawn from the first ranks in
the active concert world. Begun around 1946.

★ 3243 ★
Lake Placid - LAKE PLACID MUSIC FESTIVAL. Mid
July to late August, annual, Signal Hill Arts Center.
Contact: Lake Placid Music Festival, Box 949, Lake
Placid, New York 12946.

Lake Placid Festival Trio, the ensemble around which
the festival is organized perform in concert. Established in 1963.

★ 3244 ★
Lake Placid - OLYMPIC VILLAGE BLUEGRASS

NEW YORK (Continued)

FESTIVAL. Late July-early August, annual, 3 days. Contact: Doc Otis, Eight Hurley Avenue, Lake Placid, New York 12946.

Traditional bluegrass music and fun for all. Started in 1976.

★ 3245 ★
Lewiston - LEWISTON FESTIVAL. July-August, Lewiston State Art Park. Contact: Travel Bureau, New York Department of Commerce, 99 Washington Avenue, Albany, New York 12210.

The festival offers fifty different events of a widely varying nature, including musicals, operas, concerts and ballets.

★ 3246 ★
New York - AMERICAN FOLK-SONG FESTIVAL. Mid March, annual, 1 day, Cooper Union Great Hall. Contact: Oscar Brand, WNYC, Municipal Building, New York, New York 10007.

Traditional folk music including spirituals, hymns, sea chanties, and ballads from different nations. May also include country rock or other types of music. Begun around 1947.

★ 3247 ★
New York - BLUEGRASS AND OLD-TIME COUNTRY MUSIC BAND CONTEST AND CRAFTS FAIR. Early August, annual, 2 days, South Street Seaport. Contact: Douglas Tuchman, Bluegrass Club of New York, Box 1B, 417 East 89th Street, New York, New York 10028.

Traditional American country and bluegrass music. Prize money is awarded for the best amateur performance at the fair. Concerts and workshops. The crafts fair consists basically of handcrafts. Begun around 1973.

★ 3248 ★
New York - FESTIVAL OF CONTEMPORARY MUSIC. March, 2 weeks. Contact: New York Convention and Visitors Bureau, Incorporated, 90 East 42nd Street, New York, New York 10017; or Chamber of Commerce and Industry, 65 Liberty Street, New York, New York 10005.

A festival of performances of contemporary music.

★ 3249 ★
New York - GUGGENHEIM MEMORIAL CONCERTS. Late June-mid August, Central Park Mall, Prospect Park Music Grove, and Damrosch Park at Lincoln Center. Contact: Guggenheim Memorial Concerts, 635 Madison Avenue, Suite 800, New York, New York 10022.

The Goldman Band in performances at various city parks.

★ 3250 ★
New York - INTERNATIONAL BACH SOCIETY FESTIVAL. July, annual, Library-Museum, Lincoln Center. Contact: International Bach Society Festival, 140 West 57th Street, New York, New York 10019.

A series of recitals and lectures on the music of Bach.

★ 3251 ★
New York - JAZZ IN THE GARDENS. Mid June to mid August, annual, Museum of Modern Art. Contact: Jazz in the Garden, Museum of Modern Art, 11 West 53rd Street, New York, New York 10019.

Series of ten concerts presented in the museum's Sculpture Garden. Audience stands or sits on the ground; beer and sandwiches are available. Includes performers who have attempted to merge the styles of jazz and rock. Begun in 1960.

★ 3252 ★
New York - LINCOLN CENTER'S MID-SUMMER SERENADES. August, annual, 24 evenings, Philharmonic Hall. Contact: Lincoln Center's Mid-Summer Serenades, Philharmonic Hall, Lincoln Center, Broadway at 65th Street, New York, New York 10023.

This summer concert series has had several subnames: Mozart Festival, A Mozart and Haydn Festival, and A Mostly Mozart Festival. A concert every night from Monday through Saturday. The programs offer orchestral works, chamber music, choral works, opera, and recitals, primarily devoted to the music of Mozart. An unusually large roster of conductors, soloists, and chamber groups, along with the great number and variety of works performed, have made the festival one of the most popular. Begun in 1966.

★ 3253 ★
New York - MAY FESTIVAL OF CONTEMPORARY AMERICAN MUSIC. May, annual, Composers Theatre. Contact: May Festival of Contemporary American Music, Composers Theatre, 25 West 19th

Music

NEW YORK (Continued)

Street, New York, New York 10011.

The festival orchestra plays works by contemporary American composers representing a variety of styles. The pieces include twentieth century chamber music, new and experimental music, orchestral music, and electronic music.

★ 3254 ★
New York - METROPOLITAN OPERA FREE SUMMER-CONCERTS. June-July, annual, the parks of the five boroughs of New York City. Contact: Metropolitan Opera Free Summer Concerts, c/o Metropolitan Opera, Lincoln Center Plaza, New York, New York 10023.

The operas are presented in concert form and are performed by top metropolitan artists supported by full chorus and orchestra. Begun in 1967.

★ 3255 ★
New York - NATIONAL JEWISH MUSIC FESTIVAL. March-April, annual. Contact: Jewish Music Festival, National Jewish Music Council, 15 East 26th Street, New York, New York 10010.

The Jewish Music Council encourages a nationwide celebration of Jewish Music Month (lasting from Purim to Passover) through commissioned projects, concerts, lectures, and displays.

★ 3256 ★
New York - NAUMBURG ORCHESTRAL CONCERTS. Late May (Memorial Day), July and September, annual, 1 day each time, Central Park on the Mall. Contact: Naumburg Orchestral Concerts, c/o 175 West 93rd Street, New York, New York 10025.

The Naumburg Concerts are also offered on Independence Day, July 31, and Labor Day of each year and are free to the public. The featured ensemble is a 48-piece symphony orchestra which plays under guest conductors. Instrumental and vocal soloists also appear. The programs include concertos and orchestral works, opera in concert form, and generally a work by a contemporary American composer. Started in 1905.

★ 3257 ★
New York - NEW YORK MUSICIANS JAZZ FESTIVAL. June, annual, 1 week. Contact: Director, New York Musicians Jazz Festival, 193 Eldridge Street, New York, New York 10002.

Professional jazz ensembles perform and get together for mutual benefit and to entertain.

★ 3258 ★
New York - NEW YORK PHILHARMONIC PARK CONCERTS. Early August to early September, annual. Contact: New York Philharmonic Park Concerts, New York City Parks, Recreation and Cultural Affairs Administration, 830 Fifth Avenue, New York, New York 10021.

A series of free concerts offered in the parks of the five boroughs of New York City. The programs have a balance of orchestral works and music requiring instrumental soloists with orchestra - usually concertos. Begun in 1965.

★ 3259 ★
New York - NEWPORT JAZZ FESTIVAL. Late June-early July, annual, 10 days. Contact: Newport Jazz Festival, Post Office Box 1169, Ansonia Station, New York, New York 10023.

Indoor and outdoor concerts performed by top jazz musicians from around the nation. Styles of jazz include Dixieland, ragtime, postwar modernism, swing, bop, electronic, African, Latin, and European. Probably the most famous jazz event anywhere in the world, the festival is noted for its array of great talent. Moved to New York City in 1972, formerly held in Newport, Rhode Island - since 1954.

★ 3260 ★
New York - PROMENADE CONCERTS. May and June, annual, Tuesday through Saturday evenings, Philharmonic Hall in Lincoln Center. Contact: Promenade Concerts, Philharmonic Hall, Lincoln Center, Broadway at 65th Street, New York, New York 10023.

Concerts by New York Philharmonic. Orchestra floor converted to area with tables and chairs; beverages sold before concerts and during intermissions.

★ 3261 ★
New York - SCHAEFER MUSIC FESTIVAL IN CENTRAL PARK. Late June to late August, annual, Wollman Memorial Skating Rink Theater in Central Park. Contact: Schaefer Music Festival in Central Park, 27 East 67th Street, New York, New York 10016.

A summer event featuring many categories of popular music and famous performers. Begun in 1966.

NEW YORK (Continued)

★ 3262 ★
New York - SEAPORT DAY FESTIVAL. Early June (1st Saturday), annual, 1 day, South Street Seaport Museum. Contact: New York Pinewoods Folk Music Club, 55 Christopher Street, New York, New York 10014.

An afternoon and evening concert. The afternoon concert consists of performances mainly by members of the New York Pinewoods Folk Music Club; better known performers at the evening concert. Both concerts are outdoors. Started in 1970.

★ 3263 ★
New York - STUDIO RIVBEA SUMMER MUSIC FESTIVAL. June and July, annual. Contact: The Director, Studio Rivbea Summer Music Festival, 24 Bond Street, New York, New York 10012.

Student and professional ensembles perform jazz, new and experimental music.

★ 3264 ★
New York - WEST DOOR CONCERTS. Early July to mid August, annual, Cathedral of Saint John the Divine. Contact: West Door Concerts, Cathedral of Saint John the Divine, 1047 Amsterdam Avenue, New York, New York 10025.

Concerts take place in the cathedral on Sunday afternoons. The programs feature solo performers and chamber groups in performances of a wide range of music, and also features famous guest artists. Begun in 1965.

★ 3265 ★
Pawling - JULY MUSIC FESTIVAL. July, annual, Auditorium of Lathrop Memorial Building. Contact: July Music Festival, c/o Pawling Fine Arts Council, Taber Knolls, Pawling, New York 12564.

The Monteux Quartet performs mainly Baroque trio sonatas as well as other works using the Quartet's combination of instruments. The Monteux Chamber Players, an ensemble of 12 strings, is featured at one of the concerts. Founded in 1968.

★ 3266 ★
Petersburg - FOX HOLLOW LODGE STRING BAND FESTIVAL. Late August-early September (Labor Day weekend), 2 days, Fox Hollow Lodge. Contact: Fox Hollow Lodge String Band Festival, Fox Hollow, Petersburg, New York 12138; or Arnold S. Caplin,

16 River Street, Chatham, New York 12037.

Demonstrations and concerts by musicians representing a cross section of the varied tradition of string band music. In addition, there is contra dancing, craft demonstrations and exhibitions, workshops, song swaps, and jam sessions.

★ 3267 ★
Port Jervis - SUMMER OPERA FESTIVAL. July and August, annual, auditorium of the Port Jervis High School. Contact: Port Jervis Summer Opera Festival, c/o Lyric Arts Opera, Box 323, Milford, Pennsylvania 18337.

Port Jervis, New York, is located some eight miles northwest of Milford, Pennsylvania, at a point where the states of New York, New Jersey, and Pennsylvania meet. The operas are those from the standard French, German, and Italian repertory. The performances are sung to piano accompaniment. Founded in 1966.

★ 3268 ★
Rochester - ALL HIGH MUSIC FESTIVAL. Early June, annual, Highland Park. Contact: Gannett Rochester Newspapers, Public Service Department, 55 Exchange Street, Rochester, New York 14614.

Features massed choral groups and/or high school bands drawn from throughout the county.

★ 3269 ★
Rochester - TOURNAMENT OF DRUMS. Late June (last weekend), annual, Aquinas Stadium. Contact: United Drum Corps, 556 Westfield Street, Rochester, New York 14619.

Drum and bugle corps competition is the featured event in this festival.

★ 3270 ★
Saratoga Springs - SARATOGA FESTIVAL. Mid June-early September, annual, 8 weeks. Contact: Saratoga Festival, Box B, Saratoga Springs, New York 12866.

A summer home for two of America's major performing groups: the Philadelphia Orchestra and the New York City Ballet. Public concerts, educational programs such as choreographers' workshops, seminars for teachers, and special student and teacher matinee orchestra and ballet performances. Popular music groups and soloists. All guest performers, conductors, and groups are drawn invariably from the highest levels of the popular and classical music fields. Begun in 1966.

Music

NEW YORK (Continued)

★ 3271 ★
Saratoga Springs - SARATOGA PERFORMING ARTS
FESTIVAL. June-August (Summer), annual, Saratoga
Performing Arts Center. Contact: Saratoga Per-
forming Arts Festival, Saratoga Performing Arts Center,
Saratoga Springs, New York 12866.

Professional ensembles play chamber music, jazz,
orchestral music, ballet and popular music.

★ 3272 ★
Scarsdale - SUMMER OF MUSIC IN WESTCHESTER.
July and August, annual, Manhattanville College in
Purchase. Contact: Summer of Music in West-
chester, Post Office Box 333, Scarsdale, New York
10583.

Concerts on Saturday evenings, presented by the
Orchestral Society of Westchester.

★ 3273 ★
Schroon Lake - ADIRONDACK/CHAMPLAIN MUSIC
FESTIVAL. July and August, annual, Saranac Lake,
Lake Placid, Schroon Lake. Contact: Adirondack/
Champlain Music Festival, Schroon Lake, New York
12870.

Orchestral and chamber concerts; guest orchestras,
conductors, and soloists.

★ 3274 ★
Southampton - SOUTHAMPTON MUSIC FESTIVAL.
Late June-late August, annual, Fine Arts Theater
on the campus of Southampton College. Contact:
Southampton Music Festival, c/o Southampton College
of Long Island University, Southampton, New York
11968.

A series of chamber music concerts, held in the Fine
Arts Theater on the campus of Southampton College.
The concerts are held in conjunction with the summer
school (Some free events, such as lectures and
recitals, are also presented during the summer season.)
Begun in 1964.

★ 3275 ★
Stony Brook - STONY BROOK MUSIC FESTIVAL.
July, annual, Dogwood Hollow Amphitheatre. Con-
tact: Stony Brook Music Festival, Stony Brook, Long
Island, New York 11790.

The series consists of six concerts on Saturday evenings,
featuring famous guest artists. Established in 1953.

★ 3276 ★
Syracuse - SYRACUSE SUMMER CONCERTS. July,
annual, Crouse Auditorium of Syracuse University.
Contact: Syracuse Summer Concerts, Crouse Auditorium,
Syracuse University, Syracuse, New York 13210.

Series of chamber music and piano concerts at Crouse
Auditorium.

★ 3277 ★
Woodstock - CREATIVE MUSIC FESTIVAL. June,
annual. Contact: Creative Music Festival, Dr.
Karl Hans Berger, Post Office Box 671, Woodstock,
New York 12498.

Student and professional ensembles perform new and
experimental music and jazz.

★ 3278 ★
Woodstock - MAVERICK CONCERTS. July to
Labor Day, annual, Maverick Theater. Contact:
Maverick Concerts, Box 655, Maverick Road, Wood-
stock, New York 12498.

Heavily wooded area providing a completely rustic
atmosphere and extraordinary acoustical qualities.
Chamber music is the mainstay of the programs ranging
from the traditional instrumental combinations for the
performance of duos, trios, quartets, etc., to the
mixed groups needed for contemporary music. Established in 1916.

NORTH CAROLINA

★ 3279 ★
Angier - EASTERN NORTH CAROLINA BLUEGRASS
FESTIVAL. Early October, annual, 3 days. Contact: Chamber of Commerce, Angier, North Carolina
27501; or Travel Development Section, Department
of Natural and Economic Resources, Raleigh, North
Carolina 27611.

Traditional American music played on traditional and
modern instruments by groups, soloists, etc. Begun
in 1975.

★ 3280 ★
Asheville - HUBERT HAYES MOUNTAIN YOUTH
JAMBOREE. April, annual, 4 days, Asheville City
Auditorium. Contact: Hubert Hayes, Mountain
Youth Jamboree, 30 Maney Avenue, Asheville, North
Carolina 28804.

The jamboree's prime purpose is to present pure folk
music and dancing by means of competition among

young participants, generally those in school grades one to twelve, and noncompetitive exhibitions. Under the program theme of Folklore Dancing, Singing, Music Makin'-Pickin, the young performers, who over the years have come from nine states, compete for the various championships in smooth square dance, western square, clog dance, and the dances of other countries. Founded in 1948.

★ 3281 ★
Asheville - MOUNTAIN DANCE AND FOLK FESTIVAL. Early August (1st week), annual, 3 days, City Auditorium. Contact: Asheville Area Chamber of Commerce, Post Office Box 1011, Asheville, North Carolina 28802.

Exhibition of folk dancing and singing by people from the Smoky and Blue Ridge Mountains. Events include square dancing, buck dancing, mouth-harp, banjo and fiddle playing, and folk singing. Prizes are awarded. Started in 1928.

★ 3282 ★
Asheville - SHINDIG ON THE GREEN (MOUNTAIN FOLK FAIR). Early July-early September, annual, 2 months (every Saturday), City-County Plaza. Contact: Chamber of Commerce, Post Office Box 1011, Asheville, North Carolina 28802.

Clog and square dancing in the open air to the tunes of southern Appalachian music and ballads. The audience is invited to participate.

★ 3283 ★
Brevard - BREVARD MUSIC FESTIVAL. July to mid August, annual, 6 weeks, Brevard Music Center. Contact: Brevard Music Festival, Box 592, Brevard, North Carolina 28712.

The festival is an important part of the summer activities of the Brevard Music Center. Young, new professionals are often engaged. There are numerous performing ensembles at Brevard. In addition to the main performing group, the Brevard Music Center Orchestra, there are the various groups of the Transylvania Music Camp: the Youth Orchestra, Wind Ensemble, Symphony Orchestra, Concert Band, and Chorus; opera productions are staged by the Brevard Opera Workshop. Established in 1936.

★ 3284 ★
Buies Creek - CITY-SPIRIT - 18TH CENTURY MUSIC FESTIVAL. Late March, 1 day, Campbell College.

Contact: Anne Moore, Project Director, Campbell College, Buies Creek, North Carolina 27506.

A presentation of the music of the 1700's in a one day festival.

★ 3285 ★
Camp Springs - BLUEGRASS AND OLD TIME MUSIC FESTIVAL. May, annual, 3 days, Bluegrass (Blue Grass) Park. Contact: Carlton Haney, Box 7A, Ruffin, North Carolina 27326.

Bluegrass musicians and old time fiddlers turn out to promote and preserve their traditional music. Begun in 1974.

★ 3286 ★
Cary - CARY BAND DAY. Mid November (2nd Saturday), annual, 1 day. Contact: President, Cary Band Boosters, Post Office Box 91, Cary, North Carolina 27511.

Parade and field competition for outstanding bands from the eastern seaboard states. Nationally recognized judges officiate. Started in 1958.

★ 3287 ★
Charlotte - FESTIVAL OF MUSIC. Early April, annual, 8 days, Freedom Park. Contact: Chairman, Festival of Music in Freedom Park with High School Bands, 308 East Fifth Street, Charlotte, North Carolina 28202.

High school band performances highlight this festival.

★ 3288 ★
Davidson - SACRED MUSIC CONVOCATION. October (late Fall), annual, 2 days, Davidson College. Contact: Director of Music, Davidson College Music Department, Davidson College, Davidson, North Carolina 28036.

The purpose of the convocation is to give educators, church musicians, clergy and laity a chance to appraise and study religious music. Events include addresses, master classes on various aspects of the music, and recitals by organ and choir. Started in 1960.

★ 3289 ★
Elon College - ELON COLLEGE MUSIC FESTIVAL. July and August, annual, Elon College campus. Contact: Elon College Music Festival, Box 2159, Elon College, North Carolina 27244.

Music

NORTH CAROLINA (Continued)

Orchestral and chamber music concerts, recitals.

★ 3290 ★
Greensboro - EASTERN MUSIC FESTIVAL.   Late
June-early August, annual, 6 weeks, Guilford College.
Contact: Eastern Music Festival, Guilford College,
712 Summit Avenue, Greensboro, North Carolina
27405.

Musicians gathered for a summer institute present
nightly concerts (except on Sundays) of symphonies,
chamber music and contemporary music.   The Eastern
Philharmonic Orchestra is the prime performing ensemble of the festival and is made up of professional
musicians from the major symphonic units as well as
leading music institutions.   Established in 1962.

★ 3291 ★
Linville - SINGING ON THE MOUNTAIN (FOLK
AND FOLK SONG FESTIVAL).   Late June (last
Sunday), annual, 1 day, Grandfather Mountain
(MacRae Meadow).   Contact: Folk and Folk Song
Festival, Grandfather Mountain, Linville, North
Carolina 28646.

The day is a religious event with gospel singing and
preaching.   Many of the participants picnic on the
mountain.   Well known entertainers have participated
in the past in the renowned musical program.   Started
around 1924.

★ 3292 ★
Louisburg - FOLK MUSIC FESTIVAL.   Late March,
annual, 1 day, Louisburg College.   Contact: Allen
De Hart, Louisburg College, Louisburg, North Caroline   27549.

Presents traditional American music and dancing, with
competitions and awards in bluegrass and folk.

★ 3293 ★
Morgantown - PLAYMORE BEACH FIDDLERS
CONVENTION.   Mid September, annual, 3 days,
Playmore Beach.   Contact: Elbert Phillips, Route 5,
Box 717, Morgantown, North Carolina 28655.

Fiddlers' Convention, bluegrass music, and dancing
just outside Morgantown and near Lenoir.   Begun
around 1971.

★ 3294 ★
Mount Airy - OLD TIME FIDDLERS AND BLUEGRASS

CONVENTION.   Mid September, 1 day.   Contact:
Old Time Fiddlers and Bluegrass Convention, Post
Office Box 161, Route 9, Mount Airy, North Caro-
lina 27030.

Fiddle contest, traditional American music, traditional
dancing.

★ 3295 ★
Murphy - CLOGGING AND COUNTRY AND
BLUEGRASS MUSIC FESTIVAL.   Early June, 5 days.
Contact: Cherokee County Chamber of Commerce,
Murphy, North Carolina 28906.

A variety of old time and country music and dancing
(mountain style).

★ 3296 ★
Terrell - LAKE NORMAN FIDDLERS CONVENTION
AND BUCK DANCE CONTEST.   Late November
(Thanksgiving night), annual, 1 day, Lake Norman
Music Hall.   Contact: Mrs. Pauline Lawing, Lake
Norman Music Hall Manager, Post Office Box 326,
Terrell, North Carolina 28682.

Competition for bluegrass and old time bands, solo
guitar, banjo, fiddle, and mandolin.   Hog calling,
tall tales stories, and buck dancing contests are also
held.

★ 3297 ★
Union Grove - OLD TIME FIDDLERS CONVENTION.
Early April, annual, 2-3 days.   Contact: Annual
Old Time Fiddlers' Convention, Post Office Box 38,
Union Grove, North Carolina 28689.

The convention provides a popular form of entertainment and at the same time, raises money for the
Union Grove School.   Performers from throughout
the United States, Mexico, and Canada compete in
old time, bluegrass, and country music groups for
trophies, ribbons, and cash prizes.   The musical
emphasis is on authentic "old time" country music.
Organized in 1924.

★ 3298 ★
Winston-Salem - EARLY AMERICAN MORAVIAN
MUSIC FESTIVAL.   Mid June, biennial, 1 week.
Contact: Early American Moravian Music Festival,
Salem College, Winston Salem, North Carolina
27108.

The festivals are all under the auspices of the Moravian
Music Foundation and have as their fundamental theme
the presentation, often as first modern performances, of

NORTH CAROLINA   (Continued)

the music of the early American Moravians.   The festival programs combine chamber music with evenings of works in larger forms, organ recitals, concerts for chorus and orchestra, and seminars.   Founded in 1950.

NORTH DAKOTA

★ 3299 ★
Dunseith - INTERNATIONAL MUSIC FESTIVAL. June-August, annual, 50 days, International Peace Gardens.   Contact: Dr. Merton Utgaard, Director, International Music Camp, Bottineau, North Dakota 58318.

A cooperative arts festival between North Dakota and Manitoba, and held on the border, with students from all over the world participating in workshops and concerts in 14 different art forms, including bands, orchestras, choirs, drama and baton.   Begun in 1957.

★ 3300 ★
Dunseith - INTERNATIONAL YOUTH BAND FESTIVAL. July, 23 days, International Peace Garden.   Contact: Dr. Merton Utgaard, Director, International Music Camp, Bottineau, North Dakota 58318.

Free outdoor concerts performed by young musicians from all over the world.   Held on the United States/ Canada border between North Dakota and Manitoba.

OHIO

★ 3301 ★
Berea - BACH FESTIVAL.   Late May, 2 days, annual, Fanny Nast Gamble Auditorium in the Kulas Musical Arts Building, Baldwin-Wallace College. Contact: Bach Festival, Baldwin-Wallace College, Berea, Ohio 44017.

Although the music of Bach is the focal point of this annual event, works by composers contemporary to Bach are sometimes performed.   Festival Brass Choir performs a group of chorales from the tower of the college's Marting Hall.   A large chorus performs. Vocal soloists are usually professionals.   Established in 1933.

★ 3302 ★
Cincinnati - CINCINNATI MAY FESTIVAL.   May, annual, Cincinnati Music Hall.   Contact: Cincinnati May Festival, Cincinnati Music Hall, Cincinnati, Ohio 45210.

The essence of the festival lies in performances of works for chorus and orchestra.   The Cincinnati Symphony Orchestra under major guest conductors shares the festival with the May Festival Chorus, which often combines with adult and children voices from a variety of nearby colleges, seminaries, and junior and senior high schools.   Guest conductors. Founded in 1973.

★ 3303 ★
Cincinnati - COLLEGE CONSERVATORY JAZZ FESTIVAL.   February, annual, 2 days, campus of University of Cincinnati.   Contact: College Conservatory Jazz Festival, College Conservatory of Music, University of Cincinnati, Cincinnati, Ohio 45221.

The University of Cincinnati hosts this two day festival of jazz music.

★ 3304 ★
Cincinnati - OHIO VALLEY KOOL JAZZ FESTIVAL. Late July, annual, 2 days, Riverfront Stadium. Contact: The Kool Jazz Festivals, 3522 Erie Avenue, Cincinnati, Ohio 45208.

Some of the top names in jazz and soul music come to participate in this event.   Begun around 1960.

★ 3305 ★
Cincinnati - SUMMER OPERA FESTIVAL.   June to July, annual, 4-5 weeks, Music Hall.   Contact: Cincinnati Summer Opera Festival, 1241 Elm Street, Cincinnati, Ohio 45210.

The emphasis is on performances of the well-known works in the operatic repertory.   The productions are fully staged and feature singers from the front ranks of the operatic world.   Founded in 1920.

★ 3306 ★
Cleveland - MAY FESTIVAL OF CONTEMPORARY MUSIC.   May, annual, 4 days, Cleveland Museum Auditorium.   Contact: May Festival of Contemporary Music, The Cleveland Museum of Art, 1150 East Boulevard, Cleveland, Ohio 44106.

The contemporary music is of great variety, offering works by composers throughout the world and calling for ensembles and soloists of all kinds.   Each festival contains a program of music by Cleveland area composers.   Founded in 1959.

Music

OHIO (Continued)

★ 3307 ★
Cleveland - SUMMER POPS CONCERTS.   June to
July, annual, 4 weeks, Public Auditorium.   Contact:
Cleveland Summer Pops Concerts, c/o The Cleveland
Orchestra, Severance Hall, Cleveland, Ohio 44106.

The Pops Concerts features the Cleveland Orchestra;
consists of about 14 concerts programming classical
music, show tunes, and some jazz.

★ 3308 ★
Coshocton - DULCIMER DAYS.   Late May, annual,
2 days, Roscoe Village.   Contact: Mrs. Pat Brown,
Public Relations, 381 Hill Street, Coshocton, Ohio
43812.

The festival features a dulcimer contest and a fashion
show of the clothing of the 1800's.   Started in
1975.

★ 3309 ★
Cuyahoga Falls - BLOSSOM MUSIC FESTIVAL.   Late
June to early September, annual, 6 weeks, Blossom
Music Center.   Contact: Blossom Music Festival,
1145 West Steel's Corner Road, Northampton Town-
ship, Cuyahoga Falls, Ohio 44223.

Summer home of the Cleveland Orchestra;   guest
composers, and professional artists or teachers.
Guest conductors.   Soloists include well-known
instrumental and vocal stars.   The traditionally
styled programs give way to a series of pops concerts and ballet performances.   Also children's
matinees, a jazz-folk series, outdoor art exhibitions,
and art lectures.   Founded in 1968.

★ 3310 ★
Lakeside - GREAT COMPOSERS FESTIVAL.   July-
August, annual, 6 weeks, Hoover Auditorium.   Con-
tact: Great Composers Festival, c/o Lakeside Summer
Symphony Orchestra, Lakeside, Ohio 43440.

Programs consist of symphony concerts, chamber music,
opera, and choral works.   Begun in 1963.

★ 3311 ★
Oberlin - FESTIVAL OF CONTEMPORARY MUSIC.
May (Spring), 4 days.   Contact: Festival of Con-
temporary Music, Oberlin Conservatory of Music,
Oberlin College, Oberlin, Ohio 44074.

The festival is a series of concerts devoted to music
of the last decade with the goal of increasing the

number and improving the quality of new music performances on Oberlin's campus.   Forums, lectures,
and other talk formats are an integral part of the
festival.   Begun in 1951.   Also held in the fall

★ 3312 ★
Ottawa - HILLBROOK MUSIC FESTIVAL.   August-
September (Labor Day weekend), 3 days, Hillbrook
Recreation Area.   Contact: Henry J. Vernoff,
Post Office Box 257, Ottawa, Ohio 45875.

Bluegrass, country music, and polkas are featured at
this gala festival of American and ethnic music.

★ 3313 ★
Ottawa - HILLBROOK NATIONAL VAN FESTIVAL.
July, 3 days, Hillbrook Recreation Area.   Contact:
Hillbrook Recreation, Department M-5 Box 257,
Ottawa, Ohio 45875.

Traditional American music including country music
bands and old time fiddlers.

★ 3314 ★
Ottawa - OHIO NATIONAL BLUEGRASS FESTIVAL.
Early August, annual, 3 days, Hillbrook Recreation
Area.   Contact: Henry J. Verhoff, Box 257,
Ottawa, Ohio 45875.

Bluegrass music performed by some of the top musicians
in the field.   Begun around 1971.

★ 3315 ★
Ottawa - SPRING BLUEGRASS REUNION.   Late
April-early May, annual, 3 days, Hillbrook Recrea-
tion Area.   Contact: Hillbrook Recreation, Post
Office Box 257, Ottawa, Ohio 45875.

A festival of bluegrass music, with both indoor and
outdoor events.   Begun around 1973.

OKLAHOMA

★ 3316 ★
Edmond - CENTRAL STATE MUSIC FESTIVAL.
November, annual, Central State College.   Con-
tact: Central State Music Festival, Central State
College, Edmond, Oklahoma 73034.

Orchestral and choral concerts are held.

★ 3317 ★
Enid - TRI-STATE MUSIC FESTIVAL.   Early May,

OKLAHOMA (Continued)

annual, 1 weekend.   Contact: Tri-State Music
Festival, Box 2068, University Station, Enid,
Oklahoma 73701.

Primarily a competitive festival for high school solo
musicians and musical groups and is one of the largest
of its kind in the United States and the largest in the
southwest.   In recent years, over 12,000 high school
students have participated in each festival.   Professional musicians, composers, arrangers, conductors,
adjudicators, and music educators are engaged to
direct the various activities including rehearsals,
clinics, concerts, and so forth.   Begun in 1933.

★ 3318 ★
Hugo - BLUEGRASS AND OLD TIME MUSIC
FESTIVAL.   Early August, annual, 5 days, Salt
Creek Park.   Contact: Bluegrass and Old Time
Music Festival, Route 2, Box 11-K, Hugo, Oklahoma
74743.

Honors traditional American music with professional
concerts, plus contests for fiddle, bands, banjo,
junior banjo, mandolin, junior mandolin, guitar
and dobro.

★ 3319 ★
Langley - BLUEGRASS FESTIVAL AND OLD TIME
FIDDLERS AND BAND CONTEST.   Early July,
annual, 3 days, Powderhorn Park.   Contact: Royce
Cambell, Post Office Box 291, Langley, Oklahoma
74350; or Powderhorn Park, Post Office Box 85,
Langley, Oklahoma 74350.

Traditional American music, old-time and bluegrass,
fiddle and band concerts, and contests.   Begun in
1974 by Byron Berline.

★ 3320 ★
Tahlequah - FIDDLERS FESTIVAL.   February, 2 days,
Northeastern Oklahoma State University.   Contact:
The American Fiddlers News, 6141 Morrill Avenue,
Lincoln, Nebraska 68507.

Old time fiddling and other country and bluegrass
music.

OREGON

★ 3321 ★
Forest Grove - MUSIC IN MAY.   Mid May, annual,
1 weekend, Forest Grove Union High School Gymnasium.   Contact: Music In May, Pacific University

School of Music, Forest Grove, Oregon 94116.

The festival is a means of encouraging musical accomplishment in the public schools of the Pacific Northwest.   Students from Oregon, Washington, Idaho,
and California are drawn from the top five percent
of the total membership of the public school music
organizations.   Performing groups - band, chorus,
and orchestra.   Guest conductors.   Begun in 1947.

★ 3322 ★
Portland - CHAMBER MUSIC NORTHWEST FESTIVAL.
June-July (Summer), annual.   Contact: Chamber
Music Northwest Festival, c/o Concert Manager, Reed
College Commons, Post Office Box 751, Portland,
Oregon 97207.

Professional ensembles perform 14 concerts featuring
a resident composer of twentieth century chamber
music, new or experimental music.

PENNSYLVANIA

★ 3323 ★
Abbottstown - INDIAN SUMMER BLUEGRASS AND
FIDDLERS FESTIVAL.   September, annual, 3 days,
Adams County Fairgrounds.   Contact: Jim Clark,
Post Office Box 186, Fairfax, Virginia 22030.

Festival events include bluegrass, fiddle convention,
workshops and concerts.   Begun around 1973.

★ 3324 ★
Allentown - FESTIVAL OF THE COLONIES BANDS
COMPETITION.   Mid June, annual, 4 days, Allen-
town Fairgrounds and Allentown School District Stadium.
Contact: Department of Commerce, Bureau of Travel
Development, 431 South Office Building, Harrisburg,
Pennsylvania 17120.

Brings together one outstanding high school band from
each of the original thirteen states, in a competition
covering all phases of music education: concert, sight
reading, street marching, inspection, and field show.
Twelve Lehigh County School bands participate and
serve as hosts to the competing bands.   U.S. Navy
Band is present for opening ceremonies at the Allentown Fairgrounds.   National Service Band is present
for closing ceremonies.

★ 3325 ★
Bethlehem - BETHLEHEM BACH FESTIVAL.   Mid
May (2nd and 3rd weekend), annual, Packer Memorial
Chapel on the campus of Lehigh University.   Con-
tact: Bethlehem Bach Festival, Main and Church

Music

PENNSYLVANIA (Continued)

Street, Bethlehem, Pennsylvania 18018.

Festival features the larger Bach choral works. The program format includes both choral and instrumental works of Johann Sebastian Bach. Noted solo singers are engaged for the festival.

★ 3326 ★
Concordville - BRANDYWINE MOUNTAIN MUSIC CONVENTION. Late July (last weekend), annual, 2 days, Nathanial Newlin Grist Mill. Contact: The Brandywine Friends of Old Time Music, Box 3504, Greenville, Delaware 19807.

Traditional mountain music - different area of the country emphasized each year in concerts and jam sessions. Concessions, camping, craft show and instrument displays complete the events.

★ 3327 ★
Doylestown - MUSIC FESTIVAL. Mid May, 3 days. Contact: Department of Commerce, Bureau of Travel Development, 431 South Office Building, Harrisburg, Pennsylvania 17120.

Band competition and concerts with local and visiting groups competing.

★ 3328 ★
Philadelphia - GERMAN-AMERICAN CHORAL FESTIVAL. Late May, annual, 3 days, Ben Franklin Hotel. Contact: Department of Commerce, Bureau of Travel Development, 431 South Office Building, Harrisburg, Pennsylvania 17120.

Includes memorial concert, Independence Mall.

★ 3329 ★
Philadelphia - ROBIN HOOD DELL CONCERTS. Mid June to July, annual, 6 weeks. Contact: Robin Hood Dell Concerts, Incorporated, 1617 John F. Kennedy Boulevard, Philadelphia, Pennsylvania 19103.

A series of free evening performances. The Philadelphia Orchestra is the heart of these concerts and performs under a number of well-known guest conductors as well as the Music Director. Morning children's concerts. The programs consist primarily of symphonic music, works for solo instrument and orchestra, and solo voice with orchestra. Founded in 1930.

★ 3330 ★
Philadelphia - TEMPLE UNIVERSITY MUSIC FESTIVAL. Late June-early July, annual. Contact: Temple University Music Festival, 1949 North Broad Street, Philadelphia, Pennsylvania 19122.

The festival attempts to offer the highest possible level of combined instruction and performance. Major ensemble in-residence is the Pittsburgh Symphony Orchestra. Concerts including, besides the faculty recitals and the orchestral concerts of the Pittsburgh Symphony, pops concerts with the orchestra and guest conductors. Pennsylvania Ballet Company; Pittsburgh Chamber Orchestra; and other guest ensembles. Evenings often feature performers from the world of jazz or popular music. First held in 1968.

★ 3331 ★
Shartlesville - BLUEGRASS FESTIVAL. Mid September, annual, 3 days, Mountain Springs Camping Resort. Contact: Department of Commerce, Bureau of International Development, 431 South Office Building, Harrisburg, Pennsylvania 17120.

Music, camping, and fun for the entire family. Begun in 1975.

RHODE ISLAND

★ 3332 ★
Escoheag - NEW ENGLAND BLUEGRASS MUSIC FESTIVAL. Late August, 3 days, Stepping Stone Stables. Contact: Rhode Island Department of Economic Development, Tourist Promotion Division, One Weybosset Hill, Providence, Rhode Island 02903.

A gathering of musicians and music lovers, fiddlers, singers, etc., for three days of bluegrass music.

★ 3333 ★
Escoheag - NORTHEAST BLUEGRASS AND FOLK AND FIDDLERS FESTIVAL. June, annual, 3-4 days, Stepping Stone Ranch. Contact: Jim Clark, Post Office Box 186, Fairfax, Virginia 22030.

The festival offers traditional American music, bluegrass, and country blues. Begun around 1973.

★ 3334 ★
Newport - NEWPORT MUSIC FESTIVAL. July-August, annual. Contact: Newport Music Festival, 23 Bridge Street, Newport, Rhode Island 02840.

This festival contains many unusual elements. Three

RHODE ISLAND (Continued)

of Newport's famed mansions are made available for musical performances all providing sumptuous settings for musical programs consisting exclusively of works from the Romantic era. Chamber music, song recitals, and mixed vocal and instrumental music; chamber music and some opera performances; opera gala, a costume concert, ballet, etc.; band concerts; grand balloon regatta and ascension, and cruise concert. Film series, guest dancers, and instrumentalists.

★ 3335 ★
Pawtucket - DIAMOND HILL MUSIC FESTIVAL.
July (Summer), annual, Sunday afternoons, Diamond Hill State Park. Contact: Diamond Hill Music Festival, 150 Main Street, Pawtucket, Rhode Island 02860.

The program emphasis is on entertainment and to this end local popular music groups, concert bands, and some outside professional artists are engaged to provide music of the broadest possible appeal. Founded in 1962.

★ 3336 ★
Providence - JUNIOR CHOIR FESTIVAL. May, annual, First Universalist Church. Contact: Junior Choir Festival, First Universalist Church, 350 Washington Street, Providence, Rhode Island 02903.

Includes junior choirs from throughout Rhode Island in a gathering of melody and harmony.

★ 3337 ★
Providence - RHODE ISLAND BACH FESTIVAL.
Early May, annual, 3 days, Alumnae Hall on the campus of Pembroke College and Veterans Memorial Auditorium. Contact: Rhode Island Bach Festival, 93 Eddy Street, Providence, Rhode Island 02903.

The festival provides both instrumental and vocal music of Bach, performed with each annual event, attempting a balance of one large choral work with orchestra and vocal soloists, two or three cantatas, one or two instrumental concertos, and an orchestral suite. Founded in 1963.

SOUTH CAROLINA

★ 3338 ★
Beaufort - MUSIC FESTIVAL. Mid May, annual, 1 day, Beaufort Academy Auditorium. Contact: Mr. Robert Keller, Headmaster, Beaufort Academy, Beaufort, South Carolina 29902.

This music festival includes bands and choral groups from the academy.

★ 3339 ★
Beaufort SPRING MUSIC FESTIVAL. Early May, annual, 2 days, Beaufort Academy Auditorium. Contact: Headmaster, Beaufort Academy, Beaufort, South Carolina 29902.

This musical extravaganza highlights 250 children in dance and drama presented to the May Queen and her court.

★ 3340 ★
Columbia - COLUMBIA MUSIC FESTIVAL. July, annual, Town Auditorium. Contact: Columbia Music Festival, 1527 Senate Street, Columbia, South Carolina 29201.

Concerts - five performances, of fine music.

★ 3341 ★
Eutawville - COUNTRY AND WESTERN DAYS. Early August, annual, 2 days, Rocks Pond Campground. Contact: J. Rut Connors, Rock Ponds Campground, Eutawville, South Carolina 29048.

Bands from Nashville, Tennessee entertain in the country and western tradition.

★ 3342 ★
Eutawville - COUNTRY MUSIC DAYS. Mid June, annual, 1 day, Rocks Pond Campground. Contact: J. Rut Conners, Rock Pond Campground, Eutawville, South Carolina 29048.

Features bands from Nashville, Tennessee to delight the country music fans.

★ 3343 ★
Greenville - CHRISTIAN HIGH SCHOOL MUSIC FESTIVAL AND FORENSIC TOURNAMENT. Late February, annual, 3 days, Bob Jones University. Contact: Programs and Productions, Bob Jones University, Greenville, South Carolina 29614.

Held under the sponsorship of the University, a combination of musical events and speeches and debates.

★ 3344 ★
Greenville - FURMAN JAZZ FESTIVAL. Mid January, annual, 2 days, McAlister Auditorium, Furman University. Contact: Music Department,

Music

SOUTH CAROLINA (Continued)

Furman University, Greenville, South Carolina 29613.

Furman's jazz ensemble is host as various ensembles come together for two days of rehearsals leading up to a public concert.

★ 3345 ★
Greenville - FURMAN MUSIC FESTIVAL. Early May, annual, 8 days, Furman University. Contact: News Bureau, Furman University, Greenville, South Carolina 29613.

Music for eight days on the campus of Furman University.

★ 3346 ★
Myrtle Beach - SOUTH CAROLINA BLUEGRASS MUSIC FESTIVAL. Late November, annual, 4 days, Myrtle Beach Convention Center. Contact: Roy Martin, 105 Lakeview Drive, Chester, South Carolina 29706.

Program features top names in bluegrass. Begun around 1970.

★ 3347 ★
Spartanburg - BAROQUE/CONTEMPORARY FESTIVAL. February, annual, Converse College. Contact: Baroque/Contemporary Festival, Converse College, Spartanburg, South Carolina 29301.

A music festival featuring baroque and contemporary music.

★ 3348 ★
Spartanburg - FESTIVAL OF LESSONS AND CAROLS. Mid December, annual, 1 day, Twichell Auditorium at Converse College. Contact: Public Relations, Converse College, Spartanburg, South Carolina 29301.

The highlight of the Christmas season at the College, this is a program of song by individuals and groups at the College.

★ 3349 ★
Spartanburg - SPARTANBURG MUSIC FESTIVAL. Late April-early May, annual, Twichell Auditorium at Converse College. Contact: Spartanburg Music Festival, c/o The Music Foundation of Spartanburg, Incorporated, Box 1274, Spartanburg, South Carolina 29301.

The Spartanburg Symphony performs with featured soloists and the Converse College Opera Workshop usually performs one opera in English. Previously called the Converse College May Festival.

SOUTH DAKOTA

★ 3350 ★
Rapid City - DAKOTA DAYS BAND FESTIVAL. Late May-early June, annual, 3 days. Contact: Division of Tourism Development, State Office Building 2, Pierre, South Dakota 57501.

Participants include 50-60 bands from 12 states, and from Sweden, Norway, and Canada, plus a big name entertainer.

★ 3351 ★
Rapid City - INTERNATIONAL BAND FESTIVAL. Mid July, 3 days. Contact: David S. Bell, 428 1/2 Saint Joseph Street, Rapid City, South Dakota 57701.

This festival is designed to bring together bands not only from throughout the United States, but from the rest of the world as well for a series of concerts and contests.

★ 3352 ★
Vermillion - AMERICAN MUSIC FESTIVAL. Late April, 1 day. Contact: Division of Tourism Development, State Office Building 2, Pierre, South Dakota 57501.

Various periods in American musical history are celebrated in the music festival at the University of South Dakota Center for Fine Arts in Vermillion.

★ 3353 ★
Yankton - OLD TIME FIDDLERS CONTEST. October, annual, 3 days. Contact: Wilbur Foss, 2019 Douglas Street, Yankton, South Dakota 57078.

Invited fiddlers from all over the United States participate in the National Invitational Contest. Other events include a fiddlers' convention, a jamboree, and gospel singing.

TENNESSEE

★ 3354 ★
Bristol - BLUEGRASS AND OLD TIME MUSIC FESTIVAL. Mid May, annual, 2 days, Cherokee Bluegrass Park. Contact: Carl H. Pennington,

TENNESSEE (Continued)

540 New Bethel Road, Bristol, Virginia 24201.

Traditional American folklife with bluegrass and old time music, folk songs, and flat foot clog dancing. Contests for old time banjo, fiddle, dancing, and singing. The city of Bristol is on the Tennessee-Virginia border. Begun around 1972.

★ 3355 ★
Bristol - FALL BLUEGRASS AND OLD TIME MUSIC FESTIVAL. Mid September, annual, 2 days, Cherokee Bluegrass Park. Contact: Carl H. Pennington, 540 New Bethel Road, Bristol, Virginia 24201.

Traditional American folklife with bluegrass and old time music, folk songs, flat foot and clog dancing, apple butter and molasses making. Contests for music and dancing. The city of Bristol is on the Tennessee-Virginia border.

★ 3356 ★
Bristol - SOUTHEASTERN BAND FESTIVAL. Early October, annual, 1 day. Contact: Chamber of Commerce, Bristol, Tennessee 37620.

Bands from the area compete for honors and entertain the assembled fans.

★ 3357 ★
Church Hill - OLD TIME FIDDLING/BLUEGRASS FESTIVAL. May, annual, 2 days, Greenland Park. Contact: Vance Yeary, 214 Hulldale, Marion, Virginia 24354; or Tony Ellis, Post Office Box 213, Blountville, Tennessee 37617.

There are fiddlers and other contests and lots of bluegrass music. Begun in 1975.

★ 3358 ★
Cosby - STRING AWAKENING. Late March, 3 days. Contact: Jean and Lee Schilling, Post Office Box 8, Cosby, Tennessee 37722.

Workshops and concerts featuring the stringed instruments played in Appalachian music and the singing of traditional songs.

★ 3359 ★
Memphis - NEW MUSIC FESTIVAL. March-April, annual, 6 days, Memphis State University. Contact: Memphis State University, Department of Music, Memphis, Tennessee 38152.

The format of the festival is six evening concerts featuring the works of regional composers and the guest composer. The days of the festival are scheduled for rap sessions, open rehearsals and student recitals. Performances are given by the Memphis State University faculty solists and chamber ensembles, larger student ensembles, and guest artists attending the festival. Composers may submit pieces to be performed at the festival. Begun in 1974.

★ 3360 ★
Nashville - INTERNATIONAL COUNTRY MUSIC FANFARE. Early-mid June, annual, 5 days. Contact: International Country Music Fanfare, Post Office Box 100, Nashville, Tennessee 37202.

Features continuous music by top country/western singers.

★ 3361 ★
Nashville - INTERNATIONAL GOSPEL MUSIC FESTIVAL. Early July, annual, 4 days, Municipal Auditorium. Contact: Nashville Area Chamber of Commerce, 161 Fourth Avenue, North, Nashville, Tennessee 37219.

Performances by the nations leading gospel singing groups.

★ 3362 ★
Oak Ridge - OAK RIDGE FESTIVAL. June, annual, High school auditorium. Contact: Oak Ridge Festival, Post Office Box 155, Oak Ridge, Tennessee 37830.

Opera performances in Oak Ridge.

★ 3363 ★
Sewanee - SEWANEE SUMMER MUSIC CENTER FESTIVAL. July, annual, 4 days, campus of the University of the South. Contact: Sewanee Summer Music Center Festival, Sewanee Summer Music Center, Sewanee, Tennessee 37375.

Scenic beauty adorns this festival which draws on the talents of both faculty and students for its programs. Guest conductors. Artists on the faculty are nearly all drawn from professional sources, mainly from symphony orchestras throughout the country. Established in 1957.

Music

TEXAS

★ 3364 ★
Abilene - MUSIC IN OUR TIME.   March (Spring),
annual.   Contact: Music in Our Time, School
of Music, Hardin-Simmons University, Abilene, Texas
79601.

Devoted to contemporary music.   Students and
faculty are the performers;   guest performers and
composers are invited to participate.   Lectures com-
plement the concerts.   Founded in 1957.

★ 3365 ★
Amarillo - GREATER SOUTHWEST MUSIC FESTIVAL.
Late April (last weekend), annual, 1 weekend.
Contact: Chamber of Commerce, 301 South Polk,
Amarillo Building, Amarillo, Texas 79102;   or
Gerald Hemphill, Box 7607, Amarillo, Texas 79109.

For junior and high school bands and choirs, attracts
over 12,000 participants from five states.

★ 3366 ★
Athens - OLD FIDDLERS REUNION.   Late May
(last Friday), annual, 1 day, Court House Square.
Contact: Chamber of Commerce, 502 South Palestine,
Post Office Box 608, Athens, Texas 75751;   or
Texas Fiddlers Association, Box 1441, Athens, Texas
75751.

More than 50,000 lovers of traditional music gather.
Celebration ends with square dance on courthouse
square.   Events include a fiddle contest and children's
events.   First held in 1932.

★ 3367 ★
Brady - BAND FESTIVAL.   February or March,
annual, 2 days.   Contact: Mr. Boyd Hunt, 101
East First Street, Brady, Texas 76825.

Some 25 high school bands and 1,500 students converge for the festival, and band music and competition
is the focal interest.

★ 3368 ★
Brownwood - STAGE BAND FESTIVAL.   February,
annual, 2 days.   Contact: Chamber of Commerce,
521 East Baker, Box 880, Brownwood, Texas 76801.

Sees band competition between high school bands from
a wide area.

★ 3369 ★
Burnet - OLD FIDDLERS CONTEST.   August, annual.
Contact: Chamber of Commerce, Box 27, Burnet,
Texas 78611.

Draws country music artists and fans from throughout
the state for a musical get-together.

★ 3370 ★
Corpus Christi - ALL-TEXAS JAZZ FESTIVAL.   Mid
July, annual, 2 days, Memorial Coliseum.   Con-
tact: Beto Garcia, Jazz Society, 3629 South Saxet,
Corpus Christi, Texas 78405;   or Chamber of Com-
merce, 1201 North Shoreline Boulevard, Post Office
Box 640, Corpus Christi, Texas 78403.

Features top jazz talent from over the Southwest and
Mexico.   Begun in 1961.

★ 3371 ★
Corpus Christi - CONTEMPORARY MUSIC FESTIVAL.
February or March, annual, Del Mar College Audi-
torium.   Contact: Contemporary Music Festival,
Del Mar College, Corpus Christi, Texas 78404.

Student and professional ensembles perform twentieth
century chamber music and choral music.

★ 3372 ★
Crockett - FIDDLERS FESTIVAL.   Mid June, annual.
Contact: State Department of Highways and Public
Transportation, Travel and Information Division, Post
Office Box 5064, Austin, Texas 78763.

A famous affair attracting audiences and old fiddlers
from all parts of the country.

★ 3373 ★
Dallas - FESTIVAL OF TEXAS COMPOSERS.   Late
February, triennial, 2 days, campus of a host uni-
versity in Texas.   Contact: Fine Arts Librarian,
Dallas Public Library, 1954 Commerce Street, Dallas,
Texas 75201.

The Texas Federation of Music Clubs established a
Manuscript Archive at the Dallas Public Library and
invites serious composers of quality music to donate
at least one holograph manuscript to the Archive.
These composers are invited to participate in the
festival, held in various towns throughout Texas.
Composers must be native of Texas or have lived in
Texas or have had a similar association with the state.
Fourth festival held in 1976.

TEXAS (Continued)

★ 3374 ★
Kerrville - KERRVILLE BLUEGRASS AND COUNTRY
MUSIC FESTIVAL. Late August-early September
(Labor Day weekend), annual, 3 days, Quiet Valley
Ranch. Contact: Rod Kennedy, Box 5309, Austin,
Texas 78763.

Bluegrass, "newgrass", gospel and traditional American
music are offered in concerts, jam sessions, and a
bluegrass band contest. Begun in 1974.

★ 3375 ★
Kerrville - KERRVILLE COUNTRY AND WESTERN
JAMBOREE. Early July (July 4th weekend), annual,
3 days, Quiet Valley Ranch. Contact: Ron Kennedy,
Box 5309, Austin, Texas 78753.

The festival offers concerts of country/western music
with a big roster of Nashville performers. A
$1,000 prize is offered in a country-western song
writing contest. Held around the same time as the
Texas State Arts and Crafts Fair. Begun in 1975.

★ 3376 ★
Odessa - JAZZ FESTIVAL. May, annual, 5 nights.
Contact: Mr. Gene Garrison, Chamber of Commerce,
412 North Lincoln, Box 3626, Odessa, Texas 79760.

Outstanding artists perform jazz favorites of all eras.

★ 3377 ★
Port Arthur - FESTIVAL OF BARBERSHOP HARMONY.
April, annual, 1 day. Contact: Greater Port
Arthur Chamber of Commerce, Post Office Box 460,
Port Arthur, Texas 77640.

A day of harmony - barbershop style - in Port Arthur.

★ 3378 ★
Round Top - INTERNATIONAL MUSIC FESTIVAL-
INSTITUTE. June-July, annual, 4 weeks, Mary
Moody Northern Pavilion. Contact: Director,
International Music Festival-Institute, University of
Texas, Austin, Texas 78712.

This Texas town becomes a center for pianists and
other musicians of renown, including vocalists, string
soloists and groups, full symphony orchestras, etc.
In addition to concerts, the musicians give demonstrations and lessons and lead master classes. Begun
in 1971.

★ 3379 ★
San Antonio - FUN-TIER NIGHTS. Mid July to
early August, annual, each Wednesday, La Villita.
Contact: Chamber of Commerce, Post Office Box
1628, San Antonio, Texas 78296.

Musical shows featuring close harmony groups, Dixieland jazz, and individual vocalists. Also snack
and Mexican food booths.

★ 3380 ★
San Marcos - MUSIC ALONG THE RIVER. Mid
April, 1 day. Contact: San Marcos Chamber of
Commerce, Box 2310, San Marcos, Texas 78666.

Events include exhibits, festival, competition, and
performances.

★ 3381 ★
Sinton - OLD FIDDLERS CONTEST AND ARTS AND
CRAFTS FESTIVAL. October. Contact: Mrs.
Wanda Eakin, Box 217, Sinton, Texas 78387.

Along with lots of fiddling, there's an outstanding
arts and crafts show and parade.

★ 3382 ★
Turkey - JIM BOB WILLS DAY. April. Contact:
Lee Vardy, Turkey, Texas 79261.

Honors the late Bob Wills, country and western band
leader. Activities include a parade, barbeque and
old fiddlers' contest.

★ 3383 ★
Winnsboro - OLD FIDDLERS CONTEST. Early
July (4th), annual, 1 day. Contact: Chamber of
Commerce, 318 North Main Street, Suite 4, Winns-
boro, Texas 75494.

Festival of old time country music.

UTAH

★ 3384 ★
Provo - BRIGHAM YOUNG UNIVERSITY SUMMER
FESTIVAL. June to August, annual, Brigham Young
University campus. Contact: Brigham Young Uni-
versity Summer Festival, Music Department, Brigham
Young University, Provo, Utah 84601.

The festival offers chamber music, recitals, opera,
orchestral, band, and choral concerts. Founded
in 1939.

Music

UTAH (Continued)

★ 3385 ★
Salt Lake City - FESTIVAL OF CONTEMPORARY
MUSIC. Mid January, annual, Kingsbury Hall,
University of Utah. Contact: Festival of Con-
temporary Music, University of Utah, Salt Lake City,
Utah 84112.

Concerts presented by the University of Utah, Department of Music and the Utah Symphony at Kingsbury
Hall. The emphasis is on twentieth century chamber
music, new and experimental music, and jazz. Part
of the University of Utah Festival.

VERMONT

★ 3386 ★
Bennington - BENNINGTON CHAMBER MUSIC
FESTIVAL. August, annual. Contact: Bennington
Chamber Music Festival, Bennington College, Benning-
ton, Vermont 05201.

The festival is devoted to performances of new music.
A variety of musical aesthetics and age groups.
Many hearings and discussions of the music. Begun
in 1946.

★ 3387 ★
Burlington - CONTEMPORARY MUSIC SYMPOSIUM.
April, annual, 3 days, Ira Allen Chapel on Uni-
versity of Vermont campus. Contact: Contemporary
Music Symposium, Music Department, University of
Vermont, Burlington, Vermont 05401.

The symposium presents two lecture-demonstrations by
two guest composers, along with other composers.
Free public concert on third day. Founded in 1968.

★ 3388 ★
Burlington - LANE SUMMER SERIES. July, annual,
Ira Allen Chapel, University of Vermont. Contact:
Lane Summer Series, Ira Allen Chapel, University of
Vermont, Burlington, Vermont 05401.

Varied concerts for summertime enjoyment.

★ 3389 ★
Marlboro - MARLBOBO MUSIC FESTIVAL. Early
July-mid August, annual, 8 weeks, campus of
Marlboro College Contact: Marlboro Music
Festival, Marlboro College, Marlboro, Vermont
05344.

The festival functions as a community or workshop of

professional musicians who come by invitation each
summer from all over the world to study and perform
the classical and contemporary chamber music repertory. Wide cross-section of professional performers: concert artists, members of leading chamber
ensembles, first-chair players in major symphony
orchestras, faculty members of conservatories and
universities, etc., embodying all categories of instruments and the singing voices. Founded in 1950.

VIRGINIA

★ 3390 ★
Appomattox - NATIONAL BANJO CHAMPIONSHIP.
Late May, annual, 3 days, Joe Sweeney's Home.
Contact: String Music Association, Post Office Box
8068, Roanoke, Virginia 24014.

Held at the birthplace of the inventory of the 5-
string banjo, the festival brings together bands and
banjo pickers for competition in classical, bluegrass,
and old time banjo-picking. Gospel singing groups
also perform.

★ 3391 ★
Bedford - OLD TIME FIDDLE, BANJO STATE
CHAMPIONSHIP. Early August, 2 days, Bedford
County Lake. Contact: Bedford County Lake,
Bedford, Virginia 24523.

Hundreds of old timers and bands meet to play the
Scottish, Irish, and English music of the early pioneers
and compete for the state trophy. The park offers
camping, boating, and swimming.

★ 3392 ★
Berryville - CARLTON HANEY BLUEGRASS FESTIVAL.
Early July, annual, 4 days, Watermelon Park. Con-
tact: Jim Clark, Post Office Box 186, Fairfax,
Virginia 22030.

A wide diversity of bluegrass music in an outdoor
setting. Begun around 1967.

★ 3393 ★
Berryville - NATIONAL BLUEGRASS CHAMPIONSHIP.
July, annual, 3 days, Berryville Puritan Fairgrounds.
Contact: String Music Association, Post Office Box
8068, Roanoke, Virginia 24014.

Hundreds of musicians from all over the country compete for trophies and cash prizes. Gospel singers
also perform.

VIRGINIA (Continued)

★ 3394 ★
Bristol - BLUEGRASS AND OLD TIME MUSIC
FESTIVAL. Mid May, annual, 2 days, Cherokee
Bluegrass Park. Contact: Carl H. Pennington,
540 New Bethel Road, Bristol, Virginia 24201.

Traditional American folklife with bluegrass and old
time music, folk songs, and flat foot and clog dancing. Contests for old time banjo, fiddle, dancing,
and singing. The city of Bristol is on the Tennessee-
Virginia border. Begun in 1972.

★ 3395 ★
Bristol - FALL BLUEGRASS AND OLD TIME MUSIC
FESTIVAL. Mid September, annual, 2 days.
Cherokee Bluegrass Park. Contact: Carl H. Penning-
ton, 540 New Bethel Road, Bristol, Virginia 24201.

Traditional American folklife with bluegrass and old
time music, folk songs, flat foot and clog dancing,
apple butter and molasses making. Contests for
music and dancing. The city of Bristol is on the
Tennessee-Virginia border. Begun in 1972.

★ 3396 ★
Bristol - SOUTHEASTERN BAND FESTIVAL. October
(lst Saturday), annual, 1 day. Contact: Southeastern Band Festival, Post Office Box 1039, Bristol,
Virginia 24201.

The festival provides competition for high school
marching bands mainly from the states of Virginia
and Tennessee, with some representation from Georgia,
North Carolina, South Carolina, West Virginia, and
Kentucky. About 70 bands with over 5,000 members
have sometimes taken part in the competition. Early
morning parade, afternoon competition, and evening
massed-band performance. Started in 1951.

★ 3397 ★
Chase City - VIRGINIA FOLK MUSIC ASSOCIATION
FESTIVAL. September, annual, 2 days. Contact:
Virginia Folk Music Association Festival, Post Office
Box 108, Crewe, Virginia 23930.

Competition of so-called regular bands, bluegrass
music competition, "Sacred Music Sing-A-Long".
Devoted to folk music or folk-style music that features competitions offering usually modest prizes as
encouragement for participation by local musicians
and singers. State championships are conferred on
winners in various categories within the regular band
or "country swing band", bluegrass, and sacred music
events. The festival in Chase City features the

competition of bluegrass musicians. Also held in
Crewe. Founded in 1946.

★ 3398 ★
Chilhowie - OLD TIME FIDDLERS AND BLUEGRASS
CONVENTION. Mid June (3rd weekend), annual,
3 days. Contact: Vance M. Yeary, 214 Hulldale
Avenue, Marion, Virginia 24354.

Concerts and contests in traditional American music,
including bluegrass. There is flat foot dancing and
a fiddlers' convention in addition. Folk songs are
performed in the traditional style. Performers use
such instruments as fiddle, banjo, guitar, dobro,
mandolin, and bass fiddle. Sponsored by the Lions
Club. Begun around 1969.

★ 3399 ★
Crewe - VIRGINIA FOLK MUSIC ASSOCIATION
FESTIVAL. September, annual, 2 days. Contact:
Virginia Folk Music Association Festival, Post Office
Box 108, Crewe, Virginia 23930.

Competition of so-called regular bands, bluegrass
music competition, "Sacred Music Sing-A-Long".
Devoted to folk music or folk-style music that features competitions offering usually modest prizes as
encouragement for participation by local musicians
and singers. State championships are conferred on
winners in various categories within the regular band
or "country swing band", bluegrass, and sacred music
events. The festival in Crewe features the competition of so-called regular bands and sacred music.
Also held in Chase City.

★ 3400 ★
Dublin - PULASKI'S BLUEGRASS AND OLD TIME
FIDDLERS CONVENTION. Mid July, annual,
2 days, New River Valley Fairgrounds. Contact:
J. Foster Murray, Post Office Box 1556, Pulaski,
Virginia 24301.

Traditional American music, bluegrass, fiddle convention, dance, and contests. Begun around 1965.

★ 3401 ★
Dublin - VIRGINIA STATE STRING MUSIC FESTIVAL
OF BLUEGRASS, OLDE-TIME, FIDDLE AND BANJO-
PICKING. Mid-late June, 3 days, New River
Community College. Contact: String Music Associa-
tion, Post Office Box 8068, Roanoke, Virginia 24014.

The festival awards the State Championship Cup and
cash prizes. Competitors arrive from throughout the
state. There is also gospel singing, and arts and
crafts are on exhibit.

Music

VIRGINIA (Continued)

★ 3402 ★
Galax - OLD FIDDLERS CONVENTION.   Mid
August, annual, 1 weekend, Felts Park.   Contact:
Old Fiddlers' Convention, Box 655, Galax, Virginia
24333.

The convention offers opportunity for folk musicians
and dancers to demonstrate their skill and to compete
for modest monetary prizes.   Categories of performances and contests include folk song, guitar, banjo-
clawhammer, banjo-bluegrass, fiddle, clog or flat
foot dance, and band.   "The oldest and largest old-
time fiddlers' convention in the world".   Started in
1935.

★ 3403 ★
Hampton - HAMPTON KOOL JAZZ FESTIVAL.
Late June, annual, 3 days, Hampton Coliseum.   Con-
tact: Assistant Director of Commerce, Commerce
Department, City Hall, Hampton, Virginia 23669.

Top traditional and modern jazz artists are brought
together to perform in evening concerts.   Sponsored
by the Hampton Institute, the City of Hampton, and
George Wein's Festival Productions, Incorporated.
Begun in 1968.

★ 3404 ★
Hampton - SUSUKI FESTIVAL.   Late April (4th
Sunday), annual, 1 day, Hampton Roads Coliseum.
Contact: Travel Development Department, Virginia
State Chamber of Commerce, 611 East Franklin Street,
Richmond, Virginia 23219; or City of Hampton,
City Hall, Hampton, Virginia 23666.

A highlight of the Hampton Association for the Arts
and Humanities annual membership concert, the festival features nearly 500 students of the violin and
cello playing en masse in a varied program.

★ 3405 ★
McClure - CARTER STANLEY MEMORIAL FESTIVAL.
Late May, annual, 3 days, Old Stanley Homeplace.
Contact: Jim Clark, Post Office Box 186, Fairfax,
Virginia 22030.

Bluegrass music in an appropriate setting.   Begun
around 1971.

★ 3406 ★
Manassas - MANASSAS JAZZ FESTIVAL.   Late
November-early December, annual, 3 days.   Con-
tact: Mr. Johnson McRee, Jr., Post Office Box 458,
Manassas, Virginia 22110.

Legendary jazz greats perform traditional jazz in a
relaxed, informal concert cabaret setting.   Begun
around 1967.

★ 3407 ★
Marion - OLD TIME FIDDLERS AND BLUEGRASS
CONVENTION.   June, annual, 2 or 3 days.
Contact: Chamber of Commerce of Marion, In-
corporated, Post Office Box 602, Marion, Virginia
24354.

The events include the performance of authentic folk
songs, flat foot and clog dancing.   Visitors have an
opportunity to meet and talk with the performers.
Begun around 1969.

★ 3408 ★
Natural Bridge - WORLD CHAMPIONSHIP MUSIC
FESTIVAL.   Late August-early September (Labor
Day weekend), annual, 3 days, James River
Recreational Park.   Contact: James River Recrea-
tional Park, Natural Bridge, Virginia 24578.

Old time fiddlers, banjo pickers, and bands from all
over the world compete to select the world champions
in each category.   The park also offers swimming
and camping and other recreational activities.

★ 3409 ★
Orkney Springs - SHENANDOAH VALLEY MUSIC
FESTIVAL.   July-August, annual, 3 weeks.   Con-
tact: Shenandoah Valley Music Festival, Post Office
Box 12, Woodstock, Virginia 22664.

Takes advantage of the convocation of orchestral
musicians and conductors at the Shenandoah Valley
Music Institute to present a series of public concerts.
Pops concerts, symphony concerts, operas, jazz,
chamber music concerts, and a youth concert.   Established in 1963.

★ 3410 ★
Roanoke - STRING MUSIC FESTIVAL.   Early
August, annual, 3 days, Victory Stadium.   Contact:
String Music Association, Post Office Box 8068,
Roanoke, Virginia 24014.

The largest string festival in the world, this event
draws musicians from all over the world to compete
in the world championship.

VIRGINIA (Continued)

★ 3411 ★
Virginia Beach - VIRGINIA BEACH MUSIC FESTIVAL.
Mid June, annual, 5 days.   Contact: Virginia
Beach Music Festival, Post Office Box 390, Virginia
Beach, Virginia 23458.

High school bands from the entire eastern half of the
United States gather to compete in parades, concerts
and field shows.   Includes approximately 26 selected
bands and 3,000 musicians.   Begun in 1961.

★ 3412 ★
Warrenton - NATIONAL COUNTRY MUSIC CONTEST.
Early August (1st weekend), annual, 2 days, Lake
Whippoorwill.   Contact: Dave Meadows, Warrenton-
Farquier Jaycees, Box 508, Warrenton, Virginia
22186.

A major event in the country music world, this contest brings musicians from across the country to compete for prizes in ten different categories.   Begun
around 1951.

WASHINGTON

★ 3413 ★
Anacortes - AN-O-CHORDS.   July (last full week-
end), annual, 2 days.   Contact: Harlan Abbott,
Secretary, An-O-Chords, 1806 24th, Anacortes,
Washington 98221.

The festival brings together barbershop groups of the
northwest and national championship groups.   There
is also a novice competition and a salmon barbeque.
Begun around 1958.

★ 3414 ★
Cheney - TAMARACK SUMMER MUSIC FESTIVAL.
June, annual, campus of Eastern Washington State
College.   Contact: Director, Tamarack Festival,
Eastern Washington State College, Pence Union
Building, Cheney, Washington 99004.

Events include jazz, new and experimental music,
chamber and orchestral music as performed by both
student and professional groups (Spokane Symphony,
etc.).   There are also master classes.

★ 3415 ★
Seattle - PACIFIC NORTHWEST FESTIVAL.   July,
annual, 13 days.   Contact: Seattle Chamber of
Commerce, 215 Columbia Street, Seattle, Washington
98104.

Opera performed by the Seattle Opera company.

★ 3416 ★
Spokane - GREATER SPOKANE MUSIC AND ALLIED
ARTS FESTIVAL.   May (1st week), annual, 1 week.
Contact: Greater Spokane Music and Allied Arts
Festival, East 1321 27th, Spokane, Washington 99203.

The festival encourages the study and performance of
music and allied arts among young people.   Open to
any amateur from any state or country, and special
music and art events are organized in conjunction
with the festival: concerts and recitals by professional
or university groups.   Founded in 1945.

★ 3417 ★
Tenino - TENINO OLD TIME MUSIC FESTIVAL.
March (3rd weekend), annual, 3 days.   Contact:
Neil M. Johnston, Box 225, Tenino, Washington
98589.

The festival spotlights the traditional music of the
early settlers played on fiddles, harmonicas, banjos,
and guitars.   There are both concerts and workshops.
Begun around 1971.

WEST VIRGINIA

★ 3418 ★
Huntersville - POCOHANTAS COUNTY MUSIC
AND BLUEGRASS FESTIVAL.   Late July-early August,
3 days.   Contact: Miss B. J. Sharp, 814 Second
Avenue, Marlinton, West Virginia 24954; or West
Virginia Department of Commerce, Arts and Crafts
Division, Building 6, 1900 Washington Street East,
Charleston, West Virginia 25305.

Music in the bluegrass and country style and crafts.

★ 3419 ★
Huntersville - POCOHONTAS MUSIC AND BLUEGRASS
FESTIVAL.   Mid September, 3 days.   Contact:
Miss B. J. Sharp, 814 Second Avenue, Marlinton,
West Virginia 24954; or West Virginia Department
of Commerce, Arts and Crafts Division, Building 6,
1900 Washington Street East, Charleston, West
Virginia 25305.

A crafts show and sale is featured at this musical
celebration.

★ 3420 ★
Mannington - MOUNTAINEER DULCIMER CLUB
CONVENTION.   Mid July, 2 days, Mannington

Music

WEST VIRGINIA (Continued)

District Fairgrounds. Contact: Mannington District Fairgrounds, Russell Fluharty, Route 3, Mannington West Virginia 26582; or West Virginia Department of Commerce, Arts and Crafts Division, Building 6, 1900 Washington Street East, Charleston, West Virginia 25305.

Crafts are an important part of this dulcimer convention.

★ 3421 ★
South Charleston - UPPER AND LOWER KANAWHA MAJORETTE FESTIVAL. Late May, annual, 2 days, Oakes Field. Contact: Bob Anderson, 133 Third Avenue, South Charleston, West Virginia 25303.

Competitive entertainment from high school majorettes and band groups.

★ 3422 ★
Webster Springs - MOUNTAIN STATE BLUEGRASS FESTIVAL. Late June, 3 days. Contact: Eddie Arbogast, West McCutcheon Street, Webster Springs, West Virginia 26288; or West Virginia Department of Commerce, Arts and Crafts Division, Building 6, 1900 Washington Street East, Charleston, West Virginia 25305.

Events include bluegrass music and arts and crafts displays.

★ 3423 ★
Wheeling - OGLEBAY SUMMER CONCERTS. July-August, annual. Contact: Oglebay Summer Concerts, Oglebay Institute, Wheeling, West Virginia 26003.

Concerts and opera at Oglebay Park.

WISCONSIN

★ 3424 ★
Fish Creek - PENINSULA MUSIC FESTIVAL. Mid August, annual, 2 weeks, Gibraltar Auditorium. Contact: Peninsula Music Festival, Fish Creek, Wisconsin 54212; or Mrs. Carl T. Wilson, Chairman, Peninsula Music Festival, Box 154, Sister Bay, Wisconsin 54234.

Performances by the Chamber Symphony Orchestra and featuring rising young artists, guest soloists or groups. Works performed cover a wide range of composers - in nationality, historical period, and style. Artists engaged are uniformly of first rank. Also arts and

crafts exhibits. Sponsored by the Peninsula Arts Association. Founded in 1953.

★ 3425 ★
Madison - MADISON SUMMER SYMPHONY ORCHESTRA CONCERTS. July, annual, campus of Edgewood College. Contact: Madison Summer Symphony Orchestra Concerts, 731 State Street, Madison, Wisconsin 53703.

A varied programming is maintained; local guest instrumentalists are engaged as soloists. A number of midwest premieres have been played by the ensemble, as well as works specially commissioned. Started in 1960.

★ 3426 ★
Milwaukee - INTERNATIONAL POLKA ASSOCIATION CONVENTION AND FESTIVAL. Early August, annual, 3 days, Red Carpet Inn and Expo Center. Contact: International Polka Association, 1740 West 47th Street, Chicago, Illinois 60609.

The purpose of the convention and festival is to bring polka people together from various parts of the United States and Canada to listen and dance to the different styles of polka music (Czech, Polish, German, etc.) as performed by polka bands from all over the United States and Canada. Three people who have made contributions to the field of polka music are enrolled into the IPA Hall of Fame, and awards are given for the Best Song, Best Album, Best Vocalist Male and Female, and the Best Instrumental Group at the banquet

★ 3427 ★
Milwaukee - MUSIC UNDER THE STARS. June through August, annual. Contact: Music Under the Stars, Milwaukee County Park Commission, 4420 West Vliet Street, Milwaukee, Wisconsin 53233.

Orchestral music, opera scenes or arias, fully staged opera and operettas, ballet, and evenings of mixed musical entertainment. Guest performers of national and international renown. Established in 1938.

★ 3428 ★
Milwaukee - SUMMER EVENINGS OF MUSIC. June-July, annual, 6 weeks, University of Wisconsin-Milwaukee. Contact: Summer Evenings of Music, University of Wisconsin-Milwaukee Summer Arts Festival, Milwaukee, Wisconsin 53201.

Fine Arts Quartet and Woodwinds Arts Quintet in a series of concerts at the University of Wisconsin. Guest artists of international stature appear. In

WISCONSIN (Continued)

addition to the concerts, the artists conduct concert previews which include theme-demonstration and historical background relating to the music performed at the concerts. Prefaces to music feature lecture-demonstrations discussing backgrounds and trends in classical and contemporary music. Begun in 1954.

WYOMING

★ 3429 ★
Cheyenne - CHEYENNE SYMPHONY AND CHORAL SOCIETY FESTIVAL. April (Spring), annual. Contact: Cheyenne Symphony and Choral Society Festival, 3445 Essex Road, Cheyenne, Wyoming 82001.

Orchestral and choral concerts are featured events in this festival of music.

★ 3430 ★
Laramie - WESTERN ARTS MUSIC FESTIVAL. June-July, annual. Contact: Western Arts Music Festival, University of Wyoming, Department of Music, Laramie, Wyoming 82071.

The event consists of courses and workshops on the performance and composition of chamber and choral music. The festival also includes the Composers Symposium: New American Music: Tangents, devoted exclusively to modern music.

★ 3431 ★
Shoshoni - WYOMING STATE CHAMPIONSHIP OLD TIME FIDDLE CONTEST. Early May, Shoshoni High School Gymnasium. Contact: Wyoming Travel Commission, 2320 Capitol Avenue, Cheyenne, Wyoming 82002.

Events include a "No Holds Barred" contest in trick and fancy fiddling for fiddlers from all states, and a square dancing exhibition.

★ 3432 ★
Teton Village in Jackson Hole - GRAND TETON MUSIC FESTIVAL. July-August, annual, 6 weeks, Festival Hall. Contact: Grand Teton Music Festival, Post Office Box 20, Teton Village, Wyoming 83025.

Modern chamber music and experimental music are performed by professional groups, including full symphonies. The artists are an elite group including leading members (often first chair players) of major orchestras, established chamber music groups, faculty members of universities and conservatories, and con-

cert artists. In a rare seminar/workshop atmosphere, the weekly orchestral programs are rehearsed in depth and the weekly chamber music programs develop out of music which the participating artists have themselves chosen to work on. Works by at least 70 composers are performed. Begun in 1961.

CANADA - BRITISH COLUMBIA

★ 3433 ★
New Westminster - JAZZ FESTIVAL. Late April, 2 days. Contact: Tourist Information, 333 Brunette Street, New Westminster, British Columbia, Canada; or Tourist Information, Irving House, 302 Royal Avenue, New Westminster, British Columbia, Canada.

Includes participants from British Columbia, Washington, Oregon, and California in an event in jazz circles.

★ 3434 ★
Victoria - GREATER VICTORIA MUSIC FESTIVAL. Late April-early May, 3 weeks, various schools, churches, playhouses throughout the city. Contact: Tourist Information, 786 Government Street, Victoria, British Columbia, Canada.

The festival includes special sections and performances for strings, folk dance, choral, vocal, speech, highland dancing, piano, organ, accordion, bands, guitar, etc.

★ 3435 ★
Victoria - VICTORIA SUMMER FESTIVAL. Late July-late August, 6 days, various locations. Contact: Tourist Information, 786 Government Street, Victoria, British Columbia, Canada.

The festival offers a large number of concerts in various locations throughout the city.

CANADA - MANITOBA

★ 3436 ★
Boissevain - INTERNATIONAL MUSIC FESTIVAL. June-August, annual, 50 days, International Peace Gardens. Contact: Dr. Merton Utgaard, Director, International Music Camp, Bottineau, North Dakota 58318.

A cooperative arts festival between North Dakota and Manitoba, and held on the border, with students from all over the world participating in workshops and concerts in 14 different art forms, including bands, orchestras, choirs, drama and baton. Begun in 1957.

Music

CANADA - MANITOBA (Continued)

★ 3437 ★
Boissevain - INTERNATIONAL YOUTH BAND
FESTIVAL.   July, 23 days, International Peace
Garden.   Contact: Dr. Merton Utgaard, Director,
International Music Camp, Bottineau, North Dakota
58318;   or Manitoba Government Travel, 200 Vaughn
Street, Winnipeg, Manitoba R3C 0P8, Canada.

Free outdoor concerts performed by young musicians
from all over the world.   Held on the United
States/Canada border between Manitoba and North
Dakota.

★ 3438 ★
Fort Garry - MANITOBA OLD TIME FIDDLING
CONTEST. Mid June, 1 day.   Contact: Director,
Department of Tourism, Recreation and Cultural
Affairs, Tourist Branch, 801 Mall Centre, 491 Portage
Avenue, Winnipeg, Manitoba R3B 2E7, Canada.

A contest for fiddlers and bluegrass music performers
and fun for the audience.

★ 3439 ★
Winnipeg - MANITOBA MUSIC COMPETITION
FESTIVAL. Early March, annual.   Contact:
Director, Department of Tourism, Recreation and
Cultural Affairs, Tourist Branch, 801 Mall Centre,
491 Portage Avenue, Winnipeg, Manitoba R3B 2E7,
Canada.

Canada's largest music festival features both instrumental and vocal music in concert and in competition.

CANADA - NEW BRUNSWICK

★ 3440 ★
Edmundston - MADAWASKA FESTIVAL OF MUSIC.
Early May, 8 days.   Contact: Special Events
Co-ordination, Tourism New Brunswick, Post Office
Box 12345, Fredericton, New Brunswick, Canada.

An eight day celebration of music with a variety of
musical events.

★ 3441 ★
Fredericton - SUMMER FESTIVAL OF CHAMBER
MUSIC AND JAZZ.   Late June, annual, 11 days,
University of New Brunswick.   Contact: Special
Events Co-ordinator, Tourism New Brunswick, Post
Office Box 12345, Fredericton, New Brunswick,
Canada.

A summer music festival emphasizing chamber music
and jazz.   Begun around 1966.

★ 3442 ★
Fredericton - UNB CHAMBER MUSIC FESTIVAL.
July, annual.   Contact: UNB Chamber Music
Festival, University of New Brunswick, Fredericton,
New Brunswick, Canada.

Chamber concerts and recitals on the campus of the
University of New Brunswick.

★ 3443 ★
Moncton - MARITIME BAND FESTIVAL.   Late May,
annual, 2 days.   Contact: Special Events Co-
ordinator, Tourism New Brunswick, Post Office Box
12345, Fredericton, New Brunswick, Canada.

A competition and various concerts of band groups.

★ 3444 ★
Newcastle - MIRAMICHI FOLK SONG FESTIVAL.
Late June or early July, annual, 3 days, Beaver-
brook Theatre in the Town Hall.   Contact: Mrs.
Leo Mitchell, 356 Water Street, Newcastle, New
Brunswick, Canada.

Traditional folk songs as sung by the people of the
region.   The performers are non-professional, and
sing unaccompanied, performing songs, ballads, traditional "come all ye's" from lumber camps and river
drives, and local contemporary songs.   Old time
fiddling, mouth organ solos, and tap dancing are also
presented.   The material includes English, French,
Arabic, German and other pieces.   There is a special
matinee for performers under 16.   Begun in 1958.

★ 3445 ★
Saint John - COMPETITIVE FESTIVAL OF MUSIC.
Early May, 10 days.   Contact: Special Events
Co-ordinator, Tourism New Brunswick, Post Office
Box 12345, Fredericton, New Brunswick, Canada.

A musical competition and a series of concerts.

CANADA - NOVA SCOTIA

★ 3446 ★
Dartmouth - FESTIVAL OF PIPING.   Mid July,
annual, 1 day, Beazley Field.   Contact: Nova
Scotia Department of Tourism, Travel Division, Post
Office Box 130, Halifax, Nova Scotia B3J 2M7,
Canada.

CANADA - NOVA SCOTIA (Continued)

This festival includes pipe bands playing on a non-competitive level. The finale is a massed pipe band concert.

★ 3447 ★
Dartmouth - MARITIME OLD TIME FIDDLING CONTEST. Mid July, 2 days, Prince Andrew High School. Contact: Nova Scotia Department of Tourism, Travel Division, Post Office Box 130, Halifax, Nova Scotia B3J 2M7, Canada.

Features the best of the Scottish and old-time fiddlers competing for both trophies and prizes.

★ 3448 ★
Hardwood Lands - BLUEGRASS FESTIVAL. Late July, 2 days. Contact: Nova Scotia Department of Tourism, Travel Division, Post Office Box 130, Halifax, Nova Scotia B3J 2M7, Canada.

Bluegrass music concert performed by visiting and local musicians.

CANADA - ONTARIO

★ 3449 ★
Bancroft - CANADIAN COUNTRY MUSIC FESTIVAL. Early August, 3 days, Gemboree Grounds. Contact: The Ministry of Industry and Tourism, Parliament Buildings, Toronto, Ontario M7A 2E5, Canada.

A clap-hands, stomp-feet musical gathering of affectionatos of the country sounds.

★ 3450 ★
Shelburne - CANADIAN OLD TIME FIDDLERS CONTEST. Early August, annual, 2 days. Contact: Kenneth W. Gamble, Box 181, Shelburne, Ontario L0N 1S0, Canada.

Fiddle convention and competitions. There are several categories within the competition. Includes a parade.

CANADA - SASKATCHEWAN

★ 3451 ★
Moose Jaw - KINSMEN INTERNATIONAL BAND FESTIVAL. Mid May, annual, 4 days. Contact: Travel Information, Department of Tourism and Renewable Resources, Post Office Box 7105, Regina, Saskatchewan, S4P 0B5, Canada.

A collection of bands to compete and to entertain.

Photography
See: ARTS AND CRAFTS

Seasons

ALABAMA

★ 3452 ★
Gulf Shores - ALABAMA INVITATIONAL ANTIQUE AUTO SHOW AND SPRING FESTIVAL. April, annual. Contact: Mobile Area Chamber of Commerce, Post Office Box 2187, Mobile, Alabama 36601.

Events include a parade, luaus, fish fries, flea market, costume contest, golf, as well as the exhibition of antique cars.

★ 3453 ★
Huntsville - SPRINGFEST. Early May, annual, weekend, University of Alabama in Huntsville. Contact: Student Government Association or Office of News and Publications, The University of Alabama in Huntsville, Post Office Box 1247, Huntsville, Alabama 35807.

Tournaments in such things as chess, duplicate bridge, tennis, table tennis; fishing contest; art exhibitions; film festival; recitals; bands; debate forum and contest. First offered in 1971.

ALASKA

★ 3454 ★
Anchorage - FUR RENDEZVOUS. February, annual, 10 days. Contact: Alaska Division of Tourism, Pouch E, Juneau, Alaska 99801.

Alaska's largest winter celebration with world championship sled dog races, Lions-sponsored Miners and Trappers Ball, parades, wrestling, sports car races, Eskimo dances, blanket-toss exhibitions, art show, junior world championship sled dog races, fur hat contest, hockey, jade auction, curling, coronation pageant, Miss Alaska contest, snowshoe race, North American Ice Racing Championships, Monte Carlo Night, Chapeau Fete, Square Dance Festival, puppet show, fur auction, Pioneer Pancake Feed, carnival and midway, and more! Begun around 1937.

Seasons

ALASKA (Continued)

★ 3455 ★
Cordova - ICEWORM FESTIVAL. Late January-
early February, annual, 3 days. Contact: Alaska
Division of Tourism, Pouch E, Juneau, Alaska 99801.

This festival celebrates Iceworm's emergence from
hibernation. Iceworm is a character of Alaskan
legends and figures in Robert Service's poems. Art
show, skeet shoot, teen rodeo, airboat races, ski
events, crab-shaking contests, shooting matches, rodeo,
and queen's pageant. The parade is lead by a 150
foot iceworm; at night there is a parade of decorated
cruisers and sailboats to demonstrate that Alaska is
not as frozen solid in winter as people think. Begun around 1960.

★ 3456 ★
Dillingham - BEAVER ROUNDUP. Early March,
annual, 4-6 days. Contact: Juneau Area Office,
Bureau of Indian Affairs, U.S. Department of the
Interior, Federal Building, Box 3-8000, Juneau,
Alaska 99801.

Eskimo dances and games, and a beauty contest in
connection with the arrival of beaver trappers by
airplane, dog sled and snow traveler to sell beaver
furs in Dillingham.

★ 3457 ★
Homer - WINTER CARNIVAL. Early January or
early February, annual, 3 days. Contact: Alaska
Division of Tourism, Pouch E, Juneau, Alaska 99801.

Arts and crafts exhibit in the Society of Natural
History Museum. Baseball game on snowshoes,
snowmachine race in all classes, ice hot rod races,
parade, wrestling, and basketball.

★ 3458 ★
Palmer - MID-SUMMER FESTIVAL. June (21st,
longest day of the year), annual, 2-3 days, Fairgrounds
and environs. Contact: Alaska Division of Tourism,
Pouch E, Juneau, Alaska 99801.

On the longest day of the year, 10- to 20- foot
pre-historic monsters, Grotto Lunkers, rise out of the
ground to terrorize citizens of Matanuska Valley.
They are captured and paraded through the town to
the Fairground where prizes are awarded for the most
original and gruesome of these papier mache creations.
Miss Matanuska Valley Pageant, Woronzoff Horse Show,
horse racing, carnival, and Scottish games championship. Begun around 1973.

★ 3459 ★
Skagway - HARVEST FAIR AND BALL. September;
annual, 2 days, A. & B. Hall. Contact: Alaska
Division of Tourism, Pouch E, Juneau, Alaska 99801.

This is a revival of the Harvest Fair of the early
1900's when Skagway was famous for its fruits,
vegetables and flowers. The original festival was
discontinued during World War II and is now being
revived. First year 1974.

★ 3460 ★
Willow - WINTER CARNIVAL SLED DOG CHAMPION-
SHIP. Late January-early February, annual, 2
weekends. Contact: Alaska Division of Tourism,
Pouch E, Juneau, Alaska 99801.

Dog, sports car and motorcycle races, women Swede
saw contest, snowshoeing, annual snow-mobile race
over Hatcher Pass, cross-country ski races, pageant
and queen coronation, and Wood Choppers Ball.

ARIZONA

★ 3461 ★
Flagstaff - WINTER CARNIVAL. February, annual,
all month. Contact: Flagstaff Chamber of Commerce,
Flagstaff, Arizona 86001.

Winter sports and activities, contests highlight the
festival events.

★ 3462 ★
Payson - FALL FESTIVAL AND ARIZONA'S STATE
FIDDLERS CONTEST. Late September, 2 days,
Payson Rodeo Arena. Contact: Payson Chamber
of Commerce, Drawer A, Payson, Arizona 85541.

Contest certified by the National Fiddler's Certifica-
tion and Advisory Council; winner goes on to the
national contest. High school bands, square-dancing,
costume parade, trick and fancy fiddling contest,
singing and dancing, fireworks, and booths.

★ 3463 ★
Sedona - AUTUMN FESTIVAL AND HOMECOMING.
October, annual, 3 days. Contact: Chamber of
Commerce, Sedona, Arizona 86336.

Three days of celebration in honor of the beauty of
the season.

ARKANSAS

★ 3464 ★
Hot Springs - ARKANSAS SPRING FUN FESTIVAL.
Early June, annual, 10 days.   Contact: Hot Springs
Chamber of Commerce, Post Office Box 1500, Hot
Springs, Arkansas 71901.

On hand for enjoyment are sidewalk bands and arts
and crafts exhibits.   There are all sorts of activities
including aero races, boat races, a rock-skipping
tournament, a horse show, sports car rally, dancing,
horse-shoe pitching contest, and golf and tennis
tournaments.

★ 3465 ★
Monticello - FALL FUN FESTIVAL.   September,
1 week.   Contact: Chamber of Commerce, Monticello, Arkansas 71655; or Department of Parks
and Tourism, 149 State Capitol, Little Rock, Arkansas
72201.

A seasonal celebration extolling the joys and beauty
of the autumn in Monticello.

★ 3466 ★
Pine Bluff - FALL FESTIVAL.   October, 6 days,
Arts and Science Center.   Contact: Chamber of
Commerce, Pine Bluff, Arkansas 71601; or Depart-
ment of Parks and Tourism, 149 State Capitol, Little
Rock, Arkansas 72201.

Pine Bluff celebrates the beauty of the season.

★ 3467 ★
Pine Bluff - SPRING FESTIVAL.   April, annual,
5 days.   Contact: Chamber of Commerce, Pine
Bluff, Arkansas 71601; or Department of Parks
and Tourism, 149 State Capitol, Little Rock, Arkansas
72201.

A celebration of the beauty of spring in Pine Bluff.

CALIFORNIA

★ 3468 ★
California City - CALIFORNIA CITY SPRING
FESTIVAL.   Late May-early June, 3 days. Contact:
California Chamber of Commerce, 455 Capitol Mall,
Sacramento, California 95814.

Dancing, arts and crafts, booths, and a parade help
celebrate the glorious springtime in California City.

★ 3469 ★
Carlsbad - CARLSBAD SPRING HOLIDAY.   April
(last weekend), annual, 3 days.   Contact: San
Diego Convention and Visitors Bureau, 1200 Third
Avenue, Suite 824, San Diego, California 92101.

Community barbeque, dance, hobby and flower shows
at high school.   Begun around 1952.

★ 3470 ★
Clear Lake Oaks - FALL FESTIVAL.   October,
annual.   Contact: Redwood Empire Association,
Visitors Information Center, 476 Post Street, San
Francisco, California 94102.

A traditional community festival celebrating the beauty
of the autumn season.

★ 3471 ★
Coalinga - SPRING FIESTA.   Late April (last
Saturday), annual, 1 day.   Contact: Tourist Information Center, 1270 West Belmont, Fresno, California
93728.

A parade, a barbeque, and a carnival to celebrate
the arrival of spring in Coalinga.

★ 3472 ★
Crestline - FALL FESTIVAL.   Late September, 3
days.   Contact: California Chamber of Commerce,
455 Capitol Mall, Sacramento, California 95814.

Arts and crafts are demonstrated and displayed at this
seasonal festival.

★ 3473 ★
Julian - FALL FESTIVAL.   Early October, annual,
4 days (2 weekends, 2 days each), Town Hall.
Contact: Southern California Visitors Council, 705
West Seventh Street, Los Angeles, California 90017.

Highlights include an art show, melodramas, bazaar,
and bake sale.

★ 3474 ★
Los Alamitos - FALL FESTIVAL.   October, annual,
4 days.   Contact: Orange County Chamber of
Commerce, 401 Bank of America Tower, The City,
One City Boulevard, West, Orange, California 92668.

A carnival and a parade highlight this community
festival honoring the beauty of the autumn season.

Seasons

CALIFORNIA (Continued)

★ 3475 ★
Newman – NEWMAN FALL FESTIVAL.   Early
September, 2 days.   Contact: California Chamber
of Commerce, 455 Capitol Mall, Sacramento,
California 95814.

Parade, barbeque, carnival, junior rodeo, dancing,
and exhibits are included in this seasonal festival.

★ 3476 ★
San Juan – FIESTA DE LAS GOLANDRINAS (RETURN
OF THE SWALLOWS TO THE CITY).   Mid March
(19th), annual, 1-2 days, Mission, San Juan Capri-
strano.   Contact: Chamber of Commerce, San Juan
Capristrano, California 92675.

Fiesta celebration of the return of the swallows to
the city.   Parade.

★ 3477 ★
Santa Monica – OCTOBERFEST.   Late October, 3
days, Airport.   Contact: Southern California Visitors
Council, 705 West Seventh Street, Los Angeles,
California 90017.

An exhibit of antique airplanes highlights this traditional festival of the season.

★ 3478 ★
Stockton – SAN JOAQUIN COUNTY SPRING
FESTIVAL.   Mid May, annual, 2 days, Micke Grove
Park.   Contact: Greater Stockton Chamber of Com-
merce, 1105 North El Dorado, Stockton, California
95202.

Bonsai Club exhibit, bagpipers, Kung Fu Club demonstration, karate demonstration, dance groups representing different ethnic groups, and queens representing
different ethnic groups.   Begun around 1968.

★ 3479 ★
Ukiah – FESTIVAL INTERNATIONALE (SPRING
FESTIVAL).   Early June, annual, 3 days, Redwood
Empire Fairgrounds.   Contact: Redwood Empire
Association, Visitor Information Center, 476 Post
Street, San Francisco, California 94102.

Spring festival, parade, and festivities with an international flavor.

★ 3480 ★
Valyermo – FALL ART FESTIVAL.   Late September,
annual, 2 days, Saint Andrew's Priory.   Contact:
California Chamber of Commerce, 455 Capitol Mall,
Sacramento, California 95814.

Country fair in medieval motif on 500 acre ranch-
monastary grounds.   Events include The Little
Prince, an Indian Village, art show, dancing, games,
and gift booths.   Begun around 1958.

COLORADO

★ 3481 ★
Grand Lake – WINTER CARNIVAL AND PARADE.
Late January-early February, 3 days.   Contact:
Grand Lake Area Chamber of Commerce, Post Office
Box 57, Grand Lake, Colorado 80447.

Traditional winter carnival snow and ice events and
a parade.

★ 3482 ★
Leadville – WINTER CRYSTAL CARNIVAL.   Mid
February, 3 days.   Contact: Chamber of Commerce,
116 East Ninth Street, Leadville, Colorado 80461.

A festival of winter sports and related activities for
fun and frolic in the glorious Colorado winter.

★ 3483 ★
Steamboat Springs – WINTER CARNIVAL.   Early
February, 3 days.   Contact: Chamber of Commerce,
1201 Lincoln Avenue, Box 717, Steamboat Springs,
Colorado 80477.

Festival and competition in winter sports such as
skiing, skating, etc.

FLORIDA

★ 3484 ★
Sebring – HIGHLAND FALL ARTS FESTIVAL.   Early
November, 1 day.   Contact: Lillian Depp, 122
North Commerce Street, Sebring, Florida 33870.

Street booths, parades for pets, bicycle parades, band
concert, strolling minstrels, and a variety of food
and treasure booths.

★ 3485 ★
Tallahassee – SPRINGTIME TALLAHASSEE.   Late
March-early April (1st day of Spring-1st weekend of
April), annual, 17 days.   Contact: Earl Bacon,

FLORIDA (Continued)

Post Office Box 3123, Tallahassee, Florida 32302.

A tribute to the founding of the city and spring flowering with a series of historical and cultural events, beginning on the first day of spring and ending on the first weekend in April. Activities include tours of homes, and plantations in the area, invitational golf tournaments, fine arts festivals at Florida State University and Florida A & M University, concerts, theatrical productions, and sports events. A parade of governors, features all heads of the state from Andrew Jackson to the present, all authentically costumed and riding in the mode of transportation associated with his era of office.

GEORGIA

★ 3486 ★
Cleveland - FALL LEAF FESTIVAL. Mid to late October, 6 days, 3 successive weekends. Contact: Georgia Department of Community Development, Tourist Division, Post Office Box 38097, Atlanta, Georgia 30334.

Cleveland pays honor to the beauty of the autumn season with traditional festivities.

★ 3487 ★
Maysville - AUTUMN LEAF FESTIVAL. Early October, 3 days. Contact: Georgia Department of Community Development, Tourist Division, Post Office Box 38097, Atlanta, Georgia 30334.

A traditional community festival celebrating the beauty of the autumn season.

IDAHO

★ 3488 ★
Driggs - IDAHO STATE UNIVERSITY WINTER CARNIVAL. Late February, 2 days. Contact: Office of Public Information, Idaho State University, Driggs, Idaho 83422.

A celebration of the fun and frolic of winter and its activities on the campus of Idaho State University.

★ 3489 ★
McCall - WINTER CARNIVAL. Early February, annual, 3 days. Contact: Chamber of Commerce, Box D, McCall, Idaho 83638.

Serpentine torch parade of snowmobilers and skiers,

parade, queen contest, dancing, races, variety show, and cross country snowmobile race. Teen dance, art exhibit, fireworks, food, and snow sculpture. Begun around 1965.

★ 3490 ★
Nordman - SPRING FESTIVAL AND FLOTILLA. Late May (Memorial Day weekend), 2 days, Priest Lake. Contact: Division of Tourism and Industrial Development, Room 108, Capitol Building, Boise, Idaho 83720.

Flotilla of decorated boats, pot o' gold drawing, horseshoe tournament, golf tournament, and other events to celebrate the pleasant weather of springtime. Also held in Priest Lake.

★ 3491 ★
Pierce - WINTER CARNIVAL. Late January-early February, 5 days. Contact: Division of Tourism and Industrial Development, Room 108, Capitol Building, Boise, Idaho 83720.

Events include snowmobile races, torchlight parade, mayor's race-traveling trophy, children's snowmobile and sled dog races, all classes of snow shoe races, sled and saucer races, snow sculpture, and snowmobile motor cross.

★ 3492 ★
Priest Lake - SPRING FESTIVAL AND FLOTILLA. Late May (Memorial Day weekend), 2 days, Priest Lake. Contact: Division of Tourism and Industrial Development, Room 108, Capitol Building, Boise, Idaho 83720.

Flotilla of decorated boats, pot o' gold drawing, horseshoe tournament, golf tournament and other events to celebrate the pleasant weather of spring. Also held at Nordman.

★ 3493 ★
Priest Lake - WINTER CARNIVAL. Mid January, 2 days. Contact: Division of Tourism and Industrial Development, Room 108, Capitol Building, Boise, Idaho 83720.

Snowshoe softball and snowshoe relays are featured in this celebration of the fun and frolic of winter. Also held in Nordman.

★ 3494 ★
Rexburg - WINTER CARNIVAL. Mid January, 3 days, Ricks College. Contact: Division of

IDAHO (Continued)

Tourism and Industrial Development, Room 108, Capitol Building, Boise, Idaho 83720.

The Ricks College campus is the setting for this celebration of the fun and frolic of winter.

ILLINOIS

★ 3495 ★
Lebanon – FALL FESTIVAL.   Early October, 1 day. Contact: The Division of Tourism, Illinois Department of Business and Economic Development, 222 South College Street, Springfield, Illinois 62706.

A community festival honoring the arrival of autumn.

★ 3496 ★
Oregon – AUTUMN ON PARADE.   Mid October, 3 days.   Contact: Autumn on Parade, Box 234, Oregon, Illinois 61061.

Antique and hobby show, square dance, art fair and show, Sunday parade, scenic tours, farmer's market, crafts show and sale.

★ 3497 ★
Rockford – ROCK CUT WINTER CARNIVAL.   Mid February, 2 days, Rock Cut State Park.   Contact: Director, Division of Parks and Memorials, Program Services Section, 605 State Office Building, Springfield, Illinois 62706.

Winter recreational activities including skating, sledding, ice and snow sculpturing, cross-country skiing, winter nature awareness tours, and sleigh rides are among the events.

★ 3498 ★
Springfield – CLAYVILLE SPRING FESTIVAL.   Early May, annual, 1 day, Clayville Rural Life Center. Contact: Clayville Curator, Sangamon State University, Springfield, Illinois 62702.

Crafts and demonstrations of the early nineteenth century.   Plowing, spring farm preparation, and sewing bees.

INDIANA

★ 3499 ★
Battle Ground – OLD TIME SUMMER FAIR.   Mid August, 2 days, Tippecanoe Battlefield.   Contact:

Program Director, Battle Ground Historical Corporation, Box 225, Battle Ground, Indiana 47920.

Great American quilting bee, traditional jazz, turn-of-the-century artifacts, food, drinks, and quality art highlight the festival events.

★ 3500 ★
Canaan – CANAAN FALL FESTIVAL.   Mid September, 3 days.   Contact: President, Canaan Restoration Council, Route 1, Canaan, Indiana 47224.

Unusual contests such as the Indian Princess contest, Chief White Eye painting contest, largest frog contest, heaviest pumpkin contest, buck saw wood-cutting contest, and heaviest turkey contest.   Crafts and craftsmen, antique flea market, arts display, entertainment, old-fashioned parade, U.S. Pony Express run, foods and fashions of the mid 1800's.

★ 3501 ★
Connersville – FALL FESTIVAL.   Mid September, 2 days, Saint Gabriel Church.   Contact: Mrs. Gerald A. Mueller, 2015 Indiana Avenue, Connersville, Indiana 47331.

Artists and craftsmen display and sell their wares. Antique booths and flea markets.

★ 3502 ★
Dale – FALL FESTIVAL.   Early October, 3 days, Dale's City Park.   Contact: Bob Davis, One South Washington Street, Dale, Indiana 47523.

Queen contest, parade, demolition derby, and go-cart races.

★ 3503 ★
Martinsville – FALL FOLIAGE FESTIVAL.   Early to mid October, 9 days, Morgan County Fairgrounds. Contact: Office Manager, Chamber of Commerce, 233 East Washington Street, Martinsville, Indiana 46151.

Community sing, Central Indiana Cheerleading Contest, roaring 20's party, and a parade.   Displays of art and market wares.

★ 3504 ★
Michigan City – MICHIGAN CITY SUMMER FESTIVAL AND COUNTRY-WESTERN SHOW.   Early July, Rodgers High School Auditorium.   Contact: James S. Maule, 1011 Pine Street, Michigan City, Indiana 46360.

INDIANA (Continued)

Parade, national drum and bugle corps show, ethnic foods and dances (a different ethnic group each day), and post-festival western show.

★ 3505 ★
Milroy - FRONTIER CLUB FALL FESTIVAL. Late September, 3 days. Contact: Gene Linville, 405 North Main Street, Milroy, Indiana 46156.

Parade, queen contest, crafts exhibits, and bazaars to celebrate the season.

★ 3506 ★
Nashville - SEPTEMBER IN BROWN COUNTY. September, 27 days, Brown County's Art Gallery, Village Green. Contact: Editor and Publisher, Brown County Democrat, Incorporated, Nashville, Indiana 47448.

Free public square dances every Saturday night, fall bazaar on the Village Green, muzzle-loading rifle shoot, old settlers reunion, flower show, and fall exhibit in the art gallery.

★ 3507 ★
New Albany - HARVEST HOMECOMING. Early October. Contact: Mrs. Cora Jacobs, Southern Indiana Harvest Homecoming, Incorporated, 141 East Spring Street, New Albany, Indiana 47150.

Pumpkins are the focus of this festival. Prizes are awarded for the best carved and best baked pumpkin goods. Also included in this event are square and round dances, amusement rides, beauty pageants, music, clowns, antique cars and marching bands.

★ 3508 ★
Noblesville - SUMMER FESTIVAL. July-August, 3 days, downtown area. Contact: Executive Secretary, Noblesville Area Chamber of Commerce, 225 North Eighth Street, Post Office Box 65, Noblesville, Indiana 46060.

Flea market, fish fry, sidewalk sale, pancake breakfast, and a pork barbeque highlight this community celebration.

★ 3509 ★
Rensselaer - FALL FESTIVAL DAYS. Mid September, 2 days, Court House Square. Contact: James Hoover, 627 Dean Place, Rensselaer, Indiana 47978.

Square dancing in the street, carnival activities, arts and crafts shows, antique and flea markets, specialty booths, and amusement rides.

★ 3510 ★
Thorntown - FESTIVAL OF THE TURNING LEAVES. Late September, 2 days, Old Mill Run Park. Contact: Mrs. Martha Bowen, Rural Route 1, Colfax, Indiana 46035.

Actively re-creates glimpses of the Indian and pioneer heritage of the area. Indian dancing, pioneer crafts demonstrations, muzzle loading rifle shoots, pioneer and Indian produce, handicrafts, foods and music.

★ 3511 ★
Zionsville - COLONIAL VILLAGE FALL FESTIVAL. Early September, 2 days. Contact: Fred Nay, 650 West Poplar Street, Zionsville, Indiana 46077.

Parade, continuous entertainment, food, flea market, garden tractor pull, hobby tent, games for young and old, carnival, booths, and balloon ascension in the colonial type village.

IOWA

★ 3512 ★
Albia - FALL FESTIVAL. Early August, 5 days, Fairgrounds. Contact: Albia Chamber of Commerce, 107 South Clinton Street, Post Office Box F 306, Albia, Iowa 52531.

Activities include home economics exhibits; food sale; gadget show; dairy judging; dog jumping; other animals include horses, swine, sheep, mules, and rabbits; tractor pull; dress revue; demolition derby; flower show; country music show; educational presentations; science exhibits; mechanics and arts judging; and a livestock sale.

★ 3513 ★
Cresco - INTERNATIONAL SNOW FESTIVAL. Late January (last weekend), annual, 4 days. Contact: Cresco Chamber of Commerce, Post Office Box 403, Cresco, Iowa 52136.

More than 200 miles of marked trails for snowmobilers, snow safaris, championship snowmobile racing. Dances, hobo stew and a general fun time. Sponsored by the Chamber of Commerce. Begun in 1970.

Seasons

IOWA (Continued)

★ 3514 ★
Estherville - WINTER SPORTS FESTIVAL.   Early
February, annual, 3 days, Holiday Mountain.   Con-
tact: Estherville Chamber of Commerce, Two North
Seventh Street, Estherville, Iowa 51334.

Collegiate and open skiing races, snowmobile races,
ice sculpture contest, ice skating competition, musical
concerts and entertainment.

★ 3515 ★
Fairfield - FALL FESTIVAL.   Early October, annual,
2 days.   Contact: Chamber of Commerce, 123 West
Burlington Street, Post Office Box 945, Fairfield,
Iowa 52556.

A traditional celebration of the season and the harvest.
Begun in 1974.

★ 3516 ★
Lone Tree - FALL FESTIVAL.   Late August, 2 days,
various places in the town.   Contact: Farmer and
Merchants Savings Bank, Lone Tree, Iowa 52755.

Events include garden, flower and grain show, Fall
Festival Queen contest, firemen dunking tank, bingo,
pony pulling contest, garden tractor pulling contest,
firemen water fight, helicopter rides, bicycle races,
greased pig contest, watermelon eating and seed
spitting contest, parade, street dance, performance by
the Emerald Knights of Cedar Rapids, and a steak
supper.

★ 3517 ★
Montour - FALL FESTIVAL.   Early September
(usually Saturday after Labor Day), annual, 1 day,
Main Street and schoolhouse.   Contact: Mrs. Melvin
Lenhart, Box 128, Montour, Iowa 50173.

The events vary from year to year but include such
things as a parade with bands, drill teams, floats,
horses, honored guests, etc.; a kiddie parade, concession stands, rides, stage entertainment, pie eating
contest, water fight (volunteer firemen), treasure
hunt, country store, food stands, bingo, contests and
games, horseshoe tournament, tractor pulls, horse show,
square dancing, street dancing, and exhibition of
Indian arts and crafts by the Sac and Fox Indians.
Started in 1956.

★ 3518 ★
Spencer - SLEIGH RALLY.   Late February, annual
(if it snows), 1 day, Stub's Ranch Kitchen.   Contact:

Stub Johnson, Stub's Ranch Kitchen, Spencer, Iowa
51301.

The event attracts entrants from Iowa, Nebraska,
Minnesota and South Dakota.   The sleighs may be
antiques, authentic reproduction, or modern sleighs
of all different types such as bobsleds, cutters,
doctors' sleighs, and all pulled by different types of
horses, poines and mules.   Their riders wear appropriate costumes.   Trophies and ribbons are awarded
on the basis of appearance and handling.   Spectators
are given rides in the sleighs.   The climaxing event
is a wild two-horse chariot race.

★ 3519 ★
Stanton - SKONA MAJ (WELCOME MAY) FESTIVAL.
Late April, 1 day.   Contact: Chamber of Commerce,
Stanton, Iowa 51573.

A traditional community festival to celebrate the
coming of May and all its beauties.

★ 3520 ★
Waterloo - FALL FUN DAYS.   Mid-late September,
annual, 9 days.   Contact: Waterloo Chamber of
Commerce, 229 West Fifth Street, Waterloo, Iowa
50704.

Events include a parade, top-name entertainers, rodeo,
horse and pony pull, tractor pull, midway, horse show,
farm product exhibits, craft demonstrations and exhibits,
and livestock exhibits.   Sometimes associated with
the National Dairy Cattle Congress.

KANSAS

★ 3521 ★
Belle Plaine - BARTLETT ARBORETUM FALL COLORS
AND MUM FESTIVAL.   October, 1 month.   Con-
tact: Publications Division, Kansas Department of
Economic Development, State Office Building, Room
122S, Topeka, Kansas 66612.

A celebration of the beauties of the fall season and
the flowers that bloom.

★ 3522 ★
Winfield - SPRING THING.   Mid May, 3 days.
Contact: Walnut Valley Association, Incorporated,
Box 245, Winfield, Kansas 67156.

Featuring the National Tut Taylor Dobro Championship
and a folk arts and crafts festival.   Begun in 1976.

LOUISIANA

★ 3523 ★
Baton Rouge - LOUISIANA SPRING FAIR. Mid
April, Rebel Fairgrounds. Contact: J.W. Otzen-
berger, Post Office Box 66403, Baton Rouge,
Louisiana 70806; or Louisiana Tourist Commission,
Post Office Box 44291, Baton Rouge, Louisiana
70804.

Acadiana Day, arts and crafts (flea market), commercial exhibits, animal exhibits, bands, entertainment
acts, and a carnival highlight this seasonal festival.
Begun in 1971.

★ 3524 ★
New Orleans - SPRING FIESTA. Mid April,
annual. Contact: Executive Director, Louisiana
Tourist Commission, Post Office Box 44291, Baton
Rouge, Louisiana 70804.

Coronation of the Spring Fiesta Queen, presentation
of her court in Jackson Square, while music and
singing drifts down from the balconies of the historic
old Pontalba Apartments which flank the square.
Pageant follows. Parade - A Night in Old New
Orleans. Pirates Alley art show, tours of homes
and gardens, Festival of Flowers, etc. Begun around
1967.

MAINE

★ 3525 ★
Augusta - SNOW-FEST. Early February. Contact:
Kennebec Valley Chamber of Commerce, Memorial
Circle, Augusta, Maine 04330.

Ice fishing, winter sports, and pageantry highlight
this winter festival. Also held in other cities -
Gardiner and Winthrop.

★ 3526 ★
Gardiner - SNOW-FEST. Early February. Con-
tact: Gardiner Board of Trade, City Hall, Gardiner,
Maine 04345.

Ice fishing, winter sports, and pageantry highlight
this winter festival. Also held in Augusta and in
Winthrop.

★ 3527 ★
Kingfield - WHITE WHITE WORLD. Late January,
annual, 9 days, Sugarloaf Mountain. Contact:
Chamber of Commerce, Kingfield, Maine 04947.

In conjunction with salute to National Ski Week,
events include snow sculptures, special ski races, a
costume party each night, down east lobster bake,
clam bake, ski tours, apres ski entertainment, torchlight parade, hayrides, sleigh-rides, and Queen of
White White World Coronation at Capricorn Lodge.

★ 3528 ★
Rangeley - SNOW FOLLIES WINTER CARNIVAL.
January, 10 days, Saddleback Mountain. Contact:
Rangeley Lakes Region, Chamber of Commerce,
Rangeley, Maine 04970.

Events include night skiing, ice-skating, and other
winter sports, art photography show, live bands,
skiing demonstrations and races, snowmobiling,
carnival dance, fashion show, cookouts and luncheons,
and tours.

★ 3529 ★
Winthrop - SNOW-FEST. Early February. Contact:
Kennebec Valley Chamber of Commerce, Memorial
Circle, Augusta, Maine 04330.

Ice fishing, winter sports, and pageantry highlight
this winter festival. Also held in Augusta and
Gardiner.

MARYLAND

★ 3530 ★
Hunt Valley - HUNT VALLEY MAY FAIR. Early
May, annual, 1 day, Hunt Valley Inn. Contact:
Betty Galvin, c/o Hunt Valley Inn, Hunt Valley,
Maryland 21031.

Plants, herbs, flowers, handicrafts, lemonsticks, and
home-baked goods. The event is put on by 46
garden clubs. Begun around 1974.

★ 3531 ★
Jefferson - FALL FESTIVAL. Late September,
annual, 2 days, Jefferson Ruritan Grounds. Contact: Mrs. Charles C. Smith, Jefferson View Farm,
Jefferson, Maryland 21755.

Features exhibit, sale, and demonstrations by traditional and contemporary craftsmen including pottery,
rug braiding, quilting, spinning, weaving, apple
butter boiling, clockmaking, blacksmithing, wood
carving, apple dolls, chair caning, etc. Machinery
displays include a tractor pull, shingle mill operation,
threshing machine demonstration, corn husker and
shredder. Other activities include flea markets,
Old Timers' Ball Game, pet show, bicycle parade,

Seasons

MARYLAND (Continued)

square dance, food prepared and sold by local organizations, etc. Started in 1974 as a celebration of the town's bicentennial.

★ 3532 ★
McHenry - WINTERFEST. Late February, annual, 3 days, Wisp Ski Area. Contact: Garrett County Promotion Council, 222 East Alder Street, Oakland, Maryland 21550.

Skiing, sled dogs, sleigh rides, queen contest, snowmobiling, dances, and German food highlight the activities of this winter celebration.

★ 3533 ★
Oakland - AUTUMN GLORY FESTIVAL. Mid October (2nd weekend), annual. Contact: Garrett County Promotion Council, 222 East Alder Street, Oakland, Maryland 21550.

Events include tours, Grand Ol' Opry, fiddle convention, Maryland State Fiddlers' Championship, State 5-String Banjo Championship, antique show, antique car show, football games, Fireman's Day including firemen's parade, Autumn Glory Parade, country music show with name entertainers, Autumn Glory Rock Dance, gospel sing, Square Dance Festival at McHenry College. Activities take place throughout Garrett County. Begun around 1968.

★ 3534 ★
Ocean City - FALL FESTIVAL. Mid September, annual, 6 days, Fairgrounds - Seventh and the Boardwalk, and Convention Hall. Contact: Director of Public Relations, City Hall Building, 301 Baltimore Avenue, Ocean City, Maryland 21842.

In celebration of the "2nd season" in this ocean resort, there are a variety of events including arts and crafts shows, seaside music (barbershop quartets, bluegrass, etc.), seafood sales, sports fishing (marlin tournament and other contests), a Senior Citizens Day featuring square dancing, a Surf and Beach Day, and an antique auto parade and show. Begun in 1975.

★ 3535 ★
Thurmont - CATOCTIN WINTER FESTIVAL. February, annual, 2 days, Catoctin National Park. Contact: Frederick County Chamber of Commerce, Division of Tourism, Frederick, Maryland 21701.

Events include snowmobiling, cross-country skiing and sled dog team. Demonstrations and exhibits of sports equipment, wood-carving, and fly-tying. Begun around 1972.

★ 3536 ★
Thurmont - COLORFEST. Mid October, annual, 3 days, Catoctin National Park. Contact: Catoctin Mountain Tourist Council, Box 32, Thurmont, Maryland 21788; or Colorfest Chairman, Post Office Box 33, Thurmont, Maryland 21788.

A potpourri of activities and entertainment including arts, crafts, apple butter boilings, farm and orchard tours, cider making, country suppers. Begun in 1964.

★ 3537 ★
Towson - TOWSONTOWN SPRING FESTIVAL. Late April or early May, annual, 1 day. Contact: Thomas G. Ward, 21 West Susquehanna Avenue, Towson, Maryland 21204.

Civic and community exhibits and demonstrations, entertainment, music, antique show, arts and crafts show, costumes and pageants, wide variety of food. Begun around 1968.

MASSACHUSETTS

★ 3538 ★
Adams - SUMMER FESTIVAL. August, annual, 9 days. Contact: Adams Chamber of Commerce, Post Office Box 215, Adams, Massachusetts 01220.

Parades, fireworks, dances, and displays highlight the events celebrating the summer season.

★ 3539 ★
Ashby - WINTER SPORTS FESTIVAL AND SNOW SCULPTURE CONTEST. Early January, 1 day. Contact: Chamber of Commerce, Ashby, Massachusetts 01431.

A ceremony, performance, competition, and festival, all in honor of winter and its fun.

★ 3540 ★
Attleboro - SUMMER FESTIVAL. Early September, annual, 5 days, LaSalette Shrine. Contact: Bristol County Development Council, Incorporated, 154 North Main Street, Fall River, Massachusetts 02722.

Attractions are games, rides, food and flea market.

MASSACHUSETTS (Continued)

★ 3541 ★
East Bridgewater - WINTER CARNIVAL. Mid February, 2 days. Contact: Chamber of Commerce, East Bridgewater, Massachusetts 02333.

A festival in honor of the fun and beauty of the winter season.

★ 3542 ★
North Adams - FALL FOLIAGE FESTIVAL. Mid September, annual, 1 week. Contact: North Adams Chamber of Commerce, 24 Ashland Street, North Adams, Massachusetts 02147.

Week of festivities in preparation of foliage season. Parades, sport events, outdoor suppers, and other activities, including the crowning of the Festival Queen.

MICHIGAN

★ 3543 ★
Bellaire - AUTUMN FESTIVAL. Early October, annual, 3 days. Contact: Secretary, Chamber of Commerce at Bellaire, Bellaire, Michigan 49615; or West Michigan Tourist Association, Hospitality House, 136 Fulton East, Grand Rapids, Michigan 49502.

The festival features color tours, queen contests, competitions for children and adults, and other related autumn events.

★ 3544 ★
Central Lake - WINTER CARNIVAL. Late January, 3 days. Contact: West Michigan Tourist Association, Hospitality House, 136 Fulton East, Grand Rapids, Michigan 49502.

A lively celebration in honor of the beauty and fun of winter. Traditional winter sports activities are featured.

★ 3545 ★
Dearborn - AUTUMN HARVEST WEEKEND. Early October, 2 days, Greenfield Village. Contact: Greater Detroit Chamber of Commerce, 150 Michigan Avenue, Detroit, Michigan 48226; or Greenfield Village, Dearborn, Michigan 48121.

Demonstration of old-fashioned farming techniques and end of harvest celebrations. Includes country music and craft demonstrations.

★ 3546 ★
Grand Rapids - OCTOBERFEST. Mid October, 1 day, Blandford Nature Center. Contact: Blandford Nature Center, 1715 Hillburn, Northwest, Grand Rapids, Michigan 49504.

Crafts and hobbies are demonstrated; apple cider and corn husk dolls are made; meat smoking is demonstrated; and participants are invited to join in making caramel apples.

★ 3547 ★
Marquette - WINFESTER. Mid February (3rd week), annual, Northern Michigan University. Contact: University News Bureau, Northern Michigan University, Marquette, Michigan 49855.

A winter carnival with the traditional winter fun events. Started in 1958.

MINNESOTA

★ 3548 ★
Alexandria - ULLR FEST. Early February, 2 days. Contact: Alexandria Area Chamber of Commerce, 206 North Broadway, Alexandria, Minnesota 56308.

Events include cross-country skiing, dances, ice sculpture, bridge tournament, snow king and queen, ball, and medallion hunt.

★ 3549 ★
Austin - SNOWFLAKE FESTIVAL. Mid January, 9 days. Contact: Austin Area Chamber of Commerce, 300 North Main Street, Austin, Minnesota 55912.

Events include sports activities, treasure hunt, ice fishing contest, dog show, snowmobile contests, variety show, queen contest, parade, art show and dance.

★ 3550 ★
Bemidji - NORTH COUNTRY SKI TOURING FESTIVAL. Mid February, 3 days. Contact: Bemidji Area Chamber of Commerce, Post Office Box 806, Bemidji, Minnesota 56601.

Presidents' Day and a mass gathering of ski tourers.

★ 3551 ★
Bemidji - PAUL BUNYAN WINTER CARNIVAL. Late January-early February, 6 days, State College. Contact: Winter Carnival, State College, Bemidji, Minnesota 56601.

MINNESOTA (Continued)

Olympics, snow sculpture, skit night, dances highlight this fun festival.

★ 3552 ★
Cambridge - WINTER CARNIVAL.   Mid February,
3 days.   Contact: Craig Moline, Rum River Optimist
Club, Cambridge, Minnesota 55008.

Events include dog sled races, cross country skiing
races, ice and snow sculpture, snowmobile time trials.

★ 3553 ★
Coon Rapids - SNOWFLAKE DAYS.   Early February,
10-11 days.   Contact: Coon Rapids Chamber of
Commerce, 11400 Ilex Street, Northwest, Coon Rapids,
Michigan 55433.

Events include a snowmobile race, broomball, archery,
softball tournaments, art fair, skating, queen pageant,
snow sculpture, cross country ski tour, pancake breakfash, and motor cycle scramble.

★ 3554 ★
Menahga - MIDSUMMER CELEBRATION.   Mid July,
3 days.   Contact: Civic and Commerce Association,
Menahga, Minnesota 56464.

Festival events include queen pageant, parade, contests, water show, carnival, food, prizes, children's
activities, etc.

★ 3555 ★
Mountain Iron - MOUNT SNO WINTER CARNIVAL.
Mid February, annual, 2-3 days.   Contact: Chamber of Commerce, Mountain Iron, Minnesota 55768.

Events include a cross-country ski race, queen contest,
talent show, dance, snowshoe baseball game and
snowmobile races.   Begun around 1966.

★ 3556 ★
North Saint Paul - SNOW FROLICS.   Mid February,
5 days.   Contact: North Saint Paul Jaycees, 2035
North Margaret, North Saint Paul, Minnesota 55109.

Miss North Saint Paul pageant, parade, treasure hunt,
pancake breakfast, softball on ice highlight this
winter festival.

★ 3557 ★
Parkers Prairie - FALL FESTIVAL.   Late August,

4 days.   Contact: Commercial Club, Parkers
Prairie, Minnesota 56361.

A talent and queen contest, parades, farm produce
display, and a midway show highlight the festival
events.

★ 3558 ★
Red Lake Falls - SNO-FEST.   January or February,
annual.   Contact: Vikingland or Jaycees, Red Lake
Falls, Minnesota 56750.

Snow games, skiing, hockey, basketball, and snowmobile races.   Also a key hunt, queen coronation,
mutt races, and log sawing contest.

★ 3559 ★
Saint Paul - WINTER CARNIVAL.   Late January-
early February, annual, 10 days.   Contact: Winter
Carnival, Metro Square Building, Saint Paul, Minnesota
55101.

The carnival includes the coronations of King Boreas,
God of the North Wind, and the Queen of the Snows.
They reign in the Ice Palace, which at the end of the
carnival is destroyed by Vulcanus, god of fire and
mortal enemy of Boreas, to symbolize the triumph of
summer over winter.   Festival events include Lady
Godiva Contest, art shows, bowling tournament, snowmobile race, hockey, banquets, luncheons, balls,
parades, sports car races, square dance festival,
mutt races (spoof on husky races), horse show, polka
carnival, arts and crafts, ice cream social, coin
carnival exhibition and sale, badminton tournament,
Vulcan Victory Party, archery tournament, world's
oldest ice-fishing contest, gymnastic meet, ice
sculpting contest, amateur talent contest, table tennis
contest, ski jumping contest.   Held irregularly between
1898 and 1938, when it was revived on a permanent
basis.   Suspended during World War II, regular
schedule since 1947.

★ 3560 ★
Sauk Centre - WINTER CARNIVAL.   Late January-
early February, 3 days.   Contact: Chamber of Commerce, 405 1/2 Sinclair Lewis Avenue, Sauk Center,
Minnesota 56378.

Winter sports competition, snow and ice sculpture,
Dairyland "100" snowmobile cross country classic,
and a fishing derby highlight the events.

★ 3561 ★
Spring Grove - SNE DAG.   Late January-early
February, 3 days.   Contact: Spring Grove Commercial

MINNESOTA (Continued)

Club, Spring Grove, Minnesota 55974.

All sorts of winter sports activities including snowmobile trail rides and cross country ski event. Also a picnic, parade, queen contest, and a ball.

★ 3562 ★
Stewartville - ICE FESTIVAL. Late January-early February, annual, 7-8 days. Contact: Gary Madison, Stewartville, Minnesota 55976; or Chamber of Commerce, Stewartville, Minnesota 55976.

Snowmobile races, ice sculpture contest, Snowflake Ball, parade, festival of music, pancake dinner, square dancing, skating party, and children's events. Begun around 1971.

★ 3563 ★
Tower - WINTER SNOW FESTIVAL. Mid January, 4 days. Contact: Chamber of Commerce, Tower, Minnesota 55790

Events include dances, parade, band contest, ice fishing contest, snowmobile race, sled dog race, and coronation of a queen.

★ 3564 ★
Waseca - SLEIGH AND CUTTER FESTIVAL. Mid February, 2 days. Contact: Art McDonough, 608 Second Street, Northwest, Waseca, Minnesota 56093.

A parade of horse-drawn sleighs and cutters, winter sports activities and games highlight this festival celebrating winter fun.

★ 3565 ★
Winona - WINTER CARNIVAL. Mid February, 3 days. Contact: Winona Area Chamber of Commerce, 170 Center Street, Winona, Minnesota 55987.

Events include snowmobile races, dance, pancake breakfast, ice fishing contest for adults and children, races on ice, bowling tournament. Sponsored by the Jaycees.

MISSOURI

★ 3566 ★
Branson - AUTUMN DAZE. Late September, 4 days, streets of Branson. Contact: Branson/Lakes Area Chamber of Commerce, Post Office Box 220-0, Branson, Missouri 65616.

The town celebrates the harvest with a crafts fair, displays and demonstrations.

★ 3567 ★
Carthage - MAPLE LEAF FESTIVAL. Mid October (usually 3rd week), annual, 8 days, Memorial Hall, Central Park, K.E. Baker Stadium, city streets. Contact: The Carthage Area Chamber of Commerce, Memorial Hall, 407 South Garrison, Carthage, Missouri 64836.

A variety of events held during the peak of the hard maple autumn foliage. There is a large parade, a marching band competition, and various church activities. Started in 1967.

★ 3568 ★
Lexington - FALL FESTIVAL. Mid September, annual, 2 days, Main Street, Lions Club Park, Municipal Auditorium. Contact: Chamber of Commerce, Box 457, Lexington, Missouri 64067.

Events include parade, carnival, exhibits, and youth fair. Started in the early 1940's.

MONTANA

★ 3569 ★
Anaconda - SNO-FEST. Late January-early February, annual, 10 days. Contact: Chamber of Commerce, Hotel Marcus Daly, Anaconda, Montana 59711.

The festival offers a variety of winter sports. There are competitions in ski-racing, ski-jouring (the skier attaches himself to a skimobile and is pulled along), snowmobile races, ice skating competitions, dog sled races and slalom races. The Butte Copper Kings play an exhibition hockey game. A Miss Sno-Fest pageant is held, along with a parade and a teen dance. Begun in 1975.

★ 3570 ★
Big Sky - SKI CARNIVAL FESTIVAL. February, annual, 3 days, Mountain Village Area. Contact: Big Sky of Montana, Incorporated, Marketing Department, Big Sky, Montana 59716.

The carnival honors King Winter Sooper Sports. There is a Pro-Am race, a Winter Sooper Sports event, a Sooper Sports Parade. The activities are centered around skiing and winter. Begun around 1974.

★ 3571 ★
Big Sky - SUMMER FESTIVAL. August, annual,

Seasons

MONTANA (Continued)

Meadow Village. Contact: Big Sky of Montana, Incorporated, Marketing Department, Big Sky, Montana 59716.

The festival includes a tournament in tennis and golf, as well as Sooper Sport competition. Participants in this competition select ten events out of a possible twenty. (The Sooper Sport competition goes on for four weeks, it is not tied solely to the festival.) There is also an antique car display. Begun around 1973.

★ 3572 ★
Red Lodge – WINTER CARNIVAL. Mid February, 3 days. Contact: Chamber of Commerce, Post Office Box 998, Red Lodge, Montana 59068.

Traditional winter sports and fun activities are featured in this seasonal festival.

★ 3573 ★
Whitefish – WINTER CARNIVAL. Early February, annual, 3 days. Contact: Chamber of Commerce, Post Office Box 1309, Whitefish, Montana 59937.

Festival events include dog-sled races, cross-country ski races, ski-torchlight parade, ice-sculpture contest, costume competition, art show, sleigh rides, carnival games, street games, Grand Parade, banquets, breakfast, and horse judging.

NEVADA

★ 3574 ★
Reno – WINTER CARNIVAL. Early December, University of Nevada campus. Contact: Greater Reno Chamber of Commerce, Post Office Box 3499, Reno, Nevada 89501.

Events include skiing and a display of snow sculptures.

NEW HAMPSHIRE

★ 3575 ★
Concord – NEW HAMPSHIRE TECHNICAL INSTITUTE WINTER CARNIVAL. Early February, 3 days. Contact: Greater Concord Chamber of Commerce, 83 North Main Street, Concord, New Hampshire 03301.

A traditional festival featuring winter fun activities.

★ 3576 ★
Hampton – HAMPTON SUMMERFEST CARNIVAL. Early July, 4 days. Contact: Secretary, Hampton Summerfest Carnival, Hampton, New Hampshire 03842.

A ten mile marathon, parade, tournaments, circus, barbeque highlight the events in this community celebration.

★ 3577 ★
Hanover – DARTMOUTH WINTER CARNIVAL. Mid February, annual, 2 days. Contact: Chamber of Commerce, Post Office Box 451, Hanover, New Hampshire 03755.

A festival of winter sports, including intercollegiate skiing, basketball, hockey, swimming, and snow sculpture. Since 1911, except during World War I and World War II, when it was deactivated.

★ 3578 ★
Ossipee – FALL FESTIVAL. Late September, 2 days. Contact: New Hampshire Division of Economic Development, Concord, New Hampshire 03301.

A barbeque, family picnic, and field day highlight the events in celebration of the beauty of the season.

★ 3579 ★
Warner – FALL FOLIAGE FESTIVAL. Early October, 3 days. Contact: New Hampshire Division of Economic Development, Concord, New Hampshire 03301.

An old fashioned country fair featuring food, woodmen's contests, arts and crafts, flea markets, midway, all amid the colorful autumn foliage. Also dances, parade, and suppers.

NEW JERSEY

★ 3580 ★
Seaside Heights – SPRING FESTIVAL. Mid June, 3 days. Contact: Mayor's Office, Seaside Heights, New Jersey 08751.

A parade, sidewalk sales, and fireworks highlight this celebration of spring.

NEW MEXICO

★ 3581 ★
Albuquerque – WINTER CARNIVAL. Early April, annual, 2 days, Sandia (Peak) Ski Area. Contact:

NEW MEXICO (Continued)

Ski Area Office, Sandia Peak Ski Area, Albuquerque, New Mexico 87115.

Traditional winter sports and other events are featured to celebrate winter fun.

★ 3582 ★
Corona - SUMMER FESTIVAL.   Early August, annual, 2 days.   Contact: Tourist Division, New Mexico Department of Development, 114 Washington Avenue, Santa Fe, New Mexico 87503.

Arts and crafts fair with a parade, rodeo, fiddlers' contest, dance, and banquet.   Begun in 1975.

★ 3583 ★
Red River - WINTER SKI CARNIVAL.   February, annual, 3 days, Red River Ski area.   Contact: University of New Mexico, Albuquerque, New Mexico 87106; or Chamber of Commerce, Red River, New Mexico 87558.

The University of New Mexico sponsors this winter carnival, includes the downhill and other ski races.

★ 3584 ★
Santa Fe - SPRING FESTIVAL.   Early May (1st weekend), annual, 1-2 days, La Cienega Village Museum (El Rancho de las Golodrinas).   Contact: Father Benedicto Cuesta, Curator, La Cienega Village Museum, Santa Fe, New Mexico; or Colonial New Mexico Historical Foundation, 135 Camino Escondido, Santa Fe, New Mexico 87501.

Demonstrations of eighteenth century ranch crafts such as blacksmithing, corn grinding, and soap making. The mills, the blacksmith and the wheel wright shops are open; carding, spinning, weaving, soapmaking and other tasks are performed in the old way.   Groups of musicos perform old New Mexico music; choral groups, Spanish Colonial dancers and other groups perform.   Spanish colonial crafts market sells traditional crafts and the courtry store is open.   Alos includes the Juan Bautista de Anza Pageant.

NEW YORK

★ 3585 ★
Canandaigua - SPRING FLING! or THIS YEAR WE MADE IT.   Mid March, 1 day, Bristol Mountain Ski Center.   Contact: Finger Lakes Association, Incorporated, 309 Lake Street, Penn Yan, New York 14527; or Joseph J. Kohler III, Bristol Mountain

Ski Center, Route 64, Canandaigua, New York 14424.

Celebration of the end of winter, the coming of spring.

★ 3586 ★
Cohocton - FALL FOLIAGE FESTIVAL.   Mid October, 3 days.   Contact: Finger Lakes Association, Incorporated, 309 Lake Street, Penn Yan, New York 14527.

National Tree Sitting Contest, Grange luncheon, church dinner, flea market, pancake feast, and arts and crafts on the Village Green are a few of the festival highlights.

★ 3587 ★
Cohocton - WINTER CARNIVAL.   February, 2 days. Contact: Finger Lakes Association, 309 Lake Street, Penn Yan, New York 14527.

Winter sports events including skiing, tobogganing, bob sledding, ice skating, and a dance highlight the activities.

★ 3588 ★
Elmira - FALL FESTIVAL OF MOUNT SAVIOUR. Mid September, annual, 1 day.   Contact: Finger Lakes Association, Incorporated, 309 Lake Street, Penn Yan, New York 14527.

An arts and crafts show including ceramics, jewelry, and sculpture; choral groups, and folk dancing. Begun around 1954.

★ 3589 ★
Ithaca - FALL-IN.   Early October, annual, 1 afternoon, Cornell University.   Contact: Education Coordinator, Cornell University, 100 Judd Falls Road, Ithaca, New York 14853.

A gathering of local artists.   Booths include displays of such things as nature photography, folk dancing, pumpkin carving, sketching, dried flower arrangements, edible wild foods, herbal teas, bonsai plants, and by such groups as the University Press, the student chapter of the American Veterinary Medical Association, etc. Started in 1971.

★ 3590 ★
Monticello - WINTER CARNIVAL MONTH.   February, 3 weeks.   Contact: Chamber of Commerce, Box 51, Monticello, New York 12701.

Seasons

NEW YORK (Continued)

Traditional winter sports and other fun events are scheduled in celebration of the season.

★ 3591 ★
Saranac Lake - WINTER CARNIVAL.   Mid February (Lincoln's birthday weekend), annual, 3 days.   Contact: Chamber of Commerce, 30 Main Street, Saranac Lake, New York   12983.

Features winter sports such as ice fishing, snowshoe and snowmobile races, skiing, and a parade.   Begun around 1898.

★ 3592 ★
Skaneateles - SNOWFEST.   Late January-early February, 3 days, Austin Park.   Contact: Finger Lakes Association, 309 Lake Street, Penn Yan, New York   14527.

Events include a hockey exhibition, dog sled race, square dance, sleigh rides, sky diving, snow sculpture, figure skating, broomball game.

★ 3593 ★
Sodus - BRANTLING WINTER CARNIVAL.   Early March, annual, 2 days, Brantling Ski Area.   Contact: Finger Lakes Association, Incorporated, 309 Lake Street, Penn Yan, New York   14527.

A dual race and other winter sports and activities are featured.

NORTH CAROLINA

★ 3594 ★
Banner Elk - WATAUGA AND AVERY COUNTY WINTER FESTIVAL.   Late January-early February, annual, 11 days.   Contact: Boone Area Chamber of Commerce, 827 Blowing Rock Road, Boone, North Carolina 28607.

A celebration of winter with a round of social events, cultural activities and winter sports events. Also held (simultaneously) in Blowing Rock, Boone and Linville.

★ 3595 ★
Blowing Rock - WATAUGA AND AVERY COUNTY WINTER FESTIVAL.   Late January-early February, annual, 11 days.   Contact: Boone Area Chamber of Commerce, 827 Blowing Rock Road, Boone, North Carolina 28607.

A celebration of winter with a round of social events, cultural activities and winter sports events.   Also held (simultaneously) in Boone, Banner Elk and Linville.

★ 3596 ★
Boone - WATAUGA AND AVERY COUNTY WINTER FESTIVAL.   Late January-early February, annual, 11 days.   Contact: Boone Area Chamber of Commerce, 827 Blowing Rock Road, Boone, North Carolina 28607.

A celebration of winter with a round of social events, cultural activities and winter sports events.   Also held (simultaneously) in Blowing Rock, Banner Elk, and Linville.

★ 3597 ★
Chapel Hill - FALL FESTIVAL.   Early October, 1 day, Franklin Street.   Contact: Shirley Harper, Recreation Department, Chapel Hill, North Carolina 27514.

An old town fair, with games, bands and dancing, and refreshments.

★ 3598 ★
Garner - CIVITAN SPRING FESTIVAL.   Mid May, Forest Hills Shopping Center.   Contact: Garner Civitan Club, Post Office Box 205, Garner, North Carolina   27529.

A fun event filled with games, rides and concessions.

★ 3599 ★
Linville - WATAUGA AND AVERY COUNTY WINTER FESTIVAL.   Late January-early February, annual, 11 days.   Contact: Boone Area Chamber of Commerce, 827 Blowing Rock Road, Boone, North Carolina 28607.

A celebration of winter with a round of social events, cultural activities and winter sports events.   Also held (simultaneously) in Boone, Blowing Rock, Banner Elk.

★ 3600 ★
Mount Airy - AUTUMN LEAVES FESTIVAL.   October, annual, 3 days, downtown Main Street.   Contact: Chamber of Commerce, Post Office Box 913, Mount Airy, North Carolina   27030.

Bandstands offer country, gospel, clogging, and rock music every hour.   There are exhibits and booths featuring quilting, apple cider and butter, churning,

NORTH CAROLINA (Continued)

kraut making, refreshments and souvenirs. On exhibit are paintings, craft items and hobby displays. Started in 1967.

★ 3601 ★
Wendell - HARVEST FESTIVAL DAYS. Early October, annual. Contact: Chamber of Commerce, Post Office Box 562, Wendell, North Carolina 27591.

Events include arts and crafts displays and a parade.

NORTH DAKOTA

★ 3602 ★
Minot - WINTERFEST. Early February, annual. Contact: Chamber of Commerce, Box 940, Minot, North Dakota 58701; or Assistant Travel Director, North Dakota State Highway Department, Capitol Grounds, Bismarck, North Dakota 58505.

The festival celebrates winter with the Regina (Canada)-Minot 250 Snowmobile Race; contests such as chess, checkers, arm-wrestling and beard growing; an ethnic food fair; cultural performances; and pop entertainment.

★ 3603 ★
Valley City - NORTH DAKOTA WINTER SHOW. Mid March, annual, 10 days. Contact: Valley City Chamber of Commerce, 137 North Central Avenue, Valley City, North Dakota 58072.

The town celebrates the snow season with a bountiful program including horse and livestock shows, crop judging contests, and an indoor rodeo.

OHIO

★ 3604 ★
Bainbridge - FALL FESTIVAL OF LEAVES. Mid October, annual, 3 days. Contact: Chamber of Commerce, Bainbridge, Ohio 45612.

To celebrate the glory of the autumn foliage, the town offers old-time crafts and entertainment to recall the joys of the past.

★ 3605 ★
Mansfield - OHIO WINTER SKI CARNIVAL. February, annual, 3 days, Snow Trails Ski Area. Contact: Dave Carto, Snow Trails Ski Area, Post Office Box 163, Mansfield, Ohio 44901.

The event features races, dancing, a torchlight parade and a costume contest. Started in 1961.

PENNSYLVANIA

★ 3606 ★
Bedford - FALL FOLIAGE FESTIVAL. Mid October, annual, 2 weekends. Contact: Fall Foliage Festival Committee, Bedford, Pennsylvania 15522.

Grand parade of 200 antique autos. Bedford County wagon train, window displays, walking tours, bus tours, coin and ceramic shows, art show, and bazaars. Fiddle contest. Flea markets and apple butter making. Shawnee Rangers muzzle loading shoot. Antique show and sale.

★ 3607 ★
Bryn Mawr - MAY DAY. Early May (1st), annual, 1 day, Bryn Mawr College campus. Contact: Bryn Mawr College, Office of Public Information, Bryn Mawr, Pennsylvania 19010.

Classes are canceled for a day which begins with the sophomores making May baskets for the seniors, before awakening them with song for a breakfast of strawberries and cream and medieval festivities. Included are the procession of classes, dancing around the maypole, and Scottish and Morris dancing. Speeches are given by the May Queen and other dignitaries, and awards for the year are presented. Further entertainment is provided by a hoop race, choral and dramatic presentations (including Dragon Plays), tumblers, jesters, musicians and singers, all in costume. Begun in 1900.

★ 3608 ★
Clarion - AUTUMN LEAF FESTIVAL. October, annual, 7 days. Contact: The Clarion County Chamber of Commerce, Five North Sixth Avenue, Clarion, Pennsylvania 16214.

Fall foliage decorates the hills and is reflected in the Clarion River. Events include parade with lavish floats and outstanding bands and marching units. Native craftsmen work at finding unusual gifts and souvenirs. Making of glass is observed and beauty queens are crowned. Over 200 antique automobiles on display. Observe scenery from a helicopter or a ferris wheel. Old fashioned barbeque served.

★ 3609 ★
Conneaut Lake - SNOW BALL FESTIVAL. Early February (1st week), annual, 2 days, Community Hall. Contact: Reverend George H. Rutherford,

PENNSYLVANIA (Continued)

Box 124, Conneaut Lake, Pennsylvania 16316.

To pull the community together during the winter season, the Kiwanis Club sponsors this series of events. The junior class of the Conneaut Lake high school selects a queen to preside over the festival which includes a talent show, snowmobile safari, a fashion show, a dance, exhibits, a program arranged by the Boy Scouts, snow sculpture, art shows by elementary school children, and various other events. Begun in 1971.

★ 3610 ★
Easton - SPRING FESTIVAL. May-June, 4 weeks, Center City. Contact: Department of Commerce, Bureau of Travel Development, 431 South Office Building, Harrisburg, Pennsylvania 17120.

Festival offers hobby and craft fairs, international folk fairs, Civic Saturday, and Youth Day (all on different days).

★ 3611 ★
Lewistown - FALL FESTIVAL AND GOOSE DAY CELEBRATION. Late September-early October, annual, 5 days, throughout Mifflin County. Contact: Ms. Anita Corless, Mifflin County Tourist Promotion Agency, Lewistown, Pennsylvania 17044.

Festival events include walking and bus tours, arts and crafts, beauty pageant, parade, pig roast, fish fry, apple butter boil, and food stands.

★ 3612 ★
Lewistown - FALL FOLIAGE FESTIVAL. Mid October, annual, 4 days, Juniata Valley Area, Mifflin and Juniata Counties. Contact: Department of Commerce, Bureau of Travel Development, 431 South Office Building, Harrisburg, Pennsylvania 17120.

Tours start in Lewistown, include Amish country blacksmith, stores, historic landmarks, two covered bridges, underground railroad, museum, and fossil mine. Apple butter making, crafts displays, jazz fest, barbershop quartet, antique sales and antique auto show complete the festival events.

★ 3613 ★
Renovo - PENNSYLVANIA FLAMING FOLIAGE FESTIVAL. October, annual, 3 days. Contact: Clinton County Tourist Promotion Agency, 151 Susquehanna Avenue, Lock Haven, Pennsylvania 17745.

Parade, fireworks, beauty pageant, displays, dances and balls, and a band contest highlight the festival events, in honor of the beauty of the season.

★ 3614 ★
Selinsgrove - SUMMER FESTIVAL AND HOMECOMING. Early August, annual, 1 week. Contact: Department of Commerce, Bureau of Travel Development, 431 South Office Building, Harrisburg, Pennsylvania 17120.

Activities include pageant, "Out of This Wilderness", river regatta, tours of homes and industries, antique car show, parade, band concerts, art and craft displays, block party and dance, flintrock gun demonstration and contest, flea market, and fire company pumping contest.

★ 3615 ★
Uniontown - FAYETTE COUNTY FALL FOLIAGE FESTIVAL. October, annual, 1 month, throughout Fayette County. Contact: Fayette Festival Association, Box 1096, Uniontown, Pennsylvania 15401.

Activities include "cakes 'n' sausage" suppers, square dancing, old time fiddlin', parades, giant barbeque beef dinner and chicken and biscuit dinner. Self-conducted tours of mountainous roads through fall foliage.

★ 3616 ★
Uniontown - SPRING FESTIVAL. Early May, annual, 3 days, Fayette County Fairgrounds. Contact: Uniontown Chamber of Commerce, 11 Pittsburgh Street, Uniontown, Pennsylvania 15401.

Arts and crafts festival with heritage theme. Ethnic groups present crafts, food, dances, music, etc. Old fiddler's contest and public square dance. Held at the fairgrounds on U.S. 119, between Uniontown and Connellsville.

RHODE ISLAND

★ 3617 ★
Charlestown - RHODE ISLAND SUMMER SPECTACULAR. Late June-early September, 43 days, The Umbrella Factory, Old Post Road. Contact: Rhode Island Department of Economic Development, Tourist Promotion Division, One Weybosset Hill, Providence, Rhode Island 02903.

Professional craftsmen give demonstrations of woodcarving, pottery, leaded glass, furniture making, glassblowing, hand tooled leather, and floral drying and

RHODE ISLAND (Continued)

arranging. There is an eighteenth century farm, complete with animals.

SOUTH CAROLINA

★ 3618 ★
Myrtle Beach - INDIAN SUMMER DAYS. September-November, annual, 3 months. Contact: Greater Myrtle Beach Chamber of Commerce, Post Office Box 1326, Myrtle Beach, South Carolina 29577.

Events include golf tournaments, golf clinics, a film festival, concerts, fishing derbies, historic tours, and many other activities.

★ 3619 ★
Myrtle Beach - SPRING FLING DAYS. Mid April-early June, annual, 7 weeks. Contact: Greater Myrtle Beach Chamber of Commerce, Post Office Box 1326, Myrtle Beach, South Carolina 29577.

Golf tournaments, art exhibits, free movies, beach games, historic and garden tours, and other entertainment are offered. Begun in 1972.

★ 3620 ★
Myrtle Beach - SUN FUN FESTIVAL. Early June, annual, 4 days. Contact: Greater Myrtle Beach Chamber of Commerce, Post Office Box 1326, Myrtle Beach, South Carolina 29577.

South Carolina's largest festival, it features a variety of aquatic events and beach games including ever-popular sand building contest. Other activities include golf, dances, children's day at amusement parks, a "human checker game", a kite flying contest, historical tours and a watermelon eating contest. For entertainment, the visitor will want to see a parade, the arts and crafts show and concerts. There is also a Miss Bikina Wahine pageant and the crowning of Miss Sun Fun. Begun in 1952.

★ 3621 ★
Saint Matthews - CALHOUN COUNTY PURPLE MARTIN FESTIVAL. Late April, annual, 3 days. Contact: Calhoun County Chamber of Commerce, Post Office Box 444, Saint Matthews, South Carolina 29135.

Thousands of purple martin and people attend this festival which includes a purple martin house building contest and field day activities. Other events available are antique shows, arts and crafts displays,

historic and farm tours, flower show, and music for all ages.

★ 3622 ★
Summerville - SAINT PAUL'S SPRING FESTIVAL. Mid April, annual, 2 days. Contact: Mrs. J.C. Zimmerman, 223 Sumter Avenue, Summerville, South Carolina 29483.

Events include a food fair, house and garden tour, a sidewalk art show, and an auction. Refreshments are available.

SOUTH DAKOTA

★ 3623 ★
Aberdeen - SOUTH DAKOTA SNOW QUEEN FESTIVAL AND GOVERNOR'S CUP CROSS COUNTRY SNOW-MOBILE RACE. Early-mid January, annual, 8 days. Contact: Aberdeen Jaycees, 516 South Main Street, Aberdeen, South Dakota 57401.

The race is the first two days of the events and is run from Pierre to Aberdeen with an overnight stop in Mobridge. This is followed by the festival with the crowning of the South Dakota Snow Queen. The festival also features snowmobile parades (some in the evening by torchlight), a Junior Snow Queen Contest, and a talent show for youngsters from all over the state. Big name entertainers perform for the coronation program.

★ 3624 ★
Brookings - SUMMER FESTIVAL. Mid July, annual, 2 days. Contact: Brookings Area Chamber of Commerce, 317 Third Avenue, Post Office Box 431, Brookings, South Dakota 57006.

The town becomes a center of arts and crafts as booths offer homemade articles and businesses display works of art.

★ 3625 ★
Lennox - SUMMER FESTIVAL. Mid June, annual. Contact: Division of Tourism Development, State Office Building 2, Pierre, South Dakota 57501.

The town celebrates its progress and its crops for the year with games, parades and good food.

★ 3626 ★
Pierre - WINTER CARNIVAL. Early January, annual, 6 days. Contact: Chamber of Commerce, Post Office

Seasons

SOUTH DAKOTA (Continued)

Box 548, Pierre, South Dakota 57501.

Sponsored by the Pierre Jaycees, the carnival is a winter extravaganza on the South Dakota Great Lakes. Includes a scuba diving contest in the tailwaters of Oahe Dam, an ice sculpture contest, winter softball game and other activities.

★ 3627 ★
Sioux Falls - SNOWFLAKE DAYS.   Mid January, annual, 3 days.   Contact: Chamber of Commerce, 101 West Ninth Street, Post Office Box 1425, Sioux Falls, South Dakota 57101.

Includes skiing, ice skating, queen contest, ice sculpturing, snowmobile rides and races.   Also a parade of snowmobile floats and an outside picnic and hockey games.

TENNESSEE

★ 3628 ★
Chattanooga - FALL COLOR CRUISE.   Late October, 2 days.   Contact: Chattanooga Convention and Tourist Bureau, 349 McCallie Avenue, Chattanooga, Tennessee 37402.

Scenic float and auto tours of Chattanooga and the surrounding area.

TEXAS

★ 3629 ★
Fort Worth - MAYFEST (TRINITY RIVER FESTIVAL). Early May (1st weekend), annual, Trinity Park. Contact: Tarrant County Convention and Visitors Bureau, 700 Throckmorton Street, Fort Worth, Texas 76102.

Sponsored by a number of local organizations, the festival includes an outdoor art show, sporting events, and entertainment.   There are special children's events.

★ 3630 ★
Fort Worth - OKTOBERFEST.   Early October (1st weekend), annual, Will Rogers Memorial Complex. Contact: Tarrant County Convention and Visitors Bureau, 700 Throckmorton Street, Fort Worth, Texas 76102.

A fund raising benefit for the Student Concert Fund, the event is sponsored by the Symphony League of

Fort Worth.

★ 3631 ★
Lampasas - SPRING HO FESTIVAL.   Mid July, annual, 4 days, Hancock Park.   Contact: Chamber of Commerce, 501 East Second Street, Post Office Box 627, Lampasas, Texas 76550.

Historical tour, arts and crafts, parades, fiddle convention, band concert, dances, flea market, water activities, beauty contest, horse show, and other events highlight this happy time.   Begun around 1972.

★ 3632 ★
McAllen - INTERNATIONAL SPRING FIESTA. March, annual.   Contact: Chamber of Commerce, Ten North Broadway, Post Office Box 790, McAllen, Texas 78501.

Crowning of Duchess of Palms, International Pro-Am Golf Tournament, and other events highlight the fiesta activities.   The Ballet Folklorico performs, and there is a Mexican food fair and street dancing. Other activities include a garden exposition, an arts and crafts show, tennis and shuffleboard tournaments.

★ 3633 ★
New Braunfels - COUNTY SUMMER FAIR.   May-June.   Contact: Chamber of Commerce, Box 180, New Braunfels, Texas 78130.

The fair features an arts and crafts show, farm exhibits, German foods and refreshments.   Activities include a rodeo, western dances and horse races.

★ 3634 ★
Pecos - FALL FAIR FESTIVAL.   October, annual, 4 days.   Contact: Chamber of Commerce, 506 South Oak Street, Box 27, Pecos, Texas 79772.

Prize agricultural specimens from irrigated acres in Reeves County are exhibited and there are other festival events.

★ 3635 ★
Round Top - WINEDALE SPRING FESTIVAL.   April. Contact: L.W. Taylor, Box 11, Round Top, Texas 78954.

Arts events include a German play and crafts demonstrations at an historic inn.   Festival music includes choral, piano and organ concerts, plus early American popular music.

TEXAS (Continued)

★ 3636 ★
Winnsboro - AUTUMN TRAILS. Late September to early November, annual, weekends. Contact: Chamber of Commerce, 318 North Main Street, Suite 4, Winnsboro, Texas 75494.

Special routes through autumn beauty of forestlands. Associate attractions include an old syrup mill in operation, century-old cider mill (free cup for visitors), Queen Autumn coronation, one-act plays, gospel songfest, pilgrimage of early Texas homes, barn and square dances, turkey shoot, and a round trip horse-back trail ride to Duncanville. Art and flower shows also lend color to the popular event.

UTAH

★ 3637 ★
Cedar City - SPRING CARNIVAL. Late March, annual, 9 days, Brian Head. Contact: Chamber of Commerce, 257 North Main Street, Post Office Box 220, Cedar City, Utah 84720.

Activities include sports events such as ski racing, hot-dogging, and shokel racing. In addition, participants dress up in costume and attend dances and films.

VERMONT

★ 3638 ★
Barnet - NORTHEAST KINGDOM FALL FOLIAGE FESTIVAL. Late September-early October, annual, 6 days. Contact: Fall Festival Committee, Box 38, West Danville, Vermont 05873.

Each town features one day of activities, one after the other, and offers meals featuring regional cook-ing. Activities include such things as country auctions, Lumberjack Ball, square dancing, tours, hikes, art displays and sales, crafts displays and sales, maple sugar parties, concerts, film festival, hymn sings and costume parade.

★ 3639 ★
Brookfield - ICE HARVEST FESTIVAL AND ICE CUTTING CONTEST. Mid February, annual, 1 day, Green Trails Resort. Contact: Green Trails Ski Resort, Brookfield, Vermont 05036; or Events Editor, State of Vermont Agency of Development and Community Affairs, 61 Elm Street, Montpelier, Vermont 05602.

Winter fun activities and contests highlight this seasonal festival in Brookfield.

★ 3640 ★
Cabot - NORTHEAST KINGDOM FALL FOLIAGE FESTIVAL. Late September-early October, annual, 6 days. Contact: Fall Festival Committee, Box 38, West Danville, Vermont 05873.

Each town features one day of activities, one after the other, and offers meals featuring regional cook-ing. Activities include such things as country auctions, Lumberjack Ball, square dancing, tours, hikes, art displays and sales, crafts displays and sales, maple sugar parties, concerts, film festival, hymn sings and costume parades.

★ 3641 ★
Groton - NORTHEAST KINGDOM FALL FOLIAGE FESTIVAL. Late September-early October, annual, 6 days. Contact: Fall Festival Committee, Box 38, West Danville, Vermont 05873.

Each town features one day of activities, one after the other, and offers meals featuring regional cook-ing. Activities include such things as country auctions, Lumberjack Ball, square dancing, tours, hikes, art displays and sales, crafts displays and sales, maple sugar parties, concerts, film festival, hymn sings and costume parade.

★ 3642 ★
Peacham - NORTHEAST KINGDOM FALL FOLIAGE FESTIVAL. Late September-early October, annual, 6 days. Contact: Fall Festival Committee, Box 38, West Danville, Vermont 05873.

Each town features one day of activities, one after the other, and offers meals featuring regional cook-ing. Activities include such things as country auctions, Lumberjack Ball, square dancing, tours, hikes, art displays and sales, crafts displays and sales, maple sugar parties, concerts, film festival hymn sings and costume parade.

★ 3643 ★
Plainfield - NORTHEAST KINGDOM FALL FOLIAGE FESTIVAL. Late September-early October, annual, 6 days. Contact: Fall Festival Committee, Box 38, West Danville, Vermont 05873.

Each town features one day of activities, one after the other, and offers meals featuring regional cooking. Activities include such things as country auctions, Lumberjack Ball, square dancing, tours, hikes, art displays and sales, crafts displays and sales, maple

VERMONT (Continued)

sugar parties, concerts, film festival, hymn sings and costume parades.

★ 3644 ★
Stowe - WINTER CARNIVAL. Mid-late January, annual, 8 days. Contact: David Salembier, Stowe Area Association, Main Street, Stowe, Vermont 05672.

Winter sports including New England dog sled races, figure skating exhibitions, ice sculpture contests, ski races and torchlight ski parades, hockey, kite flying, and exhibitions of tennis. Parties at night.

★ 3645 ★
Waitsfield - NEW ENGLAND KANDAHAR. Late March, annual, 1 day, Mad River Glen Ski Area. Contact: Kenneth Quackenbush, Mad River Glen Ski Area, Waitsfield, Vermont 05673.

Winter sports enthusiasts come from all over to attend this outstanding skiing event.

★ 3646 ★
Walden - NORTHEAST KINGDOM FALL FOLIAGE FESTIVAL. Late September-early October, annual, 6 days. Contact: Fall Festival Committee, Box 38, West Danville, Vermont 05873.

Each town features one day of activities, one after the other, and offers meals featuring regional cooking. Activities include such things as country auctions, Lumberjack Ball, square dancing, tours, hikes, art displays and sales, crafts displays and sales, maple sugar parties, concerts, film festival, hymn sings, and costume parades.

VIRGINIA

★ 3647 ★
Arlington - MAY FESTIVAL FOR SENIOR ADULTS. Mid May, 1 day, Thomas Jefferson Community Center. Contact: Page N. Price, 1709 North Huntington Avenue, Arlington, Virginia 22303.

The events include music and dancing and a "Roaring 20's Costume Contest". Lunch is available at a nominal fee. Free transportation is provided with special pickups for those in wheel chairs. National, local and state dignitaries are on hand at the festival.

★ 3648 ★
Charlottesville - MERRIE OLD ENGLAND SUMMER FESTIVAL AND VILLAGE FAIR OF ARTS AND HANDICRAFTS. Late July, 1 weekend. Contact: Manager, Boar's Head Inn, Post Office Box 5185, Charlottesville, Virginia 22903.

Craft exhibits; pageantry; early English dancing, archery, and jousting tournaments; festival feasts; and special entertainment highlight this festival and fair.

★ 3649 ★
Clifton Forge - FALL FOLIAGE FESTIVAL. Mid October, annual, 3 days. Contact: The Hunt and Fun Festival, Incorporated, Post Office Box 608, Clifton Forge, Virginia 24422.

The festival highlight is the splendor of the fall foliage of the Alleghany highlands. The round of activities includes handcrafts demonstrations, an art show including sidewalk artists, a flea market and antique cars. An authentic steam powered gristmill grinds fresh corn meal, bands play and exhibition square dancers demonstrate. There is a pig roast.

★ 3650 ★
Colonial Beach - POTOMAC RIVER FESTIVAL. Mid June, annual, 3 days. Contact: Secretary, Colonial Beach Chamber of Commerce, Two Boundary Street, Colonial Beach, Virginia 22443.

This Potomac River resort town ushers in summer with land and water parades; beauty, majorette, and band contests; a dance and fireworks display. Begun around 1952.

★ 3651 ★
Front Royal - FESTIVAL OF LEAVES. Mid-late October, annual, 2 days. Contact: Chamber of Commerce, 14 West Main Street, Box 568, Front Royal, Virginia 22630.

Located at the northernmost entrance to Skyline Drive, the town celebrates the beauty of the autumn colors with a variety of activities. There are tours of Confederate homes, colonial churches, and museums. Visitors may browse the "Land Mark Art Show", a flea market, and booths selling products ranging from fresh apple butter to such crafts as hand painted jewelry and hooked rugs. Early American crafts are demonstrated. Other attractions include pony rides, antique fire engines, a Heritage feast, historical pageants, and a "Silver Tea". Sponsored by the Warren Heritage Society.

VIRGINIA (Continued)

★ 3652 ★
Monterey - HIGHLAND COUNTY FALL FOLIAGE
FESTIVAL. Mid October, annual, 4 days (2 week-
ends, 2 days each). Contact: Executive Secretary,
Highland County Chamber of Commerce, Monterey,
Virginia 24465.

Highland county's claim to special fall scenery is
based on an abundance of beautiful hardwoods plus
the beauty of the maple sugar orchards. The activities include scenic drives, homemade mountain foods
and displays.

★ 3653 ★
South Hill - HARVEST FESTIVAL. October, annual.
Contact: President, South Hill Jaycees, Post Office
Box 613, South Hill, Virginia 23970.

With the end of summer, this town welcomes fall
and the end of the harvest with a country music
show, float parade, and harvest dance. Begun
around 1954.

★ 3654 ★
Waynesboro - FALL FOLIAGE FESTIVAL. October,
annual, 24 days. Contact: Mrs. Phyllis M.
Pendergraft, General Chairman, Post Office Box
396, Waynesboro, Virginia 22980.

Activities include horse shows, parades, and concerts. The event also offers food, crafts, antiques
and an art festival.

WASHINGTON

★ 3655 ★
Bellingham - BLOSSOMTIME. May (3rd weekend),
annual. Contact: D.A.R.E. Association, Post
Office Box 958, Bellingham, Washington 98225.

Activities include a carnival, skating, parades, an
art exhibit and an aerobatic display. Sports competitions held include a hole-in-one golf tournament,
motorcycle races, a horse show, car rally, and
hydroplane races.

★ 3656 ★
Leavenworth - AUTUMN LEAF FESTIVAL. Late
September-early October, annual, 9 days. Contact:
Autumn Leaf Festival, Leavenworth, Washington 98826.

Events include an art display and show, handicraft
display, flower show, and flea market. The local

amateur theater group has several performances
during the festival. Begun around 1968.

★ 3657 ★
Lynnwood - LYNNORAMA SUMMER FESTIVAL.
July (2nd week), annual, 7 days. Contact: Don
Jenson, Chairman, Post Office Box 866, Lynnwood,
Washington 98036.

The festival's activities include a unique game of
water soccer in a state-wide competition of fire
departments using high-pressure hoses to propel the
ball. Other sporting events include field day competitions, the Junior Olympics, and old-fashioned
tree topping and cutting contests. Other attractions
include arts and crafts displays, an open air band
concert, a watermelon bust, carnival and a dance.
Begun around 1950.

★ 3658 ★
Spokane - SPOKANE VALLEY FALL FESTIVAL
PARADE. October (1st Sunday), annual, 1 day.
Contact: Spokane Valley Chamber of Commerce,
Box 14021, Opportunity Station, Spokane, Washington
99214.

Late season parade of competing floats along with
high school marching units and bands, and a nice
review of antique cars. Begun around 1968.

WEST VIRGINIA

★ 3659 ★
Davis - TUCKER COUNTY ALPINE FESTIVAL.
March, annual, 4 days, most but not all events
at either Blackwater Lodge or Canaan Valley State
Park. Contact: Alpine Festival Association, Box
16, Davis, West Virginia 26260.

Included in the events are skiing, Alpine Antics
Affair, and several ski races including the West
Virginia Governor's Cup Ski Race. Other activities
include arts and crafts demonstrations and exhibitions,
a German Fest dance, beer fest, Alpine dance and
concert, and ski movies. The Alpine Festival
Association also sponsors a number of activities
throughout the year such as the West Virginia Championship Snowmobile Race (February), Four Wheel Drive
Rally (May), Bicycle Endurance Race (July), Blackwater 100 (June), Canaan Valley Open (August), and
Blackwater Rendezvous (October). The snowmobile
races, ski races and the Blackwater rendezvous feature
Governor's Cups for the top winners.

Seasons

WEST VIRGINIA (Continued)

★ 3660 ★
Saint Albans - SNOWFLAKE FESTIVAL. Late November, 3 days. Contact: Mrs. Virginia Osborne, Five Aliff Lane, Saint Albans, West Virginia 25177; or West Virginia Department of Commerce, Arts and Crafts Division, Building 6, 1900 Washington Street East, Charleston, West Virginia 25305.

Crafts events are included in the festival celebrating the beginning of winter.

WISCONSIN

★ 3661 ★
Conover - WINTER FROLIC. Early February, 1 day. Contact: Chamber of Commerce, Phelps, Wisconsin 54554.

Sponsored by the Lions Club, a traditional winter festival with sports activities and other events. Also held in Phelps.

★ 3662 ★
Ephraim - FYR BAL FEST. Mid June. Contact: Door County Chamber of Commerce, Post Office Box 219, Sturgeon Bay, Wisconsin 54235.

The city's official welcome of summer.

★ 3663 ★
Phelps - WINTER FROLIC. Early February, 1 day. Contact: Chamber of Commerce, Phelps, Wisconsin 54554.

Sponsored by the Lions Club, a traditional winter festival with sports activities and other events. Also held in Conover.

★ 3664 ★
Phillips - WINTER FESTIVAL. Late January, 2 days. Contact: Director, Vacation and Travel Development, Department of Natural Resources, Wisconsin State Division of Tourism, Post Office Box 450, Madison, Wisconsin 53701.

Traditional winter festival events plus snowmobile races.

★ 3665 ★
Rhinelander - FESTIVAL OF THE LEAVES. Early October, 2 days. Contact: Rhinelander Area Chamber of Commerce, City Hall Square, Post Office Box 795, Rhinelander, Wisconsin 54501.

A festival in honor of the beauty of the fall season.

★ 3666 ★
Saint Germain - FAMILY WINTER FUN DAY. Early January, annual, 1 day. Contact: Chamber of Commerce, Saint Germain, Wisconsin 54558.

Sponsored by the Bo-Boen Snowmobile Club, a traditional winter celebration.

★ 3667 ★
Sister Bay - FALL FESTIVAL. Mid October, annual, 3 days. Contact: Door County Chamber of Commerce, Post Office Box 219, Sturgeon Bay, Wisconsin 54235.

Events include a large carnival featuring rides, games, music, and other activities. Local merchants and civic groups offer sales of merchandise, bazaars, and food. In addition, there may be theatrical events, a parade, and fireworks.

CANADA - ALBERTA

★ 3668 ★
Banff - ALBERTA WINTER GAMES AND BANFF WINTER FESTIVAL. Early March, 4 days. Contact: Tourist Committee, Banff-Lake Louise Chamber of Commerce, Box 1298, Banff, Alberta T0L 0C0, Canada.

A celebration of the season with games, fun, and entertainment.

★ 3669 ★
Calgary - OKTOBERFEST. Late September-early October, annual, 13 days. Contact: Travel Alberta, 10255 104th Street, Edmonton, Alberta T5J 1B1, Canada.

A celebration of the season with fun, food, entertainment, and exhibits.

★ 3670 ★
Wetaskiwin - NORTHAM INTERNATIONAL SNOW-MOBILE RACES AND CARNIVAL. Mid February, annual, 1 week. Contact: Travel Alberta, 10255 104th Street, Edmonton, Alberta T5J 1B1, Canada.

Features winter sport activities throughout the week, with snowmobile racing finals on the weekend.

CANADA - ALBERTA (Continued)

Other activities include the carnival, a parade, entertainment, beer fest, and snowshoe races.

CANADA - BRITISH COLUMBIA

★ 3671 ★
Vancouver - FALL FAIR.   Mid-late September, 1 day, Victoria Drive Community Centre.   Contact: Tourist Information, 650 Burrard Street, Vancouver, British Columbia, Canada.

The fair offers displays of floral art, flowers, fruit and vegetables.

CANADA - MANITOBA

★ 3672 ★
Altona - SUNFLOWER FESTIVAL.   Late July, annual, 2 days.   Contact: Mr. Jake Neufeld, Manitoba Sunflower Festival, Box 2000, Altona, Manitoba R0B 0B0, Canada.

Features parade, stage show, the crowning of the Sunflower Queen, log sawing, old-time fiddling, swimming and diving exhibitions, seed displays, ice cream, and seed eating contests.   There is a Low German display, and traditional Mennonite foods are served.

★ 3673 ★
Beausejour - BEAUSEJOUR WINTER FAREWELL. Late February, annual, 1 week.   Contact: Mr. Dennis Miller, Beausejour Winter Farewell, Box 393, Beausejour, Mantioba R0E 0C0, Canada.

Features the Canadian Power Toboggan Championship Races with top drivers from the United States and Canada.   These races have become a major winter event in Southern Manitoba.

★ 3674 ★
Churchill - AURORA SNOW FESTIVAL.   March, annual.   Contact: Publicity Chairman, Aurora Snow Festival, Box 188, Churchill, Manitoba R0B 0E0, Canada.

Dog team and snowmobile racing, flour-packing, snowshoe races, jigging and fiddling.   Dog sled taxi service to Fort Prince of Wales and other places of interest.

★ 3675 ★
Thompson - THOMPSON WINTER CARNIVAL.

February, annual.   Contact: Director, Department of Tourism, Recreation and Cultural Affairs, Tourist Branch, 801 Mall Centre, 491 Portage Avenue, Winnipeg, Manitoba R3B 2E7, Canada.

The official symbol of the carnival is Rudy the Raven. One of the main features is the Mr. Okimow of the North contest, testing the outdoor skills of participants.

★ 3676 ★
Paquetville - SUMMER FESTIVAL.   Mid July, 4 days.   Contact: Special Events Co-ordinator, Tourism New Brunswick, Post Office Box 12345, Fredericton, New Brunswick, Canada.

Traditional summertime events and activities during this July festival.

CANADA - NEWFOUNDLAND

★ 3677 ★
Corner Brook - WINTER CARNIVAL.   February-March, annual.   Contact: Town Council, Corner Brook, Newfoundland, Canada.

Includes skiing events and other winter activities and contests.

★ 3678 ★
Labrador - WINTER CARNIVAL.   February, annual. Contact: Town Council, Labrador City, Newfoundland, Canada.

Includes skiing events and other winter activities and contests.

★ 3679 ★
Saint John's - WINTER CARNIVAL.   February, annual, Memorial University.   Contact: Memorial University, Elizabeth Avenue, Saint John's, Newfoundland, Canada.

Traditional winter fun events and contests on the campus of Memorial University.

CANADA - NORTHWEST TERRITORIES

★ 3680 ★
Fort Smith - WOOD BUFFALO FROLICS.   Mid March, annual.   Contact: President, Fort Smith's Lion's Club, North West Territories X0E 0P0, Canada.

The event celebrates the coming of spring with a Wood Chopper's Ball and a variety night.   There are

CANADA - NORTHWEST TERRITORIES (Continued)

a variety of sports and competitive events, including cross country skiing, snowmobile racing, log chopping, a hockey tournament, and muskrat skinning.

★ 3681 ★

Frobisher Bay - TOONIK TYME.   Late April, annual, 1 week.   Contact: Secretary Manager, Hamlet Office, Frobisher Bay, Northwest Territories X0A 0H0, Canada.

Frobisher Bay welcomes spring with a carnival highlighted by the selection of Mr. Toonik and a queen. Festival-goers compete at seal skinning, igloo building and ice-sculpturing.   The event also boasts of holding the toughest power tobaggan race in the world.

★ 3682 ★

Hay River - OKTOBERFEST.   Late October.   Contact: Travel Arctic, Yellowknife, Northwest Territories X1A 2L6, Canada.

Sponsored by the Royal Canadian Legion in celebration of the season.   Begun in 1975.

★ 3683 ★

Hay River - OOKPIK CARNIVAL.   Mid March, annual, 3 days.   Contact: President, Carnival Committee, Box 1895, Hay River, Northwest Territories, Canada.

Events include an ice carnival, adult and teen dances, and a carnival queen contest.   Entertainment is provided by many sports, games of chance and competitions including snowshoe and snowmobile races, tea-making and log sawing.

★ 3684 ★

Norman Wells - WINTER CARNIVAL.   Mid March, annual.   Contact: President, Chamber of Commerce, Norman Wells, Northwest Territories, X1A 2L9, Canada.

Celebrates the coming of spring with contests and races.

★ 3685 ★

Pine Point - PINE DAYS.   Mid June, annual, 2 days.   Contact: Recreation Director, Box 180, Town of Pine Point, Northwest Territories, Canada.

A celebration of the longest day of the year with a

dance, parade, and the Firemen's Polar Lake picnic. There are plenty of games with a horseshoe tournament, children's races, canoe jousting, and softball tournament.

★ 3686 ★

Pine Point - PINE POINT KARNIVAL KAPERS. February, annual, 1 weekend.   Contact: Karnival Kapers, c/o Doug Reed, Pine Point, Northwest Territories, Canada.

The winter carnival is highlighted by a 50-mile, 2 day race for dog teams.   Prizes for the event total more than $2,000.   Other events include snowmobile races, skating races, log sawing, nail pounding, tea boiling, and other unusual activities.

★ 3687 ★

Sachs Harbour - WHITE FOX JAMBOREE.   Mid April.   Contact: Travel Arctic, Yellowknife, Northwest Territories X1A 2L9, Canada.

Celebrates the coming of spring with dog team and snowmobile races, shooting contests and caribou burgers. Sachs Harbour is the "White Fox Capital of the World".

★ 3688 ★

Yellowknife - CARIBOU CARNIVAL.   Late March, 3 days.   Contact: Caribou Carnival Committee, Post Office Box 2005, Yellowknife, Northwest Territories, Canada.

A featured attraction of this event is the Dog Derby, open to dog mushers from throughout the North American continent.   A multitude of competitions include ice sculpturing, tea making, and many more. A parade is also included in the activities.

CANADA - NOVA SCOTIA

★ 3689 ★

Canning - GLOOSCAP SUMMER FESTIVAL.   Late June, 2 days.   Contact: Nova Scotia Department of Tourism, Division of Travel, Post Office Box 130, Halifax, Nova Scotia B3J 2M7, Canada.

Festival features a parade, booths, games, pony rides, sports events, daily arts and crafts show and sale, a turkey supper, and on the second day a gymkhana.

★ 3690 ★

Margaree - SUMMER FESTIVAL.   Late July, 5 days. Contact: Nova Scotia Department of Tourism, Travel Division, Post Office Box 130, Halifax, Nova Scotia B3J 2M7, Canada.

CANADA - NOVA SCOTIA   (Continued)

This festival consists of woodsmen's competitions, canoe races, sports events, a fishing derby, a bicycle marathon, handicrafts displays, outdoor dancing, and suppers.

CANADA - QUEBEC

★ 3691 ★
Baie-Saint-Paul - BAIE-SAINT-PAUL SUMMER.   Late June-late September.   Contact: Baie-Saint-Paul Summer, Cultural Centre, Post Office Box 789, Baie-Saint-Paul, Quebec, Canada.

Exhibition of works by artists of the region; paintings, drawings, rugs, pottery, tapestries, and handicrafts. Shows, concerts, and recitals.

★ 3692 ★
Lavaltrie - WINTER CARNIVAL.   March, 1 month. Contact: The Tourist Information Division, 150 Boulevard Saint Cyrille East, Quebec, Quebec G1R 4Y3, Canada

Inaugural supper, wine and cheese tasting, masked ball, ragpickers' ball, crowning of the queen, broomball games, hockey and many other activities.

★ 3693 ★
Longueuil - LONGUEUIL SUMMER FESTIVAL. August, 10 days, Carrefour des Ancetres, corner of Chemin Chambly and rue Saint-Charles.   Contact: Festival d'Ete de Longueuil, Longueuil, Canada.

Theme is the Seigniory of Longueuil.   Social and cultural activities.   Shows with renowned artists. Terraces and terrace-cafes, a spot where the artists and crafts workers can be found.   Various types of exhibitions.   Pocket theater, children's theater festival, movies, games, and horsemanship.

★ 3694 ★
Quebec - QUEBEC WINTER CARNIVAL.   March (pre-Lenten, climaxes on Mardi Gras), annual, usually 10 days but has gone up to 3 weeks.   Contact: Tourist and Convention Bureau of Metropolitan Quebec, 60 d'Auteuil Street, Quebec, Quebec, Canada.

The symbol of the carnival is a talking snowman, Bonhomme Carnaval, who holds court in an ice palace and comes out to celebrate with the crowds. Activities and contests include an ice canoe race, day and night parades, hockey, ice and snow sculptures, motorcycle races, costumed balls, dog derby,

barrel-jumping contest, and a costumed ball.   Started in 1894, but ended about 1900, until revived in the 50's.

★ 3695 ★
Quebec - SUMMER FESTIVAL.   Mid July, 11 days. Contact: Tourist and Convention Bureau of Metropolitan Quebec, 60 d'Auteuil Street, Quebec, Quebec, Canada.

Cultural events include concerts and recitals under the stars, theatrical and film presentations, exhibitions and a horse show.

★ 3696 ★
Rimouski - RIMOUSKI FALL FESTIVAL.   October, 1 week.   Contact: Festival d'Automne de Rimouski, Post Office Box 710, Rimouski, Quebec, Canada.

Pheasant hunt, grand provincial camping-rally,   and clay pigeon contest highlight the festival events.

★ 3697 ★
Riviere-du-Loup - SUMMER FESTIVAL.   Mid July-early August, annual, 17 days.   Contact: The Tourist Information Division, 150 Boulevard Saint-Cyrille East, Quebec, Quebec G1R 4Y3, Canada.

Includes a parade, the coronation of Cinderella, art exhibition, swimming contests, dance, and rally camping.

★ 3698 ★
Ville-Marie - WINTER FESTIVAL.   March, annual. Contact: The Tourist Information Division, 150 Boulevard Saint-Syrille East, Quebec, Quebec, G1R 4Y3, Canada.

Main activities take place on weekends and include ice sports, "Pitoune" tournament, socio-cultural recreation, citizens dinner, art exhibition, and shows.

CANADA - YUKON

★ 3699 ★
Whitehorse - SOURBOUGH RENDEZVOUS.   Late February, annual, 1 week.   Contact: Klondike Visitors Association, Box 335, Dawson City, Yukon Territory, Canada.

The Yukon fights cabin fever with a winter carnival. There are races for snowmobiles, dog sleds, and snowshoes; contests for flour packing and '98 costumes and beards.   Local arts and crafts are on display;

CANADA - YUKON (Continued)

there are talent shows, can-can girls, sourdough hot cake breakfasts, Indian dances, and sports events such as curling, hockey and skiing.

Spring

See: SEASONS

State Fairs

ALABAMA

★ 3700 ★

Birmingham - ALABAMA STATE FAIR. Early October, 10 days, Alabama State Fairgrounds. Contact: Bureau of Publicity, State of Alabama, Montgomery, Alabama 36104.

Exhibitions, demonstrations, items for display and for sale, entertainment, food, contests - everything a state fair represents is available in Birmingham in October.

ALASKA

★ 3701 ★

Fairbanks - TANANA VALLEY STATE FAIR. August-September, annual, 11 days, Fairgrounds, 2-mile College Road.   Contact: Alaska Division of Tourism, Pouch E, Juneau, Alaska 99801.

Official state fair, alternate years.   Farm produce, animal exhibits, musical plays, pie-eating contests, races, arts and crafts, weaving, and flower exhibits. Begun around 1932.

★ 3702 ★

Palmer - MATAMUSKA VALLEY FAIR.   August-September, annual, 10 days. Contact: Greater Palmer Chamber of Commerce, Post Office Box 45, Palmer, Alaska 99645.

Official state fair in alternate years.   Horse show, horse racing, dog show, dog cart racing, exhibits of all phases of agriculture and homemaking, carnival and live entertainment.   The horse show is Alaska's largest with 61 classes.   Lazy Mountain Marathon Race and Bodenburg Butte Bike Race.   Begun around 1959.

ARIZONA

★ 3703 ★

Phoenix - ARIZONA STATE FAIR.   October-early November, annual, 18 days, Arizona State Fairgrounds. Contact: Phoenix Chamber of Commerce, 805 North Second Street, Phoenix, Arizona 85004.

Exhibits of all phases of agriculture and homemaking, entertainment, food, carnival, etc.

ARKANSAS

★ 3704 ★

Little Rock - ARKANSAS STATE FAIR AND LIVESTOCK SHOW.   Late September-early October, 11 days, Barton Coliseum.   Contact: Arkansas Department of Parks and Tourism, 149 State Capitol, Little Rock, Arkansas 72201.

Livestock judging, home arts competitions, midway, opening day parade, country western show, and rodeo.

CALIFORNIA

★ 3705 ★

Sacramento - CALIFORNIA STATE FAIR.   August-September, annual, 10 days.   Contact: California Chamber of Commerce, 455 Capitol Mall, Sacramento, California 95814.

Arts and crafts, carnival, horse race, open rodeo, as well as other traditional fair exhibits and entertainment.

COLORADO

★ 3706 ★

Pueblo - COLORADO STATE FAIR.   Late August-early September (last full August week), annual, 9 days, Fairgrounds, 1001 Beulah Avenue.   Contact: Pueblo Fairgrounds, 1001 Beulah Avenue, Pueblo, Colorado 81004.

Rodeo, exhibits, games, special events, wide range of industrial and agricultural exhibits, horse racing and entertainment are included as part of the traditional western state fair festivities.

CONNECTICUT

★ 3707 ★

Danbury - DANBURY STATE FAIR.   September or October, annual, 10 days.   Contact: John H. Stetson, 130 White Street, Danbury, Connecticut 06810.

CONNECTICUT (Continued)

Activities include a parade, band concerts, and a carnival. Crafts are on display; there is a livestock show and lumberjack exhibition. Regional cooking is offered.

DELAWARE

★ 3708 ★
Harrington - DELAWARE STATE FAIR. Late July, (last full week), annual, 9 days. Contact: Delaware State Fair, Incorporated, Harrington, Delaware 19952.

Old fashioned country fair with agricultural exhibits, crafts, and midway, carnival, rides, and entertainment.

FLORIDA

★ 3709 ★
Tampa - FLORIDA STATE FAIR. Early February, annual, 12 days. Contact: J. McK. Jeter, Box 1231, Tampa, Florida 33601.

Traditional state fair activities including agricultural exhibitions and demonstrations, items for display and for sale, entertainment, food, and contests.

GEORGIA

★ 3710 ★
Macon - GEORGIA STATE FAIR. Mid October, annual, 6 days. Contact: Macon Chamber of Commerce, 640 First Street, Post Office Box 169, Macon, Georgia 21202.

Traditional state fair activities and events including agricultural, 4-H, homemaking and animal contests and exhibits; carnival style entertainment; food; etc.

HAWAII

★ 3711 ★
Honolulu - FIFTIETH STATE FAIR. Late June-mid July, annual, 18 days. Contact: Hawaii Visitors Bureau, Information Services, 2270 Kalakua Avenue, Honolulu, Hawaii 96815.

Entertainers, exhibits of island products, flowers, clothes, arts and crafts. Polynesian and Oriental food. Produce and agricultural booths, and carnival midway.

IDAHO

★ 3712 ★
Blackfoot - EASTERN IDAHO FAIR. Early September, annual, 6 days. Contact: Executive Secretary, Mrs. Margaret Von Der Lieth, Blackfoot Chamber of Commerce, 11 Northwest Main Street, Blackfoot, Idaho 83221.

Traditional state fair events including agricultural, homemaking, livestock exhibits and contests and entertainment of many types - musical, carnival, etc.

★ 3713 ★
Boise - WESTERN IDAHO FAIR. Late August-early September, annual, 8 days. Contact: Executive Vice President, Norris E. Johnson, Boise Chamber of Commerce, 709 West Idaho Street, Post Office Box 2368, Boise, Idaho 83701.

Farm products and equipment demonstrated and displayed, homemaking contests, livestock judging, along with continuous entertainment and food. Fun for all.

ILLINOIS

★ 3714 ★
DuQuoin - DUQUOIN STATE FAIR. Late August-early September, annual. Contact: DuQuoin Business Association, 119 Laurel Avenue, DuQuoin, Illinois 62832.

Included in the events is the classic harness race, the Hambletonian, along with five afternoons of first class harness racing. Also included are agricultural shows, top entertainment, a carnival midway and beer gardens.

★ 3715 ★
Springfield - ILLINOIS STATE FAIR. Mid August, annual, 10 days. Contact: Illinois Division of Tourism, 205 West Wacker Drive, Chicago, Illinois 60606.

Events include rides, big name entertainment, contests, U.S.A.C. auto races, farm product expositions, horse shows, and continuous entertainment. One of the largest agricultural fairs in the nation.

INDIANA

★ 3716 ★
Indianapolis - INDIANA STATE FAIR. Mid-late

INDIANA (Continued)

August, annual, 11 days, State Fairgrounds. Contact: Publicity Supervisor, State Fairgrounds, 1200 East 38th Street, Indianapolis, Indiana 46205.

Big name entertainment, autoracing, motorcycle racing, horse racing, exhibits of all kinds, livestock judging, tractor and horse pulls, bands, drill teams, cheerleading, and baton twirling are included in the festivities.

IOWA

★ 3717 ★
Des Moines - IOWA STATE FAIR. Mid August, annual, 10-12 days. Contact: Iowa Development Commission, Tourist Division, 250 Jewett Building, Des Moines, Iowa 50309.

One of the largest state fairs in the country, includes many agricultural exhibits, industrial exhibits, cultural exhibits, commercial exhibits, renowned entertainers, horse show, midway, and rides. Many contests, including contest for the best imitator of chicken-clucking, Ladies National Nail Driving Contest, tractor pull, demolition derby, Montana Sheep Shearing Contest, horseshow pitching, and hog calling.

KANSAS

★ 3718 ★
Hutchinson - KANSAS STATE FAIR. Mid September, annual, 8 days. Contact: Chamber of Commerce, Hutchinson, Kansas 67501.

Traditional state fair festivities including exhibits of all phases of agriculture and homemaking, demonstrations, items for sale, entertainment, food, contests, and livestock shows.

KENTUCKY

★ 3719 ★
Louisville - KENTUCKY STATE FAIR. Mid August, annual, 10 days. Contact: Louisville Chamber of Commerce, 300 West Liberty Street, Louisville, Kentucky 40202.

A traditional style state fair emphasizing the agricultural and natural attributes of the state. There are contests and exhibits of farm tools and products, homemaking, livestock, etc. Entertainment for all, all of the time.

LOUISIANA

★ 3720 ★
Baton Rouge - GREATER BATON ROUGE STATE FAIR. Late October, Fairgrounds. Contact: Ed Campanella, Post Office Box 15058, Baton Rouge, Louisiana 70815.

Events and activities include big name entertainers; Two-Bit Day; Cajun Day; Manchac Canoe Races; Senior Citizens and Exceptional Children's Day; 4-H events; military, space, animal, commercial, youth, art, agriculture, educational, handicrafts, tractor and train caboose exhibits; moto-cross; horse, poultry, rabbit and dog shows; farm animal petting zoo; and carnival. Started in 1965.

★ 3721 ★
Ruston - NORTH LOUISIANA STATE FAIR. October, 6 days, Fairgrounds. Contact: Louisiana Tourist Commission, Post Office Box 44291, Baton Rouge, Louisiana 70804.

The agricultural events include exhibits and judging of beef cattle, dairy cattle, swine, horses, poultry, and rabbits. In addition, there is a forestry and wildlife exhibit; home demonstration booths; a pet and dog show including a pet parade and awards for the most unusual pet, ugliest dog, and other awards; a flower show; a kiddie show; and an open horse show.

★ 3722 ★
Shreveport - LOUISIANA STATE FAIR. October, 10 days. Contact: Shreveport Convention and Visitors Bureau, Post Office Box 1761, Shreveport, Louisiana 71166.

Events include free musical entertainment, mile-long midway with games and rides, exhibit buildings, stock shows, sporting events, top name entertainment, agricultural and industrial exhibits, gourmet delights, championship IMCA stock car and sprint car races, championship rodeo finals for the Louisiana Rodeo Association, and horse shows.

MARYLAND

★ 3723 ★
Timonium - MARYLAND STATE FAIR. Late August-early September, annual, 10 days, Timonium Fairgrounds. Contact: Howard Mosner, Timonium Fairgrounds, Timonium, Maryland 21093.

One of the nation's largest state fairs. Events include thoroughbred horse racing; livestock shows and judging; craft displays, demonstrations and judging;

MARYLAND (Continued)

4-H exhibits and judging in such things as insect collections, photography, displays, etc. Carnival rides, game booths, sale of jewelry and other craft items, agricultural and industrial displays, side show, and food. Begun around 1872.

MICHIGAN

★ 3724 ★
Detroit - MICHIGAN STATE FAIR. Late August-early September, annual, 12 days, Michigan State Fairgrounds. Contact: Michigan State Fairgrounds, Woodward/Eight Mile Road, Detroit, Michigan 48203.

The oldest in the country. Includes traditional fair events such as livestock judging, food competition, midway, agricultural products, industrial exhibits, educational exhibits, home-making exhibits, contests, and professional entertainment.

MINNESOTA

★ 3725 ★
Saint Paul - MINNESOTA STATE FAIR. Late August-early September, annual, 11 days. Contact: Saint Paul Area Chamber of Commerce, Osborn Building, Suite 300, Saint Paul, Minnesota 55102.

Traditional state fair events featuring ten different grandstand shows, displays of agricultural products, livestock shows, exhibits of local farm and craft groups, flower exhibits, commercial and industrial exhibits, Machinery Hill: world's biggest assortment of farm, yard and recreation equipment, auto racing, and professional entertainers.

MISSISSIPPI

★ 3726 ★
Jackson - MISSISSIPPI STATE FAIR. Mid October (begins 2nd Tuesday), annual, 8 days, State Fairgrounds, Jefferson Street. Contact: Director, State Fair, State Fairgrounds, Post Office Box 982, Jackson, Mississippi 39205.

Arts and crafts exhibits, popular entertainment, food, band concerts, livestock, midway, claims to have "The World's Largest Midway", exhibits of home canned products, garden club exhibits, and ice skating. Entertainment provided by famous talents. Started in 1885.

MISSOURI

★ 3727 ★
Sedalia - MISSOURI STATE FAIR. Mid August, 10 days. Contact: State Fair, Missouri Department of Agriculture, 13th Floor, Jefferson Building, Jefferson City, Missouri 65101.

One of the largest state fairs in the nation. Livestock, agricultural, horticultural, and craft exhibits; midway; auto and motorcycle races; horse shows; and performances by big name celebrities.

MONTANA

★ 3728 ★
Great Falls - MONTANA STATE FAIR. Late July-August, annual, 9 days. Contact: Chamber of Commerce, Box 2127, Great Falls, Montana 59403.

Traditional state fair festivities including exhibitions of livestock and agricultural methods, home made foods and other items, contests, entertainment, rodeos, beauty contests, parades, horse races, etc.

NEBRASKA

★ 3729 ★
Lincoln - NEBRASKA STATE FAIR. Early September, annual, 10 days. Contact: Nebraska Association of Commerce and Industry, Post Office Box 81556, Lincoln, Nebraska 68501.

Livestock, agricultural, horticultural, and craft exhibits and contests. Homemaking skills displayed and homemade foods and items for sale. Celebrities entertain in carnival atmosphere.

NEVADA

★ 3730 ★
Reno - NEVADA STATE FAIR. Early September, annual, 5 days. Contact: Greater Reno Chamber of Commerce, Post Office Box 3499, Reno, Nevada 89105.

Traditional state fair events including agricultural, livestock, and homemaking exhibits. In addition, there are a variety of western-style activities and continuous entertainment.

NEW HAMPSHIRE

★ 3731 ★
Plymouth - NEW HAMPSHIRE STATE FAIR. Late

State Fairs

NEW HAMPSHIRE (Continued)

August, annual, 4 days. Contact: Richard L. Bradley, Woodstock, New Hampshire 03293; or Chamber of Commerce, Parker Street, Post Office Box 22, Plymouth, New Hampshire 03264.

Traditional events and activities which characterize a state fair - exhibits, entertainment, etc.

NEW JERSEY

★ 3732 ★
Trenton - NEW JERSEY STATE FAIR. Mid September, annual. Contact: New Jersey Office of Tourism, Post Office Box 400, Trenton, New Jersey 08625.

Events include exhibits, arts and crafts demonstrations, and nightly entertainment by big name performers.

NEW MEXICO

★ 3733 ★
Albuquerque - NEW MEXICO STATE FAIR. September, annual, 11-16 days, Fairgrounds. Contact: Greater Albuquerque Chamber of Commerce, 401 Second Street, Northwest, Albuquerque, New Mexico 87102.

The varied events include quarterhorse and thoroughbred racing, coliseum shows, rodeo, livestock competition, food demonstrations, flower show, twirling contest, knitting contest, and cultural exhibits. There is big name entertainment and a midway. Indian and Spanish villages. During Indian Day, Miss Indian New Mexico is chosen, and there is an Indian arts and crafts show.

NEW YORK

★ 3734 ★
Syracuse - NEW YORK STATE FAIR. Late August-early September, annual, 1 week, New York State Fairgrounds. Contact: Finger Lakes Association, Incorporated, 309 Lake Street, Penn Yan, New York 14527; or Chamber of Commerce, 351 South Warren, Syracuse, New York 13202.

Exhibits of agricultural and industrial products of New York, arts and crafts exhibits, carnival, rides, contests, food, and top-name entertainment are just a few of the events and activities which highlight this state fair, sometimes called New York State Super Fair.

NORTH CAROLINA

★ 3735 ★
Raleigh - NORTH CAROLINA STATE FAIR. Mid October, annual, 9 days, State Fairgrounds. Contact: Raleigh Chamber of Commerce, 411 South Salisbury, Raleigh, North Carolina 27602.

The fair offers exhibits of food, arts, a variety of crafts, and agricultural methods and products. There are games, livestock shows, and entertainment. Begun around 1868.

NORTH DAKOTA

★ 3736 ★
Minot - NORTH DAKOTA STATE FAIR. Late July, annual, 7 days. Contact: North Dakota State Highway Department, Capitol Grounds, Bismarck, North Dakota 58505.

A typical state fair with home and garden exhibits, agricultural machinery demonstrations, livestock judging and shows, tractor pull contests, and a midway.

OHIO

★ 3737 ★
Columbus - OHIO STATE FAIR. Late August-early September, annual, 12 days. Contact: Bill Stalter, Ohio Expositions Commissions, 632 East 11th Avenue, Columbus, Ohio 43211.

The fair features livestock shows and the world's largest horse show. There is a junior fair and special events and exhibits offered by youth organizations and Ohio industries. Free grandstand entertainment by celebrities from the worlds of stage, television and the movies.

OKLAHOMA

★ 3738 ★
Oklahoma City - STATE FAIR OF OKLAHOMA. Late September-early October, annual, 10 days, State Fair Park. Contact: Director of Promotion, Oklahoma State Fair, 500 North Land Rush, Oklahoma City, Oklahoma 73107.

Besides such standard features as a midway and exhibits, the fair offers special features such as a Space Tower, Independence Arch and fountains. There is outdoor entertainment, plus an international show, a rodeo, and Ice Capades. Harness racing, automobile and motorcycle races provide additional excitement. Begun in 1907.

OREGON

★ 3739 ★
Salem - OREGON STATE FAIR. Late August-early September, annual, 10 days. Contact: Lillie M. Ward, Oregon State Fair, Salem, Oregon 97310.

Exhibits, products and displays that show Oregon and her role as one of the nation's major agricultural and recreational states. Pageantry includes thoroughbred racing, rodeo, circus, state revue, and horse show.

SOUTH CAROLINA

★ 3740 ★
Columbia - SOUTH CAROLINA STATE FAIR. Mid-late October, annual, 9 days. Contact: W. L. Abernathy, Jr., Post Office Box 393, Columbia, South Carolina 29202.

Exhibits include art and ceramics, agricultural, industrial, home-making, and flowers. There are livestock shows for cattle, swine, and poultry. Special features are the National Orchid Show and the giant midway with carnival rides and grandstand shows.

SOUTH DAKOTA

★ 3741 ★
Huron - SOUTH DAKOTA STATE FAIR. Late August-early September, annual, 6 days. Contact: State Fair Board Manager, Box 1275, Huron, South Dakota 57350.

The event showcases South Dakota's agriculture and industry with demonstrations, displays, exhibits, contests and entertainment.

TENNESSEE

★ 3742 ★
Nashville - TENNESSEE STATE FAIR. Mid September, annual, 9 days. Contact: Nashville Area Chamber of Commerce, 161 Fourth Avenue, North, Nashville, Tennessee 37219.

Over a week of activities, events, exhibits, etc. in celebration of the agricultural products of Tennessee and the achievements of its citizens. Traditional style entertainment and contests.

TEXAS

★ 3743 ★
Dallas - STATE FAIR OF TEXAS. Mid October, annual, 16 days. Contact: Dallas Chamber of Commerce, Fidelity Union Towers at Akard and Pacific Streets, Dallas, Texas 75201; or State Fair of Texas, Post Office Box 26010, Dallas, Texas 75226.

Exposition draws millions to 200-acre Fair Park. Traditional fair displays and exhibits, plus Broadway musicals, ice shows, extravaganzas, prize livestock and horse show performances, huge midway, and gridiron rivalry between Texas and Oklahoma. Big Tex, gigantic cowboy symbol, looms over all the festivities.

UTAH

★ 3744 ★
Salt Lake City - UTAH STATE FAIR. Early September, annual, 11 days, State Fairgrounds. Contact: Utah Travel Council, Council Hall, Capitol Hill, Salt Lake City, Utah 84114.

Traditional state fair activities including agricultural and homemaking exhibits, animal contests and shows, food, fun, and entertainment.

VERMONT

★ 3745 ★
Rutland - VERMONT STATE FAIR. Early September, annual, 7 days. Contact: Events Editor, State of Vermont, Agency of Development and Community Affairs, Montpelier, Vermont 05602.

Traditional New England style state fair activities and events, featuring agricultural and livestock displays and contests, homemaking exhibits, crafts, antiques, and plenty of entertainment and food.

VIRGINIA

★ 3746 ★
Richmond - STATE FAIR OF VIRGINIA. Late September, annual, 11 days. Contact: C.L. Teachworth, Fair Manager, Post Office Box 26805, Richmond, Virginia 23261.

Climaxing the local fair circuit, this event offers great agricultural and homemaking exhibits, stock shows, and entertainment. Draws over 70,000 people per year; it ranks in the nation's top ten fairs.

Theater and Drama

WEST VIRGINIA

★ 3747 ★
Lewisburg - STATE FAIR OF WEST VIRGINIA.
Mid August, annual, 9 days. Contact: E.W. Rock,
Manager, West Virginia State Fair, Box 829, Lewis-
burg, West Virginia 24901; or Lewisburg Chamber
of Commerce, Post Office Box 711, Lewisburg, West
Virginia 24901.

The fair offers agricultural exhibits, arts and handicrafts displays, and native foods. Entertainment
includes harness racing, rides and music.

WISCONSIN

★ 3748 ★
Milwaukee - WISCONSIN STATE FAIR. Mid
August, annual, 11 days, State Fair Park. Contact:
Wisconsin State Fair, State Fair Park, Milwaukee,
Wisconsin 53214.

Sights to see include a large display of dairy products, including Wisconsin's famous cheeses and a
milking parlor, livestock exhibits and veterinary
surgery demonstrations, and produce exhibits. There
are shows for flowers, fashions and arts and crafts.
A Mexican village is set up, along with a children's
world, youth and trade buildings. Entertainment
includes top performing artists, an international stage
and a large midway, claimed to be the world's
biggest.

WYOMING

★ 3749 ★
Douglas - WYOMING STATE FAIR. Late August,
annual, 6 days, Fairgrounds. Contact: State
of Wyoming, Department of Agriculture, Office of
Wyoming State Fair, Drawer 10, Douglas, Wyoming
82663.

A state fair which includes a celebration of Wyoming's
Western Heritage, along with agricultural and homemaking exhibits, and continuous entertainment. Begun in 1905.

Summer

See: SEASONS

Theater and Drama

See also: THE ARTS

ALABAMA

★ 3750 ★
Anniston - ALABAMA SHAKESPEARE FESTIVAL.
July-August, approximately 5 weeks, Anniston High
School Auditorium. Contact: Alabama Shakespeare
Festival, Post Office Box 141, Anniston, Alabama
36201.

Plays by Shakespeare and other authors are presented.

ALASKA

★ 3751 ★
Haines - DRAMA FESTIVAL. April, 3 days, Chilkat
Center for the Arts. Contact: Lynn Canal Com-
munity Players, Incorporated, Box 516, Haines,
Alaska 99827.

Presentation of plays and players. Begun around
1974.

CALIFORNIA

★ 3752 ★
Los Angeles - SHAKESPEARE FESTIVAL. Early
September, 15 days. Contact: California Chamber
of Commerce, 455 Capitol Mall, Sacramento, California 95814.

15 days of pleasure for the lovers of Shakespeare
and his works.

★ 3753 ★
Los Angeles - SUMMER DRAMA FESTIVAL. July-
August, annual, Remsen Bird Hillside Theater.
Contact: Occidental College, Director, Summer
Drama Festival, 1600 Campus Road, Los Angeles,
California 90041.

Six shows are done in reperatory. Shakespeare,
Shaw, and Gilbert and Sullivan are the mainstays.
Experimental theater is not used, only acknowledged
hits. The plays are performed by unpaid students.
Graduates of the school's drama department direct
the plays. Begun around 1960.

★ 3754 ★
San Diego - NATIONAL SHAKESPEARE FESTIVAL.
Early June-mid September, annual, 3-3 1/2 months,
Balboa Park. Contact: Old Globe Theater, San
Diego Balboa Park, Box 2171, San Diego, California
92112.

Takes place in a replica of the Globe Playhouse.

CALIFORNIA (Continued)

Each performance is preceded by a half-hour program of Elizabethan music and dances. Begun around 1949.

★ 3755 ★
San Jose - SUMMER REPERTORY THEATER FESTIVAL. July, annual, 1 month, San Jose State University Theatre and city parks. Contact: San Jose State University, School of Humanities and the Arts, Department of Theatre Arts, San Jose, California 95192.

Plays are presented on Thursdays, Fridays and Saturdays at the University Theatre and in the local parks. Begun around 1964.

★ 3756 ★
San Rafael - MARIN SHAKESPEARE FESTIVAL. Mid July-early September, annual, Forest Meadows Theatre. Contact: Marin Shakespeare Festival, Dominican College, San Rafael, California 94901.

Two plays are presented, Thursday - Sunday, in an outdoor theater. Begun around 1966.

COLORADO

★ 3757 ★
Boulder - COLORADO SHAKESPEARE FESTIVAL. Late July-mid August, annual, 17 days, University of Colorado, Mary Rippon Amphitheater. Contact: Department of Theatre and Dance, Richard Knaub, Executive Director, Festival, University of Colorado, Boulder, Colorado 80302.

Part of the Creative Arts Festival. Three Shakespearean plays are presented each summer in repertory under the stars. Begun around 1958.

★ 3758 ★
Denver - SUMMER THEATER FESTIVAL. June-August (Summer), Elitch Gardens. Contact: Adams County Chamber of Commerce, 5911 North Washington Street, Denver, Colorado 80216.

A festival of theatrical productions in the setting of Elitch Gardens.

★ 3759 ★
Steamboat Springs - WINTER THEATER FESTIVAL. December-April, annual, Thursdays, Fridays, Saturdays, Sundays, Depot Theater. Contact: Steamboat Springs Council of the Arts and Humanities, Post Office Box 1913, Steamboat Springs, Colorado 80477.

A regional theater presenting five-six plays during the course of the skiing season. Sponsored by several civic, state, and county groups.

CONNECTICUT

★ 3760 ★
New Haven - YALE FESTIVAL OF UNDERGRADUATE DRAMA. March, annual, 3 days, Yale University. Contact: Yale Festival of Undergraduate Drama, Box 902A, Yale Station, New Haven, Connecticut 06520.

An invitational tournament for college groups in the east and southeast. Sponsored by the Yale University Drama Association, it promotes the flow of ideas between groups. Begun in 1957.

★ 3761 ★
New London - PUPPETEERS OF AMERICA FESTIVAL. Early August, annual, Connecticut College campus. Contact: Puppeteers of America Festival, New London Chamber of Commerce, One Whale Oil Row, New London, Connecticut 06320.

Morning workshops and seminars covering the whole range of subjects of interest to puppeteers and enthusiasts; puppet making and manipulating, staging and directing, projecting voices, body movement, etc. Public and impromtu performances throughout the day.

★ 3762 ★
Stratford - AMERICAN SHAKESPEARE FESTIVAL. Mid June-early September, annual, 9 weeks, American Shakespeare Theatre. Contact: American Shakespeare Festival Theatre, 1850 Elm Street, Stratford, Connecticut 06497.

A professional company of actors present plays by Shakespeare and other authors. Theater also has a major collection of paintings, sculpture and Shakespearean memorabilia, a costume museum, and a training academy for young actors, students and professionals. Also road tours and a special season at the end of March.

★ 3763 ★
Westport - WHITE BARN THEATRE FESTIVAL. July-August, White Barn Theatre. Contact: White Barn Theatre Festival, Newtown Avenue, Westport, Connecticut 06880.

Internationally acclaimed theater companies who have

Theater and Drama

CONNECTICUT (Continued)

won recognition for their original contributions to
contemporary theater entertain.

DISTRICT OF COLUMBIA

★ 3764 ★
Washington, D.C. - AMERICAN COLLEGE THEATRE
FESTIVAL.   April (Spring), annual, 2 weeks,
Kennedy Center and George Washington University.
Contact: American College Theatre Festival, John
F. Kennedy Center for the Performing Arts, 2700
F Street, Northwest, Washington, D.C. 20037.

A presentation of the best in college theater productions by ten participating groups, chosen by
competitions in regional sub-tournaments. Auditions
are held in 13 regions for over 350 productions.
Each of the different productions finally chosen is
presented on two days.

★ 3765 ★
Washington, D.C. - SHAKESPEARE SUMMER
FESTIVAL.   July-August, annual, Sunday nights,
Sylvan Theater or various area parks.   Contact:
Shakespeare Summer Festival, 1000 Sixth Street,
Southwest, Washington, D.C. 20034.

Shakespearean plays are presented in outdoor settings
or theaters.

FLORIDA

★ 3766 ★
Daytona Beach - FLORIDA THEATRE FESTIVAL.
Mid June, annual, 4 days.. Contact: Bud Siefred,
681 North Halifax, Ormand Beach, Florida 32074.

Daily seminars and entertainment.   Evening presentations are offered by little theater groups in the state.

★ 3767 ★
Miami Beach - SHAKESPEARE BY THE SEA.   July-
August, annual, North Shore Community Center.
Contact: North Shore Community Center, Miami
Beach, Florida 33139.

Shakespearean plays are performed outdoors.

IDAHO

★ 3768 ★
Coeur d'Alene - ANTIQUE FESTIVAL THEATRE.

June-July (Summer), North Idaho College.   Contact:
Mary A. Nelson, North Idaho College, 1000 West
Garden Avenue, Coeur d'Alene, Idaho 83814.

Presentation of two antique plays.   Begun around
1964.

ILLINOIS

★ 3769 ★
Normal - THEATRE FESTIVAL.   Early February, 2
days, Union Ballroom, Illinois State University.
Contact: Illinois State University, .Normal, Illinois
61761.

A festival of theater and drama on the campus of
Illinois State University.

MARYLAND

★ 3770 ★
Catonsville - NEW THEATER FESTIVAL..   Mid June,
annual, 6 days, University of Maryland, Baltimore
County.   Contact: Theater Project, 45 West Preston
Street, Baltimore, Maryland 21201.

The festival presents live theater and theater workshops as done by approximately 24 American groups
and several foreign new theater troupes.   Most are
professional; around one-fourth are college companies.
The project is jointly sponsored by University of Maryland, Baltimore County, the Baltimore Theater Project,
the University of Michigan, and the U.S. International
Theater Institute.   Started in 1974 (at the University
of Michigan) as the Invitational Experimental Theater
Festival.

MASSACHUSETTS

★ 3771 ★
Plymouth - PLYMOUTH DRAMA FESTIVAL.   June
thru September.   Contact: National Association of
Dramatics, Incorporated, Drawer S, Manomet,
Massachusetts 02345.

Ten weeks of drama sponsored by the National
Association of Dramatics, Incorporated, and including
dance and instrumental and vocal music.

★ 3772 ★
Williamstown - WILLIAMSTOWN THEATRE FESTIVAL.
Early July-late August, annual, 2 months.   Contact:
Williamstown Theatre Festival, Post Office Box 517,
Williamstown, Massachusetts 01267.

MASSACHUSETTS (Continued)

The festival has a resident professional company with main stage, cabaret and second company productions. Many roles are offered which are not commonly played in ordinary commercial theater. Begun around 1955.

MICHIGAN

★ 3773 ★
Kalamazoo - FESTIVAL PLAYHOUSE. July and August, annual, 1 month, Dalton Theatre, Kalamazoo College. Contact: Theatre Arts Department, Kalamazoo College, Kalamazoo, Michigan 49007.

A series of plays using a company of semi-professional actors and local people supplementing the student body. First held in 1964.

MISSOURI

★ 3774 ★
Kansas City - STARLIGHT THEATRE SUMMER SERIES. Mid June to early September, annual, Swope Park. Contact: Starlight Theatre Summer Series, c/o Starlight Theatre Association, Post Office Box 357, Kansas City, Missouri 64141.

Consists of nightly programs of musicals and variety shows. The theater claims to have one of the most modern and elaborate outdoor theater plants in the nation. Performers engaged for the summer series include some of the leading stars of Broadway.

NEW MEXICO

★ 3775 ★
Las Cruces - NEW MEXICO SHAKESPEARE FESTIVAL. Late June-late July, annual, 1 month, New Mexico State University. Contact: Festival Director, New Mexico Shakespeare Festival, New Mexico State University, Las Cruces, New Mexico 88003.

Presents plays by Shakespeare and other playwrights. Associated with the festival is an evening of ballet. Begun around 1973.

NEW YORK

★ 3776 ★
Hempstead - SHAKESPEARE FESTIVAL. March (early Spring), annual, 5 weeks, John Cranford Adams Playhouse, Hofstra University. Contact: Department of

Drama, Hofstra University, Hempstead, New York 11550.

Presents Shakespeare's plays, plus other related activities such as concerts of English royal music, plays about Shakespeare, exhibits about Shakespearean times, and movies using Shakespeare's plays and/or themes. Takes place in a replica of the Globe Theater. Started in 1950.

★ 3777 ★
New York - SHAKESPEARE FESTIVAL. June-August, Lincoln Center or Delacorte Theater. Contact: New York Shakespeare Festival, 425 Lafayette, New York, New York 10003.

Two seasons, one in the winter in the Lincoln Center in the Mitzi E. Newman Theater and one in the summer in the Delacorte Theater in Central Park.

OREGON

★ 3778 ★
Ashland - SHAKESPEAREAN FESTIVAL. February-April, mid June-late September, annual, 6 months. Contact: Oregon Shakespearean Festival, Ashland, Oregon 97520.

America's oldest Shakespearean festival. Four plays are presented in rotation in a theater fashioned like the Fortune Theater of 1599 in London. The plays are presented as they were in Shakespeare's day with no scene breaks or intermissions. Dancing on the Green features Elizabethan-era dancing and singing prior to showtime. The educational division of the festival is the Institute of Renaissance Studies.

PENNSYLVANIA

★ 3779 ★
University Park - FESTIVAL OF AMERICAN THEATRE. June-August, annual, 6 1/2 weeks, Pennsylvania State University. Contact: Festival of American Theatre, Pennsylvania State University, 137 Arts Building, University Park, Pennsylvania 16801.

The festival has, for the last six years, concentrated on presenting outstanding plays from the American theatrical heritage. The presentations vary widely in theme and range from light comedies to provocative dramas. Held in conjunction with Nittany Mountain Summer. Begun around 1958.

Theater and Drama

SOUTH CAROLINA

★ 3780 ★
Rock Hill - SOUTH CAROLINA HIGH SCHOOL
DRAMA FESTIVAL.   Mid March, annual, 3 days,
Winthrop College campus.   Contact: Winthrop
College, Special Events, Rock Hill, South Carolina
29733.

High school students from throughout the state meet
to compete in playwriting and performance.

TEXAS

★ 3781 ★
Odessa - SHAKESPEARE FESTIVAL.   June-August,
annual, 2 months, Globe Theater.   Contact: Odessa
Chamber of Commerce, 412 North Lincoln, Box 3626,
Odessa, Texas 79760; or Shakespeare Festival,
2808 Shakespeare Road, Odessa, Texas 79760.

Festival is held at a theater which is a reproduction
of the original Globe Theatre.   Professional actors
perform in the plays, as well as students from the
University of Texas.

★ 3782 ★
Round Top - SHAKESPEARE AT WINEDALE.   June-
July.   Contact: L.W. Taylor, Box 11, Round Top,
Texas 78954.

Free performances of scenes and plays by Shakespeare
enacted by University of Texas students.

UTAH

★ 3783 ★
Cedar City - UTAH SHAKESPEAREAN FESTIVAL.
July-August, annual, 1 month, Southern Utah State
College.   Contact: Utah Shakespearean Festival,
Box Office, Cedar City, Utah 84720.

Pre-play activities, keyed to the mood of the days
performance, include local talent performing madrigal
dances and singing Elizabethan songs; a puppet show;
girls with oranges, tarts or horehound candies and
young men with programs, all singing of their wares.
Pre-professional actors, selected by applications and
auditions from top drama schools and universities
throughout the United States perform three different
plays in the course of the season.   The experience
is rounded out with Shakespeare seminars and back-
stage tours.   Begun around 1962.

WASHINGTON

★ 3784 ★
Spokane - FESTIVAL OF AMERICAN COMMUNITY
THEATERS (FACT).   Late June, biennial, 3 days,
Spokane Civic Theatre.   Contact: David M. Gooder,
ACTA President, 1341 Turvey Road, Downers Grove,
Illinois 60515.

Nine regional play festivals winners from across the
United States compete for the honor of representing
our country at the International Festival which is held
every four years.   Participants exchange ideas with
theater leaders from across the country, hear informa-
tive critiques of all the shows by nationally renowned
judges, and take a close-up look at the finest community theater groups and productions in the United
States.   The festival location and dates change each
time, this particular one is to be held June 24-26,
1977.   The nine regional festivals also vary as to
place and dates, usually performing plays of one hour
or less by American authors.

CANADA - BRITISH COLUMBIA

★ 3785 ★
Victoria - PHOENIX FESTIVAL.   Early April, annual,
3 days, Phoenix Theatre, University of Victoria.
Contact: Department of Theatre, University of
Victoria, Victoria, British Columbia, Canada.

The festival offers a variety of plays, some of which
are under-graduate projects, some are MFA thesis
productions or directing projects, some are faculty
directed production.   There are some musical events
as well.   Presented by the University of Victoria
Department of Theatre.

CANADA - NEWFOUNDLAND

★ 3786 ★
Saint John's - PROVINCIAL DRAMA FESTIVAL.
Late March-early April, annual, 6 days, Saint
John's Arts and Culture Center.   Contact: New-
foundland Department of Tourism, Confederation
Building, Saint John's, Newfoundland, Canada.

Features competition among various amateur theatre
groups.

★ 3787 ★
Saint John's - SHAKESPEAREAN PRODUCTION.
Mid April, annual, 6 days, Saint John's Arts and
Culture Centre.   Contact: Newfoundland Depart-
ment of Tourism, Confederation Building, Saint
John's, Newfoundland, Canada.

CANADA - NEWFOUNDLAND (Continued)

Six days of performances of Shakespearean plays.

CANADA - ONTARIO

★ 3788 ★
Niagra-on-the-Lake - SHAW FESTIVAL.   Mid June
through early September, annual: Contact: Shaw
Festival, Court House Theatre, Niagra-on-the-Lake,
Ontario, Canada.

Primarily a drama festival, includes a series of chamber
concerts of new music.   A newly constructed theatre
close to the Court House Theatre, its present site,
complete in the summer of 1972.   Performances of
Shaw's plays, lectures on Shaw and his works highlight the events.

★ 3789 ★
Stratford - STRATFORD FESTIVAL.   June-October,
annual.   Contact: Stratford Festival, Festival
Theater, Stratford, Ontario N5A 6V2, Canada.

Drama and music.   Opera, orchestral concerts,
chamber and choral concerts, and jazz.   Productions
of Shakespeare plays, exhibitions, special events
presented on three stages - The Festival Theatre,
The Avon, and the Third Stage (where more experimental works are performed).   Begun in 1952.

CANADA - PRINCE EDWARD ISLAND

★ 3790 ★
Charlottetown - CHARLOTTETOWN SUMMER
FESTIVAL.   Late June-early September, 9 weeks,
Confederation Centre Theatre.   Contact: Charlotte-
town Summer Festival, Box 848, Charlottetown,
Prince Edward Island, Canada.

Three live productions in repertory bring exciting
theater to the Charlottetown summer scene.

Wildlife

ALASKA

★ 3791 ★
Gambell - WALRUS CARNIVAL.   April.   Contact:
Juneau Area Office, Bureau of Indian Affairs, U.S.
Department of the Interior, Federal Building, Box
3-8000, Juneau, Alaska 99801.

Celebration of the walrus, an important source of

food for the Eskimo.   Eskimo games and dancing.
Also held in Savoonga.

★ 3792 ★
Point Barrow - WHALING FESTIVAL (NULAKATUK).
June.   Contact: Juneau Area Office, Bureau of
Indian Affairs, U.S. Department of the Interior,
Federal Building, Box 3-8000, Juneau, Alaska 99801.

Features Eskimo dancing, and in the event of a
successful whale hunt, a muktuk feast.

★ 3793 ★
Savoonga - WALRUS CARNIVAL.   April.   Contact:
Juneau Area Office, Bureau of Indian Affairs, U.S.
Department of the Interior, Federal Building, Box
3-8000, Juneau, Alaska 99801.

Celebration of the walrus, an improtant source of
food for the Eskimo.   Eskimo games and dancing.
Also held in Gambell.

★ 3794 ★
Wainwright - WHALING FESTIVAL (NULAKATUK).
June.   Contact: Juneau Area Office, Bureau of
Indian Affairs, U.S. Department of the Interior,
Federal Building, Box 3-8000, Juneau, Alaska 99801.

Features Eskimo dancing, and, if the whaling is
successful, a muktuk feast.

ARKANSAS

★ 3795 ★
Stuttgart - WORLD CHAMPIONSHIP DUCK CALLING
CONTEST AND WATERFOWL FESTIVAL.   November
(or after beginning of duck hunting season), annual,
4-5 days, Main street and the Grand Prairie War
Memorial Auditorium.   Contact: Chamber of
Commerce, Post Office Box 932, Stuttgart, Arkansas
72160.

Duck calling contest, 'Queen Mallard Beauty Pageant",
the Waterfowl Festival; an exhibit of paintings,
carvings, and any art relevant to waterfowl.   Carnival.   Sponsored by the Chamber of Commerce.
Begun around 1936.

FLORIDA

★ 3796 ★
Jensen Beach - SEA TURTLE WATCH.   Mid June,
annual, 8 days.   Contact: Jensen Beach Chamber
of Commerce, 51 Commercial Street, Jensen Beach,

FLORIDA (Continued)

Florida 33457.

This is the time when the turtles from the Atlantic Ocean make their way onto the beach to dig nests and bury their eggs.

ILLINOIS

★ 3797 ★
Lyndon – CROW FESTIVAL. Mid June, annual, 2 days. Contact: The Division of Tourism, Illinois Department of Business and Economic Development, 222 South College Street, Springfield, Illinois 62706.

The crow capital of the world celebrates the bird.

LOUISIANA

★ 3798 ★
Cameron – LOUISIANA FUR AND WILDLIFE FESTIVAL. Mid January, 2 days. Contact: Mrs. Geneva Griffith, Post Office Drawer I, Cameron, Louisiana 70631; or J B. Jones, Jr., Post Office Drawer M, Cameron, Louisiana 70631.

Events include trap shooting, trap setting contests, muskrat and nutria skinning contests, archery, duck and goose calling contest, parade, float competitions, wildlife and art exhibits, and retriever dog shows.

★ 3799 ★
Jena – CATAHOULA LAKE WATERFOWL FESTIVAL. Late October, annual, 2 days, Greer-Jones Recreation Hall, Catahoula National Wildlife Refuge. Contact: La Salle Parish Development Board, Box 122, Jena, Louisiana 71342.

Waterfowl experts from across the United States are usually on hand for this event. Events include antique duck decoy collection, contemporary waterfowl carving exhibits, a decoy and decorative bird carving contest, art exhibit, duck calling contest, and a children's fishing rodeo at the Catahoula National Wildlife Refuge.

MARYLAND

★ 3800 ★
Blackwater National Wildlife Refuge – WATERFOWL WEEK. Late November, annual, 9 days. Contact: Chincoteague National Wildlife Refuge, Box 62, Chincoteague, Virginia 23336.

The National Wildlife Refuges, strung along the Eastern Shore, provide a feeding and resting place for the thousands of waterfowl migrating southward along the Atlantic Migratory Flyway each fall. During this week, visitors are especially welcome for a memorable experience with nature. Facilities at Blackwater include a Wildlife Interpretive Center, walking and driving trails, and an observation tower. This is a chief wintering place for Canadian geese, but the birds are nocturnal feeders.

★ 3801 ★
Eastern Neck National Wildlife Refuge – WATERFOWL WEEK. Late November, annual, 9 days. Contact: Chincoteague National Wildlife Refuge, Box 62, Chincoteague, Virginia 23336.

The National Wildlife Refuges, strung along the Eastern Shore, provide a feeding and resting place for the thousands of waterfowl migrating southward along the Atlantic Migratory Flyway each fall. During this week, visitors are especially welcome for a memorable experience with nature. A boardwalk/ observation platform, wildlife trail and temporary picnic area are available. No scheduled demonstrations are planned.

★ 3802 ★
Easton – WATERFOWL FESTIVAL. Mid November (2nd weekend), annual, 3 days, public buildings around the town. Contact: Bill Perry, 239 Brookwood Avenue, Easton, Maryland 21601.

Featuring decorative and working decoys, waterfowl art, artifacts, antique gun collection. Artists and artisans from the United States and Canada. Art exhibit includes original paintings, sculptures, etchings, and prints by outstanding waterfowl artists. The carving exhibit features hand-carved birds by the best in the two nations. The work bench also features artists and craftsmen at work. There are a variety of gift shops where items may be purchased, as well as an auction. Ducks Unlimited Theater is a continuous showing of outstanding films. There is also a photographic exhibit. Begun around 1971.

MISSOURI

★ 3803 ★
Sumner – WILD GOOSE FESTIVAL. October (weekend nearest opening of goose hunting festival), annual, 3 days. Contact: Wild Goose Festival, c/o Maurice Lentz, Sumner, Missouri 64681.

The festival features a fiddlers' convention, fiddle contest, arts and crafts, and children's games. Begun around 1955.

NEW JERSEY

★ 3804 ★
Brigantine National Wildlife Refuge - WATERFOWL WEEK. Late November, annual, 9 days. Contact: Chincoteague National Wildlife Refuge, Box 62, Chincoteague, Virginia 23336.

The National Wildlife Refuges, strung along the Eastern Shore, provide a feeding and resting place for the thousands of waterfowl migrating southward along the Atlantic Migratory Flyway each fall. During this week, visitors are especially welcome for a memorable experience with nature. The refuge includes an eight-mile auto trail to observe the wide variety of waterfowl.

OHIO

★ 3805 ★
Mount Gilead - NATIONAL HUNTING AND FISHING DAY. Late September, annual, 1 day, State Lakes. Contact: Conservation Club of Morrow County, Secretary, 297 Neal Avenue, Mount Gilead, Ohio 43338.

The theme of the events is safety and conservation. Started in 1973.

SOUTH DAKOTA

★ 3806 ★
Hermosa - BUFFALO AUCTION. Early February, annual, Custer State Park. Contact: Custer State Park, Hermosa, South Dakota 57744.

In order to keep the park's herd at around 1,500 head, each year the excess buffalo are put up for auction to the visitors who come from all over the country for the event.

TEXAS

★ 3807 ★
Hamilton - HAMILTON COUNTY DOVE FESTIVAL AND FAIR. September. Contact: Chamber of Commerce, Box 429, Hamilton, Texas 76531.

Celebrating opening of the season in the Dove Capitol of Texas with a rodeo, carnival, exhibits, dances, gospel singing, and other special events and entertainment.

VIRGINIA

★ 3808 ★
Chincoteague Island - PONY ROUNDUP AND SWIM. Late July (last Wednesday and Thursday), annual, 2-3 days. Contact: Chincoteage Volunteer Fire Company, Chincoteague, Virginia 23336; or Chincoteague Chamber of Commerce, Chincoteague, Virginia 23336.

The activities are preceded by two days of roundup and corraling on Assateague Island, and followed on Friday by the ponies' swim back to Assateague. The pony penning and sale includes the swim from Assateague Island, branding, wild pony rides, pony shows, stunts and races. Begun around 1926.

★ 3809 ★
Chincoteague National Wildlife Refuge - WATERFOWL WEEK. Late November, annual, 9 days. Contact: Chincoteague National Wildlife Refuge, Box 62, Chincoteague, Virginia 23336.

The National Wildlife Refuges, strung along the Eastern Shore, provide feeding and resting places for the thousands of waterfowl migrating southward along the Atlantic Migratory Flyway each fall. During this week, visitors are especially welcome for a memorable experience with nature. The Chincoteague Refuge offers special automobile and foot trails, special exhibits, and wildlife movies.

★ 3810 ★
Presquile National Wildlife Refuge - WATERFOWL WEEK. Late November, annual, 9 days. Contact: Chincoteague National Wildlife Refuge, Box 62, Chincoteague, Virginia 23336.

The National Wildlife Refuges, strung along the Eastern Shore, provide a feeding and resting place for the thousands of waterfowl migrating southward along the Atlantic Migratory Flyway each fall. During this week, visitors are especially welcome for a memorable experience with nature. The Presquile Refuge is an island in the James River, with deer herds and many other types of wildlife. Visitors may get to the island by government ferry. There is a special hourly guided walk on certain days.

★ 3811 ★
Vienna - FALL WILDLIFE FESTIVAL. October, annual, 1 day, National Wildlife Federation. Contact: National Wildlife Federation, 8925 Leesburg Pike, Vienna, Virginia 22180.

VIRGINIA (Continued)

Typical activities include wildlife artists at work, demonstrations of bird-banding, herb gardening, fly-casting, photography, bonsai planting, radio tracking of wild animals, and wild food walks. Events vary from year to year. Begun in 1974.

★ 3812 ★
Vienna - SPRING WILDLIFE FESTIVAL. April, annual, 1 day, National Wildlife Federation. Contact: National Wildlife Federation, 8925 Leesburg Pike, Vienna, Virginia 22180.

Typical activities include wildlife artists at work, demonstrations of bird-banding, herb gardening, fly-casting, photography, bonsai planting, radio tracking of animals and wild food walks. Events vary from year to year. Begun in 1974.

WASHINGTON

★ 3813 ★
McCleary - BEAR FESTIVAL. July (3rd weekend), annual, 2 days. Contact: Donald G. Dent, Chairman, Post Office Box 388, McCleary, Washington 98557.

Events include a queen coronation, dance, parade, jeep race, art show, and bear stew. Begun around 1961.

Wine
See: FOOD AND DRINK

Winter
See: SEASONS

SECTION II
CHRONOLOGICAL LISTING
OF EVENTS

Chronological Listing of Events

419

Chronological Listing of Events

FEBRUARY (contd.)

California (contd.)

Camellia Festival (Temple City)   42
Canadian Day (Desert Hot Springs)   2007
Chinese New Year Celebration (San Francisco)
   2032
Citrus Fair and Parade (Cloverdale)   17
Clam Festival (Pismo Beach)   2877
National Date Festival (Indio)   22
Welcome of the De Anza Trek (Santa Barbara)
   2567
Welcome of the De Anza Trek (Ventura)   2569
Whiskey Flats Days (Kernville)   2553
Winter Festival (Laguna Beach)   1254

Colorado

Fasching (Georgetown)   2057
Winter Carnival (Steamboat Springs)   3483
Winter Crystal Carnival (Leadville)   3482

Florida

FSU Fine Arts Festival (Tallahassee)   512
Coconut Grove Art Festival (Miami)   817
Edison Pageant of Light (Fort Myers)   1318
Florida Citrus Festival (Winter Haven)   64
Florida State Fair (Tampa)   3709
Gasparilla Pirate Invasion (Tampa)   2578
Heart of Florida Folk Festival (Dade City)   2441
Island Shrimp Festival (Fort Myers Beach)   2880
Mardi Gras Carnival (Cape Coral)   1313
Seafood Festival (Grant)   2881
Seminole Tribal Fair (Hollywood)   2738
Swamp Cabbage Festival (La Belle)   1322
Ybor City Pirate Fiesta Days (Tampa)   2078

Georgia

Georgia Week Celebration (Savannah)   2579
Historic Savannah Foundation Fair and Festival
   (Savannah)   1337
Waterfront Festival (Savannah)   1338

Hawaii

Cherry Blossom Festival (Honolulu)   2088
Haleiwa Sea Spree (Oahu) (Haleiwa-Waialua area)
   2886

Idaho

Idaho State University Winter Carnival (Driggs)
   3488
Winter Carnival (McCall)   3489

Illinois

Black Arts Festival (DeKalb)   2100
College Choral Festival (DeKalb)   3097
Festival of Contemporary Arts (Urbana)   530
Rock Cut Winter Carnival (Rockford)   3497
Theatre Festival (Normal)   3769
Women's Week Festival (DeKalb)   525

Indiana

Parke County Maple Fair (Rockville)   114

Iowa

Sleigh Rally (Spencer)   3518
Winter Sports Festival (Estherville)   3514

Kansas

Central States Jazz Festival (Manhattan)   3131
International Pancake Day Race (Liberal)   2598

Louisiana

Frontier Days Celebration (Logansport)   1440
LSU Junior Division Livestock Show and Champi-
   onship Rodeo (Baton Rouge)   147
Mardi Gras (Acadiana)   1430
Mardi Gras (New Orleans)   1444

Maine

Snow-Fest (Augusta)   3525
Snow-Fest (Gardiner)   3526
Snow-Fest (Winthrop)   3529

Maryland

Cambridge Outdoor Show (Cambridge)   1459
Catoctin Winter Festival (Thurmont)   3535
Purim Celebration (Rockville)   2136
Winterfest (McHenry)   3532
Winter Market/Baltimore (Baltimore)   911
World Railway Film Festival (Wheaton)   2399

Massachusetts

Winter Carnival (East Bridgewater)   3541

Michigan

Winfester (Marquette)   3547

Minnesota

International Peanut Butter and Milk Festival
   (Litchfield)   1511
Mount Sno Winter Carnival (Mountain Iron)   3555

Chronological Listing of Events

FEBRUARY (contd.)

Minnesota (contd.)

North Country Ski Touring Festival (Bemidji)   3550
Sleigh and Cutter Festival (Waseca)   3564
Snowflake Days (Coon Rapids)   2157
Snow Frolics (North Saint Paul)   3556
ULLR Fest (Alexandria)   3548
Vasaloppet Cross Country Ski Race (Mora)   2169
Winter Carnival (Cambridge)   3552
Winter Carnival (Winona)   3565

Mississippi

First Monday (Ripley)   1538

Missouri

Central Missouri State University Jazz Festival
   (Warrensburg)   3214

Montana

Ski Carnival Festival (Big Sky)   3570
Winter Carnival (Red Lodge)   3572
Winter Carnival (Whitefish)   3573

Nevada

Contemporary Music Festival (Las Vegas)   3218

New Hampshire

Dartmouth Winter Carnival (Hanover)   3577
New Hampshire Technical Institute Winter Carnival
   (Concord)   3575

New Jersey

Pee Wee Russell Memorial Stomp (Martinsville)
   3225

New Mexico

Black Heritage Week Arts and Crafts Festival
   (Albuquerque)   974
Candeleria (Candlemas) Day (Cochiti)   2771
Candeleria (Candlemas) Day (San Felipe Pueblo)
   2790
Candeleria (Candlemas) Day (Santo Domingo
   Pueblo)   2805
February Festival for the Arts (Santa Fe)   3230
National Small Paintings Show (Albuquerque)   977
Winter Ski Carnival (Red River)   3583

New York

Delphic Festival (New York)   2223
Long Island Antiques Fair and Sale (Hempstead)
   459
Mid-Town Plaza Craft Show (Rochester)   1001

Winter Carnival (Cohocton)   3587
Winter Carnival (Saranac Lake)   3591
Winter Carnival Month (Monticello)   3590
Winter Festival (New York)   604

North Carolina

Festival of Contemporary Arts (Wilson)   621

North Dakota

Winterfest (Minot)   3602

Ohio

College Conservatory Jazz Festival (Cincinnati)
   3303
English Faire (Akron)   2241
Maple Syrup Weekends (Hueston Woods State Park)
   263
Ohio Winter Ski Carnival (Mansfield)   3605

Oklahoma

Fiddlers Festival (Tahlequah)   3320

Oregon

Gay 90's Festival (Forest Grove)   2646
Shakespearean Festival (Ashland)   3778

Pennsylvania

Cherries Jubilee (Valley Forge)   2660
Snow Ball Festival (Conneaut Lake)   3609

Rhode Island

Fireworks in February (Cranston)   1706

South Carolina

Baroque/Contemporary Festival (Spartanburg)   3347
Christian High School Music Festival and Forensic
   Tournament (Greenville)   3343
Festival of Arts, Hobbies, and Handcrafts (Clem-
   son)   1079
French Emphasis Festival (Charleston)   2291
George Washington Days (Myrtle Beach)   2666

South Dakota

Buffalo Auction (Hermosa)   3806

Texas

Band Festival (Brady)   3367
Contemporary Music Festival (Corpus Christi)   3371
Festival of Texas Composers (Dallas)   3373

Chronological Listing of Events

Chronological Listing of Events

MARCH (contd.)

California (contd.)

'50's Festival of Rock N' Roll (Valencia) 3045
Fine Arts Festival (Loma Linda) 748
International Broadcasting Awards Festival (Hollywood) 2379
Kite Festival (Ocean Beach) 1267
National Orange Show (San Bernardino) 32
Ojai Folk Dance Festival (Ojai) 3027
Percussive Arts Society Festival (Northridge) 3024
Saint Patrick's Frolic (San Francisco) 2035
San Diego Round Dance Festival (San Diego) 1955
South Gate Azalea Festival (South Gate) 41
Survival Faire Festival (San Jose) 2387

Connecticut

Arts and Crafts Fair (Hartford) 791
Festival of Contemporary Music (Bridgeport) 3055
Yale Festival of Undergraduate Drama (New Haven) 3760

Delaware

Great Delaware Kite Festival (Lewes) 1308
Swedish Colonial Day (Wilmington) 2061

Florida

Around the World Fair (Miami) 2072
Azalea Festival (Palatka) 60
Bach Festival of Winter Park (Winter Park) 3078
Charlotte County Historical Festival (Punta Gorda) 2577
Citrus County Fair (Inverness) 49
De Soto Celebration (Bradenton) 2064
Festival of States (Saint Petersburg) 1329
Florida Strawberry Festival (Plant City) 62
Fun 'n Sun Festival (Clearwater) 1314
Gran Romeria Hispano-Americana (Miami) 2073
Gran Romeria Ponce de Leon (Miami) 2576
Highland Games and Festival (Dunedin) 2067
King Neptune Frolics (Sarasota) 2884
Latin America Fiesta (Tampa) 2077
Orange Festival and Rodeo (Davie) 1315
Outdoor Art Festival (Jensen Beach) 814
Pioneer Days (Lake Worth) 1323
Saint Cloud Art Festival (Saint Cloud) 824
Sanibel Island Shell Fair (Sanibel) 2883
Sidewalk Art Festival (DeLand) 810
Sidewalk Art Festival (Winter Park) 514
Springtime Tallahassee (Tallahassee) 3485
Strawberry Festival (Starke) 63
Tavares Fiesta (Tavares) 2080

Georgia

Arts Festival of Atlanta (Atlanta) 515
Saint Patrick's Festival (Dublin) 2084

Hawaii

Artists of Hawaii (Part II) (Honolulu) 837
Cherry Blossom Festival (Honolulu) 2088
Hawaiian Music Festival (Honolulu) 3085
Hawaiian Song Festival and Song Composing Contest (Honolulu) 3086
Prince Kuhio Festival (Kauai Island) 2583

Idaho

Art Festival (Boise) 838
E-pah-tes War Dance Championship (Lapwai) 2744
Folk Festival of The Smokies (Idaho Falls) 2446

Illinois

Festival of the Arts (DeKalb) 2101
Fine Arts Festival (Bloomington) 523

Indiana

Ball State University Drawing and Small Sculpture Show (Muncie) 872
Collegiate Jazz Festival (Notre Dame) 3116
Purdue Festival Series (West Lafayette) 542
Sophomore Literary Festival (Notre Dame) 539

Iowa

Saint Patrick's Day Celebration (Emmetsburg) 2119
Tri-State Art Show (Rock Rapids) 893

Kansas

Messiah Festival (Lindsborg) 3130
University of Kansas Festival of the Arts (Lawrence) 548

Kentucky

Iris Festival (Cynthiana) 140

Louisiana

Dogwood Festival (Bogalusa) 148
Eva Mouton Keyboard Festival (Lafayette) 3143
Fine Arts Festival (Monroe) 909
Louisiana Industrial Arts Students Fair (Student Craftsman Fair) (Lafayette) 1436
Louisiana State University Festival of Contemporary Music (Baton Rouge) 3142

Chronological Listing of Events

Chronological Listing of Events

MARCH (contd.)

Rhode Island

Providence Art Club Painting Show (Providence) 1069

South Carolina

Canadian-American Days (Myrtle Beach) 2299
College of Charleston Fine Arts Festival (Charleston) 652
Festival of Houses (Charleston) 1715
Governor's Frog Jumping Contest (Springfield) 1723
International Egg Striking Contest (Springfield) 1724
Irish Emphasis Festival (Charleston) 2295
Myrtle Beach Square Dance Festival (Myrtle Beach) 1983
South Carolina High School Drama Festival (Rock Hill) 3780

South Dakota

Schmeckfest (Freeman) 2301

Tennessee

New Music Festival (Memphis) 3359
String Awakening (Cosby) 3358
Wearin' O' the Green (Erin) 2304

Texas

Azalea Trails and Spring Flower Show (Tyler) 369
Bluebonnet Trail Arts and Crafts Show (Kingsland) 1113
Charro Days (Brownsville) 2309
Dogwood Fiesta (Quitman) 365
Fiesta Hidalgo (Edinburg) 1765
First Mondays (Canton) 1752
Heritage Festival (Nederland) 2323
Highland Lakes Bluebonnet Art Show (Marble Falls) 1115
International Spring Fiesta (McAllen) 3632
Music In Our Time (Abilene) 3364
Rattlesnake Hunt and Antique Show (Coleman) 1755
Rattlesnake Roundup (Sweetwater) 1807
Rattlesnake Roundup and Antique Show (Brownwood) 1750
Saint Patricks Celebration (Shamrock) 2334
Southwest Hardware and Implement Association Championship Tractor Pull (Fort Worth) 352
Spring Arts Festival (Houston) 1108
Starving Artists Show (San Antonio) 1120
Tyler County Dogwood Festival (Woodville) 375
U.S.A. Film Festival (Dallas) 2421

World Championship Rattlesnake Races and Saint Patrick Day Celebration (San Patricio) 1802

Utah

Spring Carnival (Cedar City) 3637
Ute Tribal Bear Dance (Whiterocks) 2845

Vermont

Maple Sugar Square Dance Festival (Burlington) 1986
New England Kandahar (Waitsfield) 3645

Virginia

Antiques Show and Sale (Richmond) 471
City-Wide Art and Crafts Show (Richmond) 1143
Highland County Maple Sugar Festival (Monterey) 389
Kite Festival (Lorton) 1832
Virginia Craftsmen (Richmond) 1146

Washington

Puyallup Valley Daffodil Festival (Puyallup) 399
Puyallup Valley Daffodil Festival (Sumner) 405
Puyallup Valley Daffodil Festival (Tacoma) 407
Speelyi-Mi Indian Arts and Crafts Club Trade Fair (Wapato) 1161
Tenino Old Time Music Festival (Tenino) 3417

West Virginia

Tucker County Alpine Festival (Davis) 3659
White Water Weekend (Petersburg) 2978

Wisconsin

Wisconsin Painters and Sculptors (Milwaukee) 1194

Alberta, Canada

Alberta Winter Games and Banff Winter Festival (Banff) 3668

Manitoba, Canada

Aurora Snow Festival (Churchill) 3674
Brandon Film Festival (Brandon) 2426
Manitoba Music Competition Festival (Winnipeg) 3439

Newfoundland, Canada

Provincial Drama Festival (Saint John's) 3786

Chronological Listing of Events

Chronological Listing of Events

Chronological Listing of Events

Chronological Listing of Events

APRIL (contd.)

Texas (contd.)

Bear Downs Week (Waco) 1816
Bluebonnet Antique Show (Chappell Hill) 468
Brazos River Festival and Pilgrimage, Cotton
    Palace Pageant (Waco) 2681
Buccaneer Days Celebration (Corpus Christi) 2672
Cleveland Dairy Days (Cleveland) 346
Diadeloso (Waco) 1817
Farm-City Week (Marshall) 357
Festival of Arts (Abilene) 661
Festival of Barbershop Harmony (Port Arthur) 3376
Festival of Flowers (Corpus Christi) 347
Fiesta San Antonio (San Antonio) 1799
Fine Arts Festival (Breckenridge) 1096
Fine Arts Festival (Fort Worth) 663
Fine Arts Festival (Odessa) 667
First Mondays (Canton) 1752
Greater Southwest Music Festival (Amarillo) 3365
Iris Festival and Trail (Abilene) 338
Jim Bob Wills Day (Turkey) 3382
Montgomery County Texas Trek (Montgomery)
    2679
Morris County Arts and Crafts Shows (Daingerfield)
    1101
Music Along the River (San Marcos) 3380
Neches River Festival (Beaumont) 1746
Oil-O-Rama and Rattlesnake Roundup (Freer) 1772
Scandinavian Club of Houston's Spring Festival
    (Houston) 2321
Shrimp Festival and Blessing of the Fleet (Galves-
    ton) 2959
Spring Arts Festival (Longview) 1114
Strawberry Festival (Poteet) 364
Tarrant County Art Show (Fort Worth) 1103
Texas Independence Day Observance (Houston)
    2676
Winedale Spring Festival (Round Top) 3635

Utah

Americanism Week (Saint George) 1824

Vermont

Contemporary Music Symposium (Burlington) 3387
Fiddle Contest and Craft Fair (Lyndon Center)
    2499
Maple Sugar Festival (Brownsville) 382
Vermont State Maple Festival (Saint Albans) 384

Virginia

Art and Craft Show on Old Courthouse Green
    (Accomac) 1129
Art on the Green (Gloucester) 1137
Art Show (Danville) 1135

Bristol Spring Arts Festival (Bristol) 670
Cape Henry Day (Cape Henry) 2688
Dogwood Festival (Charlottesville) 385
Dogwood Festival (Vinton) 392
International Festival (Norfolk) 390
Shenandoah Apple Blossom Festival (Winchester)
    394
Spring Wildlife Festival (Vienna) 3812
Susuki Festival (Hampton) 3404
Virginia Crafts Council Craft Fair (Manassas) 1140

Washington

Washington State Apple Blossom Festival
    (Wenatchee) 408

West Virginia

Appalachian Festival (Charleston) 2507
Braxton County Art and Craft Show (Gassaway)
    1170
Crafts Center Workshop (Ripley) 1185
Fair Springtime Celebration of Arts and Crafts
    (North Charleston) 1180
Greenbrier Valley Arts and Humanities Festival
    (Lewisburg) 681
Mountain Heritage Festival (Keyser) 2509
Parkersburg College Heritage Days (Parkersburg)
    1864
Potomac Highlands Crafts Show (Petersburg) 1182
Salem College Heritage Arts Festival (Salem) 1187

Wyoming

Cheyenne Symphony and Choral Society Festival
    (Cheyenne) 3429

Alberta, Canada

Kobasa Kapers (Jasper) 1894

British Columbia, Canada

Greater Victoria Music Festival (Victoria) 3434
Jazz Festival (New Westminster) 3433
Phoenix Festival (Victoria) 3785

Manitoba, Canada

Royal Manitoba Winter Fair (Brandon) 426

Newfoundland, Canada

Shakespearean Production (Saint John's) 3787

Northwest Territories, Canada

Beluga Jamboree (Tuktoyaktuk) 2366

APRIL (contd.)

Northwest Territories, Canada (contd.)

Toonik Tyme (Frobisher Bay)   3681
White Fox Jamboree (Sachs Harbour)   3685

Ontario, Canada

Elmira Maple Sugar Festival (Elmira)   439
Guelph Spring Festival (Guelph)   691

Quebec, Canada

Maple Festival (Plessisville)   441

MAY

Alabama

First Monday (Scottsboro)   1211
Spring Bluegrass Music Festival (Steele)   2995
Springfest (Huntsville)   3453

Alaska

King Crab Festival (Kodiak)   2869
Little Norway Festival (Petersburg)   1996
Spring Fling Folk Dance Festival (Anchorage)
    1948

Arizona

Fiesta De Mayo (Nogales)   1997
Garces Celebration of the Arts (Yuma)   480
Old-Time Gospel Music Festival (Payson)   3000

Arkansas

Arkansas Blue Grass Festival (Heber Springs)   3003
Dogpatch Days (Harrison)   1216
Prints, Drawings and Crafts Exhibition (Little Rock)
    724
Sidewalk Art and Crafts Festival (Eureka Springs)
    718
Southwest Arkansas Poultry Festival (Nashville)   8
Strawberry Festival (Marshall)   7

California

American Dance Festival (San Diego)   1952
Cal Arts Spring Fair (Valencia)   498

Caleveras County Fair and Jumping Frog Jubilee
    (Angels Camp)   1220
Calico Spring Festival (Barstow)   3005
California City Spring Festival (California City)
    3468
Carlsbad Book Fair (Carlsbad)   484
Cinco de Mayo Celebration (Delano)   2006
Corpus Christi Fiesta (Pala)   2732
Early California Days Festival (Fillmore)   2551
Ferndale Arts Festival and Kinetic Art Show
    (Ferndale)   737
Festival de Cinco de Mayo (Los Angeles)   2012
Festival of Friendship (Los Angeles)   1259
Festival of the Arts (Hayward)   487
Fiesta de la Primavera (San Diego)   2027
La Fiesta de San Luis Obispo (San Luis Obispo)
    1278
Fiesta Del Artes (Hermosa Beach)   741
Frontier Days (Lake Elsinore)   2554
German Festival (Torrance)   2047
Grubstake Days (Yucca Valley)   2570
Independent Film-Makers Festival (Los Altos)   2381
International Festival (Long Beach)   2011
International Heritage Fair (Los Angeles)   2014
Inventors Workshop Expo (Ventura)   1290
Kingsburg Swedish Festival (Kingsburg)   2008
La Purisima Mission Festival (Mission Fiesta Day)
    (Lompoc)   2010
Latin-American Fiesta (San Francisco)   2034
Long Beach Heritage Week (Long Beach)   1257
Luther Burbank Rose Festival (Santa Rosa)   36
Malki Indian Fiesta and Barbeque (Banning)   2727
May Time Frolic (San Diego)   1954
Maytime Band Review (National City)   2082
Mexican Fiesta (Bakersfield)   2002
Hobo Daze (Miracle Hot Springs)   1262
Music Here and Now Festival (Claremont)   3011
Mule Days Celebration (Bishop)   1228
Novato's Pioneer Days (Novato)   1265
Ojai Festival (Ojai)   3026
Old Time Camp Meeting and Revival (Sausalito)
    3042
Old Town Fiesta de la Primavera (San Diego)
    2560
Potato and Cotton Festival (Shafter)   39
Renaissance Fair (Laytonville)   2555
Russian River Wine Fest (Healdsburg)   2517
San Fernando Fiesta Days (San Fernando)   38
San Joaquin County Spring Festival (Stockton)
    3478
Silver Dollar Fair (Chico)   1236
Strawberry Festival (Garden Grove)   20
Turtle Days (Joshua Tree)   1252
Western Festival (Elk Grove)   1246
Westwood Sidewalk Art and Crafts Show (Los
    Angeles)   753
Wildflower Show and Art Mart (Julian)   23

Chronological Listing of Events

MAY (contd.)

Kentucky (contd.)

Great Western Kentucky Bluegrass Festival (Owensboro)   3140
Kentucky Guild of Artists and Craftsmen Fair (Berea)   906
May Day Festival (Owingsville)   1426
Mountain Heritage Folk Festival (Grayson)   2453
Mountain Laurel Festival (Pineville)   142

Louisiana

Contraband Days (Lake Charles)   1439
Crayfish Festival (Breaux Bridge)   2894
Louisiana Pine Tree Festival (Walker)   1448
Southeastern Indian Festival (Baton Rouge)   2751

Maryland

Cavalier Days (Prince Frederick)   2611
Colonial Charlestown Fair (Charlestown)   915
Craft Fair (Bethesda)   912
Delmarva Chicken Festival (Easton)   175
Dimension in Music (Largo)   3156
Federal Hill Celebration (Baltimore)   1450
Festival of Fine Arts (Bowie)   558
Flower Festival (Ellicott City)   176
Goucher Country Fair (Towson)   1468
Hunt Valley May Fair (Hunt Valley)   3530
May Day Carnival (Westminster)   1470
National Capitol Area Scottish Festival (Rockville)   2135
Preakness Festival Week (Baltimore)   1453
Queen Anne's County Crafts Festival (Centreville)   914
Revolutionary War Days (Indian Head)   2610
Sheep and Wool Crafts Festival (Westminster)   923
Steam-Up and Militia Days (Westminster)   2614
Tea Party Festival (Chestertown)   2607
Towsontown Spring Festival (Towson)   3537

Massachusetts

Antique Show and Flea Market (Brimfield)   452
Hillside Folk Festival (Attleboro)   2460
National Show (Fall River)   929
Portuguese Spring Festival (Fall River)   2140
Spring Market Days (Salem)   1487
Town Fair (Wilbraham)   2619
Woods Hole Day (Woods Hole)   1491

Michigan

Blossomtime Festival (Saint Joseph and Benton Harbor)   193
Country Fair of Yesteryear (Dearborn)   2620

Ethnic Festivals (Detroit)   2147
Highland Festival (Alma)   193
Tulip Time (Holland)   190

Minnesota

Lilac Festival (Golden Valley)   200
Snoose Boulevard Festival (Minneapolis)   2164
Syttende Mai Fest (Spring Grove)   2172

Mississippi

Arts Festival (Greenwood)   575
Day Lily Festival (Osyka)   217
Delta Arts and Crafts Festival (Yazoo City)   580
Festival of Harmony (Jackson)   3181
First Monday (Ripley)   1538
Gum Tree Arts Festival (Tupelo)   579
Inverness Arts Festival (Inverness)   949
Jimmie Rodgers Festival (Meridian)   3184
Mainstream Arts and Crafts Festival (Greenville)   947

Missouri

Fair Saint Louis (Saint Louis)   1546
Maifest (Hermann)   2176
Piney River Bluegrass Music Festival (Fort Leonard Wood)   3192
Root Diggin' Days (Silver Dollar City)   1549
Spring Bluegrass Festival (Farmington)   3191
Valley of Flowers Festival (Florissant)   1540

Montana

Bucking Horse Sale (Miles City)   1555
Cherry Blossom Festival (Polson)   224
Square Dance Festival (Missoula)   1964

Nebraska

German Heritage Days (McCook)   2192
Square Dance Festival (Lincoln)   1965

Nevada

Helldorado (Las Vegas)   1560

New Hampshire

Folk Dance Weekend (Troy)   1966
Sidewalk Fair (Newmarket)   1569

New Jersey

Showcase ___ (name includes number of festival) (West Long Branch)   970

Chronological Listing of Events

Chronological Listing of Events

Chronological Listing of Events

MAY (contd.)

Texas (contd.)

Rollin' Rock Roundup (Glen Rose)   1775
Shrimp Boil (Freeport)   2958
Spanish Fiesta (Andrews)   2305
Stagecoach Days (Marshall)   2678
Texas-Louisiana Cajun Festival (Port Arthur)   2327
Village Fair (League City)   1784

Utah

Cache Valley Dairy Festival (Cache Valley)   378
Golden Spike Ceremony (Promontory)   2685
National Historic Preservation Week (Salt Lake City)   2687
The Works (Cedar City)   1122

Virginia

Arts and Crafts Fair (Bristol)   1133
Bluegrass and Old-Time Music Festival (Bristol) 3354
Carter Stanley Memorial Festival (McClure)   3405
Jamestown Day (Jamestown)   2690
Lonesome Pine Arts and Craft Festival (Big Stone Gap)   1132
Market Square Fair (Fredericksburg)   1829
May Festival for Senior Adults (Arlington)   3647
National Banjo Championship (Appomattox)   3390
National Seawall Art Show (Portsmouth)   1142
Nelson County Day (Lovingston)   1833
Northern Virginia Folk Festival and Bazaar (Arlington)   2502
Railfan Steam Weekend (Covington)   1828
Seafood Festival (Chincoteague Island)   2965
Spring Sampler (Abingdon)   1128
Virginia Artists (Richmond)   1145
Virginia Poultry Festival (Harrisonburg)   388ı

Washington

Art Fair (Seattle)   1160
Blossomtime (Bellingham)   3655
Cherry Festival (Granger)   395
Gardeners' Paradise Days (Tacoma)   406
Greater Spokane Music and Allied Arts Festival (Spokane)   3416
Irrigation Festival (Sequim)   401
Mason County Forest Festival (Shelton)   402
Northwest Regional Folklife Festival (Seattle) 2506
Quinault Derby Days (Taholah)   2854
Rhododendron Festival (Port Townsend)   398
Smoo-kee-shin Pow-wow (Spokane)   2852
Spokane Lilac Festival (Spokane)   404
Swinomish Festival (La Conner)   2847
Viking Fest (Poulsbo)   2347

West Virginia

Dogwood Festival (Huntington)   414
Hurricane Heritage Days (Hurricane)   1858
North Central West Virginia Art and Craft Festival (Fairmont)   1169
Railfan Steam Weekend (Cass)   1850
Rhododendron Outdoor Art and Crafts Festival (Charleston)   1166
Upper and Lower Kanawha Majorette Festival (South Charleston)   3421
West Virginia Country Fling (Harpers Ferry)   1855

Wisconsin

Syttende Mai Celebration (Stoughton)   2352

Wyoming

Wyoming State Championship Oldtime Fiddle Contest (Shoshoni)   3431

Alberta, Canada

Pioneer Days (Hanna)   1893

British Columbia, Canada

Beaver Valley Days Celebration (Fruitvale)   1896
Children and the Arts (Langley)   1197
Creston Valley Blossom Festival (Creston)   420
Empire Day Celebration (Nanaimo)   1899
Hyack Festival (New Westminster)   2701
Multi-Cultural Festival (Vernon)   2357
Oyster Festival (Denman Island)   2979
Port McNeill Days (Port McNeill)   1900
Rock, Gem and Mineral Show (Vancouver)   1901
Trail International Festival (Trail)   2356
Victorian Days (Victoria)   2702

Manitoba, Canada

Apple Blossom Time (Morden)   427

New Brunswick, Canada

Competitive Festival of Music (Saint John)   3445
Madawaska Festival of Music (Edmundston)   3440
Maritime Band Festival (Moncton)   3443
Oromocto Arts and Crafts Festival (Oromocto) 1199
Spring Square Dance Festival (Fredericton)   1989

Newfoundland, Canada

Lions Trade Fair (Saint John's)   433

Chronological Listing of Events

Chronological Listing of Events

Chronological Listing of Events

JUNE (contd.)

Louisiana (contd.)

Peach Festival (Ruston) 161
Summer Festival of Arts (Baton Rouge) 549

Maine

Schooner Days (Camden) 2899

Maryland

Annapolis Arts Festival (Annapolis) 555
Antiques Fair (Gaithersburg) 451
Art in the Park (Frederick) 917
Bell and History Days (Frederick) 2609
Benefit Air Fair (California) 1458
Bluegrass Festival (Callaway) 3153
Farm Visitation Day (College Park) 174
Frederick Craft Fair (Frederick) 918
Hagerstown Park Arts Festival (Hagerstown) 560
Heritage Days (Cumberland) 2608
Historic Harbor Rendezvous and Classic Yacht
    Parade (Baltimore) 2906
New Theater Festival (Catonsville) 3770
Old Time Arts and Crafts Day (Street) 922
Scottish Games (Colonial Highland Gathering)
    (Fairhill) 2133
Towsontowne Courthouse Arts Festival (Towson)
    561
U.S.A. Day Festival (Baltimore) 1455
Water Festival (North East) 2913
Ye Olde Woodlawn Crafts Festival (Woodlawn)
    924

Massachusetts

Art in the Park (Attleboro) 925
Beerfest (Northampton) 2142
Castle Hill Festival (Ipswich) 3161
Chestnut Street Days (Salem) 1484
Crown Festival (Bridgewater) 2139
Esplanade Concerts (Boston) 3158
Festival of Arts (Boston) 563
Fiesta (Gloucester) 1475
Homecoming Week (Southwick) 1490
Old Home Week (Dalton) 1474
Plymouth Drama Festival (Plymouth) 3771
Pops-in-the-Park Crafts Fair (Brockton) 927
Rail-Fans Day (South Carver) 1489
Southeastern Massachusetts University Institute
    Festival (North Dartmouth) 3164
Strawberry Festival (Falmouth) 183

Michigan

Arts and Crafts Festival (Spring Lake) 941
Bavarian Festival (Frankenmuth) 2149

Detroit Concert Band Summer Series (Grosse Pointe
    Woods) 3171
Festival (Grand Rapids) 570
International Freedom Festival (Detroit) 1496
Meadow Brook Music Festival (Rochester) 3174
Muzzle Loaders Festival (Dearborn) 2621
National Asparagus Festival (Hart) 189
Old Time Summer Festival (Dearborn) 2622

Minnesota

Aebleskiver Days (Tyler) 2173
Art Festival (Rochester) 573
Buffalo Days (Buffalo) 1503
Bullhead Days (Waterville) 1525
Carleton Summer Music Festival (Northfield) 3179
Dala Days (Mora) 2168
Danish Day at Minehaha Park (Minneapolis) 2162
International Fiesta Days (Montevideo) 2166
Kaffe Fest (Willmar) 2174
Karl Oskar Days (Lindstrom) 1510
Mound City Days (Mound) 1514
Nobles County Dairy Days (Ellsworth) 198
Northwest Dairy Days (Thief River Falls) 209
Onamia Days (Onamia) 1516
Polka Festival (Princeton) 1963
River Days (Windom) 2928
Scottish Highland Games (Mapleton) 2161
Sister City Celebration (Elbow Lake) 2156
Spud Fest Days (Big Lake) 1501
Svenskarnas Dag (Minneapolis) 2165
Swedish Festival (Cambridge) 2153
Tater Daze (Brooklyn Park) 1502
Town and Country Days (Paynesville) 1517
Water Show and Fun Days (New London) 2927
Water Ski Days (Lake City) 2924

Mississippi

Art Mart (Batesville) 943
Barter Day (Morton) 951
Bluegrass Festival (Monticello) 3185
Deep Sea Fishing Rodeo (Gulfport) 2930
Folklore Frolic (Tishomingo) 2466
First Monday (Ripley) 1538
Mainstream Festival (Greenville) 1533
Shrimp Festival and Blessing of the Shrimp Fleet
    (Biloxi) 2929

Missouri

Bluegrass Country Fair (Kansas City) 1542
Bluegrass Festival (Grassy) 3194
Central Missouri Bluegrass Music Festival (Roche-
    port) 3206
Dub Crouch's Bluegrass Festival (Hillsboro) 3196
Festival of Mountain Folks' Music (Silver Dollar
    City) 3212
Greek Plaka (Kansas City) 2178
Heart of the Ozarks Fair (West Plains) 222

JUNE (contd.)

Missouri (contd.)

Invitational Country-Bluegrass-Old Time Music
Festival (Glenwood)   3193
Mustard Seed Festival (Saint Louis)   1548
Ragtime Festival (Saint Louis)   3210
Starlight Theatre Summer Series (Kansas City)
3774

Montana

Custer Re-Enactment (Crow Agency)   2760
Red Lodge Music Festival (Student Music Festival)
(Red Lodge)   3217

Nebraska

Danish Days Celebration (Minden)   2193
Days of '56 Rodeo and Celebration (Ponca)   1559
Kolach Days (Verdigre)   2197
NEBRASKAland Days (North Platte)   1558
Polish Festival (Loup City)   2191
Swedish Festival (Stromberg)   2196

New Hampshire

Congregation of the Arts (Hanover)   587
Muster Day (New London)   2629
Strawberry Banke Chamber Music Festival (Ports-
mouth)   3223

New Jersey

Arts and Crafts Festival (Cape May)   966
Garden State Arts Center Gala (Holmdel)   3224
Irish Festival (Holmdel)   2207
Italian Festival (Holmdel)   2208
Jewish Festival of the Arts (Holmdel)   2209
June Days Folk Festival (West Orange)   2470
June Folk Festival (Middletown Folk Festival)
(Middletown)   2468
Polish Festival (Holmdel)   2210
Spring Festival (Seaside Heights)   3580
Ukrainian Festival (Holmdel)   2213
Waterloo Village Music Festival (Stanhope)   3226

New Mexico

All-State Music Festival (Las Cruces)   3227
Bandelier Indian Arts and Crafts Show (Los Alamos)
983
Chamber Music Festival (Santa Fe)   3229
Church Street Fair (Albuquerque)   975
Community House Square Dance Festival and
Pioneer Reunion (Red River)   1595
Feast Day (Sandia Pueblo)   2798
Feast Day (Taos Pueblo)   2810

Fiesta de San Juan (Los Chavez)   1590
Inter-Tribal Powwow (Albuquerque)   2769
New Mexico Arts and Crafts Fair (Albuquerque)
978
New Mexico Shakespeare Festival (Las Cruces)
3775
Ruidoso-Mescalero Apache Indian Celebration
(Mescalero)   2786
Ruidoso-Mescalero Apache Indian Celebration
Ruidoso)   2789
San Antonio Feast Day (San Ildefonso Pueblo)
2794
San Antonio Feast Day (San Juan Pueblo)   2796
San Antonio Feast Day (Santa Clara Pueblo)   2802
San Antonio Feast Day (Taos Pueblo)   2812
San Felipe de Neri Fiesta (Albuquerque)   1578
San Juan Feast Day (San Juan Pueblo)   2797
San Pedro Feast Day (Acoma Pueblo)   2767
San Pedro Feast Day (Cochiti Pueblo)   2774
San Pedro Feast Day (Isleta Pueblo)   2777
San Pedro Feast Day (San Felipe Pueblo)   2793
San Pedro Feast Day (Santa Ana Pueblo)   2800
San Pedro Feast Day (Santo Domingo Pueblo)   2806
Southwestern Crafts Biennial (Santa Fe)   988
Taos School of Music Summer Chamber Music
Concerts (Taos)   3232

New York

All High Music Festival (Rochester)   3268
American Radio Commercials Festival (New York)
2404
Antique Festival (Seneca Falls)   460
Caramoor Festival (Katonah)   3242
Chautauqua Summer Music Festival (Chautauqua)
3233
Colonial Days (Painted Post)   1611
Community Days (Big Flats)   1607
Crafts Revisited Exhibition (New York)   995
Creative Music Festival (Woodstock)   3277
Dance Films Festival (New York)   2406
Delphic Festival (New York)   2223
Gerry Days (Elbridge)   1609
Guggenheim Memorial Concerts (New York)   3249
Hudson Valley Folk Festival (Tarrytown)   2473
International Computer Art Festival (New York)
602
Jazz in the Gardens (New York)   3251
June Arts Festival (Roslyn)   607
Metropolitan Opera Free Summer Concerts (New
York)   3254
New York Musicians Jazz Festival (New York)
3257
Newport Jazz Festival (New York)   3259
Northeast Craft Fair (Rhinebeck)   999
100 American Craftsmen (Lockport)   994
Saratoga Festival (Saratoga Springs)   3270
Saratoga Performing Arts Festival (Saratoga Springs)
3271

Chronological Listing of Events

Chronological Listing of Events

JUNE (contd.)

Quebec, Canada

Baie-Saint-Paul Summer (Baie-Saint-Paul)   3691
Saint-Jean-Baptiste Day (Quebec)   1939

Prince Edward Island, Canada

Charlottetown Summer Festival (Charlottetown)
3790

JULY

Alabama

Alabama Shakespeare Festival (Anniston)   3750
Alabama State Championship Sling Shot Contest
   and Bluegrass Day (Steele)   2993
Blessing of the Shrimp Fleet (Bayou la Batre)   2866
First Monday (Scottsboro)   1211
German Folk Festival (Montgomery)   1993
Spirit of America Festival (Decatur)   1208
Square Dance Festival (Gadsden)   1946
Vacation Flat-Top Summit and Bluegrass Festival
   (Horse Pens Midsummer Blue Grass Festival)
   (Steele)   2996

Alaska

Alaska Square/Round Dance Festival (Anchorage)
   1947
Golden Days Celebration (Fairbanks)   2541
Indian Festival (Kotzebue)   2708
Soldotna Days (Soldotna)   1214
World Eskimo and Indian Olympic Games (Fair-
   banks)   2707

Arizona

Navajo Craftsmen Show (Flagstaff)   716

Arkansas

Inspiration Point Fine Arts Colony Festival (Eureka
   Springs)   3001

California

All California Show (Laguna Beach)   744
Apple Valley Pow Wow Days (Apple Valley)   1221
Art-A-Fair (Laguna Beach)   745

Art Festival (Long Beach)   749
Carmel Bach Festival (Carmel)   3008
Chula Vista Summer Arts Festival (Chula Vista)
   734
Concord Summer Festival (Concord)   3012
Crescent City Art Festival (Crescent City)   736
Crestline Mountaineer Days (Crestline)   1242
Early Valley Days (Bodfish)   2548
Easter in July Lily Festival (Smith River)   40
Festival of the Arts and Pageant of the Masters
   (Laguna Beach)   490
Festival of the Bells (San Diego)   2026
Frazier Mountain Park Fiesta Daze (Frazier Park)
   1249
Frontier Days Celebration (Willits)   1293
Georgetown Performing Arts Center Festival
   (Georgetown)   39
Hollywood Bowl Summer Festival (Los Angeles)
   3018
Los Angeles Performing Arts Festival (Hollywood)
   488
Malibu Festival (Malibu)   1261
Marin Shakespeare Festival (San Rafael)   3756
Municipal Pops Festival (San Francisco)   3035
Oban Festival (Fresno)   1951
Old Mission Hand Crafts Fair (Santa Barbara)   771
Old Town Birthday Fiesta (San Diego)   1276
San Luis Rey Fiesta and Barbecue (Oceanside)
   2020
Sawdust Art and Craft Festival (Laguna Beach)
   747
Summer Drama Festival (Los Angeles)   3753
Summer Festival Series (Music Academy of the
   West) (Santa Barbara)   3039
Summer Repertory Theater Festival (San Jose)
   3755
Sun 'n Sea Festival (Imperial Beach)   2873
Trek to The Cross (San Diego)   2562
Tyrolean Festival (Torrance)   2050
Woodcarver's Jamboree (San Diego)   767

Colorado

Colorado Mountain Fair (Carbondale)   776
Colorado Philharmonic Festival (Evergreen)   3052
Colorado Shakespeare Festival (Boulder)   3757
8-West (Grand Junction)   783
Great Rocky Mountain National Bluegrass Festival
   (Loveland)   3054
Music in the Mountains (Estes Park)   3051
Objects (Grand Junction)   784
Pack Burro Races and Festival (Breckenridge)   1296
Pack Burro Races and Festival (Fairplay)   1299
Pack Burro Races and Festival (Leadville)   1303
Southern Ute Sun Dance (Ignacio)   2737
Steamboat Summer Arts Festival (Steamboat Springs)
   502

Chronological Listing of Events

Chronological Listing of Events

Chronological Listing of Events

JULY (contd.)

Michigan (contd.)

Interlochen Summer Festival (Interlochen) 3172
National Blueberry Festival (South Haven) 194
National Cherry Festival (Traverse City) 195
National Strawberry Festival (Manistee) 191
Old Fashioned Days (Fremont) 1497
Street Art Fair (Ann Arbor) 936
Up in Central Park Music, Art, Flower Festival (Grand Haven) 569
Venetian Festival (Charlevoix) 1495
Waterfront Art Fair (Grand Haven) 939

Minnesota

All-Slav-Day (Eveleth) 2157
Aquatennial (Minneapolis) 1512
Art in the Park (Bemidji) 942
Cosmos Space Festival (Cosmos) 1505
Dutch Festival (Edgerton) 2155
Festag (Minnesota Lake) 1513
Festival of Lakes (Fairmont) 2922
Friendship Days (Nicollet) 1515
Harvest Festival (Henning) 1508
Hastings Fun Fest (Hastings) 1507
Lumberjack Days (Stillwater) 1521
Manitou Days (White Bear Lake) 1526
Midsummer Celebration (Menahga) 3554
Miss Melody Festival (Mississippi Melody Festival) (Grand Rapids) 3176
Muskie Days (Nevis) 2926
NW Water Carnival (Detroit Lakes) 2921
North Shore Art Fair (Lutsen) 571
Norway Day (Minneapolis) 2163
Panorama of Progress (Pan-O-Prog) (Lakeville) 1509
Pioneer Days (Crookston) 1500
Pork Day (Lakefield) 205
Raspberry Festival (Hopkins) 201
Sinclair Lewis Days Festival (Sauk Centre) 1520
Waterama (Glenwood) 2923
Watercade (Litchfield) 2925
Watermelon Days (Sanborn) 208
Wild Rice Festival (Kelliher) 202
Wild Rice Festival (Waskish) 210
Winona Steamboat Days (Winona) 1527
Wrong Days (in Wright) (Wright) 1528

Mississippi

Choctaw Indian Fair (Philadelphia) 2758
First Monday (Ripley) 1538
Leake County Sportsman Day (Carthage) 1531
Tobacco Spitting Championship (Raleigh) 1537
Watermelon Festival (Lucedale) 214

Missouri

Bluegrass Festival (MABC Fall Festival) (Farmington) 3190
Bluegrass Festival (Perryville) 3205
Bluegrass Festival (Saint Charles) 3202
Bluegrass Jamboree (Bismarck) 3187
Carondelet Days (Saint Louis) 1545
Fiesta Filipina (Kansas City) 2177
Herb Smith's Bluegrass Music Festival (Knob Noster) 3201
Jazz Festival (Kansas City) 3200
Mississippi River Festival (Saint Louis) 3209
Ozark Mountain Bluegrass Festival (Eminence) 3189
Saint Louis Municipal Opera (Saint Louis) 3211
Soulard Sunday (Saint Louis) 2186
Strassenfest (Saint Louis) 2187
Tom Sawyer Day Festival and National Fence Painting Contest (Hannibal) 1541

Montana

Art Festival (Billings) 959
Jim Bridger Days (Bridger) 1551
Logger Days (Libby) 1554
Marias Fair (Shelby) 1556
Montana State Fair (Great Falls) 3728
North American Indian Days (Browning) 2759
Opeta-Ye-Teca Indian Celebration (Wolf Point) 2762
Western Days (Billings) 1550
Wild Horse Stampede (Wolf Point) 1557

Nevada

National Basque Festival (Elko) 2199

New Hampshire

Arts and Crafts Festival (Andover) 585
Canterbury Fair and Auction (Canterbury) 1561
Hampton Summerfest Carnival (Hampton) 3576
Lakes Region Craftsmen Show (Gilford) 963
Monadnock Music (Jaffrey) 3222
New Hampshire Music Festival (Center Harbor) 3221
Old Muster Day (Charlestown) 2627
Regional Craftsmen's Fair (Canaan) 962
Street Fair (Hooksett) 1565
White Mountains Festival of Children's Literature (Franconia) 586
White Mountains Festival of the Seven Arts (Pike) 589

New Jersey

Black Heritage Festival (Holmdel) 2203
Festival of Art (Willingboro) 973
Hydrangea Festival (Atlantic City) 227

JULY (contd.)

New Jersey (contd.)

Irish Feis and Scottish Games Festival (Freehold) 2202

Maurice Podell Memorial Outdoor Summer Art Festival (Long Branch) 968

New Mexico

Aztec Fiesta Days (Aztec) 1579
Fiesta (Taos) 1602
Fiesta de Onate (Espanola) 2630
La Fiesta de Portales (Portales) 1593
Fourth of July Fiesta (Las Vegas) 1589
Independence Day/Frontier Days (Silver City) 1599
Little Beaver Roundup (Dulce) 1585
Mescalero Apache Gahan Ceremonial (Mescalero) 2785
Old Timers Fair and Rodeo (Magdalena) 1592
Puye Cliff Ceremonial (Santa Clara Pueblo) 2801
Saint Anne Day Grab Days (San Felipe Pueblo) 2792
Saint Anne Feast Day (Santiago's and Saint Anne's Day) (Santa Ana Pueblo) 2799
Saint Buenaventura Feast Day (Cochiti Pueblo) 2773
Saint James and Saint Anne's Day Celebration (Taos Pueblo) 2811
Santa Fe Opera Festival (Santa Fe) 3231
Sierra County Farm Bureau Cotton Extravaganza (Truth or Consequences) 231
Spanish Market (Santa Fe) 989

New York

Adirondack/Champlain Music Festival (Schroon Lake) 3273
Chautauqua Exhibition of American Art (Chautauqua) 990
Craft Day (Greenville) 991
Curbstone Art Festival (Rochester) 1000
Delphic Festival (New York) 2223
Folk Music Festival (Huntington) 3240
Forest Hills Music Festival (Forest Hills) 3235
French Festival (Cape Vincent) 2220
Gallery North Outdoor Art Show (Setauket) 1002
Hispanic Arts Festival (New York) 2227
International Bach Society Festival (New York) 3250
July Music Festival (Pawling) 3265
Lake George Opera Festival (Glen Falls) 3238
Lake Placid Music Festival (Lake Placid) 3243
Lewiston Festival (Lewiston) 3245
Maverick Concerts (Woodstock) 3278
Midsummer Faire (Petersburg) 1613

Morgan Park Summer Music Festival (Glen Cove) 3237
Olympic Village Bluegrass Festival (Lake Placid) 3244
Stony Brook Music Festival (Stony Brook) 3275
Storm King Chamber Music Series (Cornwall) 3234
Summer of Music in Westchester (Scarsdale) 3272
Summer Opera Festival (Port Jervis) 3267
Syracuse Summer Concerts (Syracuse) 3276
Utica Arts Festival (Utica) 609
West Door Concerts (New York) 3264

North Carolina

Angier Festival (Angier) 2474
Avery County Crafts Fair and Arts Festival (Banner Elk) 611
Brevard Music Festival (Brevard) 3283
Coon Dog Day (Saluda) 1628
Crepe Myrtle Festival (Angier) 242
Elon College Music Festival (Elon College) 3289
Festival of Folk Arts and Crafts (Hendersonville) 2477
Festival of the Arts (Brevard) 1620
Grandfather Mountain Highland Games (Linville) 2235
Macon County Gemboree (Franklin) 1624
Mountaineer Book Fair (Franklin) 619
Shindig on the Green (Mountain Folk Fair) (Asheville) 3282
Smoky Mountain Art and Craft Show (Murphy) 1016
Smoky Mountain Folk Festival (Waynesville) 2479
Southern Highlands Craftsmen's Fair (Asheville) 1003

North Dakota

Fort Totten Days (Fort Totten) 2821
International Youth Band Festival (Dunseith) 3300
North Dakota State Fair (Minot) 3736
Rodeo Fest (Mandan) 1631
Roughrider Days (Dickinson) 1630

Ohio

Annie Oakley Days (Greenville) 2643
Canal Days (Canal Fulton) 2642
Celina Lake Festival (Celina) 1634
Chautauqua Festival (Piqua) 1639
Great Composers Festival (Lakeside) 3310
Hillbrook National Van Festival (Hillbrook) 3313
Indian Crafts and Culture Pow-Wow (Whitehouse) 2825
Massillon Merchants Sidewalk Festival (Massillon) 1636
Ohio Artists and Craftsmen Show (Massillon) 1031
Ohio Hills Folk Festival (Quaker City) 2480

Chronological Listing of Events

JULY (contd.)

Ohio (contd.)

Ohio Valley Kool Jazz Festival (Cincinnati) 3304
Outdoor Art Festival (Willoughby) 628
Pioneer Days (Berlin) 2641
Pioneer Days and Steam Threshers Festival (Urbana) 274
Seven Hills Home Day (Seven Hills) 1640
Water Festival (Huron) 2936

Oklahoma

Bluegrass Festival and Old Time Fiddlers and Band Contest (Langley) 3319
Plains Indian Ceremonials and Dances (Anadarko) 2827
River Parks Festival (Tulsa) 1645
Tulsa Indian Pow Wow (Tulsa) 2829

Oregon

Astoria Regatta (Astoria) 2941
Bohemia Mining Days (Cottage Grove) 1648
Chief Joseph Days (Joseph) 1649
Crooked River Roundup (Prineville) 1653
Oregon Broiler Festival (Springfield) 285
Santiam Bean Festival (Stayton) 286
Turkey-Rama (McMinnville) 282
World Championship Timber Carnival (Albany) 277

Pennsylvania

Agricultural Americana Folk Festival (Amity Hall) 288
Arts and Crafts Festival (Brownsville) 1045
Brandywine Mountain Music Convention (Concordville) 3326
Butler County Music and Arts Festival (Slippery Rock) 645
Bye-Gone Days (Delmont) 2650
Central Pennsylvania Festival of the Arts (State College) 646
Colonial Festival (Greensburg) 2652
Dutch Days Festival (Richfield) 2281
Festival (Bethlehem) 1660
Folk Festival (Schaefferstown) 2487
Folk Frolic Days (Beavertown) 1659
Greek Festival (Media) 2275
Heritage Days (Waterford) 1700
Huckleberry Fair (Gallitzin) 294
Indian Heritage Days (Media) 2834
International Wine and Cheese Festival (Barnesville) 2533
Millerton Festival (Millerton) 1678
Mini-Festival (Pottstown) 1690
Nittany Mountain Summer (University Park) 647
Ohiopyle Area Festival (Ohiopyle) 1681

Old Home Days (Port Royal) 1689
Old Villages of Yesteryear Day (Hidden Valley) 1670
Palma Craft Festival and Birling Contest (Coudersport) 1046
Pennsylvania Dutch Days (Hershey) 2267
Pennsylvania Dutch Folk Festival (Lenhart) 2272
Pioneer Crafts Festival (Mill Run) 1053
Pioneer Days (Kreamer) 2654
Plainfield Farmers Fair (Bangor) 289
Pocono's Bluegrass Folk Festival (White Haven) 2491
River Festival (Monongahela) 2946
Sidewalk Festival Days (Coudersport) 1664
Spinning Wheels Day (Warminster Heights) 1699
State Craft Fair (Gettysburg) 1048
Stephen Foster Ice Cream Social and Music Festival (Athens) 1657
Summer Opera Festival (Milford) 3267
Sundance Festival (Upper Black Eddy) 649
Tamiment Festival of Music and Art (Tamiment) 647
Tinicum Art Festival (Erwinna) 1047
Tioga County Early Days (Wellsboro) 2661

Rhode Island

American Indian Federation Pow Wow (Lafayette) 2836
Charlestown Historical Society County Fair (Charlestown) 1704
Coventry Old Home Days (Coventry) 1705
Diamond Hill Music Festival (Pawtucket) 3335
Indian Festival of Songs and Dances (Newport) 2838
Newport Folk Festival (Newport) 2492
Newport Music Festival (Newport) 3334
Outdoor Art Festival (Newport) 1065
Outdoor Art Festival (Portsmouth) 1067
Rhode Island Association of Craftsmen Show (Charlestown) 1062
South County Heritage Festival (Wakefield) 1712
Westerly Art Festival (Westerly) 1073
Wickford Art Festival (Wickford) 1074

South Carolina

Beaufort Water Festival (Beaufort) 2948
Columbia Music Festival (Columbia) 3340
Hillbilly Day (Mountain Rest) 1720
Lexington County Peach Festival (Gilbert) 315
Pageland Watermelon Festival (Pageland) 320
South Carolina Festival of Flowers (Greenwood) 317

South Dakota

Black Hills Roundup (Belle Fourche) 1727
Booster Days (Valley Springs) 1738

Chronological Listing of Events

JULY (contd.)

South Dakota (contd.)

Gold Discovery Days (Custer)   2668
Heart of the Hills Days (Hill City)   1733
International Band Festival (Rapid City)   3351
Old Settlers Picnic and Rodeo (Gary)   1731
Sitting Bull Stampede (Mobridge)   1734
Summer Festival (Brookings)   3624
Tri-County Festival and Fair (Phillip)   331
Whitewood Days Celebration (Whitewood)   1740

Tennessee

International Gospel Music Festival (Nashville)
3361
Sewanee Summer Music Center Festival (Sewanee)
3363

Texas

All-Texas Jazz Festival (Corpus Christi)   3370
Arts and Crafts Fair (Kerrville)   1111
Childress County Old Settlers' Reunion (Childress)
1754
Fiesta Week (Hurst)   1782
First Mondays (Canton)   1752
Fishin' Fiesta and Shrimp Festival (Freeport)   2957
Fishing Fiesta and Shrimp Festival (Brazosport)
2954
Frontier Days (Round Rock)   1797
Fun-Tier Nights (San Antonio)   3379
Homecoming and Rodeo (Bastrop)   1745
July Jubilee (Brady)   1749
Kerrville Country and Western Jamboree (Kerrville)
3375
A Night in Old Fredericksburg (Fredericksburg)
2317
Old Fiddlers Contest (Winnsboro)   3383
Old Settlers Days (Round Rock)   1798
Old Settlers Reunion (Stanton)   1805
Panola County Western Week and Rodeo (Carthage)
1753
Parker County Frontier Days Rodeo and Livestock
Show (Weatherford)   373
Roundup Days (Glen Rose)   1776
Shrimporee (Aransas Pass)   2951
Spring Ho Festival (Lampasas)   3631
Texas Cowboy Reunion (Stamford)   1804
Western Days Celebration (Teague)   1809
Wise County Old Settlers' Reunion (Decatur)   1760

Utah

Days of '47 (Salt Lake City)   2686
Days of '47 Celebration (Pioneer Days Parade and
Rodeo) (Ogden)   2684
Festival of the American West (Logan)   2682

Freedom Festival (Provo)   1822
Great West Fair (Logan)   1123
International Days (Price)   2336
Lamb Day Celebration (Fountain Green City)   379
Northern Ute Pow Wow (Fort Duchesne)   2844
Obon Festival (Salt Lake City)   2337
Pioneer Days (Price)   1821
Raspberry Festival (Bear Lake)   376
Riverside Celebration (Riverside)   1823
Utah Shakespearean Festival (Cedar City)   3783
Ute Tribal Sun Dance (Whiterocks)   2846
Windows West (Logan)   2683

Vermont

Lane Summer Series (Burlington)   3388
Marlboro Music Festival (Marlboro)   3389

Virginia

Carlton Haney Bluegrass Festival (Berryville)   3392
Folk and Folk Song Festivals (Abingdon)   2500
Gunston Hall Arts and Crafts Show (Lorton)   1139
Lotus Festival Week (Virginia Beach)   393
Merrie Old England Summer Festival and Village
Fair of Arts and Handicrafts (Charlottesville)
3648
National Bluegrass Championship (Berryville)   3393
National Folk Festival (Vienna)   2505
Pony Roundup and Swim (Chincoteague Island)
3808
Pulaski's Bluegrass and Old Time Fiddlers Conven-
tion (Dublin)   3400
Shenandoah Valley Music Festival (Orkney Springs)
3409
Virginia Scottish Games and Gathering of the
Clans (Alexandria)   2340

Washington

Angeles Arts in Action (Port Angeles)   680
An-O-Chords (Anacortes)   3413
Ballard Halibut Feed (Seattle)   2974
Bear Festival (McCleary)   3813
Bellevue Film Festival (Bellevue)   2422
Capital Lakefair (Olympia)   2971
Fathoms O' Fun (Port Orchard)   2973
Hilander Summer Festival (Kelso)   2344
Lynnorama Summer Festival (Lynnwood)   3657
Old Settlers Days (Ferndale)   1841
Outdoor Art Festival (Olympia)   679
Pacific Northwest Arts and Crafts Fair (Bellevue)
1156
Pacific Northwest Festival (Seattle)   3415
Rotary International Air Fair (Everett)   1840
Seafair (Seattle)   2975
Slippery Gulch (Tekoa)   1845
Suds and Sun (Soap Lake)   1844

Chronological Listing of Events

Chronological Listing of Events

Chronological Listing of Events

Chronological Listing of Events

Chronological Listing of Events

Chronological Listing of Events

AUGUST (contd.)

Pennsylvania (contd.)

Philadelphia Folk Festival (Schwenksville) 2488
Polish Festival Days (Uniontown) 2283
Polka Festival (Erie) 1978
Seafaring Days (Essington, Boro of) 2945
Sidewalk Arts and Crafts Show (Allentown) 1043
Summer Festival and Homecoming (Selinsgrove) 3614
Summer Opera Festival (Milford) 3267
Sundance Festival (Upper Black Eddy) 649
Water Carnival (Easton) 2944
Woodmen's Carnival (Coudersport) 293

Rhode Island

American Dance Festival/Newport (Newport) 1982
Blessing of the Fleet (Gaililee) 2947
Blessing of the Fleet Festival (Naragansett) 1708
Burrillville Arts and Crafts Fair (Harrisville) 1064
International Ceramic Fair (Coventry) 1063
Mid-East Festival (Pawtucket) 2286
Narraganestt Indian Tribe August Meeting, Indian
    Day and Pow Wow (Charlestown) 2835
New England Blue Grass Music Festival (Escoheag) 3332
Outdoor Crafts Show (Charlestown) 1061
Rocky Hill State Fair (East Greenwich) 310
Snug Harbor Art Festival (Wakefield) 1071

South Carolina

Country and Western Days (Eutawville) 3341
Foothills Festival (Easley) 1081
Low Country Arts and Crafts Festival (Summerville) 1086
South Carolina Arts and Crafts Festival (Pendleton) 1083
Upper South Carolina State Fair (Greenville) 316

South Dakota

Central States Fair (Rapid City) 332
Corn Carnival (Canton) 326
Days of '76 (Deadwood) 2669
Fine Arts Festival (Rapid City) 1088
Harvest Festival (Salem) 333
Lakota Nation Trade Fair (Powwow) (Lower Brule) 2840
Mystic Calf Pipe and Sundance Ceremonies (Eagle
    Butte) 2839
Oahe Days (Pierre) 1736
Rosebud Sioux Fair, Pow Wow and Rodeo (Rosebud) 2841
South Dakota State Fair (Huron) 3741
Stream Threshing Jamboree (Madison) 329
White River Frontier Days (White River) 1739

Tennessee

International Banana Festival (South Fulton) 337

Texas

Aqua Festival (Austin) 2952
Black-Eyed Pea Jamboree (Athens) 340
Blanco Art Show (Blanco) 1095
Castro County Round-Up Week (Dimmit) 1762
Coronado Arts and Crafts Show (Amarillo) 1092
Cowboy Homecoming Celebration (Pleasanton) 1793
El Dia de las Misiones (The Day of the Missions)
    (San Antonio) 2680
Festival (Schulenberg) 2333
Festival USA on the Strand (Galveston) 664
First Mondays (Canton) 1752
Folk Life Festival (Livingston) 2496
Freestone County Fair and Homecoming (Fairfield) 1769
Freeze Off (Crane) 2534
Holy Cross Homecoming (Hondo) 1780
International Food Fair (Victoria) 2537
John County Pioneers and Old Settlers Reunion
    (Alvarado) 1742
Kerrville Bluegrass and Country Music Festival
    (Kerrville) 3374
Motley-Dickens Counties Old Settlers' Reunion
    (Matador) 1789
National Fair (Eagle Pass) 1764
Old Fiddlers Contest (Burnet) 3369
Old Settlers Reunion (Camp Wood) 1751
Old Settlers Reunion (Glen Rose) 1774
Peach and Melon Festival (De Leon) 349
Pioneer Celebration and Rodeo (Quanah) 1795
Pony Express Day (Fort Stockton) 1771
Race Meet and Billy Sale (Junction) 1783
Saint Louis Day Celebration (Castroville) 2310
Salado Art Fair (Salado) 1118
XIT Rodeo and Reunion (Dalhart) 1759
Texas Folklife Festival (San Antonio) 2497
West Texas Pioneers and Old Settlers Reunion
    (Crosbyton) 1757
Wood County Old Settler's Reunion and Fiddlers
    Contest (Quitman) 1796

Utah

Arts Festival (Park City) 1124
Tomato Days (Hooper) 381
Wheat and Beet Days (Garland) 380

Vermont

Bennington Chamber Music Festival (Bennington) 3386
Craftsproducers Craft Fair at Mount Snow (Mount
    Snow) 1126

Chronological Listing of Events

AUGUST (contd.)

Nova Scotia, Canada (contd.)

Natal Day (Dartmouth) 1923
Nova Scotia Festival of the Arts (Halifax/Dartmouth Metropolitan Area) 690
Rockhound Roundup (Parrsboro) 1933
Western Nova Scotia Exhibition (Yarmouth) 438

Ontario, Canada

Canadian Country Music Festival (Bancroft) 3449
Canadian Old Time Fiddlers Contest (Shelburne) 3450

Quebec, Canada

Longueuil Summer Festival (Longueuil) 3693

Yukon, Canada

Discovery Day (Dawson City) 2706

SEPTEMBER

Alabama

Arts and Crafts Show (Fort Payne) 701
Country Fair (Birmingham) 1207
Festival in the Park (Montgomery) 474
First Monday (Scottsboro) 1211
Kentuck Arts and Craft Festival (Northport) 707
Mid-South Marching Band Festival and Parade (Gadsden) 2990
Outdoor Art and Crafts Fair (Mobile) 705

Alaska

Arts Fair (Anchorage) 713
Harvest Fair and Ball (Skagway) 3459
Oktoberfest (Fairbanks) 1995

Arizona

American Indian Day (Peach Springs) 2715
American Indian Day (Salt River Indian Community) 2719
American Indian Day (Yuma) 2726
Fall Festival and Arizona's State Fiddlers Contest (Payson) 3462
Fiesta de Independencia de Mexico (Glendale) 2544

Arkansas

Arkansas State Fair and Livestock Show (Little Rock) 3704
Fall Fun Festival (Monticello) 3465
Grand Prairie Festival of Arts (Stuttgart) 483

California

Aki Matsuri (Fall Festival) (San Francisco) 2029
Antelope Valley Fair and Alfalfa Festival (Lancaster) 25
Art and Wine Festival (Millbrae) 754
Art Festival (Norwalk) 757
Arti Gras (Santa Maria) 494
Arts 'n Crafts by the Sea (Hermosa Beach) 740
Bonanza Days Wine Festival (Gilroy) 2516
Cabrillo Festival (San Diego) 2025
California State Fair (Sacramento) 3705
Country Fair (Ramona) 1270
Danish Days (Solvang) 2042
Days of the Dons (Santa Margarita) 1292
Fall Art Festival (Valyermo) 3480
Fall Festival (Crestline) 3472
Festival of Art (Catalina) 733
Festival of Arts and Crafts (Fillmore) 738
Fiesta de Lierra Vista Arts and Wine Festival (Mountain View) 756
Fiesta de la Luna (Chula Vista) 1237
Fiesta Patreias (San Ysidro) 2037
German Day (Torrance) 2046
Grecian Wine Festival (Napa) 2520
Homecoming and Labor Day Celebration (Bishop) 1226
Hungarian Press Day Festival (Los Angeles) 2013
Industrial Graphics International Festival (Los Angeles) 751
International Antiquarian Book Fair (San Francisco) 493
Irish Festival (San Francisco) 2033
Lodi Grape Festival and National Wine Show (Lodi) 2518
Mendocino County Fair and Apple Show (Boonville) 1230
Mexican Fiesta (Ojai) 2021
Mexican Fiesta Days (Los Angeles) 2015
Mexican Independence Day Celebration (Stockton) 2045
Mexican Independence Day Celebration (Valencia) 2052
Mexican Independence Parade and Fiesta (Martinez) 2018
Mission Bay Photo Festival (Mission Bay) 755
Mi-Wuk Indian Acorn Festival (Tuolumne) 2735
Montebello Fun Festival (Montebello) 1263
Monterey Jazz Festival (Monterey) 3021
National Indian Observance Day (Crescent City) 2730
National Raisin Festival (Dinuba) 18

Chronological Listing of Events

Chronological Listing of Events

SEPTEMBER (contd.)

Minnesota (contd.)

King Turkey Day (Worthington)   211
Kolacky Day (Montgomery)   2167
Lake Region Pioneer Threshermen's Association
   Show (Dalton)   197
Marigold Days (Mantorville)   206
Tri-State Band Festival (Luverne)   3177
Watermelon Festival (Kellogg)   203

Mississippi

Central Mississippi Fair, Rodeo and State Dairy
   Show (Kosciusko)   213
First Monday (Ripley)   1538

Missouri

Autumn Daze (Branson)   3566
Badenfest (Saint Louis)   2181
Bevo Day (Saint Louis)   2182
Bluegrass Festival (Grassy)   3195
Bluegrass Festival (Van Buren)   3213
Bluegrass Pickin Time (Dixon)   3188
Cotton Carnival (Sikeston)   220
Fall Festival (Lexington)   3568
Fete de Normandie (Saint Louis)   2184
Folk Music and Craft Fair (West Plains)   2467
Green Tree Festival (Kirkwood)   1543
Little Dixie Bluegrass Festival (Mexico)   3203
National Crafts Festival (Silver Dollar City)   957
Old Time Fiddlers Festival (Saint Joseph)   3208
Plaza Art Fair (Kansas City)   956
Santa-Cali-Gon (Independence)   2626

Montana

Badlands Appreciation Festival (Glendive)   1553
Herbstfest (Laurel)   2189

Nebraska

Mexican-American Festival (Scottsbluff)   2195
Nebraska State Fair (Lincoln)   3729
Northeast Nebraska Threshers Reunion (Niobrara)
   226

Nevada

Nevada State Fair (Reno)   3730

New Hampshire

Fall Festival (Ossipee)   3578
Old Home Day (Pelham Center)   1570
Swap, Talk and Brag Day and Micromounters
   Roundup (Tamworth)   1573

New Jersey

German-American Festival (Holmdel)   2204
Great Falls Festival of Paterson (Paterson)   1574
Grecian Arts Festival (Holmdel)   2205
Hungarian Festival (Holmdel)   2206
New Jersey State Fair (Trenton)   3732
Puerto Rican Heritage Festival (Holmdel)   2211
Scottish Heritage Festival (Holmdel)   2212

New Mexico

Aspen Festival and Paul Bunyan Day (Eagle Nest)
   228
Aspencade and Square Dance Festival (Red River)
   1594
Cimarron Days (Cimarron)   1581
New Mexico State Fair (Albuquerque)   3733
Pinata Festival and Quay County Fair (Tucumcari)
   1605
Saint Elizabeth Feast Day (Laguna Pueblo)   2781
Saint Joseph Feast Day (Laguna Pueblo)   2783
Saint Augustine's Day (Isleta Pueblo)   2776
San Estevan Feast Day (Saint Stephen) (Acoma
   Pueblo)   2765
San Geronimo Feast Day (Taos Pueblo)   2813
San Miguel Fiesta (Socorro)   1600
Square Dance Festival (Red River)   1969
Stone Lake Fiesta (Stone Lake)   2809

New York

Avant Garde Festival (New York)   596
Canal Town Days (Palmyra)   1612
Delphic Festival (New York)   2223
Fall Festival of Mount Saviour (Elmira)   3588
Feast of San Genarro (New York)   2224
Fox Hollow Lodge String Band Festival (Petersburg)
   3266
Grape Festival (Penn Yan)   238
International Animation Festival (New York)   2407
International Psychic Film Festival (New York)
   2410
Long Island International Film Festival (Hempstead)
   2402
New York Dance Festival (New York)   1970
New York Film Festival (New York)   2412
Oktoberfest (Rochester)   2231
One World Festival (New York)   2229

North Carolina

Albemarle Craftsman's Fair (Elizabeth City)   1007
Arts and Crafts Show (Maggie Valley)   1012
Bluegrass and Old Time Mountain Festival (Black
   Mountain)   2475
Center Fair (Center)   1621

Chronological Listing of Events

Chronological Listing of Events

SEPTEMBER (contd.)

Tennessee

    Fall Bluegrass and Old Time Music Festival
        (Bristol)   3355
    Folk Festival of the Smokies (Cosby)   2494
    Mid South Fair (Memphis)   1741
    River City Renaissance Fair (Germantown)   2670
    Tennessee State Fair (Nashville)   3742

Texas

    Autumn Trails (Winnsboro)   3636
    Bosque Arts and Crafts Show (Meridian)   1116
    Clay County Pioneer Reunion, Rodeo and Horse
        Show (Henrietta)   1779
    Cotton Carnival (Brownsville)   345
    Diez y Seis Celebration (Corpus Christi)   2311
    East Texas Fair (Tyler)   370
    Fiesta de las Flores (El Paso)   2315
    Fiestas Patrias (Houston)   2319
    First Mondays (Canton)   1752
    Forest Festival (Atlanta)   341
    Four States Fair and Rodeo (Texarkana)   1811
    Franklin County Hay Show (Mount Vernon)   360
    Hamilton County Dove Festival and Fair (Hamilton)
        3807
    Inter-State Fair (Dalhart)   348
    Jaycee Fishing Festival (Port Lavaca)   2960
    Maize Days Festival (Friona)   353
    Mexican-American Friendship Week (San Antonio)
        2331
    Mexican Independence Day (Diez y Seis) (Port
        Arthur)   2326
    Morris County Arts and Crafts Shows (Daingerfield)
        1101
    Republic of Texas Chilympiad (San Marcos)   2535
    Rice Festival (Bay City)   342
    Stratford Jamboree and Sherman County Fair
        (Stratford)   1806
    Tourist Day (Shamrock)   1803
    Trinity Community Fair (Trinity)   1813
    Tri-State Fair (Amarillo)   1743
    Turkeyfest and Jamboree (Cuero)   1758
    West Texas Fair (Abilene)   339

Utah

    Golden Onion Days and Homecoming (Payson)
        1820
    Iron County Fair (Parowan)   1819
    Oktoberfest (Snowbird)   2338
    Peach Days Art Festival (Brigham City)   1121
    Peach Days Celebration (Brigham City)   377
    Utah State Fair (Salt Lake City)   3744

Vermont

    Northeast Kingdom Fall Foliage Festival (Barnet)
        3638
    Northeast Kingdom Fall Foliage Festival (Cabot)
        3640
    Northeast Kingdom Fall Foliage Festival (Groton)
        3641
    Northeast Kingdom Fall Foliage Festival (Peacham)
        3642
    Northeast Kingdom Fall Foliage Festival (Plain-
        field)   3643
    Northeast Kingdom Fall Foliage Festival (Walden)
        3646
    Stratton Arts Festival (Stratton Mountain)   669
    Vermont State Fair (Rutland)   3745

Virginia

    Apple Harvest Arts and Crafts Festival (Winchester)
        1153
    Bluemont Fair (Bluemont)   1827
    Craft Show (Warm Springs)   1151
    Fall Bluegrass and Old Time Music Festival
        (Bristol)   3395
    Hampton Fair Day (Hampton)   1831
    International Children's Festival (Vienna)   674
    Juried Show (Alexandria)   1131
    National Tobacco Festival (Richmond)   391
    New Market Arts and Crafts Show (New Market)
        1141
    Peanut Festival (Emporia)   386
    Reston Black Arts Festival (Reston)   2342
    State Fair of Virginia (Richmond)   3746
    Virginia Beach Neptune Festival (Virginia Beach)
        1835
    Virginia Folk Music Association Festival (Chase
        City)   3397
    Virginia Folk Music Association Festival (Crewe)
        3399

Washington

    Autumn Leaf Festival (Leavenworth)   3656
    Deutsches Fest (Odessa)   2346
    Interstate Fair (Spokane)   403
    Sunfair (Yakima)   1846

West Virginia

    Apple Festival (Grafton)   412
    Harvest Moon Festival of Arts and Crafts
        (Parkersburg)   1181
    Hedgesville Heritage Festival (Hedgesville)   1856
    Heritage Weekend (Moorefield)   1860
    Pocohontas Music and Bluegrass Festival (Hunters-
        ville)   3419

Chronological Listing of Events

Chronological Listing of Events

OCTOBER (contd.)

California (contd.)

British Week Festival (San Francisco)   2030
Calico Days (Barstow)   1224
Camarillo Fiesta (Camarillo)   2005
Columbus Day Celebration (San Francisco)   2563
Cotton Festival (Corcoran)   1240
Delano Wine and Harvest Festival (Delano)   1245
Desert Festival (Borrego Springs)   2004
Early California Days (Wofford Heights)   1294
Fall Festival (Clear Lake Oaks)   3470
Fall Festival (Julian)   3473
Fall Festival (Los Alamitos)   3474
Fall Flower Festival (Ross)   30
Fiesta Day (Yorba Linda)   1295
Fiesta de Costa Mesa (Costa Mesa)   1241
Fortuna Art Festival (Fortuna)   739
Fullerton Art Fair (Fullerton)   485
Golden Days (Azusa)   1222
Golden West Bluegrass Festival (Norco)   3023
Grape Festival (San Rafael)   35
Greek Festival (Torrance)   2048
Greek Food Festival (Stockton)   2044
Hacienda Fiesta (Palmdale)   2022
Halloween Festival and Parade (Anaheim)   1219
Harvest Festival (Arroyo Grande)   12
Heritage Day Festival (Placentia)   2558
Hollywood Festival of World Television (Hollywood)   2378
Hollywood International Film Festival (Los Angeles)   2382
Inter Arts Festival (Torrance)   497
International Festival (Reedly)   1271
Johnny Appleseed Festival (Paradise)   1268
Oceanside Harbor Days (Oceanside)   2876
Octoberfest (Auburn)   743
Octoberfest (Rancho Bernardo)   2023
Octoberfest (Santa Monica)   3477
Oktoberfest (Big Bear Lake)   2003
Oktoberfest (Santa Rosa)   2041
Old-Time Fiddle Convention (Santa Barbara)   3038
Pala Mission Children's Festival (Pala)   2733
Phoenix Fine Arts Festival (Rancho Bernardo)   760
Pioneer Days Celebration (Twenty-nine Palms)   1288
Poway Pow Wow Days (Poway)   2015
Pumpkin Festival (Chatsworth)   1234
San Francisco International Film Festival (San Francisco)   2386
San Pedro Cabrillo Festival (San Pedro)   2565
Scottish Highland Games (San Diego)   2028
Sierra Art Fair (Kernville)   743
Western Folk Festival (San Francisco)   2437
Wild West Days (Lone Pine)   1255
Wine Festival (Los Angeles)   2519

Colorado

Pat Casey Day (Central City)   2054
Potato Days (Carbondale)   46

Connecticut

Apple Harvest Festival (Southington)   52
Fall Folk Music Weekend (Falls Village)   3057
Salisbury Antiques Fair and Fall Festival (Salisbury)   447
Southington Arts and Crafts Apple Harvest Art Show (Southington)   799
Yale Film Festival (New Haven)   2388

District of Columbia

Festival of Chamber Music   3071

Florida

Back to Ybor City Day (Tampa [Ybor City])   1331
Czechoslovakian Independence Day Celebration (Masaryktown)   2071
Fall Art Festival (Pensacola)   822
Florida Forest Festival (Perry)   61
Inter-American Festival (Miami, Miami Beach)   2074
Lief Eriksen Day Pageant (Jensen Beach)   2068
Oktoberfest (Cape Coral)   2065
Osceola Arts Festival (Kissimmee)   815
University of West Florida Film Festival (Pensacola)   2389
Venetian Sun Festival (Venice)   1332
Winter Park Mall Art Festival (Winter Park)   825

Georgia

Art Festival and Crafts (Saint Simons Island)   832
Arts and Crafts Festival (Blakely)   826
Atlanta Greek Festival (Atlanta)   2081
Autumn Leaf Festival (Maysville)   3487
Early County Fair and Peanut Festival (Blakely)   67
Fall Country Music Festival (Hiawassee)   3080
Fall Leaf Festival (Cleveland)   3486
Georgia State Fair (Macon)   3710
Golden Isles Arts Festival (Saint Simons Island)   518
Scottish Festival and Highland Games (Atlanta)   2083
Scottish Festival and Highland Games (Stone Mountain)   2086

Hawaii

Aloha Week (Honolulu)   2581
Waimea Highland Games (Kamuela)   2093

Chronological Listing of Events

OCTOBER (contd.)

Massachusetts (contd.)

Ethnic Festival (Springfield) 2144
Festival of the Hills (Conway) 1473
Pioneer Valley Colonial Muster Days (Northampton)
  2616
Worcester Music Festival (Worcester) 3168

Michigan

Autumn Festival (Bellaire) 3543
Autumn Harvest Weekend (Dearborn) 3545
Aviation Festival (Bellaire) 1492
Children's Book Fair (Detroit) 568
Indian Awareness Program (Marquette) 2757
Octoberfest (Grand Rapids) 3546
Red Flannel Festival (Cedar Springs) 1493

Minnesota

Mexican Independence Celebration (Saint Paul)
  2170
Twin Cities Science Fiction Festival (Minneapolis)
  572

Mississippi

Delta Cotton Wives Cotton Fair (Greenwood) 212
First Monday (Ripley) 1538
Great River Roads Craft Festival (Natchez) 952
Harvest Festival (French Camp) 1532
Mississippi-Alabama Fair (Meridian) 216
Mississippi State Fair (Jackson) 3726
Town and Country Festival (Brookhaven) 1530

Missouri

American Royal Livestock and Horse Show (Kansas
  City) 219
Bluegrass America (Kansas City) 3199
Brush Arbor Days (Rockaway Beach) 1544
Cass County Log Cabin Festival (Harrisonville)
  2625
Dutchtown Oktoberfest (Saint Louis) 2183
Go Fair (Saint Louis) 1547
Hootin' an' Hollerin' (Gainesville) 955
Maple Leaf Festival (Carthage) 3567
Multi Media Festival (Kansas City) 582
Wild Goose Festival (Sumner) 3803

Nevada

Indian Nevada Day (Nixon) 2763

New Hampshire

Fall Foliage Festival (Warner) 3579
Fort Constitution (New Castle) 2628

Hang Gliding Festival (Conway) 1563
Octoberfest (Manchester) 2200
Tri-State Collectors Exhibition (Concord) 1562

New Jersey

Assunpink Creek Folk Festival (Trenton) 2469
Oktoberfest (Waterville) 2214

New Mexico

Arts Festival (Farmington) 591
Cowboy Octoberfest (Alamogordo) 1575
Cowboy Octoberfest (Carrizozo) 1580
Cowboy Octoberfest (Cloudcroft) 1582
Cowboy Octoberfest (La Luz) 1587
Cowboy Octoberfest (Lincoln) 1591
Cowboy Octoberfest (Ruidoso) 1597
Cowboy Octoberfest (Tularosa) 1606
Festival of Arts (Taos) 593
Fiesta of Saint Francis (Ranchos de Taos) 2632
Harvest Festival (Santa Fe) 2633
International Balloon Fiesta and World Hot Air
  Balloon Championships (Albuquerque) 1576
Klobase (Bohemian Sausage) Festival (Deming)
  1584
Navajo Fair (Northern Navajo Fair and Rodeo)
  (Shiprock) 2808
Peanut Valley Festival (Portales) 230
San Francisco Feast Day (Nambe Pueblo) 2787

New York

Community Carnival (Troy) 1615
Delphic Festival (New York) 2223
Fall Foliage Festival (Cohocton) 3586
Fall-In (Ithaca) 3589
Festival of the Arts (New York) 599
International Film and Television Festival of New
  York (New York) 2408
International Wine and Cheese Tasting Festival
  (New York) 2531
Long Island Agricultural Fair (Bethpage) 235
National Arts and Antiques (New York) 996
National Student Film Festival (New York) 2411
Oktoberfest (Canandaigua) 2219
Rochester International Film Festival (Rochester)
  2415

North Carolina

Autumn Leaves Festival (Mount Airy) 3600
Bascom Lamar Lunsford Mountain Music and Dance
  Festival (Mars Hill) 2478
Eastern North Carolina Bluegrass Festival (Angier)
  3279
Fall Festival (Chapel Hill) 3597
Fall Festival (Morgantown) 1015
Fontana Fall Jubilee Festival (Fontana Dam) 1973

Chronological Listing of Events

OCTOBER (contd.)

Texas (contd.)

Old Settlers Reunion (Denver City)   1761
Rebel Days (Harlingen)   2675
River Art Show (San Antonio)   1119
Showing of Past Treasures (Alto)   467
South Texas State Fair (Beaumont)   343
State Fair of Texas (Dallas)   3743
Texas Rice Festival (Winnie)   374
Texas Rose Festival (Tyler)   371
Western Week (Beeville)   1747

Vermont

Craftproducers Foliage Festival (Mount Snow)   1127
Fall Festival of Vermont Crafts (Montpelier)   1125
Fall Foliage Square Dance Festival (Montpelier)   1987

Virginia

Art and Craft Show on Old Courthouse Green (Accomac)   1130
Blue Ridge Folklife Festival (Ferrum)   2503
Fall Craft Fair (Richmond)   1144
Fall Foliage Festival (Clifton Forge)   3649
Fall Foliage Festival (Waynesboro)   3654
Fall Wildlife Festival (Vienna)   3811
Festival of Leaves (Front Royal)   3651
Harvest Festival (South Hill)   3653
Highland County Fall Foliage Festival (Monterey)   3652
An Occasion for the Arts (Williamsburg)   676
Old Dominion University Folk Festival (Norfolk)   2504
Outdoor Art Show (Warm Springs)   1152
Oyster Festival (Chincoteague Island)   2964
Southeastern Band Festival (Bristol)   3396
Virginia Photographers (Richmond)   1148
Yorktown Day (Yorktown)   2692

Washington

Independent Film Festival Competition (Pullman)   2423
Issaquah Salmon Festival (Issaquah)   2970
Spokane Valley Fall Festival Parade (Spokane)   3658
Ten Best of the West Festival (Seattle)   2425

West Virginia

Alderson-Broaddus College Art/Craft Festival (Philippi)   1183
American Indian Fall Festival (Charleston)   2856
Apple Butter Festival (Berkeley Springs)   409

Arts and Crafts Festival (Bluefield)   1164
Black Walnut Festival (Spencer)   1872
Milton Garden Club Art and Craft Show (Milton)   1176
Monongahela Art and Craft Fair (Fairmont)   1168
Mountain Heritage Arts and Crafts Festival (Harpers Ferry)   1174
Mountain State Forest Festival (Elkins)   411
Mountaineer Week (Morgantown)   1861
West Virginia Turkey Festival (Mathias)   416
Winfield Art and Craft Festival (Winfield)   1190

Wisconsin

Apple Festival (Bayfield)   417
Applefest (Appleton)   1877
Clay-o-rama Ceramic Show (Madison)   1191
Cranberry Festival (Warrens)   419
Fall Festival (Sister Bay)   3667
Indian Summer Festival (Lake Geneva)   1878
Oktoberfest U.S.A. (LaCrosse)   2349
Pie Festival (Fort Atkinson)   2696
Festival of the Arts (Whitewater)   1196
Festival of the Leaves (Rhinelander)   3665

Manitoba, Canada

Beef and Barley Festival (Russell)   429
Oktoberfest (Winnipeg)   2364

Northwest Territories, Canada

Oktoberfest (Hay River)   3682

Nova Scotia, Canada

Atlantic Winter Fair (Halifax)   1925
Joseph Howe Festival (Halifax/Dartmouth)   1928

Quebec, Canada

Rimouski Fall Festival (Rimouski)   3696

NOVEMBER

Alabama

First Monday (Scottsboro)   1211
Hands at Work Craftsmen's Fair (Birmingham   695

NOVEMBER (contd.)

New York (contd.)

International Film and Video Festival: Cities,
   Suburbs and Small Towns (New York)   2409
PRSA Film Festival (New York)   2413

North Carolina

Cary Band Day (Cary)   3286
Charlotte International Folk Festival (Charlotte)
   2234
Davie Craft Corner (Mocksville)   1013
Lake Norman Fiddlers Convention and Buck Dance
   Contest (Terrell)   3296
Piedmont Crafts Fair (Winston-Salem)   1021

Oklahoma

Central State Music Festival (Edmond)   3316

Pennsylvania

Black Week Festival (Pittsburgh)   2279
Festival of Nations (Reading)   2280
Harvest Fair (Ulysses)   2659
New Life Folk Festival (Chester)   2481
Square Dance Festival (Pittsburgh)   1981

South Carolina

Darlington Folk Festival (Darlington)   2493
English Emphasis Festival (Charleston)   2289
Holiday Fiesta (Myrtle Beach)   1721
Kershaw County Heritage Days (Kershaw County)
   1719
South Carolina Bluegrass Music Festival (Myrtle
   Beach)   3346

South Dakota

Powder River Days (Bonesteel)   2667

Texas

Antiques Fair (Dallas)   469
Arts in Action (Amarillo)   1091
Fine Arts Festival (Austin)   661
First Mondays (Canton)   1752
Gathering of Scottish Clans of Texas (Salado)
   2328
Holiday Folk Festival (Seagraves)   2498
Pecan Perfection Day (Manchester)   359
World's Championship Chili Cook-Off (Terlingua)
   2536
Wurstfest (Sausage Festival) (New Braunfels)   2325

Virginia

Manassas Jazz Festival (Manassas)   3406
November Festival (Great Falls)   1830
Oyster Festival (Urbanna)   2966
Waterfowl Week (Chincoteague National Wildlife
   Refuge)   3809
Waterfowl Week (Presquile National Wildlife
   Refuge)   3810

West Virginia

Capital City Art and Craft Festival (Charleston)
   1165
Mountaineer Art and Craft Festival (Morgantown)
   1178
Mullens Art and Craft Festival (Mullens)   1179
Snowflake Festival (Saint Albans)   3660
Weirton Art and Craft Festival (Weirton)   1188

Wisconsin

Folk Fair (Milwaukee)   2350
Winter Art Fair (Milwaukee)   1193
Wisconsin Festival of Art (Milwaukee)   683

Northwest Territories, Canada

Northwest Territories Northern Film Festival
   (Yellowknife)   2427

DECEMBER

Alabama

First Monday (Scottsboro)   1211

California

Bazaar (Richmond)   761
Craft Festival (Point Reyes)   759
Festival of Our Lady of Guadalupe (San Juan
   Bautista)   2036
International Erotic Film Festival (San Francisco)
   2385
Richmond Art Center Festival (Richmond)   762

Colorado

Winter Theater Festival (Steamboat Springs)   3759

Chronological Listing of Events

DECEMBER (contd.)

District of Columbia

    Pageant of Peace   1312

Florida

    Exhibition of Contemporary American Paintings
        (The Society of the Four Arts) (Palm Beach)
        821
    Florida Tournament of Bands (Saint Petersburg)
        3076
    Orange Bowl Festival (Miami)   1324
    Seven Lively Arts Winter Art Show (Hollywood)
        812
    Winter Friends Festival (Saint Cloud)   1328

Hawaii

    Artists of Hawaii (Part I) (Part II in March)
        (Honolulu)   836
    Festival of Trees (Honolulu)   1340

Indiana

    Madrigal Dinners (Evansville)   3111

Louisiana

    Orange Festival (Fort Jackson)   152

Maryland

    Washington National Student Film Festival
        (College Park)   2398

Massachusetts

    Christmas Festival of Lights (South Carver)   1488

Mississippi

    First Monday (Ripley)   1538

Missouri

    SPBGMA Bluegrass Musician Convention and
        Awards Banquet, Bluegrass Festival (Lake
        Ozark)   3202

Nevada

    Winter Carnival (Reno)   3574

New York

    Delphic Festival (New York)   2223

North Carolina

    Christmas in Old Salem (Winston-Salem)   2639

Rhode Island

    Christmas in Newport (Newport)   1709

South Carolina

    Charles Towne Landing Crafts Fair (Charleston)
        1077
    Festival of Lessons and Carols (Spartanburg)   3348

Texas

    All-Valley Winter Vegetable Show (Pharr)   362
    Boll Weevil Festival (Taft)   1808
    First Mondays (Canton)   1752
    Morris County Arts and Crafts Shows (Daingerfield)
        1101
    Southwestern Sun Carnival (El Paso)   1767
    Sun Carnival Art Exhibition (El Paso)   1102

Virginia

    Merrie Old England Christmas Celebration
        (Charlottesville)   2341
    Scottish Christmas Walk in Historic Alexandria
        (Alexandria)   2339

Washington

    Christmas Around the World (Seattle)   2348
    Christmas Lighting Ceremony (Leavenworth)   2345

West Virginia

    Greenbrier Valley Artisans/Craftsmens Fair (Lewis-
        burg)   1175

SECTION III
EVENT NAME INDEX

Event Name Index

Event Name Index

Event Name Index

Baroque/Contemporary Festival 3347

Baroque Festival 3113

Barrington Fair 457

Barter Day 951

Bartlett Aboretum Fall Colors and Mum Festival 3521

Bascom Lamar Lunsford Mountain Music and Dance Festival 2478

Basque Festival 2096

Bavarian Festival 2149

Bavarian Oktoberfest 2085

Bavarian Summer Festival 2262

Bay Country Festival 2907

Bayrama Festival 2920

Bazaar 761

Beanhole Bean Festival 170

Bear Downs Week 1816

Bear Festival 3813

Beaufort Water Festival 2948

Beauregard Pioneer Festival 1433

Beausejour Winter Farewell 3673

Beaver Roundup 3456

Beaver Valley Days Celebration 1896

Bedford Limestone Festival 1372

Beef and Barley Festival 429

Beerfest 2142

Belgian American Day 2158

Bell and History Days 2609

Bella Vista Fine Arts Center Festival 481

Bellevue Film Festival 2422

Bellevue Village Mall Festival 1155

Beluga Jamboree 2366

Ben Franklin Kite Flying Contest 1467

Benefit Air Fair 1458

Bennington Chamber Music Festival 3386

Bergen County Festival 590

Berges Fest 2307

Berkshire Crafts Fair 930

Berkshire Music Festival 3162

Berry-Dairy Days 1837

Bethel College Fall and Folk Festival 2451

Bethlehem Bach Festival 3325

Bevo Day 2182

Big Bend Regatta 2937

Big Singing Day 3136

Big Thursday 1309

Big Timber Bluegrass Festival 3099

Billy Bowlegs Festival 1321

Birmingham Genealogical Society Festival 2540

Birmingham International Educational Film Festival 2376

Bishop Indian Rodeo and Pow Wow 2728

Black Arts and Heritage Festival 2122

Black Arts Festival (Colorado Springs, Colorado) 2056

Black Arts Festival (DeKalb, Illinois) 2100, 2101, 2102

Black Cultural Festival (Atlanta Black Artists Association) 2082

Black Emphasis Festival 2288

Black-Eyed Pea Jamboree 340

Black Heritage Festival 2203

Black Heritage Week Arts and Crafts Festival 974

Black Hills Roundup 1727

Black Walnut Festival 1872

Black Week Festival 2279

Blanco Art Show 1095

Blessing of the Fields (San Ysidro Feast Day) 1603

Blessing of the Fleet 2947

Blessing of the Fleet Festival 1708

Blessing of the Shrimp Fleet 2866

Blossom and Music Festival 1297

Blossom Music Festival 3309

Blossomtime 3655

Blossomtime Festival 193

Blue Hill Music Festival 3147

Blue Ridge Folklife Festival 2503

Blue River Valley Pioneer Craft Fair 877

Blue Water Festival 1498

Blueberry Harvest Festival 434

Bluebonnet Antique Show 468

Bluebonnet Trail Arts and Crafts Show 1113

Bluegrass America 3199

Bluegrass and Country Music Festival 3122

Bluegrass and Old-Time Country Music Band Contest and Crafts Fair 3247

Blue Grass and Old Time Mountain Festival 2475

Bluegrass and Old Time Music Festival (Camp Springs, North Carolina) 3285

Bluegrass and Old Time Music Festival (Hugo, Oklahoma) 3318

Bluegrass and Old Time Music Festival (Bristol, Tennessee-Virginia) 3394

Bluegrass and Old Time Music Festival (Bristol, Virginia-Tennessee) 249

Bluegrass Country Fair 1542

Bluegrass Festival (Alton, Illinois) 3089

Bluegrass Festival (Ashland, Illinois) 3090

Bluegrass Festival (Callaway, Maryland) 3153

Bluegrass Festival (Monticello, Mississippi) 3185

Bluegrass Festival (MABC Fall Festival) (Farmington, Missouri) 3190

Bluegrass Festival (Grassy, Missouri) 3194, 3195

Bluegrass Festival (Holt, Missouri) 3197

Bluegrass Festival (Kahoka, Missouri) 3198

Bluegrass Festival (Perryville, Missouri) 3205

Bluegrass Festival (Saint Charles, Missouri) 3207

Bluegrass Festival (Van Buren, Missouri) 3213

Bluegrass Festival (Shartlesville, Pennsylvania) 3331

Bluegrass Festival (Hardwood Lands, Canada) 1716

Bluegrass Festival and Old Time Fiddlers and Band Contest 3319

Bluegrass Jamboree (Cummington, Massachusetts) 3159

Bluegrass Jamboree (Bismarck, Missouri) 3187

Bluegrass Music and Folk Arts and Crafts 3135

Bluegrass Music Festival (Jacksonville, Illinois) 3101

Bluegrass Music Festival (Beanblossom, Indiana) 3107

Bluegrass Music Festival (Paola, Kansas) 3132

Bluegrass Music Festival (Boothbay, Maine) 3148

Bluegrass Music Festival of the U.S.A. 3138

Bluegrass Music Weekend 3088

Event Name Index

Event Name Index

Country Fair (Birmingham, Alabama)   1207
Country Fair (Ramona, California)   1270
Country Fair Days Art Show   891
Country Fair of Yesteryear   2620
Country Music Days   3342
Country Music Festival   3083
Country Music Festival (Old-Time Country Music Festival)   2999
County Summer Fair   3633
Covered Bridge Festival (Winterset, Iowa)   2597
Covered Bridge Festival (Centreville, Michigan)   1494
Covered Bridge Festival (Waynesburg, Pennsylvania)   1701
Coventry Old Home Days   1705
Cowboy Days   1693
Cowboy Homecoming Celebration   1793
Cowboy Octoberfest (Alamogordo, New Mexico)   1575
Cowboy Octoberfest (Carrizozo, New Mexico)   1580
Cowboy Octoberfest (Cloudcroft, New Mexico)   1582
Cowboy Octoberfest (La Luz, New Mexico)   1587
Cowboy Octoberfest (Lincoln, New Mexico)   1591
Cowboy Octoberfest (Ruidoso, New Mexico)   1597
Cowboy Octoberfest (Tularosa, New Mexico)   1606
Craft Day   991
Craft Days   1050
Craft Fair (Bethesda, Maryland)   912
Craft Fair (Spring City, Pennsylvania)   1059
Craft Festival (Point Reyes, California)   759
Craft Festival (Des Moines, Iowa)   887
Craft Show   1151
Craftman's Fair   1089
Craftproducers Foliage Festival   1127
Crafts Center Workshops   1185
Crafts Expo   789
Crafts Fair   931
Crafts Festival (Centerville, Iowa)   884
Crafts Festival (Raleigh, North Carolina)   1017
Crafts Revisited Exhibition   995
Crafts 6   976
Craftsmen Fair   993
Craftsmen's Fair (Brewster, Massachusetts)   926
Craftsmen's Fair (Newbury, New Hampshire)   965
Craftproducers Craft Fair at Cummington Farm Village   928
Craftproducers Craft Fair at Mount Snow   1126
Cranberry Festival (South Carver, Massachusetts)   185
Cranberry Festival (Warrens, Wisconsin)   419
Cranberry Festival Drum and Bugle Corps   3167
Crayfish Festival   2894
Creative Arts Festival   536
Creative Arts Week   687
Creative Music Festival   3277
Crepe Myrtle Festival   242
Crescent City Art Festival   736
Crestline Mountaineer Days   1242
Creston Valley Blossom Festival   420
Crooked River Roundup   1653
Crosstie Festival   574
Crow Festival   3797
Crow Indian Fair   2761

Crowe Springs Craftsmen Fair   827
Crown Festival   2139
Crown Resistance Day   2615
Cry of the Wild Ram   2542
Cultural Festival   598
Cummington Fair   182
Curbstone Art Festival   1000
Custer Re-Enactment   2760
Czech Days Festival   2302
Czech Fest   2324
Czech Festival (Wilber, Nebraska)   2198
Czech Festival (Yukon, Oklahoma)   2257
Czechoslovakian Independence Day Celebration   2071

D

Dairy Days in Freeport   1364
Dakota Days Band Festival   3350
Dala Days   2168
Danbury State Fair   3707
Dance Films Festival   2406
Daniel Boone Festival   2599
Danish Day at Minehaha Park   2162
Danish Days   2042
Danish Days Celebration (Minden, Nebraska)   2193
Danish Days Celebration (Viborg, South Dakota)   2303
Danish Festival   2150
Dankfest   1669
Dare Days   1626
Darlington Folk Festival   2493
Dartmouth Winter Carnival   3577
Das Awkscht Fescht   2274
Davie Craft Corner   1013
Davy's Run Homecoming Festival   1423
DAWN (Discover the Art World Now)   541
Day in Old New Castle   2060
Day in Oxford   1464
Day Lily Festival   217
The Day of the Missions (El Dia de las Misiones)   2680
Days in Spain Fiesta   2076
Days of '47   2686
Days of '47 Celebration (Pioneer Days Parade and Rodeo)   2684
Days of '56 Rodeo and Celebration   1559
Days of '76   2669
Days of the Dons   1282
Days of the Old West   1348
De Soto Celebration   2064
Deep Sea Fishing Rodeo   2930
Deep South Arts and Crafts Festival   834
Defeat of Jesse James Day   2624
Del Mar College Drawing and Small Sculpture Show   1100
Delano Wine and Harvest Festival   1245
Delaware Bluegrass Festival (Old Time Bluegrass Festival)   3068

486

Event Name Index

Event Name Index

Hang Gliding Festival (Jackson, New Hampshire) 1576

Harambee Fiesta 2058

Harbor Holidays 2969

Harpers Ferry Art Festival 1172

Hartford Festival of Music 3061

Hartt College Summer Chamber Music Festival 3065

Harvest and Grape Fiesta 422

Harvest Days 301

Harvest Fair (Schaefferstown, Pennsylvania) 305

Harvest Fair (Ulysses, Pennsylvania) 2659

Harvest Fair (Bristol, Rhode Island) 309

Harvest Fair and Ball 3459

Harvest Festival (Arroyo Grande, California) 12

Harvest Festival (Kewanna, Indiana) 107

Harvest Festival (Buffalo Lake, Minnesota) 1504

Harvest Festival (Henning, Minnesota) 1508

Harvest Festival (Remer, Minnesota) 2922

Harvest Festival (Underwood, Minnesota) 1524

Harvest Festival (French Camp, Mississippi) 1532

Harvest Festival (Santa Fe, New Mexico) 2633

Harvest Festival (Elkton, South Dakota) 1730

Harvest Festival (Salem, South Dakota) 333

Harvest Festival (Brownfield, Texas) 344

Harvest Festival (South Hill, Virginia) 3653

Harvest Festival Days 3601

Harvest Homecoming 3507

Harvest Moon Festival of Arts and Crafts 1181

Hastings Fun Fest 1507

Hattiesburg Flea Market 948

Haus und Garten Tour 2244

Havre de Grace Art Show 920

Hawaiian Music Festival 3085

Hawaiian Song Festival and Song Composing Contest 3086

Havasupai Tribal Peach Festival 2722

Head House Square Arts and Crafts Fair 1055

Head of the Lakes Jazz Festival 2169

Heard Museum Indian Fair (Indian Fair) 2717

Heart O' Texas Fair 372

Heart of Florida Folk Festival 2441

Heart of the Hills Days 1733

Heart of the Ozarks Fair 222

Hedgesville Heritage Festival 1856

Heinrichsdorf Fest 2111

Hell Hole Swamp Festival 1718

Helldorado 1560

Herb Smith's Bluegrass Music Festival 3201

Herbstfest 2189

Heritage Celebration (Tuscaloosa Heritage Week) 1213

Heritage Day 1387

Heritage Day Festival 2558

Heritage Days (Bellevue, Iowa) 1410

Heritage Days (Bath, Maine) 2603

Heritage Days (Cumberland, Maryland) 2608

Heritage Days (Salem, Massachusetts) 1485

Heritage Days (Waterford, Pennsylvania) 1700

Heritage Fair 2575

Heritage Festival 2323

Heritage Weekend (Annapolis, Maryland) 2605

Heritage Weekend (Moorefield, West Virginia) 1860

Hesperia Days 1251

Hick Festival 413

High Plains Cotton Festival 363

Highland Arts and Crafts Festival 2501

Highland County Fall Foliage Festival 3652

Highland County Maple Sugar Festival 389

Highland Fall Arts Festival 3484

Highland Festival 2145

Highland Games (Antigonish, Canada) 2367

Highland Games (Sydney, Canada) 2373

Highland Games and Festival 2067

Highland Gathering 2360

Highland Lakes Arts and Crafts Festival (Burnet, Texas) 1098

Highland Lakes Bluebonnet Art Show 1115

Highland Village Day 1930

Hilander Summer Festival 2344

Hill Day 2185

Hillbilly Days 1720

Hillbrook Music Festival 3312

Hillbrook National Van Festival 3313

Hillside Folk Festival 2460

Hispanic Arts Festival 2227

Historic Dogwood Festival 2644

Historic Fincastle Annual Arts and Crafts Festival 1136

Historic Harbor Rendezvous and Classic Yacht Parade 2906

Historic Hoosier Hills Antique and Craft Spring Festival 869

Historic Hoosier Hills Fall Antique Show 448

Historic Savannah Foundation Fair and Festival 1337

Historical Days 2593

Hobo Convention 1411

Hobo Daze 1262

Hofstra University Jazz Clinic and Festival 3239

Hog Festival 90

Holiday Festival of the Arts 688

Holiday Fiesta 1721

Holiday Folk Festival 2498

Holiday in Dixie 1447

Hollywood Bowl Summer Festival 3018

Hollywood Festival of World Television 2378

Hollywood International Film Festival 2382

Holmes County Antique Festival 465

Holy Cross Homecoming 1780

Homecoming and Labor Day Celebration 1226

Homecoming and Rodeo 1745

Homecoming-Watermelon Days 1859

Homecoming Week (Beverly, Massachusetts) 1472

Homecoming Week (Southwick, Massachusetts) 1490

Homemakers Arts and Crafts Fair 722

Homer Festival of Arts and Crafts 865

Honey Festival 265

Hoosier Heritage Handicraft Festival 860

Hoosier Mini Festival 1371

Event Name Index

Event Name Index

Event Name Index

Old Fiddlers Convention 3402
Old Fiddlers Reunion 3366
Old Guyandotte Days 1857
Old Hallowell Days 2604
Old Home Day (Pelham Center, New Hampshire) 1570
Old Home Day (Morris, Pennsylvania) 1679
Old Home Day (Roseville, Pennsylvania) 1692
Old Home Day (Tioga, Pennsylvania) 1697
Old Home Days (Rowe, Massachusetts) 1483
Old Home Days (Port Royal, Pennsylvania) 1689
Old Home Week (Dalton, Massachusetts) 1474
Old Home Week (Lancaster, Massachusetts) 1479
Old Home Week (West Newton, Pennsylvania) 1703
Old Island Days 2882
Old Lincoln Days 2631
Old Market Square Sidewalk Art Show and Festival 1107
Old Milwaukee Days 1879
Old Miner's Days 1225
Old Mission Hand Crafts Fair 771
Old Muster Day 2627
Old Orchard Art Festival 845
Old Pecos Bull Celebration 2779
Old Quawk's Day 1627
Old San Diego Art Fiesta (Old Town Art Fiesta) 764
Old Settlers Day 1732
Old Settlers Days (DeSmet, South Dakota) 1728
Old Settlers Days (Round Rock, Texas) 1798
Old Settlers Days (Ferndale, Washington) 1841
Old Settlers Picnic and Rodeo 1731
Old Settlers Reunion (Camp Wood, Texas) 1751
Old Settlers Reunion (Denver City, Texas) 1761
Old Settlers Reunion (Floydada, Texas) 1770
Old Settlers Reunion (Glen Rose, Texas) 2496
Old Settlers Reunion (Stanton, Texas) 1805
Old Soldiers and Settlers Reunion 1413
Old Spanish Days Fiesta 2038
Old Swede's Church Fair 2278
Old Time Arts and Crafts Day 922
Old Time Bluegrass Festival (Delaware Bluegrass Festival) 3068
Old Time Camp Meeting and Revival 3042
Old Time Country Music Contest and Pioneer Exposition 3123
Old-Time Country Music Festival (Country Music Festival) 2999
Old Time Fiddle, Banjo State Championship 3391
Old-Time Fiddle Convention 3038
Old Time Fiddlers and Bluegrass Convention (Mount Airy, North Carolina) 2294
Old Time Fiddlers and Bluegrass Convention (Chilhowie, Virginia) 3398
Old Time Fiddlers and Bluegrass Convention (Marion, Virginia) 3407
Old Time Fiddlers Contest 3353
Old Time Fiddlers Convention 3297
Old Time Fiddlers Festival 3208

Old Time Fiddling/Bluegrass Festival 3357
Old-Time Gospel Music Festival 3000
Old Time Railroaders Day at Tweetsie Railroad 1619
Old-Time Summer Fair 3499
Old Time Summer Festival 2622
Old Time Threshing Bee 135
Old Timers Day 1665
Old Timers Fair and Rodeo 1592
Old Town Art Fair 846
Old Town Art Fiesta (Old San Diego Art Fiesta) 764
Old Town Birthday Fiesta 1276
Old Town Festival and Outdoor Show 1266
Old Town Fiesta de la Primavera 2560
Old Villages of Yesteryear Day 1670
Olde Princess Anne Days 2612
Olde Yarmouth Antiques Fair 456
Ole Town Days 1661
Olympic Village Bluegrass Festival 3244
On-the-Avenue Festival of Art 899
On the Green Art Show and Sale (Outdoor Art Show and Sale) 790
Onamia Days 1516
100 American Craftsmen 994
One World Festival 2229
Ookpik Carnival 3683
Opasquia Indian Days 2863
Opera/South 3183
Opeta-Ye-Teca Indian Celebration 2762
Orange Bowl Festival 1324
Orange County Pumpkin Festival 103
Orange Festival 152
Orange Festival and Rodeo 1315
Oregon Broiler Festival 285
Oregon State Fair 3739
Oromocto Arts and Crafts Festival 1199
Osbornedale Arts Festival 798
Osceola Arts Festival 815
Ottumwa Heights Family Outdoor Art Festival 892
Ouachita Valley Fair 164
Outdoor Art and Crafts Fair 705
Outdoor Art Fair (Washington, D.C.) 806
Outdoor Art Fair (Des Moines, Iowa) 544
Outdoor Art Fair (Freeport, Texas) 1104
Outdoor Art Festival (San Francisco, California) 769
Outdoor Art Festival (Jensen Beach, Florida) 814
Outdoor Art Festival (Sylvania, Ohio) 1033
Outdoor Art Festival (Willoughby, Ohio) 628
Outdoor Art Festival (Newport, Rhode Island) 1065
Outdoor Art Festival (Portsmouth, Rhode Island) 1067
Outdoor Art Festival (Olympia, Washington) 679
Outdoor Art Show (Foley, Alabama) 699
Outdoor Art Show (Salisbury, Maryland) 921
Outdoor Art Show (Plymouth, Massachusetts) 933
Outdoor Art Show (Warm Springs, Virginia) 1152
Outdoor Art Show and Sale (On the Green Art Show and Sale) 790
Outdoor Crafts Show 1061

502

Event Name Index

Q

Quebec Winter Carnival   3694
Queen Anne's County Crafts Festival   914
Quilt Fair   1184
Quinault Derby Days   2854

R

Race Meet and Billy Sale   1783
Ragtime Festival   3210
Railfan Steam Weekend (Covington, Virginia)   1828
Railfan Steam Weekend (Cass, West Virginia)   1850
Rail-Fans Day   1489
Raintree Hey Days Festival   1395
Rally for Old Tippecanoe   2587
Ralph Edwards Fiesta   1604
Ramona Festival   2561
Ramp Festival   334
Raspberry Festival (Hopkins, Minnesota)   201
Raspberry Festival (Bear Lake, Utah)   376
Ratification Day   2606
Rattlesnake Hunt and Antique Show   1755
Rattlesnake Roundup   1807
Rattlesnake Roundup and Antique Show   1750
Ravinia Festival   3096
Rawling Renegade Roundup Days   1890
Raylrode Daze Festival   2665
Rebel Days   2675
Rebel Roundup Festival   1976
Red Cloud Art Show   1087
Red Flannel Festival   1493
Red Lodge Music Festival (Student Music Festival)   3217
Red River Exhibition   1913
Red River Valley Fair   1596
Red Rocks Music and Drama Festival   3050
Red Rose Festival   2656
Redbud Festival   163
ReDiscover New Mexico   1577
Redlands Bowl Summer Music Festival   3028
Redwood Empire Stage Band Festival   3030
Regional Craftsmen's Fair   962
Renaissance Crafts and Art Show   1070
Renaissance Fair (Angels Camp, California)   2547
Renaissance Fair (Laytonville, California)   2555
Renaissance Festival   2623
Renaissance Pleasure Faire (Los Angeles, California)   2556
Renaissance Pleasure Faire (San Rafael, California)   2566
Renaissance Pleasure Faire and Springtime Market   2546

Renton Art Show   1159
Republic of Texas Chilympiad   2535
Reston Black Arts Festival   2342
Reston Community Association Birthday Festival   1834
Return of the Swallows to the City (Fiesta de las Golandrinas)   3476
Revolutionary War Days   2610
Rhode Island Association of Craftsmen Show   1062
Rhode Island Bach Festival   3337
Rhode Island Independence Celebration   2662
Rhode Island Summer Spectacular   3617
Rhododendron Festival (Eureka, California)   19
Rhododendron Festival (Florence, Oregon)   280
Rhododendron Festival (Elizabethton, Tennessee)   335
Rhododendron Festival (Port Townsend, Washington)   398
Rhododendron Outdoor Art and Crafts Festival   680
Rhubarb Festival   328
Rice Festival   342
Richmond Art Center Festival   762
Richmond Rose Festival   113
Rimouski Fall Festival   3696
Rio Grande Indian Festival   2770
River Art Show   1119
River City Renaissance Fair   2670
River Days   2928
River Days Festival   2938
River Festival   2946
River Parks Festival   1645
Riverboat Days   2891
Riverfront Arts and Crafts Festival   867
Riverside Celebration   1823
Roaring Twenties Festival   2594
Robert Burns Celebration   2160
Robin Hood Dell Concerts   3329
Rochester International Film Festival   2415
Rock Cut Winter Carnival   3497
Rock, Gem and Mineral Show   1901
Rockhound Roundup   1933
Rockhounds Pow Wow   1654
Rockingham Craftsmen's Fall Fair   964
Rocky Hill State Fair   310
Rocky Mountain Bluegrass Festival   3053
Rocky Mountain Book Festival   500
Rodeo Fest   1631
Rolla Arts Festival   583
Rollin' Rock Roundup   1775
Romantic Festival   3114
Root Diggin' Days   1549
Root Festival   2831
Rose Festival (Thomasville, Georgia)   74
Rose Festival (State Center, Iowa)   137
Rose Festival (Tularosa, New Mexico)   232
Rose Festival (Portland, Oregon)   283
Rosebud Sioux Fair, Pow Wow and Rodeo   2841
Rotary International Air Fair   1840
Roughrider Days   1630
Roundup Days   1776
Royal Manitoba Winter Fair   426

Event Name Index

Event Name Index

Waterfowl Week (Blackwater National Wildlife Refuge, Maryland) 3800

Waterfowl Week (Eastern Neck National Wildlife Refuge, Maryland) 3801

Waterfowl Week (Brigantine National Wildlife Refuge, New Jersey) 3804

Waterfowl Week (Chincoteague National Wildlife Refuge, Virginia) 3809

Waterfowl Week (Presquile National Wildlife Refuge, Virginia) 3810

Waterfront Art Fair (Charlevoix, Michigan) 937

Waterfront Art Fair (Grand Haven, Michigan) 939

Waterfront Festival 1338

Waterland Festival 2967

Waterloo Village Music Festival 3226

Watermelon Day (Humeston, Iowa) 128

Watermelon Day (Pierson, Iowa) 133

Watermelon Day (Stanhope, Iowa) 136

Watermelon Days 208

Watermelon Festival (Hope, Arkansas) 6

Watermelon Festival (Cordele, Georgia) 68

Watermelon Festival (Kellogg, Minnesota) 203

Watermelon Festival (Lucedale, Mississippi) 214

Watermelon Festival (Falfurrias, Texas) 350

Watermelon Jubilee 366

Watermelon Thump and Queen Coronation 356

Wearin' O' the Green 2304

Weed Show and Art Mart 742

A Week of Jazz 3133

Weirton Art and Craft Festival 1188

Welcome of the De Anza Trek (Santa Barbara, California) 2567

Welcome of the De Anza Trek (Ventura, California) 2569

West Door Concerts 3264

West Louisiana Forestry Festival 156

West Penn Laurel Festival 290

West Texas Fair 339

West Texas Pioneers and Old Settlers Reunion 1757

West Virginia Country Fling 1855

West Virginia Oil and Gas Festival 1870

West Virginia Sports Festival 1863

West Virginia State Folk Festival 2508

West Virginia Turkey Festival 416

Westerly Art Festival 1073

Western Arts Music Festival 3430

Western Days (Valley Center, California) 1289

Western Days (Billings, Montana) 1550

Western Days and Moose Rodeo 1291

Western Days Celebration 1809

Western Festival (Elk Grove, California) 1246

Western Festival (Saint-Tite, Canada) 1940

Western Folk Festival 2046

Western Folklore Festival 2438

Western Idaho Fair 3713

Western Nova Scotia Exhibition 438

Western Nova Scotia Handcraft Demonstration 1202

Western Week (Grand Lake, Colorado) 1301

Western Week (Beeville, Texas) 1747

Western Week (Georgetown, Texas) 1773

Westminster Festival of Religious Arts 626

Westville Historical Music Day 3082

Westwood Fall Sidewalk Art and Craft Show 752

Westwood Sidewalk Art and Crafts Show 753

Wethersfield Spring Arts Festival 804

Whaling Festival (Nulakatuk) (Point Barrow, Alaska) 3792

Whaling Festival (Nulakatuk) (Wainwright, Alaska) 3794

Wheat and Beet Days 380

Wheat Threshing Steam and Gas Engine Show 177

White Barn Theatre Festival 3763

Whiskey Flats Days 2553

White Fox Jamboree 851

White Mountain All-Indian Pow Wow 2711

White Mountain Apache Tribal Fair and Rodeo 2724

White Mountains Festival of Children's Literature 586

White Mountains Festival of the Seven Arts 589

White River Arts and Crafts Fair 954

White River Carnival 2870

White River Frontier Days 1739

White Water Weekend 2978

White White World 3527

Whitehall N-SSA Skirmish and Flea Market 260

Whitewater Canal Days 1375

Whitewater Valley Canoe Races and Festival 2890

Whitewood Days Celebration 663

Wichita Jazz Festival 3134

Wichita River Festival 2893

Wickford Art Festival 1074

Wild Foods Festival 96

Wild Goose Festival 3803

Wild Horse Stampede 1557

Wild Rice Festival (Kelliher, Minnesota) 202

Wild Rice Festival (Waskish, Minnesota) 210

Wild West Days 1255

Wilderness Old Times Festival 1394

Wilhelm Tell Festival and Drama 2351

Williams Lake Stampede 1902

Williamstown Theatre Festival 3772

Willits Arts Festival 775

Winchester Days 1360

Winchester Speedway Oldtimers Festival 1408

Wind Creek Rock Swap 1206

Windjammer Days 2898

Windows West 2683

Windsor-Detroit International Freedom Festival 1938

Wine Festival 2519

Winedale Spring Festival 521

Winfester 3547

Winfield Art and Craft Festival 1190

Winnipeg Folk Festival 2513

Winona Steamboat Days 1527

Winter Art Fair 1193

Winter Carnival (Homer, Alaska) 3457

Winter Carnival (Flagstaff, Arizona) 3461

Winter Carnival (Steamboat Springs, Colorado) 3483

Winter Carnival (McCall, Idaho) 3489

SECTION IV
GEOGRAPHIC INDEX

Geographic Index

Geographic Index

Geographic Index

Geographic Index

Geographic Index

Geographic Index

Geographic Index

Geographic Index

Geographic Index

Geographic Index

Geographic Index

Geographic Index

Geographic Index

INDIANA (Continued)

Brownstown
    Jackson County Watermelon Festival   102
Cambridge City
    Whitewater Canal Days   1375
Canaan
    Canaan Fall Festival   3500
Cannelton
    Canorama   1376
Cayuga
    Pioneer Days Festival   1377
Centerville
    Arts and Crafts Festival   858
Chesterton
    Chesterton Arts and Crafts   859
Clinton
    Little Italy Festival   2107
Columbus
    May Faire   2589
Connersville
    Fall Festival   3501
Dale
    Fall Festival   3502
Dunkirk
    Glass Days Festival   1378
Dunlapsville
    Hoosier Heritage Handicraft Festival   860
Elkhart
    Boulevard of Color   861
Elwood
    Elwood Glass Festival   1379
English
    Arts and Crafts Street Fair   862
Eugene
    Pioneer Days Festival   1380
Evansville
    Art and Craft Show   863
    Freedom Festival   1394
    Madrigal Dinners   3111
    Ohio River Arts Festival   532
Fort Wayne
    Boulevard of Color   864
    Fort Wayne Fine Arts Festival   533
    Three Rivers Festival   2590
French Lick
    Orange County Pumpkin Festival   103
Friendship
    Spring Muzzle-Loading Rifle Shoots   2591
Garrett
    Garrett Days   1382
Gary
    Jazz and Bourbon Street Art Fair   534
Gas City
    Art in the Park   535
Geneva
    Wabash Valley Festival   1383
Greencastle
    Festival of Contemporary Music   3112

Greenfield
    James Whitcomb Riley Festival   1385
Greentown
    Greentown Glass Festival   1386
Hammond
    Science Fair   1384
Hesston
    Live Steam Show and Threshermen's Reunion   104
Homer
    Homer Festival of Arts and Crafts   865
Hope
    Heritage Day   1387
Indianapolis
    Baroque Festival   3113
    500 Festival   1388
    Indiana Black Expo   2108
    Indiana Rose Festival   105
    Indiana State Fair   3716
    Romantic Festival   3114
    Talbott Street Art Fair   866
Jeffersonville
    Riverfront Arts and Crafts Festival   867
Kentland
    Corn Festival   106
Kewanna
    Harvest Festival   107
Kokomo
    Creative Arts Festival   536
Lafayette
    Fiesta   2109
Leiters Ford
    Strawberry Festival   108
Liberty
    Liberty Festival   1389
Lowell
    Arts and Crafts Festival   868
Madison
    Historic Hoosier Hills Antique and Craft Spring Festival   869
    Historic Hoosier Hills Fall Antique Show   448
    Madison Chautauqua of the Arts   870
Marion
    Art in the Park   537
    Downtown Festival   1390
Martinsville
    American Donkey and Mule Society Jubilee Festival   1391
    Fall Foliage Festival   3503
Metamora
    Canal Days--Traders Rendezvous   1392
Michigan City
    Fall Rose Festival   109
    Michigan City Summer Festival and Country-Western Show   3504
Milroy
    Frontier Club Fall Festival   3505
Mishawaka
    Arts and Crafts Festival   871

532

Geographic Index

Geographic Index

Geographic Index

Geographic Index

Geographic Index

Geographic Index

Geographic Index

Geographic Index

Geographic Index

Geographic Index

Geographic Index

Geographic Index

Geographic Index

Geographic Index

Geographic Index

Geographic Index

Geographic Index

Geographic Index

Geographic Index

Geographic Index

Geographic Index

Geographic Index

Geographic Index

Geographic Index

WEST VIRGINIA (Continued)

Bluefield
    Arts and Crafts Festival   1163, 1164
Buckhannon
    Strawberry Festival   410
Cairo
    Square Dance Festival   1988
Cass
    Railfan Steam Weekend   1850
Charleston
    American Indian Fall Festival   2856
    Appalachian Festival   2507
    Capital City Art and Craft Festival   1165
    John Henry Festival   1851
    Rhododendron Outdoor Art and Crafts Festival
        1166
    Sternwheel Regatta   1856
Chloe
    Upper West Fork Art and Craft Fair   1167
Davis
    Tucker County Alpine Festival   3659
Elkins
    Mountain State Forest Festival   411
Fairmont
    Monongahela Art and Craft Fair   1168
    North Central West Virginia Art and Craft
        Festival   1169
Franklin
    Spelunkers Reunion   1853
    Treasure Mountain Festival   1854
Gassaway
    Braxton County Art and Craft Show   1170
Glenville
    West Virginia State Folk Festival   2508
Grafton
    Apple Festival   412
Grantsville
    Wood Festival   1171
Harpers Ferry
    Harpers Ferry Art Festival   1172
    Mountain Heritage Arts and Crafts Festival
        1173, 1174
    West Virginia County Fling   1855
Hedgesville
    Hedgesville Heritage Festival   1856
Hendricks
    Hick Festival   413
Hinton
    Water Festival   2977
Huntersville
    Pocohontas County Music and Bluegrass Festival
        3418
    Pocohontas Music and Bluegrass Festival   3419
Huntington
    Dogwood Festival   414
    Old Guyandotte Days   1857
Hurricane
    Hurricane Heritage Days   1858

Independence
    Homecoming--Watermelon Days   1859
Keyser
    Mountain Heritage Festival   2509
Kingwood
    Preston County Buckwheat Festival   415
Lewisburg
    Greenbrier Valley Artisans/Craftsmens Fair
        1175
    Greenbrier Valley Arts and Humanities Festival
        681
    State Fair of West Virginia   3747
Mannington
    Mountaineer Dulcimer Club Convention   3420
Marlinton
    Pocohontas County Pioneer Days   2695
Mathias
    West Virginia Turkey Festival   416
Milton
    Milton Garden Club Art and Crafts Show   1176
Moorefield
    Heritage Weekend   1860
Morgantown
    Morgantown Court House Art/Craft Show   1177
    Mountaineer Art and Craft Festival   1178
    Mountaineer Week   1861
Mullens
    Mullens Art and Craft Festival   1179
New Martinsville
    Town and Country Days   1862
North Charleston
    Fair Springtime Celebration of Arts and Crafts
        1180
Oak Hill
    West Virginia Sports Festival   1863
Parkersburg
    Harvest Moon Festival of Arts and Crafts   1181
    Parkersburg College Heritage Day   1864
Petersburg
    Potomac Highlands Craft Show   1182
    White Water Weekend   2978
Philippi
    Alderson-Broaddus College Art/Craft Festival
        1183
Pipestem
    Pipestem Folk Music Festival   2510
Princeton
    Quilt Fair   1184
Ravenswood
    Ohio River Festival   1865
Richwood
    American Heritage Week Festival   1866
    Cherry River Festival   1867
Ripley
    Crafts Center Workshops   1185
    Mountain State Art and Craft Fair   1186
Rupert
    Rupert Country Fling   1857

Geographic Index

Geographic Index

Geographic Index

Geographic Index

SECTION V
SUBJECT INDEX

ACADIAN

Louisiana

Acadian Day Festival   2368
Acadian Festival (Festival Acadien de Caraquet) 2365
Acadian Festival of Clare   2369
Cajun Festival   1434
Le Festival Willis F. Ducrest des Arts Acadiens
   et Francais   550
International Acadian Festival   2128
Lagniappe on the Bayou   1432
Louisiana Cotton Festival   2550
Madewood Arts Festival   552
Mardi Gras   1430

AGRICULTURE

See also: STATE FAIRS

Alabama

Alabama State Fair   3700
Greater Gulf State Fair   1209

Alaska

Harvest Fair and Ball   3459
Matamuska Valley Fair   3702
Tanana Valley State Fair   3701

Arizona

Arizona State Fair   3703

Arkansas

Arkansas State Fair and Livestock Show   3704
Ozark Folk Center Harvest Festival   728

California

California State Fair   3705
County Fair   1270
Delano Wine and Harvest Festival   1245
Southern California Exposition   1244

Colorado

Colorado State Fair   3706

Connecticut

Danbury State Fair   3707

Delaware

Delaware State Fair   3708

Florida

Florida State Fair   3709

Georgia

Georgia State Fair   3710

Hawaii

Fiftieth State Fair   3711

Idaho

Eastern Idaho Fair   3712
Lumberjack Days (Clearwater County Fair)
   1353
Western Idaho Fair   3713

Illinois

Clayville Spring Festival   3498
DuQuoin State Fair   3714
Illinois State Fair   3715

Indiana

Bluffton Free Street Fair   1073
Indiana State Fair   3716

Iowa

Albia Fall Festival   3512
Fall Fun Days   3520
Iowa State Fair   3717
Old Soldiers and Settlers Reunion   1413
World's Largest Street Fair   1416

Kansas

Kansas State Fair   3718

Kentucky

Kentucky State Fair   3719
Sorghum Festival   1429

Louisiana

Greater Baton Rouge State Fair   3720
Louisiana State Fair   3722
North Louisiana State Fair   3721

Subject Index

Subject Index

Subject Index

Subject Index

Subject Index

Subject Index

Subject Index

Subject Index

Subject Index

Subject Index

BLACK (contd.)

Kansas

Black Arts and Heritage Festival   2122

New Jersey

Black Heritage Festival   2893

New Mexico

Black Heritage Week Arts and Crafts Festival
974

Pennsylvania

Black Week Festival   2279

South Carolina

Black Emphasis Festival   2288

Texas

Negro Life and Achievement Week   2306

Virginia

Reston Black Arts Festival   2342

BLUEBERRY

Indiana

Marshall County Blueberry Festival   112

Maine

Maine Blueberry Festival   172

Michigan

National Blueberry Festival   194

Canada

Blueberry Harvest Festival   434

BLUEGRASS

See also: COUNTRY MUSIC

Alabama

Alabama State Championship Sling Shot Contest
and Bluegrass Day   2993
Fall Bluegrass Music Festival   2994
Spring Bluegrass Music Festival   2995
Tennessee Valley Old-Time Fiddlers Convention
2989
Vacation Flat-Top Summit and Bluegrass Festival
(Horse Pens Midsummer Bluegrass Festival)
2996

Arkansas

Arkansas Bluegrass and Country Festival   3002
Arkansas Bluegrass Festival   3003
Arkansas Folk Festival Mountain View   2434
Arkansas Onion Folk Festival   2433

California

Calico Spring Festival   3005
Golden West Bluegrass Festival   3023
Old-Time Fiddle Convention   3038
Topanga Folk Festival   3044

Colorado

Great Rocky Mountain National Bluegrass Festival
Rocky Mountain Bluegrass Festival   3053

Connecticut

Connecticut Family Folk Festival   2439

Delaware

Old Time Bluegrass Festival (Delaware Bluegrass
Festival)   3068

Georgia

Yellow Daisy Festival   73

Idaho

1860 Days   2584
National Old-Time Fiddlers Contest and Festival
3087
Smelterville Lions Frontier Days   1359
Winchester Days   1360

Illinois

Big Timer Bluegrass Festival   3099
Bluegrass Festival (Alton)   3089
Bluegrass Festival (Ashland)   3090

Subject Index

BLUEGRASS (contd.)

Illinois (contd.)

Bluegrass Music Festival   3101
Bluegrass Music Weekend   3088
Central Illinois Bluegrass Festival   3094
Country Days (Southern Illinois Country Days)
    1365
Knoxville Bluegrass Festival   3102
Lakeside Bluegrass Festival   3091
Mid-States Bluegrass Festival   3093
National Chicagoland and Northern Illinois Blue-
    grass Festival   3104
Shadey Forest Bluegrass Festival   3100
Southern Illinois Bluegrass Festival   3092

Indiana

Arts and Crafts Street Fair   862
Bluegrass Music Festival   3107
Bluegrass Reunion   3109
Fiddlers Gathering   3105
Larry Sparks Bluegrass Festival   3110
Steam Harvest Days   115
Tippecanoe and Bluegrass Too   3106

Iowa

Bluegrass and Country Music Festival   3122
Central City Bluegrass Festival   3120
Country and Old Time Music Festival   3125
Southern Iowa Bluegrass Music Festival   3119

Kansas

Bluegrass Music Festival   3132
National Guitar Flat-Picking Championship; Blue-
    grass Music, Folk Arts and Craft Festival   3135
Spring Thing   3522

Kentucky

Bluegrass Music Festival of the U.S.A.   3138
Foothills Folk Festival   2454
Fraley Family Mountain Music Festival   3139
Great Western Kentucky Bluegrass Festival   3140
Kentucky Folk Song Festival   3137

Louisiana

New Orleans Jazz and Heritage Festival   3145

Maine

Bluegrass Music Festival   3148

Maryland

Allegany Bluegrass Festival   3155
Autumn Glory Festival   3533
Bluegrass Festival   3153

Massachusetts

Bluegrass Jamboree   3159

Mississippi

Bluegrass Festival   3185
Folklore Frolic   2466

Missouri

Bluegrass America   3199
Bluegrass Country Fair   1542
Bluegrass Festival (Grassy)   3194, 3195
Bluegrass Festival (Holt)   3197
Bluegrass Festival (Kahoka)   3198
Bluegrass Festival (Perryville)   3205
Bluegrass Festival (Saint Charles(3207
Bluegrass Festival (Van Buren)   3213
Bluegrass Festival (MABC Fall Festival)   3190
Bluegrass Jamboree   3187
Bluegrass Pickin Time   3188
Central Missouri Bluegrass Music Festival   3206
Dub Crouch's Bluegrass Festival   3196
Green Tree Festival   1543
Herb Smith's Bluegrass Music Festival   3201
Invitational Country-Bluegrass-Old Time Music
    Festival   3193
Little Dixie Bluegrass Festival   3203
Missouri Bluegrass Festival   3204
Old Time Fiddlers Festival   3208
Ozark Mountain Bluegrass Festival   3189
Piney River Bluegrass Music Festival   3192
SPBGMA Bluegrass Musician Convention and
    Awards Banquet, Bluegrass Festival   3202
Spring Bluegrass Festival   3191
Summertime (Summer Bluegrass Festival)   3186

Montana

Badlands Appreciation Festival   1553

New York

Bluegrass and Old-Time Country Music Band
    Contest and Crafts Fair   3247
Olympic Village Bluegrass Festival   3244
Smokey Greene's Bluegrass Festival   3236

North Carolina

Angier Festival   2474

591

BLUEGRASS (contd.)

North Carolina (contd.)

Ohio

Oklahoma

Pennsylvania

Rhode Island

South Carolina

South Dakota

Tennessee

Texas

Virginia

West Virginia

Wyoming

Canada

Subject Index

BUFFALO

South Dakota

    Buffalo Auction   3806

CANADIAN

California

    Canadian Day   2007

Florida

    Canadian Weekend   2066
    Walt Disney World Canadian Festival   2070

South Carolina

    Canadian-American Days   2299

CANTALOUPE

California

    Cantaloupe Festival   14

CARROT

California

    Carrot Festival   21

CAVES AND CAVERNS

West Virginia

    Spelunkers Reunion   1853

CERAMICS

Florida

    Ceramics Fair   816

Louisiana

    Acadian Ceramic Show   907

Ohio

    Ohio Ceramic and Sculpture Show   1036
    Pottery Festival (Crooksville)   1026
    Pottery Festival (Roseville)   1032
    Tri-State Pottery Festival   1027

Oregon

    Ceramic and Crafts Show   1041

Rhode Island

    International Ceramic Fair   1063

Virginia

    Juried Show   1134

Wisconsin

    Clay-o-rama Ceramic Show   1191

CHAMBER MUSIC

Alaska

    Sitka Summer Music Festival   2998

California

    Claremont Music Festival   3010
    Concord Summer Festival   3012
    Contemporary Music Festival   3029
    Music Here and Now Festival   3011
    Percussive Arts Society Festival   3024

Colorado

    Music in the Mountains   3051

Connecticut

    Festival of Contemporary Music   3055
    Hartford Festival of Music   3061
    Hartt College Summer Chamber Music Festival   3065
    Music Mountain Concerts   3058
    Silvermine Chamber Music Festival   3062
    Starlight Festival of Chamber Music   3060
    Twentieth Century Arts Festival   3056
    Woodstock Academy Music Festival   3067

Subject Index

Subject Index

Subject Index

Subject Index

Subject Index

COMMUNITY (contd.)

Wisconsin

Wisconsin State Fair   3748

Wyoming

Wyoming State Fair   3749

Canada

Provincial Exhibition of Manitoba   425
Vancouver Island Exhibition   421

CORN

California

La Habra Corn Festival   24

Illinois

Corn Day Festival   83
National Sweet Corn Festival   89
Sweet Corn Festival   92
Sweetcorn-Watermelon Festival   94

Indiana

Corn Festival   106

Iowa

Corn Carnival   127
Corn Harvest Festival   122
Sweet Corn Days   126

Maine

Corn Festival   169

Maryland

Corn Roast   179

Ohio

Sweet Corn Festival   269

South Dakota

Corn Carnival   326
Corn Palace Festival   330

Canada

Corn and Apple Festival   428
Corn Festival   432

COTTON

California

Cotton Festival   1240
Potato and Cotton Festival   39

Louisiana

Louisiana Cotton Festival   162
North Louisiana Cotton Festival and Fair   146

Mississippi

Delta Cotton Wives Cotton Fair   212

Missouri

Cotton Carnival   220

New Mexico

Sierra County Farm Bureau Cotton Extravaganza   231

Tennessee

Cotton Carnival   336

Texas

Cotton Carnival   345
High Plains Cotton Festival   363

COUNTRY MUSIC

See also: BLUEGRASS, FOLK MUSIC

Arizona

Country Music Festival (Old-Time Country Music Festival)   2999
Fall Festival and Arizona's State Fiddlers Contest   3462

California

Calico Spring Festival   3005

Subject Index

CZECH

Florida

    Czechoslovakian Independence Day Celebration
      2071

Kansas

    After Harvest Czech Festival   2123

Minnesota

    Kolacky Day   2167

Nebraska

    Czech Festival   2198
    Kolach Days   2197

Oklahoma

    Czech Festival   2257
    Kolache Festival   2256

South Dakota

    Czech Days Festival   2903

Texas

    Czech Fest   2324
    National Polka Festival   2316
    Saint Mary's Annual Homecoming Festival   2335

DAIRY

Illinois

    Dairy Days in Freeport   1364

Kentucky

    Lincoln County June Dairy Day Festival   143

Louisiana

    Louisiana Dairy Festival   144
    Southeast Louisiana Dairy Festival and Livestock
      Show   154

Minnesota

    Nobles County Dairy Days   198
    Northwest Dairy Days   209

Mississippi

    Central Mississippi Fair, Rodeo and State Dairy
      Show   213

New York

    Steuben County Dairy Festival   234

Texas

    Cleveland Dairy Days   346
    East Texas Fair   370
    Hopkins County Dairy Festival   368

Utah

    Cache Valley Dairy Festival   378

Vermont

    Vermont State Dairy Festival (June Dairy Festival)
      383

DANCE

See also: SQUARE DANCE

Alabama

    Arts and Crafts Week   697

Alaska

    Arts Fair   713
    Whaling Festival (Nulakatuk) (Point Barrow)   3792
    Whaling Festival (Nulakatuk) (Wainwright)   3794

Arizona

    Ceremonial Dances   2713
    Flagstaff Summer Festival   477
    Garces Celebration of the Arts   480
    Greater Phoenix Summer Festival   478
    Indian Fair or Heard Museum Indian Fair   2717
    White Mountain Apache Tribal Fair and Rodeo
      2724

California

    Cal Arts Spring Fair   498
    Festival of the Arts   492
    Georgetown Performing Arts Center Festival   486
    Ojai Folk Dance Festival   3027
    Stanford Summer Festivals of the Arts   496

Subject Index

Subject Index

Subject Index

Subject Index

Subject Index

FROG

California

Caleveras County Fair and Jumping Frog Jubilee 1220
Jumping Frog Jamboree 1243

Louisiana

Frog Festival 1446

Oklahoma

Peach Festival 276

South Carolina

Governor's Frog Jumping Contest 1723

Canada

Frog Follies 1907

GEMS AND MINERALS

Alabama

Wind Creek Rock Swap 1206

New Hampshire

New Hampshire Gem and Mineral Festival 1572
Swap, Talk and Brag Day and Micromounters Roundup 1573

North Carolina

Macon County Gemboree 1624

Oregon

Rockhounds Pow Wow 1654
Thunderegg Days 1651

Texas

Rollin' Rock Roundup 1080

Canada

Festival of Gems 1911
Rock, Gem and Mineral Show 1901
Rockhound Roundup 1933

GENEALOGY

Alabama

Birmingham Genealogical Society Festival 2540

GERMAN

Alabama

German Folk Festival 1993

Alaska

Oktoberfest 1995

California

German Day 2046
German Festival 2047
Octoberfest (Auburn) 2001
Octoberfest (Rancho Bernardo) 2023
Oktoberfest (Big Bear Lake) 2003
Oktoberfest (Los Angeles) 2017
Oktoberfest (Santa Rosa) 2041
Oktoberfest (Torrance) 2049
Tyrolean Festival 2050
Wurst Festival 2051

Colorado

Fasching 2057

Florida

Oktoberfest 2065

Georgia

Bavarian Oktoberfest 2085

Illinois

Deutschfest 2097

Indiana

Heinrichsdorf Fest 2111
Oktoberfest (Batesville) 2106
Oktoberfest (Newburgh) 2110
Oktoberfest (Seymour) 2112
Oktoberfest (Terre Haute) 2115
Schweizer Fest 2114

Iowa

Oktoberfest 2117
Polka Fest 1961

Subject Index

GOSPEL MUSIC

Arizona

    Old-Time Gospel Music Festival   3000

Colorado

    Colorado Country Music Festival   3049

Illinois

    Knoxville Bluegrass Festival   3102

Indiana

    Bluegrass Music Festival   3107
    Larry Sparks Bluegrass Festival   3110

Mississippi

    Gospel Extravaganza   3182

Tennessee

    International Gospel Music Festival   3361

Virginia

    Virginia Folk Music Association Festival   3399

GOURDS

North Carolina

    Gourd Festival   243

GRAPEFRUIT

    See: CITRUS

GRAPES

Arkansas

    Tontitown Grape Festival   10

California

    Festival of the Grape   15
    Grape Festival (Napa)   27
    Grape Festival (San Rafael)   35
    Grecian Wine Festival   2520
    Lodi Grape Festival and National Wine Show   2518

Illinois

    Grape Festival   2522

Michigan

    Grape and Wine Festival   2530

New York

    Grape Festival   238

Ohio

    Grape Jamboree   262

South Carolina

    Golden Muscadine Festival   325

Canada

    Niagara Grape and Wine Festival   2539

GREEK

California

    Greek Festival   2048
    Greek Food Festival   2044
    Greek Theatre Festival   3017

District of Columbia

    Folk Festival   2062

Florida

    Greek Cross Day   2079

Georgia

    Atlanta Greek Festival   2081

Subject Index

Subject Index

Subject Index

Subject Index

HOBO

California

    Hobo Daze   1262

Iowa

    Hobo Convention   1411

HONEY

Ohio

    Honey Festival   265

HUCKLEBERRY

Oregon

    Huckleberry Fest   287

Pennsylvania

    Huckleberry Fair   294

HUNGARIAN

California

    Hungarian Press Day Festival   2013

Louisiana

    Hungarian Harvest Dance   2125

New Jersey

    Hungarian Festival   2206

Ohio

    Hungarian Wine Festival   2250

INDIANS (NATIVE AMERICANS)

Alabama

    Calico Fort Arts and Crafts Fair   700

Arizona

    Navajo Craftsmen Show   716
    San Xavier Fiesta   1999
    Tucson Festival   2000

California

    La Purisima Mission Festival (Mission Fiesta Day)
      2010
    Old Adobe Days Fiesta   2557
    Ramona Festival   2561
    Salmon Festival   2874
    Santa Ysabel Mission Fiesta and Pit Barbeque
      1253

Colorado

    Navajo Trails Fiesta   1298

Idaho

    Indian Days and Plummer Festival (Plummer Days)
      1355

Indiana

    Canal Days--Traders Rendezvous   1392
    Festival of the Turning Leaves   3510

Kentucky

    Daniel Boone Festival   2599

Maine

    Corn Festival   169

Mississippi

    Harvest Festival   1532

Montana

    Wild Horse Stampede   1557

Subject Index

Subject Index

JAZZ (contd.)

Indiana

    Collegiate Jazz Festival   3116
    Jazz and Bourbon Street Art Fair   534
    Old-Time Summer Fair   3499

Iowa

    Steamboat Days and Dixieland Jazz Festival
      1412

Kansas

    Central States Jazz Festival   3131
    Week of Jazz   3133
    Wichita Jazz Festival   3134

Louisiana

    Jazz and Heritage Festival   3145

Michigan

    Ann Arbor Blues and Jazz Festival   3169

Minnesota

    Head of the Lakes Jazz Festival   3175

Missouri

    Central Missouri State University Jazz Festival
      3214
    Jazz Festival   3200

Montana

    Jazz Festival   3216

Nevada

    International Jazz Festival   3220
    University of Nevada, Las Vegas, Jazz Festival
      3219

New Jersey

    Pee Wee Russell Memorial Stomp   3225

New Mexico

    Jazz Festival   3228

New York

    Hofstra University Jazz Clinic and Festival   3239
    Jazz in the Gardens   3251

    New York Musicians Jazz Festival   3257
    Newport Jazz Festival   3259
    Studio Rivbea Summer Music Festival   3263

Ohio

    College Conservatory Jazz Festival   3303
    Ohio Valley Kool Jazz Festival   3304

South Carolina

    Furman Jazz Festival   3344

Texas

    All-Texas Jazz Festival   3370
    Jazz Festival   3376

Virginia

    Hampton Kool Jazz Festival   3403
    Manassas Jazz Festival   3406

Canada

    Jazz Festival   3433
    Summer Festival of Chamber Music and Jazz
      3441

JEWISH

Maryland

    Purim Celebration   2136

New Jersey

    Jewish Festival of the Arts   2209

New York

    National Jewish Music Festival   3255

South Carolina

    Jewish Emphasis Festival   2296

KITE

California

    International Festival of Kites   1256
    Kite Festival   1267

Subject Index

LIVESTOCK

See also: WESTERN

Subject Index

Subject Index

Subject Index

Subject Index

Subject Index

Subject Index

RADIO

New York

American Radio Commercials Festival   2404

Texas

Citizens Band Radio Jamboree   1788

RAILROAD

Illinois

Abraham Lincoln National Railsplitting Contest
and Crafts Festival   1366

Indiana

Live Steam and Threshermen's Reunion   104

Maryland

World Railway Film Festival   2399

Massachusetts

Christmas Festival of Lights   1488
Rail-Fans Day   1489

Minnesota

Box Car Days   1523

North Carolina

Old Time Railroaders Day at Tweetsie Railroad
1619

South Carolina

Raylrode Daze Festival   2665

Utah

Golden Spike Ceremony   2685

Virginia

Railfan Steam Weekend   1828

West Virginia

Railfan Steam Weekend   1850

Canada

Minnedosa Fun Festival   1905

RAISIN

California

National Raisin Festival   18

RASPBERRY

Minnesota

Raspberry Festival   201

Utah

Raspberry Festival   376

RENAISSANCE

California

Renaissance Fair (Angels Camp)   2547
Renaissance Fair (Laytonville)   2555
Renaissance Pleasure Faire (Los Angeles)   2556
Renaissance Pleasure Faire (San Rafael)   2566
Renaissance Pleasure Faire and Springtime Market
2546

Indiana

May Faire   2589

Massachusetts

Martha's Vineyard Renaissance Fair   2618

Minnesota

Renaissance Festival   2623

Rhode Island

Renaissance Crafts and Art Show   1070

Tennessee

River City Renaissance Fair   3394

RENAISSANCE (contd.)

Washington

Fallshire Renaissance Faire   2693

RHUBARB

South Dakota

Rhubarb Festival   328

RICE

Louisiana

International Rice Festival   150

Minnesota

Wild Rice Festival (Kelliher)   202
Wild Rice Festival (Waskish)   210

Texas

Rice Festival   342
Texas Rice Festival   374

RILEY, JAMES WHITCOMB

Indiana

James Whitcomb Riley Festival   1385

ROCK MUSIC

California

'50's Festival of Rock N' Roll   3045

SCANDINAVIAN

Delaware

A Day in Old New Castle   2060

Iowa

Scandinavian Days   2120

Minnesota

Kaffe Fest   2174
Snoose Boulevard Festival   2164

Oregon

Scandinavian Festival   2258

Texas

Scandinavian Club of Houston's Spring Festival   2321

Washington

Midsommerfest   2343

SCIENCE

California

California Science Fair   1258
Greater San Diego Science and Engineering Fair   1275

Georgia

Georgia State Science and Engineering Fair   1333

Indiana

Science Fair   1384

Louisiana

Science Fair (Region III) (Monroe)   1441
Science Fair (Region IV) (Lafayette)   1437

Maryland

Science Fair   1454

Minnesota

Cosmos Space Festival   1505

New Mexico

State Science Fair   1601

Subject Index

Subject Index

SEAFOOD

Alabama

Alabama Seafood Festival   2865
Alabama Shrimp Festival   2868

Alaska

King Crab Festival   2869
Walrus Carnival (Gambell)   3791
Walrus Carnival (Savoonga)   3793

California

Salmon Festival (Arcata)   2871
Salmon Festival (Klamath)   2874

Florida

Island Shrimp Festival   2880
Seafood Festival (Apalachicola)   2879
Seafood Festival (Grant)   2881

Louisiana

Catfish Festival   2896
Crayfish Festival   2894
Louisiana Oyster Festival   2895
Louisiana Shrimp and Petroleum Festival   1443
Shrimp Festival   2525

Maine

Clam Festival   2903
Lobster Festival and Lobsterboat Races   2902
Maine Seafoods Festival   2901
Shrimp Festival   2897

Maryland

Chesapeake Bay Fishing Fair   2915
Frederick Seafood Festival   2910
Greater Cumberland Seafood Festival   2909
Maryland Clam Festival   2905
National Hard Crab Derby and Fair   2908
Saint Mary's Oyster Festival   2912
Seafood Festival (Hagerstown)   2911
Seafood Festival (Ocean City)   2914

Massachusetts

Bourne Bay Scallop Festival   2916

Michigan

National Trout Festival   2919

Mississippi

Shrimp Festival and Blessing of the Shrimp Fleet   2929

New Mexico

Moreno Valley Fish Fry and Square Dance Festival   1586

North Carolina

Mullet Festival   2934
North Carolina Crab Derby   2933
Shad Festival   1625

Oklahoma

National Sand Bass Festival   2940

Oregon

Indian Style Salmon Bake   2942

South Carolina

Derby Awards Night Festival   2949

Tennessee

Paris Fish Fry (World's Biggest Fish Fry)   2950

Texas

Fishing Fiesta and Shrimp Festival   2954
Fishin' Fiesta and Shrimp Festival   2957
Jaycee Fishing Festival   2960
National Sand Bass Festival   2956
Shrimp Boil   2958
Shrimp Festival and Blessing of the Fleet   2959
Shrimporee   2951

Virginia

Oyster Festival (Chincoteague Island)   2964
Oyster Festival (Urbanna)   2966
Seafood Festival   2965

Washington

Ballard Halibut Feed   2974
Festival Days   1838
Issaquah Salmon Festival   2970
Salmon Derby Days   2693

Canada

Lobster Carnival   2988
Nova Scotia Fisheries Exhibition   2987

Subject Index

Subject Index

SPRING (contd.)

Texas (contd.)

Mayfest (Trinity River Festival)   3629
Spring Ho Festival   3631
Winedale Spring Festival   3635

Utah

Spring Carnival   3637

Virginia

May Festival for Senior Adults   3647
Shenandoah Apple Blossom Festival   394

Washington

Blossomtime   3655

SQUARE DANCE

Alabama

Alabama Jubilee   1945
Lake Eufaula Festival   2867
Square Dance Festival   1946

Alaska

Alaska Square/Round Dance Festival   1947

Arizona

Bustle and Boots Square Dance Festival   1949

California

Fiesta de la Cuadrilla   1953
May Time Frolic   1954
National Square Dance Convention   1950
Stockton Square Dance Festival   1956

Colorado

Peach Festival   1300
Strawberry Days Celebration   48

Connecticut

Barnum Festival   1305

Florida

Square Dance Festival   1958

Idaho

Idaho State Square and Round Dance Festival   1960

Indiana

Early American Festival   2588
Fort Vallonia Days   1403
Harvest Homecoming   3507

Kentucky

Kentucky Folk Song Festival   3137

Missouri

Ozark Mountain Bluegrass Festival   3189

Montana

Square Dance Festival   1964

Nebraska

Square Dance Festival   1965

New Hampshire

Folk Dance Weekend   1966
Square Dance Weekend   1967

New Mexico

Aspencade and Square Dance Festival   594
Community House Square Dance Festival and
      Pioneer Reunion   1595
Noreno Valley Fish Fry and Square Dance Festival
      1586
Red River Valley Fair   1596
Square Dance Festival   1969
State Square Dance Festival and Workshop   1968

North Carolina

Accent on Rounds with Squares Festival   1972
Fontana Fall Jubilee Festival   1973
Fontana Spring Fling   1974
Fun Fest   1975
Rebel Roundup Festival   1976
Swap Shop Festival   1977

Pennsylvania

Square Dance Festival   1981
Square Dance Round-Up   1979

Subject Index

Subject Index

Subject Index

SYRUP (contd.)

Vermont

Maple Sugar Festival   382
Vermont State Maple Festival   384

Virginia

Highland County Maple Sugar Festival   389

Canada

Elmira Maple Sugar Festival   439
Maple Festival   441

TEXTILE

Canada

Textile Festival   1937

THEATER AND DRAMA

Alabama

Anniston Arts and Crafts Festival   693
Arts and Crafts Week   697
Arts Festival   475
Calico Fort Arts and Crafts Fair   700
Festival of Arts   472
Heritage Celebration (Tuscaloosa Heritage Week)
   1213

Arizona

Flagstaff Summer Festival   477
Garces Celebration of the Arts   480
Greater Phoenix Summer Festival   478

Arkansas

Ozark Frontier Trail Festival and Craft Show
   1217

California

Festival of the Arts   492
Fiesta de Artes   489
Georgetown Performing Arts Center Festival   486
Inter Arts Festival   497
Long Beach Heritage Week   1257
Medieval Festival   2552

Stanford Summer Festivals of the Arts   496
Thanksgiving Festival   491

Colorado

Central City Opera and Drama Festival   499
Colorado Craft-In   501
Red Rocks Music and Drama Festival   3050
Steamboat Summer Arts Festival   502

Connecticut

Norwich Rose-Arts Festival   505

Florida

FSU Fine Arts Festival   512
Festival Fever Days   511
Festival of the Hill   513
Seven Lively Arts Festival   509
Spring Arts Festival   508

Georgia

Dogwood Festival   66

Hawaii

Festival of the Arts of This Century   521

Illinois

Arts Festival   529
ICC Fine Arts Festival   526
Spring Arts Festival   528

Indiana

Creative Arts Festival   536
Fort Wayne Fine Arts Festival   533
Valpraiso Art Festival   540

Iowa

Riverboat Days   2891

Kentucky

Shaker Festival   2602

Maryland

Festival of Fine Arts   558
3400 on Stage   557

Massachusetts

Festival of Art   563
Summerthing   564

648

Subject Index

Subject Index

WOMEN (contd.)

Pennsylvania

Women's Cultural Festival   640

YOUTH

Iowa

Children's Day   1417
Festival of Children's Books   545

Michigan

Children's Book Fair

New York

Sarah Lawrence College Children's Fair   1608

Virginia

International Children's Festival   674